College Board AP® Topic Outline

Krugman'
2nd editi

College Board AP® Topic Outline	Krugman's 2nd edition
Basic Economic Concepts (8–12%)	**Section 1: Basic Economic Concepts**
A. Scarcity, choice, and opportunity costs	Module 1 The Study of Economics
B. Production possibilities curve	Module 3 The Production Possibilities Curve Model
C. Comparative advantage, specialization, and exchange	Module 4 Comparative Advantage and Trade
E. Macroeconomic issues: business cycle, unemployment, inflation, growth	Module 1 The Study of Economics
	Module 2 Introduction to Macroeconomics
D. Demand, supply, and market equilibrium	**Section 2: Supply and Demand**
	Module 5 Supply and Demand: Introduction and Demand
	Module 6 Supply and Demand: Supply
	Module 7 Supply and Demand: Equilibrium
II. Measurement of Economic Performance (12–16%)	**Section 3: Measurement of Economic Performance**
A. National income accounts	Module 10 The Circular Flow and Gross Domestic Product
	Module 11 Interpreting Real Gross Domestic Product
C. Unemployment	Module 12 The Meaning and Calculation of Unemployment
	Module 13 The Causes and Categories of Unemployment
B. Inflation measurement and adjustment	Module 14 Inflation: An Overview
	Module 15 The Measurement and Calculation of Inflation
III. National Income and Price Determination (10–15%)	**Section 4: National Income and Price Determination**
A. Aggregate demand	Module 16 Income and Expenditure
	Module 17 Aggregate Demand: Introduction and Determinants
B. Aggregate supply	Module 18 Aggregate Supply: Introduction and Determinants
C. Macroeconomic equilibrium	Module 19 Equilibrium in the Aggregate Demand–Aggregate Supply Model
	Module 20 Economic Policy and the Aggregate Demand–Aggregate Supply Model
	Module 21 Fiscal Policy and Multiplier Effects
IV. Financial Sector (15–20%)	**Section 5: The Financial Sector**
A. Money, banking, and financial markets	Module 22 Saving, Investment, and the Financial System
	Module 23 The Definition and Measurement of Money
	Module 24 The Time Value of Money

College Board AP® Topic Outline	Krugman's Macroeconomics for AP® 2nd edition	
	Module 25	Banking and Money Creation
	Module 28	The Money Market
B. Loanable funds market	Module 29	The Market for Loanable Funds
C. Central bank and control of the money supply	Module 26	The Federal Reserve System: History and Structure
	Module 27	The Federal Reserve: Monetary Policy
V. Stabilization Policies (20–30%)	**Section 6: Inflation, Unemployment, and Stabilization Policies**	
A. Fiscal and monetary policies	Module 30	Long-Run Implications of Fiscal Policy: Deficits and the Public Debt
	Module 31	Monetary Policy and the Interest Rate
	Module 32	Money, Output, and Prices in the Long Run
B. The Phillips curve	Module 33	Types of Inflation, Disinflation, and Deflation
	Module 34	Inflation and Unemployment: The Phillips Curve
	Module 35	History and Alternative Views of Macroeconomics
	Module 36	Consensus and Conflict in Modern Macroeconomics
VI. Economic Growth (5–10%)	**Section 7: Economic Growth and Productivity**	
A. Definition of economic growth	Module 37	Long-Run Economic Growth
B. Determinants of economic growth	Module 38	Productivity and Growth
C. Growth policy	Module 39	Growth Policy: Why Economic Growth Rates Differ
	Module 40	Economic Growth in Macroeconomic Models
VII. Open Economy: International Trade and Finance (10–15%)	**Section 8: The Open Economy: International Trade and Finance**	
A. Balance of payments accounts	Module 41	Capital Flows and the Balance of Payments
B. Foreign exchange market	Module 42	The Foreign Exchange Market
	Module 43	Exchange Rate Policy and Macroeconomic Policy
C. Imports, exports, and financial capital flows	Module 41	Capital Flows and the Balance of Payments
	Module 44	Barriers to Trade
D. Relationships between international and domestic financial and goods markets	Module 45	Putting It All Together

Krugman's Macroeconomics

for AP®

Krugman's Macroeconomics for AP® Second Edition

Margaret Ray
University of Mary Washington

David Anderson
Centre College

Adapted from *Macroeconomics*, Third Edition
by Paul Krugman and Robin Wells

Publisher: Ann Heath
Sponsoring Editor: Janie Pierce-Bratcher
Development Editor: Karen Misler
Editorial Assistant: Rachel Chlebowski
Marketing Manager: Julie Comforti
Marketing Assistant: Nont Pansringarm
Photo Editor: Cecilia Varas
Photo Researcher: Cecilia Varas
Art Director: Diana Blume
Cover Designer: Joseph DePinho
Interior Designer: Tamara Newnam
Managing Editor: Lisa Kinne
Senior Project Editor: Elizabeth Geller
Production Manager: Barbara Seixas
Composition: TSI evolve
Printing and Binding: RR Donnelley

Cover images: Kivilcim Pinar/Getty Images (market photo); Petr Vaclavek/Shutterstock (puzzle pieces); upixa/iStock/Getty Images Plus (wood background)

Library of Congress Control Number: 2014957503

ISBN-10: 1-4641-4228-9
ISBN-13: 978-1-4641-4228-4

Printed in the United States of America

Third Printing

BFW/Worth Publishers
41 Madison Ave.
New York, NY 10010

highschool.bfwpub.com/KrugmanAP2e

To beginning students everywhere,
which we all were at one time.

About the Authors

University of Mary Washington

Margaret Ray is Professor of Economics and Director of the Center for Economic Education at the University of Mary Washington, where she specializes in teaching introductory economics. She received her BS in Economics from Oklahoma State University and her PhD in Economics from the University of Tennessee. In 2012 she received her MEd in Curriculum and Instruction and became certified to teach K-12 Social Studies. She has taught AP® Economics at several high schools in Virginia and has received the Council on Economic Education's Excellence in Teaching Economics award. She has been involved in the AP® Economics program since 1992, serving as a reader and question leader, writing test items, overseeing the AP® course audit, writing College Board "Special Focus" articles, and editing the Council on Economic Education's AP® Macroeconomics resource. She has been a College Board® Endorsed Consultant for economics since 2001, and she conducts several professional development workshops and institutes each year. Her favorite hobby is showing hunter-jumper horses adopted from racehorse rescue organizations. She lives on a farm in Spotsylvania, Virginia with her two daughters.

Donna Anderson

David Anderson is the Paul G. Blazer Professor of Economics at Centre College. He received his BA in Economics from the University of Michigan and his MA and PhD in Economics from Duke University. Anderson has been involved in the AP® Economics program for two decades. For five years he led the grading of one or both of the AP® Economics exams, and he speaks regularly at AP® conferences and workshops. He has authored dozens of scholarly articles and many books, including *Cracking the AP® Economics Exam, Economics by Example, Favorite Ways to Learn Economics, Environmental Economics and Natural Resource Management, Economics in Modules*, and *Explorations in Economics*. His research is primarily on economic education, environmental economics, law and economics, and labor economics. Anderson teaches courses in each of these fields and loves teaching introductory economics. His favorite hobby is running, and he competes in marathons and triathlons. He lives in Danville, Kentucky, with his wife and two children.

Ligaya Franklin

Paul Krugman, recipient of the 2008 Nobel Memorial Prize in Economic Sciences, recently moved from Princeton University, where he taught for 14 years, to the Graduate Center of the City University of New York. In his new position, he is associated with the Luxembourg Income Study, which tracks and analyzes income inequality around the world. He received his BA from Yale and his PhD from MIT. Before Princeton, he taught at Yale, Stanford, and MIT. He also spent a year on the staff of the Council of Economic Advisers (1982–1983). His research has included pathbreaking work on international trade, economic geography, and currency crises. In 1991, Krugman received the American Economic Association's John Bates Clark medal. In addition to his teaching and academic research, Krugman writes extensively for nontechnical audiences. He is a regular op-ed columnist for the New York Times. His bestselling trade books include *The Return of Depression Economics and the Crisis of 2008,* a history of recent economic troubles and their implications for economic policy, and *The Conscience of a Liberal,* a study of the political economy of economic inequality and its relationship with political polarization from the Gilded Age to the present. His earlier books, *Peddling Prosperity* and *The Age of Diminished Expectations,* have become modern classics.

Robin Wells was a Lecturer and Researcher in Economics at Princeton University. She received her BA from the University of Chicago and her PhD from the University of California at Berkeley; she then did postdoctoral work at MIT. She has taught at the University of Michigan, the University of Southampton (United Kingdom), Stanford, and MIT.

Key Contributors and Advisors

Brian Held

Section Review Questions

Brian Held teaches AP® Economics at Loyola High School in Los Angeles, his alma mater. He holds an MA in Economics from California State University of Los Angeles. He has served as an AP® Macroeconomics reader for the past 10 years, including six as a Table Leader. In 2010, the California Council on Economic Education, CCEE, recognized Held with its Teacher of the Year Award. His students won CCEE's Capital Markets Contest in 2007.

Laura Adams

Financial Literacy Handbook

Laura Adams is an award-winning personal finance author. She earned a BS from the University of the South and an MBA from the University of Florida. She received the Excellence in Financial Literacy Education (EIFLE) Award from the Institute for Financial Literacy for her book *Money Girl's Smart Moves to Grow Rich*. Adams is the author of several e-Books and audiobooks and hosts the "Money Girl" podcast, a top-10 Internet show on iTunes that has been downloaded more than 45 million times.

Melanie Fox

Strive For a 5: Preparing for the AP® Macroeconomics Examination

Strive For a 5: Preparing for the AP® Microeconomics Examination

Melanie Fox currently teaches economics at the University of Louisville after serving as Chair of the Department of Economics and Business Administration at Austin College. She earned her BA and PhD from the University of Houston. Fox has been an AP® Macroeconomics Reader and Table Leader since 2007.

Margaret Pride

Teacher's Edition, Teacher's Resource Materials

Peggy Pride holds BA degrees in History and Economics and an MA in Business Education from Southern Illinois University. She taught AP® Economics for 35 years at St. Louis University High School. Her involvement with AP® Economics was long and varied, having served as Table Leader and Question Leader for Micro for 12 years and on the Test Development Committee for AP® Economics from 1999 to 2004. In addition, Pride was the primary author of the College Board publication *Advanced Placement Economics Teacher's Guide*. She received the GATE Teacher of the Year Award in 2005.

Richard Rankin

Section Review Questions

Dick Rankin teaches at Iolani School in Honolulu, Hawaii. He holds a BA in Economics from Virginia Military Institute and an MA in Economics from the University of Texas at Austin. Rankin is a former member and College Board Advisor to the AP® Economics Development Committee. He has been a Reader, Table Leader, and Question Leader for the AP® Economics Exams for the past 17 years, has taught AP® Economics for 20 years, and was Course Director for the Principles of Economics Course at the US Military Academy at West Point. Rankin is the 2014 Stephen L. Jackstadt Economics Award Winner.

Eric Dodge

ExamView® Assessment Suite Questions

Eric Dodge is Professor of Economics and Business Administration at Hanover College in Indiana. He received his BA from the University of Puget Sound and his MA and PhD from the University of Oregon. Dodge has been involved with AP® Economics for more than 10 years and has served as Reader, Table Leader, and Question Leader.

Dianna Miller

Teacher's Edition, Teacher's Resource Materials

Dianna Miller earned her BA in Social Studies Education and an MA in History from the University of North Florida. She currently teaches AP® Economics for Florida Virtual School, an online public school in Florida. She was a finalist for the National Online Teacher of the Year Award in 2010 and was the 2011 Florida Council for the Social Studies Trimble Award Winner. Miller has been active in AP® Economics since 2005 as a Reader and Table Leader.

Leslie Paige Wolfson

Teacher's Edition, Teacher's Resource Materials

Leslie Paige Wolfson holds a Certificate in Character Education and a Masters in Economics and Finance. She taught AP® Economics for 18 years at The Pingry School in New Jersey, and was the coordinator and instructor for the school's Financial Literacy program. Wolfson was awarded the Research Fellowship Award and the Woodruff English Faculty Honor Award.

Accuracy Reviewers

Darcy Brodison, Coronado High School, TX
Patricia Brazill, Irondequoit High School, NY
Dixie Dalton, Southside Virginia Community College, VA
David Frank, Bartram Trail High School, FL
Brian Heggood, Stanton College Prep, FL
Holly Jones, The Pennington School, NJ
Rachael Sharpe, Florida Virtual School, FL
James Watson, Independent Contractor, FL

Brief Contents

*Glosario available on Book Companion Site at bcs.worthpublishers.com/KrugmanAP2e

Contents

*Glosario available on Book Companion Site at bcs.worthpublishers.com/KrugmanAP2e

To the Student

How to Get the Most from This Program

The AP® Economics course represents a wonderful opportunity for high school students to be challenged by the rigor of a college-level course, while learning life-relevant concepts from the discipline of economics. We understand the unique challenges of teaching and learning AP® Economics and have designed this book and its support program to be the most effective possible resources to help you succeed in AP® Economics.

Intent on promoting the efficiency and effectiveness of AP® Economics courses, we started with the best available college-level introduction to economics—Krugman and Wells' *Economics*, second and third editions. We knew these would be the best foundation for an AP® adaptation. Our goal was to retain the features of *Economics* that make it a winner, while crafting it to closely follow the AP® syllabus and speak to a high school audience. *Krugman's Macroeconomics for AP®*, second edition, is designed to be easy to read and easy to use. Our hope is that you will find our explanations clear and concise, and that you will enjoy reading the book.

What's New in this Edition?

This book is your ultimate tool for success in the AP® Economics courses. With this in mind, the second edition features improvements to the organization and presentation of content, as well as to our system of supporting student learning and preparation for the AP® Exam. For a visual walk-through of the features of the book, please see page xxvi.

More AP®-focused elements and study aids

- **AP® exam tips**, found in the margin throughout the text, provide invaluable advice on where you should focus, how to avoid pitfalls, and how to be successful in the course and on the exam. These "on-the-spot" reminders help you avoid common mistakes.
- More **AP® exam practice** is provided through an increased number of multiple-choice and free-response questions (FRQs) at the end of each module and section. These assessments not only test you on the material you learned in the module, but also mimic AP® questions to train you on what you will see on the exam. The open-ended, conceptual FRQs help familiarize you with the kind of synthesis skills you'll need to master the exam.
- **A full-length AP®-style practice examination** is included at the end of the text to ensure you have nailed down the content and are ready to tackle the real test in May.

New video clips to help you study and review

Economics videos available on the Internet can be both entertaining and educational. For a complete list of these videos, look for econextras video links on the Book Companion Site at bcs.worthpublishers.com/KrugmanAP2e.

- **Module "Flip It" Concept Videos** are short, concise videos that explain a key concept covered in a module, such as the Production Possibilities Curve in Module 3 and Comparative Advantage in Module 4. Each video is short, focused, and funny. These Internet videos offer simple examples to underscore the concepts and give lots of practice in reading and interpreting graphs—skills that are important on the AP® Exam.
- **Section Review Videos** provide a great review of the key concepts in a section. These longer videos focus on explaining the big picture ideas, key graphs, and common mistakes/pitfalls for the section. Watching the Section Review Video is a smart way to make sure you understand the key ideas in the section.

What Continues?

Perhaps the most important feature is what has been left unchanged from the first edition. We adhere to the general approach of Krugman's balanced and proven *Economics* text:

> "To achieve deeper levels of understanding of the real world through economics, students must learn to appreciate the kinds of trade-offs and ambiguities that economists and policy makers face when applying their models to real-world problems. We believe this approach will make students more insightful and more effective participants in our common economic, social, and political lives."

Alignment with the College Board® Topic Outline

We have organized the book to match up with the College Board's Topic Outline for AP® Macroeconomics, so you can be sure you are receiving the best possible preparation for the AP® exam. Where the outline has recommended coverage within specific sections, you can be sure that you will find that coverage. You can find a guide correlating each module with its equivalent College Board course description topic on the front endpaper of this text.

A flexible modular approach

This book is arranged by sections that correspond to the AP® Topic Outline. Each section is divided into four to seven modules. Each module breaks the course material into a pedagogically appropriate unit that is designed to be covered in one class period. This organization takes you through the required AP® course material in a sequence and at a pace designed for optimal success.

Effective study aids

- **Learning Objectives** establish measurable goals for each module and help you direct your reading.
- **Module Reviews** allow you to practice what you've learned with AP®-style questions. These reviews help you determine your mastery of each module so you can decide if you're ready to move on or need more study.
- **Section Reviews** include detailed summaries of each module as well as page-referenced Key Terms and AP®-style multiple-choice and free-response questions.

Additional Resources to Optimize Productivity

- **Downloadable e-Book**
  This PDF-style e-Book matches the printed book page for page and is optimized for use on Windows or Apple computers, laptops, and tablets.
- **Strive for a 5: Preparing for the AP® Macroeconomics Exam**
  The *Strive for a 5* guide is designed for use with *Krugman's Macroeconomics for AP®*, second edition. It is written to help you evaluate your understanding of the material covered in the textbook, reinforce the key concepts, develop conceptual understanding and graphing skills, and prepare you to succeed on the AP® Macroeconomics Exam. The guide is divided into two sections: a study guide and a test preparation section. The study guide is written to be used throughout the course, while the prep section offers additional AP® test strategies and includes two full-length AP®-style practice exams—each with 60 multiple-choice questions and three free-response questions.

Turn the page for a tour of the text. Once you know how to use the book properly, you will be more likely to realize success in the course and on the AP® exam!

Tools for Learning...Getting the Most from this Book

Each section and its modules are structured around a common set of features designed to help you learn the concept and practice for the AP® Exam. By putting all of the pieces together as you work through the text, you will complete the entire puzzle by the end of the course.

Use the features to help you study economics and prepare for the exam.

SECTION 1

Module 1: The Study of Economics
Module 2: Introduction to Macroeconomics
Module 3: The Production Possibilities Curve Model
Module 4: Comparative Advantage and Trade
Appendix: Graphs in Economics

Economics by Example: What's to Love About Economics?

Basic Economic Concepts

Common Ground

The annual meeting of the American Economic Association draws thousands of economists, young and old, famous and obscure. There are booksellers, business meetings, and quite a few job interviews. But mainly the economists gather to talk and listen. During the busiest times, 60 or more presentations may be taking place simultaneously, on questions that range from the future of the stock market to who does the cooking in two-earner families.

What do these people have in common? An expert on the stock market probably knows very little about the economics of housework, and vice versa. Yet an economist who wanders into the wrong seminar and ends up listening to presentations on some unfamiliar topic is nonetheless likely to hear much that is familiar. The reason is that all economic analysis is based on a set of common principles that apply to many different issues.

of alternatives—limited because no one can have everything that he or she wants. Every question in economics at its most basic level involves individuals making choices.

But to understand how an economy works, you need to understand more than how individuals make choices. None of us lives like Robinson Crusoe, alone on an island—we must make decisions in an environment that is shaped by the decisions of others. Indeed, in our global economy even the simplest decisions you make—say, what to have for breakfast—are shaped by the decisions of thousands of other people, from the banana grower

Each unit is designed with a different color so that you may easily determine which AP® exam topic you are studying. For example, Section 1 is blue and Section 2 is magenta.

Review the **Learning Objectives** for an overview of the critical concepts you will be tackling in the module. Focus on mastering these skills as you work through the module.

MODULE 5

Supply and Demand: Introduction and Demand

In this Module, you will learn to:

- Explain what a competitive market is and how it is described by the supply and demand model
- Draw a demand curve and interpret its meaning
- Discuss the difference between movements along the demand curve and changes in demand
- List the factors that shift the demand curve

Read the **Opening Story**. Each section opens with a compelling story that often extends through the modules. The opening stories illustrate important concepts, to build intuition with realistic examples that are designed to pique your interest as you prepare to learn about the economic concepts in the modules.

Supply and Demand: A Model of a Competitive Market

Cotton sellers and cotton buyers constitute a *market*—a group of producers and consumers who exchange a good or service for payment. In this section, we'll focus on a particular type of market known as a *competitive market*. Roughly, a **competitive market** is one in which there are many buyers and sellers of the same good or service. More precisely, the key feature of a competitive market is that no individual's actions have a noticeable effect on the price at which the good or service is sold. It's important to understand, however, that this is not an accurate description of every market. For example, it's not an accurate description of the market for cola ...erages, Coca-Cola and Pepsi ... they are able to influence ...ut it *is* an accurate descrip... for cotton is so huge that ...nts for only a tiny fraction ... at which cotton is bought

...ifferent from other markets ..., let's just say that it's easier ...aking an exam, it's always a ... this book, we're going to do

AP® Exam Tip

Supply and demand graphs are some of the most important graphs to master for success on the AP® exam. You must be able to draw, label, and interpret the graphs for the exam. They are the basis of future graphs you will learn in the course, too.

A **competitive market** is a market in which there are many buyers and sellers of the same good or service, none of whom can influence the price at which the good or service is sold.

Pay attention to the **AP® Exam Tip** boxes. They provide helpful advice on what to read closely and what common pitfalls to avoid so you can ace the AP® exam.

Watch for the blue **Key Term** boxes, which highlight the vocabulary you'll need to master to realize success on the AP® exam. The terms are repeated in the Section Review and in the Glossary at the end of the book, as well as the Glosario on the Book Companion Site.

...dule 5 Supply and Demand: Introduction and Demand 49

Study the graphs and figures. To succeed, you must be able to interpret and draw graphs correctly.

Figure 7.1 Market Equilibrium

Market equilibrium occurs at point *E*, where the supply curve and the demand curve intersect. In equilibrium, the quantity demanded is equal to the quantity supplied. In this market, the equilibrium price is $1 per pound and the equilibrium quantity is 10 billion pounds per year.

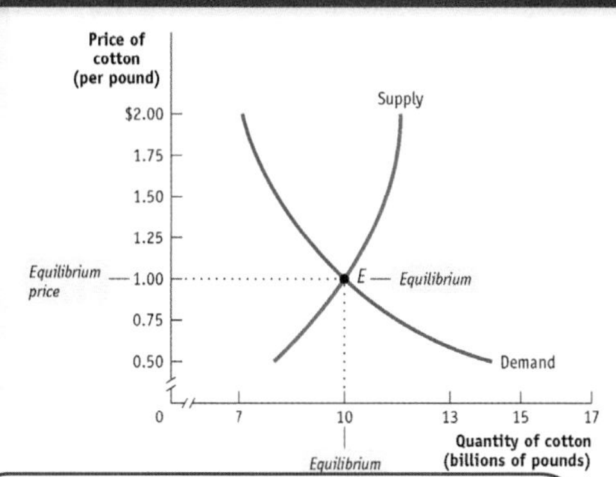

Figure 10.1 The Circular-Flow Diagram

This diagram represents the flows of money, factors of production, and goods and services in the economy. In the markets for goods and services, households purchase goods and services from firms, generating a flow of money to the firms and a flow of goods and services to the households. The money flows back to households as firms purchase factors of production from the households in factor markets.

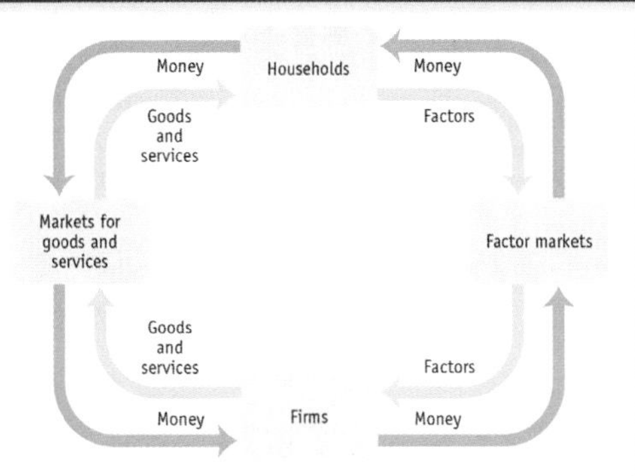

Figures and **graphs** hold volumes of information. Study them carefully and read the captions. Mastering the creation and interpretation of economic models is important to realizing success on the AP® exam. Color is used consistently to distinguish between demand (blue) and supply (red) curves.

econextras

Video List

to accompany

Krugman's Economics for AP® Second Editio

Section	Module	Name of Video	Link
Section 1			
	Module 1	Econ Overview	https://www.youtube.com/watch?v=Np-dZSdzymk&feature=c4-overview-vl&list=PL1oD
		Keynesian Theory in 5 Minutes	https://www.youtube.com/watch?v=KJ_qcvp1OB4
	Module 2	The Business Cycle	https://www.youtube.com/watch?v=DmXvUz0qAIw&feature=youtu.be
	Module 3	Scarcity, Opportunity Cost, and the PPC	https://www.youtube.com/watch?v=kmjzgB_tUJ8&feature=youtu.be
		The Law of Increasing Opportunity Cost and the PPC Model	https://www.youtube.com/watch?v=m1hY3-y0-dM&feature=youtu.be
		Production Possibilities Curve and Opportunity Cost	https://www.youtube.com/watch?feature=player_detailpage&v=SJQ56vJoy3Y&list=PL
	Module 4	Milton Friedman - I, Pencil	https://www.youtube.com/watch?v=67tHtpac5ws&feature=youtu.be
		Comparative Advantage	https://www.youtube.com/watch?v=FpTBjRf8IGs&list=PLD5BC727C84E254E5&index=3

Watch the **econextras** module video clips that provide "just in time" instruction on key concepts in each module. You can watch the videos as many times as needed to make sure that you understand the material. See the econextras list with hyperlinks to recommended videos on the book companion website, bcs.worthpublishers.com/krugmanap2e.

FYI The Price of Admission

The market equilibrium, so the theory goes, is pretty egalitarian because the equilibrium price applies to everyone. That is, all buyers pay the same price—the equilibrium price—and all ...rice. But is ...ckets is ...ontradict ...e at the ...her price ...he same ...e people ...sell them, ...ay. For ex- ...fice price ...n Miami, ... price ...n: $88.50

Puzzling as this may seem, there is no contradiction once we take opportunity costs and tastes into account. For major events, buying tickets from the box office means waiting in very long lines. Ticket buyers who use Internet resellers have decided that the opportunity cost of their time is too high to spend waiting in line. And tickets for major events being sold at face value by online box offices often sell out within minutes. In this case, some people who want to go to the concert badly but have missed out on the opportunity to buy cheaper tickets from the online box office are willing to pay the higher Internet reseller price.

Not only that—perusing the StubHub.com website, you can see that markets really do move to equilibrium. You'll notice that the prices quoted by different sellers for seats close to one another are also very close: $184.99 versus $185 for seats on the main floor of the Drake concert. As the competitive market model predicts, units of the same good end up selling for the same price. And prices move in response to demand and supply. According to an article in the *New York Times*, tickets on StubHub.com can sell for less than the face value for events with little appeal, but prices can skyrocket for events that are in high demand. (The article quotes a price of $3,530 for a Madonna concert.) Even StubHub.com's chief executive says his site is "the embodiment of supply-and-demand economics."

So the theory of competitive markets isn't just speculation. If you want to experience it for yourself, try buying tickets to a concert.

The competitive market model determines the price you pay for concert tickets.

Need a break? Read the **FYI boxes** for short but compelling applications of the major economic concepts just covered in the module. You can connect the content you're reading with these real-life examples to deepen your understanding of the concepts. Exercise your synthesis skills with these boxes!

Practice makes perfect!

Practice what you've learned at the end of each module with **Multiple-Choice Questions** and skill-building practice **Free-Response Questions**.

MODULE 4 Review

Check Your Understanding

1. In Italy, an automobile can be produced by 8 workers in one day and a washing machine by 3 workers in one day. In the United States, an automobile can be produced by 6 workers in one day, and a washing machine by 2 workers in one day.
   a. Which country has an absolute advantage in the production of automobiles? In washing machines?
   b. Which country has a comparative advantage in the production of washing machines? In automobiles?
   c. What type of specialization results in the greatest gains from trade between the two countries?
2. Refer to the story of Tom and Hank illustrated by Figure 4.1 in the text. Explain why Tom and Hank are willing to engage in a trade of 1 fish for 1½ coconuts.

Tackle the Test: Multiple-Choice Questions

Refer to the graph below to answer the following questions.

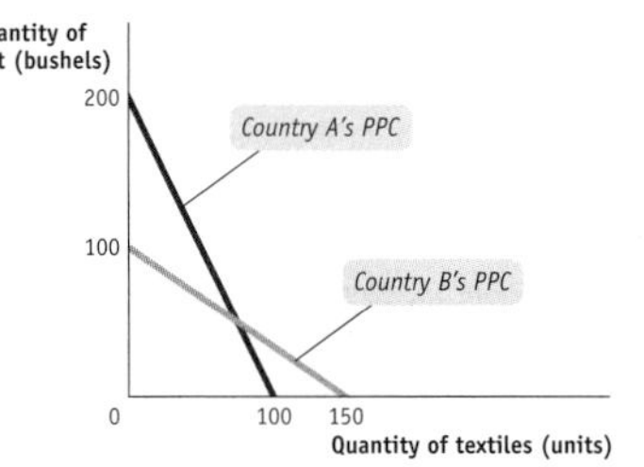

1. Use the graph to determine which country has an absolute advantage in producing each good.

	Absolute advantage in wheat production	*Absolute advantage in textile production*
a.	Country A	Country B
b.	Country A	Country A
c.	Country B	Country A
d.	Country B	Country B
e.	Country A	Neither country

30 Section 1 Basic Economic Concepts

Check Your Understanding questions at the end of each module allow you to immediately test your understanding of the content. If you're having a hard time with these questions, you'll know to go back and re-read the module.

Tackle the Test: Free-Response Questions

1. Refer to the graph below to answer the following questions.

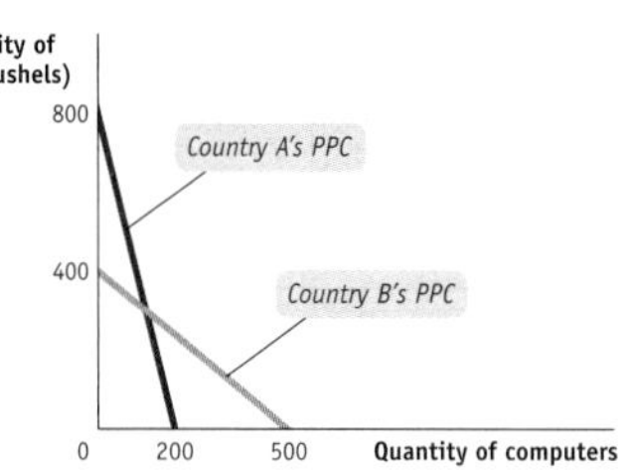

   a. What is the opportunity cost of a bushel of corn in each country?
   b. Which country has an absolute advantage in computer production? Explain.
   c. Which country has a comparative advantage in corn production? Explain.
   d. If each country specializes, what good will Country B import? Explain.
   e. What is the minimum price Country A will accept to export corn to Country B? Explain.

Rubric for FRQ 1 (9 points)

1 point: Country A, ¼ computer; Country B, 1¼ computers
1 point: Country B
1 point: Because Country B can produce more computers than Country A (500 versus 200)
1 point: Country A
1 point: Because Country A can produce corn at a lower opportunity cost (¼ versus 1¼ computers)
1 point: Corn
1 point: Country B has a comparative advantage in the production of computers, so it will produce computers and import corn (Country A has a comparative advantage in corn production, so it will specialize in corn and import computers from Country B).
1 point: ¼ computer
1 point: Country A's opportunity cost of producing corn is ¼ computer, so that is the lowest price it will accept to sell corn to Country B.

2. Refer to the table below to answer the following questions. These two countries are producing textiles and wheat using equal amounts of resources.

	Weekly output per worker Country A	 Country B
Bushels of wheat	15	10
Units of textiles	60	60

   a. What is the opportunity cost of producing a bushel of wheat for each country?
   b. Which country has the absolute advantage in wheat production?
   c. Which country has the comparative advantage in textile production? Explain.
   (5 points)

Tackle the Test presents five AP®-style multiple-choice questions to help you become comfortable with the types of questions you'll see in the multiple-choice section of the AP® exam.

In addition, two **AP®-style free-response questions** are provided. A sample grading rubric is given for the first FRQ to show you how questions are graded and to help you learn how to write thoughtful answers. The second problem asks you try a "mini FRQ" for yourself. These short, focused FRQ-style questions are one small piece of the puzzle.

Watch the review video and work through cumulative questions at the end of each section.

Start your review of each section by watching the special Section Review Video, indicated by the green play button. These reviews present the key ideas in the section using lots of visuals, down-to-earth language, and a little humor.

SECTION 1 Review

Section 1 Review Video

Module 1

1. Everyone has to make choices about what to do and what *not* to do. **Individual choice** is the basis of **economics**—if it doesn't involve choice, it isn't economics. The **economy** is a system that coordinates choices about production and consumption. In a **market economy**, these choices are made by many firms and individuals. In a **command economy**, these choices are made by a central authority. **Incentives** are rewards or punishments that motivate particular choices, and can be lacking in a command economy where producers cannot set their own prices or keep their own profits. **Property rights** create incentives in market economies by establishing ownership and granting individuals the right to trade goods and services for mutual gain. In any economy, decisions are informed by **marginal analysis**—the study of the costs and benefits of doing something a little bit more or a little bit less.
2. The reason choices must be made is that **resources**—anything that can be used to produce something else—are **scarce**. The four categories of resources are **land**,
3. Because you must choose among limited alternatives, the true cost of anything is what you must give up to get it—all costs are **opportunity costs**.
4. Economists use economic models for both **positive economics**, which describes how the economy works, and for **normative economics**, which prescribes how the economy *should* work. Positive economics often involves making forecasts. Economics can determine correct answers for positive questions, but typically not for normative questions, which involve value judgments. Exceptions occur when policies designed to achieve a certain prescription can be clearly ranked in terms of preference.
5. There are two main reasons economists disagree. One, they may disagree about which simplifications to make in a model. Two, economists may disagree—like everyone else—about values.
6. **Microeconomics** is the branch of economics that studies how people make decisions and how those decisions interact. **Macroeconomics** is concerned with the overall ups and downs of the economy, and focuses ...**ggregates** such as the unemployment ...**omestic product**, that summarize data ...ferent markets.

Read the **Section Review** and study the **Key Terms** at the end of each section.

Key Terms

Economics, p. 2
Individual choice, p. 2
Economy, p. 2
Market economy, p. 2
Command economy, p. 2
Incentives, p. 3
Property rights, p. 3
Marginal analysis, p. 3
Resource, p. 3
Land, p. 3
Labor, p. 3
Capital, p. 3
Entrepreneurship, p. 3
Scarce, p. 3
Opportunity cost, p. 4
Microeconomics, p. 5
Macroeconomics, p. 5
Economic aggregates, p. 5
Positive economics, p. 6
Normative economics, p. 6
Business cycle, p. 11
Depression, p. 11
Recessions, p. 11
Expansions, p. 11
Employment, p. 11
Unemployment, p. 11
Labor force, p. 12
Unemployment rate, p. 12
Output, p. 12
Aggregate output, p. 12
Inflation, p. 13
Deflation, p. 13
Price stability, p. 13
Economic growth, p. 13
Model, p. 14
Other things equal (*ceteris paribus*) assumption, p. 14
Trade-off, p. 16
Production possibilities curve, p. 17
Efficient, p. 18
Productive efficiency, p. 18
Allocative efficiency, p. 18
Technology, p. 21
Trade, p. 24
Gains from trade, p. 24
Specialization, p. 24
Comparative advantage, p. 27
Absolute advantage, p. 27
Terms of trade, p. 28

AP® Exam Practice Questions

Multiple-Choice Questions

1. In a market economy, most choices about production and consumption are made by which of the following?
   a. politicians
   b. many individuals and firms
   c. the government
   d. managers
   e. economists
2. Which of the following pairs indicates a category of resources and an example of that resource?

	Category	*Example*
a.	money	investment
b.	capital	money
c.	capital	minerals
d.	land	factory
e.	land	timber

3. You can either go to a movie or study for an exam. Which of the following is an opportunity cost of studying for the exam?
   a. a higher grade on the exam
   b. the price of a movie ticket
   c. the cost of paper, pens, books, and other study materials
   d. the enjoyment from seeing the movie
   e. the sense of achievement from learning

Free-Response Question

The Hatfield family lives on the east side of the Hatatoochie River and the McCoy family lives on the west side. Each family's diet consists of fried chicken and corn on the cob, and each is self-sufficient, raising its own chickens and growing its own corn.

Assume the Hatfield family has a comparative advantage in the production of corn.

1. Draw a correctly labeled graph showing a hypothetical production possibilities curve for the McCoy family.
2. Which family has the comparative advantage in the production of chickens? Explain.
3. Assuming that each family is producing efficiently, how can the two families increase their consumption of both chicken and corn?
(5 points)

Test yourself at the end of each section by tackling the **AP® Exam Practice Questions**. Here's your chance to prove that you've mastered the Economics content *and* the types of questions you'll see on the AP® exam!

The final pieces of the puzzle...Putting It All Together and the comprehensive AP® Practice Test

MODULE

45 Putting It All Together

In this Module, you will learn to:

- Use macroeconomic models to conduct policy analysis
- Improve your approach to free-response macroeconomics questions

Having completed our study of the basic macroeconomic models, analyze scenarios and evaluate policy recommendations. In this a step-by-step approach to macroeconomic analysis. You can adap problems involving any macroeconomic model, including models of and supply, production possibilities, money markets, and the Philli of this module you will be able to combine mastery of the principle ics with problem solving skills to analyze a new scenario on your ow

A Structure for Macroeconomic

Putting It All Together The final module in macroeconomics, 45, teaches you how to use what you have learned to answer comprehensive, "real-world" questions about the macroeconomy, like the type you will see in the long section FRQ on the AP® Exam.

PRACTICE EXAM

AP® Macroeconomics Exam Practice Test

Multiple-Choice Questions

Refer to the figure below to answer Question 1.

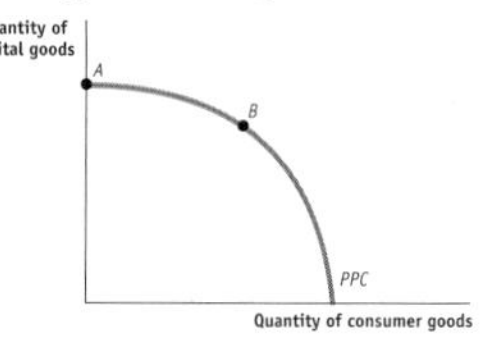

1. A movement from point *A* to point *B* illustrates which of the following?
   a. the opportunity cost of consumer goods
   b. an advance in technology
   c. an increase in available resources used to produce consumer goods

	Slope	*Opportunity cost of wheat*
a.	no change	no change
b.	decrease	decrease
c.	increase	increase
d.	no change	increase
e.	decrease	increase

3. According to the concept of comparative advantage, which of the following is true when countries specialize and trade?
   a. Both countries will be better off.
   b. Total world output increases.
   c. The production possibilities curve for both countries shifts outward.
   d. Prices fall in both countries.
   e. Deadweight loss is created.

Refer to the figure below to answer Question 4.

Quantity of corn (bushels)

800

Test your knowledge and readiness for the AP® exam by taking the end-of-book **AP®-Style Practice Exam**, which includes 60 multiple-choice questions and three FRQs, just like the official test. Time yourself to simulate the actual exam.

Interesting reading for after the Exam

ENRICHMENT MODULE

A Financial Markets and Crises

In this Module, you will learn to:

- Describe the importance of a well-functioning financial system
- List the causes of financial crises in the economy
- Identify the macroeconomic consequences of financial crises
- Explain the factors leading to the financial crisis of 2008

The Role of Financial Markets

These days, almost everyone is connected in some way to *financial markets*. When you receive a paycheck, pay a bill, borrow money, or use a credit card, the financial markets assist with the transaction. And a recent FDIC study found that about 91% of U.S. households have some form of checking or savings account.

In Module 22, we learned about the three tasks of a financial system: to reduce transactions costs, to reduce risk, and to provide liquidity. The financial system performs

Learning about Economics doesn't stop after you take the exam in May. Continue your study of Economics with an **Enrichment Module** and the **Financial Literacy Handbook** to help round out the course and to prepare you for further Economics study in college and beyond.

For additional help...

WORTH PUBLISHERS

Preparing for the
AP® Macroeconomics Exam

Melanie Fox

Use the **Strive for a 5 Guide** companion to this text. It was written to work hand-in-glove with the text and includes a study guide followed by tips and advice on taking the exam and two more full AP® practice exams.

KRUGMAN'S
Economics
for AP®
Ray | Anderson
KRUGMAN'S ECONOMICS FOR AP®
Second Edition
Margaret Ray and David Anderson

Study when and where you want...

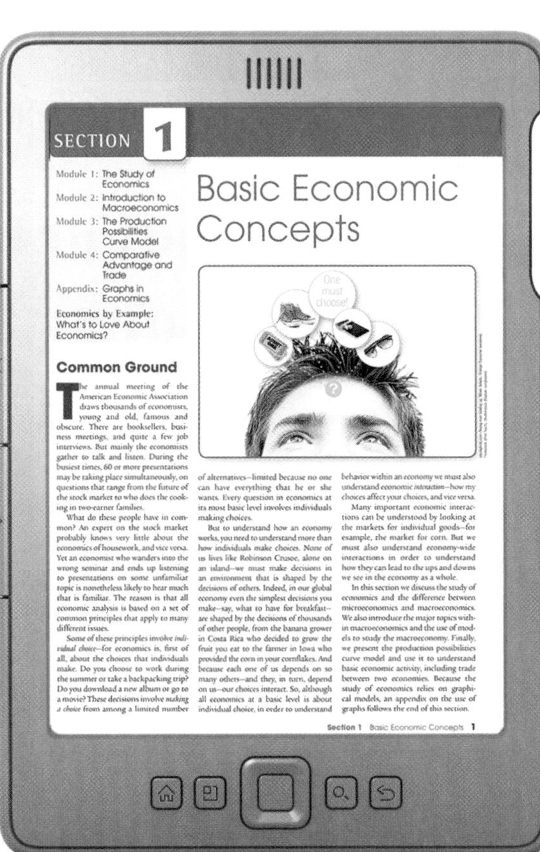

SECTION 1
Basic Economic Concepts
Module 1: The Study of Economics
Module 2: Introduction to Macroeconomics
Module 3: The Production Possibilities Curve Model
Module 4: Comparative Advantage and Trade
Appendix: Graphs in Economics
Economics by Example: What's to Love About Economics?
Common Ground
Section 1 Basic Economic Concepts 1

Take the e-Book with you anywhere! Download the text to your home computer or tablet so you can stay up to date on reading assignments.

SECTION 1

Basic Economic Concepts

istockphoto.com (Young man looking up, Movie tickets, Orange Converse sneakers); Thinkstock (iPod Touch); Shutterstock (Rayban sunglasses)

Common Ground

The annual meeting of the American Economic Association draws thousands of economists, young and old, famous and obscure. There are booksellers, business meetings, and quite a few job interviews. But mainly the economists gather to talk and listen. During the busiest times, 60 or more presentations may be taking place simultaneously, on questions that range from the future of the stock market to who does the cooking in two-earner families.

What do these people have in common? An expert on the stock market probably knows very little about the economics of housework, and vice versa. Yet an economist who wanders into the wrong seminar and ends up listening to presentations on some unfamiliar topic is nonetheless likely to hear much that is familiar. The reason is that all economic analysis is based on a set of common principles that apply to many different issues.

Some of these principles involve *individual choice*—for economics is, first of all, about the choices that individuals make. Do you choose to work during the summer or take a backpacking trip? Do you download a new album or go to a movie? These decisions involve *making a choice* from among a limited number of alternatives—limited because no one can have everything that he or she wants. Every question in economics at its most basic level involves individuals making choices.

But to understand how an economy works, you need to understand more than how individuals make choices. None of us lives like Robinson Crusoe, alone on an island—we must make decisions in an environment that is shaped by the decisions of others. Indeed, in our global economy even the simplest decisions you make—say, what to have for breakfast—are shaped by the decisions of thousands of other people, from the banana grower in Costa Rica who decided to grow the fruit you eat to the farmer in Iowa who provided the corn in your cornflakes. And because each one of us depends on so many others—and they, in turn, depend on us—our choices interact. So, although all economics at a basic level is about individual choice, in order to understand behavior within an economy we must also understand economic *interaction*—how my choices affect your choices, and vice versa.

Many important economic interactions can be understood by looking at the markets for individual goods—for example, the market for corn. But we must also understand economy-wide interactions in order to understand how they can lead to the ups and downs we see in the economy as a whole.

In this section we discuss the study of economics and the difference between microeconomics and macroeconomics. We also introduce the major topics within macroeconomics and the use of models to study the macroeconomy. Finally, we present the production possibilities curve model and use it to understand basic economic activity, including trade between two economies. Because the study of economics relies on graphical models, an appendix on the use of graphs follows the end of this section.

© 13/Tony Hopewell/Ocean/Corbis

MODULE 1

The Study of Economics

In this Module, you will learn to:

- Explain how scarcity and choice are central to the study of economics
- Discuss the importance of opportunity cost in individual choice and decision making
- Explain the difference between positive economics and normative economics
- Identify areas of agreement and disagreement among economists
- Distinguish between microeconomic concepts and macroeconomic concepts

Individual Choice: The Core of Economics

Economics is the study of scarcity and choice.

Individual choice is decisions by individuals about what to do, which necessarily involve decisions about what not to do.

An **economy** is a system for coordinating a society's productive and consumptive activities.

In a **market economy**, the decisions of individual producers and consumers largely determine what, how, and for whom to produce, with little government involvement in the decisions.

In a **command economy**, industry is publicly owned and a central authority makes production and consumption decisions.

Economics is the study of scarcity and choice. Every economic issue involves, at its most basic level, **individual choice**—decisions by individuals about what to do and what *not* to do. In fact, you might say that it isn't economics if it isn't about choice.

Step into a big store such as Walmart or Target. There are thousands of different products available, and it is extremely unlikely that you—or anyone else—could afford to buy everything you might want to have. Besides, there's only so much space in your room. Given the limitations on your budget and your living space, you must choose which products to buy and which to leave on the shelf.

The fact that those products are on the shelf in the first place involves choice—the store manager chose to put them there, and the manufacturers of the products chose to produce them. The **economy** is a system that coordinates choices about production with choices about consumption, and distributes goods and services to the people who want them. The United States has a **market economy**, in which production and consumption are the result of decentralized decisions by many firms and individuals. There is no central authority telling people what to produce or where to ship it. Each individual producer makes what he or she thinks will be most profitable, and each consumer buys what he or she chooses.

An alternative to a market economy is a **command economy**, in which industry is publicly owned and there *is* a central authority making production and consumption decisions. Command economies have been tried, most notably in the Soviet Union between 1917 and 1991, but they didn't work very well. Producers in the Soviet Union routinely found themselves unable to produce because they did not have crucial raw materials, or they succeeded in producing but then found that nobody wanted what the central authority had them produce. Consumers were often unable to find necessary items—command economies are famous for long lines at shops.

At the root of the problem with command economies is a lack of **incentives**, which are rewards or punishments that motivate particular choices. In market economies, producers are free to charge higher prices when there is a shortage of something, and to keep the resulting profits. High prices and profits provide incentives for producers to make more of the most-needed goods and services and to eliminate shortages.

In fact, economists tend to be skeptical of any attempt to change people's behavior that doesn't change their incentives. For example, a plan that calls on manufacturers to reduce pollution voluntarily probably won't be effective; a plan that gives them a financial incentive to do so is more likely to succeed.

Property rights, which establish ownership and grant individuals the right to trade goods and services with each other, create many of the incentives in market economies. With the right to own property comes the incentive to produce things of value, either to keep, or to trade for mutual gain. And ownership creates an incentive to put resources to their best possible use. Property rights to a lake, for example, give the owners an incentive not to pollute that lake if its use for recreation, serenity, or sale has greater value.

In any economy, the decisions of what to do with the next ton of pollution, the next hour of free time, and the next dollar of spending money are *marginal decisions.* They involve trade-offs at the margin: comparing the costs and benefits of doing a little bit more of an activity versus a little bit less. The gain from doing something one more time is called the *marginal benefit.* The cost of doing something one more time is the *marginal cost.* If the marginal benefit of making another car, reading another page, or buying another latte exceeds the marginal cost, the activity should continue. Otherwise, it should not. The study of such decisions, known as **marginal analysis**, plays a central role in economics because the formula of doing things until the marginal benefit no longer exceeds the marginal cost is the key to deciding "how much" to do of any activity.

All economic activities involve individual choice. Let's take a closer look at what this means for the study of economics.

Resources Are Scarce

You can't always get what you want. Almost everyone would like to have a beautiful house in a great location (and help with the housecleaning), two or three luxury cars, and frequent vacations in fancy hotels. But even in a rich country like the United States, not many families can afford all of that. So they must make choices—whether to go to Disney World this year or buy a better car, whether to make do with a small backyard or accept a longer commute in order to live where land is cheaper.

Limited income isn't the only thing that keeps people from having everything they want. Time is also in limited supply: there are only 24 hours in a day. And because the time we have is limited, choosing to spend time on one activity also means choosing not to spend time on a different activity—spending time studying for an exam means forgoing a night at the movies. Indeed, many people feel so limited by the number of hours in the day that they are willing to trade money for time. For example, convenience stores usually charge higher prices than larger supermarkets. But they fulfill a valuable role by catering to customers who would rather pay more than spend the time traveling farther to a supermarket where they might also have to wait in longer lines.

Why do individuals have to make choices? The ultimate reason is that *resources are scarce.* A **resource** is anything that can be used to produce something else. The economy's resources, sometimes called *factors of production,* can be classified into four categories: **land** (including timber, water, minerals, and all other resources that come from nature), **labor** (the effort of workers), **capital** (machinery, buildings, tools, and all other manufactured goods used to make other goods and services), and **entrepreneurship** (risk taking, innovation, and the organization of resources for production). A resource is **scarce**

Incentives are rewards or punishments that motivate particular choices.

Property rights establish ownership and grant individuals the right to trade goods and services with each other.

Marginal analysis is the study of the costs and benefits of doing a little bit more of an activity versus a little bit less.

A **resource** is anything that can be used to produce something else.

Land refers to all resources that come from nature, such as minerals, timber, and petroleum.

Labor is the effort of workers.

Capital refers to manufactured goods used to make other goods and services.

Entrepreneurship describes the efforts of entrepreneurs in organizing resources for production, taking risks to create new enterprises, and innovating to develop new products and production processes.

A **scarce** resource is not available in sufficient quantities to satisfy all the various ways a society wants to use it.

AP® Exam Tip

Students of microeconomics should pay close attention to *marginal analysis,* as it is often tested on the AP® exam. Any time you see "additional," think "marginal."

AP® Exam Tip

Be careful when you see key terms you think you already know, because economists have special meanings for many terms. For example, *scarcity* is about more than just a limited amount of a good. For an economist, scarcity involves trying to satisfy unlimited consumer wants with limited resources. The difference is the relationship to unlimited consumer wants.

AP® Exam Tip

Questions on the AP® exam generally use the term *capital* to refer to the category of factors of production made up of manufactured goods used to make other goods and services. Don't confuse this type of capital with *financial capital* such as money, stocks, and bonds.

when there is not enough of it available to satisfy the various ways a society wants to use it. For example, there are limited supplies of oil and coal, which currently provide most of the energy used to produce and deliver everything we buy. And in a growing world economy with a rapidly increasing human population, even clean air and water have become scarce resources.

Just as individuals must make choices, the scarcity of resources means that society as a whole must make choices. One way for a society to make choices is simply to allow them to emerge as the result of many individual choices. For example, there are only so many hours in a week, and Americans must decide how to spend their time. How many hours will they spend going to supermarkets to get lower prices rather than saving time by shopping at convenience stores? The answer is the sum of individual decisions: each of the millions of individuals in the economy makes his or her own choice about where to shop, and society's choice is simply the sum of those individual decisions.

For various reasons, there are some decisions that a society decides are best not left to individual choice. For example, two of the authors of this book live in an area that until recently was mainly farmland but is now being rapidly built up. Most local residents feel that the community would be a more pleasant place to live if some of the land were left undeveloped. But no individual has an incentive to keep his or her land as open space, rather than sell it to a developer. So a trend has emerged in many communities across the United States of local governments purchasing undeveloped land and preserving it as open space. Decisions about how to use scarce resources are often best left to individuals, but sometimes should be made at a higher, community-wide, level.

The real cost of an item is its **opportunity cost**: what you must give up in order to get it.

Opportunity Cost: The Real Cost of Something Is What You Must Give Up to Get It

Charles D. Winters

Suppose it is the last term before you graduate from high school and you must decide which college to attend. You have narrowed your choices to a small liberal arts college near home or a large state university several hours away. If you decide to attend the local liberal arts college, what is the cost of that decision? Of course, you will have to pay for tuition, books, and housing no matter which college you choose. Added to the cost of choosing the local college is the forgone opportunity to attend the large state university, your next best alternative. Economists call the value of what you must give up when you make a particular choice an **opportunity cost.**

Opportunity costs are crucial to individual choice because, in the end, all costs are opportunity costs. That's because with every choice, an alternative is forgone—money or time spent on one thing can't be spent on another. If you spend $15 on a pizza, you forgo the opportunity to spend that $15 on a steak. If you spend Saturday afternoon at the park, you can't spend Saturday afternoon doing homework. And if you attend one school, you can't attend another.

The park and school examples show that economists are concerned with more than just costs paid in dollars and cents. The forgone opportunity to do homework has no direct monetary cost, but it is an opportunity cost nonetheless. And if the local college and the state university have the same tuition and fees, the cost of choosing one school over the other has nothing to do with payments and everything to do with forgone opportunities.

© ZUMA Press, Inc./Alamy

LeBron James understood the concept of opportunity cost.

Now suppose tuition and fees at the state university are $5,000 less than at the local college. In that case, what you give up to attend the local college is the ability to attend the state university *plus* the enjoyment you could have gained from spending $5,000 on other things. So the opportunity cost of a choice includes all the costs—whether or not they are monetary costs—of making that choice.

The choice to go to college *at all* provides an important final example of opportunity costs. High school graduates can either go to college or seek immediate employment. Even with a full scholarship that would make college "free" in terms of monetary costs, going to college would still be an expensive proposition because most young people, if they were not in college, would have a job. By going to college, students forgo the income they could have earned if they had gone straight to work instead. Therefore, the opportunity cost of attending college is the value of all necessary monetary payments for tuition and fees *plus* the forgone income from the best available job that could take the place of going to college.

For most people the value of a college degree far exceeds the value of alternative earnings, with notable exceptions. The opportunity cost of going to college is high for people who could earn a lot during what would otherwise be their college years. Basketball star LeBron James bypassed college because the opportunity cost would have included his $13 million contract with the Cleveland Cavaliers and even more from corporate sponsors Nike and Coca-Cola. Facebook co-founder Mark Zuckerberg, Microsoft co-founder Bill Gates, and actor Matt Damon are among the high achievers who decided that the opportunity cost of completing college was too much to swallow.

Microeconomics Versus Macroeconomics

We have presented economics as the study of choices and described how, at its most basic level, economics is about individual choice. The branch of economics concerned with how individuals make decisions and how those decisions interact is called **microeconomics**. Microeconomics focuses on choices made by individuals, households, or firms—the smaller parts that make up the economy as a whole.

Macroeconomics focuses on the bigger picture—the overall ups and downs of the economy. When you study macroeconomics, you learn how economists explain these fluctuations and how governments can use economic policy to minimize the damage they cause. Macroeconomics focuses on **economic aggregates**—economic measures such as the unemployment rate, the inflation rate, and gross domestic product—that summarize data across many different markets.

Table 1.1 lists some typical questions that involve economics. A microeconomic version of the question appears on the left, paired with a similar macroeconomic question on the right. By comparing the questions, you can begin to get a sense of the difference between microeconomics and macroeconomics.

Microeconomics is the study of how individuals, households, and firms make decisions and how those decisions interact.

Macroeconomics is concerned with the overall ups and downs of the economy.

Economic aggregates are economic measures that summarize data across many different markets.

Table 1.1 Microeconomic Versus Macroeconomic Questions

Microeconomic Questions	Macroeconomic Questions
Should I go to college or get a job after high school?	How many people are employed in the economy as a whole this year?
What determines the salary that Citibank offers to a new college graduate?	What determines the overall salary levels paid to workers in a given year?
What determines the cost to a high school of offering a new course?	What determines the overall level of prices in the economy as a whole?
What government policies should be adopted to make it easier for low-income students to attend college?	What government policies should be adopted to promote employment and growth in the economy as a whole?
What determines the number of iPhones exported to France?	What determines the overall trade in goods, services, and financial assets between the United States and the rest of the world?

As these questions illustrate, microeconomics focuses on how individuals and firms make decisions, and the consequences of those decisions. For example, a school will use microeconomics to determine how much it would cost to offer a new course, which includes the instructor's salary, the cost of class materials, and so on. By weighing the costs and benefits, the school can then decide whether or not to offer the course. Macroeconomics, in contrast, examines the *overall* behavior of the economy—how the actions of all of the individuals and firms in the economy interact to produce a particular economy-wide level of economic performance. For example, macroeconomics is concerned with the general level of prices in the economy and how high or low they are relative to prices last year, rather than with the price of a particular good or service.

Positive Versus Normative Economics

Economic analysis, as we will see throughout this book, draws on a set of basic economic principles. But how are these principles applied? That depends on the purpose of the analysis. Economic analysis that is used to answer questions about the way the economy works, questions that have definite right and wrong answers, is known as **positive economics**. In contrast, economic analysis that involves saying how the economy *should* work is known as **normative economics**.

Positive economics is the branch of economic analysis that describes the way the economy actually works.

Normative economics makes prescriptions about the way the economy should work.

Imagine that you are an economic adviser to the governor of your state and the governor is considering a change to the toll charged along the state turnpike. Below are three questions the governor might ask you.

1. How much revenue will the tolls yield next year?
2. How much would that revenue increase if the toll were raised from $1.00 to $1.50?
3. Should the toll be raised, bearing in mind that a toll increase would likely reduce traffic and air pollution near the road but impose some financial hardship on frequent commuters?

AP® Exam Tip

In economics, positive statements are about *what is,* while normative statements are about *what should be.*

There is a big difference between the first two questions and the third one. The first two are questions about facts. Your forecast of next year's toll revenue without any increase will be proved right or wrong when the numbers actually come in. Your estimate of the impact of a change in the toll is a little harder to check—the increase in revenue depends on other factors besides the toll, and it may be hard to disentangle the causes of any change in revenue. Still, in principle there is only one right answer.

But the question of whether or not tolls should be raised may not have a "right" answer—two people who agree on the effects of a higher toll could still disagree about whether raising the toll is a good idea. For example, someone who lives near the turnpike but doesn't commute on it will care a lot about noise and air pollution but not so much about commuting costs. A regular commuter who doesn't live near the turnpike will have the opposite priorities.

John Greim/Loop Images/Corbis

Should the toll be raised?

This example highlights a key distinction between the two roles of economic analysis and presents another way to think about the distinction between positive and normative analysis: positive economics is about description, and normative economics is about prescription. Positive economics occupies most of the time and effort of economists.

Looking back at the three questions the governor might ask, it is worth noting a subtle but important difference between questions 1 and 2. Question 1 asks for a simple prediction about next year's revenue—a forecast. Question 2 is a "what if" question, asking how revenue would change if the toll were to increase. Economists are often called upon to answer both types of questions. Economic *models,* which provide simplified representations of reality using, for example, graphs or equations, are especially useful for answering "what if" questions.

The answers to such questions often serve as a guide to policy, but they are still predictions, not prescriptions. That is, they tell you what will happen if a policy is changed, but they don't tell you whether or not that result is good. Suppose that your economic model tells you that the governor's proposed increase in highway tolls will raise property values in communities near the road but will tax or inconvenience people who currently use the turnpike to get to work. Does that information make this proposed toll increase a good idea or a bad one? It depends on whom you ask. As we've just seen, someone who is very concerned with the communities near the road will support the increase, but someone who is very concerned with the welfare of drivers will feel differently. That's a value judgment—it's not a question of positive economic analysis.

Still, economists often do engage in normative economics and give policy advice. How can they do this when there may be no "right" answer? One answer is that economists are also citizens, and we all have our opinions. But economic analysis can often be used to show that some policies are clearly better than others, regardless of individual opinions.

Suppose that policies A and B achieve the same goal, but policy A makes everyone better off than policy B—or at least makes some people better off without making other people worse off. Then A is clearly more beneficial than B. That's not a value judgment: we're talking about how best to achieve a goal, not about the goal itself.

For example, two different policies have been used to help low-income families obtain housing: rent control, which limits the rents landlords are allowed to charge, and rent subsidies, which provide families with additional money with which to pay rent. Almost all economists agree that subsidies are the preferable policy. (In a later module we'll see why this is so.) And so the great majority of economists, whatever their personal politics, favor subsidies over rent control.

When policies can be clearly ranked in this way, then economists generally agree. But it is no secret that economists sometimes disagree.

When and Why Economists Disagree

Economists have a reputation for arguing with each other. Where does this reputation come from? One important answer is that media coverage tends to exaggerate the real differences in views among economists. If nearly all economists agree on an issue—for example, the proposition that rent controls lead to housing shortages—reporters and editors are likely to conclude that there is no story worth covering, and so the professional consensus tends to go unreported. But when there is some issue on which prominent economists take opposing sides—for example, whether cutting taxes right now would help the economy—that does make a good news story. So you hear much more about the areas of disagreement among economists than you do about the many areas of agreement.

It is also worth remembering that economics, unavoidably, is often tied up in politics. On a number of issues, powerful interest groups know what opinions they want to hear. Therefore, they have an incentive to find and promote economists who profess those opinions, which gives these economists a prominence and visibility out of proportion to their support among their colleagues.

Although the appearance of disagreement among economists exceeds the reality, it remains true that economists often *do* disagree about important things. For example, some highly respected economists argue vehemently that the U.S. government should replace the income tax with a *value-added tax* (a national sales tax, which is the main source of government revenue in many European countries). Other equally respected economists disagree. What are the sources of this difference of opinion?

One important source of differences is in values: as in any diverse group of individuals, reasonable people can differ. In comparison to an income tax, a value-added tax typically falls more heavily on people with low incomes. So an economist who values a society with more social and income equality will likely oppose a value-added tax. An economist with different values will be less likely to oppose it.

A second important source of differences arises from the way economists conduct economic analysis. Economists base their conclusions on models formed by making simplifying assumptions about reality. Two economists can legitimately disagree about which simplifications are appropriate—and therefore arrive at different conclusions.

When Economists Agree

"If all the economists in the world were laid end to end, they still couldn't reach a conclusion." So goes one popular economist joke. But do economists really disagree that much?

Not according to a classic survey of members of the American Economic Association, reported in the May 1992 issue of the *American Economic Review*. The authors asked respondents to agree or disagree with a number of statements about the economy; what they found was a high level of agreement among professional economists on many of the statements. At the top of the list, with more than 90% of the economists agreeing, were the statements "Tariffs and import quotas usually reduce general economic welfare" and "A ceiling on rents reduces the quantity and quality of housing available." What's striking about these two statements is that many noneconomists disagree: tariffs and import quotas to keep out foreign-produced goods are favored by many voters, and proposals to do away with rent control in cities like New York and San Francisco have met fierce political opposition.

So is the stereotype of quarreling economists a myth? Not entirely. Economists do disagree quite a lot on some issues, especially in macroeconomics, but they also find a great deal of common ground.

Suppose that the U.S. government was considering a value-added tax. Economist A may rely on a simplification of reality that focuses on the administrative costs of tax systems—that is, the costs of monitoring compliance, processing tax forms, collecting the tax, and so on. This economist might then point to the well-known high costs of administering a value-added tax and argue against the change. But economist B may think that the right way to approach the question is to ignore the administrative costs and focus on how the proposed law would change individual savings behavior. This economist might point to studies suggesting that value-added taxes promote higher consumer saving, a desirable result. Because the economists have made different simplifying assumptions, they arrive at different conclusions. And so the two economists may find themselves on different sides of the issue.

Most such disputes are eventually resolved by the accumulation of evidence that shows which of the various simplifying assumptions made by economists does a better job of fitting the facts. However, in economics, as in any science, it can take a long time before research settles important disputes—decades, in some cases. And since the economy is always changing in ways that make old approaches invalid or raise new policy questions, there are always new issues on which economists disagree. The policy maker must then decide which economist to believe.

MODULE 1 Review

Check Your Understanding

1. Provide an example of a resource from each of the four categories of resources.
2. What type of resource is each of the following?
   - **a.** time spent flipping hamburgers at a restaurant
   - **b.** a bulldozer
   - **c.** a river
3. You make $45,000 per year at your current job with Whiz Kids Consultants. You are considering a job offer from Brainiacs, Inc., which would pay you $50,000 per year. Is each of the following elements an opportunity cost of accepting the new job at Brainiac, Inc.? Answer yes or no, and explain your answer.
   - **a.** the increased time spent commuting to your new job
   - **b.** the $45,000 salary from your old job
   - **c.** the more spacious office at your new job
4. Identify each of the following statements as positive or normative, and explain your answer.
   - **a.** Society should take measures to prevent people from engaging in dangerous personal behavior.
   - **b.** People who engage in dangerous personal behavior impose higher costs on society through higher medical costs.

Tackle the Test: Multiple-Choice Questions

1. Which of the following is an example of a resource?
   - I. petroleum
   - II. a factory
   - III. a cheeseburger dinner

   a. I only
   b. II only
   c. III only
   d. I and II only
   e. I, II, and III

2. Which of the following is not an example of resource scarcity?
   a. There is a finite amount of petroleum in the world.
   b. Farming communities are experiencing droughts.
   c. There are not enough physicians to satisfy all desires for health care in the United States.
   d. Cassette tapes are no longer being produced.
   e. Teachers would like to have more instructional technology in their classrooms.

3. Suppose that you prefer reading a book you already own to watching TV and that you prefer watching TV to listening to music. If these are your only three choices, what is the opportunity cost of reading?
   a. watching TV and listening to music
   b. watching TV
   c. listening to music
   d. sleeping
   e. the price of the book

4. Which of the following statements is/are normative?
   - I. The price of gasoline is rising.
   - II. The price of gasoline is too high.
   - III. Gas prices are expected to fall in the near future.

   a. I only
   b. II only
   c. III only
   d. I and III only
   e. I, II, and III

5. Which of the following questions is studied in microeconomics?
   a. Should I go to college or get a job after I graduate?
   b. What government policies should be adopted to promote employment in the economy?
   c. How many people are employed in the economy this year?
   d. Has the overall level of prices in the economy increased or decreased this year?
   e. What determines the overall salary levels paid to workers in a given year?

Tackle the Test: Free-Response Questions

1. Define the term *resources*, and list the four categories of resources. What characteristic of resources results in the need to make choices?

Rubric for FRQ 1 (6 points)

1 point: Resources are anything that can be used to produce something else.

1 point each: The four categories of the economy's resources are land, labor, capital, and entrepreneurship.

1 point: The characteristic that results in the need to make choices is scarcity.

2. In what type of economic analysis do questions have a "right" or "wrong" answer? In what type of economic analysis do questions not necessarily have a "right" answer? On what type of economic analysis do economists tend to disagree most frequently? Why might economists disagree? Explain.
(5 points)

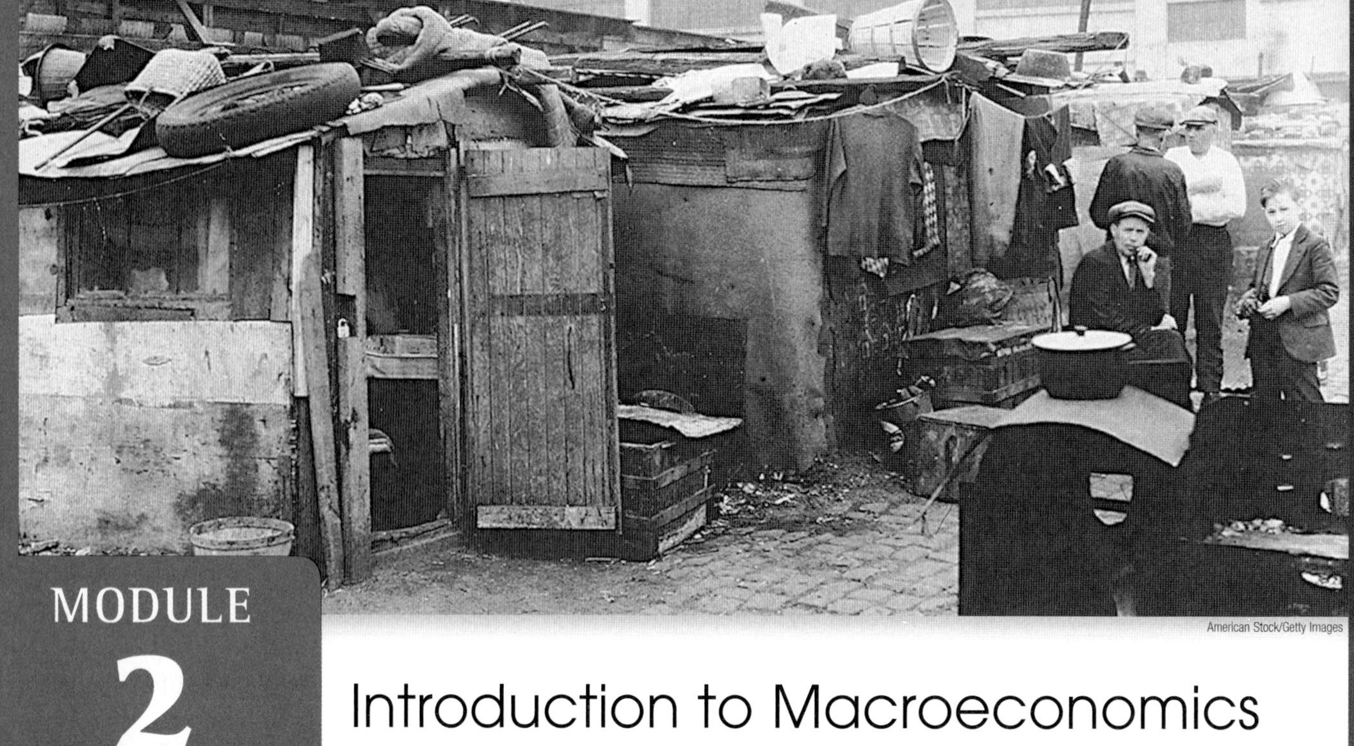
American Stock/Getty Images

MODULE 2 Introduction to Macroeconomics

In this Module, you will learn to:

- Explain what a business cycle is and why policy makers seek to diminish the severity of business cycles
- Describe how employment and unemployment are measured and how they change over the business cycle
- Define aggregate output and explain how it changes over the business cycle
- Define inflation and deflation and explain why price stability is preferred
- Explain how economic growth determines a country's standard of living
- Summarize the crucial role of models—simplified representations of reality—in economics

Today many people enjoy walking, biking, and horseback riding through New York's beautiful Central Park. But in 1932 there were many people living there in squalor. At that time, Central Park contained one of the many "Hoovervilles"–the shantytowns that had sprung up across America as a result of a catastrophic economic slump that had started in 1929. Millions of people were out of work and unable to feed, clothe, and house themselves and their families. Beginning in 1933, the U.S. economy would stage a partial recovery. But joblessness stayed high throughout the 1930s–a period that came to be known as the Great Depression.

Why the name "Hooverville"? These shantytowns were named after President Herbert Hoover, who had been elected president in 1928. When the Depression struck, people blamed the president: neither he nor his economic advisers seemed to understand what had happened or to know what to do to improve the situation. At that time, the field of macroeconomics was still in its infancy. It was only after the economy was plunged into catastrophe that economists began to closely examine how the macroeconomy works and to develop policies that might prevent such disasters in the future. To this day, the effort to understand economic slumps and find ways to prevent them is at the core of macroeconomics.

In this module, we will begin to explore the key features of macroeconomic analysis. We will look at some of the field's major concerns, including business cycles, employment, aggregate output, price stability, and economic growth.

The Business Cycle

The alternation between economic downturns and upturns in the macroeconomy is known as the **business cycle**. A **depression** is a very deep and prolonged downturn; fortunately, the United States hasn't had one since the Great Depression of the 1930s. Instead, we have experienced less prolonged economic downturns known as **recessions**, periods in which output and employment are falling. These are followed by economic upturns—periods in which output and employment are rising—known as **expansions** (sometimes called *recoveries*). According to the National Bureau of Economic Research there have been 11 recessions in the United States since World War II. During that period the average recession lasted 11 months, and the average expansion lasted 58 months. The average length of a business cycle, from the beginning of a recession to the beginning of the next recession, has been 5 years and 8 months. The shortest business cycle was 18 months, and the longest was 10 years and 8 months. The most recent economic downturn started in December 2007 and ended in June 2009. **Figure 2.1** shows the history of the U.S. unemployment rate since 1989 and the timing of business cycles. Recessions are indicated in the figure by the shaded areas.

The business cycle is an enduring feature of the economy. But even though ups and downs seem to be inevitable, most people believe that macroeconomic analysis has guided policies that help smooth out the business cycle and stabilize the economy.

What happens during a business cycle, and how can macroeconomic policies address the downturns? Let's look at three issues: employment and unemployment, aggregate output, and inflation and deflation.

The **business cycle** is the alternation between economic downturns, known as *recessions*, and economic upturns, known as *expansions*.

A **depression** is a very deep and prolonged downturn.

Recessions are periods of economic downturns when output and employment are falling.

Expansions, or recoveries, are periods of economic upturns when output and employment are rising.

AP® Exam Tip

Be prepared to identify the different phases of the business cycle so you can relate each phase to changes in employment, output, and growth.

Figure 2.1 The U.S. Unemployment Rate and the Timing of Business Cycles, 1989-2013

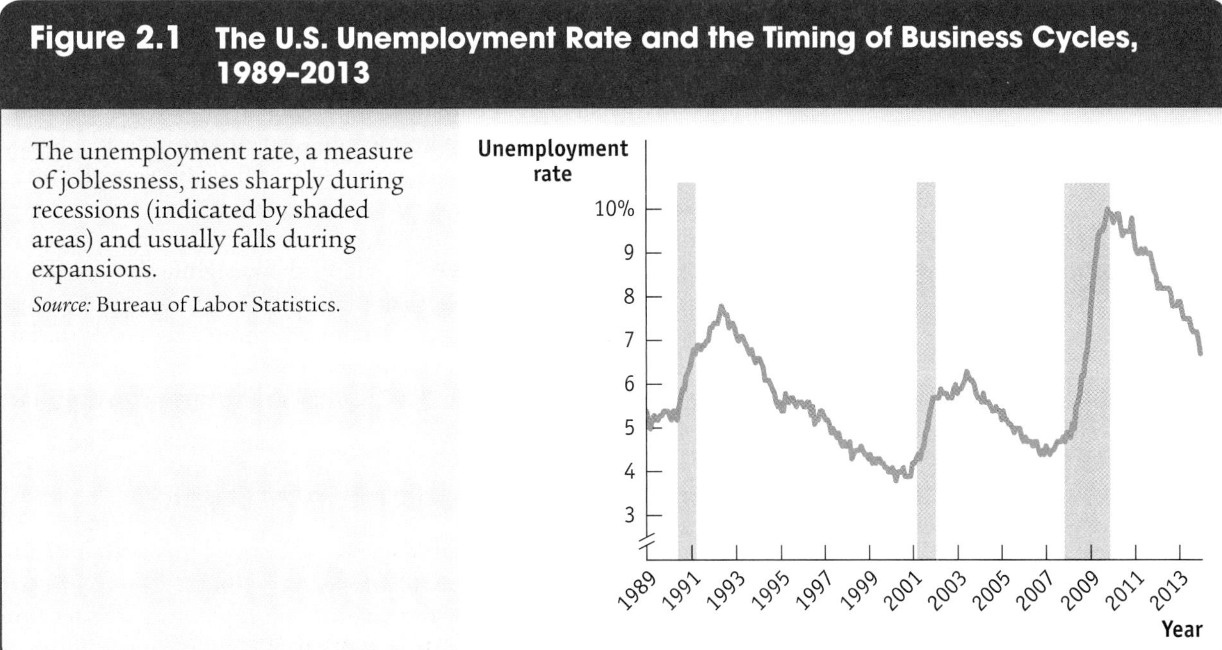

The unemployment rate, a measure of joblessness, rises sharply during recessions (indicated by shaded areas) and usually falls during expansions.

Source: Bureau of Labor Statistics.

Employment, Unemployment, and the Business Cycle

Although not as severe as a depression, a recession is clearly an undesirable event. Like a depression, a recession leads to joblessness, reduced production, reduced incomes, and lower living standards.

To understand how job loss relates to the adverse effects of recessions, we need to understand something about how the labor force is structured. **Employment** is the total number of people who are currently working for pay, and **unemployment** is the total

Employment is the number of people who are currently working for pay in the economy.

Unemployment is the number of people who are actively looking for work but aren't currently employed.

Defining Recessions and Expansions

Some readers may be wondering exactly how recessions and expansions are defined. The answer is that there is no exact definition!

In many countries, economists adopt the rule that a recession is a period of at least two consecutive quarters (a quarter is three months), during which aggregate output falls. The two-consecutive-quarter requirement is designed to avoid classifying brief hiccups in the economy's performance, with no lasting significance, as recessions.

Sometimes, however, this definition seems too strict. For example, an economy that has three months of sharply declining output, then three months of slightly positive growth, then another three months of rapid decline, should surely be considered to have endured a nine-month recession.

In the United States, we try to avoid such misclassifications by assigning the task of determining when a recession begins and ends to an independent panel of experts at the National Bureau of Economic Research (NBER). This panel looks at a variety of economic indicators, with the main focus on employment and production, but ultimately, the panel makes a judgment call.

Sometimes this judgment is controversial. In fact, there is lingering controversy over the 2001 recession. According to the NBER, that recession began in March 2001 and ended in November 2001, when output began rising. Some critics argue, however, that the recession really began several months earlier, when industrial production began falling. Other critics argue that the recession didn't really end in 2001 because employment continued to fall and the job market remained weak for another year and a half.

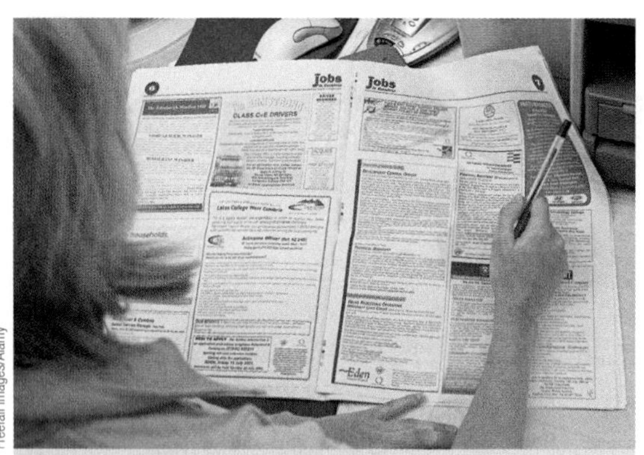

Freefall Images/Alamy

Finding a job was difficult in 2009.

number of people who are actively looking for work but aren't currently employed. A country's **labor force** is the sum of employment and unemployment.

The **unemployment rate**—the percentage of the labor force that is unemployed—is usually a good indicator of what conditions are like in the job market: a high unemployment rate signals a poor job market in which jobs are hard to find; a low unemployment rate indicates a good job market in which jobs are relatively easy to find. In general, during recessions the unemployment rate is rising, and during expansions it is falling. Look again at Figure 2.1, which shows the unemployment rate from 1989 through 2013. The graph shows significant changes in the unemployment rate. Note that even in the most prosperous times there is some unemployment. A booming economy, like that of the late 1990s, can push the unemployment rate down to 4% or even lower. But a severe recession, like the one that began in 2007, can push the unemployment rate into double digits.

The **labor force** is equal to the sum of employment and unemployment.

The **unemployment rate** is the percentage of the labor force that is unemployed.

Output is the quantity of goods and services produced.

Aggregate output is the economy's total production of goods and services for a given time period.

Aggregate Output and the Business Cycle

Rising unemployment is the most painful consequence of a recession, and falling unemployment the most urgently desired feature of an expansion. But the business cycle isn't just about jobs—it's also about **output**: the quantity of goods and services produced. During the business cycle, the economy's level of output and its unemployment rate move in opposite directions. At lower levels of output, fewer workers are needed, and the unemployment rate is relatively high. Growth in output requires the efforts of more workers, which lowers the unemployment rate. To measure the rise and fall of an economy's output, we look at **aggregate output**—the economy's total production of goods and services for a given time period, usually a year. Aggregate output normally falls during recessions and rises during expansions.

Inflation, Deflation, and Price Stability

In 1970 the average production worker in the United States was paid $3.40 an hour. By October 2013 the average hourly earnings for such a worker had risen to $19.65. Three cheers for economic progress!

But wait—American workers were paid much more in 2013, but they also faced a much higher cost of living. In 1970 a dozen eggs cost only about $0.58; by October 2013 that was up to $1.93. The price of a loaf of white bread went from about $0.20 to $1.36. And the price of a gallon of gasoline rose from just $0.33 to $3.43. If we compare the percentage increase in hourly earnings between 1970 and October 2013 with the increases in the prices of some standard items, we see that the average worker's paycheck goes just about as far today as it did in 1970. In other words, the increase in the cost of living wiped out many, if not all, of the wage gains of the typical worker from 1970 to 2013. What caused this situation?

Between 1970 and 2013, the economy experienced substantial **inflation**, a rise in the overall price level. The opposite of inflation is **deflation**, a fall in the overall price level. A change in the prices of a few goods changes the opportunity cost of purchasing those goods but does not constitute inflation or deflation. These terms are reserved for more general changes in the prices of goods and services throughout the economy.

A rising overall price level is **inflation**.

A falling overall price level is **deflation**.

Both inflation and deflation can pose problems for the economy. Inflation discourages people from holding on to cash, because if the price level is rising, cash loses value. That is, if the price level rises, a dollar will buy less than it would before. As we will see later in our more detailed discussion of inflation, in periods of rapidly rising prices, people stop holding cash altogether and instead trade goods for goods.

Deflation can cause the opposite problem. That is, if the overall price level falls, a dollar will buy more than it would before. In this situation it can be more attractive for people with cash to hold on to it rather than to invest in new factories and other productive assets. This can deepen a recession.

In later modules we will look at other costs of inflation and deflation. For now, note that economists have a general goal of **price stability**—meaning that the overall price level is changing only slowly if at all—because it avoids uncertainty about prices and helps to keep the economy stable.

The economy has **price stability** when the overall price level is changing only slowly if at all.

Economic Growth

In 1955 Americans were delighted with the nation's prosperity. The economy was expanding, consumer goods that had been rationed during World War II were available for everyone to buy, and most Americans believed, rightly, that they were better off than citizens of any other nation, past or present. Yet by today's standards Americans were quite poor in 1955. For example, in 1955 only 33% of American homes contained washing machines, and hardly anyone had air conditioning. If we turn the clock back to 1905, we find that life for most Americans was startlingly primitive by today's standards.

20th Century Advertising/Alamy

Why are the vast majority of Americans today able to afford conveniences that many lacked in 1955? The answer is **economic growth**, an increase in the maximum possible output of an economy. Unlike the short-term increases in aggregate output that occur as an economy recovers from a downturn in the business cycle, economic growth is an increase in productive capacity that permits a sustained rise in aggregate output over time. **Figure 2.2** on the next page shows annual figures for U.S. real gross domestic product (GDP) per capita—the value of final goods and services produced in the U.S. per person—from 1900 to 2013. As a result of this economic growth, the U.S. economy's aggregate output per person was more than eight times as large in 2013 as it was in 1900.

Economic growth is fundamental to a nation's prosperity. A sustained rise in output per person allows for higher wages and a rising standard of living. The need for economic growth is urgent in poorer, less developed countries, where a lack of basic necessities makes growth a central concern of economic policy.

As you will see when studying macroeconomics, the goal of economic growth can be in conflict with the goal of hastening recovery from an economic downturn. What is good for economic growth can be bad for short-run stabilization of the business cycle, and vice versa.

Economic growth is an increase in the maximum amount of goods and services an economy can produce.

We have seen that macroeconomics is concerned with the long-run trends in aggregate output as well as the short-run ups and downs of the business cycle. Now that

Figure 2.2 Growth, the Long View

Over the long run, growth in real GDP per capita has dwarfed the ups and downs of the business cycle. Except for the recession that began the Great Depression, recessions are almost invisible.

Sources: Angus Maddison, "Statistics on World Population, GDP and Per Capita GDP, 1-2006 AD," http://www.ggdc.net/maddison; Jutta Bolt and Jan Luiten van Zanden, "The First Update of the Maddison Project; Re-estimating Growth Before 1820;" Bureau of Economic Analysis.

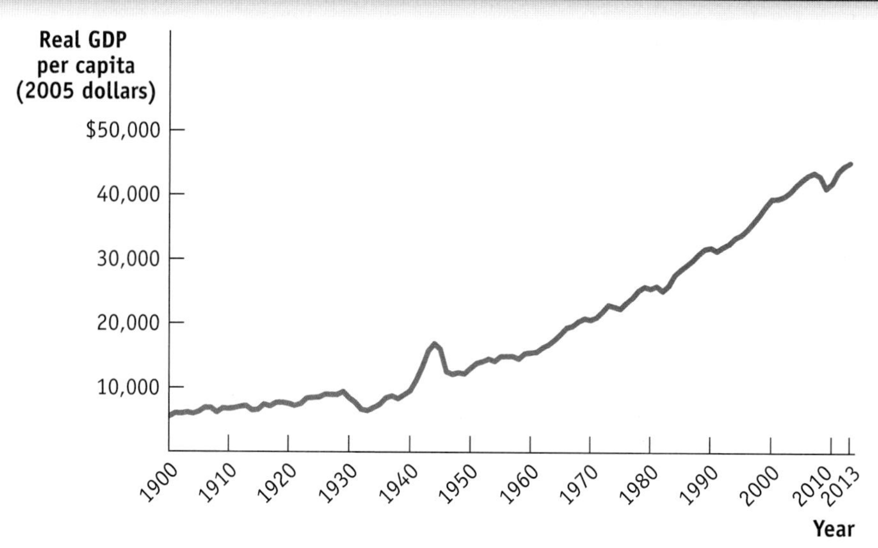

AP® Exam Tip

Economic growth is an increase in the economy's potential output. Changes in real GDP (output) do not necessarily indicate economic growth. Temporary fluctuations in economic conditions often alter real GDP when there has been no change in the economy's potential output.

we have a general understanding of the important topics studied in macroeconomics, we are almost ready to apply economic principles to real economic issues. To do this requires one more step—an understanding of how economists use *models.*

The Use of Models in Economics

In 1901, one year after their first glider flights at Kitty Hawk, the Wright brothers built something else that would change the world—a wind tunnel. This was an apparatus that let them experiment with many different designs for wings and control surfaces. These experiments gave them knowledge that would make heavier-than-air flight possible. Needless to say, testing an airplane design in a wind tunnel is cheaper and safer than building a full-scale version and hoping it will fly. More generally, models play a crucial role in almost all scientific research—economics included.

A **model** is a simplified representation used to better understand a real-life situation.

A **model** is any simplified version of reality that is used to better understand a real-life situation. But how do we create a simplified representation of an economic situation? One possibility—an economist's equivalent of a wind tunnel—is to find or create a real but simplified economy. For example, economists interested in the economic role of money have studied the system of exchange that developed in World War II prison camps, in which cigarettes became a universally accepted form of payment, even among prisoners who didn't smoke.

Another possibility is to simulate the workings of the economy on a computer. For example, when changes in tax law are proposed, government officials use *tax models*—large mathematical computer programs—to assess how the proposed changes would affect different groups of people. Models can also be depicted by graphs and equations. Starting in the next module you will see how graphical models illustrate the relationships between variables and reveal the effects of changes in the economy.

The **other things equal assumption** means that all other relevant factors remain unchanged. This is also known as the *ceteris paribus* assumption.

Models are important because their simplicity allows economists to focus on the influence of only one change at a time. That is, they allow us to hold everything else constant and to study how one change affects the overall economic outcome. So when building economic models, an important assumption is the **other things equal assumption**, which means that all other relevant factors remain unchanged. Sometimes the Latin phrase *ceteris paribus*, which means "other things equal," is used.

But it isn't always possible to find or create a small-scale version of the whole economy, and a computer program is only as good as the data it uses. (Programmers have a saying: garbage in, garbage out.) For many purposes, the most effective form of economic modeling is the construction of "thought experiments": simplified, hypothetical versions of real-life situations. And as you will see throughout this book, economists' models are very often in the form of a graph. In the next module, we will look at the *production possibilities curve*, a model that helps economists think about the choices every economy faces.

MODULE 2 Review

Check Your Understanding

1. Describe two types of models used by economists.
2. Describe who gets hurt in a recession and how they are hurt.

Tackle the Test: Multiple-Choice Questions

1. During the recession phase of a business cycle, which of the following is likely to increase?
   a. the unemployment rate
   b. the price level
   c. economic growth rates
   d. the labor force
   e. wages
2. The labor force is made up of everyone who is
   a. employed.
   b. old enough to work.
   c. actively seeking work.
   d. employed or unemployed.
   e. employed or capable of working.
3. Which of the following provides a long-term increase in the productive capacity of an economy?
   a. an expansion
   b. a recovery
   c. a recession
   d. a depression
   e. economic growth
4. Which of the following is the most likely result of inflation?
   a. falling employment
   b. a dollar will buy more than it did before
   c. people are discouraged from holding cash
   d. price stability
   e. low aggregate output per capita
5. The other things equal assumption allows economists to
   a. avoid making assumptions about reality.
   b. focus on the effects of only one change at a time.
   c. oversimplify.
   d. allow nothing to change in their model.
   e. reflect all aspects of the real world in their model.

Tackle the Test: Free-Response Questions

1. Define an expansion and economic growth, and explain the difference between the two concepts.

Rubric for FRQ 1 (3 points)

1 point: An expansion is the period of recovery after an economic downturn.

1 point: Economic growth is an increase in the productive capacity of the economy.

1 point: An expansion can occur regardless of any increase in the economy's long-term potential for production, and it only lasts until the next downturn, while economic growth increases the economy's ability to produce more goods and services over the long term.

2. Define inflation, and explain why an increase in the price of donuts does not indicate that inflation has occurred. **(2 points)**

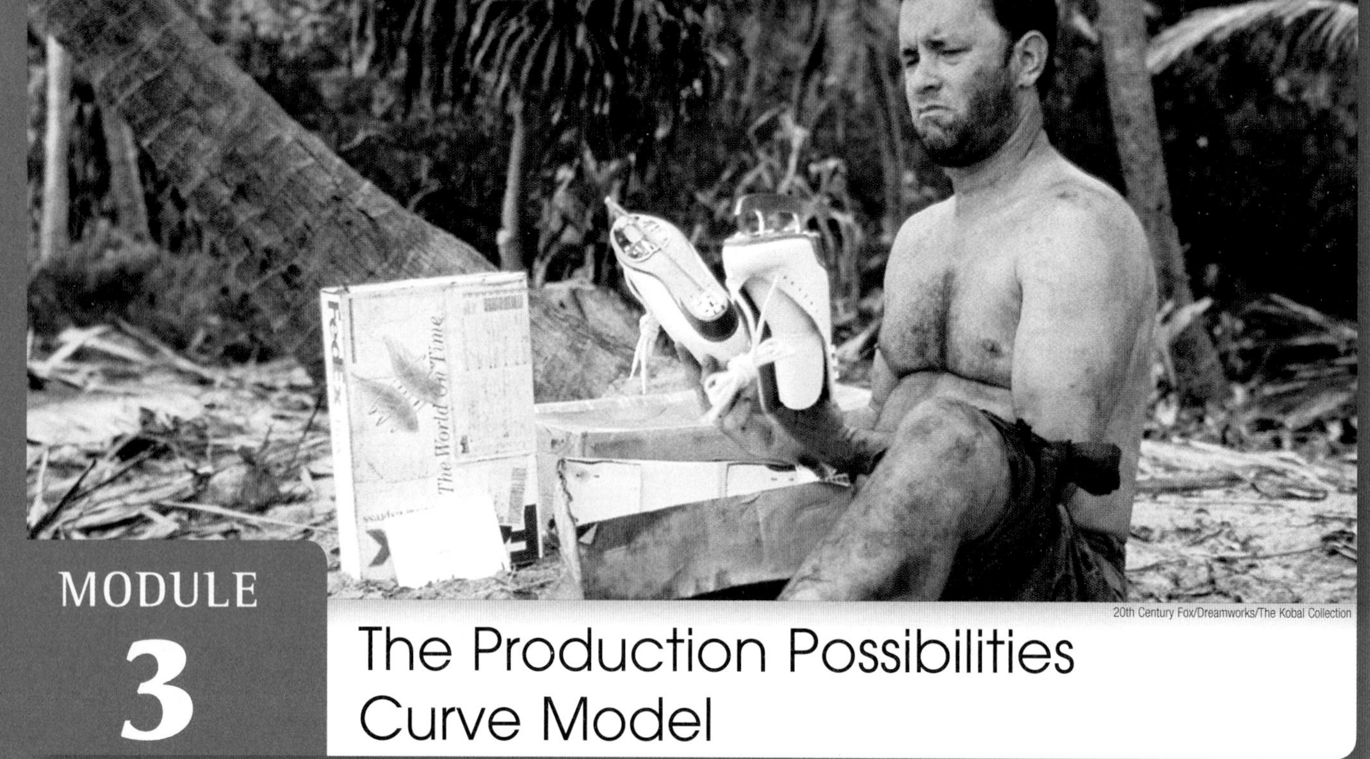

20th Century Fox/Dreamworks/The Kobal Collection

MODULE 3

The Production Possibilities Curve Model

In this Module, you will learn to:

- Explain the importance of trade-offs in economic analysis
- Describe what the production possibilities curve model tells us about efficiency, opportunity cost, and economic growth
- Explain why increases in the availability of resources and improvements in technology are the two sources of economic growth

A good economic model can be a tremendous aid to understanding. In this module, we look at the *production possibilities curve*, a model that helps economists think about the *trade-offs* every economy faces. The production possibilities curve helps us understand three important aspects of the real economy: efficiency, opportunity cost, and economic growth.

Trade-offs: The Production Possibilities Curve

The 2000 hit movie *Cast Away,* starring Tom Hanks, was an update of the classic story of Robinson Crusoe, the hero of Daniel Defoe's eighteenth-century novel. Hanks played the role of a sole survivor of a plane crash who was stranded on a remote island. As in the original story of Robinson Crusoe, the Hanks character had limited resources: the natural resources of the island, a few items he managed to salvage from the plane, and, of course, his own time and effort. With only these resources, he had to make a life. In effect, he became a one-man economy.

You make a **trade-off** when you give up something in order to have something else.

One of the important principles of economics we introduced in Module 1 was that resources are scarce. As a result, any economy—whether it contains one person or millions of people—faces trade-offs. You make a **trade-off** when you give up something in order to have something else. For example, if a castaway devotes more resources to catching fish, he benefits by catching more fish, but he cannot use those same resources to gather coconuts, so the trade-off is that he has fewer coconuts.

To think about the trade-offs necessary in any economy, economists often use the **production possibilities curve** model. The idea behind this model is to improve our understanding of trade-offs by considering a simplified economy that produces only two goods. This simplification enables us to show the trade-offs graphically.

The **production possibilities curve** illustrates the trade-offs facing an economy that produces only two goods. It shows the maximum quantity of one good that can be produced for each possible quantity of the other good produced.

Figure 3.1 shows a hypothetical production possibilities curve for Tom, a castaway alone on an island, who must make a trade-off between fish production and coconut production. The curve shows the maximum quantity of fish Tom can catch during a week *given* the quantity of coconuts he gathers, and vice versa. That is, it answers questions of the form, "What is the maximum quantity of fish Tom can catch if he also gathers 9 (or 15, or 30) coconuts?"

Figure 3.1 The Production Possibilities Curve

The production possibilities curve illustrates the trade-offs facing an economy that produces two goods. It shows the maximum quantity of one good that can be produced, given the quantity of the other good produced. Here, the maximum quantity of coconuts that Tom can gather depends on the quantity of fish he catches, and vice versa. His feasible production is shown by the area *inside* or *on* the curve. Production at point *C* is feasible but not efficient. Points *A* and *B* are feasible and *productively efficient*, but point *D* is not feasible.

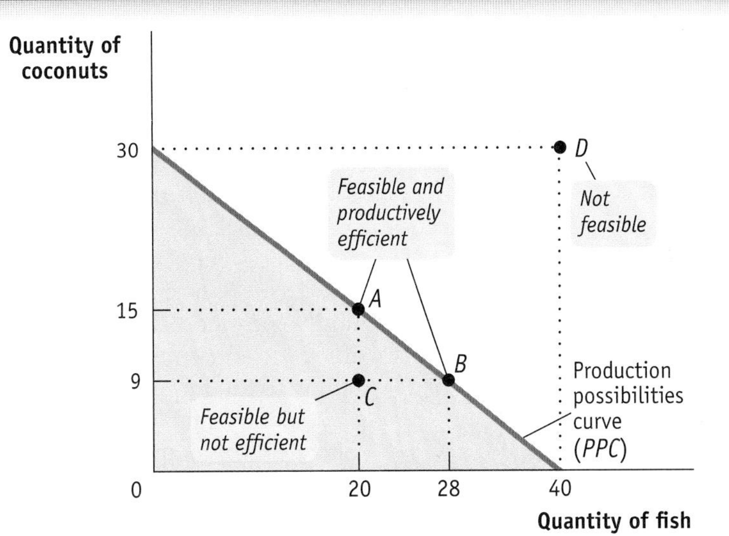

There is a crucial distinction between points *inside* or *on* the production possibilities curve (the shaded area) and points *outside* the production possibilities curve. If a production point lies inside or on the curve—like point *C*, at which Tom catches 20 fish and gathers 9 coconuts—it is feasible. After all, the curve tells us that if Tom catches 20 fish, he could also gather a maximum of 15 coconuts, so he could certainly gather 9 coconuts. However, a production point that lies outside the curve—such as point *D*, which would have Tom catching 40 fish and gathering 30 coconuts—isn't feasible.

In Figure 3.1 the production possibilities curve intersects the horizontal axis at 40 fish. This means that if Tom devoted all his resources to catching fish, he would catch 40 fish per week but would have no resources left over to gather coconuts. The production possibilities curve intersects the vertical axis at 30 coconuts. This means that if Tom devoted all his resources to gathering coconuts, he could gather 30 coconuts per week but would have no resources left over to catch fish. Thus, if Tom wants 30 coconuts, the trade-off is that he can't have any fish.

The curve also shows less extreme trade-offs. For example, if Tom decides to catch 20 fish, he would be able to gather at most 15 coconuts; this production choice is illustrated by point *A*. If Tom decides to catch 28 fish, he could gather at most 9 coconuts, as shown by point *B*.

Thinking in terms of a production possibilities curve simplifies the complexities of reality. The real-world economy produces millions of different goods. Even a castaway on an island would produce more than two different items (for example, he would need clothing and housing as well as food). But in this model we imagine an economy that produces only two goods, because in a model with many goods, it would be much harder to study trade-offs, efficiency, and economic growth.

AP® Exam Tip

Be prepared to draw a correctly labeled production possibilities curve and use it to identify opportunity cost, efficient points, inefficient points, and unattainable points. Unemployment results in production at a point below the production possibilities curve. Most production possibilities curves are concave to the origin, as shown in Figure 3.2 on page 19, due to the specialization of resources.

Efficiency

An economy is **efficient** if there is no way to make anyone better off without making at least one person worse off.

An economy achieves **productive efficiency** if it produces at a point on its production possibilities curve.

An economy achieves **allocative efficiency** if it produces at the point along its production possibilities curve that makes consumers as well off as possible.

The production possibilities curve is useful for illustrating the general economic concept of efficiency. An economy is **efficient** if there are no missed opportunities—meaning that there is no way to make some people better off without making other people worse off. For example, suppose a course you are taking meets in a classroom that is too small for the number of students—some may be forced to sit on the floor or stand—despite the fact that a larger classroom nearby is empty during the same period. Economists would say that this is an *inefficient* use of resources because there is a way to make some people better off without making anyone worse off—after all, the larger classroom is empty. The school is not using its resources efficiently. When an economy is using all of its resources efficiently, the only way one person can be made better off is by rearranging the use of resources in such a way that the change makes someone else worse off. So in our classroom example, if all larger classrooms were already fully occupied, we could say that the school was run in an efficient way; your classmates could be made better off only by making people in the larger classroom worse off—by moving them to the room that is too small.

Returning to our castaway example, as long as Tom produces a combination of coconuts and fish that is on the production possibilities curve, his production is efficient. At point *A*, the 15 coconuts he gathers are the maximum quantity he can get *given* that he has chosen to catch 20 fish; at point *B*, the 9 coconuts he gathers are the maximum he can get *given* his choice to catch 28 fish; and so on. If an economy is producing at a point on its production possibilities curve, we say that the economy has achieved **productive efficiency**.

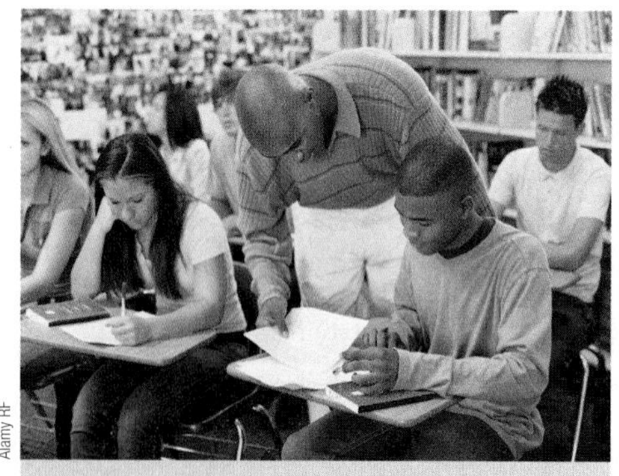

Alamy RF

A crowded classroom reflects inefficiency if switching to a larger classroom would make some students better off without making anyone worse off.

But suppose that for some reason Tom was at point *C*, producing 20 fish and 9 coconuts. Then this one-person economy would definitely not be productively efficient and would therefore be inefficient: it is missing the opportunity to produce more of both goods.

Another example of inefficiency in production occurs when people in an economy are involuntarily unemployed: they want to work but are unable to find jobs. When that happens, the economy is not productively efficient because it could produce more output if those people were employed. The production possibilities curve shows the amount that can *possibly* be produced if all resources are fully employed. In other words, changes in unemployment move the economy closer to, or further away from, the production possibilities curve (*PPC*). But the curve itself is determined by what would be possible if there were no unemployment in the economy. Greater unemployment is represented by points farther below the *PPC*—the economy is not reaching its possibilities if it is not using all of its resources. Lower unemployment is represented by points closer to the *PPC*—as unemployment decreases, the economy moves closer to reaching its possibilities.

Although the production possibilities curve helps clarify what it means for an economy to achieve productive efficiency, it's important to understand that productive efficiency is only *part* of what's required for the economy as a whole to be efficient. Efficiency also requires that the economy allocate its resources so that consumers are as well off as possible. If an economy does this, we say that it has achieved **allocative efficiency**. To see why allocative efficiency is as important as productive efficiency, notice that points *A* and *B* in Figure 3.1 both represent situations in which the economy is productively efficient, because in each case it can't produce more of one good without producing less of the other. But these two situations may not be equally desirable. Suppose that Tom prefers point *B* to point *A*—that is, he would rather consume 28 fish and 9 coconuts than 20 fish and 15 coconuts. Then point *A* is inefficient from the point of view of the economy as a whole: it's possible to make Tom better off without making anyone else worse off. (Of course, in this castaway economy there isn't anyone else; Tom is all alone.)

This example shows that efficiency for the economy as a whole requires *both* productive and allocative efficiency. To be efficient, an economy must produce as much of each good as it can, given the production of other goods, and it must also produce the mix of goods that people want to consume.

Creativ Studio Heinemann/Getty Images

Opportunity Cost

The production possibilities curve is also useful as a reminder that the true cost of any good is not only its price, but also everything else in addition to money that must be given up in order to get that good—the *opportunity cost*. If, for example, Tom decides to go from point *A* to point *B*, he will produce 8 more fish but 6 fewer coconuts. So the opportunity cost of those 8 fish is the 6 coconuts not gathered. Since 8 extra fish have an opportunity cost of 6 coconuts, 1 fish has an opportunity cost of $6/8 = 3/4$ of a coconut.

Is the opportunity cost of an extra fish in terms of coconuts always the same, no matter how many fish Tom catches? In the example illustrated by Figure 3.1, the answer is yes. If Tom increases his catch from 28 to 40 fish, an increase of 12, the number of coconuts he gathers falls from 9 to zero. So his opportunity cost per additional fish is $9/12 = 3/4$ of a coconut, the same as it was when his catch went from 20 fish to 28. However, the fact that in this example the opportunity cost of an additional fish in terms of coconuts is always the same is a result of an assumption we've made, an assumption that's reflected in the way Figure 3.1 is drawn. Specifically, whenever we assume that the opportunity cost of an additional unit of a good doesn't change regardless of the output mix, the production possibilities curve is a straight line.

Moreover, as you might have already guessed, the slope of a straight-line production possibilities curve is equal to the opportunity cost—specifically, the opportunity cost for the good measured on the horizontal axis in terms of the good measured on the vertical axis. In Figure 3.1, the production possibilities curve has a *constant slope* of $-3/4$, implying that Tom faces a *constant opportunity cost* per fish equal to $3/4$ of a coconut. (A review of how to calculate the slope of a straight line is found in the Section 1 Appendix.) This is the simplest case, but the production possibilities curve model can also be used to examine situations in which opportunity costs change as the mix of output changes.

Figure 3.2 illustrates a different assumption, a case in which Tom faces *increasing opportunity cost*. Here, the more fish he catches, the more coconuts he has to give up to catch an additional fish, and vice versa. For example, to go from producing zero fish to producing 20 fish, he has to give up 5 coconuts. That is, the opportunity cost of those 20 fish is 5 coconuts. But to increase his fish production from 20 to 40—that is, to produce an additional 20 fish—he must give up 25 more coconuts, a much higher opportunity cost. As you can see in Figure 3.2, when opportunity costs are increasing

AP® Exam Tip

Opportunity Cost = Opportunity Lost (The financial or nonfinancial cost of a choice not taken.)

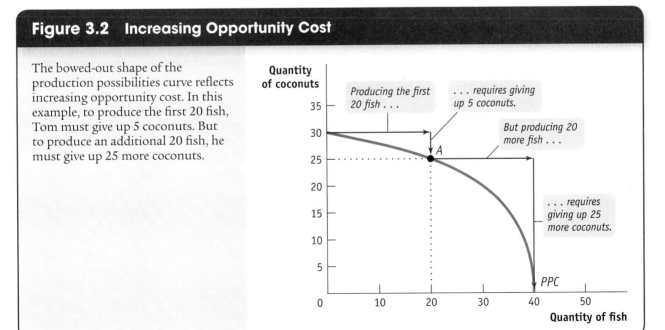

Figure 3.2 Increasing Opportunity Cost

The bowed-out shape of the production possibilities curve reflects increasing opportunity cost. In this example, to produce the first 20 fish, Tom must give up 5 coconuts. But to produce an additional 20 fish, he must give up 25 more coconuts.

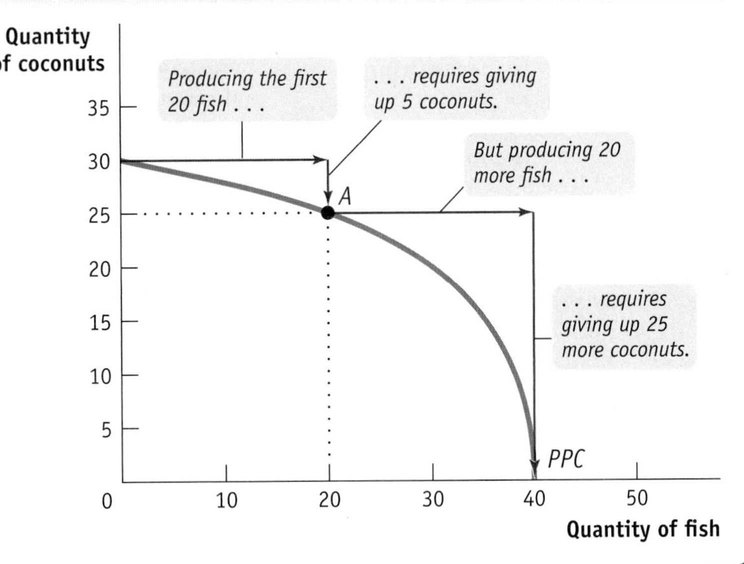

rather than constant, the production possibilities curve is a bowed-out curve rather than a straight line.

Although it's often useful to work with the simple assumption that the production possibilities curve is a straight line, economists believe that in reality, opportunity costs are typically increasing. When only a small amount of a good is produced, the opportunity cost of producing that good is relatively low because the economy needs to use only those resources that are especially well suited for its production. For example, if an economy grows only a small amount of corn, that corn can be grown in places where the soil and climate are perfect for growing corn but less suitable for growing anything else, such as wheat. So growing that corn involves giving up only a small amount of potential wheat output. Once the economy grows a lot of corn, however, land that is well suited for wheat but isn't so great for corn must be used to produce corn anyway. As a result, the additional corn production involves sacrificing considerably more wheat production. In other words, as more of a good is produced, its opportunity cost typically rises because well-suited inputs are used up and less adaptable inputs must be used instead.

Economic Growth

Finally, the production possibilities curve helps us understand what it means to talk about *economic growth*. We introduced the concept of economic growth in Module 2, saying that it allows *a sustained rise in aggregate output*. We learned that economic growth is one of the fundamental features of the economy. But are we really justified in saying that the economy has grown over time? After all, although the U.S. economy produces more of many things than it did a century ago, it produces less of other things—for example, horse-drawn carriages. In other words, production of many goods is actually down. So how can we say for sure that the economy as a whole has grown?

The answer, illustrated in **Figure 3.3**, is that economic growth means an *expansion of the economy's production possibilities:* the economy *can* produce more of everything. For example, if Tom's production is initially at point *A* (20 fish and 25 coconuts), economic growth means that he could move to point *E* (25 fish and 30 coconuts). Point *E* lies outside the original curve, so in the production possibilities curve model, growth is shown as an outward shift of the curve. Unless the *PPC* shifts outward, the points beyond the *PPC* are unattainable. Those points beyond a given *PPC* are beyond the economy's possibilities.

Figure 3.3 Economic Growth

Economic growth results in an *outward shift* of the production possibilities curve because production possibilities are expanded. The economy can now produce more of everything. For example, if production is initially at point *A* (20 fish and 25 coconuts), it could move to point *E* (25 fish and 30 coconuts).

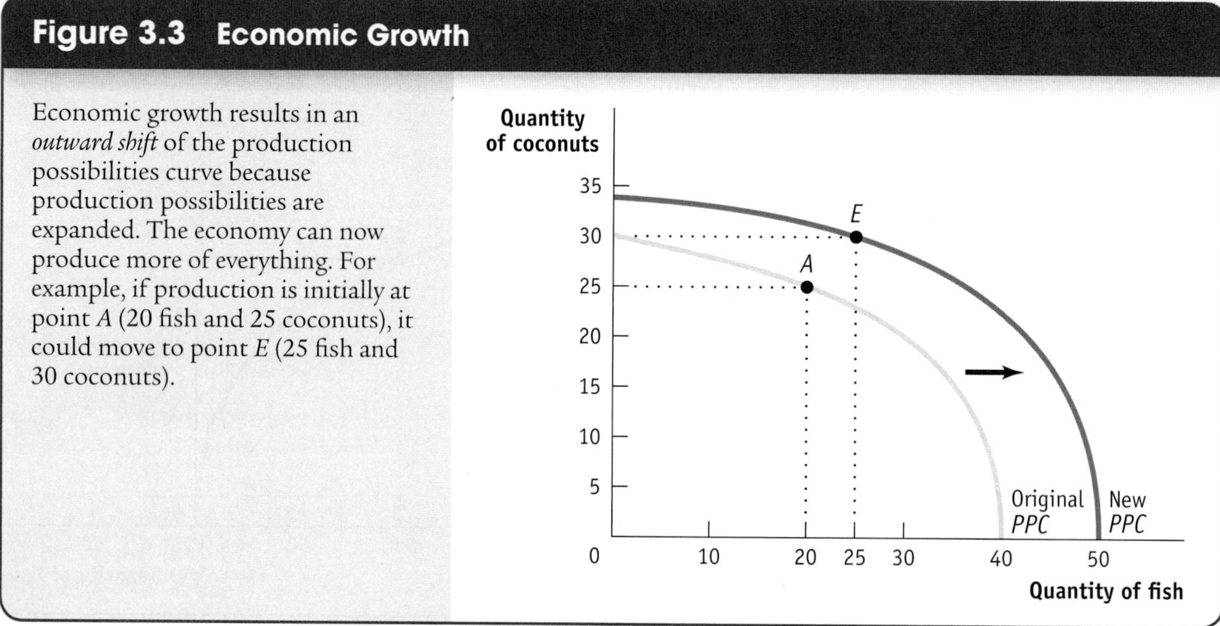

What can cause the production possibilities curve to shift outward? There are two general sources of economic growth. One is an increase in the resources used to produce goods and services: labor, land, capital, and entrepreneurship. To see how adding to an economy's resources leads to economic growth, suppose that Tom finds a fishing net washed ashore on the beach. The fishing net is a resource he can use to produce more fish in the course of a day spent fishing. We can't say how many more fish Tom will catch; that depends on how much time he decides to spend fishing now that he has the net. But because the net makes his fishing more productive, he can catch more fish without reducing the number of coconuts he gathers, or he can gather more coconuts without reducing his fish catch. So his production possibilities curve shifts outward.

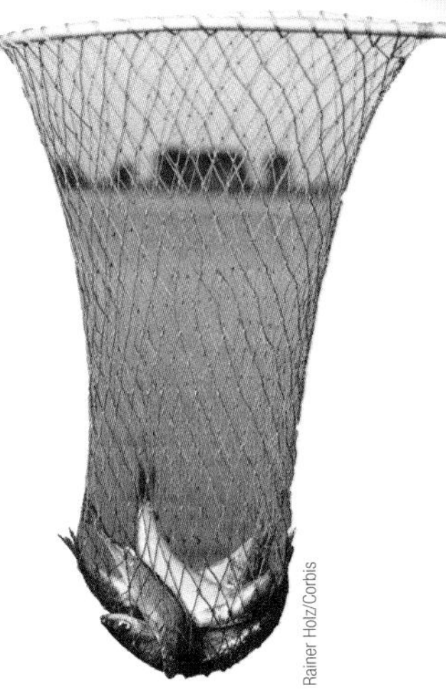
Rainer Holz/Corbis

The other source of economic growth is progress in **technology**, the technical means for the production of goods and services. Suppose Tom figures out a better way either to catch fish or to gather coconuts—say, by inventing a fishing hook or a wagon for transporting coconuts. Either invention would shift his production possibilities curve outward. However, the shift would not be a simple outward expansion of every point along the *PPC*. Technology specific to the production of only one good has no effect if all resources are devoted to the other good: a fishing hook will be of no use if Tom produces nothing but coconuts. So the point on the *PPC* that represents the number of coconuts that can be produced if there is no fishing will not change. In real-world economies, innovations in the techniques we use to produce goods and services have been a crucial force behind economic growth.

Technology is the technical means for producing goods and services.

Again, economic growth means an increase in what the economy *can* produce. What the economy actually produces depends on the choices people make. After his production possibilities expand, Tom might not choose to produce both more fish and more coconuts; he might choose to increase production of only one good, or he might even choose to produce less of one good. For example, if he gets better at catching fish, he might decide to go on an all-fish diet and skip the coconuts, just as the introduction of motor vehicles led most people to give up horse-drawn carriages. But even if, for some reason, he chooses to produce either fewer coconuts or fewer fish than before, we would still say that his economy has grown, because he *could* have produced more of everything. If an economy's production possibilities curve shifts inward, the economy has become smaller. This could happen if the economy loses resources or technology (for example, if it experiences war or a natural disaster).

The production possibilities curve is a very simplified model of an economy, yet it teaches us important lessons about real-life economies. It gives us our first clear sense of what constitutes economic efficiency, it illustrates the concept of opportunity cost, and it makes clear what economic growth is all about.

MODULE 3 Review

Check Your Understanding

1. True or false? Explain your answer.
   a. An increase in the amount of resources available to Tom for use in producing coconuts and fish does not change his production possibilities curve.
   b. A technological change that allows Tom to catch more fish relative to any amount of coconuts gathered results in a change in his production possibilities curve.
   c. Points inside a production possibilities curve are efficient and points outside a production possibilities curve are inefficient.

Tackle the Test: Multiple-Choice Questions

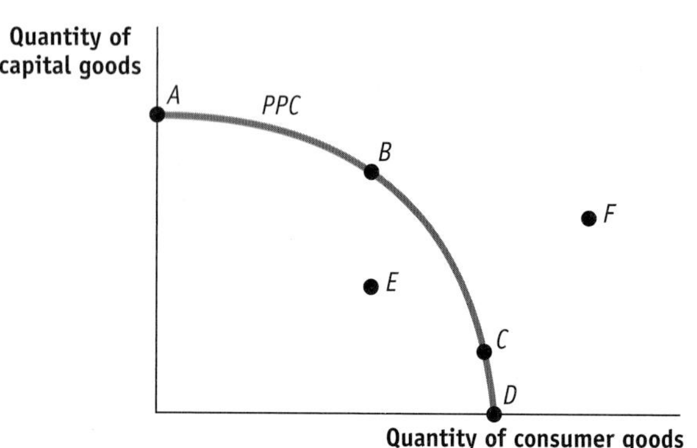

Refer to the graph above to answer the following questions.

1. Which point(s) on the graph represent productive efficiency?
   a. *B* and *C*
   b. *A* and *D*
   c. *A, B, C,* and *D*
   d. *A, B, C, D,* and *E*
   e. *A, B, C, D, E,* and *F*

2. For this economy, an increase in the quantity of capital goods produced without a corresponding decrease in the quantity of consumer goods produced
   a. cannot happen because there is always an opportunity cost.
   b. is represented by a movement from point *E* to point *A*.
   c. is represented by a movement from point *C* to point *B*.
   d. is represented by a movement from point *E* to point *B*.
   e. is only possible with an increase in resources or technology.

3. An increase in unemployment could be represented by a movement from point
   a. *D* to point *C*.
   b. *B* to point *A*.
   c. *C* to point *F*.
   d. *B* to point *E*.
   e. *E* to point *B*.

4. Which of the following might allow this economy to move from point *B* to point *F*?
   a. more workers
   b. discovery of new resources
   c. building new factories
   d. technological advances
   e. all of the above

5. This production possibilities curve shows the trade-off between consumer goods and capital goods. Since capital goods are a resource, an increase in the production of capital goods today will increase the economy's production possibilities in the future. Therefore, all other things equal (*ceteris paribus*), producing at which point today will result in the largest outward shift of the *PPC* in the future?
   a. *A*
   b. *B*
   c. *C*
   d. *D*
   e. *E*

Tackle the Test: Free-Response Questions

1. Refer to the graph below. Assume that the country is producing at point *C*.

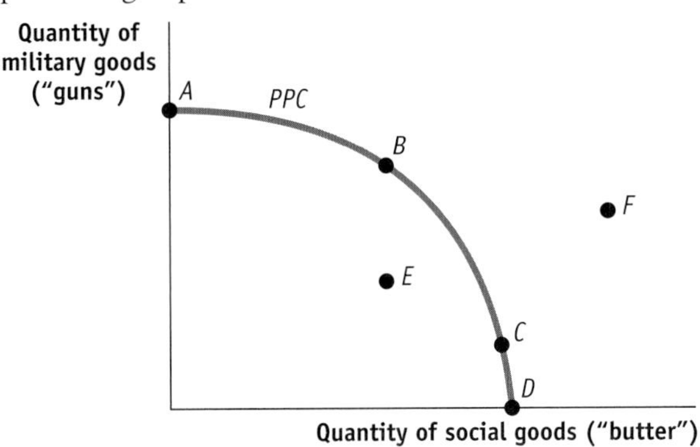

a. Does this country's production possibilities curve exhibit increasing opportunity costs? Explain.

b. If this country were to go to war, the most likely move would be from point *C* to which point? Explain.

c. If the economy entered into a recession, the country would move from point *C* to which point? Explain.

Rubric for FRQ 1 (6 points)

1 point: Yes

1 point: The *PPC* is concave (bowed outward), so with each additional unit of butter produced, the opportunity cost in terms of gun production (indicated by the slope of the line) increases. Likewise, as more guns are produced, the opportunity cost in terms of butter increases.

1 point: *B*

1 point: The country would choose an efficient point with more (but not all) military goods with which to fight the war. Point *A* would be an unlikely choice because at that point there is no production of any social goods, some of which are needed to maintain a minimal standard of living.

1 point: *E*

1 point: A recession, which causes unemployment, is represented by a point below the *PPC*.

2. Assume that an economy can choose between producing food and producing shelter at a constant opportunity cost. Draw a correctly labeled production possibilities curve for the economy. On your graph:

a. Use the letter *E* to label one of the points that is productively efficient.

b. Use the letter *U* to label one of the points at which there might be unemployment.

c. Use the letter *I* to label one of the points that is not feasible.

(5 points)

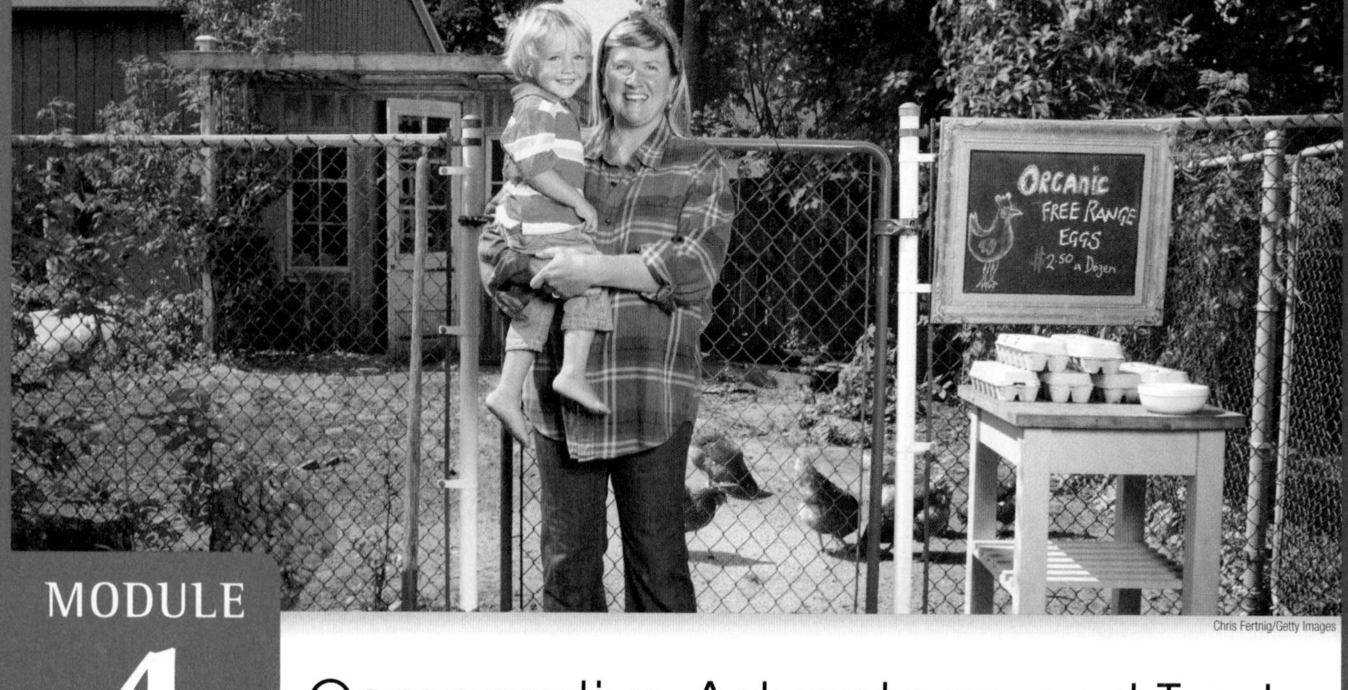

Chris Fertnig/Getty Images

MODULE 4 Comparative Advantage and Trade

In this Module, you will learn to:

- Explain how trade leads to gains for an individual or an economy
- Explain the difference between absolute advantage and comparative advantage
- Describe how comparative advantage leads to gains from trade in the global marketplace

Gains from Trade

A family could try to take care of all its own needs—growing its own food, sewing its own clothing, providing itself with entertainment, and writing its own economics textbooks. But trying to live that way would be very hard. The key to a much better standard of living for everyone is **trade**, in which people divide tasks among themselves and each person provides a good or service that other people want in return for different goods and services that he or she wants.

In a market economy, individuals engage in **trade**: they provide goods and services to others and receive goods and services in return.

There are **gains from trade**: people can get more of what they want through trade than they could if they tried to be self-sufficient. This increase in output is due to **specialization**: each person specializes in the task that he or she is good at performing.

The reason we have an economy, rather than many self-sufficient individuals, is that there are **gains from trade**: by dividing tasks and trading, two people (or 7 billion people) can each get more of what they want than they could get by being self-sufficient. Gains from trade arise, in particular, from this division of tasks, which economists call **specialization**—a situation in which different people each engage in a different task.

The advantages of specialization, and the resulting gains from trade, were the starting point for Adam Smith's 1776 book *The Wealth of Nations*, which many regard as the beginning of economics as a discipline. Smith's book begins with a description of an eighteenth-century pin factory where, rather than each of the 10 workers making a pin from start to finish, each worker specialized in one of the many steps in pin-making:

> One man draws out the wire, another straights it, a third cuts it, a fourth points it, a fifth grinds it at the top for receiving the head; to make the head requires two or three distinct operations; to put it on, is a particular business, to whiten the pins is another; it is even a trade by itself to put them into the paper; and the important business of making a pin is, in this manner, divided into about eighteen distinct operations. . . . Those ten persons, therefore, could make among them upwards of forty-eight thousand pins in a day. But if they had all wrought separately and independently, and without any of them having been educated to this particular business, they certainly could not each of them have made twenty, perhaps not one pin a day. . . .

AP® Exam Tip

Take note! The content in this module frequently shows up in the free-response and multiple-choice sections of the AP® exam.

The same principle applies when we look at how people divide tasks among themselves and trade in an economy. The economy, as a whole, can produce more when each person *specializes* in a task and *trades* with others.

The benefits of specialization are the reason a person typically focuses on the production of only one type of good or service. It takes many years of study and experience to become a doctor; it also takes many years of study and experience to become a commercial airline pilot. Many doctors might have the potential to become excellent pilots, and vice versa, but it is very unlikely that anyone who decided to pursue both careers would be as good a pilot or as good a doctor as someone who specialized in only one of those professions. So it is to everyone's advantage when individuals specialize in their career choices.

Markets are what allow a doctor and a pilot to specialize in their respective fields. Because markets for commercial flights and for doctors' services exist, a doctor is assured that she can find a flight and a pilot is assured that he can find a doctor. As long as individuals know that they can find the goods and services that they want in the market, they are willing to forgo self-sufficiency and are willing to specialize.

Comparative Advantage and Gains from Trade

Roderick Chen/Getty Images

The production possibilities curve model is particularly useful for illustrating gains from trade—trade based on *comparative advantage*. Let's stick with Tom being stranded on his island, but now let's suppose that a second castaway, who just happens to be named Hank, is washed ashore. Can Tom and Hank benefit from trading with each other?

It's obvious that there will be potential gains from trade if the two castaways do different things particularly well. For example, if Tom is a skilled fisherman and Hank is very good at climbing trees, clearly it makes sense for Tom to catch fish and Hank to gather coconuts—and for the two men to trade the products of their efforts.

But one of the most important insights in all of economics is that there are gains from trade even if one of the trading parties isn't especially good at anything. Suppose, for example, that Hank is less well suited to primitive life than Tom; he's not nearly as good at catching fish, and compared to Tom, even his coconut-gathering leaves something to be desired. Nonetheless, what we'll see is that both Tom and Hank can live better by trading with each other than either could alone.

For the purposes of this example, let's go back to the simple case of straight-line production possibilities curves. Tom's production possibilities are represented by the production possibilities curve in panel (a) of **Figure 4.1** on the next page, which is the same as the production possibilities curve in Figure 3.1 (page 17). According to this *PPC*, Tom could catch 40 fish, but only if he gathered no coconuts, and he could gather 30 coconuts, but only if he caught no fish. Recall that this means that the slope of his production possibilities curve is $-3/4$: his opportunity cost of 1 fish is $3/4$ of a coconut.

Panel (b) of Figure 4.1 shows Hank's production possibilities. Like Tom's, Hank's production possibilities curve is a straight line, implying a constant opportunity cost of fish in terms of coconuts. His production possibilities curve has a constant slope of -2. Hank is less productive all around: at most he can produce 10 fish or 20 coconuts. But he is particularly bad at fishing: whereas Tom sacrifices $3/4$ of a coconut per fish caught, for Hank the opportunity cost of a fish is 2 whole coconuts. **Table 4.1** on the next page summarizes the two castaways' opportunity costs of fish and coconuts.

Now, Tom and Hank could go their separate ways, each living on his own side of the island, catching his own fish and gathering his own coconuts. Let's suppose that they start out that way and make the consumption choices shown in Figure 4.1: in the absence of trade, Tom consumes 28 fish and 9 coconuts per week, while Hank consumes 6 fish and 8 coconuts.

Figure 4.1 Production Possibilities for Two Castaways

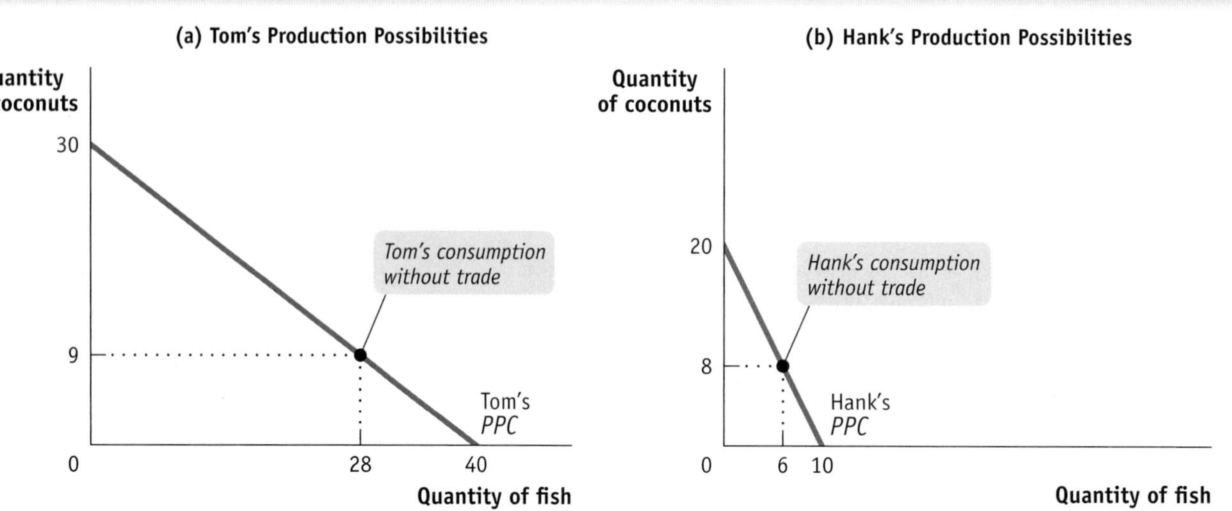

Here, each of the two castaways has a constant opportunity cost of fish and a straight-line production possibilities curve. In Tom's case, each fish has an opportunity cost of ¾ of a coconut. In Hank's case, each fish has an opportunity cost of 2 coconuts.

Table 4.1 Tom's and Hank's Opportunity Costs of Fish and Coconuts

	Tom's Opportunity Cost	Hank's Opportunity Cost
One fish	3/4 coconut	2 coconuts
One coconut	4/3 fish	1/2 fish

But is this the best they can do? No, it isn't. Given that the two castaways have different opportunity costs, they can strike a deal that makes both of them better off. **Table 4.2** shows how such a deal works: Tom specializes in the production of fish, catching 40 per week, and gives 10 to Hank. Meanwhile, Hank specializes in the production of coconuts, gathering 20 per week, and gives 10 to Tom. The result is shown in **Figure 4.2**. Tom now consumes more of both goods than before: instead of 28 fish and 9 coconuts, he consumes 30 fish and 10 coconuts. Hank also consumes more, going from 6 fish and 8 coconuts to 10 fish and 10 coconuts. As Table 4.2 also shows, both Tom and Hank experience gains from trade: Tom's consumption of fish increases by two, and his consumption of coconuts increases by one. Hank's consumption of fish increases by four, and his consumption of coconuts increases by two.

So both castaways are better off when they each specialize in what they are good at and trade with each other. It's a good idea for Tom to catch the fish for both of them, because his opportunity cost of a fish is only ¾ of a coconut not gathered versus 2 coconuts for Hank. Correspondingly, it's a good idea for Hank to gather coconuts for both of them.

Or we could describe the situation in a different way. Because Tom is so good at catching fish, his opportunity cost of gathering coconuts is high: ⁴⁄₃ of a fish not caught for every coconut gathered. Because Hank is a pretty poor fisherman, his opportunity cost of gathering coconuts is much less, only ½ of a fish per coconut.

Table 4.2 How the Castaways Gain from Trade

		Without Trade		With Trade		Gains from Trade
		Production	Consumption	Production	Consumption	
Tom	Fish	28	28	40	30	+2
	Coconuts	9	9	0	10	+1
Hank	Fish	6	6	0	10	+4
	Coconuts	8	8	20	10	+2

An individual has a **comparative advantage** in producing something if the opportunity cost of that production is lower for that individual than for other people. In other words, Hank has a comparative advantage over Tom in producing a particular good or service if Hank's opportunity cost of producing that good or service is lower than Tom's. In this case, Hank has a comparative advantage in gathering coconuts and Tom has a comparative advantage in catching fish.

Notice that Tom is actually better than Hank at producing both goods: Tom can catch more fish in a week, and he can also gather more coconuts. This means that Tom has an **absolute advantage** in both activities: he can produce more output with a given amount of input (in this case, his time) than Hank can. It might seem as though Tom has nothing to gain from trading with less competent Hank. But we've just seen that Tom can indeed benefit from a deal with Hank, because *comparative*, not *absolute*, advantage is the basis for mutual gain. It doesn't matter that it takes Hank more time to gather a coconut; what matters is that for him the opportunity cost of that coconut in terms of fish is lower. So, despite his absolute disadvantage in both activities, Hank has a comparative advantage in coconut gathering. Meanwhile Tom, who can use his time better by catching fish, has a comparative disadvantage in coconut gathering.

An individual has a **comparative advantage** in producing a good or service if the opportunity cost of producing the good or service is lower for that individual than for other people.

An individual has an **absolute advantage** in producing a good or service if he or she can make more of it with a given amount of time and resources. Having an absolute advantage is not the same thing as having a comparative advantage.

Figure 4.2 Comparative Advantage and Gains from Trade

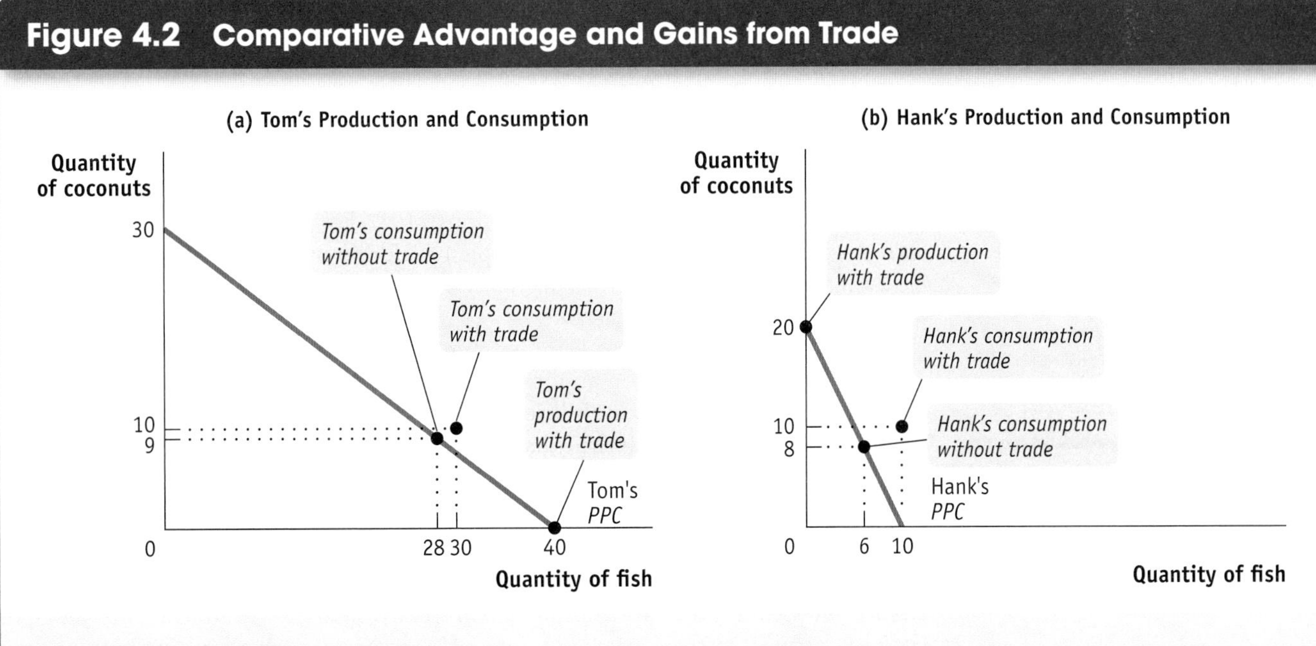

By specializing and trading, the two castaways can produce and consume more of both goods. Tom specializes in catching fish, his comparative advantage, and Hank—who has an *absolute* disadvantage in both goods but a *comparative* advantage in coconuts—specializes in gathering coconuts. The result is that each castaway can consume more of both goods than either could without trade.

The **terms of trade** indicate the rate at which one good can be exchanged for another.

Mutually Beneficial Terms of Trade

The **terms of trade** indicate the rate at which one good can be exchanged for another. In our story, Tom and Hank traded 10 coconuts for 10 fish, so each coconut traded for 1 fish. Why not some other terms of trade, such as ¾ fish per coconut? Indeed, there are many terms of trade that would make both Tom and Hank better off than if they didn't trade. But there are also terms that Tom or Hank would certainly reject. For example, Tom would not trade 2 fish per coconut, because he only gives up 4⁄3 fish per coconut without trade.

To find the range of mutually beneficial terms of trade for a coconut, look at each person's opportunity cost of producing a coconut. *Any price per coconut between the opportunity cost of the coconut producer and the opportunity cost of the coconut buyer will make both sides better off than in the absence of trade.* We know that Hank will produce coconuts because he has a comparative advantage in gathering coconuts. Hank's opportunity cost is ½ fish per coconut. Tom, the buyer of coconuts, has an opportunity cost of 4⁄3 fish per coconut. So any terms of trade between ½ fish per coconut and 4⁄3 fish per coconut would benefit both Tom and Hank.

To understand why, consider the opportunity costs summarized in Table 4.1. When Hank doesn't trade with Tom, Hank can gain ½ fish by giving up a coconut, because his opportunity cost of each coconut is ½ fish. Hank will clearly reject any deal with Tom that provides him with less than ½ fish per coconut—he's better off not trading at all and getting ½ fish per coconut. But Hank benefits from trade if he receives more than ½ fish per coconut. So the terms of 1 fish per coconut, as in our story, are acceptable to Hank.

When Tom doesn't trade with Hank, Tom gives up 4⁄3 fish to get a coconut—his opportunity cost of a coconut is 4⁄3 fish. Tom will reject any deal that requires him to pay more than 4⁄3 fish per coconut. But Tom benefits from trade if he pays less than 4⁄3 fish per coconut. The terms of 1 fish per coconut are thus acceptable to Tom as well. Both islanders would also be made better off by terms of ¾ fish per coconut or 5⁄4 fish per coconut or any other price between ½ fish and 4⁄3 fish per coconut. The islanders' negotiation skills determine where the terms of trade fall within that range.

So remember, Tom and Hank will engage in trade only if the "price" of the good each person obtains from trade is less than his own opportunity cost of producing the good. The same is true for international trade. Whenever two parties trade voluntarily, for each good, the terms of trade are found between the opportunity cost of the producer and the opportunity cost of the buyer.

The story of Tom and Hank clearly simplifies reality. Yet it teaches us some very important lessons that also apply to the real economy. First, the story provides a clear illustration of the gains from trade. By agreeing to specialize and provide goods to each other, Tom and Hank can produce more; therefore, both are better off than if each tried to be self-sufficient. Second, the story demonstrates a key point that is often overlooked in real-world arguments: as long as people have different opportunity costs, *everyone has a comparative advantage in something, and everyone has a comparative disadvantage in something, so everyone can benefit from trade.*

AP® Exam Tip

The producer with the *absolute advantage* can produce the largest quantity of the good. However, it is the producer with the *comparative advantage*, and not necessarily the one with the absolute advantage, who should specialize in the production of that good to achieve mutual gains from trade.

The idea of comparative advantage applies to many activities in the economy. Perhaps its most important application is in trade—not between individuals, but between countries. So let's look briefly at how the model of comparative advantage helps in understanding both the causes and the effects of international trade.

Comparative Advantage and International Trade

Look at the label on a manufactured good sold in the United States, and there's a good chance you will find that it was produced in some other country—in China or Japan or even in Canada. On the other hand, many U.S. industries sell a large portion of their output overseas. (This is particularly true for the agriculture, high technology, and entertainment industries.)

Should we celebrate this international exchange of goods and services, or should it cause us concern? Politicians and the public often question the desirability of international trade, arguing that the nation should produce goods for itself rather than buy them from foreigners. Industries around the world demand protection from foreign competition: Japanese farmers want to keep out American rice, and American steelworkers want to keep out European steel. These demands are often supported by public opinion.

Economists, however, have a very positive view of international trade. Why? Because they view it in terms of comparative advantage. **Figure 4.3** shows, with a simple example, how international trade can be interpreted in terms of comparative advantage. Although the example is hypothetical, it is based on an actual pattern of international trade: American exports of pork to Canada and Canadian exports of aircraft to the United States. Panels (a) and (b) illustrate hypothetical production possibilities curves for the United States and Canada, with pork measured on the horizontal axis and aircraft measured on the vertical axis. The U.S. production possibilities curve is flatter than the Canadian production possibilities curve, implying that producing one more ton of pork costs fewer aircraft in the United States than it does in Canada. This means that the United States has a comparative advantage in pork and Canada has a comparative advantage in aircraft.

Although the consumption points in Figure 4.3 are hypothetical, they illustrate a general principle: just like the example of Tom and Hank, the United States and Canada can both achieve mutual gains from trade. If the United States concentrates on producing pork and sells some of its output to Canada, while Canada concentrates on aircraft and sells some of its output to the United States, both countries can consume more than if they insisted on being self-sufficient. For example, the United States could trade 1 million tons of pork for 1,500 aircraft from Canada. This would allow both countries to consume at a point outside of their production possibilities curves.

Moreover, these mutual gains don't depend on each country's being better at producing one kind of good. Even if one country has, say, higher output per person-hour in both industries—that is, even if one country has an absolute advantage in both industries—there are still mutual gains from trade.

Figure 4.3 Comparative Advantage and International Trade

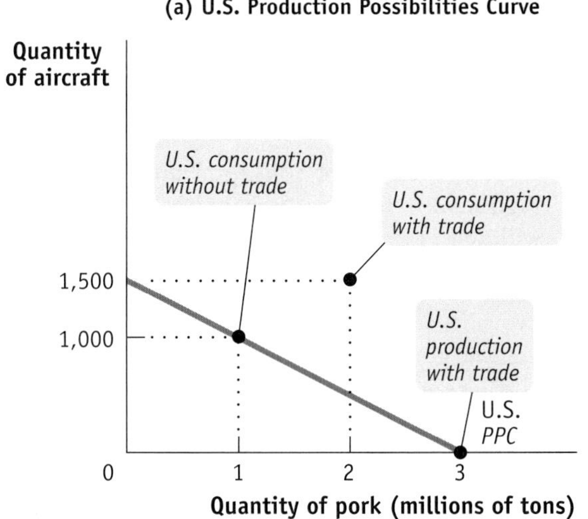

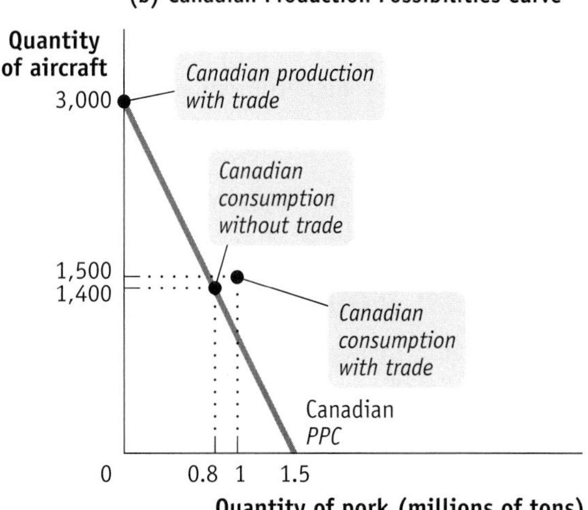

In this hypothetical example, Canada and the United States produce only two goods: pork and aircraft. Aircraft are measured on the vertical axis and pork on the horizontal axis. Panel (a) shows the U.S. production possibilities curve. It is relatively flat, implying that the United States has a comparative advantage in pork production. Panel (b) shows the Canadian production possibilities curve. It is relatively steep, implying that Canada has a comparative advantage in aircraft production. Just like two individuals, both countries gain from specialization and trade.

FYI Rich Nation, Poor Nation

Try taking off your clothes—at a suitable time and in a suitable place, of course—and take a look at the labels inside that say where the clothes were made. It's a very good bet that much, if not most, of your clothing was manufactured overseas, in a country that is much poorer than the United States is—say, in El Salvador, Sri Lanka, or Bangladesh.

Why are these countries so much poorer than the United States? The immediate reason is that their economies are much less *productive*—firms in these countries are just not able to produce as much from a given quantity of resources as comparable firms in the United States or other wealthy countries. Why countries differ so much in productivity is a deep question—indeed, one of the main questions that preoccupy economists. But in any case, the difference in productivity is a fact.

If the economies of these countries are so much less productive than ours, how is it that they make so much of our clothing? Why don't we do it for ourselves?

The answer is "comparative advantage." Just about every industry in Bangladesh is much less productive than the corresponding industry in the United States. But the productivity difference between rich and poor countries varies across goods; there is a very great difference in the production of sophisticated goods such as aircraft but not as great a difference in the production of simpler goods such as clothing. So Bangladesh's position with regard to clothing production is like Hank's position with respect to coconut gathering: he's not as good at it as his fellow castaway is, but it's the thing he does comparatively well.

Although Bangladesh is at an absolute disadvantage compared with the United States in almost everything, it has a comparative advantage in clothing production.

Robert Nickelsberg/Getty Images

Although less productive than American workers, Bangladeshi workers have a comparative advantage in clothing production.

This means that both the United States and Bangladesh are able to consume more because they specialize in producing different things, with Bangladesh supplying our clothing and the United States supplying Bangladesh with more sophisticated goods.

MODULE 4 Review

Check Your Understanding

1. In Italy, an automobile can be produced by 8 workers in one day and a washing machine by 3 workers in one day. In the United States, an automobile can be produced by 6 workers in one day, and a washing machine by 2 workers in one day.
   a. Which country has an absolute advantage in the production of automobiles? In washing machines?
   b. Which country has a comparative advantage in the production of washing machines? In automobiles?
   c. What type of specialization results in the greatest gains from trade between the two countries?
2. Refer to the story of Tom and Hank illustrated by Figure 4.1 in the text. Explain why Tom and Hank are willing to engage in a trade of 1 fish for 1½ coconuts.

Tackle the Test: Multiple-Choice Questions

Refer to the graph below to answer the following questions.

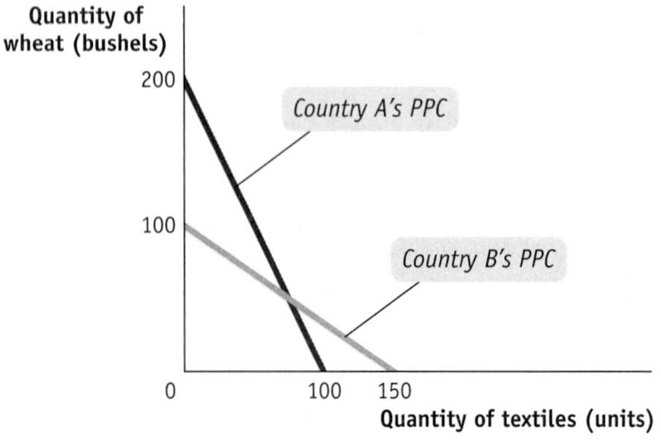

1. Use the graph to determine which country has an absolute advantage in producing each good.

	Absolute advantage in wheat production	*Absolute advantage in textile production*
a.	Country A	Country B
b.	Country A	Country A
c.	Country B	Country A
d.	Country B	Country B
e.	Country A	Neither country

2. For Country A, the opportunity cost of a bushel of wheat is
   a. ½ unit of textiles.
   b. ⅔ unit of textiles.
   c. 1⅓ units of textiles.
   d. 1½ units of textiles.
   e. 2 units of textiles.

3. Use the graph to determine which country has a comparative advantage in producing each good.

	Comparative advantage in wheat production	*Comparative advantage in textile production*
a.	Country A	Country B
b.	Country A	Country A
c.	Country B	Country A
d.	Country B	Country B
e.	Country A	Neither country

4. If the two countries specialize and trade, which of the choices below describes the countries' imports?

	Import wheat	*Import textiles*
a.	Country A	Country A
b.	Country A	Country B
c.	Country B	Country B
d.	Country B	Country A
e.	Neither country	Country B

5. What is the highest price Country B is willing to pay to buy wheat from Country A?
   a. ½ unit of textiles
   b. ⅔ unit of textiles
   c. 1 unit of textiles
   d. 1½ units of textiles
   e. 2 units of textiles

Tackle the Test: Free-Response Questions

1. Refer to the graph below to answer the following questions.

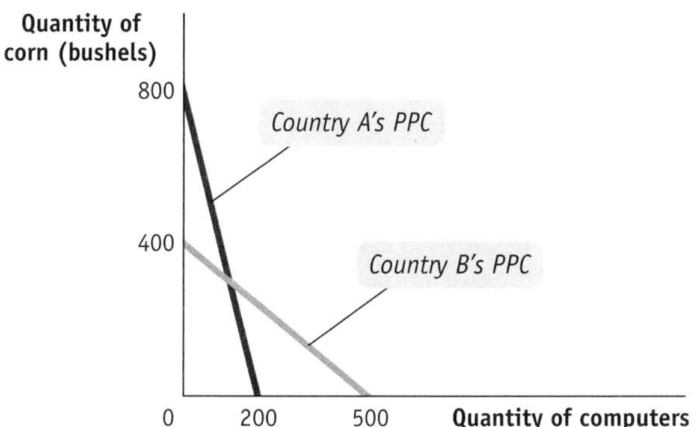

   a. What is the opportunity cost of a bushel of corn in each country?
   b. Which country has an absolute advantage in computer production? Explain.
   c. Which country has a comparative advantage in corn production? Explain.
   d. If each country specializes, what good will Country B import? Explain.
   e. What is the minimum price Country A will accept to export corn to Country B? Explain.

Rubric for FRQ 1 (9 points)

1 point: Country A, ¼ computer; Country B, 1¼ computers

1 point: Country B

1 point: Because Country B can produce more computers than Country A (500 versus 200)

1 point: Country A

1 point: Because Country A can produce corn at a lower opportunity cost (¼ versus 1¼ computers)

1 point: Corn

1 point: Country B has a comparative advantage in the production of computers, so it will produce computers and import corn (Country A has a comparative advantage in corn production, so it will specialize in corn and import computers from Country B).

1 point: ¼ computer

1 point: Country A's opportunity cost of producing corn is ¼ computer, so that is the lowest price it will accept to sell corn to Country B.

2. Refer to the table below to answer the following questions. These two countries are producing textiles and wheat using equal amounts of resources.

	Weekly output per worker	
	Country A	Country B
Bushels of wheat	15	10
Units of textiles	60	60

   a. What is the opportunity cost of producing a bushel of wheat for each country?
   b. Which country has the absolute advantage in wheat production?
   c. Which country has the comparative advantage in textile production? Explain.
   (5 points)

SECTION 1 Review

Section 1 Review Video

Module 1

1. Everyone has to make choices about what to do and what *not* to do. **Individual choice** is the basis of **economics**—if it doesn't involve choice, it isn't economics. The **economy** is a system that coordinates choices about production and consumption. In a **market economy**, these choices are made by many firms and individuals. In a **command economy**, these choices are made by a central authority. **Incentives** are rewards or punishments that motivate particular choices, and can be lacking in a command economy where producers cannot set their own prices or keep their own profits. **Property rights** create incentives in market economies by establishing ownership and granting individuals the right to trade goods and services for mutual gain. In any economy, decisions are informed by **marginal analysis**—the study of the costs and benefits of doing something a little bit more or a little bit less.
2. The reason choices must be made is that **resources**—anything that can be used to produce something else—are **scarce.** The four categories of resources are **land**, **labor**, **capital**, and **entrepreneurship**. Individuals are limited in their choices by money and time; economies are limited by their supplies of resources.
3. Because you must choose among limited alternatives, the true cost of anything is what you must give up to get it—all costs are **opportunity costs**.
4. Economists use economic models for both **positive economics**, which describes how the economy works, and for **normative economics**, which prescribes how the economy *should* work. Positive economics often involves making forecasts. Economics can determine correct answers for positive questions, but typically not for normative questions, which involve value judgments. Exceptions occur when policies designed to achieve a certain prescription can be clearly ranked in terms of preference.
5. There are two main reasons economists disagree. One, they may disagree about which simplifications to make in a model. Two, economists may disagree—like everyone else—about values.
6. **Microeconomics** is the branch of economics that studies how people make decisions and how those decisions interact. **Macroeconomics** is concerned with the overall ups and downs of the economy, and focuses on **economic aggregates** such as the unemployment rate and gross domestic product, that summarize data across many different markets.

Module 2

7. Economies experience ups and downs in economic activity. This pattern is called the **business cycle**. The downturns are known as **recessions;** the upturns are known as **expansions**. A **depression** is a long, deep downturn.
8. Workers are counted in **unemployment** figures only if they are actively seeking work but aren't currently employed. The sum of **employment** and unemployment is the **labor force**. The **unemployment rate** is the percentage of the labor force that is unemployed.
9. As the unemployment rate rises, the output for the economy as a whole—the **aggregate output**—generally falls.
10. A short-term increase in aggregate output made possible by a decrease in unemployment does not constitute **economic growth**, which is an increase in the maximum amount of output an economy can produce.
11. Rises and falls in the overall price level constitute **inflation** and **deflation**. Economists prefer that prices change only slowly if at all, because such **price stability** helps keep the economy stable.
12. Almost all economics is based on **models**, "thought experiments" or simplified versions of reality, many of which use analytical tools such as mathematics and graphs. An important assumption in economic models is the **other things equal (*ceteris paribus*) assumption**, which allows analysis of the effect of change in one factor by holding all other relevant factors unchanged.

Module 3

13. One important economic model is the **production possibilities curve**, which illustrates the **trade-offs** facing an economy that produces only two goods. The production possibilities curve illustrates three elements: opportunity cost (showing how much less of one good must be produced if more of the other good is produced), **efficiency** (an economy achieves **productive efficiency** if it produces on the production possibilities curve and **allocative efficiency** if it produces the mix of goods and services that people want to consume), and economic growth (an outward shift of the production possibilities curve).
14. There are two basic sources of growth in the production possibilities curve model: an increase in resources and improved **technology**.

Module 4

15. There are **gains from trade**: by engaging in the **trade** of goods and services with one another, the members of an economy can all be made better off. Underlying gains from trade are the advantages of **specialization**, of having individuals specialize in the tasks they are comparatively good at.

16. **Comparative advantage** explains the source of gains from trade between individuals and countries. Everyone has a comparative advantage in something—some good or service in which that person has a lower opportunity cost than everyone else. But it is often confused with **absolute advantage**, an ability to produce more of a particular good or service than anyone else. This confusion leads some to erroneously conclude that there are no gains from trade between people or countries.

17. As long as a comparative advantage exists between two parties, there are opportunities for mutually beneficial trade. The **terms of trade** indicate the rate at which one good can be exchanged for another. The range of mutually beneficial terms of trade for a good are found between the seller's opportunity cost of making the good and the buyer's opportunity cost of making the same good.

Key Terms

Economics, p. 2
Individual choice, p. 2
Economy, p. 2
Market economy, p. 2
Command economy, p. 2
Incentives, p. 3
Property rights, p. 3
Marginal analysis, p. 3
Resource, p. 3
Land, p. 3
Labor, p. 3
Capital, p. 3
Entrepreneurship, p. 3
Scarce, p. 3
Opportunity cost, p. 4
Microeconomics, p. 5
Macroeconomics, p. 5
Economic aggregates, p. 5
Positive economics, p. 6
Normative economics, p. 6
Business cycle, p. 11
Depression, p. 11
Recessions, p. 11
Expansions, p. 11
Employment, p. 11
Unemployment, p. 11
Labor force, p. 12
Unemployment rate, p. 12
Output, p. 12
Aggregate output, p. 12
Inflation, p. 13
Deflation, p. 13
Price stability, p. 13
Economic growth, p. 13
Model, p. 14
Other things equal (*ceteris paribus*) assumption, p. 14
Trade-off, p. 16
Production possibilities curve, p. 17
Efficient, p. 18
Productive efficiency, p. 18
Allocative efficiency, p. 18
Technology, p. 21
Trade, p. 24
Gains from trade, p. 24
Specialization, p. 24
Comparative advantage, p. 27
Absolute advantage, p. 27
Terms of trade, p. 28

AP® Exam Practice Questions

Multiple-Choice Questions

1. In a market economy, most choices about production and consumption are made by which of the following?
a. politicians
b. many individuals and firms
c. the government
d. managers
e. economists

2. Which of the following pairs indicates a category of resources and an example of that resource?

	Category	*Example*
a.	money	investment
b.	capital	money
c.	capital	minerals
d.	land	factory
e.	land	timber

3. You can either go to a movie or study for an exam. Which of the following is an opportunity cost of studying for the exam?
a. a higher grade on the exam
b. the price of a movie ticket
c. the cost of paper, pens, books, and other study materials
d. the enjoyment from seeing the movie
e. the sense of achievement from learning

4. Which of the following situations is explained by increasing opportunity costs?
   a. More people go to college when the job market is good.
   b. More people do their own home repairs when hourly wages fall.
   c. There are more parks in crowded cities than in suburban areas.
   d. Convenience stores cater to busy people.
   e. People with higher wages are more likely to mow their own lawns.

5. Which of the following is a normative statement?
   a. The unemployment rate is expected to rise.
   b. Individuals purchase more of a good when the price rises.
   c. The government should increase the minimum wage.
   d. An increase in the tax rate on wage earnings reduces the incentive to work.
   e. Public education generates greater benefits than costs.

6. Falling output in an economy is consistent with which of the following?
   a. a recession
   b. an expansion
   c. a recovery
   d. falling unemployment
   e. long-term economic growth

7. Which of the following is a goal for the macroeconomy?
   a. declining labor force
   b. inflation
   c. deflation
   d. rising aggregate output
   e. rising unemployment rate

Refer to the following table and information for Questions 8–11.

Suppose that Atlantis is a small, isolated island in the South Atlantic. The inhabitants grow potatoes and catch fish. The following table shows the maximum annual output combinations of potatoes and fish that can be produced.

Maximum annual output options	Quantity of potatoes (pounds)	Quantity of fish (pounds)
A	1,000	0
B	800	300
C	600	500
D	400	600
E	200	650
F	0	675

8. Atlantis can produce which of the following combinations of output?

	Pounds of potatoes	*Pounds of fish*
a.	1,000	675
b.	600	600
c.	400	600
d.	300	800
e.	200	675

9. If Atlantis is efficient in production, what is the opportunity cost of increasing the annual output of potatoes from 600 to 800 pounds?
   a. 200 pounds of fish
   b. 300 pounds of fish
   c. 500 pounds of fish
   d. 675 pounds of fish
   e. 800 pounds of fish

10. As Atlantis produces more potatoes, what is true about the opportunity cost of producing potatoes?
   a. It stays the same.
   b. It continually increases.
   c. It continually decreases.
   d. It increases and then decreases.
   e. It decreases and then increases.

11. Which of the following combinations of output is efficient?

	Pounds of potatoes	*Pounds of fish*
a.	1,000	0
b.	600	600
c.	400	500
d.	500	400
e.	0	0

Refer to the following information for Questions 12–13.

In the ancient country of Roma, only two goods—spaghetti and meatballs—are produced. There are two tribes in Roma, the Tivoli and the Frivoli. By themselves, in a given month, the Tivoli can produce 30 pounds of spaghetti and no meatballs, 50 pounds of meatballs and no spaghetti, or any combination in between. In the same month, the Frivoli can produce 40 pounds of spaghetti and no meatballs, 30 pounds of meatballs and no spaghetti, or any combination in between.

12. Which tribe has a comparative advantage in meatball and spaghetti production?

	Meatballs	*Spaghetti*
a.	Tivoli	Tivoli
b.	Frivoli	Frivoli
c.	Tivoli	Frivoli
d.	Frivoli	Tivoli
e.	neither	both

13. In A.D. 100, the Frivoli discovered a new technique for making meatballs and doubled the quantity of meatballs they could produce each month. After the discovery of this new technique in Frivoli only, which tribe had an absolute advantage in meatball production and which had a comparative advantage in meatball production?

	Absolute advantage	*Comparative advantage*
a.	Tivoli	Tivoli
b.	Frivoli	Frivoli
c.	Tivoli	Frivoli
d.	Frivoli	Tivoli
e.	Frivoli	both

14. Which of the following is a basic source of economic growth in the production possibilities model?
    - **a.** specialization
    - **b.** efficiency
    - **c.** opportunity cost
    - **d.** trade-offs
    - **e.** improved technology

15. Comparative advantage explains which of the following?
    - **a.** a country's ability to produce more of a particular good or service
    - **b.** when production is considered efficient
    - **c.** why the production possibilities curve is bowed outward
    - **d.** the source of gains from trade
    - **e.** why the production possibilities curve shifts outward

Free-Response Question

The Hatfield family lives on the east side of the Hatatoochie River and the McCoy family lives on the west side. Each family's diet consists of fried chicken and corn on the cob, and each is self-sufficient, raising its own chickens and growing its own corn.

Assume the Hatfield family has a comparative advantage in the production of corn.

1. Draw a correctly labeled graph showing a hypothetical production possibilities curve for the McCoy family.
2. Which family has the comparative advantage in the production of chickens? Explain.
3. Assuming that each family is producing efficiently, how can the two families increase their consumption of both chicken and corn?
   (5 points)

SECTION 1 APPENDIX

Graphs in Economics

In this Appendix, you will learn to:

- Recognize the importance of graphs in studying economics
- Describe the basic components of a graph
- Explain how graphs illustrate the relationship between variables
- Explain how to calculate the slope of a line or curve and discuss what the slope value means
- Describe how to calculate areas represented on graphs
- Explain how to interpret numerical graphs

Getting the Picture

Whether you're reading about economics in the *Wall Street Journal* or in your economics textbook, you will see many graphs. Visual presentations can make it much easier to understand verbal descriptions, numerical information, or ideas. In economics, graphs are the type of visual presentation used to facilitate understanding. To fully understand the ideas and information being discussed, you need to know how to interpret these visual aids. This module explains how graphs are constructed and interpreted and how they are used in economics.

Graphs, Variables, and Economic Models

A **variable** is a measure that can take on more than one value.

One reason to attend college is that a bachelor's degree provides access to higher-paying jobs. Additional degrees, such as MBAs or law degrees, increase earnings even more. If you were to read an article about the relationship between educational attainment and income, you would probably see a graph showing the income levels for workers with different levels of education. This graph would depict the idea that, in general, having more education increases a person's income. This graph, like most graphs in economics, would depict the relationship between two economic variables. A **variable** is a measure that can take on more than one value, such as the number of years of education a person has, the price of a can of soda, or a household's income.

As you learned in this section, economic analysis relies heavily on *models,* simplified representations of real situations. Most economic models describe the relationship between two variables, simplified by holding constant other variables that may affect the relationship. For example, an economic model might describe the relationship between the price of a can of soda and the number of cans of soda that consumers will buy, assuming that everything else that affects consumers' purchases of soda stays constant. This type of model can be depicted mathematically, but illustrating the relationship in a graph makes it easier to understand. Next we show how graphs that depict economic models are constructed and interpreted.

How Graphs Work

Most graphs in economics are based on a grid built around two perpendicular lines that show the values of two variables, helping you visualize the relationship between them. So a first step in understanding the use of such graphs is to see how this system works.

Two-Variable Graphs

Figure A.1 shows a typical two-variable graph. It illustrates the data in the accompanying table on outside temperature and the number of sodas a typical vendor can expect to sell at a baseball stadium during one game. The first column shows the values of outside temperature (the first variable) and the second column shows the values of the number of sodas sold (the second variable). Five combinations or pairs of the two variables are shown, denoted by points *A* through *E* in the third column.

Figure A.1 Plotting Points on a Two-Variable Graph

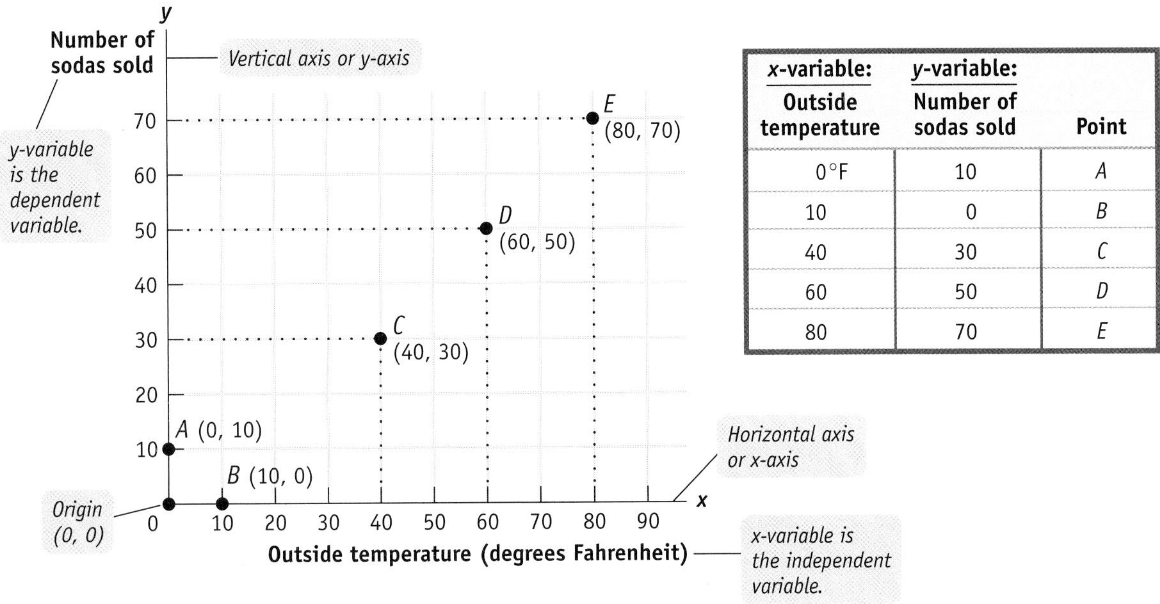

x-variable: Outside temperature	y-variable: Number of sodas sold	Point
0°F	10	*A*
10	0	*B*
40	30	*C*
60	50	*D*
80	70	*E*

The data from the table are plotted where outside temperature (the independent variable) is measured along the horizontal axis and number of sodas sold (the dependent variable) is measured along the vertical axis. Each of the five combinations of temperature and sodas sold is represented by a point: *A, B, C, D,* or *E*. Each point in the graph is identified by a pair of values. For example, point *C* corresponds to the pair (40, 30)—an outside temperature of 40°F (the value of the *x*-variable) and 30 sodas sold (the value of the *y*-variable).

Now let's turn to graphing the data in this table. In any two-variable graph, one variable is called the *x*-variable and the other is called the *y*-variable. Here we have made outside temperature the *x*-variable and number of sodas sold the *y*-variable. The solid horizontal line in the graph is called the **horizontal axis** or ***x*-axis**, and values of the *x*-variable—outside temperature—are measured along it. Similarly, the solid vertical line in the graph is called the **vertical axis** or ***y*-axis**, and values of the *y*-variable—number of sodas sold—are measured along it. At the **origin**, the point where the two axes meet, each variable is equal to zero. As you move rightward from the origin along the *x*-axis, values of the *x*-variable are positive and increasing. As you move up from the origin along the *y*-axis, values of the *y*-variable are positive and increasing.

The solid horizontal line on a graph is called the **horizontal axis** or ***x*-axis**.

The solid vertical line on a graph is called the **vertical axis** or ***y*-axis**.

The two axes meet at the **origin**.

You can plot each of the five points *A* through *E* on this graph by using a pair of numbers—the values that the *x*-variable and the *y*-variable take on for a given point. In Figure A.1, at point *C*, the *x*-variable takes on the value 40 and the *y*-variable takes on the value 30. You plot point *C* by drawing a line straight up from 40 on the *x*-axis and a horizontal line across from 30 on the *y*-axis. We write point *C* as (40, 30). We write the origin as (0, 0).

Looking at point *A* and point *B* in Figure A.1, you can see that when one of the variables for a point has a value of zero, it will lie on one of the axes. If the value of the *x*-variable is

A **causal relationship** is one in which the value taken by one variable directly influences or determines the value taken by the other variable.

In a causal relationship, the determining variable is called the **independent variable** and the determined variable is called the **dependent variable**.

A line on a graph is called a **curve**, regardless of whether it is a straight line or a curved line.

If a curve that shows the relationship between two variables is a straight line, or linear, the variables have a **linear relationship**.

When a curve is not a straight line, or nonlinear, the variables have a **nonlinear relationship**.

zero, the point will lie on the vertical axis, like point *A*. If the value of the *y*-variable is zero, the point will lie on the horizontal axis, like point *B*. (The location of point *B* was chosen to illustrate this fact and not because soda sales will really decrease when the temperature rises.)

Most graphs that depict relationships between two economic variables represent a **causal relationship**, a relationship in which the value taken by one variable directly influences or determines the value taken by the other variable. In a causal relationship, the determining variable is called the **independent variable**; the variable it determines is called the **dependent variable**. In our example of soda sales, the outside temperature is the independent variable. It directly influences the number of sodas that are sold, which is the dependent variable in this case.

By convention, we put the independent variable on the horizontal axis and the dependent variable on the vertical axis. Figure A.1 is constructed consistent with this convention: the independent variable (outside temperature) is on the horizontal axis and the dependent variable (number of sodas sold) is on the vertical axis. An important exception to this convention is in graphs showing the economic relationship between the price of a product and quantity of the product: although price is generally the independent variable that determines quantity, it is always measured on the vertical axis.

Curves on a Graph

Panel (a) of **Figure A.2** contains some of the same information as Figure A.1, with a line drawn through the points *B*, *C*, *D*, and *E*. Such a line on a graph is called a **curve**, regardless of whether it is a straight line or a curved line. If the curve that shows the relationship between two variables is a straight line, or linear, the variables have a **linear relationship**. When the curve is not a straight line, or nonlinear, the variables have a **nonlinear relationship**.

Figure A.2 Drawing Curves

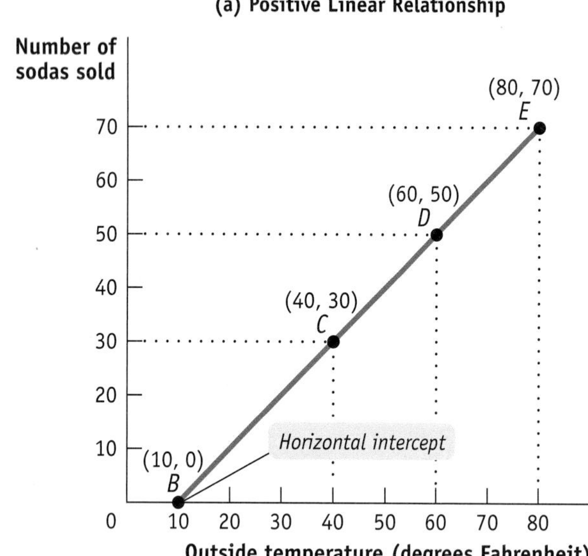

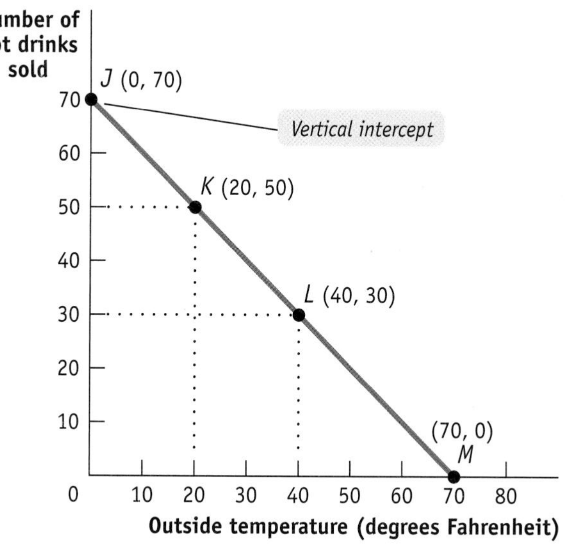

The curve in panel (a) illustrates the relationship between the two variables, outside temperature and number of sodas sold. The two variables have a positive linear relationship: positive because the curve has an upward tilt, and linear because it is a straight line. The curve implies that an increase in the *x*-variable (outside temperature) leads to an increase in the *y*-variable (number of sodas sold). The curve in panel (b) is also a straight line, but it tilts downward. The two variables here, outside temperature and number of hot drinks sold, have a negative linear relationship: an increase in the *x*-variable (outside temperature) leads to a decrease in the *y*-variable (number of hot drinks sold). The curve in panel (a) has a horizontal intercept at point B, where it hits the horizontal axis. The curve in panel (b) has a vertical intercept at point *J*, where it hits the vertical axis, and a horizontal intercept at point *M*, where it hits the horizontal axis.

A point on a curve indicates the value of the y-variable for a specific value of the x-variable. For example, point D indicates that at a temperature of 60°F, a vendor can expect to sell 50 sodas. The shape and orientation of a curve reveal the general nature of the relationship between the two variables. The upward tilt of the curve in panel (a) of Figure A.2 suggests that vendors can expect to sell more sodas at higher outside temperatures.

When variables are related in this way—that is, when an increase in one variable is associated with an increase in the other variable—the variables are said to have a **positive relationship**. It is illustrated by a curve that slopes upward from left to right. Because this curve is also linear, the relationship between outside temperature and number of sodas sold illustrated by the curve in panel (a) of Figure A.2 is a positive linear relationship.

When an increase in one variable is associated with a decrease in the other variable, the two variables are said to have a **negative relationship**. It is illustrated by a curve that slopes downward from left to right, like the curve in panel (b) of Figure A.2. Because this curve is also linear, the relationship it depicts is a negative linear relationship. Two variables that might have such a relationship are the outside temperature and the number of hot drinks a vendor can expect to sell at a baseball stadium.

Return for a moment to the curve in panel (a) of Figure A.2, and you can see that it hits the horizontal axis at point B. This point, known as the **horizontal intercept**, shows the value of the x-variable when the value of the y-variable is zero. In panel (b) of Figure A.2, the curve hits the vertical axis at point J. This point, called the **vertical intercept**, indicates the value of the y-variable when the value of the x-variable is zero.

When an increase in one variable is associated with an increase in the other variable, the variables are said to have a **positive relationship**.

When an increase in one variable is associated with a decrease in the other variable, the two variables are said to have a **negative relationship**.

The **horizontal intercept** indicates the value of the x-variable when the value of the y-variable is zero.

The **vertical intercept** indicates the value of the y-variable when the value of the x-variable is zero.

The **slope** of a curve is a measure of how steep it is; the slope indicates how sensitive the y-variable is to a change in the x-variable.

A Key Concept: The Slope of a Curve

The **slope** of a curve is a measure of how steep it is; the slope indicates how sensitive the y-variable is to a change in the x-variable. In our example of outside temperature and the number of cans of soda a vendor can expect to sell, the slope of the curve would indicate how many more cans of soda the vendor could expect to sell with each 1° increase in temperature. Interpreted this way, the slope gives meaningful information. Even without numbers for x and y, it is possible to arrive at important conclusions about the relationship between the two variables by examining the slope of a curve at various points.

The Slope of a Linear Curve

Along a linear curve the slope, or steepness, is measured by dividing the "rise" between two points on the curve by the "run" between those same two points. The rise is the amount that y changes, and the run is the amount that x changes. Here is the formula:

$$\frac{\text{Change in } y}{\text{Change in } x} = \frac{\Delta y}{\Delta x} = \text{slope}$$

In the formula, the symbol Δ (the Greek uppercase delta) stands for "change in." When a variable increases, the change in that variable is positive; when a variable decreases, the change in that variable is negative.

The slope of a curve is positive when the rise (the change in the y-variable) has the same sign as the run (the change in the x-variable). That's because when two numbers have the same sign, the ratio of those two numbers is positive. The curve in panel (a) of Figure A.2 has a positive slope: along the curve, both the y-variable and the x-variable increase. The slope of a curve is negative when the rise and the run have different signs. That's because when two numbers have different signs, the ratio of those two numbers is negative. The curve in panel (b) of Figure A.2 has a negative slope: along the curve, an increase in the x-variable is associated with a decrease in the y-variable.

Figure A.3 on the next page illustrates how to calculate the slope of a linear curve. Let's focus first on panel (a). From point A to point B the value of the y-variable changes from 25 to 20 and the value of the x-variable changes from 10 to 20. So the slope of the line between these two points is

$$\frac{\text{Change in } y}{\text{Change in } x} = \frac{\Delta y}{\Delta x} = \frac{-5}{10} = -\frac{1}{2} = -0.5$$

Figure A.3 Calculating the Slope

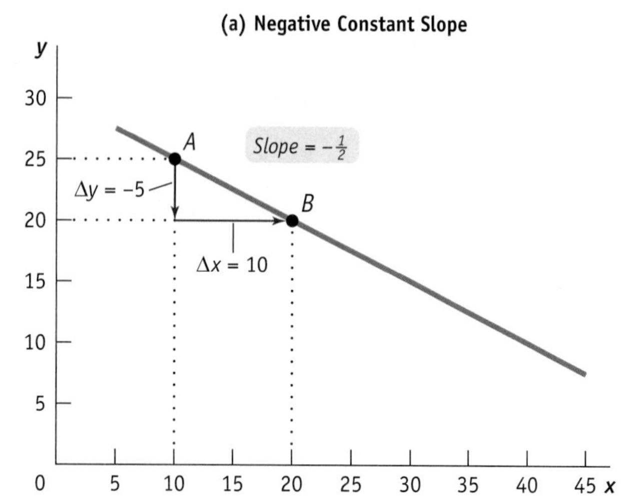

Panels (a) and (b) show two linear curves. Between points A and B on the curve in panel (a), the change in y (the rise) is -5 and the change in x (the run) is 10. So the slope from A to B is $\frac{\Delta y}{\Delta x} = \frac{-5}{10} = -\frac{1}{2} = -0.5$, where the negative sign indicates that the curve is downward sloping. In panel (b), the curve has a slope from A to B of $\frac{\Delta y}{\Delta x} = \frac{10}{2} = 5$. The slope from C to D is $\frac{\Delta y}{\Delta x} = \frac{20}{4} = 5$. The slope is positive, indicating that the curve is upward sloping. Furthermore, the slope between A and B is the same as the slope between C and D, making this a linear curve. The slope of a linear curve is constant: it is the same regardless of where it is calculated along the curve.

Because a straight line is equally steep at all points, the slope of a straight line is the same at all points. In other words, a straight line has a constant slope. You can check this by calculating the slope of the linear curve between points A and B and between points C and D in panel (b) of Figure A.3.

$$\frac{\Delta y}{\Delta x} = \frac{10}{2} = 5$$

$$\frac{\Delta y}{\Delta x} = \frac{20}{4} = 5$$

Horizontal and Vertical Curves and Their Slopes

When a curve is horizontal, the value of y along that curve never changes—it is constant. Everywhere along the curve, the change in y is zero. Now, zero divided by any number is zero. So regardless of the value of the change in x, the slope of a horizontal curve is always zero.

If a curve is vertical, the value of x along the curve never changes—it is constant. Everywhere along the curve, the change in x is zero. This means that the slope of a vertical line is a ratio with zero in the denominator. A ratio with zero in the denominator is equal to infinity—that is, an infinitely large number. So the slope of a vertical line is equal to infinity.

A vertical or a horizontal curve has a special implication: it means that the x-variable and the y-variable are unrelated. Two variables are unrelated when a change in one variable (the independent variable) has no effect on the other variable (the dependent variable). To put it a slightly different way, two variables are unrelated when the dependent variable is constant regardless of the value of the independent variable. If, as is usual, the y-variable is the dependent variable, the curve is horizontal. If the dependent variable is the x-variable, the curve is vertical.

The Slope of a Nonlinear Curve

A **nonlinear curve** is one along which the slope changes. Panels (a), (b), (c), and (d) of **Figure A.4** show various nonlinear curves. Panels (a) and (b) show nonlinear curves whose slopes change as you follow the line's progression, but the slopes always remain positive. Although both curves tilt upward, the curve in panel (a) gets steeper as the line moves from left to right in contrast to the curve in panel (b), which gets flatter. A curve

A **nonlinear curve** is one along which the slope changes.

Figure A.4 Nonlinear Curves

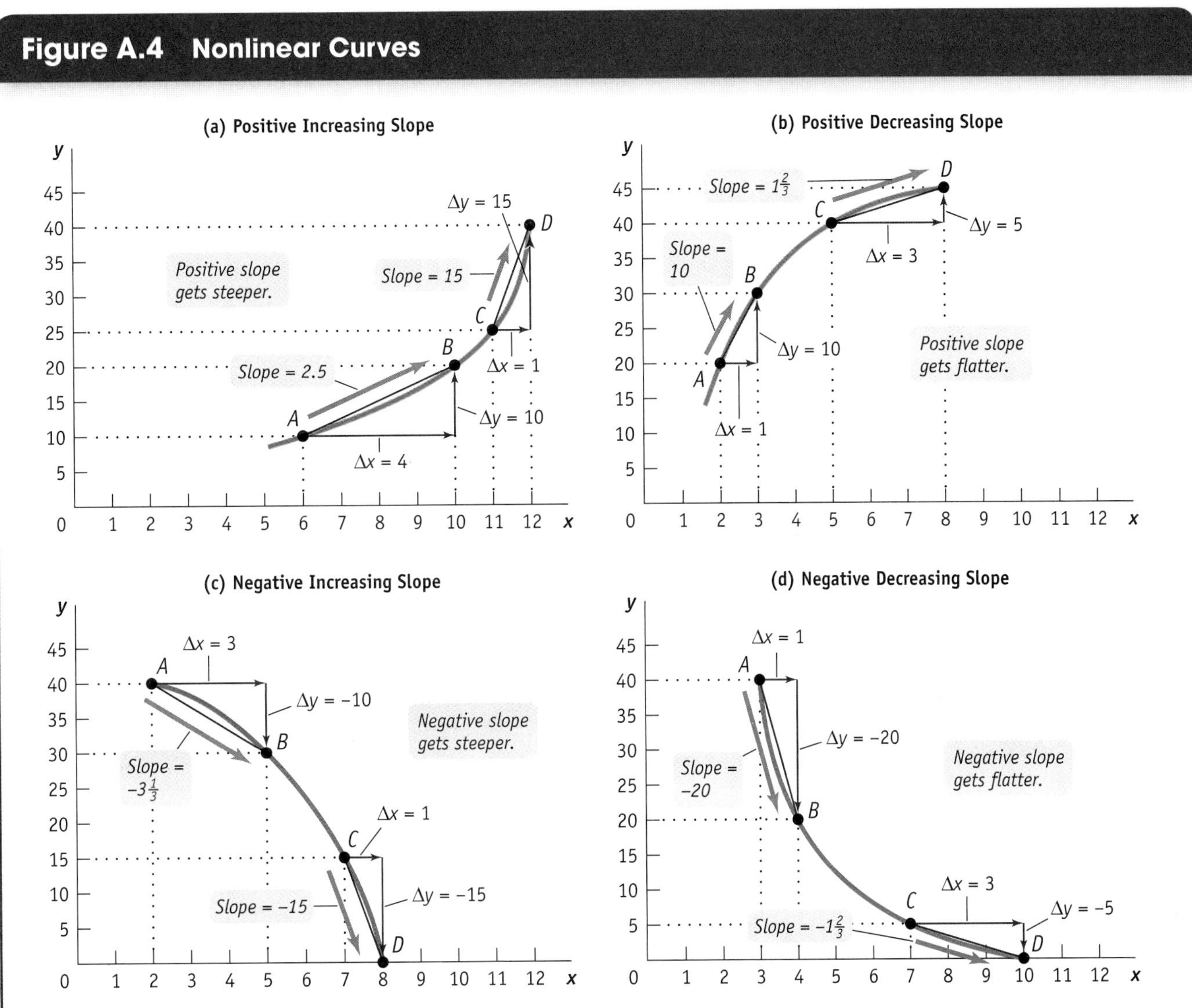

In panel (a) the slope of the curve from A to B is $\frac{\Delta y}{\Delta x} = \frac{10}{4} =$ 2.5, and from C to *D* it is $\frac{\Delta y}{\Delta x} = \frac{15}{1} = 15$. The slope is positive and increasing; it gets steeper as it moves to the right. In panel (b) the slope of the curve from A to B is $\frac{\Delta y}{\Delta x} = \frac{10}{1} = 10$, and from C to *D* it is $\frac{\Delta y}{\Delta x} = \frac{5}{3} = 1\frac{2}{3}$. The slope is positive and decreasing; it gets flatter as it moves to the right. In panel (c) the slope from *A* to *B* is $\frac{\Delta y}{\Delta x} = \frac{-10}{3} = -3\frac{1}{3}$, and from C to *D* it is $\frac{\Delta y}{\Delta x} = \frac{-15}{1} = -15$. The slope is negative and increasing; it gets steeper as it moves to the right. And in panel (d) the slope from *A* to *B* is $\frac{\Delta y}{\Delta x} = \frac{-20}{1} = -20$, and from C to *D* it is $\frac{\Delta y}{\Delta x} = \frac{-5}{3} = -1\frac{2}{3}$. The slope is negative and decreasing; it gets flatter as it moves to the right. The slope in each case has been calculated by using the *arc method*—that is, by drawing a straight line connecting two points along a curve. The average slope between those two points is equal to the slope of the straight line between those two points.

that is upward sloping and gets steeper, as in panel (a), is said to have *positive increasing* slope. A curve that is upward sloping but gets flatter, as in panel (b), is said to have *positive decreasing* slope.

When we calculate the slope along these nonlinear curves, we obtain different values for the slope at different points. How the slope changes along the curve determines the curve's shape. For example, in panel (a) of Figure A.4, the slope of the curve is a positive number that steadily increases as the line moves from left to right, whereas in panel (b), the slope is a positive number that steadily decreases.

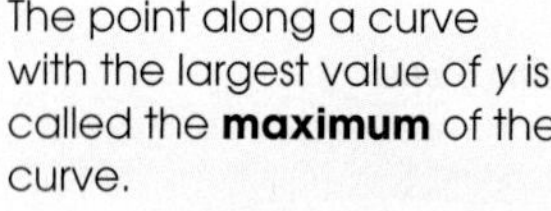

The **absolute value** of a number is the value of that number without a minus sign, whether or not the number was negative to begin with.

The slopes of the curves in panels (c) and (d) are negative numbers. Economists often prefer to express a negative number as its **absolute value**, which is the value of the negative number without the minus sign. In general, we denote the absolute value of a number by two parallel bars around the number; for example, the absolute value of −4 is written as $|-4| = 4$. In panel (c), the absolute value of the slope steadily increases as the line moves from left to right. The curve therefore has *negative increasing* slope. And in panel (d), the absolute value of the slope of the curve steadily decreases along the curve. This curve therefore has *negative decreasing* slope.

Maximum and Minimum Points

The slope of a nonlinear curve can change from positive to negative or vice versa. When the slope of a curve changes from positive to negative, it creates what is called a *maximum* point of the curve. When the slope of a curve changes from negative to positive, it creates a *minimum* point.

The point along a curve with the largest value of *y* is called the **maximum** of the curve.

Panel (a) of **Figure A.5** illustrates a curve in which the slope changes from positive to negative as the line moves from left to right. When x is between 0 and 50, the slope of the curve is positive. When x equals 50, the curve attains its highest point—the largest value of y along the curve. This point is called the **maximum** of the curve. When x exceeds 50, the slope becomes negative as the curve turns downward. Many important curves in economics, such as the curve that represents how the profit of a firm changes as it produces more output, are hill-shaped like this one.

Figure A.5 Maximum and Minimum Points

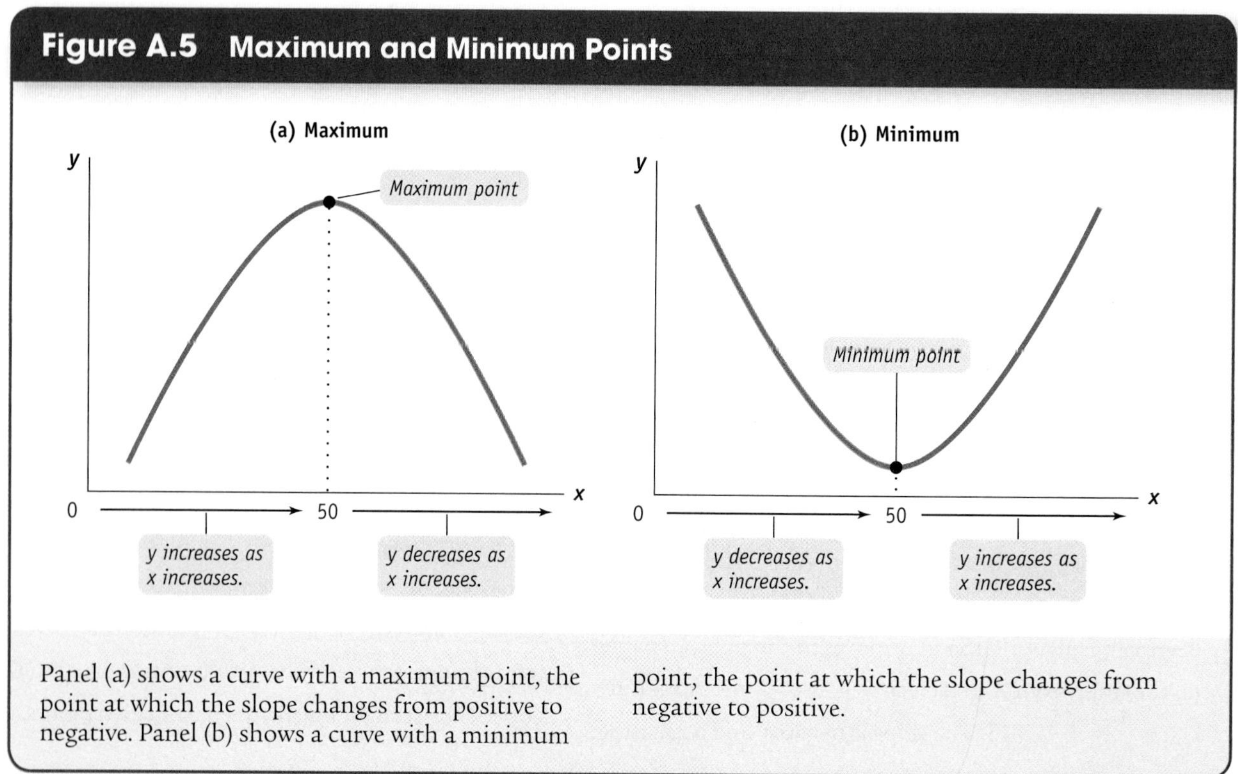

Panel (a) shows a curve with a maximum point, the point at which the slope changes from positive to negative. Panel (b) shows a curve with a minimum point, the point at which the slope changes from negative to positive.

In contrast, the curve shown in panel (b) of Figure A.5 is U-shaped: it has a slope that changes from negative to positive. When x equals 50, the curve reaches its lowest point—the smallest value of y along the curve. This point is called the **minimum** of the curve. Various important curves in economics, such as the curve that represents how a firm's cost per unit changes as output increases, are U-shaped like this one.

The point along a curve with the smallest value of y is called the **minimum** of the curve.

Calculating the Area Below or Above a Curve

Sometimes it is useful to be able to measure the size of the area below or above a curve. To keep things simple, we'll only calculate the area below or above a linear curve.

How large is the shaded area below the linear curve in panel (a) of **Figure A.6**? First, note that this area has the shape of a right triangle. A right triangle is a triangle in which two adjacent sides form a 90° angle. We will refer to one of these sides as the *height* of the triangle and the other side as the *base* of the triangle. For our purposes, it doesn't matter which of these two sides we refer to as the base and which as the height. Calculating the area of a right triangle is straightforward: multiply the height of the triangle by the base of the triangle, and divide the result by 2. The height of the triangle in panel (a) of Figure A.6 is 10 – 4 = 6. And the base of the triangle is 3 – 0 = 3. So the area of that triangle is

Figure A.6 Calculating the Area Below and Above a Linear Curve

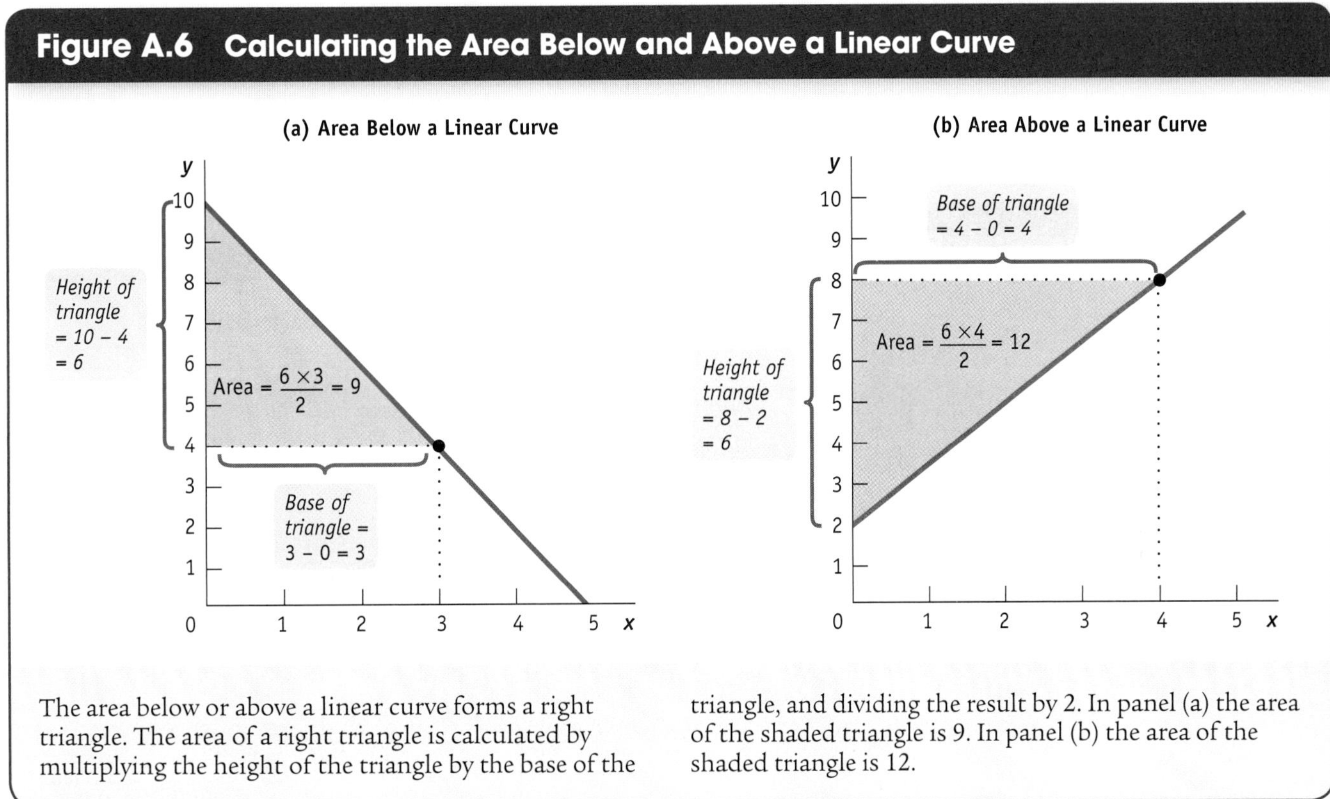

The area below or above a linear curve forms a right triangle. The area of a right triangle is calculated by multiplying the height of the triangle by the base of the triangle, and dividing the result by 2. In panel (a) the area of the shaded triangle is 9. In panel (b) the area of the shaded triangle is 12.

$$\frac{6 \times 3}{2} = 9$$

How about the shaded area above the linear curve in panel (b) of Figure A.6? We can use the same formula to calculate the area of this right triangle. The height of the triangle is 8 – 2 = 6. And the base of the triangle is 4 – 0 = 4. So the area of that triangle is

$$\frac{6 \times 4}{2} = 12$$

Graphs That Depict Numerical Information

Graphs can also be used as a convenient way to summarize and display data without assuming some underlying causal relationship. Graphs that simply display numerical information are called *numerical graphs*. Here we will consider four types of numerical graphs: *time-series graphs, scatter diagrams, pie charts,* and *bar graphs*. These are widely used to display real empirical data about different economic variables, because they often help economists and policy makers identify patterns or trends in the economy.

Types of Numerical Graphs

A **time-series graph** has successive dates on the horizontal axis and the values of a variable that occurred on those dates on the vertical axis.

You have probably seen graphs in newspapers that show what has happened over time to economic variables such as the unemployment rate or stock prices. A **time-series graph** has successive dates on the horizontal axis and the values of a variable that occurred on those dates on the vertical axis. For example, **Figure A.7** shows the unemployment rate in the United States from 1989 to late 2013. A line connecting the points that correspond to the unemployment rate for each month during those years gives a clear idea of the overall trend in unemployment during that period. Note the two short diagonal lines toward the bottom of the y-axis in Figure A.7. This *truncation sign* indicates that a piece of the axis—here, unemployment rates below 4%—was cut to save space.

Figure A.7 Time-Series Graph

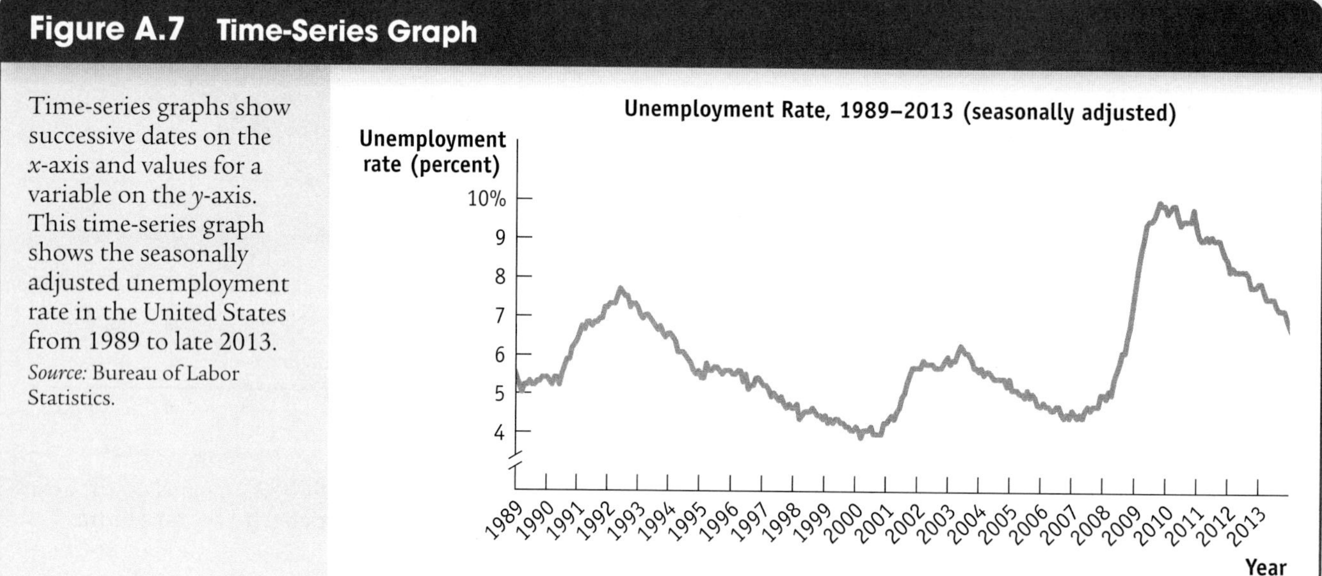

Time-series graphs show successive dates on the x-axis and values for a variable on the y-axis. This time-series graph shows the seasonally adjusted unemployment rate in the United States from 1989 to late 2013.
Source: Bureau of Labor Statistics.

Figure A.8 is an example of a different kind of numerical graph. It represents information from a sample of 168 countries on average life expectancy and gross national product (GNP) per capita—a rough measure of a country's standard of living. Each point in the graph indicates an average resident's life expectancy and the log of GNP per capita for a given country. (Economists have found that the log of GNP rather than the simple level of GNP is more closely tied to average life expectancy.) The points lying in the upper right of the graph, which show combinations of high life expectancy and high log of GNP per capita, represent economically advanced countries such as the United States. Points lying in the bottom left of the graph, which show combinations of low life expectancy and low log of GNP per capita, represent economically less advanced countries such as Afghanistan and Sierra Leone. The pattern of points indicates that there is a positive relationship between life expectancy and log of GNP per capita: on the whole, people live longer in countries with a higher standard of living. This type

Figure A.8 Scatter Diagram

In a scatter diagram, each point represents the corresponding values of the *x*- and *y*-variables for a given observation. Here, each point indicates the observed average life expectancy and the log of GNP per capita of a given country for a sample of 168 countries. The upward-sloping fitted line here is the best approximation of the general relationship between the two variables.

Source: World Bank (2012).

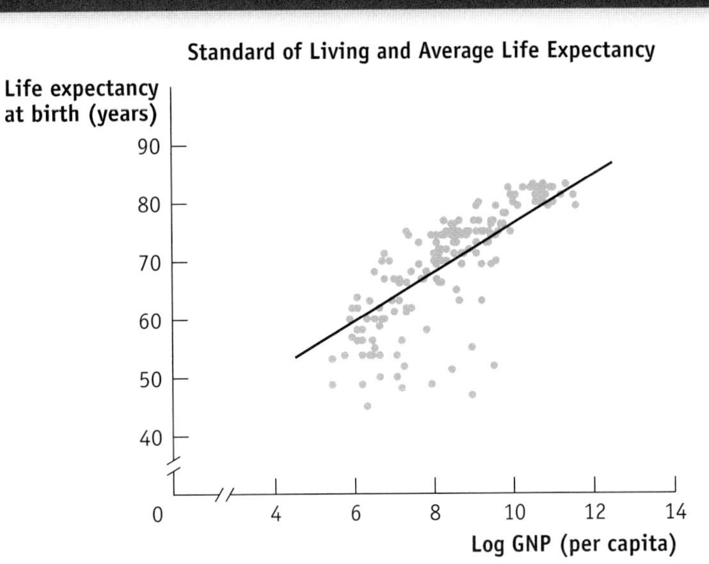

of graph is called a **scatter diagram**, a diagram in which each point corresponds to an actual observation of the *x*-variable and the *y*-variable. In scatter diagrams, a curve is typically fitted to the scatter of points; that is, a curve is drawn that approximates as closely as possible the general relationship between the variables. As you can see, the fitted curve in Figure A.8 is upward-sloping, indicating the underlying positive relationship between the two variables. Scatter diagrams are often used to show how a general relationship can be inferred from a set of data.

Each point on a **scatter diagram** corresponds to an actual observation of the *x*-variable and the *y*-variable.

A **pie chart** shows the share of a total amount that is accounted for by various components, usually expressed in percentages.

A **pie chart** shows the share of a total amount that is accounted for by various components, usually expressed in percentages. For example, **Figure A.9** is a pie chart that depicts the various sources of revenue for the U.S. government budget in 2012, expressed in percentages of the total revenue amount, $2,663 billion. As you can see, social insurance receipts (the revenues collected to fund Social Security, Medicare, and unemployment insurance) accounted for 35% of total government revenue, and individual income tax receipts accounted for 43%.

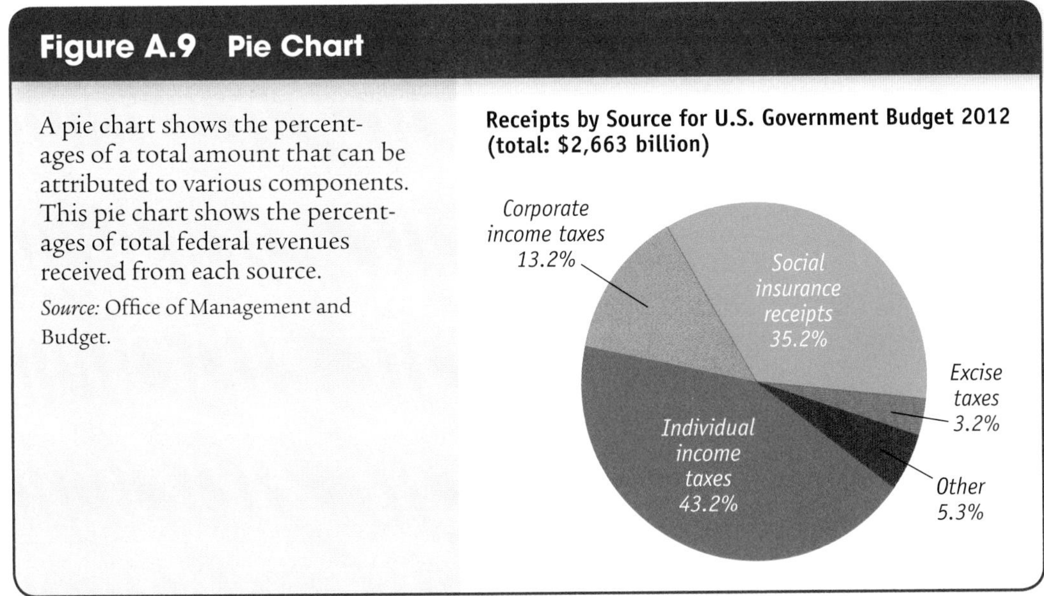

A pie chart shows the percentages of a total amount that can be attributed to various components. This pie chart shows the percentages of total federal revenues received from each source.

Source: Office of Management and Budget.

A **bar graph** uses bars of various heights or lengths to indicate values of a variable.

A **bar graph** uses bars of various heights or lengths to indicate values of a variable. In the bar graph in **Figure A.10**, the bars show the percent change in the number of unemployed workers in the United States from 2012 to 2013, indicated separately for White, Black or African-American, and Asian workers. Exact values of the variable that is being measured may be written at the end of the bar, as in this figure. For instance, the number of unemployed Asian workers in the United States decreased by 15% between 2012 and 2013. But even without the precise values, comparing the heights or lengths of the bars can give useful insight into the relative magnitudes of the different values of the variable.

Figure A.10 Bar Graph

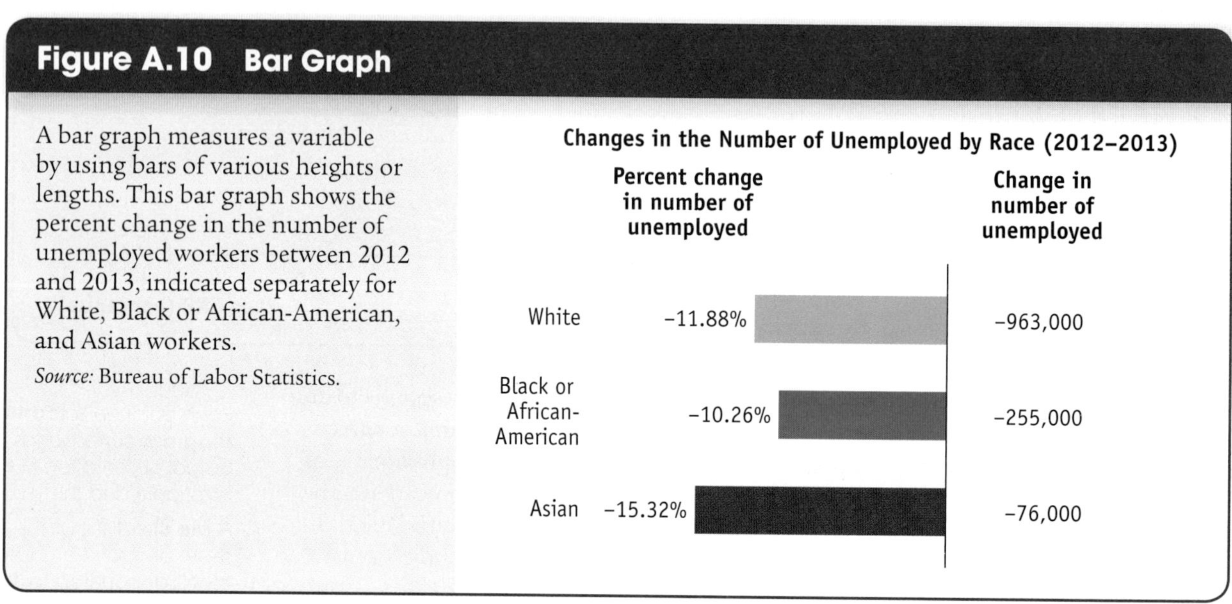

A bar graph measures a variable by using bars of various heights or lengths. This bar graph shows the percent change in the number of unemployed workers between 2012 and 2013, indicated separately for White, Black or African-American, and Asian workers.

Source: Bureau of Labor Statistics.

SECTION 1 Appendix Review

Check Your Understanding

1. Study the four accompanying diagrams. Consider the following statements and indicate which diagram matches each statement. For each statement, tell which variable would appear on the horizontal axis and which on the vertical. In each of these statements, is the slope positive, negative, zero, or infinity?

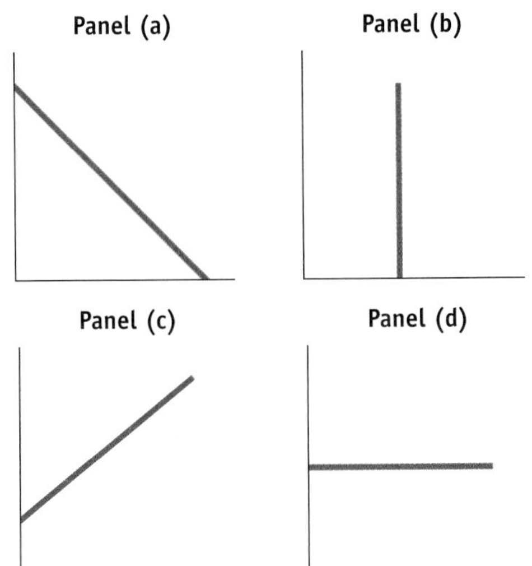

   a. If the price of movies increases, fewer consumers go to see movies.
   b. Workers with more experience typically have higher incomes than less experienced workers.
   c. Regardless of the temperature outside, Americans consume the same number of hot dogs per day.
   d. Consumers buy more frozen yogurt when the price of ice cream goes up.
   e. Research finds no relationship between the number of diet books purchased and the number of pounds lost by the average dieter.
   f. Regardless of its price, there is no change in the quantity of salt that Americans buy.

2. During the Reagan administration, economist Arthur Laffer argued in favor of lowering income tax rates in order to increase tax revenues. Like most economists, he believed that at tax rates above a certain level, tax revenue would fall (because high taxes would discourage some people from working) and that people would refuse to work at all if they received no income after paying taxes. This relationship between tax rates and tax revenue is graphically summarized in what is widely known as the Laffer curve. Plot the Laffer curve relationship, assuming that it has the shape of a nonlinear curve. The following questions will help you construct the graph.
   a. Which is the independent variable? Which is the dependent variable? On which axis do you therefore measure the income tax rate? On which axis do you measure income tax revenue?
   b. What would tax revenue be at a 0% income tax rate?
   c. The maximum possible income tax rate is 100%. What would tax revenue be at a 100% income tax rate?
   d. Estimates now show that the maximum point on the Laffer curve is (approximately) at a tax rate of 80%. For tax rates less than 80%, how would you describe the relationship between the tax rate and tax revenue, and how is this relationship reflected in the slope? For tax rates higher than 80%, how would you describe the relationship between the tax rate and tax revenue, and how is this relationship reflected in the slope?

Key Terms

Variable, p. 36
Horizontal axis/*x*-axis, p. 37
Vertical axis/*y*-axis, p. 37
Origin, p. 37
Causal relationship, p. 38
Independent variable, p. 38
Dependent variable, p. 38
Curve, p. 38
Linear relationship, p. 38
Nonlinear relationship, p. 38
Positive relationship, p. 39
Negative relationship, p. 39
Horizontal intercept, p. 39
Vertical intercept, p. 39
Slope, p. 39
Nonlinear curve, p. 41
Absolute value, p. 42
Maximum, p. 42
Minimum, p. 43
Time-series graph, p. 44
Scatter diagram, p. 45
Pie chart, p. 45
Bar graph, p. 46

SECTION 2

Supply and Demand

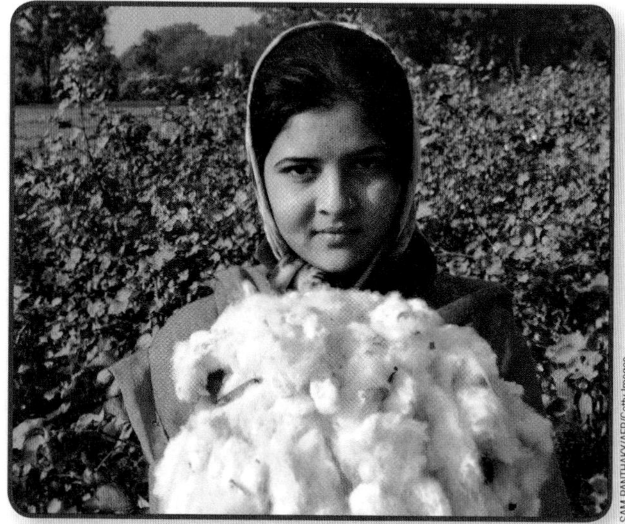

SAM PANTHAKY/AFP/Getty Images

Blue Jean Blues

If you bought a pair of blue jeans in 2012, you may have been shocked at the price. Or maybe not: fashions change, and maybe you thought you were paying the price for being fashionable. But you weren't—you were paying for cotton. Jeans are made of denim, a particular weave of cotton. In 2011, when jeans manufacturers were buying supplies for the coming year, the price of cotton climbed to more than triple its level just two years earlier. In March 2011, the price of a pound of cotton hit a 141-year high, the highest cotton price since record keeping began in 1870.

Why were cotton prices so high? On one side, demand for clothing of all kinds was surging. In 2008–2009, as the world struggled with the effects of a financial crisis, nervous consumers cut back on clothing purchases. But by 2011, with the worst apparently over, buyers were back in force. On the supply side, severe weather events hit world cotton production. Most notably, Pakistan, the world's fourth-largest cotton producer, was hit by devastating floods that put one-fifth of the country underwater and virtually destroyed its cotton crop.

Fearing that consumers had limited tolerance for large increases in the price of cotton clothing, apparel makers began scrambling to find ways to reduce costs without offending consumers' fashion sense. They adopted changes like smaller buttons, cheaper linings, and—yes—polyester, doubting that consumers would be willing to pay more for cotton goods. In fact, some experts on the cotton market warned that the sky-high prices of cotton in 2011 might lead to a permanent shift in tastes, with consumers becoming more willing to wear synthetics even when cotton prices came down.

At the same time, it was not all bad news for everyone connected with the cotton trade. In the United States, cotton producers had not been hit by bad weather and were relishing the higher prices. American farmers responded to the sky-high cotton prices by sharply increasing the acreage they devoted to the crop. None of these measures were enough, however, to produce immediate price relief.

Wait a minute: how, exactly, does flooding in Pakistan translate into higher jeans prices and more polyester in your T-shirts? It's a matter of supply and demand—but what does that mean? Many people use "supply and demand" as a catchphrase to mean "the laws of the marketplace at work." To economists, however, the concept of supply and demand has a precise meaning: it is a *model* of market behavior that is extremely useful for understanding many—but not all—markets.

In this section, we lay out the pieces that make up the *supply and demand model*, put them together, and show how this model can be used to understand how most markets behave.

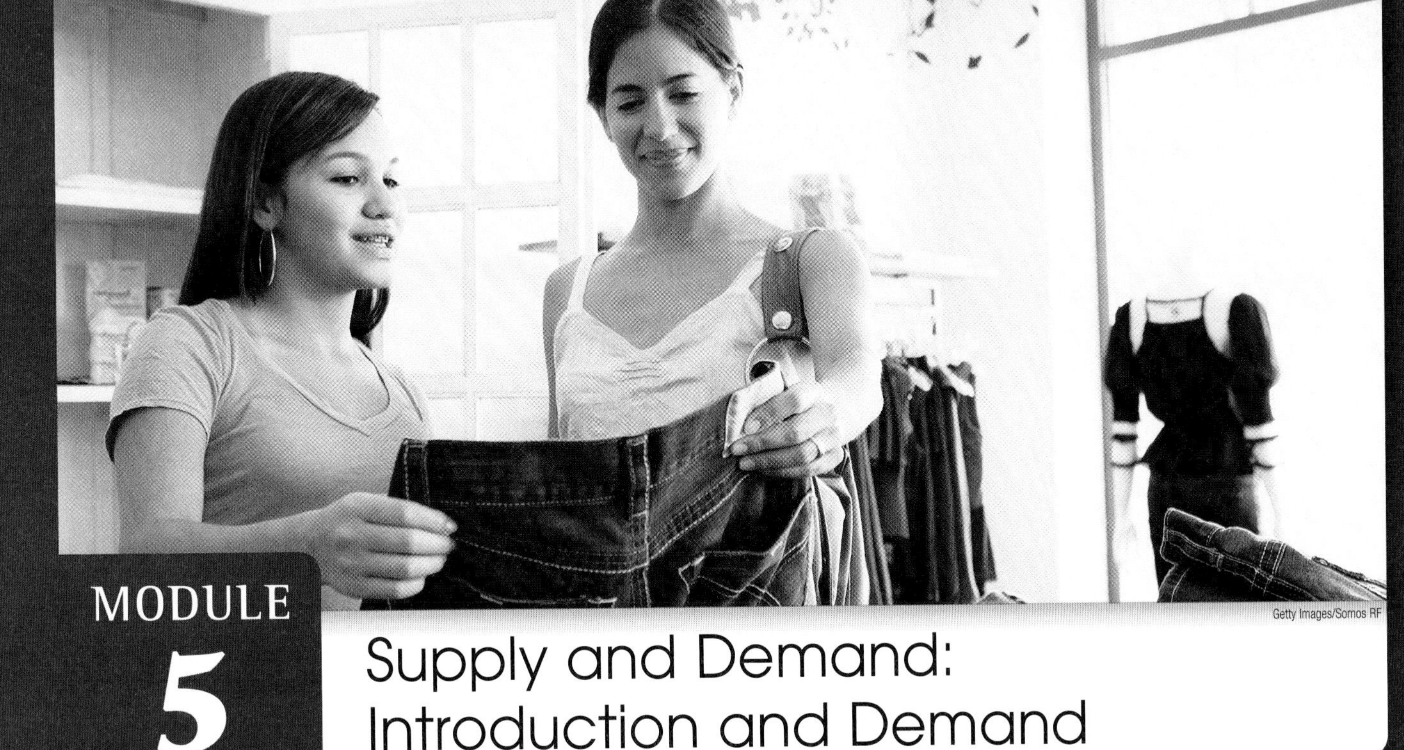

Getty Images/Somos RF

MODULE 5 Supply and Demand: Introduction and Demand

In this Module, you will learn to:

- Explain what a competitive market is and how it is described by the supply and demand model
- Draw a demand curve and interpret its meaning
- Discuss the difference between movements along the demand curve and changes in demand
- List the factors that shift the demand curve

Supply and Demand: A Model of a Competitive Market

Cotton sellers and cotton buyers constitute a *market*—a group of producers and consumers who exchange a good or service for payment. In this section, we'll focus on a particular type of market known as a *competitive market*. Roughly, a **competitive market** is one in which there are many buyers and sellers of the same good or service. More precisely, the key feature of a competitive market is that no individual's actions have a noticeable effect on the price at which the good or service is sold. It's important to understand, however, that this is not an accurate description of every market. For example, it's not an accurate description of the market for cola beverages. That's because in the market for cola beverages, Coca-Cola and Pepsi account for such a large proportion of total sales that they are able to influence the price at which cola beverages are bought and sold. But it *is* an accurate description of the market for cotton. The global marketplace for cotton is so huge that even a jeans retailer as large as Levi Strauss & Co. accounts for only a tiny fraction of transactions, making it unable to influence the price at which cotton is bought and sold.

It's a little hard to explain why competitive markets are different from other markets until we've seen how a competitive market works. For now, let's just say that it's easier to model competitive markets than other markets. When taking an exam, it's always a good strategy to begin by answering the easier questions. In this book, we're going to do the same thing. So we will start with competitive markets.

AP® Exam Tip

Supply and demand graphs are some of the most important graphs to master for success on the AP® exam. You must be able to draw, label, and interpret the graphs for the exam. They are the basis of future graphs you will learn in the course, too.

A **competitive market** is a market in which there are many buyers and sellers of the same good or service, none of whom can influence the price at which the good or service is sold.

The **supply and demand model** is a model of how a competitive market works.

When a market is competitive, its behavior is well described by the **supply and demand model**. Because many markets *are* competitive, the supply and demand model is a very useful one indeed.

There are five key elements in this model:

- The *demand curve*
- The *supply curve*
- The set of factors that cause the demand curve to shift and the set of factors that cause the supply curve to shift
- The *market equilibrium*, which includes the *equilibrium price* and *equilibrium quantity*
- The way the market equilibrium changes when the supply curve or demand curve shifts

To explain the supply and demand model, we will examine each of these elements in turn. In this module we begin with demand.

The Demand Curve

How many pounds of cotton, packaged in the form of blue jeans, do consumers around the world want to buy in a given year? You might at first think that we can answer this question by multiplying the number of pairs of blue jeans purchased around the world each day by the amount of cotton it takes to make a pair of jeans, and then multiplying by 365. But that's not enough to answer the question because how many pairs of jeans—in other words, how many pounds of cotton—consumers want to buy depends on the price of cotton. When the price of cotton rises, as it did in 2011, some people will respond to the higher price of cotton clothing by buying fewer cotton garments or, perhaps, by switching completely to garments made from other materials, such as synthetics or linen. In general, the quantity of cotton clothing, or of any good or service that people want to buy (taking "want" to mean they are willing and able to buy it), depends on the price. The higher the price, the less of the good or service people want to purchase; alternatively, the lower the price, the more they want to purchase.

So the answer to the question "How many pounds of cotton do consumers want to buy?" depends on the price of a pound of cotton. If you don't yet know what the price will be, you can start by making a table of how many pounds of cotton people would want to buy at a number of different prices. Such a table is known as a *demand schedule*. This, in turn, can be used to draw a *demand curve*, which is one of the key elements of the supply and demand model.

The Demand Schedule and the Demand Curve

A **demand schedule** shows how much of a good or service consumers will be willing and able to buy at different prices.

A **demand schedule** is a table that shows how much of a good or service consumers will want to buy at different prices. On the right side of **Figure 5.1**, we show a hypothetical demand schedule for cotton. It's hypothetical in that it doesn't use actual data on the world demand for cotton, and it assumes that all cotton is of equal quality.

According to the table, if cotton costs $1 a pound, consumers around the world will want to purchase 10 billion pounds of cotton over the course of a year. If the price is $1.25 a pound, they will want to buy only 8.9 billion pounds; if the price is only $0.75 a pound, they will want to buy 11.5 billion pounds; and so on. So the higher the price, the fewer pounds of cotton consumers will want to purchase. In other words, as the price rises, the **quantity demanded** of cotton—the actual amount consumers are willing and able to buy at some specific price—falls.

The **quantity demanded** is the actual amount of a good or service consumers are willing and able to buy at some specific price.

The graph in Figure 5.1 is a visual representation of the information in the table. The vertical axis shows the price of a pound of cotton and the horizontal axis shows the quantity of cotton in pounds. Each point on the graph corresponds to one of the

Figure 5.1 The Demand Schedule and the Demand Curve

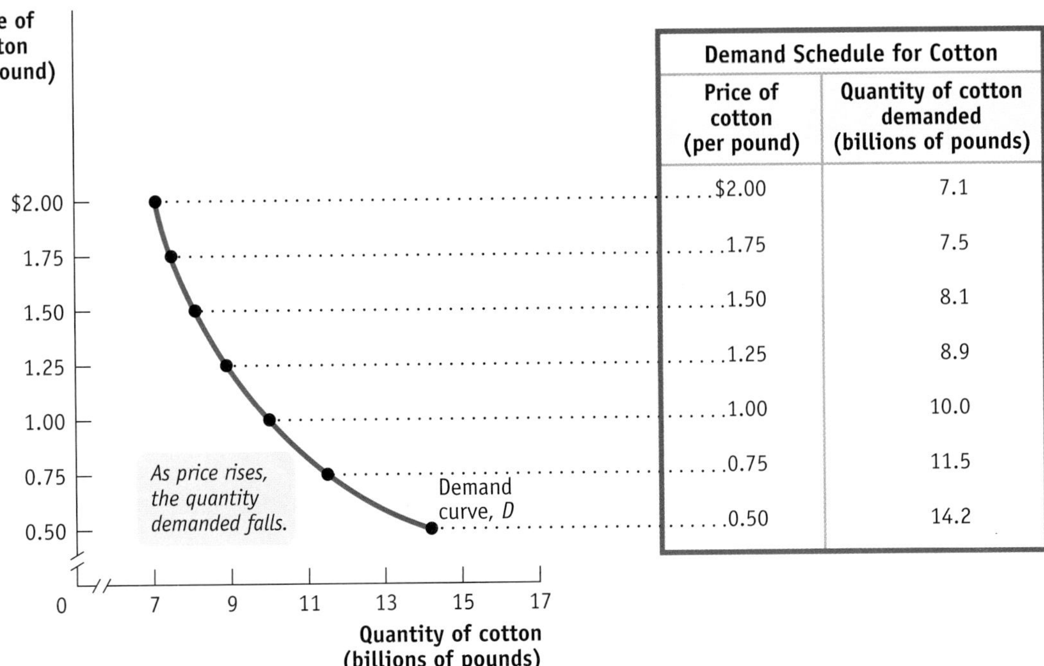

Demand Schedule for Cotton	
Price of cotton (per pound)	Quantity of cotton demanded (billions of pounds)
$2.00	7.1
1.75	7.5
1.50	8.1
1.25	8.9
1.00	10.0
0.75	11.5
0.50	14.2

The demand schedule for cotton yields the corresponding demand curve, which shows how much of a good or service consumers want to buy at any given price. The demand curve and the demand schedule reflect the law of demand: As price rises, the quantity demanded falls. Similarly, a decrease in price raises the quantity demanded. As a result, the demand curve is downward-sloping.

entries in the table. The curve that connects these points is a **demand curve**, a graphical representation of the demand schedule, which is another way of showing the relationship between the quantity demanded and the price.

Note that the demand curve shown in Figure 5.1 slopes downward. This reflects the general proposition that a higher price reduces the quantity demanded. For example, jeans-makers know they will sell fewer pairs of jeans when the price of jeans is higher, reflecting a $2 price per pound of cotton, compared to the number they will sell when the price of jeans is lower, reflecting a price of only $1 per pound of cotton. When the price of jeans is relatively high, some people buy pants less often, and some people buy pants made of wool, linen, or synthetics instead of cotton. In the real world, demand curves almost always slope downward. It is so likely that, all other things being equal, a higher price for a good will lead people to demand a smaller quantity of it, that economists are willing to call it a "law"—the **law of demand**.

A **demand curve** is a graphical representation of the demand schedule. It shows the relationship between quantity demanded and price.

The **law of demand** says that a higher price for a good or service, all other things being equal, leads people to demand a smaller quantity of that good or service.

Shifts of the Demand Curve

Even though cotton prices were higher in 2013 than they had been in 2012, total world consumption of cotton was higher in 2013. How can we reconcile this fact with the law of demand, which says that a higher price reduces the quantity demanded, all other things being equal?

The answer lies in the crucial phrase *all other things being equal*. In this case, all other things weren't equal: there were changes between 2012 and 2013 that increased the quantity of cotton demanded at any given price. For one thing, the world's population

AP® Exam Tip

In several common economics graphs including the graph of supply and demand, the dependent variable is on the vertical axis and the independent variable is on the horizontal axis. You learned the opposite convention in math and science classes, so graphing in economics may be a little difficult at first.

Figure 5.2 An Increase in Demand

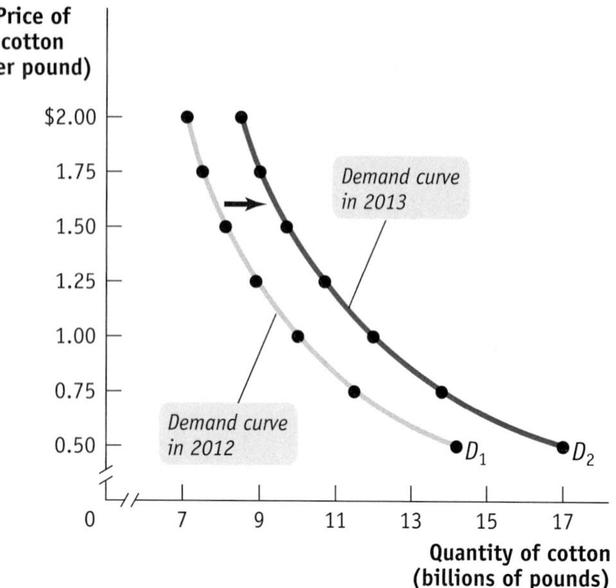

Demand Schedules for Cotton		
Price of cotton (per pound)	Quantity of cotton demanded (billions of pounds)	
	in 2012	in 2013
$2.00	7.1	8.5
1.75	7.5	9.0
1.50	8.1	9.7
1.25	8.9	10.7
1.00	10.0	12.0
0.75	11.5	13.8
0.50	14.2	17.0

Increases in population and income, among other changes, generate an increase in demand—a rise in the quantity demanded at any given price. This is represented by the two demand schedules—one showing demand in 2012, before the rise in population and income, the other showing demand in 2013, after the rise in population and income—and their corresponding demand curves. The increase in demand shifts the demand curve to the right.

AP® Exam Tip

A price change causes a change in the quantity demanded, shown by a movement along the demand curve. When a nonprice factor of demand changes, this changes demand, and therefore shifts the demand curve. It would be correct to say that an increase in the price of apples decreases the quantity of apples demanded; it would be incorrect to say that an increase in the price of apples decreases the demand for apples.

A **change in demand** is a shift of the demand curve, which changes the quantity demanded at any given price.

A **movement along the demand curve** is a change in the quantity demanded of a good that is the result of a change in that good's price.

increased by 77 million, and therefore the number of potential wearers of cotton clothing increased. In addition, higher incomes in countries like China allowed people to buy more clothing than before. These changes led to an increase in the quantity of cotton demanded at any given price. **Figure 5.2** illustrates this phenomenon using the demand schedule and demand curve for cotton. (As before, the numbers in Figure 5.2 are hypothetical.)

The table in Figure 5.2 shows two demand schedules. The first is a demand schedule for 2012, the same one shown in Figure 5.1. The second is a demand schedule for 2013. It differs from the 2012 demand schedule due to factors such as a larger population and higher incomes, factors that led to an increase in the quantity of cotton demanded at any given price. So at each price, the 2013 schedule shows a larger quantity demanded than the 2012 schedule. For example, the quantity of cotton consumers wanted to buy at a price of $1 per pound increased from 10 billion to 12 billion pounds per year, the quantity demanded at $1.25 per pound went from 8.9 billion to 10.7 billion pounds, and so on.

What is clear from this example is that the changes that occurred between 2012 and 2013 generated a *new* demand schedule, one in which the quantity demanded was greater at any given price than in the original demand schedule. The two curves in Figure 5.2 show the same information graphically. As you can see, the demand schedule for 2013 corresponds to a new demand curve, D_2, that is to the right of the demand curve for 2012, D_1. This **change in demand** shows the increase in the quantity demanded at any given price, represented by the shift in position of the original demand curve, D_1, to its new location at D_2.

It's crucial to make the distinction between such changes in demand and **movements along the demand curve**, changes in the quantity demanded of a good that result from a change in that good's price. **Figure 5.3** illustrates the difference.

Figure 5.3 A Movement Along the Demand Curve Versus a Shift of the Demand Curve

The rise in the quantity demanded when going from point *A* to point *B* reflects a movement along the demand curve: it is the result of a fall in the price of the good. The rise in the quantity demanded when going from point *A* to point *C* reflects a change in demand: this shift to the right is the result of a rise in the quantity demanded at any given price.

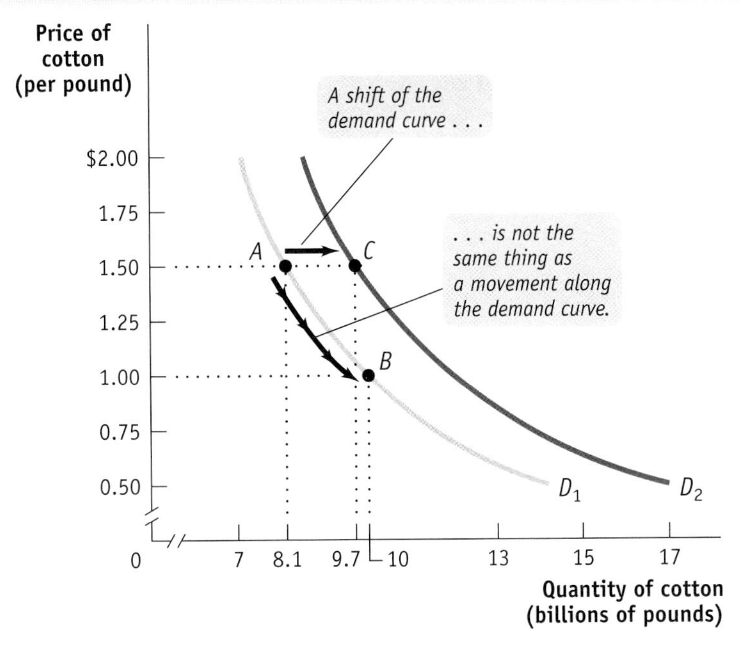

The movement from point *A* to point *B* is a movement along the demand curve: the quantity demanded rises due to a fall in price as you move down D_1. Here, a fall in the price of cotton from \$1.50 to \$1 per pound generates a rise in the quantity demanded from 8.1 billion to 10 billion pounds per year. But the quantity demanded can also rise when the price is unchanged if there is an *increase in demand*—a rightward shift of the demand curve. This is illustrated in Figure 5.3 by the shift of the demand curve from D_1 to D_2. Holding the price constant at \$1.50 a pound, the quantity demanded rises from 8.1 billion pounds at point *A* on D_1 to 9.7 billion pounds at point *C* on D_2.

When economists talk about a "change in demand," saying "the demand for *X* increased" or "the demand for *Y* decreased," they mean that the demand curve for *X* or *Y* shifted—*not* that the quantity demanded rose or fell because of a change in the price.

AP® Exam Tip

When shifting curves, *left is less and right is more.*

Understanding Shifts of the Demand Curve

Figure 5.4 on the next page illustrates the two basic ways in which demand curves can shift. When economists talk about an "increase in demand," they mean a *rightward* shift of the demand curve: at any given price, consumers demand a larger quantity of the good or service than before. This is shown by the rightward shift of the original demand curve D_1 to D_2. And when economists talk about a "decrease in demand," they mean a *leftward* shift of the demand curve: at any given price, consumers demand a smaller quantity of the good or service than before. This is shown by the leftward shift of the original demand curve D_1 to D_3.

What caused the demand curve for cotton to shift? We have already mentioned two reasons: changes in population and income. If you think about it, you can come up with other things that would be likely to shift the demand curve for cotton. For example, suppose that the price of polyester rises. This will induce some people who previously bought polyester clothing to buy cotton clothing instead, increasing the demand for cotton.

Khomulo Anna/Shutterstock

Figure 5.4 Shifts of the Demand Curve

Any event that increases demand shifts the demand curve to the right, reflecting a rise in the quantity demanded at any given price. Any event that decreases demand shifts the demand curve to the left, reflecting a fall in the quantity demanded at any given price.

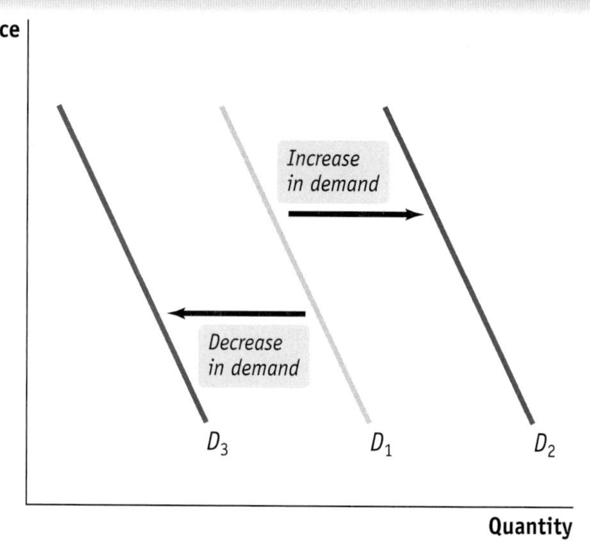

There are five principal factors that shift the demand curve for a good or service:

- Changes in the prices of related goods or services
- Changes in income
- Changes in tastes
- Changes in expectations
- Changes in the number of consumers

Although this is not an exhaustive list, it contains the five most important factors that can shift demand curves. So when we say that the quantity of a good or service demanded falls as its price rises, all other things being equal, we are in fact stating that the factors that shift demand are remaining unchanged. Let's now explore, in more detail, how those factors shift the demand curve.

Two goods are **substitutes** if a rise in the price of one of the goods leads to an increase in the demand for the other good.

Two goods are **complements** if a rise in the price of one of the goods leads to a decrease in the demand for the other good.

Changes in the Prices of Related Goods or Services While there's nothing quite like a comfortable pair of all-cotton blue jeans, for some purposes khakis—typically made from polyester blends—aren't a bad alternative. Khakis are what economists call a *substitute* for jeans. A pair of goods are **substitutes** if a rise in the price of one good (jeans) makes consumers more willing to buy the other good (polyester-blend khakis). Substitutes are usually goods that in some way serve a similar function: coffee and tea, muffins and doughnuts, train rides and airplane rides. A rise in the price of the alternative good induces some consumers to purchase the original good *instead* of it, shifting demand for the original good to the right.

But sometimes a fall in the price of one good makes consumers *more* willing to buy another good. Such pairs of goods are known as **complements**. Complements are usually goods that in some sense are consumed together: computers and software, cookies and milk, cars and gasoline. Because consumers like to consume a good and its complement together, a change in the price of one of the goods will affect the demand for its complement. In particular, when the price of one good rises, the demand for its complement decreases, shifting the demand curve for the complement to the left. So a rise in the price of cookies is likely to precipitate a leftward shift in the demand curve for milk, as people consume fewer snacks of cookies and milk. Likewise, when the price of one good falls, the quantity demanded of its complement rises, shifting the demand curve for the complement to the right.

This means that if, for some reason, the price of cookies falls, we should see a rightward shift in the demand curve for milk, as people consume more cookies *and* more milk.

Changes in Income When individuals have more income, they are normally more likely to purchase a good at any given price. For example, if a family's income rises, it is more likely to take that summer trip to Disney World—and therefore also more likely to buy plane tickets. So a rise in consumer incomes will cause the demand curves for most goods to shift to the right.

Why do we say "most goods," rather than "all goods"? Most goods are **normal goods**—the demand for them increases when consumer income rises. However, the demand for some products falls when income rises. Goods for which demand decreases when income rises are known as **inferior goods**. Usually an inferior good is one that is considered less desirable than more expensive alternatives—such as a bus ride versus a taxi ride. When they can afford to, people stop buying an inferior good and switch their consumption to the preferred, more expensive alternative. So when a good is inferior, a rise in income shifts the demand curve to the left. And, not surprisingly, a fall in income shifts the demand curve to the right.

When a rise in income increases the demand for a good—the normal case—it is a **normal good**.

When a rise in income decreases the demand for a good, it is an **inferior good**.

One example of the distinction between normal and inferior goods that has drawn considerable attention in the business press is the difference between so-called casual-dining restaurants such as Applebee's and Olive Garden and fast-food chains such as McDonald's and KFC. When their incomes rise, Americans tend to eat out more at casual-dining restaurants. However, some of this increased dining out comes at the expense of fast-food venues—to some extent, people visit McDonald's less once they can afford to move upscale. So casual dining is a normal good, while fast-food appears to be an inferior good.

Changes in Tastes Why do people want what they want? Fortunately, we don't need to answer that question—we just need to acknowledge that people have certain preferences, or tastes, that determine what they choose to consume and that these tastes can change. Economists usually lump together changes in demand due to fads, beliefs, cultural shifts, and so on under the heading of changes in *tastes,* or *preferences.*

For example, once upon a time men wore hats. Up until around World War II, a respectable man wasn't fully dressed unless he wore a dignified hat along with his suit. But the returning soldiers adopted a more informal style, perhaps due to the rigors of the war. And President Eisenhower, who had been supreme commander of Allied Forces before becoming president, often went hatless. After World War II, it was clear that the demand curve for hats had shifted leftward, reflecting a decrease in the demand for hats.

Chimpinski/Shutterstock

Economists have little to say about the forces that influence consumers' tastes. (Marketers and advertisers, however, have plenty to say about them!) However, a *change* in tastes has a predictable impact on demand. When tastes change in favor of a good, more people want to buy it at any given price, so the demand curve shifts to the right. When tastes change against a good, fewer people want to buy it at any given price, so the demand curve shifts to the left.

Changes in Expectations When consumers have some choice about when to make a purchase, current demand for a good is often affected by expectations about its future price. For example, savvy shoppers often wait for seasonal sales—say, buying next year's holiday gifts during the post-holiday markdowns. In this case, expectations of a future drop in price lead to a decrease in demand today. Alternatively, expectations of a future rise in price are likely to cause an increase in demand today. For example, if you heard that the price of jeans would increase next year, you might go out and buy an extra pair now.

Changes in expectations about future income can also lead to changes in demand. If you learned today that you would inherit a large sum of money sometime in the future, you might borrow some money today and increase your demand for certain goods. On the other hand, if you learned that you would earn less in the future than you thought, you might reduce your demand for some goods and save more money today.

Figure 5.5 Individual Demand Curves and the Market Demand Curve

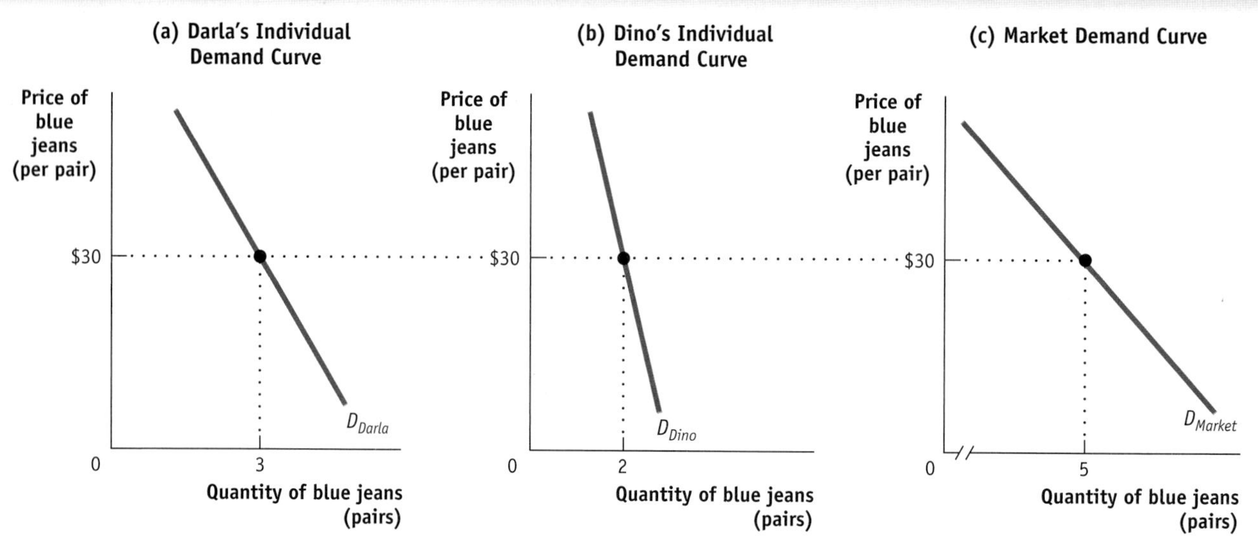

Darla and Dino are the only two consumers of blue jeans in the market. Panel (a) shows Darla's individual demand curve: the number of pairs of jeans she will buy per year at any given price. Panel (b) shows Dino's individual demand curve. Given that Darla and Dino are the only two consumers, the *market demand* curve, which shows the quantity of blue jeans demanded by all consumers at any given price, is shown in panel (c). The market demand curve is the *horizontal sum* of the individual demand curves of all consumers. In this case, at any given price, the quantity demanded by the market is the sum of the quantities demanded by Darla and Dino.

Changes in the Number of Consumers As we've already noted, one of the reasons for rising cotton demand between 2012 and 2013 was a growing world population. Because of population growth, overall demand for cotton would have risen even if the demand of each individual wearer of cotton clothing had remained unchanged.

An **individual demand curve** illustrates the relationship between quantity demanded and price for an individual consumer.

Let's introduce a new concept: the **individual demand curve**, which shows the relationship between quantity demanded and price for an individual consumer. For example, suppose that Darla is a consumer of cotton blue jeans; also suppose that all blue jeans are the same, so they sell for the same price. Panel (a) of **Figure 5.5** shows how many pairs of jeans she will buy per year at any given price per pound. Then D_{Darla} is Darla's individual demand curve.

The *market demand curve* shows how the combined quantity demanded by all consumers depends on the market price of that good. (Most of the time, when economists refer to the demand curve, they mean the market demand curve.) The market demand curve is the *horizontal sum* of the individual demand curves of all consumers in that market. To see what we mean by the term *horizontal sum*, assume for a moment that there are only two consumers of blue jeans, Darla and Dino. Dino's individual demand curve, D_{Dino}, is shown in panel (b). Panel (c) shows the market demand curve. At any given price, the quantity demanded by the market is the sum of the quantities demanded by Darla and Dino. For example, at a price of $30 per pair, Darla demands 3 pairs of jeans per year and Dino demands 2 pairs per year. So the quantity demanded by the market is 5 pairs per year.

Clearly, the quantity demanded by the market at any given price is larger with Dino present than it would be if Darla were the only consumer. The quantity demanded at any given price would be even larger if we added a third consumer, then a fourth, and so on. So an increase in the number of consumers leads to an increase in demand.

For an overview of the factors that shift demand, see **Table 5.1**.

AP® Exam Tip

A mnemonic to help you remember the factors that shift demand is TRIBE. Demand is shifted by changes in . . .
Tastes and preferences,
prices of **R**elated goods
Income,
the number of **B**uyers, and
Expectations.

Table 5.1 Factors That Shift Demand

When this happens . . .	. . . demand increases		But when this happens . . .	. . . demand decreases	
When the price of a substitute rises . . .	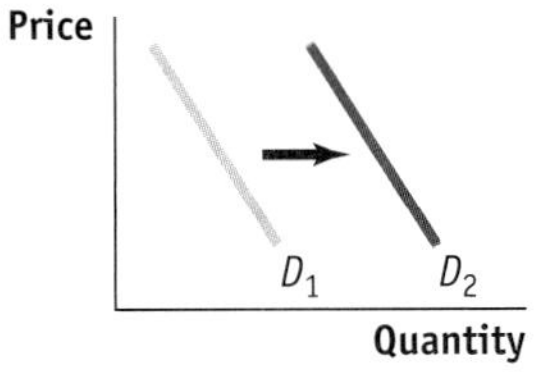 Price; Quantity; D_1 → D_2	. . . demand for the original good increases.	When the price of a substitute falls . . .	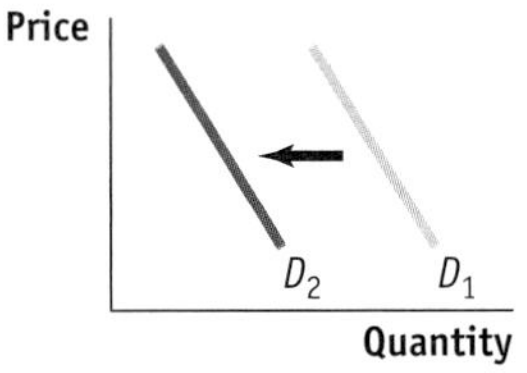 Price; Quantity; D_2 ← D_1	. . . demand for the original good decreases.
When the price of a complement falls . . .	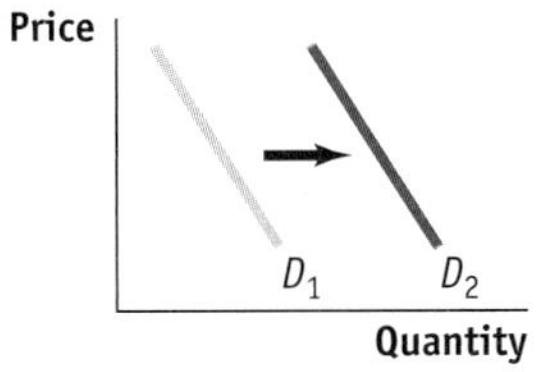 Price; Quantity; D_1 → D_2	. . . demand for the original good increases.	When the price of a complement rises . . .	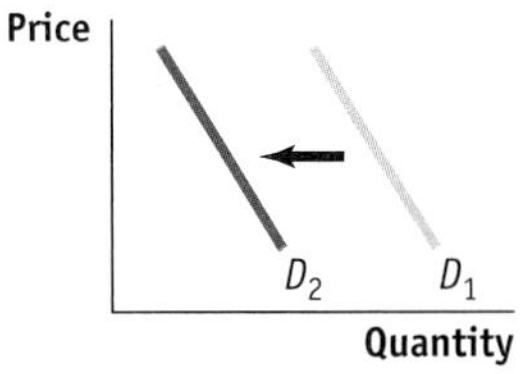 Price; Quantity; D_2 ← D_1	. . . demand for the original good decreases.
When income rises . . .	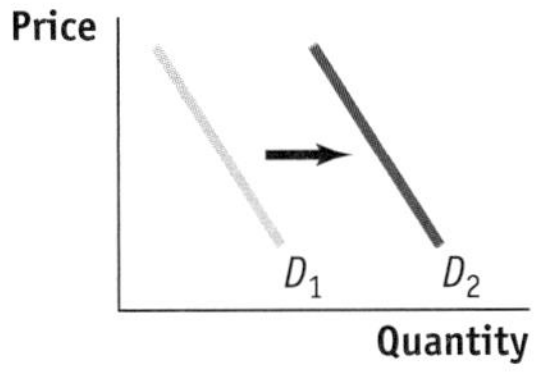 Price; Quantity; D_1 → D_2	. . . demand for a normal good increases.	When income falls . . .	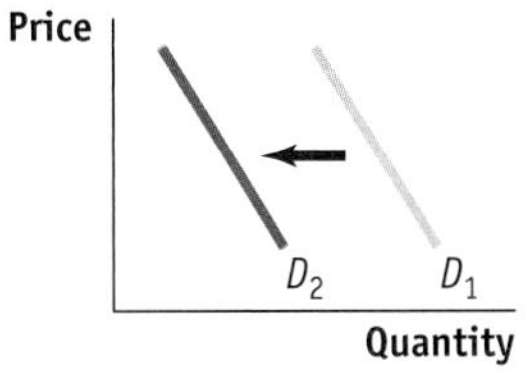 Price; Quantity; D_2 ← D_1	. . . demand for a normal good decreases.
When income falls . . .	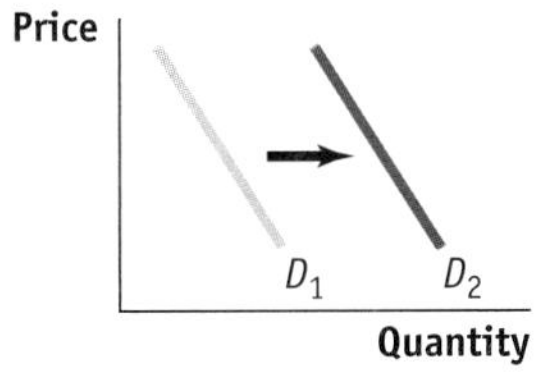 Price; Quantity; D_1 → D_2	. . . demand for an inferior good increases.	When income rises . . .	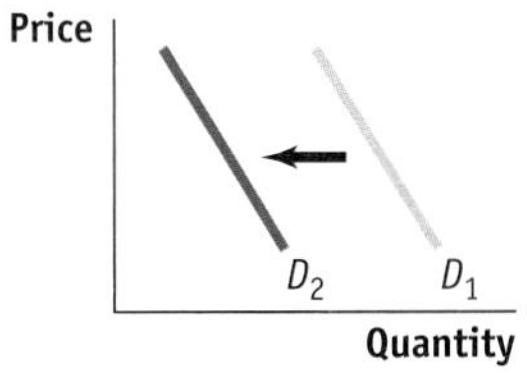 Price; Quantity; D_2 ← D_1	. . . demand for an inferior good decreases.
When tastes change in favor of a good . . .	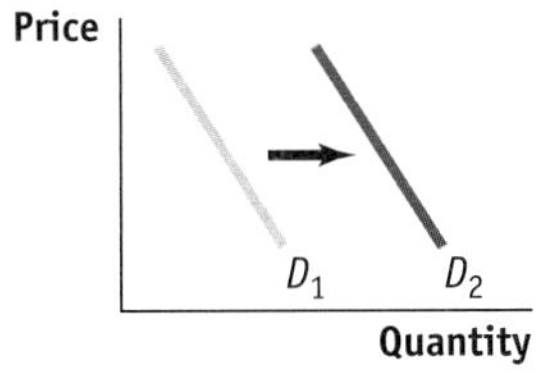 Price; Quantity; D_1 → D_2	. . . demand for the good increases.	When tastes change against a good . . .	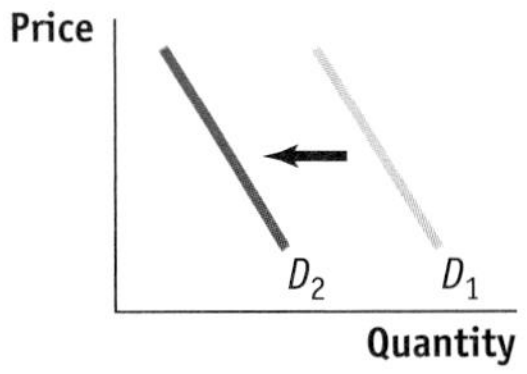 Price; Quantity; D_2 ← D_1	. . . demand for the good decreases.
When the price is expected to rise in the future . . .	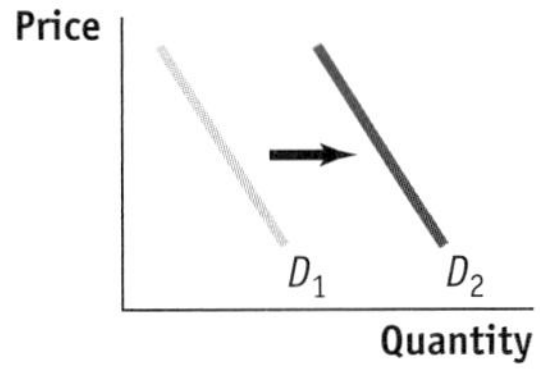 Price; Quantity; D_1 → D_2	. . . demand for the good increases today.	When the price is expected to fall in the future . . .	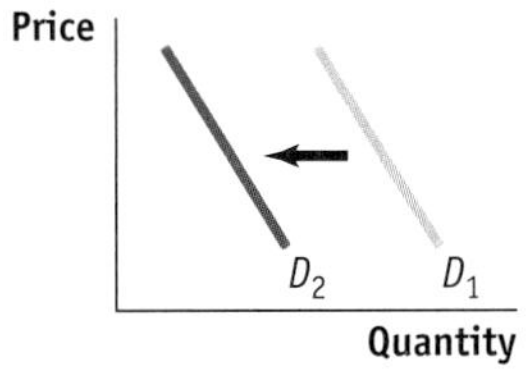 Price; Quantity; D_2 ← D_1	. . . demand for the good decreases today.
When the number of consumers rises . . .	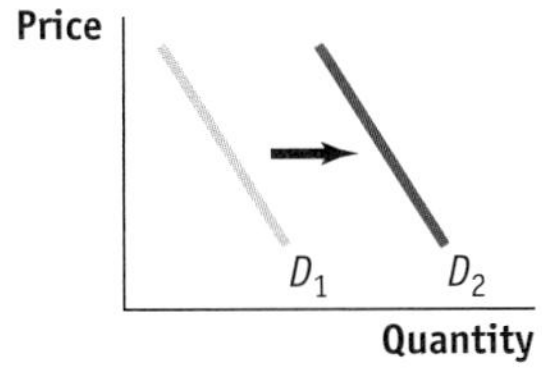 Price; Quantity; D_1 → D_2	. . . market demand for the good increases.	When the number of consumers falls . . .	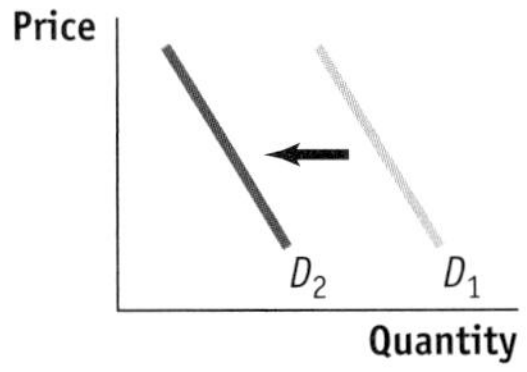 Price; Quantity; D_2 ← D_1	. . . market demand for the good decreases.

Beating the Traffic

All big cities have traffic problems, and many local authorities try to discourage driving in the crowded city center. If we think of an auto trip to the city center as a good that people consume, we can use the economics of demand to analyze anti-traffic policies.

One common strategy of local governments is to reduce the demand for auto trips by lowering the prices of substitutes. Many metropolitan areas subsidize bus and rail service, hoping to lure commuters out of their cars.

An alternative strategy is to raise the price of complements: several major U.S. cities impose high taxes on commercial parking garages, both to raise revenue and to discourage people from driving into the city. High tolls for bridges and tunnels going into cities such as New York serve the same purposes.

However, few cities have been willing to adopt the politically controversial direct approach: reducing congestion by raising the price of simply driving in the city. So it was a shock when, in 2003, London imposed a "congestion charge" on all cars entering the city center during business hours—currently £10 (about $16) for drivers who pay on the same day they travel.

Compliance is monitored with automatic cameras that photograph license plates. People can either pay the charge in advance or pay it by midnight of the day they have driven. If they pay on the day after they have driven, the charge increases to £12 (about $20). And if they don't pay and are caught, a fine of £130 (about $212) is imposed for each transgression. (A full description of the rules can be found at www.cclondon.com.)

Not surprisingly, the result of the new policy confirms the law of demand: three years after the charge was put in place, traffic in central London was about 10 percent lower than before the charge. In February 2007, the British government doubled the area of London covered by the congestion charge, and it suggested that it might institute congestion charging across the country by 2015. Several American and European municipalities, having seen the success of London's congestion charge, have said that they are seriously considering adopting a congestion charge as well.

London's bold policy to charge cars a fee to enter the city center proved effective in reducing traffic congestion.

MODULE 5 Review

Check Your Understanding

1. Explain whether each of the following events represents (i) a *change in demand* (a *shift* of the demand curve) or (ii) a *movement along* the demand curve (a *change in the quantity demanded*).
   - **a.** A store owner finds that customers are willing to pay more for umbrellas on rainy days.
   - **b.** When XYZ Telecom, a long-distance telephone service provider, offered reduced rates on weekends, its volume of weekend calling increased sharply.
   - **c.** People buy more long-stem roses the week of Valentine's Day, even though the prices are higher than at other times during the year.
   - **d.** A sharp rise in the price of gasoline leads many commuters to join carpools in order to reduce their gasoline purchases.

Tackle the Test: Multiple-Choice Questions

1. Which of the following would increase demand for a normal good? A decrease in
- **a.** price
- **b.** income
- **c.** the price of a substitute
- **d.** consumer taste for a good
- **e.** the price of a complement

2. A decrease in the price of butter would most likely decrease the demand for
- **a.** margarine.
- **b.** bagels.
- **c.** jelly.
- **d.** milk.
- **e.** syrup.

3. If an increase in income leads to a decrease in demand, the good is
- **a.** a complement.
- **b.** a substitute.
- **c.** inferior.
- **d.** abnormal.
- **e.** normal.

4. Which of the following will occur if consumers expect the price of a good to fall in the coming months?
- **a.** The quantity demanded will rise today.
- **b.** The quantity demanded will remain the same today.
- **c.** Demand will increase today.
- **d.** Demand will decrease today.
- **e.** No change will occur today.

5. Which of the following will increase the demand for disposable diapers?
- **a.** a new "baby boom"
- **b.** concern over the environmental effect of landfills
- **c.** a decrease in the price of cloth diapers
- **d.** a move toward earlier potty training of children
- **e.** a decrease in the price of disposable diapers

Tackle the Test: Free-Response Questions

1. Create a table with two hypothetical prices for a good and two corresponding quantities demanded. Choose the prices and quantities so that they illustrate the law of demand. Using your data, draw a correctly labeled graph showing the demand curve for the good. Using the same graph, illustrate an increase in demand for the good.

Rubric for FRQ 1 (6 points)

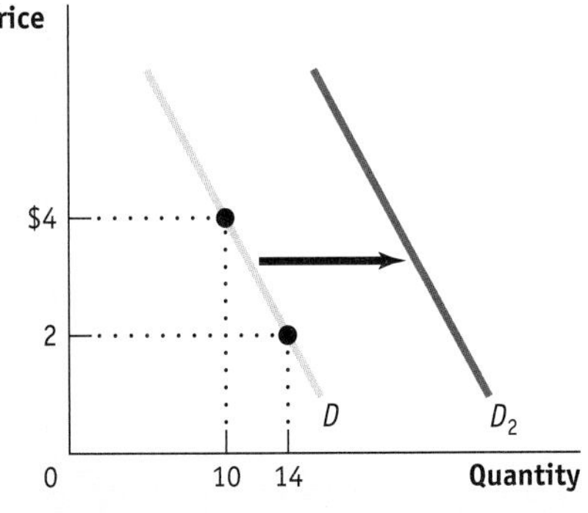

Price	Quantity
$4	10
2	14

1 point: Table with data labeled "Price" (or "*P*") and "Quantity" (or "*Q*")

1 point: Values in the table show a negative relationship between *P* and *Q*

1 point: Graph with "Price" on the vertical axis and "Quantity" on the horizontal axis

1 point: Negatively sloped curve labeled "Demand" or "*D*"

1 point: Demand curve correctly plots the data from the table

1 point: A second demand curve (with a label such as D_2) shown to the right of the original demand curve

2. Draw a correctly labeled graph showing the demand for apples. On your graph, illustrate what happens to the demand for apples if a new report from the Surgeon General finds that an apple a day really *does* keep the doctor away.
(3 points)

Bonnie Taylor Barry/Shutterstock

MODULE 6 Supply and Demand: Supply

In this Module, you will learn to:

- Draw a supply curve and interpret its meaning
- Discuss the difference between movements along the supply curve and changes in supply
- List the factors that shift the supply curve

The Supply Curve

AP® Exam Tip

A change in demand does not affect the supply schedule, and it does not affect the supply curve, which represents the supply schedule on a graph. A change in demand does cause a change in the price, so it will affect the quantity supplied by causing a movement along the supply curve.

Some parts of the world are especially well suited to growing cotton, and the United States is one of those. But even in the United States, some land is better suited to growing cotton than other land. Whether American farmers restrict their cotton-growing to only the most ideal locations or expand it to less suitable land depends on the price they expect to get for their cotton. Moreover, there are many other areas in the world where cotton could be grown—such as Pakistan, Brazil, Turkey, and China. Whether farmers there actually grow cotton depends, again, on the price.

So just as the quantity of cotton that consumers want to buy depends on the price they have to pay, the quantity that producers are willing to produce and sell—the **quantity supplied**—depends on the price they are offered.

The Supply Schedule and the Supply Curve

The **quantity supplied** is the actual amount of a good or service people are willing to sell at some specific price.

A **supply schedule** shows how much of a good or service producers would supply at different prices.

A **supply curve** shows the relationship between the quantity supplied and the price.

The table in **Figure 6.1** shows how the quantity of cotton made available varies with the price—that is, it shows a hypothetical **supply schedule** for cotton.

A supply schedule works the same way as the demand schedule shown in Figure 5.1: in this case, the table shows the number of pounds of cotton farmers are willing to sell at different prices. At a price of $0.50 per pound, farmers are willing to sell only 8 billion pounds of cotton per year. At $0.75 per pound, they're willing to sell 9.1 billion pounds. At $1, they're willing to sell 10 billion pounds, and so on.

In the same way that a demand schedule can be represented graphically by a demand curve, a supply schedule can be represented by a **supply curve**, as shown in Figure 6.1. Each point on the curve represents an entry from the table.

Suppose that the price of cotton rises from $1 to $1.25; we can see that the quantity of cotton farmers are willing to sell rises from 10 billion to 10.7 billion pounds. This is

Figure 6.1 The Supply Schedule and the Supply Curve

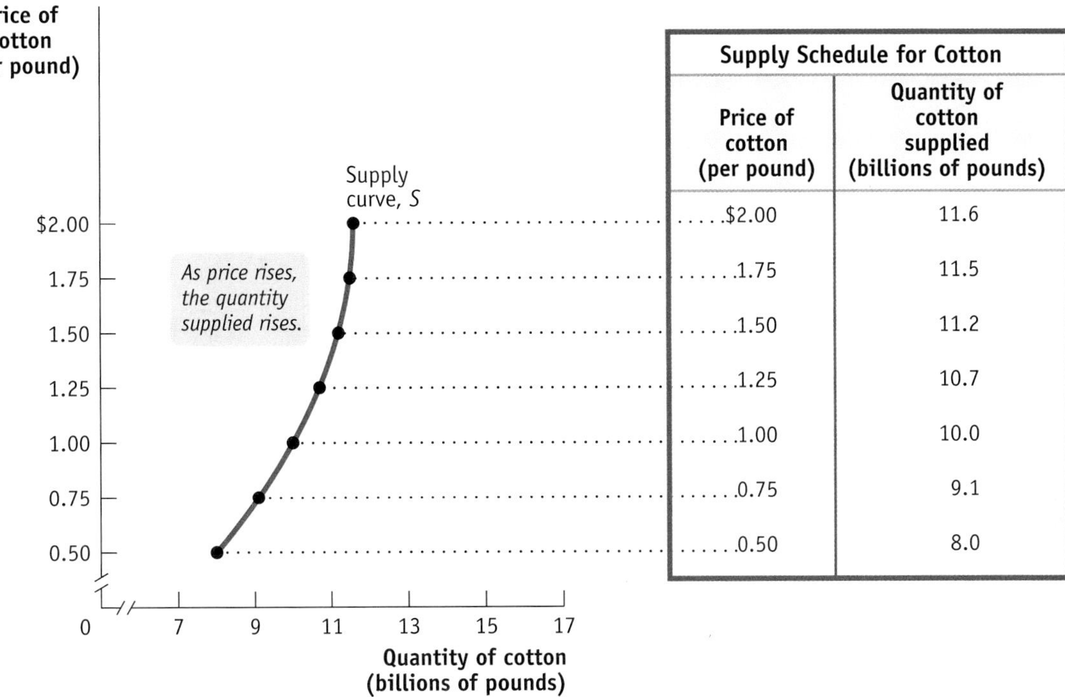

Supply Schedule for Cotton	
Price of cotton (per pound)	Quantity of cotton supplied (billions of pounds)
$2.00	11.6
1.75	11.5
1.50	11.2
1.25	10.7
1.00	10.0
0.75	9.1
0.50	8.0

The supply schedule for cotton is plotted to yield the corresponding supply curve, which shows how much of a good producers are willing to sell at any given price. The supply curve and the supply schedule reflect the fact that supply curves are usually upward sloping: the quantity supplied rises when the price rises.

the normal situation for a supply curve, that a higher price leads to a higher quantity supplied. Some economists refer to this positive relationship as the **law of supply**. So just as demand curves normally slope downward, supply curves normally slope upward: the higher the price being offered, the more of any good or service producers will be willing to sell.

The **law of supply** says that, other things being equal, the price and quantity supplied of a good are positively related.

Shifts of the Supply Curve

Until recently, cotton remained relatively cheap over the past several decades. One reason is that the amount of land cultivated for cotton expanded over 35% from 1945 to 2007. However, the major factor accounting for cotton's relative cheapness was advances in the production technology, with output per acre more than quadrupling from 1945 to 2007. **Figure 6.2** on the next page illustrates these events in terms of the supply schedule and the supply curve for cotton.

The table in Figure 6.2 shows two supply schedules. The schedule before improved cotton-growing technology was adopted is the same one as in Figure 6.1. The second schedule shows the supply of cotton *after* the improved technology was adopted. Just as a change in demand schedules leads to a shift of the demand curve, a change in supply schedules leads to a shift of the supply curve—a **change in supply**. This is shown in Figure 6.2 by the shift of the supply curve before the adoption of new cotton-growing technology, S_1, to its new position after the adoption of new cotton-growing technology, S_2. Notice that S_2 lies to the right of S_1, a reflection of the fact that the quantity supplied rises at any given price.

AP® Exam Tip

The supply curve itself shows the relationship between the price and the quantity supplied, so you should not shift the supply curve to show the effect of a change in the price. When there is a change in a nonprice determinant of supply, such as production costs or the number of firms, supply changes and the supply curve shifts.

A **change in supply** is a shift of the supply curve, which changes the quantity supplied at any given price.

Figure 6.2 An Increase in Supply

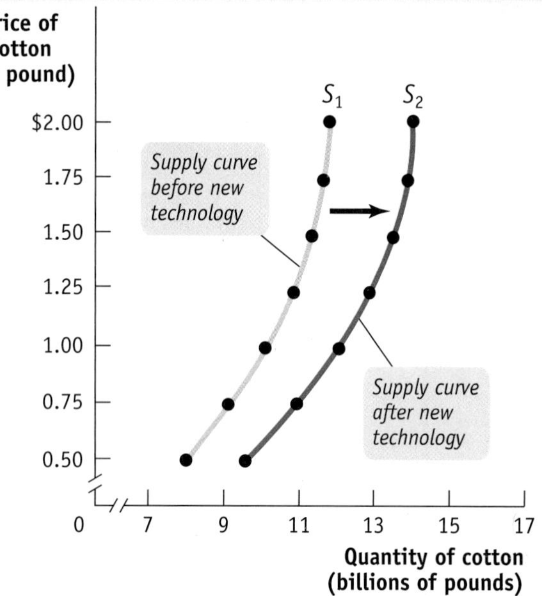

Supply Schedules for Cotton

Price of cotton (per pound)	Quantity of cotton supplied (billions of pounds)	
	Before new technology	After new technology
$2.00	11.6	13.9
1.75	11.5	13.8
1.50	11.2	13.4
1.25	10.7	12.8
1.00	10.0	12.0
0.75	9.1	10.9
0.50	8.0	9.6

The adoption of improved cotton-growing technology generated an increase in supply—a rise in the quantity supplied at any given price. This event is represented by the two supply schedules—one showing supply before the new technology was adopted, the other showing supply after the new technology was adopted—and their corresponding supply curves. The increase in supply shifts the supply curve to the right.

A **movement along the supply curve** is a change in the quantity supplied of a good arising from a change in the good's price.

As in the analysis of demand, it's crucial to draw a distinction between such changes in supply and **movements along the supply curve**—changes in the quantity supplied arising from a change in price. We can see this difference in **Figure 6.3**. The movement from point *A* to point *B* is a movement along the supply curve: the quantity supplied rises along S_1 due to a rise in price. Here, a rise in price from $1 to $1.50 leads to a rise in the quantity supplied from 10 billion to 11.2 billion pounds of cotton. But the quantity supplied can also rise when the price is unchanged if there is an increase in supply—a rightward shift of the supply curve. This is shown by the rightward shift of the supply curve from S_1 to S_2. Holding the price constant at $1, the quantity supplied rises from 10 billion pounds at point *A* on S_1 to 12 billion pounds at point *C* on S_2.

Understanding Shifts of the Supply Curve

Figure 6.4 illustrates the two basic ways in which supply curves can shift. When economists talk about an "increase in supply," they mean a *rightward* shift of the supply curve: at any given price, producers supply a larger quantity of the good than before. This is shown in Figure 6.4 by the rightward shift of the original supply curve S_1 to S_2. And when economists talk about a "decrease in supply," they mean a *leftward* shift of the supply curve: at any given price, producers supply a smaller quantity of the good than before. This is represented by the leftward shift of S_1 to S_3.

Shifts of the supply curve for a good or service are mainly the result of five factors (though, as in the case of demand, there are other possible causes):

- Changes in input prices
- Changes in the prices of related goods or services

AP® Exam Tip

Looks can be deceiving. An increase in supply is not a shift down; it is a shift to the right, indicating an increase in the quantity supplied at every price. A decrease in supply is not a shift up, but a shift to the left, indicating a decrease in the quantity supplied at every price.

Figure 6.3 A Movement Along the Supply Curve Versus a Shift of the Supply Curve

The increase in quantity supplied when going from point *A* to point *B* reflects a movement along the supply curve: it is the result of a rise in the price of the good. The increase in quantity supplied when going from point *A* to point *C* reflects a shift of the supply curve: it is the result of an increase in the quantity supplied at any given price.

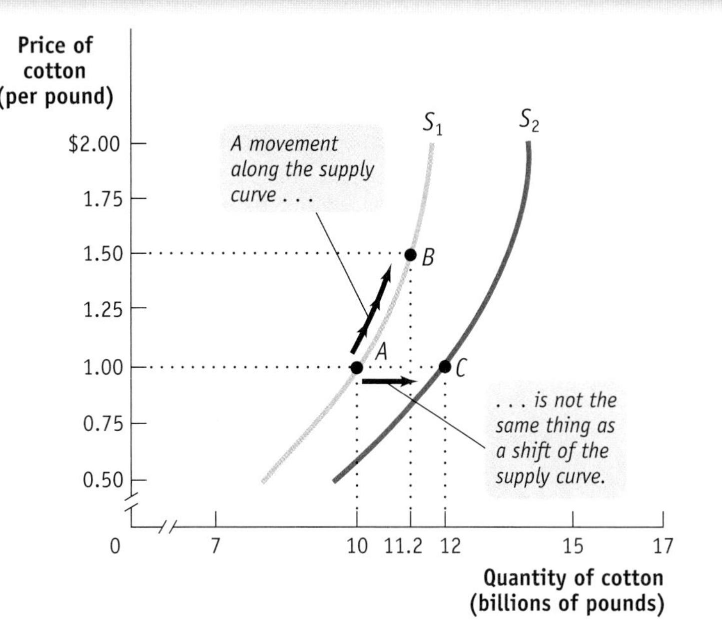

- Changes in technology
- Changes in expectations
- Changes in the number of producers

Changes in Input Prices To produce output, you need *inputs*. For example, to make vanilla ice cream, you need vanilla beans, cream, sugar, and so on. An **input** is any good or service that is used to produce another good or service. Inputs, like outputs, have prices. And an increase in the price of an input makes the production of the final

An **input** is a good or service that is used to produce another good or service.

Figure 6.4 Shifts of the Supply Curve

Any event that increases supply shifts the supply curve to the right, reflecting a rise in the quantity supplied at any given price. Any event that decreases supply shifts the supply curve to the left, reflecting a fall in the quantity supplied at any given price.

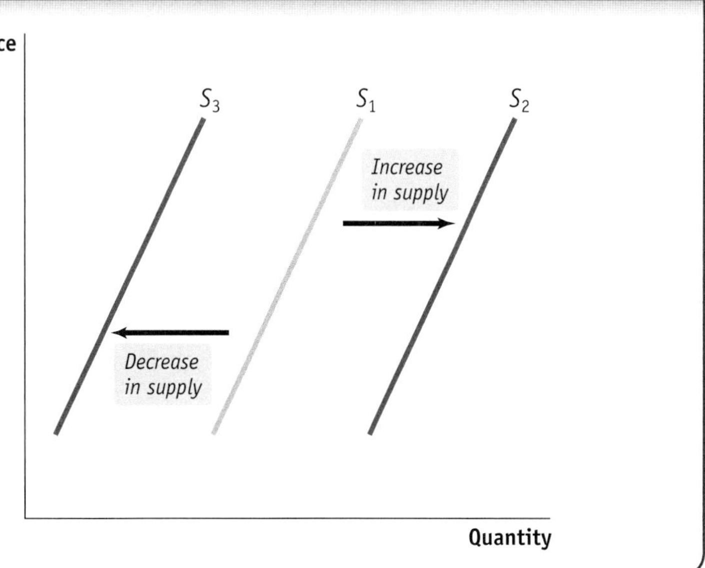

good more costly for those who produce and sell it. So producers are less willing to supply the final good at any given price, and the supply curve shifts to the left. For example, fuel is a major cost for airlines. When oil prices surged in 2007–2008, airlines began cutting back on their flight schedules and some went out of business. Similarly, a fall in the price of an input makes the production of the final good less costly for sellers. They are more willing to supply the good at any given price, and the supply curve shifts to the right.

Changes in the Prices of Related Goods or Services A single producer often produces a mix of goods rather than a single product. For example, an oil refinery produces gasoline from crude oil, but it also produces heating oil and other products from the same raw material. When a producer sells several products, the quantity of any one good it is willing to supply at any given price depends on the prices of its other co-produced goods.

This effect can run in either direction. An oil refiner will supply less gasoline at any given price when the price of heating oil rises, shifting the supply curve for gasoline to the left. But it will supply more gasoline at any given price when the price of heating oil falls, shifting the supply curve for gasoline to the right. This means that gasoline and other co-produced oil products are *substitutes in production* for refiners.

In contrast, due to the nature of the production process, other goods can be *complements in production*. For example, producers of crude oil—oil-well drillers—often find that oil wells also produce natural gas as a by-product of oil extraction. The higher the price at which a driller can sell its natural gas, the more oil wells it will drill and the more oil it will supply at any given price for oil. As a result, natural gas is a complement in production for crude oil.

Changes in Technology When economists talk about "technology," they don't necessarily mean high technology—they mean all the methods people can use to turn inputs into useful goods and services. In that sense, the whole complex sequence of activities that turn cotton from Pakistan into the pair of jeans hanging in your closet is technology.

Improvements in technology enable producers to spend less on inputs yet still produce the same output. When a better technology becomes available, reducing the cost of production, supply increases, and the supply curve shifts to the right. As we have already mentioned, improved technology enabled farmers to more than quadruple cotton output per acre planted over the past several decades. Improved technology is the main reason that, until recently, cotton remained relatively cheap even as worldwide demand grew.

Changes in Expectations Just as changes in expectations can shift the demand curve, they can also shift the supply curve. When suppliers have some choice about when they put their good up for sale, changes in the expected future price of the good can lead a supplier to supply less or more of the good today.

For example, consider the fact that gasoline and other oil products are often stored for significant periods of time at oil refineries before being sold to consumers. In fact, storage is normally part of producers' business strategy. Knowing that the demand for gasoline peaks in the summer, oil refiners normally store some of their gasoline produced during the spring for summer sale. Similarly, knowing that the demand for heating oil peaks in the winter, they normally store some of their heating oil produced during the fall for winter sale. In each case, there's a decision to be made between selling the product now versus storing it for later sale. Which choice a producer makes depends on a comparison of the current price versus the expected future price. This example illustrates how changes in expectations can alter supply: an increase in the anticipated future price of a good or service reduces supply today, a leftward shift of the supply curve. But a fall in the anticipated future price increases supply today, a rightward shift of the supply curve.

Changes in the Number of Producers Just as changes in the number of consumers affect the demand curve, changes in the number of producers affect the supply curve. Let's examine the **individual supply curve**, by looking at panel (a) in **Figure 6.5**. The individual supply curve shows the relationship between quantity supplied and price for an individual producer. For example, suppose that Mr. Silva is a Brazilian cotton farmer and that panel (a) of Figure 6.5 shows how many pounds of cotton he will supply per year at any given price. Then S_{Silva} is his individual supply curve.

An **individual supply curve** illustrates the relationship between quantity supplied and price for an individual producer.

The *market supply curve* shows how the combined total quantity supplied by all individual producers in the market depends on the market price of that good. Just as the market demand curve is the horizontal sum of the individual demand curves of all consumers, the market supply curve is the horizontal sum of the individual supply curves of all producers. Assume for a moment that there are only two producers of cotton, Mr. Silva and Mr. Liu, a Chinese cotton farmer. Mr. Liu's individual supply curve is shown in panel (b). Panel (c) shows the market supply curve. At any given price, the quantity supplied to the market is the sum of the quantities supplied by Mr. Silva and Mr. Liu. For example, at a price of $2 per pound, Mr. Silva supplies 3,000 pounds of cotton per year and Mr. Liu supplies 2,000 pounds per year, making the quantity supplied to the market 5,000 pounds.

AP® Exam Tip

A mnemonic to help you remember the factors that shift supply is *I-RENT.* Supply is shifted by changes in . . .
Input (resource) prices,
prices of **R**elated goods and services,
Expectations,
the **N**umber of producers, and
Technology.

Clearly, the quantity supplied to the market at any given price is larger with Mr. Liu present than it would be if Mr. Silva were the only supplier. The quantity supplied at a given price would be even larger if we added a third producer, then a fourth, and so on. So an increase in the number of producers leads to an increase in supply and a rightward shift of the supply curve.

For an overview of the factors that shift supply, see **Table 6.1** on the next page.

Figure 6.5 Individual Supply Curves and the Market Supply Curve

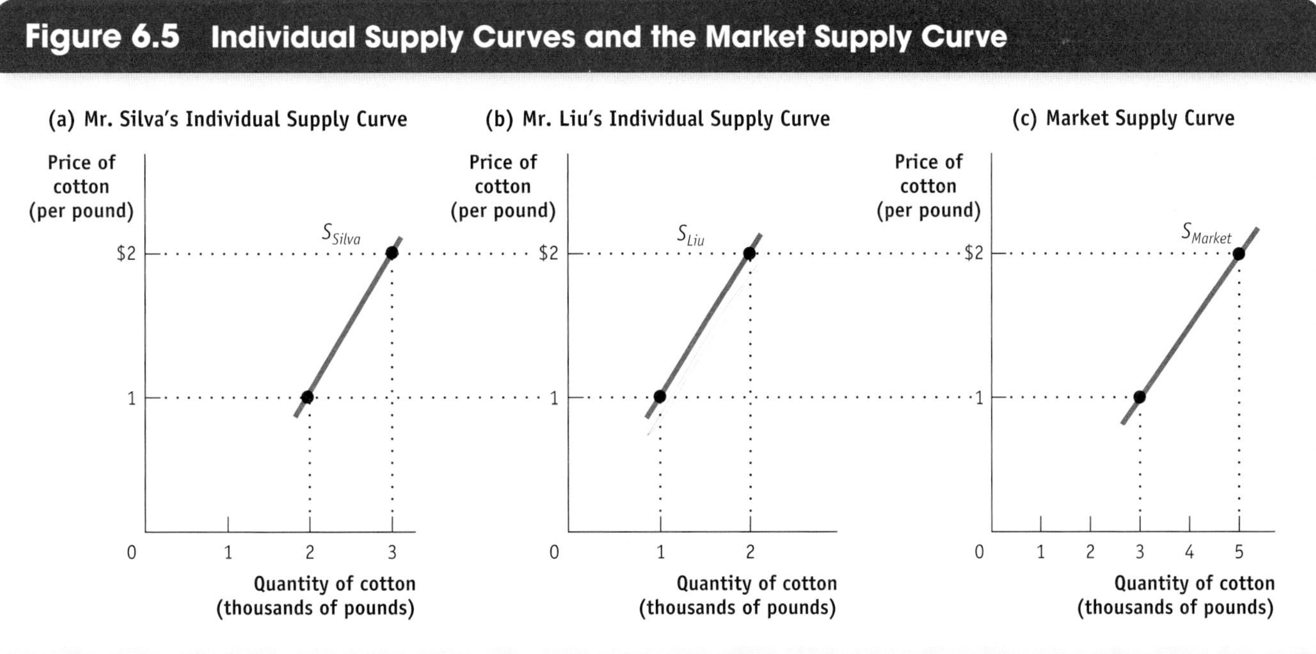

Panel (a) shows the individual supply curve for Mr. Silva, S_{Silva}, the quantity of cotton he will sell at any given price. Panel (b) shows the individual supply curve for Mr. Liu, S_{Liu}. The market supply curve, which shows the quantity of cotton supplied by all producers at any given price, is shown in panel (c). The market supply curve is the horizontal sum of the individual supply curves of all producers.

Table 6.1 Factors That Shift Supply

When this happens . . .	. . . supply increases		But when this happens . . .	. . . supply decreases	
When the price of an input falls . . .	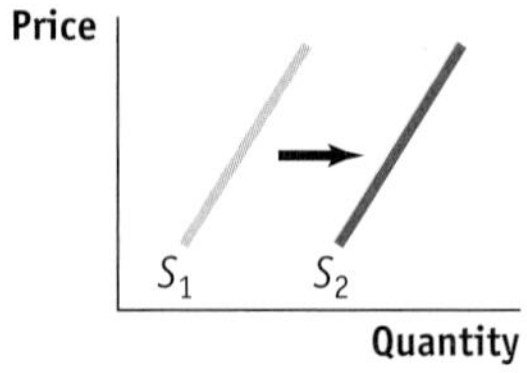 Price / Quantity graph: S_1 → S_2	. . . supply of the good increases.	When the price of an input rises . . .	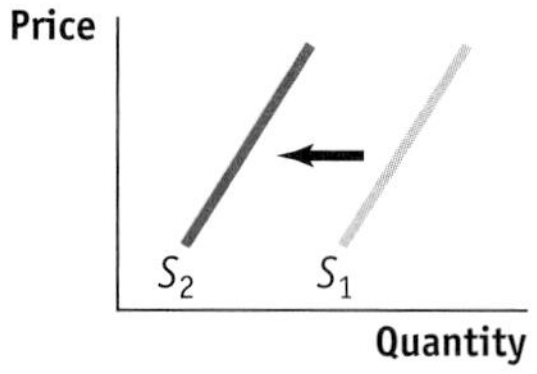 Price / Quantity graph: S_2 ← S_1	. . . supply of the good decreases.
When the price of a substitute in production falls . . .	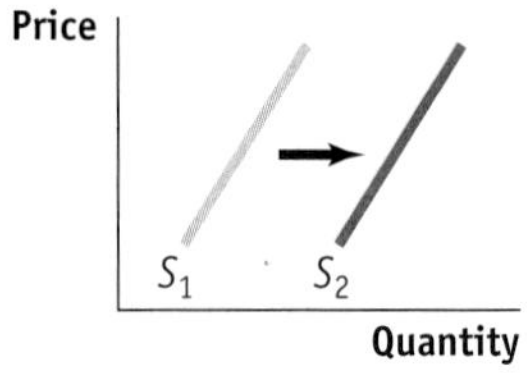 Price / Quantity graph: S_1 → S_2	. . . supply of the original good increases.	When the price of a substitute in production rises . . .	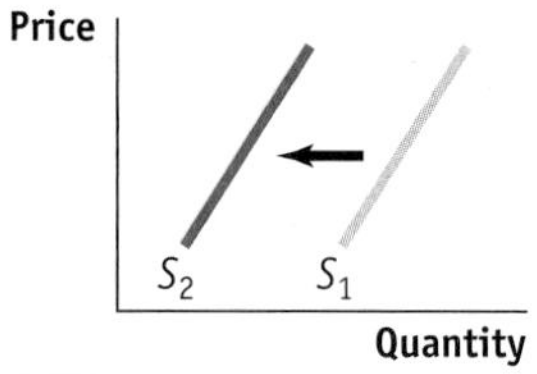 Price / Quantity graph: S_2 ← S_1	. . . supply of the original good decreases.
When the price of a complement in production rises . . .	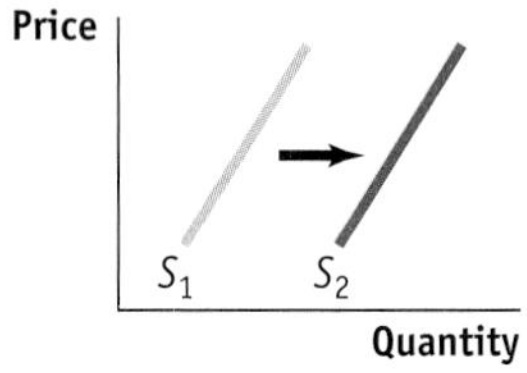 Price / Quantity graph: S_1 → S_2	. . . supply of the original good increases.	When the price of a complement in production falls . . .	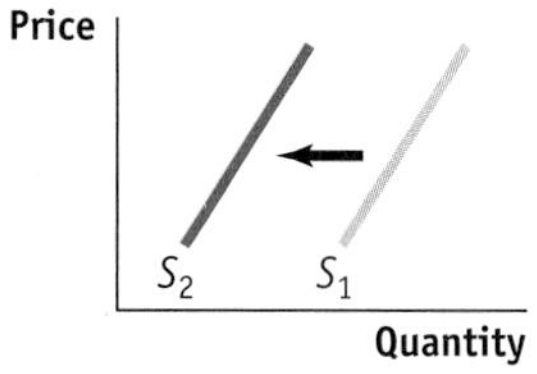 Price / Quantity graph: S_2 ← S_1	. . . supply of the original good decreases.
When the technology used to produce the good improves . . .	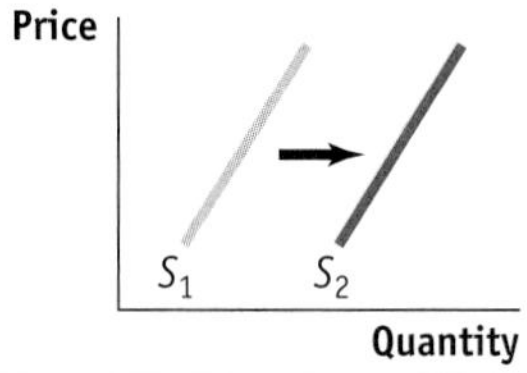 Price / Quantity graph: S_1 → S_2	. . . supply of the good increases.	When the best technology used to produce the good is no longer available . . .	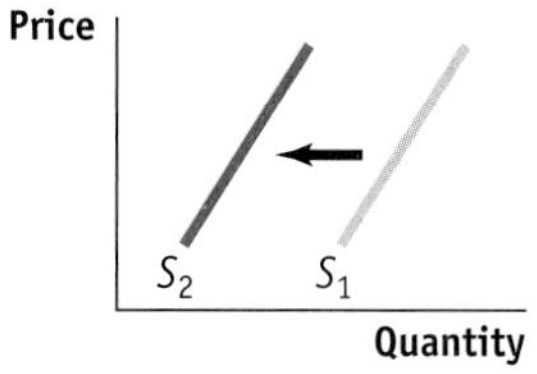 Price / Quantity graph: S_2 ← S_1	. . . supply of the good decreases.
When the price is expected to fall in the future . . .	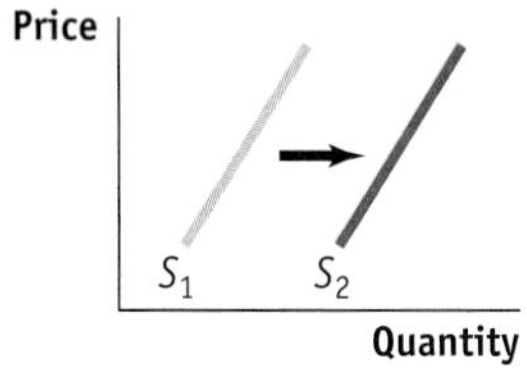 Price / Quantity graph: S_1 → S_2	. . . supply of the good increases today.	When the price is expected to rise in the future . . .	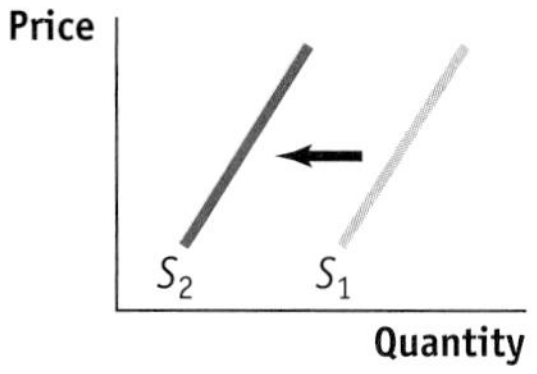 Price / Quantity graph: S_2 ← S_1	. . . supply of the good decreases today.
When the number of producers rises . . .	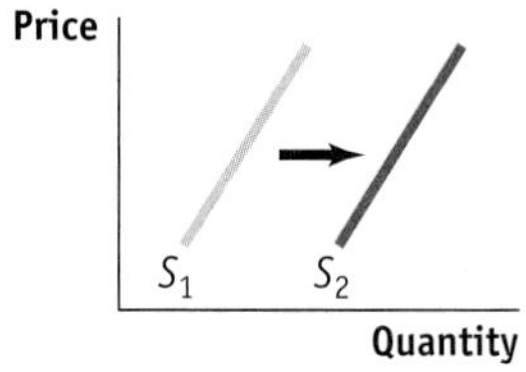 Price / Quantity graph: S_1 → S_2	. . . market supply of the good increases.	When the number of producers falls . . .	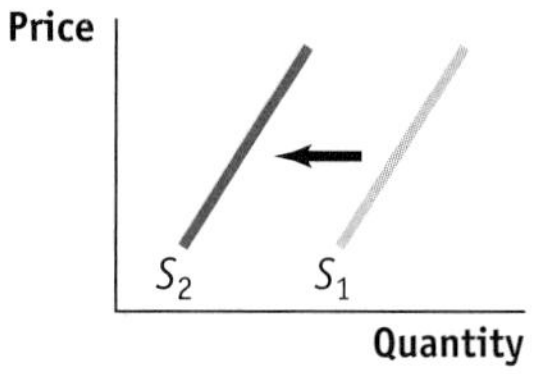 Price / Quantity graph: S_2 ← S_1	. . . market supply of the good decreases.

Only Creatures Small and Pampered

During the 1970s, British television featured a popular show titled *All Creatures Great and Small.* It chronicled the real life of James Herriot, a country veterinarian who tended to cows, pigs, sheep, horses, and the occasional house pet, often under arduous conditions, in rural England during the 1930s. The show made it clear that, in those days, the local vet was a critical member of farming communities, saving valuable farm animals and helping farmers survive financially. And it was also clear that Mr. Herriot considered his life's work well spent.

But that was then and this is now. According to a recent article in the *New York Times,* the United States has experienced a severe decline in the number of farm veterinarians over the past two decades. The source of the problem is competition. As the number of household pets has increased and the incomes of pet owners have grown, the demand for pet veterinarians has increased sharply. As a result, vets are being drawn away from the business of caring for farm animals into the more lucrative business of caring for pets. As one vet stated, she began her career caring for farm animals but changed her mind after "doing a C-section on a cow and it's 50 bucks. Do a C-section on a Chihuahua and you get $300. It's the money. I hate to say that."

How can we translate this into supply and demand curves? Farm veterinary services and pet veterinary services are like gasoline and fuel oil: they're related goods that are substitutes in production. A veterinarian typically specializes in one type of practice or the other, and that decision often depends on the going price for the service. America's growing pet population, combined with the increased willingness of doting owners to spend on their companions' care, has driven up the price of pet veterinary services. As a result, fewer and fewer veterinarians have gone into farm animal practice. So the supply curve of farm veterinarians has shifted leftward—fewer farm veterinarians are offering their services at any given price.

In the end, farmers understand that it is all a matter of dollars and cents: they get fewer veterinarians because they are unwilling to pay more. As one farmer, who had recently lost an expensive cow due to the unavailability of a veterinarian, stated, "The fact that there's nothing you can do, you accept it as a business expense now. You didn't used to. If you have livestock, sooner or later you're going to have deadstock." (Although we should note that this farmer could have chosen to pay more for a vet who would then have saved his cow.)

iStockphoto/Thinkstock

Higher spending on pets means fewer veterinarians are available to tend to farm animals.

MODULE 6 Review

Check Your Understanding

1. Explain whether each of the following events represents (i) a *change in* supply or (ii) a *movement along* the supply curve.
   a. During a real estate boom that causes house prices to rise, more homeowners put their houses up for sale.
   b. Many strawberry farmers open temporary roadside stands during harvest season, even though prices are usually low at that time.
   c. Immediately after the school year begins, fewer young people are available to work. Fast-food chains must raise wages, which represent the price of labor, to attract workers.
   d. Many construction workers temporarily move to areas that have suffered hurricane damage, lured by higher wages.
   e. Since new technologies have made it possible to build larger cruise ships (which are cheaper to run per passenger), Caribbean cruise lines have offered more cabins, at lower prices, than before.
2. After each of the following events, will the supply curve for the good that is mentioned shift to the left, shift to the right, or remain unchanged?
   a. The coffee berry borer beetle destroys large quantities of coffee berries.
   b. Consumers demand more bike helmets than ever.
   c. The number of tea producers increases.
   d. The price of leather, an input in wallet production, increases.

Tackle the Test: Multiple-Choice Questions

1. Which of the following will decrease the supply of rice?
   a. There is a technological advance that affects the production of *all* goods.
   b. The price of rice falls.
   c. The price of corn (which consumers regard as a substitute for rice) decreases.
   d. The wages of workers producing rice increase.
   e. The demand for rice decreases.
2. An increase in the demand for steak, which increases the price of steak, will lead to an increase in which of the following?
   a. the supply of steak
   b. the supply of hamburger (a substitute in production)
   c. the supply of chicken (a substitute in consumption)
   d. the supply of leather (a complement in production)
   e. the demand for leather
3. A technological advance in textbook production will lead to which of the following?
   a. a decrease in textbook supply
   b. an increase in textbook demand
   c. an increase in textbook supply
   d. a movement along the supply curve for textbooks
   e. an increase in textbook prices
4. Expectations among hiking boot makers that boot prices will rise significantly in the future will lead to which of the following now?
   a. an increase in boot supply
   b. no change in boot supply
   c. a decrease in boot supply
   d. a movement to the left along the boot supply curve
   e. a movement to the right along the boot supply curve
5. Starch from the stalks of potato plants is used to make packing peanuts, a complement in production. A decrease in potato demand that lowers potato prices will cause which of the following in the packing-peanut market?
   a. an increase in supply and no change in demand
   b. an increase in supply and a decrease in demand
   c. a decrease in both demand and supply
   d. a decrease in supply and no change in demand
   e. a decrease in supply and an increase in demand

Tackle the Test: Free-Response Questions

1. Tesla Motors makes sports cars powered by lithium batteries.
   a. Draw a correctly labeled graph showing a hypothetical supply curve for Tesla sports cars.
   b. On the same graph, show the effect of a major new discovery of lithium that lowers the price of lithium.
   c. Suppose Tesla Motors expects to be able to sell its cars for a higher price next month. Explain the effect that will have on the supply of Tesla cars this month.

Rubric for FRQ 1 (4 points)

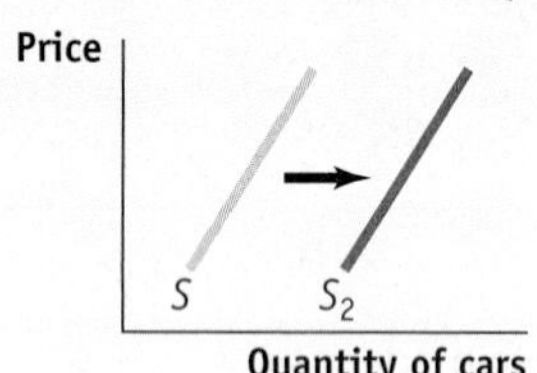

1 point: Graph with "Price" or "*P*" on the vertical axis and "Quantity" or "*Q*" on the horizontal axis

1 point: Positively-sloped curve labeled "Supply" or "*S*"

1 point: A second supply curve shown to the right of the original supply curve with a label such as S_2 indicating that it is the new supply curve

1 point: Correct explanation that the expectation of higher prices next month would lead to a decrease in the supply of Tesla cars this month because the company will want to sell more of its cars when the price is higher

2. Suppose AP® Economics students at your school offer tutoring services to students in regular economics courses.
   a. Draw a correctly labeled graph showing the supply curve for tutoring services measured in hours. Label the supply curve "S_1".
   b. Suppose the wage paid for babysitting, an alternative activity for AP® Economics students, increases. Show the effect of this wage increase on the graph you drew for part a. Label the new supply curve "S_2".
   c. Suppose instead that the number of AP® Economics students increases. Show the effect of this increase in AP® Economics students on the same graph you drew for parts a and b. Label the new supply curve "S_3".

   (3 points)

STR/AFP/Getty Images

MODULE 7 Supply and Demand: Equilibrium

In this Module, you will learn to:

- Explain how supply and demand curves determine a market's equilibrium price and equilibrium quantity
- Describe how price moves the market back to equilibrium in the case of a shortage or surplus
- Explain how equilibrium price and quantity are affected when there is a change in either supply or demand
- Explain how equilibrium price and quantity are affected when there is a simultaneous change in both supply and demand

Supply, Demand, and Equilibrium

We have now covered the first three key elements in the supply and demand model: the demand curve, the supply curve, and the set of factors that shift each curve. The next step is to put these elements together to show how they can be used to predict the actual price at which the good is bought and sold, as well as the actual quantity transacted.

In competitive markets this interaction of supply and demand tends to move toward what economists call *equilibrium*. Imagine a busy afternoon at your local supermarket; there are long lines at the checkout counters. Then one of the previously closed registers opens. The first thing that happens is a rush to the newly opened register. But soon enough things settle down and shoppers have rearranged themselves so that the line at the newly opened register is about as long as all the others. This situation—all the checkout lines are now the same length, and none of the shoppers can be better off by doing something different—is what economists call **equilibrium**.

An economic situation is in **equilibrium** when no individual would be better off doing something different.

The concept of equilibrium helps us understand the price at which a good or service is bought and sold as well as the quantity transacted of the good or service. A competitive market is in equilibrium when the price has moved to a level at which the quantity of a good demanded equals the quantity of that good supplied. At that price, no individual seller could make herself better off by offering to sell either more or less of the good and no individual buyer could make himself better off by offering to buy more or less of the good. Recall the shoppers at the supermarket who cannot make themselves better off (cannot save time) by changing lines. Similarly, at the market equilibrium, the price has moved to a level that exactly matches the quantity demanded by consumers to the quantity supplied by sellers.

AP® Exam Tip

Equilibrium is a term you will hear often throughout the course. When a market is in equilibrium, the quantity supplied equals the quantity demanded. There are no shortages or surpluses pushing the price up or down, and therefore there is no tendency for the price or the quantity to change.

A competitive market is in equilibrium when the price has moved to a level at which the quantity demanded of a good equals the quantity supplied of that good. The price at which this takes place is the **equilibrium price**, also referred to as the **market-clearing price**. The quantity of the good bought and sold at that price is the **equilibrium quantity**.

The price that matches the quantity supplied and the quantity demanded is the **equilibrium price**; the quantity bought and sold at that price is the **equilibrium quantity**. The equilibrium price is also known as the **market-clearing price**: it is the price that "clears the market" by ensuring that every buyer willing to pay that price finds a seller willing to sell at that price, and vice versa. So how do we find the equilibrium price and quantity?

Finding the Equilibrium Price and Quantity

The easiest way to determine the equilibrium price and quantity in a market is by putting the supply curve and the demand curve on the same diagram. Since the supply curve shows the quantity supplied at any given price and the demand curve shows the quantity demanded at any given price, the price at which the two curves cross is the equilibrium price: the price at which quantity supplied equals quantity demanded.

Figure 7.1 combines the demand curve from Figure 5.1 and the supply curve from Figure 6.1. They *intersect* at point *E*, which is the equilibrium of this market; $1 is the equilibrium price and 10 billion pounds is the equilibrium quantity.

Let's confirm that point *E* fits our definition of equilibrium. At a price of $1 per pound, cotton farmers are willing to sell 10 billion pounds a year and cotton consumers want to buy 10 billion pounds a year. So at the price of $1 a pound, the quantity of cotton supplied equals the quantity demanded. Notice that at any other price the market would not clear: every willing buyer would not be able to find a willing seller, or vice versa. More specifically, if the price were more than $1, the quantity supplied would exceed the quantity demanded; if the price were less than $1, the quantity demanded would exceed the quantity supplied.

The model of supply and demand, then, predicts that given the demand and supply curves shown in Figure 7.1, 10 billion pounds of cotton would change

Figure 7.1 Market Equilibrium

Market equilibrium occurs at point *E*, where the supply curve and the demand curve intersect. In equilibrium, the quantity demanded is equal to the quantity supplied. In this market, the equilibrium price is $1 per pound and the equilibrium quantity is 10 billion pounds per year.

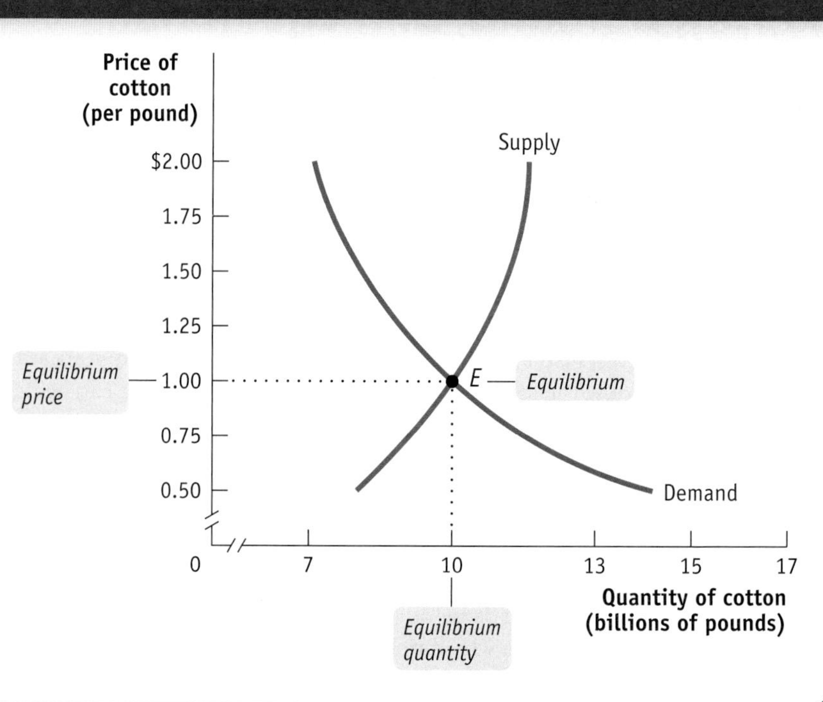

hands at a price of $1 per pound. But how can we be sure that the market will arrive at the equilibrium price? We begin by answering three simple questions:

1. Why do all sales and purchases in a market take place at the same price?
2. Why does the market price fall if it is above the equilibrium price?
3. Why does the market price rise if it is below the equilibrium price?

Why Do All Sales and Purchases in a Market Take Place at the Same Price?

There are some markets where the same good can sell for many different prices, depending on who is selling or who is buying. For example, have you ever bought a souvenir in a "tourist trap" and then seen the same item on sale somewhere else (perhaps even in the shop next door) for a lower price? Because tourists don't know which shops offer the best deals and don't have time for comparison shopping, sellers in tourist areas can charge different prices for the same good.

But in any market in which the buyers and sellers have both been around for some time, sales and purchases tend to converge at a generally uniform price, so we can safely talk about *the* market price. It's easy to see why. Suppose a seller offered a potential buyer a price noticeably above what the buyer knew other people were paying. The buyer would clearly be better off shopping elsewhere—unless the seller were prepared to offer a better deal. Conversely, a seller would not be willing to sell for significantly less than the amount he knew most buyers were paying; he would be better off waiting to get a more reasonable customer. So in any well-established, ongoing market, all sellers receive and all buyers pay approximately the same price. This is what we call the *market price.*

Why Does the Market Price Fall If It Is Above the Equilibrium Price?

Suppose the supply and demand curves are as shown in Figure 7.1 but the market price is above the equilibrium level of $1—say, $1.50. This situation is illustrated in **Figure 7.2** on the next page. Why can't the price stay there?

As the figure shows, at a price of $1.50 there would be more pounds of cotton available than consumers wanted to buy: 11.2 billion pounds versus 8.1 billion pounds. The difference of 3.1 billion pounds is the **surplus**—also known as the *excess supply*—of cotton at $1.50.

This surplus means that some cotton farmers are frustrated: at the current price, they cannot find consumers who want to buy their cotton. The surplus offers an incentive for those frustrated would-be sellers to offer a lower price in order to poach business from other producers and entice more consumers to buy. The result of this price cutting will be to push the prevailing price down until it reaches the equilibrium price. So the price of a good will fall whenever there is a surplus—that is, whenever the market price is above its equilibrium level.

There is a **surplus** of a good or service when the quantity supplied exceeds the quantity demanded. Surpluses occur when the price is above its equilibrium level.

There is a **shortage** of a good or service when the quantity demanded exceeds the quantity supplied. Shortages occur when the price is below its equilibrium level.

Why Does the Market Price Rise If It Is Below the Equilibrium Price?

Now suppose the price is below its equilibrium level—say, at $0.75 per pound, as shown in **Figure 7.3** on the next page. In this case, the quantity demanded, 11.5 billion pounds, exceeds the quantity supplied, 9.1 billion pounds, implying that there are would-be buyers who cannot find cotton: there is a **shortage**, also known as an *excess demand,* of 2.4 billion pounds.

Figure 7.2 Price Above Its Equilibrium Level Creates a Surplus

The market price of $1.50 is above the equilibrium price of $1. This creates a surplus: at a price of $1.50, producers would like to sell 11.2 billion pounds but consumers want to buy only 8.1 billion pounds, so there is a surplus of 3.1 billion pounds. This surplus will push the price down until it reaches the equilibrium price of $1.

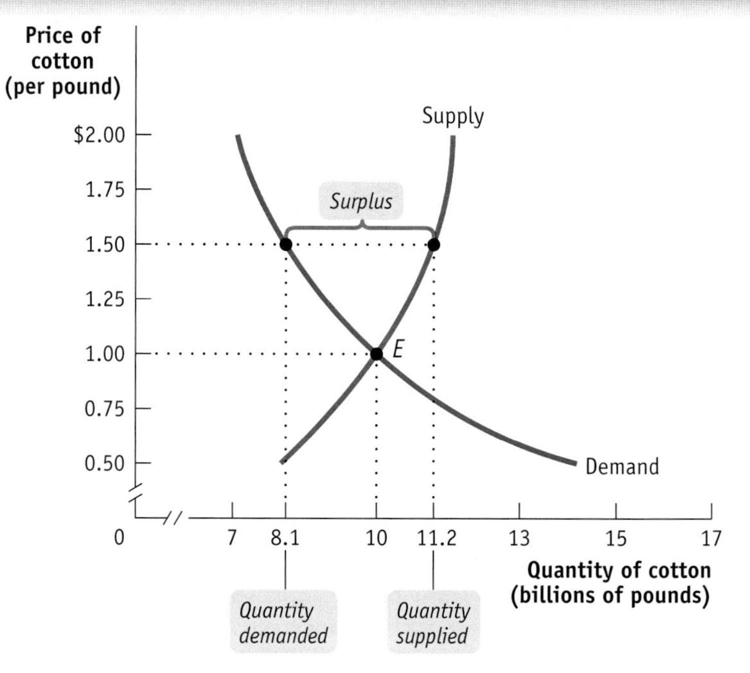

Figure 7.3 Price Below Its Equilibrium Level Creates a Shortage

The market price of $0.75 is below the equilibrium price of $1. This creates a shortage: consumers want to buy 11.5 billion pounds, but only 9.1 billion pounds are for sale, so there is a shortage of 2.4 billion pounds. This shortage will push the price up until it reaches the equilibrium price of $1.

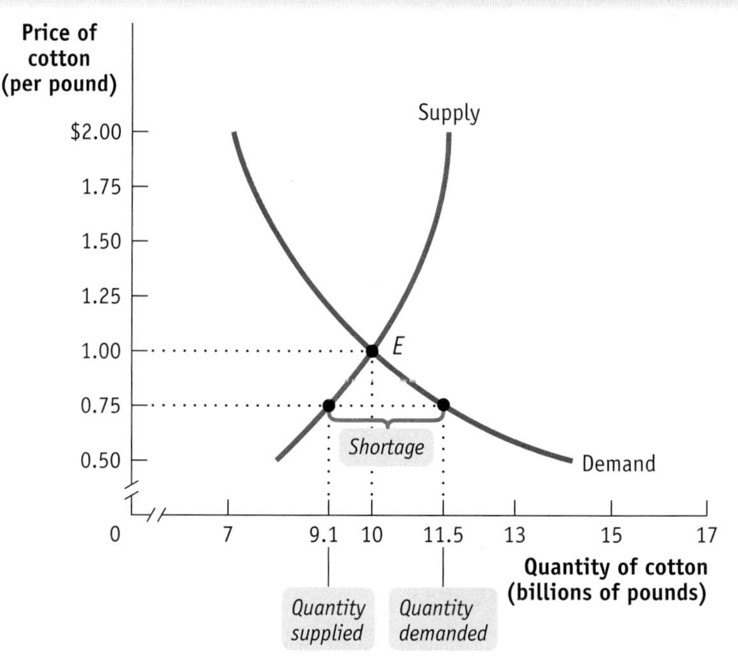

The Price of Admission

The market equilibrium, so the theory goes, is pretty egalitarian because the equilibrium price applies to everyone. That is, all buyers pay the same price—the equilibrium price—and all sellers receive that same price. But is this realistic?

The market for concert tickets is an example that seems to contradict the theory—there's one price at the box office, and there's another price (typically much higher) for the same event on Internet sites where people who already have tickets resell them, such as StubHub.com or eBay. For example, compare the box office price for a recent Drake concert in Miami, Florida, to the StubHub.com price for seats in the same location: \$88.50 versus \$155.

Puzzling as this may seem, there is no contradiction once we take opportunity costs and tastes into account. For major events, buying tickets from the box office means waiting in very long lines. Ticket buyers who use Internet resellers have decided that the opportunity cost of their time is too high to spend waiting in line. And tickets for major events being sold at face value by online box offices often sell out within minutes. In this case, some people who want to go to the concert badly but have missed out on the opportunity to buy cheaper tickets from the online box office are willing to pay the higher Internet reseller price.

Not only that—perusing the StubHub.com website, you can see that markets really do move to equilibrium. You'll notice that the prices quoted by different sellers for seats close to one another are also very close: \$184.99 versus \$185 for seats on the main floor of the Drake concert. As the competitive market model predicts, units of the same good end up selling for the same price. And prices move in response to demand and supply. According to an article in the *New York Times*, tickets on StubHub.com can sell for less than the face value for events with little appeal, but prices can skyrocket for events that are in high demand. (The article quotes a price of \$3,530 for a Madonna concert.) Even StubHub.com's chief executive says his site is "the embodiment of supply-and-demand economics."

So the theory of competitive markets isn't just speculation. If you want to experience it for yourself, try buying tickets to a concert.

Claire R. Greenway/Getty Images

The competitive market model determines the price you pay for concert tickets.

When there is a shortage, there are frustrated would-be buyers—people who want to purchase cotton but cannot find willing sellers at the current price. In this situation, either buyers will offer more than the prevailing price or sellers will realize that they can charge higher prices. Either way, the result is to drive up the prevailing price. This bidding up of prices happens whenever there are shortages—and there will be shortages whenever the price is below its equilibrium level. So the market price will always rise if it is below the equilibrium level.

Using Equilibrium to Describe Markets

We have now seen that a market tends to have a single price, the equilibrium price. If the market price is above the equilibrium level, the ensuing surplus leads buyers and sellers to take actions that lower the price. And if the market price is below the equilibrium level, the ensuing shortage leads buyers and sellers to take actions that raise the price. So the market price always *moves toward* the equilibrium price, the price at which there is neither surplus nor shortage.

Changes in Supply and Demand

The 2010 floods in Pakistan came as a surprise, but the subsequent increase in the price of cotton was no surprise at all. Suddenly there was a fall in supply: the quantity of cotton available at any given price fell. Predictably, a fall in supply raises the equilibrium price.

The flooding in Pakistan is an example of an event that shifted the supply curve for a good without having much effect on the demand curve. There are many such events. There are also events that shift the demand curve without shifting the supply curve. For example, a medical report that chocolate is good for you increases the demand for chocolate but does not affect the supply. Events often shift either the supply curve or the demand curve, but not both; it is therefore useful to ask what happens in each case.

We have seen that when a curve shifts, the equilibrium price and quantity change. We will now concentrate on exactly how the shift of a curve alters the equilibrium price and quantity.

What Happens When the Demand Curve Shifts

AP® Exam Tip

A shift of the demand curve changes the price, which changes the quantity supplied. A shift of the supply curve also changes the price, which changes the quantity demanded. Note that these price changes cause movements *along* the curve that didn't shift. A shift of the demand curve never causes a shift of the supply curve, and a shift of the supply curve never causes a shift of the demand curve.

Cotton and polyester are substitutes: if the price of polyester rises, the demand for cotton will increase, and if the price of polyester falls, the demand for cotton will decrease. But how does the price of polyester affect the *market equilibrium* for cotton?

Figure 7.4 shows the effect of a rise in the price of polyester on the market for cotton. The rise in the price of polyester increases the demand for cotton. Point E_1 shows the equilibrium corresponding to the original demand curve, with P_1 the equilibrium price and Q_1 the equilibrium quantity bought and sold.

An increase in demand is indicated by a *rightward* shift of the demand curve from D_1 to D_2. At the original market price P_1, this market is no longer in equilibrium: a shortage occurs because the quantity demanded exceeds the quantity supplied. So the price of cotton rises and generates an increase in the quantity supplied, an upward *movement along the supply curve.* A new equilibrium is established at point E_2, with a higher equilibrium price, P_2, and higher equilibrium quantity, Q_2. This sequence of events reflects a general principle: *When demand for a good or service increases, the equilibrium price and the equilibrium quantity of the good or service both rise.*

What would happen in the reverse case, a fall in the price of polyester? A fall in the price of polyester reduces the demand for cotton, shifting the demand curve to the *left.* At the original price, a surplus occurs as quantity supplied exceeds quantity demanded. The price falls and leads to a decrease in the quantity supplied, resulting in a lower

Figure 7.4 Equilibrium and Shifts of the Demand Curve

The original equilibrium in the market for cotton is at E_1, at the intersection of the supply curve and the original demand curve, D_1. A rise in the price of polyester, a substitute, shifts the demand curve rightward to D_2. A shortage exists at the original price, P_1, causing both the price and quantity supplied to rise, a movement along the supply curve. A new equilibrium is reached at E_2, with a higher equilibrium price, P_2, and a higher equilibrium quantity, Q_2. When demand for a good or service increases, the equilibrium price and the equilibrium quantity of the good or service both rise.

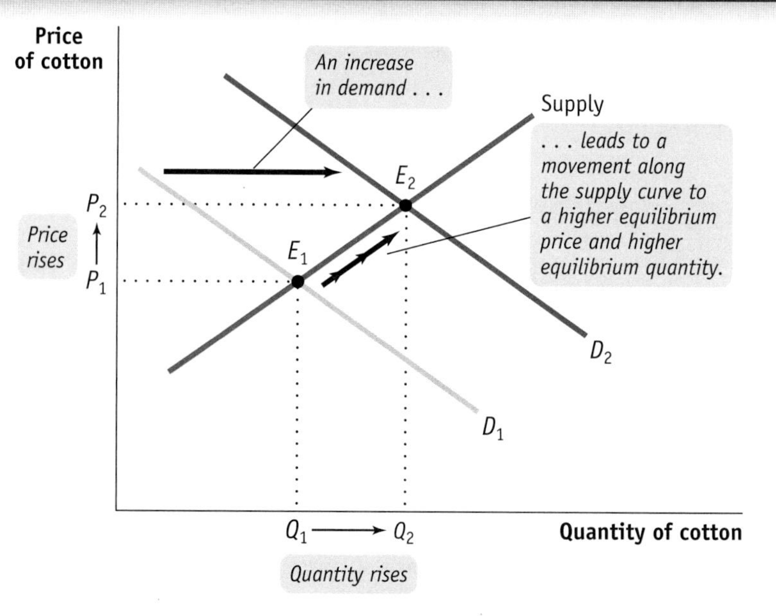

equilibrium price and a lower equilibrium quantity. This illustrates another general principle: *When demand for a good or service decreases, the equilibrium price and the equilibrium quantity of the good or service both fall.*

To summarize how a market responds to a change in demand: *An increase in demand leads to a rise in both the equilibrium price and the equilibrium quantity. A decrease in demand leads to a fall in both the equilibrium price and the equilibrium quantity.*

What Happens When the Supply Curve Shifts

In the real world, it is a bit easier to predict changes in supply than changes in demand. Physical factors that affect supply, like weather or the availability of inputs, are easier to get a handle on than the fickle tastes that affect demand. Still, with supply as with demand, what we can best predict are the *effects* of shifts of the supply curve.

As we mentioned earlier, devastating floods in Pakistan sharply reduced the supply of cotton in 2010. **Figure 7.5** shows how this shift affected the market equilibrium. The original equilibrium is at E_1, the point of intersection of the original supply curve, S_1, and the demand curve, with an equilibrium price P_1 and equilibrium quantity Q_1. As a result of the bad weather, supply falls and S_1 shifts *leftward* to S_2. At the original price P_1, a shortage of cotton now exists and the market is no longer in equilibrium. The shortage causes a rise in price and a fall in quantity demanded, an upward movement along the demand curve. The new equilibrium is at E_2, with an equilibrium price P_2 and an equilibrium quantity Q_2. In the new equilibrium, E_2, the price is higher and the equilibrium quantity lower than before. This can be stated as a general principle: *When supply of a good or service decreases, the equilibrium price of the good or service rises and the equilibrium quantity of the good or service falls.*

What happens to the market when supply increases? An increase in supply leads to a *rightward* shift of the supply curve. At the original price, a surplus now exists; as a result, the equilibrium price falls and the quantity demanded rises. This describes what happened to the market for cotton as new technology increased cotton yields. We can formulate a general principle: *When supply of a good or service increases, the equilibrium price of the good or service falls and the equilibrium quantity of the good or service rises.*

AP® Exam Tip

The graph never lies! If asked to determine what happens to price and quantity when supply or demand shifts, draw the graph first and then look where the old equilibrium was and compare it to the new equilibrium. Draw quick graphs whenever you can to help you answer multiple choice questions about changes in quantity and price.

Figure 7.5 Equilibrium and Shifts of the Supply Curve

The original equilibrium in the market for cotton is at E_1. Bad weather in cotton-growing areas causes a fall in the supply of cotton and shifts the supply curve leftward from S_1 to S_2. A new equilibrium is established at E_2, with a higher equilibrium price, P_2, and a lower equilibrium quantity, Q_2.

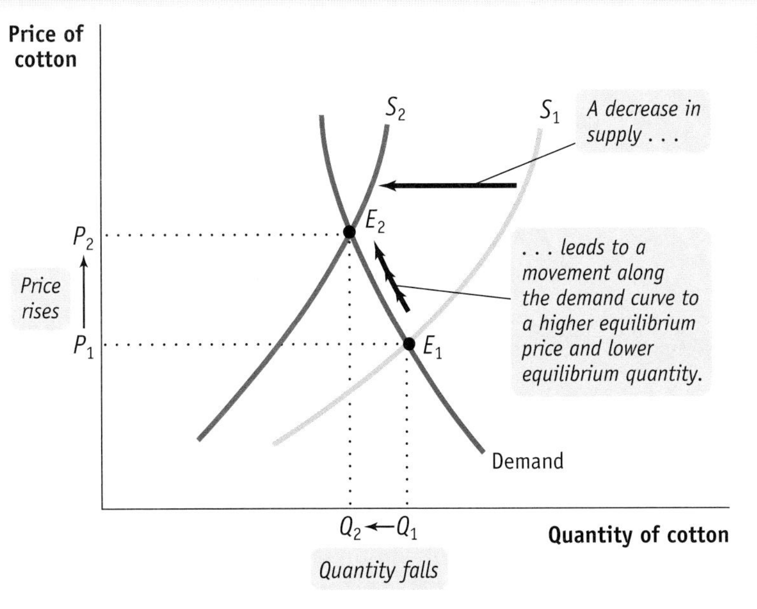

AP® Exam Tip

You can do supply and demand analysis in three easy steps. First, draw the graph before the change. Be sure to label the equilibrium price and quantity on the appropriate axes. Second, identify which line shifts and add the shift to your graph. Third, label the new equilibrium price and quantity on the appropriate axes and note how each value changed.

To summarize how a market responds to a change in supply: *An increase in supply leads to a fall in the equilibrium price and a rise in the equilibrium quantity. A decrease in supply leads to a rise in the equilibrium price and a fall in the equilibrium quantity.*

Simultaneous Shifts of Supply and Demand Curves

Finally, it sometimes happens that events shift *both* the demand and supply curves at the same time. This is not unusual; in real life, supply curves and demand curves for many goods and services shift quite often because the economic environment continually changes. **Figure 7.6** illustrates two examples of simultaneous shifts. In both panels there is an increase in demand—that is, a rightward shift of the demand curve, from D_1 to D_2—say, for example, representing an increase in the demand for cotton due to changing tastes. Notice that the rightward shift in panel (a) is larger than the one in panel (b): we can suppose that panel (a) represents a year in which many more people than usual choose to buy jeans and cotton T-shirts and panel (b) represents a normal year. Both panels also show a decrease in supply—that is, a leftward shift of the supply curve from S_1 to S_2. Also notice that the leftward shift in panel (b) is relatively larger than the one in panel (a): we can suppose that panel (b) represents the effect of particularly bad weather in Pakistan and panel (a) represents the effect of a much less severe weather event.

In both cases, the equilibrium price rises from P_1 to P_2, as the equilibrium moves from E_1 to E_2. But what happens to the equilibrium quantity, the quantity of cotton

Figure 7.6 Simultaneous Shifts of the Demand and Supply Curves

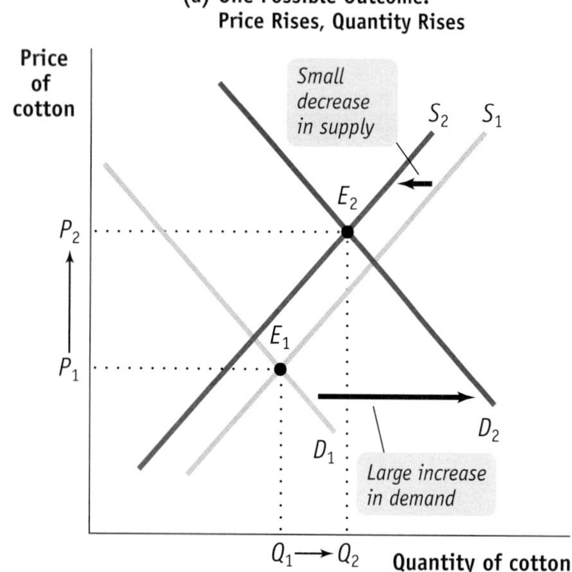

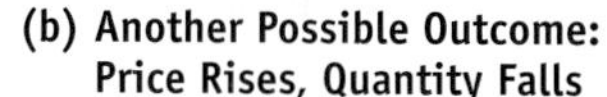

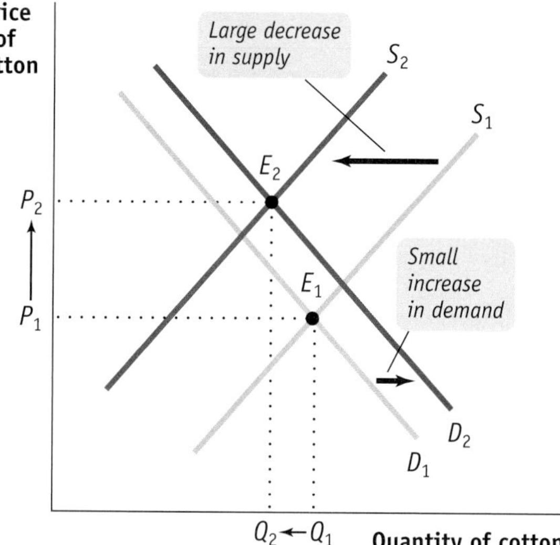

In panel (a) there is a simultaneous rightward shift of the demand curve and leftward shift of the supply curve. Here the increase in demand is relatively larger than the decrease in supply, so the equilibrium price and equilibrium quantity both rise. In panel (b) there is also a simultaneous rightward shift of the demand curve and leftward shift of the supply curve. Here the decrease in supply is relatively larger than the increase in demand, so the equilibrium price rises and the equilibrium quantity falls.

bought and sold? In panel (a) the increase in demand is large relative to the decrease in supply, and the equilibrium quantity rises as a result. In panel (b), the decrease in supply is large relative to the increase in demand, and the equilibrium quantity falls as a result. That is, when demand increases and supply decreases, the actual quantity bought and sold can go either way, depending on *how much* the demand and supply curves have shifted.

In general, when supply and demand shift in opposite directions, we can't predict what the ultimate effect will be on the quantity bought and sold. What we can say is that a curve that shifts a disproportionately greater distance than the other curve will have a disproportionately greater effect on the quantity bought and sold. That said, we can make the following prediction about the outcome when the supply and demand curves shift in opposite directions:

- When demand increases and supply decreases, the equilibrium price rises but the change in the equilibrium quantity is ambiguous.
- When demand decreases and supply increases, the equilibrium price falls but the change in the equilibrium quantity is ambiguous.

But suppose that the demand and supply curves shift in the same direction. Before 2010, this was the case in the global market for cotton, where both supply and demand had increased over the past decade. Can we safely make any predictions about the changes in price and quantity? In this situation, the change in quantity bought and sold can be predicted, but the change in price is ambiguous. The two possible outcomes when the supply and demand curves shift in the same direction (which you should check for yourself) are as follows:

- When both demand and supply increase, the equilibrium quantity rises but the change in the equilibrium price is ambiguous.
- When both demand and supply decrease, the equilibrium quantity falls but the change in the equilibrium price is ambiguous.

FYI Makin' Bacon?

"Pork plight looming: Worldwide bacon shortage 'unavoidable' after drought, pig farmers warn." So read a recent headline in Canada's *National Post*. Behind the gloom and doom were droughts in 2012 that reduced the supply of corn. Why was the supply of bacon threatened? Because of what happens to the equilibrium price of corn, a key ingredient in a pig's dinner, when its supply decreases. High corn prices make it more expensive to raise the pigs whose bellies become bacon. This added expense reduced the supply of bacon. And with that, the price of bacon rose by 26 percent between mid-2012 and mid-2013.

Was there a shortage? No. There would have been a shortage if something prevented the price from rising to the equilibrium level. But as we have seen in our models, rising prices close the gap between the quantity supplied and the quantity demanded. Or, as explained by Andrew Dickson, general manager of the Manitoba Pork Council, "Is there less pork in the world? Probably, but I wouldn't call it a shortage. You give me the right price, and I will produce as much bacon as you want."

Lisovskaya Natalia/Shutterstock

A decrease in the supply of bacon may cause consumers to squeal, but it won't cause a lasting shortage, because higher bacon prices will decrease the quantity demanded and increase the quantity supplied.

MODULE 7 Review

Check Your Understanding

1. In the following three situations, the market is initially in equilibrium. After each event described below, does a surplus or shortage exist at the original equilibrium price? What will happen to the equilibrium price as a result?
   - **a.** In 2014 there was a bumper crop of wine grapes.
   - **b.** After a hurricane, Florida hoteliers often find that many people cancel their upcoming vacations, leaving them with empty hotel rooms.
   - **c.** After a heavy snowfall, many people want to buy second-hand snowblowers at the local tool shop.
2. For each of the following examples, explain how the indicated change affects supply or demand for the good in question and how the shift you describe affects the equilibrium price and quantity.
   - **a.** As the price of gasoline fell in the United States during the 1990s, more people bought large cars.
   - **b.** Technological innovation in the use of recycled paper has lowered the cost of paper production.
   - **c.** When a local cable company offers cheaper pay-per-view films, local movie theaters have more unfilled seats.
3. Periodically, a computer chip maker like Intel introduces a new chip that is faster than the previous one. In response, demand for computers using the earlier chip decreases as customers put off purchases in anticipation of machines containing the new chip. Simultaneously, computer makers increase their production of computers containing the earlier chip in order to clear out their stocks of those chips.

   Draw two diagrams of the market for computers containing the earlier chip: (a) one in which the equilibrium quantity falls in response to these events and (b) one in which the equilibrium quantity rises. What happens to the equilibrium price in each diagram?

Tackle the Test: Multiple-Choice Questions

1. Which of the following describes what will happen in the market for tomatoes if a salmonella outbreak is attributed to tainted tomatoes?
   - **a.** Supply will decrease and price will increase.
   - **b.** Supply will decrease and price will decrease.
   - **c.** Demand will decrease and price will increase.
   - **d.** Demand will decrease and price will decrease.
   - **e.** Supply and demand will both decrease.
2. Which of the following will lead to an increase in the equilibrium price of product "X"? A(n)
   - **a.** increase in consumer incomes if product "X" is an inferior good
   - **b.** increase in the price of machinery used to produce product "X"
   - **c.** technological advance in the production of good "X"
   - **d.** decrease in the price of good "Y" (a substitute for good "X")
   - **e.** expectation by consumers that the price of good "X" is going to fall
3. The equilibrium price will rise, but the equilibrium quantity may increase, decrease, or stay the same if
   - **a.** demand increases and supply decreases.
   - **b.** demand increases and supply increases.
   - **c.** demand decreases and supply increases.
   - **d.** demand decreases and supply decreases.
   - **e.** demand increases and supply does not change.
4. An increase in the number of buyers and a technological advance will cause
   - **a.** demand to increase and supply to increase.
   - **b.** demand to increase and supply to decrease.
   - **c.** demand to decrease and supply to increase.
   - **d.** demand to decrease and supply to decrease.
   - **e.** no change in demand and an increase in supply.
5. Which of the following is certainly true if demand and supply increase at the same time?
   - **a.** The equilibrium price will increase.
   - **b.** The equilibrium price will decrease.
   - **c.** The equilibrium quantity will increase.
   - **d.** The equilibrium quantity will decrease.
   - **e.** The equilibrium quantity may increase, decrease, or stay the same.

Tackle the Test: Free-Response Questions

1. Draw a correctly labeled graph showing the market for tomatoes in equilibrium. Label the equilibrium price "P_E" and the equilibrium quantity "Q_E." On your graph, draw a horizontal line indicating a price, labeled "P_C", that would lead to a shortage of tomatoes. Label the size of the shortage on your graph.

Rubric for FRQ 1 (6 points)

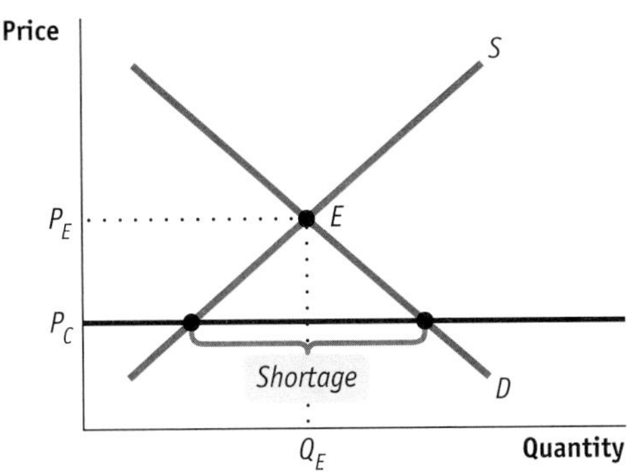

1 point: Graph with the vertical axis labeled "Price" or "*P*" and the horizontal axis labeled "Quantity" or "*Q*"

1 point: Downward-sloping demand curve labeled "Demand" or "*D*"

1 point: Upward-sloping supply curve labeled "Supply" or "*S*"

1 point: Equilibrium price "P_E" labeled on the vertical axis and quantity "Q_E" labeled on the horizontal axis at the intersection of the supply and demand curves

1 point: Price line at a price "P_C" below the equilibrium price

1 point: Correct indication of the shortage, which is the horizontal distance between the quantity demanded and the quantity supplied at the height of P_C

2. Draw a correctly labeled graph showing the market for cups of coffee in equilibrium. On your graph, show the effect of a decrease in the price of coffee beans on the equilibrium price and the equilibrium quantity in the market for cups of coffee.

(5 points)

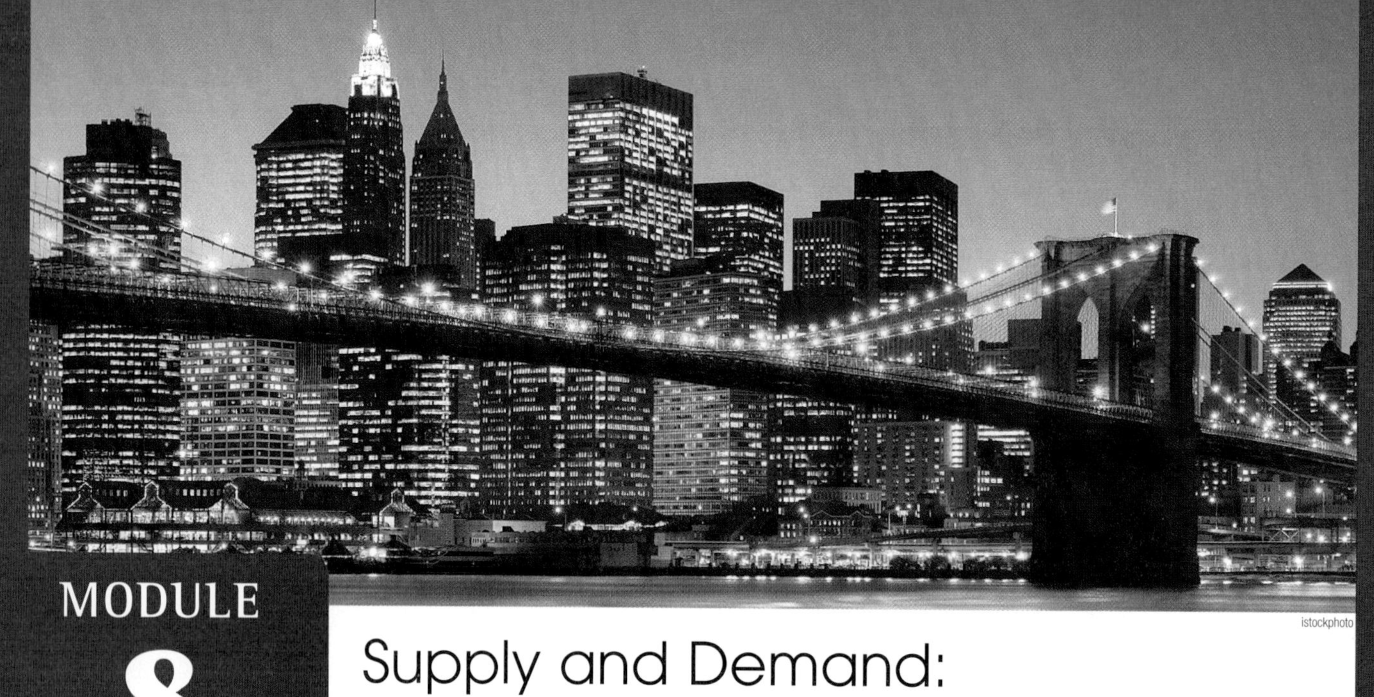

MODULE 8

Supply and Demand: Price Controls (Ceilings and Floors)

In this Module, you will learn to:

- Explain the workings of price controls, one way government intervenes in markets
- Describe how price controls can create problems and make a market inefficient
- Explain why economists are often deeply skeptical of attempts to intervene in markets
- Identify who benefits and who loses from price controls

Why Governments Control Prices

In Module 7, you learned that a market moves to equilibrium—that is, the market price moves to the level at which the quantity supplied equals the quantity demanded. But this equilibrium price does not necessarily please either buyers or sellers.

After all, buyers would always like to pay less if they could, and sometimes they can make a strong moral or political case that they should pay lower prices. For example, what if the equilibrium between supply and demand for apartments in a major city leads to rental rates that an average working person can't afford? In that case, a government might well be under pressure to impose limits on the rents landlords can charge.

Sellers, however, would always like to get more money for what they sell, and sometimes they can make a strong moral or political case that they should receive higher prices. For example, consider the labor market: the price for an hour of a worker's time is the wage rate. What if the equilibrium between supply and demand for less skilled workers leads to wage rates that yield an income below the poverty level? In that case, a government might well be pressured to require employers to pay a rate no lower than some specified minimum wage.

Price controls are legal restrictions on how high or low a market price may go. They can take two forms: a **price ceiling**, a maximum price sellers are allowed to charge for a good or service, or a **price floor**, a minimum price buyers are required to pay for a good or service.

In other words, there is often a strong political demand for governments to intervene in markets. And powerful interests can make a compelling case that a market intervention favoring them is "fair." When a government intervenes to regulate prices, we say that it imposes **price controls**. These controls typically take the form of either an upper limit, a **price ceiling**, or a lower limit, a **price floor**.

Unfortunately, it's not that easy to tell a market what to do. As we will now see, when a government tries to legislate prices—whether it legislates them *down* by imposing a price ceiling or *up* by imposing a price floor—there are certain predictable and unpleasant side effects.

We make an important assumption in this module: the markets in question are efficient before price controls are imposed. Markets can sometimes be inefficient—for example, a market dominated by a monopolist, a single seller who has the power to influence the market price. When markets are inefficient, price controls don't necessarily cause problems and can potentially move the market closer to efficiency. In practice, however, price controls often *are* imposed on efficient markets—like the New York City apartment market. And so the analysis in this module applies to many important real-world situations.

Price Ceilings

Aside from rent control, there are not many price ceilings in the United States today. But at times they have been widespread. Price ceilings are typically imposed during crises—wars, harvest failures, natural disasters—because these events often lead to sudden price increases that hurt many people but produce big gains for a lucky few. The U.S. government imposed ceilings on many prices during World War II: the war sharply increased demand for raw materials, such as aluminum and steel, and price controls prevented those with access to these raw materials from earning huge profits. Price controls on oil were imposed in 1973, when an embargo by Arab oil-exporting countries seemed likely to generate huge profits for U.S. oil companies. Price controls were imposed on California's wholesale electricity market in 2001, when a shortage created big profits for a few power-generating companies but led to higher electricity bills for consumers.

Believe it or not, rent control in New York is a legacy of World War II: it was imposed because wartime production created an economic boom, which increased demand for apartments at a time when the labor and raw materials that might have been used to build them were being used to win the war instead. Although most price controls were removed soon after the war ended, New York's rent limits were retained and gradually extended to buildings not previously covered, leading to some very strange situations.

You can rent a one-bedroom apartment in Manhattan on fairly short notice—if you are able and willing to pay several thousand dollars a month and live in a less-than-desirable area. Yet some people pay only a small fraction of this amount for comparable apartments, and others pay hardly more for bigger apartments in better locations.

Aside from producing great deals for some renters, however, what are the broader consequences of New York's rent control system? To answer this question, we turn to the supply and demand model.

Modeling a Price Ceiling

To see what can go wrong when a government imposes a price ceiling on an efficient market, consider **Figure 8.1** on the next page, which shows a simplified model of the market for apartments in New York. For the sake of simplicity, we imagine that all apartments are exactly the same and so would rent for the same price in an unregulated market. The table in the figure shows the demand and supply schedules; the demand and supply curves are shown on the left. We show the quantity of apartments on the horizontal axis and the monthly rent per apartment on the vertical axis. You can see that in an unregulated market the equilibrium would be at point *E*: 2 million apartments would be rented for $1,000 each per month.

Now suppose that the government imposes a price ceiling, limiting rents to a price below the equilibrium price—say, no more than $800. **Figure 8.2** on the next page shows the effect of the price ceiling, represented by the line at $800. At the enforced rental rate of $800, landlords have less incentive to offer apartments, so they won't be willing to supply as many as they would at the equilibrium rate of $1,000. They will choose point *A* on the supply curve, offering only 1.8 million apartments for rent, 200,000 fewer than in the unregulated market. At the same time, more people will want to rent apartments at a price of $800 than at the equilibrium price of $1,000; as shown at point *B* on the demand curve,

Figure 8.1 The Market for Apartments in the Absence of Government Controls

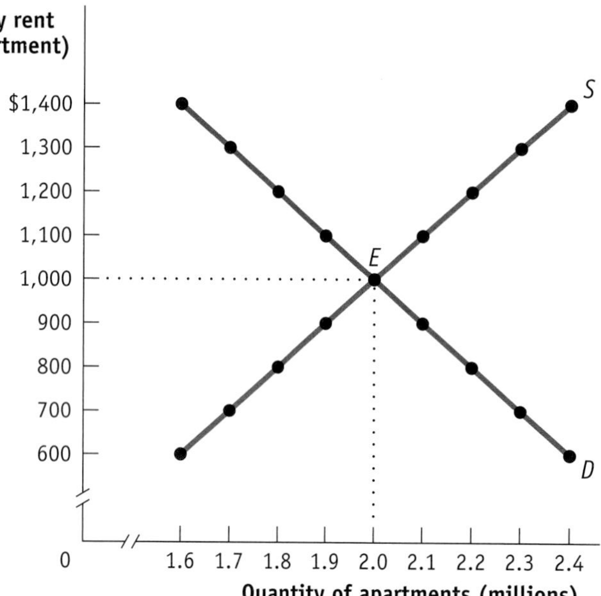

Monthly rent (per apartment)	Quantity of apartments (millions)	
	Quantity demanded	Quantity supplied
$1,400	1.6	2.4
1,300	1.7	2.3
1,200	1.8	2.2
1,100	1.9	2.1
1,000	2.0	2.0
900	2.1	1.9
800	2.2	1.8
700	2.3	1.7
600	2.4	1.6

Without government intervention, the market for apartments reaches equilibrium at point *E* with a market rent of $1,000 per month and 2 million apartments rented.

Figure 8.2 The Effects of a Price Ceiling

The black horizontal line represents the government-imposed price ceiling on rents of $800 per month. This price ceiling reduces the quantity of apartments supplied to 1.8 million, point *A*, and increases the quantity demanded to 2.2 million, point *B*. This creates a persistent shortage of 400,000 units: 400,000 of the people who want apartments at the legal rent of $800 cannot get them.

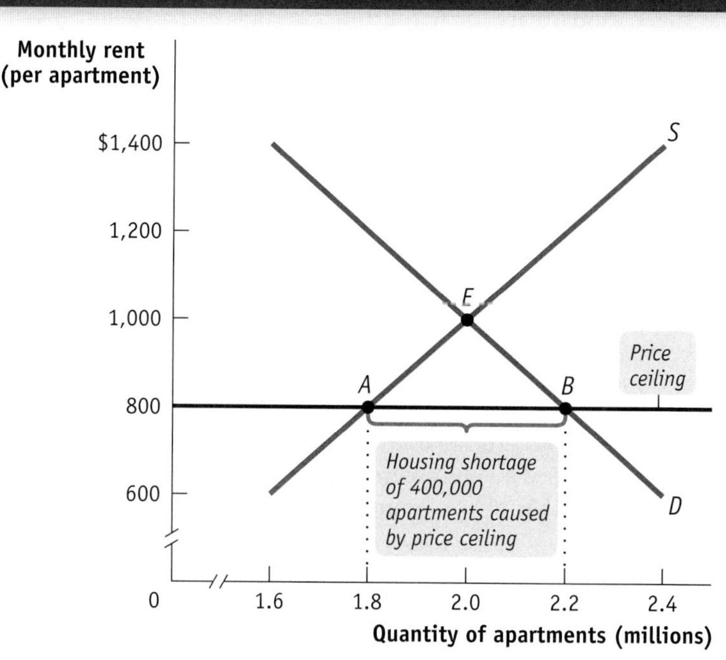

at a monthly rent of $800 the quantity of apartments demanded rises to 2.2 million, 200,000 more than in the unregulated market and 400,000 more than are actually available at the price of $800. So there is now a persistent shortage of rental housing: at that price, there are 400,000 more people who want to rent than are able to find apartments.

Do price ceilings always cause shortages? No. If a price ceiling is set above the equilibrium price, it won't have any effect. Suppose that the equilibrium rental rate on apartments is $1,000 per month and the city government sets a ceiling of $1,200. Who cares? In this case, the price ceiling won't be binding—it won't actually constrain market behavior—and it will have no effect.

Inefficient Allocation to Consumers Rent control doesn't just lead to too few apartments being available. It can also lead to misallocation of the apartments that are available: people who badly need a place to live may not be able to find an apartment, while some apartments may be occupied by people with much less urgent needs.

In the case shown in Figure 8.2, 2.2 million people would like to rent an apartment at $800 per month, but only 1.8 million apartments are available. Of those 2.2 million who are seeking an apartment, some want an apartment badly and are willing to pay a high price to get one. Others have a less urgent need and are only willing to pay a low price, perhaps because they have alternative housing. An efficient allocation of apartments would reflect these differences: people who really want an apartment will get one and people who aren't all that eager to find an apartment won't. In an inefficient distribution of apartments, the opposite will happen: some people who are not especially eager to find an apartment will get one and others who are very eager to find an apartment won't. Because people usually get apartments through luck or personal connections under rent control, it generally results in an **inefficient allocation to consumers** of the few apartments available.

Price ceilings often lead to inefficiency in the form of **inefficient allocation to consumers**: people who want the good badly and are willing to pay a high price don't get it, and those who care relatively little about the good and are only willing to pay a relatively low price do get it.

To see the inefficiency involved, consider the plight of the Lees, a family with young children who have no alternative housing and would be willing to pay up to $1,500 for an apartment—but are unable to find one. Also consider George, a retiree who lives most of the year in Florida but still has a lease on the New York apartment he moved into 40 years ago. George pays $800 per month for this apartment, but if the rent were even slightly more—say, $850—he would give it up and stay with his children when he is in New York.

This allocation of apartments—George has one and the Lees do not—is a missed opportunity: there is a way to make the Lees and George both better off at no additional cost. The Lees would be happy to pay George, say, $1,200 a month to sublease his apartment, which he would happily accept since the apartment is worth no more than $849 a month to him. George would prefer the money he gets from the Lees to keeping his apartment; the Lees would prefer to have the apartment rather than the money. So both would be made better off by this transaction—and nobody else would be made worse off.

Generally, if people who really want apartments could sublease them from people who are less eager to live there, both those who gain apartments and those who trade their occupancy for money would be better off. However, subletting is illegal under rent control because it would occur at prices above the price ceiling. The fact that subletting is illegal doesn't mean it never happens. In fact, chasing down illegal subletting is a major business for New York private investigators. A 2007 report in the *New York Times* described how private investigators use hidden cameras and other tricks to prove that the legal tenants in rent-controlled apartments actually live in the suburbs, or even in other states, and have sublet their apartments at two or three times the controlled rent. This subletting is a kind of illegal activity, which we will discuss shortly. For now, just notice that the aggressive pursuit of illegal subletting surely discourages the practice, so there isn't enough subletting to eliminate the inefficient allocation of apartments.

Wasted Resources Another reason a price ceiling causes inefficiency is that it leads to **wasted resources**: people expend money, effort, and time to cope with the shortages caused by the price ceiling. Back in 1979, U.S. price controls on gasoline led to shortages that forced millions of Americans to spend hours each week waiting in lines at gas stations. The opportunity cost of the time spent in gas lines—the wages not earned, the leisure time not enjoyed—constituted wasted resources from the point of

Price ceilings typically lead to inefficiency in the form of **wasted resources**: people expend money, effort, and time to cope with the shortages caused by the price ceiling.

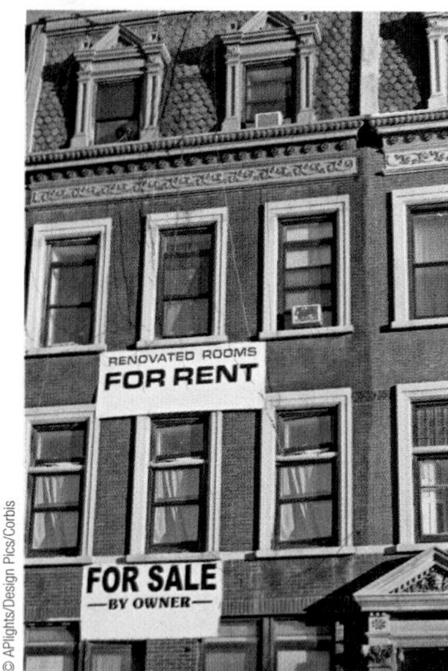

© APlights/Design Pics/Corbis

Signs advertising apartments to rent or sublet are common in New York City.

view of consumers and of the economy as a whole. Because of rent control, the Lees will spend all their spare time for several months searching for an apartment, time they would rather have spent working or engaged in family activities. That is, there is an opportunity cost to the Lees' prolonged search for an apartment—the leisure or income they had to forgo. If the market for apartments worked freely, the Lees would quickly find an apartment at the equilibrium rent of $1,000, leaving them time to earn more or to enjoy themselves—an outcome that would make them better off without making anyone else worse off. Again, rent control creates missed opportunities.

Inefficiently Low Quality Yet another way a price ceiling causes inefficiency is by causing goods to be of inefficiently low quality. **Inefficiently low quality** means that sellers offer low-quality goods at a low price even though buyers would rather have higher quality and are willing to pay a higher price for it.

Again, consider rent control. Landlords have no incentive to provide better conditions because they cannot raise rents to cover their repair costs but are able to find tenants easily. In many cases, tenants would be willing to pay much more for improved conditions than it would cost for the landlord to provide them—for example, the upgrade of an antiquated electrical system that cannot safely run air conditioners or computers. But any additional payment for such improvements would be legally considered a rent increase, which is prohibited. Indeed, rent-controlled apartments are notoriously badly maintained, rarely painted, subject to frequent electrical and plumbing problems, sometimes even hazardous to inhabit. As one former manager of Manhattan buildings explained, "At unregulated apartments we'd do most things that the tenants requested. But on the rent-regulated units, we did absolutely only what the law required. . . . We had a perverse incentive to make those tenants unhappy. With regulated apartments, the ultimate objective is to get people out of the building [because rents can be raised for new tenants]."

Price ceilings often lead to inefficiency in that the goods being offered are of **inefficiently low quality**: sellers offer low quality goods at a low price even though buyers would prefer a higher quality at a higher price.

A **black market** is a market in which goods or services are bought and sold illegally—either because it is illegal to sell them at all or because the prices charged are legally prohibited by a price ceiling.

This whole situation is a missed opportunity—some tenants would be happy to pay for better conditions, and landlords would be happy to provide them for payment. But such an exchange would occur only if the market were allowed to operate freely.

Black Markets And that leads us to a last aspect of price ceilings: the incentive they provide for illegal activities, specifically the emergence of **black markets**. We have already described one kind of black market activity—illegal subletting by tenants. But it does not stop there. Clearly, there is a temptation for a landlord to say to a potential tenant, "Look, you can have the place if you slip me an extra few hundred in cash each month"—and for the tenant to agree, if he or she is one of those people who would be willing to pay much more than the maximum legal rent.

What's wrong with black markets? In general, it's a bad thing if people break *any* law because it encourages disrespect for the law in general. Worse yet, in this case illegal activity worsens the position of those who try to be honest. If the Lees are scrupulous about upholding the rent control law but other people—who may need an apartment less than the Lees—are willing to bribe landlords, the Lees may *never* find an apartment.

So Why Are There Price Ceilings?

We have seen three common results of price ceilings:

- a persistent shortage of the good
- inefficiency arising from this persistent shortage in the form of inefficiently low quantity, inefficient allocation of the good to consumers, resources wasted in searching for the good, and the inefficiently low quality of the good offered for sale
- the emergence of illegal, black market activity

Given these unpleasant consequences, why do governments still sometimes impose price ceilings? Why does rent control, in particular, persist in New York?

One answer is that although price ceilings may have adverse effects, they do benefit some people. In practice, New York's rent control rules—which are more complex than our simple model—hurt most residents but give a small minority of renters much cheaper housing than they would get in an unregulated market. And those who benefit from the controls may be better organized and more vocal than those who are harmed by them.

Also, when price ceilings have been in effect for a long time, buyers may not have a realistic idea of what would happen without the price ceilings. In our previous example, the rental rate in an unregulated market (Figure 8.1) would be only 25% higher than in the regulated market (Figure 8.2): $1,000 instead of $800. But how would renters know that? Indeed, they might have heard about black market transactions at much higher prices—the Lees or some other family paying George $1,200 or more—and would not realize that these black market prices are much higher than the price that would prevail in a fully unregulated market.

A last answer is that government officials often do not understand supply and demand analysis! It is a great mistake to suppose that economic policies in the real world are always sensible or well informed.

AP® Exam Tip

When it comes to price controls, the ceiling is down low and the floor is up high. That is, to have any effect, a price ceiling must be below the equilibrium price, and a price floor must be above the equilibrium price.

Price Floors

Sometimes governments intervene to push market prices up instead of down. *Price floors* have been widely legislated for agricultural products, such as wheat and milk, as a way to support the incomes of farmers. Historically, there were also price floors on such services as trucking and air travel, although these were phased out by the U.S. government in the 1970s. If you have ever worked in a fast-food restaurant, you are likely to have encountered a price floor: governments in the United States and many other countries maintain a lower limit on the hourly wage rate paid for a worker's labor—that is, a floor on the price of labor—called the **minimum wage**.

The **minimum wage** is a legal floor on the hourly wage rate paid for a worker's labor.

Just like price ceilings, price floors are intended to help some people but generate predictable and undesirable side effects. **Figure 8.3** shows hypothetical supply and demand

Figure 8.3 The Market for Butter in the Absence of Government Controls

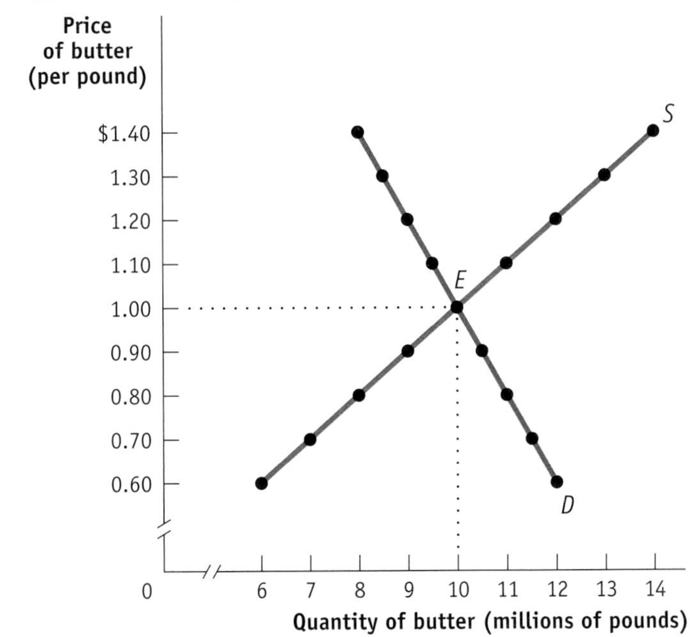

Price of butter (per pound)	Quantity of butter (millions of pounds) Quantity demanded	Quantity supplied
$1.40	8.0	14.0
1.30	8.5	13.0
1.20	9.0	12.0
1.10	9.5	11.0
1.00	10.0	10.0
0.90	10.5	9.0
0.80	11.0	8.0
0.70	11.5	7.0
0.60	12.0	6.0

Without government intervention, the market for butter reaches equilibrium at a price of $1 per pound with 10 million pounds of butter bought and sold.

curves for butter. Left to itself, the market would move to equilibrium at point *E*, with 10 million pounds of butter bought and sold at a price of $1 per pound.

Now suppose that the government, in order to help dairy farmers, imposes a price floor on butter of $1.20 per pound. Its effects are shown in **Figure 8.4**, where the line at $1.20 represents the price floor. At a price of $1.20 per pound, producers would want to supply 12 million pounds (point *B* on the supply curve) but consumers would want to buy only 9 million pounds (point *A* on the demand curve). So the price floor leads to a persistent surplus of 3 million pounds of butter.

Does a price floor always lead to an unwanted surplus? No. Just as in the case of a price ceiling, the floor may not be binding—that is, it may be irrelevant. If the equilibrium price of butter is $1 per pound but the floor is set at only $0.80, the floor has no effect.

But suppose that a price floor *is* binding: what happens to the unwanted surplus? The answer depends on government policy. In the case of agricultural price floors, governments buy up unwanted surplus. As a result, the U.S. government has at times found itself warehousing thousands of tons of butter, cheese, and other farm products. (The European Commission, which administers price floors for a number of European countries, once found itself the owner of a so-called butter mountain, equal in weight to the entire population of Austria.) The government then has to find a way to dispose of these unwanted goods.

Some countries pay exporters to sell products at a loss overseas; this is standard procedure for the European Union. The United States gives surplus food away to schools, which use the products in school lunches. In some cases, governments have actually destroyed the surplus production. To avoid the problem of dealing with the unwanted surplus, the U.S. government typically pays farmers not to produce the products at all.

When the government is not prepared to purchase the unwanted surplus, a price floor means that would-be sellers cannot find buyers. This is what happens when there is a price floor on the wage rate paid for an hour of labor, the *minimum wage:* when the minimum wage is above the equilibrium wage rate, some people who are willing to work—that is, sell labor—cannot find buyers—that is, employers—willing to give them jobs.

Figure 8.4 The Effects of a Price Floor

The dark horizontal line represents the government-imposed price floor of $1.20 per pound of butter. The quantity of butter demanded falls to 9 million pounds, and the quantity supplied rises to 12 million pounds, generating a persistent surplus of 3 million pounds of butter.

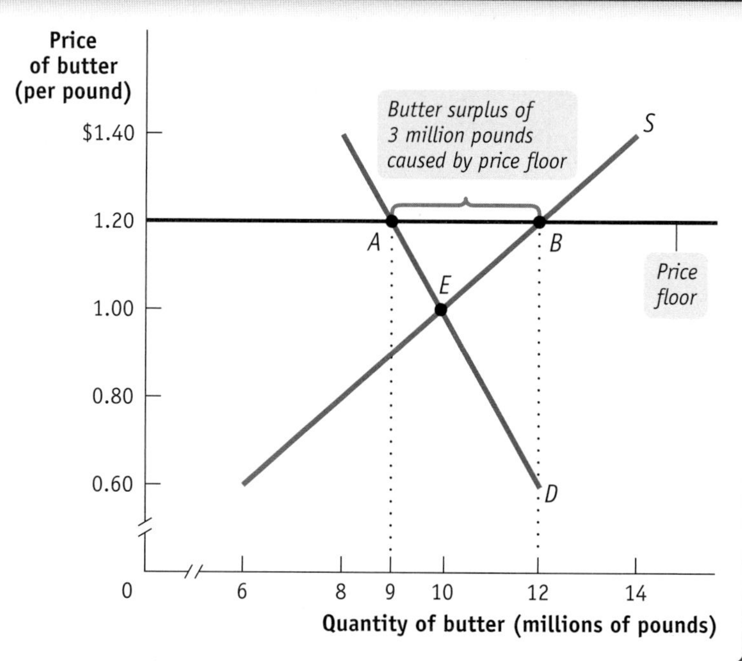

Price Floors and School Lunches

When you were in grade school, did your school offer free or very cheap lunches? If so, you were probably a beneficiary of price floors.

Where did all the cheap food come from? During the 1930s, when the U.S. economy was going through the Great Depression, a prolonged economic slump, prices were low and farmers were suffering severely. In an effort to help rural Americans, the U.S. government imposed price floors on a number of agricultural products. The system of agricultural price floors—officially called price support programs—continues to this day. Among the products subject to price support are sugar and various dairy products; at times grains, beef, and pork have also had a minimum price.

The big problem with any attempt to impose a price floor is that it creates a surplus. To some extent the U.S. Department of Agriculture has tried to head off surpluses by taking steps to reduce supply; for example, by paying farmers *not* to grow crops. As a last resort, however, the U.S. government has been willing to buy up the surplus, taking the excess supply off the market.

But then what? The government has to find a way to get rid of the agricultural products it has bought. It can't just sell them: that would depress market prices, forcing the government to buy the stuff right back. So it has to give it away in ways that don't depress market prices. One of the ways it does this is by giving surplus food, free, to school lunch programs. These gifts are known as "bonus foods." Along with financial aid, bonus foods are what allow many school districts to provide free or very cheap lunches to their students. Is this a story with a happy ending?

Not really. Nutritionists, concerned about growing child obesity in the United States, place part of the blame on those bonus foods. Schools get whatever the government has too much of—and that has tended to include a lot of dairy products, beef, and corn, and not much in the way of fresh vegetables or fruit. As a result, school lunches that make extensive use of bonus foods tend to be very high in fat and calories. So this is a case in which there is such a thing as a free lunch—but this lunch may be bad for your health.

Mike Flippo/Shutterstock

How a Price Floor Causes Inefficiency

The persistent surplus that results from a price floor creates missed opportunities—inefficiencies—that resemble those created by the shortage that results from a price ceiling.

Inefficiently Low Quantity Because a price floor raises the price of a good to consumers, it reduces the quantity of that good demanded; because sellers can't sell more units of a good than buyers are willing to buy, a price floor reduces the quantity of a good bought and sold below the market equilibrium quantity. Notice that this is the *same* effect as a price ceiling. You might be tempted to think that a price floor and a price ceiling have opposite effects, but both have the effect of reducing the quantity of a good bought and sold.

Inefficient Allocation of Sales Among Sellers Like a price ceiling, a price floor can lead to *inefficient allocation*—but in this case **inefficient allocation of sales among sellers** rather than inefficient allocation to consumers.

Price floors lead to **inefficient allocation of sales among sellers**: those who would be willing to sell the good at the lowest price are not always those who manage to sell it.

Suppose you would be willing to sell your English tutoring services for $5 per hour, but the minimum wage is $9 per hour. The job might go to someone else who would tutor for $9 per hour but not for less. In this case, the price floor on wages prevents the worker who would sell tutoring services for the lowest amount from being able to do so.

Wasted Resources Also like a price ceiling, a price floor generates inefficiency by *wasting resources.* The most graphic examples involve government purchases of the unwanted surpluses of agricultural products caused by price floors. When the surplus production is simply destroyed, and when the stored produce goes, as officials euphemistically put it, "out of condition" and must be thrown away, it is pure waste.

Price floors also lead to wasted time and effort. Consider the minimum wage. Would-be workers who spend many hours searching for jobs, or waiting in line in the hope of getting jobs, play the same role in the case of price floors as hapless families searching for apartments in the case of price ceilings.

Inefficiently High Quality Again like price ceilings, price floors lead to inefficiency in the quality of goods produced.

We've seen that when there is a price ceiling, suppliers produce goods that are of inefficiently low quality: buyers prefer higher-quality products and are willing to pay for them, but sellers refuse to improve the quality of their products because the price ceiling prevents their being compensated for doing so. This same logic applies to price floors, but in reverse: suppliers offer goods of **inefficiently high quality**.

Price floors often lead to inefficiency in that goods of **inefficiently high quality** are offered: sellers offer high-quality goods at a high price, even though buyers would prefer a lower quality at a lower price.

How can this be? Isn't high quality a good thing? Yes, but only if it is worth the cost. Suppose that suppliers spend a lot to make goods of very high quality but that this quality isn't worth much to consumers, who would rather receive the money spent on that quality in the form of a lower price. This represents a missed opportunity: suppliers and buyers could make a mutually beneficial deal in which buyers got goods of lower quality for a much lower price.

A good example of the inefficiency of excessive quality comes from the days when transatlantic airfares were set artificially high by international treaty. Forbidden to compete for customers by offering lower ticket prices, airlines instead offered expensive services, like lavish in-flight meals that went largely uneaten. At one point the regulators tried to restrict this practice by defining maximum service standards—for example, that snack service should consist of no more than a sandwich. One airline then introduced what it called a "Scandinavian Sandwich," a towering affair that forced the convening of another conference to define *sandwich*. All of this was wasteful, especially considering that what passengers really wanted was less food and lower airfares.

istockphoto

Since the deregulation of U.S. airlines in the 1970s, American passengers have experienced a large decrease in ticket prices accompanied by a decrease in the quality of in-flight service—smaller seats, lower-quality food, and so on. Everyone complains about the service—but thanks to lower fares, the number of people flying on U.S. carriers has grown several hundred percent since airline deregulation.

Illegal Activity Finally, like price ceilings, price floors provide incentives for illegal activity. For example, in countries where the minimum wage is far above the equilibrium wage rate, workers desperate for jobs sometimes agree to work off the books for employers who conceal their employment from the government—or bribe the government inspectors. This practice, known in Europe as "black labor," is especially common in southern European countries such as Italy and Spain.

So Why Are There Price Floors?

To sum up, a price floor creates various negative side effects:

- a persistent surplus of the good
- inefficiency arising from the persistent surplus in the form of inefficiently low quantity, inefficient allocation of sales among sellers, wasted resources, and an inefficiently high level of quality offered by suppliers
- the temptation to engage in illegal activity, particularly bribery and corruption of government officials

So why do governments impose price floors when they have so many negative side effects? The reasons are similar to those for imposing price ceilings. Government officials often disregard warnings about the consequences of price floors either because they believe that the relevant market is poorly described by the supply and demand model or, more often, because they do not understand the model. Above all, just as price ceilings are often imposed because they benefit some influential buyers of a good, price floors are often imposed because they benefit some influential sellers.

MODULE 8 Review

Check Your Understanding

1. On game days, homeowners near Middletown University's stadium used to rent parking spaces in their driveways to fans at a going rate of $11. A new town ordinance now sets a maximum parking fee of $7. Use the accompanying supply and demand diagram to show how each of the following can result from the price ceiling.

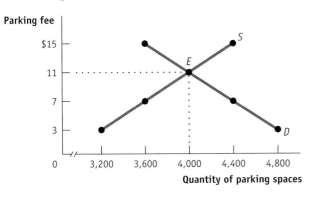

a. Some homeowners now think it's not worth the hassle to rent out spaces.
b. Some fans who used to carpool to the game now drive alone.
c. Some fans can't find parking and leave without seeing the game.

Explain how each of the following adverse effects arises from the price ceiling.

d. Some fans now arrive several hours early to find parking.
e. Friends of homeowners near the stadium regularly attend games, even if they aren't big fans. But some serious fans have given up because of the parking situation.
f. Some homeowners rent spaces for more than $7 but pretend that the buyers are nonpaying friends or family.

2. True or false? Explain your answer. A price ceiling below the equilibrium price in an otherwise efficient market does the following:

a. increases quantity supplied
b. makes some people who want to consume the good worse off
c. makes all producers worse off

3. The state legislature mandates a price floor for gasoline of P_F per gallon. Assess the following statements and illustrate your answer using the figure provided.

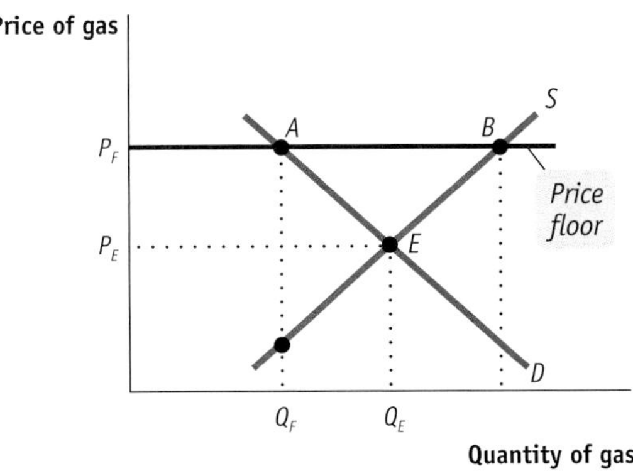

a. Proponents of the law claim it will increase the income of gas station owners. Opponents claim it will hurt gas station owners because they will lose customers.
b. Proponents claim consumers will be better off because gas stations will provide better service. Opponents claim consumers will be generally worse off because they prefer to buy gas at cheaper prices.
c. Proponents claim that they are helping gas station owners without hurting anyone else. Opponents claim that consumers are hurt and will end up doing things like buying gas in a nearby state or on the black market.

Tackle the Test: Multiple-Choice Questions

1. To be effective, a price ceiling must be set
   - **I.** above the equilibrium price.
   - **II.** in the housing market.
   - **III.** to achieve the equilibrium market quantity.

   a. I
   b. II
   c. III
   d. I, II, and III
   e. None of the above

2. Refer to the graph provided. A price floor set at $5 will result in

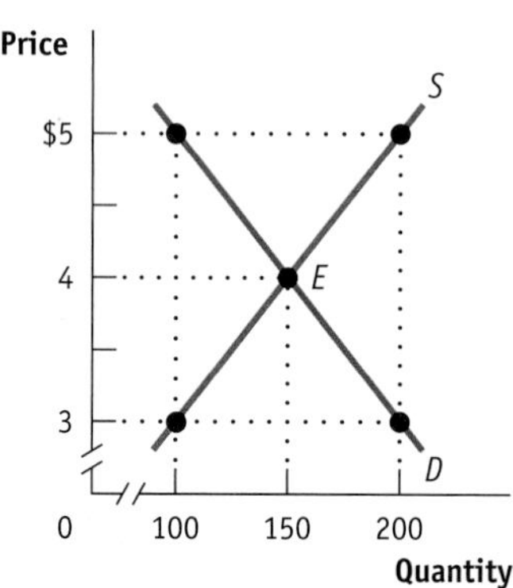

   a. a shortage of 100 units.
   b. a surplus of 100 units.
   c. a shortage of 200 units.
   d. a surplus of 200 units.
   e. a surplus of 50 units.

3. Effective price ceilings are inefficient because they
   a. create shortages.
   b. lead to wasted resources.
   c. decrease quality.
   d. create black markets.
   e. do all of the above.

4. Refer to the graph provided. If the government establishes a minimum wage at $10, how many workers will benefit from the higher wage?

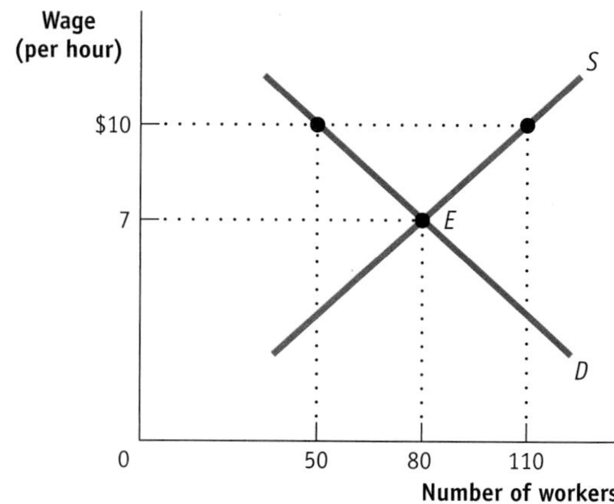

   a. 30
   b. 50
   c. 60
   d. 80
   e. 110

5. Refer to the graph for Question 4. With a minimum wage of $10, how many workers are unemployed (would like to work, but are unable to find a job)?
   a. 30
   b. 50
   c. 60
   d. 80
   e. 110

Tackle the Test: Free-Response Questions

1. Refer to the graph provided to answer the following questions.

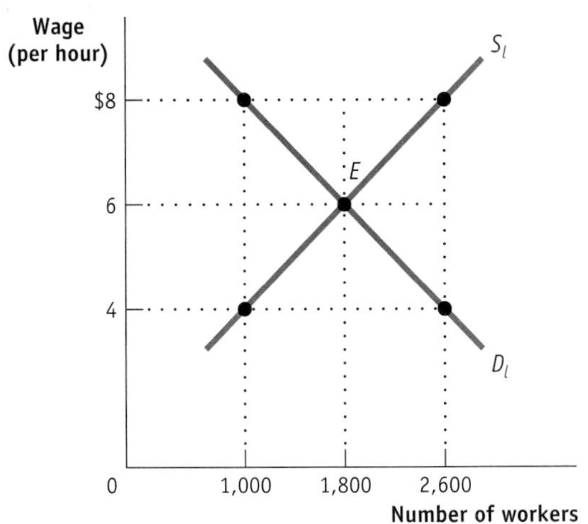

a. What are the equilibrium wage and quantity of workers in this market?

b. For it to have an effect, where would the government have to set a minimum wage?

c. If the government set a minimum wage at $8,

i. how many workers would supply their labor?

ii. how many workers would be hired?

iii. how many workers would want to work that did *not* want to work for the equilibrium wage?

iv. how many previously employed workers would no longer have a job?

Rubric for FRQ 1 (6 points)

1 point: equilibrium wage = $6, quantity of labor = 1,800

1 point: The minimum wage will have an effect if it is set anywhere above $6.

1 point: 2,600 workers would supply their labor

1 point: 1,000 workers would be hired

1 point: 800 (the number of workers who would want to work for $8 but did not supply labor for $6)

1 point: 800 (at the equilibrium wage of $6, 1,800 workers were hired; at a wage of $8, 1,000 workers would be hired. 1,800 – 1,000 = 800)

2. Draw a correctly labeled graph of a housing market in equilibrium. On your graph, illustrate an effective legal limit (ceiling) on rent. Identify the quantity of housing demanded, the quantity of housing supplied, and the size of the resulting surplus or shortage.
(6 points)

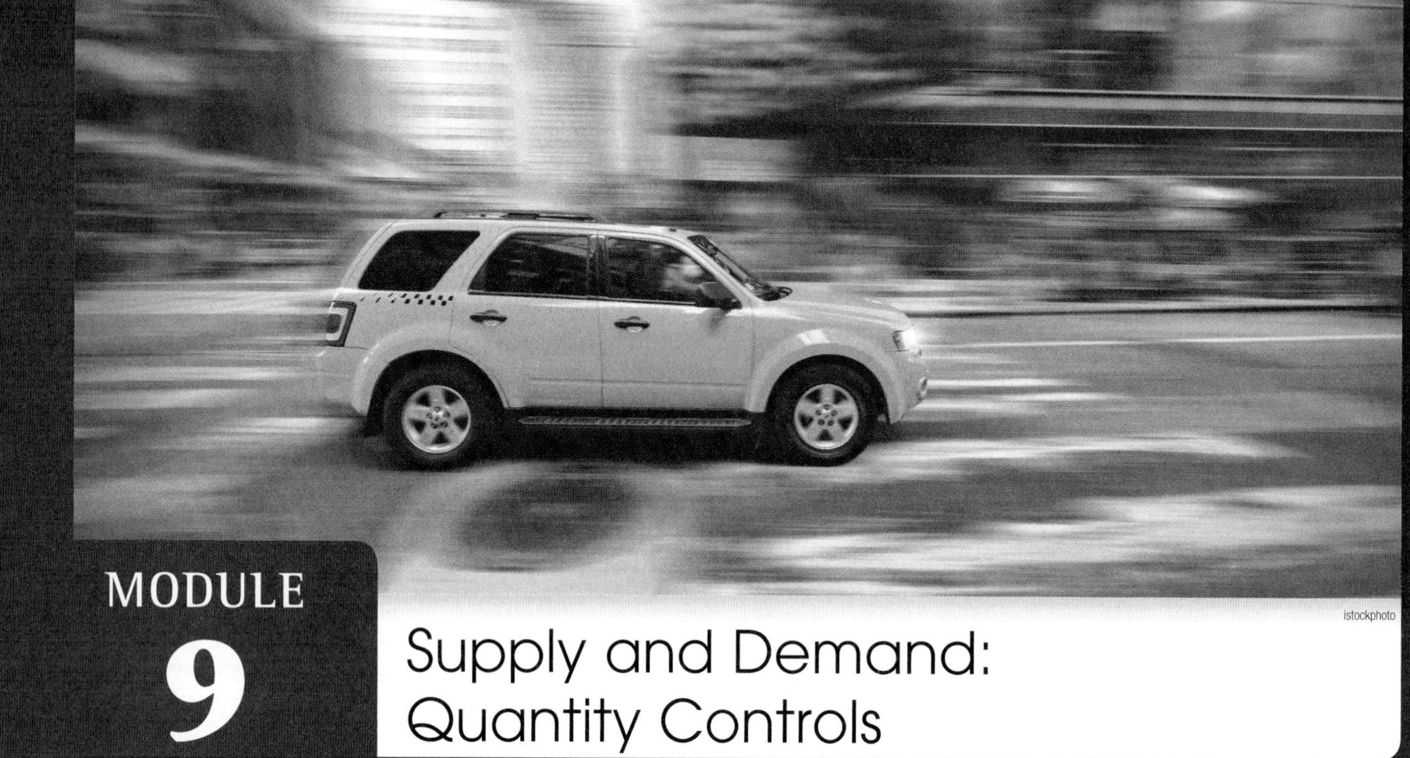
istockphoto

MODULE 9 Supply and Demand: Quantity Controls

In this Module, you will learn to:

- Explain the workings of quantity controls, another way government intervenes in markets
- Describe how quantity controls create problems and can make a market inefficient
- Explain who benefits and who loses from quantity controls

Controlling Quantities

In the 1930s, New York City instituted a system of licensing for taxicabs: only taxis with a "medallion" were allowed to pick up passengers. Because this system was intended to ensure quality, medallion owners were supposed to maintain certain standards, including safety and cleanliness. A total of 11,787 medallions were issued, with taxi owners paying $10 for each medallion.

AP® Exam Tip

Quantity controls and price controls are graphed differently. Graph a quota as a vertical line at the quantity limit. Graph a price ceiling or floor as a horizontal line at the price limit.

In 1995, there were still only 11,787 licensed taxicabs in New York, even though the city had meanwhile become the financial capital of the world, a place where hundreds of thousands of people in a hurry tried to hail a cab every day. (An additional 400 medallions were issued in 1995; after several rounds of sales of additional medallions, today there are 13,257 medallions.) The result of this restriction on the number of taxis was that a New York City taxi medallion became very valuable: if you wanted to operate a taxi in New York, you had to lease a medallion from someone else or buy one for a going price of several hundred thousand dollars.

It turns out that this story is not unique; other cities introduced similar medallion systems in the 1930s and, like New York, have issued few new medallions since. In San Francisco and Boston, as in New York, taxi medallions trade for six-figure prices.

A **quantity control**, or **quota**, is an upper limit on the quantity of some good that can be bought or sold.

A **license** gives its owner the right to supply a good or service.

A taxi medallion system is a form of **quantity control**, or **quota**, by which the government regulates the quantity of a good that can be bought and sold rather than regulating the price. Typically, the government limits quantity in a market by issuing **licenses**; only people with a license can legally supply the good. A taxi medallion is just such a license. The government of New York City limits the number of taxi rides that can be sold by limiting the number of taxis to only those who hold medallions. There are many other cases of quantity controls, ranging from limits on how much foreign currency (for instance, British pounds or Mexican pesos) people are allowed to buy to the quantity of clams New Jersey fishing boats are allowed to catch. Section 8 discusses quotas on goods imported from other countries.

Some attempts to control quantities are undertaken for good economic reasons, some for bad ones. In many cases, as we will see, quantity controls introduced to address a temporary problem become politically hard to remove later because the beneficiaries don't want them abolished, even after the original reason for their existence is long gone. But whatever the reasons for such controls, they have certain predictable—and usually undesirable—economic consequences.

The Anatomy of Quantity Controls

To understand why a New York taxi medallion is worth so much money, we consider a simplified version of the market for taxi rides, shown in **Figure 9.1**. Just as we assumed in the analysis of rent control that all apartments were the same, we now suppose that all taxi rides are the same—ignoring the real-world complication that some taxi rides are longer, and therefore more expensive, than others. The table in the figure shows supply and demand schedules. The equilibrium—indicated by point *E* in the figure and by the shaded entries in the table—is a fare of $5 per ride, with 10 million rides taken per year. (You'll see in a minute why we present the equilibrium this way.)

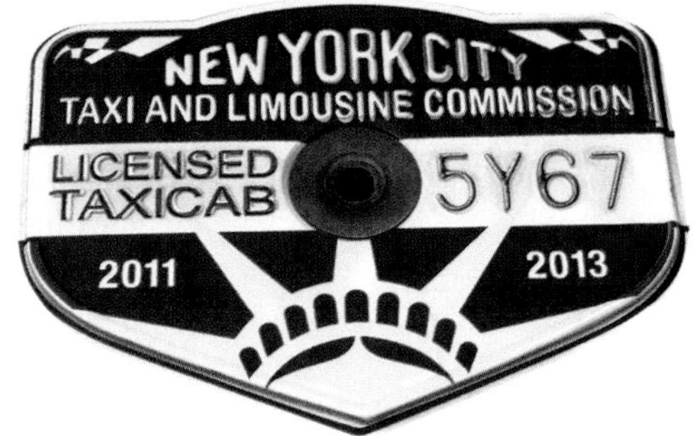

The New York medallion system limits the number of taxis, but each taxi driver can offer as many rides as he or she can manage. (Now you know why New York taxi drivers are so aggressive!) To simplify our analysis, however, we will assume that a medallion system limits the number of taxi rides that can legally be given to 8 million per year.

Until now, we have derived the demand curve by answering questions of the form: "How many taxi rides will passengers want to take if the price is $5 per ride?" But it is possible to reverse the question and ask instead: "At what price will consumers want to buy 10 million rides per year?" The price at which consumers want to buy a given quantity—in this case, 10 million rides at $5 per ride—is the **demand price** of that quantity. You can see from the demand schedule in Figure 9.1 that the demand price of 6 million rides is $7 per ride, the demand price of 7 million rides is $6.50 per ride, and so on.

The **demand price** of a given quantity is the price at which consumers will demand that quantity.

Figure 9.1 The Market for Taxi Rides in the Absence of Government Controls

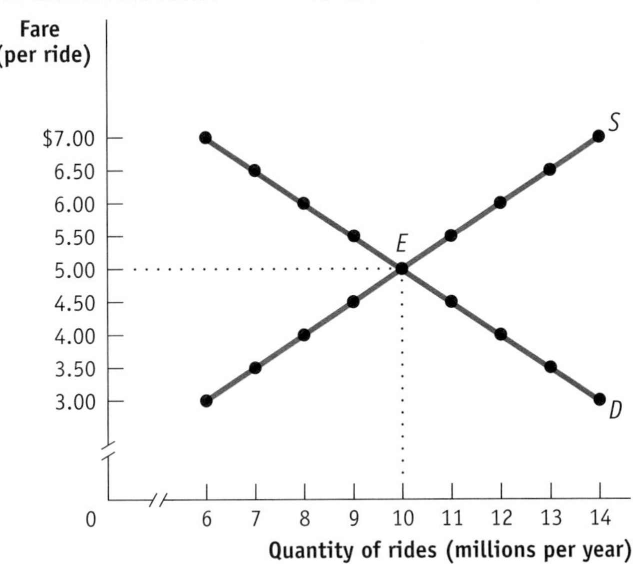

Fare (per ride)	Quantity of rides (millions per year): Quantity demanded	Quantity supplied
$7.00	6	14
6.50	7	13
6.00	8	12
5.50	9	11
5.00	10	10
4.50	11	9
4.00	12	8
3.50	13	7
3.00	14	6

Without government intervention, the market reaches equilibrium with 10 million rides taken per year at a fare of $5 per ride.

The **supply price** of a given quantity is the price at which producers will supply that quantity.

Similarly, the supply curve represents the answer to questions of the form: "How many taxi rides would taxi drivers supply at a price of $5 each?" But we can also reverse this question to ask: "At what price will producers be willing to supply 10 million rides per year?" The price at which producers will supply a given quantity—in this case, 10 million rides at $5 per ride—is the **supply price** of that quantity. We can see from the supply schedule in Figure 9.1 that the supply price of 6 million rides is $3 per ride, the supply price of 7 million rides is $3.50 per ride, and so on.

Now we are ready to analyze a quota. We have assumed that the city government limits the quantity of taxi rides to 8 million per year. Medallions, each of which carries the right to provide a certain number of taxi rides per year, are made available to selected people in such a way that a total of 8 million rides will be provided. Medallion holders may then either drive their own taxis or rent their medallions to others for a fee.

Figure 9.2 shows the resulting market for taxi rides, with the black vertical line at 8 million rides per year representing the quota. Because the quantity of rides is limited to 8 million, consumers must be at point *A* on the demand curve, corresponding to the shaded entry in the demand schedule: the demand price of 8 million rides is $6 per ride. Meanwhile, taxi drivers must be at point *B* on the supply curve, corresponding to the shaded entry in the supply schedule: the supply price of 8 million rides is $4 per ride.

But how can the price received by taxi drivers be $4 when the price paid by taxi riders is $6? The answer is that in addition to the market in taxi rides, there is also a market in medallions. Medallion-holders may not always want to drive their taxis: they may be ill or on vacation. Those who do not want to drive their own taxis will sell the right to use the medallion to someone else. So we need to consider two sets of transactions here, and so two prices: (1) the transactions in taxi rides and the price at which these will occur

Figure 9.2 Effect of a Quota on the Market for Taxi Rides

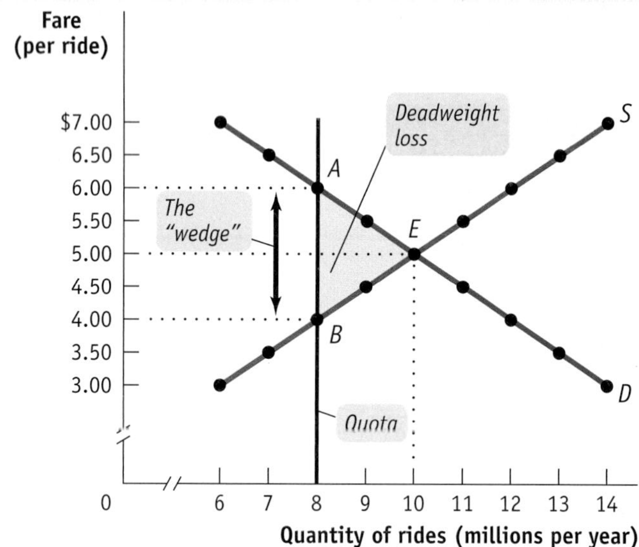

Fare (per ride)	Quantity of rides (millions per year): Quantity demanded	Quantity supplied
$7.00	6	14
6.50	7	13
6.00	8	12
5.50	9	11
5.00	10	10
4.50	11	9
4.00	12	8
3.50	13	7
3.00	14	6

The table shows the demand price and the supply price corresponding to each quantity: the price at which that quantity would be demanded and supplied, respectively. The city government imposes a quota of 8 million rides by selling enough medallions for only 8 million rides, represented by the black vertical line. The price paid by consumers rises to $6 per ride, the demand price of 8 million rides, shown by point *A*. The supply price of 8 million rides is only $4 per ride, shown by point *B*. The difference between these two prices is the quota rent per ride, the earnings that accrue to the owner of a medallion. The quota rent drives a wedge between the demand price and the supply price. Because the quota discourages mutually beneficial transactions, it creates a deadweight loss equal to the shaded triangle.

and (2) the transactions in medallions and the price at which these will occur. It turns out that since we are looking at two markets, the $4 and $6 prices will both be right.

To see how all of this works, consider two imaginary New York taxi drivers, Sunil and Harriet. Sunil has a medallion but can't use it because he's recovering from a severely sprained wrist. So he's looking to rent his medallion out to someone else. Harriet doesn't have a medallion but would like to rent one. Furthermore, at any point in time there are many other people like Harriet who would like to rent a medallion. Suppose Sunil agrees to rent his medallion to Harriet. To make things simple, assume that any driver can give only one ride per day and that Sunil is renting his medallion to Harriet for one day. What rental price will they agree on?

To answer this question, we need to look at the transactions from the viewpoints of both drivers. Once she has the medallion, Harriet knows she can make $6 per day—the demand price of a ride under the quota. And she is willing to rent the medallion only if she makes at least $4 per day—the supply price of a ride under the quota. So Sunil cannot demand a rent of more than $2—the difference between $6 and $4. And if Harriet offered Sunil less than $2—say, $1.50—there would be other eager drivers willing to offer him more, up to $2. So, in order to get the medallion, Harriet must offer Sunil at least $2. Since the rent can be no more than $2 and no less than $2, it must be exactly $2.

Sam Edwards/Getty Images

New York City: An empty cab is hard to find.

It is no coincidence that $2 is exactly the difference between $6, the demand price of 8 million rides, and $4, the supply price of 8 million rides. In every case in which the supply of a good is legally restricted, there is a **wedge** between the demand price of the quantity transacted and the supply price of the quantity transacted. This wedge, illustrated by the double-headed arrow in Figure 9.2, has a special name: the **quota rent**. It is the earnings that accrue to the medallion holder from ownership of a valuable commodity, the medallion. In the case of Sunil and Harriet, the quota rent of $2 goes to Sunil because he owns the medallion, and the remaining $4 from the total fare of $6 goes to Harriet.

A quantity control, or quota, drives a **wedge** between the demand price and the supply price of a good; that is, the price paid by buyers ends up being higher than that received by sellers.

The difference between the demand and supply price at the quota amount is the **quota rent**, the earnings that accrue to the license-holder from ownership of the right to sell the good. It is equal to the market price of the license when the licenses are traded.

So Figure 9.2 also illustrates the quota rent in the market for New York taxi rides. The quota limits the quantity of rides to 8 million per year, a quantity at which the demand price of $6 exceeds the supply price of $4. The wedge between these two prices, $2, is the quota rent that results from the restrictions placed on the quantity of taxi rides in this market.

But wait a second. What if Sunil doesn't rent out his medallion? What if he uses it himself? Doesn't this mean that he gets a price of $6? No, not really. Even if Sunil doesn't rent out his medallion, he could have rented it out, which means that the medallion has an *opportunity cost* of $2: if Sunil decides to use his own medallion and drive his own taxi rather than renting his medallion to Harriet, the $2 represents his opportunity cost of not renting out his medallion. That is, the $2 quota rent is now the rental income he forgoes by driving his own taxi. In effect, Sunil is in two businesses—the taxi-driving business and the medallion-renting business. He makes $4 per ride from driving his taxi and $2 per ride from renting out his medallion. It doesn't make any difference that in this particular case he has rented his medallion to himself! So regardless of whether the medallion owner uses the medallion himself or herself, or rents it to others, it is a valuable asset. And this is represented in the going price for a New York City taxi medallion.

Notice, by the way, that quotas—like price ceilings and price floors—don't always have a real effect. If the quota were set at 12 million rides—that is, above the equilibrium quantity in an unregulated market—it would have no effect because it would not be binding.

AP® Exam Tip

Drawing a quick graph using the data given will aid you in answering questions on quotas. For example, quota rent is simply the difference between the height of the demand curve and the height of the supply curve at the quota amount.

The Costs of Quantity Controls

Like price controls, quantity controls can have some predictable and undesirable side effects. The first is the by-now-familiar problem of inefficiency due to missed opportunities: quantity controls prevent mutually beneficial transactions from occurring, transactions that would benefit both buyers and sellers. Looking back at Figure 9.2, you can see that starting at the quota of 8 million rides, New Yorkers would be willing to pay at least $5.50 per ride for an additional 1 million rides and that taxi drivers would be willing to provide those rides as long as they got at least $4.50 per ride. These are rides that would have taken place if there had been no quota. The same is true for the next 1 million rides: New Yorkers would be willing to pay at least $5 per ride when the quantity of rides is increased from 9 to 10 million, and taxi drivers would be willing to provide those rides as long as they got at least $5 per ride. Again, these rides would have occurred without the quota. Only when the market has reached the unregulated market equilibrium quantity of 10 million rides are there no "missed-opportunity rides"—the quota of 8 million rides has caused 2 million "missed-opportunity rides." A buyer would be willing to buy the good at a price that the seller would be willing to accept, but such a transaction does not occur because it is forbidden by the quota. Economists have a special term for the lost gains from missed opportunities such as these: **deadweight loss**. Generally, when the demand price exceeds the supply price, there is a deadweight loss. Figure 9.2 illustrates the deadweight loss with a shaded triangle between the demand and supply curves. This triangle represents the missed gains from taxi rides prevented by the quota, a loss that is experienced by both disappointed would-be riders and frustrated would-be drivers.

Deadweight loss is the value of foregone mutually beneficial transactions.

Because there are transactions that people would like to make but are not allowed to, quantity controls generate an incentive to evade them or even to break the law. New York's taxi industry again provides clear examples. Taxi regulation applies only to those drivers who are hailed by passengers on the street. A car service that makes prearranged pickups does not need a medallion. As a result, such hired cars provide much of the service that might otherwise be provided by taxis, as in other cities. In addition, there are substantial numbers of unlicensed cabs that simply defy the law by picking up passengers without a medallion. Because these cabs are illegal, their drivers are completely unregulated, and they generate a disproportionately large share of traffic accidents in New York City.

In fact, in 2004 the hardships caused by the limited number of New York taxis led city leaders to authorize an increase in the number of licensed taxis. In a series of sales, the city sold more than 1,000 new medallions, to bring the total number up to the current 13,257 medallions—a move that certainly cheered New York riders. But those who already owned medallions were less happy with the increase; they understood that the nearly 1,000 new taxis would reduce or eliminate the shortage of taxis. As a result, taxi drivers anticipated a decline in their revenues as they would no longer always be assured of finding willing customers. And, in turn, the value of a medallion would fall. So to placate the medallion owners, city officials also raised taxi fares: by 25% in 2004, and again—by a smaller percentage—in 2006 and 2012. Although taxis are now easier to find, a ride now costs more—and that price increase slightly diminished the newfound cheer of New York taxi riders.

The Clams of New Jersey

Forget the refineries along the Jersey Turnpike; one industry that New Jersey *really* dominates is clam fishing. In 2012 the Garden State supplied 50% of the country's surf clams, whose tongues are used in fried-clam dinners, and 53% of the quahogs, which are used to make clam chowder.

In the 1980s, however, excessive fishing threatened to wipe out New Jersey's clam beds. To save the resource, the U.S. government introduced a clam quota, which sets an overall limit on the number of bushels of clams that may be caught and allocates licenses to owners of fishing boats based on their historical catches.

Laura Stone/Shutterstock

A fried clam feast is a favorite on the Jersey shore.

Notice, by the way, that this is an example of a quota that is probably justified by broader economic and environmental considerations—unlike the New York taxicab quota, which has long since lost any economic rationale. Still, whatever its rationale, the New Jersey clam quota works the same way as any other quota.

Once the quota system was established, many boat owners stopped fishing for clams. They realized that rather than operate a boat part time, it was more profitable to sell or rent their licenses to someone else, who could then assemble enough licenses to operate a boat full time. Today, there are approximately 50 New Jersey boats fishing for clams; the license required to operate one is worth more than the boat itself.

Source: NOAA

MODULE 9 Review

Check Your Understanding

1. Suppose that the supply and demand for taxi rides is given by Figure 9.1 and a quota is set at 6 million rides. Replicate the graph from Figure 9.1, and identify each of the following on your graph:
   a. the price of a ride
   b. the quota rent
   c. the deadweight loss resulting from the quota.
   Suppose the quota on taxi rides is increased to 9 million.
   d. What happens to the quota rent and the deadweight loss?

2. Again replicate the graph from Figure 9.1. Suppose that the quota is 8 million rides and that demand decreases due to a decline in tourism. Show on your graph the smallest parallel leftward shift in demand that would result in the quota no longer having an effect on the market.

Tackle the Test: Multiple-Choice Questions

Refer to the graph provided for Questions 1–3.

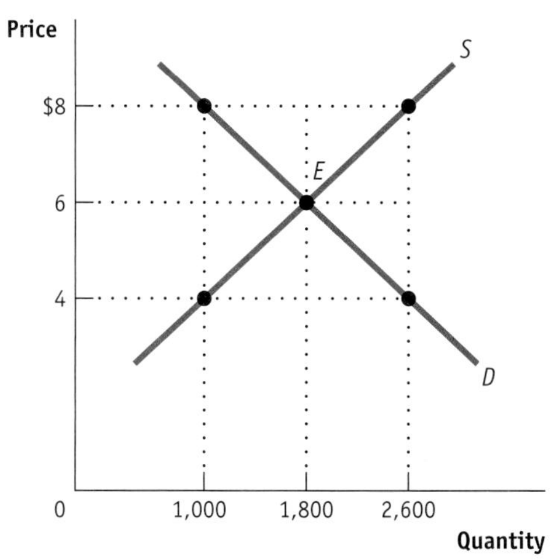

1. If the government established a quota of 1,000 in this market, the demand price would be
   a. less than $4.
   b. $4.
   c. $6.
   d. $8.
   e. more than $8.

2. If the government established a quota of 1,000 in this market, the supply price would be
   a. less than $4.
   b. $4.
   c. $6.
   d. $8.
   e. more than $8.

3. If the government established a quota of 1,000 in this market, the quota rent would be
   a. $2.
   b. $4.
   c. $6.
   d. $8.
   e. more than $8.

4. Quotas lead to which of the following?
   I. inefficiency due to missed opportunities
   II. incentives to evade or break the law
   III. a surplus in the market
   a. I
   b. II
   c. III
   d. I and II
   e. I, II, and III

5. Which of the following would decrease the effect a quota has on the quantity sold in a market?
   a. decrease in demand
   b. increase in supply
   c. increase in demand
   d. price ceiling above the equilibrium price
   e. none of the above

Tackle the Test: Free-Response Questions

1. Draw a correctly labeled graph illustrating hypothetical supply and demand curves for the U.S. automobile market. Label the equilibrium price and quantity. Suppose the government institutes a quota to limit automobile production. Draw a vertical line labeled "$Q_{ineffective}$" to show the level of a quota that would have no effect on the market. Draw a vertical line labeled "$Q_{effective}$" to show the level of a quota that would have an effect on the market. Shade in and label the deadweight loss resulting from the effective quota.

Rubric for FRQ 1 (5 points)

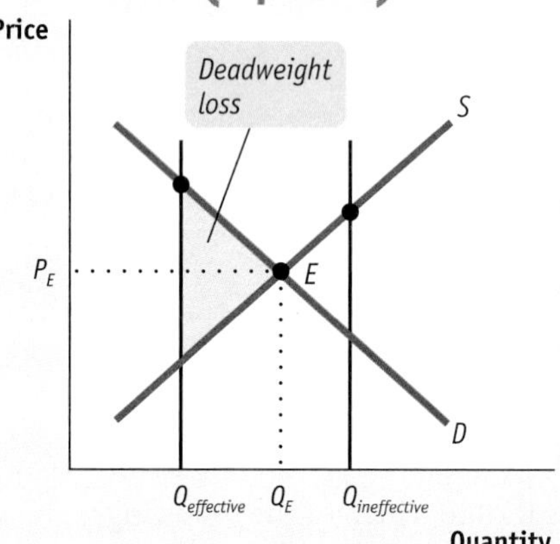

1 point: Correctly labeled supply and demand diagram (vertical axis labeled "Price" or "P," horizontal axis labeled "Quantity" or "Q," upward-sloping supply curve with label, downward-sloping demand curve with label)

1 point: Equilibrium at the intersection of supply and demand with the equilibrium price labeled on the vertical axis and the equilibrium quantity labeled on the horizontal axis

1 point: Vertical line to the right of equilibrium quantity labeled $Q_{ineffective}$

1 point: Vertical line to the left of equilibrium quantity labeled $Q_{effective}$

1 point: The triangle to the right of the effective quota line and to the left of supply and demand shaded in and labeled as the deadweight loss

2. Draw a correctly labeled graph of the market for taxicab rides. On the graph, draw and label a vertical line showing the level of an effective quota. Label the demand price, the supply price, and the quota rent. **(6 points)**

SECTION 2 Review

Section 2 Review Video

Module 5

1. The **supply and demand model** illustrates how a **competitive market**, one with many buyers and sellers of the same product, works.
2. The **demand schedule** shows the **quantity demanded** at each price and is represented graphically by a **demand curve**. The **law of demand** says that demand curves slope downward, meaning that as price decreases, the quantity demanded increases.
3. A **movement along the demand curve** occurs when the price changes and causes a change in the quantity demanded. When economists talk of **changes in demand**, they mean shifts of the demand curve—a change in the quantity demanded at any given price. An increase in demand causes a rightward shift of the demand curve. A decrease in demand causes a leftward shift.
4. There are five main factors that shift the demand curve:
   - A change in the prices of related goods, such as substitutes or complements
   - A change in income: when income rises, the demand for **normal goods** increases and the demand for **inferior goods** decreases
   - A change in tastes
   - A change in expectations
   - A change in the number of consumers

Module 6

5. The **supply schedule** shows the **quantity supplied** at each price and is represented graphically by a **supply curve**. According to the **law of supply**, supply curves slope upward, meaning that as price increases, the quantity demanded increases.
6. A **movement along the supply curve** occurs when the price changes and causes a change in the quantity supplied. When economists talk of **changes in supply**, they mean shifts of the supply curve—a change in the quantity supplied at any given price. An increase in supply causes a rightward shift of the supply curve. A decrease in supply causes a leftward shift.
7. There are five main factors that shift the supply curve:
   - A change in **input** prices
   - A change in the prices of related goods and services
   - A change in technology
   - A change in expectations
   - A change in the number of producers

Module 7

8. An economic situation is in **equilibrium** when no individual would be better off doing something different. The supply and demand model is based on the principle that the price in a market moves to its **equilibrium price**, or **market-clearing price**, the price at which the quantity demanded is equal to the quantity supplied. This quantity is the **equilibrium quantity**. When the price is above its market-clearing level, there is a **surplus** that pushes the price down. When the price is below its market-clearing level, there is a **shortage** that pushes the price up.
9. An increase in demand increases both the equilibrium price and the equilibrium quantity; a decrease in demand has the opposite effect. An increase in supply reduces the equilibrium price and increases the equilibrium quantity; a decrease in supply has the opposite effect.
10. Shifts of the demand curve and the supply curve can happen simultaneously. When they shift in opposite directions, the change in price is predictable but the change in quantity is not. When they shift in the same direction, the change in quantity is predictable but the change in price is not. In general, the curve that shifts the greater distance has a greater effect on the changes in price and quantity.

Module 8

11. Even when a market is efficient, governments often intervene to pursue greater fairness or to please a powerful interest group. Interventions can take the form of **price controls** or quantity controls, both of which generate predictable and undesirable side effects, consisting of various forms of inefficiency and illegal activity.
12. A **price ceiling**, a maximum market price below the equilibrium price, benefits successful buyers but creates persistent shortages. Because the price is maintained below the equilibrium price, the quantity demanded is increased and the quantity supplied is decreased compared to the equilibrium quantity. This leads to predictable problems including **inefficient allocation to consumers**, **wasted resources**, and **inefficiently low quality**. It also encourages illegal activity as people turn to **black markets** to get the good. Because of these problems, price ceilings have generally lost favor as an economic policy tool. But some governments continue to impose them either because they don't understand the effects or because the price ceilings benefit some influential group.
13. A **price floor**, a minimum market price above the equilibrium price, benefits successful sellers but creates a persistent surplus: because the price is maintained above the equilibrium price, the quantity demanded is decreased and the quantity supplied is increased compared to the equilibrium quantity. This leads to predictable problems: inefficiencies in the form of **inefficient allocation of sales among sellers**, wasted resources, and **inefficiently high quality**. It also encourages illegal activity and black markets. The most well-known kind of price floor is the **minimum wage**, but price floors are also commonly applied to agricultural products.

Module 9

14. Quantity controls, or **quotas**, limit the quantity of a good that can be bought or sold. The government issues **licenses** to individuals, the right to sell a given quantity of the good. The owner of a license earns a **quota rent**, earnings that accrue from ownership of the right to sell the good. It is equal to the difference between the **demand price** at the quota amount, what consumers are willing to pay for that amount, and the **supply price** at the quota amount, what suppliers are willing to accept for that amount. Economists say that a quota drives a **wedge** between the demand price and the supply price; this wedge is equal to the quota rent. By limiting mutually beneficial transactions, quantity controls generate inefficiency. Like price controls, quantity controls lead to **deadweight loss** and encourage illegal activity.

Key Terms

Competitive market, p. 49
Supply and demand model, p. 50
Demand schedule, p. 50
Quantity demanded, p. 50
Demand curve, p. 51
Law of demand, p. 51
Change in demand, p. 52
Movement along the demand curve, p. 52
Substitutes, p. 54
Complements, p. 54
Normal good, p. 55
Inferior good, p. 55
Individual demand curve, p. 56
Quantity supplied, p. 60
Supply schedule, p. 60
Supply curve, p. 60
Law of supply, p. 61
Change in supply, p. 61
Movement along the supply curve, p. 62
Input, p. 63
Individual supply curve, p. 65
Equilibrium, p. 69
Equilibrium price, p. 70
Market-clearing price, p. 70
Equilibrium quantity, p. 70
Surplus, p. 71
Shortage, p. 71
Price controls, p. 80
Price ceiling, p. 80
Price floor, p. 80
Inefficient allocation to consumers, p. 83
Wasted resources, p. 83
Inefficiently low quality, p. 84
Black market, p. 84
Minimum wage, p. 85
Inefficient allocation of sales among sellers, p. 87
Inefficiently high quality, p. 88
Quantity control or quota, p. 92
License, p. 92
Demand price, p. 93
Supply price, p. 94
Wedge, p. 95
Quota rent, p. 95
Deadweight loss, p. 96

AP® Exam Practice Questions

Multiple-Choice Questions

1. Which of the following changes will most likely result in an increase in the demand for hamburgers in your hometown?
  a. The price of hotdogs decreases.
  b. The price of drinks sold at hamburger restaurants increases.
  c. Income in your town decreases and hamburgers are a normal good.
  d. The local newspaper publishes a story on health problems caused by red meat.
  e. The number of vegetarians in your town decreases and the population size remains the same.

2. Which of the following changes will most likely result in a decrease in the supply of guitars?
  a. The popularity of guitar music increases.
  b. Consumer incomes decrease.
  c. A new firm enters the guitar industry.
  d. The guitar-making process is reengineered to be more efficient.
  e. The wages of guitar makers increase.

3. Which of the following will most likely result in a decrease in the quantity of lemons demanded?
  a. an increase in the price of lemons
  b. an increase in the price of limes
  c. an increase in the price of lemonade
  d. an increase in the number of lemonade stands
  e. a decrease in consumer income

4. Which of the following will occur if consumer incomes increase?
   a. The demand for inferior goods will increase.
   b. The demand for normal goods will increase.
   c. The demand for all goods will increase.
   d. The demand for normal goods will decrease.
   e. The demand for all goods will decrease.
5. If two goods are complements, an increase in the price of one good will cause which of the following?
   a. a decrease in the demand for the other
   b. a decrease in the quantity demanded of the other
   c. an increase in the demand for the other
   d. an increase in the quantity demanded of the other
   e. no change in the demand for the other
6. An increase in the wages of workers producing a good will most likely lead to which of the following?
   a. a decrease in the quantity of the good supplied
   b. a decrease in the supply of the good
   c. an increase in the quantity of the good supplied
   d. an increase in the supply of the good
   e. no change in the supply of the good
7. Which of the following is true at the equilibrium price in a market?
   a. Consumers who purchase the good may be better off buying something else instead.
   b. The market has not yet cleared.
   c. There is a tendency for the price to decrease over time.
   d. There may be either a surplus or a shortage of the good.
   e. The quantity demanded of the good equals the quantity supplied.
8. A survey indicated that chocolate is America's favorite ice cream flavor. Which of the following will lead to a decrease in the price of chocolate ice cream?
   a. A drought in the Midwest causes farmers to reduce the number of dairy cows they raise.
   b. A new report from the American Medical Association concludes that chocolate has significant health benefits.
   c. The price of vanilla ice cream increases.
   d. New freezer technology lowers the cost of producing ice cream.
   e. The price of ice cream toppings decreases.
9. Which of the following events will increase both the price and the quantity of pizza?
   a. The price of mozzarella cheese increases.
   b. New health hazards of eating pizza are widely publicized.
   c. The price of pizza ovens rises.
   d. Consumers expect the price of pizza to fall next week.
   e. Consumer income falls and pizza is an inferior good.

Use the following situation and diagram to answer Questions 10–15.

For the last 70 years, the U.S. government has used price supports to provide income assistance to U.S. farmers. At times, the government has used price floors, which it maintains by buying up the surplus farm products. At other times, it has used target prices, giving the farmer an amount equal to the difference between the market price and the target price for each unit sold.

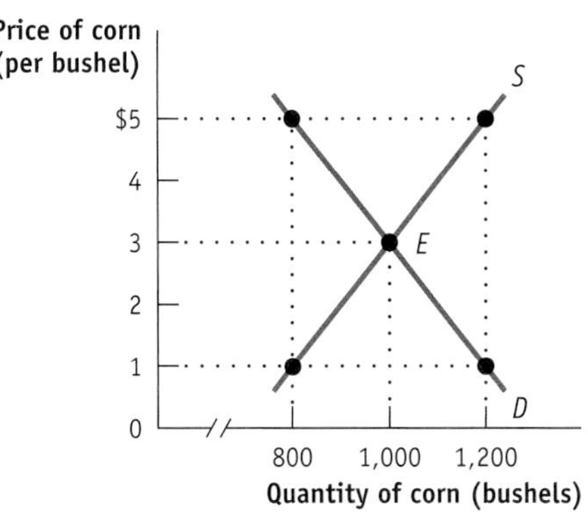

10. What are the equilibrium price and quantity in the market for corn?

	Price	Quantity
a.	$1	800
b.	$1	1,200
c.	$3	1,000
d.	$5	800
e.	$5	1,200

11. If the government sets a price floor of $5 per bushel, how many bushels of corn are produced?
   a. 0
   b. 400
   c. 800
   d. 1,000
   e. 1,200
12. If the government sets a price floor of $5 per bushel, how many bushels of corn are purchased by consumers?
   a. 0
   b. 400
   c. 800
   d. 1,000
   e. 1,200
13. How many bushels of corn are purchased by the government if it maintains a price floor of $5 by buying all surplus corn?
   a. 0
   b. 400
   c. 800
   d. 1,000
   e. 1,200

14. How much does a price floor of $5 cost the government if it maintains the price floor by buying any surplus corn?

a. $0
b. $2,000
c. $4,000
d. $5,000
e. $6,000

15. How much revenue do corn farmers receive if there is a price floor at $5?

a. $0
b. $1,200
c. $3,000
d. $4,000
e. $6,000

Use the following diagram to answer Questions 16–20.

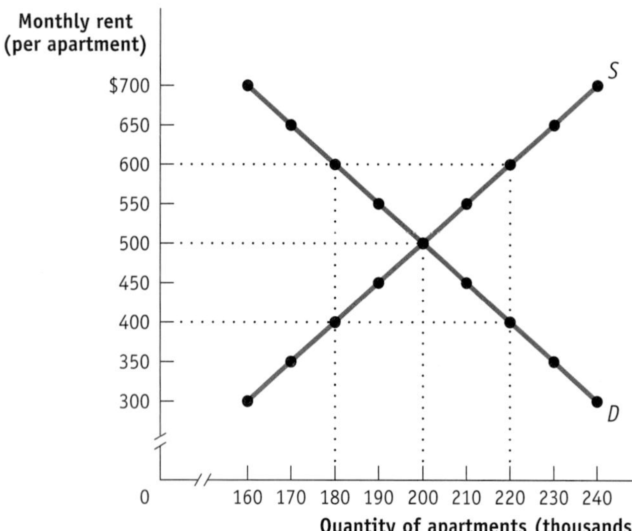

16. Where must an effective price ceiling in this market be set?

a. at $500
b. above $400
c. above $500
d. below $600
e. below $500

17. If the government sets a price ceiling at $400, how many apartments will be demanded by consumers?

a. 0
b. 40,000
c. 180,000
d. 200,000
e. 220,000

18. How many apartments will be offered for rent if the government sets a price ceiling at $400?

a. 0
b. 40,000
c. 180,000
d. 200,000
e. 220,000

19. A price ceiling set at $400 will result in which of the following in the market for apartments?

a. a surplus of 40,000 apartments
b. a surplus of 220,000 apartments
c. no surplus or shortage
d. a shortage of 40,000 apartments
e. a shortage of 220,000 apartments

20. A price ceiling set at $600 will result in which of the following in the market for apartments?

a. a surplus of 40,000 apartments
b. a surplus of 220,000 apartments
c. no surplus or shortage
d. a shortage of 40,000 apartments
e. a shortage of 220,000 apartments

Refer to the following table and information to answer Questions 21–24.

Only fishing boats licensed by the U.S. government are allowed to catch swordfish in the waters off the North Atlantic coast. The following table shows hypothetical demand and supply schedules for swordfish caught in the United States each year.

	Quantity of swordfish (millions of pounds per year)	
Price of swordfish (per pound)	**Quantity demanded**	**Quantity supplied**
$20	6	15
18	7	13
16	8	11
14	9	9
12	10	7

21. If the government establishes a quota of 7 million pounds in the market, what will the demand price of swordfish be (per pound)?
- **a.** $20
- **b.** $18
- **c.** $16
- **d.** $14
- **e.** $12

22. If the government establishes a quota of 7 million pounds in the market, what will the supply price of swordfish be (per pound)?
- **a.** $20
- **b.** $18
- **c.** $16
- **d.** $14
- **e.** $12

23. What is the quota rent per pound of swordfish received by licensed fishing boats when the government sets a quota of 7 million pounds?
- **a.** $0
- **b.** $6
- **c.** $12
- **d.** $18
- **e.** $30

24. If there is a quota of 7 million pounds and swordfish fishing licenses are traded in a market, how much will the price of a fishing license be per pound?
- **a.** $0
- **b.** $6
- **c.** $12
- **d.** $18
- **e.** $30

25. When transactions do not occur due to price or quantity controls, what is the term for the lost gains?
- **a.** wasted resources
- **b.** inefficient quality
- **c.** price wedge
- **d.** black market losses
- **e.** deadweight loss

Free-Response Question

1. Pablo Picasso died having painted only 1,000 paintings during his "Blue Period."
- **a.** Draw a correctly labeled graph of the market for Picasso "Blue Period" paintings showing each of the following:
  - **i.** the supply and demand curves for paintings
  - **ii.** the equilibrium price and quantity of paintings
- **b.** List the five principal factors that will lead to a change in the price of paintings in this market.
- **c.** Show the effect on price in your market for paintings if wealthy art collectors decide that it is essential to acquire Picasso "Blue Period" paintings for their collections.

(5 points)

SECTION 3

Measurement of Economic Performance

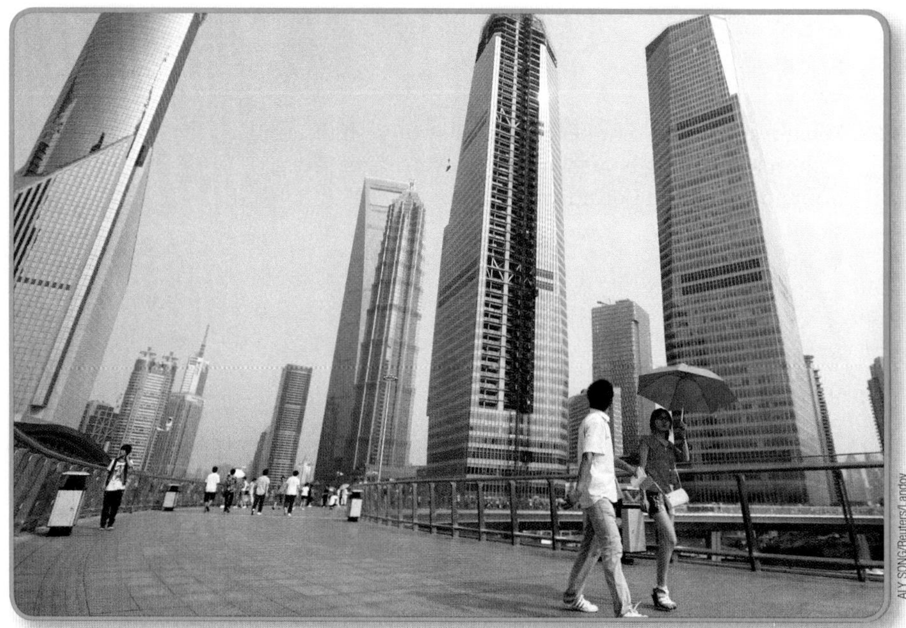
ALY SONG/Reuters/Landov

The New #2

"China Passes Japan as Second-Largest Economy." That was the headline in the *New York Times* on August 15, 2010. Citing evidence that Japan's economy was weakening while China's was roaring ahead, the article predicted—correctly, as it turned out—that 2010 would mark the first year in which the surging Chinese economy finally overtook Japan's, taking second place to the United States on the world economic stage. "The milestone," wrote the *Times*, "though anticipated for some time, is the most striking evidence yet that China's ascendance is for real and that the rest of the world will have to reckon with a new economic superpower."

But wait a minute—what does it mean to say that China's economy is larger than Japan's? After all, the two economies are producing very different mixes of goods. Despite its rapid advance, China is still a fairly poor country whose greatest strength is in relatively low-tech production. Japan, by contrast, is very much a high-tech nation, and it dominates world output of some sophisticated goods, like electronic sensors for automobiles. That's why the 2011 earthquake in northeastern Japan, which put many factories out of action, temporarily caused major production disruptions for auto factories around the world.

How can you compare the sizes of two economies when they aren't producing the same things? The answer is that comparisons of national economies are based on the *value* of their production. When news reports declared that China's economy had overtaken Japan's, they meant that China's *gross domestic product*, or *GDP*—a measure of the overall value of goods and services produced—had surpassed Japan's GDP.

GDP is one of the most important measures used to track the macroeconomy—that is, to quantify movements in the overall level of output and prices. Measures like GDP and *price indexes* play a central role in the formulation of economic policy, because policy makers need to know what's going on, and anecdotes are no substitute for hard data. These measures are also important for business decisions—to such an extent that corporations and other players are willing to pay consulting firms such as Macroeconomic Advisors for early estimates of what official economic measurements will find.

In this section we explain three of the most useful macroeconomic measures: gross domestic product, unemployment, and inflation.

Spencer Platt/Getty Images

MODULE 10 The Circular Flow and Gross Domestic Product

In this Module, you will learn to:

- Explain how economists use aggregate measures to track the performance of the economy
- Interpret the circular-flow diagram of the economy
- Define and calculate gross domestic product, or GDP

The National Accounts

Almost all countries calculate a set of numbers known as the *national income and product accounts*. In fact, the accuracy of a country's accounts is a remarkably reliable indicator of its state of economic development—in general, the more reliable the accounts, the more economically advanced the country. When international economic agencies seek to help a less developed country, typically the first order of business is to send a team of experts to audit and improve the country's accounts.

In the United States, these numbers are calculated by the Bureau of Economic Analysis, a division of the U.S. government's Department of Commerce. The **national income and product accounts**, often referred to simply as the **national accounts**, keep track of the spending of consumers, sales of producers, business investment spending, government purchases, and a variety of other flows of money among different sectors of the economy. Let's see how they work.

National income and product accounts, or **national accounts**, keep track of the flows of money among different sectors of the economy.

The Circular-Flow Diagram

To understand the principles behind the national accounts, it helps to look at a graphic called a *circular-flow diagram*. This diagram is a simplified representation of the macroeconomy. It shows the flows of money, goods and services, and factors of production through the economy. It allows us to visualize the key concepts behind the national accounts. The underlying principle is that the flow of money into each market or sector is equal to the flow of money coming out of that market or sector.

AP® Exam Tip

Be prepared to draw the simple circular-flow diagram with two markets and three sectors on the AP® exam. Make sure you use the proper terms between markets, firms, and households.

The Simple Circular-Flow Diagram The U.S. economy is a vastly complex entity, with more than a hundred million workers employed by millions of companies, producing millions of different goods and services. Yet you can learn some very important

Figure 10.1 The Circular-Flow Diagram

This diagram represents the flows of money, factors of production, and goods and services in the economy. In the markets for goods and services, households purchase goods and services from firms, generating a flow of money to the firms and a flow of goods and services to the households. The money flows back to households as firms purchase factors of production from the households in factor markets.

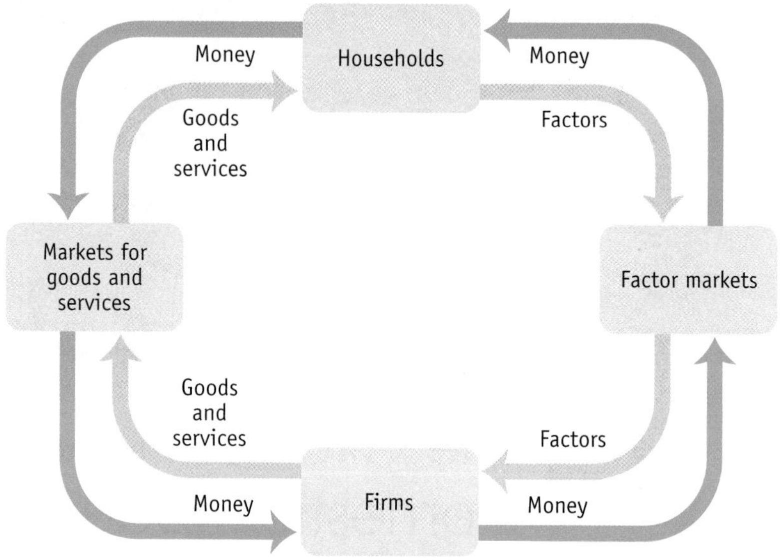

things about the economy by considering a simple diagram, shown in **Figure 10.1**. This simple model of the macroeconomy represents the transactions that take place by two kinds of flows around a circle: flows of physical things such as goods, services, labor, or raw materials in one direction, and flows of money that pay for these things in the opposite direction. In this case, the physical flows are shown in yellow and the money flows are shown in green.

The simplest circular-flow diagram illustrates an economy that contains only two kinds of "inhabitants": households and firms. A **household** consists of either an individual or a group of people who share their income. A **firm** is an organization that produces goods and services for sale—and that employs members of households.

As you can see in Figure 10.1, there are two kinds of markets in this simple economy. On one side (here the left side) there are markets for goods and services (also known as **product markets**) in which households buy the goods and services they want from firms. This produces a flow of goods and services to the households and a return flow of money to the firms.

On the other side, there are **factor markets** in which firms buy the resources they need to produce goods and services. The best known factor market is the *labor market,* in which workers are paid for their time. Besides labor, we can think of households as owning the other factors of production and selling them to firms.

A **household** is a person or group of people who share income.

A **firm** is an organization that produces goods and services for sale.

Product markets are where goods and services are bought and sold.

Factor markets are where resources, especially capital and labor, are bought and sold.

Consumer spending is household spending on goods and services.

This simple circular-flow diagram omits a number of real-world complications in the interest of simplicity. However, the diagram is a useful aid to thinking about the economy—and we can use it as the starting point for developing a more realistic (and therefore more complicated) circular-flow diagram.

The Expanded Circular-Flow Diagram **Figure 10.2** is a revised and expanded circular-flow diagram. This diagram shows only the flows of money in the economy, but is expanded to include extra elements that were ignored in the interest of simplicity in Figure 10.1. The underlying principle that the inflow of money into each market or sector must equal the outflow of money coming from that market or sector still applies in this model.

In Figure 10.2, the circular flow of money between households and firms illustrated in Figure 10.1 remains. In the product markets, households engage in **consumer spending**,

Figure 10.2 An Expanded Circular-Flow Diagram: How Money Flows Through the Economy

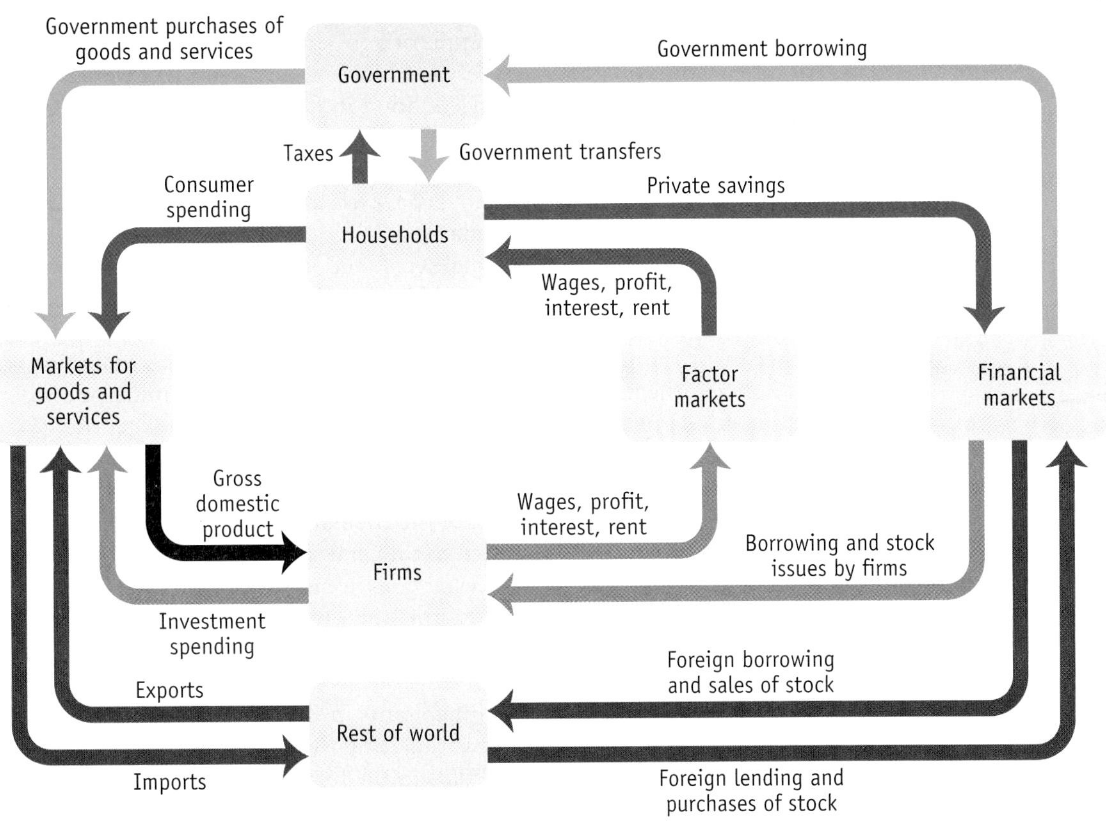

A circular flow of funds connects the four sectors of the economy—households, firms, government, and the rest of the world—via three types of markets: the factor markets, the markets for goods and services, and the *financial markets*. Funds flow from firms to households in the form of wages, profit, interest, and rent through the factor markets. After paying taxes to the government and receiving *government transfers*, households allocate the remaining income—*disposable income*—to private savings and consumer spending. Via the financial markets, *private savings* and funds from the rest of the world are channeled into investment spending by firms, government borrowing, foreign borrowing and lending, and foreign transactions of stocks. In turn, funds flow from the government and households to firms to pay for purchases of goods and services. Finally, exports to the rest of the world generate a flow of funds into the economy and imports lead to a flow of funds out of the economy. We can determine the total flow of funds by adding all spending—consumer spending on goods and services, investment spending by firms, government purchases of goods and services, and exports—and then subtracting the value of imports. This is the value of all the final goods and services produced in the United States—that is, the *gross domestic product* of the economy.

buying goods and services from both domestic firms and firms in the rest of the world. Households receive money as owners of the factors of production—land, labor, and capital. They sell the use of these factors of production to firms, receiving rent, wages, and interest payments in return. Firms buy, and pay households for, the use of those factors of production in factor markets, represented to the right of center in the diagram. Most households derive the bulk of their income from wages earned by selling labor. Some households derive additional income from their indirect ownership of the physical capital used by firms, mainly in the form of **stocks**—shares in the ownership of a company—and **bonds**—loans to firms in the form of an IOU that pays interest. In other words, the income households receive from the factor markets includes profit distributed to

A **stock** is a share in the ownership of a company held by a shareholder.

A **bond** is a loan in the form of an IOU that pays interest.

Government transfers are payments that the government makes to individuals without expecting a good or service in return.

Disposable income, equal to income plus government transfers minus taxes, is the total amount of household income available to spend on consumption and to save.

Private savings, equal to disposable income minus consumer spending, is disposable income that is not spent on consumption.

The banking, stock, and bond markets, which channel private savings and foreign lending into investment spending, government borrowing, and foreign borrowing, are known as the **financial markets**.

Government borrowing is the amount of funds borrowed by the government in the financial markets.

Government purchases of goods and services are total expenditures on goods and services by federal, state, and local governments.

Goods and services sold to other countries are **exports**. Goods and services purchased from other countries are **imports**.

company shareholders and the interest payments on any bonds that they hold. Finally, households receive rent from firms in exchange for the use of land or structures that the households own. So in factor markets, households receive income in the form of wages, profit, interest, and rent.

Some households receive **government transfers**—payments that the government makes to individuals without expecting a good or service in return. Unemployment insurance payments are one example of a government transfer. Households spend most of their income on goods and services. However, in Figure 10.2 we see two reasons why the markets for goods and services don't in fact absorb *all* of a household's income. First, households don't get to keep all the income they receive. They must pay part of their income to the government in the form of taxes, such as income taxes and sales taxes. The total income households have left after receiving government transfers and paying taxes is **disposable income**.

The second reason that the markets for goods and services do not absorb all household income is that many households set aside a portion of their income for **private savings**. These private savings go into **financial markets** where individuals, banks, and other institutions buy and sell stocks and bonds as well as make loans. As Figure 10.2 shows, the financial markets (on the far right of the circular-flow diagram) also receive funds from the rest of the world and provide funds to the government, to firms, and to the rest of the world.

Before going further, we can use the box representing households to illustrate an important general characteristic of the circular-flow diagram: the total sum of flows of money out of a given box is equal to the total sum of flows of money into that box. It's simply a matter of accounting: what goes in must come out. So, for example, the total flow of money out of households—the sum of taxes paid, consumer spending, and private savings—must equal the total flow of money into households—the sum of wages, profit, interest, rent, and government transfers.

Now let's look at the other inhabitants in the circular-flow diagram, including the government and the rest of the world. The government returns a portion of the money it collects from taxes to households in the form of government transfers. However, it uses much of its tax revenue, plus additional funds borrowed in the financial markets through **government borrowing**, to buy goods and services. **Government purchases of goods and services**, the total of purchases made by federal, state, and local governments, includes everything from military spending on ammunition to your local public school's spending on chalk, erasers, and teacher salaries.

The rest of the world participates in the U.S. economy in three ways. First, some of the goods and services produced in the United States are sold to residents of other countries. For example, more than half of America's annual wheat and cotton crops are sold abroad. Goods and services sold to other countries are known as **exports**. Export sales lead to a flow of funds from the rest of the world into the United States to pay for them. Second, some of the goods and services purchased by residents of the United States are produced abroad. For example, many consumer goods are now made in China. Goods and services purchased from other countries are known as **imports**. Import purchases lead to a flow of funds out of the United States to pay for them. Third, foreigners can participate in U.S. financial markets. Foreign lending—lending by foreigners to borrowers in the United States and purchases by foreigners of shares of stock in American companies—generates a flow of funds into the United States from the rest of the world. Conversely, foreign borrowing—borrowing by foreigners from U.S. lenders and purchases by Americans of stock in foreign companies—leads to a flow of funds out of the United States to the rest of the world.

Thinkstock/Comstock/Getty Images

Supplies used in public schools, such as the chalk shown here, are among the goods and services purchased by the government.

Notice that, like households, firms also buy goods and services in our economy. For example, an automobile company that is building a new factory will buy investment goods—machinery like stamping presses and welding robots—from companies that manufacture these items. It will also accumulate an *inventory* of finished cars in preparation for shipment to dealers. **Inventories**, then, are goods and raw materials that firms hold to facilitate their operations. The national accounts count this **investment spending**—spending on new productive physical capital, such as machinery and buildings, and on changes in inventories—as part of total spending on goods and services.

You might ask why changes in inventories are included in investment spending—after all, finished cars aren't used to produce more cars. Changes in inventories of finished goods are counted as investment spending because, like machinery, they change the ability of a firm to make future sales. So spending on additions to inventories is a form of investment spending by a firm. Conversely, a drawing-down of inventories is counted as a fall in investment spending because it leads to lower future sales. It's also important to understand that investment spending includes spending on the construction of any structure, regardless of whether it is an assembly plant or a new house. Why include the construction of homes? Because, like a plant, a new house produces a future stream of output—housing services for its occupants.

Suppose we add up consumer spending on goods and services, investment spending, government purchases of goods and services, and the value of exports, then subtract the value of imports. This gives us a measure of the overall market value of the goods and services the economy produces. That measure has a name: it's a country's *gross domestic product*. But before we can formally define gross domestic product, or GDP, we have to examine an important distinction between classes of goods and services: the difference between *final goods and services* versus *intermediate goods and services*.

Gross Domestic Product

A consumer's purchase of a new car from a dealer is one example of a sale of **final goods and services**: goods and services sold to the final, or end, user. But an automobile manufacturer's purchase of steel from a steel foundry or glass from a glassmaker is an example of a sale of **intermediate goods and services**: goods and services that are inputs into the production of final goods and services. In the case of intermediate goods and services, the purchaser—another firm—is *not* the final user.

Gross domestic product, or **GDP**, is the total value of all *final goods and services* produced in an economy during a given period, usually a year. In 2013 the GDP of the United States was $16,803 billion, or about $53,086 per person.

There are three approaches to the calculation of GDP. The **value-added approach** is to survey firms and add up their contributions to the value of final goods and services. The **expenditure approach** is to add up **aggregate spending** on domestically produced final goods and services in the economy—the sum of consumer spending, investment spending, government purchases of goods and services, and exports minus imports. The **income approach** is to add up the total factor income earned by households from firms in the economy, including rent, wages, interest, and profit.

Government statisticians use all three methods. To illustrate how they work, we will consider a hypothetical economy, shown in **Figure 10.3** on the next page. This economy consists of three firms—American Motors, Inc., which produces one car per year; American Steel, Inc., which produces the steel that goes into the car; and American Ore, Inc., which mines the iron ore that goes into the steel. GDP in this economy is $21,500, the value of the one car per year the economy produces. Let's look at how the three different methods of calculating GDP yield the same result.

The Value-Added Approach The first method for calculating GDP is to add up the value of all the final goods and services produced in the economy—a calculation that excludes the value of intermediate goods and services. Why are intermediate goods and services excluded? After all, don't they represent a very large and valuable portion of the economy?

Inventories are stocks of goods and raw materials held to facilitate business operations.

Investment spending is spending on new productive physical capital, such as machinery and structures, and on changes in inventories.

Final goods and services are goods and services sold to the final, or end, user.

Intermediate goods and services are goods and services bought from one firm by another firm to be used as inputs into the production of final goods and services.

Gross domestic product, or **GDP**, is the total value of all final goods and services produced in the economy during a given year.

The **value-added approach** to calculating GDP is to survey firms and add up their contributions to the value of final goods and services.

The **expenditure approach** to calculating GDP is to add up *aggregate spending* on domestically produced final goods and services in the economy—the sum of consumer spending, investment spending, government purchases of goods and services, and exports minus imports.

Aggregate spending—the total spending on domestically produced final goods and services in the economy—is the sum of consumer spending, investment spending, government purchases of goods and services, and exports minus imports.

The **income approach** to calculating GDP is to add up the total factor income earned by households from firms in the economy, including rent, wages, interest, and profit.

Figure 10.3 Calculating GDP

In this hypothetical economy consisting of three firms, GDP can be calculated in three different ways: measuring GDP as the value of production of final goods and services by summing each firm's value added; measuring GDP as aggregate spending on domestically produced final goods and services; and measuring GDP as factor income earned by households from firms in the economy.

Aggregate spending on domestically produced final goods and services = $21,500

	American Ore, Inc.	American Steel, Inc.	American Motors, Inc.	Total factor income
Value of sales	$4,200 (ore)	$9,000 (steel)	$21,500 (car)	
Intermediate goods	0	4,200 (iron ore)	9,000 (steel)	
Wages	2,000	3,700	10,000	$15,700
Interest payments	1,000	600	1,000	2,600
Rent	200	300	500	1,000
Profit	1,000	200	1,000	2,200
Total expenditure by firm	4,200	9,000	21,500	
Value added per firm = Value of sales − cost of intermediate goods	4,200	4,800	12,500	

Total payments to factors = $21,500

Sum of value added = $21,500

AP® Exam Tip

The trick to measuring GDP is to avoid double-counting. Each approach to calculating GDP includes a way to avoid counting the value of inputs twice—once at the production stage and again in the value of the final product. Likewise, the value of used goods should not be counted because their value was part of GDP when the goods were new.

The **value added** of a producer is the value of its sales minus the value of its purchases of inputs.

To understand why only final goods and services are included in GDP, look at the simplified economy described in Figure 10.3. Should we measure the GDP of this economy by adding up the total sales of the iron ore producer, the steel producer, and the auto producer? If we did, we would in effect be counting the value of the steel twice—once when it is sold by the steel plant to the auto plant and again when the steel auto body is sold to a consumer as a finished car. And we would be counting the value of the iron ore *three* times—once when it is mined and sold to the steel company, a second time when it is made into steel and sold to the auto producer, and a third time when the steel is made into a car and sold to the consumer. So counting the full value of each producer's sales would cause us to count the same items several times and artificially inflate the calculation of GDP.

In Figure 10.3, the total value of all sales, intermediate and final, is $34,700: $21,500 from the sale of the car, plus $9,000 from the sale of the steel, plus $4,200 from the sale of the iron ore. Yet we know that GDP—the total value of all final goods and services in a given year—is only $21,500. To avoid double-counting, we count only each producer's **value added** in the calculation of GDP: the difference between the value of its sales and the value of the inputs it purchases from other businesses. That is, at each stage of the production process we subtract the cost of inputs—the intermediate goods—at that stage. In this case, the value added of the auto producer is the dollar value of the cars it manufactures *minus* the cost of the steel it buys, or $12,500. The value added of the steel producer is the dollar value of the steel it produces *minus* the cost of the ore it buys, or $4,800. Only the ore producer, who we have assumed doesn't buy any inputs, has value added equal to its total sales, $4,200. The sum of the three producers' value added is $12,500 + $4,800 + $4,200 = $21,500, equal to GDP.

The Expenditure Approach Another way to calculate GDP is by adding up aggregate spending on domestically produced final goods and services. That is, GDP can be measured by the flow of funds into firms. Like the method that estimates GDP as the value of domestic production of final goods and services, this measurement must be carried out in a way that avoids double-counting. In terms of our steel and auto example, we don't want to count both consumer spending on a car (represented in Figure 10.3 by the sales price of the car) and the auto producer's spending on steel (represented in Figure 10.3 by the price of a car's worth of steel). If we counted both, we would be counting the steel embodied in the car twice. We solve this problem by counting only the value of sales to *final buyers*, such as consumers, firms that purchase investment goods, the government, or foreign buyers. In other words, in order to avoid the double-counting of spending, we omit sales of inputs from one business to another when estimating GDP using spending data. You can see from Figure 10.3 that aggregate spending on final goods and services—the finished car—is $21,500.

Digitalvision

Steel is an intermediate good because it is sold to other product manufacturers like automakers or refrigerator makers, and rarely to the final consumer.

As we've already pointed out, the national accounts *do* include investment spending by firms as a part of final spending. That is, an auto company's purchase of steel to make a car isn't considered a part of final spending, but the company's purchase of new machinery for its factory *is* considered a part of final spending. What's the difference? Steel is an input that is used up in production; machinery will last for a number of years. Since purchases of capital goods that will last for a considerable time aren't closely tied to current production, the national accounts consider such purchases a form of final sales.

What types of spending make up GDP? Look again at the markets for goods and services in Figure 10.2, and you will see that one source of sales revenue for firms is consumer spending. Let's denote consumer spending with the symbol *C*. Figure 10.2 shows three other components of sales: sales of investment goods to other businesses, or investment spending, which we will denote by *I*; government purchases of goods and services, which we will denote by *G*; and sales to foreigners—that is, exports—which we will denote by *X*.

In reality, not all of this final spending goes toward domestically produced goods and services. We must take account of spending on imports, which we will denote by *IM*. Income spent on imports is income not spent on domestic goods and services—it is income that has "leaked" across national borders. So to calculate domestic production using spending data, we must subtract spending on imports. Putting this all together gives us the following equation, which breaks GDP down by the four sources of aggregate spending:

$$\textbf{(10-1)}\quad GDP = C + I + G + X - IM$$

Note that the value of $X - IM$—the difference between the value of exports and the value of imports—is known as **net exports**. We'll be seeing a lot of Equation 10-1 in later modules!

Net exports are the difference between the value of exports and the value of imports ($X - IM$).

The Income Approach A final way to calculate GDP is to add up all the income earned by factors of production in the economy—the wages earned by labor; the interest earned by those who lend their savings to firms and the government; the rent earned by those who lease their land or structures to firms; and the profit earned by the shareholders, the owners of the firms' physical capital. This is a valid measure because the money firms earn by selling goods and services must go somewhere; whatever isn't paid as wages, interest, or rent is profit. And part of profit is paid out to shareholders as *dividends*.

Figure 10.3 shows how this calculation works for our simplified economy. The shaded column at the far right shows the total wages, interest, and rent paid by all these firms, as well as their total profit. Adding up all of these yields a total factor income of $21,500—again, equal to GDP.

We won't emphasize the income approach as much as the other two approaches to calculating GDP. It's important to keep in mind, however, that all the money spent on domestically produced goods and services generates factor income to households—that is, there really is a circular flow.

The Components of GDP Now that we know how GDP is calculated in principle, let's see what it looks like in practice.

Figure 10.4 shows the first two methods of calculating GDP side by side. The height of each bar above the horizontal axis represents the GDP of the U.S. economy in 2013: $16,803 billion. Each bar is divided to show the breakdown of that total in terms of where the value was added and how the money was spent.

In the left bar in Figure 10.4, we see the breakdown of GDP by value added according to sector, the first method of calculating GDP. Of the $16,803 billion, $12,688 billion consisted of value added by businesses. Another $1,830 billion of value added was contributed by households and institutions. Finally, $2,036 billion consisted of value added by government, in the form of military, education, and other government services.

The right bar in Figure 10.4 corresponds to the second method of calculating GDP, showing the breakdown by the four types of aggregate spending. The total height of the right bar is greater than the total height of the left bar, a difference of $494 billion (which, as you can see, extends below the horizontal axis). That's because the total height of the right bar represents total spending in the economy, spending on both domestically produced and foreign-produced—imported—final goods and services. Within the bar, consumer spending (*C*), which is 66.5% of GDP, dominates the picture. But some of that spending was absorbed by foreign-produced goods and services. In 2013, the value of net exports, the difference between the value of exports and the value of imports (*X* − *IM* in Equation 10-1), was negative—the United States was a net importer of foreign goods and services. The 2013 value of *X* − *IM* was −$494 billion, or −2.9% of GDP. Thus, a portion of the right bar extends below the horizontal axis by $494 billion to represent

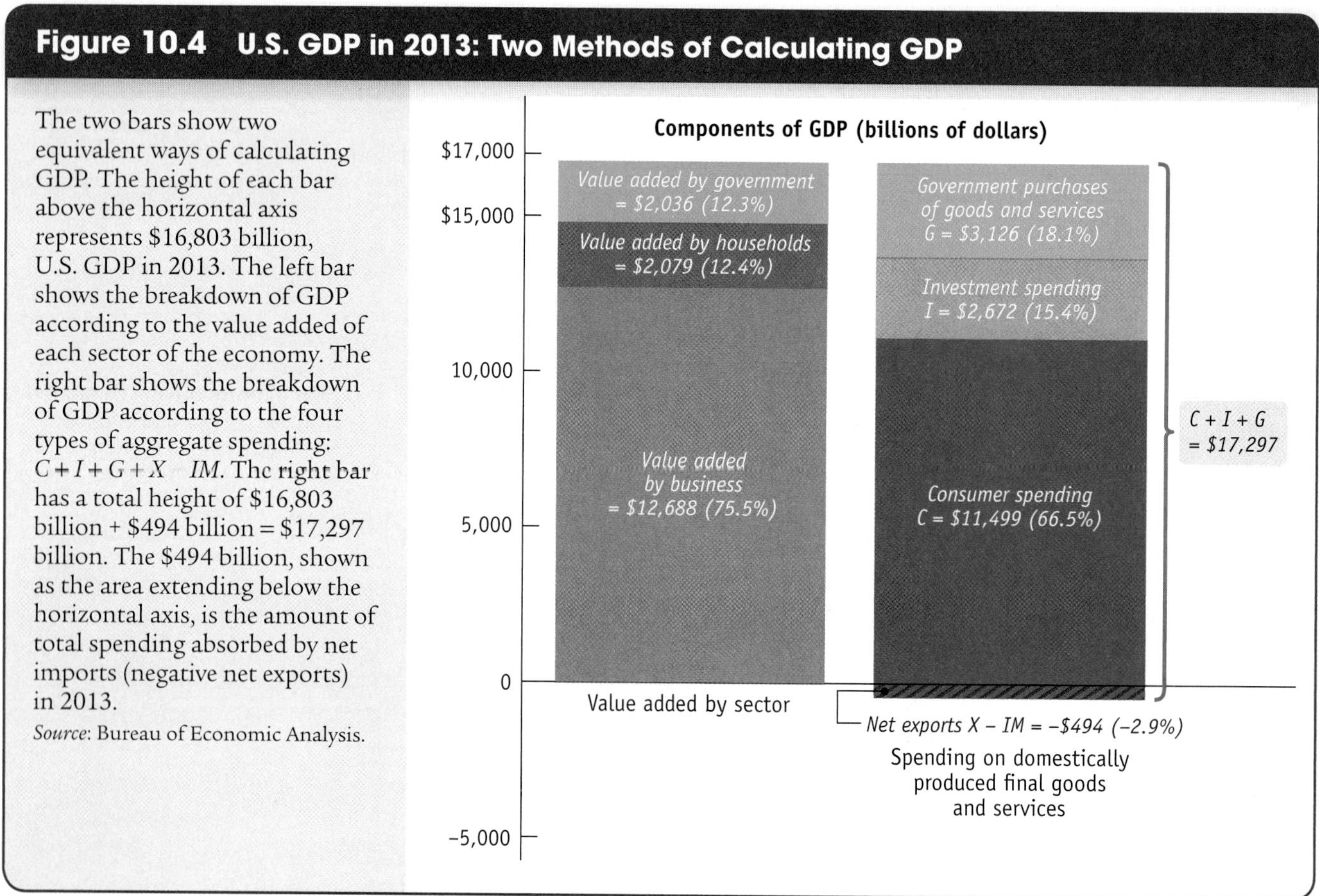

Figure 10.4 U.S. GDP in 2013: Two Methods of Calculating GDP

The two bars show two equivalent ways of calculating GDP. The height of each bar above the horizontal axis represents $16,803 billion, U.S. GDP in 2013. The left bar shows the breakdown of GDP according to the value added of each sector of the economy. The right bar shows the breakdown of GDP according to the four types of aggregate spending: *C* + *I* + *G* + *X* *IM*. The right bar has a total height of $16,803 billion + $494 billion = $17,297 billion. The $494 billion, shown as the area extending below the horizontal axis, is the amount of total spending absorbed by net imports (negative net exports) in 2013.

Source: Bureau of Economic Analysis.

the amount of total spending that was absorbed by net imports and so did not lead to higher U.S. GDP. Investment spending (*I*) constituted 15.4% of GDP; government purchases of goods and services (*G*) constituted 18.1% of GDP.

GDP: What's In and What's Out? It's easy to confuse what is included and what isn't included in GDP. So let's stop here and make sure the distinction is clear. Don't confuse investment spending with spending on inputs. Investment spending—spending on productive physical capital, the construction of structures (residential as well as commercial), and changes to inventories—is included in GDP. But spending on inputs is not. Why the difference? Recall the distinction between resources that are *used up* and those that are *not used up* in production. An input, like steel, is used up in production. A metal-stamping machine, an investment good, is not. It will last for many years and will be used repeatedly to make many cars. Since spending on productive physical capital—investment goods—and the construction of structures is not directly tied to current output, economists consider such spending to be spending on final goods. Spending on changes to inventories is considered a part of investment spending so it is also included in GDP. Why? Because, like a machine, additional inventory is an investment in future sales. And when a good is released for sale from inventories, its value is subtracted from the value of inventories and so from GDP. Used goods are not included in GDP because, as with inputs, to include them would be to double-count: counting them once when sold as new and again when sold as used.

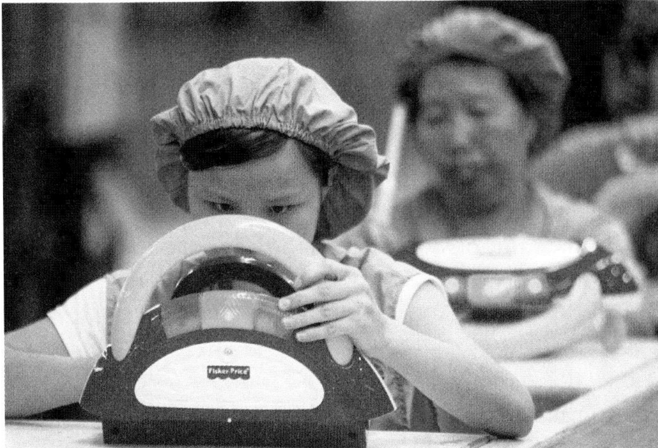
Photo by Feng Li/Getty Images

The United States is a net importer of goods and services, such as these toys made on a production line in China.

Also, financial assets such as stocks and bonds are not included in GDP because they don't represent either the production or the sale of final goods and services. Rather, a bond represents a promise to repay with interest, and a stock represents a proof of ownership. And for obvious reasons, foreign-produced goods and services are not included in calculations of gross *domestic* product.

Here is a summary of what's included and not included in GDP:

Included

- Domestically produced final goods and services, including capital goods, new construction of structures, and changes to inventories

Not Included

- Intermediate goods and services
- Inputs
- Used goods
- Financial assets such as stocks and bonds
- Foreign-produced goods and services

AP® Exam Tip

Use this mnemonic to help you remember what isn't counted in GDP: **IF IF U**
Intermediate goods and services
Financial assets and transfer payments
Inputs used up in production
Foreign-produced goods and services
Used goods

MODULE 10 Review

Check Your Understanding

1. Explain why the three methods of calculating GDP produce the same estimate of GDP.
2. Identify each of the sectors to which firms make sales. What are the various ways in which households are linked with other sectors of the economy?
3. Consider Figure 10.3. Explain why it would be incorrect to calculate total value added as $30,500, the sum of the sales price of a car and a car's worth of steel.

Tackle the Test: Multiple-Choice Questions

1. The circular-flow diagram is a simple model of the macroeconomy in which
   a. the flow of money into each market or sector exceeds the flow of money coming out of that market or sector.
   b. the value of stocks equals the value of bonds.
   c. households own the factors of production.
   d. there is only one household and one firm.
   e. goods and services are sold in factor markets.
2. GDP is equal to
   a. the total value of all goods and services produced in an economy during a given period.
   b. $C + I + G + IM$.
   c. the total value of intermediate goods plus final goods.
   d. the total income received by producers of final goods and services.
   e. none of the above.
3. Which of the following is included in GDP?
   a. changes to inventories
   b. intermediate goods
   c. used goods
   d. financial assets (stocks and bonds)
   e. foreign-produced goods
4. Which of the following is *not* included in GDP?
   a. capital goods such as machinery
   b. imports
   c. the value of domestically produced services
   d. government purchases of goods and services
   e. the construction of structures
5. Which of the following components makes up the largest percentage of GDP measured by aggregate spending?
   a. consumer spending
   b. investment spending
   c. government purchases of goods and services
   d. exports
   e. imports

Tackle the Test: Free-Response Questions

1. Will each of the following transactions be included in GDP for the United States? Explain why or why not.
   a. Coca-Cola builds a new bottling plant in the United States.
   b. Delta sells one of its existing airplanes to Korean Air.
   c. Ms. Moneybags buys an existing share of Disney stock.
   d. A California winery produces a bottle of Chardonnay and sells it to a customer in Montreal, Canada.
   e. An American buys a bottle of French perfume in Tulsa.
   f. A book publisher produces too many copies of a new book; the books don't sell this year, so the publisher adds the surplus books to inventories.

Rubric for FRQ 1 (6 points)

1 point: Yes. New structures built in the United States are included in U.S. GDP.

1 point: No. The airplane is used, and sales of used goods are not included in GDP.

1 point: No. This is a transfer of ownership—not new production.

1 point: Yes. This is an export.

1 point: No. This is an import—it was not produced in the United States.

1 point: Yes. Additions to inventories are considered investments.

2. Draw a correctly labeled circular-flow diagram showing the flows of funds between the markets for goods and services and the factor markets. Add the government to your diagram, and show how money leaks out of the economy to the government and how money is injected back into the economy by the government. **(5 points)**

Michael Hitoshi/Getty Images

MODULE 11 Interpreting Real Gross Domestic Product

In this Module, you will learn to:

- Differentiate between real GDP and nominal GDP
- Explain why real GDP is the appropriate measure of real economic activity

What GDP Tells Us

Now we've seen the various ways that gross domestic product is calculated. But what does the measurement of GDP tell us?

The most important use of GDP is as a measure of the size of the economy, providing us a scale against which to compare the economic performance of other years or other countries. For example, in 2013, as we've seen, U.S. GDP was $16,803 billion. By comparison, Japan's GDP was $4,902 billion, and the combined GDP of the 28 countries that make up the European Union was $17,371 billion. This comparison tells us that Japan, although it has the world's third-largest national economy, carries considerably less economic weight than does the United States. When taken in aggregate, Europe's economy is larger than the U.S. economy.

Lim Yong Hian/Shutterstock

Still, one must be careful when using GDP numbers, especially when making comparisons over time. That's because part of the increase in the value of GDP over time represents increases in the *prices* of goods and services rather than an increase in output. For example, U.S. GDP was $7,751 billion in 1996 and had more than doubled to $16,803 billion by 2013. But U.S. production didn't actually double over that period. To measure actual changes in aggregate output, we need a modified version of GDP that is adjusted for price changes, known as *real GDP*. We'll see how real GDP is calculated next.

Real GDP: A Measure of Aggregate Output

At the beginning of this section we described how China passed Japan as the world's second-largest economy in 2010. At the time, Japan's economy was weakening: during the second quarter of 2010, output declined by an annual rate of 6.3%. Oddly, however,

Creating the National Accounts

The national accounts, like modern macroeconomics, owe their creation to the Great Depression. As the economy plunged into depression, government officials found their ability to respond crippled not only by the lack of adequate economic theories but also by the lack of adequate information. All they had were scattered statistics: railroad freight car loadings, stock prices, and incomplete indexes of industrial production. They could only guess at what was happening to the economy as a whole.

In response to this perceived lack of information, the Department of Commerce commissioned Simon Kuznets, a young Russian-born economist, to develop a set of national income accounts. (Kuznets later won the Nobel Prize in economics for his work.) The first version of these accounts was presented to Congress in 1937 and in a research report titled *National Income, 1929–35*.

Kuznets's initial estimates fell short of the full modern set of accounts because they focused on income rather than production. The push to complete the national accounts came during World War II, when policy makers were in even more need of comprehensive measures of the economy's performance. The federal government began issuing estimates of gross domestic product and gross national product in 1942.

In January 2000, in its publication *Survey of Current Business*, the Department of Commerce ran an article titled "GDP: One of the Great Inventions of the 20th Century." This may seem a bit over the top, but national income accounting, invented in the United States, has since become a tool of economic analysis and policy making around the world.

GDP was up. In fact, Japan's GDP measured in yen, its national currency, rose by an annual rate of 4.8% during the quarter. How was that possible? The answer is that Japan was experiencing inflation at the time. As a result, the yen value of Japan's GDP rose although output actually fell.

The moral of this story is that the commonly cited GDP number is an interesting and useful statistic, one that provides a good way to compare the size of different economies, but it's not a good measure of the economy's growth over time. GDP can grow because the economy grows, but it can also grow simply because of inflation. Even if an economy's output doesn't change, GDP will go up if the prices of the goods and services the economy produces increase. Likewise, GDP can fall either because the economy is producing less or because prices have fallen.

Aggregate output is the total quantity of final goods and services produced within an economy.

To measure the economy's growth with accuracy, we need a measure of **aggregate output**: the total quantity of final goods and services the economy produces. As we noted above, the measure that is used for this purpose is known as real GDP. By tracking real GDP over time, we avoid the problem of changes in prices distorting the value of changes in production over time. Let's look first at how real GDP is calculated and then at what it means.

AP® Exam Tip

Aggregate output is another name for GDP. You may see (or hear) it referred to as output, economic output, or aggregate output.

Calculating Real GDP

To understand how real GDP is calculated, imagine an economy in which only two goods, apples and oranges, are produced and in which both goods are sold only to final consumers. The outputs and prices of the two fruits for two consecutive years are shown in **Table 11.1**.

The first thing we can say about these data is that the value of sales increased from year 1 to year 2. In the first year, the total value of sales was (2,000 billion × \$0.25) + (1,000 billion × \$0.50) = \$1,000 billion; in the second, it was (2,200 billion × \$0.30) + (1,200 billion × \$0.70) = \$1,500 billion, which is 50% larger. But it is also clear from the table that this increase in the dollar value of GDP overstates the real growth in the economy. Although the quantities of both apples and oranges increased, the prices of both apples and oranges also rose. So part of the 50% increase in the dollar value of GDP simply reflects higher prices, not increased production.

Table 11.1 Calculating GDP and Real GDP in a Simple Economy

	Year 1	Year 2
Quantity of apples (billions)	2,000	2,200
Price of an apple	$0.25	$0.30
Quantity of oranges (billions)	1,000	1,200
Price of an orange	$0.50	$0.70
GDP (billions of dollars)	$1,000	$1,500
Real GDP (billions of year 1 dollars)	$1,000	$1,150

To estimate the true increase in aggregate output produced, we have to ask the following question: How much would GDP have gone up if prices had *not* changed? To answer this question, we need to find the value of output in year 2 expressed in year 1 prices. In year 1, the price of apples was $0.25 each and the price of oranges $0.50 each. So year 2 output *at year 1 prices* is (2,200 billion × $0.25) + (1,200 billion × $0.50) = $1,150 billion. Since output in year 1 at year 1 prices was $1,000 billion, GDP measured in year 1 prices rose 15%—from $1,000 billion to $1,150 billion.

Now we can define **real GDP**: it is the total value of all final goods and services produced in the economy during a year, calculated as if prices had stayed constant at the level of some given base year in order to remove the effects of price changes. A real GDP number always comes with information about what the base year is. A GDP number that has not been adjusted for changes in prices is calculated using the prices in the year in which the output is produced. Economists call this measure **nominal GDP**, or GDP at current prices. If we had used nominal GDP to measure the change in output from year 1 to year 2 in our apples and oranges example, we would have overstated the true growth in output: we would have claimed it to be 50%, when in fact it was only 15%. By comparing output in the two years using a common set of prices—the year 1 prices in this example—we are able to focus solely on changes in the quantity of output by eliminating the influence of changes in prices.

Alamy

Real GDP is the total value of all final goods and services produced in the economy during a given year, calculated using the prices of a selected base year in order to remove the effects of price changes.

Nominal GDP is the total value of all final goods and services produced in the economy during a given year, calculated with the prices current in the year in which the output is produced.

Table 11.2 shows a real-life version of our apples and oranges example. The second column shows nominal GDP in 2000, 2005, and 2013. The third column shows real GDP for each year in 2005 dollars (that is, using the value of the dollar in the year 2005). For 2005 the nominal GDP and the real GDP are the same. But real GDP in 2000 expressed in 2005 dollars was higher than nominal GDP in 2000, reflecting the fact that prices were in general higher in 2005 than in 2000. Real GDP in 2013 expressed in 2005 dollars, however, was less than nominal GDP in 2013 because prices in 2005 were lower than in 2013.

Table 11.2 Nominal versus Real GDP in 2000, 2005, and 2013

	Nominal GDP (billions of current dollars)	Real GDP (billions of 2005 dollars)
2000	$9,951.5	$11,286
2005	12,683	12,638
2013	16,803	14,504

Source: Bureau of Economic Analysis.

You might have noticed that there is an alternative way to calculate real GDP using the data in Table 11.1. Why not measure it using the prices of year 2 rather than year 1 as the base-year prices? This procedure seems equally valid. According to that calculation, real GDP in year 1 at year 2 prices is (2,000 billion × $0.30) + (1,000 billion × $0.70) = $1,300 billion; real GDP in year 2 at year 2 prices is $1,500 billion, the same as nominal GDP in year 2. So using year 2 prices as the base year, the growth rate of real GDP is equal to ($1,500 billion – $1,300 billion)/$1,300 billion = 0.154, or 15.4%. This is slightly higher than the figure we got from the previous calculation, in which year 1 prices were the base-year prices. In that calculation, we found that real GDP increased by 15.0%. Neither answer, 15.4% versus 15.0%, is more "correct" than the other. In reality, the government economists who put together the U.S. national accounts have adopted a method to measure the change in real GDP known as **chain-linking**, which uses the average between the GDP growth rate calculated using an early base year and the GDP growth rate calculated using a late base year. As a result, U.S. statistics on real GDP are always expressed in *chained dollars*, which splits the difference between using early and late base years.

Chain-linking is the method of calculating changes in real GDP using the average between the growth rate calculated using an early base year and the growth rate calculated using a late base year.

What Real GDP Doesn't Measure

GDP is a measure of a country's aggregate output. Other things equal, a country with a larger population will have higher GDP simply because there are more people working. So if we want to compare GDP across countries but want to eliminate the effect of differences in population size, we use the measure **GDP per capita**—GDP divided by the size of the population, equivalent to the average GDP per person. Correspondingly, real GDP per capita is the average real GDP per person.

GDP per capita is GDP divided by the size of the population; it is equivalent to the average GDP per person.

Real GDP per capita can be a useful measure in some circumstances, such as in a comparison of labor productivity between two countries. However, despite the fact that it is a rough measure of the average real output per person, real GDP per capita has well-known limitations as a measure of a country's living standards. Every once in a while, economists are accused of believing that growth in real GDP per capita is the only thing that matters—that is, thinking that increasing real GDP per capita is a goal in itself. In fact, economists rarely make that mistake; the idea that economists care only about real GDP per capita is a sort of urban legend. Let's take a moment to be clear about why a country's real GDP per capita is not a sufficient measure of human welfare in that country and why growth in real GDP per capita is not an appropriate policy goal in itself.

istockphoto

Real GDP does not include many of the things that contribute to happiness, such as leisure time, volunteerism, housework, and natural beauty. And real GDP increases with expenditures on some things that make people unhappy, including disease, divorce, crime, and natural disasters.

Real GDP per capita is a measure of an economy's average aggregate output per person—an indication of the economy's potential for certain achievements. Having studied the income approach to calculating GDP, you know that the value of output corresponds to the value of income. A country with a relatively high GDP per capita can afford relatively high expenditures on health, education, and other goods and services that contribute to a high quality of life. But how output is actually used is another matter. To put it differently, your income might be higher this year than last year, but whether you use that higher income to actually improve your quality of life is up to you. There is not a one-to-one match between real GDP and the quality of life. The real GDP per capita measure does not indicate how income is distributed. It doesn't include some sources of well-being, and it does include some things that are detriments to well-being.

FYI Miracle in Venezuela?

The South American nation of Venezuela has a distinction that may surprise you: in recent years, it has had one of the world's fastest-growing nominal GDPs. Between 2000 and 2012, Venezuelan nominal GDP grew by an average of 27% each year—much faster than nominal GDP in the United States or even in booming economies like China.

So is Venezuela experiencing an economic miracle? No, it's just suffering from unusually high inflation. The figure shows Venezuela's nominal and real GDP from 2000 to 2012, with real GDP measured in 2000 prices. Real GDP did grow over the period, but at an annual rate of only 2.0%. That's about the same as the U.S. growth rate over the same period and far short of China's 10% growth.

Source: World Bank.

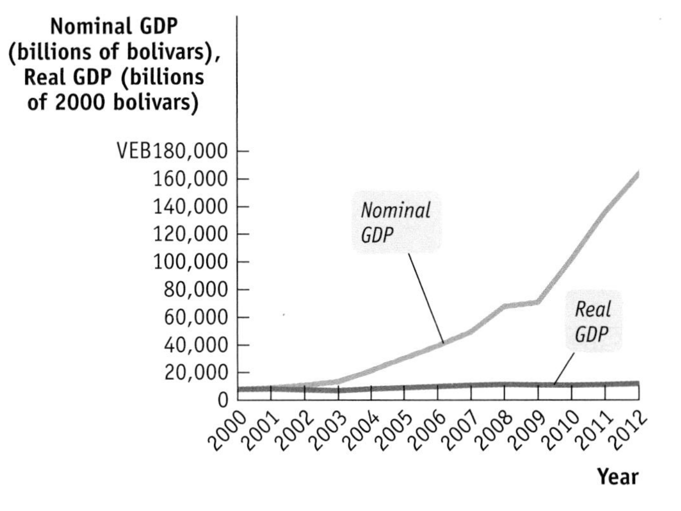

MODULE 11 Review

Check Your Understanding

1. Assume there are only two goods in the economy, french fries and onion rings. In 2013, 1,000,000 servings of french fries were sold for $0.40 each and 800,000 servings of onion rings were sold for $0.60 each. From 2013 to 2014, the price of french fries rose to $0.50 and the servings sold fell to 900,000; the price of onion rings fell to $0.51 and the servings sold rose to 840,000.
   a. Calculate nominal GDP in 2013 and 2014. Calculate real GDP in 2014 using 2013 prices.
   b. Why would an assessment of growth using nominal GDP be misguided?

2. Indicate the effect of each of the following on real GDP:
   a. Chevrolet increases its production of Corvettes.
   b. Consumer expenditures increase as a result of inflation.
   c. $50 billion is spent on hurricane cleanup.
   d. Citizens spend 10,000 hours as neighborhood watch volunteers.

Tackle the Test: Multiple-Choice Questions

1. Which of the following is true of real GDP?
   I. It is adjusted for changes in prices.
   II. It is always equal to nominal GDP.
   III. It increases whenever aggregate output increases.
   a. I only
   b. II only
   c. III only
   d. I and III
   e. I, II, and III

2. The best measure for comparing a country's aggregate output over time is
   a. nominal GDP.
   b. real GDP.
   c. nominal GDP per capita.
   d. real GDP per capita.
   e. average GDP per capita.

3. Use the information provided in the table below for an economy that produces only apples and oranges. Assume year 1 is the base year.

	Year 1	Year 2
Quantity of apples	3,000	4,000
Price of an apple	$0.20	$0.30
Quantity of oranges	2,000	3,000
Price of an orange	$0.40	$0.50

What was the value of real GDP in each year?

	Year 1	*Year 2*
a.	$1,400	$2,700
b.	1,900	2,700
c.	1,400	2,000
d.	1,900	2,000
e.	1,400	1,900

4. Real GDP per capita is an imperfect measure of the quality of life in part because it
   - **a.** includes the value of leisure time.
   - **b.** excludes expenditures on education.
   - **c.** includes expenditures on natural disasters.
   - **d.** excludes expenditures on entertainment.
   - **e.** includes the value of housework.

5. Refer to the 2013 data in the table below.

	Nominal GDP in billions of dollars
United States	$16,803
Japan	4,902
European Union	17,371

Which of the following can be determined with the information in the table?

- **I.** Residents of Japan were worse off than residents of the United States or the European Union.
- **II.** The European Union had a higher nominal GDP per capita than the United States.
- **III.** The European Union had a larger economy than the United States.

- **a.** I only
- **b.** II only
- **c.** III only
- **d.** II and III
- **e.** I, II, and III

Tackle the Test: Free-Response Questions

1. The economy of Britannica produces three goods: computers, DVDs, and pizza. The accompanying table shows the prices and output of the three goods for the years 2012 and 2014.

	Computers		DVDs		Pizza	
Year	Price	Quantity	Price	Quantity	Price	Quantity
2012	$900	10	$10	100	$15	2
2014	1,050	12	14	110	17	3

- **a.** Calculate the nominal GDP in Britannica for 2012.
- **b.** Calculate the real GDP in Britannica for 2012 using 2012 as the base year.
- **c.** Calculate the real GDP in Britannica for 2014 using 2012 as the base year.

Rubric for FRQ 1 (3 points)

1 point: ($900 × 10) + ($10 × 100) + ($15 × 2) = $9,000 + $1,000 + $30 = $10,030

1 point: Real GDP equals nominal GDP in the base year, so this answer is the same as in part a.

1 point: ($900 × 12) + ($10 × 110) + ($15 × 3) = $10,800 + $1,100 + $45 = $11,945

2. The country of Hungry produces only pizzas and the country of Thirsty produces only smoothies. Use the information in the table below to answer the following questions:
   - **a.** Calculate the number of pizzas made in Hungry and the number of smoothies made in Thirsty in each year.
   - **b.** Calculate the real GDP in each country in year 2 using year 1 prices.
   - **c.** In which country did real GDP increase the most between year 1 and year 2?
   - **d.** In which country did real GDP per capita decrease the most between year 1 and year 2? Show your work.

	Nominal GDP	Price	Population
Hungry			
Year 1	$10,000	$10	5
Year 2	20,000	10	16
Thirsty			
Year 1	$10,000	$10	5
Year 2	30,000	20	10

(6 points)

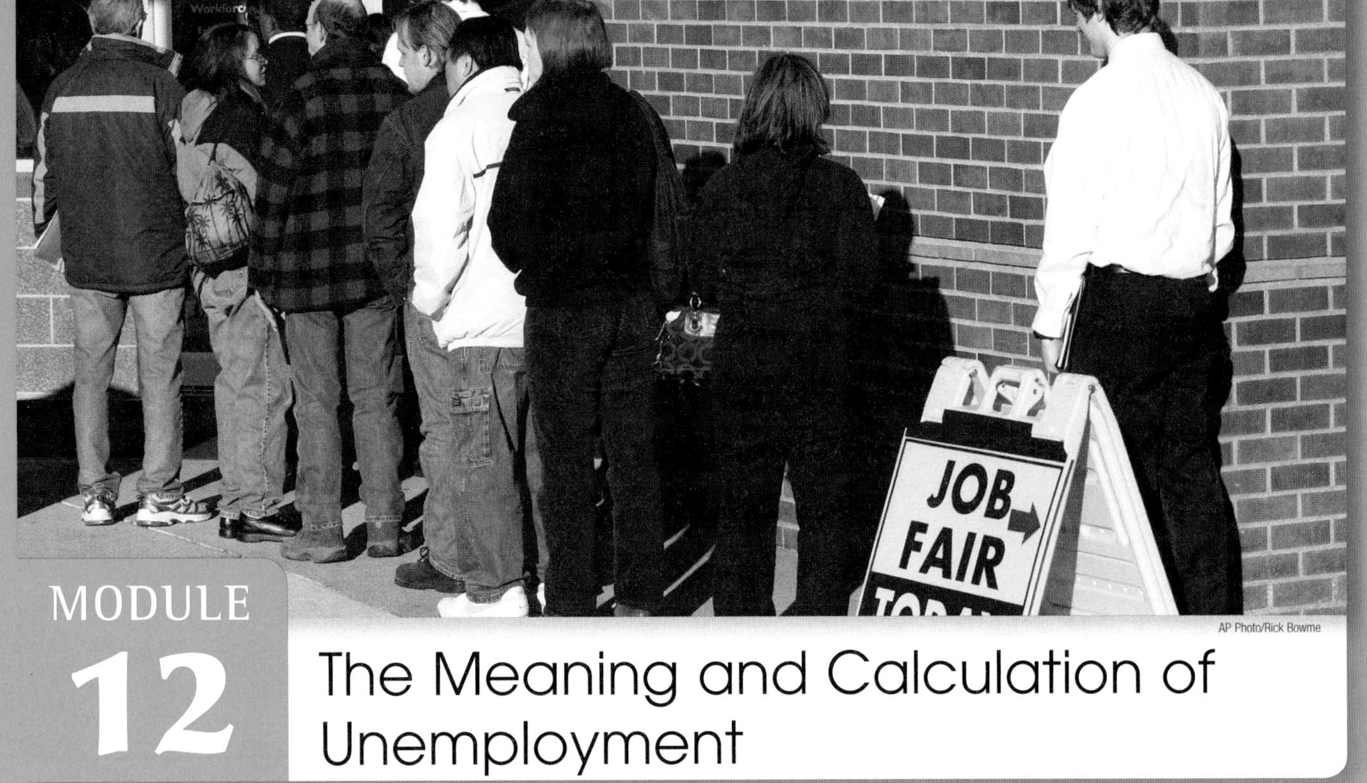

AP Photo/Rick Bowme

MODULE 12 The Meaning and Calculation of Unemployment

In this Module, you will learn to:

- Explain how unemployment is measured
- Calculate the unemployment rate
- Summarize the significance of the unemployment rate for the economy
- Explain the relationship between the unemployment rate and economic growth

The Unemployment Rate

The economy—and unemployment in particular—topped the list of issues important to voters in the 2012 presidential election. **Figure 12.1** on the next page shows the U.S. unemployment rate from 1948 to the early part of 2013. As you can see, the labor market hit a difficult patch starting in mid-2008, with the unemployment rate rising from 4.8% in February 2008 to 10.1% in October 2009. What did the rise in the unemployment rate mean, and why was it still a major concern for U.S. citizens in 2012 and beyond? To make sense of the attention paid to employment and unemployment, we need to understand how they are both defined and measured.

Defining and Measuring Unemployment

It's easy to define employment: you're **employed** if and only if you have a job.

Employed people are currently holding a job in the economy, either full time or part time.

Unemployment, however, is a more subtle concept. Just because a person isn't working doesn't mean that we consider that person *unemployed*. For example, in April 2014 there were 38 million retired workers in the United States receiving Social Security checks. Most of them were probably happy that they were no longer working, so we wouldn't consider someone who has settled into a comfortable, well-earned retirement to be unemployed. There were also 8 million disabled U.S. workers receiving benefits because they were unable to work. Again, although they weren't working, we wouldn't normally consider them to be unemployed.

The U.S. Census Bureau, the federal agency that collects data on unemployment, considers the unemployed to be those who are "jobless, looking for jobs, and available for work." Retired people don't count because they aren't looking for jobs; the disabled don't count because they aren't available for work. More specifically, an individual is

Figure 12.1 The U.S. Unemployment Rate, 1948-2013

The unemployment rate has fluctuated widely over time. It always rises during recessions, which are shown by the shaded bars. It usually, but not always, falls during periods of economic expansion.

Source: Bureau of Labor Statistics; National Bureau of Economic Research.

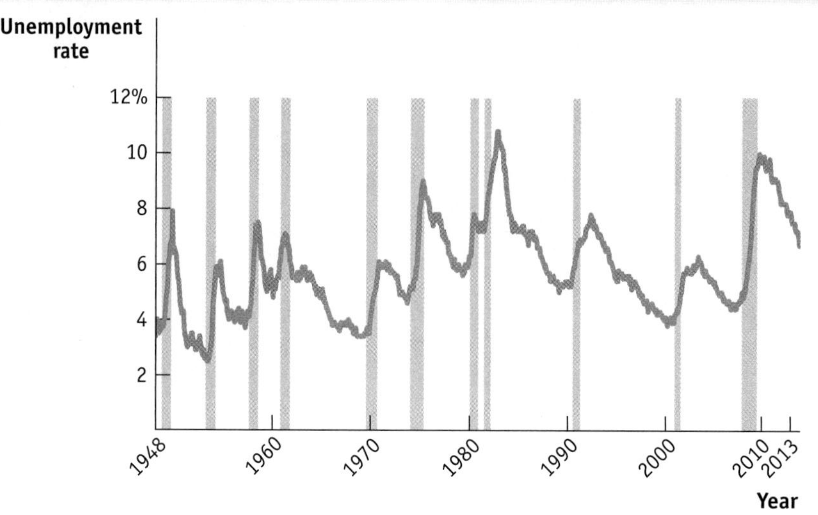

considered unemployed if he or she doesn't currently have a job and has been actively seeking a job during the past four weeks. So the **unemployed** are people who are actively looking for work but aren't currently employed.

A country's **labor force** is the sum of the employed and the unemployed—that is, the people who are currently working and the people who are currently looking for work. The **labor force participation rate**, defined as the share of the working-age population that is in the labor force, is calculated as follows:

AP® Exam Tip

A formula sheet is not provided during the AP® exam. You will need to remember these formulas to calculate the size of the labor force and the unemployment rate.

$$\textbf{(12-1)}\quad \text{Labor force participation rate} = \frac{\text{Labor force}}{\text{Population age 16 and older}} \times 100$$

The **unemployment rate**, defined as the percentage of the total number of people in the labor force who are unemployed, is calculated as follows:

$$\textbf{(12-2)}\quad \text{Unemployment rate} = \frac{\text{Number of unemployed workers}}{\text{Labor force}} \times 100$$

To estimate the numbers that go into calculating the unemployment rate, the U.S. Census Bureau carries out a monthly survey called the Current Population Survey, which involves interviewing a random sample of 60,000 American families. People are asked whether they are currently employed. If they are not employed, they are asked whether they have been looking for a job during the past four weeks. The results are then scaled up, using estimates of the total population, to estimate the total number of employed and unemployed Americans.

Unemployed people are actively looking for work but aren't currently employed.

The **labor force** is equal to the sum of the employed and the unemployed.

The **labor force participation rate** is the percentage of the population aged 16 or older that is in the labor force.

The **unemployment rate** is the percentage of the total number of people in the labor force who are unemployed.

The Significance of the Unemployment Rate

In general, the unemployment rate is a good indicator of how easy or difficult it is to find a job given the current state of the economy. When the unemployment rate is low, nearly everyone who wants a job can find one. In 2000, when the unemployment rate averaged 4%, jobs were so abundant that employers spoke of a "mirror test" for getting a job: if you were breathing (therefore, your breath would fog a mirror), you could find work. By contrast, in 2009, the unemployment rate in 17 states rose to over 10% (over 15% in Michigan), with many highly qualified workers having lost their jobs and having a hard time finding new ones. Although the unemployment rate is a good indicator of current labor market conditions, it is not a perfect measure.

How the Unemployment Rate Can Overstate the True Level of Unemployment If you are searching for work, it's normal to take at least a few weeks to find a suitable job. Yet a worker who is quite confident of finding a job, but has not yet accepted a position, is counted as unemployed. As a consequence, the unemployment rate never falls to zero, even in boom times when jobs are plentiful. Even in the buoyant labor market of 2000, when it was easy to find work, the unemployment rate was still 4%. Later, we'll discuss in greater depth the reasons that measured unemployment persists even when jobs are abundant.

How the Unemployment Rate Can Understate the True Level of Unemployment Frequently, some of the people who would like to work but aren't working still don't get counted as unemployed. In particular, an individual who has given up looking for a job for the time being because there are no jobs available isn't counted as unemployed because he or she has not been searching for a job during the previous four weeks. Individuals who want to work but aren't currently searching because they see little prospect of finding a job given the state of the job market are known as **discouraged workers**. Because it does not count discouraged workers, the measured unemployment rate may understate the percentage of people who want to work but are unable to find jobs.

Discouraged workers are nonworking people who are capable of working but have given up looking for a job due to the state of the job market.

Marginally attached workers would like to be employed and have looked for a job in the recent past but are not currently looking for work.

The **underemployed** are workers who would like to work more hours or who are overqualified for their jobs.

Discouraged workers are part of a larger group known as **marginally attached workers**. These are people who say they would like to have a job and have looked for work in the recent past but are not currently looking for work. The difference between discouraged workers and other marginally attached workers is that the other marginally attached workers ended their job search for a reason other than a belief that no job was available for them. For example, they may have gone back to school or become disabled. Marginally attached workers are also not included when calculating the unemployment rate.

Finally, another category of workers who are frustrated in their ability to find work but aren't counted as unemployed are the **underemployed**: workers who would like to work more hours or who are overqualified for their jobs. For example, some part-time workers would like to work full time, and some college graduates work as fast-food clerks. Again, they aren't counted in the unemployment rate.

The Bureau of Labor Statistics is the federal agency that calculates the official unemployment rate. It also calculates broader "measures of labor underutilization" that include the three categories of frustrated workers. **Figure 12.2** on the next page shows what happens to the measured unemployment rate once marginally attached workers (including discouraged workers) and the underemployed are counted. The broadest measure of unemployment and underemployment, known as *U6*, is the sum of these three measures plus the unemployed; it is substantially higher than the rate usually quoted by the news media. But U6 and the unemployment rate move very much in parallel, so changes in the unemployment rate remain a good guide to what's happening in the overall labor market.

Finally, it's important to realize that the unemployment rate varies greatly among demographic groups. Other things equal, jobs are generally easier to find for more experienced workers and for workers during their "prime" working years, from ages 25 to 54. For younger workers, as well as workers nearing retirement age, jobs are typically harder to find. **Figure 12.3** on the next page shows unemployment rates for different

Figure 12.2 Alternative Measures of Unemployment, 1994–2013

The unemployment number usually quoted in the news media counts someone as unemployed only if he or she has been looking for work during the past four weeks. Broader measures also count discouraged workers, other marginally attached workers, and the underemployed. These broader measures show a higher unemployment rate—but they move closely in parallel with the standard rate.

Source: Bureau of Labor Statistics.

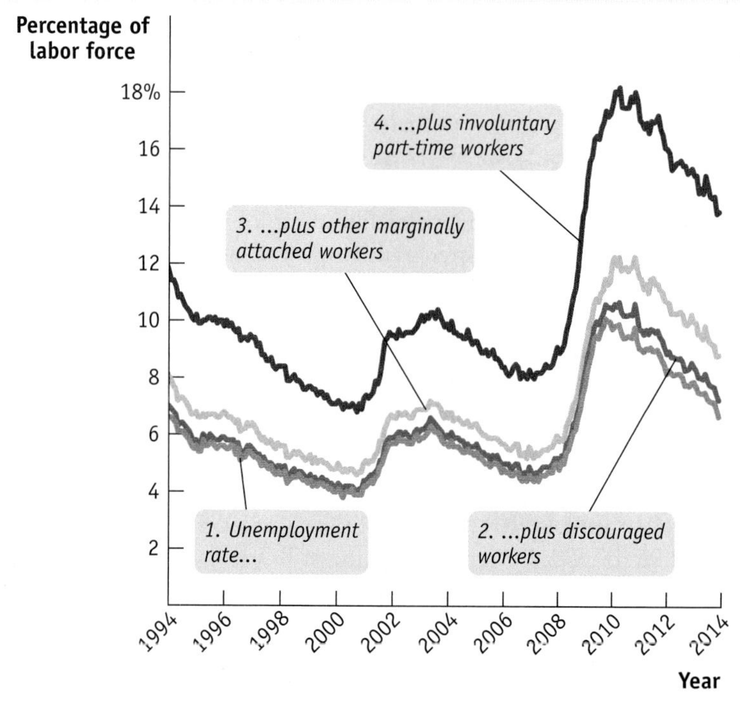

groups in December 2013, when the overall unemployment rate of 6.7% was low by historical standards. As you can see, in December 2013 the unemployment rate for African-American workers was much higher than the national average; the unemployment rate for White teenagers (ages 16–19) was almost three times the national average; and the unemployment rate for African-American teenagers, at more than 35%, was over five times the national average. (Bear in mind that a teenager isn't considered unemployed, even if he or she isn't working, unless that teenager is looking for work but can't find it.) So even at a time when the overall unemployment rate was relatively low, jobs were hard to find for some groups.

Figure 12.3 Unemployment Rates of Different Groups, 2013

Unemployment rates vary greatly among different demographic groups. For example, although the overall unemployment rate in December 2013 was 6.7%, the unemployment rate among African-American teenagers was 35.5%. As a result, even during periods of low overall unemployment, unemployment remains a serious problem for some groups.

Source: Bureau of Labor Statistics.

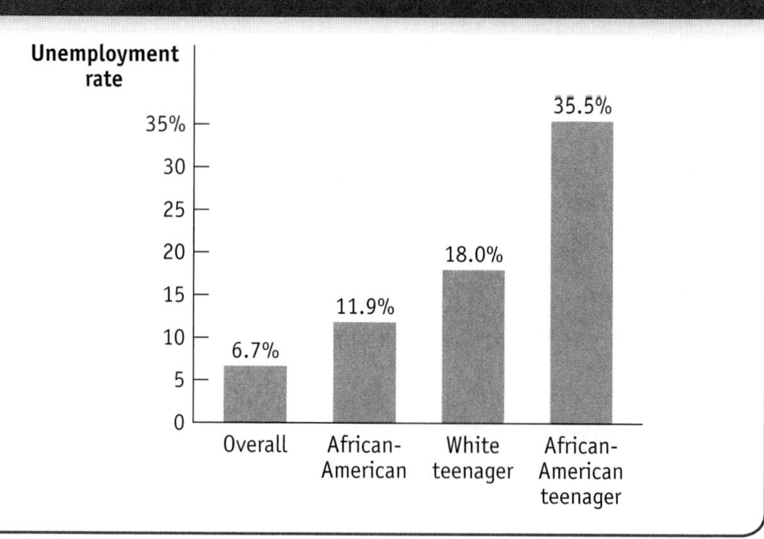

Although the unemployment rate is not an exact, literal measure of the percentage of people unable to find jobs, it is a good indicator of overall labor market conditions. The ups and downs of the unemployment rate closely reflect economic changes that have a significant impact on people's lives. Let's turn now to the causes of these fluctuations.

Growth and Unemployment

Compared to Figure 12.1, **Figure 12.4** shows the U.S. unemployment rate over a somewhat shorter period, the 33 years from 1980 to 2013. The shaded bars represent periods of recession. As you can see, during every recession, without exception, the unemployment rate rose. The recession of 1981–1982, the most severe one shown, pushed the unemployment rate into double digits: unemployment peaked in November 1982 at 10.8%. And during the most recent recession shown, in late 2009 the unemployment rate rose to above 10%.

Correspondingly, during periods of economic expansion the unemployment rate usually falls. The long economic expansion of the 1990s eventually brought the unemployment rate below 4%. However, it's important to recognize that *economic expansions aren't always periods of falling unemployment.* Look at the periods immediately following two recent recessions, those of 1990–1991 and 2001. In each case the unemployment rate continued to rise for more than a year after the recession was officially over. The explanation in both cases is that, although the economy was growing, it was not growing fast enough to reduce the unemployment rate.

Figure 12.5 on the next page is a scatter diagram showing U.S. data for the period from 1949 to 2013.The horizontal axis measures the annual rate of growth in real GDP—the percent by which each year's real GDP changed compared to the previous year's real GDP. (Notice that there were nine years in which growth was negative—that is, real GDP shrank.) The vertical axis measures the *change* in the unemployment rate over the previous year in percentage points. Each dot represents the observed growth rate of real GDP and change in the unemployment rate for a given year. For example, in 2000 the average unemployment rate fell to 4.0% from 4.2% in 1999; this is shown as a value of –0.2 along the vertical axis for the year 2000. Over the same period, real GDP grew by 4.1%; this is the value shown along the horizontal axis for the year 2000.

AP® Exam Tip

Unemployment always rises during recessions and usually falls during expansions. If a question indicates that real GDP is falling and asks about the effect on unemployment, you can conclude that it is rising.

Figure 12.4 Unemployment and Recessions, 1980–2013

This figure shows a close-up of the unemployment rate since the 1980s, with the shaded bars indicating recessions. It's clear that unemployment always rises during recessions and *usually* falls during expansions. But in both the early 1990s and the early 2000s, unemployment continued to rise for some time after the recession was officially declared over.
Source: Bureau of Labor Statistics; National Bureau of Economic Research.

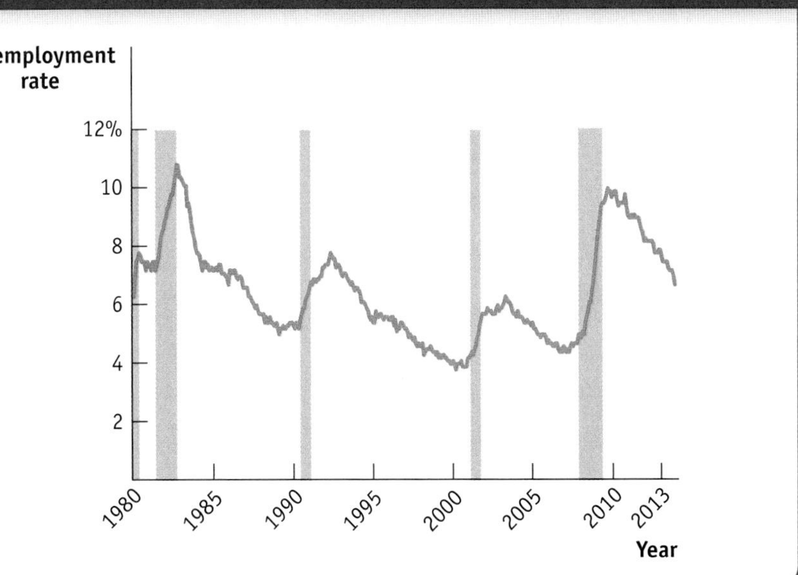

Figure 12.5 Growth and Changes in Unemployment, 1949-2013

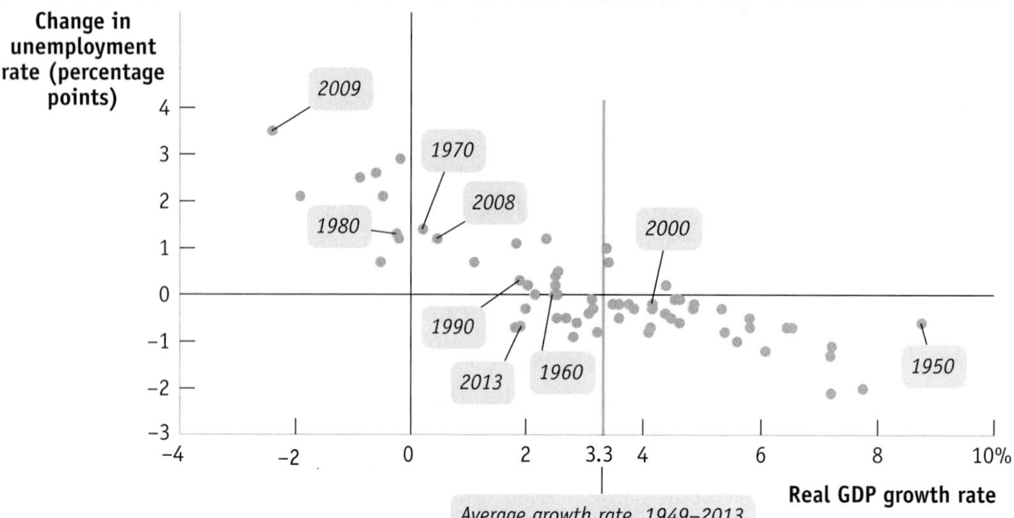

Each dot shows the growth rate of the economy and the change in the unemployment rate for a specific year between 1949 and 2013. For example, in 2000 the economy grew 4.1% and the unemployment rate fell 0.2 percentage points, from 4.2% to 4.0%. In general, the unemployment rate fell when growth was above its average rate of 3.3% a year and rose when growth was below average. Unemployment always rose when real GDP fell.

Source: Bureau of Labor Statistics; Bureau of Economic Analysis.

The downward trend of the scatter points in Figure 12.5 shows that there is a generally strong negative relationship between growth in the economy and the rate of unemployment. Years of high growth in real GDP were also years in which the unemployment rate fell, and years of low or negative growth in real GDP were years in which the unemployment rate rose. The green vertical line in Figure 12.5 at the value of 3.3% indicates the average growth rate of real GDP over the period from 1949 to 2013. Points lying to the right of the vertical line are years of above-average growth. In these years, the value on the vertical axis is usually negative, meaning that the unemployment rate fell. That is, years of above-average growth were usually years in which the unemployment rate was falling. Conversely, points lying to the left of the vertical line were years of below-average growth. In these years, the value on the vertical axis is usually positive, meaning that the unemployment rate rose. That is, years of below-average growth were usually years in which the unemployment rate was rising. There are periods in which GDP is growing, but at a below-average rate; these are periods in which the economy isn't in a recession but unemployment is still rising—sometimes called a "growth recession." But true recessions, periods when real GDP falls, are especially painful for workers. As illustrated by the points to the left of the vertical axis in Figure 12.5, falling real GDP is always associated with a rising rate of unemployment, causing a great deal of hardship to families.

Failure to Launch

In March 2010, when the U.S. job situation was near its worst, the *Harvard Law Record* published a brief note titled "Unemployed law student will work for $160K plus benefits." In a self-mocking tone, the author admitted to having graduated from Harvard Law School the previous year but not landing a job offer. "What mark on our résumé is so bad that it outweighs the crimson H?" the note asked.

The answer, of course, is that it wasn't about the résumé—it was about the economy. Times of high unemployment are especially hard on new graduates, who often find it hard to get any kind of full-time job. How bad was it in March 2010, around the time that note was written? Researchers at the San Francisco Fed analyzed the employment experience of college graduates, ages 21–23, and their findings are in the figure to the right.

Although the overall unemployment rate for college graduates 25 and older, even at its peak, was only about 5%, unemployment among recent graduates aged 21–23 peaked in 2010 at 10.7%. And many of those who *were* employed had been able to get only part-time jobs. In December 2007, at the beginning of the 2007–2009 recession, 83% of college graduates under the age of 24 who weren't still in school were employed full time. By December 2009, that number was down to just 72%. Quite simply, many college graduates were having a hard time getting their working lives started.

A year later, the situation was starting to improve, but slowly: in December 2010, 74% of recent graduates had full-time jobs. The U.S. labor market had a long way to go before being able to offer college graduates—and young people in general—the kinds of opportunities they deserved.

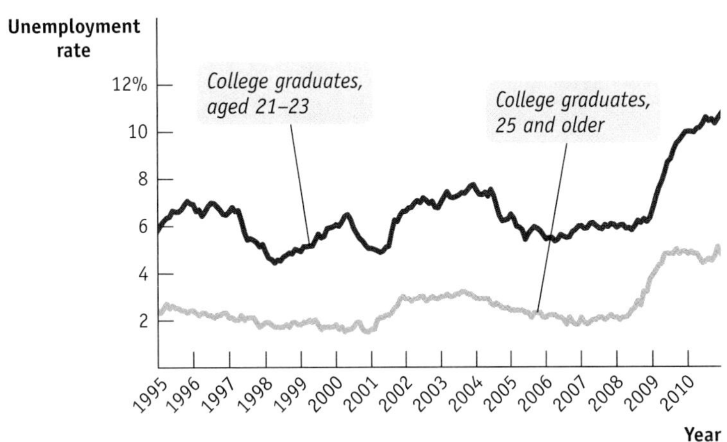

Source: Federal Reserve Bank of San Francisco, 2010; Bureau of Labor Statistics.

MODULE 12 Review

Check Your Understanding

1. Suppose that employment websites enable job-seekers to find suitable jobs more quickly. What effect will this have on the unemployment rate over time? Also suppose that these websites encourage job-seekers who had given up their searches to begin looking again. What effect will this have on the unemployment rate?

2. In which of the following cases would the worker be counted as unemployed? Explain.
   - **a.** Rosa, an older worker, has been laid off and gave up looking for work months ago.
   - **b.** Anthony, a schoolteacher, has chosen not to work during his three-month summer break.
   - **c.** Grace, an investment banker, has been laid off and is currently searching for another position.
   - **d.** Sergio, a classically trained musician, can only find work playing for local parties.
   - **e.** Natasha, a graduate student, went back to school because jobs were scarce.

3. Which of the following are consistent with the observed relationship between growth in real GDP and changes in the unemployment rate? Which are not?
   - **a.** A rise in the unemployment rate accompanies a fall in real GDP.
   - **b.** An exceptionally strong business recovery is associated with a greater percentage of the labor force being employed.
   - **c.** Negative real GDP growth is associated with a fall in the unemployment rate.

Tackle the Test: Multiple-Choice Questions

1. To be considered unemployed, a person must
   - **I.** not be working.
   - **II.** be actively seeking a job.
   - **III.** be available for work.

   a. I only
   b. II only
   c. III only
   d. II and III
   e. I, II, and III

Use the information for a hypothetical economy presented in the following table to answer questions 2, 3, and 4.

Population age 16 and older = 200,000
Labor force = 100,000
Number of people working part time = 20,000
Number of people working full time = 70,000

2. What is the labor force participation rate?
   a. 70%
   b. 50%
   c. 20%
   d. 10%
   e. 5%

3. How many people are unemployed?
   a. 10,000
   b. 20,000
   c. 30,000
   d. 100,000
   e. 110,000

4. What is the unemployment rate?
   a. 70%
   b. 50%
   c. 20%
   d. 10%
   e. 5%

5. The unemployment problem in an economy may be understated by the unemployment rate due to
   a. people lying about seeking a job.
   b. discouraged workers.
   c. job candidates with one offer but waiting for more.
   d. overemployed workers.
   e. none of the above.

Tackle the Test: Free-Response Questions

1. Use the data provided below to calculate each of the following. Show how you calculate each.
   a. the size of the labor force
   b. the labor force participation rate
   c. the unemployment rate

   Population age 16 and older = 12 million
   Employment = 5 million
   Unemployment = 1 million

Rubric for FRQ 1 (6 points)

1 point: 6 million

1 point: employment + unemployment = 5 million + 1 million = 6 million

1 point: 50%

1 point: (labor force/population) × 100 = ((5 million + 1 million)/12 million) × 100 = (6 million/12 million) × 100 = 50%

1 point: 17%

1 point: (unemployment/labor force) × 100 = (1 million/(5 million + 1 million)) × 100 = (1 million/6 million) × 100 = 17%

2. What is the labor market classification of each of the following individuals? Be as specific as possible, and explain your answer.
   a. Julie has a graduate degree in mechanical engineering. She works full-time mowing lawns.
   b. Jeff was laid off from his previous job. He would very much like to work at any job, but, after looking for work for a year, he has stopped looking for work.
   c. Ian is working 25 hours per week at a bookstore and has no desire to work full time.
   d. Raj has decided to take a year off from work to stay home with his daughter.
   (4 points)

Adam Gault.Photodisc/Getty Images

MODULE 13 The Causes and Categories of Unemployment

In this Module, you will learn to:

- Explain the three different types of unemployment and their causes
- Identify the factors that determine the natural rate of unemployment

The Natural Rate of Unemployment

Fast economic growth tends to reduce the unemployment rate. So how low can the unemployment rate go? You might be tempted to say zero, but that isn't feasible. Over the past half century, the national unemployment rate has never dropped below 2.9%.

Can there be unemployment even when many businesses are having a hard time finding workers? To answer this question, we need to examine the nature of labor markets and why they normally lead to substantial measured unemployment even when jobs are plentiful. Our starting point is the observation that, even in the best of times, jobs are constantly being created and destroyed.

Job Creation and Job Destruction

In early 2010 the unemployment rate hovered close to 10%. Even during good times, most Americans know someone who has lost his or her job. The U.S. unemployment rate in July 2007 was only 4.7%, relatively low by historical standards, yet in that month there were 4.5 million "job separations"—terminations of employment that occurred because a worker was either fired or quit voluntarily.

There are many reasons for such job loss. One is structural change in the economy: industries rise and fall as new technologies emerge and consumers' tastes change. For example, employment in high-tech industries such as telecommunications surged in the late 1990s but slumped severely after 2000. However, structural change also brings the creation of new jobs: since 2000, the number of jobs in the American health care sector has surged as new medical technologies have emerged and the aging of the population has increased the demand for medical care. Poor management performance or bad luck at individual companies also leads to job loss for their employees. For example, in 2013, smartphone maker BlackBerry announced plans to eliminate about 4,500 jobs after years of lagging sales, even as companies such as Apple and Samsung faced growing demand for their phones.

AP® Exam Tip

Be prepared to identify the type of unemployment given a specific scenario in both the multiple-choice and free-response questions on the AP® exam.

istockphoto

During the housing slump of 2009 when unemployment was running very high, many construction workers resorted to more traditional methods of finding work.

This constant churning of the workforce is an inevitable feature of the modern economy. And this churning, in turn, is one source of *frictional unemployment*—one main reason that there is a considerable amount of unemployment even when jobs are abundant.

Frictional Unemployment

Workers who lose a job involuntarily due to job destruction often choose not to take the first new job offered. For example, suppose a skilled programmer, laid off because her software company's product line was unsuccessful, sees a help-wanted ad for clerical work in the local newspaper. She might respond to the ad and get the job—but that would be foolish. Instead, she should take the time to look for a job that takes advantage of her skills and pays accordingly. In addition, individual workers are constantly leaving jobs voluntarily, typically for personal reasons—family moves, dissatisfaction, and better job prospects elsewhere.

Economists say that workers who spend time looking for employment are engaged in **job search**. If all workers and all jobs were alike, job search wouldn't be necessary; if information about jobs and workers were perfect, job search would be very quick. In practice, however, it's normal for a worker who loses a job, or a young worker seeking a first job, to spend at least a few weeks searching.

Frictional unemployment is unemployment due to the time workers spend in job search. A certain amount of frictional unemployment is inevitable, for two reasons. One is the constant process of job creation and job destruction. The other is the fact that new workers are always entering the labor market. For example, in January 2014, out of 10.2 million workers counted as unemployed, 1.2 million were new entrants to the workforce and another 2.9 million were "re-entrants"—people who had come back after being out of the workforce for a time.

A limited amount of frictional unemployment is relatively harmless and may even be a good thing. The economy is more productive if workers take the time to find jobs that are well matched to their skills, and workers who are unemployed for a brief period while searching for the right job don't experience great hardship. In fact, when there is a low unemployment rate, periods of unemployment tend to be quite short, suggesting that much of the unemployment is frictional. **Figure 13.1** shows the composition of unemployment in 2000, when the unemployment rate was only 4%. Forty-five percent of the unemployed had been unemployed for less than 5 weeks and only 23% had been unemployed for 15 or more weeks. Just 11% were considered to be "long-term unemployed"—unemployed for 27 or more weeks. The picture looked very different in January 2010, after unemployment had been high for an extended period of time.

Workers who spend time looking for employment are engaged in **job search**.

Frictional unemployment is unemployment due to the time workers spend in job search.

AP® Exam Tip

Frictional unemployment always exists in an economy. There are always people looking for better jobs or even their first job.

Figure 13.1 Distribution of the Unemployed by Duration of Unemployment, 2000 and 2010

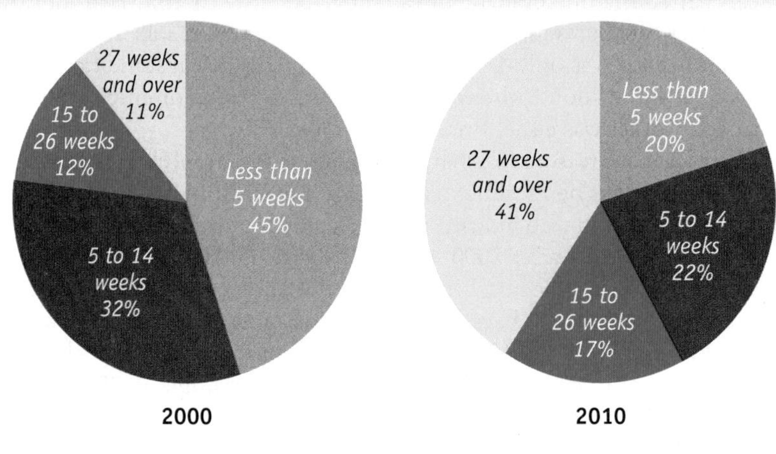

In years when the unemployment rate is low, most unemployed workers are unemployed for only a short period. In 2000, a year of low unemployment, 45% of the unemployed had been unemployed for less than 5 weeks and 77% for less than 15 weeks. The short duration of unemployment for most workers suggests that most unemployment in 2000 was frictional. In early 2010, by contrast, only 20% of the unemployed had been unemployed for less than 5 weeks, but 41% had been unemployed for 27 or more weeks, indicating that during periods of high unemployment, a smaller share of unemployment is frictional.
Source: Bureau of Labor Statistics.

In periods of higher unemployment, workers tend to be jobless for longer periods of time, suggesting that a smaller share of unemployment is frictional. By early 2010, when unemployment had been high for several months, for instance, the fraction of unemployed workers considered "long-term unemployed" had jumped to 41%.

Public policy designed to help workers who lose their jobs can lead to frictional unemployment as an unintended side effect. Most economically advanced countries provide benefits to laid-off workers as a way to tide them over until they find a new job. In the United States, these benefits typically replace only a small fraction of a worker's income and expire after 26 weeks. In other countries, particularly in Europe, benefits are more generous and last longer. The drawback to this generosity is that it reduces the incentive to quickly find a new job. By keeping more people searching for longer, the benefits increase frictional unemployment. Generous unemployment benefits in some European countries are widely believed to be one of the main causes of "Eurosclerosis," the persistent high unemployment that afflicts a number of European economies.

Structural Unemployment

Frictional unemployment exists even when the number of people seeking jobs is equal to the number of jobs being offered—that is, the existence of frictional unemployment doesn't mean that there is a surplus of labor. Sometimes, however, there is a *persistent surplus* of job-seekers in a particular labor market. For example, there may be more workers with a particular skill than there are jobs available using that skill, or there may be more workers in a particular geographic region than there are jobs available in that region. **Structural unemployment** is unemployment that results when workers lack the skills required for the available jobs, or there are more people seeking jobs in a labor market than there are jobs available at the current wage rate.

The supply and demand model tells us that the price of a good, service, or factor of production tends to move toward an equilibrium level that matches the quantity supplied with the quantity demanded. This is equally true, in general, of labor markets. **Figure 13.2** shows a typical market for labor. The labor demand curve indicates that when the price of labor—the wage rate—increases, employers demand less labor. The labor supply curve indicates that when the price of labor increases, more workers are willing to supply labor at the prevailing wage rate. These two forces coincide to lead to

Structural unemployment is unemployment that results when workers lack the skills required for the available jobs, or there are more people seeking jobs in a labor market than there are jobs available at the current wage rate.

AP® Exam Tip

Structural unemployment is common in an economy. Its causes include lack of skills, automation, geographic migration, minimum wages, and insufficient product demand.

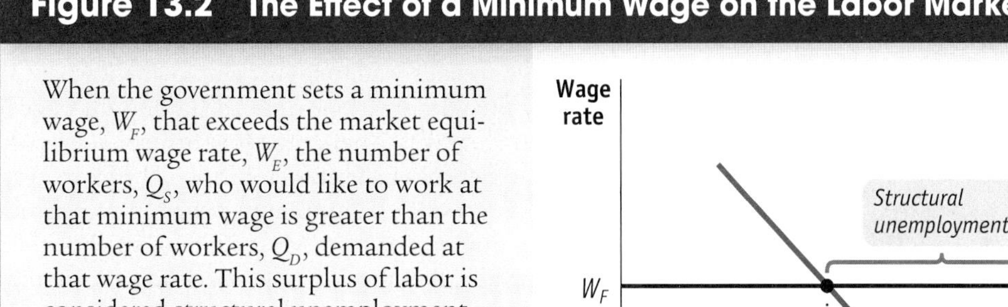

Figure 13.2 The Effect of a Minimum Wage on the Labor Market

When the government sets a minimum wage, W_F, that exceeds the market equilibrium wage rate, W_E, the number of workers, Q_S, who would like to work at that minimum wage is greater than the number of workers, Q_D, demanded at that wage rate. This surplus of labor is considered structural unemployment.

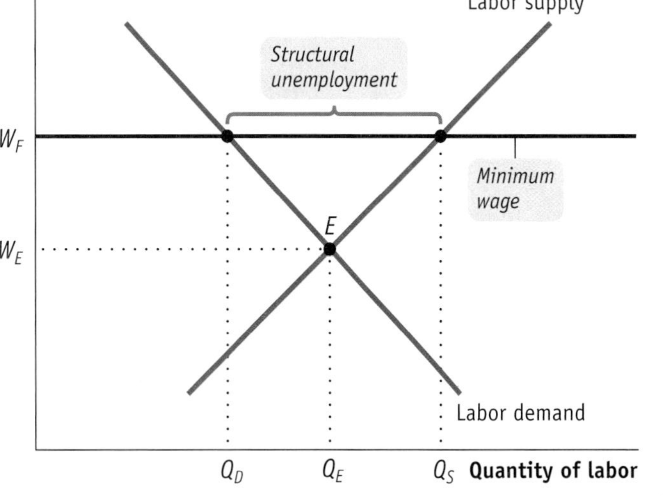

an equilibrium wage rate for any given type of labor in a particular location. That equilibrium wage rate is shown as W_E.

Even at the equilibrium wage rate, W_E, there will still be some frictional unemployment. That's because there will always be some workers engaged in job search even when the number of jobs available is equal to the number of workers seeking jobs. But there wouldn't be any structural unemployment caused by a surplus of labor, as there is when the wage rate, for some reason, is persistently above W_E. Several factors can lead to a wage rate in excess of W_E, the most important being minimum wages, labor unions, *efficiency wages,* and the side effects of government policies.

Minimum Wages As explained in Module 8, a minimum wage is a government-mandated floor on the price of labor. In the United States, the national minimum wage in mid-2014 was $7.25 an hour. For many American workers, the minimum wage is irrelevant; the market equilibrium wage for these workers is well above this price floor. But for less skilled workers, the minimum wage may be binding—it affects the wages that people are actually paid and can lead to structural unemployment. In countries that have higher minimum wages, the range of workers for whom the minimum wage is binding is larger.

Figure 13.2 shows the effect of a binding minimum wage. In this market, there is a legal floor on wages, W_F, which is above the equilibrium wage rate, W_E. This leads to a persistent surplus in the labor market: the quantity of labor supplied, Q_S, is larger than the quantity demanded, Q_D. In other words, more people want to work than can find jobs at the minimum wage, leading to structural unemployment.

Given that minimum wages—that is, binding minimum wages—generally lead to structural unemployment, you might wonder why governments impose them. The rationale is to help ensure that people who work can earn enough income to afford at least a minimally comfortable lifestyle. However, this may come at a cost, because it may eliminate employment opportunities for some workers who would have willingly worked for lower wages. As illustrated in Figure 13.2, not only are there more sellers of labor than there are buyers, but there are also fewer people working at a minimum wage (Q_D) than there would have been with no minimum wage at all (Q_E).

Although economists broadly agree that a high minimum wage has the employment-reducing effects shown in Figure 13.2, there is some question about whether this is a good description of how the minimum wage actually works in the United States. The minimum wage in the United States is quite low compared with that in other wealthy countries. For three decades, from the 1970s to the mid-2000s, the U.S. minimum wage was so low that it was not binding for the vast majority of workers—employers paid most workers more than the minimum wage. In addition, some researchers have produced evidence that increases in the minimum wage actually lead to higher employment when, as was the case in the United States at one time, the minimum wage is low compared to average wages. They argue that firms that employ low-skilled workers sometimes restrict their hiring in order to keep wages low and that, as a result, the minimum wage can sometimes be increased without any loss of jobs. Most economists, however, agree that a sufficiently high minimum wage *does* lead to structural unemployment.

Bill Pugliano/Stringer/Getty Images

Members of the United Auto Workers (UAW) union march on a picket line during a strike to protest unfair labor practices.

Labor Unions The actions of *labor unions* can have effects similar to those of minimum wages, leading to structural unemployment. By bargaining collectively for all of a firm's workers, unions can often win higher wages from employers than workers would have obtained by bargaining individually. This process, known as *collective bargaining,* is intended to tip the scales of bargaining power more toward workers and away from employers. Labor unions exercise bargaining power by threatening firms with a *labor strike,* a collective refusal to work. The threat of a strike can have very serious consequences for firms that have difficulty replacing striking workers.

In such cases, workers acting collectively can exercise more power than they could if they acted individually.

When workers have greater bargaining power, they tend to demand and receive higher wages. Unions also bargain over benefits, such as health care and pensions, which we can think of as additional wages. Indeed, economists who study the effects of unions on wages find that unionized workers earn higher wages and more generous benefits than non-union workers with similar skills. The result of these increased wages can be the same as the result of a minimum wage: labor unions push the wage that workers receive above the equilibrium wage. Consequently, there are more people willing to work at the wage being paid than there are jobs available. Like a binding minimum wage, this leads to structural unemployment.

Efficiency Wages Actions by firms may also contribute to structural unemployment. Firms may choose to pay **efficiency wages**—wages that employers set above the equilibrium wage rate as an incentive for their workers to deliver better performance.

Employers may feel the need for such incentives for several reasons. For example, employers often have difficulty directly observing how hard an employee works. They can, however, elicit more work effort by paying above-market wages: employees receiving these higher wages are more likely to work harder to ensure that they aren't fired, which would cause them to lose their higher wages.

When many firms pay efficiency wages, the result is a pool of workers who want jobs but can't find them. So the use of efficiency wages by firms leads to structural unemployment.

Efficiency wages are wages that employers set above the equilibrium wage rate as an incentive for better employee performance.

The **natural rate of unemployment** is the unemployment rate that arises from the effects of frictional plus structural unemployment.

Cyclical unemployment is the deviation of the actual rate of unemployment from the natural rate.

The Natural Rate of Unemployment

Because some frictional unemployment is inevitable and because many economies also suffer from structural unemployment, a certain amount of unemployment is normal, or "natural." Actual unemployment fluctuates around this normal level. The **natural rate of unemployment** is the rate of unemployment that arises from the effects of frictional plus structural unemployment. It is the normal unemployment rate around which the actual unemployment rate fluctuates. **Figure 13.3** on the next page provides estimates of the natural rates of unemployment in the 34 relatively wealthy countries that belong to the Organization for Economic Cooperation and Development (OECD). **Cyclical unemployment** is the deviation of the actual rate of unemployment from the natural rate; that is, it is the difference between the actual and natural rates of unemployment. As the name suggests, cyclical unemployment is the share of unemployment that arises from the business cycle. We'll see later that public policy cannot keep the unemployment rate persistently below the natural rate without leading to accelerating inflation.

We can summarize the relationships between the various types of unemployment as follows:

(13-1) Natural unemployment =
Frictional unemployment + Structural unemployment

(13-2) Actual unemployment =
Natural unemployment + Cyclical unemployment

AP® Exam Tip

The natural rate of unemployment is never zero because frictional employment always exists in an economy.

Perhaps because of its name, people often imagine that the natural rate of unemployment is a constant that doesn't change over time and can't be affected by policy. Neither proposition is true. Let's take a moment to stress two facts: the natural rate of unemployment changes over time, and it can be affected by economic policies.

Changes in the Natural Rate of Unemployment

Private-sector economists and government agencies need estimates of the natural rate of unemployment both to make forecasts and to conduct policy analyses. Almost all these estimates show that the U.S. natural rate rises and falls over time. For example,

Figure 13.3 Natural Unemployment in OECD Countries

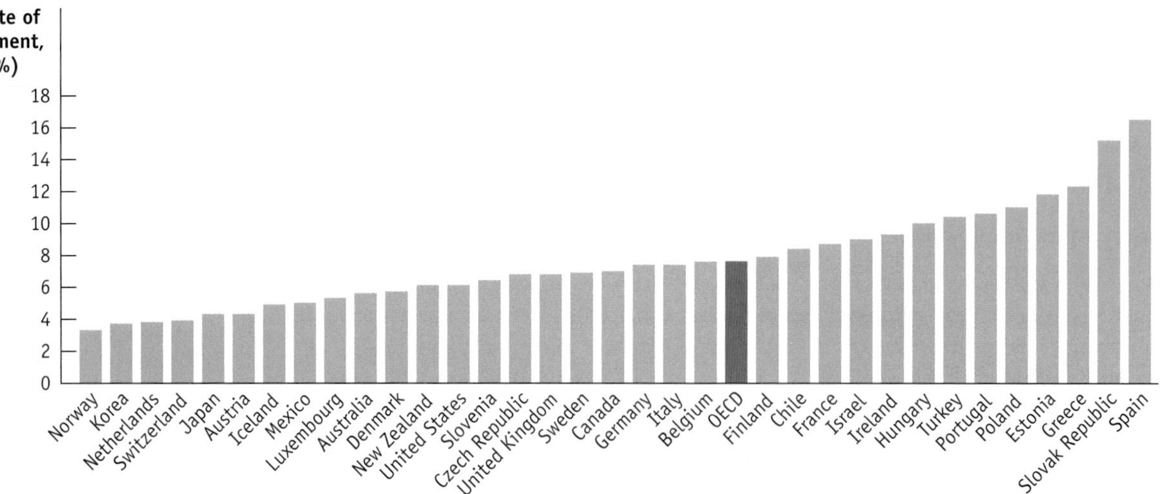

Among members of the OECD, estimates of the natural rates of unemployment in 2013 ranged from 3.3% in Norway to 16.5% in Spain. The blue bar shows the average across all the OECD countries, 7.6%. The U.S. natural rate of unemployment, 6.1%, is low relative to both the average rate and the rates in the major European economies of the United Kingdom, Germany, Italy, France, and Spain. As mentioned earlier, the rates in Europe may be elevated by frictional unemployment caused by generous unemployment benefits. In addition, high minimum wages in Europe can discourage employers from offering jobs and lead to higher rates of structural unemployment.

Source: OECD.

the Congressional Budget Office, the independent agency that conducts budget and economic analyses for Congress, believes that the U.S. natural rate of unemployment was 5.3% in 1950, rose to 6.3% by the end of the 1970s, and fell back to 5.0% from late 1999 until early 2008. In 2013, the estimated rate was back up to 6%. European countries have experienced even larger swings in their natural rates of unemployment.

What causes the natural rate of unemployment to change? The most important factors are changes in the characteristics of the labor force, changes in labor market institutions, and changes in government policies. Let's look briefly at each factor.

Changes in Labor Force Characteristics In January 2014 the overall rate of unemployment in the United States was 6.6%. Young workers, however, had much higher unemployment rates: 20.7% for teenagers and 12.9% for workers aged 20 to 24. Workers aged 25 to 54 had an unemployment rate of only 6.1%.

In general, unemployment rates tend to be lower for experienced than for inexperienced workers. Because experienced workers tend to stay in a given job longer than do inexperienced ones, they have lower frictional unemployment. Also, because older workers are more likely than young workers to be family breadwinners, they have a stronger incentive to find and keep jobs.

One reason the natural rate of unemployment rose during the 1970s was a large rise in the number of new workers—children of the post–World War II baby boom entered the labor force, as did a rising percentage of married women. As **Figure 13.4** shows, both the percentage of the labor force less than 25 years old and the percentage of women in the labor force surged in the 1970s. By the end of the 1990s, however, the share of women in the labor force had leveled off and the percentage of workers under 25 had fallen sharply. As a result, the labor force as a whole is more experienced today than it was in the 1970s, one likely reason that the natural rate of unemployment is lower today than in the 1970s.

Figure 13.4 The Changing Makeup of the U.S. Labor Force, 1948-2013

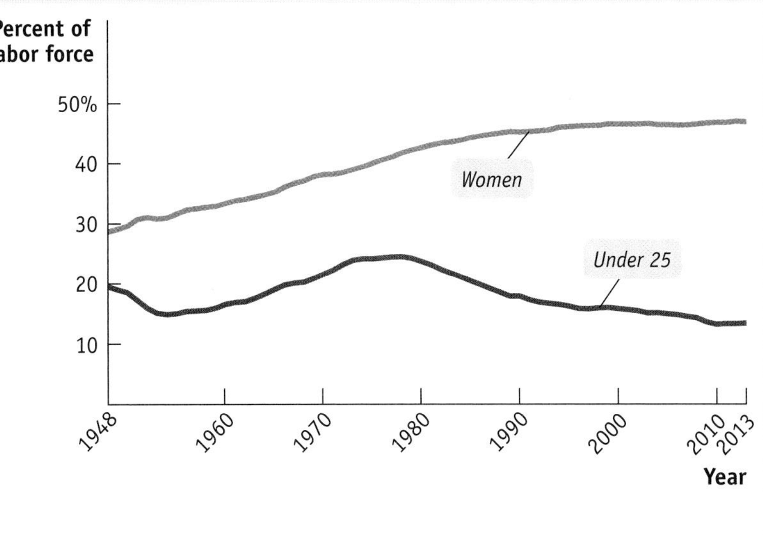

In the 1970s the percentage of the labor force consisting of women rose rapidly, as did the percentage under age 25. These changes reflected the entry of large numbers of women into the paid labor force for the first time and the fact that baby boomers were reaching working age. The natural rate of unemployment may have risen because many of these workers were relatively inexperienced. Today, the labor force is much more experienced, which is one possible reason the natural rate has fallen since the 1970s.
Source: Bureau of Labor Statistics.

Changes in Labor Market Institutions As we pointed out earlier, unions that negotiate wages above the equilibrium level can be a source of structural unemployment. Some economists believe that strong labor unions are one of the reasons for the high natural rate of unemployment in Europe. In the United States, a sharp fall in union membership after 1980 may have been one reason the natural rate of unemployment fell between the 1970s and the 1990s.

Other institutional changes may also have been at work. For example, some labor economists believe that temporary employment agencies, which have proliferated in recent years, have reduced frictional unemployment by matching workers to jobs. Furthermore, Internet websites such as monster.com may have reduced frictional unemployment by making information about job openings and job-seekers more widely available, thereby helping workers avoid a prolonged job search.

Technological change, coupled with labor market institutions, can also affect the natural rate of unemployment. Technological change probably leads to an increase in the demand for skilled workers who are familiar with the relevant technology and a reduction in the demand for unskilled workers. Economic theory predicts that wages should increase for skilled workers and decrease for unskilled workers. But if wages for unskilled workers cannot go down—say, due to a binding minimum wage—increased structural unemployment, and therefore a higher natural rate of unemployment, will result.

© NetPhotos/Alamy

Websites such as monster.com may have reduced frictional unemployment by helping to match employers with job-seekers.

Changes in Government Policies A high minimum wage can cause structural unemployment. Generous unemployment benefits can increase frictional unemployment. So government policies intended to help workers can have the undesirable side effect of raising the natural rate of unemployment.

Some government policies, however, may reduce the natural rate. Two examples are job training and employment subsidies. Job -training programs are supposed to provide unemployed workers with skills that widen the range of jobs they can perform. Employment subsidies are payments either to workers or to employers that provide a financial incentive to accept or offer jobs.

FYI Structural Unemployment in Eastern Germany

In one of the most dramatic events in world history, a spontaneous popular uprising in 1989 overthrew the communist dictatorship in East Germany. Citizens quickly tore down the wall that had divided Berlin, and in short order East and West Germany became a united, democratic nation.

Then the trouble started.

After reunification, employment in East Germany plunged and the unemployment rate soared. This high unemployment rate has persisted: despite receiving massive aid from the federal German government, the economy of the former East Germany has remained persistently depressed, with an unemployment rate of 10.1% in December 2013, compared to West Germany's unemployment rate of 6%. Other parts of formerly communist Eastern Europe have done much better. For example, the Czech Republic, which was often cited along with East Germany as a relatively successful communist economy, had a comparatively lower unemployment rate of only 7.7% in December 2013. What went wrong in East Germany?

The answer is that, through nobody's fault, East Germany found itself suffering from severe structural unemployment. When Germany was reunified, it became clear that workers in East Germany were much less productive than their cousins in the west. Yet unions initially demanded wage rates equal to those in West Germany, and these wage rates have been slow to come down because East German workers don't want to be treated as inferior to their West German counterparts. Meanwhile, productivity in the former East Germany has remained well below West German levels, in part because of decades of misguided investment. The result has been a persistently large mismatch between the number of workers demanded and the number of those seeking jobs.

Robert Wallis/Corbis

After reunification in 1989, East Germany found itself suffering from severe structural unemployment that continues to this day.

MODULE 13 Review

Check Your Understanding

1. Explain the following.
   a. Frictional unemployment always exists.
   b. Frictional unemployment accounts for a larger share of total unemployment when the unemployment rate is low.
2. Why does collective bargaining have the same general effect on unemployment as a minimum wage? Illustrate your answer with a diagram.
3. Suppose the United States dramatically increases benefits for unemployed workers. Explain what will happen to the natural rate of unemployment.

Tackle the Test: Multiple-Choice Questions

1. A person who moved to a new state and took two months to find a new job experienced which type of unemployment?
a. frictional
b. structural
c. cyclical
d. natural
e. none of the above

2. What type of unemployment is created by a recession?
a. frictional
b. structural
c. cyclical
d. natural
e. none of the above

3. A person who is unemployed because of a mismatch between the quantity of labor supplied and the quantity of labor demanded is experiencing what type of unemployment?
a. frictional
b. structural
c. cyclical
d. natural
e. none of the above

4. Which of the following is true of the natural rate of unemployment?
I. It includes frictional unemployment.
II. It includes structural unemployment.
III. It is equal to 0%.
a. I only
b. II only
c. III only
d. I and II
e. I, II, and III

5. Which of the following can affect the natural rate of unemployment in an economy over time?
a. labor force characteristics such as age and work experience
b. the existence of labor unions
c. advances in technologies that help workers find jobs
d. government job-training programs
e. all of the above

Tackle the Test: Free-Response Questions

1. a. The natural rate of unemployment is made up of which of the types of unemployment?
b. Explain how cyclical unemployment relates to the natural rate of unemployment.
c. List three factors that can lead to a change in the natural rate of unemployment.

Rubric for FRQ 1 (6 points)

1 point: The natural rate of unemployment is made up of frictional unemployment . . .

1 point: . . . plus structural unemployment.

1 point: Cyclical unemployment is the deviation of the actual rate of unemployment from the natural rate. *Or*, cyclical unemployment is the difference between the actual and natural rates of unemployment.

1 point: Changes in labor force characteristics

1 point: Changes in labor market institutions such as unions

1 point: Changes in government policies

2. In each of the following situations, what type of unemployment is Melanie facing? Explain.
a. After completing a complex programming project, Melanie is laid off. Her prospects for a new job requiring similar skills are good, and she has signed up with a programmer placement service. She has passed up offers for low-paying jobs.
b. Melanie loses her programming job because the development of new packaged software programs means employers no longer need to hire as many programmers.
c. Due to the current slump in investment spending, Melanie has been laid off from her programming job. Her employer promises to rehire her when business picks up.
(6 points)

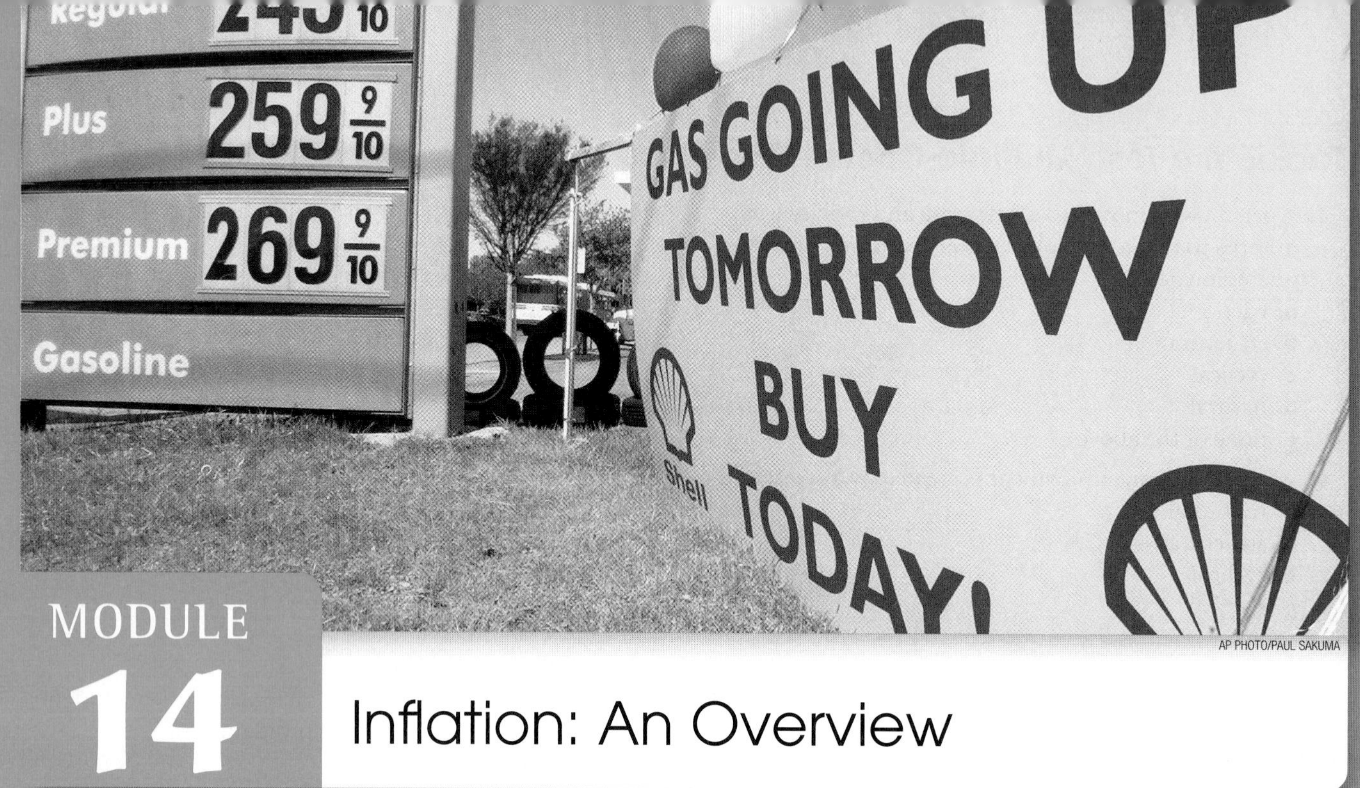

AP PHOTO/PAUL SAKUMA

MODULE 14 Inflation: An Overview

In this Module, you will learn to:

- Calculate the rate of inflation
- Specify the economic costs of inflation
- Identify who is helped and who is hurt by inflation
- Explain why policy makers try to maintain a stable rate of inflation
- Differentiate between real and nominal values of income, wages, and interest rates
- Discuss the problems of deflation and disinflation

Inflation and Deflation

In 1980 Americans were dismayed about the state of the economy for two reasons: the unemployment rate was high, and so was inflation. In fact, the high rate of inflation, not the high rate of unemployment, was the principal concern of policy makers at the time—so much so that Paul Volcker, the chairman of the Federal Reserve Board (which controls monetary policy), more or less deliberately created a deep recession in order to bring inflation under control. Only in 1982, after inflation had dropped sharply and the unemployment rate had risen to more than 10%, did fighting unemployment become the chief priority.

Why is inflation something to worry about? Why do policy makers even now get anxious when they see the inflation rate moving upward? The answer is that inflation can impose costs on the economy—but not in the way most people think.

The Level of Prices Doesn't Matter . . .

The most common complaint about inflation, an increase in the price level, is that it makes everyone poorer—after all, a given amount of money buys less. But inflation does *not* make everyone poorer. To see why, it's helpful to imagine what would happen if the United States did something other countries have done from time to time—replaced the dollar with a new currency.

An example of this kind of currency conversion happened in 2002, when France, like a number of other European countries, replaced its national currency, the franc, with the new Pan-European currency, the euro. People turned in their franc coins and notes, and received euro coins and notes in exchange, at a rate of precisely 6.55957 francs per euro. At the same time, all contracts were restated in euros at the same rate of exchange.

For example, if a French citizen had a home mortgage debt of 500,000 francs, this became a debt of 500,000/6.55957 = 76,224.51 euros. If a worker's contract specified that he or she should be paid 100 francs per hour, it became a contract specifying a wage of 100/6.55957 = 15.2449 euros per hour, and so on.

You could imagine doing the same thing here, replacing the dollar with a "new dollar" at a rate of exchange of, say, 7 to 1. If you owed $140,000 on your home, that would become a debt of 20,000 new dollars. If you had a wage rate of $14 an hour, it would become 2 new dollars an hour, and so on. This would bring the overall U.S. price level back to about what it was when John F. Kennedy was president.

So would everyone be richer as a result because prices would be only one-seventh as high? Of course not. Prices would be lower, but so would wages and incomes in general. If you cut a worker's wage to one-seventh of its previous value, but also cut all prices to one-seventh of their previous level, the worker's **real wage**—the wage rate divided by the price level to adjust for the effects of inflation or deflation—doesn't change. In fact, bringing the overall price level back to what it was during the Kennedy administration would have no effect on overall purchasing power, because doing so would reduce income exactly as much as it reduced prices. Conversely, the rise in prices that has actually taken place since the early 1960s hasn't made America poorer, because it has also raised incomes by the same amount: **real income**—income divided by the price level to adjust for the effects of inflation or deflation—hasn't been affected by the rise in overall prices.

The **real wage** is the wage rate divided by the price level to adjust for the effects of inflation or deflation.

Real income is income divided by the price level to adjust for the effects of inflation or deflation.

The moral of this story is that the *level* of prices doesn't matter: the United States would be no richer than it is now if the overall level of prices was still as low as it was in 1961; conversely, the rise in prices over the past 45 years hasn't made us poorer.

AP® Exam Tip

Inflation is an increase in the general price level that causes the real value of money to decrease. That means your dollar will buy less today than it could buy in previous years.

. . . But the Rate of Change of Prices Does

The conclusion that the level of prices doesn't matter might seem to imply that the inflation rate doesn't matter either. But that's not true.

To see why, it's crucial to distinguish between the *level of prices* and the *inflation rate*. In the next module, we will discuss precisely how the level of prices in the economy is measured using price indexes such as the consumer price index. For now, let's look at the **inflation rate**, the percentage increase in the overall level of prices per year. The inflation rate is calculated as follows:

The **inflation rate** is the percentage increase in the overall level of prices per year.

$$\text{Inflation rate} = \frac{\text{Price level in year 2} - \text{Price level in year 1}}{\text{Price level in year 1}} \times 100$$

Figure 14.1 on the next page highlights the difference between the price level and the inflation rate in the United States since 1969, with the price level measured along the left vertical axis and the inflation rate measured along the right vertical axis. In the 2000s, the overall level of prices in the United States was much higher than it was in 1969—but that, as we've learned, didn't matter. The inflation rate in the 2000s, however, was much lower than in the 1970s—and that almost certainly made the economy richer than it would have been if high inflation had continued.

Economists believe that high rates of inflation impose significant economic costs. The most important of these costs are *shoe-leather costs*, *menu costs*, and *unit-of-account costs*. We'll discuss each in turn.

Shoe-Leather Costs People hold money—cash in their wallets and bank deposits on which they can write checks—for convenience in making transactions. A high inflation rate, however, discourages people from holding money, because the purchasing power of the cash in their wallets and the funds in their bank accounts steadily erodes as the overall level of prices rises. This leads people to search for ways to reduce the amount of money they hold, often at considerable economic cost.

During the most famous of all inflations, the German *hyperinflation* of 1921–1923, merchants employed runners to take their cash to the bank many times a day to convert

Figure 14.1 The Price Level Versus the Inflation Rate, 1969–2013

Over the past 44 years, the price level has continuously gone up. But the *inflation rate*—the rate at which consumer prices are rising—has had both ups and downs.

Source: Bureau of Labor Statistics.

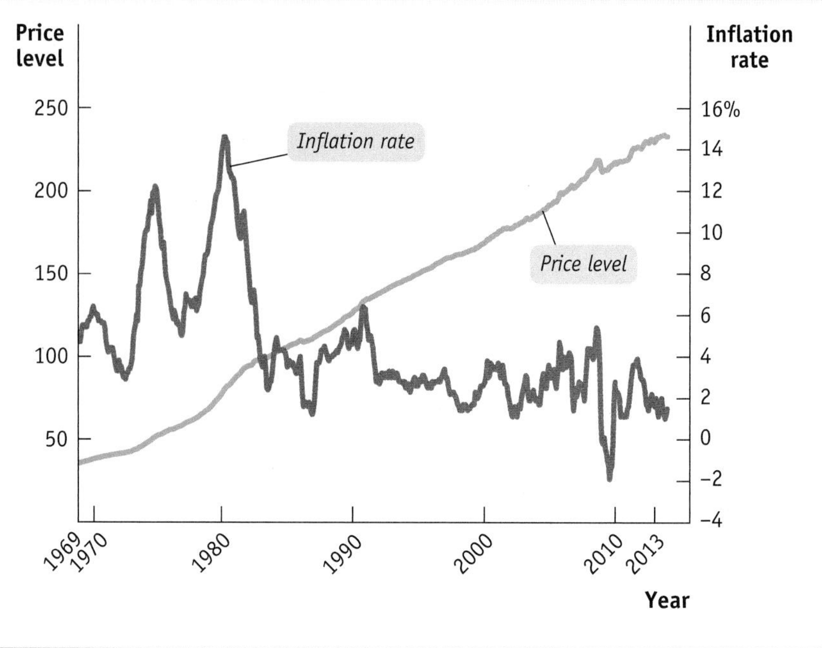

During the German hyperinflation of the early 1920s, people burned worthless paper money in their stoves.

Shoe-leather costs are the increased costs of transactions caused by inflation.

Menu costs are the real costs of changing listed prices.

it into something that would hold its value, such as a stable foreign currency. In an effort to avoid having the purchasing power of their money eroded, people used up valuable resources—the time and labor of the runners—that could have been used productively elsewhere. During the German hyperinflation, so many banking transactions were taking place that the number of employees at German banks nearly quadrupled—from around 100,000 in 1913 to 375,000 in 1923. More recently, Brazil experienced hyperinflation during the early 1990s; during that episode, the Brazilian banking sector grew so large that it accounted for 15% of GDP, more than twice the size of the financial sector in the United States measured as a share of GDP. The large increase in the Brazilian banking sector that was needed to cope with the consequences of inflation represented a loss of real resources to its society.

Increased costs of transactions caused by inflation are known as **shoe-leather costs**, an allusion to the wear and tear caused by the extra running around that takes place when people are trying to avoid holding money. Shoe-leather costs are substantial in economies with very high inflation rates, as anyone who has lived in such an economy—say, one suffering inflation of 100% or more per year—can attest. Most estimates suggest, however, that the shoe leather costs of inflation at the rates seen in the United States—which in peacetime has never had inflation above 15%—are quite small.

Menu Costs In a modern economy, most of the things we buy have a listed price. There's a price listed under each item on a supermarket shelf, a price printed on the front page of your newspaper, a price listed for each dish on a restaurant's menu. Changing a listed price has a real cost, called a **menu cost**. For example, to change a price in a supermarket may require a clerk to change the price listed under the item on the shelf and an office worker to change the price associated with the item's UPC code in the store's computer. In the face of inflation, of course, firms are forced to change prices more often than they would if the price level was more or less stable. This means higher costs for the economy as a whole.

In times of very high inflation rates, menu costs can be substantial. During the Brazilian inflation of the early 1990s, for instance, supermarket workers reportedly spent half of their time replacing old price stickers with new ones. When the inflation

Israel's Experience with Inflation

It's hard to see the costs of inflation clearly because serious inflation is often associated with other problems that disrupt the economy and life in general, notably war or political instability (or both). In the mid-1980s, however, Israel experienced a "clean" inflation: there was no war, the government was stable, and there was order in the streets. Yet a series of policy errors led to very high inflation, with prices often rising more than 10% a month.

As it happens, one of the authors spent a month visiting Tel Aviv University at the height of the inflation, so we can give a first-hand account of the effects.

First, the shoe-leather costs of inflation were substantial. At the time, Israelis spent a lot of time in lines at the bank, moving money in and out of accounts that provided high enough interest rates to offset inflation. People walked around with very little cash in their wallets; they had to go to the bank whenever they needed to make even a moderately large cash payment. Banks responded by opening a lot of branches, a costly business expense.

Ricki Rosen/Corbis Saba

The shoe-leather costs of inflation in Israel: when the inflation rate hit 500% in 1985, people spent a lot of time in line at banks.

Second, although menu costs weren't that visible to a visitor, what you could see were the efforts businesses made to minimize them. For example, restaurant menus often didn't list prices. Instead, they listed numbers that you had to multiply by another number, written on a chalkboard and changed every day, to figure out the price of a dish.

Finally, it was hard to make decisions because prices changed so much and so often. It was a common experience to walk out of a store because prices were 25% higher than at one's usual shopping destination, only to discover that prices had just been increased 25% there, too.

rate is high, merchants may decide to stop listing prices in terms of the local currency and use either an artificial unit—in effect, measuring prices relative to one another—or a more stable currency, such as the U.S. dollar. This is exactly what the Israeli real estate market began doing in the mid-1980s: prices were quoted in U.S. dollars, even though payment was made in Israeli shekels. And this is also what happened in Zimbabwe when, in May 2008, official estimates of the inflation rate reached 1,694,000%.

Menu costs are also present in low-inflation economies, but they are not severe. In low-inflation economies, businesses might update their prices only sporadically—not daily or even more frequently, as is the case in high-inflation or hyperinflation economies. Also, with technological advances, menu costs are becoming less and less important, since prices can be changed electronically and fewer merchants attach price stickers to merchandise.

© Graham Oliver/Alamy

To fight menu costs, some restaurants list their prices with chalk.

Unit-of-Account Costs In the Middle Ages, contracts were often specified "in kind": for example, a tenant might be obliged to provide his landlord with a certain number of cattle each year (the phrase *in kind* actually comes from an ancient word for *cattle*). This may have made sense at the time, but it would be an awkward way to conduct modern business. Instead, we state contracts in monetary terms: a renter owes a certain number of dollars per month, a company that issues a bond promises to pay the bondholder the dollar value of the bond when it comes due, and so on. We also tend to make our economic calculations in dollars: a family planning its budget, or a small business owner trying to figure out how well the business is doing, makes estimates of the amount of money coming in and going out.

This role of the dollar as a basis for contracts and calculation is called the *unit-of-account* role of money. It's an important aspect of the modern economy. Yet it's a role that can be degraded by inflation, which causes the purchasing power of a dollar to change over time—a dollar next year is worth less than a dollar this year. The effect, many economists argue, is to reduce the quality of economic decisions: the economy as a whole makes less efficient use of its resources because of the uncertainty caused by changes in the unit of account, the dollar. The **unit-of-account costs** of inflation are the costs arising from the way inflation makes money a less reliable unit of measurement.

Unit-of-account costs arise from the way inflation makes money a less reliable unit of measurement.

Unit-of-account costs may be particularly important in the tax system, because inflation can distort the measures of income on which taxes are collected. Here's an example: assume that the inflation rate is 10%, so that the overall level of prices rises 10% each year. Suppose that a business buys an asset, such as a piece of land, for $100,000 and then resells it a year later at a price of $110,000. In a fundamental sense, the business didn't make a profit on the deal: in real terms, it got no more for the land than it paid for it, because the $110,000 would purchase no more goods than the $100,000 would have a year earlier. But U.S. tax law would say that the business made a capital gain of $10,000, and it would have to pay taxes on that phantom gain.

During the 1970s, when the United States had a relatively high inflation rate, the distorting effects of inflation on the tax system were a serious problem. Some businesses were discouraged from productive investment spending because they found themselves paying taxes on phantom gains. Meanwhile, some unproductive investments became attractive because they led to phantom losses that reduced tax bills. When the inflation rate fell in the 1980s—and tax rates were reduced—these problems became much less important.

Winners and Losers from Inflation

As we've just learned, a high inflation rate imposes overall costs on the economy. In addition, inflation can produce winners and losers within the economy. The main reason inflation sometimes helps some people while hurting others is that economic transactions, such as loans, often involve contracts that extend over a period of time and these contracts are normally specified in nominal—that is, in dollar—terms. In the case of a loan, the borrower receives a certain amount of funds at the beginning, and the loan contract specifies how much he or she must repay at some future date. But what that dollar repayment is worth in real terms—that is, in terms of purchasing power—depends greatly on the rate of inflation over the intervening years of the loan.

AP® Exam Tip

In general, borrowers are helped by inflation because it decreases the real value of what they must repay. Lenders, savers, and people with fixed incomes are hurt by inflation because it decreases the real value of the money available to them in the future.

The *interest rate* on a loan is the percentage of the loan amount that the borrower must pay to the lender, typically on an annual basis, in addition to the repayment of the loan amount itself. Economists summarize the effect of inflation on borrowers and lenders by distinguishing between *nominal* interest rates and *real* interest rates. The **nominal interest rate** is the interest rate that is actually paid for a loan, unadjusted for the effects of inflation. For example, the interest rates advertised on student loans and every interest rate you see listed by a bank is a nominal rate. The **real interest rate** is the nominal interest rate adjusted for inflation. This adjustment is achieved by simply subtracting the inflation rate from the nominal interest rate. For example, if a loan carries a nominal interest rate of 8%, but the inflation rate is 5%, the real interest rate is 8% − 5% = 3%.

The **nominal interest rate** is the interest rate actually paid for a loan.

The **real interest rate** is the nominal interest rate minus the rate of inflation.

When a borrower and a lender enter into a loan contract, the contract normally specifies a nominal interest rate. But each party has an expectation about the future rate of inflation and therefore an expectation about the real interest rate on the loan. If the actual inflation rate is *higher* than expected, borrowers gain at the expense of lenders: borrowers will repay their loans with funds that have a lower real value than had been expected—they can purchase fewer goods and services than expected due to the surprisingly high inflation rate. Conversely, if the inflation rate is *lower* than expected, lenders will gain at the expense of borrowers: borrowers must repay their loans with funds that have a higher real value than had been expected.

Historically, the fact that inflation creates winners and losers has sometimes been a major source of political controversy. In 1896 William Jennings Bryan electrified the Democratic presidential convention with a speech in which he declared, "You shall not crucify mankind on a cross of gold." What he was actually demanding was an inflationary policy. At the time, the U.S. dollar had a fixed value in terms of gold. Bryan wanted the U.S. government to abandon the gold standard and print more money, which would have raised the level of prices and, he believed, helped the nation's farmers who were deeply in debt.

In modern America, home mortgages (loans for the purchase of homes) are the most important source of gains and losses from inflation. Americans who took out mortgages in the early 1970s quickly found their real payments reduced by higher-than-expected inflation: by 1983, the purchasing power of a dollar was only 45% of what it had been in 1973. Those who took out mortgages in the early 1990s were not so lucky, because the inflation rate fell to lower-than-expected levels in the following years: in 2003 the purchasing power of a dollar was 78% of what it had been in 1993.

Because gains for some and losses for others result from inflation that is either higher or lower than expected, yet another problem arises: uncertainty about the future inflation rate discourages people from entering into any form of long-term contract. This is an additional cost of high inflation, because high rates of inflation are usually unpredictable, too. In countries with high and uncertain inflation, long-term loans are rare. This, in turn, makes it difficult for people to commit to long-term investments.

One last point: unexpected deflation—a surprise fall in the price level—creates winners and losers, too. Between 1929 and 1933, as the U.S. economy plunged into the Great Depression, the price level fell by 35%. This meant that debtors, including many farmers and homeowners, saw a sharp rise in the real value of their debts, which led to widespread bankruptcy and helped create a banking crisis, as lenders found their customers unable to pay back their loans.

Inflation Is Easy; Disinflation Is Hard

There is not much evidence that a rise in the inflation rate from, say, 2% to 5% would do a great deal of harm to the economy. Still, policy makers generally move forcefully to bring inflation back down when it creeps above 2% or 3%. Why? Because experience shows that bringing the inflation rate down—a process called **disinflation**—is very difficult and costly once a higher rate of inflation has become well established in the economy.

Disinflation is the process of bringing the inflation rate down.

Figure 14.2 shows the inflation rate and the unemployment rate in the United States over a crucial decade, from 1978 to 1988. The decade began with an alarming rise in the

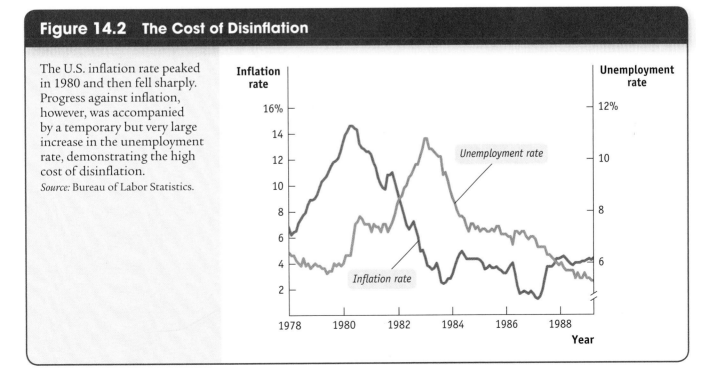

Figure 14.2 The Cost of Disinflation

The U.S. inflation rate peaked in 1980 and then fell sharply. Progress against inflation, however, was accompanied by a temporary but very large increase in the unemployment rate, demonstrating the high cost of disinflation.

Source: Bureau of Labor Statistics.

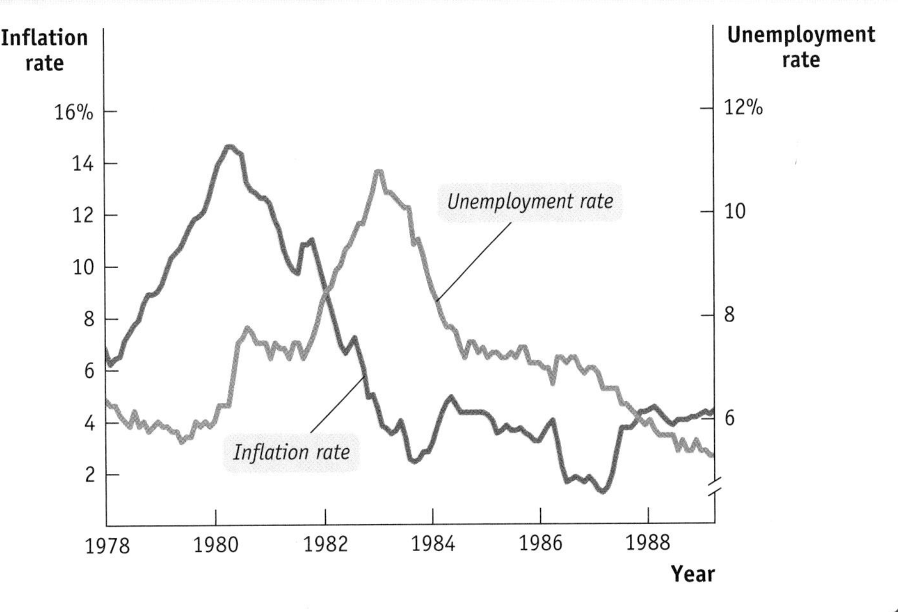

inflation rate, but by the end of the period inflation averaged only about 4%. This was considered a major economic achievement—but it came at a high cost. Much of the fall in inflation probably resulted from the very severe recession of 1981–1982, which drove the unemployment rate to 10.8%—its highest level since the Great Depression.

Many economists believe that this period of high unemployment was necessary, because they believe that the only way to reduce inflation that has become deeply embedded in the economy is through policies that temporarily depress the economy. The best way to avoid having to put the economy through a wringer to reduce inflation, however, is to avoid having a serious inflation problem in the first place. So, policy makers respond forcefully to signs that inflation may be accelerating as a form of preventive medicine for the economy.

MODULE 14 Review

Check Your Understanding

1. The widespread use of technology has revolutionized the banking industry, making it much easier for customers to access and manage their money. Does this mean that the shoe-leather costs of inflation are higher or lower than they used to be? Explain.

2. Most people in the United States have grown accustomed to a modest inflation rate of around 2–3%. Who would gain and who would lose if inflation came to a complete stop for several years? Explain.

Tackle the Test: Multiple-Choice Questions

1. Which of the following is true regarding prices in an economy?
   - I. An increase in the price level is called inflation.
   - II. The level of prices doesn't matter.
   - III. The rate of change in prices matters.

   a. I only
   b. II only
   c. III only
   d. II and III only
   e. I, II, and III

2. If your nominal wage doubles at the same time as prices double, your real wage will
   a. increase.
   b. decrease
   c. not change.
   d. double.
   e. be impossible to determine.

3. If inflation causes people to frequently convert their dollars into other assets, the economy experiences what type of cost?
   a. price level
   b. shoe-leather
   c. menu
   d. unit-of-account
   e. none of the above

4. Because dollars are used as the basis for contracts, inflation leads to which type of cost?
   a. price level
   b. shoe-leather
   c. menu
   d. unit-of-account
   e. none of the above

5. Changing the listed price when inflation leads to a price increase is an example of which type of cost?
   a. price level
   b. shoe-leather
   c. menu
   d. unit-of-account
   e. none of the above

Tackle the Test: Free-Response Questions

1. In the following examples: (i) indicate whether inflation imposes a net cost on the economy; (ii) explain your answer; and (iii) identify the type of net cost involved if there is one.
   a. When inflation is expected to be high, workers get paid more frequently and make more trips to the bank.
   b. Lanwei is reimbursed by her company for her work-related travel expenses. Sometimes, however, the company takes a long time to reimburse her. So when inflation is high, she is less willing to travel for her job.
   c. Hector Homeowner has a mortgage loan that he took out five years ago with a fixed 6% nominal interest rate. Over the years, the inflation rate has crept up unexpectedly to its present level of 7%.
   d. In response to unexpectedly high inflation, the manager of Cozy Cottages of Cape Cod must reprint and resend expensive color brochures correcting the price of rentals this season.

Rubric for FRQ 1 (11 points)

1 point: There is a net cost to the economy.

1 point: There is an increase in the cost of financial transactions imposed by inflation.

1 point: This type of cost is called a shoe-leather cost.

1 point: There is a net cost to the economy.

1 point: Lanwei's forgone output is a cost to the economy.

1 point: This type of cost is called a unit-of-account cost.

1 point: There is no net cost to the economy.

1 point: Hector gains and the bank loses because the money Hector pays back is worth less than expected.

1 point: There is a net cost to the economy.

1 point: Cozy Cottages must reprint and resend the expensive brochure when inflation causes rental prices to rise.

1 point: This type of cost is called a menu cost.

2. You borrow $1,000 for one year at 5% interest to buy a couch. Although you did not anticipate any inflation, there is unexpected inflation of 5% over the life of your loan.
   a. What was the real interest rate on your loan?
   b. Explain how you gained from the inflation.
   c. Who lost as a result of the situation described? Explain.
   (4 points)

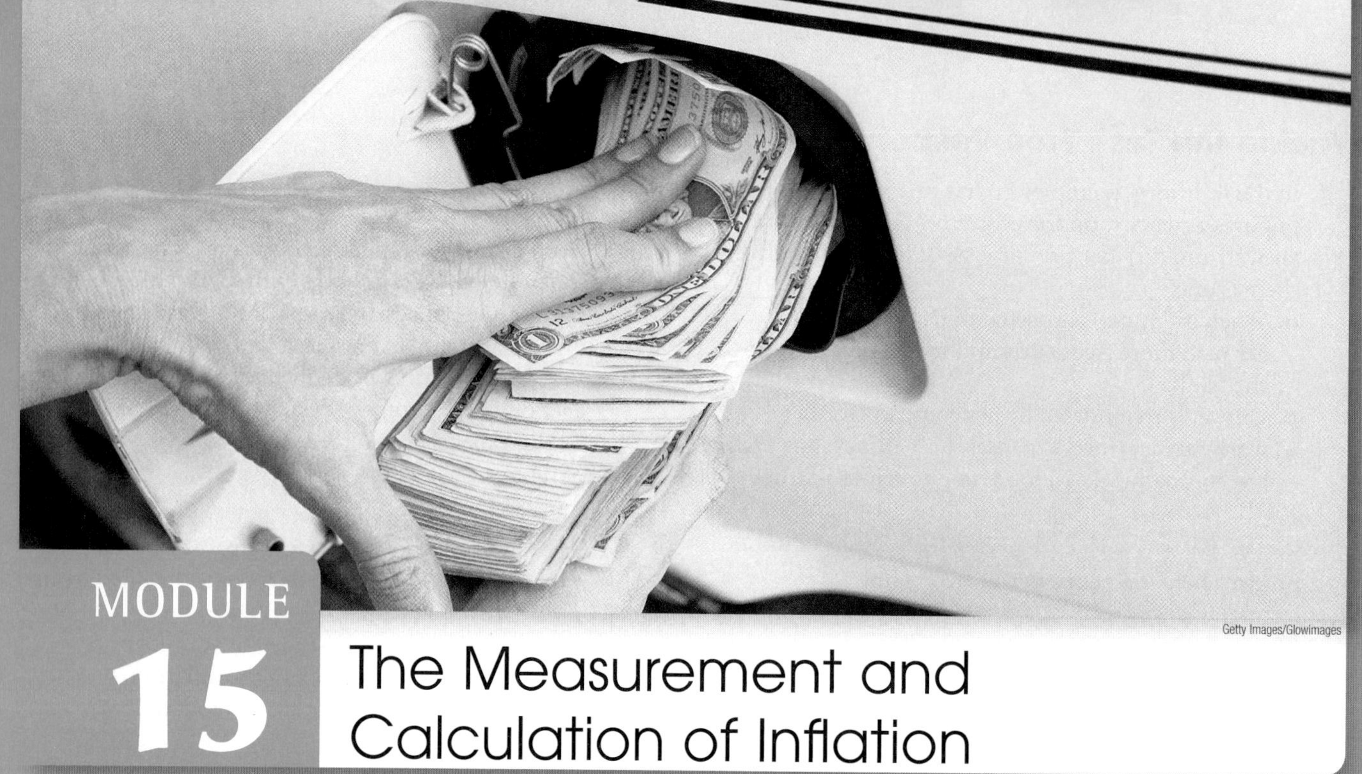

Getty Images/Glowimages

MODULE 15

The Measurement and Calculation of Inflation

In this Module, you will learn to:

- Explain what a price index is and how it is calculated
- Calculate the inflation rate using the values of a price index
- Describe the importance of the consumer price index and other price indexes

Price Indexes and the Aggregate Price Level

In the summer of 2008, Americans were facing sticker shock at the gas pump: the price of a gallon of regular gasoline had risen from about $3 in late 2007 to more than $4 in most places. Many other prices were also up. Some prices, though, were heading down: the prices of some foods, like eggs, were coming down from a run-up earlier in the year, and virtually anything involving electronics was also getting cheaper. Yet practically everyone felt that the overall cost of living seemed to be rising. But how fast?

Clearly there was a need for a single number that would summarize what was happening to consumer prices. Just as macroeconomists find it useful to have a single number to represent the overall level of output, they also find it useful to have a single number to represent the overall level of prices: the **aggregate price level**. Yet a huge variety of goods and services are produced and consumed in the economy. How can we summarize the prices of all these goods and services with a single number? The answer lies in the concept of a *price index*—a concept best introduced with an example.

The **aggregate price level** is a measure of the overall level of prices in the economy.

Market Baskets and Price Indexes

Suppose that a frost in Florida destroys most of the citrus harvest. As a result, the price of oranges rises from $0.20 each to $0.40 each, the price of grapefruit rises from $0.60 to $1.00, and the price of lemons rises from $0.25 to $0.45. How much has the price of citrus fruit increased?

One way to answer that question is to state three numbers—the changes in prices for oranges, grapefruit, and lemons. But this is a very cumbersome method. Rather than having to recite three numbers in an effort to track changes in the prices of citrus fruit, we would prefer to have some kind of overall measure of the *average* price change.

To measure average price changes for consumer goods and services, economists track changes in the cost of a typical consumer's *consumption bundle*—the typical basket of goods and services purchased before the price changes. A hypothetical consumption bundle, used to measure changes in the overall price level, is known as a **market basket**. For our market basket in this example we will suppose that, before the frost, a typical consumer bought 200 oranges, 50 grapefruit, and 100 lemons over the course of a year.

A **market basket** is a hypothetical set of consumer purchases of goods and services.

Table 15.1 shows the pre-frost and post-frost costs of this market basket. Before the frost, it cost \$95; after the frost, the same basket of goods cost \$175. Since \$175/\$95 = 1.842, the post-frost basket costs 1.842 times the cost of the pre-frost basket, a cost increase of 84.2%. In this example, the average price of citrus fruit has increased 84.2% since the base year as a result of the frost, where the base year is the initial year used in the measurement of the price change.

© PhotoAlto/Alamy

Table 15.1 Calculating the Cost of a Market Basket

	Pre-frost	Post-frost
Price of orange	\$0.20	\$0.40
Price of grapefruit	0.60	1.00
Price of lemon	0.25	0.45
Cost of market basket (200 oranges, 50 grapefruit, 100 lemons)	(200 × \$0.20) + (50 × \$0.60) + (100 × \$0.25) = \$95.00	(200 × \$0.40) + (50 × \$1.00) + (100 × \$0.45) = \$175.00

AP® Exam Tip

Don't let the term *market basket* confuse you. It simply means a group of goods and services that represents what consumers buy. On the AP® exam, market baskets usually consist of three or four goods, a simplification of the real market basket used to compute a price index.

Economists use the same method to measure changes in the overall price level: they track changes in the cost of buying a given market basket. Working with a market basket and a base year, we obtain what is known as a **price index**, a measure of the overall price level. It is always cited along with the year for which the aggregate price level is being measured and the base year. A price index can be calculated using the following formula:

A **price index** measures the cost of purchasing a given market basket in a given year. The index value is normalized so that it is equal to 100 in the selected base year.

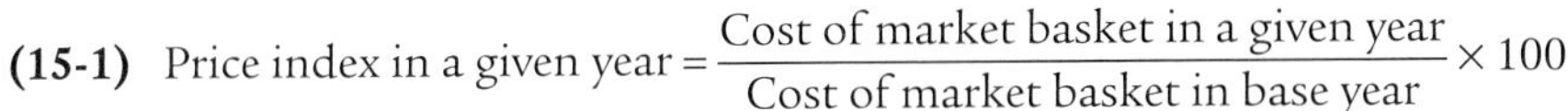

$$\textbf{(15-1)}\quad \text{Price index in a given year} = \frac{\text{Cost of market basket in a given year}}{\text{Cost of market basket in base year}} \times 100$$

In our example, the citrus fruit market basket cost \$95 in the base year, the year before the frost. So by applying Equation 15-1, we define the price index for citrus fruit as (cost of market basket in the current year/\$95) × 100, yielding an index of 100 for the period before the frost and 184.2 after the frost. You should note that applying Equation 15-1 to calculate the price index for the base year always results in a price index of (cost of market basket in base year/cost of market basket in base year) × 100 = 100. Choosing a price index formula that always normalizes the index value to 100 in the base year avoids the need to keep track of the cost of the market basket, for example, \$95, in such and such a year.

The price index makes it clear that the average price of citrus has risen 84.2% as a consequence of the frost. Because of its simplicity and intuitive appeal, the method we've just described is used to calculate a variety of price indexes to track average price changes among a variety of different groups of goods and services. Examples include the *consumer price index* and the *producer price index,* which we'll discuss shortly. Price indexes are also the basis for measuring inflation. The price level mentioned in the inflation rate formula in Module 14 is simply a price index value, and the inflation rate is determined as the annual percentage change in an official price index. The inflation rate from year 1 to year 2 is thus calculated using the following formula, with year 1 and year 2 being consecutive years.

The **consumer price index**, or **CPI**, measures the cost of the market basket of a typical urban American family.

$$\text{(15-2)}\quad \text{Inflation rate} = \frac{\text{Price index in year 2} - \text{Price index in year 1}}{\text{Price index in year 1}} \times 100$$

Typically, a news report that cites "the inflation rate" is referring to the annual percentage change in the consumer price index.

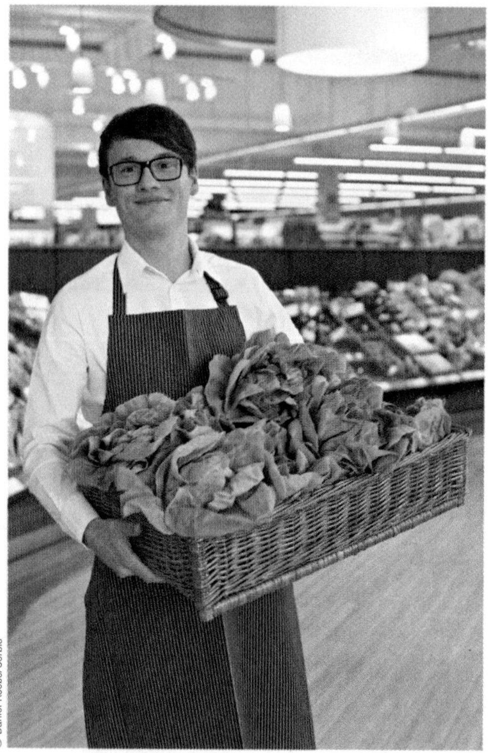

© Daniel Koebe/Corbis

The Consumer Price Index

The most widely used measure of the overall price level in the United States is the **consumer price index** (often referred to simply as the **CPI**), which is intended to show how the cost of all purchases by a typical urban family has changed over time. It is calculated by surveying market prices for a market basket that is constructed to represent the consumption of a typical family of four living in a typical American city. Rather than having a single base year, the CPI currently has a base period of 1982–1984.

The market basket used to calculate the CPI is far more complex than the three-fruit market basket we described above. In fact, to calculate the CPI, the Bureau of Labor Statistics sends its employees out to survey supermarkets, gas stations, hardware stores, and so on—some 23,000 retail outlets in 87 cities. Every month it tabulates about 80,000 prices, on everything from romaine lettuce to a medical checkup. **Figure 15.1** shows the weight of major categories in the consumer price index as of December 2012. For example, motor fuel, mainly gasoline, accounted for 5% of the CPI in December 2012.

Figure 15.2 shows how the CPI has changed since measurement began in 1913. Since 1940, the CPI has risen steadily, although its annual percentage increases in recent years have been much smaller than those of the 1970s and early 1980s. A logarithmic scale is used so that equal percentage changes in the CPI appear the same.

AP® Exam Tip

The CPI is the most commonly used price index on the AP® exam. Make sure you learn how to calculate both the index value in a given year and the inflation rate using the index value.

Figure 15.1 The Makeup of the Consumer Price Index in 2012

This chart shows the percentage shares of major types of spending in the CPI as of December 2012. Housing, food, transportation, and motor fuel made up about 73% of the CPI market basket.

Source: Bureau of Labor Statistics.

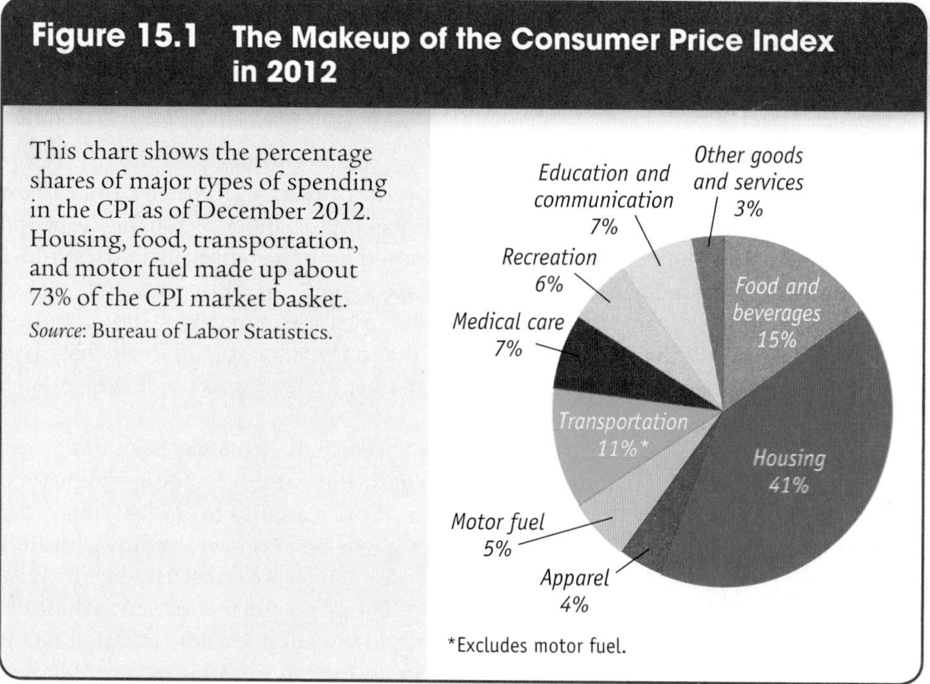

Figure 15.2 The CPI, 1913-2013

Since 1940, the CPI has risen steadily. But the annual percentage increases in recent years have been much smaller than those of the 1970s and early 1980s. (The vertical axis is measured on a logarithmic scale so that equal percentage changes in the CPI appear the same.)

Source: Bureau of Labor Statistics.

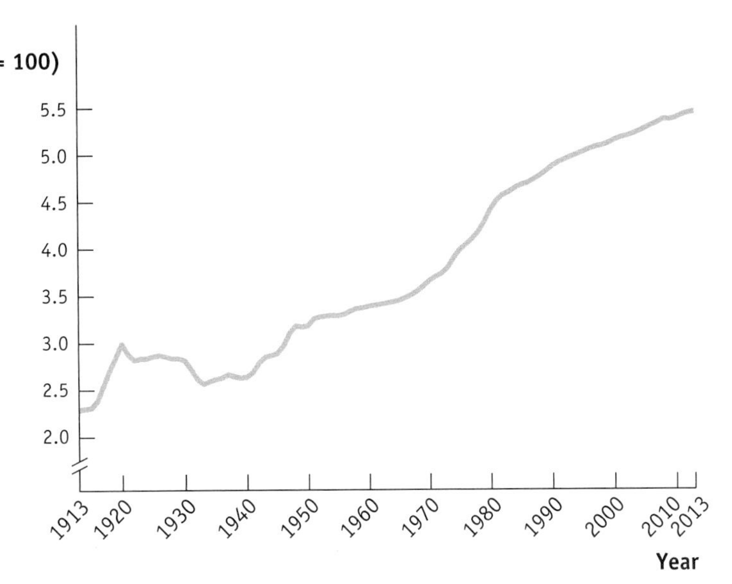

Some economists believe that the consumer price index systematically overstates the actual rate of inflation. Why? Suppose the price of everything in the market basket used to calculate the CPI increased by 10% over the past year. The typical consumer might not need to spend 10% more this year to be as well off as last year, for three reasons.

First, each item remains in the studied market basket for four years. Yet consumers frequently alter the mix of goods and services they buy, reducing purchases of products that have become relatively more expensive and increasing purchases of products that have become relatively cheaper. For example, suppose that the price of hamburgers suddenly doubled. Americans currently eat a lot of hamburgers, but in the face of such a price rise many of them would switch to chicken sandwiches, pizza, or other substitutes whose prices hadn't increased as much. As a result, a price index based on a market basket with a lot of hamburgers in it would overstate the true rise in the cost of living.

The second reason arises from product improvements. It's likely that over the years your favorite toothpaste, laundry detergent, and snack foods have both increased in price and come out in "new and improved" versions. If what you're getting is really better than before, you aren't paying more for the same product. Rather, you're paying more and getting more. The Bureau of Labor Statistics does its best to make adjustments for changes in product quality, but it is hard to measure the extent to which consumers are getting more as opposed to simply paying more.

The third reason that inflation rate estimates may be misleading is innovation. Every new year brings new items, such as new electronic gadgets, new smartphone apps, new health care solutions, and new clothing options. By widening the range of consumer choice, innovation makes a given amount of money worth more. That is, innovation creates benefits similar to those of a fall in consumer prices. For all of these reasons, changes in the CPI may overstate changes in the cost of maintaining a particular standard of living. However, with more frequent updates of the market basket, among other tweaks in its methods, the Bureau of Labor Statistics has improved the accuracy of the CPI in recent years. And, despite some remaining controversy, the CPI remains the basis for most estimates of inflation.

The United States is not the only country that calculates a consumer price index. In fact, nearly every country calculates one. As you might expect, the market baskets that make up these indexes differ quite a lot from country to country. In poor countries, where people must spend a high proportion of their income just to feed themselves, food makes up a large share of the price index. Among high-income countries, differences in consumption patterns lead to differences in the price indexes: the Japanese price index puts a larger weight on raw fish and a smaller weight on beef than ours does, and the French price index puts a larger weight on wine.

Other Price Measures

The **producer price index**, or **PPI**, measures the prices of goods and services purchased by producers.

There are two other price measures that are also widely used to track economy-wide price changes. One is the **producer price index** (or **PPI**, which used to be known as the *wholesale price index*). As its name suggests, the producer price index measures the cost of a typical basket of goods and services—containing raw commodities such as steel, electricity, coal, and so on—purchased by producers. Because commodity producers are relatively quick to raise prices when they perceive a change in overall demand for their goods, the PPI often responds to inflationary or deflationary pressures more quickly than the CPI. As a result, the PPI is often regarded as an "early warning signal" of changes in the inflation rate.

The **GDP deflator** for a given year is 100 times the ratio of nominal GDP to real GDP in that year.

The other widely used price measure is the *GDP deflator;* it isn't exactly a price index, although it serves the same purpose. Recall how we distinguished between nominal GDP (GDP in current prices) and real GDP (GDP calculated using the prices of a base year). The **GDP deflator** for a given year is 100 times the ratio of nominal GDP to real GDP in that year. Since the Bureau of Economic Analysis—the source of the GDP deflator—calculates real GDP using a base year of 2005, the nominal GDP and the real GDP for 2005 are the same. This makes the GDP deflator for 2005 equal to 100. For this reason, later in this book you will see measures of the aggregate price level with the designation "GDP Deflator, 2005 = 100." And in many cases you will see real GDP measured in 2005 dollars. Inflation raises nominal GDP but not real GDP, causing the GDP deflator to rise. If nominal GDP doubles but real GDP does not change, the GDP deflator indicates that the aggregate price level has doubled.

Perhaps the most important point about the different inflation rates generated by these three measures of prices is that they usually move closely together (although the producer price index tends to fluctuate more than either of the other two measures). **Figure 15.3** shows the annual percentage changes in the three indexes since 1930. By all three measures, the U.S. economy experienced deflation during the early years of

Figure 15.3 The CPI, the PPI, and the GDP Deflator

As the figure shows, these three different measures of inflation usually move closely together. Each reveals a drastic acceleration of inflation during the 1970s and a return to relative price stability in the 1990s.

Source: Bureau of Labor Statistics; Bureau of Economic Analysis.

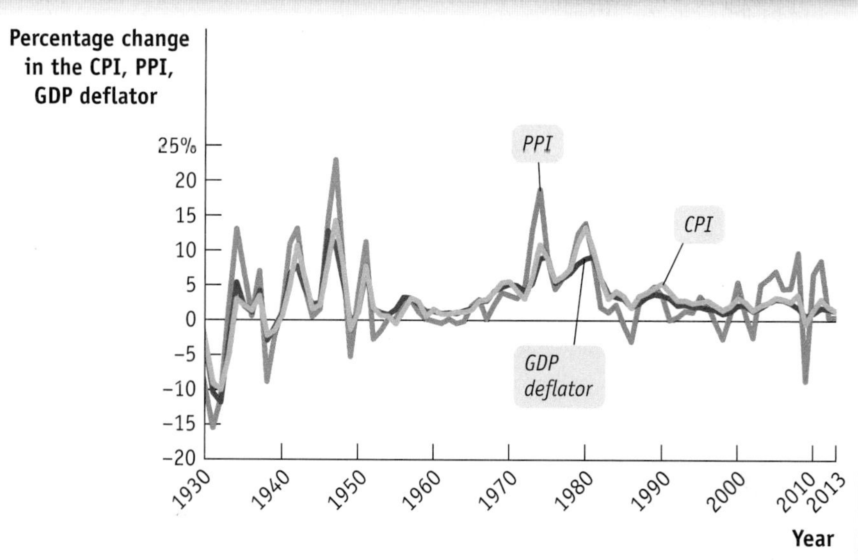

the Great Depression, inflation during World War II, accelerating inflation during the 1970s, and a return to relative price stability in the 1990s. Notice, by the way, the dramatic ups and downs in producer prices from 2000 to 2012. This reflects large swings in energy and food prices, which play a much bigger role in the PPI than they do in either the CPI or the GDP deflator.

Indexing to the CPI

Although GDP is a very important number for shaping economic policy, official statistics on GDP don't have a direct effect on people's lives. The CPI, by contrast, has a direct and immediate impact on millions of Americans. The reason is that many payments are tied, or "indexed," to the CPI—the amount paid rises or falls when the CPI rises or falls.

The practice of indexing payments to consumer prices goes back to the dawn of the United States as a nation. In 1780 the Massachusetts State Legislature recognized that the pay of its soldiers fighting the British needed to be increased because of inflation that occurred during the Revolutionary War. The legislature adopted a formula that made a soldier's pay proportional to the cost of a market basket consisting of 5 bushels of corn, 68 $\frac{4}{7}$ pounds of beef, 10 pounds of sheep's wool, and 16 pounds of sole leather.

Today, 58 million people, most of them old or disabled, receive checks from Social Security, a national retirement program that accounts for almost a quarter of current total federal spending—more than the defense budget. The amount of an individual's check is determined by a formula that reflects his or her previous payments into the system as well as other factors. In addition, all Social Security payments are adjusted each year to offset any increase in consumer prices over the previous year. The CPI is used to calculate the official estimate of the inflation rate used to adjust these payments annually. So every percentage point added to the official estimate of the rate of inflation adds 1% to the checks received by tens of millions of individuals.

Other government payments are also indexed to the CPI. In addition, income tax brackets, the bands of income levels that determine a taxpayer's income tax rate, are indexed to the CPI. (An individual in a higher income bracket pays a higher income tax rate in a progressive tax system like ours.) Indexing also extends to the private sector, where many private contracts, including some wage settlements, contain cost-of-living allowances (called COLAs) that adjust payments in proportion to changes in the CPI.

Because the CPI plays such an important and direct role in people's lives, it's a politically sensitive number. The Bureau of Labor Statistics, which calculates the CPI, takes great care in collecting and interpreting price and consumption data. It uses a complex method in which households are surveyed to determine what they buy and where they shop, and a carefully selected sample of stores are surveyed to get representative prices. As explained in the preceding section, however, there is still controversy about whether the CPI accurately measures inflation.

Superstock

A small change in the CPI has large consequences for those who depend on Social Security payments.

MODULE 15 Review

Check Your Understanding

1. Consider Table 15.1 but suppose that the market basket is composed of 100 oranges, 50 grapefruit, and 200 lemons. How does this change the pre-frost and post-frost consumer price indexes? Explain. Generalize your answer to explain how the construction of the market basket affects the CPI.
2. For each of the following events, explain how the use of a 10-year-old market basket would bias measurements of price changes over the past decade.
   a. A typical family owns more cars than it would have a decade ago. Over that time, the average price of a car has increased more than the average prices of other goods.
   b. Virtually no households had tablet PCs a decade ago. Now many households have them, and their prices have been falling.
3. The consumer price index in the United States (base period 1982–1984) was 214.537 in 2009 and 218.056 in 2010. Calculate the inflation rate from 2009 to 2010.

Tackle the Test: Multiple-Choice Questions

1. If the cost of a market basket of goods increases from $100 in year 1 to $108 in year 2, the consumer price index in year 2 equals ___ if year 1 is the base year.
   a. 8
   b. 10
   c. 100
   d. 108
   e. 110
2. If the consumer price index increases from 80 to 120 from one year to the next, the inflation rate over that time period was
   a. 20%
   b. 40%
   c. 50%
   d. 80%
   e. 120%
3. Which of the following is true of the CPI?
   I. It is the most common measure of the price level.
   II. It measures the price of a typical market basket of goods.
   III. It currently uses a base period of 1982–1984.
   a. I only
   b. II only
   c. III only
   d. I and II only
   e. I, II, and III
4. The value of a price index in the base year is
   a. 0.
   b. 100.
   c. 200.
   d. the inflation rate.
   e. the average cost of a market basket of goods.
5. If your wage doubles at the same time as the consumer price index goes from 100 to 300, your real wage
   a. doubles.
   b. falls.
   c. increases.
   d. stays the same.
   e. cannot be determined.

Tackle the Test: Free-Response Questions

1. Suppose the year 2000 is the base year for a price index. Between 2000 and 2020 prices double and at the same time your nominal income increases from $40,000 to $80,000.
   a. What is the value of the price index in 2000?
   b. What is the value of the price index in 2020?
   c. What is the percentage increase in your nominal income between 2000 and 2020?
   d. What has happened to your real income between 2000 and 2020? Explain.

Rubric for FRQ 1 (5 points)

1 point: 100
1 point: 200
1 point: 100%
1 point: It stayed the same.
1 point: Real income is a measure of the purchasing power of my income, and because my income and the price level both doubled, the purchasing power of my income has not been affected: $40,000/100 = $80,000/200.

2. The accompanying table contains the values of the CPI for 2012 and 2013.
   a. What does the CPI measure?
   b. Calculate the inflation rate from 2012 to 2013.

Year	CPI
2012	229.6
2013	233.0

(2 points)

SECTION 3 Review

Section 3 Review Video

Module 10

1. Economists keep track of the flows of money between sectors with the **national income and product accounts**, or **national accounts. Households** earn income via the **factor markets** from wages, interest on **bonds**, profit accruing to owners of **stocks**, and rent on land. In addition, they receive **government transfers. Disposable income**, total household income minus taxes plus government transfers, is allocated to **consumer spending** (*C*) in the **product markets** and **private savings**. Via the **financial markets**, private savings and foreign lending are channeled to **investment spending** (*I*), government borrowing, and foreign borrowing. **Government purchases of goods and services** (*G*) are paid for by tax revenues and **government borrowing**. **Exports** (*X*) generate an inflow of funds into the country from the rest of the world, but **imports** (*IM*) lead to an outflow of funds to the rest of the world. Foreigners can also buy stocks and bonds in the U.S. financial markets.

2. **Gross domestic product**, or **GDP**, measures the value of all **final goods and services** produced in the economy. It does not include the value of **intermediate goods and services**, but it does include **inventories** and **net exports** ($X - IM$). There are three approaches to calculating GDP: the **value-added approach** of adding up the **value added** by all producers; the **expenditure approach** of adding up all spending on domestically produced final goods and services, leading to the equation $GDP = C + I + G + X - IM$, also known as **aggregate spending**; and the **income approach** of adding up all the income paid by domestic **firms** to factors of production. These three methods are equivalent because in the economy as a whole, total income paid by domestic firms to factors of production must equal total spending on domestically produced final goods and services.

Module 11

3. **Real GDP** is the value of the final goods and services produced, calculated using the prices of a selected base year. Except in the base year, real GDP is not the same as **nominal GDP**, the value of **aggregate output** calculated using current prices. Analysis of the growth rate of aggregate output must use real GDP because doing so eliminates any change in the value of aggregate output due solely to price changes. Real **GDP per capita** is a measure of average aggregate output per person but is not in itself an appropriate policy goal. U.S. statistics on real GDP are always expressed in "chained dollars," which means they are calculated with the **chain-linking** method of averaging the GDP growth rate found using an early base year and the GDP growth rate found using a late base year.

Module 12

4. **Employed** people currently hold a part-time or full-time job; **unemployed** people do not hold a job but are actively looking for work. Their sum is equal to the **labor force**; the **labor force participation rate** is the percentage of the population age 16 or older that is in the labor force.

5. The **unemployment rate**, the percentage of the labor force that is unemployed and actively looking for work, can overstate or understate the true level of unemployment. It can overstate because it counts as unemployed those who are continuing to search for a job despite having been offered one (that is, workers who are frictionally unemployed). It can understate because it ignores frustrated workers, such as **discouraged workers**, **marginally attached workers**, and the **underemployed**. In addition, the unemployment rate varies greatly among different groups in the population; it is typically higher for younger workers and for workers near retirement age than for workers in their prime working years.

6. The unemployment rate is affected by the business cycle. The unemployment rate generally falls when the growth rate of real GDP is above average and generally rises when the growth rate of real GDP is below average.

Module 13

7. Job creation and destruction, as well as voluntary job separations, lead to **job search** and **frictional unemployment**. In addition, a variety of factors, such as minimum wages, unions, and **efficiency wages**, result in a situation in which there is a surplus of labor at the market wage rate, creating **structural unemployment**. As a result, the **natural rate of unemployment**, the sum of frictional and structural unemployment, is well above zero, even when jobs are plentiful.

8. The actual unemployment rate is equal to the natural rate of unemployment, the share of unemployment that is independent of the business cycle, plus **cyclical unemployment**, the share of unemployment that depends on fluctuations in the business cycle.

9. The natural rate of unemployment changes over time, largely in response to changes in labor force characteristics, labor market institutions, and government policies.

Module 14

10. Inflation does not, as many assume, make everyone poorer by raising the level of prices. That's because if wages and incomes are adjusted to take into account a rising price level, **real wages** and **real income** remain unchanged. However, a high **inflation rate** imposes overall costs on the economy: **shoe-leather costs**, **menu costs**, and **unit-of-account costs**.

11. Inflation can produce winners and losers within the economy, because long-term contracts are generally written in dollar terms. Loans typically specify a **nominal interest rate**, which differs from the **real interest rate** due to inflation. A higher-than-expected inflation rate is good for borrowers and bad for lenders. A lower-than-expected inflation rate is good for lenders and bad for borrowers.

12. **Disinflation**, the process of bringing the inflation rate down, usually comes at the cost of a higher unemployment rate. So policy makers try to prevent inflation from becoming excessive in the first place.

Module 15

13. To measure the **aggregate price level**, economists calculate the cost of purchasing a **market basket**. A **price index** is the ratio of the current cost of that market basket to the cost in a selected base year, multiplied by 100.

14. The inflation rate is calculated as the annual percentage change in a price index, typically based on the **consumer price index**, or **CPI**, the most common measure of the aggregate price level. A similar index for goods and services purchased by firms is the **producer price index**, or **PPI**. Finally, economists also use the **GDP deflator**, which measures the price level by calculating the ratio of nominal to real GDP times 100.

Key Terms

National income and product accounts, p. 105
National accounts, p. 105
Household, p. 106
Firm, p. 106
Product markets, p. 106
Factor markets, p. 106
Consumer spending, p. 106
Stock, p. 107
Bond, p. 107
Government transfers, p. 108
Disposable income, p. 108
Private savings, p. 108
Financial markets, p. 108
Government borrowing, p. 108
Government purchases of goods and services, p. 108
Exports, p. 108
Imports, p. 108
Inventories, p. 109
Investment spending, p. 109
Final goods and services, p. 109
Intermediate goods and services, p. 109
Gross domestic product (GDP), p. 109
Value-added approach, p. 109
Expenditure approach, p. 109
Aggregate spending, p. 109
Income approach, p. 109
Value added, p. 110
Net exports, p. 111
Aggregate output, p. 116
Real GDP, p. 117
Nominal GDP, p. 117
Chain-linking, p. 118
GDP per capita, p. 118
Employed, p. 121
Unemployed, p. 122
Labor force, p. 122
Labor force participation rate, p. 122
Unemployment rate, p. 122
Discouraged workers, p. 123
Marginally attached workers, p. 123
Underemployed, p. 123
Job search, p. 130
Frictional unemployment, p. 130
Structural unemployment, p. 131
Efficiency wages, p. 133
Natural rate of unemployment, p. 133
Cyclical unemployment, p. 133
Real wage, p. 139
Real income, p. 139
Inflation rate, p. 139
Shoe-leather costs, p. 140
Menu costs, p. 140
Unit-of-account costs, p. 142
Nominal interest rate, p. 142
Real interest rate, p. 142
Disinflation, p. 143
Aggregate price level, p. 146
Market basket, p. 147
Price index, p. 147
Consumer price index (CPI), p. 148
Producer price index (PPI), p. 150
GDP deflator, p. 150

AP® Exam Practice Questions

Multiple-Choice Questions

Refer to the following diagram for Questions 1–3.

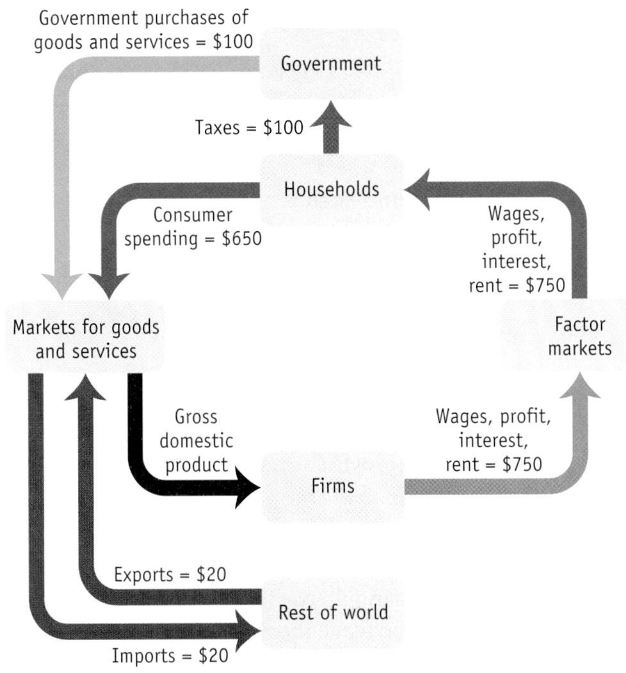

1. What is the value of GDP?
   a. $550
   b. $650
   c. $750
   d. $770
   e. $790

2. What is the value of disposable income?
   a. $750
   b. $650
   c. $550
   d. $530
   e. $510

3. The $750 of wages, profit, interest, and rent shown by the red arrow pointing into the factor markets box illustrates the calculation of GDP using which approach?
   a. value-added
   b. aggregate spending
   c. expenditure
   d. income
   e. resource

Refer to the following table for Questions 4–6.

Category	Components of GDP (billions of dollars)
Consumer spending	
Durable goods	$1,000
Nondurable goods	2,000
Services	7,000
Private Investment Spending	
Fixed investment spending	1,700
Nonresidential	1,400
Structures	500
Equipment and software	900
Residential	300
Change in private inventories	−100
Net exports	
Exports	1,500
Imports	2,000
Government purchases of goods and services and investment spending	
Federal	1,400
State and local	1,600

4. What is the value of GDP?
   a. $10,000
   b. $11,600
   c. $14,100
   d. $15,100
   e. $18,100

5. What is the value of net exports?
   a. $3,500
   b. $2,000
   c. $1,500
   d. $500
   e. −$500

6. Which of the following refers to a loan in the form of an IOU that pays interest?
   a. stock
   b. bond
   c. disposable income
   d. government transfer
   e. investment

7. Investment spending includes spending on which of the following?
   a. stocks
   b. physical capital
   c. inputs
   d. services
   e. reductions in inventories
8. Which of the following is included in the calculation of GDP?
   a. intermediate goods and services
   b. used goods
   c. stocks and bonds
   d. foreign-produced goods and services
   e. domestically produced capital goods
9. Which of the following is true for this year if real GDP is greater than nominal GDP?
   a. The price level has decreased since the base year.
   b. The consumer price index has increased since the base year.
   c. The economy is experiencing inflation.
   d. There has been economic growth.
   e. Net exports are positive.
10. A country's labor force is equal to which of the following?
   a. the number of people aged 16 and above
   b. the number of people employed plus the number retired
   c. the number of people employed plus the number unemployed
   d. the number of people working for pay
   e. the number of people employed for pay plus the number who have given up looking for work
11. The number of people who are considered unemployed is equal to the number of people who are not working and
   a. are receiving unemployment compensation.
   b. have given up seeking work.
   c. plan to look for work in the future.
   d. have looked for work in the recent past.
   e. are actively seeking work.
12. The unemployment rate is the number of people unemployed divided by the number
   a. employed.
   b. employed plus the number discouraged.
   c. in the labor force.
   d. in the population aged 16 and above.
   e. in the population.
13. The number of people counted as unemployed includes which of the following types of workers?
   a. discouraged workers
   b. aspiring workers seeking their first job
   c. underemployed workers
   d. retired workers
   e. part-time workers
14. A worker who is not working while engaged in a job search after moving to a new city is considered which of the following?
   a. frictionally unemployed
   b. structurally unemployed
   c. cyclically unemployed
   d. underemployed
   e. a discouraged worker
15. A worker who is not working because his or her skills are no longer demanded in the labor market is considered which of the following?
   a. frictionally unemployed
   b. structurally unemployed
   c. cyclically unemployed
   d. underemployed
   e. a discouraged worker
16. The normal unemployment rate around which the actual unemployment rate fluctuates is known as which of the following?
   a. frictional unemployment rate
   b. structural unemployment rate
   c. cyclical unemployment rate
   d. natural rate of unemployment
   e. maximum unemployment rate
17. Which of the following is true if the real wage rate is equal to the nominal wage rate?
   a. Real income is constant.
   b. The price level for the current year is the same as the price level in the base year.
   c. The CPI is increasing.
   d. The demand for labor is increasing.
   e. The economy is experiencing deflation.
18. A worker who is unemployed due to fluctuations in the business cycle is considered which of the following?
   a. frictionally unemployed
   b. structurally unemployed
   c. cyclically unemployed
   d. underemployed
   e. a discouraged worker
19. When inflation makes money a less reliable unit of measurement, the economy is experiencing which of the following costs of inflation?
   a. unit-of-account
   b. shoe-leather
   c. menu
   d. measurement
   e. monetary
20. Bringing down the inflation rate is known as
   a. negative inflation.
   b. deflation.
   c. bubble popping.
   d. disinflation.
   e. contraction.

21. The real interest rate is equal to the nominal interest rate
- **a.** minus the inflation rate.
- **b.** plus the inflation rate.
- **c.** divided by the inflation rate.
- **d.** times the inflation rate.
- **e.** plus the real interest rate divided by the inflation rate.

22. Who loses from unanticipated inflation?
- **a.** borrowers
- **b.** the government
- **c.** investors
- **d.** mortgage owners
- **e.** people on fixed incomes

23. Assume a country has a population of 1,000. If 400 people are employed and 100 people are unemployed, what is the country's unemployment rate?
- **a.** 50%
- **b.** 40%
- **c.** 25%
- **d.** 20%
- **e.** 10%

24. Which of the following changes will result in an increase in the natural rate of unemployment?
- **a.** More teenagers focus on their studies and do not look for jobs until after college.
- **b.** The government increases the time during which an unemployed worker can receive benefits.
- **c.** Greater access to the Internet makes it easier for job-seekers to find a job.
- **d.** Union membership declines.
- **e.** Opportunities for job training improve.

25. If the consumer price index rises from 120 to 132, what is the inflation rate?
- **a.** 8%
- **b.** 10%
- **c.** 12%
- **d.** 20%
- **e.** 32%

Free-Response Question

1. Assume the country of Technologia invests in an online system that efficiently matches job-seekers with employers and significantly reduces the time required for job searches.
- **a.** Which type of unemployment will Technologia's investment affect?
- **b.** Will unemployment increase or decrease?
- **c.** Given the change in unemployment from part b. what will happen to the natural rate of unemployment in Technologia? Explain.
- **d.** Given your answer to part b. what will happen to real GDP in Technologia? Explain.

(6 points)

SECTION 4

National Income and Price Determination

Ethan Miller/Getty Images

From Boom to Bust

Ft. Myers, Florida, was a boom town in 2005. Jobs were plentiful: the unemployment rate was less than 3%. The shopping malls were humming, and new stores were opening everywhere.

But then the boom went bust. Jobs became scarce, and by 2010, the unemployment rate was above 13%. Stores had few customers, and many were closing. One new business was flourishing, however. Marc Joseph, a real estate agent, began offering "foreclosure tours": visits to homes that had been seized by banks after the owners were unable to make mortgage payments.

What happened? Ft. Myers boomed because of a surge in home construction, fueled in part by speculators who bought houses not to live in, but because they believed they could resell those houses at much higher prices. Home construction gave jobs to construction workers, electricians, real estate agents, and others. And these workers, in turn, spent money locally, creating jobs for sales workers, waiters, gardeners, pool cleaners, and more. These workers also spent money locally, creating further expansion, and so on.

The boom turned into a bust when home construction came to a virtual halt. It turned out that speculation had been feeding on itself: people were buying houses as investments, then selling them to other people who were also buying houses as investments, and the prices had risen to levels far beyond what people who actually wanted to live in houses were willing to pay.

The abrupt collapse of the housing market pulled the local economy down with it, as the process that had created the earlier boom operated in reverse.

The boom and bust in Ft. Myers illustrates, on a small scale, the way booms and busts often happen for the economy as a whole. The business cycle is often driven by ups or downs in investment spending—either residential investment spending (spending on home construction) or nonresidential investment spending (such as spending on construction of office buildings, factories, and shopping malls). Changes in investment spending, in turn, indirectly lead to changes in consumer spending, which magnify—or *multiply*—the effect of the investment spending changes on the economy as a whole.

In this section we'll study how this process works on a grand scale. As a first step, we introduce *multiplier* analysis and show how it helps us understand the business cycle. We then explore how *aggregate supply* and *aggregate demand* determine the levels of prices and real output in an economy. Finally, we use the aggregate demand–aggregate supply model to visualize the state of the economy and examine the effects of economic policy.

Maria Teijeiro/Digital Vision/Getty Images

MODULE 16 Income and Expenditure

In this Module, you will learn to:

- Describe the multiplier process by which initial changes in spending lead to further changes in spending
- Use the consumption function to show how current disposable income affects consumer spending
- Explain how expected future income and aggregate wealth affect consumer spending
- Identify the determinants of investment spending
- Explain why investment spending is considered a leading indicator of the future state of the economy

The Spending Multiplier: An Informal Introduction

The story of the boom and bust in Ft. Myers involves a sort of chain reaction in which an initial rise or fall in spending leads to changes in income, which lead to further changes in spending, and so on. Let's examine that chain reaction more closely, this time thinking through the effects of changes in spending on the economy as a whole.

For the sake of this analysis, we'll make the following four simplifying assumptions that we will have to reconsider in later modules:

1. We assume that *producers are willing to supply additional output at a fixed price.* That is, if consumers or businesses buying investment goods decide to spend an additional \$1 billion, that will translate into the production of \$1 billion worth of additional goods and services without driving up the overall level of prices. As a result, *changes in overall spending translate into changes in aggregate output,* as measured by real GDP. This assumption isn't too unrealistic in the short run, but in this section we'll learn that it needs to be changed when we think about the long-run effects of changes in demand.
2. We take the interest rate as given.
3. We assume that there is no government spending and no taxes.
4. We assume that exports and imports are zero.

Given these simplifying assumptions, consider what happens if there is a change in investment spending. Specifically, imagine that for some reason home builders decide to spend an extra \$100 billion on home construction over the next year.

The direct effect of this increase in investment spending will be to increase income and the value of aggregate output by the same amount. That's because each dollar spent on home construction translates into a dollar's worth of income for construction workers, suppliers of building materials, electricians, and so on. If the process stopped there, the increase in residential investment spending would raise overall income by exactly $100 billion.

But the process doesn't stop there. The increase in aggregate output leads to an increase in disposable income that flows to households in the form of profits and wages. The increase in households' disposable income leads to a rise in consumer spending, which, in turn, induces firms to increase output yet again. This generates another rise in disposable income, which leads to another round of consumer spending increases, and so on. So there are multiple rounds of increases in aggregate output.

Juice Images/Alamy

Many businesses, such as those that support home improvement and interior design, benefit during housing booms.

How large is the total effect on aggregate output if we sum the effect from all these rounds of spending increases? To answer this question, we need to introduce the concept of the **marginal propensity to consume**, or ***MPC***: the increase in consumer spending when disposable income rises by $1. When consumer spending changes because of a rise or fall in disposable income, *MPC* is the change in consumer spending divided by the change in disposable income:

$$\textbf{(16-1)}\quad MPC = \frac{\Delta \text{ Consumer spending}}{\Delta \text{ Disposable income}}$$

where the symbol Δ (delta) means "change in." For example, if consumer spending goes up by $6 billion when disposable income goes up by $10 billion, *MPC* is $6 billion/$10 billion = 0.6.

Because consumers normally spend part but not all of an additional dollar of disposable income, *MPC* is a number between 0 and 1. The additional disposable income that consumers don't spend is saved; the **marginal propensity to save**, or ***MPS***, is the fraction of an additional $1 of disposable income that is saved. *MPS* is equal to $1 - MPC$.

AP® Exam Tip

You will need to be able to calculate the multiplier. Learn the *MPC* formula: $\frac{\Delta \text{ Consumer spending}}{\Delta \text{ Disposable income}}$, as well as the multiplier formula itself: $\frac{1}{(1 - MPC)}$. For the *MPS*, substitute the change in savings for the change in consumer spending.

With the assumption of no taxes and no international trade, each $1 increase in spending raises both real GDP and disposable income by $1. So the $100 billion increase in investment spending initially raises real GDP by $100 billion. The corresponding $100 billion increase in disposable income leads to a second-round increase in consumer spending, which raises real GDP by a further $MPC \times$ $100 billion. It is followed by a third-round increase in consumer spending of $MPC \times MPC \times$ $100 billion, and so on. After an infinite number of rounds, the total effect on real GDP is:

Increase in investment spending	=	$100 billion
+ Second-round increase in consumer spending	=	$MPC \times$ $100 billion
+ Third-round increase in consumer spending	=	$MPC^2 \times$ $100 billion
+ Fourth-round increase in consumer spending	=	$MPC^3 \times$ $100 billion
•		•
•		•
•		•

Total increase in real GDP = $(1 + MPC + MPC^2 + MPC^3 + \ldots) \times$ $100 billion

The **marginal propensity to consume**, or ***MPC***, is the increase in consumer spending when disposable income rises by $1.

The **marginal propensity to save**, or ***MPS***, is the increase in household savings when disposable income rises by $1.

So the $100 billion increase in investment spending sets off a chain reaction in the economy. The net result of this chain reaction is that a $100 billion increase in investment spending leads to a change in real GDP that is a *multiple* of the size of that initial change in spending.

How large is this multiple? It's a mathematical fact that an infinite series of the form $1 + x + x^2 + x^3 + \ldots$, where x is between 0 and 1, is equal to $1/(1 - x)$. So the total effect of a $100 billion increase in investment spending, *I*, taking into account all the subsequent increases in consumer spending (and assuming no taxes and no international trade), is given by:

(16-2) Total increase in real GDP from $100 billion rise in

$$I = \frac{1}{(1 - MPC)} \times \$100 \text{ billion}$$

Let's consider a numerical example in which $MPC = 0.6$: each $1 in additional disposable income causes a $0.60 rise in consumer spending. In that case, a $100 billion increase in investment spending raises real GDP by $100 billion in the first round. The second-round increase in consumer spending raises real GDP by another 0.6 × $100 billion, or $60 billion. The third-round increase in consumer spending raises real GDP by another 0.6 × $60 billion, or $36 billion. This process goes on and on until the amount of spending in another round would be virtually zero. In the end, real GDP rises by $250 billion as a consequence of the initial $100 billion rise in investment spending:

$$\frac{1}{(1 - 0.6)} \times \$100 \text{ billion} = 2.5 \times \$100 \text{ billion} = \$250 \text{ billion}$$

Notice that even though there can be a nearly endless number of rounds of expansion of real GDP, the total rise in real GDP is limited to $250 billion. The reason is that at each stage some of the rise in disposable income "leaks out" because it is saved, leaving less and less to be spent in the next round. How much of an additional dollar of disposable income is saved depends on *MPS*, the marginal propensity to save.

We've described the effects of a change in investment spending, but the same analysis can be applied to any other change in spending. The important thing is to distinguish between the initial change in aggregate spending, before real GDP rises, and the additional change in aggregate spending caused by the change in real GDP as the chain reaction unfolds. For example, suppose that a boom in housing prices makes consumers feel richer and that, as a result, they become willing to spend more at any given level of disposable income. This will lead to an initial rise in consumer spending, before real GDP rises. But it will also lead to second and later rounds of higher consumer spending as real GDP and disposable income rise.

An initial rise or fall in aggregate spending at a given level of real GDP is called an **autonomous change in aggregate spending**. It's autonomous—which means "self-governing"—because it's the cause, not the result, of the chain reaction we've just described. Formally, the **spending multiplier** is the ratio of the total change in real GDP caused by an autonomous change in aggregate spending to the size of that autonomous change. If we let ΔAAS stand for the autonomous change in aggregate spending and ΔY stand for the total change in real GDP, then the spending multiplier is equal to $\Delta Y/\Delta AAS$. We've already seen how to find the value of the spending multiplier. Assuming no taxes and no trade, the total change in real GDP caused by an autonomous change in aggregate spending is:

(16-3) $$\Delta Y = \frac{1}{(1 - MPC)} \times \Delta AAS$$

So the spending multiplier is:

(16-4) $$\frac{\Delta Y}{\Delta AAS} = \frac{1}{(1 - MPC)}$$

Notice that the size of the spending multiplier depends on *MPC*. If the marginal propensity to consume is high, so is the spending multiplier. This is true because the size of *MPC* determines how large each round of expansion is compared with the previous round. To put it another way, the higher *MPC* is, the less disposable income "leaks out" into savings at each round of expansion.

An **autonomous change in aggregate spending** is an initial rise or fall in aggregate spending that is the cause, not the result, of a series of income and spending changes.

The **spending multiplier** is the ratio of the total change in real GDP caused by an autonomous change in aggregate spending to the size of that autonomous change. It indicates the total rise in real GDP that results from each $1 of an initial rise in spending.

The Spending Multiplier and the Great Depression

The concept of the spending multiplier was originally devised by economists trying to understand the greatest economic disaster in history, the collapse of output and employment from 1929 to 1933, which began the Great Depression. Most economists believe that the slump from 1929 to 1933 was driven by a collapse in investment spending. But as the economy shrank, consumer spending also fell sharply, multiplying the effect on real GDP.

The table below shows what happened to investment spending, consumer spending, and GDP during those four terrible years. All data are in 2005 dollars for consistency with most of the other data in this section that are adjusted for inflation to 2005, the base year for the GDP deflator. What we see is that investment spending imploded, falling by more than 80%. But consumer spending also fell drastically and actually accounted for more of the fall in real GDP. (The total fall in real GDP was larger than the combined fall in consumer and investment spending, mainly because of technical accounting issues.)

Investment Spending, Consumer Spending, and Real GDP in the Great Depression (billions of 2005 dollars)

	1929	1933	Change
Investment spending	$101.7	$18.9	−$82.8
Consumer spending	736.6	601.1	−135.5
Real GDP	977.0	716.4	−260.6

Source: Bureau of Economic Analysis.

The numbers in the table suggest that at the time of the Great Depression, the spending multiplier was around 3. Most current estimates put the size of the spending multiplier considerably lower—but there's a reason for that change. In 1929, the government of the United States was very small by modern standards: taxes were low and major government programs like Social Security and Medicare had not yet come into being. In the modern U.S. economy, taxes are much higher, and so is government spending. Why does this matter? Because taxes and some government programs act as *automatic stabilizers*, reducing the size of the spending multiplier. For example, when incomes are relatively high, tax payments are relatively high as well, thus moderating increases in expenditures. And when incomes are relatively low, the unemployment insurance program pays more money out to individuals, thus boosting expenditures higher than they would otherwise be.

In later modules we'll use the concept of the spending multiplier to analyze the effects of fiscal and monetary policies. We'll also see that the spending multiplier changes when we introduce various complications, including taxes and foreign trade. First, however, we need to look more deeply at what determines consumer spending.

Consumer Spending

Should you splurge on a restaurant meal or save money by eating at home? Should you buy a new car and, if so, how expensive a model? Should you redo that bathroom or live with it for another year? In the real world, households are constantly confronted with such choices—not just about the consumption mix but also about how much to spend in total. These choices, in turn, have a powerful effect on the economy: consumer spending normally accounts for two-thirds of total spending on final goods and services. But what determines how much consumers spend?

Current Disposable Income and Consumer Spending

The most important factor affecting a family's consumer spending is its current disposable income—income after taxes are paid and government transfers are received. It's obvious from daily life that people with high disposable incomes on average drive more expensive cars, live in more expensive houses, and spend more on meals and clothing than people with lower disposable incomes. And the relationship between current disposable income and spending is clear in the data.

The Bureau of Labor Statistics (BLS) collects annual data on family income and spending. Families are grouped by levels of before-tax income; after-tax income for each group is also reported. Since the income figures include transfers from the government, what the BLS calls a household's after-tax income is equivalent to its current disposable income.

Figure 16.1 is a scatter diagram that illustrates the relationship between household current disposable income and household consumer spending for U.S. households by income group in 2012. For example, point *A* shows that in 2012 the middle fifth of the population had an average current disposable income of $46,777 and average spending of $43,004. The pattern of the dots slopes upward from left to right, making it clear that households with higher current disposable income had higher consumer spending.

A **consumption function** uses an equation or a graph to show how a household's consumer spending varies with the household's current disposable income.

A **consumption function** shows how a household's consumer spending varies with the household's current disposable income.

Autonomous consumer spending is the amount of money a household would spend if it had no disposable income.

Figure 16.2 on the next page provides the graph of a consumption function. The vertical intercept is the household's **autonomous consumer spending**: the amount the household would spend if its current disposable income were zero. Autonomous consumer spending is greater than zero because a household with no disposable income can buy some things by borrowing or using its savings.

Recall that the marginal propensity to consume, or *MPC*, is the amount the household spends out of each additional $1 of current disposable income. The slope of any line is "rise over run"; for the consumption function, the rise is the increase in consumer spending and the run is the increase in current disposable income. For each $1 "run" in income, the "rise" is the *MPC*, so the slope of the consumption function is $MPC/1 = MPC$.

According to the data on U.S. households in Figure 16.1, the best estimate of autonomous consumption for that population in 2012 was $18,478 and the best estimate of *MPC* was $0.52. This implies that the marginal propensity to save (*MPS*)—the amount of an additional $1 of disposable income that is saved—is approximately $1 - 0.52 = 0.48$ and the spending multiplier is $1/(1 - MPC) = 1/MPS =$ approximately $1/0.48 = 2.08$.

An individual household's consumption function shows a microeconomic relationship between the household's current disposable income and its spending on goods

Figure 16.1 Current Disposable Income and Consumer Spending for U.S. Households in 2012

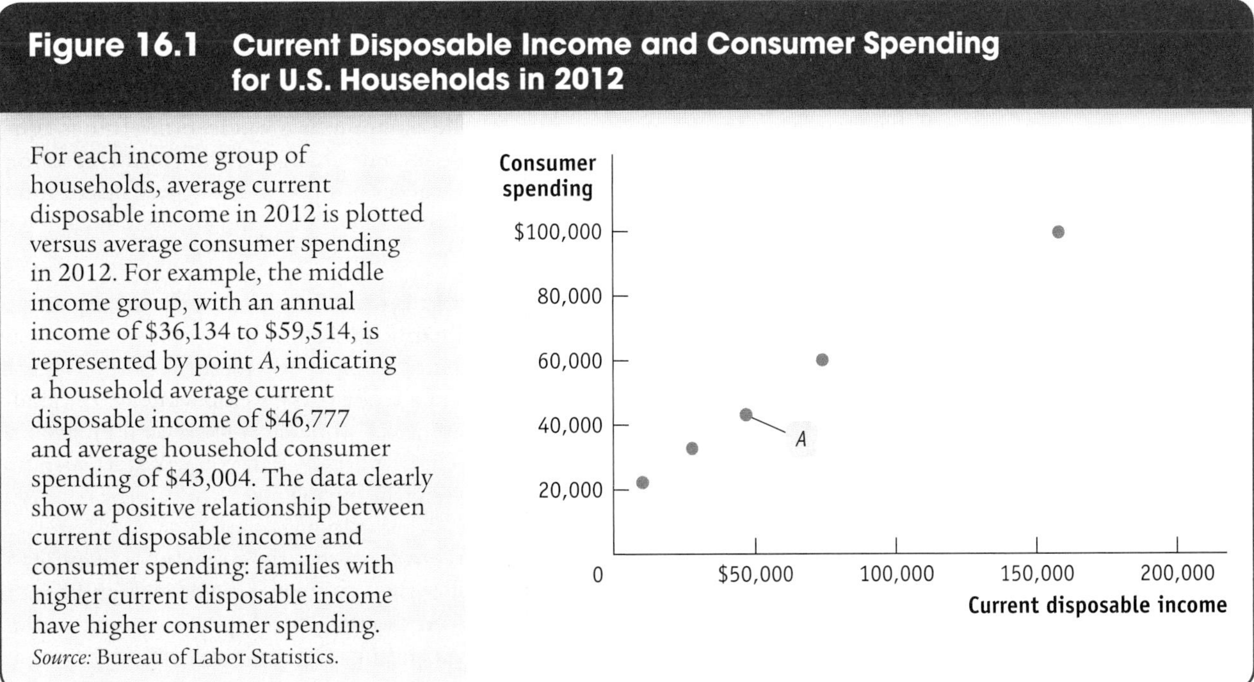

For each income group of households, average current disposable income in 2012 is plotted versus average consumer spending in 2012. For example, the middle income group, with an annual income of $36,134 to $59,514, is represented by point *A*, indicating a household average current disposable income of $46,777 and average household consumer spending of $43,004. The data clearly show a positive relationship between current disposable income and consumer spending: families with higher current disposable income have higher consumer spending.

Source: Bureau of Labor Statistics.

Figure 16.2 The Consumption Function

The consumption function relates a household's current disposable income to its consumer spending. The vertical intercept is the household's autonomous consumer spending: the amount the household would spend if its current disposable income were zero. The slope of the consumption function is the marginal propensity to consume, or *MPC*: the amount the household spends out of each additional $1 of current disposable income.

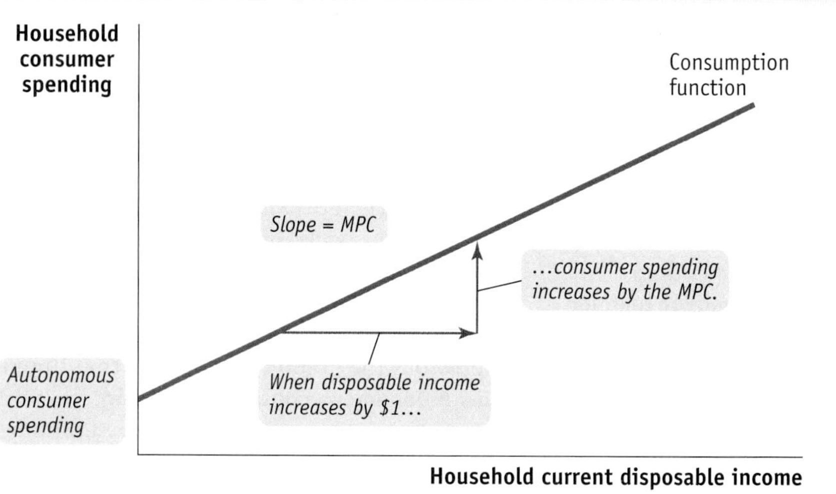

The **aggregate consumption function** is the relationship for the economy as a whole between aggregate current disposable income and aggregate consumer spending.

and services. Macroeconomists study the **aggregate consumption function**, which shows the relationship between current disposable income and consumer spending for the economy as a whole. We can represent this relationship with the following equation:

$$\textbf{(16-5)}\quad C = A + MPC \times Y_D$$

Here, C is aggregate consumer spending, Y_D is aggregate current disposable income, and A is aggregate autonomous consumer spending, the amount of consumer spending when disposable income is zero. **Figure 16.3** shows two aggregate consumption functions as graphs, analogous to the graph of the household consumption function in Figure 16.2.

Shifts of the Aggregate Consumption Function

The aggregate consumption function shows the relationship between current disposable income and consumer spending for the economy as a whole, other things equal. When things other than current disposable income change, the aggregate consumption function shifts. There are two principal causes of shifts of the aggregate consumption function: changes in expected future disposable income and changes in aggregate wealth.

Changes in Expected Future Disposable Income Milton Friedman argued that consumer spending ultimately depends primarily on the income people expect to have over the long term rather than on their current income. This argument is known as the *permanent income hypothesis*. Suppose you land a really good, well-paying job on graduating from college—but the job, and the paychecks, won't start for several months. So your disposable income hasn't risen yet. Even so, it's likely that you will start spending more on final goods and services right away—maybe buying nicer work clothes than you originally planned—because you know that higher income is coming.

Conversely, suppose you have a good job but learn that the company is planning to downsize your division, raising the possibility that you may lose your job and have to take a lower-paying one somewhere else. Even though your disposable income hasn't gone down yet, you might well cut back on spending even while still employed, to save for a rainy day.

Figure 16.3 Shifts of the Aggregate Consumption Function

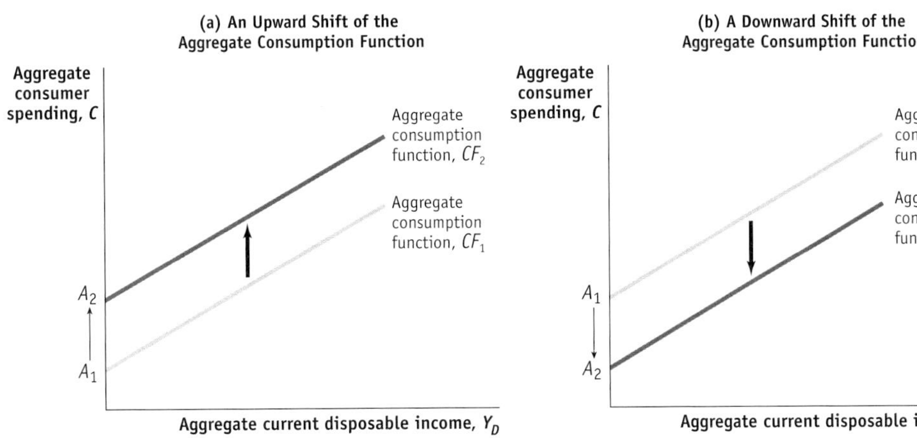

Panel (a) illustrates the effect of an increase in expected aggregate future disposable income. Consumers will spend more at every given level of aggregate current disposable income, Y_D. As a result, the initial aggregate consumption function CF_1, with aggregate autonomous consumer spending A_1, shifts up to a new position at CF_2 with aggregate autonomous consumer spending A_2. An increase in aggregate wealth will also shift the aggregate consumption function up. Panel (b), by contrast, illustrates the effect of a reduction in expected aggregate future disposable income. Consumers will spend less at every given level of aggregate current disposable income, Y_D. Consequently, the initial aggregate consumption function CF_1, with aggregate autonomous consumer spending A_1, shifts down to a new position at CF_2 with aggregate autonomous consumer spending A_2. A reduction in aggregate wealth will have the same effect.

Both of these examples show how expectations about future disposable income can affect consumer spending. The two panels of Figure 16.3, which plot aggregate current disposable income against aggregate consumer spending, show how changes in expected future disposable income affect the aggregate consumption function. In both panels, CF_1 is the initial aggregate consumption function. Panel (a) shows the effect of good news: information that leads consumers to expect higher disposable income in the future than they had expected before. Consumers will now spend more at any given level of aggregate current disposable income Y_D, corresponding to an increase in A, aggregate autonomous consumer spending, from A_1 to A_2. The effect is to shift the aggregate consumption function up, from CF_1 to CF_2. Panel (b) shows the effect of bad news: information that leads consumers to expect lower disposable income in the future than they had expected before. Consumers will now spend less at any given level of aggregate current disposable income, Y_D, corresponding to a fall in A from A_1 to A_2. The effect is to shift the aggregate consumption function down, from CF_1 to CF_2.

Changes in Aggregate Wealth Imagine two individuals, Maria and Mark, both of whom expect to earn $30,000 this year. Suppose, however, that they have different histories. Maria has been working steadily for the past 10 years, owns her own home, and has $200,000 in the bank. Mark is the same age as Maria, but he has been in and out of work, hasn't managed to buy a house, and has very little in savings. In this case, Maria has something that Mark doesn't have: wealth. Even though they have the same disposable income, other things equal, you'd expect Maria to spend more on consumption than Mark. That is, *wealth* has an effect on consumer spending.

Mike Kemp/Rubberball/Getty Images

The effect of wealth on spending is emphasized by an influential economic model of how consumers make choices about spending versus saving called the *life-cycle hypothesis*. According to this hypothesis, consumers plan their spending over their lifetime, not just in response to their current disposable income. As a result, people try to *smooth* their consumption over their lifetimes—they save some of their current disposable income during their years of peak earnings (typically occurring during a worker's 40s and 50s) and live off the wealth they accumulated while working during their retirement. We won't go into the details of this hypothesis but will simply point out that it implies an important role for wealth in determining consumer spending. For example, a middle-aged couple who have accumulated a lot of wealth—who have paid off the mortgage on their house and already own plenty of stocks and bonds—will, other things equal, spend more on goods and services than a couple who have the same current disposable income but still need to save for their retirement.

Because wealth affects household consumer spending, changes in wealth across the economy can shift the aggregate consumption function. A rise in aggregate wealth—say, because of a booming stock market—increases the vertical intercept *A*, aggregate autonomous consumer spending. This, in turn, shifts the aggregate consumption function up in the same way as does an expected increase in future disposable income. A decline in aggregate wealth—say, because of a fall in housing prices as occurred in 2008—reduces *A* and shifts the aggregate consumption function down.

Investment Spending

Although consumer spending is much greater than investment spending, booms and busts in investment spending tend to drive the business cycle. In fact, most recessions originate as a fall in investment spending. **Figure 16.4** illustrates this point; it shows the annual percentage change of investment spending and consumer spending in the United States, both measured in 2005 dollars, during six recessions from 1973 to 2009. As you can see, swings in investment spending are much more dramatic than those in consumer spending. In addition, economists believe that declines in consumer spending are usually the result of slumps in investment spending that trigger the spending multiplier process. Soon we'll examine in more detail how investment spending affects consumer spending.

Planned investment spending is the investment spending that businesses intend to undertake during a given period.

Before we do that, however, let's analyze the factors that determine investment spending, which are somewhat different from those that determine consumer spending. **Planned investment spending** is the investment spending that firms *intend* to undertake during a given period. For reasons explained shortly, the level of investment spending

Figure 16.4 Fluctuations in Investment Spending and Consumer Spending

The bars illustrate the annual percent change in investment spending and consumer spending during six recent recessions. As the heights of the bars show, swings in investment spending were much larger in percentage terms than those in consumer spending. The pattern has led economists to believe that recessions typically originate as a slump in investment spending.

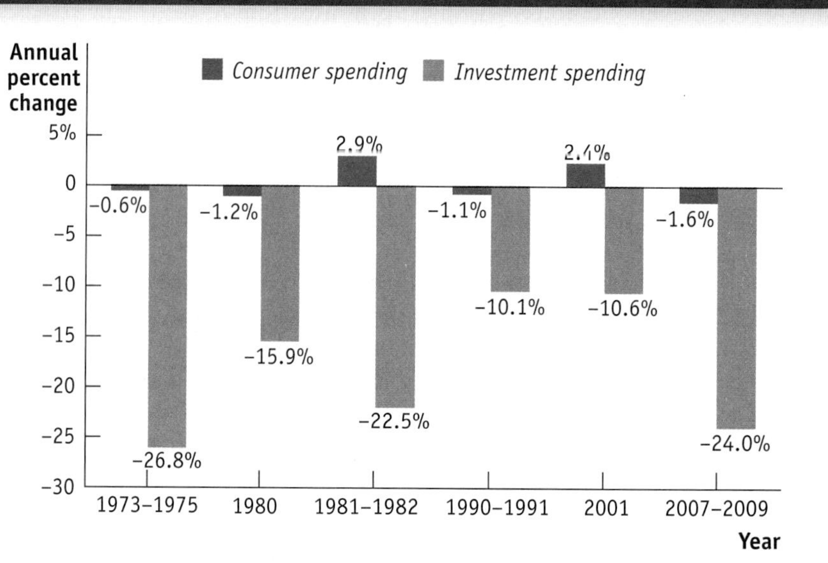

that businesses *actually* carry out is sometimes not the same level as was planned. Planned investment spending depends on three principal factors: the interest rate, the expected future level of real GDP, and the current level of production capacity. First, we'll analyze the effect of the interest rate.

The Interest Rate and Investment Spending

Interest rates have their clearest effect on one particular form of investment spending: spending on residential construction—that is, on the construction of homes. The reason is straightforward: home builders only build houses they think they can sell, and houses are more affordable—and so more likely to sell—when the interest rate is low. Consider a potential home-buying family that needs to borrow $150,000 to buy a house. At an interest rate of 7.5%, a 30-year home mortgage will mean payments of $1,048 per month. At an interest rate of 5.5%, those payments would be only $851 per month, making houses significantly more affordable. Interest rates actually did drop from roughly 7.5% to 5.5% between the late 1990s and 2003, helping set off a housing boom.

Dmitry Kalinovsky/Shutterstock

Interest rates have a direct impact on whether or not construction companies decide to invest in the construction of new homes.

Interest rates also affect other forms of investment spending. Firms with investment spending projects will go ahead with a project only if they expect a rate of return higher than the cost of the funds they would have to borrow to finance that project. If the interest rate rises, fewer projects will pass that test, and, as a result, investment spending will be lower.

You might think that the trade-off a firm faces is different if it can fund its investment project with its past profits rather than through borrowing. Past profits used to finance investment spending are called *retained earnings*. But even if a firm pays for investment spending out of retained earnings, the trade-off it must make in deciding whether or not to fund a project remains the same because it must take into account the opportunity cost of its funds. For example, instead of purchasing new equipment, the firm could lend out the funds and earn interest. The forgone interest earned is the opportunity cost of using retained earnings to fund an investment project. So the trade-off the firm faces when comparing a project's rate of return to the market interest rate has not changed when it uses retained earnings rather than borrowed funds. Either way, a rise in the market interest rate makes any given investment project less profitable. Conversely, a fall in the interest rate makes some investment projects that were unprofitable before profitable at the new lower interest rate. As a result, some projects that had been unfunded before will be funded now.

So planned investment spending—spending on investment projects that firms voluntarily decide whether or not to undertake—is negatively related to the interest rate. Other things equal, a higher interest rate leads to a lower level of planned investment spending.

Expected Future Real GDP, Production Capacity, and Investment Spending

Suppose a firm has enough capacity to continue to produce the amount it is currently selling but doesn't expect its sales to grow in the future. Then it will engage in investment spending only to replace existing equipment and structures that wear out or are rendered obsolete by new technologies. But if, instead, the firm expects its sales to grow rapidly in the future, it will find its existing production capacity insufficient for its future production needs. So the firm will undertake investment spending to meet those needs. This implies that, other things equal, firms will undertake more investment spending when they expect their sales to grow.

Now suppose that the firm currently has considerably more capacity than necessary to meet current production needs. Even if it expects sales to grow, it won't have to undertake investment spending for a while—not until the growth in sales catches up with its excess capacity. This illustrates the fact that, other things equal, the current level of productive capacity has a negative effect on investment spending: other things equal, the higher the current capacity, the lower the investment spending.

If we put together the effects on investment spending of (1) growth in expected future sales and (2) the size of current production capacity, we can see one situation in which firms will most likely undertake high levels of investment spending: when they expect sales to grow rapidly. In that case, even excess production capacity will soon be used up, leading firms to resume investment spending.

What is an indicator of high expected growth in future sales? It's a high expected future growth rate of real GDP. A higher expected future growth rate of real GDP results in a higher level of planned investment spending, but a lower expected future growth rate of real GDP leads to lower planned investment spending.

Inventories and Unplanned Investment Spending

AP® Exam Tip

An increase in unplanned inventories is preceded by a decrease in consumer spending. A decrease in unplanned inventories is preceded by an increase in consumer spending.

Most firms maintain inventories, stocks of goods held to satisfy future sales. Firms hold inventories so they can quickly satisfy buyers—a consumer can purchase an item off the shelf rather than waiting for it to be manufactured. In addition, businesses often hold inventories of their inputs to be sure they have a steady supply of necessary materials and spare parts. At the end of 2013, the overall value of inventories in the U.S. economy was estimated at $2.5 trillion, more than 14% of GDP.

A firm that increases its inventories is engaging in a form of investment spending. Suppose, for example, that the U.S. auto industry produces 800,000 cars per month but sells only 700,000. The remaining 100,000 cars are added to the inventory at auto company warehouses or car dealerships, ready to be sold in the future.

Inventory investment is the value of the change in total inventories held in the economy during a given period.

Positive **unplanned inventory investment** occurs when actual sales are lower than businesses expected, leading to unplanned increases in inventories. Sales in excess of expectations result in negative unplanned inventory investment.

Actual investment spending is the sum of planned investment spending and unplanned inventory investment.

Inventory investment is the value of the change in total inventories held in the economy during a given period. Unlike other forms of investment spending, inventory investment can actually be negative. If, for example, the auto industry reduces its inventory over the course of a month, we say that it has engaged in negative inventory investment.

To understand inventory investment, think about a manager stocking the canned goods section of a supermarket. The manager tries to keep the store fully stocked so that shoppers can almost always find what they're looking for. But the manager does not want the shelves too heavily stocked because shelf space is limited and products can spoil. Similar considerations apply to many firms and typically lead them to manage their inventories carefully. However, sales fluctuate. And because firms cannot always accurately predict sales, they often find themselves holding larger or smaller inventories than they had intended. When a firm's inventories are higher than intended due to an unforeseen decrease in sales, the result is **unplanned inventory investment.** An unexpected increase in sales depletes inventories and causes the value of unplanned inventory investment to be negative.

So in any given period, **actual investment spending** is equal to planned investment spending plus unplanned inventory investment. If we let $I_{Unplanned}$ represent unplanned inventory investment, $I_{Planned}$ represent planned investment spending, and I represent actual investment spending, then the relationship among all three can be represented as:

$$\textbf{(16-6)}\quad I = I_{Unplanned} + I_{Planned}$$

Getty Images

To see how unplanned inventory investment can occur, let's continue to focus on the auto industry and make the following assumptions. First, let's assume that the industry must determine each month's production volume in advance, before it knows the volume of actual sales. Second, let's assume that it anticipates selling 800,000 cars next month and that it plans neither to add to nor subtract from existing inventories. In that case, it will produce 800,000 cars to match anticipated sales.

Interest Rates and the U.S. Housing Boom

Interest rates in the United States dropped from roughly 7.5% to 5.5% between the late 1990s and 2003, helping set off a nationwide housing boom. There is little question that this housing boom was caused, in the first instance, by low interest rates.

The figure below shows the interest rate on 30-year home mortgages—the traditional way to borrow money for a home purchase—and the number of housing starts—the number of homes for which construction is started per month—from 1995 to the end of 2013 in the United States. Panel (a), which shows the mortgage rate, gives you an idea of how much interest rates fell. In the second half of the 1990s, mortgage rates generally fluctuated between 7% and 8%; by 2003, they were down to between 5% and 6%. These lower rates were largely the result of Federal Reserve policy: the Fed cut rates in response to the 2001 recession and continued cutting them into 2003 out of concern that the economy's recovery was too weak to generate sustained job growth.

The low interest rates led to a large increase in residential investment spending, reflected in a surge of housing starts, shown in panel (b). This rise in investment spending drove an overall economic expansion, both through its direct effects and through the spending multiplier process.

Unfortunately, the housing boom eventually turned into too much of a good thing. By 2006, it was clear that the U.S. housing market was experiencing a bubble: people were buying housing based on unrealistic expectations about future price increases. When the bubble burst, housing—and the U.S. economy—took a fall. The fall was so severe that, even when the Fed cut interest rates to near zero and mortgage rates consequently dropped to below 5% beginning in 2009, housing starts merely stabilized. As of early 2014, housing starts had not yet fully recovered.

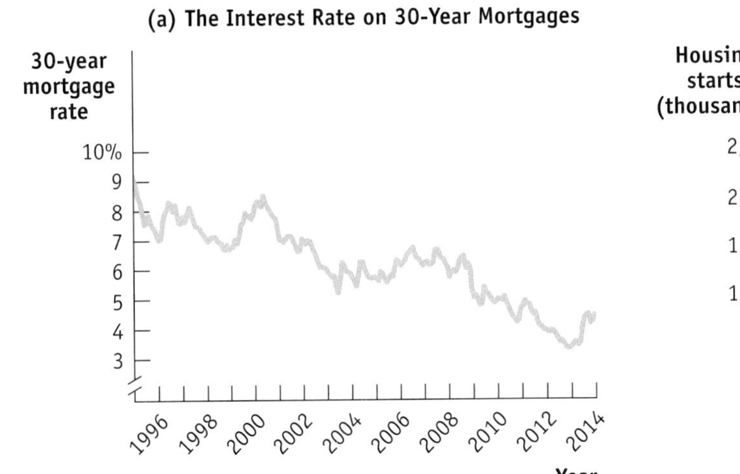

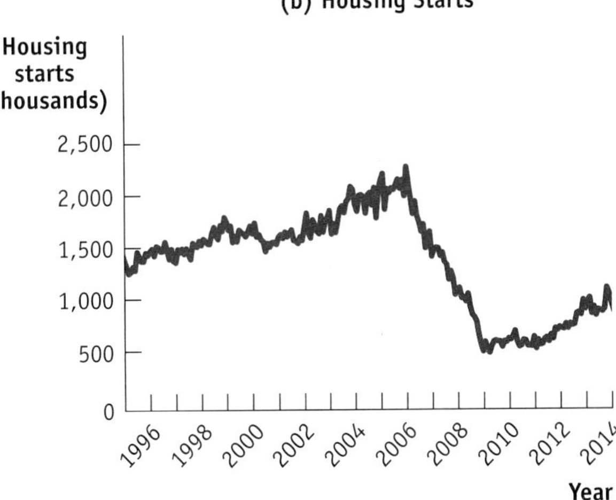

Source: Federal Reserve Bank of St. Louis.

Now imagine that next month's actual sales are less than expected, only 700,000 cars. As a result, the value of 100,000 cars will be added to investment spending as unplanned inventory investment.

The auto industry will, of course, eventually adjust to this slowdown in sales and the resulting unplanned inventory investment. It is likely that it will cut next month's production volume in order to reduce inventories. In fact, economists who study macroeconomic variables in an attempt to determine the future path of the economy pay careful attention to changes in inventory levels. Rising inventories typically indicate positive unplanned inventory investment and a slowing economy, as sales are less than had been forecast. Falling inventories typically indicate negative unplanned inventory investment and a growing economy, as sales are greater than forecast. In the next section, we will see how production adjustments in response to fluctuations in sales and inventories ensure that the value of final goods and services actually produced is equal to desired purchases of those final goods and services.

MODULE 16 Review

Check Your Understanding

1. Explain why a decline in investment spending caused by a change in business expectations leads to a fall in consumer spending.
2. What is the spending multiplier if the marginal propensity to consume is 0.5? What is it if *MPC* is 0.8?
3. Suppose a crisis in the capital markets makes consumers unable to borrow and unable to save money. What implication does this have for the effects of expected future disposable income on consumer spending?
4. For each event, explain whether the initial effect is a change in planned investment spending or a change in unplanned inventory investment, and indicate the direction of the change.
   a. an unexpected increase in consumer spending
   b. a sharp rise in the interest rate
   c. a sharp increase in the economy's growth rate of real GDP
   d. an unanticipated fall in sales

Tackle the Test: Multiple-Choice Questions

1. Changes in which of the following leads to a shift of the aggregate consumption function?
   I. expected future disposable income
   II. aggregate wealth
   III. current disposable income
   a. I only
   b. II only
   c. III only
   d. I and II only
   e. I, II, and III
2. The slope of a household's consumption function is equal to
   a. the real interest rate.
   b. the inflation rate.
   c. the marginal propensity to consume.
   d. the rate of increase in household current disposable income.
   e. the tax rate.
3. Given the aggregate consumption function $C = \$1.6$ trillion $+ 0.5Y_D$, if aggregate current disposable income is \$2.0 trillion, aggregate consumption spending will equal
   a. \$3.6 trillion.
   b. \$2.6 trillion.
   c. \$2.0 trillion.
   d. \$1.6 trillion.
   e. \$0.6 trillion.
4. The level of planned investment spending is negatively related to
   a. the rate of return on investment.
   b. the level of consumer spending.
   c. the level of actual investment spending.
   d. the interest rate.
   e. all of the above.
5. Actual investment spending in any period is equal to
   a. planned investment spending + unplanned inventory investment.
   b. planned investment spending − unplanned inventory investment.
   c. planned investment spending + inventory decreases.
   d. unplanned inventory investment + inventory increases.
   e. unplanned inventory investment − inventory increases.

Tackle the Test: Free-Response Questions

1. Use the aggregate consumption function provided to answer the following questions:

$$C = \$1.5 \text{ trillion} + 0.8Y_D$$

   a. What is the value of the marginal propensity to consume?
   b. Suppose aggregate current disposable income is \$4.0 trillion. Calculate the amount of aggregate consumer spending.
   c. Draw a correctly labeled graph showing this aggregate consumption function.
   d. What is the slope of this aggregate consumption function?
   e. On your graph from part c, show what would happen if expected future income decreases.

Rubric for FRQ 1 (7 points)

1 point: 0.8

1 point: $4.7 trillion

1 point: Vertical axis labeled "Aggregate consumer spending" and horizontal axis labeled "Aggregate current disposable income"

1 point: Vertical intercept of $1.5 trillion

1 point: Upward-sloping aggregate consumption function

1 point: 0.8

1 point: Aggregate consumption function shifts downward

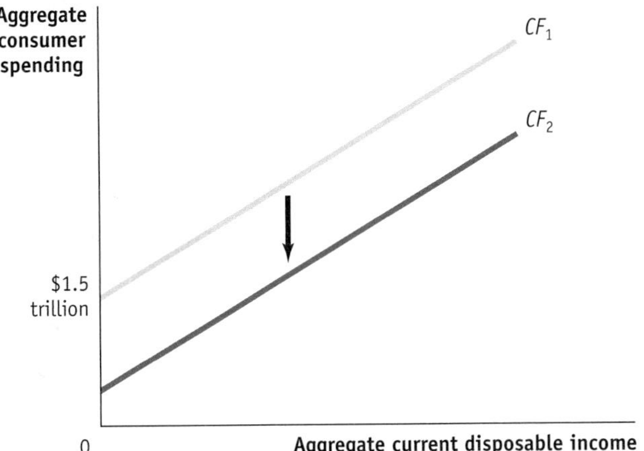

2. List the three most important factors affecting planned investment spending. Explain how each is related to actual investment spending.

(6 points)

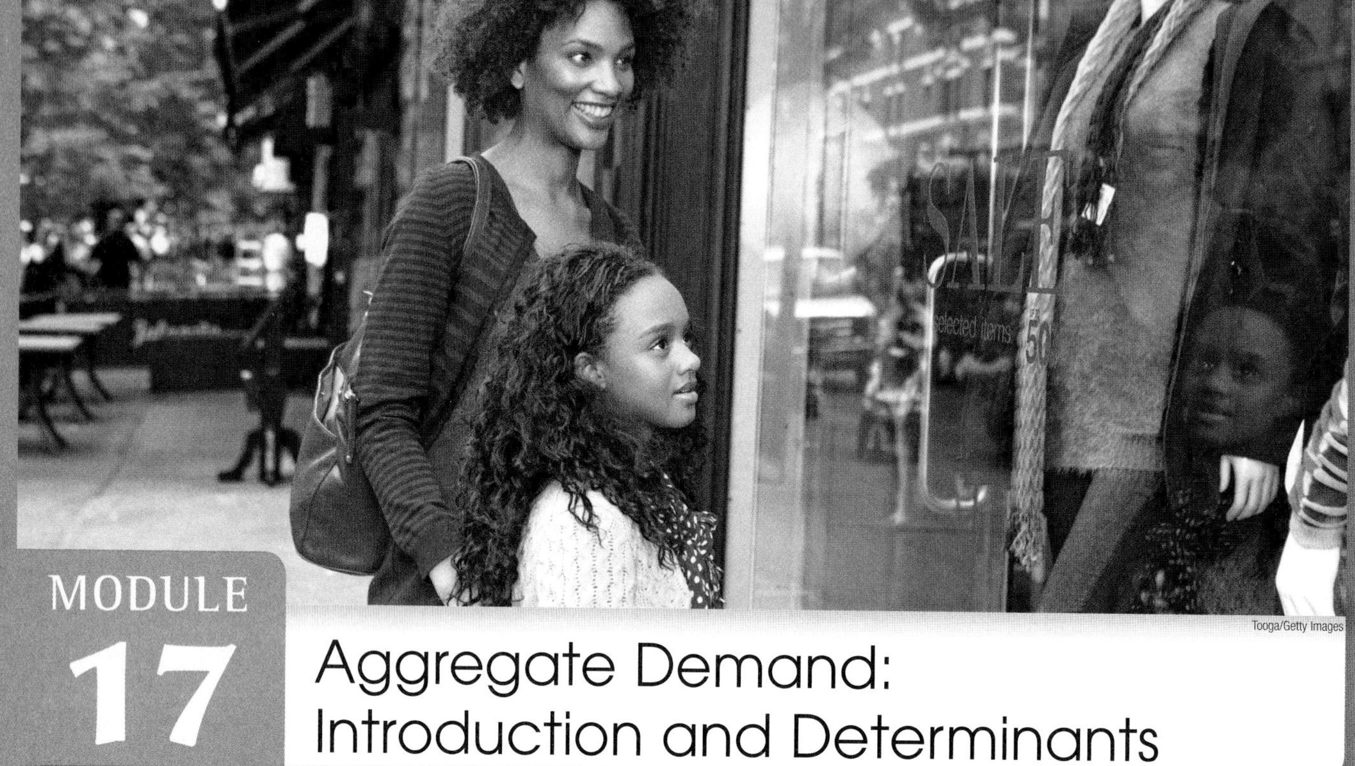

Tooga/Getty Images

MODULE 17 Aggregate Demand: Introduction and Determinants

In this Module, you will learn to:

- Use the aggregate demand curve to illustrate the relationship between the aggregate price level and the quantity of aggregate output demanded in the economy
- Explain how the wealth effect and the interest rate effect give the aggregate demand curve a negative slope
- Identify the factors that can shift the aggregate demand curve

Aggregate Demand

AP® Exam Tip

Aggregate demand is the demand for all goods and services in all markets rather than the demand for one good or service in one market.

The Great Depression, the great majority of economists agree, was the result of a massive negative demand shock. What does that mean? When economists talk about a fall in the demand for a particular good or service, they're referring to a leftward shift of the demand curve. Similarly, when economists talk about a negative demand shock to the economy as a whole, they're referring to a leftward shift of the **aggregate demand curve**, a curve that shows the relationship between the aggregate price level and the quantity of aggregate output demanded by households, firms, the government, and the rest of the world.

Figure 17.1 shows what the aggregate demand curve may have looked like in 1933, at the end of the 1929–1933 recession. The horizontal axis shows the total quantity of domestic goods and services demanded, measured in 2005 dollars. We use real GDP to measure aggregate output and will use the two terms interchangeably. The vertical axis shows the aggregate price level, measured by the GDP deflator. With these variables on the axes, we can draw a curve, *AD*, that shows how much aggregate output would have been demanded at any given aggregate price level. Since *AD* is meant to illustrate aggregate demand in 1933, one point on the curve corresponds to actual data for 1933, when the aggregate price level was 7.9 and the total quantity of domestic final goods and services purchased was $716 billion in 2005 dollars.

The **aggregate demand curve** shows the relationship between the aggregate price level and the quantity of aggregate output demanded by households, businesses, the government, and the rest of the world.

As drawn in Figure 17.1, the aggregate demand curve is downward sloping, indicating a negative relationship between the aggregate price level and the quantity of aggregate output demanded. A higher aggregate price level, other things equal, reduces the quantity of aggregate output demanded; a lower aggregate price level, other things equal,

Figure 17.1 The Aggregate Demand Curve

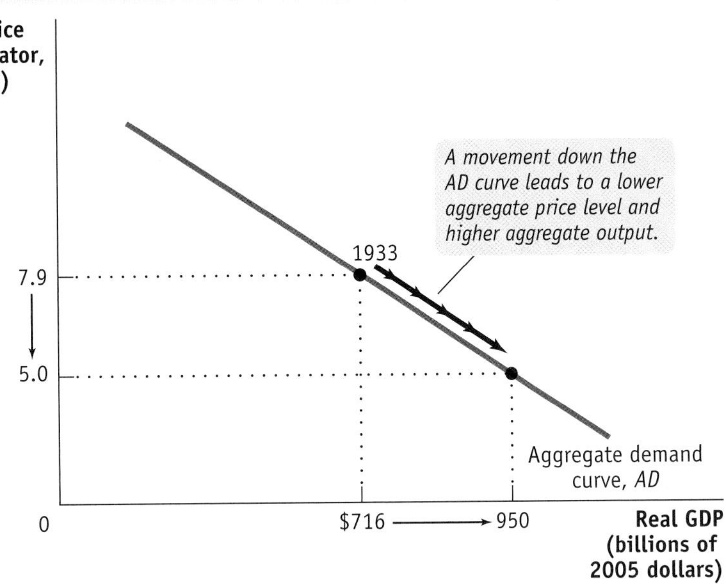

The aggregate demand curve shows the relationship between the aggregate price level and the quantity of aggregate output demanded. The curve is downward sloping due to the wealth effect of a change in the aggregate price level and the interest rate effect of a change in the aggregate price level. Corresponding to the actual 1933 data, here the total quantity of goods and services demanded at an aggregate price level of 7.9 is $716 billion in 2005 dollars. According to our hypothetical curve, however, if the aggregate price level had been only 5.0, the quantity of aggregate output demanded would have risen to $950 billion.

increases the quantity of aggregate output demanded. According to Figure 17.1, if the price level in 1933 had been 5.0 instead of 7.9, the total quantity of domestic final goods and services demanded would have been $950 billion in 2005 dollars instead of $716 billion.

The first key question about the aggregate demand curve involves its negative slope.

AP® Exam Tip

Notice the axis labels in Figure 17.1. These will be important when you create *AD–AS* graphs. Points are awarded for correctly drawn and labeled graphs on the AP® exam.

Why Is the Aggregate Demand Curve Downward Sloping?

In Figure 17.1, the curve *AD* slopes downward. Why? Recall the basic equation of national income accounting:

$$\textbf{(17-1)}\quad GDP = C + I + G + X - IM$$

where C is consumer spending, I is investment spending, G is government purchases of goods and services, X is exports to other countries, and IM is imports. If we measure these variables in constant dollars—that is, in prices of a base year—then $C + I + G + X - IM$ represents the quantity of domestically produced final goods and services demanded during a given period. G is decided by the government, but the other variables are private-sector decisions. To understand why the aggregate demand curve slopes downward, we need to understand why a rise in the aggregate price level reduces C, I, and $X - IM$.

You might think that the downward slope of the aggregate demand curve is a natural consequence of the *law of demand*. That is, since the demand curve for any one good is downward-sloping, isn't it natural that the demand curve for aggregate output is also downward-sloping? This turns out, however, to be a misleading parallel. The demand curve for any individual good shows how the quantity demanded depends on the price of that good, *holding the prices of other goods and services constant.* The main reason the quantity of a good demanded falls when the price of that good rises—that is, the quantity of a good demanded falls as we move up the demand curve—is that people switch their consumption to other goods and services that have become relatively less expensive.

But when we consider movements up or down the aggregate demand curve, we're considering *a simultaneous change in the prices of all final goods and services.* Furthermore, changes in the composition of goods and services in consumer spending aren't relevant to the aggregate demand curve: if consumers decide to buy fewer clothes but more cars, this doesn't necessarily change the total quantity of final goods and services they demand.

Why, then, does a rise in the aggregate price level lead to a fall in the quantity of all domestically produced final goods and services demanded? There are two main reasons: the *wealth effect* and the *interest rate effect* of a change in the aggregate price level.

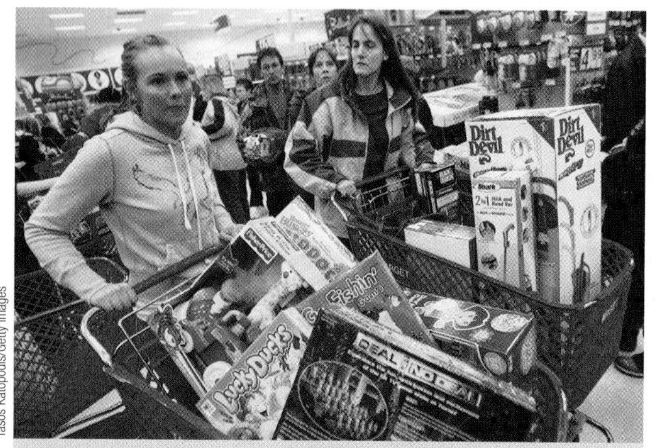

Tasos Katopodis/Getty Images

When the aggregate price level falls, the purchasing power of consumers' assets rises, leading shoppers to place more items in their carts.

The Wealth Effect An increase in the aggregate price level, other things equal, reduces the purchasing power of many assets. Consider, for example, someone who has \$5,000 in a bank account. If the aggregate price level were to rise by 25%, that \$5,000 would buy only as much as \$4,000 would have bought previously. With the loss in purchasing power, the owner of that bank account would probably scale back his or her consumption plans. Millions of other people would respond the same way, leading to a fall in spending on final goods and services, because a rise in the aggregate price level reduces the purchasing power of everyone's bank account.

Correspondingly, a fall in the aggregate price level increases the purchasing power of consumers' assets and leads to more consumer demand. The **wealth effect of a change in the aggregate price level** is the change in consumer spending caused by the altered purchasing power of consumers' assets. Because of the wealth effect, consumer spending, *C*, falls when the aggregate price level rises, leading to a downward-sloping aggregate demand curve.

AP® Exam Tip

You may see a question about the wealth or interest rate effects on the AP® exam. They will help you explain why *AD* is downward-sloping.

The Interest Rate Effect Economists use the term *money* in its narrowest sense to refer to cash and bank deposits on which people can write checks. People and firms hold money because it reduces the cost and inconvenience of making transactions. An increase in the aggregate price level, other things equal, reduces the purchasing power of a given amount of money holdings. To purchase the same basket of goods and services as before, people and firms now need to hold more money. So, in response to an increase in the aggregate price level, the public tries to increase its money holdings, either by borrowing more or by selling assets such as bonds. This reduces the funds available for lending to other borrowers and drives interest rates up. A rise in the interest rate reduces investment spending because it makes the cost of borrowing higher. It also reduces consumer spending because households save more of their disposable income. So a rise in the aggregate price level depresses investment spending, *I*, and consumer spending, *C*, through its effect on the purchasing power of money holdings, an effect known as the **interest rate effect of a change in the aggregate price level**. This also leads to a downward-sloping aggregate demand curve.

The **wealth effect of a change in the aggregate price level** is the change in consumer spending caused by the altered purchasing power of consumers' assets.

The **interest rate effect of a change in the aggregate price level** is the change in investment and consumer spending caused by altered interest rates that result from changes in the demand for money.

Shifts of the Aggregate Demand Curve

When we introduced the analysis of supply and demand in the market for an individual good, we stressed the importance of the distinction between *movements along* the demand curve and *shifts of* the demand curve. The same distinction applies to the aggregate demand curve. Figure 17.1 shows a *movement along* the aggregate demand

Figure 17.2 Shifts of the Aggregate Demand Curve

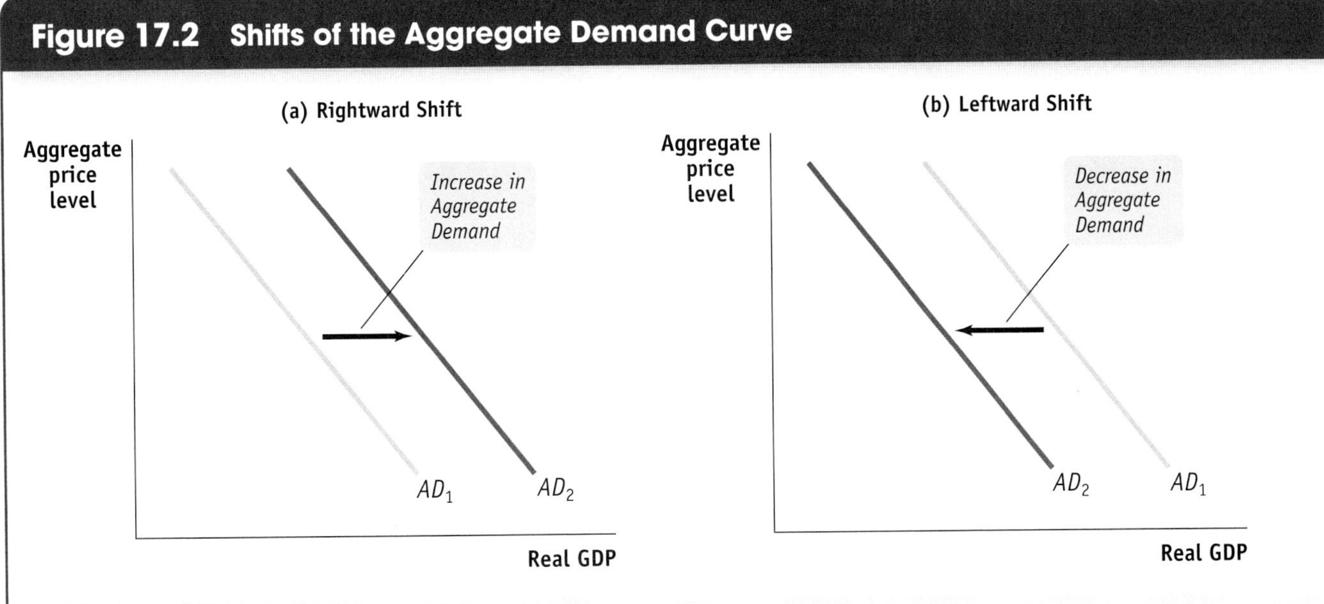

Panel (a) shows the effect of events that increase the quantity of aggregate output demanded at any given aggregate price level, such as a rise in consumer optimism about future income or a rise in government spending. Such changes shift the aggregate demand curve to the right, from AD_1 to AD_2. Panel (b) shows the effect of events that decrease the quantity of aggregate output demanded at any given aggregate price level, such as a fall in wealth caused by a stock market decline. This shifts the aggregate demand curve leftward from AD_1 to AD_2.

curve, a change in the aggregate quantity of goods and services demanded as the aggregate price level changes. But there can also be *shifts of* the aggregate demand curve, changes in the quantity of goods and services demanded at any given price level, as shown in **Figure 17.2**. When we talk about an increase in aggregate demand, we mean a shift of the aggregate demand curve to the right, as shown in panel (a) by the shift from AD_1 to AD_2. A rightward shift occurs when the quantity of aggregate output demanded increases at any given aggregate price level. A decrease in aggregate demand means that the *AD* curve shifts to the left, as in panel (b). A leftward shift implies that the quantity of aggregate output demanded falls at any given aggregate price level.

A number of factors can shift the aggregate demand curve. Among the most important factors are changes in expectations, changes in wealth, and the size of the existing stock of physical capital. In addition, both fiscal and monetary policy can shift the aggregate demand curve. All five factors set the spending multiplier process in motion. By causing an initial rise or fall in real GDP, they change disposable income, which leads to additional changes in aggregate spending, which lead to further changes in real GDP, and so on. For an overview of factors that shift the aggregate demand curve, see **Table 17.1** on the next page.

Changes in Expectations Both consumer spending and planned investment spending depend in part on people's expectations about the future. Consumers base their spending not only on the income they have now but also on the income they expect to have in the future. Firms base their planned investment spending not only on current conditions but also on the sales they expect to make in the future. As a result, changes in expectations can push consumer spending and planned investment spending up or down. If consumers and firms become more optimistic, aggregate spending rises; if they become more pessimistic, aggregate spending falls. In fact, short-run economic forecasters pay careful attention to surveys of consumer and business sentiment. In particular, forecasters watch the Consumer Confidence Index, a monthly measure calculated by the Conference Board, and the Michigan Consumer Sentiment Index, a similar measure calculated by the University of Michigan.

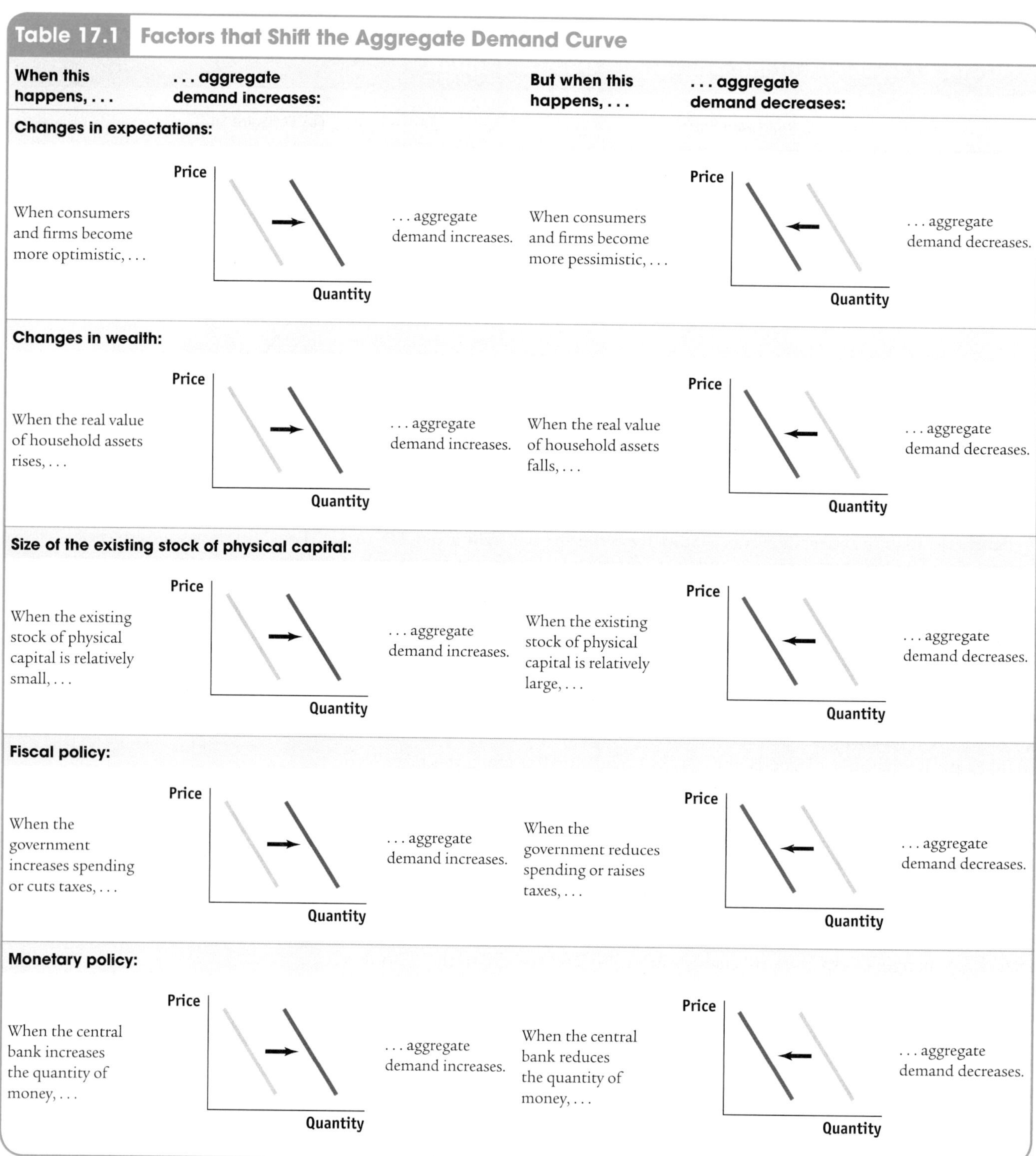

Table 17.1 Factors that Shift the Aggregate Demand Curve

When this happens, . . .	. . . aggregate demand increases:	But when this happens, . . .	. . . aggregate demand decreases:
Changes in expectations:			
When consumers and firms become more optimistic, . . .	. . . aggregate demand increases.	When consumers and firms become more pessimistic, . . .	. . . aggregate demand decreases.
Changes in wealth:			
When the real value of household assets rises, . . .	. . . aggregate demand increases.	When the real value of household assets falls, . . .	. . . aggregate demand decreases.
Size of the existing stock of physical capital:			
When the existing stock of physical capital is relatively small, . . .	. . . aggregate demand increases.	When the existing stock of physical capital is relatively large, . . .	. . . aggregate demand decreases.
Fiscal policy:			
When the government increases spending or cuts taxes, . . .	. . . aggregate demand increases.	When the government reduces spending or raises taxes, . . .	. . . aggregate demand decreases.
Monetary policy:			
When the central bank increases the quantity of money, . . .	. . . aggregate demand increases.	When the central bank reduces the quantity of money, . . .	. . . aggregate demand decreases.

Changes in Wealth Consumer spending depends in part on the value of household assets. When the real value of these assets rises, the purchasing power they embody also rises, leading to an increase in aggregate spending. For example, in the 1990s, there was a significant rise in the stock market that increased aggregate demand. And when the real value of household assets falls—for example, because of a stock market crash—the purchasing power they embody is reduced and aggregate demand also falls. The stock market crash of 1929 was a significant factor leading to the Great Depression. Similarly, a sharp decline in real estate values was a major factor depressing consumer spending in 2008.

Size of the Existing Stock of Physical Capital Firms engage in planned investment spending to add to their stock of physical capital. Their incentive to spend depends in part on how much physical capital they already have: the more they have, the less they will feel a need to add more, other things equal. The same applies to other types of investment spending—for example, if a large number of houses have been built in recent years, this will depress the demand for new houses and, as a result, will also tend to reduce residential investment spending. In fact, that's part of the reason for the deep slump in residential investment spending that began in 2006. The housing boom of the previous few years had created an oversupply of houses: by spring 2008, the inventory of unsold houses on the market was equal to more than 11 months of sales, and prices had fallen more than 20% from their peak. This gave the construction industry little incentive to build even more homes.

BROOKLYN DAILY EAGLE
And Complete Long Island News
LATE NEWS
WALL STREET 1:15 PRICES ★★
NEW YORK CITY, THURSDAY, OCTOBER 24, 1929.
32 PAGES

WALL ST. IN PANIC AS STOCKS CRASH

Attempt Made to Kill Italy's Crown Prince

ASSASSIN CAUGHT IN BRUSSELS MOB: PRINCE UNHURT

Royal Suitor Was About to Lay Wreath on Unknown Soldiers' Tomb.

Princess, Deeply Moved, Falls Into Fiance's Arms and Kisses Him

ATTEMPT MADE ON LIFE

Crown Prince Humbert.

Hollywood Fire Destroys Films Worth Millions

Consolidated Studios Are Swept by Flames Fatal to One—Master Pictures Burned Include Many New Talkie Productions.

FEAR 52 PERISHED IN LAKE MICHIGAN; FERRY IS MISSING

Wreckage Picked Up Indicates Craft Went Down With All Aboard.

PIECE OF PLANE LIKE DITEMAN'S IS FOUND AT SEA

Black and Orange Wreckage Indicates Daring Flier Went to Death.

High Duty Group Gave $700,000 to Coolidge Drive

Grundy Agrees Rates Went Up Due to His Activities as Propagandist. Favors More Lobbying to 'Carry Out Voters' Wish.'

FOR MORE LOBBYISTS

JOSEPH R. GRUNDY

STOCKS CRASH IN RUSH TO SELL; BILLIONS LOST

Morgan, Mitchell Buying Stocks in Effort to Check Rush to Unload.

CARNEGIE CHARGE OF PAID ATHLETES

HOOVER'S TRAIN HALTED BY AUTO

WARDER SOUGHT TO KEEP SEA TRIP

SOMERS NAMED AS HEAD OF NEW

FPG/Getty Images

The loss of wealth resulting from the stock market crash of 1929 was a significant factor leading to the Great Depression.

Government Policies and Aggregate Demand One of the key insights of macroeconomics is that the government can have a powerful influence on aggregate demand and that, in some circumstances, this influence can be used to improve economic performance.

The two main ways the government can influence the aggregate demand curve are through *fiscal policy* and *monetary policy*. We'll briefly discuss their influence on aggregate demand, leaving a full-length discussion for later.

Fiscal Policy **Fiscal policy** is the use of either government spending—government purchases of final goods and services and government transfers—or tax policy to stabilize the economy. In practice, governments often respond to recessions by increasing spending, cutting taxes, or both. They often respond to inflation by reducing spending or increasing taxes.

Fiscal policy is the use of government purchases of goods and services, government transfers, or tax policy to stabilize the economy.

The effect of government purchases of final goods and services, *G*, on the aggregate demand curve is *direct* because government purchases are themselves a component of aggregate demand. So an increase in government purchases shifts the aggregate demand curve to the right and a decrease shifts it to the left. History's most dramatic example of how increased government purchases affect aggregate demand was the effect of wartime government spending during World War II. Because of the war, purchases by the U.S. federal government surged 400%. This increase in purchases is usually credited with ending the Great Depression. In the 1990s, Japan used large public works projects—such as government-financed construction of roads, bridges, and dams—in an effort to increase aggregate demand in the face of a slumping economy.

In contrast, changes in either tax rates or government transfers influence the economy *indirectly* through their effect on disposable income. A lower tax rate means that consumers get to keep more of what they earn, increasing their disposable income. An increase in government transfers also increases consumers' disposable income. In either case, this increases consumer spending and shifts the aggregate demand curve to the right. A higher tax rate or a reduction in transfers reduces the amount of disposable income received by consumers. This reduces consumer spending and shifts the aggregate demand curve to the left.

Monetary Policy In the next section, we will study the Federal Reserve System and monetary policy in detail. At this point, we just need to note that the Federal Reserve controls **monetary policy**—the use of changes in the quantity of money or the interest rate to stabilize the economy. We've just discussed how a rise in the aggregate price level, by reducing the purchasing power of money holdings, causes a rise in the interest rate. That, in turn, reduces both investment spending and consumer spending.

Monetary policy is the central bank's use of changes in the quantity of money or the interest rate to stabilize the economy.

But what happens if the quantity of money in the hands of households and firms changes? In modern economies, the quantity of money in circulation is largely determined by the decisions of a *central bank* created by the government. As we'll learn in more detail later, the Federal Reserve, the U.S. central bank, is a special institution that is neither exactly part of the government nor exactly a private institution. When the central bank increases the quantity of money in circulation, households and firms have more money, which they are willing to lend out. The effect is to drive the interest rate down at any given aggregate price level, leading to higher investment spending and higher consumer spending. That is, increasing the quantity of money shifts the aggregate demand curve to the right. Reducing the quantity of money has the opposite effect: households and firms have less money holdings than before, leading them to borrow more and lend less. This raises the interest rate, reduces investment spending and consumer spending, and shifts the aggregate demand curve to the left.

MODULE 17 Review

Check Your Understanding

1. Determine the effect on aggregate demand of each of the following events. Explain whether it represents a movement along the aggregate demand curve (up or down) or a shift of the curve (leftward or rightward).

a. a rise in the interest rate caused by a change in monetary policy

b. a fall in the real value of money in the economy due to a higher aggregate price level

c. news of a worse-than-expected job market next year

d. a fall in tax rates

e. a rise in the real value of assets in the economy due to a lower aggregate price level

f. a rise in the real value of assets in the economy due to a surge in real estate values

Tackle the Test: Multiple-Choice Questions

1. Which of the following explains the slope of the aggregate demand curve?

I. the wealth effect of a change in the aggregate price level

II. the interest rate effect of a change in the aggregate price level

III. the product-substitution effect of a change in the aggregate price level

a. I only

b. II only

c. III only

d. I and II only

e. I, II, and III

2. Which of the following will shift the aggregate demand curve to the right?

a. a decrease in wealth

b. pessimistic consumer expectations

c. a decrease in the existing stock of capital

d. contractionary fiscal policy

e. a decrease in the quantity of money

3. The Consumer Confidence Index is used to measure which of the following?

a. the level of consumer spending

b. the rate of return on investments

c. consumer expectations

d. planned investment spending

e. the level of current disposable income

4. Decreases in the stock market decrease aggregate demand by decreasing which of the following?

a. consumer wealth

b. the price level

c. the stock of existing physical capital

d. interest rates

e. tax revenues

5. Which of the following government policies will shift the aggregate demand curve to the left?

a. a decrease in the quantity of money

b. an increase in government purchases of goods and services

c. a decrease in taxes

d. a decrease in interest rates

e. an increase in government transfers

Tackle the Test: Free-Response Questions

1. **a.** Draw a correctly labeled graph showing aggregate demand.
   b. On your graph from part a, illustrate an increase in aggregate demand.
   c. List the four factors that shift aggregate demand.
   d. Describe a change in each determinant of aggregate demand that would lead to the shift you illustrated in part b.

Rubric for FRQ 1 (12 points)

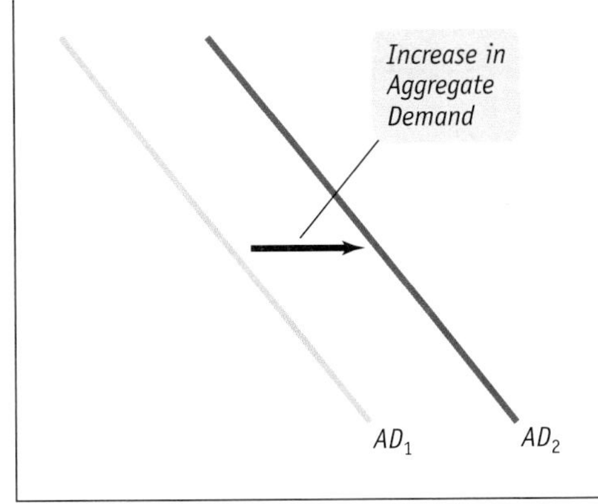

1 point: Vertical axis labeled "Aggregate price level" (or "Price level")

1 point: Horizontal axis labeled "Real GDP"

1 point: Downward-sloping curve labeled "*AD*" (or "AD_1")

1 point: *AD* curve shifted to the right

1 point: Expectations

1 point: Wealth

1 point: Size of existing stock of physical capital

1 point: Government policies

1 point: Consumers/Producers more confident

1 point: Increase in wealth

1 point: Lower existing stock of physical capital

1 point: An increase in government spending or in the money supply

2. Identify the two effects that cause the aggregate demand curve to have a downward slope. Explain each. **(4 points)**

Digital Vision

MODULE 18 Aggregate Supply: Introduction and Determinants

In this Module, you will learn to:

- Use the aggregate supply curve to illustrate the relationship between the aggregate price level and the quantity of aggregate output supplied in the economy
- Identify the factors that can shift the aggregate supply curve
- Explain why the aggregate supply curve is different in the short run from in the long run

Aggregate Supply

Between 1929 and 1933, there was a sharp fall in aggregate demand—a reduction in the quantity of goods and services demanded at any given price level. One consequence of the economy-wide decline in demand was a fall in the prices of most goods and services. By 1933, the GDP deflator (one of the price indexes) was 26% below its 1929 level, and other indexes were down by similar amounts. A second consequence was a decline in the output of most goods and services: by 1933, real GDP was 27% below its 1929 level. A third consequence, closely tied to the fall in real GDP, was a surge in the unemployment rate from 3% to 25%.

The **aggregate supply curve** shows the relationship between the aggregate price level and the quantity of aggregate output supplied in the economy.

The association between the plunge in real GDP and the plunge in prices wasn't an accident. Between 1929 and 1933, the U.S. economy was moving down its **aggregate supply curve**, which shows the relationship between the economy's aggregate price level (the overall price level of final goods and services in the economy) and the total quantity of final goods and services, or aggregate output, producers are willing to supply. (As you will recall, we use real GDP to measure aggregate output, and we'll often use the two terms interchangeably.) More specifically, between 1929 and 1933, the U.S. economy moved down its *short-run aggregate supply curve.*

The Short-Run Aggregate Supply Curve

The period from 1929 to 1933 demonstrated that there is a positive relationship in the short run between the aggregate price level and the quantity of aggregate output supplied. That is, a rise in the aggregate price level is associated with a rise in the quantity of aggregate output supplied, other things equal; a fall in the aggregate price level is associated with a fall in the quantity of aggregate output supplied, other things equal. To understand why this positive relationship exists, consider the most basic question facing a producer: is producing a unit of output profitable or not? Let's define profit per unit:

(18-1) Profit per unit of output =
Price per unit of output − Production cost per unit of output

Thus, the answer to the question depends on whether the price the producer receives for a unit of output is greater or less than the cost of producing that unit of output. At any given point in time, many of the costs producers face are fixed per unit of output and can't be changed for an extended period of time. Typically, the largest source of inflexible production cost is the wages paid to workers. *Wages* here refers to all forms of worker compensation, including employer-paid health care and retirement benefits in addition to earnings.

Wages are typically an inflexible production cost because the dollar amount of any given wage paid, called the **nominal wage**, is often determined by contracts that were signed some time ago. And even when there are no formal contracts, there are often informal agreements between management and workers, making companies reluctant to change wages in response to economic conditions. For example, companies usually will not reduce wages during poor economic times—unless the downturn has been particularly long and severe—for fear of generating worker resentment. Correspondingly, they typically won't raise wages during better economic times—until they are at risk of losing workers to competitors—because they don't want to encourage workers to routinely demand higher wages. As a result of both formal and informal agreements, then, the economy is characterized by **sticky wages**: nominal wages that are slow to fall even in the face of high unemployment and slow to rise even in the face of labor shortages. It's important to note, however, that nominal wages cannot be sticky forever: ultimately, formal contracts and informal agreements will be renegotiated to take into account changed economic circumstances. How long it takes for nominal wages to become flexible is an integral component of what distinguishes the short run from the long run.

AP® Exam Tip

Because wages are "sticky," they fall very slowly even when the unemployment rate is high. This is important to know when you look at how the economy reacts with no government involvement.

To understand how the fact that many costs are fixed in nominal terms gives rise to an upward-sloping short-run aggregate supply curve, it's helpful to know that prices are set somewhat differently in different kinds of markets. In *perfectly competitive markets,* producers take prices as given; in *imperfectly competitive markets,* producers have some ability to choose the prices they charge. In both kinds of markets, there is a positive relationship between prices and output in the short run, but for slightly different reasons.

The **nominal wage** is the dollar amount of the wage paid.

Sticky wages are nominal wages that are slow to fall even in the face of high unemployment and slow to rise even in the face of labor shortages.

Let's start with the behavior of producers in perfectly competitive markets; remember, they take the price as given. Imagine that, for some reason, the aggregate price level falls, which means that the price received by the typical producer of a final good or service falls. Because many production costs are fixed in the short run, the production cost per unit of output doesn't fall in proportion to the price of output. So the profit per unit of output declines, leading perfectly competitive producers to reduce the quantity supplied in the short run.

On the other hand, suppose that for some reason the aggregate price level rises. As a result, the typical producer receives a higher price for its final good or service. Again, many production costs are fixed in the short run, so the production cost per unit of output doesn't rise in proportion to the rise in the price of a unit. And since the typical perfectly competitive producer takes the price as given, profit per unit of output rises and output increases.

Now consider an imperfectly competitive producer that is able to set its own price. If there is a rise in the demand for this producer's product, it will be able to sell more at any given price. Given stronger demand for its products, it will probably choose to increase its prices as well as its output, as a way of increasing profit per unit of output.

In fact, industry analysts often talk about variations in an industry's "pricing power": when demand is strong, firms with pricing power are able to raise prices—and they do.

Conversely, if there is a fall in demand, firms will normally try to limit the fall in their sales by cutting prices.

Both the responses of firms in perfectly competitive industries and those of firms in imperfectly competitive industries lead to an upward-sloping relationship between aggregate output and the aggregate price level. The positive relationship between the aggregate price level and the quantity of aggregate output producers are willing to supply during the time period when many production costs, particularly nominal wages, can be taken as fixed is illustrated by the **short-run aggregate supply curve**. The positive relationship between the aggregate price level and aggregate output in the short run gives the short-run aggregate supply curve its upward slope. **Figure 18.1** shows a hypothetical short-run aggregate supply curve, *SRAS,* that matches actual U.S. data for 1929 and 1933. On the horizontal axis is aggregate output (or, equivalently, real GDP)—the total quantity of final goods and services supplied in the economy—measured in 2005 dollars. On the vertical axis is the aggregate price level as measured by the GDP deflator, with the value for the year 2005 equal to 100. In 1929, the aggregate price level was 10.6 and real GDP was $977 billion. In 1933, the aggregate price level was 7.9 and real GDP was only $716 billion. The movement down the *SRAS* curve corresponds to the deflation and fall in aggregate output experienced over those years.

The **short-run aggregate supply curve** shows the relationship between the aggregate price level and the quantity of aggregate output supplied that exists in the short run, the time period when many production costs can be taken as fixed.

Shifts of the Short-Run Aggregate Supply Curve

Figure 18.1 shows a *movement along* the short-run aggregate supply curve, as the aggregate price level and aggregate output fell from 1929 to 1933. But there can also be *shifts of* the short-run aggregate supply curve, as shown in **Figure 18.2**. Panel (a) shows

Figure 18.1 The Short-Run Aggregate Supply Curve

The short-run aggregate supply curve shows the relationship between the aggregate price level and the quantity of aggregate output supplied in the short run, the period in which many production costs such as nominal wages are fixed. It is upward sloping because a higher aggregate price level leads to higher profit per unit of output and higher aggregate output given fixed nominal wages. Here we show numbers corresponding to the Great Depression, from 1929 to 1933: when deflation occurred and the aggregate price level fell from 10.6 (in 1929) to 7.9 (in 1933), firms responded by reducing the quantity of aggregate output supplied from $977 billion to $716 billion measured in 2005 dollars.

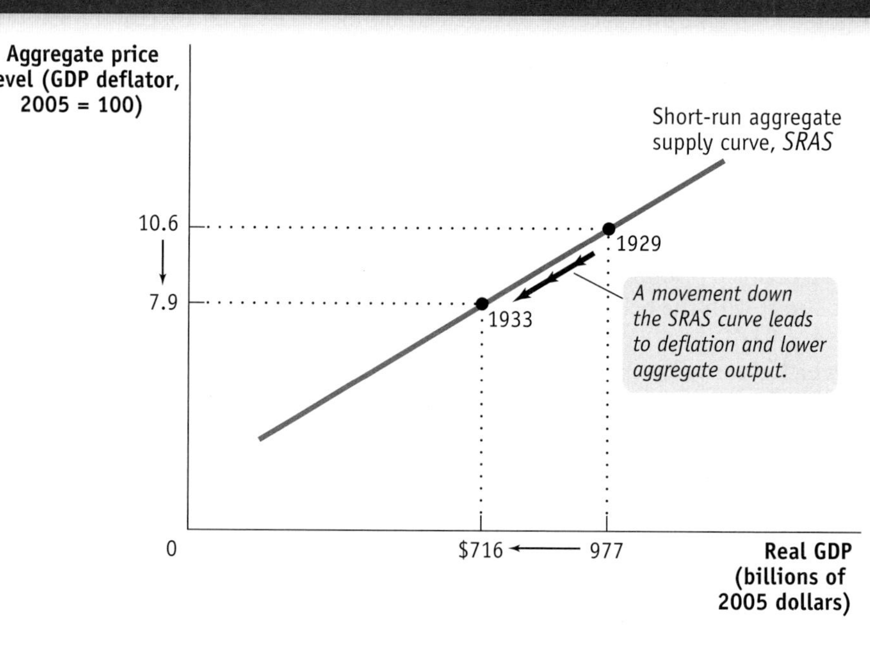

Figure 18.2 Shifts of the Short-Run Aggregate Supply Curve

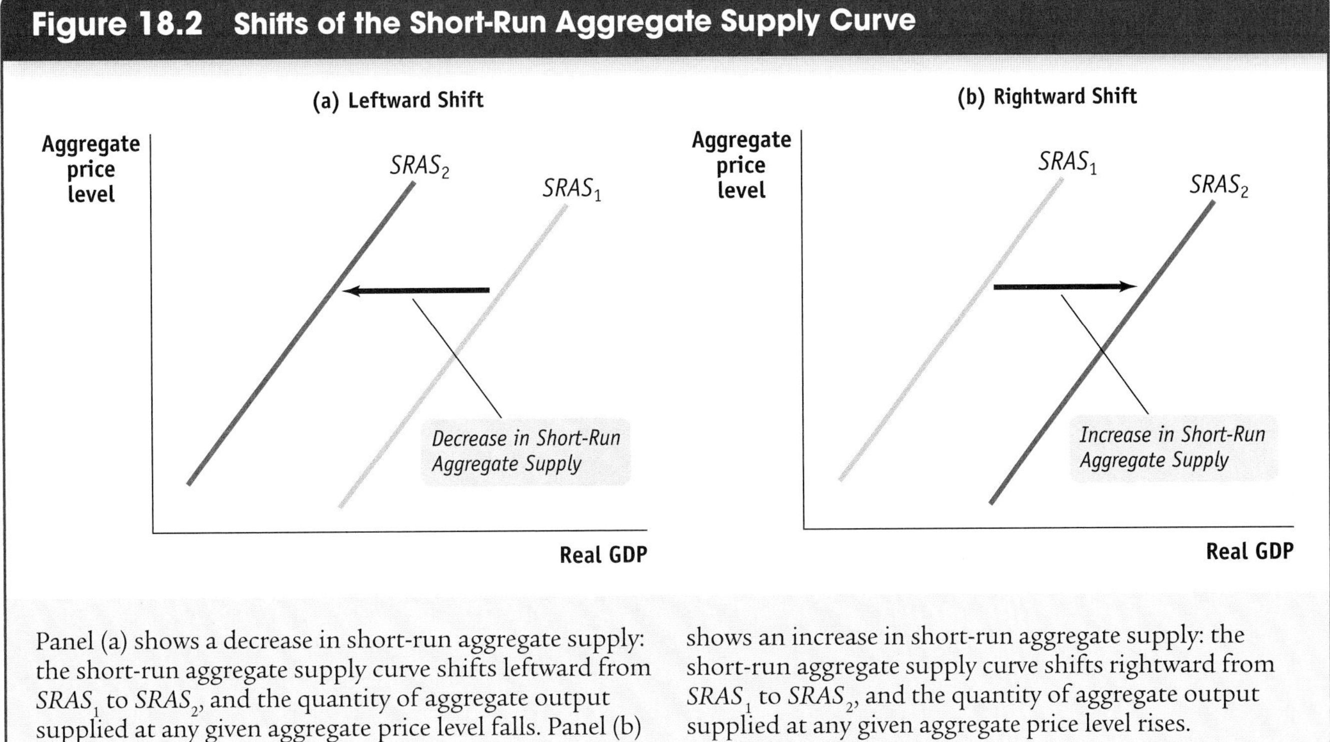

Panel (a) shows a decrease in short-run aggregate supply: the short-run aggregate supply curve shifts leftward from $SRAS_1$ to $SRAS_2$, and the quantity of aggregate output supplied at any given aggregate price level falls. Panel (b) shows an increase in short-run aggregate supply: the short-run aggregate supply curve shifts rightward from $SRAS_1$ to $SRAS_2$, and the quantity of aggregate output supplied at any given aggregate price level rises.

a *decrease in short-run aggregate supply*—a leftward shift of the short-run aggregate supply curve. Aggregate supply decreases when producers reduce the quantity of aggregate output they are willing to supply at any given aggregate price level. Panel (b) shows an *increase in short-run aggregate supply*—a rightward shift of the short-run aggregate supply curve. Aggregate supply increases when producers increase the quantity of aggregate output they are willing to supply at any given aggregate price level.

To understand why the short-run aggregate supply curve can shift, it's important to recall that producers make output decisions based on their profit per unit of output. The short-run aggregate supply curve illustrates the relationship between the aggregate price level and aggregate output: because some production costs are fixed in the short run, a change in the aggregate price level leads to a change in producers' profit per unit of output and, in turn, leads to a change in aggregate output. But other factors besides the aggregate price level can affect profit per unit and, in turn, aggregate output. It is changes in these other factors that will shift the short-run aggregate supply curve.

To develop some intuition, suppose something happens that raises production costs—say, an increase in the price of oil. At any given price of output, a producer now earns a smaller profit per unit of output. As a result, producers reduce the quantity supplied at any given aggregate price level, and the short-run aggregate supply curve shifts to the left. If, by contrast, something happens that lowers production costs—say, a fall in the nominal wage—a producer now earns a higher profit per unit of output at any given price of output. This leads producers to increase the quantity of aggregate output supplied at any given aggregate price level, and the short-run aggregate supply curve shifts to the right.

Now we'll look more closely at the link between important factors that affect producers' profit per unit and shifts in the short-run aggregate supply curve.

Changes in Commodity Prices A surge in the price of oil caused problems for the U.S. economy in the 1970s and in early 2008. Oil is a *commodity,* a standardized input bought and sold in bulk quantities. An increase in the price of a commodity—in

AP® Exam Tip

Remember, left is less and right is more. Shifting *SRAS* can be confusing because it appears as if left would be more because the line is higher on the graph. Look at the horizontal axis to see the resulting change in quantity to help you get this right.

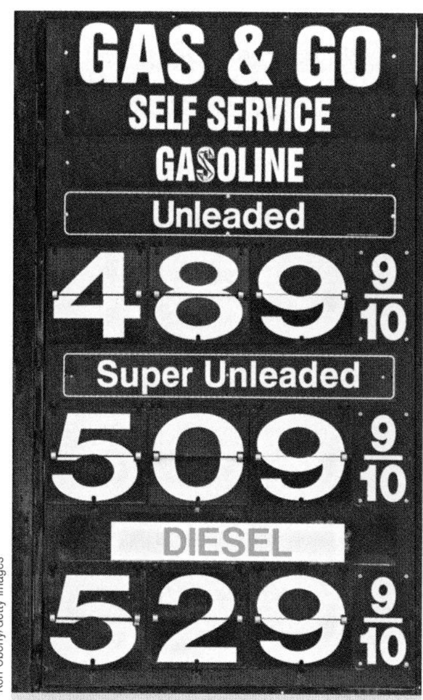

Keri Oberly/Getty Images

Signs of the times: high oil prices caused high gasoline prices in 2008.

this case, oil—raised production costs across the economy and reduced the quantity of aggregate output supplied at any given aggregate price level, shifting the short-run aggregate supply curve to the left. Conversely, a decline in commodity prices reduces production costs, leading to an increase in the quantity supplied at any given aggregate price level and a rightward shift of the short-run aggregate supply curve.

Why isn't the influence of commodity prices already captured by the short-run aggregate supply curve? Because commodities—unlike, say, soft drinks—are not a final good, their prices are not included in the calculation of the aggregate price level. Furthermore, commodities represent a significant cost of production to most suppliers, just like nominal wages do. So changes in commodity prices have large impacts on production costs. And in contrast to noncommodities, the prices of commodities can sometimes change drastically due to industry-specific shocks to supply—such as wars in the Middle East or rising Chinese demand that leaves less oil for the United States.

AP® Exam Tip

Think of a PEAR to remember the factors that shift *SRAS*:
Productivity
Expectations about inflation
Actions by the government (business taxes and subsidies)
Resource (input) prices like wages and commodities

Changes in Nominal Wages At any given point in time, the dollar wages of many workers are fixed because they are set by contracts or informal agreements made in the past. Nominal wages can change, however, once enough time has passed for contracts and informal agreements to be renegotiated. Suppose, for example, that there is an economy-wide rise in the cost of health care insurance premiums paid by employers as part of employees' wages. From the employers' perspective, this is equivalent to a rise in nominal wages because it is an increase in employer-paid compensation. So this rise in nominal wages increases production costs and shifts the short-run aggregate supply curve to the left. Conversely, suppose there is an economy-wide fall in the cost of such premiums. This is equivalent to a fall in nominal wages from the point of view of employers; it reduces production costs and shifts the short-run aggregate supply curve to the right.

An important historical fact is that during the 1970s, the surge in the price of oil had the indirect effect of also raising nominal wages. This "knock-on" effect occurred because many wage contracts included *cost-of-living allowances* that automatically raised the nominal wage when consumer prices increased. Through this channel, the surge in the price of oil—which led to an increase in overall consumer prices—ultimately caused a rise in nominal wages. So the economy, in the end, experienced two leftward shifts of the aggregate supply curve: the first generated by the initial surge in the price of oil and the second generated by the induced increase in nominal wages. The negative effect on the economy of rising oil prices was greatly magnified through the cost-of-living allowances in wage contracts. Today, cost-of-living allowances in wage contracts are rare.

Shutterstock

Almost every good purchased today has a UPC bar code on it, which allows stores to scan and track merchandise with great speed.

Changes in Productivity An increase in productivity means that a worker can produce more units of output with the same quantity of inputs. For example, the introduction of bar-code scanners in retail stores greatly increased the ability of a single worker to stock, inventory, and resupply store shelves. As a result, the cost to a store of "producing" a dollar of sales fell and profit rose. And, correspondingly, the quantity supplied increased. (Think of Walmart and the increase in the number of its stores as an increase in aggregate supply.) So a rise in productivity, whatever the source, increases producers' profits and shifts the short-run aggregate supply curve to the right.

Conversely, a fall in productivity—say, due to new regulations that require workers to spend more time filling out forms—reduces the number of units of output a worker can produce with the same quantity of inputs. Consequently, the cost per unit of output rises, profit falls, and quantity supplied falls. This shifts the short-run aggregate supply curve to the left.

Changes in Expectations about Inflation If inflation is expected to be higher than previously thought, workers will seek higher nominal wages to keep pace with the higher prices. Suppose you saw prices rising more rapidly than in the recent past. You might expect a particularly high inflation rate over the coming year. To prevent the expected inflation from eroding your real wages, you and other workers would pressure employers to raise nominal wages. As we've discussed, nominal wages are temporarily inflexible due to wage contracts, but when contracts are renewed and nominal wages rise, the short-run aggregate supply curve shifts to the left. Likewise, if inflation is expected to be lower than previously thought, workers will accept lower nominal wages and the short-run aggregate supply curve will shift to the right.

For a summary of the factors that shift the short-run aggregate supply curve, see **Table 18.1**.

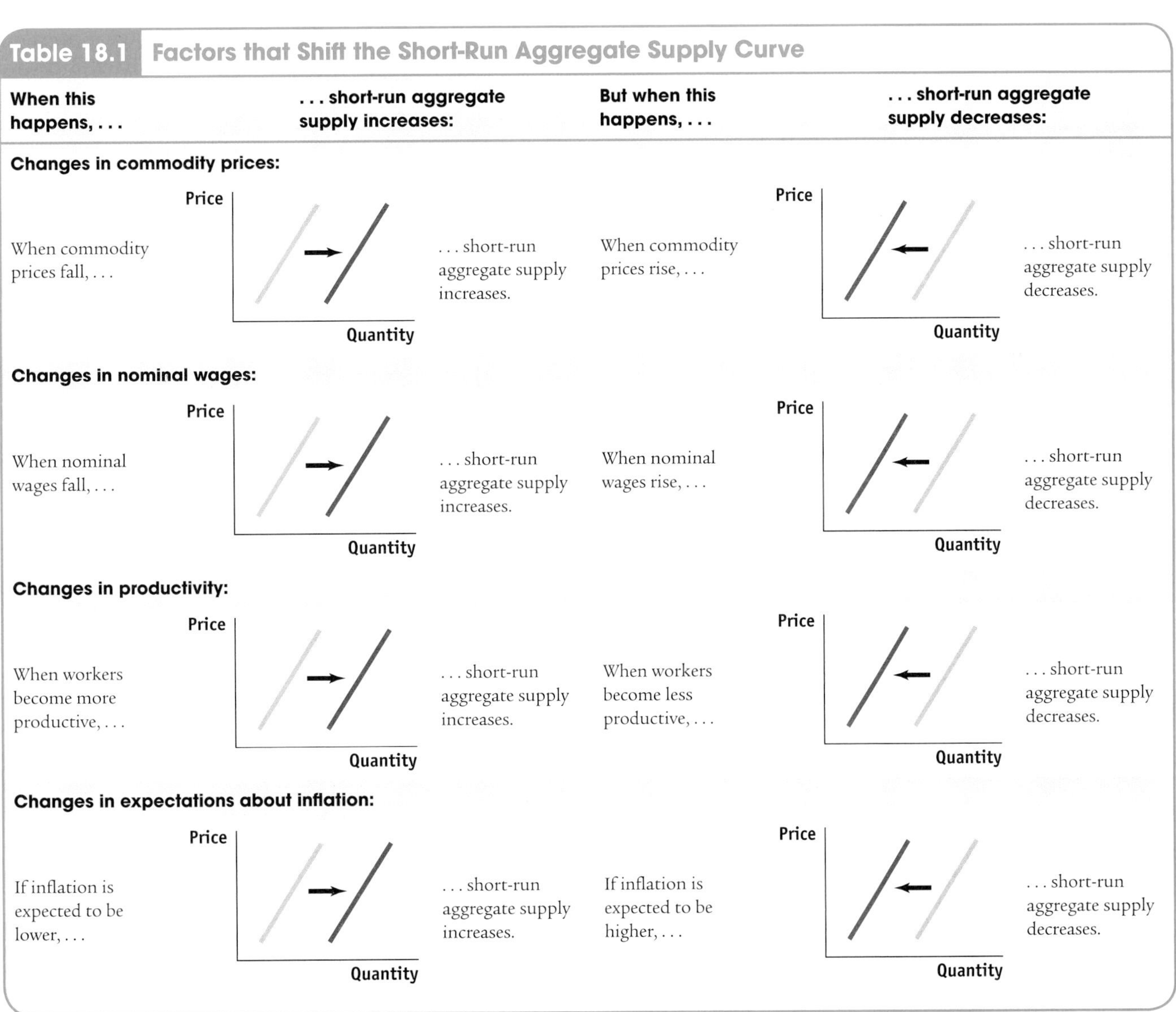

Table 18.1 Factors that Shift the Short-Run Aggregate Supply Curve

When this happens, . . .		. . . short-run aggregate supply increases:	But when this happens, . . .		. . . short-run aggregate supply decreases:
Changes in commodity prices:					
When commodity prices fall, . . .	Price / Quantity (curve shifts right)	. . . short-run aggregate supply increases.	When commodity prices rise, . . .	Price / Quantity (curve shifts left)	. . . short-run aggregate supply decreases.
Changes in nominal wages:					
When nominal wages fall, . . .	Price / Quantity (curve shifts right)	. . . short-run aggregate supply increases.	When nominal wages rise, . . .	Price / Quantity (curve shifts left)	. . . short-run aggregate supply decreases.
Changes in productivity:					
When workers become more productive, . . .	Price / Quantity (curve shifts right)	. . . short-run aggregate supply increases.	When workers become less productive, . . .	Price / Quantity (curve shifts left)	. . . short-run aggregate supply decreases.
Changes in expectations about inflation:					
If inflation is expected to be lower, . . .	Price / Quantity (curve shifts right)	. . . short-run aggregate supply increases.	If inflation is expected to be higher, . . .	Price / Quantity (curve shifts left)	. . . short-run aggregate supply decreases.

The Long-Run Aggregate Supply Curve

We've just seen that in the short run, a fall in the aggregate price level leads to a decline in the quantity of aggregate output supplied. This is the result of nominal wages that are sticky in the short run. But as we mentioned earlier, contracts and informal agreements are renegotiated in the long run. So in the long run, nominal wages—like the aggregate price level—are flexible, not sticky. Wage flexibility greatly alters the long-run relationship between the aggregate price level and aggregate supply. In fact, in the long run the aggregate price level has *no* effect on the quantity of aggregate output supplied.

To see why, let's conduct a thought experiment. Imagine that you could wave a magic wand—or maybe a magic bar-code scanner—and cut *all prices* in the economy in half at the same time. By "all prices" we mean the prices of all inputs, including nominal wages, as well as the prices of final goods and services. What would happen to aggregate output, given that the aggregate price level has been halved and all input prices, including nominal wages, have been halved?

The answer is: nothing. Consider Equation 18-1 again: each producer would receive a lower price for its product, but costs would fall by the same proportion. As a result, every unit of output that was profitable to produce before the change in prices would still be profitable to produce after the change in prices. So a halving of *all* prices in the economy has no effect on the economy's aggregate output. In other words, changes in the aggregate price level now have no effect on the quantity of aggregate output supplied.

In reality, of course, no one can change all prices by the same proportion at the same time. But now, we'll consider the *long run,* the period of time over which all prices are fully flexible. In the long run, inflation or deflation has the same effect as someone changing all prices by the same proportion. As a result, changes in the aggregate price level do not change the quantity of aggregate output supplied in the long run. That's because changes in the aggregate price level, in the long run, will be accompanied by equal proportional changes in *all* input prices, including nominal wages.

The **long-run aggregate supply curve** shows the relationship between the aggregate price level and the quantity of aggregate output supplied that would exist if all prices, including nominal wages, were fully flexible.

The **long-run aggregate supply curve**, illustrated in **Figure 18.3** by the curve *LRAS,* shows the relationship between the aggregate price level and the quantity of aggregate output supplied that would exist if all prices, including nominal wages, were fully flexible. The long-run aggregate supply curve is vertical because changes in the

Figure 18.3 The Long -Run Aggregate Supply Curve

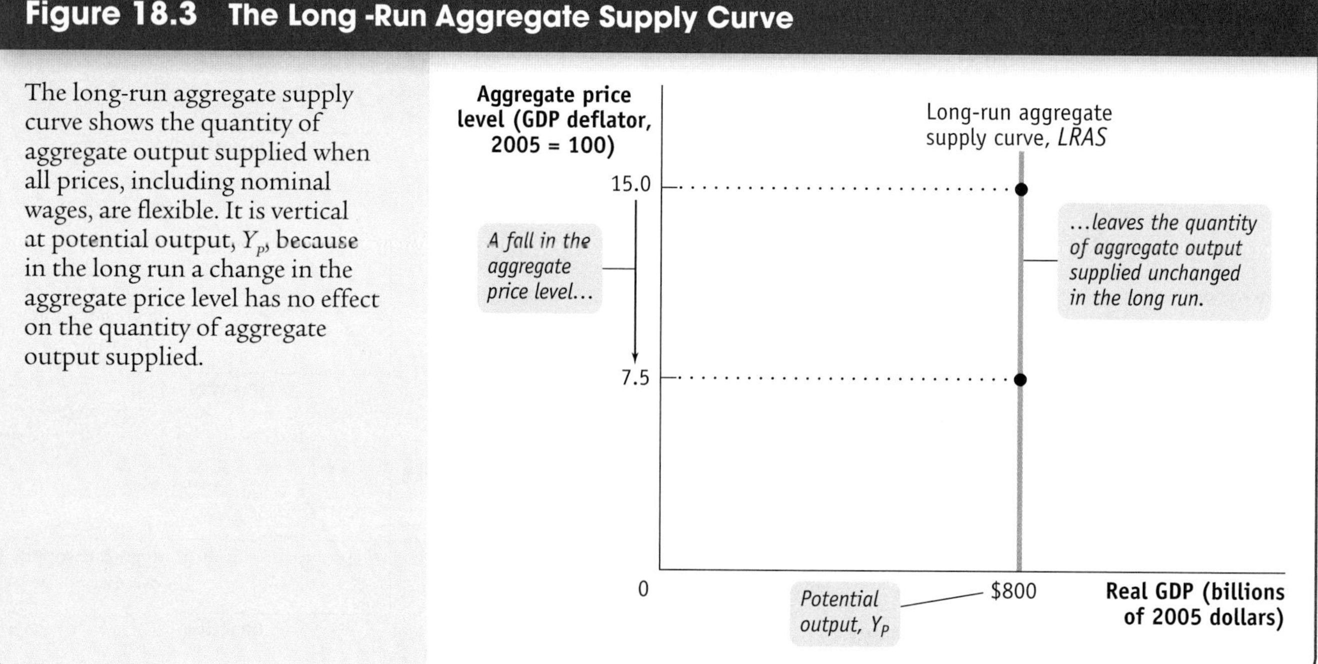

The long-run aggregate supply curve shows the quantity of aggregate output supplied when all prices, including nominal wages, are flexible. It is vertical at potential output, Y_P, because in the long run a change in the aggregate price level has no effect on the quantity of aggregate output supplied.

aggregate price level have *no* effect on aggregate output in the long run. At an aggregate price level of 15.0, the quantity of aggregate output supplied is $800 billion in 2005 dollars. If the aggregate price level falls by 50% to 7.5, the quantity of aggregate output supplied is unchanged in the long run at $800 billion in 2005 dollars.

It's important to understand not only that the *LRAS* curve is vertical but also that its position along the horizontal axis marks an important benchmark for output. The horizontal intercept in Figure 18.3, where *LRAS* touches the horizontal axis ($800 billion in 2005 dollars), is the economy's **potential output**, Y_P: the level of real GDP the economy would produce if all prices, including nominal wages, were fully flexible.

Potential output is the level of real GDP the economy would produce if all prices, including nominal wages, were fully flexible.

In reality, the actual level of real GDP is almost always either above or below potential output. We'll see why later, when we discuss the *AD–AS* model. Still, an economy's potential output is an important number because it defines the trend around which actual aggregate output fluctuates from year to year.

In the United States, the Congressional Budget Office (CBO) estimates annual potential output for the purpose of federal budget analysis. In **Figure 18.4**, the CBO's estimates of U.S. potential output from 1989 to 2013 are represented by the orange line and the actual values of U.S. real GDP over the same period are represented by the blue line. Years shaded purple on the horizontal axis correspond to periods in which actual aggregate output fell short of potential output, while years shaded green correspond to periods in which actual aggregate output exceeded potential output.

Figure 18.4 Actual and Potential Output from 1989 to 2013

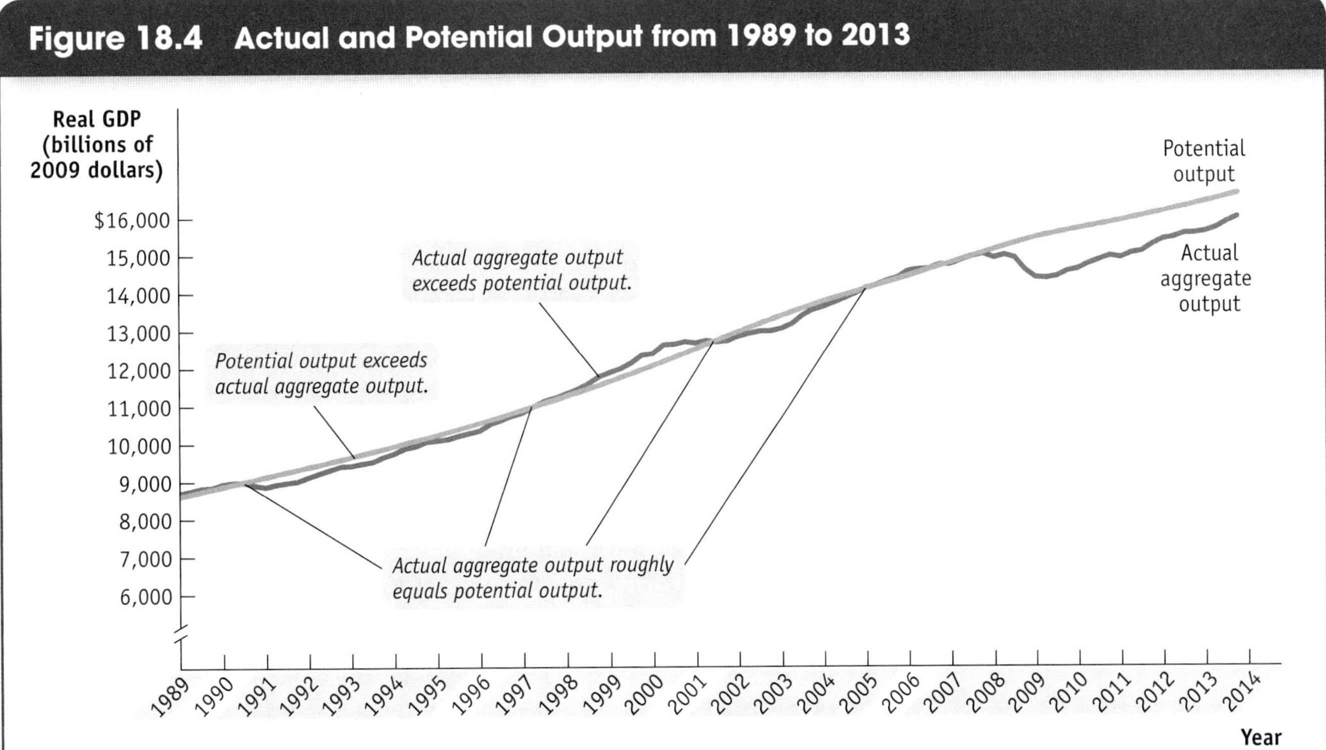

This figure shows the performance of actual and potential output in the United States from 1989 to 2013. The orange line shows estimates, produced by the Congressional Budget Office, of U.S. potential output, and the blue line shows actual aggregate output. The purple-shaded years are periods in which actual aggregate output fell below potential output, while the green-shaded years are periods in which actual aggregate output exceeded potential output. As shown, significant shortfalls occurred in the recessions of the early 1990s and after 2000—particularly during the recession that began in 2007. Actual aggregate output was significantly above potential output in the boom of the late 1990s.

Source: Congressional Budget Office; Bureau of Economic Analysis.

As you can see, U.S. potential output has risen steadily over time—implying a series of rightward shifts of the *LRAS* curve. What has caused these rightward shifts? The answer lies in the factors related to long-run growth:

- increases in the quantity of resources, including land, labor, capital, and entrepreneurship
- increases in the quality of resources, such as a better-educated workforce
- technological progress

Over the long run, as the size of the labor force and the productivity of labor both rise, for example, the level of real GDP that the economy is capable of producing also rises. Indeed, one way to think about economic growth is that it is the growth in the economy's potential output. We generally think of the long-run aggregate supply curve as shifting to the right over time as an economy experiences long-run growth.

From the Short Run to the Long Run

As you can see in Figure 18.4, the economy normally produces more or less than potential output: actual aggregate output was below potential output in the early 1990s, above potential output in the late 1990s, and below potential output for most of the 2000s. So the economy is normally operating at a point on its short-run aggregate supply curve—but not at a point on its long-run aggregate supply curve. Why, then, is the long-run curve relevant? Does the economy ever move from the short run to the long run? And if so, how?

The first step to answering these questions is to understand that the economy is always in one of only two states with respect to the short-run and long-run aggregate supply curves. It can be on both curves simultaneously by being at a point where the curves cross (as in the few years in Figure 18.4 in which actual aggregate output and potential output roughly coincided). Or it can be on the short-run aggregate supply curve but not the long-run aggregate supply curve (as in the years in which actual aggregate output and potential output *did not* coincide). But that is not the end of the story. If the economy is on the short-run but not the long-run aggregate supply curve, the short-run aggregate supply curve will shift over time until the economy is at a point where both curves cross—a point where actual aggregate output is equal to potential output.

Figure 18.5 illustrates how this process works. In both panels *LRAS* is the long-run aggregate supply curve, $SRAS_1$ is the initial short-run aggregate supply curve, and the aggregate price level is at P_1. In panel (a) the economy starts at the initial production point, A_1, which corresponds to a quantity of aggregate output supplied, Y_1, that is higher than potential output, Y_P. Producing an aggregate output level (such as Y_1) that is higher than potential output (Y_P) is possible only because nominal wages have not yet fully adjusted upward. Until this upward adjustment in nominal wages occurs, producers are earning high profits and producing a high level of output. But a level of aggregate output higher than potential output means a low level of unemployment. Because jobs are abundant and workers are scarce, nominal wages will rise over time, gradually shifting the short-run aggregate supply curve leftward. Eventually, it will be in a new position, such as $SRAS_2$. (Later, we'll show where the short-run aggregate supply curve ends up. As we'll see, that depends on the aggregate demand curve as well.)

In panel (b), the initial production point, A_1, corresponds to an aggregate output level, Y_1, that is lower than potential output, Y_P. Producing an aggregate output level (such as Y_1) that is lower than potential output (Y_P) is possible only because nominal wages have not yet fully adjusted downward. Until this downward adjustment occurs, producers are earning low (or negative) profits and producing a low level of output. An aggregate output level lower than potential output means high unemployment. Because workers are abundant and jobs are scarce, nominal wages will fall over time, shifting the short-run aggregate supply curve gradually to the right. Eventually, it will be in a new position, such as $SRAS_2$.

We'll see shortly that these shifts of the short-run aggregate supply curve will return the economy to potential output in the long run.

Figure 18.5 From the Short Run to the Long Run

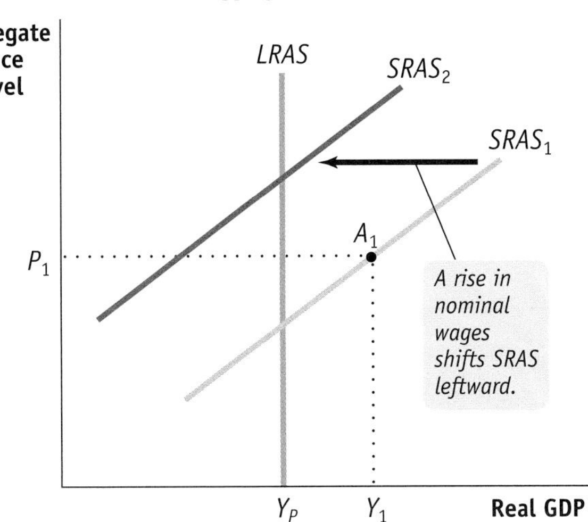

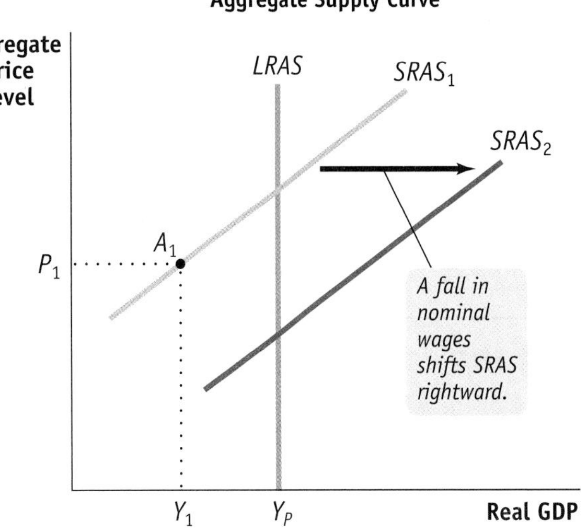

In panel (a), the initial short-run aggregate supply curve is $SRAS_1$. At the aggregate price level, P_1, the quantity of aggregate output supplied, Y_1, exceeds potential output, Y_P. Eventually, low unemployment will cause nominal wages to rise, leading to a leftward shift of the short-run aggregate supply curve from $SRAS_1$ to $SRAS_2$.

In panel (b), the reverse happens: at the aggregate price level, P_1, the quantity of aggregate output supplied is less than potential output. High unemployment eventually leads to a fall in nominal wages over time and a rightward shift of the short-run aggregate supply curve.

FYI Prices and Output During the Great Depression

The figure shows the actual track of the aggregate price level, as measured by the GDP deflator, and real GDP, from 1929 to 1942. As you can see, aggregate output and the aggregate price level fell together from 1929 to 1933 and rose together from 1933 to 1937. This is what we'd expect to see if the economy were moving down the short-run aggregate supply curve from 1929 to 1933 and moving up it (with a brief reversal in 1937–1938) thereafter.

But even in 1942 the aggregate price level was still lower than it was in 1929; yet real GDP was much higher. What happened?

The answer is that the short-run aggregate supply curve shifted to the right over time. This shift partly reflected rising productivity—a rightward shift of the underlying long-run aggregate supply curve. But since the U.S. economy was producing below potential output and had high unemployment during this period, the rightward shift of the short-run aggregate supply curve also reflected the adjustment process shown in panel (b) of Figure 18.5. So the movement of aggregate output from 1929 to 1942 reflected both movements along and shifts of the short-run aggregate supply curve.

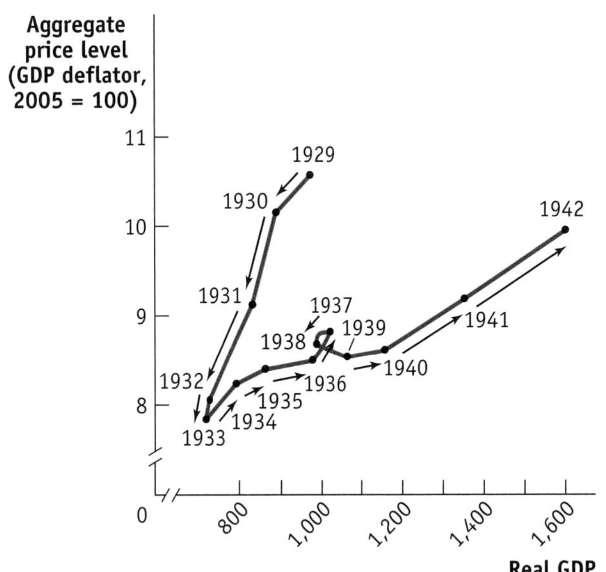

MODULE 18 Review

Check Your Understanding

1. Determine the effect on short-run aggregate supply of each of the following events. Explain whether it represents a movement along the *SRAS* curve or a shift of the *SRAS* curve.
   a. A rise in the consumer price index (CPI) leads producers to increase output.
   b. A fall in the price of oil leads producers to increase output.
   c. A rise in legally mandated retirement benefits paid to workers leads producers to reduce output.

2. Suppose the economy is initially at potential output and the quantity of aggregate output supplied increases. What information would you need to determine whether this was due to a movement along the *SRAS* curve or a shift of the LRAS curve?

Tackle the Test: Multiple-Choice Questions

1. Which of the following will shift the short-run aggregate supply curve? A change in
   a. profit per unit at any given price level
   b. commodity prices
   c. nominal wages
   d. productivity
   e. all of the above

2. Because changes in the aggregate price level have no effect on aggregate output in the long run, the long-run aggregate supply curve is
   a. vertical.
   b. horizontal.
   c. fixed.
   d. negatively sloped.
   e. positively sloped.

3. The horizontal intercept of the long-run aggregate supply curve is
   a. at the origin.
   b. negative.
   c. at potential output.
   d. equal to the vertical intercept.
   e. always the same as the horizontal intercept of the short-run aggregate supply curve.

4. A decrease in which of the following will cause the short-run aggregate supply curve to shift to the left?
   a. commodity prices
   b. the cost of health care insurance premiums paid by employers
   c. nominal wages
   d. productivity
   e. the use of cost-of-living allowances in labor contracts

5. That employers are reluctant to decrease nominal wages during economic downturns and raise nominal wages during economic expansions is one reason nominal wages are described as
   a. long-run.
   b. unyielding.
   c. flexible.
   d. real.
   e. sticky.

Tackle the Test: Free-Response Questions

1. **a.** Draw a correctly labeled graph illustrating a long-run aggregate supply curve.
   b On your graph from part a, label potential output.
   c. On your graph from part a, illustrate an increase in long-run aggregate supply.
   d. What could have caused the change you illustrated in part c? List three possible causes.

Rubric for FRQ 1 (8 points)

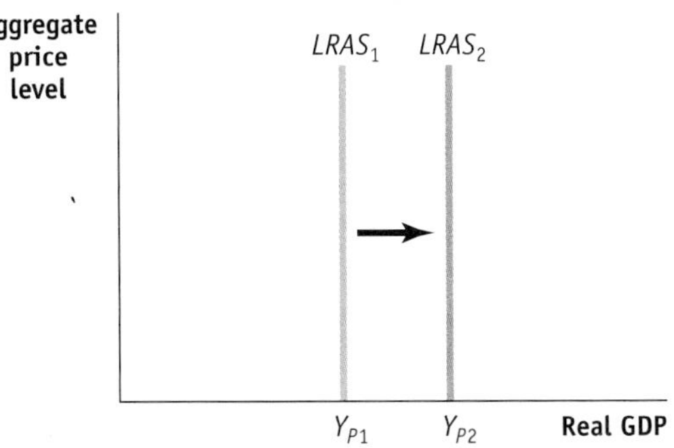

1 point: Vertical axis labeled "Aggregate price level" (or "Price level")

1 point: Horizontal axis labeled "Real GDP"

1 point: Vertical curve labeled "*LRAS*" (or "$LRAS_1$")

1 point: Potential output labeled Y_P (or Y_{P1}) on the horizontal axis at the intercept of the long-run aggregate supply curve

1 point: Long-run aggregate supply curve shifted to the right

1 point: An increase in the quantity of resources (land, labor, capital, or entrepreneurship)

1 point: An increase in the quality of resources

1 point: Technological progress

2. **a.** Draw a correctly labeled short-run aggregate supply curve.
   b. On your graph from part a, illustrate a decrease in short-run aggregate supply.
   c. List three types of changes, including the factor that changes and the direction of the change, that could lead to a decrease in short-run aggregate supply.

   (6 points)

Kurt Brady/Alamy

MODULE 19 Equilibrium in the Aggregate Demand–Aggregate Supply Model

In this Module, you will learn to:

- Explain the difference between short-run and long-run macroeconomic equilibrium
- Describe the causes and effects of demand shocks and supply shocks
- Determine if an economy is experiencing a recessionary gap or an inflationary gap and explain how to calculate the size of an output gap

AP® Exam Tip

The *AD–AS* model is one of the most important models you will study. Make sure you can correctly draw, label, and interpret the model, and practice using it to show the effects of policies.

The *AD–AS* Model

From 1929 to 1933, the U.S. economy moved down the short-run aggregate supply curve as the aggregate price level fell. In contrast, from 1979 to 1980, the U.S. economy moved up the aggregate demand curve as the aggregate price level rose. In each case, the cause of the movement along the curve was a shift of the other curve. In 1929–1933, it was a leftward shift of the aggregate demand curve—a major fall in consumer spending. In 1979–1980, it was a leftward shift of the short-run aggregate supply curve—a dramatic fall in short-run aggregate supply caused by the oil *price shock*.

So to understand the behavior of the economy, we must put the aggregate supply curve and the aggregate demand curve together. The result is the ***AD–AS* model**, the basic model we use to understand economic fluctuations.

In the ***AD–AS* model**, the aggregate supply curve and the aggregate demand curve are used together to analyze economic fluctuations.

The economy is in **short-run macroeconomic equilibrium** when the quantity of aggregate output supplied is equal to the quantity demanded.

Short-Run Macroeconomic Equilibrium

We'll begin our analysis by focusing on the short run. **Figure 19.1** shows the aggregate demand curve and the short-run aggregate supply curve on the same diagram. The point at which the *AD* and *SRAS* curves intersect, E_{SR}, is the **short-run macroeconomic equilibrium**: the point at which the quantity of aggregate output supplied is equal to the quantity demanded by domestic households, businesses, the government, and the rest of the world. The aggregate price level at E_{SR}, P_E, is the

Figure 19.1 The *AD–AS* Model

The *AD–AS* model combines the aggregate demand curve and the short-run aggregate supply curve. Their point of intersection, E_{SR}, is the point of short-run macroeconomic equilibrium where the quantity of aggregate output demanded is equal to the quantity of aggregate output supplied. P_E is the short-run equilibrium aggregate price level, and Y_E is the short-run equilibrium level of aggregate output.

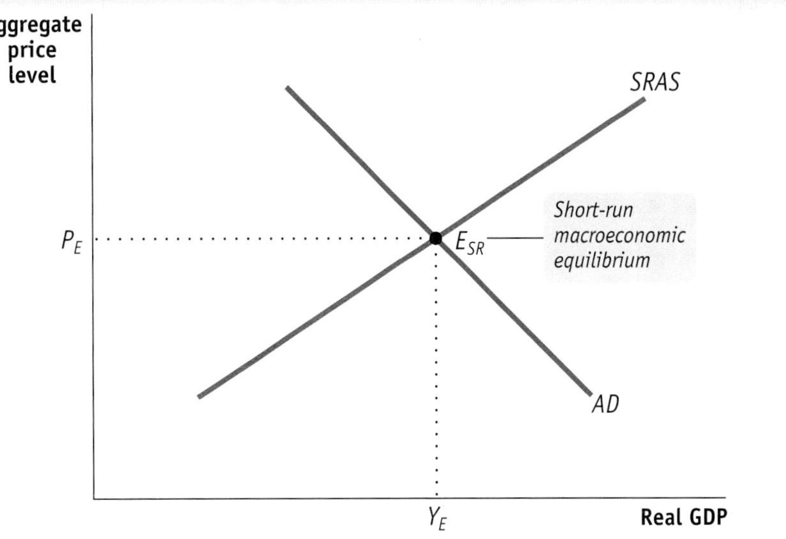

short-run equilibrium aggregate price level. The level of aggregate output at E_{SR}, Y_E, is the **short-run equilibrium aggregate output**.

We have seen that a shortage of any individual good causes its market price to rise and a surplus of the good causes its market price to fall. These forces ensure that the market reaches equilibrium. The same logic applies to short-run macroeconomic equilibrium. If the aggregate price level is above its equilibrium level, the quantity of aggregate output supplied exceeds the quantity of aggregate output demanded. This leads to a fall in the aggregate price level and pushes it toward its equilibrium level. If the aggregate price level is below its equilibrium level, the quantity of aggregate output supplied is less than the quantity of aggregate output demanded. This leads to a rise in the aggregate price level, again pushing it toward its equilibrium level. In the discussion that follows, we'll assume that the economy is always in short-run macroeconomic equilibrium.

The **short-run equilibrium aggregate price level** is the aggregate price level in the short-run macroeconomic equilibrium.

Short-run equilibrium aggregate output is the quantity of aggregate output produced in the short-run macroeconomic equilibrium.

We'll also make another important simplification based on the observation that, in reality, there is a long-term upward trend in both aggregate output and the aggregate price level. We'll assume that a fall in either variable really means a fall compared to the long-run trend. For example, if the aggregate price level normally rises 4% per year, a year in which the aggregate price level rises only 3% would count, for our purposes, as a 1% decline. In fact, since the Great Depression there have been very few years in which the aggregate price level of any major nation actually declined—Japan's period of deflation from 1995 to 2005 is one of the few exceptions (which we will explain later). However, there have been many cases in which the aggregate price level fell relative to the long-run trend.

AP® Exam Tip

When asked to graph the effect of a change, graph the first thing that happens in the short-run unless the question tells you to look at the long-run.

The short-run equilibrium aggregate output and the short-run equilibrium aggregate price level can change because of shifts of either the *AD* curve or the *SRAS* curve. Let's look at each case in turn.

Shifts of Aggregate Demand: Short-Run Effects

An event that shifts the aggregate demand curve, such as a change in expectations or wealth, the effect of the size of the existing stock of physical capital, or the use of fiscal or monetary policy, is known as a **demand shock**. The Great Depression was caused by a negative demand shock, the collapse of wealth and of business and consumer confidence that followed the stock market crash of 1929 and the banking

An event that shifts the aggregate demand curve is a **demand shock**.

crises of 1930–1931. The Depression was ended by a positive demand shock—the huge increase in government purchases during World War II. In 2008, the U.S. economy experienced another significant negative demand shock as the housing market turned from boom to bust, leading consumers and firms to scale back their spending.

Figure 19.2 shows the short-run effects of negative and positive demand shocks. A negative demand shock shifts the aggregate demand curve, *AD*, to the left, from AD_1 to AD_2, as shown in panel (a). The economy moves down along the *SRAS* curve from E_1 to E_2, leading to lower short-run equilibrium aggregate output and a lower short-run equilibrium aggregate price level. A positive demand shock shifts the aggregate demand curve, *AD*, to the right, as shown in panel (b). Here, the economy moves up along the *SRAS* curve, from E_1 to E_2. This leads to higher short-run equilibrium aggregate output and a higher short-run equilibrium aggregate price level. Demand shocks cause aggregate output and the aggregate price level to move in the same direction.

Figure 19.2 Demand Shocks

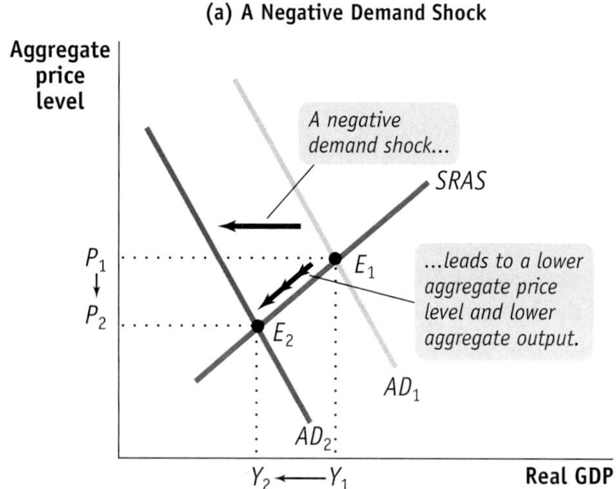

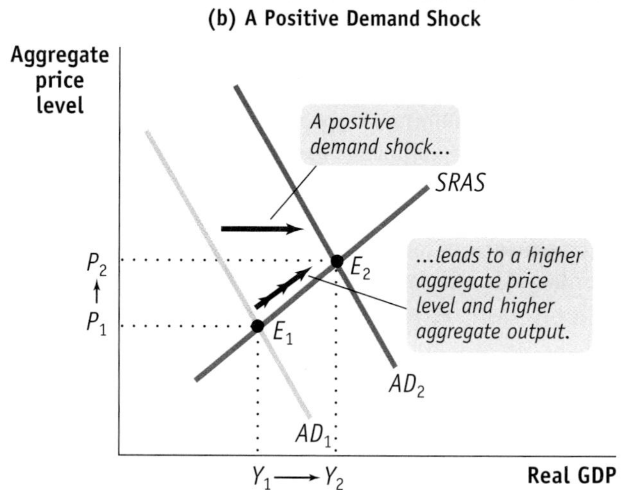

A demand shock shifts the aggregate demand curve, moving the aggregate price level and aggregate output in the same direction. In panel (a), a negative demand shock shifts the aggregate demand curve leftward from AD_1 to AD_2, reducing the aggregate price level from P_1 to P_2 and aggregate output from Y_1 to Y_2. In panel (b), a positive demand shock shifts the aggregate demand curve rightward, increasing the aggregate price level from P_1 to P_2 and aggregate output from Y_1 to Y_2.

Shifts of the *SRAS* Curve

An event that shifts the short-run aggregate supply curve, such as a change in commodity prices, nominal wages, or productivity, is known as a **supply shock**. A *negative* supply shock raises production costs and reduces the quantity producers are willing to supply at any given aggregate price level, leading to a leftward shift of the short-run aggregate supply curve. The U.S. economy experienced severe negative supply shocks following disruptions to world oil supplies in 1973 and 1979. In contrast, a *positive* supply shock reduces production costs and increases the quantity supplied at any given aggregate price level, leading to a rightward shift of the short-run aggregate supply curve. The United States experienced a positive supply shock between 1995 and 2000, when the increasing use of the Internet and other information technologies caused productivity growth to surge.

An event that shifts the short-run aggregate supply curve is a **supply shock**.

The effects of a negative supply shock are shown in panel (a) of **Figure 19.3**. The initial equilibrium is at E_1, with aggregate price level P_1 and aggregate output Y_1. The disruption in the oil supply causes the short-run aggregate supply curve to shift to the left, from $SRAS_1$ to $SRAS_2$. As a consequence, aggregate output falls and the aggregate price level rises, an upward movement along the *AD* curve. At the new equilibrium, E_2, the short-run equilibrium aggregate price level, P_2, is higher, and the short-run equilibrium aggregate output level, Y_2, is lower than before.

The combination of inflation and falling aggregate output shown in panel (a) has a special name: **stagflation**, for "stagnation plus inflation." When an economy experiences stagflation, it's very unpleasant: falling aggregate output leads to rising unemployment, and people feel that their purchasing power is squeezed by rising prices. Stagflation in the 1970s led to a mood of national pessimism. As we'll see shortly, it also poses a dilemma for policy makers.

Producers are vulnerable to dramatic changes in the price of oil, a cause of supply shocks.

A positive supply shock, shown in panel (b), has exactly the opposite effects. A rightward shift of the *SRAS* curve, from $SRAS_1$ to $SRAS_2$ results in a rise in aggregate output and a fall in the aggregate price level, a downward movement along the *AD* curve. The favorable supply shocks of the late 1990s led to a combination of full employment and declining inflation. That is, the aggregate price level fell compared with the long-run trend. For a few years, this combination produced a great wave of national optimism.

Stagflation is the combination of inflation and stagnating (or falling) aggregate output.

The distinctive feature of supply shocks, both negative and positive, is that, unlike demand shocks, they cause the aggregate price level and aggregate output to move in *opposite* directions.

Figure 19.3 Supply Shocks

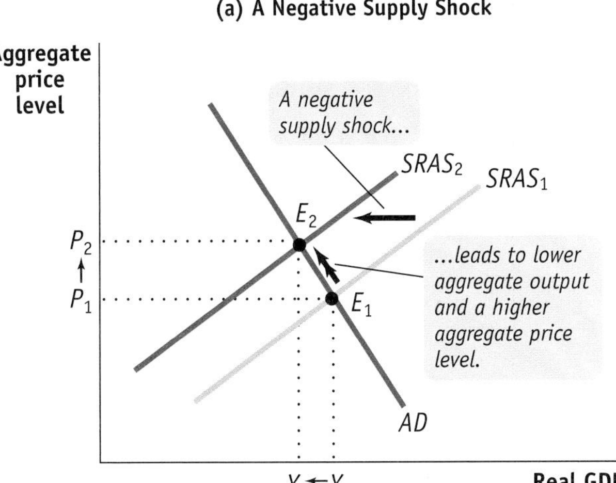

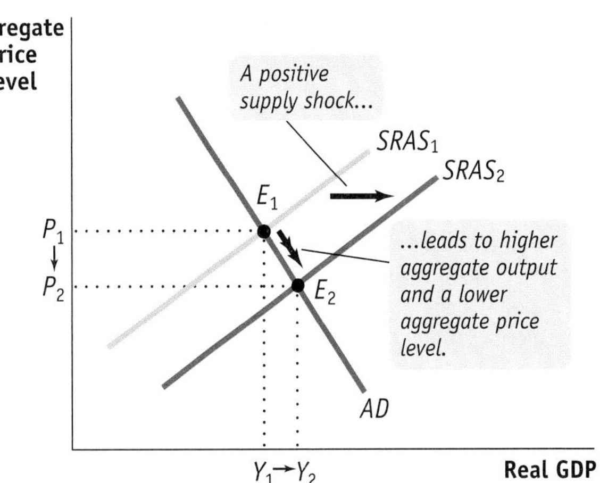

A supply shock shifts the short-run aggregate supply curve, moving the aggregate price level and aggregate output in opposite directions. Panel (a) shows a negative supply shock, which shifts the short-run aggregate supply curve leftward and causes stagflation—lower aggregate output and a higher aggregate price level. Here, the short-run aggregate supply curve shifts from $SRAS_1$ to $SRAS_2$, and the economy moves from E_1 to E_2. The aggregate price level rises from P_1 to P_2, and aggregate output falls from Y_1 to Y_2. Panel (b) shows a positive supply shock, which shifts the short-run aggregate supply curve rightward, generating higher aggregate output and a lower aggregate price level. The short-run aggregate supply curve shifts from $SRAS_1$ to $SRAS_2$, and the economy moves from E_1 to E_2. The aggregate price level falls from P_1 to P_2, and aggregate output rises from Y_1 to Y_2.

There's another important contrast between supply shocks and demand shocks. As we've seen, monetary policy and fiscal policy enable the government to shift the *AD* curve, meaning that governments are in a position to create the kinds of shocks shown in Figure 19.2. It's much harder for governments to shift the *AS* curve. Are there good policy reasons to shift the *AD* curve? We'll turn to that question soon. First, however, let's look at the difference between short-run macroeconomic equilibrium and long-run macroeconomic equilibrium.

Long-Run Macroeconomic Equilibrium

Figure 19.4 combines the aggregate demand curve with both the short-run and long-run aggregate supply curves. The aggregate demand curve, *AD*, crosses the short-run aggregate supply curve, *SRAS*, at E_{LR}. Here we assume that enough time has elapsed that the economy is also on the long-run aggregate supply curve, *LRAS*. As a result, E_{LR} is at the intersection of all three curves—*SRAS*, *LRAS*, and *AD*. So short-run equilibrium aggregate output is equal to potential output, Y_P. Such a situation, in which the point of short-run macroeconomic equilibrium is on the long-run aggregate supply curve, is known as **long-run macroeconomic equilibrium**.

The economy is in **long-run macroeconomic equilibrium** when the point of short-run macroeconomic equilibrium is on the long-run aggregate supply curve.

To see the significance of long-run macroeconomic equilibrium, let's consider what happens if a demand shock moves the economy away from long-run macroeconomic equilibrium. In **Figure 19.5**, we assume that the initial aggregate demand curve is AD_1 and the initial short-run aggregate supply curve is $SRAS_1$. So the initial macroeconomic equilibrium is at E_1, which lies on the long-run aggregate supply curve, *LRAS*. The economy, then, starts from a point of short-run and long-run macroeconomic equilibrium, and short-run equilibrium aggregate output equals potential output at Y_1.

Now suppose that for some reason—such as a sudden worsening of business and consumer expectations—aggregate demand falls and the aggregate demand curve shifts leftward to AD_2. This results in a lower equilibrium aggregate price level at P_2 and a lower equilibrium aggregate output level at Y_2 as the economy settles in the

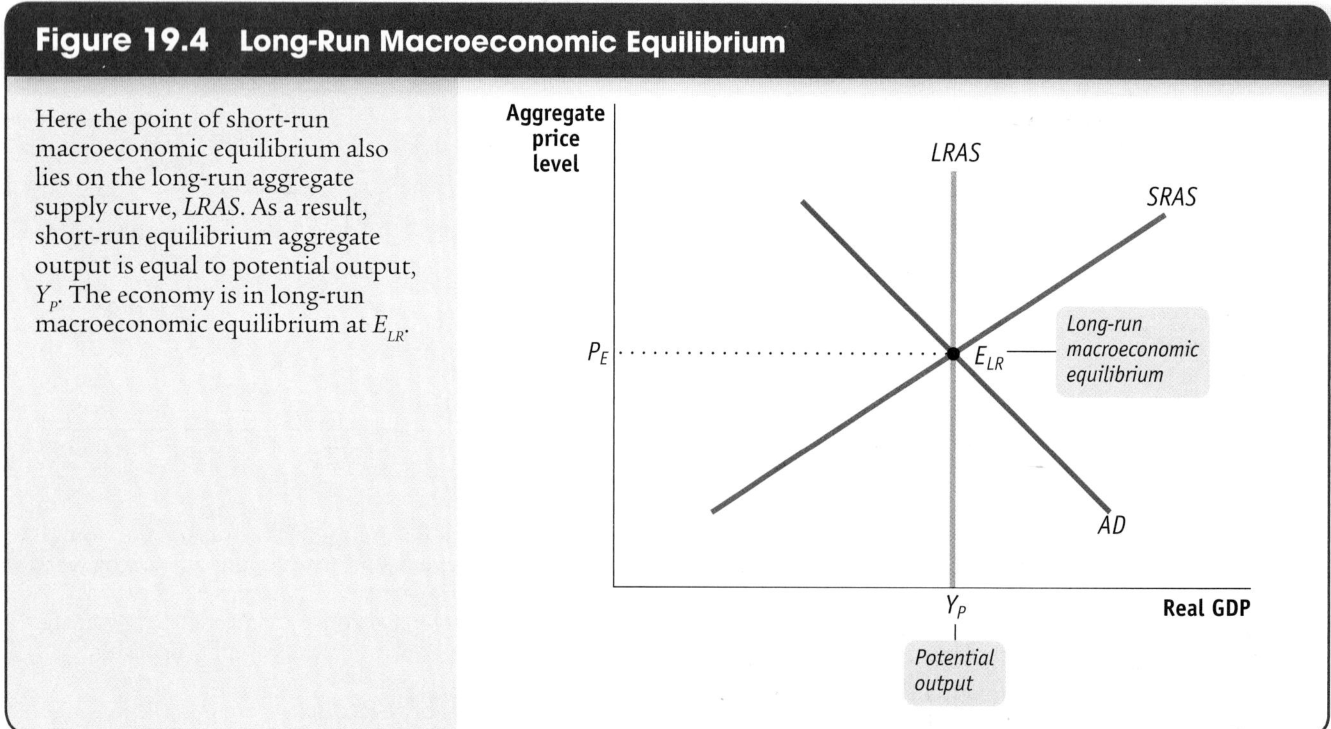

Figure 19.4 Long-Run Macroeconomic Equilibrium

Here the point of short-run macroeconomic equilibrium also lies on the long-run aggregate supply curve, *LRAS*. As a result, short-run equilibrium aggregate output is equal to potential output, Y_P. The economy is in long-run macroeconomic equilibrium at E_{LR}.

Figure 19.5 Short-Run Versus Long-Run Effects of a Negative Demand Shock

In the long run the economy is self-correcting: demand shocks have only a short-run effect on aggregate output. Starting at E_1, a negative demand shock shifts AD_1 leftward to AD_2. In the short run the economy moves to E_2 and a recessionary gap arises: the aggregate price level declines from P_1 to P_2, aggregate output declines from Y_1 to Y_2, and unemployment rises. But in the long run nominal wages fall in response to high unemployment at Y_2, and $SRAS_1$ shifts rightward to $SRAS_2$. Aggregate output rises from Y_2 to Y_1, and the aggregate price level declines again, from P_2 to P_3. Long-run macroeconomic equilibrium is eventually restored at E_3.

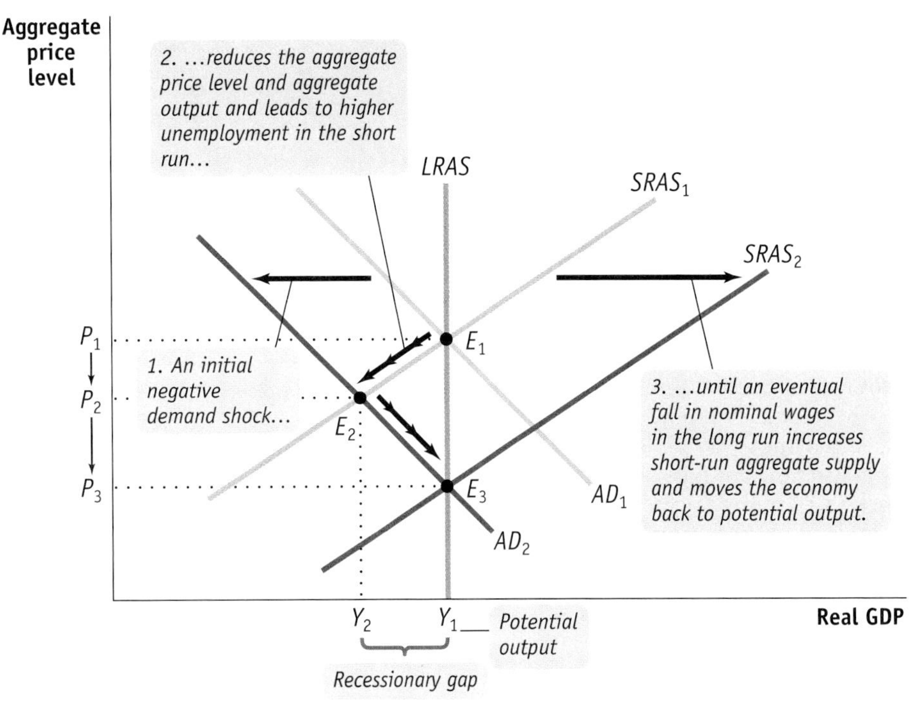

Aggregate price level
2. ...reduces the aggregate price level and aggregate output and leads to higher unemployment in the short run...
LRAS
SRAS1
SRAS2
P1
P2
P3
E1
E2
E3
1. An initial negative demand shock...
3. ...until an eventual fall in nominal wages in the long run increases short-run aggregate supply and moves the economy back to potential output.
AD1
AD2
Y2
Y1
Potential output
Recessionary gap
Real GDP

short run at E_2. The short-run effect of such a fall in aggregate demand is what the U.S. economy experienced in 1929–1933: a falling aggregate price level and falling aggregate output.

Aggregate output in this new short-run equilibrium, E_2, is below potential output. When this happens, the economy faces a **recessionary gap**. A recessionary gap inflicts a great deal of pain because it corresponds to high unemployment. The large recessionary gap that had opened up in the United States by 1933 caused intense social and political turmoil. And the devastating recessionary gap that opened up in Germany at the same time played an important role in Hitler's rise to power.

There is a **recessionary gap** when aggregate output is below potential output.

But this isn't the end of the story. In the face of high unemployment, nominal wages eventually fall, as do any other sticky prices, ultimately leading producers to increase output. As a result, a recessionary gap causes the short-run aggregate supply curve to gradually shift to the right. This process continues until $SRAS_1$ reaches its new position at $SRAS_2$, bringing the economy to equilibrium at E_3, where AD_2, $SRAS_2$, and *LRAS* all intersect. At E_3, the economy is back in long-run macroeconomic equilibrium; it is back at potential output Y_1 but at a lower aggregate price level, P_3, reflecting a long-run fall in the aggregate price level. The economy is *self-correcting* in the long run.

AP® Exam Tip

If you have drawn a recessionary gap correctly, the intersection of *AD* and *SRAS* will be to the left of *LRAS* and potential output.

What if, instead, there was an increase in aggregate demand? The results are shown in **Figure 19.6** on the next page, where we again assume that the initial aggregate demand curve is AD_1 and the initial short-run aggregate supply curve is $SRAS_1$. The initial macroeconomic equilibrium, at E_1, lies on the long-run aggregate supply curve, *LRAS*. Initially, then, the economy is in long-run macroeconomic equilibrium.

Now suppose that aggregate demand rises, and the *AD* curve shifts rightward to AD_2. This results in a higher aggregate price level, at P_2, and a higher aggregate output level,

Figure 19.6 Short-Run Versus Long-Run Effects of a Positive Demand Shock

Starting at E_1, a positive demand shock shifts AD_1 rightward to AD_2, and the economy moves to E_2 in the short run. This results in an inflationary gap as aggregate output rises from Y_1 to Y_2, the aggregate price level rises from P_1 to P_2, and unemployment falls to a low level. In the long run, $SRAS_1$ shifts leftward to $SRAS_2$ as nominal wages rise in response to low unemployment at Y_2. Aggregate output falls back to Y_1, the aggregate price level rises again to P_3, and the economy self-corrects as it returns to long-run macroeconomic equilibrium at E_3.

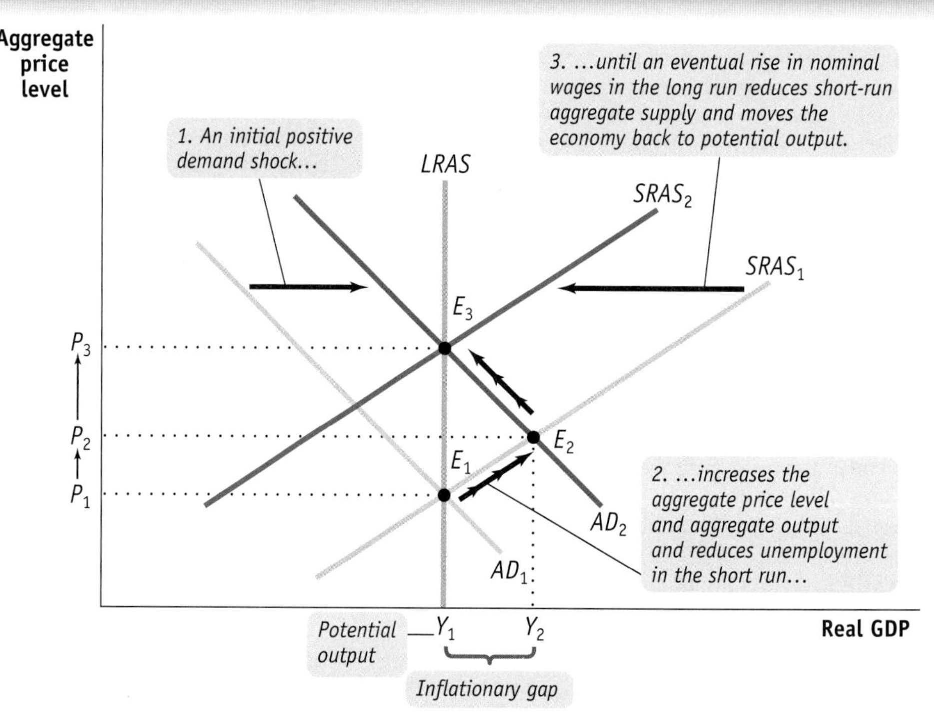

Aggregate price level
3. ...until an eventual rise in nominal wages in the long run reduces short-run aggregate supply and moves the economy back to potential output.
1. An initial positive demand shock...
LRAS
SRAS2
SRAS1
E3
P3
P2
P1
E2
E1
2. ...increases the aggregate price level and aggregate output and reduces unemployment in the short run...
AD2
AD1
Potential output
Y1
Y2
Inflationary gap
Real GDP

There is an **inflationary gap** when aggregate output is above potential output.

The **output gap** is the percentage difference between actual aggregate output and potential output.

at Y_2, as the economy settles in the short run at E_2. Aggregate output in this new short-run equilibrium is above potential output, and unemployment is low in order to produce this higher level of aggregate output. When this happens, the economy experiences an **inflationary gap**. As in the case of a recessionary gap, this isn't the end of the story. In the face of low unemployment, nominal wages will rise, as will other sticky prices. An inflationary gap causes the short-run aggregate supply curve to shift gradually to the left as producers reduce output in the face of rising nominal wages. This process continues until $SRAS_1$ reaches its new position at $SRAS_2$, bringing the economy into equilibrium at E_3, where AD_2, $SRAS_2$, and $LRAS$ all intersect. At E_3, the economy is back in long-run macroeconomic equilibrium. It is back at potential output, but at a higher price level, P_3, reflecting a long-run rise in the aggregate price level. Again, the economy is self-correcting in the long run.

To summarize the analysis of how the economy responds to recessionary and inflationary gaps, we can focus on the **output gap**, the percentage difference between actual aggregate output and potential output. The output gap is calculated as follows:

AP® Exam Tip

If you have drawn an inflationary gap correctly, the intersection of *AD* and *SRAS* will be to the right of *LRAS* and potential output.

$$\textbf{(19-1)}\quad \text{Output gap} = \frac{\text{Actual aggregate output} - \text{Potential output}}{\text{Potential output}} \times 100$$

Our analysis says that the output gap always tends toward zero.

If there is a recessionary gap, so that the output gap is negative, nominal wages eventually fall, moving the economy back to potential output and bringing the output gap back to zero. If there is an inflationary gap, so that the output gap is positive, nominal wages eventually rise, also moving the economy back to potential output and again bringing the output gap back to zero. So in the long run the economy is **self-correcting**: shocks to aggregate demand affect aggregate output in the short run but not in the long run.

The economy is **self-correcting** when shocks to aggregate demand affect aggregate output in the short run, but not the long run.

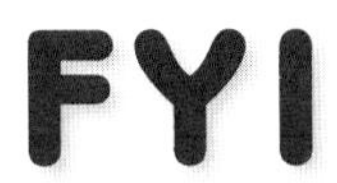

Supply Shocks Versus Demand Shocks in Practice

How often do supply shocks and demand shocks, respectively, cause recessions? The verdict of most, though not all, macroeconomists is that recessions are mainly caused by demand shocks. But when a negative supply shock does happen, the resulting recession tends to be particularly severe.

Let's get specific. Officially there have been twelve recessions in the United States since World War II. However, two of these, in 1979–1980 and 1981–1982, are often treated as a single "double-dip" recession, bringing the total number down to 11. Of these 11 recessions, only two—the recession of 1973–1975 and the double-dip recession of 1979–1982—showed the distinctive combination of falling aggregate output and a surge in the price level that we call stagflation. In each case, the cause of the supply shock was political turmoil in the Middle East—the Arab-Israeli war of 1973 and the Iranian revolution of 1979—that disrupted world oil supplies and sent oil prices skyrocketing. In fact, economists sometimes refer to the two slumps as "OPEC I" and "OPEC II," after the Organization of Petroleum Exporting Countries, the world oil cartel. A third recession that began in December 2007and ended in June 2009 was at least partially caused by a spike in oil prices.

So 8 of 11 postwar recessions were purely the result of demand shocks, not supply shocks. The few supply-shock recessions, however, were the worst as measured by the unemployment rate. The figure shows the U.S. unemployment rate since 1948, with the dates of the 1973 Arab–Israeli war, the 1979 Iranian revolution, and the 2007 oil price shock marked on the graph. As you can see, the three highest unemployment rates since World War II came after these big negative supply shocks.

There's a reason the aftermath of a supply shock tends to be particularly severe for the economy: macroeconomic policy has a much harder time dealing with supply shocks than with demand shocks, as explained in the next module.

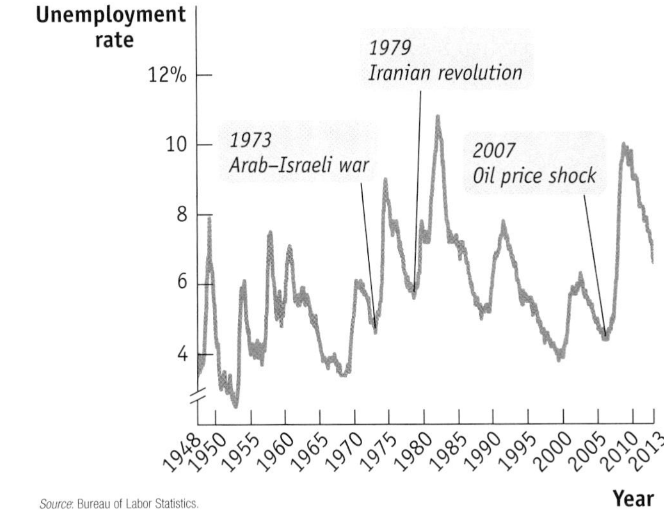

Source: Bureau of Labor Statistics.

MODULE 19 Review

Check Your Understanding

1. Describe the short-run effects of each of the following shocks on the aggregate price level and on aggregate output:
   a. The government sharply increases the minimum wage, raising the wages of many workers.
   b. Solar energy firms launch a major program of investment spending.
   c. Congress raises taxes and cuts spending.
   d. Severe weather destroys crops around the world.

2. Suppose a rise in productivity increases potential output and creates a recessionary gap. Explain how the economy can self-correct in the long run.

Tackle the Test: Multiple-Choice Questions

1. Which of the following causes a negative supply shock?
   - **I.** a technological advance
   - **II.** increasing productivity
   - **III.** an increase in oil prices

   a. I only
   b. II only
   c. III only
   d. I and III only
   e. I, II, and III

2. Which of the following causes a positive demand shock?
   a. an increase in wealth
   b. pessimistic consumer expectations
   c. a decrease in government spending
   d. an increase in taxes
   e. a relatively high existing stock of capital

3. During stagflation, what happens to the aggregate price level and real GDP?

	Aggregate price level	*Real GDP*
a.	decreases	increases
b.	decreases	decreases
c.	increases	increases
d.	increases	decreases
e.	stays the same	stays the same

Refer to the graph for Questions 4 and 5.

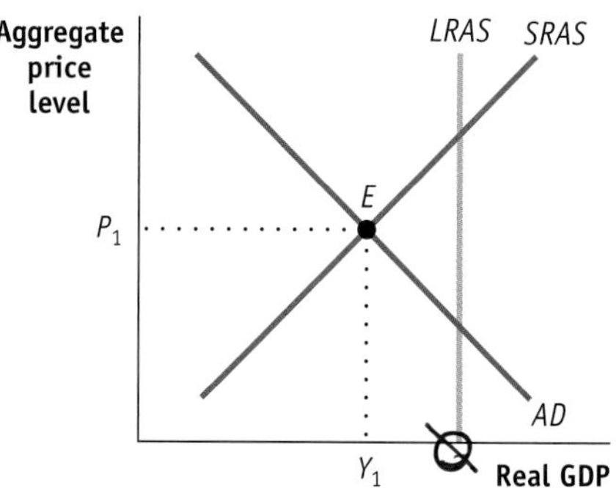

4. Which of the following statements is true if this economy is operating at P_1 and Y_1?
   - **I.** The level of aggregate output equals potential output.
   - **II.** It is in short-run macroeconomic equilibrium.
   - **III.** It is in long-run macroeconomic equilibrium.

   a. I only
   b. II only
   c. III only
   d. II and III
   e. I and III

5. The economy depicted in the graph is experiencing a(n)
   a. contractionary gap.
   b. recessionary gap.
   c. inflationary gap.
   d. demand gap.
   e. supply gap.

Tackle the Test: Free-Response Questions

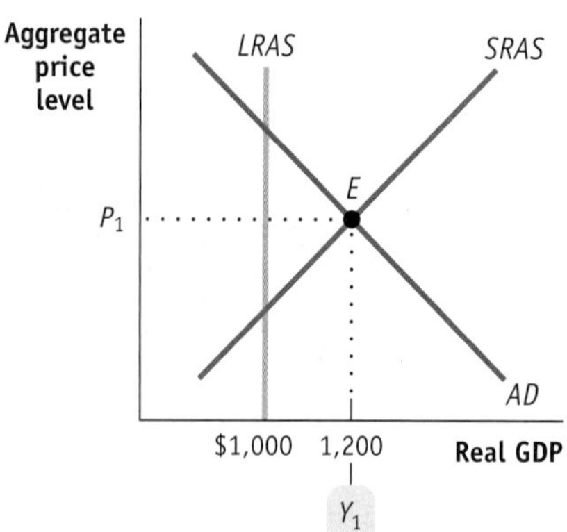

1. Refer to the graph above, with the economy operating at P_1 and Y_1.
   a. Is the economy in short-run macroeconomic equilibrium? Explain.
   b. Is the economy in long-run macroeconomic equilibrium? Explain.
   c. What type of gap exists in this economy?
   d. Calculate the size of the output gap.
   e. What will happen to the size of the output gap in the long run?

Rubric for FRQ 1 (7 points)

1 point: Yes

1 point: The economy is in short-run equilibrium because it operates at the point where short-run aggregate supply and aggregate demand intersect.

1 point: No

1 point: Short-run equilibrium occurs at a level of aggregate output that is not equal to potential output

1 point: Inflationary gap

1 point: $[(\$1,200 - \$1,000)/\$1,000] \times 100 = 20\%$

1 point: It will decrease (or approach zero).

2. Draw a correctly labeled aggregate demand and aggregate supply graph illustrating an economy in long-run macroeconomic equilibrium.
   (5 points)

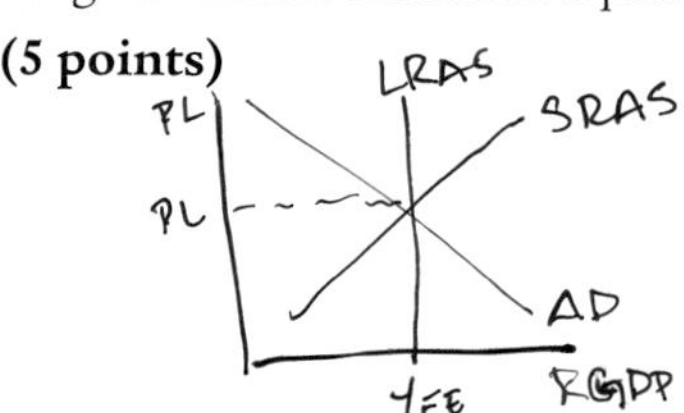

Mark Wilson/Getty Images

MODULE 20 Economic Policy and the Aggregate Demand–Aggregate Supply Model

In this Module, you will learn to:

- Discuss how the *AD–AS* model is used to formulate macroeconomic policy
- Explain the rationale for stabilization policy
- Describe the importance of fiscal policy as a tool for managing economic fluctuations
- Identify the policies that constitute expansionary fiscal policy and those that constitute contractionary fiscal policy

Macroeconomic Policy

We've just seen that the economy is self-correcting in the long run: it will eventually trend back to potential output. Most macroeconomists believe, however, that the process of self-correction typically takes a decade or more. In particular, if aggregate output is below potential output, the economy can suffer an extended period of depressed aggregate output and high unemployment before it returns to normal.

This belief is the background to one of the most famous quotations in economics: John Maynard Keynes's declaration, "In the long run we are all dead." Economists usually interpret Keynes as having recommended that governments not wait for the economy to correct itself. Instead, it is argued by many economists, but not all, that the government should use fiscal policy to get the economy back to potential output in the aftermath of a shift of the aggregate demand curve. This is the rationale for active **stabilization policy**, which is the use of government policy to reduce the severity of recessions and rein in excessively strong expansions.

Tim Gidal/ Picture Post/ Getty Images

Some people use *Keynesian economics* as a synonym for *left-wing economics*—but the truth is that the ideas of John Maynard Keynes have been accepted across a broad range of the political spectrum.

Stabilization policy is the use of government policy to reduce the severity of recessions and rein in excessively strong expansions.

Can stabilization policy improve the economy's performance? As we saw in Figure 18.4, the answer certainly appears to be yes. Under active stabilization policy, the U.S. economy returned to potential output in 1996 after an approximately five-year recessionary gap. Likewise, in 2001, it also returned to potential output after an approximately four-year inflationary gap. These periods are much shorter than the decade or more that economists believe it would take for the economy to self-correct in the absence of active stabilization policy. However, as we'll see shortly, the ability to improve the economy's performance is not always guaranteed. It depends on the kinds of shocks the economy faces.

Policy in the Face of Demand Shocks

Imagine that the economy experiences a negative demand shock, like the one shown by the shift from AD_1 to AD_2 in Figure 19.5. Monetary and fiscal policy shift the aggregate demand curve. If policy makers react quickly to the fall in aggregate demand, they can use monetary or fiscal policy to shift the aggregate demand curve back to the right. And if policy were able to perfectly anticipate shifts of the aggregate demand curve and counteract them, it could short-circuit the whole process shown in Figure 19.5. Instead of going through a period of low aggregate output and falling prices, the government could manage the economy so that it would stay at E_1.

Why might a policy that short-circuits the adjustment shown in Figure 19.5 and maintains the economy at its original equilibrium be desirable? For two reasons: First, the temporary fall in aggregate output that would happen without policy intervention is a bad thing, particularly because such a decline is associated with high unemployment. Second, *price stability* is generally regarded as a desirable goal. So preventing deflation—a fall in the aggregate price level—is a good thing.

Does this mean that policy makers should always act to offset declines in aggregate demand? Not necessarily. As we'll see, some policy measures to increase aggregate demand, especially those that increase budget deficits, may have long-term costs in terms of lower long-run growth. Furthermore, in the real world policy makers aren't perfectly informed, and the effects of their policies aren't perfectly predictable. This creates the danger that stabilization policy will do more harm than good; that is, attempts to stabilize the economy may end up creating more instability. We'll describe the long-running debate over macroeconomic policy in later modules. Despite these qualifications, most economists believe that a good case can be made for using macroeconomic policy to offset major negative shocks to the *AD* curve.

Should policy makers also try to offset positive shocks to aggregate demand? It may not seem obvious that they should. After all, even though inflation may be a bad thing, isn't more output and lower unemployment a good thing? Again, not necessarily. Most economists now believe that any short-run gains from an inflationary gap must be paid back later. So policy makers today usually try to offset positive as well as negative demand shocks. For reasons we'll explain later, attempts to eliminate recessionary gaps and inflationary gaps usually rely on monetary rather than fiscal policy. For now, let's explore how macroeconomic policy can respond to supply shocks.

Responding to Supply Shocks

In panel (a) of Figure 19.3, we showed the effects of a negative supply shock: in the short run such a shock leads to lower aggregate output but a higher aggregate price level. As we've noted, policy makers can respond to a negative *demand* shock by using monetary and fiscal policy to return aggregate demand to its original level. But what can or should they do about a negative *supply* shock?

In contrast to the case of a demand shock, there are no easy remedies for a supply shock. That is, there are no government policies that can easily counteract the changes in production costs that shift the short-run aggregate supply curve. So the policy response to a negative supply shock cannot aim to simply push the curve that shifted back to its original position.

In addition, if you consider using monetary or fiscal policy to shift the aggregate demand curve in response to a supply shock, the right response isn't obvious. Two bad things are

FYI Is Stabilization Policy Stabilizing?

We've described the theoretical rationale for stabilization policy as a way of responding to demand shocks. But does stabilization policy actually stabilize the economy? One way we might try to answer this question is to look at the long-term historical record. Before World War II, the U.S. government didn't really have a stabilization policy, largely because macroeconomics as we know it didn't exist, and there was no consensus about what to do. Since World War II, and especially since 1960, active stabilization policy has become standard practice.

So here's the question: has the economy actually become more stable since the government began trying to stabilize it? The answer is a qualified yes. It's qualified because data from the pre–World War II era are less reliable than more modern data. But there still seems to be a clear reduction in the size of economic fluctuations.

The figure on the right shows the number of unemployed as a percentage of the nonfarm labor force since 1890. (We focus on nonfarm workers because farmers, though they often suffer economic hardship, are rarely reported as unemployed.) Even ignoring the huge spike in unemployment during the Great Depression, unemployment seems to have varied a lot more before World War II than after. It's also worth noticing that the peaks in postwar unemployment in 1975 and 1982 corresponded to major supply shocks—the kind of shock for which stabilization policy has no good answer.

It's possible that the greater stability of the economy reflects good luck rather than policy. But on the face of it, the evidence suggests that stabilization policy is indeed stabilizing.

Source: C. Romer, "Spurious Volatility in Historical Unemployment Data," *Journal of Political Economy* 94, no. 1 (1986): 1–37 (years 1890–1928); Bureau of Labor Statistics (years 1929–2013).

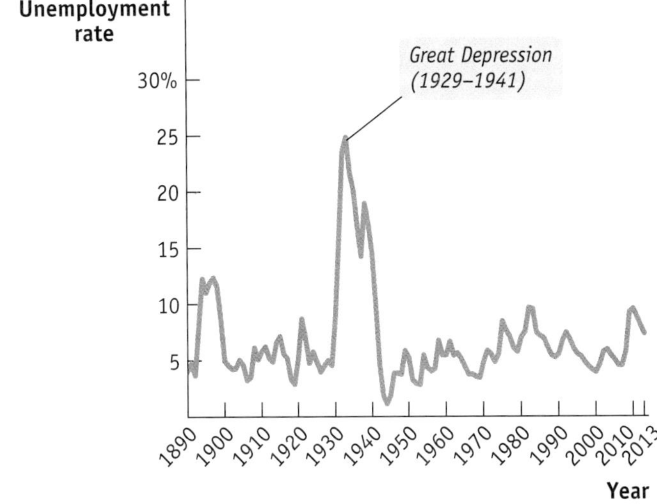

happening simultaneously: a fall in aggregate output, leading to a rise in unemployment, *and* a rise in the aggregate price level. Any policy that shifts the aggregate demand curve alleviates one problem only by making the other problem worse. If the government acts to increase aggregate demand and limit the rise in unemployment, it reduces the decline in output but causes even more inflation. If it acts to reduce aggregate demand, it curbs inflation but causes a further rise in unemployment.

It's a trade-off with no good answer. In the end, the United States and other economically advanced nations suffering from the supply shocks of the 1970s eventually chose to stabilize prices even at the cost of higher unemployment. But being an economic policy maker in the 1970s, or in early 2008, meant facing even harder choices than usual.

Bloomberg via Getty Images

Negative supply shocks cause inflation and unemployment. This makes for difficult policy choices for Federal Reserve Chairman Janet Yellen because any policy that alleviates one problem worsens the other.

Fiscal Policy: The Basics

Let's begin with the obvious: modern governments spend a great deal of money and collect a lot in taxes. **Figure 20.1** on the next page shows government spending and tax revenue as percentages of GDP for a selection of high-income countries in 2012. As you can see, the French government sector is relatively large, accounting for more than half of the French economy. The government of the United States plays a smaller role in the economy than do the governments of Canada or most European countries. But that role is still sizable. As a result, changes in the

Figure 20.1 Government Spending and Tax Revenue for Some High-Income Countries in 2012

Government spending and tax revenue are represented as a percentage of GDP. France has a particularly large government sector, representing nearly 60% of its GDP. The U.S. government sector, although sizable, is smaller than the government sectors of Canada and most European countries.
Source: OECD (data for Japan is for year 2011).

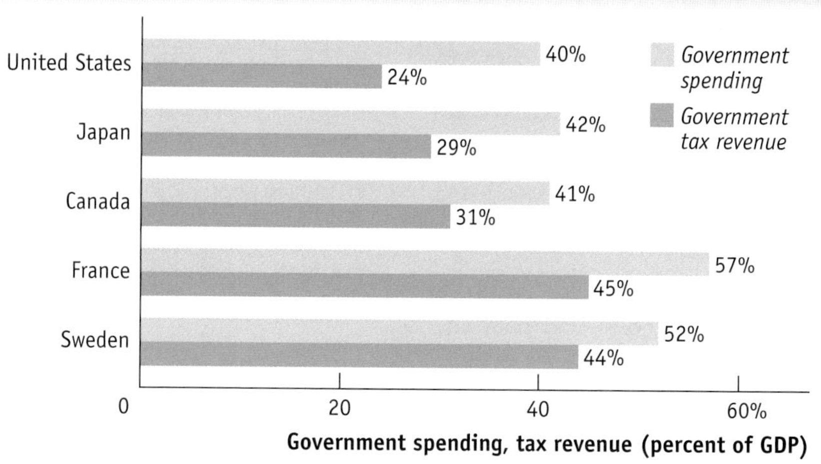

federal budget—changes in government spending or in taxation—can have large effects on the U.S. economy.

To analyze these effects, we begin by showing how taxes and government spending affect the economy's flow of income. Then we can see how changes in spending and tax policy affect aggregate demand.

AP® Exam Tip

When the government increases spending or transfer payments or decreases taxes (to give consumers more income), the economy expands. When the government decreases spending or transfer payments or increases taxes, the economy contracts.

Taxes, Government Purchases of Goods and Services, Transfers, and Borrowing

In the circular-flow diagram discussed in Module 10, we showed the circular flow of income and spending in the economy as a whole. One of the sectors represented in that figure was the government. Funds flow *into* the government in the form of taxes and government borrowing; funds flow *out* in the form of government purchases of goods and services and government transfers to households.

What kinds of taxes do Americans pay, and where does the money go? **Figure 20.2** shows the composition of U.S. tax revenue in 2013. Taxes, of course, are required

Figure 20.2 Sources of Tax Revenue in the United States, 2013

Personal income taxes, taxes on corporate profits, and social insurance taxes account for most government tax revenue. The rest is a mix of property taxes, sales taxes, and other sources of revenue.
Source: Bureau of Economic Analysis.

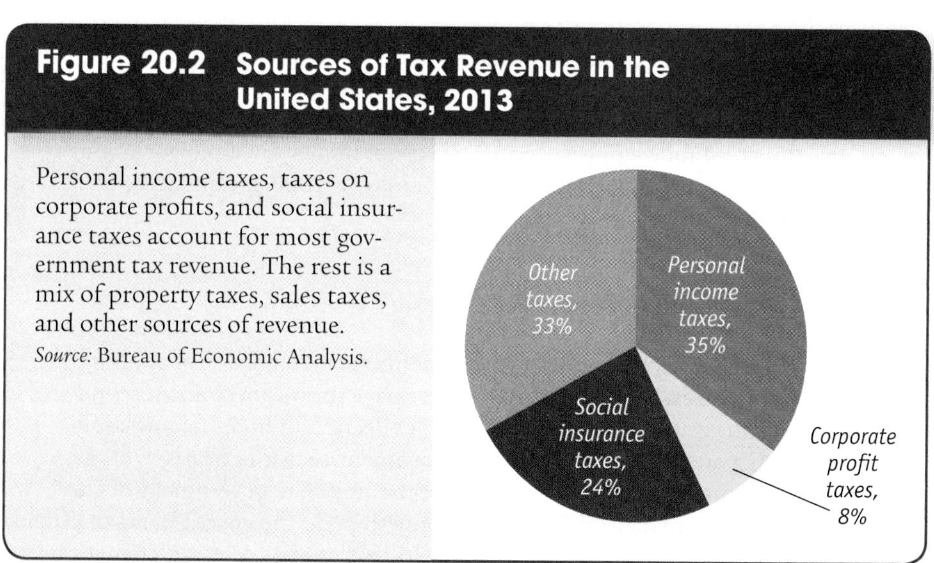

Figure 20.3 Government Spending in the United States, 2013

The two types of government spending are purchases of goods and services and government transfers. The big items in government purchases are national defense and education. The big items in government transfers are Social Security and the Medicare and Medicaid health care programs.

Source: Bureau of Economic Analysis.

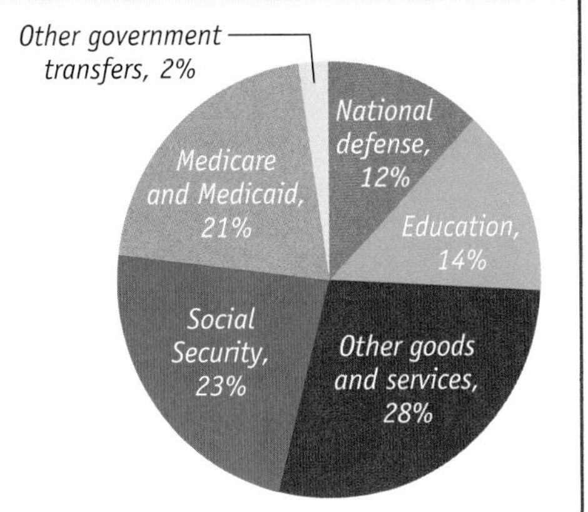

payments to the government. In the United States, taxes are collected at the national level by the federal government; at the state level by each state government; and at local levels by counties, cities, and towns. At the federal level, the main taxes are income taxes on both personal income and corporate profits as well as *social insurance* taxes, which we'll explain shortly. At the state and local levels, the picture is more complex: these governments rely on a mix of sales taxes, property taxes, income taxes, and fees of various kinds. Overall, taxes on personal income and corporate profits accounted for 43% of total government revenue in 2013; social insurance taxes accounted for 24%; and a variety of other taxes, collected mainly at the state and local levels, accounted for the rest.

Figure 20.3 shows the composition of total U.S. government spending in 2013, which takes two forms. One form is purchases of goods and services. This includes everything from ammunition for the military to the salaries of public schoolteachers (who are treated in the national accounts as providers of a service–education). The big items here are national defense and education. The large category labeled "Other goods and services" consists mainly of state and local spending on a variety of services, from police and firefighters to highway construction and maintenance.

Social insurance programs are government programs intended to protect families against economic hardship.

The other form of government spending is government transfers, which are payments by the government to households for which no good or service is provided in return. In the modern United States, as well as in Canada and Europe, government transfers represent a very large proportion of the budget. Most U.S. government spending on transfer payments is accounted for by three big programs:

- Social Security, which provides guaranteed income to older Americans, disabled Americans, and the surviving spouses and dependent children of deceased beneficiaries
- Medicare, which covers much of the cost of health care for Americans over age 65
- Medicaid, which covers much of the cost of health care for Americans with low incomes

The term **social insurance** is used to describe government programs that are intended to protect families

William Thomas Cain/Getty Images

Government transfers on their way: Social Security checks are run through a printer at the U.S. Treasury printing facility in Philadelphia, Pennsylvania.

against economic hardship. These include Social Security, Medicare, and Medicaid, as well as smaller programs such as unemployment insurance and food stamps. In the United States, social insurance programs are largely paid for with special, dedicated taxes on wages—the social insurance taxes we mentioned earlier.

But how do tax policy and government spending affect the economy? The answer is that taxation and government spending have a strong effect on aggregate spending.

The Government Budget and Total Spending

Let's recall the basic equation of national income accounting:

$$\textbf{(20-1)}\quad GDP = C + I + G + X - IM$$

The left-hand side of this equation is GDP, the value of all final goods and services produced in the economy. The right-hand side is aggregate spending, the total spending on final goods and services produced in the economy. It is the sum of consumer spending (C), investment spending (I), government purchases of goods and services (G), and the value of exports (X) minus the value of imports (IM). It includes all the sources of aggregate demand.

The government directly controls one of the variables on the right-hand side of Equation 20-1: government purchases of goods and services (G). But that's not the only effect fiscal policy has on aggregate spending in the economy. Through changes in taxes and transfers, it also influences consumer spending (C) and, in some cases, investment spending (I).

To see why the budget affects consumer spending, recall that *disposable income,* the total income households have available to spend, is equal to the total income they receive from wages, dividends, interest, and rent, *minus* taxes, *plus* government transfers. So either an increase in taxes or a decrease in government transfers *reduces* disposable income. And a fall in disposable income, other things equal, leads to a fall in consumer spending. Conversely, either a decrease in taxes or an increase in government transfers *increases* disposable income. And a rise in disposable income, other things equal, leads to a rise in consumer spending.

The government's ability to affect investment spending is a more complex story, which we won't discuss in detail. The important point is that the government taxes profits, and changes in the rules that determine how much a business owes can increase or decrease the incentive to spend on investment goods.

Because the government itself is one source of spending in the economy, and because taxes and transfers can affect spending by consumers and firms, the government can use changes in taxes or government spending to *shift the aggregate demand curve*, and there can be good reasons for doing so. In early 2008, for example, there was bipartisan agreement that the U.S. government should act to prevent a fall in aggregate demand—that is, to move the aggregate demand curve to the right of where it would otherwise be. The resulting Economic Stimulus Act of 2008 was a classic example of fiscal policy: the use of taxes, government transfers, or government purchases of goods and services to stabilize the economy by shifting the aggregate demand curve.

Expansionary and Contractionary Fiscal Policy

Why would the government want to shift the aggregate demand curve? Because it wants to close either a recessionary gap, created when aggregate output falls below potential output, or an inflationary gap, created when aggregate output exceeds potential output.

Figure 20.4 shows the case of an economy facing a recessionary gap. *SRAS* is the short-run aggregate supply curve, *LRAS* is the long-run aggregate supply curve, and AD_1 is the initial aggregate demand curve. At the initial short-run macroeconomic equilibrium, E_1, aggregate output is Y_1, below potential output, Y_P. What the government would like to do is increase aggregate demand, shifting the aggregate demand curve rightward to AD_2. This would increase aggregate output, making it equal to potential

Figure 20.4 Expansionary Fiscal Policy Can Close a Recessionary Gap

At E_1 the economy is in short-run macroeconomic equilibrium where the aggregate demand curve, AD_1, intersects the *SRAS* curve. At E_1, there is a recessionary gap of $Y_P - Y_1$. An expansionary fiscal policy—an increase in government purchases of goods and services, a reduction in taxes, or an increase in government transfers—shifts the aggregate demand curve rightward. It can close the recessionary gap by shifting AD_1 to AD_2, moving the economy to a new short-run macroeconomic equilibrium, E_2, which is also a long-run macroeconomic equilibrium.

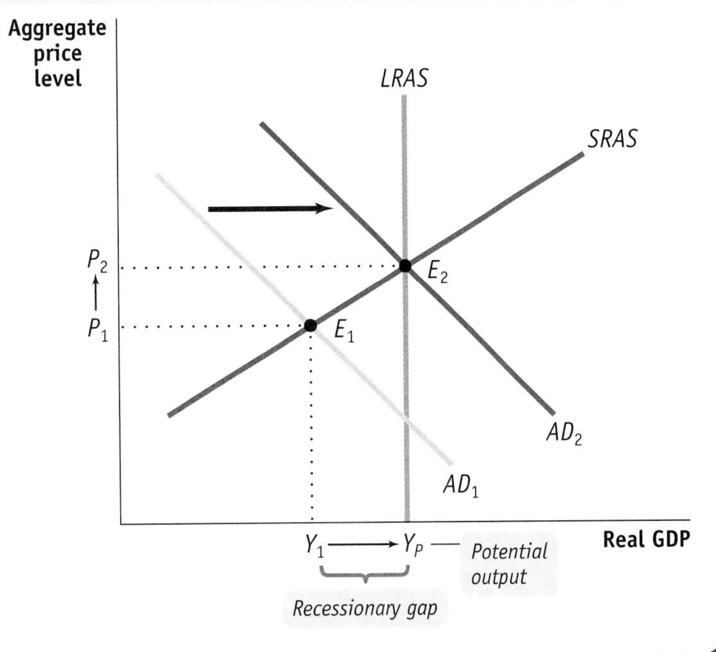

output. Fiscal policy that increases aggregate demand, called **expansionary fiscal policy**, normally takes one of three forms:

- an increase in government purchases of goods and services
- a cut in taxes
- an increase in government transfers

Expansionary fiscal policy increases aggregate demand.

Figure 20.5 on the next page shows the opposite case—an economy facing an inflationary gap. At the initial equilibrium, E_1, aggregate output is Y_1, above potential output, Y_P. Policy makers often try to head off inflation by eliminating inflationary gaps. To eliminate the inflationary gap shown in Figure 20.5, fiscal policy must reduce aggregate demand and shift the aggregate demand curve leftward to AD_2. This reduces aggregate output and makes it equal to potential output. Fiscal policy that reduces aggregate demand, called **contractionary fiscal policy**, is implemented by:

- a reduction in government purchases of goods and services
- an increase in taxes
- a reduction in government transfers

AP® Exam Tip

If a question on the AP® exam asks you to identify a policy that would be appropriate to close a recessionary gap or an inflationary gap, don't simply say "expansionary" or "contractionary." Your answer should specify a policy (a change in spending, transfer payments, or taxes) that would close the gap described in the question.

A classic example of contractionary fiscal policy occurred in 1968, when U.S. policy makers grew worried about rising inflation. President Lyndon Johnson imposed a temporary 10% surcharge on income taxes—everyone's income taxes were increased by 10%. He also tried to scale back government purchases of goods and services, which had risen dramatically because of the cost of the Vietnam War.

Contractionary fiscal policy reduces aggregate demand.

A Cautionary Note: Lags in Fiscal Policy

Looking at Figures 20.4 and 20.5, it may seem obvious that the government should actively use fiscal policy—always adopting an expansionary fiscal policy when the economy faces a recessionary gap and always adopting a contractionary fiscal policy when the economy faces an inflationary gap. But many economists caution against an extremely active stabilization policy, arguing that a government that tries too hard to stabilize

Figure 20.5 Contractionary Fiscal Policy Can Close an Inflationary Gap

At E_1 the economy is in short-run macroeconomic equilibrium where the aggregate demand curve, AD_1, intersects the *SRAS* curve. At E_1, there is an inflationary gap of $Y_1 - Y_P$. A contractionary fiscal policy—such as reduced government purchases of goods and services, an increase in taxes, or a reduction in government transfers—shifts the aggregate demand curve leftward. It closes the inflationary gap by shifting AD_1 to AD_2, moving the economy to a new short-run macroeconomic equilibrium, E_2, which is also a long-run macroeconomic equilibrium.

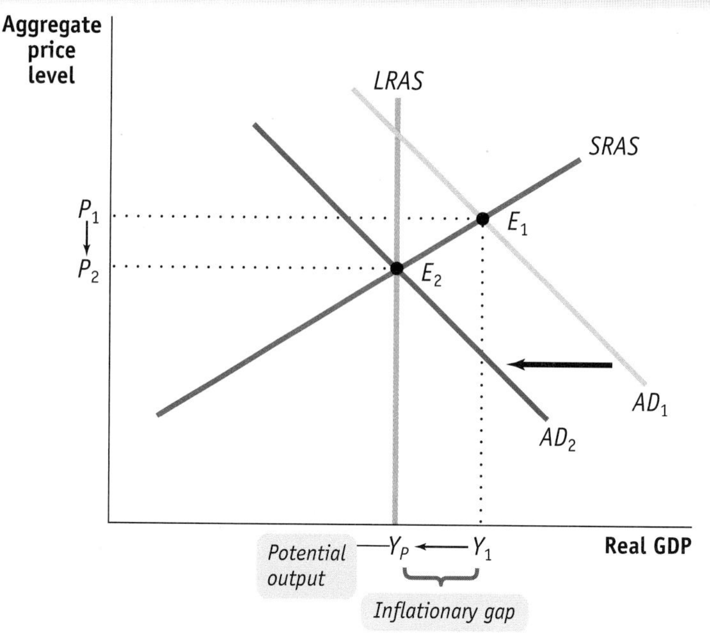

the economy through fiscal policy, or a central bank that does the same with monetary policy, can end up making the economy less stable.

We'll leave discussion of the warnings associated with monetary policy to later modules. In the case of fiscal policy, one key reason for caution is that there are important *time lags* in its use. To understand the nature of these lags, think about what has to happen before the government increases spending to fight a recessionary gap. First, the government has to realize that the recessionary gap exists: economic data take time to collect and analyze, and recessions are often recognized only months after they have begun. Second, the government has to develop a spending plan, which can itself take months, particularly if politicians take time debating how the money should be spent and passing legislation. Finally, it takes time to spend money. For example, a road construction project begins with activities such as surveying that don't involve spending large sums. It may be quite some time before the big spending begins.

AP Photo/Ron Edmonds

Will the stimulus come in time to be worthwhile? President Barack Obama listens to a question during a news conference in the East Room of the White House in Washington, D.C.

Because of these lags, an attempt to increase spending to fight a recessionary gap may take so long to get going that the economy has already recovered on its own. In fact, the recessionary gap may have turned into an inflationary gap by the time the fiscal policy takes effect. In that case, the fiscal policy will make things worse instead of better.

This doesn't mean that fiscal policy should never be actively used. In early 2008, for example, there was good reason to believe that the U.S. economy had begun a lengthy slowdown caused by turmoil in the financial markets, so a fiscal stimulus designed to arrive within a few months would almost surely push aggregate demand in the right direction. But the problem of lags makes the actual use of both fiscal and monetary policy harder than you might think from a simple analysis like the one we have just given.

MODULE 20 Review

Check Your Understanding

1. In each of the following cases, determine whether the policy is an expansionary or contractionary fiscal policy:
   a. Several military bases around the country, which together employ tens of thousands of people, are closed.
   b. The number of weeks an unemployed person is eligible for unemployment benefits is increased.
   c. The federal tax on gasoline is increased.
2. Explain why federal disaster relief, which quickly disburses funds to victims of natural disasters such as hurricanes, floods, and large-scale crop failures, will stabilize the economy more effectively after a disaster than relief that must be legislated.
3. Suppose someone says, "Using monetary or fiscal policy to pump up the economy is counterproductive—you get a brief high, but then you have the pain of inflation."
   a. Explain what this means in terms of the *AD–AS* model.
   b. Is this a valid argument against stabilization policy? Why or why not?

Tackle the Test: Multiple-Choice Questions

1. Which of the following contributes to the lag in implementing fiscal policy?
   I. It takes time for Congress and the president to pass spending and tax changes.
   II. Current economic data take time to collect and analyze.
   III. It takes time to realize an output gap exists.
   a. I only
   b. II only
   c. III only
   d. I and III only
   e. I, II, and III
2. Which of the following is a government transfer program?
   a. Social Security
   b. Medicare/Medicaid
   c. unemployment insurance
   d. food stamps
   e. all of the above
3. Which of the following is an example of expansionary fiscal policy?
   a. increasing taxes
   b. increasing government spending
   c. decreasing government transfers
   d. decreasing interest rates
   e. increasing the money supply
4. Which of the following is a fiscal policy that is appropriate to combat inflation?
   a. decreasing taxes
   b. decreasing government spending
   c. increasing government transfers
   d. increasing interest rates
   e. expansionary fiscal policy
5. A cut in income taxes is an example of
   a. an expansionary fiscal policy.
   b. a contractionary fiscal policy.
   c. an expansionary monetary policy.
   d. a contractionary monetary policy.
   e. none of the above.

Tackle the Test: Free-Response Questions

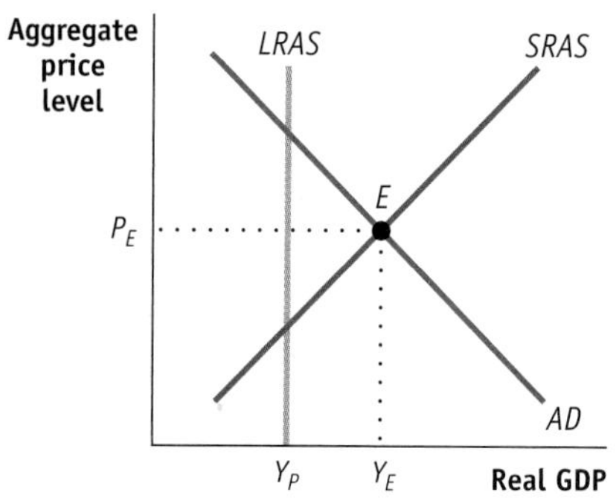

1. Refer to the graph above.
   a. What type of gap exists in this economy?
   b. What type of fiscal policy is appropriate in this situation?
   c. List the three variables the government can change to implement fiscal policy.
   d. How would the government change each of the three variables to implement the policy you listed in part b?

Rubric for FRQ 1 (8 points)

1 point: Inflationary
1 point: Contractionary
1 point: Taxes
1 point: Government transfers
1 point: Government purchases of goods and services
1 point: Increase taxes
1 point: Decrease government transfers
1 point: Decrease government purchases of goods and services

2. a. Draw a correctly labeled graph showing an economy experiencing a recessionary gap.
   b. What type of fiscal policy is appropriate in this situation?
   c. Give an example of what the government could do to implement the type of policy you listed in part b.

   (6 points)

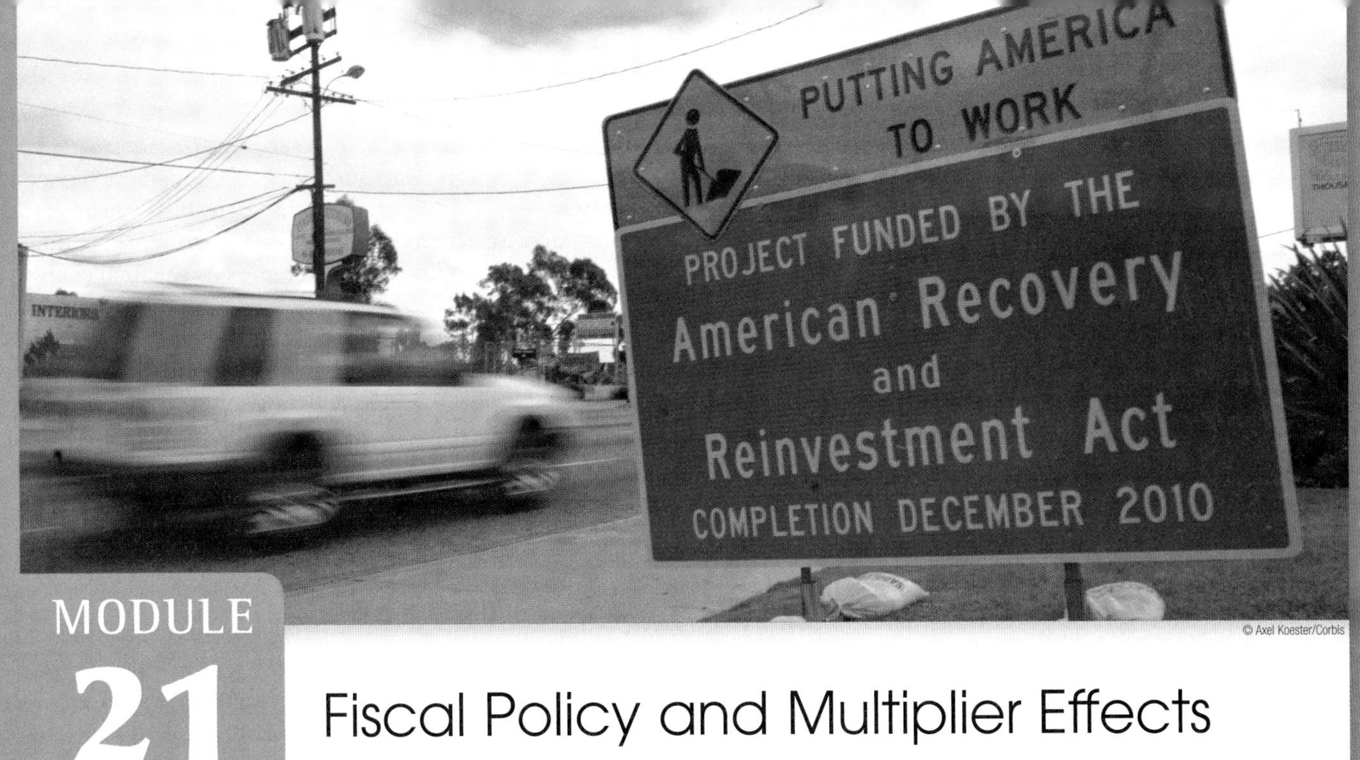

© Axel Koester/Corbis

MODULE 21 Fiscal Policy and Multiplier Effects

In this Module, you will learn to:

- Explain why fiscal policy has a multiplier effect
- Describe how automatic stabilizers influence the multiplier effect

The Spending Multiplier and Estimates of the Influence of Government Policy

An expansionary fiscal policy, like the American Recovery and Reinvestment Act, pushes the aggregate demand curve to the right. A contractionary fiscal policy, like Lyndon Johnson's tax surcharge, pushes the aggregate demand curve to the left. For policy makers, however, knowing the direction of the shift isn't enough: they need estimates of *how much* the aggregate demand curve will be shifted by a given policy. To get these estimates, they use the concept of the multiplier.

Multiplier Effects of Changes in Government Purchases

Suppose that a government decides to spend $50 billion to build bridges and roads. The government's purchases of goods and services will directly increase total spending on final goods and services by $50 billion. But there will also be an indirect effect because the government's purchases will start a chain reaction throughout the economy. The firms producing the goods and services purchased by the government will earn revenues that flow to households in the form of wages, profit, interest, and rent. This increase in disposable income will lead to a rise in consumer spending. The rise in consumer spending, in turn, will induce firms to increase output, leading to a further rise in disposable income, which will lead to another round of consumer spending increases, and so on.

In Module 16 we learned about the *spending multiplier*: the factor by which we multiply the amount of an autonomous change in aggregate spending to find the resulting change in real GDP. An increase in government purchases of goods and services is

NASA/Tony Gray, Tom Farrar

When the government hires Boeing to build spacecraft, Boeing employees spend their earnings on things like cars, and the automakers spend their earnings on things like education, and so on, creating a multiplier effect.

an example of an autonomous increase in aggregate spending. Any increase in government purchases of goods and services will lead to a series of additional purchases, resulting in an even larger final increase in real GDP. The initial change in spending, multiplied by the spending multiplier gives us the final change in real GDP.

Let's consider a simple case that does not involve taxes or international trade. In this case, any change in GDP accrues entirely to households. Assume that the aggregate price level is fixed, so that any increase in nominal GDP is also a rise in real GDP, and that the interest rate is fixed. In that case, the spending multiplier is $1/(1 - MPC)$. Recall that *MPC* is the *marginal propensity to consume,* the fraction of an additional $1 in disposable income that is spent. For example, if the marginal propensity to consume is 0.5, the spending multiplier is $1/(1 - 0.5) = 1/0.5 = 2$. Given a spending multiplier of 2, a $50 billion increase in government purchases of goods and services would increase real GDP by $100 billion. Of that $100 billion, $50 billion is the initial effect from the increase in *G,* and the remaining $50 billion is the subsequent effect of more production leading to more income which leads to more consumer spending, which leads to more production, and so on.

What happens if government purchases of goods and services are reduced instead? The math is exactly the same, except that there's a minus sign in front: if government purchases of goods and services fall by $50 billion and the marginal propensity to consume is 0.5, real GDP falls by $100 billion. This is the result of less production leading to less income, which leads to less consumption, which leads to less production, and so on.

Multiplier Effects of Changes in Government Transfers and Taxes

Expansionary or contractionary fiscal policy need not take the form of changes in government purchases of goods and services. Governments can also change transfer payments or taxes. In general, however, a change in government transfers or taxes shifts the aggregate demand curve by *less* than an equal-sized change in government purchases, resulting in a smaller effect on real GDP.

To see why, imagine that instead of spending $50 billion on building bridges, the government simply hands out $50 billion in the form of government transfers. In this case, there is no direct effect on aggregate demand as there was with government purchases of goods and services. Real GDP and income grow only because households spend some of that $50 billion—and they probably won't spend it all. In fact, they will spend additional income according to the *MPC*. If the *MPC* is 0.5, households will spend only 50 cents of every additional dollar they receive in transfers.

Table 21.1 shows a hypothetical comparison of two expansionary fiscal policies assuming an *MPC* equal to 0.5 and a multiplier equal to 2: one in which the government directly purchases $50 billion in goods and services and one in which the government makes transfer payments instead, sending out $50 billion in checks to consumers. In each case, there is a first-round effect on real GDP, either from purchases by the government or from purchases by the consumers who received the checks. This first round is followed by a series of additional rounds as rising real GDP raises income (all of which is disposable under our assumption of no taxes), which in turn raises consumption.

However, the first-round effect of the transfer program is smaller; because we have assumed that the *MPC* is 0.5, only $25 billion of the $50 billion is spent, with the other $25 billion saved. As a result, all the further rounds are smaller, too. In the end, the transfer payment increases real GDP by only $50 billion. In comparison, a $50 billion increase in government purchases produces a $100 billion increase in real GDP.

Table 21.1 Hypothetical Effects of a Fiscal Policy with a Multiplier of 2

Effect on real GDP	$50 billion rise in government purchases of goods and services	$50 billion rise in government transfer payments
First round	$50 billion	$25 billion
Second round	$25 billion	$12.5 billion
Third round	$12.5 billion	$6.25 billion
•	•	•
•	•	•
•	•	•
Eventual effect	$100 billion	$50 billion

A tax cut has an effect similar to the effect of a transfer. It increases disposable income, leading to a series of increases in consumer spending. But the overall effect is smaller than that of an equal-sized increase in government purchases of goods and services: the autonomous increase in aggregate spending is smaller because households save part of the amount of the tax cut. They save a fraction of the tax cut equal to their *MPS* (which equals 1−*MPC*). So, for each $1 decrease in taxes, spending increases only by the portion of the dollar that is not saved: the *MPC*. A tax increase has the opposite effect. For each $1 of additional taxes collected, savings decrease by the *MPS* and spending decreases by the *MPC*.

The **tax multiplier** is the factor by which we multiply a change in tax collections to find the total change in real GDP. Recall that the spending multiplier is 1/(1−*MPC*). The tax multiplier has "*MPC*" in place of "1" in the numerator to reflect the initial spending decrease of *MPC* for each $1 of taxes collected. And the tax multiplier is negative because spending decreases when taxes increase, and spending increases when taxes decrease. This makes the tax multiplier:

The **tax multiplier** is the factor by which a change in tax collections changes real GDP.

$$-MPC/(1-MPC)$$

For example, if the *MPC* is 0.80, then the tax multiplier is −0.80/(1−0.80) = −4. So a $10 billion increase in taxes would cause a change in spending of −4 × $10 billion = −$40 billion.

The multiplier for a change in transfers is the same as the tax multiplier, except the multiplier is positive, because when transfers increase, spending increases, and when transfers decrease, spending decreases. In our example above, the *MPC* was 0.5, so the multiplier was 0.5/(1−0.5) = 1. This explains why the $50 billion increase in transfers led to a $50 billion total increase in real GDP. If the *MPC* had been 0.75, the multiplier would have been 0.75/(1−0.75) = 3, and the $50 billion increase in transfers would have led to a 3 × $50 billion = $150 billion total increase in real GDP.

When a government collects taxes to cover its expenditures, it activates both the spending multiplier and the tax multiplier. The spending multiplier applies to the government spending and the tax multiplier applies to the equivalent taxes. By combining these multipliers, the **balanced budget multiplier** is the factor by which we multiply a change in both spending and taxes to find the total change in real GDP. We can find the balanced budget multiplier by adding the spending and tax multipliers together: 1/(1−*MPC*) + (−*MPC*)/(1−*MPC*) = (1−*MPC*)/(1−*MPC*) = 1. So each $1 of government spending funded with new tax collections increases aggregate spending by $1.

The **balanced budget multiplier** is the factor by which a change in both spending and taxes changes real GDP.

Lump-sum taxes are taxes that don't depend on the taxpayer's income.

While a balanced budget simplifies the multiplier story, the existence of taxes that depend on real GDP complicate it. In the real world, governments rarely impose **lump-sum taxes**, for which the amount owed is independent of the taxpayer's income. Instead, the great majority of tax revenue is raised with taxes that depend positively on

the level of real GDP. As we'll discuss shortly, these taxes make the spending and tax multipliers smaller.

In practice, economists often argue that *who* among the population gets tax cuts or increases in government transfers also matters. For example, compare the effects of an increase in unemployment benefits with a cut in taxes on profits distributed to shareholders as dividends. Consumer surveys suggest that the average unemployed worker will spend a higher share of any increase in his or her disposable income than would the average recipient of dividend income. That is, people who are unemployed tend to have a higher *MPC* than people who own a lot of stocks, because the latter tend to be wealthier and tend to save more of any increase in disposable income. If that's true, a dollar spent on unemployment benefits increases aggregate demand more than a dollar's worth of dividend tax cuts. Such arguments played an important role in the final provisions of the 2008 stimulus package.

AP® Exam Tip

Simplify your calculations! The tax multiplier is always 1 less than the spending multiplier, and the opposite sign. When taxes and government spending both increase or decrease by the same amount, the net change in real GDP is simply the change in government spending. That is, the *balanced budget multiplier* is simply 1.

How Taxes Affect the Multiplier

Government taxes capture some part of the increase in real GDP that occurs in each round of the multiplier process, since most government taxes depend positively on real GDP. As a result, disposable income increases by considerably less than $1 for each $1 spent once we include taxes in the model.

The increase in government tax revenue when real GDP rises isn't the result of a deliberate decision or action by the government. It's a consequence of the way the tax laws are written, which causes most sources of government revenue to increase *automatically* when real GDP goes up. For example, income tax receipts increase when real GDP rises because the amount each individual owes in taxes depends positively on his or her income, and households' taxable income rises when real GDP rises. Sales tax receipts increase when real GDP rises because people with more income spend more on goods and services. And corporate profit tax receipts increase when real GDP rises because profits increase when the economy expands.

An historical example of discretionary fiscal policy was the Works Progress Administration (WPA), a relief measure established during the Great Depression that put the unemployed to work building bridges, roads, buildings, and parks.

The effect of these automatic increases in tax revenue is to reduce the size of the spending and tax multipliers. Remember, the multipliers are the result of a chain reaction in which higher real GDP leads to higher disposable income, which leads to higher consumer spending, which leads to further increases in real GDP. The fact that the government siphons off some of any increase in real GDP means that at each stage of this process, the increase in consumer spending is smaller than it would be if taxes weren't part of the picture. As a result, these multipliers become smaller.

Many macroeconomists believe it's a good thing that taxes reduce the multipliers in real life. Most, though not all, recessions are the result of negative demand shocks. The same mechanism that causes tax revenue to increase when the economy expands causes it to decrease when the economy contracts. Since tax receipts decrease when real GDP falls, the effects of these negative demand shocks are smaller than they would be if there were no taxes. The decrease in tax revenue reduces the adverse effect of the initial fall in aggregate demand. The automatic decrease in government tax revenue generated by a fall in real GDP—caused by a decrease in the amount of taxes households pay—acts like an automatic expansionary fiscal policy implemented in the face of a recession. Similarly, when the economy expands, the government finds itself automatically pursuing a contractionary fiscal policy—a tax increase. Government spending and taxation rules that cause fiscal policy to be automatically expansionary when the economy contracts and automatically contractionary when the economy expands, without requiring any deliberate action by policy makers, are called **automatic stabilizers.**

Automatic stabilizers are government spending and taxation rules that cause fiscal policy to be automatically expansionary when the economy contracts and automatically contractionary when the economy expands.

The rules that govern tax collection aren't the only automatic stabilizers, although they are the most important ones. Some types of government transfers also play a stabilizing role. For example, more people receive unemployment insurance when the economy is depressed than when it is booming. The same is true of Medicaid and food stamps. So transfer payments tend to rise when the economy is contracting and fall when the economy is expanding. Like changes in tax revenue, these automatic changes in transfers tend to reduce the size of the multipliers because the total change in disposable income that results from a given rise or fall in real GDP is smaller.

As in the case of government tax revenue, many macroeconomists believe that it's a good thing that government transfers reduce the spending and tax multipliers. Expansionary and contractionary fiscal policies that are the result of automatic stabilizers are widely considered helpful to macroeconomic stabilization, because they blunt the extremes of the business cycle. But what about fiscal policy that *isn't* the result of automatic stabilizers? **Discretionary fiscal policy** is fiscal policy that is the direct result of deliberate actions by policy makers rather than automatic adjustment. For example, during a recession, the government may pass legislation that cuts taxes and increases government spending in order to stimulate the economy. In general, mainly due to problems with time lags as discussed in Module 10, economists tend to support the use of discretionary fiscal policy only in special circumstances, such as during an especially severe recession.

Discretionary fiscal policy is fiscal policy that is the result of deliberate actions by policy makers rather than rules.

About That Stimulus Package . . .

In early 2008, there was broad bipartisan agreement that the U.S. economy needed a fiscal stimulus. However, there was sharp partisan disagreement about what form that stimulus should take. The eventual bill was a compromise that left both sides unhappy and arguably made the stimulus less effective than it could have been.

Initially, there was little support for an increase in government purchases of goods and services—that is, neither party wanted to build bridges and roads to stimulate the economy. Both parties believed that the economy needed a quick boost, and ramping up spending would take too long. But there was a fierce debate over whether the stimulus should take the form of a tax cut, which would deliver its biggest benefits to those who paid the most taxes, or an increase in transfer payments targeted at those Americans who were most in economic distress.

The eventual compromise gave most taxpayers a flat $600 rebate, $1,200 for married couples. Very high-income taxpayers were not entitled to a rebate; low earners who didn't make enough to pay income taxes, but did pay other taxes, received $300. In effect, the plan was a combination of tax cuts for most Americans and transfer payments to Americans with low incomes.

How well designed was the stimulus plan? Many economists believed that only a fraction of the rebate checks would actually be spent, so that the eventual multiplier would be fairly low. White House economists appeared to agree: they estimated that the stimulus would raise employment by half a million jobs above what it would have been otherwise, the same number offered by independent economists who believed that the multiplier on the plan would be around 0.75. Some economists were critical, arguing that Congress should have insisted on a plan that yielded more "bang for the buck."

Both Democratic and Republican economists working for Congress defended the plan, arguing that the perfect is the enemy of the good—that it was the best that could be negotiated on short notice and was likely to be of real help in fighting the economy's weakness. But by late summer 2008, with the U.S. economy still in the doldrums, there was widespread agreement that the plan's results had been disappointing. And by late 2008, with the economy shrinking further, policy makers were working on a new, much larger stimulus plan that relied more heavily on government purchases. The American Recovery and Reinvestment Act was passed in February 2009. The bill called for $787 billion in expenditures on stimulus in three areas: help for the unemployed and those receiving Medicaid and food stamps; investments in infrastructure, energy, and health care; and tax cuts for families and small businesses.

Despite controversies over specifics, the general consensus about active stabilization policy is apparent: when at first you don't succeed, try, try again.

RECESSION
S.S. STIMULUS
"WE'RE GONNA NEED A BIGGER BOAT."

MODULE 21 Review

Check Your Understanding

1. Explain why a $500 million increase in government purchases of goods and services will generate a larger rise in real GDP than a $500 million increase in government transfers.
2. Explain why the tax multiplier is smaller than the spending multiplier for a decrease in government purchases.
3. The country of Boldovia has no unemployment insurance benefits and a tax system that uses only lump-sum taxes. The neighboring country of Moldovia has generous unemployment benefits and a tax system in which residents must pay a percentage of their income. Which country will experience greater variation in real GDP in response to demand shocks, positive and negative? Explain.

Tackle the Test: Multiple-Choice Questions

1. The marginal propensity to consume
   - **I.** has a negative relationship to the spending multiplier.
   - **II.** is equal to 1.
   - **III.** represents the proportion of consumers' disposable income that is spent.

   a. I only
   b. II only
   c. III only
   d. I and III only
   e. I, II, and III
2. Assume that taxes and interest rates remain unchanged when government spending increases, and that both savings and consumer spending increase when income increases. The ultimate effect on real GDP of a $100 million increase in government purchases of goods and services will be
   a. an increase of $100 million.
   b. an increase of more than $100 million.
   c. an increase of less than $100 million.
   d. an increase of either more than or less than $100 million, depending on the *MPC*.
   e. a decrease of $100 million.
3. The presence of income taxes has what effect on the spending multiplier? They
   a. increase it.
   b. decrease it.
   c. destabilize it.
   d. negate it.
   e. have no effect on it.
4. A lump-sum tax is
   a. higher as income increases.
   b. lower as income increases.
   c. independent of income.
   d. the most common form of tax.
   e. a type of business tax.
5. Which of the following is NOT an automatic stabilizer?
   a. income taxes
   b. unemployment insurance
   c. Medicaid
   d. food stamps
   e. monetary policy

Tackle the Test: Free-Response Questions

1. Assume the *MPC* in an economy is 0.8 and the government increases government purchases of goods and services by $60 million. Also assume the absence of taxes, international trade, and changes in the aggregate price level.
   a. What is the value of the spending multiplier?
   b. By how much will real GDP change as a result of the increase in government purchases?
   c. What would happen to the size of the effect on real GDP if the *MPC* fell? Explain.
   d. If we relax the assumption of no taxes, automatic changes in tax revenue as income changes will have what effect on the size of the spending multiplier?
   e. Suppose the government collects $60 million in taxes to balance its $60 million in expenditures. By how much would real GDP change as a result of this increase in both government spending and taxes?

Rubric for FRQ 1 (6 points)

1 point: Spending multiplier = $1/(1 - MPC) = 1/(1 - 0.8) = 1/0.2 = 5$

1 point: $60 million × 5 = $300 million

1 point: It would decrease.

1 point: The spending multiplier is $1/(1 - MPC)$. A fall in *MPC* increases the denominator, $(1 - MPC)$, and therefore decreases the spending multiplier.

1 point: Decrease it

1 point: $60 million × 1 = $60 million

2. A change in government purchases of goods and services results in a change in real GDP equal to $200 million. Assume the absence of taxes, international trade, and changes in the aggregate price level.
   a. Suppose that the *MPC* is equal to 0.75. What was the size of the change in government purchases of goods and services that resulted in the increase in real GDP of $200 million?
   b. Now suppose that the change in government purchases of goods and services was $20 million. What value of the spending multiplier would result in an increase in real GDP of $200 million?
   c. Given the value of the spending multiplier you calculated in part b, what marginal propensity to save would have led to that value of the spending multiplier?
   (3 points)

SECTION  Review

 Section 4 Review Video

MODULE 16

1. An **autonomous change in aggregate spending** leads to a chain reaction in which the total change in real GDP is equal to the spending multiplier times the initial change in aggregate spending. The size of the **spending multiplier**, $1/(1 - MPC)$, depends on the **marginal propensity to consume, *MPC***, the fraction of an additional dollar of disposable income spent on consumption. The larger the *MPC*, the larger the multiplier and the larger the change in real GDP for any given autonomous change in aggregate spending. The fraction of an additional dollar of disposable income that is saved is called the **marginal propensity to save, *MPS***.

2. The **consumption function** shows how an individual household's consumer spending is determined by its current disposable income. Autonomous consumer spending is the amount a household would spend if it had no disposable income. The **aggregate consumption function** shows the relationship for the entire economy. According to the life-cycle hypothesis, households try to smooth their consumption over their lifetimes. As a result, the aggregate consumption function shifts in response to changes in expected future disposable income and changes in aggregate wealth.

3. **Planned investment spending** depends negatively on the interest rate and on existing production capacity; it depends positively on expected future real GDP.

4. Firms hold inventories of goods so that they can satisfy consumer demand quickly. **Inventory investment** is positive when firms add to their inventories, negative when they reduce them. Often, however, changes in inventories are not a deliberate decision but the result of mistakes in forecasts about sales. The result is **unplanned inventory investment**, which can be either positive or negative. **Actual investment spending** is the sum of planned investment spending and unplanned inventory investment.

MODULE 17

5. The **aggregate demand curve** shows the relationship between the aggregate price level and the quantity of aggregate output demanded.

6. The aggregate demand curve is downward sloping for two reasons. The first is the **wealth effect of a change in the aggregate price level**—a higher aggregate price level reduces the purchasing power of households' wealth and reduces consumer spending. The second is the **interest rate effect of a change in the aggregate price level**—a higher aggregate price level reduces the purchasing power of households' and firms' money holdings, leading to a rise in interest rates and a fall in investment spending and consumer spending.

7. The aggregate demand curve shifts because of changes in expectations, changes in wealth not due to changes in the aggregate price level, and the effect of the size of the existing stock of physical capital. Policy makers can also influence aggregate demand. **Fiscal policy** is the use of taxes, government transfers, or government purchases of goods and services to shift the aggregate demand curve. **Monetary policy** is the Fed's use of changes in the quantity of money or the interest rate to stabilize the economy, which involves shifting the aggregate demand curve.

MODULE 18

8. The **aggregate supply curve** shows the relationship between the aggregate price level and the quantity of aggregate output supplied.
9. The **short-run aggregate supply curve** is upward sloping because **nominal wages** are **sticky** in the short run: a higher aggregate price level leads to higher profit per unit of output and increased aggregate output in the short run.
10. Changes in commodity prices, nominal wages, and productivity lead to changes in producers' profits and shift the short-run aggregate supply curve.
11. In the long run, all prices, including nominal wages, are flexible and the economy produces at its **potential output**. If actual aggregate output exceeds potential output, nominal wages will eventually rise in response to low unemployment and aggregate output will fall. If potential output exceeds actual aggregate output, nominal wages will eventually fall in response to high unemployment and aggregate output will rise. So the **long-run aggregate supply curve** is vertical at potential output.

MODULE 19

12. In the ***AD–AS* model**, the intersection of the short-run aggregate supply curve and the aggregate demand curve is the point of **short-run macroeconomic equilibrium**. It determines the **short-run equilibrium aggregate price level** and the level of **short-run equilibrium aggregate output**.
13. Economic fluctuations occur because of a shift of the aggregate demand curve (a *demand shock*) or the short-run aggregate supply curve (a *supply shock*). A **demand shock** causes the aggregate price level and aggregate output to move in the same direction as the economy moves along the short-run aggregate supply curve. A **supply shock** causes them to move in opposite directions as the economy moves along the aggregate demand curve. A particularly nasty occurrence is **stagflation**—inflation and falling aggregate output—which is caused by a negative supply shock.
14. Demand shocks have only short-run effects on aggregate output because the economy is **self-correcting** in the long run. In a **recessionary gap**, an eventual fall in nominal wages moves the economy to **long-run macroeconomic equilibrium**, in which aggregate output is equal to potential output. In an **inflationary gap**, an eventual rise in nominal wages moves the economy to long-run macroeconomic equilibrium. We can use the **output gap**, the percentage difference between actual aggregate output and potential output, to summarize how the economy responds to recessionary and inflationary gaps. Because the economy tends to be self-correcting in the long run, the output gap always tends toward zero.

MODULE 20

15. The high cost—in terms of unemployment—of a recessionary gap and the future adverse consequences of an inflationary gap lead many economists to advocate active **stabilization policy**: using fiscal or monetary policy to offset demand shocks. There can be drawbacks, however, because such policies may contribute to a long-term rise in the budget deficit, leading to lower long-run growth. Also, poorly timed policies can increase economic instability.
16. Negative supply shocks pose a policy dilemma: a policy that counteracts the fall in aggregate output by increasing aggregate demand will lead to higher inflation, but a policy that counteracts inflation by reducing aggregate demand will deepen the output slump.
17. The government plays a large role in the economy, collecting a large share of GDP in taxes and spending a large share both to purchase goods and services and to make transfer payments, largely for **social insurance**. Fiscal policy is the government's tool for stabilizing the economy, although many economists caution that a very active fiscal policy may in fact make the economy less stable due to time lags in policy formulation and implementation.
18. Government purchases of goods and services directly affect aggregate demand, and changes in taxes and government transfers affect aggregate demand indirectly by changing households' disposable income. **Expansionary fiscal policy** shifts the aggregate demand curve rightward; **contractionary fiscal policy** shifts the aggregate demand curve leftward.

MODULE 21

19. Fiscal policy has a multiplier effect on the economy, the size of which depends upon the fiscal policy. Except in the case of lump-sum taxes, taxes reduce the size of the spending and tax multipliers. Expansionary fiscal policy leads to an increase in real GDP, while contractionary fiscal policy leads to a decrease in real GDP. Because part of any change in taxes or transfers is absorbed by savings in the first round of spending, changes in government purchases of goods and services have a more powerful effect on the economy than equal-size changes in taxes or transfers.
20. The **tax multiplier** indicates the total change in aggregate spending that results from each $1 increase in tax collections. It is smaller than the spending multiplier because some of the tax collections would have been saved, not spent. Smaller still, with a value of 1, is the **balanced budget multiplier**, which indicates the total increase in aggregate spending that results from each $1 increase in both government spending and taxes.
21. Rules governing taxes—with the exception of **lump-sum taxes**—and some transfers act as **automatic stabilizers**, reducing the size of the spending multiplier and automatically reducing the size of fluctuations in the business cycle. In contrast, **discretionary fiscal policy** arises from deliberate actions by policy makers rather than from the business cycle.

Key Terms

AP® Exam Practice Questions

Multiple-Choice Questions

1. Which of the following will occur if the federal government reduces defense spending?
   a. Aggregate demand will increase.
   b. Aggregate demand will decrease.
   c. There will be no change in aggregate demand or supply.
   d. Aggregate supply will increase.
   e. Aggregate supply will decrease.
2. Which of the following will occur if an increase in interest rates leads to a decrease in investment spending?
   a. Aggregate demand will increase.
   b. Aggregate demand will decrease.
   c. There will be no change in aggregate demand or supply.
   d. Aggregate supply will increase.
   e. Aggregate supply will decrease.

3. Which of the following will occur as a result of an increase in the aggregate price level?
   a. Aggregate demand will increase.
   b. Aggregate demand will decrease.
   c. There will be no change in aggregate demand or supply.
   d. Aggregate supply will increase.
   e. Aggregate supply will decrease.
4. Which of the following will occur if the price of steel decreases as a result of the discovery of new deposits of iron ore used to make steel?
   a. Aggregate demand will increase.
   b. Aggregate demand will decrease.
   c. There will be no change in aggregate demand or supply.
   d. Aggregate supply will increase.
   e. Aggregate supply will decrease.
5. Sticky nominal wages in the short run cause the short-run aggregate supply curve to
   a. shift to the right.
   b. shift to the left.
   c. slope upward.
   d. slope downward.
   e. be vertical.
6. As a result of the wealth effect, a higher aggregate price level will reduce which of the following?
   a. households' purchasing power
   b. interest rates
   c. investment spending
   d. nominal wages
   e. aggregate demand
7. The interest rate effect of a decrease in the aggregate price level will increase which of the following?
   a. the purchasing power of money holdings
   b. investment spending
   c. interest rates
   d. aggregate supply
   e. aggregate demand
8. Which of the following types of shocks poses a policy dilemma due to the inability to use stabilization policy to address inflation and unemployment at the same time?
   a. negative supply shock
   b. positive supply shock
   c. negative demand shock
   d. positive demand shock
   e. negative budget shock
9. A higher aggregate price level leads to higher profit per unit of output and increased output in the short run because of which of the following?
   a. the wealth effect
   b. the interest rate effect
   c. sticky nominal wages
   d. productivity gains
   e. stabilization policy
10. If potential output is equal to actual aggregate output, which of the following is true?
    a. The economy is experiencing inflation.
    b. The economy is experiencing cyclical unemployment.
    c. Nominal wages are sticky.
    d. The economy is in long-run equilibrium.
    e. The aggregate price level is rising.
11. Which of the following is true about the long-run aggregate supply curve?
    a. It is horizontal.
    b. It is the result of nominal wages being fully flexible.
    c. It is the result of sticky prices.
    d. It is upward sloping.
    e. It intersects the horizontal axis at the actual level of real GDP.
12. Short-run equilibrium aggregate output is the quantity of aggregate output produced when
    a. the aggregate demand curve and the short-run aggregate supply curve are identical.
    b. the quantity of aggregate output supplied is equal to the quantity demanded.
    c. the economy reaches its potential output.
    d. the short-run aggregate supply curve is vertical.
    e. all prices, including nominal wages, are fully flexible.
13. The collapse of wealth and business and consumer confidence that caused the Great Depression is an example of which type of shock?
    a. negative supply shock
    b. positive supply shock
    c. negative demand shock
    d. positive demand shock
    e. negative recessionary shock
14. Which of the following is an example of a positive demand shock?
    a. a large increase in defense spending
    b. the stock market crash of 1929
    c. the discovery of a large, previously unknown oil field
    d. a reduction in the aggregate price level
    e. an increase in nominal wages
15. A positive supply shock will lead to which of the following?
    a. stagflation
    b. an increase in the aggregate price level
    c. a recession
    d. a rightward shift of the short-run aggregate supply curve
    e. an increase in aggregate output along with inflation
16. Which of the following is an example of a negative supply shock?
    a. Production costs decrease.
    b. Information technologies lead to productivity growth.
    c. The stock market collapses.
    d. The government runs a budget deficit.
    e. World oil supplies are disrupted.

17. Which of the following is true when the economy is experiencing a recessionary gap?
a. Potential output is below aggregate output.
b. Aggregate demand is below aggregate supply.
c. There is high unemployment.
d. The aggregate price level is rising.
e. The economy has self-corrected.

18. When the economy is experiencing an inflationary gap, the output gap is
a. positive.
b. negative.
c. zero.
d. decreasing.
e. increasing.

19. Which of the following leads to self-correction when the economy is experiencing a recessionary gap?
a. Nominal wages and prices rise.
b. The short-run aggregate supply curve decreases.
c. The long-run aggregate supply curve decreases.
d. The short-run aggregate supply curve shifts to the right.
e. Unemployment leads to an increase in aggregate demand.

20. Which type of policy can be used to address a decrease in aggregate output to below potential output?
a. expansionary
b. contractionary
c. indiscretionary
d. recessionary
e. inflationary

21. If the marginal propensity to consume is equal to 0.80, the spending multiplier is
a. 0.80
b. 1.25
c. 4.00
d. −4.00
e. 5.00

22. If the marginal propensity to consume is 0.75, an initial increase in aggregate spending of $1,000 will lead to a total change in real GDP equal to
a. $750
b. $1,000
c. $1,333
d. $4,000
e. $7,500

23. If the marginal propensity to consume is 0.9, every $10 billion increase in taxes will cause a change in spending equal to
a. $100 billion.
b. $90 billion.
c. $9 billion.
d. −$10 billion.
e. −$90 billion.

24. Compared to an increase in taxes, an equal-sized increase in government spending will have what effect on real GDP?
a. a larger, negative effect
b. a smaller, negative effect
c. a larger, positive effect
d. a smaller, positive effect
e. an equal, offsetting effect

25. Which of the following is an example of an automatic stabilizer?
a. the Works Progress Administration established during the Great Depression
b. lump-sum taxes
c. a balanced budget requirement for the government
d. sales taxes
e. economic stimulus checks from the government

Free-Response Questions

1. Consider an economy operating at full employment.
a. Draw a correctly labeled aggregate supply and aggregate demand graph for the economy. On your graph, show each of the following:
i. equilibrium price level, labeled P_1
ii. equilibrium output level, labeled Y_1
b. Assume the government increases transfer payments to families with dependent children.
i. Show the effect of the increase in transfer payments on your graph.
ii. Label the new short-run equilibrium price level P_2 and the new short-run equilibrium output level Y_2.
c. Refer to the new short-run equilibrium shown on your graph in response to part b.
i. The new short-run equilibrium illustrates what type of output gap?
ii. What type of fiscal policy would be appropriate for an economy facing a persistent gap of the type you identified in part i?

(7 points)

SECTION 5

The Financial Sector

Pixtal/SuperStock

Funny Money

On October 2, 2004, FBI and Secret Service agents seized a shipping container that had just arrived in Newark, New Jersey, on a ship from China. Inside the container, under cardboard boxes containing plastic toys, they found what they were looking for: more than $300,000 in counterfeit $100 bills. Two months later, another shipment with $3 million in counterfeit bills was intercepted. Government and law enforcement officials began alleging publicly that these bills—which were high-quality fakes, very hard to tell from the real thing—were being produced by the government of North Korea.

The funny thing is that elaborately decorated pieces of paper have little or no intrinsic value. Indeed, a $100 bill printed with blue or orange ink literally wouldn't be worth the paper it was printed on. But if the ink on that decorated piece of paper is just the right shade of green, people will think that it's *money* and will accept it as payment for very real goods and services. Why? Because they believe, correctly, that they can do the same thing: exchange that piece of green paper for real goods and services.

In fact, here's a riddle: If a fake $100 bill from North Korea enters the United States, and nobody ever realizes it's fake, who gets hurt? Accepting a fake $100 bill isn't like buying a car that turns out to be a lemon or a meal that turns out to be inedible; as long as the bill's counterfeit nature remains undiscovered, it will pass from hand to hand just like a real $100 bill. The answer to the riddle is that the real victims of North Korean counterfeiting are U.S. taxpayers because counterfeit dollars reduce the revenues available to pay for the operations of the U.S. government. Accordingly, the Secret Service diligently monitors the integrity of U.S. currency, promptly investigating any reports of counterfeit dollars.

The efforts of the Secret Service attest to the fact that money isn't like ordinary goods and services. In this section we'll look at the role money plays, the workings of a modern monetary system, and the institutions that sustain and regulate it. We'll then see how models of the money and loanable funds markets help us understand *monetary policy* as carried out by our central bank—the *Federal Reserve*.

Michael Belardo/Alamy

MODULE 22 Saving, Investment, and the Financial System

In this Module, you will learn to:

- Describe the relationship between savings and investment spending
- Explain how financial intermediaries help investors achieve diversification
- Identify the purposes of the four principal types of financial assets: stocks, bonds, loans, and bank deposits

Matching Up Savings and Investment Spending

Two instrumental sources of economic growth are increases in the skills and knowledge of the workforce, known as *human capital*, and increases in capital—goods used to make other goods—which can also be called *physical capital* to distinguish it from human capital. Human capital is largely provided by the government through public education. (In countries with a large private education sector, like the United States, private post-secondary education is also an important source of human capital.) But physical capital, with the exception of infrastructure such as roads and bridges, is mainly created through private investment spending—that is, spending by firms rather than by the government.

AP® Exam Tip

The amount of savings is equal to the amount of investment.

Who pays for private investment spending? In some cases it's the people or corporations who actually do the spending—for example, a family that owns a business might use its own savings to buy new equipment or a new building, or a corporation might reinvest some of its own profits to build a new factory. In the modern economy, however, individuals and firms who create physical capital often do it with other people's money—money that they borrow or raise by selling stock. If they borrow money to create physical capital, they are charged an *interest rate*. The **interest rate** is the price, calculated as a percentage of the amount borrowed, charged by lenders to borrowers for the use of their savings for one year.

The **interest rate** is the price, calculated as a percentage of the amount borrowed, charged by lenders to borrowers for the use of their savings for one year.

To understand how investment spending is financed, we need to look first at how savings and investment spending are related for the economy as a whole.

The Savings-Investment Spending Identity

According to the **savings-investment spending identity**, savings and investment spending are always equal for the economy as a whole.

The most basic point to understand about savings and investment spending is that they are always equal. This is not a theory; it's a fact of accounting called the **savings-investment spending identity**.

To see why the savings-investment spending identity must be true, first imagine a highly simplified economy in which there is no government and no interaction with other countries. The overall income of this simplified economy, by definition, would be equal to total spending in the economy. Why? Because the only way people could earn income would be by selling something to someone else, and every dollar spent in the economy would create income for somebody. So, in this simplified economy,

(22-1) Total income = Total spending

Now, what can people do with income? They can either spend it on consumption or save it. So it must be true that

(22-2) Total income = Consumer spending + Savings

Meanwhile, spending consists of either consumer spending or investment spending:

(22-3) Total spending = Consumer spending + Investment spending

Putting these together, we get:

(22-4) Consumer spending + Savings = Consumer spending + Investment spending

Subtract consumer spending from both sides, and we get:

(22-5) Savings = Investment spending

As we said, then, it's a basic accounting fact that savings equals investment spending for the economy as a whole.

So far, however, we've looked only at a simplified economy in which there is no government and no economic interaction with the rest of the world. Bringing these realistic complications back into the story changes things in two ways.

The **budget surplus** is the difference between tax revenue and government spending when tax revenue exceeds government spending.

The **budget deficit** is the difference between tax revenue and government spending when government spending exceeds tax revenue.

The **budget balance** is the difference between tax revenue and government spending.

National savings, the sum of private savings and the budget balance, is the total amount of savings generated within the economy.

First, households are not the only parties that can save in an economy. In any given year, the government can save, too, if it collects more tax revenue than it spends. When this occurs, the difference is called a **budget surplus** and is equivalent to savings by the government. If, alternatively, government spending exceeds tax revenue, there is a **budget deficit**—a negative budget surplus. In this case, we often say that the government is "dissaving". By spending more than its tax revenues, the government is engaged in the opposite of saving. We'll define the term **budget balance** to refer to both cases, with the understanding that the budget balance can be positive (a budget surplus) or negative (a budget deficit). **National savings** is equal to the sum of private savings and the budget balance, whereas private savings is disposable income (income after taxes) minus consumption.

Second, the fact that any one country is part of a wider world economy means that savings need not be spent on physical capital located in the same country in which the savings are generated. That's because the savings of people who live in any one country can be used to finance investment spending that takes place in other countries. So any given country can receive *inflows* of funds—foreign savings that finance investment spending in the country. Any given country can also generate *outflows* of funds—domestic savings that finance investment spending in another country.

The net effect of international inflows and outflows of funds on the total savings available for investment spending in any given country is known as the **capital inflow** into that country, equal to the total inflow of foreign funds minus the total outflow of domestic funds to other countries. Like the budget balance, a capital inflow can be negative—that is, more capital can flow out of a country than flows into it. In recent years, the United States has experienced a consistent net inflow of capital from foreigners, who view our economy as an attractive place to put their savings. In 2012, for example, capital inflows into the United States were $446 billion.

Capital inflow is equal to the total inflow of foreign funds minus the total outflow of domestic funds to other countries.

It's important to note that, from a national perspective, a dollar generated by national savings and a dollar generated by capital inflow are not equivalent. Yes, they can both finance the same dollar's worth of investment spending, but any dollar borrowed from a saver must eventually be repaid with interest. A dollar that comes from national savings is repaid with interest to someone domestically—either a private party or the government. But a dollar that comes as capital inflow must be repaid with interest to a foreigner. So a dollar of investment spending financed by a capital inflow comes at a higher *national* cost—the interest that must eventually be paid to a foreigner—than a dollar of investment spending financed by national savings.

The corner of Wall and Broad Streets is at the center of New York City's financial district.

So the application of the savings-investment spending identity to an economy that is open to inflows or outflows of capital means that investment spending is equal to savings, where savings is equal to national savings *plus* capital inflow. That is, in an economy with a positive capital inflow, some investment spending is funded by the savings of foreigners. And, in an economy with a negative capital inflow (a net outflow), some portion of national savings is funding investment spending in other countries. In the United States in 2012, investment spending totaled $2,475.2 billion. Private savings were $1,491.7 billion, offset by a budget deficit of $1,109.7 billion and supplemented by capital inflows of $446 billion. Notice that these numbers don't quite add up; because data collection isn't perfect, there is a "statistical discrepancy" of $17 billion. But we know that this is an error in the data, not in the theory, because the savings-investment spending identity must hold in reality.

The Financial System

Financial markets are where households invest their current savings and their accumulated savings, or **wealth**, by purchasing *financial assets*.

A **financial asset** is a paper claim that entitles the buyer to future income from the seller. For example, when a saver lends funds to a company, the loan is a financial asset sold by the company that entitles the lender (the buyer) to future income from the company. A household can also invest its current savings or wealth by purchasing a **physical asset**, a claim on a tangible object, such as a preexisting house or a preexisting piece of equipment. It gives the owner the right to dispose of the object as he or she wishes (for example, rent it or sell it).

If you were to go to your local bank and get a loan—say, to buy a new car—you and the bank would be creating a financial asset: your loan. A *loan* is one important kind of financial asset in the real world, one that is owned by the lender—in this case, your local bank. In creating that loan, you and the bank would also be creating a **liability**, a requirement to pay money in the future. So, although your loan is a financial asset from the bank's point of view, it is a liability from your point of view: a requirement that you repay the loan, including any interest. In addition to loans, there are three other important kinds of financial assets: stocks, bonds, and *bank deposits*. Because a financial asset is a claim to future income that someone has to pay, it is also someone else's liability. Shortly, we'll explain in detail who bears the liability for each type of financial asset.

AP® Exam Tip

When other nations buy financial assets from the United States, there is a capital inflow. When Americans buy financial assets in other countries, there is a capital outflow.

A household's **wealth** is the value of its accumulated savings.

A **financial asset** is a paper claim that entitles the buyer to future income from the seller.

A **physical asset** is a claim on a tangible object that gives the owner the right to dispose of the object as he or she wishes.

A **liability** is a requirement to pay money in the future.

These four types of financial assets exist because the economy has developed a set of specialized markets, such as the stock market and the bond market, and specialized institutions, such as banks, that facilitate the flow of funds from lenders to borrowers. A well-functioning financial system is a critical ingredient in achieving long-run growth because it encourages greater savings and investment spending. It also ensures that savings and investment spending are undertaken efficiently. To understand how this occurs, we first need to know what tasks the financial system needs to accomplish. Then we can see how the job gets done.

Three Tasks of a Financial System

There are three important problems facing borrowers and lenders: *transaction costs*, financial risk, and the desire for *liquidity*. The three tasks of a financial system are to reduce these problems in a cost-effective way. Doing so enhances the efficiency of financial markets: it makes it more likely that lenders and borrowers will make mutually beneficial trades—trades that make society as a whole richer.

Transaction costs are the expenses of negotiating and executing a deal.

Reducing Transaction Costs **Transaction costs** are the expenses of actually putting together and executing a deal. For example, arranging a loan requires spending time and money negotiating the terms of the deal, verifying the borrower's ability to pay, drawing up and executing legal documents, and so on. Suppose a large business decided that it wanted to raise $1 billion for investment spending. No individual would be willing to lend that much. And negotiating individual loans from thousands of different people, each willing to lend a modest amount, would impose very large total costs because each individual transaction would incur a cost. Total costs would be so large that the entire deal would probably be unprofitable for the business.

Fortunately, that's not necessary: when large businesses want to borrow money, they either get a loan from a bank or sell bonds in the bond market. Obtaining a loan from a bank avoids large transaction costs because it involves only a single borrower and a single lender. We'll explain more about how bonds work in the next section. For now, it is enough to know that the principal reason there is a bond market is that it allows companies to borrow large sums of money without incurring large transaction costs.

Financial risk is uncertainty about future outcomes that involve financial losses and gains.

Reducing Risk A second problem that real-world borrowers and lenders face is **financial risk**, uncertainty about future outcomes that involve financial losses or gains. Financial risk (which from now on we'll simply call "risk") is a problem because the future is uncertain; it holds the potential for losses as well as gains.

Most people are risk-averse, although to differing degrees. A well-functioning financial system helps people reduce their exposure to risk. Suppose the owner of a business expects to make a greater profit if she buys additional capital equipment but isn't completely sure of this result. She could pay for the equipment by using her savings or selling her house. But if the profit is significantly less than expected, she will have lost her savings, or her house, or both. That is, she would be exposing herself to a lot of risk due to uncertainty about how well or poorly the business performs. So, being risk-averse, this business owner wants to share the risk of purchasing new capital equipment with someone, even if that requires sharing some of the profit if all goes well. How can she do this? By selling shares of her company to other people and using the money she receives from selling shares, rather than money from the sale of her other assets, to finance the equipment purchase. By selling shares in her company, she reduces her personal losses if the profit is less than expected: she won't have lost her other assets. But if things go well, the shareholders earn a share of the profit as a return on their investment.

An individual can engage in **diversification** by investing in several different assets with unrelated risks.

By selling a share of her business, the owner has been able to invest in several things in a way that lowers her total risk. She has maintained her investment in her bank account, a financial asset; in ownership of her house, a physical asset; and in ownership of the unsold portion of her business, also a physical asset. By engaging in **diversification**—investing in several assets with unrelated, or independent, risks—our business owner has lowered her total risk of loss. The desire of individuals to reduce their total risk by engaging in diversification is why we have stocks and a stock market.

Providing Liquidity The third and final task of the financial system is to provide investors with *liquidity*, which—like risk—becomes relevant because the future is uncertain. Suppose that you want to start a new business at some point. Even if you have no concerns about the risk of the business failing, you probably won't want to invest all of your savings into the business. This is because you might suddenly find yourself in need of cash—say, to pay for a medical emergency. Money invested in a business is not easily converted into cash in the event that it is needed for other purposes. For this reason, savvy investors like you are reluctant to lock up too much money in businesses among other large purchases.

istockphoto

An asset is **liquid** if, as with money deposited in a bank, it can be quickly converted into cash without much loss of value. An asset is **illiquid** if, as with a business, car, or home, it cannot. The reluctance to invest heavily in illiquid assets would deter business growth and many major purchases if financial systems offered no remedy. As we'll see, however, the initial sale of stocks and bonds can resolve some liquidity problems by raising money for new and expanding projects. And, by taking deposits and lending them out, banks allow individuals to own liquid assets (their deposits) while financing investments in illiquid assets such as businesses and homes.

An asset is **liquid** if it can be quickly converted into cash without much loss of value.

An asset is **illiquid** if it cannot be quickly converted into cash without much loss of value.

To help lenders and borrowers make mutually beneficial deals, then, the economy needs ways to reduce transaction costs, to reduce and manage risk through diversification, and to provide liquidity. How does it achieve these tasks? With a variety of financial assets.

Types of Financial Assets

In the modern economy there are four main types of financial assets: *loans*, bonds, stocks, and *bank deposits*. In addition, financial innovation has allowed the creation of a wide range of *loan-backed securities*. Each type of asset serves a somewhat different purpose. We'll explain loans, bonds, stocks, and loan-backed securities first. Then we'll turn to bank deposits when we explain the role banks play as financial intermediaries.

A **loan** is a lending agreement between an individual lender and an individual borrower.

Loans A **loan** is a lending agreement between an individual lender and an individual borrower. Most people encounter loans in the form of bank loans to finance the purchase of a car or a house. And small businesses usually use bank loans to buy new equipment.

United States of America

UNITED STATES TREASURY DEPARTMENT

BEARER BOND

PAYABLE TO THE BEARER UPON DEMAND

ONE HUNDRED THOUSAND DOLLARS

© PhotoSpin, Inc/Alamy

The good aspect of loans is that a given loan is usually tailored to the needs of the borrower. Before a small business can get a loan, it usually has to discuss its business plans, its profits, and so on with the lender. This results in a loan that meets the borrower's needs and ability to repay.

The bad aspect of loans is that making a loan to an individual person or a business typically involves a lot of transaction costs, such as the cost of negotiating the terms of the loan, investigating the borrower's credit history and ability to repay, and so on. To minimize these costs, large borrowers such as major corporations and governments often take a more streamlined approach: they sell (or issue) bonds.

Bonds A bond is an IOU issued by the borrower. Normally, the seller of the bond promises to pay a fixed sum of interest each year and to repay the principal—the value stated on the face of the bond—to the owner of the bond on a particular date. So a bond is a financial asset from its owner's point of view and a liability from its issuer's point of view. A bond issuer sells a number of bonds with a given interest rate and maturity date to whoever is willing to buy them, a process that avoids costly negotiation of the terms of a loan with many individual lenders.

Bond purchasers can acquire information free of charge on the quality of the bond issuer, such as the bond issuer's credit history, from *bond-rating agencies* rather than having to incur the expense of investigating it themselves. A particular concern for investors is the possibility of **default**, the risk that the bond issuer might fail to make payments as specified by the bond contract. Once a bond's risk of default has been rated, it can be sold on the bond market as a more or less standardized product—a product with clearly defined terms and quality. In general, bonds with a higher default risk must pay a higher interest rate to attract investors.

A **default** occurs when a borrower fails to make payments as specified by the loan or bond contract.

Another important advantage of bonds is that they are easy to resell. This provides liquidity to bond purchasers. Indeed, a bond will often pass through many hands before it finally comes due. Loans, in contrast, are much more difficult to resell because, unlike bonds, they are not standardized: they differ in size, quality, terms, and so on. This makes them a lot less liquid than bonds.

A **loan-backed security** is an asset created by pooling individual loans and selling shares in that pool.

Loan-backed Securities **Loan-backed securities**, assets created by pooling individual loans and selling shares in that pool (a process called *securitization*), have become extremely popular over the past two decades. Mortgage-backed securities, created by pooling thousands of individual home mortgage loans and selling shares to investors, are the best known example. Securitization has also been widely applied to student loans, credit card loans, and auto loans. These loan-backed securities trade on financial markets like bonds. They are appealing to investors because they provide more diversification and liquidity than individual loans. However, with so many loans packaged together, it can be difficult to assess the true quality of the asset. That difficulty came to haunt investors during the financial crisis of 2007–2008, when the bursting of the housing bubble led to widespread defaults on mortgages and large losses for holders of "supposedly safe" mortgage-backed securities, causing pain that spread throughout the entire financial system.

AP® Exam Tip

It is worthwhile to understand the categories of assets so you can understand their use in different macroeconomic models.

Stocks A stock is a share in the ownership of a company. A share of stock is a financial asset from its owner's point of view and a liability from the company's point of view.

Not all companies sell shares of their stock; "privately held" companies are owned by an individual or a few partners, who get to keep all of the company's profit. Most large companies, however, do sell stock. For example, as this book goes to press, Microsoft has more than 8 billion shares outstanding; if you buy one of those shares, you are entitled to about one-eight billionth of the company's profit, as well as 1 of 8 billion votes on company decisions.

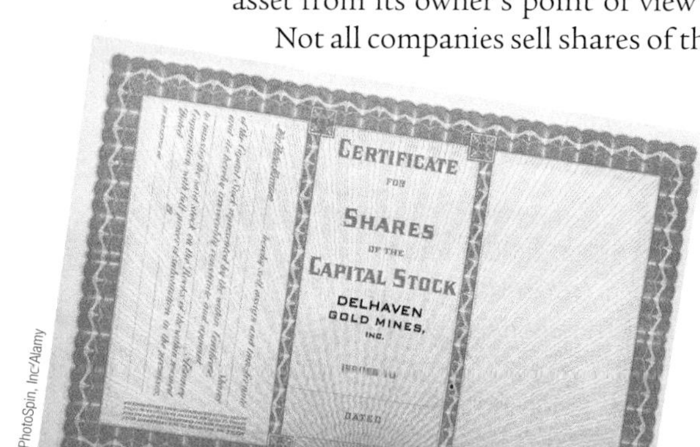

© PhotoSpin, Inc/Alamy

Why does Microsoft, historically a very profitable company, allow you to buy a share in its ownership? Why don't Bill Gates and Paul Allen, the two founders of Microsoft, keep complete ownership for themselves and just sell bonds for their investment spending needs? The reason, as we have just learned, is risk: few individuals are risk-tolerant enough to face the risk involved in being the sole owner of a large company.

Reducing the risk that business owners face, however, is not the only way in which the existence of stocks improves society's welfare: it also improves the welfare of investors who buy stocks (that is, shareowners, or shareholders). Shareowners are able to enjoy the higher returns over time that stocks generally offer in comparison to bonds. Over the past century, the average annual return on U.S. stocks has been about 7% after adjusting for inflation; for U.S. bonds the average annual return during the same time period has been only about 2%. But as investment companies warn you, "Past performance is no guarantee of future performance." And there is a downside: owning the stock of a given company is riskier than owning a bond issued by the same company. Why? Loosely speaking, a bond is a promise while a stock is a hope: by law, a company must pay what it owes its lenders (bondholders) before it distributes any profit to its shareholders. And if the company should fail (that is, be unable to pay its interest obligations and declare bankruptcy), its physical and financial assets go to its bondholders—its lenders—while its shareholders typically receive nothing. So, although a stock generally provides a higher return to an investor than a bond, it also carries higher risk.

The financial system has devised ways to help investors as well as business owners simultaneously manage risk and enjoy somewhat higher returns. It does that through the services of institutions known as *financial intermediaries*.

Financial Intermediaries

A **financial intermediary** is an institution that transforms funds gathered from many individuals into financial assets. The most important types of financial intermediaries are *mutual funds*, *pension funds*, *life insurance companies*, and *banks*. About three-quarters of the financial assets Americans own are held through these intermediaries rather than directly.

A **financial intermediary** is an institution that transforms the funds it gathers from many individuals into financial assets.

Mutual Funds As we've explained, owning shares of a company entails risk in return for a higher potential reward. But it should come as no surprise that stock investors can lower their total risk by engaging in diversification. By owning a *diversified portfolio* of stocks—a group of stocks in which risks are unrelated to, or offset, one another—rather than concentrating investment in the shares of a single company or a group of related companies, investors can reduce their risk. In addition, financial advisers, aware that most people are risk-averse, almost always advise their clients to diversify not only their stock portfolio but also their entire wealth by holding other assets in addition to stock—assets such as bonds, real estate, and cash. (And, for good measure, to have plenty of insurance in case of accidental losses!)

Jay Brousseau/Getty Images

The daily performance of hundreds of different mutual funds is listed in the business section of most large city newspapers.

However, for individuals who don't have a large amount of money to invest—say $1 million or more—building a diversified stock portfolio can incur high transaction costs (particularly fees paid to stockbrokers) because they are buying a few shares of a lot of companies. Fortunately for such investors, mutual funds help solve the problem of achieving diversification without high transaction costs. A **mutual fund** is a financial intermediary that creates a stock portfolio by buying and holding shares in companies and then selling *shares of the stock portfolio* to individual investors. By buying these shares, investors with a relatively small amount of money to invest can indirectly hold a diversified portfolio, achieving a better return for any given level of risk than they could otherwise achieve.

A **mutual fund** is a financial intermediary that creates a stock portfolio and then resells shares of this portfolio to individual investors.

The mutual fund industry represents a huge portion of the modern U.S. economy, not just of the U.S. financial system. In total, U.S. mutual funds had assets of $13 trillion at the end of 2012. The largest mutual fund company at the end of 2013 was Vanguard Group, Inc., which managed almost $2.4 trillion in funds.

We should mention, by the way, that mutual funds do charge fees for their services. These fees are quite small for mutual funds that simply hold a diversified portfolio of stocks, without trying to pick winners. But the fees charged by mutual funds that claim to have special expertise in investing your money can be quite high.

Pension Funds and Life Insurance Companies In addition to mutual funds, many Americans have holdings in **pension funds**, nonprofit institutions that collect the savings of their members and invest those funds in a wide variety of assets, providing their members with income when they retire. Although pension funds are subject to

A **pension fund** is a nonprofit institution that invests the savings of members and provides them with income when they retire.

some special rules and receive special treatment for tax purposes, they function much like mutual funds. They invest in a diverse array of financial assets, allowing their members to achieve more cost-effective diversification and conduct more market research than they would be able to individually. At the end of 2013, pension funds in the United States held more than $18.9 trillion in assets.

A **life insurance company** sells policies that guarantee a payment to a policyholder's beneficiaries when the policyholder dies.

Americans also have substantial holdings in the policies of **life insurance companies**, which guarantee a payment to the policyholder's beneficiaries (typically, the family) when the policyholder dies. By enabling policyholders to cushion their beneficiaries from financial hardship arising from their death, life insurance companies also improve welfare by reducing risk.

Banks Recall the problem of liquidity: other things equal, people want assets that can be readily converted into cash. Bonds and stocks are much more liquid than physical assets or loans, yet the transaction cost of selling bonds or stocks to meet a sudden expense can be large. Furthermore, for many small and moderate-sized companies, the cost of issuing bonds and stocks is too large, given the modest amount of money they seek to raise. A *bank* is an institution that helps resolve the conflict between lenders' needs for liquidity and the financing needs of borrowers who don't want to use the stock or bond markets.

A bank works by first accepting funds from *depositors*: when you put your money in a bank, you are essentially becoming a lender by lending the bank your money. In return, you receive credit for a **bank deposit**—a claim on the bank, which is obliged to give you your cash if and when you demand it. So a bank deposit is a financial asset owned by the depositor and a liability of the bank that holds it.

A **bank deposit** is a claim on a bank that obliges the bank to give the depositor his or her cash when demanded.

A bank, however, keeps only a fraction of its customers' deposits in the form of ready cash. Most of its deposits are lent out to businesses, buyers of new homes, and other borrowers. These loans come with a long-term commitment by the bank to the borrower: as long as the borrower makes his or her payments on time, the loan cannot be recalled by the bank and converted into cash. So a bank enables those who wish to borrow for long lengths of time to use the funds of those who wish to lend but simultaneously want to maintain the ability to get their cash back on demand. More formally, a **bank** is a financial intermediary that provides liquid financial assets in the form of deposits to lenders and uses their funds to finance borrowers' investment spending on illiquid assets.

A **bank** is a financial intermediary that provides liquid assets in the form of bank deposits to lenders and uses those funds to finance borrowers' investment spending on illiquid assets.

In essence, a bank is engaging in a kind of mismatch: lending for long periods of time but also subject to the condition that its depositors could demand their funds back at any time. How can it manage that?

The bank counts on the fact that, on average, only a small fraction of its depositors will want their cash at the same time. On any given day, some people will make withdrawals and others will make new deposits; these will roughly cancel each other out. So the bank needs to keep only a limited amount of cash on hand to satisfy its depositors. In addition, if a bank becomes financially incapable of paying its depositors, individual bank deposits are currently guaranteed to depositors up to $250,000 by the Federal Deposit Insurance Corporation, or FDIC, a federal agency. This reduces the risk to a depositor of holding a bank deposit, in turn reducing the incentive to withdraw funds if concerns about the financial state of the bank should arise. So, under normal conditions, banks need hold only a fraction of their depositors' cash.

By reconciling the needs of savers for liquid assets with the needs of borrowers for long-term financing, banks play a key economic role.

MODULE 22 Review

Check Your Understanding

1. Rank the following assets from the lowest level to the highest level of (i) transaction costs, (ii) risk, and (iii) liquidity. Ties are acceptable for items that have indistinguishable rankings.
   a. a bank deposit with a guaranteed interest rate
   b. a share of a highly diversified mutual fund, which can be quickly sold
   c. a share of the family business, which can be sold only if you find a buyer and all other family members agree to the sale

2. What relationship would you expect to find between the level of development of a country's financial system and the country's level of economic development? Explain in terms of the country's levels of savings and investment spending.

Tackle the Test: Multiple-Choice Questions

1. Decreasing which of the following is a task of the financial system?
   I. transaction costs
   II. risk
   III. liquidity
   a. I only
   b. II only
   c. III only
   d. I and II only
   e. I, II, and III

2. Which of the following is NOT a type of financial asset?
   a. bonds
   b. stocks
   c. bank deposits
   d. loans
   e. houses

3. The federal government is said to be "dissaving" when
   a. there is a budget deficit.
   b. there is a budget surplus.
   c. there is no budget surplus or deficit.
   d. savings does not equal investment spending.
   e. national savings equals private savings.

4. A nonprofit institution collects the savings of its members and invests those funds in a wide variety of assets in order to provide its members with income after retirement. This describes a
   a. mutual fund.
   b. bank.
   c. savings and loan.
   d. pension fund.
   e. life insurance company.

5. A financial intermediary that provides liquid financial assets in the form of deposits to lenders and uses their funds to finance borrowers' investment spending on illiquid assets is called a
   a. mutual fund.
   b. bank.
   c. corporation.
   d. pension fund.
   e. life insurance company.

Tackle the Test: Free-Response Questions

1. Identify and describe the three tasks of a well-functioning financial system.

Rubric for FRQ 1 (6 points)

1 point: Decrease transaction costs

1 point: A well-functioning financial system facilitates investment spending by allowing companies to borrow large sums of money without incurring large transaction costs.

1 point: Decrease risk

1 point: A well-functioning financial system helps people reduce their exposure to risk, so that they are more willing to engage in investment spending in the face of uncertainty in the economy.

1 point: Provide liquidity

1 point: A well-functioning financial system allows the fast, low-cost conversion of assets into cash.

2. List and describe the four most important types of financial intermediaries.
   (4 points)

Shutterstock

MODULE 23 The Definition and Measurement of Money

In this Module, you will learn to:

- Identify the functions of money
- Explain the various roles money plays and the many forms it takes in the economy
- Describe how the amount of money in the economy is measured

AP® Exam Tip

You'll need to know the functions and characteristics of money for the AP® exam.

The Meaning of Money

In everyday conversation, people often use the word *money* to mean "wealth." If you ask, "How much money does Bill Gates have?" the answer will be something like, "Oh, $50 billion or so, but who's counting?" That is, the number will include the value of the stocks, bonds, real estate, and other assets he owns.

But the economist's definition of money doesn't include all forms of wealth. The dollar bills in your wallet are money; other forms of wealth—such as cars, houses, and stocks—aren't money. Let's examine what, according to economists, distinguishes money from other forms of wealth.

What Is Money?

Money is any asset that can easily be used to purchase goods and services.

Money is defined in terms of what it does: **money** is any asset that can easily be used to purchase goods and services. For ease of use, money must be widely accepted by sellers. It is also desirable for money to be durable, portable, uniform, in limited supply, and divisible into smaller units, as with dollars and cents. In Module 22 we defined an asset as *liquid* if it can easily be converted into cash. Money consists of cash itself, which is liquid by definition, as well as other assets that are highly liquid.

You can see the distinction between money and other assets by asking yourself how you pay for groceries. The person at the cash register will accept dollar bills in return for milk and frozen pizza—but he or she won't accept stock certificates or a collection of vintage baseball cards. If you want to convert stock certificates or vintage baseball cards into groceries, you have to sell them—trade them for money—and then use the money to buy groceries.

Of course, many stores allow you to write a check on your bank account in payment for goods (or to pay with a debit card that is linked to your bank account). Does that make your bank account money, even if you haven't converted it into cash? Yes. **Currency in circulation**—actual cash in the hands of the public—is considered money. So are **checkable bank deposits**—bank accounts on which people can write checks.

Currency in circulation is cash held by the public.

Checkable bank deposits are bank accounts on which people can write checks.

The **money supply** is the total value of financial assets in the economy that are considered money.

Are currency and checkable bank deposits the only assets that are considered money? It depends. As we'll see later, there are two widely used definitions of the **money supply**, the total value of financial assets in the economy that are considered money. The narrower definition considers only the most liquid assets to be money: currency in circulation, traveler's checks, and checkable bank deposits. The broader definition includes these three categories plus other assets that are "almost" checkable, such as savings account deposits that can be transferred into a checking account online with a few mouse clicks. Both definitions of the money supply, however, make a distinction between those assets that can easily be used to purchase goods and services, and those that can't.

Money plays a crucial role in generating *gains from trade* because it makes indirect exchange possible. Think of what happens when a cardiac surgeon buys a new refrigerator. The surgeon has valuable services to offer—namely, performing heart operations. The owner of the store has valuable goods to offer: refrigerators and other appliances. It would be extremely difficult for both parties if, instead of using money, they had to directly barter the goods and services they sell. In a barter system, a cardiac surgeon and an appliance store owner could trade only if the store owner happened to want a heart operation *and* the surgeon happened to want a new refrigerator. This is known as the problem of finding a "double coincidence of wants": in a barter system, two parties can trade only when each wants what the other has to offer. Money solves this problem: individuals can trade what they have to offer for money and trade money for what they want.

Because the ability to make transactions with money rather than relying on bartering makes it easier to achieve gains from trade, the existence of money increases welfare, even though money does not directly produce anything. As Adam Smith put it, money "may very properly be compared to a highway, which, while it circulates and carries to market all the grass and corn of the country, produces itself not a single pile of either."

Let's take a closer look at the roles money plays in the economy.

A **medium of exchange** is an asset that individuals acquire for the purpose of trading for goods and services rather than for their own consumption.

Roles of Money

Money plays three main roles in any modern economy: it is a *medium of exchange*, a *store of value*, and a *unit of account*.

Medium of Exchange Our cardiac surgeon/appliance store owner example illustrates the role of money as a **medium of exchange**—an asset that individuals use to trade for goods and services rather than for consumption. People can't eat dollar bills; rather, they use dollar bills to trade for food among other goods and services.

In normal times, the official money of a given country—the dollar in the United States, the peso in Mexico, and so on—is also the medium of exchange in virtually all transactions in that country. During troubled economic times, however, other goods or assets often play that role instead. For example, during economic turmoil people often turn to other countries' moneys as the medium of exchange: U.S. dollars have played this role in troubled Latin American countries, as have euros in troubled Eastern European countries. In a famous example, cigarettes functioned as the medium of exchange in World War II prisoner-of-war camps. Even nonsmokers traded goods and services for cigarettes because the cigarettes could in turn be easily traded for other items. During the extreme German inflation of 1923, goods such as eggs and lumps of coal briefly became mediums of exchange.

Gambling at the Stalag 383 prisoner of war camp during World War II was carried out using cigarettes as currency.

A **store of value** is a means of holding purchasing power over time.

Store of Value In order to act as a medium of exchange, money must also be a **store of value**—a means of holding purchasing power over time. To see why this is necessary, imagine trying to operate an economy in which ice cream cones were the medium of exchange. Such an economy would quickly suffer from, well, monetary meltdown: your medium of exchange would often turn into a sticky puddle before you could use it to buy something else. Of course, money is by no means the only store of value. Any asset that holds its purchasing power over time is a store of value. Examples include farmland and classic cars. So the store-of-value role is a necessary but not a distinctive feature of money.

A **unit of account** is a measure used to set prices and make economic calculations.

Unit of Account Finally, money normally serves as the **unit of account**—the commonly accepted measure individuals use to set prices and make economic calculations. To understand the importance of this role, consider a historical fact: during the Middle Ages, peasants typically were required to provide landowners with goods and labor rather than money in exchange for a place to live. For example, a peasant might be required to work on the landowner's land one day a week and also hand over one-fifth of his harvest. Today, rents, like other prices, are almost always specified in money terms. That makes things much clearer: imagine how hard it would be to decide which apartment to rent if modern landowners followed medieval practice. Suppose, for example, that Mr. Smith says he'll let you have a place if you clean his house twice a week and bring him a pound of steak every day, whereas Ms. Jones wants you to clean her house just once a week but wants four pounds of chicken every day. Who's offering the better deal? It's hard to say. If, on the other hand, Mr. Smith wants $600 a month and Ms. Jones wants $700, the comparison is easy. In other words, without a commonly accepted measure, the terms of a transaction are harder to determine, making it more difficult to make transactions and achieve gains from trade.

Types of Money

Commodity money is a good used as a medium of exchange that has intrinsic value in other uses.

In some form or another, money has been in use for thousands of years. For most of that period, people used **commodity money**: the medium of exchange was a good, normally gold or silver, that had intrinsic value in other uses. These alternative uses gave commodity money value independent of its role as a medium of exchange. For example, the cigarettes that served as money in World War II POW camps were valuable because many prisoners smoked. Gold was valuable because it was used for jewelry and ornamentation, aside from the fact that it was minted into coins.

By 1776, the year in which the United States declared its independence and Adam Smith published *The Wealth of Nations*, there was widespread use of paper money in addition to gold and silver coins. Unlike modern dollar bills, however, this paper money consisted of notes issued by private banks, which promised to exchange their notes for gold or silver coins on demand. So the paper currency that initially replaced commodity money was **commodity-backed money**, a medium of exchange with no intrinsic value whose ultimate value was guaranteed by a promise that it could always be converted into valuable goods on demand.

Commodity-backed money is a medium of exchange with no intrinsic value whose ultimate value is guaranteed by a promise that it can be converted into valuable goods.

The big advantage of commodity-backed money over simple commodity money, like gold and silver coins, was that it tied up fewer valuable resources. Although a note-issuing bank still had to keep some gold and silver on hand, it had to keep only enough to satisfy demands for redemption of its notes. And it could rely on the fact that only a fraction of its paper notes would be redeemed on a normal day. So the bank needed to keep only a portion of the total value of its notes in circulation in the form of gold and silver in its vaults. It could lend out the remaining gold and silver to those who wished to use it. This allowed society to use the remaining gold and silver for other purposes, all with no loss in the ability to achieve gains from trade.

In a famous passage in *The Wealth of Nations*, Adam Smith described paper money as a "waggon-way through the air." Smith was making an analogy between money and an

The History of the Dollar

U.S. dollar bills are pure fiat money: they have no intrinsic value, and they are not backed by anything that does. But American money wasn't always like that. In the early days of European settlement, the colonies that would become the United States used commodity money, partly consisting of gold and silver coins minted in Europe. But such coins were scarce on this side of the Atlantic, so the colonists relied on a variety of other forms of commodity money. For example, settlers in Virginia used tobacco as money and settlers in the Northeast used "wampum," a type of clamshell.

Later in American history, commodity-backed paper money came into widespread use. But this wasn't paper money as we now know it, issued by the U.S. government and bearing the signature of the Secretary of the Treasury. Before the Civil War, the U.S. government didn't issue any paper money. Instead, dollar bills were issued by private banks, which promised that their bills could be redeemed for silver coins on demand. These promises weren't always credible because banks sometimes failed, leaving holders of their bills with worthless pieces of paper. Understandably, people were reluctant to accept currency from any bank rumored to be in financial trouble. In other words, in this private money system, some dollars were less valuable than others.

A curious legacy of that time was notes issued by the Citizens' Bank of Louisiana, based in New Orleans. They became among the most widely used bank notes in the southern states. These notes were printed in English on one side and French on the other. (At the time, many people in New Orleans, originally a colony of France, spoke French.) Thus, the $10 bill read *Ten* on one side and *Dix*, the French word for "ten," on the other. These $10 bills became known as "dixies," probably the source of the nickname of the U.S. South.

The U.S. government began issuing official paper money, called "greenbacks," during the Civil War, as a way to help pay for the war. At first greenbacks had no fixed value in terms of commodities. After 1873, however, the U.S. government guaranteed the value of a dollar in terms of gold, effectively turning dollars into commodity-backed money.

In 1933, when President Franklin D. Roosevelt broke the link between dollars and gold, his own federal budget director—who feared that the public would lose confidence in the dollar if it wasn't ultimately backed by gold—declared ominously, "This will be the end of Western civilization." It wasn't. The link between the dollar and gold was restored a few years later, and then dropped again—seemingly for good—in August 1971. Despite the warnings of doom, the U.S. dollar is still the world's most widely used currency.

imaginary highway that did not absorb the valuable land beneath it. An actual highway provides a useful service but at a cost: land that could be used to grow crops is instead paved over. If the highway could be built through the air, it wouldn't destroy useful land. As Smith understood, when banks replaced gold and silver money with paper notes, they accomplished a similar feat: they reduced the amount of real resources used by society to provide the functions of money.

Fiat money is a medium of exchange whose value derives entirely from its official status as a means of payment.

At this point you may ask, why make any use at all of gold and silver in the monetary system, even to back paper money? In fact, today's monetary system goes even further than the system Smith admired, having eliminated any role for gold and silver. A U.S. dollar bill isn't commodity money, and it isn't even commodity-backed. Rather, its value arises entirely from the fact that it is generally accepted as a means of payment, a role that is ultimately decreed by the U.S. government. Money whose value derives entirely from its official status as a means of exchange is known as **fiat money** because it exists by government *fiat,* a historical term for a policy declared by a ruler.

Fiat money has two major advantages over commodity-backed money. First, it is even more of a "waggon-way through the air"—it doesn't tie up any real resources, except for the paper it's printed on. Second, the money supply can be managed based on the needs of the economy, instead of being determined by the amount of gold and silver prospectors happen to discover.

AP Photo/Don Heupel

The image of a valid U.S. five-dollar bill shows a pattern in the background of the Lincoln Memorial image as seen through a Document Security Systems, Inc. document verifier.

On the other hand, fiat money poses some risks. One such risk is counterfeiting. Counterfeiters usurp a privilege of the U.S. government, which has the sole legal right to print dollar bills. And the benefit that counterfeiters get by exchanging fake bills for real goods and services comes at the expense of the U.S. federal government, which covers a small but nontrivial part of its own expenses by issuing new currency to meet a growing demand for money.

The larger risk is that government officials who have the authority to print money will be tempted to abuse the privilege by printing so much money that they create inflation.

Measuring the Money Supply

AP® Exam Tip

When you see "money supply" on the AP® exam, that usually refers to the M1 measure of the money supply.

A **monetary aggregate** is an overall measure of the money supply.

Near-moneys are financial assets that can't be directly used as a medium of exchange but can be readily converted into cash or checkable bank deposits.

The Federal Reserve (an institution we'll talk more about shortly) calculates the size of two **monetary aggregates**, overall measures of the money supply, which differ in how strictly money is defined. The two aggregates are known, rather cryptically, as M1 and M2. (There used to be a third aggregate named—you guessed it—M3, but in 2006 the Federal Reserve concluded that measuring it was no longer useful.) M1, the narrowest definition, contains only currency in circulation (also known as cash), traveler's checks, and checkable bank deposits. M2 starts with M1 and adds several other kinds of assets, often referred to as **near-moneys**—financial assets that aren't directly usable as a medium of exchange but can be readily converted into cash or checkable bank deposits. Examples include savings accounts and time deposits such as small-denomination certificates of deposit (CDs), which aren't checkable but can be withdrawn at any time before their maturity date by paying a penalty. Other types of assets in M2 include money market funds, which are mutual funds that invest only in liquid assets and bear a close resemblance to bank deposits. These near-moneys pay interest while cash (currency in circulation) does not; in addition, they typically pay higher interest rates than any offered on checkable bank deposits. Because currency and checkable deposits are directly usable as a medium of exchange, however, M1 is the most liquid measure of money.

In January 2014, M1 was valued at $2,698.2 billion, with approximately 43% accounted for by currency in circulation, approximately 57% accounted for by checkable bank deposits, and a tiny slice accounted for by traveler's checks. In turn, M1 made up 24% of M2, valued at $11,039.1 billion.

FYI What's with All the Currency?

Alert readers may be a bit startled at one of the numbers in the money supply: $1,159 billion of currency in circulation in January 2014. That's $3,652 in cash for every man, woman, and child in the United States. How many people do you know who carry $3,652 in their wallets? Not many. So where is all that cash?

Part of the answer is that it isn't in individuals' wallets: it's in cash registers. Businesses as well as individuals need to hold cash.

Economists also believe that cash plays an important role in transactions that people want to keep hidden. Small businesses and the self-employed sometimes prefer to be paid in cash so they can avoid paying taxes by hiding income from the Internal Revenue Service. Also, drug dealers and other criminals obviously don't want bank records of their dealings. In fact, some analysts have tried to infer the amount of illegal activity in the economy from the total amount of cash held by the public. The most important reason for those huge currency holdings, however, is foreign use of dollars. The Federal Reserve estimates that 60% of U.S. currency is actually held outside the United States—largely in countries in which residents are so distrustful of their national currencies that the U.S. dollar has become a widely accepted medium of exchange.

Steven Puetzer/Getty Images

MODULE 23 Review

Check Your Understanding

1. Suppose you hold a gift certificate, good for certain products at participating stores. Is this gift certificate money? Why or why not?
2. Although most bank accounts pay some interest, depositors can get a higher interest rate by buying a certificate of deposit, or CD. The difference between a CD and a checking account is that the depositor pays a penalty for withdrawing the money before the CD comes due—a period of months or even years. Small CDs are counted in M2, but not in M1. Explain why they are not part of M1.
3. Explain why a system of commodity-backed money uses resources more efficiently than a system of commodity money.

Tackle the Test: Multiple-Choice Questions

1. When you use money to purchase the $6 lunch special, money is serving which role(s)?
   - I. medium of exchange
   - II. store of value
   - III. unit of account
   - a. I only
   - b. II only
   - c. III only
   - d. I and III only
   - e. I, II, and III
2. When you decide you want "$10 worth" of a product, money is serving which role(s)?
   - I. medium of exchange
   - II. store of value
   - III. unit of account
   - a. I only
   - b. II only
   - c. III only
   - d. I and II only
   - e. I, II, and III
3. In the United States, the dollar is
   - a. backed by silver.
   - b. backed by gold and silver.
   - c. commodity-backed money.
   - d. commodity money.
   - e. fiat money.
4. Which of the following is the most liquid monetary aggregate?
   - a. M1
   - b. M2
   - c. M3
   - d. near-moneys
   - e. dollar bills
5. Which of the following is the best example of using money as a store of value?
   - a. A customer pays in advance for $10 worth of gasoline at a gas station.
   - b. A babysitter puts her earnings in a dresser drawer while she saves to buy a bicycle.
   - c. Travelers buy meals on board an airline flight.
   - d. Foreign visitors to the United States convert their currency to dollars at the airport.
   - e. You use $1 bills to purchase soda from a vending machine.

Tackle the Test: Free-Response Questions

1. a. What does it mean for an asset to be "liquid"?
   b. Which of the assets listed below is the most liquid? Explain.
   A Federal Reserve note (dollar bill)
   A savings account deposit
   A house
   c. Which of the assets listed above is the least liquid? Explain.
   d. In which monetary aggregate(s) calculated by the Federal Reserve are checkable deposits included?

Rubric for FRQ 1 (6 points)

1 point: It can easily be converted into cash.

1 point: A Federal Reserve note

1 point: It is already cash.

1 point: A house

1 point: It takes time and resources to sell a house.

1 point: M1 and M2 (They were part of M3 as well, but the Fed no longer uses this measure.)

2. a. The U.S. dollar derives its value from what? That is, what "backs" U.S. currency?
   b. What is the term used to describe the type of money used in the United States today?
   c. What two other types of money have been used in the past? Define each.
   (5 points)

Oli Scarff/Getty Images

MODULE 24 The Time Value of Money

In this Module, you will learn to:

- Explain why a dollar today is worth more than a dollar a year from now
- Use the concept of present value to make better decisions about costs and benefits that come in the future

The Concept of Present Value

Individuals often face financial decisions that will have consequences long into the future. For example, when you decide to attend college, you are committing yourself to years of study, which you expect will pay off for the rest of your life. So the decision to attend college is a decision to embark on a long-term project.

The basic rule in deciding whether or not to undertake a project is that you should compare the benefits of that project with its costs, implicit as well as explicit. But making these comparisons can sometimes be difficult because the benefits and costs of a project may not arrive at the same time. Sometimes the costs of a project come at an earlier date than the benefits. For example, going to college involves large immediate costs: tuition, income forgone because you are in school, and so on. The benefits, such as a higher salary in your future career, come later, often much later. In other cases, the benefits of a project come at an earlier date than the costs. If you take out a loan to pay for a vacation cruise, the satisfaction of the vacation will come immediately, but the burden of making payments will come later.

How, specifically, is time an issue in economic decision making?

Borrowing, Lending, and Interest

In general, having a dollar today is worth more than having a dollar a year from now. To see why, let's consider two examples.

First, suppose that you get a new job that comes with a $1,000 bonus, which will be paid at the end of the first year. But you would like to spend the extra money now—say, on new clothes for work. Can you do that? The answer is yes—you can borrow money today and use the bonus to repay the debt a year from now. But if that is your plan, you cannot borrow the full $1,000 today. You must borrow *less* than that because a year from now you will have to repay the amount borrowed *plus interest.*

Now consider a different scenario. Suppose that you are paid a bonus of $1,000 today, and you decide that you don't want to spend the money until a year from now. What do you do with it? You put it in the bank; in effect, you are lending the $1,000 to the bank, which in turn lends it out to its customers who wish to borrow. At the end of a year, you will get *more* than $1,000 back—you will receive the $1,000 plus the interest earned.

All of this means that having $1,000 today is worth more than having $1,000 a year from now. As any borrower and lender know, this is what allows a lender to charge a borrower interest on a loan: borrowers are willing to pay interest in order to have money today rather than waiting until they acquire that money later on. Most interest rates are stated as the percentage of the borrowed amount that must be paid to the lender for each year of the loan. Whether money is actually borrowed for 1 month or 10 years, and regardless of the amount, the same principle applies: money in your pocket today is worth more than money in your pocket tomorrow. To keep things simple in the discussions that follow, we'll restrict ourselves to examples of loans of $1.

Because the value of money depends on when it is paid or received, you can't evaluate a project by simply adding up the costs and benefits when those costs and benefits arrive at different times. You must take time into account when evaluating the project because $1 that is paid to you today is worth more than $1 that is paid to you a year from now. Similarly, $1 that you must pay today is more burdensome than $1 that you must pay next year. Fortunately, there is a simple way to adjust for these complications so that we can correctly compare the value of dollars received and paid out at different times.

Next we'll see how the interest rate can be used to convert future benefits and costs into what economists call *present values*. By using present values when evaluating a project, you can evaluate a project *as if* all relevant costs and benefits were occurring today rather than at different times. This allows people to "factor out" the complications created by time. We'll start by defining the concept of present value.

Defining Present Value

The key to the concept of present value is to understand that you can use the interest rate to compare the value of a dollar realized (paid or received) today with the value of a dollar realized later. Why the interest rate? Because the interest rate correctly measures the cost to you of delaying the receipt of a dollar of benefit and, correspondingly, the benefit to you of delaying the payment of a dollar of cost. Let's illustrate this with some examples.

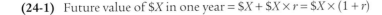

Suppose that you are evaluating whether or not to take a job in which your employer promises to pay you a bonus at the end of the first year. What is the value to you today of $1 of bonus money to be paid one year in the future? Or, to put the question somewhat differently, what amount would you be willing to accept today as a substitute for receiving $1 one year from now?

Jorg Greuel/Getty Images

To answer this question, begin by observing that you need *less* than $1 today in order to be assured of having $1 one year from now. Why? Because any money that you have today can be lent out at interest—say, by depositing it in a bank account so that the bank can then lend it out to its borrowers. The accumulation of interest turns any amount you have today into a greater sum, called the **future value** of today's amount, at the end of the loan period.

Let's work this out mathematically. We'll use the symbol r to represent the interest rate, expressed in decimal terms—that is, if the interest rate is 10%, then $r = 0.10$. If you lend out $\$X$ for one year, at the end of that year you will receive your $\$X$ back, plus the interest on your $\$X$, which is $\$X \times r$. Thus, at the end of the year you will receive:

The **future value** of some current amount of money is the amount to which it will grow as interest accumulates over a specified period of time.

(24-1) Future value of $\$X$ in one year $= \$X + \$X \times r = \$X \times (1 + r)$

The next step is to find out how much you would have to lend out today to have \$1 a year from now. To do that, we just need to set the future value in Equation 24-1 equal to \$1 and solve for \$*X*. That is, we solve the following equation for \$*X*:

$$\textbf{(24-2)}\quad \$X \times (1 + r) = \$1$$

When we rearrange Equation 24-2 to solve for \$*X*, we find the amount you need to lend out today in order to receive \$1 one year from now. Economists have a special name for \$*X*—it's called the **present value** of \$1:

The **present value** of \$1 realized one year from now is \$1/(1 + r): the amount of money you must lend out today in order to have \$1 in one year. It is the value to you today of \$1 realized one year from now.

$$\textbf{(24-3)}\quad \text{Present value of \$1 realized in one year} = \$X = \$1/(1 + r)$$

This means that you would be willing to accept \$*X* today in place of each \$1 to be paid to you one year in the future. The reason is that, if you were to lend out \$*X* today, you would be assured of receiving \$1 one year from now.

Now let's find the value of \$*X*. To do this we simply need to plug the actual value of *r* (a value determined by the financial markets) into Equation 24-3. Let's assume that the interest rate is 10%, which means that $r = 0.10$. In that case:

$$\textbf{(24-4)}\quad \$X = \$1/(1 + 0.10) = \$1/1.10 = \$0.91$$

So you would be willing to accept \$0.91 today in exchange for every \$1 to be paid to you one year in the future. That is, the present value of \$1 realized in one year is \$0.91. Note that the present value of any given amount will change as the interest rate changes.

To see that this technique works for evaluating future costs as well as evaluating future benefits, consider the following example. Suppose you enter into an agreement that obliges you to pay \$1 one year from now—say, to pay off a car loan from your parents when you graduate in a year. How much money would you need today to ensure that you have \$1 in a year? The answer is \$*X*, the present value of \$1, which in our example is \$0.91. The reason \$0.91 is the right answer is that if you lend it out for one year at an interest rate of 10%, you will receive \$1 in return at the end. So if, for example, you must pay back \$5,000 one year from now, then you need to deposit \$5,000 × 0.91 = \$4,550 into a bank account today earning an interest rate of 10% in order to have \$5,000 one year from now. (There is a slight discrepancy due to rounding.) In other words, today you need to have the present value of \$5,000, which equals \$4,550, in order to be assured of paying off your debt in a year.

Baerbel Schmidt/Getty Images

Having it someday isn't the same as having it now.

These examples show us that the present value concept provides a way to calculate the value today of \$1 that is realized in a year—regardless of whether that \$1 is realized as a benefit (the bonus) or a cost (the car loan payback). To evaluate a project today that has benefits, costs, or both to be realized in a year, we just use the relevant interest rate to convert those future dollars into their present values. In that way we have "factored out" the complication that time creates for decision making.

Below we will use the present value concept to evaluate a project. But before we do that, it is worthwhile to note that the present value method can be used for projects in which the \$1 is realized more than a year later—say, two, three, or even more years. Suppose you are considering a project that will pay you \$1 *two* years from today. What is the value to you today of \$1 received two years into the future? We can find the answer with extensions of the formulas we've already seen.

Let's call \$*V* the amount of money you need to lend today at an interest rate of *r* in order to have \$1 in two years. So if you lend \$*V* today, in one year you will receive:

$$\textbf{(24-5)}\quad \text{Future value of \$V in one year} = \$V \times (1 + r)$$

And if you re-lend that sum for another year, at the end of the second year you will receive:

(24-6) Future value of $\$V$ in two years $= \$V \times (1 + r) \times (1 + r) = \$V \times (1 + r)^2$

For example, if $r = 0.10$, then $\$V \times (1.10)^2 = \$V \times 1.21$.

Now we are ready to find the present value of \$1 realized in two years. First we set the future value in Equation 24-6 equal to \$1:

(24-7) Condition satisfied when \$1 is received two years from now as a result of lending $\$V$ today: $\$V \times (1 + r)^2 = \$1$

Rearranging Equation 24-7, we can solve for $\$V$:

(24-8) $\$V = \$1/(1 + r)^2$

Given $r = 0.10$ and using Equation 24-8, we arrive at $\$V = \$1/1.21 = \$0.83$.

(24-9) $\$V = \$1/(1.10)^2 = \$1/1.21 = \$0.83$

So, when the interest rate is 10%, \$1 realized two years from today is worth \$0.83 today because by lending out \$0.83 today you can be assured of having \$1 in two years. And that means that the present value of \$1 realized two years into the future is \$0.83.

Equation 24-9 points the way toward a general expression for present value, where \$1 is paid after N years:

(24-10) Present value of \$1 received in N years $= \$1/(1 + r)^N$

Likewise, each \$1 lent today for N years has a future value of:

(24-11) Future value of today's \$1 in N years $= \$1(1 + r)^N$

For example, \$1 lent for 5 years at an interest rate of 6% has a future value of $\$1(1 + 0.06)^5 = \$1.34$.

Using Present Value

Suppose you have three choices for a project to undertake. Project A costs nothing and has an immediate payoff to you of \$100. Project B requires that you pay \$10 today in order to receive \$115 a year from now. Project C gives you an immediate payoff of \$119 but requires that you pay \$20 a year from now. Let's assume that the annual interest rate is 10%—that is, $r = 0.10$.

The problem in evaluating these three projects is that their costs and benefits are realized at different times. That is, of course, where the concept of present value becomes extremely helpful: by using present value to convert any dollars realized in the future into today's value, you factor out the issue of time. Appropriate comparisons can be made using the **net present value** of a project—the present value of current and future benefits minus the present value of current and future costs. The best project to undertake is the one with the highest net present value.

The **net present value** of a project is the present value of current and future benefits minus the present value of current and future costs.

Table 24.1 on the next page shows how to calculate net present value for each of the three projects. The second and third columns show how many dollars are realized and when they are realized; costs are indicated by a minus sign. The fourth column shows the equations used to convert the flows of dollars into their present

Table 24.1 The Net Present Value of Three Hypothetical Projects

Project	Dollars realized today	Dollars realized one year from today	Present value formula	Net present value given r = 0.10
A	$100	—	$100	$100.00
B	–$10	$115	$-\$10 + \$115/(1 + r)$	$94.55
C	$119	–$20	$\$119 - \$20/(1 + r)$	$100.82

value, and the fifth column shows the actual amounts of the total net present value for each of the three projects.

For instance, to calculate the net present value of project B, we need to calculate the present value of $115 received in one year. The present value of $1 received in one year would be $\$1/(1 + r)$. So the present value of $115 is equal to $115 \times \$1/(1 + r)$; that is, $\$115/(1 + r)$. The net present value of project B is the present value of today's and future benefits minus the present value of today's and future costs: $-\$10 + \$115/(1 + r)$.

From the fifth column, we can immediately see which is the preferred project—it is project C. That's because it has the highest net present value, $100.82, which is higher than the net present value of project A ($100) and much higher than the net present value of project B ($94.55).

This example shows how important the concept of present value is. If we had failed to use the present value calculations and instead simply added up the dollars generated by each of the three projects, we could easily have been misled into believing that project B was the best project and project C was the worst when the reverse is actually the case.

How Big Is That Jackpot, Anyway?

For a clear example of present value at work, consider the case of lottery jackpots.

On March 30, 2012, Mega Millions set the record for the largest jackpot ever in North America, with a payout of $656 million. Well, sort of. That $656 million was available only if you chose to take your winnings in the form of an "annuity," consisting of an annual payment for the next 26 years. If you wanted cash up front, the jackpot was only $471 million and change.

Why was Mega Millions so stingy about quick payoffs? It was all a matter of present value. If the winner had been willing to take the annuity, the lottery would have invested the jackpot money, buying U.S. government bonds (in effect lending the money to the federal government). The money would have been invested in such a way that the investments would pay just enough to cover the annuity. This worked, of course, because at the interest rates prevailing at the time, the present value of a $656 million annuity spread over 26 years was just about $471 million. To put it another way, the opportunity cost to the lottery of that annuity in present value terms was $471 million.

So why didn't they just call it a $471 million jackpot? Well, $656 million sounds more impressive! But receiving $656 million over 26 years is essentially the same as receiving $471 million today.

David Gould/Photographers Choice RF/Getty Images

MODULE 24 Review

Check Your Understanding

1. Consider the three hypothetical projects shown in Table 24.1. This time, however, suppose that the interest rate is only 2%.
   a. Calculate the net present values of the three projects. Which one is now preferred?
   b. Explain why the preferred choice is different with a 2% interest rate than with a 10% interest rate.

Tackle the Test: Multiple-Choice Questions

1. Suppose, for simplicity, that a bank uses a single interest rate for loans and deposits, there is no inflation, and all unspent money is deposited in the bank. The interest rate measures which of the following?
   I. the cost of using a dollar today rather than a year from now
   II. the benefit of delaying the use of a dollar from today until a year from now
   III. the price of borrowing money calculated as a percentage of the amount borrowed
   a. I only
   b. II only
   c. III only
   d. I and II only
   e. I, II, and III

2. If the interest rate is zero, then the present value of a dollar received at the end of the year is
   a. more than $1.
   b. equal to $1.
   c. less than $1.
   d. zero.
   e. infinite.

3. If the interest rate is 10%, the present value of $1 paid to you one year from now is
   a. $0.
   b. $0.89.
   c. $0.91.
   d. $1.
   e. more than $1.

4. If the interest rate is 5%, the future value of $100 lent today is
   a. $90.
   b. $95.
   c. $100.
   d. $105.
   e. $110.

5. What is the present value of $100 realized two years from now if the interest rate is 10%?
   a. $80
   b. $83
   c. $90
   d. $100
   e. $110

Tackle the Test: Free-Response Questions

1. **a.** Calculate the net present value of each of the three hypothetical projects described below. Assume the interest rate is 5%.
   Project A: You receive an immediate payoff of $1,000.
   Project B: You pay $100 today in order to receive $1,200 a year from now.
   Project C: You receive $1,200 today but must pay $200 one year from now.
   b. Which of the three projects would you choose to undertake based on your net present value calculations? Explain.

Rubric for FRQ 1 (5 points)

1 point: Project A net present value: $1,000

1 point: Project B net present value: –$100 + ($1,200/1.05) = $1,042.86

1 point: Project C net present value: $1,200 – ($200/1.05) = $1,009.52

1 point: Choose project B.

1 point: It has the highest net present value.

2. **a.** What is the future value of a 3-year loan of $1,000 at 5% interest? Show your work.
   b. What is the present value of $1,000 received in three years if the interest rate is 5%? Show your work.
   (4 points)

Spencer Platt/Getty Images

Banking and Money Creation

In this Module, you will learn to:

- Describe the role of banks in the economy
- Identify the reasons for and types of banking regulation
- Explain how banks create money

The Monetary Role of Banks

More than half of M1, the narrowest definition of the money supply, consists of currency in circulation—those bills and coins held by the public. It's obvious where currency comes from: it's printed or minted by the U.S. Treasury. But the rest of M1 consists of bank deposits, and deposits account for the great bulk of M2, the broader definition of the money supply. By either measure, then, bank deposits are a major component of the money supply. And this fact brings us to our next topic: the monetary role of banks.

What Banks Do

A bank is a *financial intermediary* that uses bank deposits, which you will recall are liquid assets, to finance borrowers' investments in illiquid assets such as businesses and homes. Banks can lend depositors' money to investors and thereby create liquidity because it isn't necessary for a bank to keep all of its deposits on hand. Except in the case of a *bank run*—which we'll discuss shortly—all of a bank's depositors won't want to withdraw their funds at the same time.

However, banks can't lend out *all* the funds placed in their hands by depositors because they have to satisfy any depositor who wants to withdraw his or her funds. In order to meet these demands, a bank must keep substantial quantities of liquid assets on hand. In the modern U.S. banking system, these assets take the form of either currency in the bank's vault or deposits held in the bank's own account at the Federal Reserve. As we'll see shortly, the latter can be converted into currency more or less instantly. Currency in bank vaults and bank deposits held at the Federal Reserve are called **bank reserves**. Because bank reserves are in bank vaults and at the Federal Reserve, not held by the public, they are not part of currency in circulation.

Bank reserves are the currency that banks hold in their vaults plus their deposits at the Federal Reserve.

Figure 25.1 A T-Account for Samantha's Smoothies

A T-account summarizes a business's financial position. Its assets, in this case consisting of a building and some smoothie-making machinery, are on the left side. Its liabilities, consisting of the money it owes to a local bank, are on the right side.

Assets		Liabilities	
Building	$30,000	Loan from bank	$20,000
Smoothie-making machines	$15,000		

To understand the role of banks in determining the money supply, we start by introducing a simple tool for analyzing a bank's financial position: a **T-account**. A business's T-account summarizes its financial position by showing, in a single table, the business's assets and liabilities, with assets on the left and liabilities on the right. **Figure 25.1** shows the T-account for a hypothetical business that *isn't* a bank—Samantha's Smoothies. According to Figure 25.1, Samantha's Smoothies owns a building worth $30,000 and has $15,000 worth of smoothie-making equipment. These are assets, so they're on the left side of the table. To finance its opening, the business borrowed $20,000 from a local bank. That's a liability, so the loan is on the right side of the table. By looking at the T-account, you can immediately see what Samantha's Smoothies owns and what it owes. This type of table is called a T-account because the lines in the table make a T-shape.

A **T-account** is a tool for analyzing a business's financial position by showing, in a single table, the business's assets (on the left) and liabilities (on the right).

AP® Exam Tip

Make sure you understand T-accounts as they do show up on the AP® exam.

Samantha's Smoothies is an ordinary, nonbank business. Now let's look at the T-account for a hypothetical bank, First Street Bank, which is the repository of $1 million in bank deposits.

Figure 25.2 shows First Street's financial position. The loans First Street has made are on the left side because they're assets: they represent funds that those who have borrowed from the bank are expected to repay. The bank's only other assets, in this simplified example, are its reserves, which, as we've learned, can take the form of either cash in the bank's vault or deposits at the Federal Reserve. On the right side we show the bank's liabilities, which in this example consist entirely of deposits made by customers at First Street. These are liabilities because they represent funds that must ultimately be repaid to depositors. Notice, by the way, that in this example First Street's assets are larger than its liabilities. That's the way it's supposed to be! In fact, as we'll see shortly, banks are required by law to maintain assets larger than their liabilities by a specific percentage.

In this example, First Street Bank holds reserves equal to 10% of its customers' bank deposits. The fraction of bank deposits that a bank holds as reserves is its **reserve ratio**.

In the modern American system, the Federal Reserve—which, among other things, regulates banks operating in the United States—sets a **required reserve ratio**, which is the smallest fraction of bank deposits that a bank must hold. To understand why banks are regulated, let's consider a problem banks can face: *bank runs.*

The **reserve ratio** is the fraction of bank deposits that a bank holds as reserves.

The **required reserve ratio** is the smallest fraction of deposits that the Federal Reserve allows banks to hold.

Figure 25.2 Assets and Liabilities of First Street Bank

First Street Bank's assets consist of $1,000,000 in loans and $100,000 in reserves. Its liabilities consist of $1,000,000 in deposits—money owed to people who have placed funds in First Street's hands.

Assets		Liabilities	
Loans	$1,000,000	Deposits	$1,000,000
Reserves	$100,000		

The Problem of Bank Runs

A bank can lend out most of the funds deposited in its care because in normal times only a small fraction of its depositors want to withdraw their funds on any given day. But what would happen if, for some reason, all or at least a large fraction of its depositors *did* try to withdraw their funds during a short period of time, such as a couple of days?

The answer is that the bank wouldn't be able to raise enough cash to meet those demands. The reason is that banks convert most of their depositors' funds into loans made to borrowers; that's how banks earn revenue—by charging interest on loans. Bank loans, however, are illiquid: they can't easily be converted into cash on short notice. To see why, imagine that First Street Bank has lent $100,000 to Drive-a-Peach Used Cars, a local dealership. To raise cash to meet demands for withdrawals, First Street can sell its loan to Drive-a-Peach to someone else—another bank or an individual investor. But if First Street tries to sell the loan quickly, potential buyers will be wary: they will suspect that First Street wants to sell the loan because there is something wrong and the loan might not be repaid. As a result, First Street Bank can sell the loan quickly only by offering it for sale at a deep discount—say, a discount of 50%, or $50,000.

The upshot is that, if a significant number of First Street's depositors suddenly decided to withdraw their funds, the bank's efforts to raise the necessary cash quickly would force it to sell off its assets very cheaply. Inevitably, this would lead to a *bank failure*: the bank would be unable to pay off its depositors in full.

What might start this whole process? That is, what might lead First Street's depositors to rush to pull their money out? A plausible answer is a spreading rumor that the bank is in financial trouble. Even if depositors aren't sure the rumor is true, they are likely to play it safe and get their money out while they still can. And it gets worse: a depositor who simply thinks that *other* depositors are going to panic and try to get their money out will realize that this could "break the bank." So he or she joins the rush. In other words, fear about a bank's financial condition can be a self-fulfilling prophecy:

It's a Wonderful Banking System

Next Christmastime, it's a sure thing that at least one TV channel will show the 1946 film *It's a Wonderful Life*, featuring Jimmy Stewart as George Bailey, a small-town banker whose life is saved by an angel. The movie's climactic scene is a run on Bailey's bank, as fearful depositors rush to take their funds out.

When the movie was made, such scenes were still fresh in Americans' memories. There was a wave of bank runs in late 1930, a second wave in the spring of 1931, and a third wave in early 1933. By the end, more than a third of the nation's banks had failed. To bring the panic to an end, on March 6, 1933, the newly inaugurated president, Franklin Delano Roosevelt, closed all banks for a week to give bank regulators time to shut down unhealthy banks and certify healthy ones.

Since then, regulation has protected the United States and other wealthy countries against most bank runs. In fact, the scene in *It's a Wonderful Life* was already out of date when the movie was made. But the last decade has seen several waves of bank runs in developing countries. For example, bank runs played a role in an economic crisis that swept Southeast Asia in 1997–1998 and in the severe economic crisis in Argentina, which began in late 2001.

Gabriel Bouys/AFP/Getty Images

In July 2008, panicky IndyMac depositors lined up to pull their money out of the troubled California bank.

Notice that we said "most bank runs." There are some limits on deposit insurance; in particular, currently only the first $250,000 of any bank account is insured. As a result, there can still be a rush to pull money out of a bank perceived as troubled. In fact, that's exactly what happened to IndyMac, a Pasadena-based lender that had made a large number of questionable home loans, in July 2008. As questions about IndyMac's financial soundness were raised, depositors began pulling out funds, forcing federal regulators to step in and close the bank. Unlike in the bank runs of the 1930s, however, most depositors got all their funds back—and the panic at IndyMac did not spread to other institutions.

depositors who believe that other depositors will rush to the exit will rush to the exit themselves.

A **bank run** is a phenomenon in which many of a bank's depositors try to withdraw their funds due to fears of a bank failure. Moreover, bank runs aren't bad only for the bank in question and its depositors. Historically, they have often proved contagious, with a run on one bank leading to a loss of faith in other banks, causing additional bank runs. The FYI "It's a Wonderful Banking System" describes an actual case of just such a contagion, the wave of bank runs that swept across the United States in the early 1930s. In response to that experience and similar experiences in other countries, the United States and most other modern governments have established a system of bank regulations that protects depositors and prevents most bank runs.

A **bank run** is a phenomenon in which many of a bank's depositors try to withdraw their funds due to fears of a bank failure.

Bank Regulation

Should you worry about losing money in the United States due to a bank run? No. After the banking crises of the 1930s, the United States and most other countries put into place a system designed to protect depositors and the economy as a whole against bank runs. This system has three main features: *deposit insurance, capital requirements,* and *reserve requirements.* In addition, banks have access to the *discount window,* a source of loans from the Federal Reserve when they're needed.

Deposit Insurance Almost all banks in the United States advertise themselves as a "member of the FDIC"—the Federal Deposit Insurance Corporation. The FDIC provides **deposit insurance**, a guarantee that depositors will be paid even if the bank can't come up with the funds, up to a maximum amount per account. As this book was going to press, the FDIC guaranteed the first $250,000 of each account.

It's important to realize that deposit insurance doesn't just protect depositors if a bank actually fails. The insurance also eliminates the main reason for bank runs: since depositors know their funds are safe even if a bank fails, they have no incentive to rush to pull them out because of a rumor that the bank is in trouble.

Deposit insurance guarantees that a bank's depositors will be paid even if the bank can't come up with the funds, up to a maximum amount per account.

Capital Requirements Deposit insurance, although it protects the banking system against bank runs, creates a well-known incentive problem. Because depositors are protected from loss, they have no incentive to monitor their bank's financial health, allowing risky behavior by the bank to go undetected. At the same time, the owners of banks have an incentive to engage in overly risky investment behavior, such as making questionable loans at high interest rates. That's because if all goes well, the owners profit; and if things go badly, the government covers the losses through federal deposit insurance.

To reduce the incentive for excessive risk-taking, regulators require that the owners of banks hold substantially more assets than the value of bank deposits. That way, the bank will have assets larger than its deposits even if some of its loans go bad, and losses will accrue against the bank owners' assets, rather than against the government. The excess of a bank's assets over its bank deposits and other liabilities is called the *bank's capital.* For example, First Street Bank has capital of $100,000, equal to 9% of the total value of its assets. In practice, banks' capital is required to equal at least 7% of the value of their assets.

Reserve Requirements Another regulation used to reduce the risk of bank runs is **reserve requirements**, rules set by the Federal Reserve that establish the required reserve ratio for banks. For example, in the United States, the required reserve ratio for checkable bank deposits is currently between zero and 10%, depending on the amount deposited at the bank.

Reserve requirements are rules set by the Federal Reserve that determine the required reserve ratio for banks.

The **discount window** is the channel through which the Federal Reserve lends money to banks.

The Discount Window One final protection against bank runs is the fact that the Federal Reserve stands ready to lend money to banks through a channel known as the **discount window**. The ability to borrow money means a bank can avoid being forced to sell its assets at fire-sale prices in order to satisfy the demands of a sudden rush of depositors demanding cash. Instead, it can turn to the Federal Reserve and borrow the funds it needs to pay off depositors.

Determining the Money Supply

Without banks, there would be no checkable deposits, and so the quantity of currency in circulation would equal the money supply. In that case, the money supply would be determined solely by whoever controls government minting and printing presses. But banks do exist, and through their creation of checkable bank deposits, they affect the money supply in two ways. First, banks remove some currency from circulation: dollar bills that are sitting in bank vaults, as opposed to sitting in people's wallets, aren't part of the money supply. Second, and much more importantly, banks create money by accepting deposits and making loans—that is, they make the money supply larger than just the value of currency in circulation. Our next topic is how banks create money and what determines the amount of money they create.

AP® Exam Tip

The money that banks create is recorded in accounts. Banks do not print money—only the Treasury can do that.

How Banks Create Money

To see how banks create money, let's examine what happens when someone decides to deposit currency in a bank. Consider the example of Silas, a miser, who keeps a shoebox full of cash under his bed. Suppose Silas realizes that it would be safer, as well as more convenient, to deposit that cash in the bank and to use his debit card when shopping. Assume that he deposits $1,000 into a checkable account at First Street Bank. What effect will Silas's actions have on the money supply?

Jonathan Kitchen/Photographer's Choice RF/Getty Images

Panel (a) of **Figure 25.3** shows the initial effect of his deposit. First Street Bank credits Silas with $1,000 in his account, so the economy's checkable bank deposits rise by $1,000. Meanwhile, Silas's cash goes into the vault, raising First Street's reserves by $1,000 as well.

This initial transaction has no effect on the money supply. Currency in circulation, part of the money supply, falls by $1,000; checkable bank deposits, also part of the money supply, rise by the same amount.

Figure 25.3 Effect on the Money Supply of Turning Cash into a Checkable Deposit at First Street Bank

(a) Initial Effect Before Bank Makes a New Loan

Assets		Liabilities	
Loans	No change	Checkable deposits	+$1,000
Reserves	+$1,000		

(b) Effect When Bank Makes a New Loan

Assets		Liabilities
Loans	+$900	No change
Reserves	−$900	

When Silas deposits $1,000 (which had been stashed under his bed) into a checkable bank account, there is initially no effect on the money supply: currency in circulation falls by $1,000, but checkable bank deposits rise by $1,000. The corresponding entries on the bank's T-account, depicted in panel (a), show deposits initially rising by $1,000 and the bank's reserves initially rising by $1,000. In the second stage, depicted in panel (b), the bank holds 10% of Silas's deposit ($100) as reserves and lends out the rest ($900) to Mary. As a result, its reserves fall by $900 and its loans increase by $900. Its liabilities, including Silas's $1,000 deposit, are unchanged. The money supply, the sum of checkable bank deposits and currency in circulation, has now increased by $900—the $900 now held by Mary.

But this is not the end of the story because First Street Bank can now lend out part of Silas's deposit. Assume that it holds 10% of Silas's deposit—$100—in reserves and lends the rest out in cash to Silas's neighbor, Mary. The effect of this second stage is shown in panel (b) of Figure 25.3. First Street's deposits remain unchanged, and so does the value of its assets. But the composition of its assets changes: by making the loan, it reduces its reserves by $900, so that they are only $100 larger than they were before Silas made his deposit. In the place of the $900 reduction in reserves, the bank has acquired an IOU, its $900 cash loan to Mary. So by putting $900 of Silas's cash back into circulation by lending it to Mary, First Street Bank has, in fact, increased the money supply. That is, the sum of currency in circulation and checkable bank deposits has risen by $900 compared to what it had been when Silas's cash was still under his bed. Although Silas is still the owner of $1,000, now in the form of a checkable deposit, Mary has the use of $900 in cash from her borrowings.

This may not be the end of the story either. Suppose that Mary uses her cash to buy a television and a Blu-ray player from Acme Merchandise. What does Anne Acme, the store's owner, do with the cash? If she holds on to it, the money supply doesn't increase any further. But suppose she deposits the $900 into a checkable bank deposit—say, at Second Street Bank. Second Street Bank, in turn, will keep only part of that deposit in reserves, lending out the rest, creating still more money.

Assume that Second Street Bank, like First Street Bank, keeps 10% of any bank deposit in reserves and lends out the rest. Then it will keep $90 in reserves and lend out $810 of Anne's deposit to another borrower, further increasing the money supply.

Table 25.1 shows the process of money creation we have described so far. At first the money supply consists only of Silas's $1,000. After he deposits the cash into a checkable bank deposit and the bank makes a loan, the money supply rises to $1,900. After the second deposit and the second loan, the money supply rises to $2,710. And the process will, of course, continue from there. (Although we have considered the case in which Silas places his cash in a checkable bank deposit, the results would be the same if he put it into any type of near-money.)

Table 25.1 How Banks Create Money

	Currency in circulation	Checkable bank deposits	Money supply
First stage: Silas keeps his cash under his bed.	$1,000	$0	$1,000
Second stage: Silas deposits cash in First Street Bank, which lends out $900 to Mary, who then pays it to Anne Acme.	900	1,000	1,900
Third stage: Anne Acme deposits $900 in Second Street Bank, which lends out $810 to another borrower.	810	1,900	2,710

This process of money creation may sound familiar. Recall the *spending multiplier process* that we described in Module 16: an initial increase in spending leads to a rise in real GDP, which leads to a further rise in spending, which leads to a further rise in real GDP, and so on. What we have here is another kind of multiplier—the *money multiplier.* Next, we'll learn what determines the size of this multiplier.

Reserves, Bank Deposits, and the Money Multiplier

In tracing out the effect of Silas's deposit in Table 25.1, we assumed that the funds a bank lends out always end up being deposited either in the same bank or in another bank—so funds disbursed as loans come back to the banking system, even if not to the lending bank itself. In reality, some of these loaned funds may be held by borrowers in their wallets and not deposited in a bank, meaning that some of the loaned amount "leaks" out of the banking system. Such leaks reduce the size of the money multiplier, just as leaks of real income into savings reduce the size of the real GDP multiplier. (Bear in mind, however, that the "leak" here comes from the fact that borrowers keep some of their funds in currency, rather than the fact that consumers save some of their income.) But let's set that complication aside for a moment and consider how the money supply is determined in a "checkable-deposits-only" monetary system, in which funds are always deposited in bank accounts and none are held in wallets as currency. That is, in our checkable-deposits-only monetary system, any and all funds borrowed from a bank are immediately deposited into a checkable bank account. We'll assume that banks are required to satisfy a minimum reserve ratio of 10% and that every bank lends out all of its **excess reserves**, reserves over and above the amount needed to satisfy the minimum reserve ratio.

Excess reserves are a bank's reserves over and above its required reserves.

Now suppose that for some reason a bank suddenly finds itself with \$1,000 in excess reserves. What happens? The answer is that the bank will lend out that \$1,000, which will end up as a checkable bank deposit somewhere in the banking system, launching a money multiplier process very similar to the process shown in Table 25.1. In the first stage, the bank lends out its excess reserves of \$1,000, which becomes a checkable bank deposit somewhere. The bank that receives the \$1,000 deposit keeps 10%, or \$100, as reserves and lends out the remaining 90%, or \$900, which again becomes a checkable bank deposit somewhere. The bank receiving this \$900 deposit again keeps 10%, which is \$90, as reserves and lends out the remaining \$810. The bank receiving this \$810 keeps \$81 in reserves and lends out the remaining \$729, and so on. As a result of this process, the total increase in checkable bank deposits is equal to a sum that looks like:

AP® Exam Tip

Excess reserves are important because these reserves are what banks can loan out to borrowers.

$$\$1{,}000 + \$900 + \$810 + \$729 + \ldots$$

We'll use the symbol *rr* for the reserve ratio. More generally, the total increase in checkable bank deposits that is generated when a bank lends out \$1,000 in excess reserves is:

$$\textbf{(25-1)}\quad \$1{,}000 + \$1{,}000 \times (1 - rr) + \$1{,}000 \times (1 - rr)^2 + \$1{,}000 \times (1 - rr)^3 + \ldots$$

As we have seen, an infinite series of this form can be simplified to $\$1{,}000/rr$. We must introduce another term before formally defining the money multiplier, but we can now see its usefulness: it is the factor by which we multiply an initial increase in excess reserves to find the total resulting increase in checkable bank deposits:

$$\textbf{(25-2)}\quad \text{Money multiplier} = \frac{1}{rr}$$

AP® Exam Tip

The money multiplier is $\frac{1}{rr}$ where *rr* is the reserve ratio. Be sure to know this frequently tested formula.

Given a reserve ratio of 10%, or 0.1, a \$1,000 increase in excess reserves will increase the total value of checkable bank deposits by $\$1{,}000 \times 1/rr = \$1{,}000/0.1 = \$10{,}000$. In fact, in a checkable-deposits-only monetary system, the total value of checkable bank deposits will be equal to the value of bank reserves divided by the reserve ratio. Or to put it a different way, if the reserve ratio is 10%, each \$1 of reserves held by a bank supports $\$1/rr = \$1/0.1 = \$10$ of checkable bank deposits.

The Money Multiplier in Reality

In reality, the determination of the money supply is more complicated than our simple model suggests because it depends not only on the ratio of reserves to bank deposits but also on the fraction of the money supply that individuals choose to hold in the form of currency. In fact, we already saw this in our example of Silas depositing the cash instead of holding it under his bed: when he chose to hold a checkable bank deposit instead of currency, he set in motion an increase in the money supply.

To define the money multiplier in practice, we need to understand that the Federal Reserve controls the **monetary base**, the sum of currency in circulation and the reserves held by banks. The Federal Reserve does not determine how that sum is allocated between bank reserves and currency in circulation. Consider Silas and his deposit one more time: by taking the cash from under his bed and depositing it in a bank, he reduced the quantity of currency in circulation but increased bank reserves by an equal amount. So while the allocation of the monetary base changes—the amount in reserves grows and the amount in circulation shrinks—the total of these two, the monetary base, remains unchanged.

© Steve Hamblin/Alamy

Currency held as bank reserves isn't part of the money supply, but it is part of the monetary base.

The monetary base is different from the money supply in two ways. First, bank reserves, which are part of the monetary base, aren't considered part of the money supply. A \$1 bill in someone's wallet is considered money because it's available for an individual to spend, but a \$1 bill held as bank reserves in a bank vault or deposited at the Federal Reserve isn't considered part of the money supply because it's not available for spending. Second, checkable bank deposits, which are part of the money supply because they are available for spending, aren't part of the monetary base.

Figure 25.4 shows the two concepts schematically. The circle on the left represents the monetary base, consisting of bank reserves plus currency in circulation. The circle on the right represents the money supply, consisting mainly of currency in circulation plus checkable or near-checkable bank deposits. As the figure indicates, currency in circulation is part of both the monetary base and the money supply. But bank reserves aren't part of the money supply, and checkable or near-checkable bank deposits aren't part of the monetary base. In normal times, most of the monetary base actually consists of currency in circulation, which also makes up about half of the money supply.

The **monetary base** is the sum of currency in circulation and bank reserves.

The **money multiplier** is the ratio of the money supply to the monetary base. It indicates the total number of dollars created in the banking system by each \$1 addition to the monetary base.

Now we can formally define the **money multiplier**: it's the ratio of the money supply to the monetary base. Most importantly, this tells us the total number of dollars created in the banking system by each \$1 addition to the monetary base. We have seen that in a simple situation in which banks hold no excess reserves and all cash is deposited in banks, the money multiplier is $1/rr$. So if the reserve requirement is 0.1 (the minimum required ratio for most checkable deposits in the United States), the money multiplier is $1/0.1 = 10$; if the Federal Reserve adds \$100 to the monetary base, the money supply will increase by $10 \times \$100 = \$1{,}000$. During normal times, the actual money multiplier in the United States, using M1 as our measure of money, is about 1.9. That's a lot smaller than 10. Normally, the reason the actual money multiplier is so small arises from the fact that people hold significant amounts of cash, and a dollar of currency in circulation, unlike a dollar in reserves, doesn't support multiple dollars of the money supply. In fact, currency in circulation normally accounts for more than 90% of the monetary base.

Figure 25.4 The Monetary Base and the Money Supply

The monetary base is equal to bank reserves plus currency in circulation. It is different from the money supply, consisting mainly of checkable or near-checkable bank deposits plus currency in circulation. Each dollar of bank reserves backs several dollars of bank deposits, making the money supply larger than the monetary base.

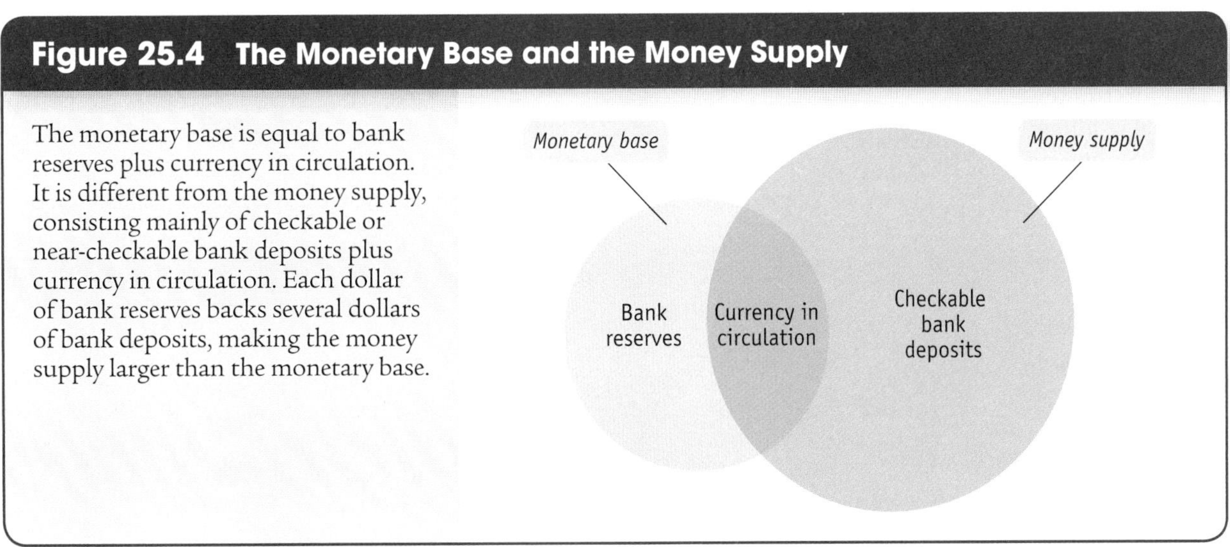

MODULE 25 Review

Check Your Understanding

1. Suppose you are a depositor at First Street Bank. You hear a rumor that the bank has suffered serious losses on its loans. Every depositor knows that the rumor isn't true, but each thinks that most other depositors believe the rumor. Why, in the absence of deposit insurance, could this lead to a bank run? How does deposit insurance change the situation?
2. A con artist has a great idea: he'll open a bank without investing any capital and lend all the deposits at high interest rates to real estate developers. If the real estate market booms, the loans will be repaid and he'll make high profits. If the real estate market goes bust, the loans won't be repaid and the bank will fail—but he will not lose any of his own wealth. How would modern bank regulation frustrate his scheme?
3. Assume that total reserves are equal to $200 and total checkable bank deposits are equal to $1,000. Also assume that the public does not hold any currency and banks hold no excess reserves. Now suppose that the required reserve ratio falls from 20% to 10%. Trace out how this leads to an expansion in bank deposits.
4. Take the example of Silas depositing his $1,000 in cash into First Street Bank and assume that the required reserve ratio is 10%. But now assume that each recipient of a bank loan keeps half the loan in cash and deposits the rest. Trace out the resulting expansion in the money supply through at least three rounds of deposits.

Tackle the Test: Multiple-Choice Questions

1. Bank reserves include which of the following?
   - I. currency in bank vaults
   - II. bank deposits held in accounts at the Federal Reserve
   - III. customer deposits in bank checking accounts

   a. I only
   b. II only
   c. III only
   d. I and II only
   e. I, II, and III
2. The fraction of bank deposits actually held as reserves is the
   a. reserve ratio.
   b. required reserve ratio.
   c. excess reserve ratio.
   d. reserve requirement.
   e. monetary base.
3. Bank regulation includes which of the following?
   - I. deposit insurance
   - II. capital requirements
   - III. reserve requirements

   a. I only
   b. II only
   c. III only
   d. I and II
   e. I, II, and III
4. Which of the following changes would be the most likely to reduce the size of the money multiplier?
   a. a decrease in the required reserve ratio
   b. a decrease in excess reserves
   c. an increase in cash holding by consumers
   d. a decrease in bank runs
   e. an increase in deposit insurance
5. The monetary base equals
   a. currency in circulation.
   b. bank reserves.
   c. currency in circulation − bank reserves.
   d. currency in circulation + bank reserves.
   e. currency in circulation/bank reserves.

Tackle the Test: Free-Response Questions

1. How will each of the following affect the money supply through the money multiplier process? Explain.
   a. People hold more cash.
   b. Banks hold more excess reserves.
   c. The Fed increases the required reserve ratio.

Rubric for FRQ 1 (6 points)

1 point: It will decrease.

1 point: Money held as cash does not support multiple dollars in the money supply.

1 point: It will decrease.

1 point: Excess reserves are not loaned out and therefore do not expand the money supply.

1 point: It will decrease.

1 point: Banks will have to hold more as reserves and therefore loan out less.

2. Suppose the required reserve ratio is 5%.
   a. If a bank has deposits of $100,000 and holds $10,000 as reserves, how much are its excess reserves? Explain.
   b. If a bank holds no excess reserves and it receives a new deposit of $1,000, how much of that $1,000 can the bank lend out and how much is the bank required to add to its reserves? Explain.
   c. By how much can an increase in excess reserves of $2,000 change the money supply in a checkable-deposits-only system? Explain.
   (4 points)

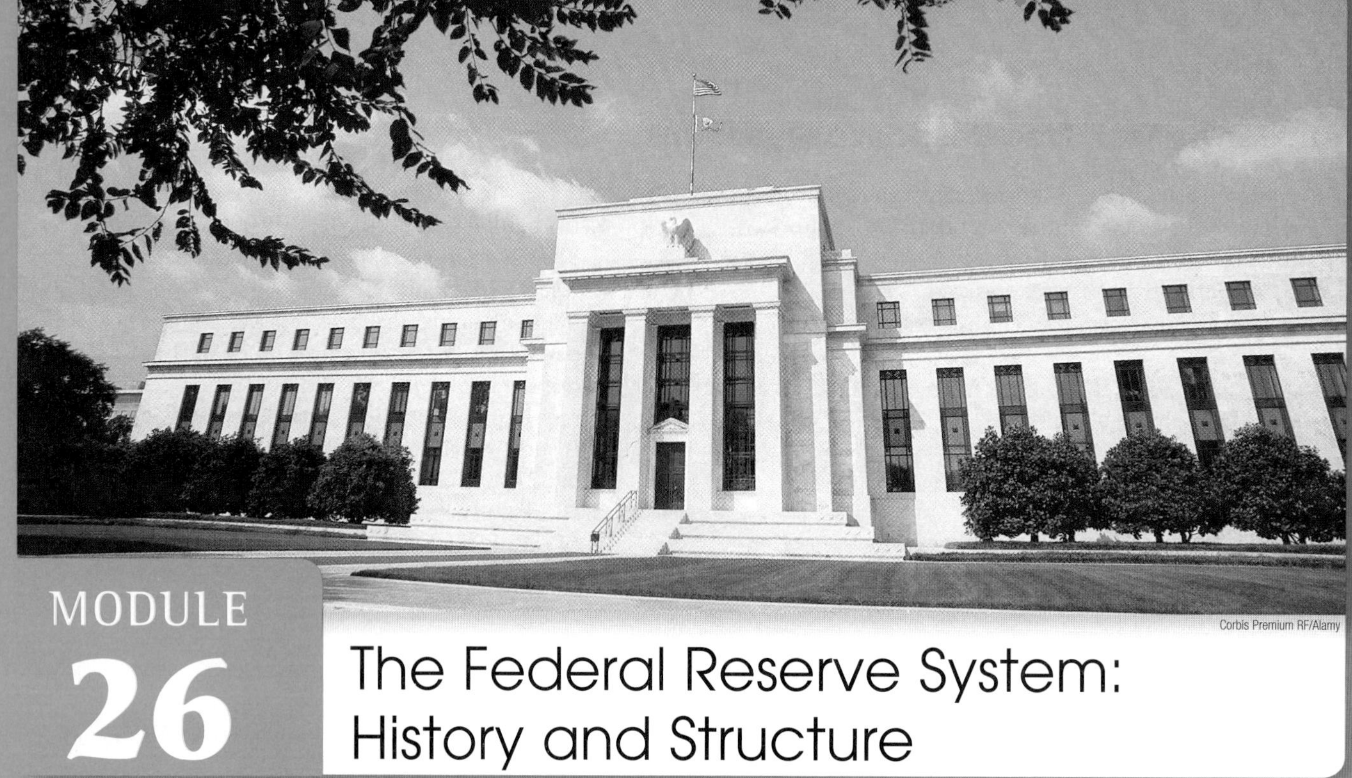
Corbis Premium RF/Alamy

MODULE 26 The Federal Reserve System: History and Structure

In this Module, you will learn to:

- Discuss the history of the Federal Reserve System
- Describe the structure of the Federal Reserve System
- Explain how the Federal Reserve has responded to major financial crises

AP® Exam Tip

The Federal Reserve is responsible for conducting monetary policy for the United States. Other nations have central banks with different names, and the AP® exam may simply refer to the "central bank" rather than identifying a particular central bank.

The Federal Reserve System

Who's in charge of ensuring that banks maintain enough reserves? Who decides how large the monetary base will be? The answer, in the United States, is an institution known as the Federal Reserve (or, informally, as "the Fed"). The Federal Reserve is a **central bank**—an institution that oversees and regulates the banking system and controls the monetary base. Other central banks include the Bank of England, the Bank of Japan, and the European Central Bank, or ECB.

A **central bank** is an institution that oversees and regulates the banking system and controls the monetary base.

An Overview of the Twenty-first Century American Banking System

Under normal circumstances, banking is a rather staid and unexciting business. Fortunately, bankers and their customers like it that way. However, there have been repeated episodes in which "sheer panic" would be the best description of banking conditions—the panic induced by a bank run and the specter of the collapse of a bank or multiple banks, leaving depositors penniless, bank shareholders wiped out, and borrowers unable to get credit. In this section, we'll give an overview of the behavior and regulation of the American banking system over the last century.

The creation of the Federal Reserve System in 1913 was largely a response to lessons learned in the Panic of 1907. In 2008, the United States found itself in the midst of a financial crisis that in many ways mirrored the Panic of 1907, which occurred almost exactly 100 years earlier.

Crisis in American Banking at the Turn of the Twentieth Century

The creation of the Federal Reserve System in 1913 marked the beginning of the modern era of American banking. From 1864 until 1913, American banking was dominated by a federally regulated system of national banks. They alone were allowed to issue currency, and the currency notes they issued were printed by the federal government with uniform size and design. How much currency a national bank could issue depended on its capital. Although this system was an improvement on the earlier period in which banks issued their own notes with no uniformity and virtually no regulation, the national banking regime still suffered numerous bank failures and major financial crises—at least one and often two per decade.

The main problem afflicting the system was that the money supply was not sufficiently responsive: it was difficult to shift currency around the country to respond quickly to local economic changes. In particular, there was often a tug-of-war between New York City banks and rural banks for adequate amounts of currency. Rumors that a bank had insufficient currency to satisfy demands for withdrawals would quickly lead to a bank run. A bank run would then spark a contagion, setting off runs at other nearby banks, sowing widespread panic and devastation in the local economy. In response, bankers in some locations pooled their resources to create local clearinghouses that would jointly guarantee a member's liabilities in the event of a panic, and some state governments began offering deposit insurance on their banks' deposits.

The Pierpont Morgan Library/Art Resource, NY

In both the Panic of 1907 and the financial crisis of 2008, large losses from risky speculation destabilized the banking system.

However, the cause of the Panic of 1907 was different from those of previous crises; in fact, its cause was eerily similar to the roots of the 2008 crisis. Ground zero of the 1907 panic was New York City, but the consequences devastated the entire country, leading to a deep four-year recession. The crisis originated in institutions in New York known as trusts, bank-like institutions that accepted deposits but that were originally intended to manage only inheritances and estates for wealthy clients. Because these trusts were supposed to engage only in low-risk activities, they were less regulated, had lower reserve requirements, and had lower cash reserves than national banks. However, as the American economy boomed during the first decade of the twentieth century, trusts began speculating in real estate and the stock market, areas of speculation forbidden to national banks.

Being less regulated than national banks, trusts were able to pay their depositors higher returns. Yet trusts took a free ride on national banks' reputation for soundness, with depositors considering them equally safe. As a result, trusts grew rapidly: by 1907, the total assets of trusts in New York City were as large as those of national banks. Meanwhile, the trusts declined to join the New York Clearinghouse, a consortium of New York City national banks that guaranteed one another's soundness; that would have required the trusts to hold higher cash reserves, reducing their profits.

The Panic of 1907 began with the failure of the Knickerbocker Trust, a large New York City trust that failed when it suffered massive losses in unsuccessful stock market speculation. Quickly, other New York trusts came under pressure, and frightened depositors began queuing in long lines to withdraw their funds. The New York Clearinghouse declined to step in and lend to the trusts, and even healthy trusts came under serious assault. Within two days, a dozen major trusts had gone under. Credit markets froze, and the stock market fell dramatically as stock traders were unable to get credit to finance their trades and business confidence evaporated.

Fortunately, one of New York City's wealthiest men, the banker J. P. Morgan, quickly stepped in to stop the panic. Understanding that the crisis was spreading and would soon engulf healthy institutions, trusts and banks alike, he worked with other bankers, wealthy men such as John D. Rockefeller, and the U.S. Secretary of the Treasury to shore up the reserves of banks and trusts so they could withstand the onslaught of withdrawals. Once people were assured that they could withdraw their money, the panic ceased. Although the panic itself lasted little more than a week, it and the stock market collapse decimated the economy. A four-year recession ensued, with production falling 11% and unemployment rising from 3% to 8%.

Responding to Banking Crises: The Creation of the Federal Reserve

Concerns over the frequency of banking crises and the unprecedented role of J. P. Morgan in saving the financial system prompted the federal government to initiate banking reform. In 1913 the national banking system was eliminated and the Federal Reserve System was created as a way to compel all deposit-taking institutions to hold adequate reserves and to open their accounts to inspection by regulators. The Panic of 1907 convinced many that the time for centralized control of bank reserves had come. The Federal Reserve was given the sole right to issue currency in order to make the money supply sufficiently responsive to satisfy economic conditions around the country.

The Structure of the Fed

The legal status of the Fed is unusual: it is not exactly part of the U.S. government, but it is not really a private institution either. Strictly speaking, the Federal Reserve System consists of two parts: the Board of Governors and the 12 regional Federal Reserve Banks.

The Board of Governors, which oversees the entire system from its offices in Washington, D.C., is constituted like a government agency: its seven members are appointed by the president and must be approved by the Senate. However, they are appointed for 14-year terms, to insulate them from political pressure in their conduct of monetary policy. Although the chair is appointed more frequently—every four years—it is traditional for the chair to be reappointed and serve much longer terms. For example, William McChesney Martin was chair of the Fed from 1951 until 1970. Alan Greenspan, appointed in 1987, served as the Fed's chair until 2006.

The 12 Federal Reserve Banks each serve a region of the country, known as a *Federal Reserve district,* providing various banking and supervisory services. One of their jobs, for example, is to audit the books of private-sector banks to ensure their financial health. Each regional bank is run by a board of directors chosen from the local banking and business community. The Federal Reserve Bank of New York plays a special role: it carries out *open-market operations,* usually the main tool of monetary policy. **Figure 26.1** shows the 12 Federal Reserve districts and the city in which each regional Federal Reserve Bank is located.

Decisions about monetary policy are made by the Federal Open Market Committee, which consists of the Board of Governors plus five of the regional bank presidents. The president of the Federal Reserve Bank of New York is always on the committee, and the other four seats rotate among the 11 other regional bank presidents. The chair of the Board of Governors normally also serves as the chair of the Federal Open Market Committee.

The effect of this complex structure is to create an institution that is ultimately accountable to the voting public because the Board of Governors is chosen by the president and confirmed by the Senate, all of whom are themselves elected officials. But the long terms served by board members, as well as the indirectness of their appointment process, largely insulate them from short-term political pressures.

Figure 26.1 The Federal Reserve System

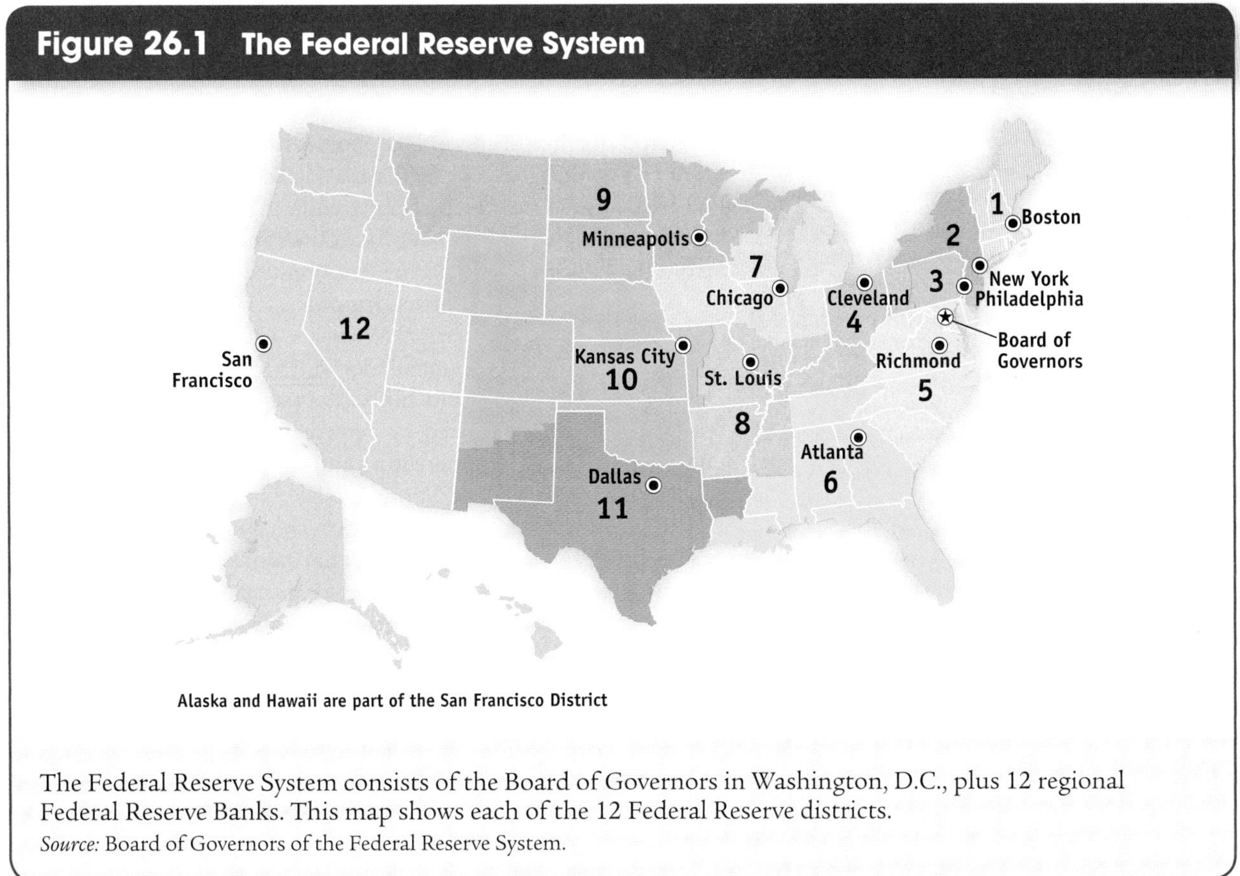

The Federal Reserve System consists of the Board of Governors in Washington, D.C., plus 12 regional Federal Reserve Banks. This map shows each of the 12 Federal Reserve districts.
Source: Board of Governors of the Federal Reserve System.

The Effectiveness of the Federal Reserve System

Although the Federal Reserve System standardized and centralized the holding of bank reserves, it did not eliminate the potential for bank runs because banks' reserves were still less than the total value of their deposits. The potential for more bank runs became a reality during the Great Depression. Plunging commodity prices hit American farmers particularly hard, precipitating a series of bank runs in 1930, 1931, and 1933, each of which started at midwestern banks and then spread throughout the country. After the failure of a particularly large bank in 1930, federal officials realized that the economy-wide effects compelled them to take a less hands-off approach and to intervene more vigorously. In 1932, the Reconstruction Finance Corporation (RFC) was established and given the authority to make loans to banks in order to stabilize the banking sector. In addition, the Glass-Steagall Act of 1933, which increased the ability of banks to borrow from the Federal Reserve System, was passed. A loan to a leading Chicago bank from the Federal Reserve appears to have stopped a major banking crisis in 1932. However, the beast had not yet been tamed. Banks became fearful of borrowing from the RFC because doing so signaled weakness to the public.

In the midst of the catastrophic bank run of 1933, the new U.S. president, Franklin Delano Roosevelt, was inaugurated. He immediately declared a "bank holiday," closing all banks until regulators could get a handle on the problem. In March 1933, emergency measures were adopted that gave the RFC extraordinary powers to stabilize and restructure the banking industry by providing capital to banks either by loans or by outright purchases of bank shares. With the new regulations, regulators closed nonviable banks and recapitalized viable ones by allowing the RFC to buy preferred shares in banks (shares that gave the U.S. government more rights than regular shareholders) and by greatly expanding banks' ability to borrow from the Federal Reserve. By 1933,

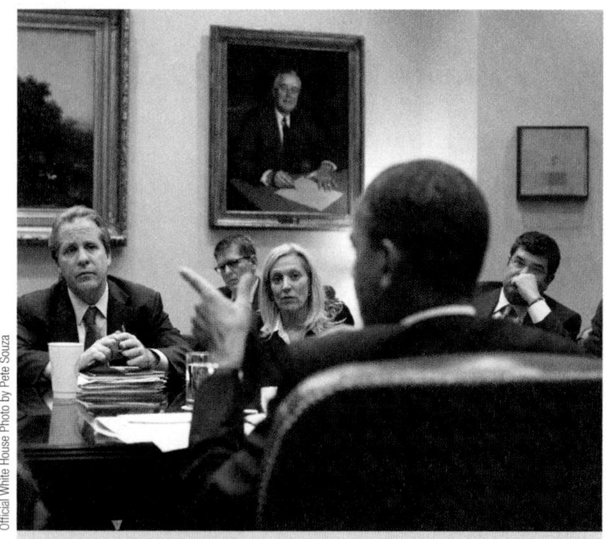

Like Franklin Delano Roosevelt, President Obama, shown here meeting with economic advisers, was faced with a major financial crisis upon taking office.

the RFC had invested over $17 billion (2013 dollars) in bank capital—one-third of the total capital of all banks in the United States at that time—and purchased shares in almost one-half of all banks. The RFC loaned more than $34 billion (2013 dollars) to banks during this period. Economic historians uniformly agree that the banking crises of the early 1930s greatly exacerbated the severity of the Great Depression, rendering monetary policy ineffective as the banking sector broke down and currency, withdrawn from banks and stashed under beds, reduced the money supply.

Although the powerful actions of the RFC stabilized the banking industry, new legislation was needed to prevent future banking crises. The Glass-Steagall Act of 1933 separated banks into two categories, **commercial banks**, depository banks that accepted deposits and were covered by deposit insurance, and **investment banks**, which engaged in creating and trading financial assets such as stocks and corporate bonds but were not covered by deposit insurance because their activities were considered more risky. Regulation Q prevented commercial banks from paying interest on checking accounts, in the belief that this would promote unhealthy competition between banks. In addition, investment banks were much more lightly regulated than commercial banks. The most important measure for the prevention of bank runs, however, was the adoption of federal deposit insurance (with an original limit of $2,500 per deposit).

A **commercial bank** accepts deposits and is covered by deposit insurance.

An **investment bank** trades in financial assets and is not covered by deposit insurance.

A **savings and loan (thrift)** is another type of deposit-taking bank, usually specialized in issuing home loans.

These measures were clearly successful, and the United States enjoyed a long period of financial and banking stability. As memories of the bad old days dimmed, Depression-era bank regulations were lifted. Regulation Q was eliminated in 1980 and by 1999, the Glass-Steagall Act had been so weakened that commercial banks could deal in stocks and bonds among other financial assets.

The Savings and Loan Crisis of the 1980s

Along with banks, the banking industry also included **savings and loans** (also called S&Ls or **thrifts**), institutions established to accept savings and turn them into long-term mortgages for home-buyers. S&Ls were covered by federal deposit insurance and were tightly regulated for safety. However, trouble hit in the 1970s, as high inflation led savers to withdraw their funds from low-interest-paying S&L accounts and put them into higher-paying money market accounts. In addition, the high inflation rate severely eroded the value of the S&Ls' assets, the long-term mortgages they held on their books.

In order to improve S&Ls' competitive position versus banks, Congress eased regulations to allow S&Ls to undertake much more risky investments in addition to long-term home mortgages. However, the new freedom did not bring with it increased oversight, leaving S&Ls with less oversight than banks.

Not surprisingly, during the real estate boom of the 1970s and 1980s, S&Ls engaged in overly risky real estate lending. Also, corruption occurred as some S&L executives used their institutions as private piggy banks. By the early 1980s, a large number of S&Ls had failed. Because accounts were covered by federal deposit insurance, the liabilities of a failed S&L were now liabilities of the federal government. From 1986 through 1995, the federal government closed over 1,000 failed S&Ls, costing U.S. taxpayers over $124 billion.

In a classic case of shutting the barn door after the horse has escaped, in 1989 Congress put in place comprehensive oversight of S&L activities. It also empowered Fannie Mae and Freddie Mac to take over much of the home mortgage lending previously done by S&Ls. Fannie Mae and Freddie Mac are quasi-governmental agencies created during the Great Depression to make homeownership more affordable for low- and moderate-income households. There is evidence that the S&L crisis helped cause a steep slowdown in the finance and real estate industries, leading to the recession of the early 1990s.

Back to the Future: The Financial Crisis of 2008

The financial crisis of 2008 shared features of previous crises. Like the Panic of 1907 and the S&L crisis, it involved institutions that were not as strictly regulated as deposit-taking banks, as well as excessive speculation. And like the crises of the early 1930s, it involved a U.S. government that was reluctant to take aggressive action until the scale of the devastation became clear. Enrichment Module A: Financial Markets and Crises provides a detailed account of the financial crisis of 2008. To summarize the situation briefly, historically low interest rates helped cause a boom in housing between 2003 and 2006. With home prices rising steadily, loans to home buyers with questionable finances seemed deceptively safe, and the number of such loans exploded. But then housing prices started falling in 2006, leaving many borrowers with homes that were worth less than the mortgage loans used to buy them. The resulting losses for lenders caused a collapse of trust in the financial system. Lending institutions were reluctant to make loans, and firms had difficulty obtaining enough money to continue their operations.

Beginning in mid-2007, the Federal Reserve took ambitious steps to make more cash available in the economy. It provided liquidity to the troubled financial system through discount window lending, and bought large quantities of other assets, mainly long-term government debt and the debt of Fannie Mae and Freddie Mac. The Fed and the Treasury Department also rescued several firms whose collapse could have been catastrophic for the economy, including the investment bank Bear Stearns and the insurance company AIG.

By the fall of 2010, the financial system was relatively stable, and major institutions had repaid much of the money the federal government had injected during the crisis. It was generally expected that taxpayers would end up losing little if any money. However, the recovery of the banks was not matched by a successful turnaround for the overall economy: although the recession that began in December 2007 officially ended in June 2009, unemployment remained stubbornly high.

Like earlier crises, the crisis of 2008 led to changes in banking regulation, most notably the Dodd-Frank financial regulatory reform bill enacted in 2010. We describe that bill briefly in the FYI box that follows.

Regulation After the 2008 Crisis

In July 2010, President Obama signed the Wall Street Reform and Consumer Protection Act—generally known as Dodd-Frank, after its sponsors in the Senate and House, respectively—into law. It was the biggest financial reform enacted since the 1930s—not surprising given that the nation had just gone through the worst financial crisis since the 1930s. How did it change regulation?

For the most part, it left regulation of traditional deposit-taking banks more or less as it was. The main change these banks would face was the creation of a new agency, the Consumer Financial Protection Bureau, whose mission was to protect borrowers from being exploited through seemingly attractive financial deals they didn't understand.

The major changes came in the regulation of financial institutions other than banks—institutions that, as the fall of Lehman Brothers showed, could trigger banking crises. The new law gave a special government committee, the Financial Stability Oversight Council, the right to designate certain institutions as "systemically important" even if they weren't ordinary deposit-taking banks. These systemically important institutions would be subjected to bank-style regulation, including relatively high capital requirements and limits on the kinds of risks they could take. In addition, the federal government would acquire "resolution authority," meaning the right to seize troubled financial institutions in much the same way that it routinely takes over troubled banks.

Beyond this, the law established new rules on the trading of derivatives, those complex financial instruments that played an important role in the 2008 crisis: most derivatives would henceforth have to be bought and sold on exchanges, where everyone could observe their prices and the volume of transactions. The idea was to make the risks taken by financial institutions more transparent.

Overall, Dodd-Frank is probably best seen as an attempt to extend the spirit of old-fashioned bank regulation to the more complex financial system of the twenty-first century. Will it succeed in heading off future banking crises? Stay tuned.

Oli Scarff/Getty Images

MODULE 26 Review

Check Your Understanding

1. What are the similarities between the Panic of 1907, the S&L crisis, and the crisis of 2008?

2. Why did the creation of the Federal Reserve fail to prevent the bank runs of the Great Depression? What measures did stop the bank runs?

Tackle the Test: Multiple-Choice Questions

1. Which of the following contributed to the creation of the Federal Reserve System?
   - I. the bank panic of 1907
   - II. the Great Depression
   - III. the savings and loan crisis of the 1980s

   a. I only
   b. II only
   c. III only
   d. I and II only
   e. I, II, and III

2. Which of the following controls the monetary base?
   a. the central bank
   b. the Treasury
   c. Congress
   d. commercial banks
   e. investment banks

3. Which of the following is NOT a role of the Federal Reserve System?
   a. controlling bank reserves
   b. printing currency (Federal Reserve notes)
   c. carrying out monetary policy
   d. supervising and regulating banks
   e. holding reserves for commercial banks

4. Who oversees the Federal Reserve System?
   a. Congress
   b. the president of the United States
   c. the Federal Open Market Committee
   d. the Board of Governors of the Federal Reserve System
   e. the Reconstruction Finance Corporation

5. Which of the following contributed to the financial crisis of 2008?
   a. excessive speculation
   b. inadequate regulation
   c. delays in aggressive action by the government
   d. low interest rates leading to a housing boom
   e. all of the above

Tackle the Test: Free-Response Questions

1. a. What group determines monetary policy?
   b. How many members serve in this group?
   c. Who always serves in this group?
   d. Who sometimes serves in this group? Explain.

Rubric for FRQ 1 (5 points)

1 point: The Federal Open Market Committee (FOMC)

1 point: 12

1 point: Members of the Board of Governors and the New York Federal Reserve Bank president

1 point: 4 of the other 11 Federal Reserve Bank presidents

1 point: The 11 other Federal Reserve Bank presidents rotate their service on the FOMC.

2. a. What does the Board of Governors of the Federal Reserve System do?
   b. How many members serve on the group?
   c. Who appoints members?
   d. How long do members serve?
   e. Why do they serve a term of this length?
   f. How long does the chair serve?
   (6 points)

Drew Angerer/Getty Images

MODULE 27

The Federal Reserve System: Monetary Policy

In this Module, you will learn to:

- Describe the functions of the Federal Reserve System
- Explain the primary tools the Federal Reserve uses to influence the economy

The Federal Reserve System

In the previous module, you learned that the Federal Reserve System serves as the central bank of the United States. It has two parts: the Board of Governors, which is part of the U.S. government, and the 12 regional Federal Reserve Banks, which are privately owned. But what are the functions of the Federal Reserve System, and how does it serve them?

The Functions of the Federal Reserve System

Today, the Federal Reserve's functions fall into four basic categories: providing financial services to depository institutions, supervising and regulating banks and other financial institutions, maintaining the stability of the financial system, and conducting monetary policy. Let's look at each in turn.

AP® Exam Tip

Among the most important functions of the Federal Reserve is the conduct of monetary policy.

Provide Financial Services The 12 regional Federal Reserve Banks provide financial services to depository institutions such as banks and other large institutions, including the U.S. government. The Federal Reserve is sometimes referred to as the "banker's bank" because it holds reserves, clears checks, provides cash, and transfers funds for commercial banks—all services that banks provide for their customers. The Federal Reserve also acts as the banker and fiscal agent for the federal government. The U.S. Treasury has its checking account with the Federal Reserve, so when the federal government writes a check, it is written on an account at the Fed.

Supervise and Regulate Banking Institutions The Federal Reserve System is charged with ensuring the safety and soundness of the nation's banking and financial system. Each regional Federal Reserve Bank examines and regulates commercial banks in its district. The Board of Governors also engages in regulation and supervision of financial institutions.

Maintain the Stability of the Financial System As we have seen, one of the major reasons the Federal Reserve System was created was to provide the nation with a safe and stable monetary and financial system. The Fed is charged with maintaining the integrity of the financial system. As part of this function, Federal Reserve Banks provide liquidity to financial institutions to ensure their safety and soundness.

Conduct Monetary Policy One of the Federal Reserve's most important functions is the conduct of monetary policy. As we will see, the Federal Reserve uses the tools of monetary policy to prevent or address extreme macroeconomic fluctuations in the U.S. economy.

What the Fed Does

How does the Fed perform its functions? The Federal Reserve has three main policy tools at its disposal: *reserve requirements,* the *discount rate,* and, perhaps most importantly, *open-market operations.* These tools play a part in how the Fed performs each of its functions as outlined below.

The **federal funds market** allows banks that fall short of the reserve requirement to borrow funds from banks with excess reserves.

The **federal funds rate** is the interest rate that banks charge other banks for loans, as determined in the federal funds market.

The **discount rate** is the interest rate the Fed charges on loans to banks.

The Reserve Requirement

In our discussion of bank runs, we noted that the Fed sets a minimum required reserve ratio, currently between zero and 10% for checkable bank deposits. Banks that fail to maintain at least the required reserve ratio on average over a two-week period face penalties.

What does a bank do if it has insufficient reserves to meet the Fed's reserve requirement? Normally, it borrows additional reserves from other banks via the **federal funds market**, a financial market that allows banks that fall short of the reserve requirement to borrow reserves (usually just overnight) from banks that are holding excess reserves. The interest rate in this market is determined by supply and demand, but the supply and demand for bank reserves are both strongly affected by Federal Reserve actions. Later we will see how the **federal funds rate**, the interest rate at which funds are borrowed and lent among banks in the federal funds market, plays a key role in modern monetary policy.

In order to alter the money supply, the Fed can change reserve requirements. If the Fed reduces the required reserve ratio, banks will lend a larger percentage of their deposits, leading to more loans and an increase in the money supply via the money multiplier. Alternatively, if the Fed increases the required reserve ratio, banks are forced to reduce their lending, leading to a fall in the money supply via the money multiplier. Under current practice, however, the Fed doesn't use changes in reserve requirements to actively manage the money supply. The last significant change in reserve requirements was in 1992.

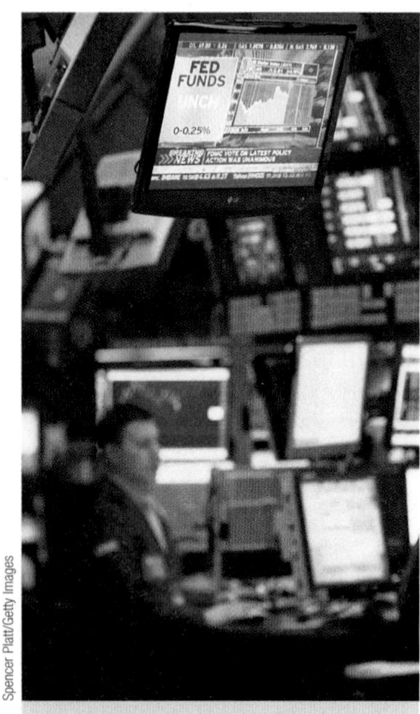

Spencer Platt/Getty Images

A trader works on the floor of the New York Stock Exchange as the Federal Reserve announces that it will be keeping its key interest rate near zero.

The Discount Rate

Banks in need of reserves can also borrow from the Fed itself via the *discount window.* The **discount rate** is the interest rate the Fed charges on those loans. Normally, the discount rate is set 1 percentage point above the federal funds rate in order to discourage banks from turning to the Fed when they are in need of reserves.

In order to alter the money supply, the Fed can change the discount rate. Beginning in the fall of 2007, the Fed reduced the spread between the federal funds rate and the discount rate as part of its response to the ongoing financial crisis. As a result, by the spring of 2008 the discount rate was only 0.25 percentage points above the federal funds rate.

If the Fed reduces the spread between the discount rate and the federal funds rate, the cost to banks of being short of reserves falls. Banks respond by increasing their lending, and the money supply increases via the money multiplier. If the Fed increases the spread between the discount rate and the federal funds rate, bank lending falls—and so will the money supply via the money multiplier.

The Fed normally doesn't use the discount rate to actively manage the money supply. As we mentioned earlier, however, there was a temporary surge in lending through the discount window in 2007 in response to the financial crisis. Today, normal monetary policy is conducted almost exclusively using the Fed's third policy tool: open-market operations.

Open-Market Operations

Like the banks it oversees, the Federal Reserve has assets and liabilities. The Fed's assets consist of its holdings of debt issued by the U.S. government, mainly short-term U.S. government bonds with a maturity of less than one year, known as U.S. Treasury bills. Remember, the Fed and the U.S. government are not one entity; U.S. Treasury bills held by the Fed are a liability of the government but an asset of the Fed. The Fed's liabilities consist of currency in circulation and bank reserves. **Figure 27.1** summarizes the normal assets and liabilities of the Fed in the form of a T-account.

Figure 27.1 The Federal Reserve's Assets and Liabilities

The Federal Reserve holds its assets mostly in short-term government bonds called U.S. Treasury bills. Its liabilities are the monetary base—currency in circulation plus bank reserves.

Assets	Liabilities
Government debt (Treasury bills)	Monetary base (Currency in circulation + bank reserves)

In an **open-market operation**, the Federal Reserve buys or sells U.S. Treasury bills, normally through a transaction with *commercial banks*—banks that mainly make business loans, as opposed to home loans. The Fed never buys U.S. Treasury bills directly from the federal government. There's a good reason for this: when a central bank buys government debt directly from the government, it is lending directly to the government—in effect, the central bank is issuing "printing money" to finance the government's budget deficit. As we'll see later in the book, this has historically been a formula for disastrous levels of inflation.

An **open-market operation** is a purchase or sale of government debt by the Fed.

The two panels of **Figure 27.2** on the next page show the changes in the financial position of both the Fed and commercial banks that result from open-market operations. When the Fed buys U.S. Treasury bills from a commercial bank, it pays by crediting the bank's reserve account by an amount equal to the value of the Treasury bills. This is illustrated in panel (a): the Fed buys $100 million of U.S. Treasury bills from commercial banks, which increases the monetary base by $100 million because it increases bank reserves by $100 million. When the Fed sells U.S. Treasury bills to commercial banks, it debits the banks' accounts, reducing their reserves. This is shown in panel (b), where the Fed sells $100 million of U.S. Treasury bills. Here, bank reserves and the monetary base decrease.

You might wonder where the Fed gets the funds to purchase U.S. Treasury bills from banks. The answer is that it simply creates them with a stroke of the pen—or, these days, a click of the mouse—that credits the banks' accounts with extra reserves. The Fed issues currency to pay for Treasury bills only when banks want the additional reserves

Figure 27.2 Open-Market Operations by the Federal Reserve

(a) An Open-Market Purchase of $100 Million

	Assets		Liabilities	
Federal Reserve	Treasury bills	+$100 million	Monetary base	+$100 million

	Assets		Liabilities
Commercial banks	Treasury bills	−$100 million	No change
	Reserves	+$100 million	

(b) An Open-Market Sale of $100 Million

	Assets		Liabilities	
Federal Reserve	Treasury bills	−$100 million	Monetary base	−$100 million

	Assets		Liabilities
Commercial banks	Treasury bills	+$100 million	No change
	Reserves	−$100 million	

In panel (a), the Federal Reserve increases the monetary base by purchasing U.S. Treasury bills from private commercial banks in an open-market operation. Here, a $100 million purchase of U.S. Treasury bills by the Federal Reserve is paid for by a $100 million increase in the monetary base. This will ultimately lead to an increase in the money supply via the money multiplier as banks lend out some of these new reserves. In panel (b), the Federal Reserve reduces the monetary base by selling U.S. Treasury bills to private commercial banks in an open-market operation. Here, a $100 million sale of U.S. Treasury bills leads to a $100 million reduction in commercial bank reserves, resulting in a $100 million decrease in the monetary base. This will ultimately lead to a fall in the money supply via the money multiplier as banks reduce their loans in response to a fall in their reserves.

in the form of currency. Remember, the modern dollar is fiat money, which isn't backed by anything. So the Fed can add to the monetary base at its own discretion.

The change in bank reserves caused by an open-market operation doesn't directly affect the money supply. Instead, it starts the money multiplier in motion. After the $100 million increase in reserves shown in panel (a), commercial banks would lend out their additional reserves, immediately increasing the money supply by $100 million. Some of those loans would be deposited back into the banking system, increasing reserves again and permitting a further round of loans, and so on, leading to a rise in the money supply. An open-market sale has the reverse effect: bank reserves fall, requiring banks to reduce their loans, leading to a fall in the money supply.

Economists often say, loosely, that the Fed controls the money supply—checkable deposits plus currency in circulation. In fact, it controls only the monetary base—bank reserves plus currency in circulation. But by increasing or decreasing the monetary base, the Fed can exert a powerful influence on both the money supply and interest rates. This influence is the basis of monetary policy, discussed in detail in Modules 28 and 29.

The European Central Bank

As we noted earlier, the Fed is only one of a number of central banks around the world, and it's much younger than Sweden's Sveriges Rijksbank and Britain's Bank of England. In general, other central banks operate in much the same way as the Fed. That's especially true of the only other central bank that rivals the Fed in terms of importance to the world economy: the European Central Bank.

The European Central Bank, known as the ECB, was created in January 1999 when 11 European nations abandoned their national currencies, adopted the euro as their

Who Gets the Interest on the Fed's Assets?

As we've just learned, the Fed owns a lot of assets—Treasury bills—which it bought from commercial banks in exchange for the monetary base in the form of credits to banks' reserve accounts. These assets pay interest. Yet the Fed's liabilities consist mainly of the monetary base, liabilities on which the Fed *doesn't* pay interest. So the Fed, in effect, is an institution that has the privilege of borrowing funds at a zero interest rate and lending them out at a positive interest rate. That sounds like a pretty profitable business. Who gets the profits?

You do—or rather, U.S. taxpayers do. The Fed keeps some of the interest it receives to finance its operations but turns most of it over to the U.S. Treasury. For example, in 2013 the Federal Reserve System received $79.5 billion in income—largely in interest on its holdings of Treasury bills, of which $77.7 billion was returned to the Treasury.

We can now finish the story of the impact of those forged $100 bills allegedly printed in North Korea. When a fake $100 bill enters circulation, it has the same economic effect as a real $100 bill printed by the U.S. government. That is, as long as nobody catches the forgery, the fake bill, for all practical purposes, serves as part of the monetary base. Meanwhile, the Fed decides on the size of the monetary base based on economic considerations—in particular, the Fed doesn't let the monetary base get too large because that can cause inflation. So every fake $100 bill that enters circulation basically means that the Fed issues one less real $100 bill. When the Fed issues a $100 bill legally, however, it gets Treasury bills in return—and the interest on those bills helps pay for the U.S. government's expenses. So a counterfeit $100 bill reduces the amount of Treasury bills the Fed can acquire and thereby reduces the interest payments going to the Fed and the U.S. Treasury. So taxpayers bear the real cost of counterfeiting.

common currency, and placed their joint monetary policy in the ECB's hands. (Six more countries have joined since 1999.) The ECB instantly became an extremely important institution: although no single European nation has an economy anywhere near as large as that of the United States, the combined economies of the eurozone, the group of countries that have adopted the euro as their currency, are roughly as big as the U.S. economy. As a result, the ECB and the Fed are the two giants of the monetary world.

Like the Fed, the ECB has a special status: it's not a private institution, but it's not exactly a government agency either. In fact, it can't be a government agency because there is no pan-European government! Luckily for puzzled Americans, there are strong analogies between European central banking and the Federal Reserve System.

First of all, the ECB, which is located in the German city of Frankfurt, isn't really the counterpart of the whole Federal Reserve System: it's the equivalent of the Board of Governors in Washington. The European counterparts of the regional Federal Reserve Banks are Europe's national central banks: the Bank of France, the Bank of Italy, and so on. Until 1999, each of these national banks was its country's equivalent to the Fed. For example, the Bank of France controlled the French monetary base.

Today these national banks, like regional Feds, provide various financial services to local banks and businesses and conduct open-market operations, but the making of monetary policy has moved upstream to the ECB. Still, the various European national central banks aren't small institutions: in total, they employ more than 50,000 people; in December 2012, the ECB employed only 1,638.

In the eurozone, each country chooses who runs its own national central bank. The ECB's Executive Board is the counterpart of the Fed's Board of Governors; its members are chosen by unanimous consent of the eurozone national governments. The counterpart of the Federal Open Market Committee is the ECB's Governing Council. Just as the Fed's Open Market Committee consists of the Board of Governors plus a rotating group of regional Fed presidents, the ECB's Governing Council consists of the Executive Board plus the heads of the national central banks.

Like the Fed, the ECB is ultimately answerable to voters. Given the fragmentation of political forces across national boundaries, however, it appears to be even more insulated than the Fed from short-term political pressures.

MODULE 27 Review

Check Your Understanding

1. Assume that any money lent by a bank is deposited back into the banking system as a checkable deposit and that the reserve ratio is 10%. Trace out the effects of a $100 million open-market purchase of U.S. Treasury bills by the Fed on the value of checkable bank deposits. What is the size of the money multiplier?

Tackle the Test: Multiple-Choice Questions

1. Which of the following is a function of the Federal Reserve System?
   - I. examine commercial banks
   - II. conduct fiscal policy
   - III. conduct monetary policy

   a. I only
   b. II only
   c. III only
   d. I and III only
   e. I, II, and III

2. Which of the following financial services does the Federal Reserve provide for commercial banks?
   - I. clearing checks
   - II. holding reserves
   - III. making loans

   a. I only
   b. II only
   c. III only
   d. I and II
   e. I, II, and III

3. When the Fed makes a loan to a commercial bank, it charges
   a. no interest.
   b. the prime rate.
   c. the federal funds rate.
   d. the discount rate.
   e. the market interest rate.

4. If the Fed purchases U.S. Treasury bills from a commercial bank, what happens to bank reserves and the money supply?

	Bank reserves	*Money supply*
a.	increase	decrease
b.	increase	increase
c.	decrease	decrease
d.	decrease	increase
e.	increase	no change

5. When banks make loans to each other, they charge the
   a. prime rate.
   b. discount rate.
   c. federal funds rate.
   d. CD rate.
   e. mortgage rate.

Tackle the Test: Free-Response Questions

1. a. What are the three major tools of the Federal Reserve System?
   b. What would the Fed do with each tool to increase the money supply? Explain for each.

Rubric for FRQ 1 (9 points)

1 point: The discount rate

1 point: The reserve requirement

1 point: Open-market operations

1 point: Decrease the discount rate

1 point: A lower discount rate makes it cheaper to borrow from the Fed so the money supply increases.

1 point: Decrease the reserve requirement

1 point: A lower reserve requirement allows banks to loan more, increasing the money supply.

1 point: Buy U.S. Treasury bills

1 point: When the Fed buys U.S. Treasury bills, banks' excess reserves increase. When lent out, these excess reserves increase the money supply with the assistance of the money multiplier.

2. What are the four basic functions of the Federal Reserve System and what part of the system is responsible for each?
(8 points)

istockphoto

MODULE 28 The Money Market

In this Module, you will learn to:

- Illustrate the relationship between the demand for money and the interest rate with a graph
- Explain why the liquidity preference model determines the interest rate in the short run

The Demand for Money

Remember that M1, the most commonly used definition of the money supply, consists of currency in circulation (cash), plus checkable bank deposits, plus traveler's checks. M2, a broader definition of the money supply, consists of M1 plus deposits that can easily be transferred into checkable deposits. You also learned why people hold money—to make it easier to purchase goods and services. Now we'll go deeper, examining what determines *how much* money individuals and firms want to hold at any given time.

The Opportunity Cost of Holding Money

Most economic decisions involve trade-offs at the margin. That is, individuals decide how much of a good to consume by determining whether the benefit they'd gain from consuming a bit more of that good is worth the cost. The same decision process is used when deciding how much money to hold.

Individuals and firms find it useful to hold some of their assets in the form of money because of the convenience money provides: money can be used to make purchases directly, while other assets can't. But there is a price to be paid—an opportunity cost—for that convenience: money held in your wallet earns no interest.

As an example of how convenience makes it worth incurring some opportunity costs, consider the fact that even today—with the prevalence of credit cards, debit cards, and ATMs—people continue to keep cash in their wallets rather than leave the funds in an interest-bearing account. They do this because they don't want to have to go to an ATM to withdraw money every time they want to make a small purchase. In other words, the convenience of keeping some cash in your wallet is more valuable than the interest you would earn by keeping that money in the bank.

Table 28.1 Selected Interest Rates, June 2007

One-month CDs	5.30%
Interest-bearing demand deposits	2.30
Currency	0

Source: Federal Reserve Bank of St. Louis.

Even holding money in a checking account involves a trade-off between convenience and interest payments. That's because you can earn a higher interest rate by putting your money in assets other than a checking account. For example, many banks offer certificates of deposit, or CDs, which pay a higher interest rate than ordinary bank accounts. But CDs also carry a penalty if you withdraw the funds before a certain amount of time—say, six months—has elapsed. An individual who keeps funds in a checking account is forgoing the higher interest rate those funds would have earned if placed in a CD in return for the convenience of having cash readily available when needed.

Table 28.1 illustrates the opportunity cost of holding money in a specific month. Because interest rates are currently at abnormally low levels, we refer back to June 2007. The first row shows the interest rate on one-month certificates of deposit—that is, the interest rate individuals could get if they were willing to tie their funds up for one month. In June 2007, one-month CDs yielded 5.30%. The second row shows the interest rate on interest-bearing bank accounts (specifically, those included in M1). Funds in these accounts were more accessible than those in CDs, but the price of that convenience was a much lower interest rate, only 2.30%. Finally, the last row shows the interest rate on currency—cash in your wallet—which, of course, was zero.

Table 28.1 shows the opportunity cost of holding money at one point in time, but the opportunity cost of holding money changes when the overall level of interest rates changes. Specifically, when the overall level of interest rates falls, the opportunity cost of holding money falls, too.

Table 28.2 illustrates this point by showing how selected interest rates changed between June 2007 and June 2008, a period when the Federal Reserve was slashing rates in an effort to fight off recession. Between June 2007 and June 2008, the federal funds rate, which is the rate the Fed controls most directly, fell by 3.25 percentage points. The interest rate on one-month CDs fell almost as much, 2.8 percentage points. That's not an accident: all **short-term interest rates**—rates on financial assets that come due, or mature, within a year—tend to move together, with rare exceptions. The reason short-term interest rates tend to move together is that CDs and other short-term assets (like one-month and three-month U.S. Treasury bills) are in effect competing for the same business. Any short-term asset that offers a lower-than-average interest rate will be sold by investors, who will move their wealth into a higher-yielding short-term asset. The selling of the asset, in turn, forces its interest rate up because investors must be rewarded with a higher rate in order to induce them to buy it. Conversely, investors will move their wealth into any short-term financial asset that offers an above-average interest rate. The purchase of the asset drives its interest rate down when sellers find they can lower the rate of return on the asset and still find willing buyers. So interest rates on short-term financial assets tend to be roughly the same because no asset will consistently offer a higher-than-average or a lower-than-average interest rate.

Short-term interest rates are the interest rates on financial assets that mature within a year.

Table 28.2 Interest Rates and the Opportunity Cost of Holding Money

	June 2007	June 2008
Federal funds rate	5.25%	2.00%
One-month certificates of deposit (CD)	5.30	2.50
Interest-bearing demand deposits	2.30	1.24
Currency	0	0
CDs minus interest-bearing demand deposits	3.00	1.26
CDs minus currency	5.30	2.50

Source: Federal Reserve Bank of St. Louis.

FYI Long-Term Interest Rates

Long-term interest rates—rates on bonds or loans that mature in several years—don't necessarily move with short-term interest rates. How is that possible?

Consider the case of Millie, who has already decided to place $1,000 in CDs for the next two years. However, she hasn't decided whether to put the money in a one-year CD, at a 4% rate of interest, or a two-year CD, at a 5% rate of interest.

You might think that the two-year CD is a clearly better deal—but it may not be. Suppose that Millie expects the rate of interest on one-year CDs to rise sharply next year. If she puts her funds in a one-year CD this year, she will be able to reinvest the money at a much higher rate next year. And this could give her a two-year rate of return that is higher than if she put her funds into the two-year CD. For example, if the rate of interest on one-year CDs rises from 4% this year to 8% next year, putting her funds in a one-year CD will give her an annual rate of return over the next two years of about 6%, better than the 5% rate on two-year CDs.

The same considerations apply to investors deciding between short-term and long-term bonds. If they expect short-term interest rates to rise, investors may buy short-term bonds even if long-term bonds offer a higher interest rate. If they expect short-term interest rates to fall, investors may buy long-term bonds even if short-term bonds offer a higher interest rate.

In practice, long-term interest rates reflect the average expectation in the market about what's going to happen to short-term rates in the future. When long-term rates are higher than short-term rates, as they were in 2014, the market is signaling that it expects short-term rates to rise in the future.

But as short-term interest rates fell between June 2007 and June 2008, the interest rates on money didn't fall by the same amount. The interest rate on currency, of course, remained at zero. The interest rate paid on demand deposits did fall, but by much less than short-term interest rates. As a result, the opportunity cost of holding money fell. The last two rows of Table 28.2 show the differences between the interest rates on demand deposits and currency and the interest rate on CDs. These differences declined sharply between June 2007 and June 2008. This reflects a general result: the higher the short-term interest rate, the higher the opportunity cost of holding money; the lower the short-term interest rate, the lower the opportunity cost of holding money.

Table 28.2 contains only short-term interest rates. At any given moment, **long-term interest rates**—interest rates on financial assets that mature, or come due, a number of years in the future—may be different from short-term interest rates. The difference between short-term and long-term interest rates is sometimes important as a practical matter. Moreover, it's short-term rates rather than long-term rates that affect money demand, because the decision to hold money involves trading off the convenience of holding cash versus the payoff from holding assets that mature in the short-term—a year or less. For our current purposes, however, it's useful to ignore the distinction between short-term and long-term rates and assume that there is only one interest rate.

Long-term interest rates are interest rates on financial assets that mature a number of years in the future.

The Money Demand Curve

Because the overall level of interest rates affects the opportunity cost of holding money, the quantity of money individuals and firms want to hold, other things equal, is negatively related to the interest rate. In **Figure 28.1** on the next page, the horizontal axis shows the quantity of money demanded and the vertical axis shows the nominal interest rate, r, which you can think of as a representative short-term interest rate such as the rate on one-month CDs. Why do we place the nominal interest rate and not the real interest rate on the vertical axis? Because the opportunity cost of holding money includes both the real return that could be earned on a bank deposit and the erosion in purchasing power caused by inflation. The nominal interest rate includes both the forgone real return and the expected loss due to inflation. Hence, r in Figure 28.1 and all subsequent figures is the nominal interest rate.

Figure 28.1 The Money Demand Curve

The money demand curve illustrates the relationship between the interest rate and the quantity of money demanded. It slopes downward: a higher interest rate leads to a higher opportunity cost of holding money and reduces the quantity of money demanded.

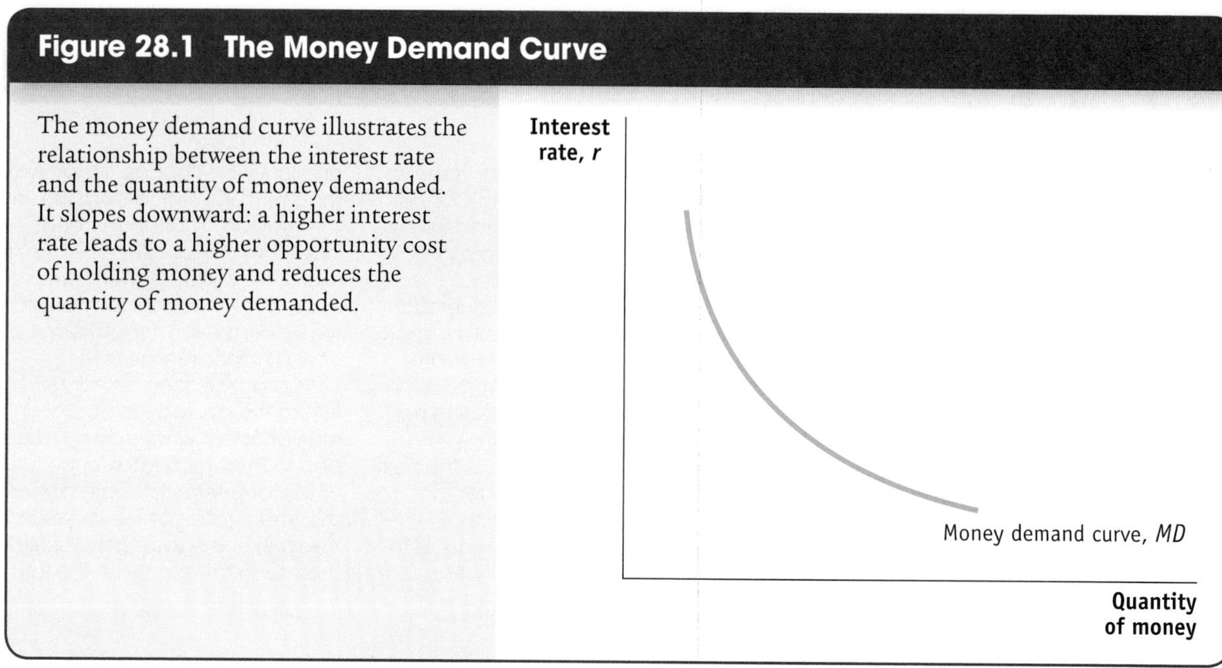

The **money demand curve** shows the relationship between the quantity of money demanded and the interest rate.

The relationship between the interest rate and the quantity of money demanded by the public is illustrated by the **money demand curve**, *MD*, in Figure 28.1. The money demand curve slopes downward because, other things equal, a higher interest rate increases the opportunity cost of holding money, leading the public to reduce the quantity of money it demands. For example, if the interest rate is very low—say, 0.15%, a common rate for one-month CDs in 2014—the interest forgone by holding money is relatively small. As a result, individuals and firms will tend to hold relatively large amounts of money to avoid the cost and nuisance of converting other assets into money when making purchases. By contrast, if the interest rate is relatively high—say, 15%, a level it reached in the United States in the early 1980s—the opportunity cost of holding money is high. People will respond by keeping only small amounts in cash and deposits, converting assets into money only when needed.

AP® Exam Tip

The money market graph is one of the essential graphs you must be able to correctly draw, label, and interpret for the AP® exam. The interest rate measured along the vertical axis is the nominal interest rate.

You might ask why we draw the money demand curve with the interest rate—as opposed to rates of return on other assets, such as stocks or real estate—on the vertical axis. The answer is that, for most people, the relevant question in deciding how much money to hold is whether to put the funds in the form of other assets that can be turned fairly quickly and easily into money. Stocks don't fit that definition because there are significant broker's fees when you sell stock (which is why stock market investors are advised not to buy and sell too often); selling real estate involves even larger fees and can take a long time as well. So the relevant comparison is with assets that are "close to" money—fairly liquid assets like CDs. And, as we've already seen, the interest rates on all these assets normally move closely together.

Shifts of the Money Demand Curve

Like the demand curve for an ordinary good, the money demand curve can be shifted by a number of factors. **Figure 28.2** shows shifts of the money demand curve: an increase in the demand for money corresponds to a rightward shift of the *MD* curve, raising the quantity of money demanded at any given interest rate; a fall in the demand for money corresponds to a leftward shift of the *MD* curve, reducing the quantity of money demanded at any given interest rate. The most important factors causing the money demand curve to shift are changes in the aggregate price level, changes in real GDP, changes in banking technology, and changes in banking institutions.

Figure 28.2 Increases and Decreases in the Demand for Money

A rise in money demand shifts the money demand curve to the right, from MD_1 to MD_2, and the quantity of money demanded rises at any given interest rate. A fall in money demand shifts the money demand curve to the left, from MD_1 to MD_3, and the quantity of money demanded falls at any given interest rate.

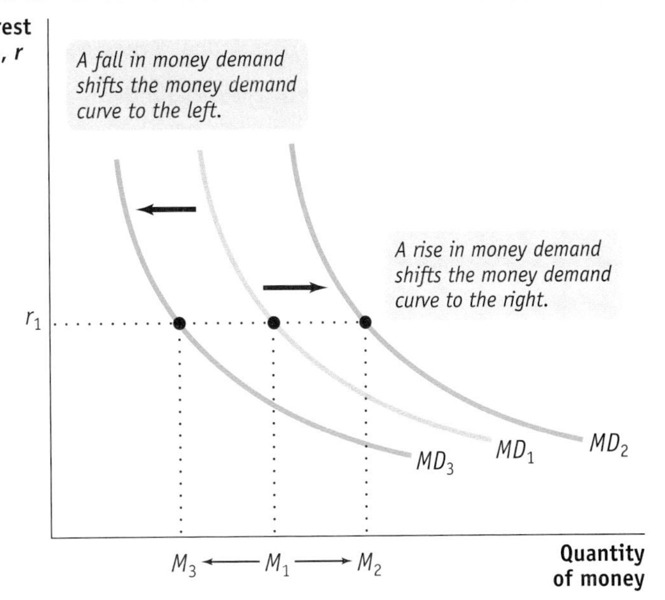

Changes in the Aggregate Price Level Americans keep a lot more cash in their wallets and funds in their checking accounts today than they did in the 1950s. One reason is that they have to if they want to be able to buy anything: almost everything costs more now than it did when you could get a burger, fries, and a drink at McDonald's for 45 cents and a gallon of gasoline for 29 cents. So higher prices increase the demand for money (a rightward shift of the *MD* curve), and lower prices decrease the demand for money (a leftward shift of the *MD* curve).

We can actually be more specific than this: other things equal, the demand for money is *proportional* to the price level. That is, if the aggregate price level rises by 20%, the quantity of money demanded at any given interest rate, such as r_1 in Figure 28.2, also rises by 20%—the movement from M_1 to M_2. Why? Because if the price of everything rises by 20%, it takes 20% more money to buy the same basket of goods and services. And if the aggregate price level falls by 20%, at any given interest rate the quantity of money demanded falls by 20%—shown by the movement from M_1 to M_3 at the interest rate r_1. As we'll see later, the fact that money demand is proportional to the price level has important implications for the long-run effects of monetary policy.

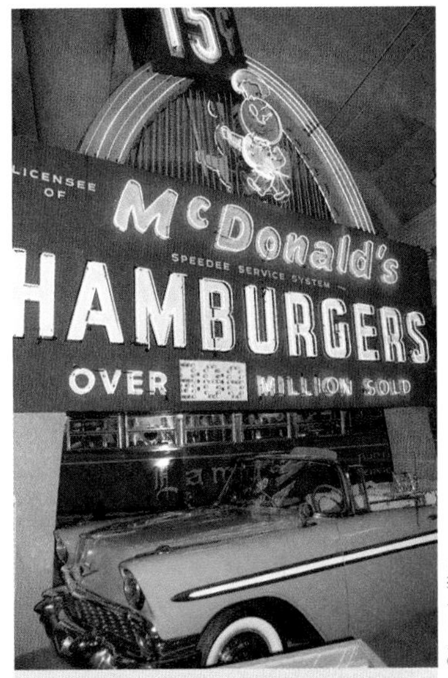

A re-creation of a McDonald's in the 1950s at the Ford Museum in Detroit, Michigan.

Changes in Real GDP Households and firms hold money as a way to facilitate purchases of goods and services. The larger the quantity of goods and services they buy, the larger the quantity of money they will want to hold at any given interest rate. So an increase in real GDP—the total quantity of goods and services produced and sold in the economy—shifts the money demand curve rightward. A fall in real GDP shifts the money demand curve leftward.

Changes in Technology There was a time, not so long ago, when withdrawing cash from a bank account required a visit during the bank's hours of operation. Since most people tried to do their banking during lunch hour, they often found themselves standing in line. So people limited the number of times they needed to withdraw funds by keeping substantial amounts of cash on hand. Not surprisingly, this tendency diminished greatly with the advent of ATMs in the 1970s. As a result, the demand for money fell and the money demand curve shifted leftward.

These events illustrate how changes in technology can affect the demand for money. In general, advances in information technology have tended to reduce the demand

AP® Exam Tip

Changes in the aggregate price level, real GDP, technology, and banking institutions shift the money demand curve. On the AP® exam you may be given scenarios in which you must determine the direction of a shift in this curve.

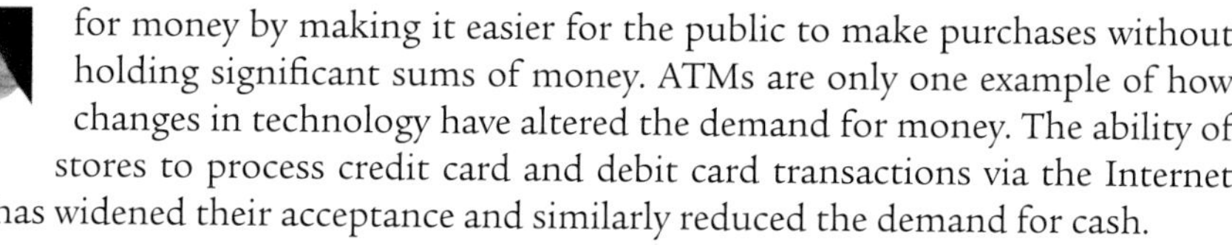

istockphoto

for money by making it easier for the public to make purchases without holding significant sums of money. ATMs are only one example of how changes in technology have altered the demand for money. The ability of stores to process credit card and debit card transactions via the Internet has widened their acceptance and similarly reduced the demand for cash.

Changes in Institutions Changes in institutions can increase or decrease the demand for money. For example, until Regulation Q was eliminated in 1980, U.S. banks weren't allowed to offer interest on checking accounts. So the interest you would forgo by holding funds in a checking account instead of an interest-bearing asset made the opportunity cost of holding funds in checking accounts very high. When banking regulations changed, allowing banks to pay interest on checking account funds, the demand for money rose and shifted the money demand curve to the right.

Money and Interest Rates

The Federal Open Market Committee decided today to lower its target for the federal funds rate 75 basis points to 2¼ percent.

Recent information indicates that the outlook for economic activity has weakened further. Growth in consumer spending has slowed and labor markets have softened. Financial markets remain under considerable stress, and the tightening of credit conditions and the deepening of the housing contraction are likely to weigh on economic growth over the next few quarters.

So read the beginning of a press release from the Federal Reserve issued on March 18, 2008. (A basis point is equal to 0.01 percentage point. So the statement implies that the Fed lowered the target from 3% to 2.25%.) Remember that the federal funds rate is the rate at which banks lend reserves to each other to meet the required reserve ratio. As the statement implies, at each of its eight-times-a-year meetings, the Federal Open Market Committee sets a target value for the federal funds rate. It's then up to Fed officials to achieve that target. This is done by the Open Market Desk at the Federal Reserve Bank of New York, which buys and sells short-term U.S. government debt, known as Treasury bills, to achieve that target.

As we've already seen, other short-term interest rates, such as the rates on CDs, move with the federal funds rate. So when the Fed reduced its target for the federal funds rate from 3% to 2.25% in March 2008, many other short-term interest rates also fell by about three-quarters of a percentage point.

How does the Fed go about achieving a *target federal funds rate*? And more to the point, how is the Fed able to affect interest rates at all?

The Equilibrium Interest Rate

According to the **liquidity preference model of the interest rate**, the interest rate is determined by the supply and demand for money.

The **money supply curve** shows the relationship between the quantity of money supplied and the interest rate.

Recall that, for simplicity, we've assumed that there is only one interest rate paid on nonmonetary financial assets, both in the short run and in the long run. To understand how the interest rate is determined, consider **Figure 28.3**, which illustrates the **liquidity preference model of the interest rate**; this model says that the interest rate is determined by the supply and demand for money in the market for money. Figure 28.3 combines the money demand curve, *MD*, with the **money supply curve**, *MS*, which shows the relationship between the quantity of money supplied by the Federal Reserve and the interest rate.

The Federal Reserve can increase or decrease the money supply: it usually does this through *open-market operations*, buying or selling Treasury bills, but it can also lend via the *discount window* or change *reserve requirements*. Let's assume for simplicity that the Fed, using one or more of these methods, simply chooses the level of the money supply that it believes will achieve its interest rate target. Then the money supply curve is a vertical line, *MS* in Figure 28.3, with a horizontal intercept corresponding to the money supply chosen by the Fed, $\overline{M}$. The money market equilibrium is at *E*, where *MS*

Figure 28.3 Equilibrium in the Money Market

The money supply curve, *MS*, is vertical at the money supply chosen by the Federal Reserve, $\overline{M}$. The money market is in equilibrium at the interest rate r_E: the quantity of money demanded by the public is equal to $\overline{M}$, the quantity of money supplied. At a point such as *L*, the interest rate, r_L, is below r_E and the corresponding quantity of money demanded, M_L, exceeds the money supply, $\overline{M}$. In an attempt to shift their wealth out of nonmoney interest-bearing financial assets and raise their money holdings, investors drive the interest rate up to r_E. At a point such as *H*, the interest rate r_H is above r_E and the corresponding quantity of money demanded, M_H, is less than the money supply, $\overline{M}$. In an attempt to shift out of money holdings into nonmoney interest-bearing financial assets, investors drive the interest rate down to r_E.

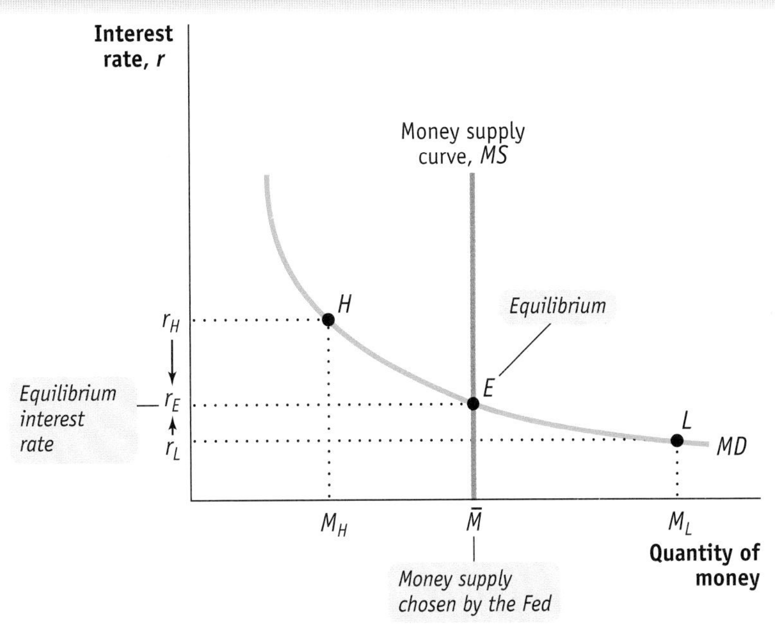

and *MD* cross. At this point the quantity of money demanded equals the money supply, $\overline{M}$, leading to an equilibrium interest rate of r_E.

To understand why r_E is the equilibrium interest rate, consider what happens if the money market is at a point like *L*, where the interest rate, r_L, is below r_E. At r_L the public wants to hold the quantity of money M_L, an amount larger than the actual money supply, $\overline{M}$. This means that at point *L*, the public wants to shift some of its wealth out of interest-bearing assets such as high-denomination CDs (which aren't money) into money. This has two implications. One is that the quantity of money demanded is *more* than the quantity of money supplied. The other is that the quantity of interest-bearing nonmoney assets demanded is *less* than the quantity supplied. So those trying to sell nonmoney assets will find that they have to offer a higher interest rate to attract buyers. As a result, the interest rate will be driven up from r_L until the public wants to hold the quantity of money that is actually available, *M*. That is, the interest rate will rise until it is equal to r_E.

Now consider what happens if the money market is at a point such as *H* in Figure 28.3, where the interest rate r_H is above r_E. In that case the quantity of money demanded, M_H, is less than the quantity of money supplied, $\overline{M}$. Correspondingly, the quantity of interest-bearing nonmoney assets demanded is greater than the quantity supplied. Those trying to sell interest-bearing nonmoney assets will find that they can offer a lower interest rate and still find willing buyers. This leads to a fall in the interest rate from r_H. It falls until the public wants to hold the quantity of money that is actually available, $\overline{M}$. Again, the interest rate will end up at r_E.

Two Models of the Interest Rate

Here we have developed the liquidity preference model of the interest rate. In this model, the equilibrium interest rate is the rate at which the quantity of money demanded equals the quantity of money supplied in the money market. This model is different from, but consistent with, another model known as the loanable funds model of the interest rate, which is developed in the next module. In the loanable funds model, we will see that the interest rate matches the quantity of loanable funds supplied by savers with the quantity of loanable funds demanded for investment spending.

MODULE 28 Review

Check Your Understanding

1. Explain how each of the following would affect the quantity of money demanded, and indicate whether each change would cause a movement along the money demand curve or a shift of the money demand curve.
   a. The short-term interest rate rises from 5% to 30%.
   b. All prices fall by 10%.
   c. New wireless technology automatically charges supermarket purchases to credit cards, eliminating the need to stop at the cash register.
   d. In order to avoid paying taxes, a vast underground economy develops in which workers are paid their wages in cash rather than with checks.

2. How will each of the following affect the opportunity cost or benefit of holding cash? Explain.
   a. Merchants charge a 1% fee on debit/credit card transactions for purchases of less than $50.
   b. To attract more deposits, banks raise the interest paid on six-month CDs.
   c. The cost of food rises significantly.

Tackle the Test: Multiple-Choice Questions

1. A change in which of the following will shift the money demand curve?
   I. the aggregate price level
   II. real GDP
   III. the interest rate
   a. I only
   b. II only
   c. III only
   d. I and II only
   e. I, II, and III

2. Which of the following will decrease the demand for money?
   a. an increase in the interest rate
   b. inflation
   c. an increase in real GDP
   d. an increase in the availability of ATMs
   e. the adoption of Regulation Q

3. What will happen to the money supply and the equilibrium interest rate if the Federal Reserve sells Treasury securities?

	Money supply	*Equilibrium interest rate*
a.	increase	increase
b.	decrease	increase
c.	increase	decrease
d.	decrease	decrease
e.	decrease	no change

4. Which of the following is true regarding short-term and long-term interest rates?
   a. Short-term interest rates are always above long-term interest rates.
   b. Short-term interest rates are always below long-term interest rates.
   c. Short-term interest rates are always equal to long-term interest rates.
   d. Short-term interest rates are more important for determining the demand for money.
   e. Long-term interest rates are more important for determining the demand for money.

5. The quantity of money demanded rises (that is, there is a movement along the money demand curve) when
   a. the aggregate price level increases.
   b. the aggregate price level falls.
   c. real GDP increases.
   d. new technology makes banking easier.
   e. short-term interest rates fall.

Tackle the Test: Free-Response Questions

1. Draw three correctly labeled graphs of the money market. Show the effect of each of the following three changes on a separate graph.
   a. The aggregate price level increases.
   b. Real GDP falls.
   c. There is a dramatic increase in online banking.

Rubric for FRQ 1 (6 points)

1 point: The vertical axis is labeled "Interest rate" or "r" and the horizontal axis is labeled "Quantity of money."

1 point: The money supply curve is vertical and labeled.

1 point: The money demand curve is negatively sloped and labeled.

1 point: The money demand curve shifts right.

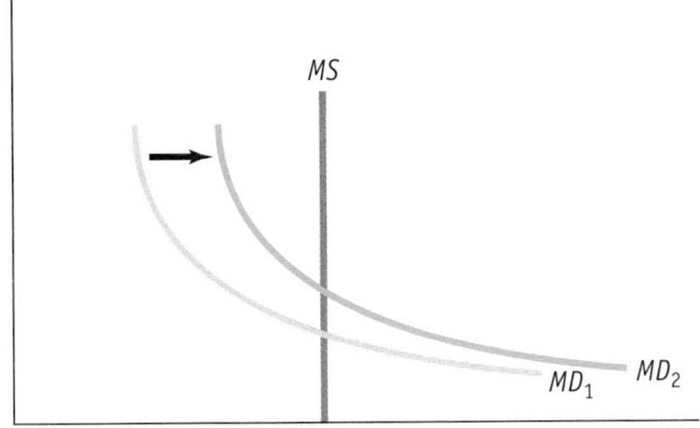

1 point: The money demand curve shifts left.

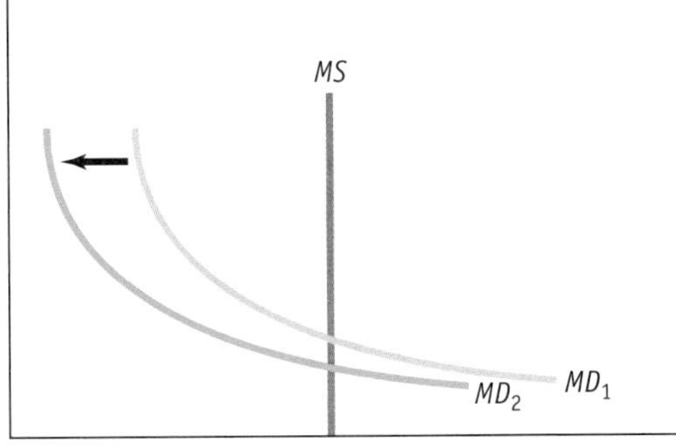

1 point: The money demand curve shifts left.

Interest rate, r

MS

MD_2 MD_1

Quantity of money

2. Draw a correctly labeled graph showing equilibrium in the money market. Label the equilibrium interest rate r_E and label an interest rate below the equilibrium interest rate r_L. Explain what occurs in the market when the interest rate is r_L and how the market will eventually return to equilibrium.
(7 points)

Brad Schloss/Icon SMI/Corbis

MODULE 29 The Market for Loanable Funds

In this Module, you will learn to:

- Describe how the loanable funds market matches savers and investors
- Identify the determinants of supply and demand in the loanable funds market
- Explain how the two models of interest rates can be reconciled

The Market for Loanable Funds

Recall that, for the economy as a whole, savings always equals investment spending. In a closed economy, savings is equal to national savings. In an open economy, savings is equal to national savings plus capital inflow. At any given time, however, savers, the people with funds to lend, are usually not the same as borrowers, the people who want to borrow to finance their investment spending. How are savers and borrowers brought together?

Savers and borrowers are matched up with one another in much the same way producers and consumers are matched up: through markets governed by supply and demand. In the circular-flow diagram, we noted that the *financial markets* channel the savings of households to businesses that want to borrow in order to purchase capital equipment. It's now time to take a look at how those financial markets work.

The **loanable funds market** is a hypothetical market that brings together those who want to lend money and those who want to borrow money.

The Equilibrium Interest Rate There are a large number of different financial markets in the financial system, such as the bond market and the stock market. However, economists often work with a simplified model in which they assume that there is just one market that brings together those who want to lend money (savers) and those who want to borrow money (firms with investment spending projects). This hypothetical market is known as the **loanable funds market**. The price that is determined in the loanable funds market is the interest rate, denoted by *r*. It is the return a lender receives for allowing borrowers the use of a dollar for one year, calculated as a percentage of the amount borrowed.

Recall that in the money market, the *nominal* interest rate is of central importance and always serves as the "price" measured on the vertical axis. The interest rate in the loanable funds market can be measured in either real or nominal terms—with or without the inclusion of expected inflation that makes nominal rates differ from real rates. Investors and savers care about the *real* interest rate, which tells them the price paid for the use of money aside from the amount paid to keep up with inflation. However, in the real world neither borrowers nor lenders know what the future inflation rate will be when they make a deal, so actual loan contracts specify a nominal interest rate rather than a real interest rate. For this reason, and because it facilitates comparisons between the money market and the loanable funds market, the figures in this section are drawn with the vertical axis measuring the *nominal interest rate for a given expected future inflation rate.* As long as the expected inflation rate is unchanged, changes in the nominal interest rate also lead to changes in the real interest rate. We take up the influence of inflation later in this module.

We should also note at this point that, in reality, there are many different kinds of nominal interest rates because there are many different kinds of loans—short-term loans, long-term loans, loans made to corporate borrowers, loans made to governments, and so on. In the interest of simplicity, we'll ignore those differences and assume that there is only one type of loan. **Figure 29.1** illustrates the hypothetical demand for loanable funds. On the horizontal axis we show the quantity of loanable funds demanded. On the vertical axis we show the interest rate, which is the "price" of borrowing. To see why the demand curve for loanable funds, *D*, slopes downward, imagine that there are many businesses, each of which has one potential investment project. How does a given business decide whether or not to borrow money to finance its project? The decision depends on the interest rate the business faces and the **rate of return** on its project—the profit earned on the project expressed as a percentage of its cost. This can be expressed in a formula as:

The **rate of return** on a project is the profit earned on the project expressed as a percentage of its cost.

$$\textbf{(29-1)}\quad \text{Rate of return} = \frac{\text{Revenue from project} - \text{Cost of project}}{\text{Cost of project}} \times 100$$

For example, a project that costs \$300,000 and produces revenue of \$315,000 provides a rate of return of [(\$315,000 – \$300,000)/\$300,000] × 100 = 5%.

A business will want a loan when the rate of return on its project is greater than or equal to the interest rate. So, for example, at an interest rate of 12%, only businesses with projects that yield a rate of return greater than or equal to 12% will want a loan. A business will not pay 12% interest to fund a project with a 5% rate of return. The demand curve in Figure 29.1 shows that if the interest rate is 12%, businesses will want to borrow \$150 billion (point *A*); if the interest rate is only 4%, businesses will want to borrow a

AP® Exam Tip

When expectations about the future inflation rate remain unchanged, the real interest rate and the nominal interest rate rise and fall together, and either rate can appear on the vertical axis of the loanable funds graph. We use the nominal interest rate here for comparability with the money market graph. If a question asks you to draw conclusions about the real interest rate on the basis of the loanable funds graph, simply label the vertical axis "real interest rate."

Figure 29.1 The Demand for Loanable Funds

The demand curve for loanable funds slopes downward: the lower the interest rate, the greater the quantity of loanable funds demanded. Here, reducing the interest rate from 12% to 4% increases the quantity of loanable funds demanded from \$150 billion to \$450 billion.

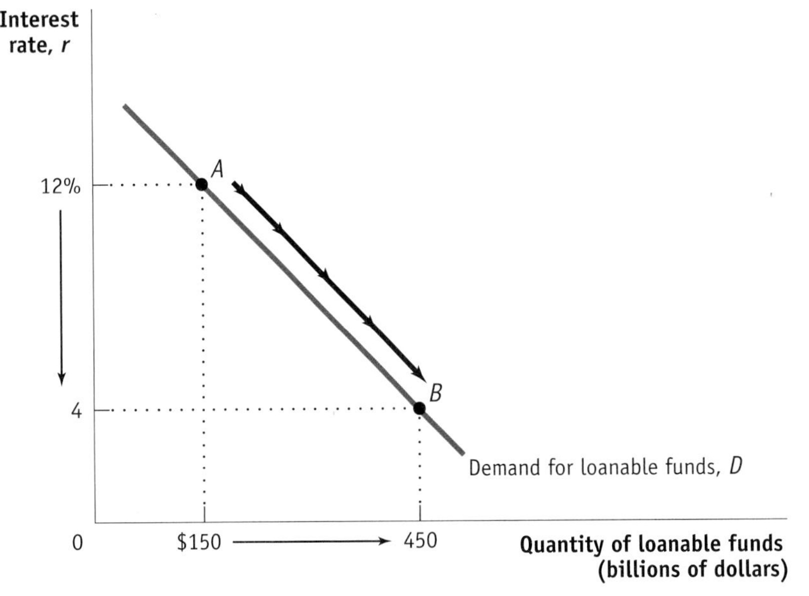

Figure 29.2 The Supply of Loanable Funds

The supply curve for loanable funds slopes upward: the higher the interest rate, the greater the quantity of loanable funds supplied. Here, increasing the interest rate from 4% to 12% increases the quantity of loanable funds supplied from \$150 billion to \$450 billion.

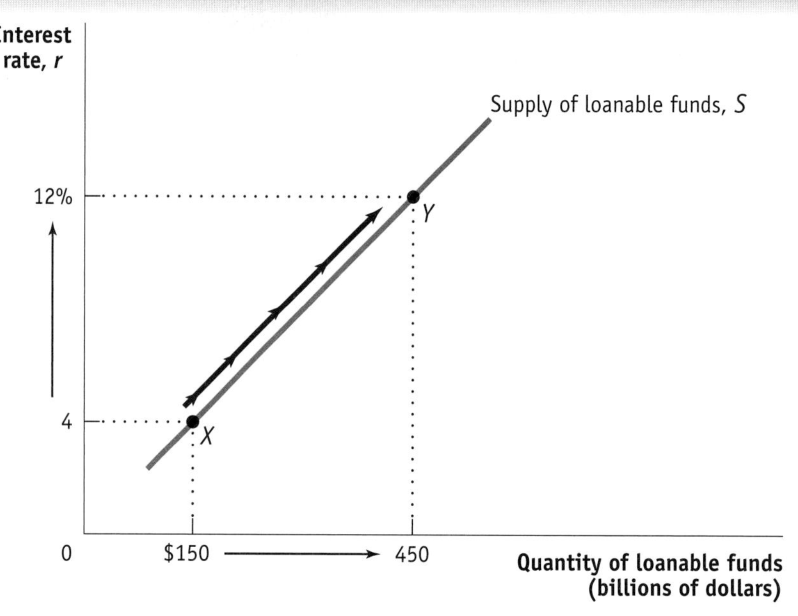

larger amount, \$450 billion (point *B*). That's a consequence of our assumption that the demand curve slopes downward: the lower the interest rate, the larger the total quantity of loanable funds demanded. Why do we make that assumption? Because, in reality, the number of potential investment projects that yield at least 4% is always greater than the number that yield at least 12%.

Figure 29.2 shows the hypothetical supply of loanable funds. Again, the interest rate plays the same role that the price plays in ordinary supply and demand analysis. Savers incur an opportunity cost when they lend to a business; the funds could instead be spent on consumption—say, a nice vacation. Whether a given individual becomes a lender by making funds available to borrowers depends on the interest rate received in return. By saving your money today and earning interest on it, you are rewarded with higher consumption in the future when your loan is repaid with interest. So it is a good assumption that more people are willing to forgo current consumption and make a loan when the interest rate is higher. As a result, our hypothetical supply curve of loanable funds slopes upward. In Figure 29.2, lenders will supply \$150 billion to the loanable funds market at an interest rate of 4% (point *X*); if the interest rate rises to 12%, the quantity of loanable funds supplied will rise to \$450 billion (point *Y*).

AP® Exam Tip

The loanable funds graph is another essential graph for the AP® exam. The incentive to lend money is higher when the interest rate is higher, so the supply curve for loanable funds has an upward slope.

The equilibrium interest rate is the interest rate at which the quantity of loanable funds supplied equals the quantity of loanable funds demanded. As you can see in **Figure 29.3**, the equilibrium interest rate, r_E, and the total quantity of lending, Q_E, are determined by the intersection of the supply and demand curves, at point *E*. Here, the equilibrium interest rate is 8%, at which \$300 billion is lent and borrowed. Investment spending projects with a rate of return of 8% or more are funded; projects with a rate of return of less than 8% are not. Correspondingly, only lenders who are willing to accept an interest rate of 8% or less will have their offers to lend funds accepted.

Figure 29.3 shows how the market for loanable funds matches up desired savings with desired investment spending: in equilibrium, the quantity of funds that savers want to lend is equal to the quantity of funds that firms want to borrow. The figure also shows that this match-up is efficient in two senses. First, the right investments get made: the investment spending projects that are actually financed have higher rates of return than those that do not get financed. Second, the right people do the saving: the potential savers who actually lend funds are willing to lend for lower interest rates than

Figure 29.3 Equilibrium in the Loanable Funds Market

At the equilibrium interest rate, the quantity of loanable funds supplied equals the quantity of loanable funds demanded. Here, the equilibrium interest rate is 8%, with $300 billion of funds lent and borrowed. Investment spending projects with a rate of return of 8% or higher receive funding; those with a lower rate of return do not. Lenders who demand an interest rate of 8% or lower have their offers of loans accepted; those who demand a higher interest rate do not.

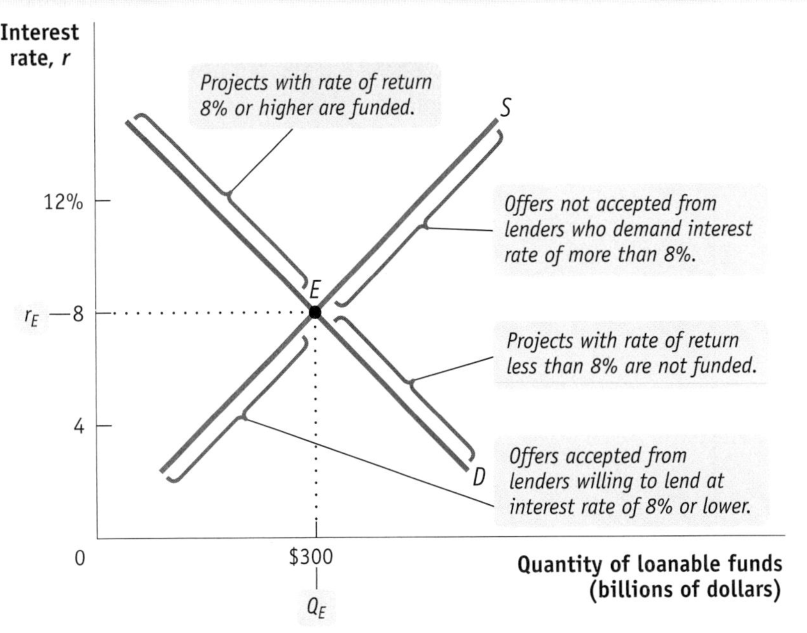

those who do not. The insight that the loanable funds market leads to an efficient use of savings, although drawn from a highly simplified model, has important implications for real life. As we'll see shortly, it is the reason that a well-functioning financial system increases an economy's long-run economic growth rate.

Before we get to that, however, let's look at how the market for loanable funds responds to shifts of demand and supply.

Shifts of the Demand for Loanable Funds The equilibrium interest rate changes when there are shifts of the demand curve for loanable funds, the supply curve for loanable funds, or both. Let's start by looking at the causes and effects of changes in demand.

The factors that can cause the demand curve for loanable funds to shift include the following:

- *Changes in perceived business opportunities*. A change in beliefs about the rate of return on investment spending can increase or reduce the amount of desired spending at any given interest rate. For example, during the 1990s there was great excitement over the business possibilities created by the Internet, which had just begun to be widely used. As a result, businesses rushed to buy computer equipment, put fiber-optic cables in the ground, and so on. This shifted the demand for loanable funds to the right. By 2001, the failure of many dot-com businesses led to disillusionment with technology-related investment; this shifted the demand for loanable funds back to the left.
- *Changes in the government's borrowing*. Governments that run budget deficits are major sources of the demand for loanable funds. As a result, changes in the budget deficit can shift the demand curve for loanable funds. For example, between 2000 and 2003, as the U.S. federal government went from a budget surplus to a budget deficit, net federal borrowing went from *minus* $189 billion—that is, in 2000 the federal government was actually providing loanable funds to the market because it was paying off some of its debt—to *plus* $416 billion because in 2003 the government had to borrow large sums to pay its bills. This change in the federal budget position had the effect, other things equal, of shifting the demand curve for loanable funds to the right.

Brand-X Pictures

Figure 29.4 An Increase in the Demand for Loanable Funds

If the quantity of funds demanded by borrowers rises at any given interest rate, the demand for loanable funds shifts rightward from D_1 to D_2. As a result, the equilibrium interest rate rises from r_1 to r_2.

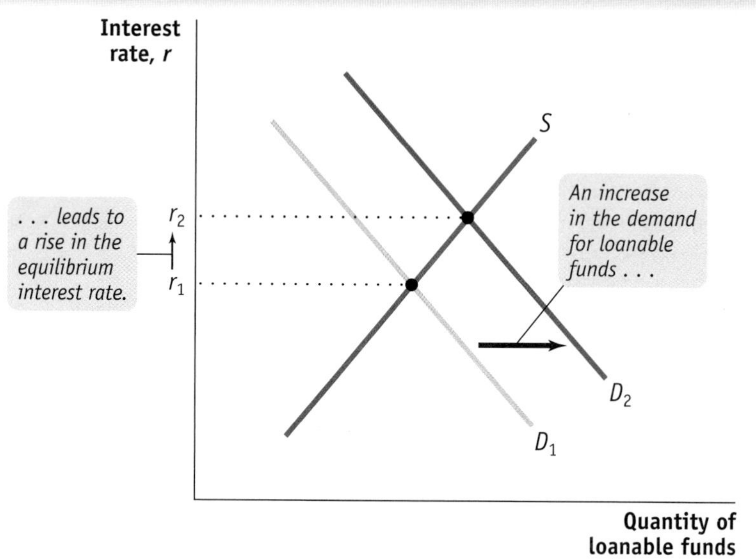

Figure 29.4 shows the effects of an increase in the demand for loanable funds. *S* is the supply of loanable funds, and D_1 is the initial demand curve. The initial equilibrium interest rate is r_1. An increase in the demand for loanable funds means that the quantity of funds demanded rises at any given interest rate, so the demand curve shifts rightward to D_2. As a result, the equilibrium interest rate rises to r_2.

The fact that, other things equal, an increase in the demand for loanable funds leads to a rise in the interest rate has one especially important implication: beyond concern about repayment, there are other reasons to be wary of government budget deficits. As we've already seen, an increase in the government's deficit shifts the demand curve for loanable funds to the right, which leads to a higher interest rate. If the interest rate rises, businesses will cut back on their investment spending. So a rise in the government budget deficit tends to reduce overall investment spending. Economists call the negative effect of government budget deficits on investment spending **crowding out**. The threat of crowding out is a key source of concern about persistent budget deficits.

Crowding out occurs when a government deficit drives up the interest rate and leads to reduced investment spending.

Shifts of the Supply of Loanable Funds Like the demand for loanable funds, the supply of loanable funds can shift. Among the factors that can cause the supply of loanable funds to shift are the following:

- *Changes in private saving behavior.* A number of factors can cause the level of private savings to change at any given rate of interest. For example, between 2000 and 2006 rising home prices in the United States made many homeowners feel richer, making them willing to spend more and save less. This had the effect of shifting the supply of loanable funds to the left. The drop in home prices between 2006 and 2009 had the opposite effect, shifting the supply of loanable funds to the right.

Photodisc

- *Changes in capital inflows.* Capital flows into a country can change as investors' perceptions of that country change. For example, Brazil experienced large capital inflows during much of the last decade because international investors believed that years of economic reforms made it a safe place to put their funds. As we've already seen, the United States has received large capital inflows in recent years, with much of the money coming from China and the Middle East. Those inflows helped fuel a big increase in residential investment spending—newly constructed homes—from 2003 to 2006. As a result of the worldwide slump, those inflows trailed off in 2008 and remained relatively low through early 2014.

Figure 29.5 An Increase in the Supply of Loanable Funds

If the quantity of funds supplied by lenders rises at any given interest rate, the supply of loanable funds shifts rightward from S_1 to S_2. As a result, the equilibrium interest rate falls from r_1 to r_2.

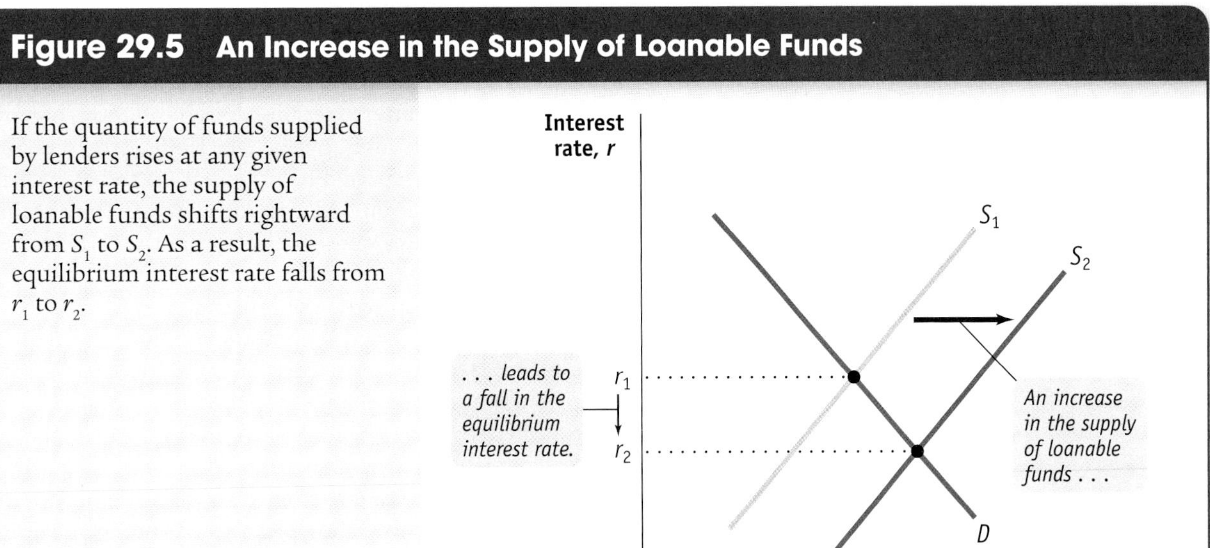
Interest rate, r
S1
S2
. . . leads to a fall in the equilibrium interest rate.
r1
r2
An increase in the supply of loanable funds . . .
D
Quantity of loanable funds

Figure 29.5 shows the effects of an increase in the supply of loanable funds. D is the demand for loanable funds, and S_1 is the initial supply curve. The initial equilibrium interest rate is r_1. An increase in the supply of loanable funds means that the quantity of funds supplied rises at any given interest rate, so the supply curve shifts rightward to S_2. As a result, the equilibrium interest rate falls to r_2.

Inflation and Interest Rates Anything that shifts either the supply of loanable funds curve or the demand for loanable funds curve changes the interest rate. Historically, major changes in interest rates have been driven by many factors, including changes in government policy and technological innovations that created new investment opportunities. However, arguably the most important factor affecting interest rates over time—the reason, for example, why interest rates today are much lower than they were in the late 1970s and early 1980s—is changing expectations about future inflation, which shift both the supply of and the demand for loanable funds.

To understand the effect of expected inflation on interest rates, recall our discussion in Module 14 of the way inflation creates winners and losers—for example, the way that high U.S. inflation in the 1970s and 1980s reduced the real value of homeowners' mortgages, which was good for the homeowners but bad for the banks. We know that economists capture the effect of inflation on borrowers and lenders by distinguishing between the *nominal interest rate* and the *real interest rate*, where the distinction is as follows:

$$\text{Real interest rate} = \text{Nominal interest rate} - \text{Inflation rate}$$

The true cost of borrowing is the real interest rate, not the nominal interest rate. To see why, suppose a firm borrows $10,000 for one year at a 10% nominal interest rate. At the end of the year, it must repay $11,000—the amount borrowed plus the interest. But suppose that over the course of the year the average level of prices increases by 10%, so that the real interest rate is zero. Then the $11,000 repayment has the same purchasing power as the original $10,000 loan. In effect, the borrower has received a zero-interest loan.

Similarly, the true payoff to lending is the real interest rate, not the nominal rate. The bank that makes the one-year $10,000 loan at a 10% nominal interest rate receives an $11,000 repayment at the end of the year. But the 10% increase in the average level of prices means that the purchasing power of the money the bank gets back is no more than that of the money it lent out. In effect, the bank has made a zero-interest loan.

The expectations of borrowers and lenders about future inflation rates are normally based on recent experience. In the late 1970s, after a decade of high inflation, borrowers and lenders expected future inflation to be high. By the late 1990s, after a decade of fairly low inflation, borrowers and lenders expected future inflation to be low. And these changing expectations about future inflation had a strong effect on the nominal interest rate, largely explaining why interest rates were much lower in the early years of the twenty-first century than they were in the early 1980s.

Let's look at how changes in the expected future rate of inflation are reflected in the loanable funds model. In **Figure 29.6**, the curves S_0 and D_0 show the supply of and demand for loanable funds given that the expected future rate of inflation is 0%. In that case, equilibrium is at E_0 and the equilibrium nominal interest rate is 4%. Because expected future inflation is 0%, the equilibrium expected real interest rate over the life of the loan, the real interest rate expected by borrowers and lenders when the loan is contracted, is also 4%.

Now suppose that the expected future inflation rate rises to 10%. The demand curve for funds shifts upward to D_{10}: borrowers are now willing to borrow as much at a nominal interest rate of 14% as they were previously willing to borrow at 4%. That's because with a 10% inflation rate, a borrower who pays a 14% nominal interest rate pays a 4% real interest rate. Similarly, the supply curve of funds shifts upward to S_{10}: lenders require a nominal interest rate of 14% to persuade them to lend as much as they would previously have lent at 4%. That's because with a 10% inflation rate, a lender who receives a 14% nominal interest rate receives a 4% real interest rate. The new equilibrium is at E_{10}: the result of an increase in the expected future inflation rate from 0% to 10% is that the equilibrium nominal interest rate rises from 4% to 14%.

According to the **Fisher effect**, an increase in expected future inflation drives up the nominal interest rate by the same number of percentage points, leaving the expected real interest rate unchanged.

This situation can be summarized as a general principle, named the **Fisher effect** after the American economist Irving Fisher, who proposed it in 1930: an increase in expected inflation drives up the nominal interest rate by the same number of percentage points, leaving the expected real interest rate unchanged. The central point is that both lenders and borrowers base their decisions on the expected real interest rate. As a result, a change in the expected rate of inflation does not affect the equilibrium quantity of loanable funds or the expected real interest rate; all it affects is the equilibrium nominal interest rate.

Figure 29.6 The Fisher Effect

D_0 and S_0 are the demand and supply curves for loanable funds when the expected future inflation rate is 0%. At an expected inflation rate of 0%, the equilibrium nominal interest rate is 4%. An increase in expected future inflation pushes both the demand and supply curves upward by 1 percentage point for every percentage point increase in expected future inflation. D_{10} and S_{10} are the demand and supply curves for loanable funds when the expected future inflation rate is 10%. The 10 percentage point increase in expected future inflation raises the equilibrium nominal interest rate to 14%. The expected real interest rate remains at 4%, and the equilibrium quantity of loanable funds also remains unchanged.

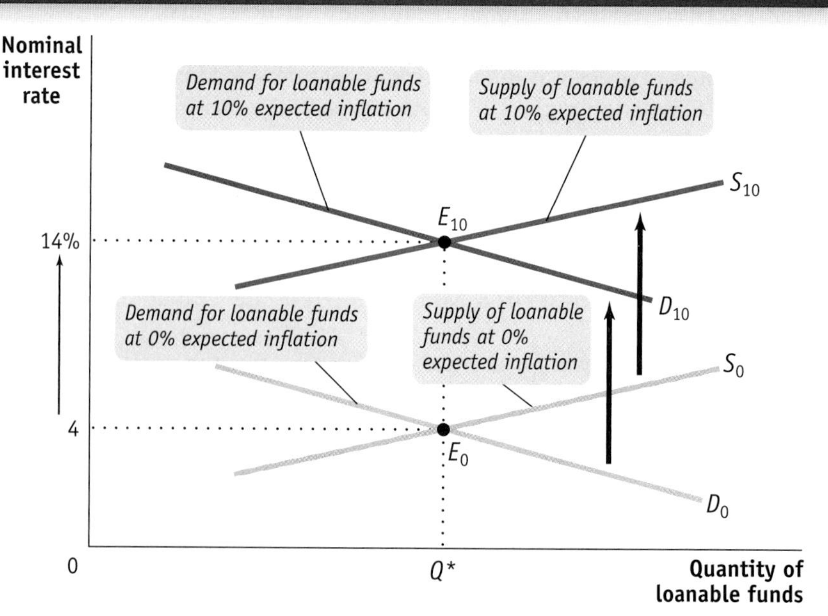

Reconciling the Two Interest Rate Models

In Module 28 we developed what is known as the liquidity preference model of the interest rate. In that model, the equilibrium interest rate is the rate at which the quantity of money demanded equals the quantity of money supplied in the money market. In the loanable funds model, we see that the interest rate matches the quantity of loanable funds supplied by savers with the quantity of loanable funds demanded for investment spending. How do the two models compare?

The Interest Rate in the Short Run

As we explained using the liquidity preference model, a fall in the interest rate leads to a rise in investment spending, *I*, which then leads to a rise in both real GDP and consumer spending, *C*. The rise in real GDP doesn't lead only to a rise in consumer spending, however. It also leads to a rise in savings: at each stage of the multiplier process, part of the increase in disposable income is saved. How much do savings rise? According to the *savings–investment spending identity*, total savings in the economy is always equal to investment spending. This tells us that when a fall in the interest rate leads to higher investment spending, the resulting increase in real GDP generates exactly enough additional savings to match the rise in investment spending. To put it another way, after a fall in the interest rate, the quantity of savings supplied rises exactly enough to match the quantity of savings demanded.

Figure 29.7 shows how our two models of the interest rate are reconciled in the short run by the links among changes in the interest rate, changes in real GDP, and changes in savings. Panel (a) represents the liquidity preference model of the interest rate. MS_1 and MD_1 are the initial supply and demand curves for money. According to the liquidity preference model, the equilibrium interest rate in the economy is the rate at which the quantity of money supplied is equal to the quantity of money demanded

Figure 29.7 The Short-Run Determination of the Interest Rate

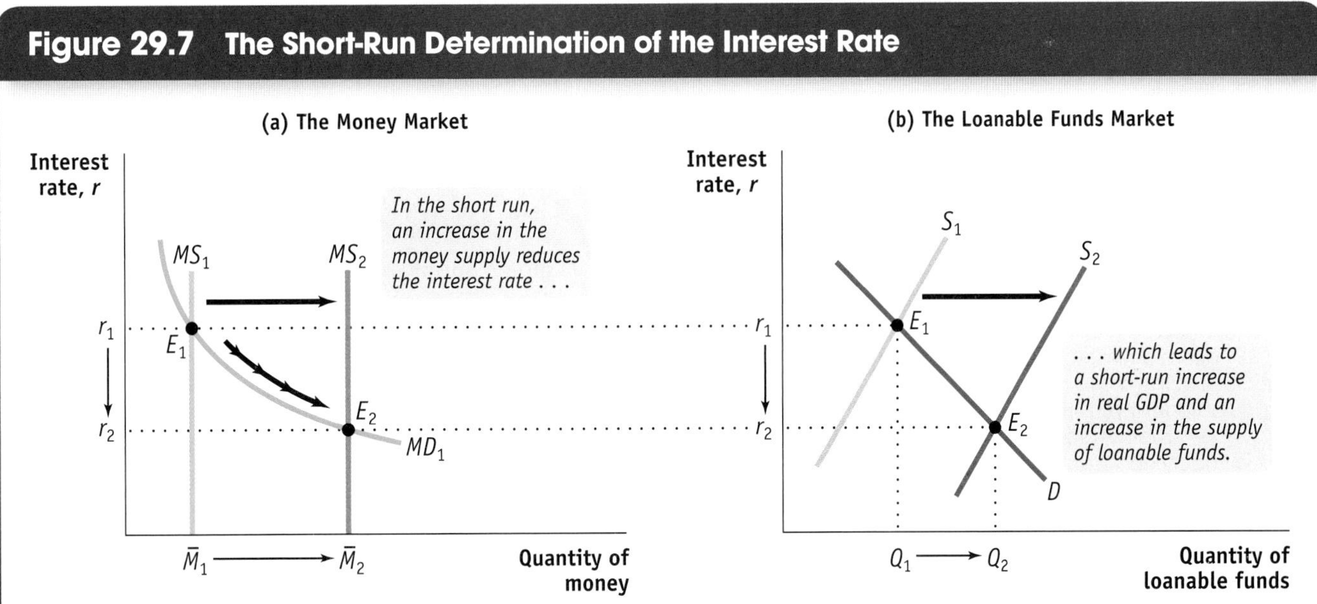

Panel (a) shows the liquidity preference model of the interest rate: the equilibrium interest rate matches the money supply to the quantity of money demanded. In the short run, the interest rate is determined in the money market, where an increase in the money supply, from $\overline{M}_1$ to $\overline{M}_2$, pushes the equilibrium interest rate down, from r_1 to r_2. Panel (b) shows the loanable funds model of the interest rate. The fall in the interest rate in the money market leads, through the multiplier effect, to an increase in real GDP and savings; to a rightward shift of the supply curve of loanable funds, from S_1 to S_2; and to a fall in the interest rate, from r_1 to r_2. As a result, the new equilibrium interest rate in the loanable funds market matches the new equilibrium interest rate in the money market at r_2.

in the money market. Panel (b) represents the loanable funds model of the interest rate. S_1 is the initial supply curve and D is the demand curve for loanable funds. According to the loanable funds model, the equilibrium interest rate in the economy is the rate at which the quantity of loanable funds supplied is equal to the quantity of loanable funds demanded in the market for loanable funds.

In Figure 29.7 both the money market and the market for loanable funds are initially in equilibrium at E_1 with the same interest rate, r_1. You might think that this would happen only by accident, but in fact it will always be true. To see why, let's look at what happens when the Fed increases the money supply from $\overline{M}_1$ to $\overline{M}_2$. This pushes the money supply curve rightward to MS_2, causing the equilibrium interest rate in the market for money to fall to r_2, and the economy moves to a short-run equilibrium at E_2. What happens in panel (b), in the market for loanable funds? In the short run, the fall in the interest rate due to the increase in the money supply leads to a rise in real GDP, which generates a rise in savings through the multiplier process. This rise in savings shifts the supply curve for loanable funds rightward, from S_1 to S_2, moving the equilibrium in the loanable funds market from E_1 to E_2 and also reducing the equilibrium interest rate in the loanable funds market. And we know that savings rise by exactly enough to match the rise in investment spending. This tells us that the equilibrium rate in the loanable funds market falls to r_2, the same as the new equilibrium interest rate in the money market.

In the short run, then, the supply and demand for money determine the interest rate, and the loanable funds market follows the lead of the money market. When a change in the supply of money leads to a change in the interest rate, the resulting change in real GDP causes the supply of loanable funds to change as well. As a result, the equilibrium interest rate in the loanable funds market is the same as the equilibrium interest rate in the money market.

Notice our use of the phrase "in the short run." Changes in aggregate demand affect aggregate output only in the short run. In the long run, aggregate output is equal to potential output. So our story about how a fall in the interest rate leads to a rise in aggregate output, which leads to a rise in savings, applies only to the short run. In the long run, as we'll see next, the determination of the interest rate is quite different because the roles of the two markets are reversed. In the long run, the loanable funds market determines the equilibrium interest rate, and it is the market for money that follows the lead of the loanable funds market.

The Interest Rate in the Long Run

AP® Exam Tip

To determine which graph to draw for an AP® exam question, watch for mentions of the money market, which indicate that you should draw a *money market* graph with a vertical supply curve, or mentions of loanable funds, which suggest that you should draw a *loanable funds* market graph with an upward-sloping supply curve.

In the short run an increase in the money supply leads to a fall in the interest rate, and a decrease in the money supply leads to a rise in the interest rate. In the long run, however, changes in the money supply don't affect the interest rate.

Figure 29.8 shows why. As in Figure 29.7, panel (a) shows the liquidity preference model of the interest rate and panel (b) shows the supply and demand for loanable funds. We assume that in both panels the economy is initially at E_1, in long-run macroeconomic equilibrium at potential output with the money supply equal to $\overline{M}_1$. The demand curve for loanable funds is D, and the initial supply curve for loanable funds is S_1. The initial equilibrium interest rate in both markets is r_1.

Now suppose the money supply rises from $\overline{M}_1$ to $\overline{M}_2$. As we saw in Figure 29.7, this initially reduces the interest rate to r_2. However, in the long run the aggregate price level will rise by the same proportion as the increase in the money supply (due to the *neutrality of money*, a topic presented in detail in the next section). A rise in the aggregate price level increases money demand by the same proportion. So in the long run the money demand curve shifts out to MD_2, and the equilibrium interest rate rises back to its original level, r_1.

Panel (b) of Figure 29.8 shows what happens in the market for loanable funds. We saw earlier that an increase in the money supply leads to a short-run rise in real GDP and that this rise shifts the supply of loanable funds rightward from S_1 to S_2. In the long run, however, real GDP falls back to its original level as wages and other nominal prices rise. As a result, the supply of loanable funds, S, which initially shifted from S_1 to S_2, shifts back to S_1.

Figure 29.8 The Long-Run Determination of the Interest Rate

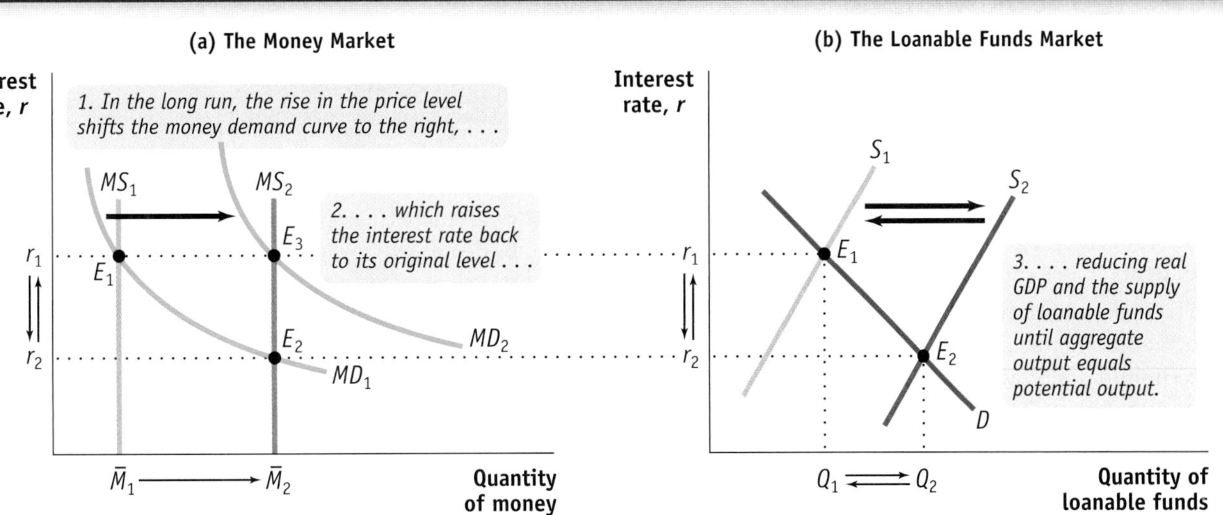

Panel (a) shows the liquidity preference model long-run adjustment to an increase in the money supply from $\bar{M}_1$ to $\bar{M}_2$; panel (b) shows the corresponding long-run adjustment in the loanable funds market. As we discussed in Figure 29.7, the increase in the money supply reduces the interest rate from r_1 to r_2, increases real GDP, and increases savings in the short run. This is shown in panel (a) and panel (b) as the movement from E_1 to E_2. In the long run, however, the increase in the money supply raises wages and other nominal prices; this shifts the money demand curve in panel (a) from MD_1 to MD_2, leading to an increase in the interest rate from r_1 to r_2 as the economy moves from E_2 to E_3. The rise in the interest rate causes a fall in real GDP and a fall in savings, shifting the loanable funds supply curve back to S_1 from S_2 and moving the loanable funds market from E_2 back to E_1. In the long run, the equilibrium interest rate is the rate that matches the supply and demand for loanable funds when real GDP equals potential output.

In the long run, then, changes in the money supply do not affect the interest rate. So what determines the interest rate in the long run—that is, what determines r_1 in Figure 29.8? The answer is the supply and demand for loanable funds. More specifically, in the long run the equilibrium interest rate is the rate that matches the supply of loanable funds with the demand for loanable funds when real GDP equals potential output.

MODULE 29 Review

Check Your Understanding

1. Use a diagram of the loanable funds market to illustrate the effect of the following events on the equilibrium interest rate and quantity of loanable funds.
   a. An economy is opened to international movements of capital, and a capital inflow occurs.
   b. Retired people generally save less than working people at any interest rate. The proportion of retired people in the population goes up.
2. Explain what is wrong with the following statement: "Savings and investment spending may not be equal in the economy as a whole in equilibrium because when the interest rate rises, households will want to save more money than businesses will want to invest."
3. Suppose that expected inflation rises from 3% to 6%.
   a. How will the real interest rate be affected by this change?
   b. How will the nominal interest rate be affected by this change?
   c. What will happen to the equilibrium quantity of loanable funds?

Tackle the Test: Multiple-Choice Questions

1. A business will decide whether or not to borrow money to finance a project based on a comparison of the interest rate with the _____ from its project.
   a. expected revenue
   b. profit
   c. rate of return
   d. cost generated
   e. demand generated
2. The real interest rate equals the
   a. nominal interest rate plus the inflation rate.
   b. nominal interest rate minus the inflation rate.
   c. nominal interest rate divided by the inflation rate.
   d. nominal interest rate times the inflation rate.
   e. federal funds rate.
3. Which of the following will increase the demand for loanable funds?
   a. a federal government budget surplus
   b. an increase in perceived business opportunities
   c. a decrease in the interest rate
   d. positive capital inflows
   e. decreased private saving rates
4. Which of the following will increase the supply of loanable funds?
   a. an increase in perceived business opportunities
   b. decreased government borrowing
   c. an increased private saving rate
   d. an increase in the expected inflation rate
   e. a decrease in capital inflows
5. Both lenders and borrowers base their decisions on
   a. expected real interest rates.
   b. expected nominal interest rates.
   c. real interest rates.
   d. nominal interest rates.
   e. nominal interest rates minus real interest rates.

Tackle the Test: Free-Response Questions

1. Draw a correctly labeled graph showing equilibrium in the loanable funds market.

Rubric for FRQ 1 (6 points)

1 point: Vertical axis labeled "Interest rate" or "r"

1 point: Horizontal axis labeled "Quantity of loanable funds"

1 point: Downward-sloping demand curve for loanable funds (labeled)

1 point: Upward-sloping supply curve for loanable funds (labeled)

1 point: Equilibrium quantity of loanable funds shown on horizontal axis below where curves intersect

1 point: Equilibrium interest rate shown on vertical axis across from where curves intersect

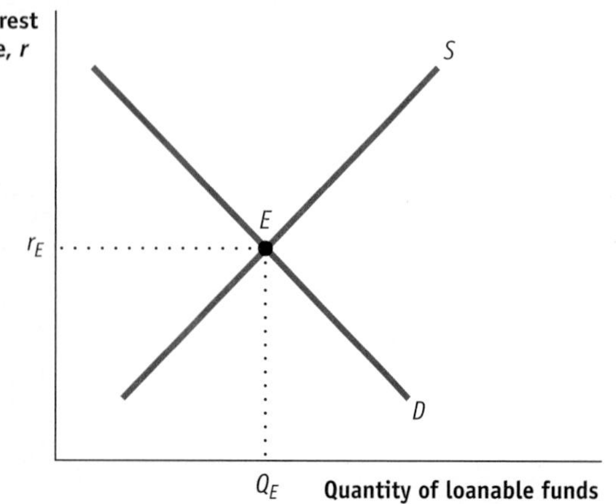

2. Does each of the following affect either the supply or the demand for loanable funds, and if so, does the affected curve increase (shift to the right) or decrease (shift to the left)?
   a. There is an increase in capital inflows into the economy.
   b. Businesses are pessimistic about future business conditions.
   c. The government increases borrowing.
   d. The private saving rate decreases.

   (4 points)

SECTION 5 Review

Section 5 Review Video

Module 22

1. Investment in physical capital is necessary for long-run economic growth. So in order for an economy to grow, it must channel savings into investment spending. The price charged per year by lenders to investors and other borrowers for the use of their savings is the **interest rate**, which is calculated as a percentage of the amount borrowed.
2. According to the **savings-investment spending identity**, savings and investment spending are always equal for the economy as a whole. The government is a source of savings when it runs a positive **budget balance**, also known as a **budget surplus**; it is a source of dissavings when it runs a negative budget balance, also known as a **budget deficit**. In a closed economy, savings is equal to **national savings**, the sum of private savings plus the budget balance. In an open economy, savings is equal to national savings plus **capital inflow** of foreign savings. When a capital outflow, or negative capital inflow, occurs, some portion of national savings is funding investment spending in other countries.
3. Households invest their current savings or **wealth**—their accumulated savings—by purchasing assets. Assets come in the form of either a **financial asset**, a paper claim that entitles the buyer to future income from the seller, or a **physical asset**, a claim on a tangible object that gives the owner the right to dispose of it as desired. A financial asset is also a **liability** from the point of view of its seller. There are four main types of financial assets: loans, bonds, stocks, and **bank deposits**. Each of them serves a different purpose in addressing the three fundamental tasks of a financial system: reducing **transaction costs**—the cost of making a deal; reducing **financial risk**—uncertainty about future outcomes that involves financial gains and losses; and providing **liquid** assets—assets that can be quickly converted into cash without much loss of value (in contrast to **illiquid** assets, which are not easily converted).
4. Although many small and moderate-size borrowers use bank **loans** to fund investment spending, larger companies typically issue bonds. Bonds with a higher risk of **default** must typically pay a higher interest rate. Business owners reduce their risk by selling stock. Although stocks usually generate a higher return than bonds, investors typically wish to reduce their risk by engaging in **diversification**, owning a wide range of assets whose returns are based on unrelated, or independent, events. Most people are risk-averse, viewing the loss of a given amount of money as a significant hardship but viewing the gain of an equal amount of money as a much less significant benefit. **Loan-backed securities**, a recent innovation, are assets created by pooling individual loans and selling shares of that pool to investors. Because they are more diversified and more liquid than individual loans, trading on financial markets like bonds, they are preferred by investors. It can be difficult, however, to assess their quality.
5. **Financial intermediaries**—institutions such as **mutual funds**, **pension funds**, **life insurance companies**, and **banks**—are critical components of the financial system. Mutual funds and pension funds allow small investors to diversify and life insurance companies allow families to reduce risk.
6. A bank allows individuals to hold liquid bank deposits that are then used to finance investments in illiquid assets. Banks can perform this mismatch because on average only a small fraction of depositors withdraw their savings at any one time. Banks are a key ingredient in long-run economic growth.

Module 23

7. **Money** is any asset that can easily be used to purchase goods and services. **Currency in circulation** and **checkable bank deposits** are both considered part of the **money supply**. Money plays three roles: it is a **medium of exchange** used for transactions, a **store of value** that holds purchasing power over time, and a **unit of account** in which prices are stated.
8. Over time, **commodity money**, which consists of goods possessing value aside from their role as money, such as gold and silver coins, was replaced by **commodity-backed money**, such as paper currency backed by gold. Today the dollar is pure **fiat money**, whose value derives solely from its official role.
9. The Federal Reserve calculates two measures of the money supply. M1 is the narrowest **monetary aggregate**; it contains only currency in circulation, traveler's checks, and checkable bank deposits. M2 includes a wider range of assets called **near-moneys**, mainly other forms of bank deposits, that can easily be converted into checkable bank deposits.

Module 24

10. The accumulation of interest causes any amount of money loaned today to grow into a larger amount, called the **future value**, over the loan period.

11. In order to evaluate a project in which costs or benefits are realized in the future, you must first transform them into their **present values** using the interest rate, r. The present value of \$1 realized one year from now is \$1/(1 + r), the amount of money you must lend out today to have \$1 one year from now. Once this transformation is done, you should choose the project with the highest **net present value**.

Module 25

12. Banks allow depositors immediate access to their funds, but they also lend out most of the funds deposited in their care. To meet demands for cash, they maintain **bank reserves** composed of both currency held in vaults and deposits at the Federal Reserve. The **reserve ratio** is the ratio of bank reserves to bank deposits. A **T-account** summarizes a bank's financial position, with loans and reserves counted as assets, and deposits counted as liabilities.

13. Banks have sometimes been subject to **bank runs**, most notably in the early 1930s. To avert this danger, depositors are now protected by **deposit insurance**, bank owners face capital requirements that reduce the incentive to make overly risky loans with depositors' funds, banks must satisfy **reserve requirements**—a legally mandated **required reserve ratio**, and the Federal Reserve stands ready to lend money to banks through the **discount window**.

14. When currency is deposited in a bank, it starts a multiplier process in which banks lend out **excess reserves**, leading to an increase in the money supply—so banks create money. If the entire money supply consisted of checkable bank deposits, the money supply would be equal to the value of reserves divided by the reserve ratio. In reality, much of the **monetary base** consists of currency in circulation, and the **money multiplier** is the ratio of the money supply to the monetary base.

Module 26

15. The Federal Reserve or "the Fed" is the **central bank** of the United States. In response to the Panic of 1907, the Fed was created to centralize holding of reserves, inspect banks' books, and make the money supply sufficiently responsive to varying economic conditions.

16. The Great Depression sparked widespread bank runs in the early 1930s, which greatly worsened and lengthened the depth of the Depression. Federal deposit insurance was created, and the government recapitalized banks by lending to them and by buying shares of banks. By 1933, banks had been separated into two categories: **commercial** (covered by deposit insurance) and **investment** (not covered). Public acceptance of deposit insurance finally stopped the bank runs of the Great Depression.

17. The **savings and loan (thrift)** crisis of the 1980s arose because insufficiently regulated S&Ls engaged in overly risky speculation and incurred huge losses. Depositors in failed S&Ls were compensated with taxpayer funds because they were covered by deposit insurance. However, the crisis caused steep losses in the financial and real estate sectors, resulting in a recession in the early 1990s.

18. As housing prices rose between 2003 and 2006, lenders made large quantities of questionable mortgage loans. When housing prices tumbled, massive losses by banks and nonbank financial institutions led to widespread collapse in the financial system. To prevent another Great Depression, the Fed and the U.S. Treasury expanded lending to bank and nonbank institutions, provided capital through the purchase of bank shares, and purchased private debt. Because much of the crisis originated in nontraditional bank institutions, the crisis of 2008 raised the question of whether a wider safety net and broader regulation were needed in the financial sector.

Module 27

19. The Fed regulates banks and sets reserve requirements. To meet those requirements, banks borrow and lend reserves in the **federal funds market** at the **federal funds rate**. Banks can also borrow from the Fed at the **discount rate**.

20. **Open-market operations** by the Fed are the principal tool of monetary policy: the Fed can increase or reduce the monetary base by buying U.S. Treasury bills from banks or selling U.S. Treasury bills to banks.

Module 28

21. The **money demand curve** arises from a trade-off between the opportunity cost of holding money and the liquidity that money provides. The opportunity cost of holding money depends on **short-term interest rates**, not **long-term interest rates**. Changes in the aggregate price level, real GDP, technology, and institutions shift the money demand curve.

22. According to the **liquidity preference model of the interest rate**, the interest rate is determined in the money market by the money demand curve and the **money supply curve**. The Federal Reserve can change the interest rate in the short run by shifting the money supply curve. In practice, the Fed uses open-market operations to achieve a target federal funds rate, which other short-term interest rates generally follow.

Module 29

23. The hypothetical **loanable funds market** shows how loans from savers are allocated among borrowers with investment spending projects. In equilibrium, only those projects with a **rate of return** greater than or equal to the equilibrium interest rate will be funded. By showing how gains from trade between lenders and borrowers are maximized, the loanable funds market shows why a well-functioning financial system leads to greater long-run economic growth. Government budget deficits can raise the interest rate and can lead to **crowding out** of investment spending. Changes in perceived business opportunities and in government borrowing shift the demand curve for loanable funds; changes in private savings and capital inflows shift the supply curve.

24. Because neither borrowers nor lenders can know the future inflation rate, loans specify a nominal interest rate rather than a real interest rate. For a given expected future inflation rate, shifts of the demand and supply curves of loanable funds result in changes in the underlying real interest rate, leading to changes in the nominal interest rate. According to the **Fisher effect**, an increase in expected future inflation raises the nominal interest rate by the same number of percentage points, so that the expected real interest rate remains unchanged.

Key Terms

AP® Exam Practice Questions

Multiple-Choice Questions

1. The interest rate is
   a. the opportunity cost of lending money.
   b. the price borrowers pay for the use of lenders' savings.
   c. a percentage of the amount saved by borrowers.
   d. the rate charged by banks to hold savings for one year.
   e. the amount earned by using profits to build a new factory.
2. Which of the following identities is true in a simplified economy with no government and no interaction with other countries?
   a. consumer spending = investment spending
   b. total income = consumer spending − investment spending
   c. total spending = investment spending + savings
   d. investment spending = total spending − savings
   e. savings = investment spending
3. A budget surplus exists when the government does which of the following?
   a. saves
   b. collects less tax revenue than it spends
   c. has a negative budget balance
   d. increases the national debt
   e. uses expansionary fiscal policy
4. Which of the following is a task of an economy's financial system?
   a. maximizing risk
   b. increasing transactions costs
   c. decreasing diversification
   d. eliminating liquidity
   e. enhancing the efficiency of financial markets
5. A financial intermediary that resells shares of a stock portfolio is a
   a. mutual fund.
   b. pension fund.
   c. loan-backed security.
   d. bond broker.
   e. depository institution.
6. Which of the following assets is most liquid?
   a. stock
   b. bond
   c. loan
   d. mutual fund
   e. cash
7. When money acts as a means of holding purchasing power over time, it is serving which function?
   a. medium of exchange
   b. source of liquidity
   c. store of value
   d. unit of account
   e. source of wealth
8. Which of the following is an example of using money as a unit of account?
   a. buying a new T-shirt
   b. purchasing $10 worth of candy
   c. keeping the dollar you receive each year for your birthday for 10 years
   d. putting money into your savings account
   e. paying for lunch with your debit card
9. Which of the following is a desirable characteristic of money?
   a. fixed supply
   b. large denominations
   c. made of precious metal
   d. widely accepted
   e. backed by commodities
10. Fiat money derives its value from which of the following?
    a. its official status
    b. the good being used as a medium of exchange
    c. a promise it can be converted into something valuable
    d. gold or silver
    e. exchange rates
11. The M1 money supply includes which of the following?
    a. near-moneys
    b. checkable deposits
    c. savings accounts
    d. time deposits
    e. mutual funds
12. The present value of $1 you receive one year from now is equal to
    a. $\$1(1 + r)$.
    b. $\$1/(1 - r)$.
    c. $\$1/(1 + r)$.
    d. $\$1(1 + r^2)$.
    e. $\$1(1 + r)^2$.
13. If the interest rate is 2%, the amount received 1 year from now as a result of lending $1,000 today is
    a. $980.
    b. $1,000.
    c. $1,020.
    d. $1,200.
    e. $2,000.
14. The liquid assets banks keep in their vaults are known as bank
    a. deposits.
    b. savings.
    c. reserves.
    d. money.
    e. returns.

15. The required reserve ratio is
- **a.** the most cash that banks are allowed to hold in their vault.
- **b.** set by the Federal Reserve.
- **c.** responsible for most bank runs.
- **d.** equal to 5% of bank deposits.
- **e.** the fraction of bank loans held as reserves.

16. If *rr* is the reserve requirement, the money multiplier is equal to
- **a.** rr.
- **b.** $1-rr$.
- **c.** $1/rr$.
- **d.** rr^2.
- **e.** $1/rr^2$.

17. Which of the following is part of the money supply but not part of the monetary base?
- **a.** checkable bank deposits
- **b.** bank reserves
- **c.** currency in circulation
- **d.** deposits at the Fed
- **e.** savings accounts

18. The Federal Reserve is a(n)
- **a.** single central bank located in New York.
- **b.** government agency overseen by the Secretary of the Treasury.
- **c.** system of 10 regional banks.
- **d.** institution that oversees the banking system.
- **e.** depository institution that lends to large corporations.

19. The Federal Reserve is charged with doing all of the following EXCEPT
- **a.** providing financial services to commercial banks.
- **b.** supervising and regulating banks.
- **c.** maintaining the stability of the financial system.
- **d.** conducting monetary policy.
- **e.** insuring bank deposits.

20. Which of the following will increase the demand for money?
- **a.** a fall in the aggregate price level
- **b.** an increase in real GDP
- **c.** technological advances
- **d.** open-market operations by the Fed
- **e.** a decrease in the interest rate

21. The money supply curve is
- **a.** upward sloping.
- **b.** vertical.
- **c.** horizontal.
- **d.** downward sloping.
- **e.** U-shaped.

22. When banking regulations were changed so that banks could pay interest on checking accounts, what was the effect on interest rates and the equilibrium quantity of money?

Interest rate	*Quantity of money*
a. increase	decrease
b. decrease	increase
c. increase	increase
d. decrease	decrease
e. increase	no change

23. Which of the following will shift the supply curve for loanable funds to the right?
- **a.** an increase in the rate of return on investment spending
- **b.** an increase in the government budget deficit
- **c.** a decrease in the national saving rate
- **d.** an increase in expected inflation
- **e.** capital inflows from abroad

24. Crowding out is illustrated by which of the following changes in the loanable funds market?
- **a.** a decreasing equilibrium interest rate
- **b.** an increase in the demand for loanable funds
- **c.** a decrease in the demand for loanable funds
- **d.** an increase in the supply of loanable funds
- **e.** a decrease in the supply of loanable funds

25. The supply curve for loanable funds is
- **a.** upward sloping.
- **b.** vertical.
- **c.** horizontal.
- **d.** downward sloping.
- **e.** U-shaped.

Free-Response Question

1. a. Draw a correctly labeled graph of the market for loanable funds. On your graph, indicate each of the following:
- **i.** the equilibrium interest rate, labeled r_1
- **ii.** the equilibrium quantity of loanable funds, labeled Q_1

b. Use your graph from (a) to show how an increase in government spending affects the loanable funds market. On the graph, indicate each of the following:
- **i.** the new equilibrium interest rate, labeled r_2
- **ii.** the new equilibrium quantity of loanable funds, labeled Q_2

c. Explain how the new interest rate (r_2) affects the level of real GDP.
(5 points)

SECTION 6

Inflation, Unemployment, and Stabilization Policies

The Fed as First Responder

Jim Cramer's *Mad Money* is one of the most popular shows on CNBC, a cable TV network that specializes in business and financial news. In January of 2014, Cramer touted the "invisible positives" in the economy, such as companies with enough financial strength to pay billions of dollars to acquire other companies. It was a different story on August 3, 2007, when Cramer was so alarmed about negatives he felt were invisible to the Federal Reserve that he screamed about Fed leaders:

"Bernanke is being an academic! It is no time to be an academic. . . . **He has no idea how bad it is out there. He has no idea! He has no idea!** . . . and Bill Poole? Has no idea what it's like out there! . . . They're nuts! **They know nothing!** . . . The Fed is asleep! Bill Poole is a shame! He's shameful!!"

Who are Bernanke and Bill Poole? In the previous chapter, we described the role of the Federal Reserve System, the U.S. central bank. At the time of Cramer's tirade, Ben Bernanke, a former Princeton professor of economics, was the chair of the Fed's Board of Governors, and William Poole, a former Brown professor of economics, was the president of the Federal Reserve Bank of St. Louis. Both men, because of their positions, are members of the Federal Open Market Committee, which meets eight times a year to set monetary policy. In 2007, Cramer was crying out for the Fed to change monetary policy in order to address what he perceived to be a growing financial crisis.

Why was Cramer screaming at the Federal Reserve rather than, say, the U.S. Treasury—or, for that matter, the president? The answer is that the Fed's control of monetary policy makes it the first line of response to macroeconomic difficulties—very much including the financial crisis that had Cramer so upset. Indeed, within a few weeks, the Fed swung into action with a dramatic reversal of its previous policies.

G. Paul Burnett/The New York Times/Redux

In Section 4, we developed the aggregate demand and supply model and introduced the use of fiscal policy to stabilize the economy. In Section 5, we introduced money, banking, and the Federal Reserve System, and began to look at how monetary policy is used to stabilize the economy. In this section, we use the models introduced in Sections 4 and 5 to further develop our understanding of stabilization policies (both fiscal and monetary), including their long-run effects on the economy. In addition, we introduce the Phillips curve—a short-run trade-off between unexpected inflation and unemployment—and investigate the role of expectations in the economy. We end the section with a brief summary of the history of macroeconomic thought and how the modern consensus view of stabilization policy has developed.

Marmaduke St. John/Alamy

MODULE 30 Long-Run Implications of Fiscal Policy: Deficits and the Public Debt

In this Module, you will learn to:

- Explain why governments calculate the cyclically adjusted budget balance
- Identify problems posed by a large public debt
- Discuss why implicit liabilities of the government are also a cause for concern

In Module 20 we discussed how discretionary fiscal policy can be used to stabilize the economy in the short run. During a recession, an expansionary fiscal policy—raising government spending, lowering taxes, or both—can be used to shift the aggregate demand curve to the right. And when there are inflationary pressures in the economy, a contractionary fiscal policy—lowering government spending, raising taxes, or both—can be used to shift the aggregate demand curve to the left. But how do these policies affect the economy over a longer period of time? In this module we will look at some of the long-term effects of fiscal policy, including budget balance, debt, and liabilities.

The Budget Balance

Headlines about the government's budget tend to focus on just one point: whether the government is running a budget surplus or a budget deficit and, in either case, how big. People usually think of surpluses as good: when the federal government ran a record surplus in 2000, many people regarded it as a cause for celebration. Conversely, people usually think of deficits as bad: when the Congressional Budget Office projected a $675 billion federal deficit in 2014, many people regarded it as a cause for concern.

How do surpluses and deficits fit into the analysis of fiscal policy? Are deficits ever a good thing and surpluses ever a bad thing? To answer those questions, let's look at the causes and consequences of surpluses and deficits.

AP® Exam Tip

The budget balance is the difference between the government's tax revenue and its spending, both on goods and services and on government transfers, in a given year.

The Budget Balance as a Measure of Fiscal Policy

What do we mean by surpluses and deficits? The budget balance, which we have previously defined, is the difference between the government's tax revenue and its spending, both on goods and services and on government transfers, in a given year. That is, the budget balance—savings by government—is defined by Equation 30-1:

$$\textbf{(30-1)} \quad S_{Government} = T - G - TR$$

AP® Exam Tip

The budget deficit almost always rises when the unemployment rate rises and falls when the unemployment rate falls.

where *T* is the value of tax revenues, *G* is government purchases of goods and services, and *TR* is the value of government transfers. A budget surplus is a positive budget balance, and a budget deficit is a negative budget balance.

Other things equal, expansionary fiscal policies—increased government purchases of goods and services, higher government transfers, or lower taxes—reduce the budget balance for that year. That is, expansionary fiscal policies make a budget surplus smaller or a budget deficit bigger. Conversely, contractionary fiscal policies—reduced government purchases of goods and services, lower government transfers, or higher taxes—increase the budget balance for that year, making a budget surplus bigger or a budget deficit smaller.

You might think this means that changes in the budget balance can be used to measure fiscal policy. In fact, economists often do just that: they use changes in the budget balance as a "quick-and-dirty" way to assess whether current fiscal policy is expansionary or contractionary. But they always keep in mind two reasons this quick-and-dirty approach is sometimes misleading:

- Two different changes in fiscal policy that have equal-sized effects on the budget balance may have quite unequal effects on the economy. As we have already seen, changes in government purchases of goods and services have a larger effect on real GDP than equal-sized changes in taxes and government transfers.
- Often, changes in the budget balance are themselves the result, not the cause, of fluctuations in the economy.

To understand the second point, we need to examine the effects of the business cycle on the budget.

The Business Cycle and the Cyclically Adjusted Budget Balance

Historically, there has been a strong relationship between the federal government's budget balance and the business cycle. The budget tends to move into deficit when the economy experiences a recession, but deficits tend to get smaller or even turn into surpluses when the economy is expanding. **Figure 30.1** shows the federal budget deficit as a percentage of GDP from 1970 to 2013. Shaded areas indicate recessions; unshaded areas indicate expansions. As you can see, the federal budget deficit increased around the time of each recession and usually declined during expansions. In fact, in the late stages of the long expansion from 1991 to 2000, the deficit actually became negative—the budget deficit became a budget surplus.

The relationship between the business cycle and the budget balance is even more clear if we compare the budget deficit as a percentage of GDP with the unemployment rate, as we do in **Figure 30.2**. The budget deficit almost always rises when the unemployment rate rises and falls when the unemployment rate falls.

Is this relationship between the business cycle and the budget balance evidence that policy makers engage in discretionary fiscal policy? Not necessarily. It is largely automatic stabilizers that drive the relationship shown in Figure 30.2. As we learned in the discussion of automatic stabilizers in Module 21, government tax revenue tends to rise and some government transfers, like unemployment insurance payments, tend to fall when the economy expands. Conversely, government tax revenue tends to fall and some government transfers tend to rise when the economy contracts. So the budget tends to move toward surplus during expansions and toward deficit during recessions even without any deliberate action on the part of policy makers.

In assessing budget policy, it's often useful to separate movements in the budget balance due to the business cycle from movements due to discretionary fiscal policy changes.

Figure 30.1 The U.S. Federal Budget Deficit and the Business Cycle

The budget deficit as a percentage of GDP tends to rise during recessions (indicated by shaded areas) and fall during expansions.

Source: Bureau of Economic Analysis; National Bureau of Economic Research.

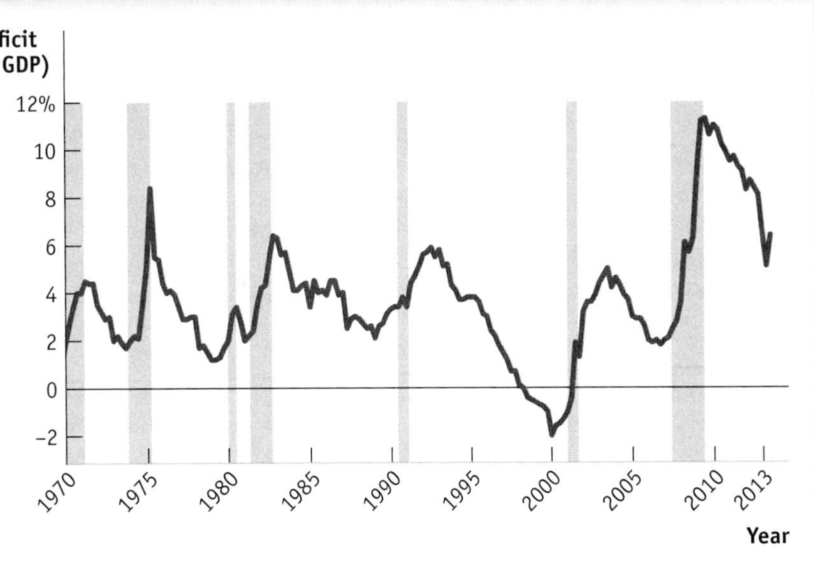

Figure 30.2 The U.S. Federal Budget Deficit and the Unemployment Rate

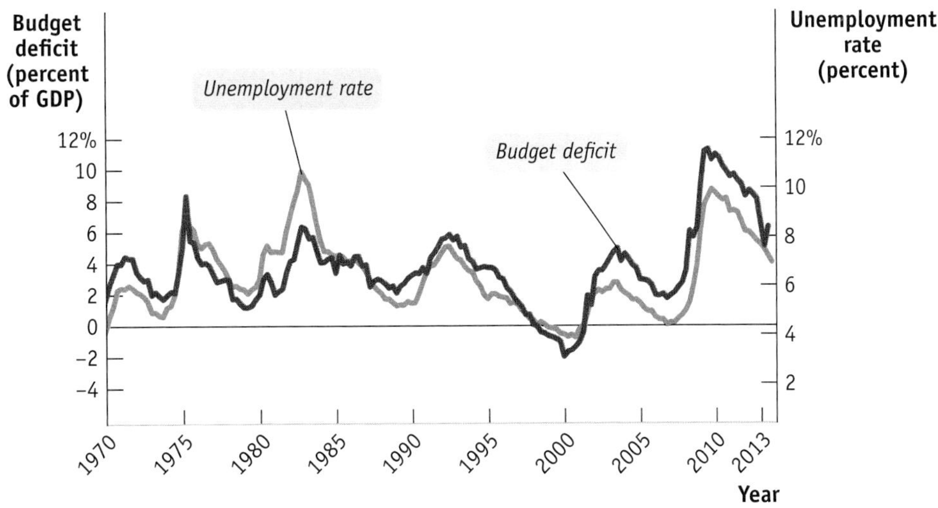

There is a close relationship between the budget balance and the business cycle: a recession moves the budget balance toward deficit, but an expansion moves it toward surplus. Here, the unemployment rate serves as an indicator of the business cycle, and we should expect to see a higher unemployment rate associated with a higher budget deficit. This is confirmed by the figure: the budget deficit as a percentage of GDP moves closely in tandem with the unemployment rate.

Source: Bureau of Economic Analysis; Bureau of Labor Statistics.

The former are affected by automatic stabilizers and the latter by deliberate changes in government purchases, government transfers, or taxes. It's important to realize that business-cycle effects on the budget balance are temporary: both recessionary gaps (in which real GDP is below potential output) and inflationary gaps (in which real GDP is above potential output) tend to be eliminated in the long run. Removing their effects on the budget balance sheds light on whether the government's taxing and spending policies are sustainable in the long run. In other words, do the government's tax policies yield enough revenue to fund its spending in the long run? As we'll learn shortly, this is a fundamentally more important question than whether the government runs a budget surplus or deficit in the current year.

To separate the effect of the business cycle from the effects of other factors, many governments produce an estimate of what the budget balance would be if there were neither a recessionary nor an inflationary gap. The **cyclically adjusted budget balance** is an estimate of what the budget balance would be if real GDP were exactly equal to potential output. It takes into account the extra tax revenue the government would collect and the transfers it would save if a recessionary gap were eliminated—or the revenue the government would lose and the extra transfers it would make if an inflationary gap were eliminated.

The **cyclically adjusted budget balance** is an estimate of what the budget balance would be if real GDP were exactly equal to potential output.

Figure 30.3 shows the actual budget deficit and the Congressional Budget Office estimate of the cyclically adjusted budget deficit, both as a percentage of GDP, since 1970. As you can see, the cyclically adjusted budget deficit doesn't fluctuate as much as the actual budget deficit. In particular, large actual deficits, such as those of 1975 and 1983, are usually caused in part by a depressed economy.

Should the Budget Be Balanced?

Persistent budget deficits can cause problems for both the government and the economy. Yet politicians are always tempted to run deficits because this allows them to cater to voters by cutting taxes without cutting spending or by increasing

Figure 30.3 The Actual Budget Deficit Versus the Cyclically Adjusted Budget Deficit

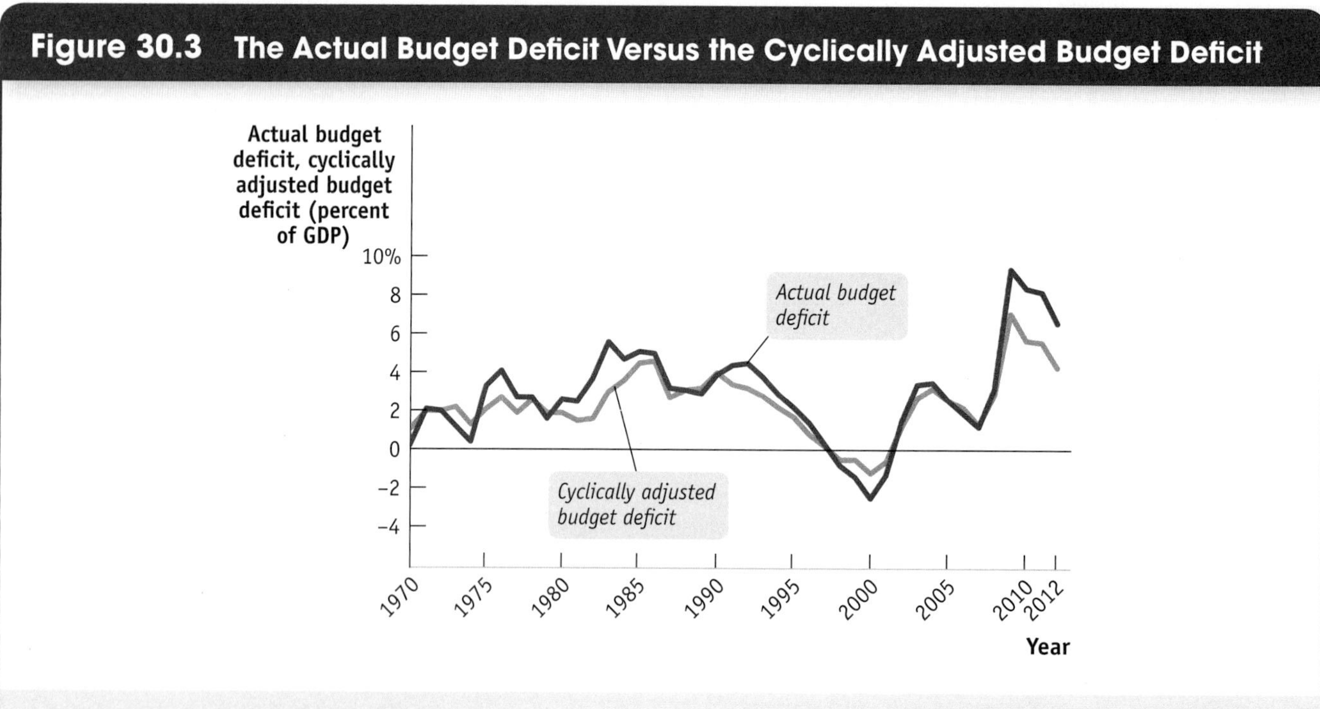

The cyclically adjusted budget deficit is an estimate of what the budget deficit would be if the economy were at potential output. It fluctuates less than the actual budget deficit, because years of large budget deficits also tend to be years when the economy has a large recessionary gap.
Source: Congressional Budget Office.

spending without increasing taxes. As a result, there are occasional attempts by policy makers to force fiscal discipline by introducing legislation—even a constitutional amendment—forbidding the government from running budget deficits. This is usually stated as a requirement that the budget be "balanced"—that revenues at least equal spending each fiscal year. Would it be a good idea to require a balanced budget annually?

Most economists don't think so. They believe that the government should only balance its budget on average—that it should be allowed to run deficits in bad years, offset by surpluses in good years. They don't believe the government should be forced to run a balanced budget *every year* because this would undermine the role of taxes and transfers as automatic stabilizers. As we learned earlier, the tendency of tax revenue to fall and transfers to rise when the economy contracts helps to limit the size of recessions. But falling tax revenue and rising transfer payments push the budget toward deficit. If constrained by a balanced-budget rule, the government would have to respond to this deficit with contractionary fiscal policies that would tend to deepen a recession.

Nonetheless, policy makers concerned about excessive deficits sometimes feel that rigid rules prohibiting—or at least setting an upper limit on—deficits are necessary.

Colin Anderson/Brand X Pictures/Getty Images

Long-Run Implications of Fiscal Policy

During the 1990s, the Japanese government engaged in massive deficit spending in an effort to increase aggregate demand. That policy was partly successful: although Japan's economy was sluggish during the 1990s, it avoided a severe slump comparable to what happened to many countries in the 1930s. Yet the fact that Japan was running large budget deficits year after year made many observers uneasy, as Japan's **government debt**—the accumulation of past budget deficits, minus past budget surpluses—climbed to alarming levels. Now that we understand how budget deficits and surpluses arise, let's take a closer look at their long-run effects on the economy.

Government debt is the accumulation of past budget deficits, minus past budget surpluses.

Deficits, Surpluses, and Debt

When a family spends more than it earns over the course of a year, it has to raise the extra funds either by selling assets or by borrowing. And if a family borrows year after year, it will eventually end up with a lot of debt.

The same is true for governments. With a few exceptions, governments don't raise large sums by selling assets such as national parkland. Instead, when a government spends more than the tax revenue it receives—when it runs a budget deficit—it almost always borrows the extra funds. And governments that run persistent budget deficits end up with substantial debts.

AP® Exam Tip

A budget deficit occurs when the government's revenue is less than its spending in a given year.

To interpret the numbers that follow, you need to know a slightly peculiar feature of federal government accounting. For historical reasons, the U.S. government does not keep the books by calendar years. Instead, budget totals are kept by **fiscal years**, which run from October 1 to September 30 and are labeled by the calendar year in which they end. For example, fiscal 2013 began on October 1, 2012, and ended on September 30, 2013.

At the end of fiscal 2013, the total debt of the U.S. federal government was $16.7 trillion, or about 100% of gross domestic product. However, part of that debt represented special accounting rules specifying that the federal government as a whole owes funds to certain government programs, especially Social Security. We'll explain those rules shortly. For now, however, let's focus on **public debt**: government debt held by individuals and institutions outside the government. At the end of fiscal 2013, the federal government's public debt was "only" $12.0 trillion, or about 72% of GDP. If we include the debts of state and local governments, total government public debt was approximately 88% of GDP.

A **fiscal year** runs from October 1 to September 30 and is labeled according to the calendar year in which it ends.

Public debt is government debt held by individuals and institutions outside the government.

U.S. federal government public debt at the end of fiscal 2013 was larger than it was at the end of fiscal 2012 because the federal government ran a budget deficit during fiscal 2013. A government that runs persistent budget deficits will experience a rising level of debt. Why is this a problem?

Problems Posed by Rising Government Debt

There are two reasons to be concerned when a government runs persistent budget deficits. We described one reason previously: when the economy is at potential output and the government borrows funds in the financial markets, it is competing with firms that plan to borrow funds for investment spending. As a result, the government's borrowing may crowd out private investment spending, thereby increasing interest rates and reducing the economy's long-run rate of growth.

The second reason: today's deficits, by increasing the government's debt, place financial pressure on future budgets. The impact of current deficits on future budgets is straightforward. Like individuals, governments must pay their bills, including interest payments on their accumulated debt. When a government is deeply in debt, those interest payments can be substantial. In fiscal 2013, the U.S. federal government paid 2.4% of GDP—$415.7 billion—in interest on its debt. And although this is a relatively large fraction of GDP, other countries pay even greater fractions of their GDP to service their debt. For example, in 2013, Greece paid interest of about 3.6% of GDP.

Other things equal, a government paying large sums in interest must raise more revenue from taxes or spend less than it would otherwise be able to afford—or it must borrow even more to cover the gap. And a government that borrows to pay interest on its outstanding debt pushes itself even deeper into debt. This process can eventually push a government to the point at which lenders question its ability to repay. Like consumers who have maxed out their credit cards, the government will find that lenders are unwilling to lend any more funds. The result can be that the government defaults on its debt—it stops paying what it owes. Default is often followed by deep financial and economic turmoil.

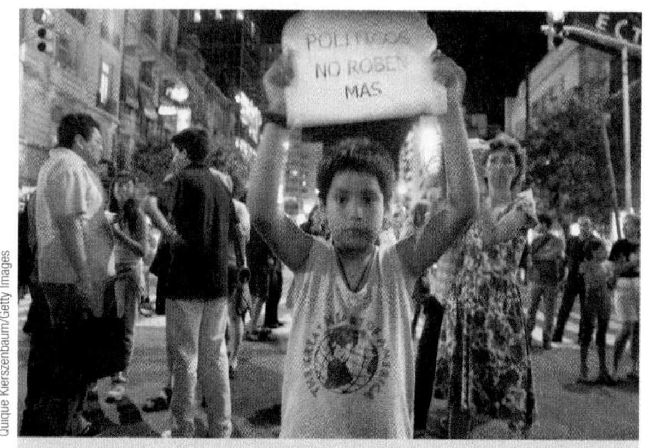

Quique Kierszenbaum/Getty Images

Lautario Palacios, 7, holds a sign that calls for politicians to stop robbing, during a January 9, 2002 demonstration in Buenos Aires, Argentina.

The idea of a government defaulting sounds far-fetched, but it is not impossible. In the 1990s, Argentina, a relatively high-income developing country, was widely praised for its economic policies—and it was able to borrow large sums from foreign lenders. By 2001, however, Argentina's interest payments were spiraling out of control, and the country stopped paying the sums that were due. In the end, Argentina reached a settlement with most of its lenders under which it paid less than a third of the amount originally due. Similarly, the government of Greece faced default in 2012, and bond holders agreed to trade their bonds for new ones worth less than half as much. In the same year, concerns about economic frailty forced the governments of Ireland, Portugal, Italy, and Spain to pay high interest rates on their debt to compensate for the risk of default.

Default creates havoc in a country's financial markets and badly shakes public confidence in both the government and the economy. For example, Argentina's debt default was accompanied by a crisis in the country's banking system and a very severe recession. And even if a highly indebted government avoids default, a heavy debt burden typically forces it to slash spending or raise taxes, politically unpopular measures that can also damage the economy.

One question some people ask is: can't a government that has trouble borrowing just print money to pay its bills? Yes, it can, but this leads to another problem: inflation. In fact, budget problems are the main cause of very severe inflation, as we'll see later. The point for now is that governments do not want to find themselves in a position where the choice is between defaulting on their debts and inflating those debts away.

Concerns about the long-run effects of deficits need not rule out the use of fiscal policy to stimulate the economy when it is depressed. However, these concerns do mean that governments should try to offset budget deficits in bad years with budget surpluses in good years. In other words, governments should run a budget that is approximately balanced over time. Have they actually done so?

Deficits and Debt in Practice

Figure 30.4 shows how the U.S. federal government's budget deficit and its debt have evolved since 1940. Panel (a) shows the federal deficit as a percentage of GDP. As you can see, the federal government ran huge deficits during World War II. It briefly ran surpluses after the war, but it has normally run deficits ever since, especially after 1980. This seems inconsistent with the advice that governments should offset deficits in bad times with surpluses in good times.

However, panel (b) of Figure 30.4 shows that these deficits have not led to runaway debt. To assess the ability of governments to pay their debt, we often use the **debt-GDP ratio**, the government's debt as a percentage of GDP. We use this measure, rather than simply looking at the size of the debt because GDP, which measures the size of the economy as a whole, is a good indicator of the potential taxes the government can collect. If the government's debt grows more slowly than GDP, the burden of paying that debt is actually falling compared with the government's potential tax revenue.

The **debt-GDP ratio** is the government's debt as a percentage of GDP.

What we see from panel (b) is that, although the federal debt has grown in almost every year, the debt-GDP ratio fell for 30 years after the end of World War II. This shows that the debt-GDP ratio can fall, even when debt is rising, as long as GDP grows faster than debt. Growth and inflation sometimes allow a government that runs persistent budget deficits to have a declining debt-GDP ratio nevertheless.

Figure 30.4 U.S. Federal Deficits and Debt

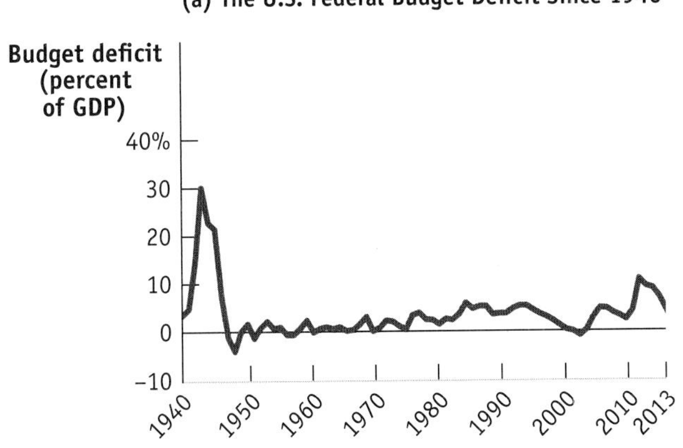

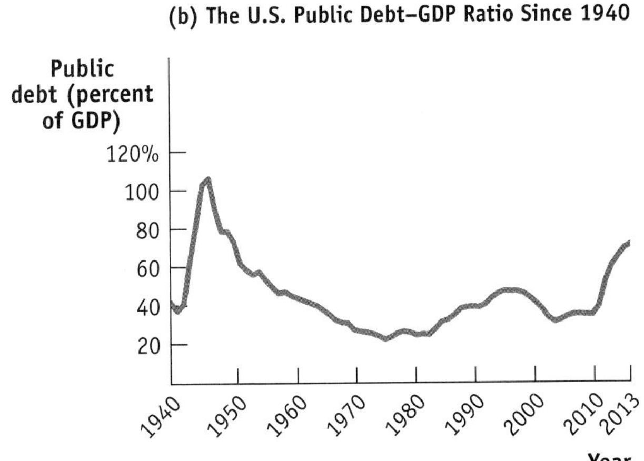

Panel (a) shows the U.S. federal budget deficit as a percentage of GDP since 1940. The U.S. government ran huge deficits during World War II and has usually run smaller deficits ever since. Panel (b) shows the U.S. debt–GDP ratio. Comparing panels (a) and (b), you can see that in many years the debt–GDP ratio has declined in spite of government deficits. This seeming paradox reflects the fact that the debt–GDP ratio can fall, even when debt is rising, as long as GDP grows faster than debt.
Source: Office of Management and Budget.

Figure 30.5 Japanese Deficits and Debt

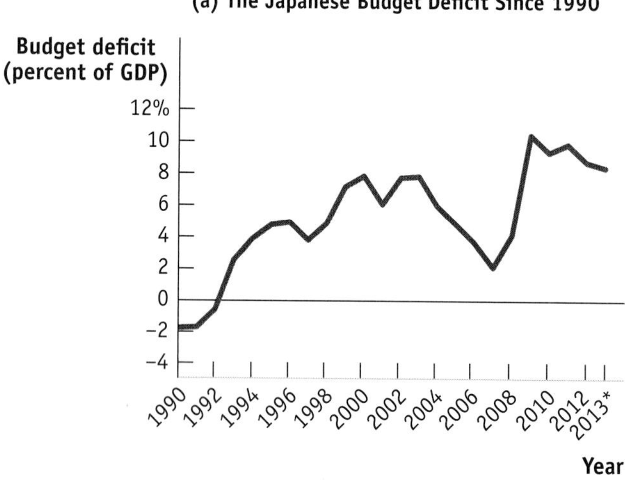

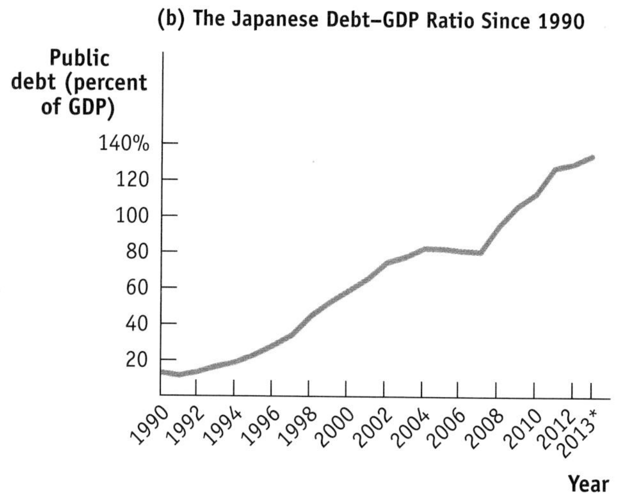

Panel (a) shows the budget deficit of Japan as a percentage of GDP since 1990 and panel (b) shows its debt–GDP ratio. The large deficits that the Japanese government began running in the early 1990s have led to a rapid rise in its debt–GDP ratio as debt has grown more quickly than GDP. This has led some analysts to express concern about the long-run fiscal health of the Japanese economy.
Source: International Monetary Fund.

Still, a government that runs persistent *large* deficits will have a rising debt–GDP ratio when debt grows faster than GDP. Panel (a) of **Figure 30.5** shows Japan's budget deficit as a percentage of GDP, and panel (b) shows Japan's debt–GDP ratio, both since 1990. As we have already mentioned, Japan began running large deficits in the early 1990s, a by-product of its effort to prop up aggregate demand with government spending. This has led to a rapid rise in the debt–GDP ratio. For this reason, some economic analysts are concerned about the long-run fiscal health of the Japanese economy.

Implicit Liabilities

Looking at Figure 30.4, you might be tempted to conclude that, until the 2008 economic crisis struck, the U.S. federal budget was in fairly decent shape: the return to budget deficits after 2001 caused the debt–GDP ratio to rise a bit, but that ratio was

What Happened to the Debt from World War II?

As you can see from Figure 30.4, the government paid for World War II by borrowing on a huge scale. By the war's end, the public debt was more than 100% of GDP, and many people worried about how it could ever be paid off.

The truth is that it never was paid off. In 1946, the public debt was $242 billion; that number dipped slightly in the next few years, as the United States ran postwar budget surpluses, but the government budget went back into deficit in 1950 with the start of the Korean War. By 1962, the public debt was back up to $248 billion.

But by that time nobody was worried about the fiscal health of the U.S. government because the debt–GDP ratio had fallen by more than half. The reason? Vigorous economic growth, plus mild inflation, had led to a rapid rise in GDP. The experience was a clear lesson in the peculiar fact that modern governments can run deficits forever, as long as they aren't too large.

still low compared with both historical experience and some other wealthy countries. However, experts on long-run budget issues view the situation of the United States (and other countries with high public debt, such as Japan and Greece) with alarm. The reason is the problem of *implicit liabilities*. **Implicit liabilities** are spending promises made by governments that are effectively a debt despite the fact that they are not included in the usual debt statistics.

Implicit liabilities are spending promises made by governments that are effectively a debt despite the fact that they are not included in the usual debt statistics.

The largest implicit liabilities of the U.S. government arise from two transfer programs that principally benefit older Americans: Social Security and Medicare. The third-largest implicit liability, Medicaid, benefits low-income families. In each of these cases, the government has promised to provide transfer payments to future as well as current beneficiaries. So these programs represent a future debt that must be honored, even though the debt does not currently show up in the usual statistics. Together, these three programs currently account for almost 40% of federal spending.

The implicit liabilities created by these transfer programs worry fiscal experts. **Figure 30.6** shows why. It shows actual spending on Social Security and on Medicare and Medicaid as percentages of GDP from 1980 to 2013, with Congressional Budget Office projections of spending through 2085. According to these projections, spending on Social Security will rise substantially over the next few decades and spending on the two health care programs will soar. Why?

In the case of Social Security, the answer is demography. Social Security is a "pay-as-you-go" system: current workers pay payroll taxes that fund the benefits of current retirees. So the ratio of the number of retirees drawing benefits to the number of workers paying into Social Security has a major impact on the system's finances. There was a huge surge in the U.S. birth rate between 1946 and 1964, the years of the baby boom. Baby boomers are currently of working age—which means they are paying taxes, not collecting benefits. But some are starting to retire, and as more and more of them do so, they will stop earning income that is taxed and start collecting benefits. As a result, the ratio of retirees receiving benefits to workers paying into the Social Security system

Figure 30.6 Future Demands on the Federal Budget

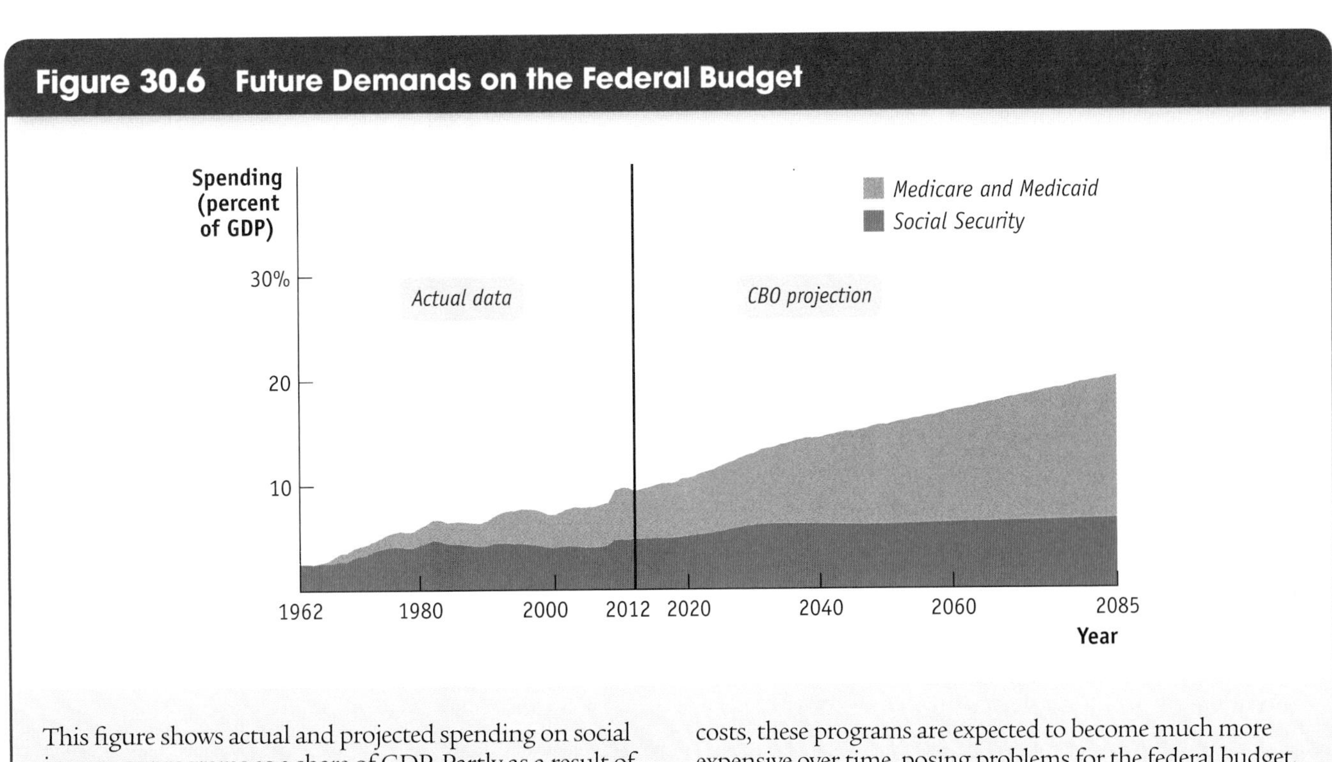

This figure shows actual and projected spending on social insurance programs as a share of GDP. Partly as a result of an aging population, but mainly because of rising health care costs, these programs are expected to become much more expensive over time, posing problems for the federal budget. *Source:* Congressional Budget Office.

will rise. In 2010, there were 34 retirees for every 100 workers paying into the system. By 2030, according to the Social Security Administration, that number will rise to 46; by 2050, it will rise to 48; and by 2080 that number will be 51. This will raise benefit payments relative to the size of the economy.

The aging of the baby boomers, by itself, poses a problem, but the projected rise in Medicare and Medicaid spending is a much more serious concern. The main story behind projections of higher Medicare and Medicaid spending is the long-run tendency of health care spending to rise faster than overall spending, both for government-funded and for private-funded health care.

To some extent, the implicit liabilities of the U.S. government are already reflected in debt statistics. We mentioned earlier that the government had a total debt of $16.7 trillion at the end of fiscal 2013, but that only $12.0 trillion of that total was owed to the public. The main explanation for that discrepancy is that both Social Security and part of Medicare (the hospital insurance program) are supported by *dedicated taxes*: their expenses are paid out of special taxes on wages. At times, these dedicated taxes yield more revenue than is needed to pay current benefits. In particular, since the mid-1980s the Social Security system has been taking in more revenue than it currently needs in order to prepare for the retirement of the baby boomers. This surplus in the Social Security system has been used to accumulate a *Social Security trust fund*, which was $2.8 trillion at the end of fiscal 2013.

The money in the trust fund is held in the form of U.S. government bonds, which are included in the $16.7 trillion in total debt. You could say that there's something funny about counting bonds in the Social Security trust fund as part of government debt. After all, these bonds are owed by one part of the government (the government outside the Social Security system) to another part of the government (the Social Security system itself). But the debt corresponds to a real, if implicit, liability: promises by the government to pay future retirement benefits. So, many economists argue that the gross debt of $16.7 trillion, the sum of public debt and government debt held by Social Security and other trust funds, is a more accurate indication of the government's fiscal health than the smaller amount owed to the public alone.

MODULE 30 Review

Check Your Understanding

1. Why is the cyclically adjusted budget balance a better measure of the long-run sustainability of government policies than the actual budget balance?
2. Explain why states required by their constitutions to balance their budgets are likely to experience more severe economic fluctuations than states that are not held to that requirement.
3. Explain how each of the following events would affect the public debt or implicit liabilities of the U.S. government, other things equal. Would the public debt or implicit liabilities be larger or smaller if they occurred?
   a. The growth rate of real GDP increases.
   b. Retirees live longer.
   c. Tax revenue decreases.
   d. The government borrows to pay interest on its current public debt.
4. Suppose the economy is in a slump and the current public debt is quite large. Explain the trade-off of short-run versus long-run objectives that policy makers face when deciding whether or not to engage in deficit spending.

Tackle the Test: Multiple-Choice Questions

1. If government spending exceeds tax revenues, which of the following is necessarily true? There is a
   - I. positive budget balance.
   - II. budget deficit.
   - III. recession.

   a. I only
   b. II only
   c. III only
   d. I and II only
   e. I, II, and III

2. Which of the following fiscal policies is expansionary?

	Taxes	*Government spending*
a.	increase by $100 million	increases by $100 million
b.	decrease by $100 million	decreases by $100 million
c.	increase by $100 million	decreases by $100 million
d.	decrease by $100 million	increases by $100 million
e.	both (a) and (d)	

3. The cyclically adjusted budget deficit is an estimate of what the budget balance would be if real GDP were
   a. greater than potential output.
   b. equal to nominal GDP.
   c. equal to potential output.
   d. falling.
   e. calculated during a recession.

4. During a recession in the United States, what happens automatically to tax revenues and government spending?

	Tax revenues	*Government spending*
a.	increase	increases
b.	decrease	decreases
c.	increase	decreases
d.	decrease	increases
e.	decrease	does not change

5. Which of the following is a reason to be concerned about persistent budget deficits?
   a. crowding out
   b. government default
   c. the opportunity cost of future interest payments
   d. higher interest rates leading to decreased long-run growth
   e. all of the above

Tackle the Test: Free-Response Questions

1. Consider the information provided below for the hypothetical country of Zeta.

   Tax revenues = $2,000

   Government purchases of goods and services = $1,500

   Government transfers = $1,000

   Real GDP = $20,000

   Potential output = $18,000

   a. Is the budget balance in Zeta positive or negative? What is the amount of the budget balance?
   b. Zeta is currently in what phase of the business cycle? Explain.
   c. Is Zeta implementing the appropriate fiscal policy given the current state of the economy? Explain.
   d. How does Zeta's cyclically adjusted budget deficit compare with its actual budget deficit? Explain.

Rubric for FRQ 1 (8 points)

1 point: Negative

1 point: –$500

1 point: Expansion

1 point: Real GDP > potential output

1 point: No

1 point: Zeta is running a budget deficit during an expansion.

1 point: It is larger.

1 point: Because if real GDP equaled potential output, tax revenues would be lower and government transfers would be higher.

2. In Module 29 you learned about the market for loanable funds, which is intimately related to our current topic of budget deficits. Use a correctly labeled graph of the market for loanable funds to illustrate the effect of a persistent budget deficit. Identify and explain the effect persistent budget deficits can have on private investment.

   (6 points)

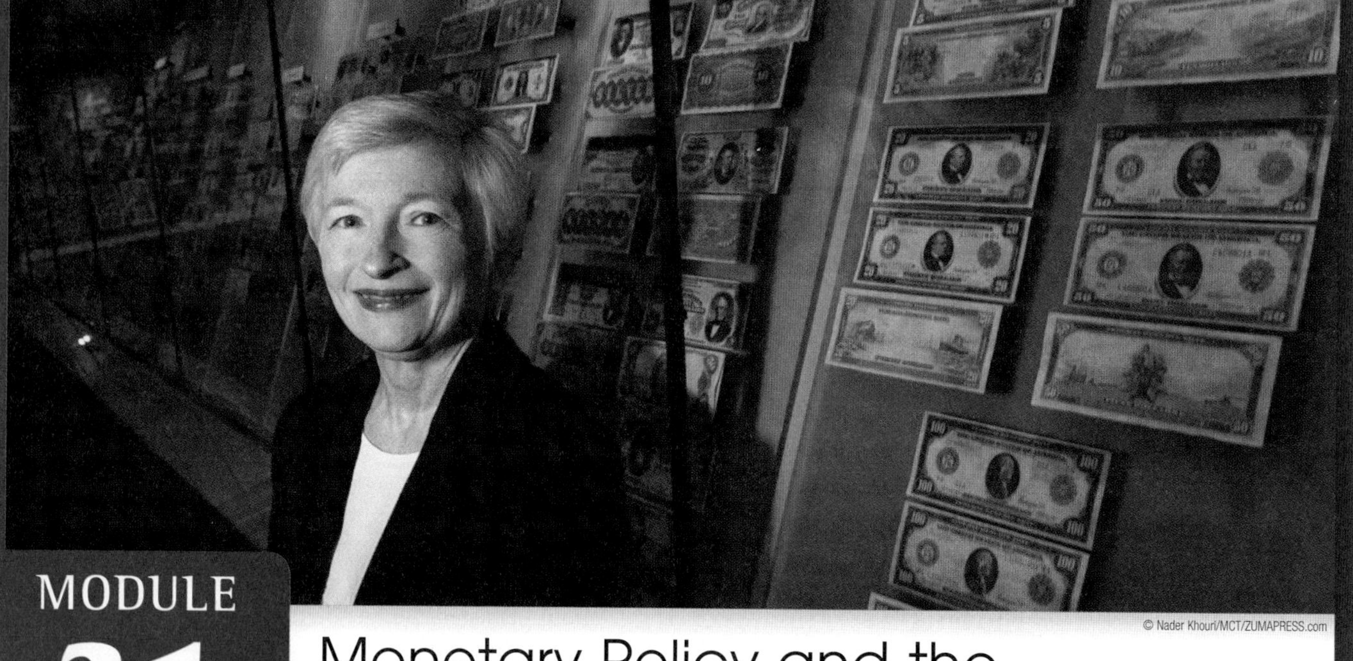

MODULE

31 Monetary Policy and the Interest Rate

In this Module, you will learn to:

- Describe how the Federal Reserve implements monetary policy, moving the interest rate to affect aggregate output
- Explain why monetary policy is the main tool for stabilizing the economy

In Modules 28 and 29 we developed models of the money market and the loanable funds market. We also saw how these two markets are consistent and related. In the short run, the interest rate is determined in the money market and the loanable funds market adjusts in response to changes in the money market. However, in the long run, the interest rate is determined by matching the supply and demand of loanable funds that arise when real GDP equals potential output. Now we are ready to use these models to explain how the Federal Reserve can use monetary policy to stabilize the economy in the short run.

Monetary Policy and the Interest Rate

Let's examine how the Federal Reserve can use changes in the money supply to change the interest rate. **Figure 31.1** shows what happens when the Fed increases the money supply from $\overline{M}_1$ to $\overline{M}_2$. The economy is originally in equilibrium at E_1, with the equilibrium interest rate r_1 and the money supply $\overline{M}_1$. When the Fed increases the money supply to $\overline{M}_2$, the money supply curve shifts to the right, from MS_1 to MS_2, and the equilibrium interest rate falls to r_2. Why? Because r_2 is the only interest rate at which the public is willing to hold the quantity of money actually supplied, $\overline{M}_2$. So an increase in the money supply drives the interest rate down. Similarly, a reduction in the money supply drives the interest rate up. By adjusting the money supply up or down, the Fed can set the interest rate.

AP® Exam Tip

Don't confuse the federal funds rate with the discount rate. The Fed can only target the federal funds rate because it is set through the interaction of supply and demand.

The Federal Reserve can move the interest rate through open-market operations that shift the money supply curve. In practice, the Fed sets a **target federal funds rate** and uses open-market operations to achieve that target.

In practice, at each meeting the Federal Open Market Committee decides on the interest rate to prevail for the next six weeks, until its next meeting. The Fed sets a **target federal funds rate**, a desired level for the federal funds rate. This target is then enforced by the Open Market Desk of the Federal Reserve Bank of New York, which adjusts the money supply through *open-market operations*—the purchase or sale of Treasury bills—until the actual federal funds rate equals the target rate. The other tools of

Figure 31.1 The Effect of an Increase in the Money Supply on the Interest Rate

The Federal Reserve can lower the interest rate by increasing the money supply. Here, the equilibrium interest rate falls from r_1 to r_2 in response to an increase in the money supply from $\overline{M}_1$ to $\overline{M}_2$. In order to induce people to hold the larger quantity of money, the interest rate must fall from r_1 to r_2.

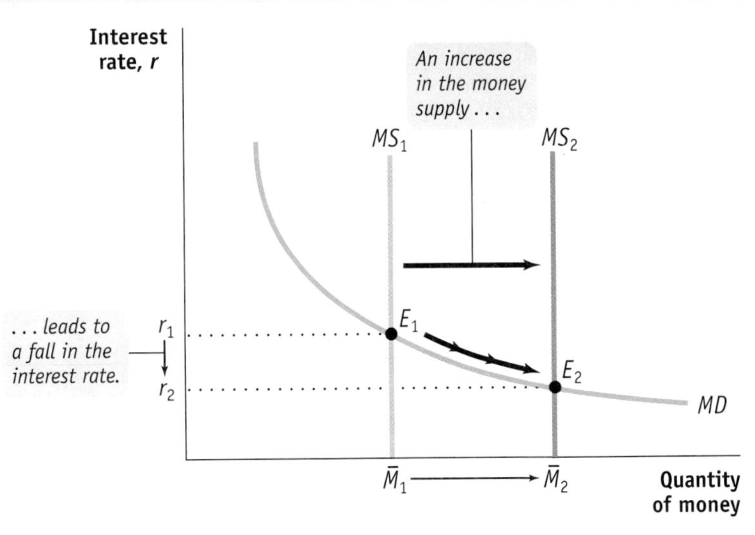

monetary policy, lending through the discount window and changes in reserve requirements, aren't used on a regular basis (although the Fed used discount window lending in its efforts to address the 2008 financial crisis).

Figure 31.2 shows how interest rate targeting works. In both panels, r_T is the target federal funds rate. In panel (a), the initial money supply curve is MS_1 with money supply

Figure 31.2 Setting the Federal Funds Rate

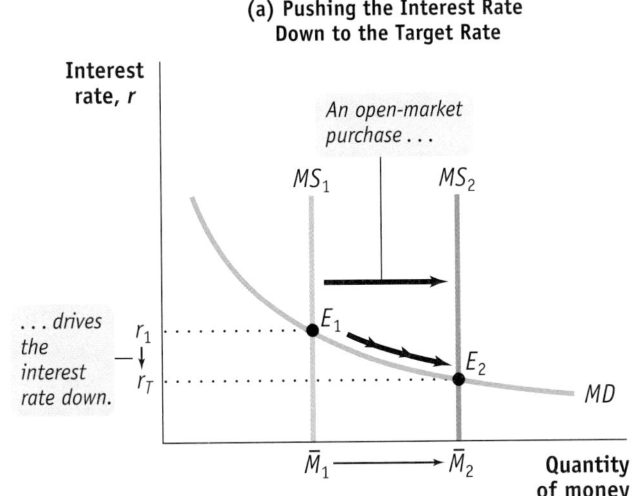

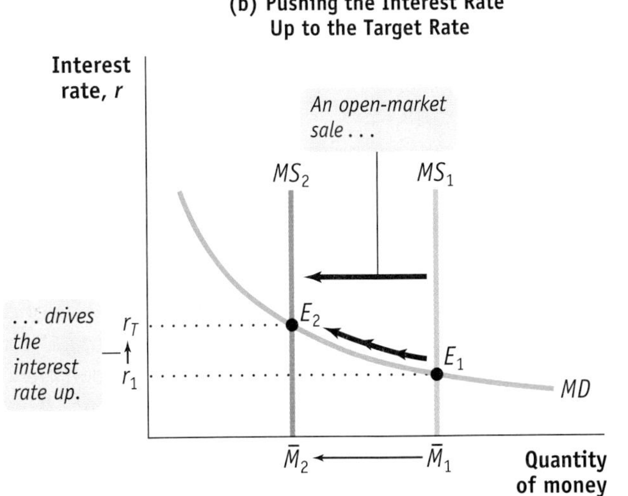

The Federal Reserve sets a target for the federal funds rate and uses open-market operations to achieve that target. In both panels the target rate is r_T. In panel (a) the initial equilibrium interest rate, r_1, is above the target rate. The Fed increases the money supply by making an open-market purchase of Treasury bills, pushing the money supply curve rightward, from MS_1 to MS_2, and driving the interest rate down to r_T. In panel (b) the initial equilibrium interest rate, r_1, is below the target rate. The Fed reduces the money supply by making an open-market sale of Treasury bills, pushing the money supply curve leftward, from MS_1 to MS_2, and driving the interest rate up to r_T.

The Fed Reverses Course

During the summer of 2007, many called for a change in Federal Reserve policy. At first the Fed remained unmoved. On August 7, 2007, the Federal Open Market Committee decided to make no change in its interest rate policy. The official statement, however, did concede that "financial markets have been volatile in recent weeks" and that "credit conditions have become tighter for some households and businesses."

Just three days later, the Fed issued a special statement basically assuring market players that it was paying attention; on August 17 it issued another statement declaring that it was "monitoring the situation," which is Fed-speak for "we're getting nervous." And on September 18, the Fed did what CNBC analyst Jim Cramer wanted: it cut the target federal funds rate "to help forestall some of the adverse effects on the broader economy that might otherwise arise from the disruptions in financial markets." In effect, it conceded that Cramer's worries were at least partly right.

It was the beginning of a major change in monetary policy. The figure on the right shows two interest rates from the beginning of 2004 to 2013: the target federal funds rate decided by the Federal Open Market Committee, which dropped in a series of steps starting in September 2007, and the average effective rate that prevailed in the market each day. The figure shows that the interest rate cut six weeks after Cramer's diatribe was only the first of several cuts. As you can see, this was a reversal of previous policy: previously the Fed had generally been raising rates, not reducing them, out of concern that inflation might become a problem. But starting in September 2007, fighting the financial crisis took priority. By the way, notice how beginning late in 2008, it looks as if there are two target federal funds rates. What happened? The Federal Open Market Committee set a target *range* for the federal funds rate, between 0% and 0.25%. That target range was still in effect at the time of writing in 2014.

The figure also shows that the Fed doesn't always hit its target. There were a number of days, especially in 2008, when the actual federal funds rate was significantly above or below the target rate. But these episodes didn't last long, and overall the Fed got what it wanted, at least as far as short-term interest rates were concerned.

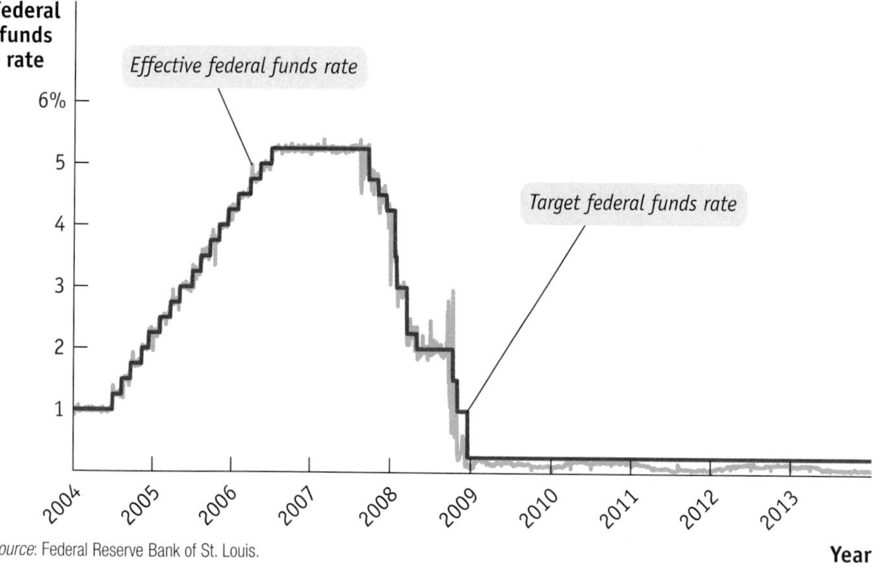

Source: Federal Reserve Bank of St. Louis.

$\overline{M}_1$, and the equilibrium interest rate, r_1, is above the target rate. To lower the interest rate to r_T, the Fed makes an open-market purchase of Treasury bills, which leads to an increase in the money supply via the money multiplier. This is illustrated in panel (a) by the rightward shift of the money supply curve from MS_1 to MS_2 and an increase in the money supply to $\overline{M}_2$. This drives the equilibrium interest rate *down* to the target rate, r_T.

Panel (b) shows the opposite case. Again, the initial money supply curve is MS_1 with money supply $\overline{M}_1$. But this time the equilibrium interest rate, r_1, is below the target federal funds rate, r_T. In this case, the Fed will make an open-market sale of Treasury bills, leading to a fall in the money supply to $\overline{M}_2$ via the money multiplier. The money supply curve shifts leftward from MS_1 to MS_2, driving the equilibrium interest rate *up* to the target federal funds rate, r_T.

AP® Exam Tip

Remember that the aggregate demand curve shifts in the same direction as the money supply curve when the Fed conducts monetary policy.

Monetary Policy and Aggregate Demand

We have seen how fiscal policy can be used to stabilize the economy. Now we will see how monetary policy—changes in the money supply or the interest rate, or both—can play the same role.

Expansionary and Contractionary Monetary Policy

Previously we said that monetary policy shifts the aggregate demand curve. We can now explain how that works: through the effect of monetary policy on the interest rate.

Figure 31.3 illustrates the process. Suppose that the Federal Reserve wants to reduce interest rates, so it expands the money supply. As we've seen, this leads to a lower interest rate. A lower interest rate, in turn, will lead to more investment spending, which will lead to higher real GDP, which will lead to higher consumer spending, and so on through the multiplier process. So the total quantity of goods and services demanded at any given aggregate price level rises when the quantity of money increases, and the *AD* curve shifts to the right. Monetary policy that shifts the *AD* curve to the right, as illustrated in the top portion of Figure 31.3, is known as **expansionary monetary policy**.

Expansionary monetary policy is monetary policy that increases aggregate demand.

Figure 31.3 Expansionary and Contractionary Monetary Policy

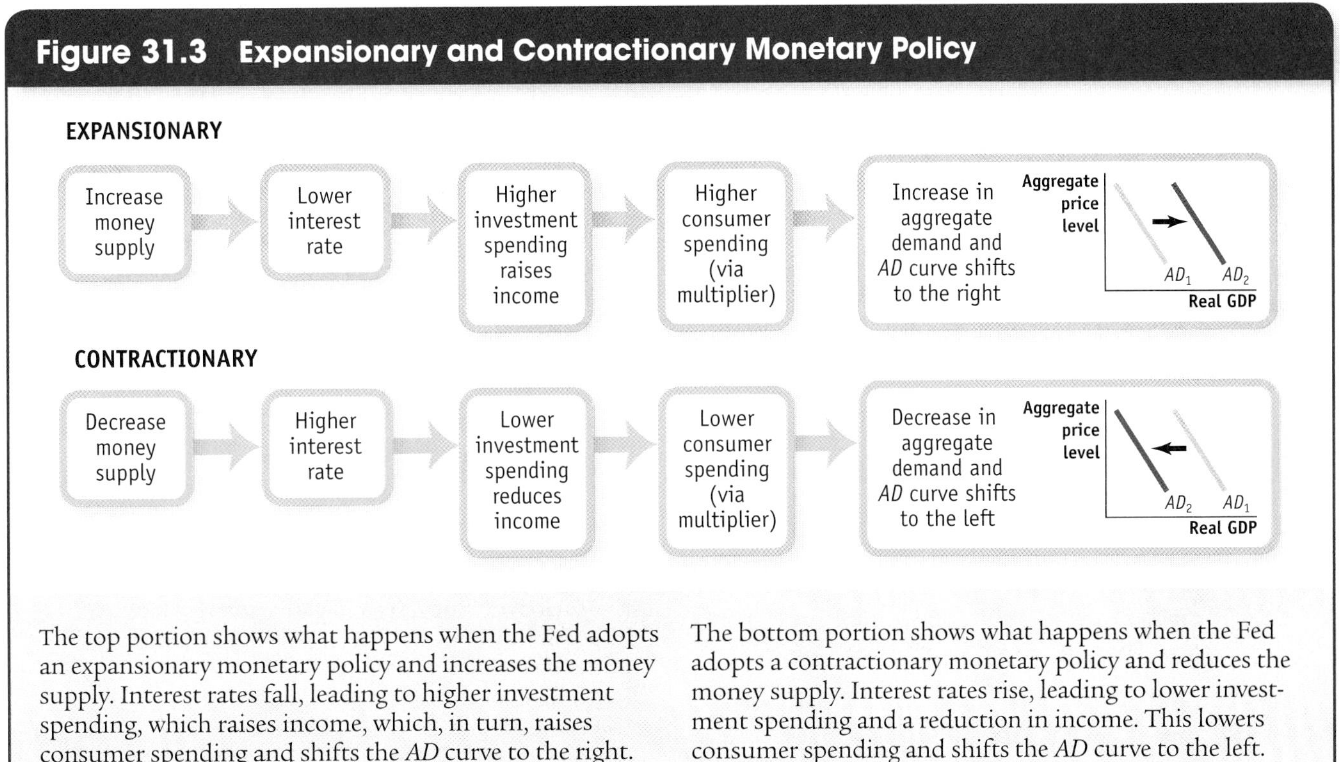

The top portion shows what happens when the Fed adopts an expansionary monetary policy and increases the money supply. Interest rates fall, leading to higher investment spending, which raises income, which, in turn, raises consumer spending and shifts the *AD* curve to the right.

The bottom portion shows what happens when the Fed adopts a contractionary monetary policy and reduces the money supply. Interest rates rise, leading to lower investment spending and a reduction in income. This lowers consumer spending and shifts the *AD* curve to the left.

Suppose, alternatively, that the Federal Reserve contracts the money supply. This leads to a higher interest rate. The higher interest rate leads to lower investment spending, which leads to lower real GDP, which leads to lower consumer spending, and so on. So the total quantity of goods and services demanded falls when the money supply is reduced, and the *AD* curve shifts to the left. Monetary policy that shifts the *AD* curve to the left, as illustrated in the lower portion of Figure 31.3, is called **contractionary monetary policy**.

Contractionary monetary policy is monetary policy that reduces aggregate demand.

AP® Exam Tip

On the AP® exam, if you are asked what policy the central bank could use to correct a particular problem in the economy, don't just say "expansionary policy" or "contractionary policy." Identify a specific policy tool (open-market operations, the reserve ratio, or the discount rate) and indicate how that tool would be applied to remedy the situation.

Monetary Policy in Practice

We have learned that policy makers try to fight recessions. They also try to ensure *price stability*: low (though usually not zero) inflation. Actual monetary policy reflects a combination of these goals.

In general, the Federal Reserve and other central banks tend to engage in expansionary monetary policy when actual real GDP is below potential output. Panel (a) of **Figure 31.4** on the next page shows the U.S. output gap, which we defined as the

Figure 31.4 Tracking Monetary Policy Using the Output Gap, Inflation, and the Taylor Rule

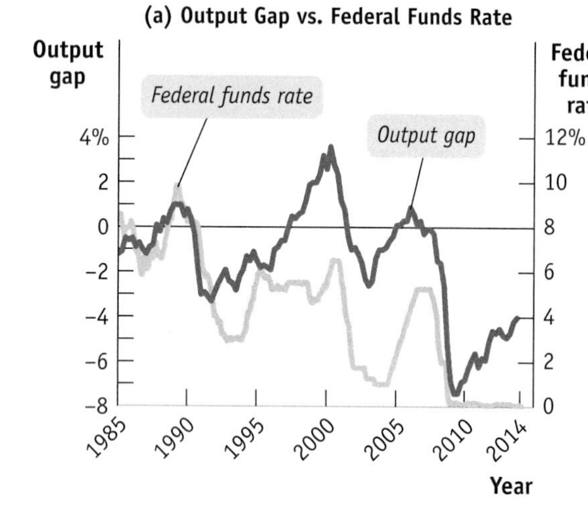

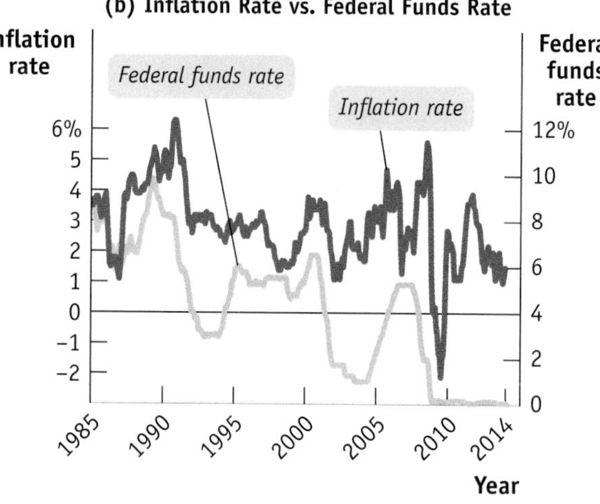

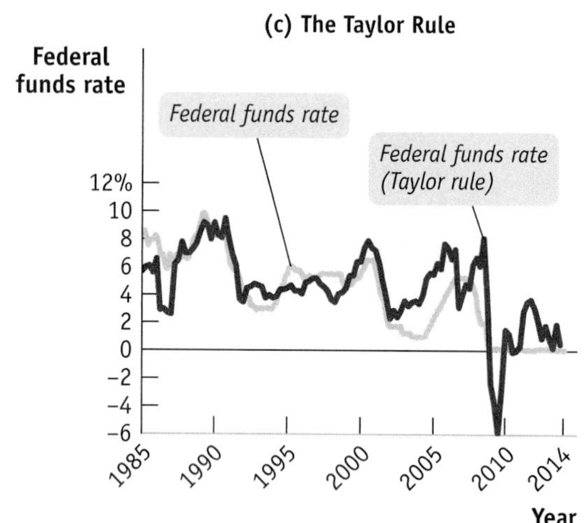

Panel (a) shows that the federal funds rate usually rises when the output gap is positive—that is, when actual real GDP is above potential output—and falls when the output gap is negative. Panel (b) illustrates that the federal funds rate tends to be high when inflation is high and low when inflation is low. Panel (c) shows the Taylor rule in action. The green line shows the actual federal funds rate from 1985 to 2010. The purple line shows the interest rate the Fed *should* have set according to the Taylor rule. The fit isn't perfect—in fact, for a period after 2009 the Taylor rule suggests a negative interest rate, an impossibility—but the Taylor rule does a better job of tracking U.S. monetary policy than either the output gap or the inflation rate alone.

Sources: Federal Reserve Bank of St. Louis; Bureau of Economic Analysis; Bureau of Labor Statistics.

percentage difference between actual real GDP and potential output, versus the federal funds rate since 1985. (Recall that the output gap is positive when actual real GDP exceeds potential output.) As you can see, the Fed has tended to raise interest rates when the output gap is rising—that is, when the economy is developing an inflationary gap—and cut rates when the output gap is falling. The big exception was the late 1990s, when the Fed left rates steady for several years even as the economy developed a positive output gap (which went along with a low unemployment rate).

One reason the Fed was willing to keep interest rates low in the late 1990s was that inflation was low. Panel (b) of Figure 31.4 compares the inflation rate, measured as the rate of change in consumer prices excluding food and energy, with the federal funds rate. You can see how low inflation during the mid-1990s and early 2000s helped encourage loose monetary policy both in the late 1990s and in 2002–2003.

The **Taylor rule for monetary policy** is a rule for setting the federal funds rate that takes into account both the inflation rate and the output gap.

In 1993, Stanford economist John Taylor suggested that monetary policy should follow a simple rule that takes into account concerns about both the business cycle and inflation. The **Taylor rule for monetary policy** is a rule for setting the federal funds rate that takes into account both the inflation rate and the output gap. He also suggested that actual monetary policy often looks as if the Federal Reserve was, in fact, more or less following the proposed rule. The rule Taylor originally suggested was as follows:

$$\text{Federal funds rate} = 1 + (1.5 \times \text{inflation rate}) + (0.5 \times \text{output gap})$$

Panel (c) of Figure 31.4 compares the federal funds rate specified by the Taylor rule with the actual federal funds rate from 1985 to 2010. With the exception of a period beginning in 2009, the Taylor rule does a pretty good job of predicting the Fed's actual behavior—better than looking at either the output gap alone or the inflation rate alone. Furthermore, the direction of changes in interest rates predicted by an application of the Taylor rule to monetary policy and the direction of changes in actual interest rates have always been the same—further evidence that the Fed is using some form of the Taylor rule to set monetary policy. But, what happened in 2009? A combination of low inflation and a large and negative output gap put the Taylor's rule of prediction of the federal funds into negative territory. But, of course, a negative federal funds rate is impossible. So the Fed did the best it could—it cut rates aggressively and the federal funds rate fell to almost zero.

Stanford economist John Taylor suggested a simple rule for monetary policy.

Monetary policy, rather than fiscal policy, is the main tool of stabilization policy. Like fiscal policy, it is subject to lags: it takes time for the Fed to recognize economic problems and time for monetary policy to affect the economy. However, since the Fed moves much more quickly than Congress, monetary policy is typically the preferred tool.

Inflation Targeting

Until 2012, the Fed did not explicitly commit itself to achieving a particular inflation rate. However, in January 2012, Ben Bernanke, the chair of the Federal Reserve at the time, announced that the Fed would set its policy to maintain an approximately 2% inflation rate per year. With that statement, the Fed joined a number of other central banks that have explicit *inflation targets*. So rather than using the Taylor rule to set monetary policy, they instead announce the inflation rate that they want to achieve—the inflation target—and set policy in an attempt to hit that target. This method of setting monetary policy is called **inflation targeting**. The central bank of New Zealand, which was the first country to adopt inflation targeting, specified a range for that target of 1% to 3%. Other central banks commit themselves to achieving a specific number. For example, the Bank of England is supposed to keep inflation at 2%. In practice, there doesn't seem to be much difference between these versions: central banks with a target range for inflation seem to aim for the middle of that range, and central banks with a fixed target tend to give themselves considerable wiggle room.

Inflation targeting occurs when the central bank sets an explicit target for the inflation rate and sets monetary policy in order to hit that target.

One major difference between inflation targeting and the Taylor rule is that inflation targeting is forward-looking rather than backward-looking. That is, the Taylor rule adjusts monetary policy in response to *past* inflation, but inflation targeting is based on a forecast of *future* inflation.

Advocates of inflation targeting argue that it has two key advantages, *transparency* and *accountability*. First, economic uncertainty is reduced because the public knows the objective of an inflation-targeting central bank. Second, the central bank's success can be judged by seeing how closely actual inflation rates have matched the inflation target, making central bankers accountable.

Critics of inflation targeting argue that it's too restrictive because there are times when other concerns—like the stability of the financial system—should take priority over achieving any particular inflation rate. Indeed, in late 2007 and early 2008 the Fed cut interest rates much more than either the Taylor rule or inflation targeting would have dictated because it feared that turmoil in the financial markets would lead to a major recession (which it did).

What the Fed Wants, the Fed Gets

What's the evidence that the Fed can actually cause an economic contraction or expansion? You might think that finding such evidence is just a matter of looking at what happens to the economy when interest rates go up or down. But it turns out that there's a big problem with that approach: the Fed usually changes interest rates in an attempt to tame the business cycle, raising rates if the economy is expanding and reducing rates if the economy is slumping. So, in the actual data, it often looks as if low interest rates go along with a weak economy and high rates go along with a strong economy.

In a famous 1994 paper titled "Monetary Policy Matters," the macroeconomists Christina Romer and David Romer solved this problem by focusing on episodes in which monetary policy *wasn't* a reaction to the business cycle. Specifically, they used minutes from the Federal Open Market Committee and other sources to identify episodes "in which the Federal Reserve in effect decided to attempt to create a recession to reduce inflation." Contractionary monetary policy is sometimes used to eliminate inflation that has become *embedded* in the economy, rather than just as a tool of macroeconomic stabilization. In this case, the Fed needs to create a recessionary gap—not just eliminate an inflationary gap—to wring embedded inflation out of the economy.

The figure shows the unemployment rate between 1952 and 1984 (orange) and identifies five dates on which, according to Romer and Romer, the Fed decided that it wanted a recession (vertical red lines). In four out of the five cases, the decision to contract the economy was followed, after a modest lag, by a rise in the unemployment rate. On average, Romer and Romer found, the unemployment rate rises by 2 percentage points after the Fed decides that unemployment needs to go up.

So yes, the Fed gets what it wants.

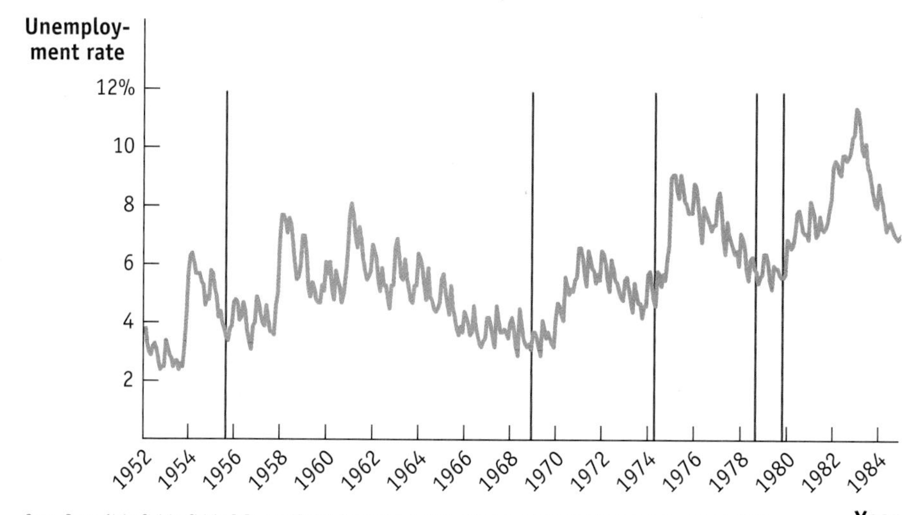

Sources: Bureau of Labor Statistics; Christina D. Romer and David H. Romer, "Monetary Policy Matters," *Journal of Monetary Economics* 34 (August 1994): 75-88.

MODULE 31 Review

Check Your Understanding

1. Assume that there is an increase in the demand for money at every interest rate. Using a diagram, show what effect this will have on the equilibrium interest rate for a given money supply.
2. Now assume that the Fed is following a policy of targeting the federal funds rate. What will the Fed do in the situation described in Question 1 to keep the federal funds rate unchanged? Illustrate with a diagram.
3. Suppose the economy is currently suffering from a recessionary gap and the Federal Reserve uses an expansionary monetary policy to close that gap. Describe the short-run effect of this policy on the following.
   a. the money supply curve
   b. the equilibrium interest rate
   c. investment spending
   d. consumer spending
   e. aggregate output

Tackle the Test: Multiple-Choice Questions

1. At each meeting of the Federal Open Market Committee, the Federal Reserve sets a target for which of the following?
   I. the federal funds rate
   II. the prime interest rate
   III. the market interest rate
   a. I only
   b. II only
   c. III only
   d. I and III only
   e. I, II, and III
2. Which of the following actions can the Fed take to decrease the equilibrium interest rate?
   a. increase the money supply
   b. increase money demand
   c. decrease the money supply
   d. decrease money demand
   e. both (a) and (d)
3. Contractionary monetary policy attempts to _______ aggregate demand by _______ interest rates.

a.	decrease	increasing
b.	increase	decreasing
c.	decrease	decreasing
d.	increase	increasing
e.	increase	maintaining

4. Which of the following is a goal of monetary policy?
   a. zero inflation
   b. deflation
   c. price stability
   d. increased potential output
   e. decreased actual real GDP
5. When implementing monetary policy, the Federal Reserve attempts to achieve
   a. an explicit target real GDP growth rate.
   b. zero inflation.
   c. a low rate of deflation.
   d. an explicit target inflation rate.
   e. 4–5% inflation.

Tackle the Test: Free-Response Questions

1. a. Give the equation for the Taylor rule.
   b. How well does the Taylor rule fit the Fed's actual behavior? Explain.
   c. Suppose the inflation rate is 1% and the output gap is 3%. What federal funds rate does the Taylor rule predict?
   d. Suppose the inflation rate increases by 2 percentage points. If the Fed follows the Taylor rule, what specific change in the target federal funds rate will the Fed seek? Identify the general type of policy the Fed uses to achieve that sort of change.

Rubric for FRQ 1 (6 points)

1 point: Federal funds rate = $1 + (1.5 \times \text{inflation rate}) + (0.5 \times \text{output gap})$

1 point: It's not a perfect fit but it is usually a close approximation.

1 point: It does better than any one measure alone, and it has always correctly predicted the direction of change of interest rates.

1 point: $1 + (1.5 \times 1) + (0.5 \times 3) = 4\%$

1 point: An increase of 3 (1.5×2) percentage points

1 point: Contractionary monetary policy

2. a. What can the Fed do with each of its three primary tools to implement expansionary monetary policy during a recession?
   b. Use a correctly labeled graph of the money market to explain how the Fed's use of expansionary monetary policy affects interest rates in the short run.
   c. Explain how the interest rate change you graphed in part b affects aggregate supply and demand in the short run.
   d. Use a correctly labeled aggregate demand and supply graph to show how expansionary monetary policy affects aggregate output in the short run.
   (11 points)

MODULE 32 Money, Output, and Prices in the Long Run

In this Module, you will learn to:

- Identify the effects of an inappropriate monetary policy
- Explain the concept of monetary neutrality and its relationship to the long-term economic effects of monetary policy

In the previous module we discussed how expansionary and contractionary monetary policy can be used to stabilize the economy. The Federal Reserve can use its monetary policy tools to change the money supply and cause the equilibrium interest rate in the money market to increase or decrease. But what if a central bank pursues a monetary policy that is not appropriate? That is, what if a central bank pursues expansionary policy during an expansion or contractionary policy during a recession? In this module we consider how a counterproductive action by a central bank can actually destabilize the economy in the short run. We also introduce the long-run effects of monetary policy. As we learned in the last section, the money market (where monetary policy has its effect on the money supply) determines the interest rate only in the short run. In the long run, the interest rate is determined in the market for loanable funds. Here we look at long-run adjustments and consider the long-run effects of monetary policy.

Money, Output, and Prices

Because of its expansionary and contractionary effects, monetary policy is generally the policy tool of choice to help stabilize the economy. However, not all actions by central banks are productive. In particular, as we'll see later, central banks sometimes print money not to fight a recessionary gap but to help the government pay its bills, an action that typically destabilizes the economy.

What happens when a change in the money supply pushes the economy away from, rather than toward, long-run equilibrium? The economy is self-correcting in the long run: a demand shock has only a temporary effect on aggregate output. If the demand shock is the result of a change in the money supply, we can make a stronger statement: in the long run, changes in the quantity of money affect the aggregate price level, but they do not change real aggregate output or the interest rate. To see why, let's look at what happens if the central bank permanently increases the money supply.

Short-Run and Long-Run Effects of an Increase in the Money Supply

To analyze the long-run effects of monetary policy, it's helpful to think of the central bank as choosing a target for the money supply rather than for the interest rate. In assessing the effects of an increase in the money supply, we return to the analysis of the long-run effects of an increase in aggregate demand.

Figure 32.1 shows the short-run and long-run effects of an increase in the money supply when the economy begins at potential output, Y_1. The initial short-run aggregate supply curve is $SRAS_1$, the long-run aggregate supply curve is *LRAS*, and the initial aggregate demand curve is AD_1. The economy's initial equilibrium is at E_1, a point of both short-run and long-run macroeconomic equilibrium because it is on both the short-run and the long-run aggregate supply curves. Real GDP is at potential output, Y_1.

Now suppose there is an increase in the money supply. Other things equal, an increase in the money supply reduces the interest rate, which increases investment spending, which leads to a further rise in consumer spending, and so on. So an increase in the money supply increases the demand for goods and services, shifting the *AD* curve rightward to AD_2. In the short run, the economy moves to a new short-run macroeconomic equilibrium at E_2. The price level rises from P_1 to P_2, and real GDP rises from Y_1 to Y_2. That is, both the aggregate price level and aggregate output increase in the short run.

But the aggregate output level, Y_2, is above potential output. Production at a level above potential output leads to low unemployment, which brings about a rise in nominal wages over time, causing the short-run aggregate supply curve to shift leftward. This process stops only when the *SRAS* curve ends up at $SRAS_2$ and the economy ends up at

Figure 32.1 The Short-Run and Long-Run Effects of an Increase in the Money Supply

An increase in the money supply generates a positive short-run effect, but no long-run effect, on real GDP. Here, the economy begins at E_1, a point of short-run and long-run macroeconomic equilibrium. An increase in the money supply shifts the *AD* curve rightward, and the economy moves to a new short-run equilibrium at E_2 and a new real GDP of Y_2. But E_2 is not a long-run equilibrium: Y_2 exceeds potential output, Y_1, leading to an increase in nominal wages over time. In the long run, the increase in nominal wages shifts the short-run aggregate supply curve leftward, to a new position at $SRAS_2$. The economy reaches a new short-run and long-run macroeconomic equilibrium at E_3 on the *LRAS* curve, and output falls back to potential output, Y_1. The only long-run effect of an increase in the money supply is an increase in the aggregate price level from P_1 to P_3.

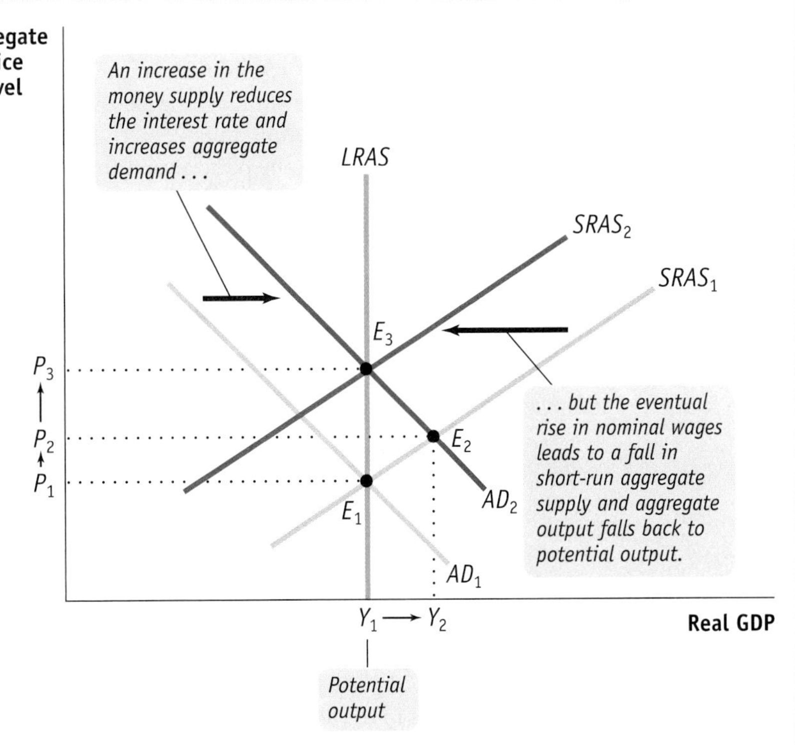

point E_3, a point of both short-run and long-run macroeconomic equilibrium. The long-run effect of an increase in the money supply, then, is that the aggregate price level has increased from P_1 to P_3, but aggregate output is back at potential output, Y_1. In the long run, a monetary expansion raises the aggregate price level but has no effect on real GDP.

If the money supply decreases, the story we have just told plays out in reverse. Other things equal, a decrease in the money supply raises the interest rate, which decreases investment spending, which leads to a further decrease in consumer spending, and so on. So a decrease in the money supply decreases the demand for goods and services at any given aggregate price level, shifting the aggregate demand curve to the left. In the short run, the economy moves to a new short-run macroeconomic equilibrium at a level of real GDP below potential output and a lower aggregate price level. That is, both the aggregate price level and aggregate output decrease in the short run. But what happens over time? When the aggregate output level is below potential output, nominal wages fall. When this happens, the short-run aggregate supply curve shifts rightward. This process stops only when the *SRAS* curve ends up at a point of both short-run and long-run macroeconomic equilibrium. The long-run effect of a decrease in the money supply, then, is that the aggregate price level decreases, but aggregate output is back at potential output. In the long run, a monetary contraction decreases the aggregate price level but has no effect on real GDP.

Monetary Neutrality

How much does a change in the money supply change the aggregate price level in the long run? The answer is that a change in the money supply leads to a proportional change in the aggregate price level in the long run. For example, if the money supply falls 25%, the aggregate price level falls 25% in the long run; if the money supply rises 50%, the aggregate price level rises 50% in the long run.

How do we know this? Consider the following thought experiment: suppose all prices in the economy—prices of final goods and services and also factor prices, such as nominal wage rates—double. And suppose the money supply doubles at the same time. What difference does this make to the economy in real terms? None. All real variables in the economy—such as real GDP and the real value of the money supply (the amount of goods and services it can buy)—are unchanged. So there is no reason for anyone to behave any differently.

We can state this argument in reverse: if the economy starts out in long-run macroeconomic equilibrium and the money supply changes, restoring long-run macroeconomic equilibrium requires restoring all real values to their original values. This includes restoring the real value of the money supply to its original level. So if the money supply falls 25%, the aggregate price level must fall 25%; if the money supply rises 50%, the price level must rise 50%; and so on.

According to the concept of **monetary neutrality**, changes in the money supply have no real effects on the economy.

This analysis demonstrates the concept known as **monetary neutrality**, in which changes in the money supply have no real effects on the economy. In the long run, the only effect of an increase in the money supply is to raise the aggregate price level by an equal percentage. Economists argue that *money is neutral in the long run.*

However, this is a good time to recall the dictum of John Maynard Keynes: "In the long run we are all dead." In the long run, changes in the money supply don't have any effect on real GDP, interest rates, or anything else except the price level. But it would be foolish to conclude from this that the Fed is irrelevant. Monetary policy does have powerful real effects on the economy in the short run, often making the difference between recession and expansion. And that matters a lot for society's welfare.

Changes in the Money Supply and the Interest Rate in the Long Run

In the short run, an increase in the money supply leads to a fall in the interest rate, and a decrease in the money supply leads to a rise in the interest rate. Module 29 explained that in the long run it's a different story: changes in the money supply don't affect the interest rate at all. Here we'll review that story and discuss the reasons behind it in greater detail.

Figure 32.2 The Long-Run Determination of the Interest Rate

In the short run, an increase in the money supply from $\overline{M}_1$ to $\overline{M}_2$ pushes the interest rate down from r_1 to r_2 and the economy moves to E_2, a short-run equilibrium. In the long run, however, the aggregate price level rises in proportion to the increase in the money supply, leading to an increase in money demand at any given interest rate in proportion to the increase in the aggregate price level, as shown by the shift from MD_1 to MD_2. The result is that the quantity of money demanded at any given interest rate rises by the same amount as the quantity of money supplied. The economy moves to long-run equilibrium at E_3 and the interest rate returns to r_1.

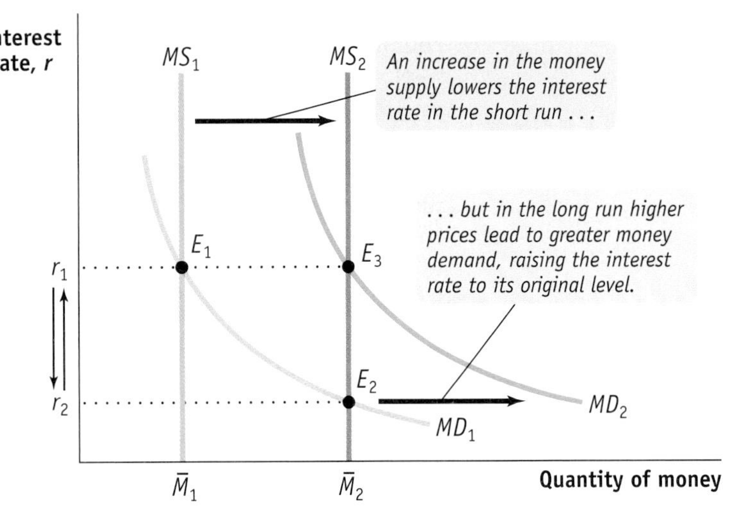

Figure 32.2 shows the money supply curve and the money demand curve before and after the Fed increases the money supply. We assume that the economy is initially at E_1, in long-run macroeconomic equilibrium at potential output, and with money supply $\overline{M}_1$. The initial equilibrium interest rate, determined by the intersection of the money demand curve MD_1 and the money supply curve MS_1, is r_1.

International Evidence of Monetary Neutrality

These days monetary policy is quite similar among wealthy countries. Each major nation (or, in the case of the euro, the eurozone) has a central bank that is insulated from political pressure. All of these central banks try to keep the aggregate price level roughly stable, which usually means inflation of at most 2% to 3% per year.

But if we look at a longer period and a wider group of countries, we see large differences in the growth of the money supply. Between 1970 and the present, the money supply rose only a few percentage points per year in countries such as Switzerland and the United States, but rose much more rapidly in some poorer countries, such as South Africa. These differences allow us to see whether it is really true that increases in the money supply, in the long run, lead to equal percentage increases in the aggregate price level.

The figure shows the annual percentage increases in the money supply and average annual increases in the aggregate price level—that is, the average rate of inflation—for a sample of countries during the period 1970–2012, with each point representing a country. If the relationship between increases in the money supply and changes in the aggregate price level were exact, the points would lie precisely on a 45-degree line. In fact, the relationship isn't exact because other factors besides money affect the aggregate price level. But the scatter of points clearly lies close to a 45-degree line, showing a more or less proportional relationship between money and the aggregate price level. That is, the data support the concept of monetary neutrality in the long run.

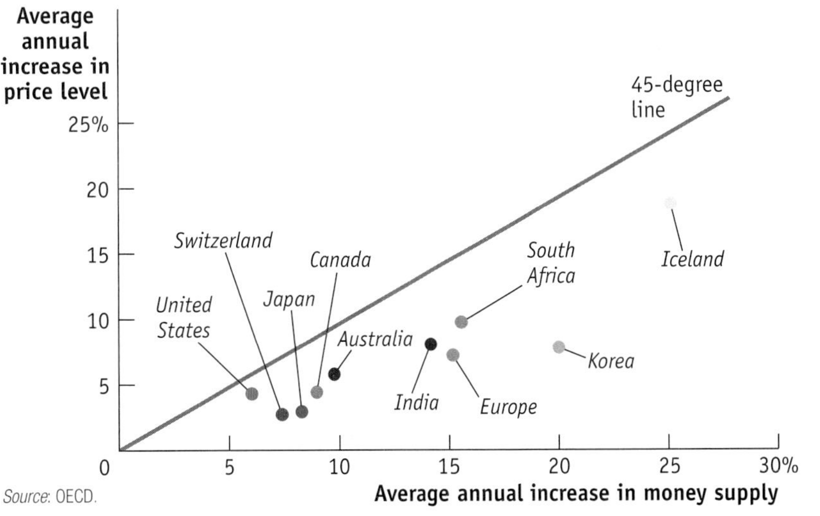

Source: OECD.

Now suppose that the money supply increases from $\overline{M}_1$ to $\overline{M}_2$. In the short run, the economy moves from E_1 to E_2 and the interest rate falls from r_1 to r_2. Over time, however, the aggregate price level rises, and this raises money demand, shifting the money demand curve rightward from MD_1 to MD_2. The economy moves to a new long-run equilibrium at E_3, and the interest rate rises to its original level of r_1.

How do we know that the long-run equilibrium interest rate is the original interest rate, r_1? Because the eventual increase in money demand is proportional to the increase in money supply, thus counteracting the initial downward effect on interest rates. Let's follow the chain of events to see why. With monetary neutrality, an increase in the money supply is matched by a proportional increase in the price level in the long run. If the money supply rises by, say, 50%, the price level will also rise by 50%. Changes in the price level, in turn, cause proportional changes in the demand for money. So a 50% increase in the money supply raises the aggregate price level by 50%, which increases the quantity of money demanded at any given interest rate by 50%. Thus, at the initial interest rate of r_1, the quantity of money demanded rises exactly as much as the money supply, and r_1 is again the equilibrium interest rate. In the long run, then, changes in the money supply do not affect the interest rate.

MODULE 32 Review

Check Your Understanding

1. Suppose the economy begins in long-run macroeconomic equilibrium. What is the long-run effect on the aggregate price level of a 5% increase in the money supply? Explain.

2. Suppose the economy begins in long-run macroeconomic equilibrium. What is the long-run effect on the interest rate of a 5% increase in the money supply? Explain.

Tackle the Test: Multiple-Choice Questions

1. In the long run, changes in the quantity of money affect which of the following?
   - **I.** real aggregate output
   - **II.** interest rates
   - **III.** the aggregate price level

   a. I only
   b. II only
   c. III only
   d. I and II only
   e. I, II, and III

2. An increase in the money supply will lead to which of the following in the short run?
   a. higher interest rates
   b. decreased investment spending
   c. decreased consumer spending
   d. increased aggregate demand
   e. lower real GDP

3. A 10% decrease in the money supply will change the aggregate price level in the long run by
   a. zero.
   b. less than 10%.
   c. 10%.
   d. 20%.
   e. more than 20%.

4. Monetary neutrality means that, in the long run, changes in the money supply
   a. cannot happen.
   b. have no effect on the economy.
   c. have no real effect on the economy.
   d. increase real GDP.
   e. change real interest rates.

5. A graph of percentage increases in the money supply and average annual increases in the price level for various countries provides evidence that
   a. changes in the two variables are exactly equal.
   b. the money supply and aggregate price level are unrelated.
   c. money neutrality holds only in wealthy countries.
   d. monetary policy is ineffective.
   e. money is neutral in the long run.

Tackle the Test: Free-Response Questions

1. Assume the central bank increases the quantity of money by 25%, even though the economy is initially in both short-run and long-run macroeconomic equilibrium. Describe the effects, in the short run and in the long run (giving numbers where possible), on the following:
   a. aggregate output
   b. the aggregate price level
   c. the real value of the money supply (its purchasing power for goods and services)
   d. the interest rate

Rubric for FRQ 1 (8 points)

1 point: Aggregate output rises in the short run.

1 point: Aggregate output falls back to potential output in the long run.

1 point: The aggregate price level rises in the short run (by less than 25%).

1 point: The aggregate price level rises by 25% in the long run.

1 point: The real value of the money supply increases in the short run.

1 point: The real value of the money supply does not change (relative to its original value) in the long run.

1 point: The interest rate falls in the short run.

1 point: The interest rate rises back to its original level in the long run.

2. a. Draw a correctly labeled graph of aggregate demand and aggregate supply showing an economy in long-run macroeconomic equilibrium.
   b. On your graph, show what happens in the short run if the central bank increases the money supply to pay off a government deficit. Explain.
   c. On your graph, show what will happen in the long run. Explain.
   (6 points)

RBZ unveils $100 trillion note

Herald Reporter

THE Reserve Bank of Zimbabwe has introduced a new family of trillion-dollar banknotes in denominations of $100 trillion, $50 trillion, $20 trillion and $10 trillion that go into circulation today, starting with the $10 trillion note.

The $20 trillion, $50 trillion and $100 trillion notes will be introduced gradually.

In a statement yesterday, the Reserve Bank of Zimbabwe said the notes would ensure that those in formal employment withdraw their salaries with minimal hassle.

"In a move meant to ensure that the public has access to their money from banks, the Reserve Bank of Zimbabwe has introduced a new family of banknotes which will gradually come into circulation, starting with the Z$10 trillion," read the statement from the RBZ.

With effect from January 12, workers can now withdraw their entire January salary in cash as long as they produce their current payslips.

The new notes have the same security features as the existing ones: a colour shift stripe with RBZ printed on it, the Zimbabwe Bird colour shift on the front, and see-through of the values on either side which are in perfect register.

The $10 trillion note has the image of the RBZ Building and the Conical Tower at the Great Zimbabwe National Monuments.

The $100 trillion note has the image of a buffalo and the Victoria Falls, the $50 trillion the Kariba Dam spilling and an elephant, while a mineworker drilling in an underground shaft and the GMB grain silos appear on the new $20 trillion note.

RBZ last week introduced $10 billion, $20 billion and $50 billion notes with a view to enabling workers to access their full salaries.

THE new $10 trillion, $20 trillion, $50 trillion and $100 trillion banknotes which go into circulation in phases beginning today. The introductio of the higher denomination notes is meant to ensure that those in formal employment can withdraw their salaries with minimal hassle.

DESMOND KWANDE/AFP/Getty Images

MODULE **33**

Types of Inflation, Disinflation, and Deflation

In this Module, you will learn to:

- Use the classical model of the price level
- Explain why efforts to collect an inflation tax by printing money can lead to high rates of inflation and even hyperinflation
- Define the types of inflation: cost-push and demand-pull

We have seen that monetary policy affects economic welfare in the short-run. Let's take a closer look at two phenomena that involve monetary policy: inflation and deflation.

Money and Inflation

In the summer of 2008, the African nation of Zimbabwe achieved the unenviable distinction of having the world's highest inflation rate: 11 million percent a year. Although the United States has not experienced the inflation levels that some countries have seen, in the late 1970s and early 1980s, consumer prices were rising at an annual rate as high as 13%. The policies that the Federal Reserve instituted to reduce this high level led to the deepest recession since the Great Depression. As we'll see later, moderate levels of inflation such as those experienced in the United States—even the double-digit inflation of the late 1970s—can have complex causes. Very high inflation, the type suffered by Zimbabwe, is associated with rapid increases in the money supply, but the causes of moderate inflation, the type experienced in the United States, are quite different.

To understand what causes inflation, we need to revisit the effect of changes in the money supply on the overall price level. Then we'll turn to the reasons why governments sometimes increase the money supply very rapidly.

The Classical Model of Money and Prices

Author's Image Ltd/Alamy

The Turkish currency is the *lira*. When Turkey made 1,000,000 "old" lira equivalent to 1 "new" lira, real GDP was unaffected because of the neutrality of money.

We learned that in the short run an increase in the money supply increases real GDP by lowering the interest rate and stimulating investment spending and consumer spending. However, in the long run, as nominal wages and other sticky prices rise, real GDP falls back to its original level. So in the long run, an increase in the money supply does not change real GDP. Instead, other things equal, it leads to an equal percentage rise in the overall price level; that is, the prices of all goods and services in the economy, including nominal wages and the prices of intermediate goods, rise by the same percentage as the money supply. And when the overall price level rises, the aggregate price level—the prices of all final goods and services—rises as well. As a result, in the long run, a change in the *nominal* money supply, M, leads to a change in the aggregate price level, P, that leaves the *real* quantity of money, M/P, at its original level. As a result, there is no long-run effect on aggregate demand or real GDP. For example, when Turkey dropped six zeros from its currency, the Turkish lira, in January 2005, Turkish real GDP did not change. The only thing that changed was the number of zeros in prices: instead of something costing 2,000,000 lira, it cost 2 lira.

To repeat, this is what happens in the long run. When analyzing large changes in the aggregate price level, however, macroeconomists often find it useful to ignore the distinction between the short run and the long run. Instead, they work with a simplified model in which the effect of a change in the money supply on the aggregate price level takes place instantaneously rather than over a long period of time. You might be concerned about this assumption given the emphasis we've placed on the difference between the short run and the long run. However, for reasons we'll explain shortly, this is a reasonable assumption to make in the case of high inflation.

According to the **classical model of the price level**, the real quantity of money is always at its long-run equilibrium level.

The simplified model in which the real quantity of money, M/P, is always at its long-run equilibrium level is known as the **classical model of the price level** because it was commonly used by "classical" economists prior to the influence of John Maynard Keynes. To understand the classical model and why it is useful in the context of high inflation, let's revisit the *AD–AS* model and what it says about the effects of an increase in the money supply. (Unless otherwise noted, we will always be referring to changes in the *nominal* supply of money.)

AP® Exam Tip

In the Keynesian model, sticky prices and wages slow the economy's process of self correction. Classical economists believe that prices and wages are flexible enough to allow the economy to correct itself quickly.

Figure 33.1 reviews the effects of an increase in the money supply according to the *AD–AS* model. The economy starts at E_1, a point of short-run and long-run

Figure 33.1 The Classical Model of the Price Level

Starting at E_1, an increase in the money supply shifts the aggregate demand curve rightward, as shown by the movement from AD_1 to AD_2. There is a new short-run macroeconomic equilibrium at E_2 and a higher price level at P_2. In the long run, nominal wages adjust upward and push the *SRAS* curve leftward to $SRAS_2$. The total percent increase in the price level from P_1 to P_3 is equal to the percent increase in the money supply. In the *classical model of the price level*, we ignore the transition period and think of the price level as rising to P_3 immediately. This is a good approximation under conditions of high inflation.

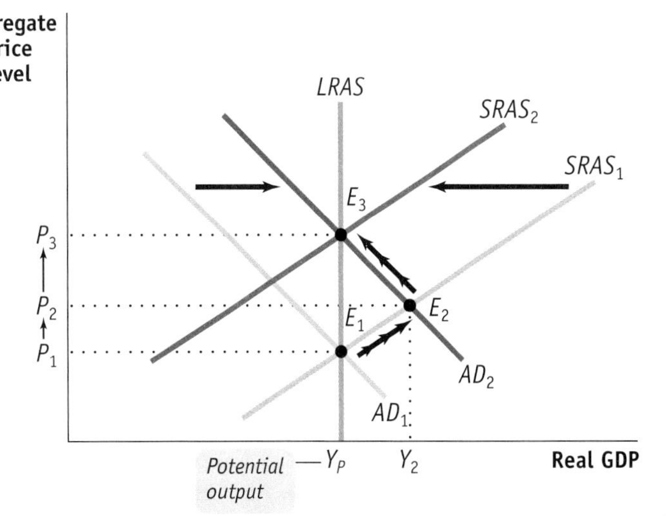

macroeconomic equilibrium. It lies at the intersection of the aggregate demand curve, AD_1, and the short-run aggregate supply curve, $SRAS_1$. It also lies on the long-run aggregate supply curve, *LRAS*. At E_1, the equilibrium aggregate price level is P_1.

Now suppose there is an increase in the money supply. This is an expansionary monetary policy, which shifts the aggregate demand curve to the right, to AD_2, and moves the economy to a new short-run macroeconomic equilibrium at E_2. Over time, however, nominal wages adjust upward in response to low unemployment and the rise in the aggregate price level, and the *SRAS* curve shifts to the left, to $SRAS_2$. The new long-run macroeconomic equilibrium is at E_3, and real GDP returns to its initial level. The long-run increase in the aggregate price level from P_1 to P_3 is proportional to the increase in the money supply. As a result, in the long run, changes in the money supply have no effect on the real quantity of money, M/P, or on real GDP. In the long run, money—as we learned—is *neutral.*

The classical model of the price level ignores the short-run movement from E_1 to E_2, assuming that the economy moves directly from one long-run equilibrium to another long-run equilibrium. In other words, it assumes that the economy moves directly from E_1 to E_3 and that real GDP never changes in response to a change in the money supply. In effect, in the classical model the effects of money supply changes are analyzed as if the short-run as well as the long-run aggregate supply curves were vertical.

In reality, this is a poor assumption during periods of low inflation. With a low inflation rate, it may take a while for workers and firms to react to a monetary expansion by raising wages and prices. In this scenario, some nominal wages and the prices of some goods are sticky in the short run. As a result, under low inflation there is an upward-sloping *SRAS* curve, and changes in the money supply can indeed change real GDP in the short run.

Denise Bober

With a low inflation rate, it may take a while for workers and firms to react to a monetary expansion by raising wages and prices.

But what about periods of high inflation? In the face of high inflation, economists have observed that the short-run stickiness of nominal wages and prices tends to vanish. Workers and businesses, sensitized to inflation, are quick to raise their wages and prices in response to changes in the money supply. This implies that under high inflation there is a quicker adjustment of wages and prices of intermediate goods than occurs in the case of low inflation. So the short-run aggregate supply curve shifts leftward more quickly and there is a more rapid return to long-run equilibrium under high inflation. As a result, the classical model of the price level is much more likely to be a good approximation of reality for economies experiencing persistently high inflation.

The consequence of this rapid adjustment of all prices in the economy is that in countries with persistently high inflation, changes in the money supply are quickly translated into changes in the inflation rate. Let's look at Zimbabwe. **Figure 33.2** shows the annual rate of growth in the money supply and the annual rate of change of consumer prices from 2003 through January 2008. As you can see, the surge in the growth rate of the money supply coincided closely with a roughly equal surge in the inflation rate. Note that to fit these very large percentage increases—exceeding 100,000%—onto the figure, we have drawn the vertical axis using a logarithmic scale.

In late 2008, Zimbabwe's inflation rate reached 231 million percent. What leads a country to increase its money supply so much that the result is an inflation rate in the millions of percent?

The Inflation Tax

Modern economies use fiat money—pieces of paper that have no intrinsic value but are accepted as a medium of exchange. In the United States and most other wealthy countries, the decision about how many pieces of paper to issue is placed in the hands of a central bank that is somewhat independent of the political process. However, this

Figure 33.2 Money Supply Growth and Inflation in Zimbabwe

This figure, drawn on a logarithmic scale, shows the annual rates of change of the money supply and the price level in Zimbabwe from 2003 through January 2008. The surges in the money supply were quickly reflected in a roughly equal surge in the price level.
Source: International Monetary Fund.

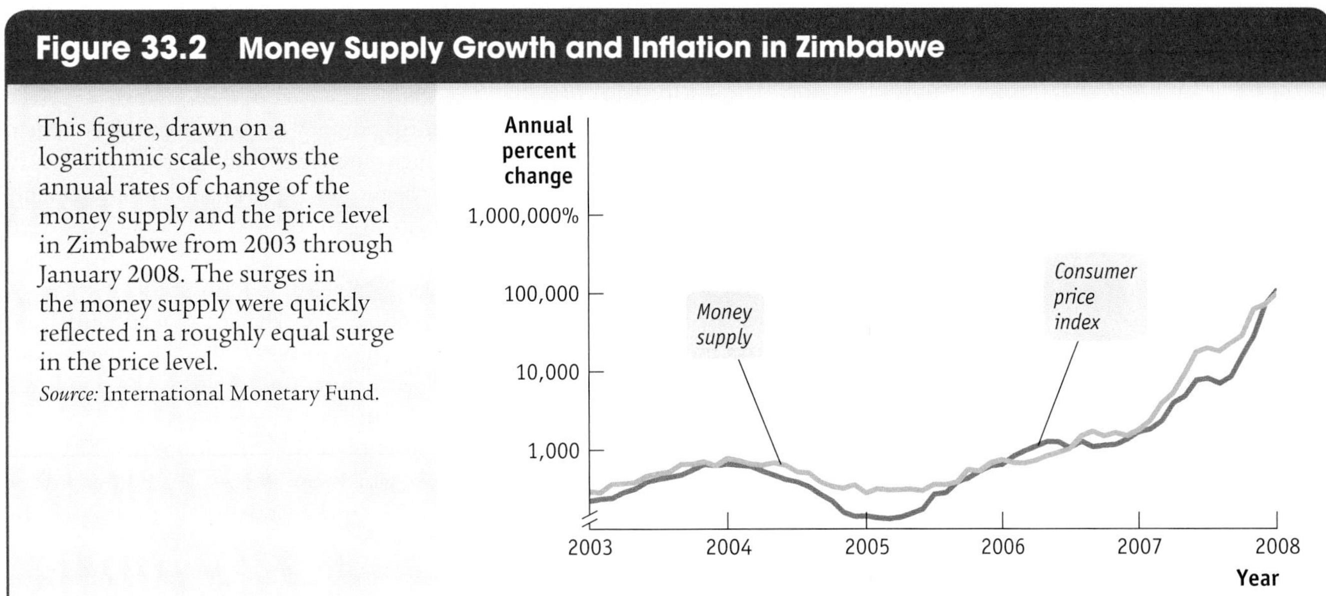

independence can always be taken away if politicians decide to seize control of monetary policy.

So what is to prevent a government from paying for some of its expenses not by raising taxes or borrowing but simply by printing money? Nothing. In fact, governments, including the U.S. government, do it all the time. How can the U.S. government do this, given that the Federal Reserve, not the U.S. Treasury, issues money? The answer is that the Treasury and the Federal Reserve work in concert. The Treasury issues debt to finance the government's purchases of goods and services, and the Fed *monetizes* the debt by creating money and buying the debt back from the public through open-market purchases of Treasury bills. In effect, the U.S. government can and does raise revenue by printing money.

For example, in February 2010, the U.S. monetary base—bank reserves plus currency in circulation—was $559 billion larger than it had been a year earlier. This occurred because, over the course of that year, the Federal Reserve had issued $559 billion in money or its electronic equivalent and put it into circulation mainly through open-market operations. To put it another way, the Fed created money out of thin air and used it to buy valuable government securities from the private sector. It's true that the U.S. government pays interest on debt owned by the Federal Reserve—but the Fed, by law, hands the interest payments it receives on government debt back to the Treasury, keeping only enough to fund its own operations. In effect, then, the Federal Reserve's actions enabled the government to pay off $559 billion in outstanding government debt by printing money.

An alternative way to look at this is to say that the right to print money is itself a source of revenue. Economists refer to the revenue generated by the government's right to print money as *seignorage,* an archaic term that goes back to the Middle Ages. It refers to the right to stamp gold and silver into coins, and charge a fee for doing so, that medieval lords—seigneurs, in France—reserved for themselves.

Seignorage accounts for only a tiny fraction (less than 1%) of the U.S. government's budget. Furthermore, concerns about seignorage don't have any influence on the Federal Reserve's decisions about how much money to print; the Fed is worried about inflation and unemployment, not revenue. But this hasn't always been true, even in the United States: both sides relied on seignorage to help cover budget deficits during the Civil War. And there have been many occasions in history when governments turned to their printing presses as a crucial source of revenue. According to the usual scenario, a government finds itself running a large budget deficit—and lacks either the competence or the political will to eliminate this deficit by raising taxes or cutting spending. Furthermore, the government can't borrow to cover the gap because potential lenders won't extend loans, given the fear that the government's weakness will continue and leave it unable to repay its debts.

In such a situation, governments end up printing money to cover the budget deficit. But by printing money to pay its bills, a government increases the quantity of money in circulation. And as we've just seen, increases in the money supply translate into equally large increases in the aggregate price level. So printing money to cover a budget deficit leads to inflation.

Who ends up paying for the goods and services the government purchases with newly printed money? The people who currently hold money pay. They pay because inflation erodes the purchasing power of their money holdings. In other words, a government imposes an **inflation tax**, a reduction in the value of the money held by the public, by printing money to cover its budget deficit and creating inflation.

An **inflation tax** is a reduction in the value of money held by the public caused by inflation.

It's helpful to think about what this tax represents. If the inflation rate is 5%, then a year from now $1 will buy goods and services worth only about $0.95 today. So a 5% inflation rate in effect imposes a tax rate of 5% on the value of all money held by the public.

But why would any government push the inflation tax to rates of hundreds or thousands of percent? We turn next to the process by which high inflation turns into explosive hyperinflation.

The Logic of Hyperinflation

Keystone/ Getty Images

In the 1920s, hyperinflation made German currency worth so little that children made kites from banknotes.

Inflation imposes a tax on individuals who hold money. And, like most taxes, it will lead people to change their behavior. In particular, when inflation is high, people have a strong incentive to either spend money quickly or acquire interest-bearing assets. The goal is to avoid holding money and thereby reduce the burden of the inflation tax. During the German hyperinflation, people began using eggs or lumps of coal as a medium of exchange. They did this because lumps of coal maintained their real value over time but money did not. Indeed, during the peak of German hyperinflation, people often burned paper money, which was less valuable than wood.

We are now prepared to understand how countries can get themselves into situations of extreme inflation. Suppose the government prints enough money to pay for a given quantity of goods and services each month. The increase in the money supply causes the inflation rate to rise, which means the government must print more money each month to buy the same quantity of goods and services. If the desire to reduce money holdings causes people to spend money faster than the government prints money, prices increase faster than the money supply. As a result, the government must accelerate the rate of growth of the money supply, which leads to an even higher rate of inflation. As this process becomes self-reinforcing, it can easily spiral out of control.

Here's an analogy: imagine a city government that tries to raise a lot of money with a special fee on taxi rides. The fee will raise the cost of taxi rides, and this will cause people to turn to substitutes, such as walking or taking the bus. As taxi use declines, the government finds that its tax revenue declines and it must impose a higher fee to raise the same amount of revenue as before. You can imagine the ensuing vicious circle: the government imposes fees on taxi rides, which leads to less taxi use, which causes the government to raise the fee on taxi rides, which leads to even less taxi use, and so on.

Shutterstock

Substitute the real money supply for taxi rides and the inflation rate for the increase in the fee on taxi rides, and you have the story of hyperinflation. A race develops between the government printing presses and the public: the presses churn out money at a faster and faster rate to try to compensate for the fact that the

Zimbabwe's Inflation

Zimbabwe offers a recent example of a country experiencing very high inflation. Figure 33.2 showed that surges in Zimbabwe's money supply growth were matched by almost simultaneous surges in its inflation rate. But looking at rates of change doesn't give a true feel for just how much prices went up.

The figure here shows Zimbabwe's consumer price index from 1999 to June 2008, with the 2000 level set equal to 100. As in Figure 33.2, we use a logarithmic scale, which lets us draw equal-sized percentage changes as the same size. Over the course of about nine years, consumer prices rose by approximately 4.5 trillion percent.

Why did Zimbabwe's government pursue policies that led to runaway inflation? The reason boils down to political instability, which in turn had its roots in Zimbabwe's history. Until the 1970s, Zimbabwe had been ruled by its small white minority; even after the shift to majority rule, many of the country's farms remained in the hands of whites. Eventually Robert Mugabe, Zimbabwe's president, tried to solidify his position by seizing these farms and turning them over to his political supporters. But because this seizure disrupted production, the result was to undermine the country's economy and its tax base. It became impossible for the country's government to balance its budget either by raising taxes or by cutting spending. At the same time, the regime's instability left Zimbabwe unable to borrow money in world markets. Like many others before it, Zimbabwe's government turned to the printing press to cover the gap—leading to massive inflation.

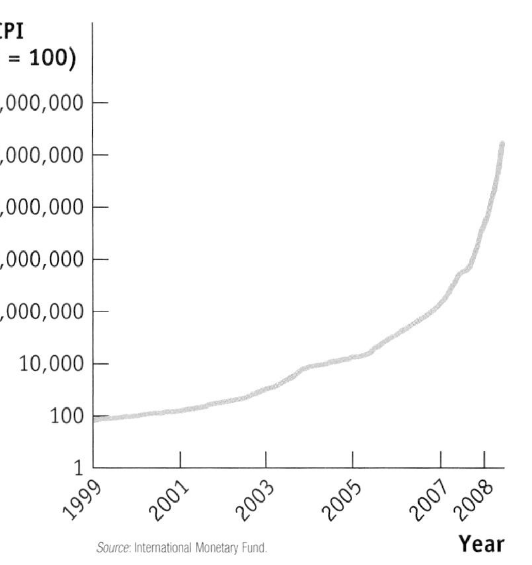

public is reducing its real money holdings. At some point the inflation rate explodes into hyperinflation, and people are unwilling to hold any money at all (and resort to trading in eggs and lumps of coal). The government is then forced to abandon its use of the inflation tax and shut down the printing presses.

Moderate Inflation and Disinflation

The governments of wealthy, politically stable countries like the United States and Britain don't find themselves forced to print money to pay their bills. Yet over the past 40 years, both countries, along with a number of other nations, have experienced uncomfortable episodes of inflation. In the United States, the inflation rate peaked at 13% in 1980. In Britain, the inflation rate reached 26% in 1975. Why did policy makers allow this to happen?

Using the aggregate demand and supply model, we can see that there are two possible changes that can lead to an increase in the aggregate price level: a decrease in aggregate supply or an increase in aggregate demand. Inflation that is caused by a significant increase in the price of an input with economy-wide importance is called **cost-push inflation**. For example, it is argued that the oil crisis in the 1970s led to an increase in energy prices in the United States, causing a leftward shift of the aggregate supply curve, increasing the aggregate price level. However, aside from crude oil, it is difficult to think of examples of inputs with economy-wide importance that experience significant price increases.

Cost-push inflation is inflation that is caused by a significant increase in the price of an input with economy-wide importance.

Demand-pull inflation is inflation that is caused by an increase in aggregate demand.

Inflation that is caused by an increase in aggregate demand is known as **demand-pull inflation**. When a rightward shift of the aggregate demand curve leads to an increase in the aggregate price level, the economy experiences demand-pull inflation. This is sometimes described by the phrase "too much money chasing too few goods," which means that the aggregate demand for goods and services is outpacing the aggregate supply and driving up the prices of goods.

AP® Exam Tip

Make sure you can graph and explain cost-push inflation and demand-pull inflation, as these are both tested frequently on the AP® exam. Remember that cost-push inflation is a leftward shift of *AS* and demand-pull inflation is a rightward shift of *AD*.

In the short run, policies that produce a booming economy also tend to lead to higher inflation, and policies that reduce inflation tend to depress the economy. This creates both temptations and dilemmas for governments.

Imagine yourself as a politician facing an election in a year, and suppose that inflation is fairly low at the moment. You might well be tempted to pursue expansionary policies that will push the unemployment rate down, as a way to please voters, even if your economic advisers warn that this will eventually lead to higher inflation. You might also be tempted to find different economic advisers, who will tell you not to worry: in politics, as in ordinary life, wishful thinking often prevails over realistic analysis.

Conversely, imagine yourself as a politician in an economy suffering from inflation. Your economic advisers will probably tell you that the only way to bring inflation down is to push the economy into a recession, which will lead to temporarily higher unemployment. Are you willing to pay that price? Maybe not.

This political asymmetry—inflationary policies often produce short-term political gains, but policies to bring inflation down carry short-term political costs—explains how countries with no need to impose an inflation tax sometimes end up with serious inflation problems. For example, that 26% rate of inflation in Britain was largely the result of the British government's decision in 1971 to pursue highly expansionary monetary and fiscal policies. Politicians disregarded warnings that these policies would be inflationary and were extremely reluctant to reverse course even when it became clear that the warnings had been correct.

But why do expansionary policies lead to inflation? To answer that question, we need to look first at the relationship between output and unemployment. Then we'll add inflation to the story in Module 34.

The Output Gap and the Unemployment Rate

Earlier we introduced the concept of *potential output*, the level of real GDP that the economy would produce once all prices had fully adjusted. Potential output typically grows steadily over time, reflecting long-run growth. However, as we learned from the aggregate demand–aggregate supply model, actual aggregate output fluctuates around potential output in the short run: a recessionary gap arises when actual aggregate output falls short of potential output; an inflationary gap arises when actual aggregate output exceeds potential output. Recall that the percentage difference between the actual level of real GDP and potential output is called the *output gap*. A positive or negative output gap occurs when an economy is producing more or less than what would be "expected" because all prices have not yet adjusted. And, as we've learned, wages are the prices in the labor market.

Meanwhile, we learned that the unemployment rate is composed of cyclical unemployment and natural unemployment, the portion of the unemployment rate unaffected by the business cycle. So there is a relationship between the unemployment rate and the output gap. This relationship is defined by two rules:

- When actual aggregate output is equal to potential output, the actual unemployment rate is equal to the natural rate of unemployment.
- When the output gap is positive (an inflationary gap), the unemployment rate is *below* the natural rate. When the output gap is negative (a recessionary gap), the unemployment rate is *above* the natural rate.

In other words, fluctuations of aggregate output around the long-run trend of potential output correspond to fluctuations of the unemployment rate around the natural rate.

This makes sense. When the economy is producing less than potential output—when the output gap is negative—it is not making full use of its productive resources.

Among the resources that are not fully used is labor, the economy's most important resource. So we would expect a negative output gap to be associated with unusually high unemployment. Conversely, when the economy is producing more than potential output, it is temporarily using resources at higher-than-normal rates. With this positive output gap, we would expect to see lower-than-normal unemployment.

Figure 33.3 confirms this rule. Panel (a) shows the actual and natural rates of unemployment, as estimated by the Congressional Budget Office (CBO). Panel (b) shows two series. One is cyclical unemployment: the difference between the actual unemployment rate and the CBO estimate of the natural rate of unemployment, measured on the left. The other is the CBO estimate of the output gap, measured on the right. To make the relationship clearer, the output gap series is inverted—shown upside down—so that the line goes down if actual output rises above potential output and up if actual output falls below potential output. As you can see, the two series move together quite closely, showing the strong relationship between the output gap and cyclical unemployment. Years of high cyclical unemployment, like 1982 or 2009, were also years of a strongly negative output gap. Years of low cyclical unemployment, like the late 1960s or 2000, were years of a strongly positive output gap.

Figure 33.3 Cyclical Unemployment and the Output Gap

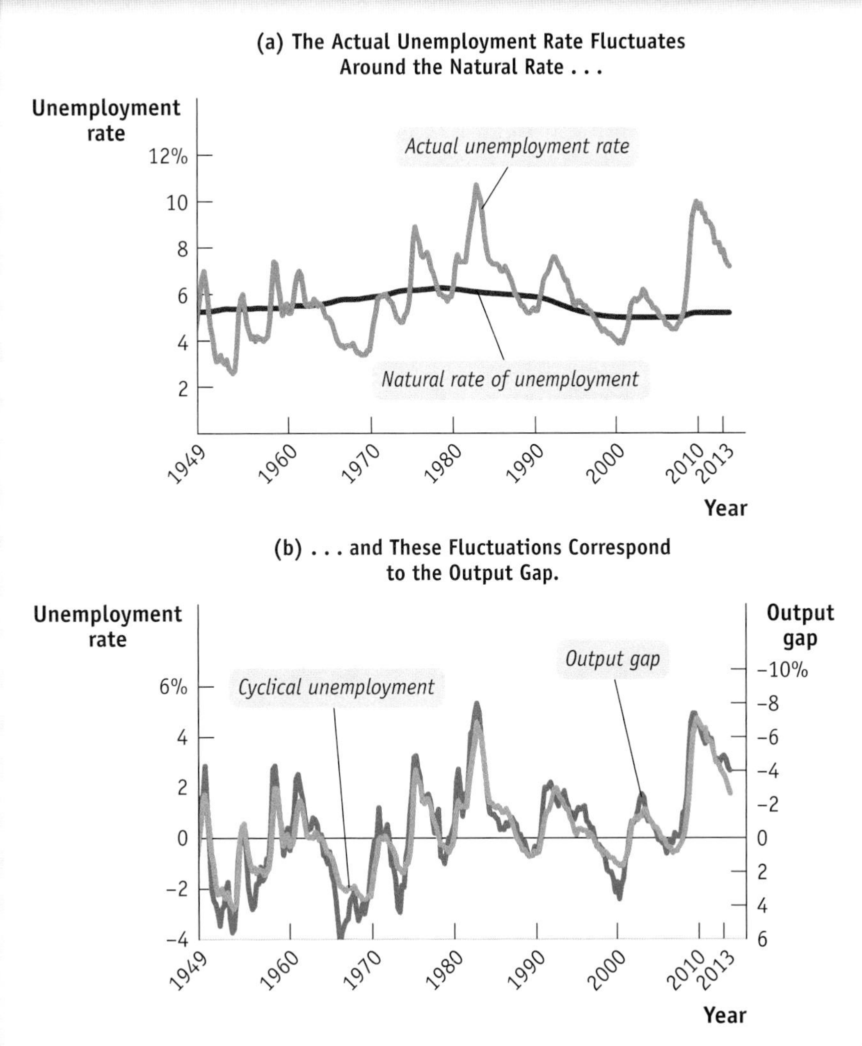

Panel (a) shows the actual U.S. unemployment rate from 1949 to 2013, together with the Congressional Budget Office (CBO) estimate of the natural rate of unemployment. The actual rate fluctuates around the natural rate, often for extended periods. Panel (b) shows cyclical unemployment—the difference between the actual unemployment rate and the natural rate of unemployment—and the output gap, also estimated by the CBO. The unemployment rate is measured on the left vertical axis, and the output gap is measured with an inverted scale on the right vertical axis. With an inverted scale, it moves in the same direction as the unemployment rate: when the output gap is positive, the actual unemployment rate is below its natural rate; when the output gap is negative, the actual unemployment rate is above its natural rate. The two series track one another closely, showing the strong relationship between the output gap and cyclical unemployment.

Sources: Congressional Budget Office; Bureau of Labor Statistics; Bureau of Economic Analysis.

MODULE 33 Review

Check Your Understanding

1. Explain why a large increase in the money supply causes a larger short-run increase in real GDP in an economy that previously had low inflation than in an economy that previously had high inflation. What does this say about situations in which the classical model of the price level applies?
2. Suppose that all wages and prices in an economy are indexed to inflation, meaning that they increase at the same rate as the price level. Can there still be an inflation tax?

Tackle the Test: Multiple-Choice Questions

1. The real quantity of money is
   - I. equal to M/P.
   - II. the money supply adjusted for inflation.
   - III. higher in the long run when the Fed buys government securities.
   - a. I only
   - b. II only
   - c. III only
   - d. I and II only
   - e. I, II, and III
2. In the classical model of the price level
   - a. only the short-run aggregate supply curve is vertical.
   - b. both the short-run and long-run aggregate supply curves are vertical.
   - c. only the long-run aggregate supply curve is vertical.
   - d. both the short-run aggregate demand and supply curves are vertical.
   - e. both the long-run aggregate demand and supply curves are vertical.
3. The classical model of the price level is most applicable in
   - a. the United States.
   - b. periods of high inflation.
   - c. periods of low inflation.
   - d. recessions.
   - e. depressions.
4. An inflation tax is
   - a. imposed by governments to offset price increases.
   - b. paid directly as a percentage of the sale price on purchases.
   - c. the result of a decrease in the value of money held by the public.
   - d. generally levied by states rather than the federal government.
   - e. higher during periods of low inflation.
5. Revenue generated by the government's right to print money is known as
   - a. seignorage.
   - b. an inflation tax.
   - c. hyperinflation.
   - d. fiat money.
   - e. monetary funds.

Tackle the Test: Free-Response Questions

1. Use a correctly labeled aggregate demand and aggregate supply graph to illustrate cost-push inflation. Give an example of what might cause cost-push inflation in the economy.

Rubric for FRQ 1 (9 points)

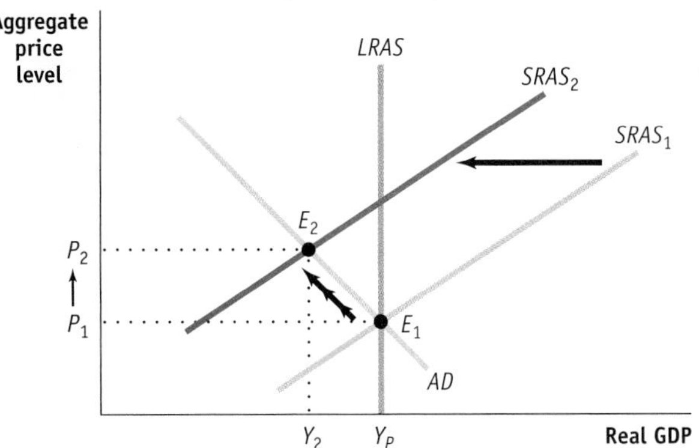

1 point: Graph labeled "Aggregate price level" or "*PL*" on the vertical axis and "Real GDP" on the horizontal axis

1 point: *AD* downward-sloping and labeled

1 point: *SRAS* upward-sloping and labeled

1 point: *LRAS* vertical and labeled

1 point: Potential output labeled at horizontal intercept of *LRAS*

1 point: Long-run macroeconomic equilibrium aggregate price level labeled on vertical axis at intersection of *SRAS*, *LRAS*, and *AD*

1 point: Leftward shift of the SRAS curve

1 point: Higher equilibrium aggregate price level at new intersection of *SRAS* and *AD*

1 point: This could be caused by anything that would shift the short-run aggregate supply curve to the left, such as an increase in the price of energy, labor, or another input with economy-wide importance.

2. Draw a correctly labeled aggregate demand and aggregate supply graph showing an economy in long-run macroeconomic equilibrium. On your graph, show the effect of an increase in the money supply, according to the classical model of the price level.
(4 points)

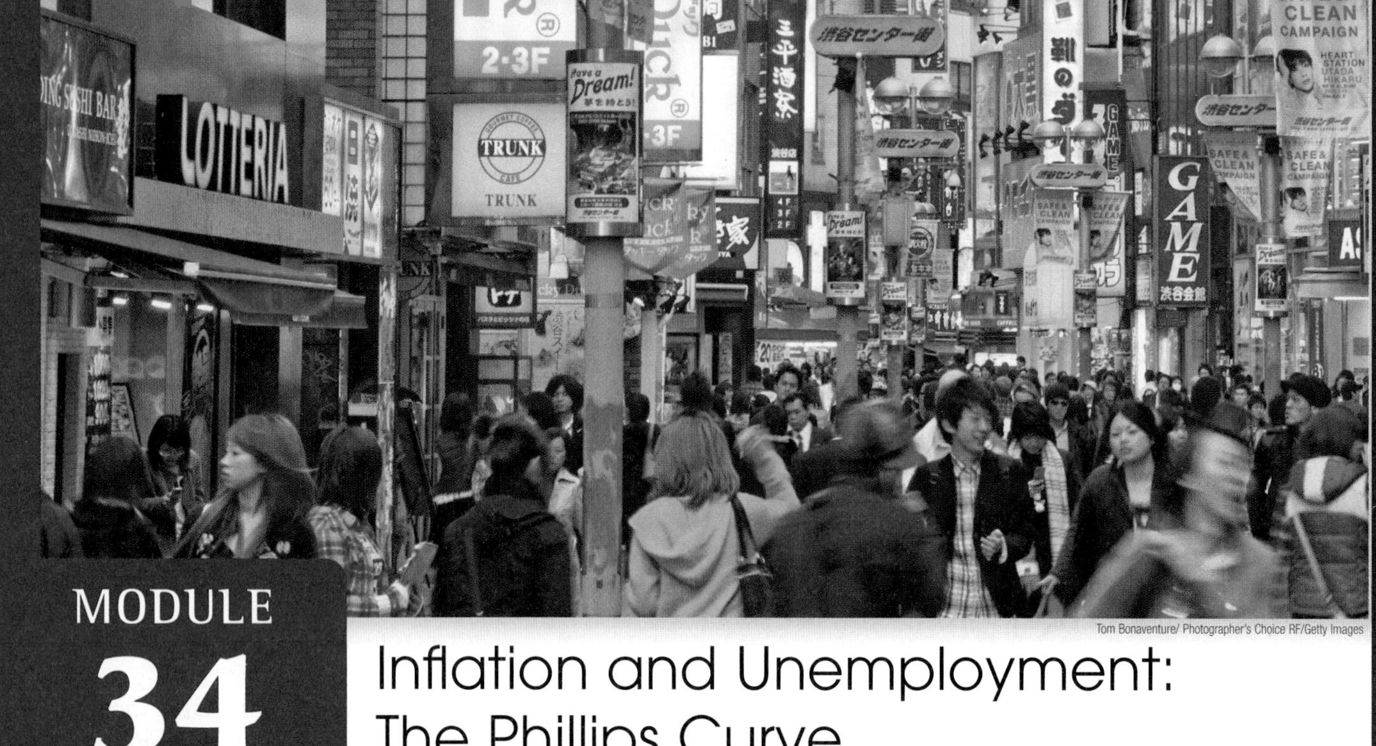

Tom Bonaventure/ Photographer's Choice RF/Getty Images

MODULE 34 Inflation and Unemployment: The Phillips Curve

In this Module, you will learn to:

- Use the Phillips curve to show the nature of the short-run trade-off between inflation and unemployment
- Explain why there is no long-run trade-off between inflation and unemployment
- Discuss why expansionary policies are limited due to the effects of expected inflation
- Explain why even moderate levels of inflation can be hard to end
- Identify the problems with deflation that lead policy makers to prefer a low but positive inflation rate

The Short-Run Phillips Curve

We've just seen that expansionary policies lead to a lower unemployment rate. Our next step in understanding the temptations and dilemmas facing governments is to show that there is a short-run trade-off between unemployment and inflation—lower unemployment tends to lead to higher inflation, and vice versa. The key concept is that of the *Phillips curve.*

The origins of this concept lie in a famous 1958 paper by the New Zealand–born economist Alban W. H. Phillips. Looking at historical data for Britain, he found that when the unemployment rate was high, the wage rate tended to fall, and when the unemployment rate was low, the wage rate tended to rise. Using data from Britain, the United States, and elsewhere, other economists soon found a similar apparent relationship between the unemployment rate and the rate of inflation—that is, the rate of change in the aggregate price level. For example, **Figure 34.1** shows the U.S. unemployment rate and the rate of consumer price inflation over each subsequent year from 1955 to 1968, with each dot representing one year's data.

The **short-run Phillips curve** represents the negative short-run relationship between the unemployment rate and the inflation rate.

Looking at evidence like Figure 34.1, many economists concluded that there is a negative short-run relationship between the unemployment rate and the inflation rate, represented by the **short-run Phillips curve**, or *SRPC.* (We'll explain the difference between the short-run and the long-run Phillips curve soon.) **Figure 34.2** shows a hypothetical short-run Phillips curve.

Figure 34.1 Unemployment and Inflation, 1955–1968

Each dot shows the average U.S. unemployment rate for one year and the percentage increase in the consumer price index over the subsequent year. Data like this lay behind the initial concept of the Phillips curve.

Source: Bureau of Labor Statistics.

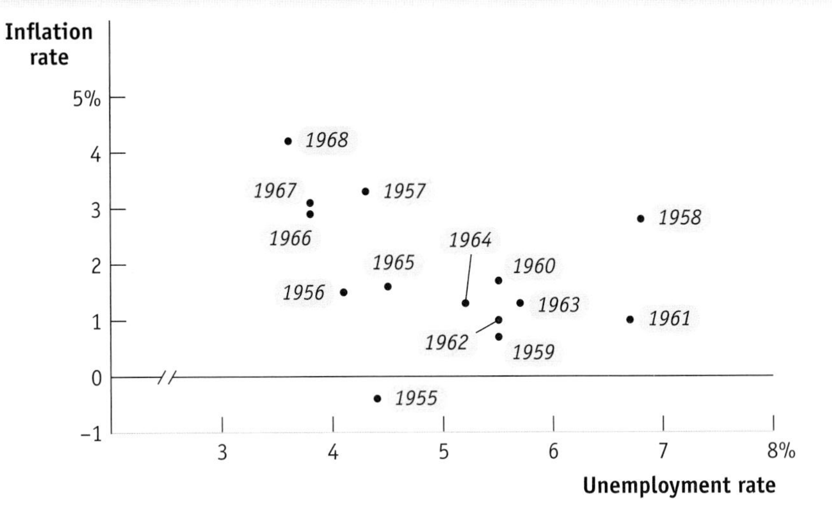

We can better understand the shape of the Phillips curve by examining its ties to the *AD–AS* model. Panel (a) of **Figure 34.3** on the next page shows how changes in the aggregate price level and the output gap depend on changes in aggregate demand. Assume that in year 1 the aggregate demand curve is AD_1, the long-run aggregate supply curve is *LRAS*, and the short-run aggregate supply curve is *SRAS*. The initial macroeconomic equilibrium is at E_1, where the price level is 100 and real GDP is $10 trillion. Notice that at E_1 real GDP is equal to potential output, so the output gap is zero.

Now consider what happens if aggregate demand shifts rightward to AD_2 and the economy moves to E_2. At E_2, Real GDP is $10.4 trillion, $0.4 trillion more than potential output—forming a 4% output gap. Meanwhile, at E_2 the aggregate price level has risen to 102—a 2% increase. So panel (a) indicates that in this example a zero output gap is associated with zero inflation and a 4% output gap is associated with 2% inflation.

Panel (b) shows what this implies for the relationship between unemployment and inflation: an increase in aggregate demand leads to a fall in the unemployment rate and

Figure 34.2 The Short-Run Phillips Curve

The short-run Phillips curve, *SRPC*, slopes downward because the relationship between the unemployment rate and the inflation rate is negative.

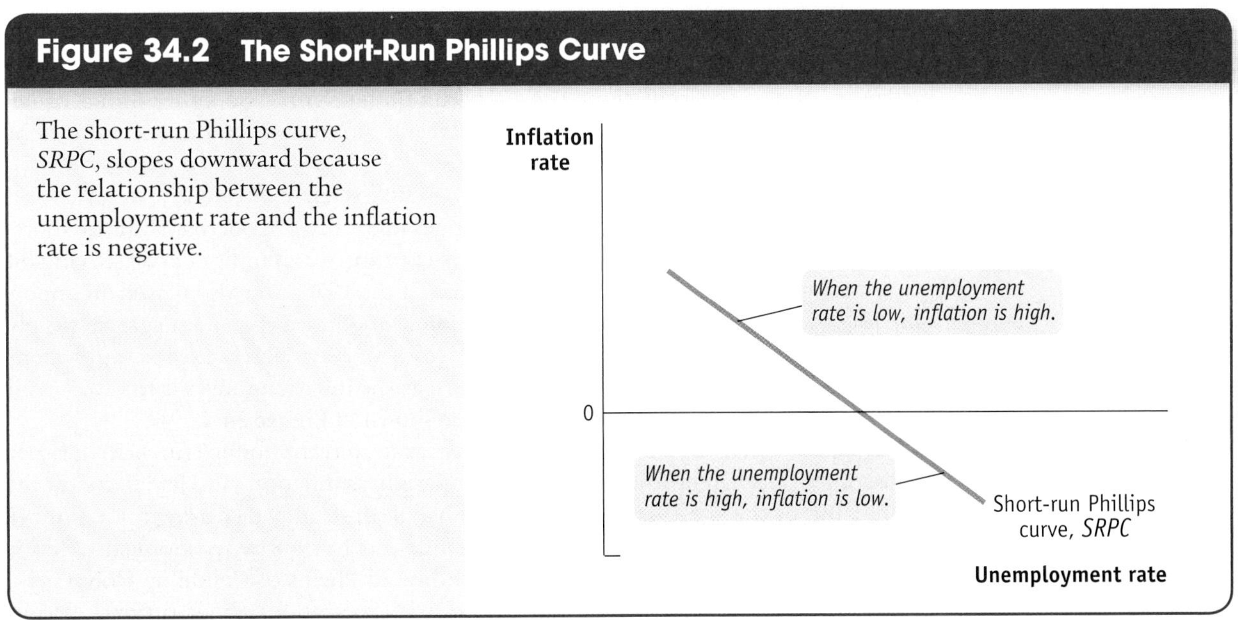

Figure 34.3 The *AD-AS* Model and the Short-Run Phillips Curve

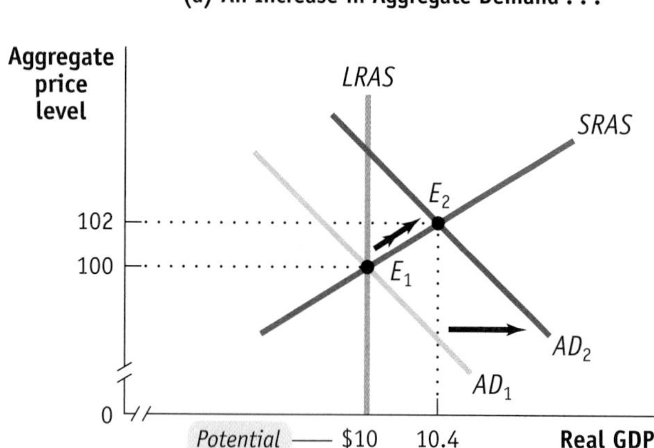

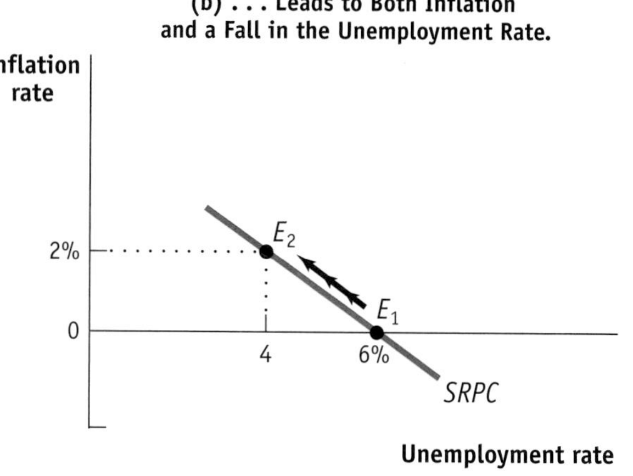

Shifts in aggregate demand lead to movements along the Phillips curve. In panel (a), the economy is initially in equilibrium at E_1, with the aggregate price level at 100 and aggregate output at \$10 trillion, which we assume is potential output. Now consider two possibilities. If the aggregate demand curve remains at AD_1, there is an output gap of zero and 0% inflation. If the aggregate demand curve shifts out to AD_2, the positive output gap reduces unemployment to 4%, and inflation rises to 2%. Assuming that the natural rate of unemployment is 6%, the implications for unemployment and inflation are shown in panel (b): with aggregate demand at AD_1, 6% unemployment and 0% inflation will result; if aggregate demand increases to AD_2, 4% unemployment and 2% inflation will result.

an increase in the inflation rate. Assume that the natural rate of unemployment is 6% and that a rise of 1 percentage point in the output gap causes a fall of ½ percentage point in the unemployment rate (this is a predicted relationship between the output gap and the unemployment rate known as *Okun's law*). Then E_1 and E_2 in panel (a) correspond to E_1 and E_2 in panel (b). At E_1, the unemployment rate is 6% and the inflation rate is 0%. At E_2, the unemployment rate is 4%, because an output gap of 4% reduces the unemployment rate by $4\% \times 0.5 = 2\%$ below its natural rate of 6%—and the inflation rate is 2%. This is an example of the negative relationship between unemployment and inflation.

Going in the other direction, a decrease in aggregate demand leads to a rise in the unemployment rate and a fall in the inflation rate. This corresponds to a movement downward and to the right along the short-run Phillips curve. So, other things equal, increases and decreases in aggregate demand result in movements to the left and right along the short-run Phillips curve.

Changes in aggregate supply also affect the Phillips curve. Previously, we discussed the effect of *supply shocks,* such as sudden changes in the price of oil, that shift the short-run aggregate supply curve. Such shocks shift the short-run Phillips curve: surging oil prices were an important factor in the inflation of the 1970s and also played an important role in the acceleration of inflation in 2007–2008. In general, a negative supply shock shifts *SRPC* up, as the inflation rate increases for every level of the unemployment rate, and a positive supply shock shifts it down as the inflation rate falls for every level of the unemployment rate. Both outcomes are shown in **Figure 34.4**.

But supply shocks are not the only factors that can shift the Phillips curve. In the early 1960s, Americans had little experience with inflation, as inflation rates had been low for decades. But by the late 1960s, after inflation had been steadily increasing for a number of years, Americans had come to expect future inflation. In 1968 two economists—Milton Friedman of the University of Chicago and Edmund Phelps of Columbia University—independently set forth a crucial hypothesis: that expectations about future inflation

Figure 34.4 The Short-Run Phillips Curve and Supply Shocks

A negative supply shock shifts the *SRPC* up, and a positive supply shock shifts the *SRPC* down.

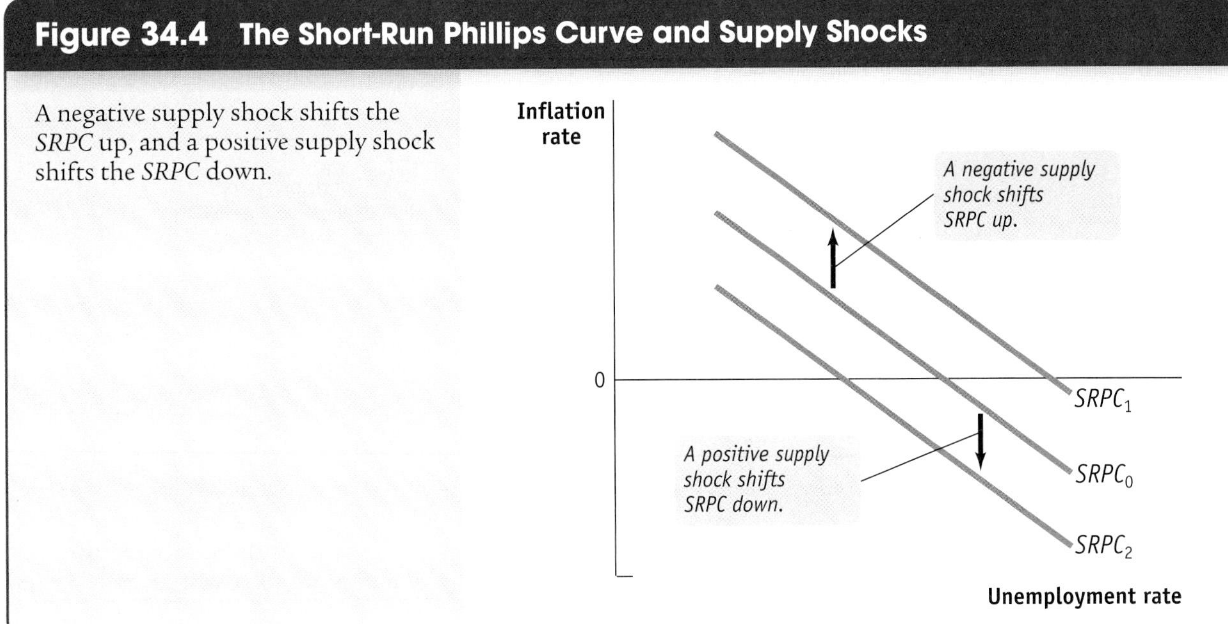

directly affect the present inflation rate. Today most economists accept that the *expected inflation rate*—the rate of inflation that employers and workers expect in the near future—is the most important factor, other than the unemployment rate, affecting inflation.

Inflation Expectations and the Short-Run Phillips Curve

The expected rate of inflation is the rate that employers and workers expect in the near future. One of the crucial discoveries of modern macroeconomics is that changes in the expected rate of inflation affect the short-run trade-off between unemployment and inflation and shift the short-run Phillips curve.

Why do changes in expected inflation affect the short-run Phillips curve? Put yourself in the position of a worker or employer about to sign a contract setting the worker's wages over the next year. For a number of reasons, the wage rate they agree to will be higher if everyone expects high inflation (including rising wages) than if everyone expects prices to be stable. The worker will want a wage rate that takes into account future declines in the purchasing power of earnings. He or she will also want a wage rate that won't fall behind the wages of other workers. And the employer will be more willing to agree to a wage increase now if hiring workers later will be even more expensive. Also, rising prices will make paying a higher wage rate more affordable for the employer because the employer's output will sell for more.

For these reasons, an increase in expected inflation shifts the short-run Phillips curve upward: the actual rate of inflation at any given unemployment rate is higher when the expected inflation rate is higher. In fact, macroeconomists believe that the relationship between changes in expected inflation and changes in actual inflation is one-to-one. That is, when the expected inflation rate increases, the actual inflation rate at any given unemployment rate will increase by the same amount. When the expected inflation rate falls, the actual inflation rate at any given level of unemployment will fall by the same amount.

Figure 34.5 on the next page shows how the expected rate of inflation affects the short-run Phillips curve. First, suppose that the expected rate of inflation is 0%. $SRPC_0$ is the short-run Phillips curve when the public expects 0% inflation. According to $SRPC_0$, the actual inflation rate will be 0% if the unemployment rate is 6%; it will be 2% if the unemployment rate is 4%.

Alternatively, suppose the expected rate of inflation is 2%. In that case, employers and workers will build this expectation into wages and prices: at any given unemployment

AP® Exam Tip

Inflationary expectations shift the short-run *AS* curve as well as the short-run Phillips curve.

Figure 34.5 Expected Inflation and the Short-Run Phillips Curve

An increase in expected inflation shifts the short-run Phillips curve up. $SRPC_0$ is the initial short-run Phillips curve with an expected inflation rate of 0%; $SRPC_2$ is the short-run Phillips curve with an expected inflation rate of 2%. Each additional percentage point of expected inflation raises the actual inflation rate at any given unemployment rate by 1 percentage point.

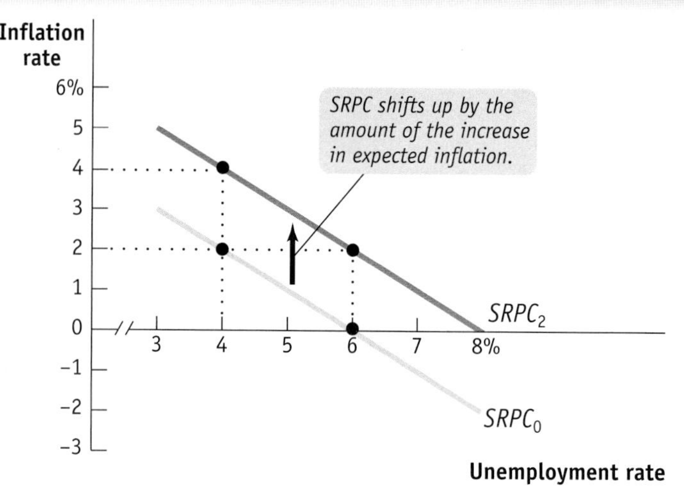

FYI From the Scary Seventies to the Nifty Nineties

Figure 34.1 showed that the American experience during the 1950s and 1960s supported the belief in the existence of a short-run Phillips curve for the U.S. economy, with a short-run trade-off between unemployment and inflation.

After 1969, however, that relationship appeared to fall apart according to the data. The figure here plots the course of U.S. unemployment and inflation rates from 1961 to 1990. As you can see, the course looks more like a tangled piece of yarn than like a smooth curve.

Through much of the 1970s and early 1980s, the economy suffered from a combination of above-average unemployment rates coupled with inflation rates unprecedented in modern American history. This condition came to be known as *stagflation*—for stagnation combined with high inflation. In the late 1990s, by contrast, the economy was experiencing a blissful combination of low unemployment and low inflation. What explains these developments?

Part of the answer can be attributed to a series of negative supply shocks that the U.S. economy suffered during the 1970s. The price of oil, in particular, soared as wars and revolutions in the Middle East led to a reduction in oil supplies and as oil-exporting countries deliberately curbed production to drive up prices. Compounding the oil price shocks, there was also a slowdown in labor productivity growth. Both of these factors shifted the short-run Phillips curve upward. During the 1990s, by contrast, supply shocks were positive. Prices of oil and other raw materials were generally falling, and productivity growth accelerated. As a result, the short-run Phillips curve shifted downward.

Equally important, however, was the role of expected inflation. As mentioned earlier, inflation accelerated during the 1960s. During the 1970s, the public came to expect high inflation, and this also shifted the short-run Phillips curve up. It took a sustained and costly effort during the 1980s to get inflation back down. The result, however, was that expected inflation was very low by the late 1990s, allowing actual inflation to be low even with low rates of unemployment.

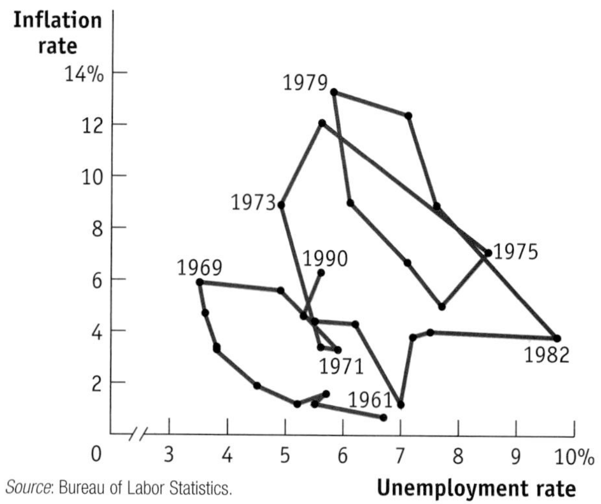

Source: Bureau of Labor Statistics.

rate, the actual inflation rate will be 2 percentage points higher than it would be if people expected 0% inflation. $SRPC_2$, which shows the Phillips curve when the expected inflation rate is 2%, is $SRPC_0$ shifted upward by 2 percentage points at every level of unemployment. According to $SRPC_2$, the actual inflation rate will be 2% if the unemployment rate is 6%; it will be 4% if the unemployment rate is 4%.

What determines the expected rate of inflation? In general, people base their expectations about inflation on experience. If the inflation rate has hovered around 0% in the last few years, people will expect it to be around 0% in the near future. But if the inflation rate has averaged around 5% lately, people will expect inflation to be around 5% in the near future.

Since expected inflation is an important part of the modern discussion about the short-run Phillips curve, you might wonder why it was not in the original formulation of the Phillips curve. The answer lies in history. Think back to what we said about the early 1960s: at that time, people were accustomed to low inflation rates and reasonably expected that future inflation rates would also be low. It was only after 1965 that persistent inflation became a fact of life. So only then did it become clear that expected inflation would play an important role in price-setting.

Inflation and Unemployment in the Long Run

The short-run Phillips curve says that at any given point in time there is a trade-off between unemployment and inflation. According to this view, policy makers have a choice: they can choose to accept the price of high inflation in order to achieve low unemployment, or they can reject high inflation and pay the price of high unemployment. In fact, during the 1960s many economists believed that this trade-off represented a real choice.

However, this view was greatly altered by the later recognition that expected inflation affects the short-run Phillips curve. In the short run, expectations often diverge from reality. In the long run, however, any consistent rate of inflation will be reflected in expectations. If inflation is consistently high, as it was in the 1970s, people will come to expect more of the same; if inflation is consistently low, as it has been in recent years, that, too, will become part of expectations. So what does the trade-off between inflation and unemployment look like in the long run, when actual inflation is incorporated into expectations? Most macroeconomists believe that, in fact, there is no long-run trade-off. That is, it is not possible to achieve lower unemployment in the long run by accepting higher inflation. To see why, we need to introduce another concept: the *long-run Phillips curve.*

The Long-Run Phillips Curve

Figure 34.6 on the next page reproduces the two short-run Phillips curves from Figure 34.5, $SRPC_0$ and $SRPC_2$. It also adds an additional short-run Phillips curve, $SRPC_4$, representing a 4% expected rate of inflation. In a moment, we'll explain the significance of the vertical long-run Phillips curve, *LRPC.*

Suppose that the economy has had a 0% inflation rate in the past. In that case, the current short-run Phillips curve will be $SRPC_0$, reflecting a 0% expected inflation rate. If the unemployment rate is 6%, the actual inflation rate will be 0%.

Also suppose that policy makers decide to trade off lower unemployment for a higher rate of inflation. They use monetary policy, fiscal policy, or both to drive the unemployment rate down to 4%. This puts the economy at point *A* on $SRPC_0$, leading to an actual inflation rate of 2%.

Over time, the public will come to expect a 2% inflation rate. *This increase in inflationary expectations will shift the short-run Phillips curve upward* to $SRPC_2$. Now, when the unemployment rate is 6%, the actual inflation rate will be 2%. Given this new short-run Phillips curve, policies adopted to keep the unemployment rate at 4% will lead to a 4% actual inflation rate—point *B* on $SRPC_2$—rather than point *A* with a 2% actual inflation rate.

Figure 34.6 The NAIRU and the Long-Run Phillips Curve

$SRPC_0$ is the short-run Phillips curve when the expected inflation rate is 0%. At a 4% unemployment rate, the economy is at point *A* with an actual inflation rate of 2%. The higher inflation rate will be incorporated into expectations, and the *SRPC* will shift upward to $SRPC_2$. If policy makers act to keep the unemployment rate at 4%, the economy will be at *B* and the actual inflation rate will rise to 4%. Inflationary expectations will be revised upward again, and *SRPC* will shift to $SRPC_4$. At a 4% unemployment rate, the economy will be at *C* and the actual inflation rate will rise to 6%. Here, an unemployment rate of 6% is the NAIRU, or nonaccelerating inflation rate of unemployment. As long as unemployment is at the NAIRU, the actual inflation rate will match expectations and remain constant. An unemployment rate below 6% requires ever-accelerating inflation. The long-run Phillips curve, *LRPC*, which passes through E_0, E_2, and E_4, is vertical: no long-run trade-off between unemployment and inflation exists.

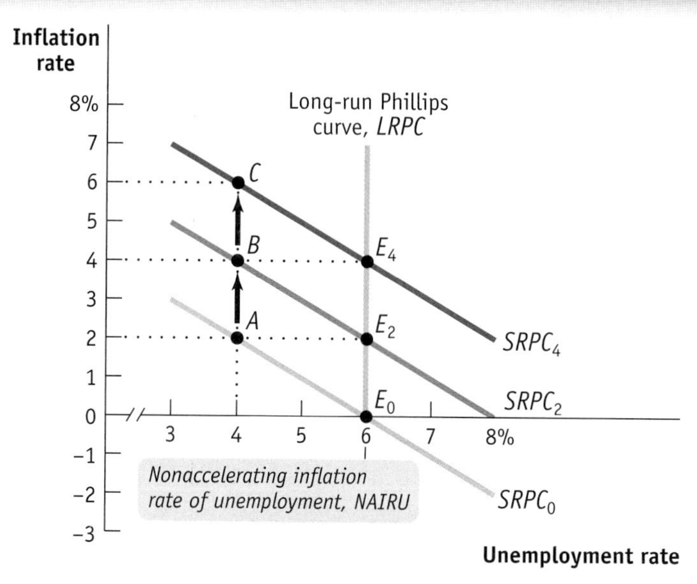

The **nonaccelerating inflation rate of unemployment**, or **NAIRU**, is the unemployment rate at which inflation does not change over time.

The **long-run Phillips curve** shows the relationship between unemployment and inflation after expectations of inflation have had time to adjust to experience.

Eventually, the 4% actual inflation rate gets built into expectations about the future inflation rate, and the short-run Phillips curve shifts upward yet again to $SRPC_4$. To keep the unemployment rate at 4% would now require accepting a 6% actual inflation rate, point *C* on $SRPC_4$, and so on. In short, a persistent attempt to trade off lower unemployment for higher inflation leads to *accelerating* inflation over time.

To avoid accelerating inflation over time, the unemployment rate must be high enough that the actual rate of inflation matches the expected rate of inflation. This is the situation at E_0 on $SRPC_0$: when the expected inflation rate is 0% and the unemployment rate is 6%, the actual inflation rate is 0%. It is also the situation at E_2 on $SRPC_2$: when the expected inflation rate is 2% and the unemployment rate is 6%, the actual inflation rate is 2%. And it is the situation at E_4 on $SRPC_4$: when the expected inflation rate is 4% and the unemployment rate is 6%, the actual inflation rate is 4%. As we'll learn shortly, this relationship between accelerating inflation and the unemployment rate is known as the *natural rate hypothesis.*

The unemployment rate at which inflation does not change over time—6% in Figure 34.6—is known as the **nonaccelerating inflation rate of unemployment**, or **NAIRU** for short. Keeping the unemployment rate below the NAIRU leads to ever-accelerating inflation and cannot be maintained. Most macroeconomists believe that there is a NAIRU and that there is no long-run trade-off between unemployment and inflation.

We can now explain the significance of the vertical line *LRPC*. It is the **long-run Phillips curve**, which shows the relationship between unemployment and inflation in the long run, after expectations of inflation have had time to adjust to experience. It is vertical because any unemployment rate below the NAIRU leads to ever-accelerating inflation. In other words, the long-run Phillips curve shows that there are limits to expansionary policies because an unemployment rate below the NAIRU cannot be maintained in the long run. Moreover, there is a corresponding point we have not yet emphasized: any unemployment rate above the NAIRU leads to decelerating inflation.

Andy Sacks/Stone/Getty Images

The nonaccelerating inflation rate of unemployment, or NAIRU, is the unemployment rate at which inflation does not change over time.

The Natural Rate of Unemployment, Revisited

Recall the concept of the natural rate of unemployment, the portion of the unemployment rate unaffected by the swings of the business cycle. Now we have introduced the concept of the NAIRU. How do these two concepts relate to each other?

The answer is that the NAIRU is another name for the natural rate. The level of unemployment the economy "needs" in order to avoid accelerating inflation is equal to the natural rate of unemployment.

In fact, economists estimate the natural rate of unemployment by looking for evidence about the NAIRU from the behavior of the inflation rate and the unemployment rate over the course of the business cycle. For example, the way major European countries learned, to their dismay, that their natural rates of unemployment were 9% or more was through unpleasant experience. In the late 1980s, and again in the late 1990s, European inflation began to accelerate as European unemployment rates, which had been above 9%, began to fall, approaching 8%.

In Figure 33.3 we cited Congressional Budget Office estimates of the U.S. natural rate of unemployment. The CBO has a model that predicts changes in the inflation

The Great Disinflation of the 1980s

As we've mentioned, the United States ended the 1970s with a high rate of inflation, at least by its own peacetime historical standards—13% in 1980. Part of this inflation was the result of one-time events, especially a world oil crisis. But expectations of future inflation at 10% or more per year appeared to be firmly embedded in the economy.

By the mid-1980s, however, inflation was running at about 4% per year. Panel (a) of the figure shows the annual rate of change in the "core" consumer price index (CPI)—also called the *core inflation rate*. This index, which excludes volatile energy and food prices, is widely regarded as a better indicator of underlying inflation trends than the overall CPI. By this measure, inflation fell from about 12% at the end of the 1970s to about 4% by the mid-1980s.

How was this disinflation achieved? At great cost. Beginning in late 1979, the Federal Reserve imposed strongly contractionary monetary policies, which pushed the economy into its worst recession since the Great Depression. Panel (b) shows the Congressional Budget Office estimate of the U.S. output gap from 1979 to 1989: by 1982, actual output was 7% below potential output, corresponding to an unemployment rate of more than 9%. Aggregate output didn't get back to potential output until 1987.

Our analysis of the Phillips curve tells us that a temporary rise in unemployment, like that of the 1980s, is needed to break the cycle of inflationary expectations. Once expectations of inflation are reduced, the economy can return to the natural rate of unemployment at a lower inflation rate. And that's just what happened.

At what cost? If you add up the output gaps over 1980–1987, you find that the economy sacrificed approximately 18% of an average year's output over the period. If we had to do the same thing today, that would mean giving up roughly $2.6 trillion worth of goods and services.

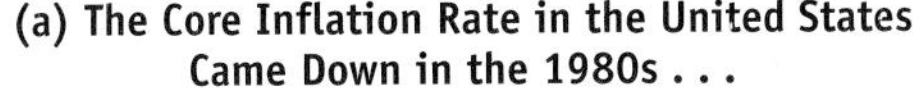

(a) The Core Inflation Rate in the United States Came Down in the 1980s . . .

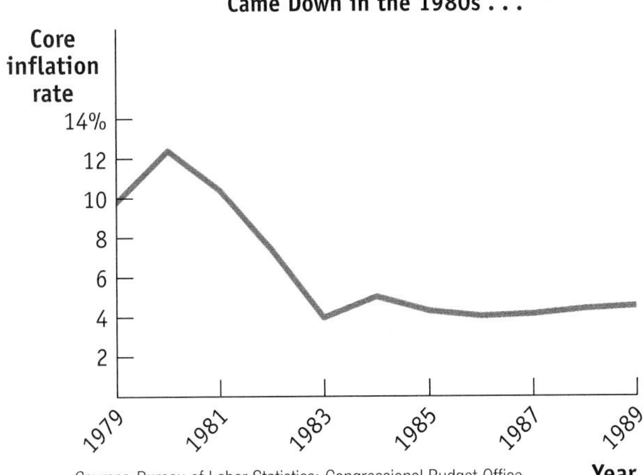

Sources: Bureau of Labor Statistics; Congressional Budget Office.

(b) . . . but Only at the Expense of a Huge Sacrifice of Output and High Unemployment.

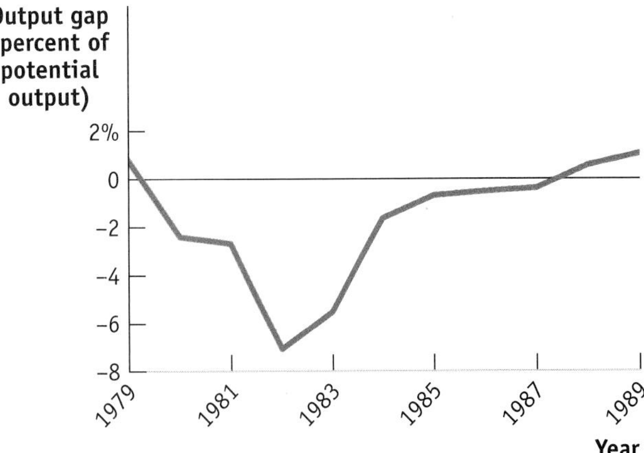

rate based on the deviation of the actual unemployment rate from the natural rate. Given data on actual unemployment and inflation, this model can be used to deduce estimates of the natural rate—and that's where the CBO numbers come from.

The Costs of Disinflation

Through experience, policy makers have found that bringing inflation down is a much harder task than increasing it. The reason is that once the public has come to expect continuing inflation, bringing inflation down is painful.

A persistent attempt to keep unemployment below the natural rate leads to accelerating inflation that becomes incorporated into expectations. To reduce inflationary expectations, policy makers need to run the process in reverse, adopting contractionary policies that keep the unemployment rate above the natural rate for an extended period of time. The process of bringing down inflation that has become embedded in expectations is known as *disinflation.*

Disinflation can be very expensive. The U.S. retreat from high inflation at the beginning of the 1980s appears to have cost the equivalent of about 18% of a year's real GDP, the equivalent of roughly $2.6 trillion today. The justification for paying these costs is that they lead to a permanent gain. Although the economy does not recover the short-term production losses caused by disinflation, it no longer suffers from the costs associated with persistently high inflation. In fact, the United States, Britain, and other wealthy countries that experienced inflation in the 1970s eventually decided that the benefit of bringing inflation down was worth the required suffering—the large reduction in real GDP in the short term.

Some economists argue that the costs of disinflation can be reduced if policy makers explicitly state their determination to reduce inflation. A clearly announced, credible policy of disinflation, they contend, can reduce expectations of future inflation and so shift the short-run Phillips curve downward. Some economists believe that the clear determination of the Federal Reserve to combat the inflation of the 1970s was credible enough that the costs of disinflation, huge though they were, were lower than they might otherwise have been.

Deflation

Before World War II, *deflation*—a falling aggregate price level—was almost as common as inflation. In fact, the U.S. consumer price index on the eve of World War II was 30% lower than it had been in 1920. After World War II, inflation became the norm in all countries. But in the 1990s, deflation reappeared in Japan and proved difficult to reverse. Concerns about potential deflation played a crucial role in U.S. monetary policy in the early 2000s and again in late 2008. In fact, in late 2008, the U.S. experienced a brief period of deflation.

Why is deflation a problem? And why is it hard to end?

Debt Deflation

Deflation, like inflation, produces both winners and losers—but in the opposite direction. Due to the falling price level, a dollar in the future has a higher real value than a dollar today. So lenders, who are owed money, gain under deflation because the real value of borrowers' payments increases. Borrowers lose because the real burden of their debt rises.

In a famous analysis at the beginning of the Great Depression, Irving Fisher claimed that the effects of deflation on borrowers and lenders can worsen an economic slump. In effect, deflation takes real resources away from borrowers and redistributes them to lenders. Fisher argued that borrowers, who lose from deflation, are typically short of cash and will be forced to cut their spending sharply when their debt burden rises. However, lenders are less likely to increase spending sharply when the values of the loans they own rise. The overall effect, said Fisher, is that deflation reduces aggregate demand, deepening an economic slump, which, in a vicious circle, may lead to further deflation. The effect of deflation in reducing aggregate demand, known as **debt deflation**, probably played a significant role in the Great Depression.

Debt deflation is the reduction in aggregate demand arising from the increase in the real burden of outstanding debt caused by deflation.

Effects of Expected Deflation

Like expected inflation, expected deflation affects the nominal interest rate. Consider Figure 29.6 from Section 5 (repeated here as **Figure 34.7**), which demonstrates how expected inflation affects the equilibrium interest rate. As shown, the equilibrium nominal interest rate is 4% if the expected inflation rate is 0%. Clearly, if the expected inflation rate is −3%—meaning that the public expects deflation at 3% per year—the equilibrium nominal interest rate will be 4% − 3% = 1%.

But what would happen if the expected rate of inflation were −5%? Would the nominal interest rate fall to −1%, meaning that lenders are paying borrowers 1% on their debt? No. Nobody would lend money at a negative nominal rate of interest because they could do better by simply holding cash. This illustrates what economists call the **zero bound** on the nominal interest rate: it cannot go below zero.

There is a **zero bound** on the nominal interest rate: it cannot go below zero.

This zero bound can limit the effectiveness of monetary policy. Suppose the economy is depressed, with output below potential output and the unemployment rate above the natural rate. Normally, the central bank can respond by cutting interest rates so as to increase aggregate demand. If the nominal interest rate is already zero, however, the central bank cannot push it down any further. Banks refuse to lend and consumers and firms refuse to spend because, with a negative inflation rate and a 0% nominal interest rate, holding cash yields a positive real rate of return. Any further increases in the monetary base will either be held in bank vaults or held as cash by individuals and firms, without being spent.

A situation in which conventional monetary policy to fight a slump—cutting interest rates—can't be used because nominal interest rates are up against the zero bound is known as a **liquidity trap**. A liquidity trap can occur whenever there is a sharp reduction

A **liquidity trap** is a situation in which conventional monetary policy is ineffective because nominal interest rates are up against the zero bound.

Figure 34.7 The Fisher Effect

D_0 and S_0 are the demand and supply curves for loanable funds when the expected future inflation rate is 0%. At an expected inflation rate of 0%, the equilibrium nominal interest rate is 4%. An increase in expected future inflation pushes both the demand and supply curves upward by 1 percentage point for every percentage point increase in expected future inflation. D_{10} and S_{10} are the demand and supply curves for loanable funds when the expected future inflation rate is 10%. The 10 percentage point increase in expected future inflation raises the equilibrium nominal interest rate to 14%. The expected real interest rate remains at 4%, and the equilibrium quantity of loanable funds also remains unchanged.

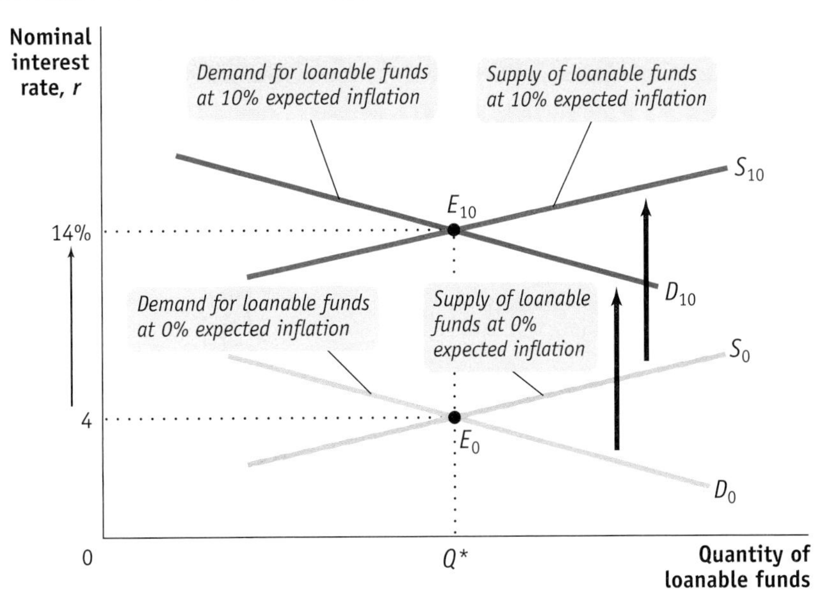

Figure 34.8 The Zero Bound in U.S. History

This figure shows U.S. short-term interest rates, specifically the interest rate on three-month Treasury bills, since 1920. As shown by the shaded area on the left, for much of the 1930s, interest rates were very close to zero, leaving little room for expansionary monetary policy. After World War II, persistent inflation generally kept rates well above zero. However, starting in late 2008, in the wake of the housing bubble bursting and the financial crisis, the interest rate on three-month Treasury bills was again virtually zero.

Source: Federal Reserve Bank of St. Louis.

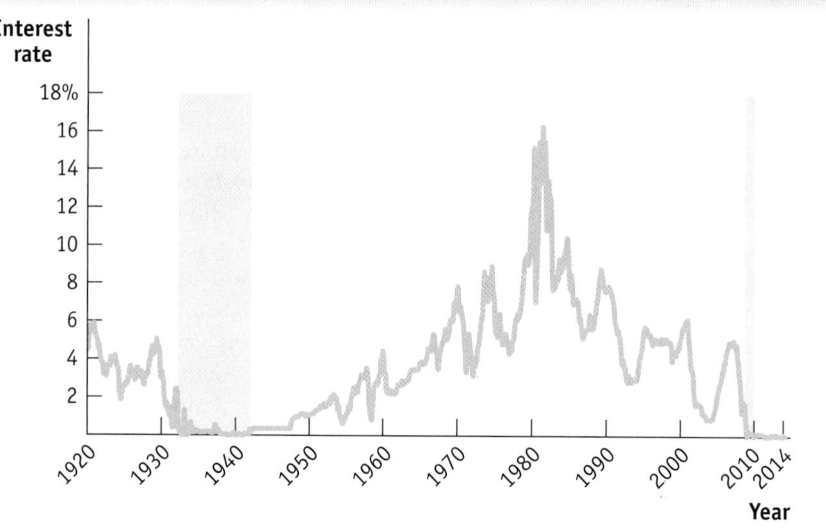

in demand for loanable funds—which is exactly what happened during the Great Depression. **Figure 34.8** shows the interest rate on short-term U.S. government debt from 1920 to February 2014. As you can see, starting in 1933 and ending when World War II brought a full economic recovery, the U.S. economy was either close to or up against the zero bound. After World War II, when inflation became the norm around the world, the zero bound problem largely vanished as the public came to expect inflation rather than deflation.

However, the recent history of the Japanese economy, shown in **Figure 34.9**, provides a modern illustration of the problem of deflation and the liquidity trap. Japan experienced a huge boom in the prices of both stocks and real estate in the late 1980s, and then saw both bubbles burst. The result was a prolonged period of economic

Figure 34.9 Japan's Lost Decade

A prolonged economic slump in Japan led to deflation from the late 1990s on. The Bank of Japan responded by cutting interest rates—but eventually ran up against the zero bound.

Sources: Japanese Ministry of Internal Affairs and Communications, Statistics Bureau; Bank of Japan.

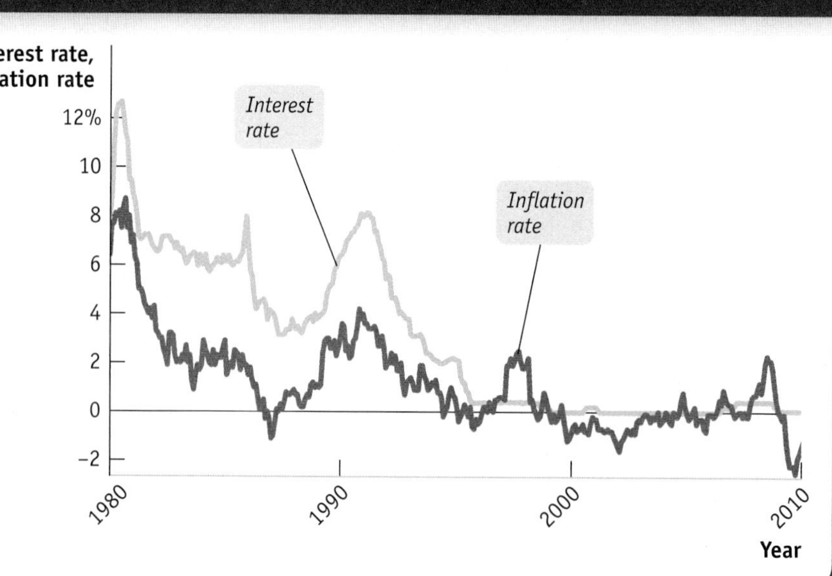

stagnation, the so-called Lost Decade, which gradually reduced the inflation rate and eventually led to persistent deflation. In an effort to fight the weakness of the economy, the Bank of Japan—the equivalent of the Federal Reserve—repeatedly cut interest rates. Eventually, it arrived at the "ZIRP": the zero interest rate policy. The "call money rate," the equivalent of the U.S. federal funds rate, was literally set equal to zero. Because the economy was still depressed, it would have been desirable to cut interest rates even further. But that wasn't possible: Japan was up against the zero bound.

From 2008 until at least 2014, the Federal Reserve also found itself up against the zero bound. In the aftermath of the bursting of the housing bubble and the ensuing financial crisis, the interest on short-term U.S. government debt fell to virtually zero.

MODULE 34 Review

Check Your Understanding

1. Explain why a decrease in aggregate demand causes a movement along the short-run Phillips curve.
2. Why is there no long-run trade-off between unemployment and inflation?
3. Why is disinflation so costly for an economy? Are there ways to reduce these costs?
4. Why won't anyone lend money at a negative nominal rate of interest? How can this pose problems for monetary policy?

Tackle the Test: Multiple-Choice Questions

1. The long-run Phillips curve is
   - I. the same as the short-run Phillips curve.
   - II. vertical.
   - III. the short-run Phillips curve plus expected inflation.

   a. I only
   b. II only
   c. III only
   d. I and II only
   e. I, II, and III

2. The short-run Phillips curve shows a ____________ relationship between ____________.

a.	negative	the aggregate price level and aggregate output
b.	positive	the aggregate price level and aggregate output
c.	negative	unemployment and inflation
d.	positive	unemployment and aggregate output
e.	positive	unemployment and the aggregate price level

3. An increase in expected inflation will shift
   a. the short-run Phillips curve downward.
   b. the short-run Phillips curve upward.
   c. the long-run Phillips curve upward.
   d. the long-run Phillips curve downward.
   e. neither the short-run nor the long-run Phillips curve.

4. Bringing down inflation that has become embedded in expectations is called
   a. deflation.
   b. negative inflation.
   c. anti-inflation.
   d. unexpected inflation.
   e. disinflation.

5. Debt deflation is
   a. the effect of deflation in decreasing aggregate demand.
   b. an idea proposed by Irving Fisher.
   c. a contributing factor in causing the Great Depression.
   d. due to differences in how borrowers/lenders respond to inflation losses/gains.
   e. all of the above.

Tackle the Test: Free-Response Questions

1. **a.** Draw a correctly labeled graph showing a short-run Phillips curve with an expected inflation rate of 0% and the corresponding long-run Phillips curve.
   b. On your graph, label the nonaccelerating inflation rate of unemployment.
   c. On your graph, show what happens in the long run if the government decides to decrease the unemployment rate below the nonaccelerating inflation rate of unemployment. Explain.

Rubric for FRQ 1 (8 points)

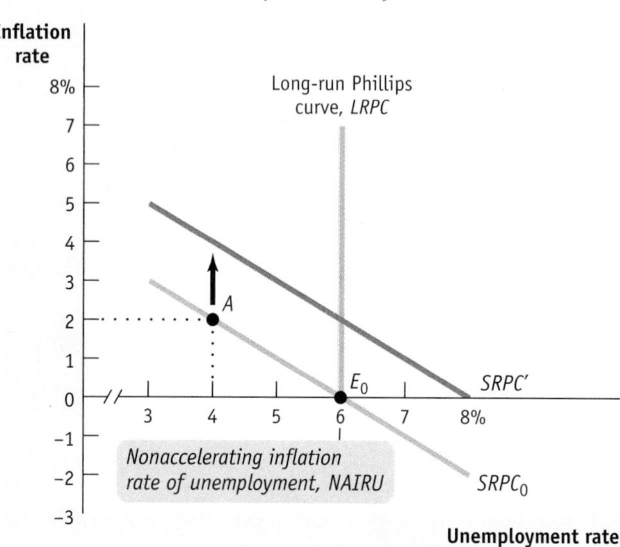

1 point: Vertical axis labeled "Inflation rate"

1 point: Horizontal axis labeled "Unemployment rate"

1 point: Downward-sloping curve labeled "$SRPC_0$"

1 point: Vertical curve labeled "*LRPC*"

1 point: $SRPC_0$ crosses horizontal axis where it crosses *LRPC*

1 point: NAIRU is labeled where $SRPC_0$ crosses *LRPC* and horizontal axis

1 point: New *SRPC* is labeled, for example as "*SRPC*′," and shown above the original $SRPC_0$

1 point: When the unemployment rate moves below the NAIRU, it creates inflation and moves the economy to a point such as *A*. This leads to positive inflationary expectations, which shift the *SRPC* up as shown by *SRPC*′.

2. Consider the accompanying figure.

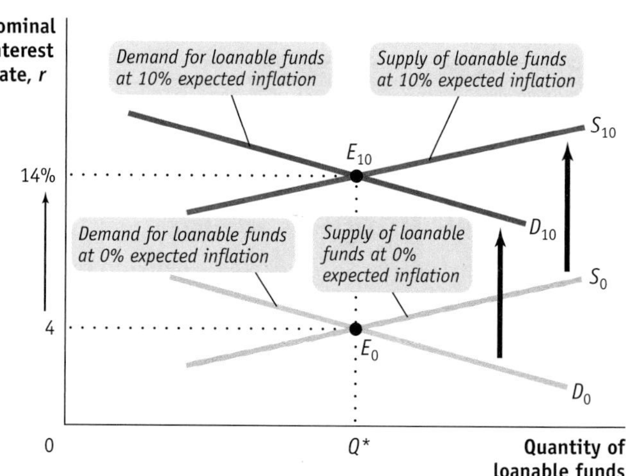

   a. What is the nominal interest rate if expected inflation is 0%?
   b. What would the nominal interest rate be if the expected inflation rate were –2%? Explain.
   c. What would the nominal interest rate be if the expected inflation rate were –6%? Explain.
   d. What would a negative nominal interest rate mean for lenders? How much lending would take place at a negative nominal interest rate? Explain.
   e. What effect does a nominal interest rate of zero have on monetary policy? What is this situation called? **(6 points)**

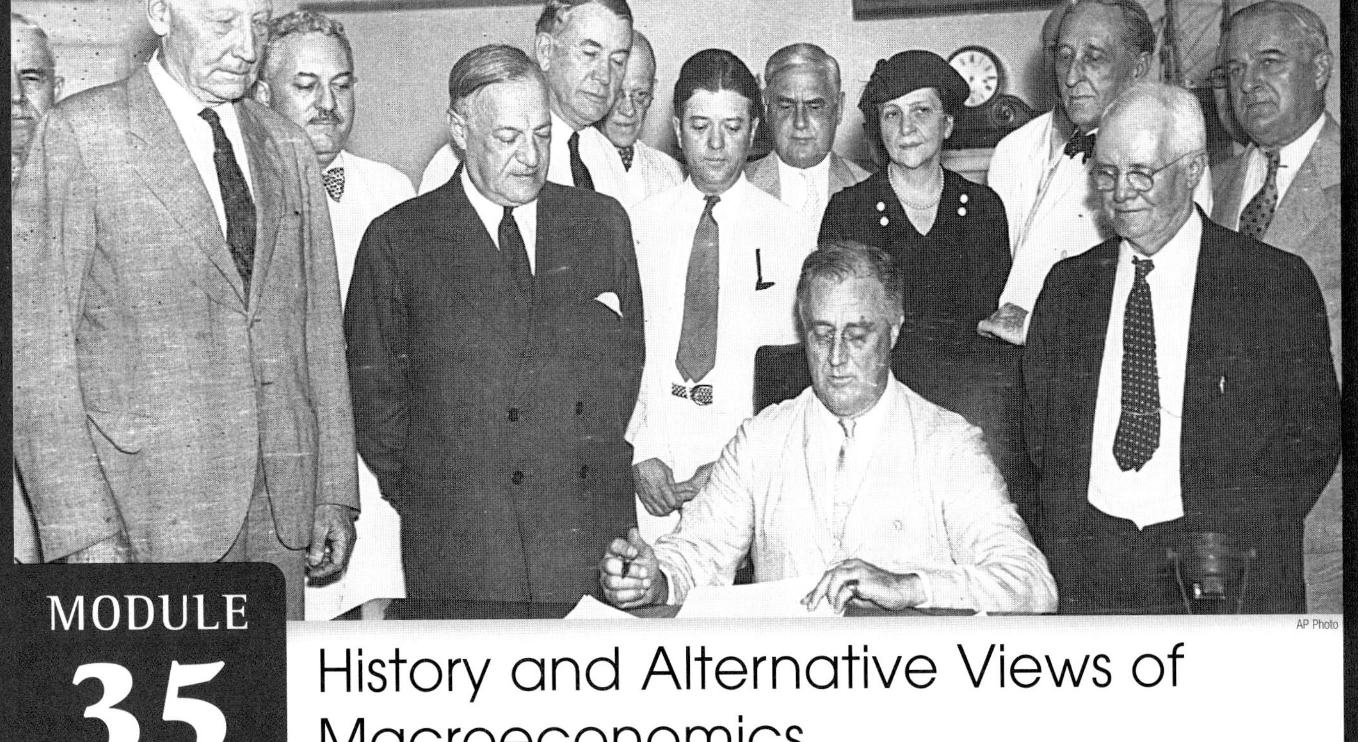
AP Photo

MODULE 35 History and Alternative Views of Macroeconomics

In this Module, you will learn to:

- Explain why classical macroeconomics wasn't adequate for the problems posed by the Great Depression
- Discuss how Keynes and the experience of the Great Depression legitimized macroeconomic policy activism
- Define monetarism and identify monetarist views on the limits of discretionary monetary policy
- Describe how challenges led to a revision of Keynesian ideas and the emergence of the new classical macroeconomics

Classical Macroeconomics

The term *macroeconomics* appears to have been coined in 1933 by the Norwegian economist Ragnar Frisch. The timing, during the worst year of the Great Depression, was no accident. Still, there were economists analyzing what we now consider macroeconomic issues—the behavior of the aggregate price level and aggregate output—before then.

Money and the Price Level

Previously, we described the *classical model of the price level.* According to the classical model, prices are flexible, making the aggregate supply curve vertical even in the short run. In this model, other things equal, an increase in the money supply leads to a proportional rise in the aggregate price level, with no effect on aggregate output. As a result, increases in the money supply lead to inflation, and that's all. Before the 1930s, the classical model of the price level dominated economic thinking about the effects of monetary policy.

Did classical economists really believe that changes in the money supply affected only aggregate prices, without any effect on aggregate output? Probably not. Historians of economic thought argue that before 1930 most economists were aware that changes in the money supply affected aggregate output as well as aggregate prices in the short run—or, to use modern terms, they were aware that the short-run aggregate supply curve sloped upward. But they regarded such short-run effects as unimportant, stressing the long run instead. It was this attitude that led John Maynard Keynes to scoff at the focus on the long run, in which, as he said, "we are all dead."

The Business Cycle

Of course, classical economists were also aware that the economy did not grow smoothly. The American economist Wesley Mitchell pioneered the quantitative study of business cycles. In 1920, he founded the National Bureau of Economic Research, an independent, nonprofit organization that to this day has the official role of declaring the beginnings of recessions and expansions. Thanks to Mitchell's work, the *measurement* of business cycles was well advanced by 1930. But there was no widely accepted *theory* of business cycles.

In the absence of any clear theory, views about how policy makers should respond to a recession were conflicting. Some economists favored expansionary monetary and fiscal policies to fight a recession. Others believed that such policies would worsen the slump or merely postpone the inevitable. For example, in 1934 Harvard's Joseph Schumpeter, now famous for his early recognition of the importance of technological change, warned that any attempt to alleviate the Great Depression with expansionary monetary policy "would, in the end, lead to a collapse worse than the one it was called in to remedy." When the Great Depression hit, the policy-making process was paralyzed by this lack of consensus. In many cases, economists now believe, policy makers took steps in the wrong direction.

Necessity, however, was the mother of invention. As we'll explain next, the Great Depression provided a strong incentive for economists to develop theories that could serve as a guide to policy—and economists responded.

The Great Depression and the Keynesian Revolution

Alfred Eisenstaedt/Time & Life Pictures/Getty Images

The work of John Maynard Keynes (right), seen here with U.S. Treasury Secretary Henry Morgenthau, Jr., legitimized the use of monetary and fiscal policy to smooth out the business cycle.

The Great Depression demonstrated, once and for all, that economists cannot safely ignore the short run. Not only was the economic pain severe, it threatened to destabilize societies and political systems. In particular, the economic plunge helped Adolf Hitler rise to power in Germany.

The whole world wanted to know how this economic disaster could be happening and what should be done about it. But because there was no widely accepted theory of the business cycle, economists gave conflicting and, we now believe, often harmful advice. Some believed that only a huge change in the economic system—such as having the government take over much of private industry and replace markets with a command economy—could end the slump. Others argued that slumps were natural—even beneficial—and that nothing should be done.

Some economists, however, argued that the slump both could have and should have been cured—without giving up on the basic idea of a market economy. In 1930, the British economist John Maynard Keynes compared the problems of the U.S. and British economies to those of a car with a defective alternator. Getting the economy running, he argued, would require only a modest repair, not a complete overhaul.

Nice metaphor. But what was the nature of the trouble?

Keynes's Theory

In 1936, Keynes presented his analysis of the Great Depression—his explanation of what was wrong with the economy's alternator—in a book titled *The General Theory of Employment, Interest, and Money.* In 1946, the great American economist Paul Samuelson wrote that "it is a badly written book, poorly organized. . . . Flashes of insight and intuition intersperse tedious algebra. . . . We find its analysis to be obvious and at the same time new. In short, it is a work of genius." *The General Theory* isn't easy reading, but it stands with Adam Smith's *The Wealth of Nations* as one of the most influential books on economics ever written.

As Samuelson's description suggests, Keynes's book is a vast stew of ideas. **Keynesian economics** mainly reflected two innovations. First, Keynes emphasized the short-run effects of shifts in aggregate demand on aggregate output, rather than the long-run determination of the aggregate price level. As Keynes's famous remark about being dead in the long run suggests, until his book appeared, most economists had treated short-run macroeconomics as a minor issue. Keynes focused the attention of economists on situations in which the short-run aggregate supply curve slopes upward and shifts in the aggregate demand curve affect aggregate output and employment as well as aggregate prices.

Keynesian economics focuses on the ability of shifts in aggregate demand to influence aggregate output in the short run.

Figure 35.1 illustrates the difference between Keynesian and classical macroeconomics. Both panels of the figure show the short-run aggregate supply curve, *SRAS*; in both it is assumed that for some reason the aggregate demand curve shifts leftward from AD_1 to AD_2—let's say in response to a fall in stock market prices that leads households to reduce consumer spending.

Figure 35.1 Classical Versus Keynesian Macroeconomics

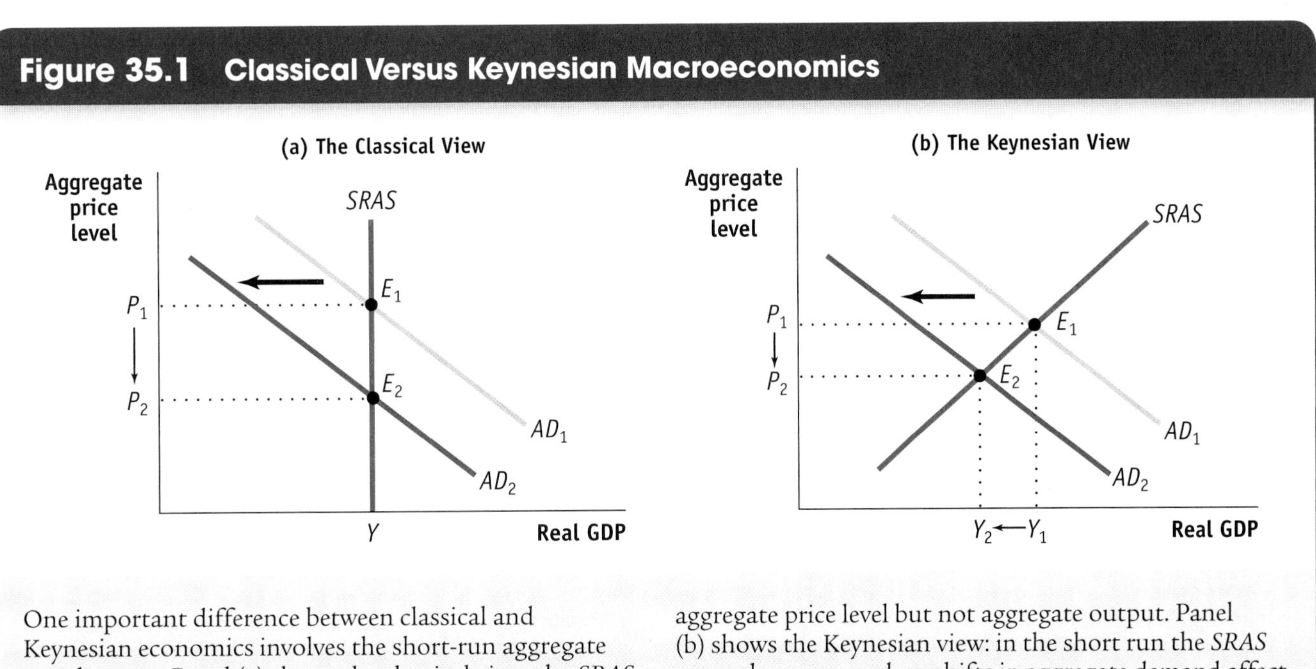

One important difference between classical and Keynesian economics involves the short-run aggregate supply curve. Panel (a) shows the classical view: the *SRAS* curve is vertical, so shifts in aggregate demand affect the aggregate price level but not aggregate output. Panel (b) shows the Keynesian view: in the short run the *SRAS* curve slopes upward, so shifts in aggregate demand affect aggregate output as well as aggregate prices.

Panel (a) shows the classical view: the short-run aggregate supply curve is vertical. The decline in aggregate demand leads to a fall in the aggregate price level, from P_1 to P_2, but no change in aggregate output. Panel (b) shows the Keynesian view: the short-run aggregate supply curve slopes upward, so the decline in aggregate demand leads to both a fall in the aggregate price level, from P_1 to P_2, and a fall in aggregate output, from Y_1 to Y_2. As we've already explained, many classical macroeconomists would have agreed that panel (b) was an accurate story in the short run—but they regarded the short run as unimportant. Keynes disagreed. (Just to be clear, there isn't any diagram that looks like panel (b) of Figure 35.1 in Keynes's *The General Theory*. But Keynes's discussion of aggregate supply, translated into modern terminology, clearly implies an upward-sloping *SRAS* curve.)

Second, classical economists emphasized the role of changes in the money supply in shifting the aggregate demand curve, paying little attention to other factors. Keynes, however, argued that other factors, especially changes in "animal spirits"—these days usually referred to with the bland term *business confidence*—are mainly responsible for business cycles. Before Keynes, economists often argued that a decline in business confidence would have no effect on either the aggregate price level or aggregate output, as long as the money supply stayed constant. Keynes offered a very different picture.

Keynes's ideas have penetrated deeply into the public consciousness, to the extent that many people who have never heard of Keynes, or have heard of him but think they disagree with his theory, use Keynesian ideas all the time. For example, suppose that a business commentator says something like this: "Because of a decline in business confidence, investment spending slumped, causing a recession." Whether the commentator knows it or not, that statement is pure Keynesian economics.

Keynes himself more or less predicted that his ideas would become part of what "everyone knows." In another famous passage, this from the end of *The General Theory*, he wrote: "Practical men, who believe themselves to be quite exempt from any intellectual influences, are usually the slaves of some defunct economist."

Policy to Fight Recessions

Macroeconomic policy activism is the use of monetary and fiscal policy to smooth out the business cycle.

The main practical consequence of Keynes's work was that it legitimized **macroeconomic policy activism**—the use of monetary and fiscal policy to smooth out the business cycle.

Macroeconomic policy activism wasn't something completely new. Before Keynes, many economists had argued for using monetary expansion to fight economic downturns—though others were fiercely opposed. Some economists had even argued that temporary budget deficits were a good thing in times of recession—though others disagreed strongly. In practice, during the 1930s many governments followed policies that we would now call Keynesian. In the United States, the administration of Franklin Roosevelt engaged in modest deficit spending in an effort to create jobs.

But these efforts were half-hearted. Roosevelt's advisers were deeply divided over the appropriate policies to adopt. In fact, in 1937 Roosevelt gave in to advice from

FYI The End of the Great Depression

It would make a good story if Keynes's ideas had led to a change in economic policy that brought the Great Depression to an end. Unfortunately, that's not what happened. Still, the way the Depression ended did a lot to convince economists that Keynes was right.

The basic message many of the young economists who adopted Keynes's ideas in the 1930s took from his work was that economic recovery requires aggressive fiscal expansion—deficit spending on a large scale to create jobs. And that is what they eventually got, but it wasn't because politicians were persuaded. Instead, what happened was a very large and expensive war, World War II.

The figure here shows the U.S. unemployment rate and the federal budget deficit as a share of GDP from 1930 to 1947. As you can see, deficit spending during the 1930s was on a modest scale. In 1940, as the risk of war grew larger, the United States began a large military buildup, and the budget moved deep into deficit. After the attack on Pearl Harbor on December 7, 1941, the country began deficit spending on an enormous scale: in fiscal 1943, which began in July 1942, the deficit was 30% of GDP. Today that would be a deficit of $4.3 trillion.

And the economy recovered. World War II wasn't intended as a Keynesian fiscal policy, but it demonstrated that expansionary fiscal policy can, in fact, create jobs in the short run.

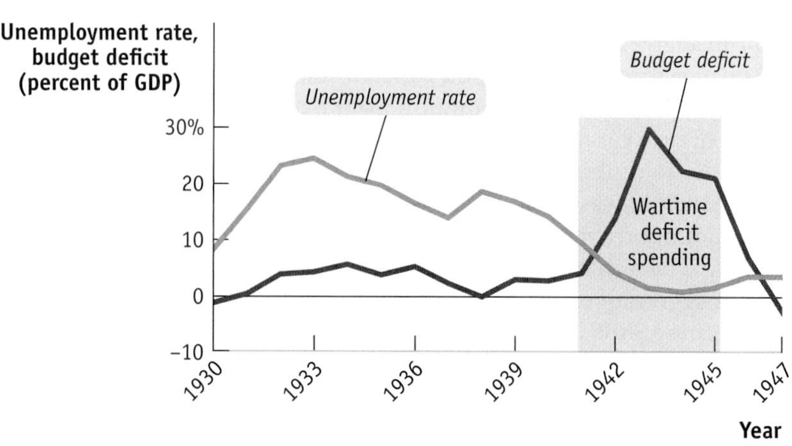

Source: U.S. Census Bureau.

non-Keynesian economists who urged him to balance the budget and raise interest rates, even though the economy was still depressed. The result was a renewed slump.

Today, by contrast, there is broad consensus about the useful role monetary and fiscal policy can play in fighting recessions. The 2004 Economic Report of the President was issued by a conservative Republican administration that was generally opposed to government intervention in the economy. Yet its view on economic policy in the face of recession was far more like that of Keynes than like that of most economists before 1936.

It would be wrong, however, to suggest that Keynes's ideas have been fully accepted by modern macroeconomists. In the decades that followed the publication of *The General Theory*, Keynesian economics faced a series of challenges, some of which succeeded in modifying the macroeconomic consensus in important ways.

Challenges to Keynesian Economics

Keynes's ideas fundamentally changed the way economists think about business cycles. However, they did not go unquestioned. In the decades that followed the publication of *The General Theory*, Keynesian economics faced a series of challenges. As a result, the consensus of macroeconomists retreated somewhat from the strong version of Keynesianism that prevailed in the 1950s. In particular, economists became much more aware of the limits to macroeconomic policy activism.

The Revival of Monetary Policy

Keynes's *The General Theory* suggested that monetary policy wouldn't be very effective in depression conditions. Many modern macroeconomists agree: earlier we introduced the concept of a *liquidity trap*, a situation in which monetary policy is ineffective because the interest rate is down against the zero bound. In the 1930s, when Keynes wrote, interest rates, in fact, were very close to 0%. (The term *liquidity trap* was first introduced by the British economist John Hicks in a 1937 paper, "Mr. Keynes and the Classics: A Suggested Interpretation," that summarized Keynes's ideas.)

But even when the era of near-0% interest rates came to an end after World War II, many economists continued to emphasize fiscal policy and downplay the usefulness of monetary policy. Eventually, however, macroeconomists reassessed the importance of monetary policy. A key milestone in this reassessment was the 1963 publication of *A Monetary History of the United States, 1867–1960* by Milton Friedman, of the University of Chicago, and Anna Schwartz, of the National Bureau of Economic Research. Friedman and Schwartz showed that business cycles had historically been associated with fluctuations in the money supply. In particular, the money supply fell sharply during the onset of the Great Depression. Friedman and Schwartz persuaded many, though not all, economists that the Great Depression could have been avoided if the Federal Reserve had acted to prevent that monetary contraction. They persuaded most economists that monetary policy should play a key role in economic management.

Roger Ressmeyer/Corbis

Teresa Zabala/The New York Times

Milton Friedman and his co-author Anna Schwartz played a key role in convincing macroeconomists of the importance of monetary policy.

The revival of interest in monetary policy was significant because it suggested that the burden of managing the economy could be shifted away from fiscal policy—meaning that economic management could largely be taken out of the hands of politicians. Fiscal policy, which must involve changing tax rates or government spending, necessitates political choices. If the government tries to stimulate the economy by cutting taxes, it must decide whose taxes will be cut. If it tries to stimulate the economy with government spending, it must decide what to spend the money on.

Monetary policy, by contrast, does not involve such choices: when the central bank cuts interest rates to fight a recession, it cuts everyone's interest rate at the same time. So a shift from relying on fiscal policy to relying on monetary policy makes macroeconomics a more technical, less political issue. In fact, monetary policy in most major economies is set by an independent central bank that is insulated from the political process.

Monetarism

Monetarism asserts that GDP will grow steadily if the money supply grows steadily.

After the publication of *A Monetary History*, Milton Friedman led a movement, called *monetarism*, that sought to eliminate macroeconomic policy activism while maintaining the importance of monetary policy. **Monetarism** asserted that GDP will grow steadily if the money supply grows steadily. The monetarist policy prescription was to have the central bank target a constant rate of growth of the money supply, such as 3% per year, and maintain that target regardless of any fluctuations in the economy.

It's important to realize that monetarism retained many Keynesian ideas. Like Keynes, Friedman asserted that the short run is important and that short-run changes in aggregate demand affect aggregate output as well as aggregate prices. Like Keynes, he argued that policy should have been much more expansionary during the Great Depression.

Discretionary monetary policy is the use of changes in the interest rate or the money supply by the central bank to stabilize the economy.

However, monetarists argued that most of the efforts of policy makers to smooth out the business cycle actually make things worse. We have already discussed concerns over the usefulness of *discretionary fiscal policy*—changes in taxes or government spending, or both—in response to the state of the economy. As we explained, government perceptions about the economy often lag behind reality, and there are further lags in changing fiscal policy and in its effects on the economy. As a result, discretionary fiscal policies intended to fight a recession often end up feeding a boom, and vice versa. According to monetarists, **discretionary monetary policy**, changes in the interest rate or the money supply by the central bank in order to stabilize the economy, faces the same problem of lags as fiscal policy, but to a lesser extent.

Friedman also argued that if the central bank followed his advice and refused to change the money supply in response to fluctuations in the economy, fiscal policy would be much less effective than Keynesians believed. Earlier we analyzed the phenomenon of *crowding out*, in which government deficits drive up interest rates and lead to reduced investment spending. Friedman and others pointed out that if the money supply is held fixed while the government pursues an expansionary fiscal policy, crowding out will limit the effect of the fiscal expansion on aggregate demand.

Figure 35.2 illustrates this argument. Panel (a) shows aggregate output and the aggregate price level. AD_1 is the initial aggregate demand curve and *SRAS* is the short-run aggregate supply curve. At the initial equilibrium, E_1, the level of aggregate output is Y_1 and the aggregate price level is P_1. Panel (b) shows the money market. *MS* is the money supply curve and MD_1 is the initial money demand curve, so the initial interest rate is r_1.

Now suppose the government increases purchases of goods and services. We know that this will shift the *AD* curve rightward, as illustrated by the shift from AD_1 to AD_2; that aggregate output will rise, from Y_1 to Y_2, and that the aggregate price level will rise, from P_1 to P_2. Both the rise in aggregate output and the rise in the aggregate price level, however, will increase the demand for money, shifting the money demand curve rightward from MD_1 to MD_2. This drives up the equilibrium interest rate to r_2. Friedman's point was that this rise in the interest rate reduces investment spending, partially offsetting the initial rise in government spending. As a result, the rightward shift of the *AD* curve is smaller than multiplier analysis indicates. And Friedman argued that with a constant money supply, the multiplier is so small that there's not much point in using fiscal policy.

But Friedman didn't favor activist monetary policy either. He argued that the problem of time lags that limit the ability of discretionary fiscal policy to stabilize the economy also apply to discretionary monetary policy. Friedman's solution was

Figure 35.2 Fiscal Policy with a Fixed Money Supply

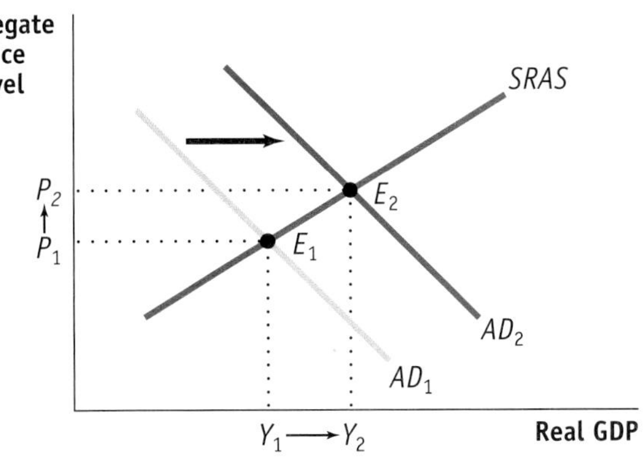

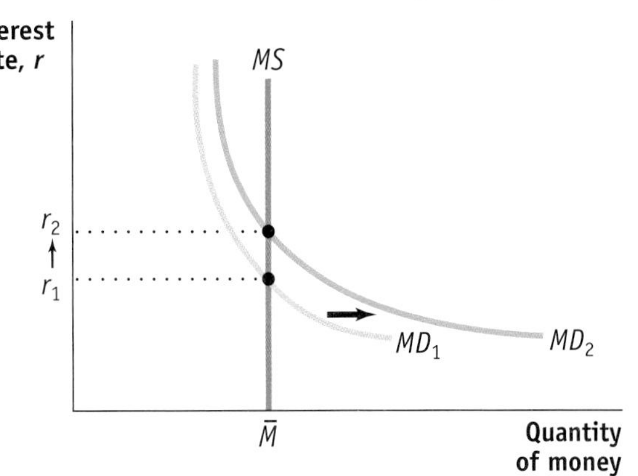

In panel (a) an expansionary fiscal policy shifts the *AD* curve rightward, driving up both the aggregate price level and aggregate output. However, this leads to an increase in the demand for money. If the money supply is held fixed, as in panel (b), the increase in money demand drives up the interest rate, reducing investment spending and offsetting part of the fiscal expansion. So the shift of the *AD* curve is less than it would otherwise be: fiscal policy becomes less effective when the money supply is held fixed.

to put monetary policy on "autopilot." The central bank, he argued, should follow a **monetary policy rule**, a formula that determines its actions and leaves it relatively little discretion. During the 1960s and 1970s, most monetarists favored a monetary policy rule of slow, steady growth in the money supply. Underlying this view was the **Quantity Theory of Money**, which relies on the concept of the **velocity of money**, the ratio of nominal GDP to the money supply. Velocity is a measure of the number of times the average dollar bill in the economy turns over per year between buyers and sellers (e.g., I tip the Starbucks barista a dollar, she uses it to buy lunch, and so on). This concept gives rise to the *velocity equation*:

A **monetary policy rule** is a formula that determines the central bank's actions.

The **Quantity Theory of Money** emphasizes the positive relationship between the price level and the money supply. It relies on the velocity equation ($M \times V = P \times Y$).

The **velocity of money** is the ratio of nominal GDP to the money supply. It is a measure of the number of times the average dollar bill is spent per year.

$$\textbf{(35-1)} \quad M \times V = P \times Y$$

Where M is the money supply, V is velocity, P is the aggregate price level, and Y is real GDP.

Monetarists believed, with considerable historical justification, that the velocity of money was stable in the short run and changed only slowly in the long run. As a result, they claimed, steady growth in the money supply by the central bank would ensure steady growth in spending, and therefore in GDP.

Monetarism strongly influenced actual monetary policy in the late 1970s and early 1980s. It quickly became clear, however, that steady growth in the money supply didn't ensure steady growth in the economy: the velocity of money wasn't stable enough for such a simple policy rule to work. **Figure 35.3** on the next page shows how events eventually undermined the monetarists' view. The figure shows the velocity of money, as measured by the ratio of nominal GDP to M1, from 1960 to the middle of 2013. As you can see, until 1980, velocity followed a fairly smooth, seemingly predictable trend. After the Fed began to adopt monetarist ideas in the late 1970s and early 1980s, however, the velocity of money began moving erratically—probably due to financial market innovations.

Figure 35.3 The Velocity of Money

From 1960 to 1980, the velocity of money was stable, leading monetarists to believe that steady growth in the money supply would lead to a stable economy. After 1980, however, velocity began moving erratically, undermining the case for traditional monetarism. As a result, traditional monetarism fell out of favor.

Sources: Bureau of Economic Analysis; Federal Reserve Bank of St. Louis.

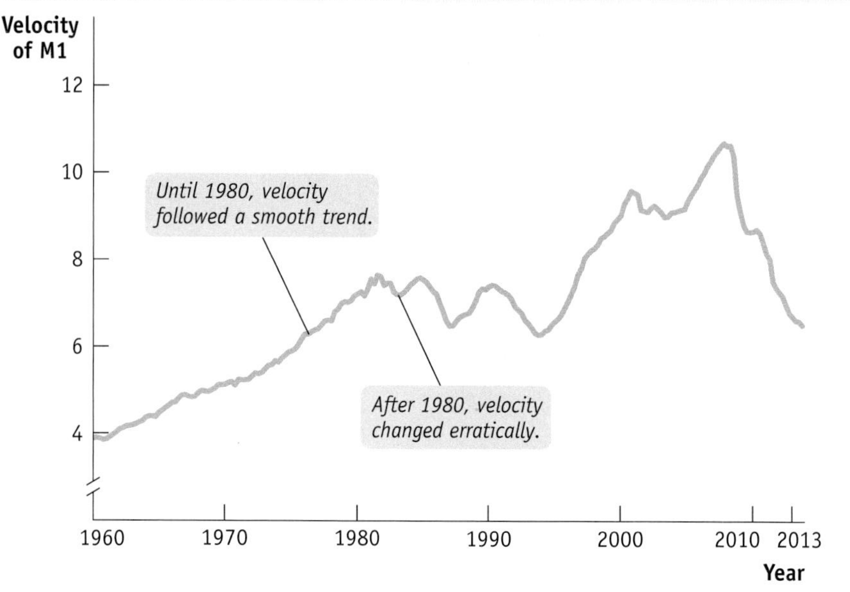

Traditional monetarists are hard to find among today's macroeconomists. As we'll see later, however, the concern that originally motivated the monetarists—that too much discretionary monetary policy can actually destabilize the economy—has become widely accepted.

Inflation and the Natural Rate of Unemployment

At the same time that monetarists were challenging Keynesian views about how macroeconomic policy should be conducted, a somewhat broader group of economists was emphasizing the limits to what activist macroeconomic policy could achieve.

In the 1940s and 1950s, many Keynesian economists believed that expansionary fiscal policy could be used to achieve full employment on a permanent basis. In the 1960s, however, many economists realized that expansionary policies could cause problems with inflation, but they still believed policy makers could choose to trade off low unemployment for higher inflation even in the long run.

In 1968, however, Edmund Phelps of Columbia University and Milton Friedman, working independently, proposed the concept of the natural rate of unemployment. In Module 34 we saw that the natural rate of unemployment is also the nonaccelerating inflation rate of unemployment, or NAIRU. According to the **natural rate hypothesis**, because inflation is eventually embedded in expectations, to avoid accelerating inflation over time, the unemployment rate must be high enough that the actual inflation rate equals the expected rate of inflation. Attempts to keep the unemployment rate below the natural rate will lead to an ever-rising inflation rate.

According to the **natural rate hypothesis**, to avoid accelerating inflation over time, the unemployment rate must be high enough that the actual inflation rate equals the expected inflation rate.

The natural rate hypothesis limits the role of activist macroeconomic policy compared to earlier theories. Because the government can't keep unemployment below the natural rate, its task is not to keep unemployment low but to keep it *stable*—to prevent large fluctuations in unemployment in either direction.

The Friedman–Phelps hypothesis made a strong prediction: that the apparent tradeoff between unemployment and inflation would not survive an extended period of rising prices. Once inflation was embedded in the public's expectations, inflation would continue even in the face of high unemployment. Sure enough, that's exactly what happened in the 1970s. This accurate prediction was one of the triumphs of macroeconomic analysis, and it convinced the great majority of economists that the natural rate hypothesis was correct. In contrast to traditional monetarism, which declined in influence as more evidence accumulated, the natural rate hypothesis has become almost universally accepted among macroeconomists, with a few qualifications. (Some macroeconomists believe that at very low or negative rates of inflation the hypothesis doesn't work.)

The Political Business Cycle

One final challenge to Keynesian economics focused not on the validity of the economic analysis but on its political consequences. A number of economists and political scientists pointed out that activist macroeconomic policy lends itself to political manipulation.

Statistical evidence suggests that election results tend to be determined by the state of the economy in the months just before the election. In the United States, if the economy is growing rapidly and the unemployment rate is falling in the six months or so before Election Day, the incumbent party tends to be re-elected even if the economy performed poorly in the preceding three years.

A **political business cycle** results when politicians use macroeconomic policy to serve political ends.

This creates an obvious temptation to abuse activist macroeconomic policy: pump up the economy in an election year, and pay the price in higher inflation and/or higher unemployment later. The result can be unnecessary instability in the economy, a **political business cycle** caused by the use of macroeconomic policy to serve political ends.

An often-cited example is the combination of expansionary fiscal and monetary policy that led to rapid growth in the U.S. economy just before the 1972 election and a sharp acceleration in inflation after the election. Kenneth Rogoff, a respected macroeconomist who served as chief economist at the International Monetary Fund, proclaimed Richard Nixon, the president at the time, "the all-time hero of political business cycles."

One way to avoid a political business cycle is to place monetary policy in the hands of an independent central bank, insulated from political pressure. The political business cycle is also a reason to limit the use of discretionary fiscal policy to extreme circumstances.

Win McNamee/Getty Images

Election results tend to be determined by the state of the economy in the months just before the election.

Rational Expectations, Real Business Cycles, and New Classical Macroeconomics

As we have seen, one key difference between classical economics and Keynesian economics is that classical economists believed that the short-run aggregate supply curve is vertical, but Keynes emphasized the idea that the aggregate supply curve slopes upward in the short run. As a result, Keynes argued that demand shocks—shifts in the aggregate demand curve—can cause fluctuations in aggregate output.

The challenges to Keynesian economics that arose in the 1950s and 1960s—the renewed emphasis on monetary policy and the natural rate hypothesis—didn't question the view that an increase in aggregate demand leads to a rise in aggregate output in the short run nor that a decrease in aggregate demand leads to a fall in aggregate output in the short run. In the 1970s and 1980s, however, some economists developed an approach to the business cycle known as **new classical macroeconomics**, which returned to the classical view that shifts in the aggregate demand curve affect only the aggregate price level, not aggregate output. The new approach evolved in two steps. First, some economists challenged traditional arguments about the slope of the short-run aggregate supply curve based on the concept of *rational expectations*. Second, some

New classical macroeconomics is an approach to the business cycle that returns to the classical view that shifts in the aggregate demand curve affect only the aggregate price level, not aggregate output.

economists suggested that changes in productivity caused economic fluctuations, a view known as *real business cycle theory*.

Rational Expectations

Rational expectations is the view that individuals and firms make decisions optimally, using all available information.

In the 1970s, a concept known as *rational expectations* had a powerful impact on macroeconomics. **Rational expectations**, a theory originally introduced by John Muth in 1961, is the view that individuals and firms make decisions optimally, using all available information.

For example, workers and employers bargaining over long-term wage contracts need to estimate the inflation rate they expect over the life of that contract. Rational expectations says that in making estimates of future inflation, they won't just look at past rates of inflation; they will also take into account available information about monetary and fiscal policy. Suppose that prices didn't rise last year, but that the monetary and fiscal policies announced by policy makers made it clear to economic analysts that there would be substantial inflation over the next few years. According to rational expectations, long-term wage contracts will be adjusted today to reflect this future inflation, even though prices didn't rise in the past.

Rational expectations can make a major difference to the effects of government policy. According to the original version of the natural rate hypothesis, a government attempt to trade off higher inflation for lower unemployment would work in the short run but would eventually fail because higher inflation would get built into expectations. According to rational expectations, we should remove the word *eventually*: if it's clear that the government intends to trade off higher inflation for lower unemployment, the public will understand this, and expected inflation will immediately rise.

In the 1970s, Robert Lucas of the University of Chicago, in a series of highly influential papers, used this logic to argue that monetary policy can change the level of unemployment only if it comes as a surprise to the public. If his analysis was right, monetary policy isn't useful in stabilizing the economy after all. In 1995 Lucas won the Nobel Prize in economics for this work, which remains widely admired. However, many—perhaps most—macroeconomists, especially those advising policy makers, now believe that his conclusions were overstated. The Federal Reserve certainly thinks that it can play a useful role in economic stabilization.

According to **new Keynesian economics**, market imperfections can lead to price stickiness for the economy as a whole.

Why, in the view of many macroeconomists, doesn't the rational expectations hypothesis accurately describe how the economy behaves? **New Keynesian economics**, a set of ideas that became influential in the 1990s, provides an explanation. It argues that market imperfections interact to make many prices in the economy temporarily sticky. For example, one new Keynesian argument points out that monopolists don't have to be too careful about setting prices exactly "right": if they set a price a bit too high, they'll lose some sales but make more profit on each sale; if they set the price too low, they'll reduce the profit per sale but sell more. As a result, even small costs to changing prices can lead to substantial price stickiness and make the economy as a whole behave in a Keynesian fashion.

Over time, new Keynesian ideas combined with actual experience have reduced the practical influence of the rational expectations concept. Nonetheless, the idea of rational expectations served as a useful caution for macroeconomists who had become excessively optimistic about their ability to manage the economy.

Real Business Cycles

Real business cycle theory claims that fluctuations in the rate of growth of total factor productivity cause the business cycle.

Earlier we introduced the concept of *total factor productivity*, the amount of output that can be generated with a given level of factor inputs. Total factor productivity grows over time, but that growth isn't smooth. In the 1980s, a number of economists argued that slowdowns in productivity growth, which they attributed to pauses in technological progress, are the main cause of recessions. **Real business cycle theory** claims that fluctuations in the rate of growth of total factor productivity cause the business cycle.

Believing that the aggregate supply curve is vertical, real business cycle theorists attribute the source of business cycles to shifts of the aggregate supply curve: a recession occurs when a slowdown in productivity growth shifts the aggregate supply curve leftward, and a recovery occurs when a pickup in productivity growth shifts the aggregate supply curve rightward. In the early days of real business cycle theory, the theory's proponents denied that changes in aggregate demand had any effect on aggregate output.

This theory was strongly influential, as shown by the fact that two of the founders of real business cycle theory, Finn Kydland of Carnegie Mellon University and Edward Prescott of the Federal Reserve Bank of Minneapolis, won the 2004 Nobel Prize in economics. The current status of real business cycle theory, however, is somewhat similar to that of rational expectations. The theory is widely recognized as having made valuable contributions to our understanding of the economy, and it serves as a useful caution against too much emphasis on aggregate demand. But many of the real business cycle theorists themselves now acknowledge that their models need an upward-sloping aggregate supply curve to fit the economic data—and that this gives aggregate demand a potential role in determining aggregate output. And as we have seen, policy makers strongly believe that aggregate demand policy has an important role to play in fighting recessions.

MODULE 35 Review

Check Your Understanding

1. The figure below shows the behavior of M1 before, during, and after the 2001 recession. What would a classical economist have said about the Fed's policy?

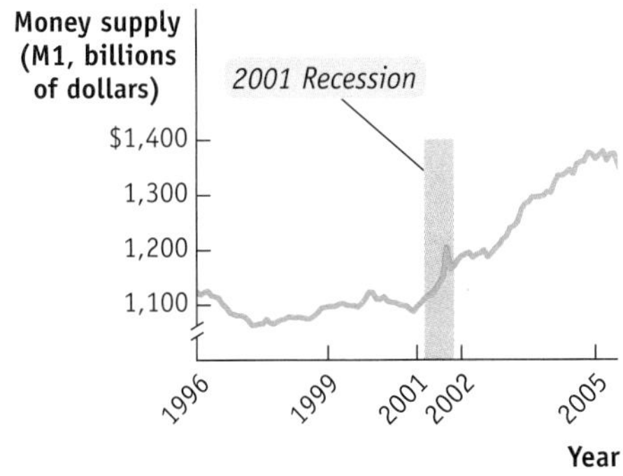

2. What would the figure in Question 1 have looked like if the Fed had been following a monetarist policy since 1996?

3. Now look at Figure 35.3, which shows the path of the velocity of money. What problems do you think the United States would have had since 1996 if the Fed had followed a monetarist policy?

4. In addition to praising aggressive monetary policy, the 2004 Economic Report of the President says that "tax cuts can boost economic activity by raising after-tax income and enhancing incentives to work, save, and invest." Which part of the report is a Keynesian statement and which part is not? Explain your answer.

5. In early 2001, as it became clear that the United States was experiencing a recession, the Fed stated that it would fight the recession with an aggressive monetary policy. By 2004, most observers concluded that this aggressive monetary expansion should be given credit for ending the recession.
   a. What would rational expectations theorists say about this conclusion?
   b. What would real business cycle theorists say?

Tackle the Test: Multiple-Choice Questions

1. Which of the following was a point made in Keynes's influential work?
   I. In the short run, shifts in aggregate demand affect aggregate output.
   II. Animal spirits are an important determinant of business cycles.
   III. In the long run we're all dead.

   a. I only
   b. II only
   c. III only
   d. I and II only
   e. I, II, and III

2. Which of the following is a central point of monetarism?
   a. Business cycles are associated with fluctuations in money demand.
   b. Activist monetary policy is the best way to address business cycles.
   c. Discretionary monetary policy is effective while discretionary fiscal policy is not.
   d. The Fed should follow a monetary policy rule.
   e. All of the above.
3. The natural rate hypothesis says that the unemployment rate should be
   a. below the NAIRU.
   b. high enough that the actual rate of inflation equals the expected rate.
   c. as close to zero as possible.
   d. 5%.
   e. left wherever the economy sets it.
4. The main difference between the classical model of the price level and Keynesian economics is that
   a. the classical model assumes a vertical short-run aggregate supply curve.
   b. Keynesian economics assumes a vertical short-run aggregate supply curve.
   c. the classical model assumes an upward-sloping long-run aggregate supply curve.
   d. Keynesian economics assumes a vertical long-run aggregate supply curve.
   e. the classical model assumes that aggregate demand cannot change in the long run.
5. That fluctuations in total factor productivity growth cause the business cycle is the main tenet of which theory?
   a. Keynesian
   b. classical
   c. rational expectations
   d. real business cycle
   e. natural rate

Tackle the Test: Free-Response Questions

1. a. According to monetarism, business cycles are associated with fluctuations in what?
   b. Does monetarism advocate discretionary fiscal policy? Discretionary monetary policy?
   c. What monetary policy does monetarism suggest?
   d. What is the velocity equation? Indicate what each letter in the equation stands for.
   e. Use the velocity equation to explain the major conclusion of monetarism.

Rubric for FRQ 1 (10 points)

1 point: The money supply
1 point: No
1 point: No
1 point: A monetary policy rule
1 point: $M \times V = P \times Y$
1 point: M is the money supply.
1 point: V is the velocity of money.
1 point: P is the aggregate price level.
1 point: Y is real GDP.
1 point: Since V is stable, a steady growth of M will lead to a steady growth in GDP.

2. For each of the following economic theories, identify its fundamental conclusion.
   a. the classical model of the price level
   b. Keynesian economics
   c. monetarism
   d. the natural rate hypothesis
   e. rational expectations
   f. real business cycle theory
   (6 points)

Pete Souza/The White House via Getty Images

MODULE 36 Consensus and Conflict in Modern Macroeconomics

In this Module, you will learn to:

- List and describe the elements of the modern macroeconomic consensus
- Explain the main remaining disputes

The Modern Consensus

The 1970s and the first half of the 1980s were a stormy period for the U.S. economy (and for other major economies, too). There was a severe recession in 1974–1975, then two back-to-back recessions in 1979–1982 that sent the unemployment rate to almost 11%. At the same time, the inflation rate soared into double digits—and then plunged. As we have seen, these events left a strong mark on macroeconomic thought.

After about 1985, however, the economy settled down. The recession of 1990–1991 was much milder than the 1974–1975 recession or the double-dip slump from 1979 to 1982, and the inflation rate generally stayed below 4%. The period of relative calm in the economy from 1985 to 2007 came to be known as the *Great Moderation*. To a large extent, the calmness of the economy was marked by a similar calm in macroeconomic policy discussion. In fact, it seemed that a broad consensus had emerged about several key macroeconomic issues.

Unfortunately, the Great Moderation was followed by the *Great Recession*, the severe and persistent slump that followed the 2008 financial crisis. We'll talk shortly about the policy disputes caused by the Great Recession. First, however, let's examine the apparent consensus that emerged during the Great Moderation. It combines a belief in monetary policy as the main tool of stabilization, with skepticism toward the use of fiscal policy, and an acknowledgement of the policy constraints imposed by the natural rate of unemployment and the political business cycle.

To understand the modern consensus, where it came from, and what still remains in dispute, we'll look at how macroeconomists have changed their answers to five key questions about macroeconomic policy. The five questions, and the answers given by macroeconomists over the past 70 years, are summarized in **Table 36.1** on the next page. (In the table, new classical economics is subsumed under classical economics, and new Keynesian economics is subsumed under the modern consensus.) Notice that

Table 36.1 Five Key Questions About Macroeconomic Policy	Classical macroeconomics	Keynesian macroeconomics	Monetarism	Modern consensus
Is expansionary monetary policy helpful in fighting recessions?	No	Not very	Yes	Yes, except in special circumstances
Is expansionary fiscal policy effective in fighting recessions?	No	Yes	No	Yes
Can monetary and/or fiscal policy reduce unemployment in the long run?	No	Yes	No	No
Should fiscal policy be used in a discretionary way?	No	Yes	No	No, except in special circumstances
Should monetary policy be used in a discretionary way?	No	Yes	No	Still in dispute

classical macroeconomics said no to each question; basically, classical macroeconomists didn't think macroeconomic policy could accomplish very much. But let's go through the questions one by one.

Is Expansionary Monetary Policy Helpful in Fighting Recessions?

As we've seen, classical macroeconomists generally believed that expansionary monetary policy was ineffective or even harmful in fighting recessions. In the early years of Keynesian economics, macroeconomists weren't against monetary expansion during recessions, but they tended to believe that it was of doubtful effectiveness. Milton Friedman and his followers convinced economists that monetary policy was effective after all.

Nearly all macroeconomists now agree that monetary policy can be used to shift the aggregate demand curve and to reduce economic instability. The classical view that changes in the money supply affect only aggregate prices, not aggregate output, has few supporters today. The view once held by some Keynesian economists—that changes in the money supply have little effect—has equally few supporters. Now, it is generally agreed that monetary policy is ineffective only in the case of a liquidity trap.

Is Expansionary Fiscal Policy Effective in Fighting Recessions?

Classical macroeconomists were, if anything, even more opposed to fiscal expansion than to monetary expansion. Keynesian economists, on the other hand, gave fiscal policy a central role in fighting recessions. Monetarists argued that fiscal policy was ineffective as long as the money supply was held constant. But that strong view has become relatively rare.

Most macroeconomists now agree that fiscal policy, like monetary policy, can shift the aggregate demand curve. Most macroeconomists also agree that the government should not seek to balance the budget regardless of the state of the economy: they agree that the role of the budget as an automatic stabilizer helps keep the economy on an even keel.

Can Monetary and/or Fiscal Policy Reduce Unemployment in the Long Run?

Classical macroeconomists didn't believe the government could do anything about unemployment. Some Keynesian economists moved to the opposite extreme, arguing that expansionary policies could be used to achieve a permanently low unemployment rate, perhaps at the cost of some inflation. Monetarists believed that unemployment could not be kept below the natural rate.

Almost all macroeconomists now accept the natural rate hypothesis and agree on the limitations of monetary and fiscal policy. They believe that effective monetary and fiscal policy can limit the size of fluctuations of the actual unemployment rate around the natural rate but can't keep unemployment below the natural rate.

Should Fiscal Policy Be Used in a Discretionary Way?

As we've already seen, views about the effectiveness of fiscal policy have gone back and forth, from rejection by classical macroeconomists, to a positive view by Keynesian economists, to a negative view once again by monetarists. Today, most macroeconomists believe that tax cuts and spending increases are at least somewhat effective in increasing aggregate demand. However, *discretionary fiscal policy* is subject to the various types of lags discussed in Module 20. All too often, policies intended to fight a slump affect aggregate demand after the economy has turned around, and end up intensifying a boom.

As a result, the macroeconomic consensus gives monetary policy the lead role in economic stabilization. Discretionary fiscal policy plays the leading role only in special circumstances when monetary policy is ineffective and fiscal policy is likely to take effect before the economy has recovered. For example, many macroeconomists favored the use of discretionary fiscal policy in 2008–2010, when interest rates were near the zero bound and the economy was likely to remain depressed for an extended period.

Should Monetary Policy Be Used in a Discretionary Way?

Classical macroeconomists didn't think that monetary policy should be used to fight recessions; Keynesian economists didn't oppose discretionary monetary policy, but they were skeptical about its effectiveness. Monetarists argued that discretionary monetary policy was doing more harm than good. Where are we today? This remains an area of dispute. Today there is a broad consensus among macroeconomists on these points:

- Monetary policy should play the main role in stabilization policy.
- The central bank should be independent, insulated from political pressures, in order to avoid a political business cycle.
- Discretionary fiscal policy should be used sparingly, both because of policy lags and because of the risks of a political business cycle.

However, the Great Moderation was upended by events that posed very difficult questions—questions that rage on to this day. We'll now examine what happened and why the ongoing debate is so fierce.

Crisis and Aftermath

The Great Recession shattered any sense among macroeconomists that they had entered a permanent era of agreement over key policy questions. Given the nature of the slump, however, this should have come as no surprise. Why? Because the severity of the slump arguably made the policies that seemed to work during the Great Moderation inadequate.

During the Great Moderation, there had been broad agreement that the job of stabilizing the economy was best carried out by having the Federal Reserve and its counterparts abroad raise or lower interest rates as the economic situation warranted. But what should be done if the economy is deeply depressed, while the interest rates the Fed normally controls are already close to zero and can go no lower (that is, when the economy is in a liquidity trap)? Some economists called for aggressive discretionary fiscal policy and/or unconventional monetary policies that might achieve results despite the zero lower bound. Others strongly opposed these measures, arguing either that they would be ineffective or that they would produce undesirable side effects.

Brendan Smialowski/Bloomberg via Getty Images

In 2008, the Fed took a series of unconventional monetary policy actions in response to the deepening recession and financial crisis.

The Debate over Fiscal Policy In 2009, a number of governments, including that of the United States, responded with expansionary fiscal policy, or "stimulus," generally taking the form of a mix of temporary spending measures and temporary tax cuts. From the start, however, these efforts were highly controversial.

FYI Supply-Side Economics

During the 1970s, a group of economic writers began propounding a view of economic policy that came to be known as "supply-side economics." The core of this view was the belief that reducing tax rates, and so increasing the incentives to work and invest, would have a powerful positive effect on the growth rate of potential output. The supply-siders urged the government to cut taxes without worrying about matching spending cuts: economic growth, they argued, would offset any negative effects from budget deficits. Some supply-siders even argued that a cut in tax *rates* would have such an effect on economic growth that tax *revenues*—the total amount taxpayers pay to the government—would actually rise. That is, some supply-siders argued that the United States was on the wrong side of the *Laffer curve*, a hypothetical relationship between tax rates and total tax revenue that slopes upward (meaning higher taxes bring higher tax revenues) at low tax rates but turns downward (meaning higher taxes bring lower tax revenues) when tax rates are very high, as shown in the figure.

In the 1970s, supply-side economics was enthusiastically supported by the editors of the *Wall Street Journal* and other figures in the media, and it became popular with politicians. In 1980, Ronald Reagan made supply-side economics the basis of his presidential campaign.

Because supply-side economics emphasizes supply rather than demand, and because the supply-siders themselves are harshly critical of Keynesian economics, it might seem as if supply-side theory belongs in our discussion of new classical macroeconomics. But unlike rational expectations and real business cycle theory, supply-side economics is generally dismissed by economic researchers.

The main reason for this dismissal is lack of evidence. Almost all economists agree that tax cuts increase incentives to work and invest, but attempts to estimate these incentive effects indicate that at current U.S. tax levels they aren't nearly strong enough to support the strong claims made by supply-siders. In particular, the supply-side doctrine implies that large tax cuts, such as those implemented by Ronald Reagan in the early 1980s, should sharply raise potential output. Yet estimates of potential output by the Congressional Budget Office and others show no sign of an acceleration in growth after the Reagan tax cuts.

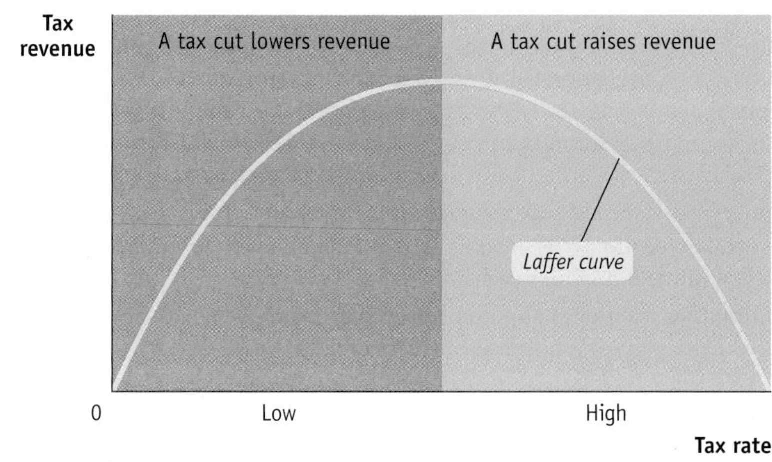

"I'll pause for a moment so you can let this information sink in."

Supporters of fiscal stimulus offered three main arguments for breaking with the normal presumption against discretionary fiscal policy:

1. They argued that discretionary fiscal expansion was needed because the usual tool for stabilizing the economy, monetary policy, could no longer be used now that interest rates were near zero.
2. They argued that one normal concern about expansionary fiscal policy—that deficit spending would drive up interest rates, crowding out private investment spending—was unlikely to be a problem in a depressed economy. Again, this was because interest rates were close to zero and likely to stay there as long as the economy was depressed.
3. Finally, they argued that another concern about discretionary fiscal policy—that it might take a long time to get going—was less of a concern than usual given the likelihood that the economy would be depressed for an extended period. These arguments generally won the day in early 2009.

However, opponents of fiscal stimulus raised two main objections:

1. They argued that households and firms would see any rise in government spending as a sign that tax burdens were likely to rise in the future, leading to a fall in

private spending that would undo any positive effect. This is known as the *Ricardian equivalence* argument.

2. They also warned that spending programs might undermine investors' faith in the government's ability to repay its debts, leading to an increase in long-term interest rates despite increases in the money supply.

In fact, by 2010 a number of economists were arguing that the best way to boost the economy was actually to cut government spending, which they argued would increase private-sector confidence and lead to a rise in output and employment. This notion, often referred to as the doctrine of "expansionary austerity," was especially popular in Europe, where it was supported by officials at the European Central Bank and became the official policy of the Cameron government in Britain, which took office in the spring of 2010.

Critics of fiscal stimulus pointed out that the U.S. stimulus had failed to deliver a convincing fall in unemployment; stimulus advocates, however, had warned from the start that this was likely to happen because the stimulus was too small compared with the depth of the slump. Meanwhile, austerity programs in Britain and elsewhere had also failed to deliver an economic turnaround and, in fact, had seemed to deepen the slump. Supporters of these programs, however, argued that they were nonetheless necessary to head off a potential collapse of confidence.

One thing that was clear, however, was that those who had predicted a sharp rise in U.S. interest rates due to budget deficits, leading to conventional crowding out, had been wrong: by the fall of 2011, U.S. long-term rates were hitting record lows despite continuing large deficits.

MODULE 36 Review

Check Your Understanding

1. What debates has the modern consensus resolved? What debates has it not resolved?

Tackle the Test: Multiple-Choice Questions

1. Which of the following is an example of an opinion on which economists have reached a broad consensus?
   - I. The natural rate hypothesis holds true.
   - II. Discretionary fiscal policy is usually counterproductive.
   - III. Monetary policy is effective, especially in a liquidity trap.

   a. I only
   b. II only
   c. III only
   d. I and II only
   e. I, II, and III

2. In the FYI box in this module, you learned about supply-side economics. Which of the following is stressed by supply-siders?
   a. Taxes should be increased.
   b. Lower taxes will lead to lower tax revenues.
   c. It is important to increase incentives to work, save, and invest.
   d. The economy operates on the upward-sloping section of the Laffer curve.
   e. Supply-side views are widely supported by empirical evidence.

3. Which of the following was one of the main arguments against using fiscal stimulus during the Great Recession?
   a. Monetary policy could no longer be used because interest rates were so low.
   b. The crowding out of private investment was no longer a problem in the depressed economy.
   c. Implementation lags were less of a concern than usual because the economy was likely to be depressed for an extended period.

d. Consumers would see an increase in government spending as a signal that the tax burden would decrease in the future, and therefore they would spend more.
e. Spending programs might undermine investors' faith in the government's ability to repay its debts, leading to an increase in long-term interest rates.

4. Which of the following is a major source of disagreement among macroeconomists?
   a. The Fed conducted the appropriate amount of quantitative easing during the Great Recession.
   b. The central bank should be independent, insulated from political pressures.
   c. Discretionary fiscal policy should be used sparingly.
   d. Monetary policy should play the main role in stabilization policy.
   e. Budget deficits caused high rates of inflation shortly after the Great Recession.

5. Which of the following best describes the 23 years prior to the Great Recession?
   a. a period of growing disagreement among macroeconomists
   b. a period of high inflation
   c. a period of consensus building among economists
   d. a period of consistently high unemployment
   e. the Great Depression

Tackle the Test: Free-Response Questions

1. What is the consensus view of macroeconomists on each of the following?
   a. monetary policy and aggregate demand
   b. when monetary policy is ineffective
   c. fiscal policy and aggregate demand
   d. a balanced budget mandate
   e. the effectiveness of discretionary fiscal policy

Rubric for FRQ 1 (5 points)

1 point: Monetary policy can shift aggregate demand in the short run.

1 point: Monetary policy is ineffective when in a liquidity trap.

1 point: Fiscal policy can shift aggregate demand.

1 point: This is not a good idea. Fluctuations in the budget act as an automatic stabilizer for the economy.

1 point: It is usually counterproductive (for example, due to lags in implementation).

2. Draw a correctly labeled graph of the Laffer curve. Use an "x" to identify a point on the curve at which a reduction in tax rates would lead to increased tax revenue. **(3 points)**

SECTION  6 Review

 Section 6 Review Video

Module 30

1. Some of the fluctuations in the budget balance are due to the effects of the business cycle. In order to separate the effects of the business cycle from the effects of discretionary fiscal policy, governments estimate the **cyclically adjusted budget balance**, an estimate of the budget balance if the economy were at potential output.
2. U.S. government budget accounting is calculated on the basis of **fiscal years** that run from October 1 to September 30. Annual budget deficits, minus budget surpluses, accumulate into **government debt**. Persistent budget deficits have long-run consequences because they lead to an increase in **public debt**—government debt held by the individuals and institutions outside the government. This can be a problem for two reasons. Public debt may crowd out investment spending, which reduces long-run economic growth. And in extreme cases, rising debt may lead to government default, resulting in economic and financial turmoil.

3. A widely used measure of fiscal health is the **debt-GDP ratio**. This number can remain stable or fall even in the face of moderate budget deficits if GDP rises over time. However, a stable debt–GDP ratio may give a misleading impression that all is well because modern governments often have large **implicit liabilities**. The largest implicit liabilities of the U.S. government come from Social Security, Medicare, and Medicaid, the costs of which are increasing due to the aging of the population and rising medical costs.

Module 31

4. The Federal Reserve can use monetary policy to change the interest rate. In practice, this involves setting a **target federal funds rate**. **Expansionary monetary policy** reduces the interest rate by increasing the money supply. This increases investment spending and consumer spending, which in turn increases aggregate demand and real GDP in the short run. **Contractionary monetary policy** raises the interest rate by reducing the money supply. This reduces investment spending and consumer spending, which in turn reduces aggregate demand and real GDP in the short run.
5. The Federal Reserve and other central banks try to stabilize their economies, limiting fluctuations of actual output to around potential output, while also keeping inflation low but positive. Under the **Taylor rule for monetary policy**, the target interest rate rises when there is inflation, or a positive output gap, or both; the target interest rate falls when inflation is low or negative, or when the output gap is negative, or both. Some central banks engage in **inflation targeting**, which is a forward-looking policy rule, whereas the Taylor rule is a backward-looking policy rule. In practice, the Fed appears to operate on a loosely defined version of the Taylor rule. In 2012, the Fed adopted an explicit inflation target as well. Because monetary policy is subject to fewer implementation lags than fiscal policy, monetary policy is the preferred policy tool for stabilizing the economy.

Module 32

6. In the long run, changes in the money supply affect the aggregate price level but not real GDP or the interest rate. Data show that the concept of **monetary neutrality** holds: changes in the money supply have no real effect on the economy in the long run.

Module 33

7. In analyzing high inflation, economists use the **classical model of the price level**, which says that changes in the money supply lead to proportional changes in the aggregate price level even in the short run.
8. Governments sometimes print money in order to finance budget deficits. When they do, they impose an **inflation tax**, generating tax revenue equal to the inflation rate times the money supply, on those who hold money. Revenue from the real inflation tax, the inflation rate times the real money supply, is the real value of resources captured by the government. In order to avoid paying the inflation tax, people reduce their real money holdings and force the government to increase inflation to capture the same amount of real inflation tax revenue. In some cases, this leads to a vicious circle of a shrinking real money supply and a rising rate of inflation, leading to hyperinflation and a fiscal crisis.
9. Countries that don't need to print money to cover government deficits can still stumble into moderate inflation. When an increase in the price of a key input such as oil decreases aggregate supply, the result is **cost-push inflation**. Inflation caused by an increase in aggregate demand is called **demand-pull inflation**.
10. A positive output gap is associated with lower-than-normal unemployment; a negative output gap is associated with higher-than-normal unemployment.

Module 34

11. At a given point in time, there is a downward-sloping relationship between unemployment and inflation known as the **short-run Phillips curve**. This curve is shifted by changes in the expected rate of inflation. The **long-run Phillips curve**, which shows the relationship between unemployment and inflation once expectations have had time to adjust, is vertical. It defines the **nonaccelerating inflation rate of unemployment**, or **NAIRU**, which is equal to the natural rate of unemployment.

12. Once inflation has become embedded in expectations, getting inflation back down can be difficult because disinflation can be very costly, requiring the sacrifice of large amounts of aggregate output and imposing high levels of unemployment. However, policy makers in the United States and other wealthy countries were willing to pay that price of bringing down the high inflation of the 1970s.

13. Deflation poses several problems. It can lead to **debt deflation**, in which a rising real burden of outstanding debt intensifies an economic downturn. Also, interest rates are more likely to run up against the **zero bound** in an economy experiencing deflation. When this happens, the economy enters a **liquidity trap**, rendering conventional monetary policy ineffective.

Module 35

14. Classical macroeconomics asserted that monetary policy affected only the aggregate price level, not aggregate output, and that the short run was unimportant. By the 1930s, measurement of business cycles was a well-established subject, but there was no widely accepted theory of business cycles.

15. **Keynesian economics** attributed the business cycle to shifts of the aggregate demand curve, often the result of changes in business confidence. Keynesian economics also offered a rationale for **macroeconomic policy activism**.

16. In the decades that followed Keynes's work, economists came to agree that monetary policy as well as fiscal policy is effective under certain conditions. **Monetarism** is a doctrine that called for a **monetary policy rule** as opposed to **discretionary monetary policy**. On the basis of the **Quantity Theory of Money** and a belief that the **velocity of money** was stable, monetarists argued that GDP would grow steadily if the money supply grew steadily. This idea was influential for a time but was eventually rejected by many macroeconomists.

17. The **natural rate hypothesis** became almost universally accepted, limiting the role of macroeconomic policy to stabilizing the economy rather than seeking a permanently low unemployment rate. Fears of a **political business cycle** concocted to advance the careers of the politicians in power led to a consensus that monetary policy should be insulated from politics.

18. **Rational expectations** suggests that even in the short run there might not be a trade-off between inflation and unemployment because expected inflation would change immediately in the face of expected changes in policy. **Real business cycle theory** claims that changes in the rate of growth of total factor productivity are the main cause of business cycles. Both of these versions of **new classical macroeconomics** received wide attention and respect, but policy makers and many economists haven't accepted the conclusion that monetary and fiscal policy are ineffective in changing aggregate output.

19. **New Keynesian economics** argues that market imperfections can lead to price stickiness, so that changes in aggregate demand have effects on aggregate output after all.

Module 36

20. The modern consensus is that monetary and fiscal policy are both effective in the short run but that neither can reduce the unemployment rate in the long run. Discretionary fiscal policy is considered generally unadvisable, except in special circumstances.

21. There are continuing debates about the appropriate role of monetary policy. Some economists advocate the explicit use of an inflation target, but others oppose it. There's also a debate about what kind of unconventional monetary policy, if any, should be adopted to address a liquidity trap.

Key Terms

Cyclically adjusted budget balance, p. 296
Government debt, p. 297
Fiscal year, p. 297
Public debt, p. 297
Debt–GDP ratio, p. 299
Implicit liabilities, p. 301
Target federal funds rate, p. 304
Expansionary monetary policy, p. 307
Contractionary monetary policy, p. 307
Taylor rule for monetary policy, p. 308
Inflation targeting, p. 309
Monetary neutrality, p. 314
Classical model of the price level, p. 319
Inflation tax, p. 322
Cost-push inflation, p. 323
Demand-pull inflation, p. 323
Short-run Phillips curve, p. 328
Nonaccelerating inflation rate of unemployment (NAIRU), p. 334
Long-run Phillips curve, p. 334
Debt deflation, p. 337
Zero bound, p. 337
Liquidity trap, p. 337
Keynesian economics, p. 343
Macroeconomic policy activism, p. 344
Monetarism, p. 346
Discretionary monetary policy, p. 346
Monetary policy rule, p. 347
Quantity Theory of Money, p. 347
Velocity of money, p. 347
Natural rate hypothesis, p. 348
Political business cycle, p. 349
New classical macroeconomics, p. 349
Rational expectations, p. 350
New Keynesian economics, p. 350
Real business cycle theory, p. 350

AP® Exam Practice Questions

Multiple-Choice Questions

1. The budget balance is equal to
   a. total spending by the government.
   b. taxes minus transfer payments.
   c. taxes minus government spending and transfer payments.
   d. the sum of deficits and surpluses over time.
   e. total tax revenues collected.
2. The cyclically adjusted budget deficit adjusts the actual budget deficit for the effect of
   a. discretionary fiscal policy.
   b. discretionary monetary policy.
   c. inflation.
   d. transfer payments.
   e. the business cycle.
3. The public debt increases when
   a. the government collects more in taxes than it spends.
   b. the government runs a budget deficit.
   c. taxes exceed transfer payments.
   d. the budget balance is positive.
   e. individuals borrow for goods like houses and cars.
4. Which of the following is a potential problem with persistent increases in government debt?
   a. Government borrowing may crowd out private investment.
   b. Government debt is caused by budget deficits, which are always bad for the economy.
   c. It will always lead the government to default.
   d. It creates inflation because the government has to print money to pay it off.
   e. It causes automatic stabilizers to raise taxes in the future.
5. The Federal Open Market Committee sets a target for which of the following?
   a. the income tax rate
   b. the federal funds rate
   c. the money supply
   d. the prime interest rate
   e. the unemployment rate
6. Which of the following will occur if the Federal Reserve buys Treasury bills?
   a. The money supply will increase.
   b. The money supply curve will shift to the left.
   c. The money demand curve will shift to the right.
   d. Interest rates will rise.
   e. Aggregate demand will decrease.
7. Which of the following actions would the Federal Reserve use to address inflation?
   a. make an open-market sale of Treasury bills
   b. increase the money supply
   c. lower the discount rate
   d. decrease money demand
   e. raise taxes

8. The Taylor rule sets the target federal funds rate based on which of the following?
   a. the inflation rate only
   b. the unemployment rate only
   c. the output gap only
   d. both the inflation rate and the unemployment rate
   e. both the output gap and the inflation rate

9. An increase in the money supply will generate which of the following?
   a. a negative short-run effect on real GDP
   b. an increase in real GDP in the long run
   c. a decrease in real GDP in the long run
   d. a decrease in the aggregate price level in the long run
   e. an increase in the aggregate price level in the short run and the long run

10. According to the concept of money neutrality, changes in the money supply will affect which of the following in the long run?
    a. only real values
    b. the aggregate price level
    c. employment
    d. aggregate output
    e. aggregate demand

11. An inflation tax is the result of
    a. the federal government running a budget surplus.
    b. the Federal Reserve raising the federal funds rate.
    c. an increase in the demand for money.
    d. printing money to cover a budget deficit.
    e. contractionary fiscal policy.

12. An increase in the aggregate price level caused by a significant increase in the price of an input with economy-wide importance is called
    a. demand-pull inflation.
    b. seignorage inflation.
    c. supply-push inflation.
    d. cost-push inflation.
    e. input-pull inflation.

13. Which of the following is true when the output gap is negative?
    a. Aggregate output is above potential output.
    b. The unemployment rate is below the natural rate.
    c. The economy is experiencing inflation.
    d. Potential output is above aggregate output.
    e. The natural rate of unemployment is decreasing.

14. The short-run Phillips curve shows the relationship between the inflation rate and the
    a. GDP growth rate.
    b. unemployment rate.
    c. employment rate.
    d. real interest rate.
    e. nominal interest rate.

15. An increase in expected inflation has what effect on the short-run Phillips curve?
    a. a movement up and to the left along the curve
    b. a movement down and to the right along the curve
    c. an upward shift of the curve
    d. a downward shift of the curve
    e. an increase in the slope of the curve

16. The long-run Phillips curve is
    a. horizontal.
    b. vertical.
    c. upward sloping.
    d. downward sloping.
    e. U-shaped.

17. The long-run Phillips curve illustrates which of the following?
    a. a positive relationship between unemployment and inflation
    b. a negative relationship between unemployment and inflation
    c. that unemployment will always return to the NAIRU
    d. that unemployment will adjust so that the economy experiences 2% inflation
    e. that output will adjust so that there is no unemployment or inflation in the long run

18. The process of bringing down the rate of inflation that has become embedded in expectations is known as
    a. disinflation.
    b. deflation.
    c. negative inflation.
    d. debt deflation.
    e. monetary policy.

19. A liquidity trap occurs when conventional monetary policy is ineffective because
    a. the short-run Phillips curve is negatively sloped.
    b. the public will not buy or sell Treasury bills.
    c. the unemployment rate can't go below 5%.
    d. the nominal interest rate can't be negative.
    e. the real interest rate can't be negative.

20. According to the Quantity Theory of Money,
    a. the money supply times velocity is equal to nominal GDP.
    b. velocity varies significantly with the business cycle.
    c. changes in the money supply have no long-run effect on the economy.
    d. activist monetary policy is necessary to promote economic growth.
    e. monetary policy rules promote business-cycle fluctuations.

Free-Response Question

1. Draw a correctly labeled graph showing a short-run Phillips curve.
   a. On your graph, show a long-run Phillips curve and label
      i. the NAIRU
      ii. the equilibrium inflation rate
   b. On your graph, show the effect of an increase in the expected inflation rate.

   (6 points)

SECTION 7

Economic Growth and Productivity

Grown in China

China is growing—and so are the Chinese. According to official statistics, children in China are almost 2½ inches taller now than they were 30 years ago. The average Chinese citizen is still a lot shorter than the average American, but at the current rate of growth the difference may be largely gone in a couple of generations.

If that does happen, China will be following in Japan's footsteps. Older Americans tend to think of the Japanese as short, but today young Japanese men are more than 5 inches taller on average than they were in 1900, which makes them almost as tall as their American counterparts.

There's no mystery about why the Japanese grew taller—it's because they grew richer. In the early twentieth century, Japan was a relatively poor country in which many families couldn't afford to give their children adequate nutrition. As a result, their children grew up to be short adults. However, since World War II, Japan has become an economic powerhouse in which food is ample and young adults are much taller than before.

The same phenomenon is now happening in China. Although it continues to be a relatively poor country, China has made great economic strides over the past 30 years. Its recent history is probably the world's most dramatic example of economic growth—a sustained increase in the productive capacity of an economy. Yet despite its impressive performance, China is currently playing catch-up with economically advanced countries like the United States and Japan. It's still relatively poor because these other nations began their own processes of economic growth many decades ago—and in the case of the United States and European countries, more than a century ago.

Unlike a short-run increase in real GDP caused by an increase in aggregate demand or short-run aggregate supply, we'll see that economic growth pushes the production possibilities curve outward and shifts the long-run aggregate supply curve to the right. Because economic growth is a long-run concept, we often refer to it as *long-run economic growth* for clarity. Many economists have argued that long-run economic growth—why it happens and how to achieve it—is the single most important issue in macroeconomics. In this section, we present some facts about long-run growth, look at the factors that economists believe determine its pace, examine how government policies can help or hinder growth, and address questions about the environmental sustainability of growth.

AP Photo/EyePress

Stockbyte/Getty Images

MODULE 37

Long-Run Economic Growth

In this Module, you will learn to:

- Interpret measures of long-run economic growth
- Describe how real GDP has changed over time
- Explain how real GDP varies across countries
- Identify the sources of long-run economic growth
- Explain how productivity is driven by physical capital, human capital, and technological progress

Comparing Economies Across Time and Space

Before we analyze the sources of long-run economic growth, it's useful to have a sense of just how much the U.S. economy has grown over time and how large the gaps are between wealthy countries like the United States and countries that have yet to achieve a comparable standard of living. So let's take a look at the numbers.

Real GDP per Capita

The key statistic used to track economic growth is *real GDP per capita*—real GDP divided by the population size. We focus on GDP because, as we have learned, GDP measures the total value of an economy's production of final goods and services as well as the income earned in that economy in a given year. We use *real* GDP because we want to separate changes in the quantity of goods and services from the effects of a rising price level. We focus on real GDP *per capita* because we want to isolate the effect of changes in the population. For example, other things equal, an increase in the population lowers the standard of living for the average person—there are now more people to share a given amount of real GDP. An increase in real GDP that only matches an increase in population leaves the real GDP per capita unchanged.

Although we learned that growth in real GDP per capita should not be a policy goal in and of itself, it does serve as a very useful summary measure of a country's economic progress over time. **Figure 37.1** on the next page shows real GDP per capita for the United States, India, and China, measured in 2005 dollars, from 1910 to 2010. (We'll talk about India and China in a moment.) The vertical axis is drawn on a logarithmic scale so that

Figure 37.1 Economic Growth in the United States, India, and China over the Past Century

Real GDP per capita from 1910 to 2010, measured in 2005 dollars, is shown for the United States, India, and China. Equal percentage changes in real GDP per capita are drawn the same size. India and China currently have a much higher growth rate than the United States. However, China has only recently attained the standard of living achieved in the United States in 1910, while India is still poorer than the United States was in 1910.

Sources: Angus Maddison, January 2003; J. Bolt and J. L. van Zanden, "The First Update of the Maddison Project; Re-Estimating Growth Before 1820," Maddison Project Working Paper 4, January 2003, http://www.ggdc.net/maddison/maddison-project/home.htm.

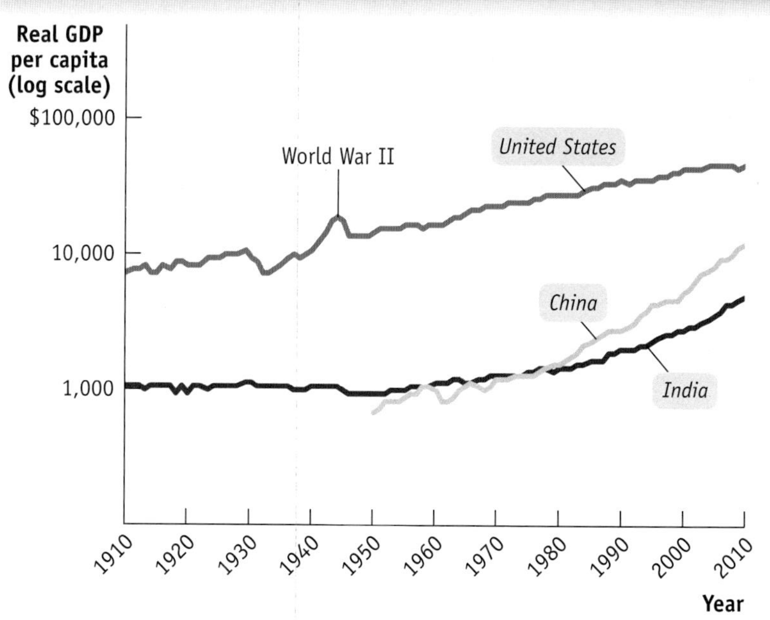

equal percentage changes in real GDP per capita across countries are the same size in the graph.

To give a sense of how much the U.S. economy grew during the last century, **Table 37.1** shows real GDP per capita at 20-year intervals, expressed two ways: as a percentage of the 1910 level and as a percentage of the 2010 level. In 1930, the U.S. economy already produced 125% as much per person as it did in 1910. In 2010, it produced 614% as much per person as it did in 1910. Alternatively, in 1910, the U.S. economy produced only 16% as much per person as it did in 2010.

The income of the typical family normally grows more or less in proportion to per capita income. For example, a 1% increase in real GDP per capita corresponds, roughly, to a 1% increase in the income of the median or typical family—a family at the center of the income distribution. In 2010, the median American household had an income of about $45,600. Since Table 37.1 tells us that real GDP per capita in 1910 was only 16% of its 2010 level, a typical family in 1910 probably had purchasing power only 16% as large as the purchasing power of a typical family in 2010. That's around $7,400 in

Table 37.1 U.S. Real GDP per Capita

Year	Percentage of 1910 real GDP per capita	Percentage of 2010 real GDP per capita
1910	100%	16%
1930	125	20
1950	192	31
1970	302	49
1990	467	76
2010	614	100

Sources: Angus Maddison, January 2003; J. Bolt and J. L. van Zanden, "The First Update of the Maddison Project; Re-Estimating Growth Before 1820," Maddison Project Working Paper 4, January 2003, http://www.ggdc.net/maddison/maddison-project/home.htm.

Figure 37.2 Incomes Around the World, 2013

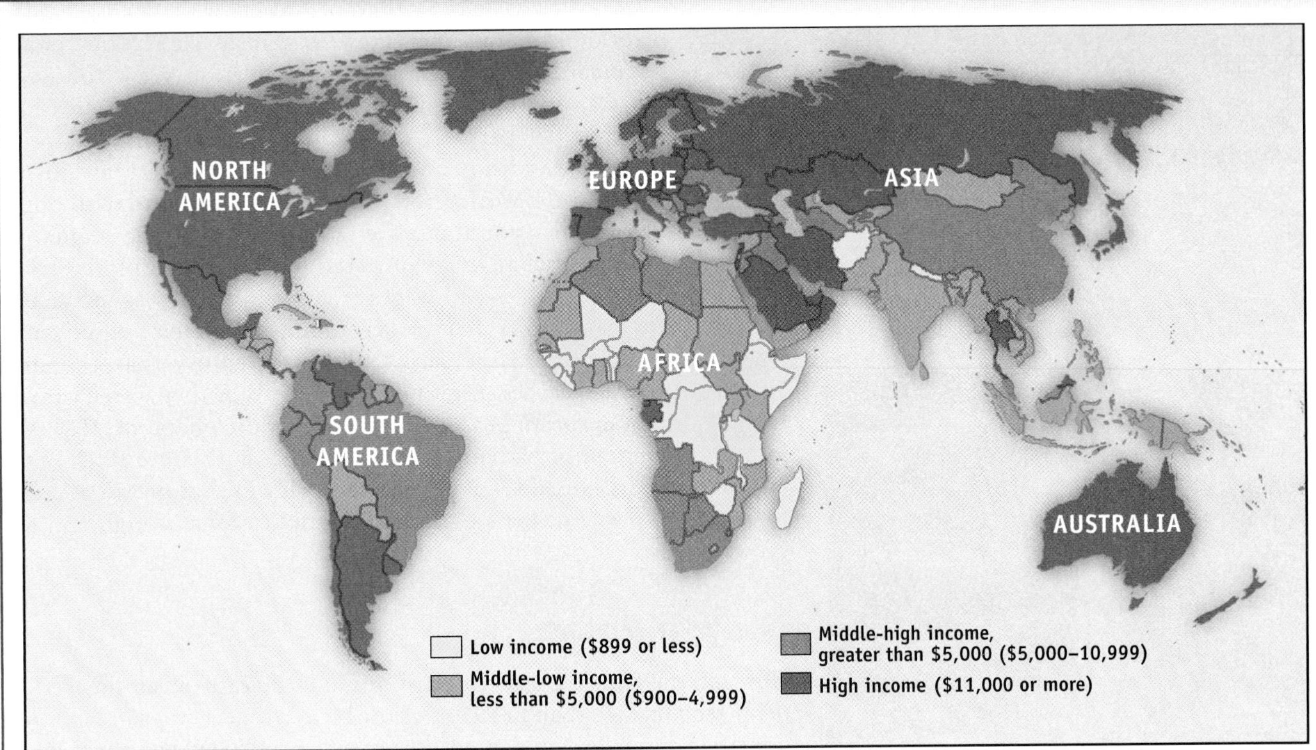

Although the countries of Europe and North America—along with a few in East Asia—have high incomes, much of the world is still very poor. Today, more than 50% of the world's population lives in countries with a lower standard of living than the United States had a century ago.
Source: International Monetary Fund.

today's dollars, representing a standard of living that we would now consider severe poverty. Today's typical American family, if transported back to the United States of 1910, would feel quite deprived.

Yet many people in the world have a standard of living equal to or lower than that of the United States a century ago. That's the message about China and India in Figure 37.1: despite dramatic economic growth in China over the last three decades and the less dramatic acceleration of economic growth in India, China has only recently attained the standard of living that the United States enjoyed in 1910, while India is still poorer than the United States was in 1910. And much of the world today is poorer than China or India.

You can get a sense of how poor much of the world remains by looking at **Figure 37.2**, a map of the world in which countries are classified according to their 2013 levels of GDP per capita, in U.S. dollars. As you can see, large parts of the world have very low incomes. Generally speaking, the countries of Europe and North America, as well as a few in the Pacific, have high incomes. The rest of the world, containing most of its population, is dominated by countries with GDP less than $7,000 per capita—and often much less. In fact, today more than 50% of the world's people live in countries with a lower standard of living than the United States had a century ago.

When Did Long-Run Growth Begin?

In 2013, the United States was much richer than it was in 1953; in 1953, it was much richer than it had been in 1903. But how did 1853 compare with 1803? Or 1753? How far back does long-run economic growth go?

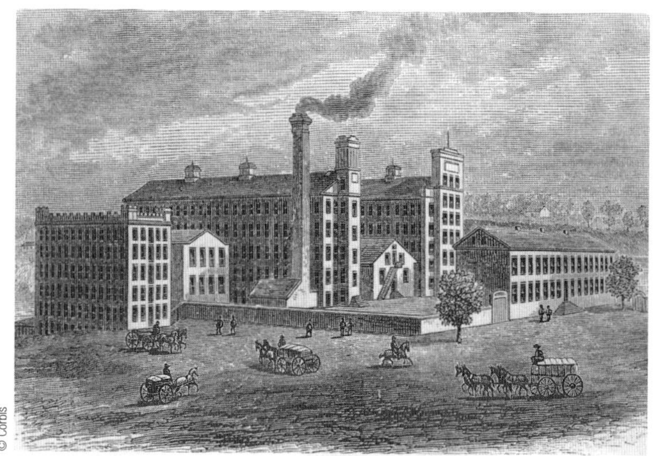

© Corbis

Thinkstock

The answer is that long-run growth is a relatively modern phenomenon. The U.S. economy was already growing steadily by the mid-nineteenth century—think railroads. But if you go back to the period before 1800, you find a world economy that grew extremely slowly by today's standards. Furthermore, the population grew almost as fast as the economy, so there was very little increase in output per person. According to the economic historian Angus Maddison, from 1000 to 1800, real aggregate output around the world grew less than 0.2% per year, with population rising at about the same rate. Economic stagnation meant unchanging living standards. For example, information on prices and wages from sources such as monastery records shows that workers in England weren't significantly better off in the early eighteenth century than they had been five centuries earlier. And it's a good bet that they weren't much better off than Egyptian peasants in the age of the pharaohs. However, long-run economic growth has increased significantly since 1800. In the last 50 years or so, real GDP per capita worldwide has grown at a rate of about 2% per year. Let's examine the implications of high and low growth rates.

Growth Rates

How did the United States manage to produce nearly seven times more per person in 2010 than in 1910? A little bit at a time. Long-run economic growth is normally a gradual process in which real GDP per capita grows at most a few percent per year. From 1910 to 2010, real GDP per capita in the United States increased an average of 2.1% each year.

FYI India Takes Off

India achieved independence from Great Britain in 1947, becoming the world's most populous democracy—a status it has maintained to this day. For more than three decades after independence, however, this happy political story was partly overshadowed by economic disappointment. Despite ambitious economic development plans, India's performance was consistently sluggish. In 1980, India's real GDP per capita was only about 50% higher than it had been in 1947; the gap between Indian living standards and those in wealthy countries like the United States had been growing rather than shrinking.

Since then, however, India has done much better. As Figure 37.3 shows, real GDP per capita has grown at an average rate of 3% a year, tripling between 1980 and 2013. India now has a large and rapidly growing middle class. And yes, the well-fed children of that middle class are much taller than their parents.

What went right in India after 1980? Many economists point to policy reforms. For decades after independence, India had a tightly controlled, highly regulated economy. Today, things are very different: a series of reforms opened the economy to international trade and freed up domestic competition. Some economists, however, argue that this can't be the main story because the big policy reforms weren't adopted until 1991, yet growth accelerated around 1980.

Regardless of the explanation, India's economic rise has transformed it into a major new economic power—and allowed hundreds of millions of people to have a much better life, better than their grandparents could have imagined.

Verity Steel/Alamy

India's high rate of economic growth since 1980 has raised living standards and led to the emergence of a rapidly growing middle class.

To have a sense of the relationship between the annual growth rate of real GDP per capita and the long-run change in real GDP per capita, it's helpful to keep in mind the **Rule of 70**, a mathematical formula that tells us how long it takes real GDP per capita, or any other variable that grows gradually over time, to double. The approximate answer is:

The **Rule of 70** tells us that the time it takes a variable that grows gradually over time to double is approximately 70 divided by that variable's annual growth rate.

$$\textbf{(37-1)} \quad \text{Number of years for variable to double} = \frac{70}{\text{Annual growth rate of variable}}$$

(Note that the Rule of 70 can only be applied to a positive growth rate.) So if real GDP per capita grows at 1% per year, it will take 70 years to double. If it grows at 2% per year, it will take only 35 years to double. Applying the Rule of 70 to the 2.1% average growth rate in the United States implies that it should have taken 33.3 years for real GDP per capita to double; it would have taken 100 years—three periods of 33.3 years each—for U.S. real GDP per capita to double three times. That is, the Rule of 70 implies that over the course of 100 years, U.S. real GDP per capita should have increased by a factor of $2 \times 2 \times 2 = 8$. And this does turn out to be a pretty good approximation of reality. Between 1910 and 2013—a period of 103 years—real GDP per capita rose just about eightfold.

Figure 37.3 shows the average annual rate of growth of real GDP per capita for selected countries from 1980 to 2012. Some countries were notable success stories: we've already mentioned China, which has made spectacular progress. India, although not matching China's performance, has also achieved impressive growth.

Figure 37.3 Comparing Recent Growth Rates

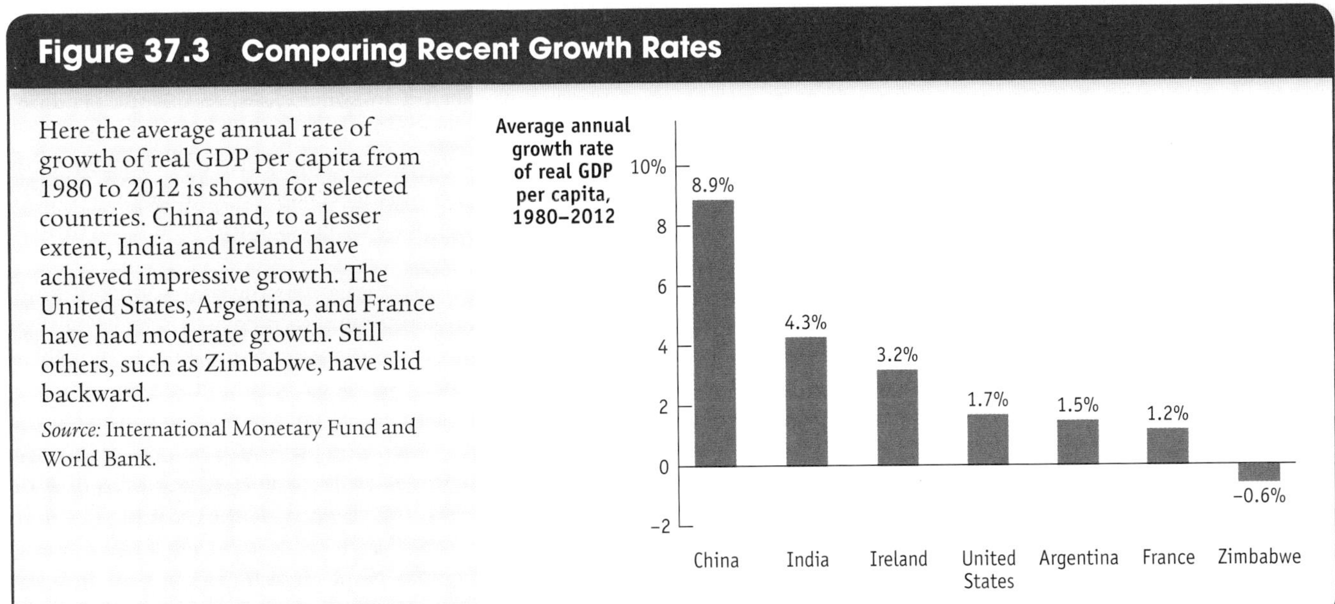

Here the average annual rate of growth of real GDP per capita from 1980 to 2012 is shown for selected countries. China and, to a lesser extent, India and Ireland have achieved impressive growth. The United States, Argentina, and France have had moderate growth. Still others, such as Zimbabwe, have slid backward.

Source: International Monetary Fund and World Bank.

Some countries, though, have had very disappointing growth. This includes many of the countries in Africa and South America, where growth rates below 1% are common. A few countries, such as Zimbabwe, have actually slid backward.

What explains these differences in growth rates? To answer that question, we need to examine the sources of long-run growth.

The Sources of Long-Run Growth

Long-run economic growth depends almost entirely on one ingredient: rising *productivity*. However, a number of factors affect the growth of productivity. Let's look first at why productivity is the key ingredient. After that, we'll examine what affects it.

The Walmart Effect

After 20 years of being sluggish, U.S. productivity growth accelerated sharply in the late 1990s. What caused that acceleration? Was it the rise of the Internet?

Not according to analysts at McKinsey and Co., a famous business consulting firm. They found that a major source of productivity improvement after 1995 was a surge in output per worker in retailing—stores were selling much more merchandise per worker. And why did productivity surge in retailing in the United States? "The reason can be explained in just two syllables: Walmart," wrote McKinsey.

Walmart has been a pioneer in using modern technology to improve productivity. For example, it was one of the first companies to use computers to track inventory, to use bar-code scanners, to establish direct electronic links with suppliers, and so on. It continued to set the pace in the 1990s, but, increasingly, other companies have imitated Walmart's business practices.

There are two lessons from the "Walmart effect," as McKinsey calls it. One is that how you apply a technology makes all the difference: everyone in the retail business knew about computers, but Walmart figured out what to do with them. The other is that a lot of economic growth comes from everyday improvements rather than glamorous new technologies.

PAUL J. RICHARDS/AFP/Getty Images

AP® Exam Tip

Productivity is the most important factor that changes economic growth. Productivity is impacted by improvements in human capital (worker education) and technology.

Labor productivity, often referred to simply as **productivity**, is output per worker.

The Crucial Importance of Productivity

Sustained growth in real GDP per capita occurs only when the amount of output produced by the average worker increases steadily. The term **labor productivity**, or **productivity** for short, is used to refer either to output per worker or, in some cases, to output per hour (the number of hours worked by an average worker differs to some extent across countries, although this isn't an important factor in the difference between living standards in, say, India and the United States). In this book we'll focus on output per worker. For the economy as a whole, productivity—output per worker—is simply real GDP divided by the number of people working.

You might wonder why we say that higher productivity is the only source of long-run growth in real GDP per capita. Can't an economy also increase its real GDP per capita by putting more of the population to work? The answer is, yes, but . . . . For short periods of time, an economy can experience a burst of growth in output per capita by putting a higher percentage of the population to work. That happened in the United States during World War II, when millions of women who previously worked only in the home entered the paid workforce. The percentage of adult civilians employed outside the home rose from 50% in 1941 to 58% in 1944, and you can see the resulting bump in real GDP per capita during those years in Figure 37.1.

Over the longer run, however, the rate of employment growth is never very different from the rate of population growth. Over the course of the twentieth century, for example, the population of the United States rose at an average rate of 1.3% per year and employment rose 1.5% per year. Real GDP per capita rose 1.9% per year; of that, 1.7%—that is, almost 90% of the total—was the result of rising productivity. In general, overall real GDP can grow because of population growth, but any large increase in real GDP *per capita* must be the result of increased output *per worker*. That is, it must be due to higher productivity.

We have just seen that increased productivity is the key to long-run economic growth. But what leads to higher productivity?

AP® Exam Tip

If you're asked to identify a source of economic growth, "increased investment in physical capital" is a good answer. Don't just say "increased investment," because the meaning of that is more ambiguous.

Explaining Growth in Productivity

There are three main reasons why the average U.S. worker today produces far more than his or her counterpart a century ago. First, the modern worker has far more *physical capital*, such as tools and office space, to work with. Second, the modern worker is much better educated and so possesses much more *human capital*. Finally, modern firms have the advantage of a century's accumulation of technical advancements reflecting a great deal of *technological progress*.

Let's look at each of these factors in turn.

Physical Capital Module 22 explained that capital—manufactured goods used to produce other goods and services—is often described as **physical capital** to distinguish it from human capital and other types of capital. Physical capital such as buildings and machinery makes workers more productive. For example, a worker operating a backhoe can dig a lot more feet of trench per day than one equipped with only a shovel.

The average U.S. private-sector worker today makes use of approximately $130,000 worth of physical capital—far more than a U.S. worker had 100 years ago and far more than the average worker in most other countries has today.

Physical capital consists of human-made goods such as buildings and machines used to produce other goods and services.

Human capital is the improvement in labor created by the education and knowledge of members of the workforce.

Technology is the technical means for the production of goods and services.

Human Capital It's not enough for a worker to have good equipment—he or she must also know what to do with it. **Human capital** refers to the improvement in labor created by the education and knowledge embodied in the workforce.

The human capital of the United States has increased dramatically over the past century. A century ago, although most Americans were able to read and write, very few had an extensive education. In 1910, only 13.5% of Americans over 25 had graduated from high school and only 3% had four-year college degrees. By 2013, the percentages were 88% and 31%, respectively. It would be impossible to run today's economy with a population as poorly educated as that of a century ago.

Analyses based on *growth accounting*, described later in this section, suggest that education—and its effect on productivity—is an even more important determinant of growth than increases in physical capital.

iStockphoto/Thinkstock

If you've ever had doubts about attending college, consider this: factory workers with only high school degrees will make much less than college grads. The present discounted value of the difference in lifetime earnings is as much as $300,000.

Technology Probably the most important driver of productivity growth is progress in **technology**, which is broadly defined as the technical means for the production of goods and services. We'll see shortly how economists measure the impact of technology on growth.

Workers today are able to produce more than those in the past, even with the same amount of physical and human capital, because technology has advanced over time. It's important to realize that economically important technological progress need not be flashy or rely on cutting-edge science. Historians have noted that past economic growth has been driven not only by major inventions, such as the railroad or the semiconductor chip, but also by thousands of modest innovations, such as the flat-bottomed paper bag, patented in 1870, which made packing groceries and many other goods much easier, and the Post-it note, introduced in 1981, which has had surprisingly large benefits for office productivity. Experts attribute much of the productivity surge that took place in the United States late in the twentieth century to new technology adopted by retail companies like Walmart rather than to high-technology companies.

Corbis Super RF/Alamy

MODULE 37 Review

Check Your Understanding

1. Why do economists focus on real GDP per capita as a measure of economic progress rather than on some other measure, such as nominal GDP per capita or real GDP?
2. Apply the Rule of 70 to the data in Figure 37.3 to determine how long it will take each of the countries listed there to double its real GDP per capita. Will India's real GDP per capita exceed that of the United States in the future if growth rates remain the same? Why or why not?
3. Although China and India currently have growth rates much higher than the U.S. growth rate, the typical Chinese or Indian household is far poorer than the typical American household. Explain why.

Tackle the Test: Multiple-Choice Questions

1. Which of the following is true regarding growth rates for countries around the world compared to the United States?
    - **I.** More than fifty percent of the world's people live in countries with a lower standard of living than the U.S. had a century ago.
    - **II.** The U.S. growth rate is six times the growth rate in the rest of the world.
    - **III.** China has only recently attained the same standard of living the U.S. had a century ago.

    a. I only
    b. II only
    c. III only
    d. I and III only
    e. I, II, and III

2. Which of the following is the key statistic used to track economic growth?
    a. GDP
    b. real GDP
    c. real GDP per capita
    d. median real GDP
    e. median real GDP per capita

3. According to the "Rule of 70," if a country's real GDP per capita grows at a rate of 2% per year, it will take how many years for real GDP per capita to double?
    a. 3.5
    b. 20
    c. 35
    d. 70
    e. It will never double at that rate.

4. If a country's real GDP per capita doubles in 10 years, what was its average annual rate of growth of real GDP per capita?
    a. 3.5%
    b. 7%
    c. 10%
    d. 70%
    e. 700%

5. Long-run economic growth depends almost entirely on
    a. technological change.
    b. rising productivity.
    c. increased labor force participation.
    d. rising real GDP per capita.
    e. population growth.

Tackle the Test: Free-Response Questions

1. Refer to Figure 37.3, reproduced below, to answer each of the questions that follow.

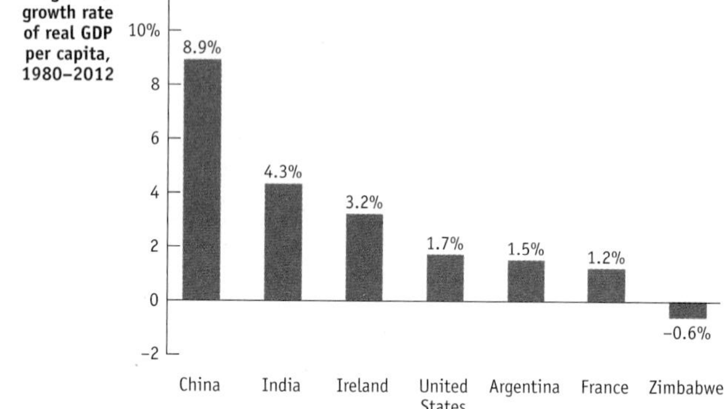

a. If growth continued at the rates shown in the figure, which of the seven countries would have had a lower real GDP per capita in 2014 than in 2013? Explain.
b. If growth continued at the rates shown in the figure, which of the seven countries would have had the highest real GDP per capita in 2014? Explain.
c. If growth continues at the rates shown in the figure, real GDP per capita for which of the seven countries will at least double over the next 10 years? Explain.

Rubric for FRQ 1 (6 points)

1 point: Zimbabwe

1 point: It has a negative average annual growth rate of real GDP per capita.

1 point: It cannot be determined.

1 point: The figure provides data for growth rates, but not for the level of real GDP per capita. Higher growth rates do not indicate higher levels.

1 point: China

1 point: A country has to have an average annual growth rate of 7% or higher for real GDP to at least double in 10 years. China has a growth rate of 8.9%.

2. Increases in real GDP per capita result primarily from changes in what variable? (Hint: This is a general source of long-run growth and not a particular input such as capital.) Define that variable. Increases in what other variable could also lead to increased real GDP per capita? Why is this other factor less significant? **(4 points)**

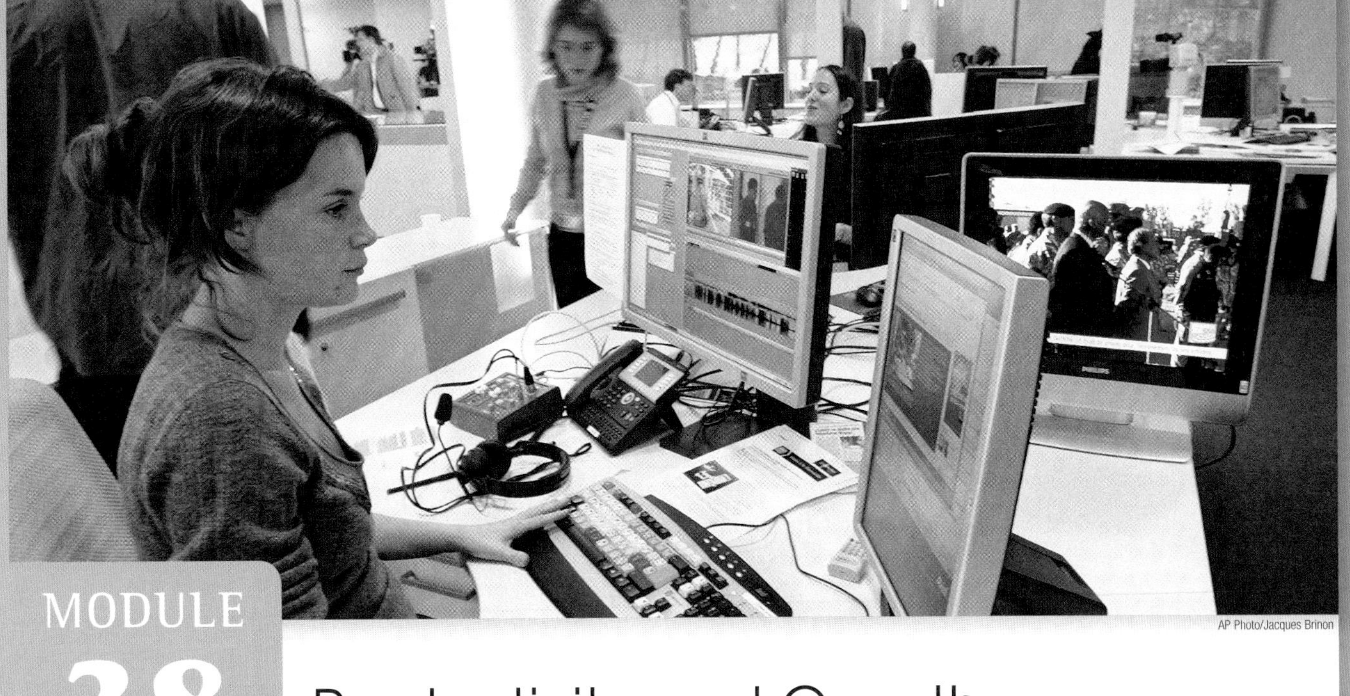
AP Photo/Jacques Brinon

MODULE 38

Productivity and Growth

In this Module, you will learn to:

- Illustrate changes in productivity using an aggregate production function
- Discuss how growth has varied among several important regions of the world and explain why the convergence hypothesis applies to economically advanced countries

Accounting for Growth: The Aggregate Production Function

Productivity is higher, other things equal, when workers are equipped with more physical capital, more human capital, better technology, or any combination of the three. But can we put numbers to these effects? To do this, economists make use of estimates of the **aggregate production function**, which shows how productivity depends on the quantities of physical capital per worker and human capital per worker as well as the state of technology. In general, all three factors tend to rise over time, as workers are equipped with more machinery, receive more education, and benefit from technological advances. What the aggregate production function does is allow economists to disentangle the effects of these three factors on overall productivity.

The **aggregate production function** is a hypothetical function that shows how productivity (output per worker) depends on the quantities of physical capital per worker and human capital per worker as well as the state of technology.

An example of an aggregate production function applied to real data comes from a comparative study of Chinese and Indian economic growth conducted by the economists Barry Bosworth and Susan Collins of the Brookings Institution. They used the following aggregate production function:

$$\text{GDP per worker} = T \times (\text{physical capital per worker})^{0.4} \times (\text{human capital per worker})^{0.6}$$

where T represented an estimate of the level of technology and they assumed that each year of education raised workers' human capital by 7%. Using this function, they tried to explain why China grew faster than India between 1978 and 2004. They found that

Table 38.1 A Hypothetical Example: How Physical Capital per Worker Affects Productivity, Holding Human Capital and Technology Fixed	
Physical capital investment per worker	**Real GDP per worker**
$0	$0
15,000	30,000
30,000	45,000
45,000	55,000

about half the difference was due to China's higher levels of investment spending, which raised its level of physical capital per worker faster than India's. The other half was due to faster Chinese technological progress.

An aggregate production function exhibits **diminishing returns to physical capital** when, holding the amount of human capital per worker and the state of technology fixed, each successive increase in the amount of physical capital per worker leads to a smaller increase in productivity.

In analyzing historical economic growth, economists have discovered a crucial fact about the estimated aggregate production function: it exhibits **diminishing returns to physical capital**. That is, when the amount of human capital per worker and the state of technology are held fixed, each successive increase in the amount of physical capital per worker leads to a smaller increase in productivity. **Table 38.1** gives a hypothetical example of how the level of physical capital per worker might affect the level of real GDP per worker, holding human capital per worker and the state of technology fixed. In this example, we measure the quantity of physical capital in terms of the dollars worth of investment.

As you can see from the table, there is a big payoff from the first $15,000 invested in physical capital: real GDP per worker rises by $30,000. The second $15,000 worth of physical capital also raises productivity, but not by as much: real GDP per worker goes up by only $15,000. The third $15,000 worth of physical capital raises real GDP per worker by only $10,000.

AP® Exam Tip

Recognize that diminishing returns to physical capital can only be measured accurately if other factors like technology and human capital per worker are held constant.

To see why the relationship between physical capital per worker and productivity exhibits diminishing returns, think about how having farm equipment affects the productivity of farm workers. A little bit of equipment makes a big difference: a worker equipped with a tractor can do much more than a worker without one. And, other things equal, a worker using more expensive equipment will be more productive: a worker with a $30,000 tractor will normally be able to cultivate more farmland in a given amount of time than a worker with a $15,000 tractor because the more expensive machine will be more powerful, perform more tasks, or both.

But will a worker with a $30,000 tractor, holding human capital and technology constant, be twice as productive as a worker with a $15,000 tractor? Probably not: there's a huge difference between not having a tractor at all and having even an inexpensive tractor; there's much less difference between having an inexpensive tractor and having a better tractor. And we can be sure that a worker with a $150,000 tractor won't be 10 times as productive: a tractor can be improved only so much. Because the same is true of other kinds of equipment, the aggregate production function shows diminishing returns to physical capital.

Figure 38.1 is a graphical representation of the aggregate production function with diminishing returns to physical capital. As the *productivity curve* illustrates, more physical capital per worker leads to more output per worker. But each $30,000 increment in physical capital per worker adds less to productivity. By comparing points *A*, *B*, and *C*, you can also see that, as physical capital per worker rises, output per worker also rises—but at a diminishing rate. Going from point *A* to point *B*, representing a $30,000 increase in physical capital per worker, leads to an increase of $20,000 in real GDP per worker. Going from point *B* to point *C*, a second $30,000 increase in physical capital per worker, leads to an increase of only $10,000 in real GDP per worker.

It's important to realize that diminishing returns to physical capital is an "other things equal" phenomenon: additional amounts of physical capital are less productive

Figure 38.1 Physical Capital and Productivity

Other things equal, a greater quantity of physical capital per worker leads to higher real GDP per worker but is subject to diminishing returns: each successive addition to physical capital per worker produces a smaller increase in productivity. Starting at point *A*, with $20,000 in physical capital per worker, a $30,000 increase in physical capital per worker leads to an increase of $20,000 in real GDP per worker. At point *B*, with $50,000 in physical capital per worker, a $30,000 increase in physical capital per worker leads to an increase of only $10,000 in real GDP per worker.

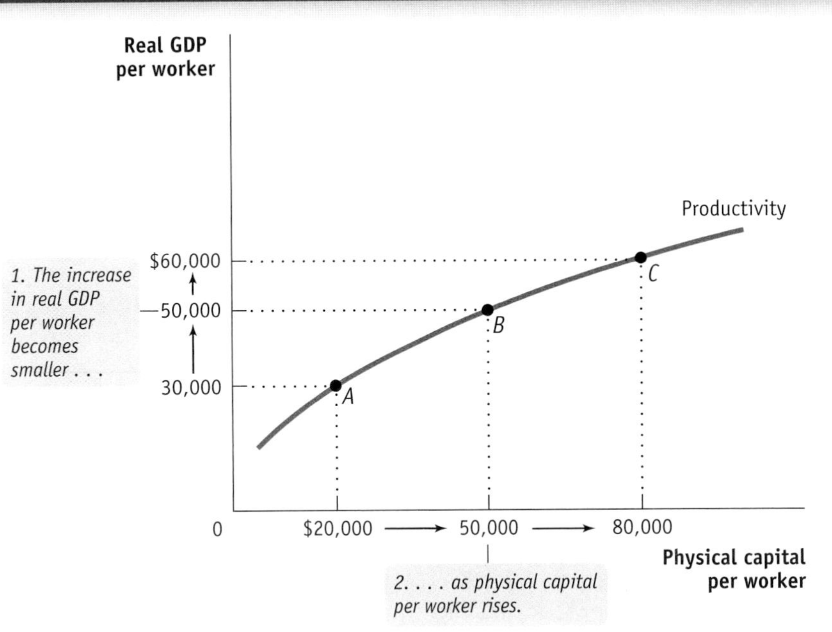

when the amount of human capital per worker and the technology are held fixed. Diminishing returns may disappear if we increase the amount of human capital per worker, or improve the technology, or both when the amount of physical capital per worker is increased. For example, a worker with a $30,000 tractor who has also been trained in the most advanced cultivation techniques may in fact be more than twice as productive as a worker with only a $15,000 tractor and no additional human capital. But diminishing returns to any one input—regardless of whether it is physical capital, human capital, or labor—is a pervasive characteristic of production. Typical estimates suggest that, in practice, a 1% increase in the quantity of physical capital per worker increases output per worker by only one-third of 1%, or 0.33%.

In practice, all the factors contributing to higher productivity rise during the course of economic growth: both physical capital and human capital per worker increase, and technology advances as well. To disentangle the effects of these factors, economists use **growth accounting** to estimate the contribution of each major factor in the aggregate production function to economic growth. For example, suppose the following are true:

Economists use **growth accounting** to estimate the contribution of each major factor in the aggregate production function to economic growth.

- The amount of physical capital per worker grows 3% a year.
- According to estimates of the aggregate production function, each 1% rise in physical capital per worker, holding human capital and technology constant, raises output per worker by one-third of 1%, or 0.33%.

In that case, we would estimate that growing physical capital per worker is responsible for 1 percentage point (3% × 0.33) of productivity growth per year. A similar but more complex procedure is used to estimate the effects of growing human capital. The procedure is more complex because there aren't simple dollar measures of the quantity of human capital.

Growth accounting allows us to calculate the effects of greater amounts of physical and human capital on economic growth. But how can we estimate the effects of technological progress? We can do so by estimating what is left over after the effects of physical and human capital have been taken into account. For example, let's imagine that there was no increase in human capital per worker so that we can focus on changes in physical capital

Figure 38.2 Technological Progress and Productivity Growth

Technological progress shifts the productivity curve upward. Here we hold human capital per worker fixed. We assume that the lower curve (the same curve as in Figure 38.1) reflects technology in 1940 and the upper curve reflects technology in 2010. Holding technology and human capital fixed, quadrupling physical capital per worker from $20,000 to $80,000 leads to a doubling of real GDP per worker, from $30,000 to $60,000. This is shown by the movement from point *A* to point *C*, reflecting an approximately 1% per year rise in real GDP per worker. In reality, technological progress shifted the productivity curve upward and the actual rise in real GDP per worker is shown by the movement from point *A* to point *D*. Real GDP per worker grew 2% per year, leading to a quadrupling during the period. The extra 1% in growth of real GDP per worker is due to higher total factor productivity.

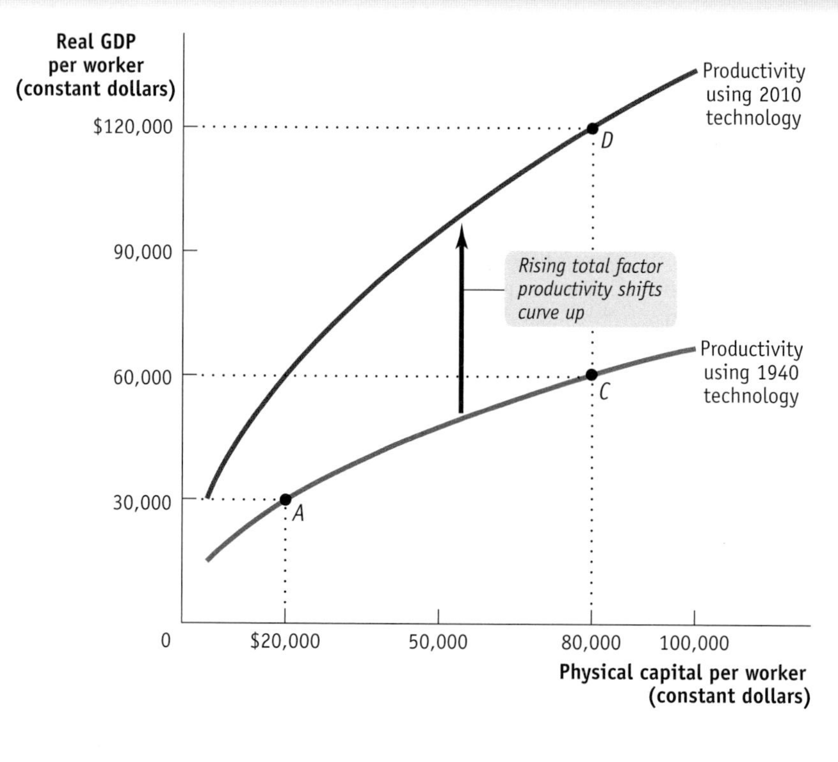

Total factor productivity is the amount of output that can be achieved with a given amount of factor inputs.

and in technology. In **Figure 38.2**, the lower curve shows the same hypothetical relationship between physical capital per worker and output per worker shown in Figure 38.1. Let's assume that this was the relationship given the technology available in 1940. The upper curve also shows a relationship between physical capital per worker and productivity, but this time given the technology available in 2010. (We've chosen a 70-year stretch to allow us to use the Rule of 70.) The 2010 curve is shifted up compared to the 1940 curve because technologies developed over the previous 70 years make it possible to produce more output for a given amount of physical capital per worker than was possible with the technology available in 1940. (Note that the two curves are measured in constant dollars.)

"Productivity is up nine per cent since I made everyone a vice-president."

Ed Fisher/The New Yorker Collection/www.cartoonbank.com

Let's assume that between 1940 and 2010 the amount of physical capital per worker rose from $20,000 to $80,000. If this increase in physical capital per worker had taken place without any technological progress, the economy would have moved from *A* to *C*: output per worker would have risen, but only from $30,000 to $60,000, or 1% per year (using the Rule of 70 tells us that a 1% growth rate over 70 years doubles output). In fact, however, the economy moved from *A* to *D*: output rose from $30,000 to $120,000, or 2% per year. There was an increase in both physical capital per worker and technological progress, which shifted the aggregate production function.

In this case, 50% of the annual 2% increase in productivity—that is, 1% in annual productivity growth—is due to higher **total factor productivity**, the amount of output that can be produced with a given amount of factor inputs. So when total factor productivity increases, the economy can produce more output with the same quantity of physical capital, human capital, and labor.

Most estimates find that increases in total factor productivity are central to a country's economic growth. We believe that observed increases in total factor productivity in fact measure the economic effects of technological progress. All of this implies that technological change is crucial to economic growth. The Bureau of Labor Statistics estimates the growth rate of both labor productivity and total factor productivity for nonfarm business in the United States. According to the Bureau's estimates, over the period from 1948 to 2010, American labor productivity rose 2.3% per year. Only 49% of that rise is explained by increases in physical and human capital per worker; the rest is explained by rising total factor productivity—that is, by technological progress.

What About Natural Resources?

In our discussion so far, we haven't mentioned natural resources, which certainly have an effect on productivity. Other things equal, countries that are abundant in valuable natural resources, such as highly fertile land or rich mineral deposits, have higher real GDP per capita than less fortunate countries. The most obvious modern example is the Middle East, where enormous oil deposits have made a few sparsely populated countries very rich. For instance, Kuwait has about the same level of real GDP per capita as South Korea, but Kuwait's wealth is based on oil, not manufacturing, the source of South Korea's high output per worker.

But other things are often not equal. In the modern world, natural resources are a much less important determinant of productivity than human or physical capital for the great majority of countries. For example, some nations with very high real GDP per capita, such as Japan, have very few natural resources. Some resource-rich nations, such as Nigeria (which has sizable oil deposits), are very poor.

Historically, natural resources played a much more prominent role in determining productivity. In the nineteenth century, the countries with the highest real GDP per capita were those abundant in rich farmland and mineral deposits: the United States, Canada, Argentina, and Australia. As a consequence, natural resources figured prominently in the development of economic thought. In a famous book published in 1798, *An Essay on the Principle of Population*, the English economist Thomas Malthus made the fixed quantity of land in the world the basis of a pessimistic prediction about future productivity. As population grew, he pointed out, the amount of land per worker would decline. And, other things equal, this would cause productivity to fall. In fact, his view was that improvements in technology or increases in physical capital would lead only to temporary improvements in productivity because they would always be offset by the pressure of rising population and more workers on the supply of land. In the long run, he concluded, the great majority of people were condemned to living on the edge of starvation. Only then would death rates be high enough and birth rates low enough to prevent rapid population growth from outstripping productivity growth.

© Frans Lemmens/Alamy

The offerings at markets such as this one in Lagos, Nigeria, are shaped by the available natural resources, human and physical capital, and technology.

It hasn't turned out that way, although many historians believe that Malthus's prediction of falling or stagnant productivity was valid for much of human history. Population pressure probably did prevent large productivity increases until the eighteenth century. But in the time since Malthus wrote his book, any negative effects on productivity from population growth have been far outweighed by other, positive factors—advances in technology, increases in human and physical capital, and the opening up of enormous amounts of cultivatable land in the New World.

It remains true, however, that we live on a finite planet, with limited supplies of resources such as oil and limited ability to absorb environmental damage. We address the concerns these limitations pose for economic growth later in this section.

The Information Technology Paradox

From the early 1970s through the mid-1990s, the United States went through a slump in total factor productivity growth. The figure shows Bureau of Labor Statistics estimates of annual total factor productivity growth since 1949. As you can see, there was a large fall in the productivity growth rate beginning in the early 1970s. Because higher total factor productivity plays such a key role in long-run growth, the economy's overall growth was also disappointing, leading to a widespread sense that economic progress had ground to a halt.

Many economists were puzzled by the slowdown in total factor productivity growth after 1973, since in other ways the era seemed to be one of rapid technological progress. Modern information technology really began with the development of the first microprocessor—a computer on a chip—in 1971. In the 25 years that followed, a series of inventions that seemed revolutionary became standard equipment in the business world: fax machines, desktop computers, cell phones, and e-mail. Yet the rate of growth of productivity remained stagnant. In a famous remark, MIT economics professor and Nobel laureate Robert Solow, a pioneer in the analysis of economic growth, declared that the information technology revolution could be seen everywhere except in the economic statistics.

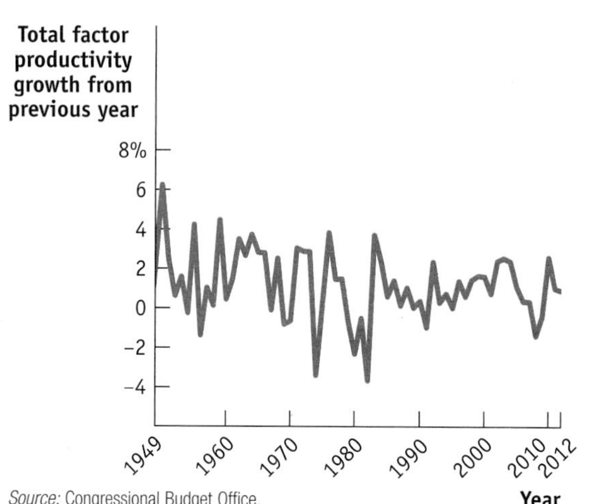

Source: Congressional Budget Office.

Why didn't information technology show large rewards? Paul David, a Stanford University economic historian, offered a theory and a prediction. He pointed out that 100 years earlier another miracle technology—electric power—had spread through the economy, again with surprisingly little impact on productivity growth at first. The reason, he suggested, was that a new technology doesn't yield its full potential if you use it in old ways.

For example, a traditional factory around 1900 was a multistory building, with the machinery tightly crowded together and designed to be powered by a steam engine in the basement. This design had problems: it was very difficult to move people and materials around. Yet owners who electrified their factories initially maintained the multistory, tightly packed layout. Only with the switch to spread-out, one-story factories that took advantage of the flexibility of electric power—most famously Henry Ford's auto assembly line—did productivity take off.

David suggested that the same phenomenon was happening with information technology. Productivity, he predicted, would take off when people really changed their way of doing business to take advantage of the new technology—such as replacing letters and phone calls with e-mail. Sure enough, productivity growth accelerated dramatically in the second half of the 1990s. And, a lot of that may have been due to the discovery by companies like Walmart of how to effectively use information technology.

Success, Disappointment, and Failure

Rates of long-run economic growth differ markedly around the world. Let's look at three regions that have had quite different experiences with economic growth over the last few decades.

Figure 38.3 shows trends since 1960 in real GDP per capita in 2005 dollars for three countries: Argentina, Nigeria, and South Korea. (As in Figure 37.1, the vertical axis is drawn in logarithmic scale.) We have chosen these countries because each is a particularly striking example of what has happened in its region. South Korea's amazing rise is part of a larger success story in East Asia. Argentina's slow progress, interrupted by repeated setbacks, is more or less typical of the disappointment that has characterized Latin America. And Nigeria's unhappy story–real GDP per capita is barely higher now than it was in 1960–is, unfortunately, an experience shared by many African countries.

East Asia's Miracle

In 1960, South Korea was a very poor country. In fact, in 1960 its real GDP per capita was lower than that of India today. But, as you can see from Figure 38.3, beginning in the early 1960s, South Korea began an extremely rapid economic ascent: real GDP per

Figure 38.3 Success and Disappointment

Real GDP per capita from 1960 to 2012, measured in 2005 dollars, is shown for Argentina, South Korea, and Nigeria, using a logarithmic scale. South Korea and some other East Asian countries have been highly successful at achieving economic growth. Argentina, like much of Latin America, has had several setbacks, slowing its growth. Nigeria's standard of living in 2012 was only barely higher than it had been in 1960, an experience shared by many African countries.

Source: World Bank.

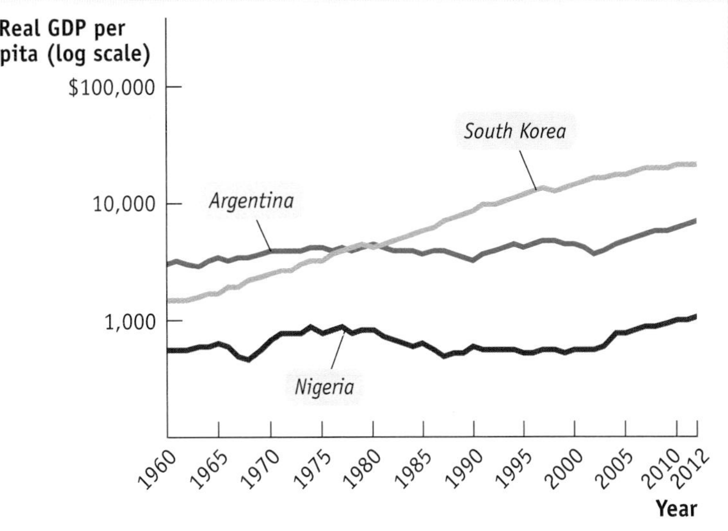

capita grew about 7% per year for more than 30 years. Today South Korea, though still somewhat poorer than Europe or the United States, looks very much like an economically advanced country.

South Korea's economic growth is unprecedented in history: it took the country only 35 years to achieve growth that required centuries elsewhere. Yet South Korea is only part of a broader phenomenon, often referred to as the East Asian economic miracle. High growth rates first appeared in South Korea, Taiwan, Hong Kong, and Singapore but then spread across the region, most notably to China. Since 1975, the whole region has increased real GDP per capita by 6% per year, three times America's historical rate of growth.

Countries in East Asia have enjoyed unprecedented growth since the 1970s, thanks largely to the adoption of modern technology and the accumulation of human capital.

amana images inc./Alamy

How have the Asian countries achieved such high growth rates? The answer is that all of the sources of productivity growth have been firing on all cylinders. Very high savings rates, the percentage of GDP that is saved nationally in any given year, have allowed the countries to significantly increase the amount of physical capital per worker. Very good basic education has permitted a rapid improvement in human capital. And these countries have experienced substantial technological progress.

Why hasn't any economy achieved this kind of growth in the past? Most economic analysts think that East Asia's growth spurt was possible because of its *relative* backwardness. That is, by the time that East Asian economies began to move into the modern world, they could benefit from adopting the technological advances that had been generated in technologically advanced countries such as the United States. In 1900, the United States could not have moved quickly to a modern level of productivity because much of the technology that powers the modern economy, from jet planes to computers, hadn't been invented yet. In 1970, South Korea probably still had lower labor productivity than the United States had in 1900, but it could rapidly upgrade its productivity by adopting technology that had been developed in the United States, Europe, and Japan over the previous century. This was aided by a huge investment in human capital through widespread schooling.

The East Asian experience demonstrates that economic growth can be especially fast in countries that are playing catch-up to other countries with higher GDP per capita.

According to the **convergence hypothesis**, international differences in real GDP per capita tend to narrow over time.

On this basis, many economists have suggested a general principle known as the **convergence hypothesis**. It says that differences in real GDP per capita among countries tend to narrow over time because countries that start with lower real GDP per capita tend to have higher growth rates. We'll look at the evidence for the convergence hypothesis later in this section.

Even before we get to that evidence, however, we can say right away that starting with a relatively low level of real GDP per capita is no guarantee of rapid growth, as the examples of Latin America and Africa both demonstrate.

Latin America's Disappointment

In 1900, Latin America was not regarded as an economically backward region. Natural resources, including both minerals and cultivatable land, were abundant. Some countries, notably Argentina, attracted millions of immigrants from Europe in search of a better life. Measures of real GDP per capita in Argentina, Uruguay, and southern Brazil were comparable to those in economically advanced countries.

David R. Frazier Photolibrary, Inc./Alamy

Relatively low rates of savings, investment spending, and education, along with political instability, have hampered economic growth in Latin America.

Since about 1920, however, growth in Latin America has been disappointing. As Figure 38.3 shows in the case of Argentina, it has remained disappointing to this day. The fact that South Korea is now much richer than Argentina would have seemed inconceivable a few generations ago.

Why has Latin America stagnated? Comparisons with East Asian success stories suggest several factors. The rates of savings and investment spending in Latin America have been much lower than in East Asia, partly as a result of irresponsible government policy that has eroded savings through high inflation, bank failures, and other disruptions. Education—especially broad basic education—has been underemphasized: even Latin American nations rich in natural resources often failed to channel that wealth into their educational systems. And political instability, leading to irresponsible economic policies, has taken a toll.

In the 1980s, many economists came to believe that Latin America was suffering from excessive government intervention in markets. They recommended opening the economies to imports, selling off government-owned companies, and, in general, freeing up individual initiative. The hope was that this would produce an East Asian–type economic surge. So far, however, only one Latin American nation, Chile, has achieved rapid growth. It now seems that pulling off an economic miracle is harder than it looks.

Africa's Troubles

Africa south of the Sahara is home to about 930 million people, nearly three times the population of the United States. On average, they are very poor, nowhere close to U.S. living standards 100 or even 200 years ago. And economic progress has been both slow and uneven, as the example of Nigeria, the most populous nation in the region, suggests. In fact, real GDP per capita in sub-Saharan Africa actually fell 13 percent from 1980 to 1994, although it has recovered since then. The consequence of this poor growth performance has been intense and continuing poverty.

This is a very disheartening picture. What explains it?

Perhaps first and foremost is the problem of political instability. In the years since 1975, large parts of Africa have experienced savage civil wars (often with outside powers backing rival sides) that have killed millions of people and made productive investment spending impossible. The threat of war and general anarchy has also inhibited other important preconditions for growth, such as education and provision of necessary infrastructure.

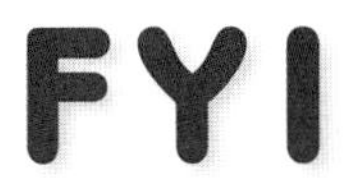

Are Economies Converging?

In the 1950s, much of Europe seemed quaint and backward to American visitors, and Japan seemed very poor. Today, a visitor to Paris or Tokyo sees a city that looks about as rich as New York. Although real GDP per capita is still somewhat higher in the United States, the differences in the standards of living among the United States, Europe, and Japan are relatively small.

Many economists have argued that this convergence in living standards is normal; the convergence hypothesis says that relatively poor countries should have higher rates of growth of real GDP per capita than relatively rich countries. And if we look at today's relatively well-off countries, the convergence hypothesis seems to be true. Panel (a) of the figure shows data for a number of today's wealthy economies measured in 2005 dollars. On the horizontal axis is real GDP per capita in 1955; on the vertical axis is the average annual growth rate of real GDP per capita from 1955 to 2010. There is a clear negative relationship. The United States was the richest country in this group in 1955 and had the slowest rate of growth. Japan and Spain were the poorest countries in 1955 and had the fastest rates of growth. These data suggest that the convergence hypothesis is true.

But economists who looked at similar data realized that these results depended on the countries selected. If you look at successful economies that have a high standard of living today, you find that real GDP per capita has converged. But looking across the world as a whole, including countries that remain poor, there is little evidence of convergence. Panel (b) of the figure illustrates this point using data for regions rather than individual countries (other than the United States). In 1955, East Asia and Africa were both very poor regions. Over the next 55 years, the East Asian regional economy grew quickly, as the convergence hypothesis would have predicted, but the African regional economy grew very slowly. In 1955, Western Europe had substantially higher real GDP per capita than Latin America. But, contrary to the convergence hypothesis, the Western European regional economy grew more quickly over the next 55 years, widening the gap between the regions.

So is the convergence hypothesis all wrong? No: economists still believe that countries with relatively low real GDP per capita tend to have higher rates of growth than countries with relatively high real GDP per capita, *other things equal*. But other things—education, infrastructure, rule of law, and so on—are often not equal. Statistical studies find that when you adjust for differences in these other factors, poorer countries do tend to have higher growth rates. This result is known as *conditional convergence*.

Because other factors differ, however, there is no clear tendency toward convergence in the world economy as a whole. Western Europe, North America, and parts of Asia are becoming more similar in real GDP per capita, but the gap between these regions and the rest of the world is growing.

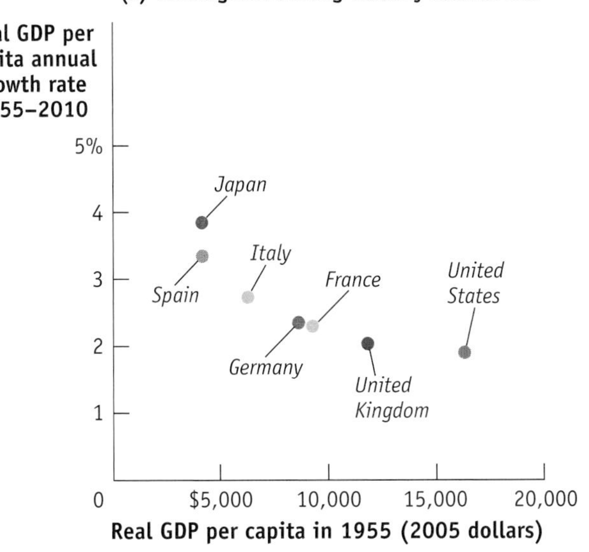

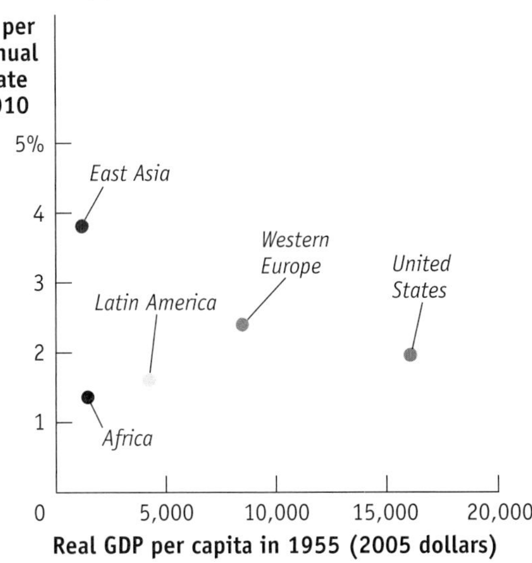

Sources: Angus Maddison, January 2003; J. Bolt and J. L. van Zanden, "The First Update of the Maddison Project; Re-Estimating Growth Before 1820," Maddison Project Working Paper 4, January 2003, http://www.ggdc.net/ maddison/maddison-project/home.htm.

Property rights are also a problem. The lack of legal safeguards means that property owners are often subject to extortion because of government corruption, making them averse to owning property or improving it. This is especially damaging in a country that is very poor.

While many economists see political instability and government corruption as the leading causes of underdevelopment in Africa, some—most notably Jeffrey Sachs of

Columbia University and the United Nations—believe the opposite. They argue that Africa is politically unstable because Africa is poor. And Africa's poverty, they go on to claim, stems from its extremely unfavorable geographic conditions—much of the continent is landlocked, hot, infested with tropical diseases, and cursed with poor soil.

Sachs, along with economists from the World Health Organization, has highlighted the importance of health problems in Africa. In poor countries, worker productivity is often severely hampered by malnutrition and disease. In particular, tropical diseases such as malaria can be controlled only with an effective public health infrastructure, something that is lacking in much of Africa. At the time of this writing, economists are studying certain regions of Africa to determine whether modest amounts of aid given directly to residents for the purposes of increasing crop yields, reducing malaria, and increasing school attendance can produce self-sustaining gains in living standards.

Although the example of African countries represents a warning that long-run economic growth cannot be taken for granted, there are some signs of hope. Mauritius has developed a successful textile industry. Several African countries that are dependent on exporting commodities such as coffee and oil have benefited from the higher prices of those commodities. And Africa's economic performance since the mid-1990s has been generally much better than it was in preceding decades.

MODULE 38 Review

Check Your Understanding

1. Describe the shift in, or movement along, the productivity curve caused by each of the following:
   a. The amounts of physical and human capital per worker are unchanged, but there is significant technological progress.
   b. The amount of physical capital per worker grows, but the level of human capital per worker and technology are unchanged.
2. The real GDP of Erehwon has grown 5% per year over the past 30 years. The amount of physical capital has grown 4% per year. The size of the labor force hasn't changed. Estimates by economists say that each 1% increase in the amount of physical capital per worker, other things equal, raises productivity by 0.3%.
   a. How much has growing physical capital per worker contributed to productivity growth? What percentage of total productivity growth is that?
   b. How would your answer to part a change if the labor force had grown by 4% per year?
3. Multinomics, Inc., is a large company with many offices around the country. It has just adopted a new computer system that will affect virtually every function performed within the company. Why might a period of time pass before employees' productivity is improved by the new computer system? Why might there be a temporary decrease in employees' productivity?

Tackle the Test: Multiple-Choice Questions

1. Which of the following is a source of productivity growth?
   I. increased physical capital
   II. increased human capital
   III. technological progress
   a. I only
   b. II only
   c. III only
   d. I and II only
   e. I, II, and III
2. Which of the following is an example of physical capital?
   a. machinery
   b. health care
   c. education
   d. money
   e. all of the above

3. The following statement describes which area of the world? "This area has experienced growth rates unprecedented in history and now looks like an economically advanced country."
   a. North America
   b. Latin America
   c. Europe
   d. East Asia
   e. Africa

4. Which of the following is cited as an important factor preventing long-run economic growth in Africa?
   a. political instability
   b. lack of property rights
   c. unfavorable geographic conditions
   d. poor health
   e. all of the above

5. The "convergence hypothesis"
   a. states that differences in real GDP per capita among countries widen over time.
   b. states that low levels of real GDP per capita are associated with higher growth rates.
   c. states that low levels of real GDP per capita are associated with lower growth rates.
   d. contradicts the "Rule of 70."
   e. has been proven by evidence from all parts of the world.

Tackle the Test: Free-Response Questions

1. A productivity curve is a graphical representation of an aggregate production function.
   a. Draw a correctly labeled graph of a productivity curve that illustrates diminishing returns to physical capital.
   b. Explain what it is about your productivity curve that indicates that there are diminishing returns to physical capital.
   c. On your graph, illustrate the effect of technological progress.
   d. How is the level of human capital per worker addressed on your graph?

Rubric for FRQ 1 (7 points)

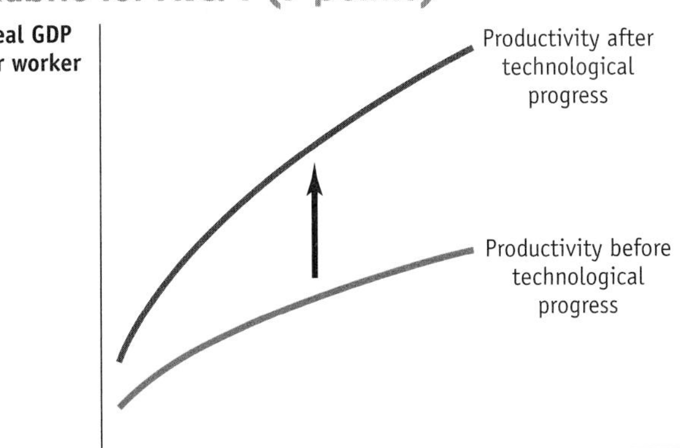

1 point: Vertical axis is labeled "Real GDP per worker."

1 point: Horizontal axis is labeled "Physical capital per worker."

1 point: Upward-sloping curve is labeled "Aggregate production function" or "Productivity."

1 point: Curve increases at a decreasing rate (the slope is positive and decreasing).

1 point: Equal increases in physical capital per worker lead to smaller increases in real GDP per worker.

1 point: Upward shift of production function is labeled to indicate technological progress.

1 point: Human capital per worker is held constant.

2. Croatia is a small country in Eastern Europe.
   a. Suppose that in Croatia each successive increase in the amount of physical capital per worker leads to the same increase in productivity. Use a correctly labeled graph to show what Croatia's productivity curve would look like.
   b. Suppose instead that each successive increase in the amount of physical capital per worker leads to a larger increase in productivity. Use a correctly labeled graph to show what Croatia's productivity curve would look like.
   c. Between 1991 and 1995, Croatia fought a war for independence from Yugoslavia. This war destroyed a significant portion of the physical capital in Croatia. Supposing all other things remained unchanged, explain how the effect of this change would be illustrated on your graph from part a.
   d. After the war, Croatia invested in education that increased each worker's ability to make productive use of any given amount of capital. Explain how this affected Croatia's productivity curve.
   (5 points)

FocusJapan/Alamy

MODULE 39 Growth Policy: Why Economic Growth Rates Differ

In this Module, you will learn to:

- Discuss the factors that explain why long-run growth rates differ so much among countries
- Explain the challenges to growth posed by the scarcity of natural resources, environmental degradation, and efforts to make growth sustainable

Why Growth Rates Differ

In 1820, according to estimates by the economic historian Angus Maddison, Mexico had somewhat higher real GDP per capita than Japan. Today, Japan has higher real GDP per capita than most European nations and Mexico is a poor country, though by no means among the poorest. The difference? Over the long run, real GDP per capita grew at 1.9% per year in Japan but at only 1.2% per year in Mexico.

As this example illustrates, even small differences in growth rates have large consequences over the long run. So why do growth rates differ across countries and across periods of time?

Explaining Differences in Growth Rates

As one might expect, economies with rapid growth tend to be economies that add physical capital, increase their human capital, or experience rapid technological progress. Striking economic success stories, like Japan in the 1950s and 1960s or China today, tend to be countries that do all three: rapidly add to their physical capital, upgrade their educational level, and make fast technological progress.

Adding to Physical Capital One reason for differences in growth rates among countries is that some countries are increasing their stock of physical capital much more rapidly than others, through high rates of investment spending. In the 1960s, Japan was the fastest-growing major economy; it also spent a much higher share of its GDP on investment goods than other major economies. Today, China is the fastest-growing major economy, and it similarly spends a very large share of its GDP on investment goods. In 2013, investment spending was 54.4% of China's GDP, compared with only 19% in the United States.

Where does the money for high investment spending come from? We have already analyzed how financial markets channel savings into investment spending. The key point is that investment spending must be paid for either out of savings from domestic households or by an inflow of foreign capital—that is, savings from foreign households. Foreign capital has played an important role in the long-run economic growth of some countries, including the United States, which relied heavily on foreign funds during its early industrialization. For the most part, however, countries that invest a large share of their GDP are able to do so because they have high domestic savings. One reason for differences in growth rates, then, is that countries have different rates of savings and investment spending.

AP® Exam Tip

Growth rates between nations differ due to differing levels of physical capital, human capital, and technology. Past AP® exams have tested economic growth concepts but not actual growth rates.

Adding to Human Capital Just as countries differ substantially in the rate at which they add to their physical capital, there have been large differences in the rate at which countries add to their human capital through education.

A case in point is the comparison between Argentina and China. In both countries, the average educational level has risen steadily over time, but it has risen much faster in China. **Figure 39.1** shows the average years of education of adults in China, which we have highlighted as a spectacular example of long-run growth, and in Argentina, a country whose growth has been disappointing. Compared to China, 60 years ago, Argentina had a much more educated population, while many Chinese were still illiterate. Today, the average educational level in China is still slightly below that in Argentina—but that's mainly because there are still many elderly adults who never received basic education. In terms of high school and college education, China has outstripped once-rich Argentina.

Research and development, or **R&D**, is spending to create and implement new technologies.

Figure 39.1 China's Students Are Catching Up

In both China and Argentina, the average educational level—measured by the number of years the average adult aged 25 or older has spent in school—has risen over time. Although China is still lagging behind Argentina, it is catching up—and China's success at adding human capital is one key to its spectacular long-run growth.

Source: Robert Barro and Jong-Wha Lee, "A New Data Set of Educational Attainment in the World, 1950-2010," NBER Working Paper No. 15902 (April 2010).

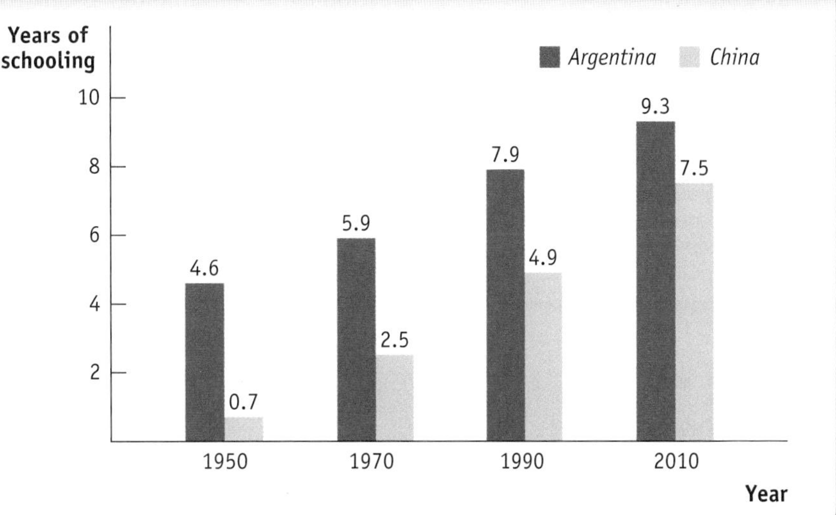

Technological Progress The advance of technology is a key force behind economic growth. What drives technology?

Scientific advances make new technologies possible. To take the most spectacular example in today's world, the semiconductor chip—which is the basis for all modern information technology—could not have been developed without the theory of quantum mechanics in physics.

But science alone is not enough: scientific knowledge must be translated into useful products and processes. And that often requires devoting a lot of resources to **research and development**, or **R&D**, spending to create new technologies and prepare them for practical use.

Photodisc

FYI Inventing R&D

Thomas Edison is best known as the inventor of the lightbulb and the phonograph. But his biggest invention may surprise you: he invented research and development.

Before Edison's time, of course, there had been many inventors. Some of them worked in teams. But in 1875 Edison created something new: his Menlo Park, New Jersey, laboratory. It employed 25 men full-time to generate new products and processes for business. In other words, he did not set out to pursue a particular idea and then cash in. He created an organization whose purpose was to create new ideas year after year.

Edison's Menlo Park lab is now a museum. "To name a few of the products that were developed in Menlo Park," says the museum's website, "we can list the following: the carbon button mouthpiece for the telephone, the phonograph, the incandescent lightbulb and the electrical distribution system, the electric train, ore separation, the Edison effect bulb, early experiments in wireless, the grasshopper telegraph, and improvements in telegraphic transmission."

You could say that before Edison's lab, technology just sort of happened: people came up with ideas, but businesses didn't plan to make continuous technological progress. Now R&D operations, often much bigger than Edison's original team, are standard practice throughout the business world.

© Bettmann/CORBIS

Thomas Alva Edison in his laboratory in East Orange, New Jersey, in 1901.

Roads, power lines, ports, information networks, and other underpinnings for economic activity are known as **infrastructure**.

AP® Exam Tip

Don't automatically assume that government spending will have an impact on economic growth. Some government spending is on things that are not sources of economic growth.

Although some research and development is conducted by governments, much R&D is paid for by the private sector, as discussed in the FYI box. The United States became the world's leading economy in large part because American businesses were among the first to make systematic research and development a part of their operations.

Developing new technology is one thing; applying it is another. There have often been notable differences in the pace at which different countries take advantage of new technologies. America's surge in productivity growth after 1995, as firms learned to make use of information technology, was at least initially not matched in Europe.

The Role of Government in Promoting Economic Growth

Governments can play an important role in promoting—or blocking—all three sources of long-term economic growth: physical capital, human capital, and technological progress.

ED OUDENAARDEN/AFP/Getty Images

Governments play a vital role in health maintenance. A child is vaccinated against the influenza A (H1N1) virus during a mass vaccination in Schiedam, Netherlands.

Governments and Physical Capital Governments play an important direct role in building **infrastructure**: roads, power lines, ports, information networks, and other parts of an economy's physical capital that provide an underpinning, or foundation, for economic activity. Although some infrastructure is provided by private companies, much of it is either provided by the government or requires a great deal of government regulation and support. Ireland, whose economy really took off in the 1990s, is often cited as an example of the importance of government-provided infrastructure: the government invested in an excellent telecommunications infrastructure in the 1980s, and this helped make Ireland a favored location for high-technology companies.

Poor infrastructure—for example, a power grid that often fails, cutting off electricity to homes and businesses—is a major obstacle to economic growth in some countries. To provide good infrastructure, an economy must be able to afford it, but it must also have the political discipline to maintain it and provide for the future.

Perhaps the most crucial infrastructure is something we rarely think about: basic public health measures in the form of a clean water supply and disease control. As we'll see in the next section, poor health infrastructure is a major obstacle to economic growth in poor countries, especially those in Africa.

Governments also play an important indirect role in making high rates of private investment spending possible. Both the amount of savings and the ability of an economy to direct savings into productive investment spending depend on the economy's institutions, notably its financial system. In particular, a well-functioning banking system is very important for economic growth because, in most countries, it is the principal way in which savings are channeled into business investment spending. If a country's citizens trust their banks, they will place their savings in bank deposits, which the banks will then lend to their business customers. But if people don't trust their banks, they will hoard gold or foreign currency, keeping their savings in safe deposit boxes or under their mattresses, where it cannot be turned into productive investment spending. A well-functioning financial system requires appropriate government regulation that assures depositors that their funds are protected.

Governments and Human Capital An economy's physical capital is created mainly through investment spending by individuals and private companies. Much of an economy's human capital, by contrast, is the result of government spending on education. Governments pay for the great bulk of primary and secondary education, although individuals pay a significant share of the costs of higher education.

As a result, differences in the rate at which countries add to their human capital largely reflect government policy. For example, East Asia now has a more educated population than Latin America. This isn't because East Asia is richer than Latin America and so can afford to spend more on education. Until very recently, East Asia, on average, was poorer than Latin America. Instead, it reflects the fact that Asian governments made broad education of the population a higher priority.

Governments and Technology Technological progress is largely the result of private initiative. But much important R&D is done by government agencies. For example, Brazil's agricultural boom was made possible by government researchers who discovered that adding crucial nutrients to the soil would allow crops to be grown on previously unusable land. They also developed new varieties of soybeans and breeds of cattle that flourish in Brazil's tropical climate.

Political Stability, Property Rights, and Excessive Government Intervention There's not much point in investing in a business if rioting mobs are likely to destroy it. And why save your money if someone with political connections can steal it? Political stability and protection of property rights are crucial ingredients in long-run economic growth.

Long-run economic growth in successful economies, like that of the United States, has been possible because there are good laws, institutions that enforce those laws, and a stable political system that maintains those institutions. The law must say that your property is really yours so that someone else can't take it away. The courts and the police must be honest so that they can't be bribed to ignore the law. And the political system must be stable so that the law doesn't change capriciously.

Americans take these preconditions for granted, but they are by no means guaranteed. Aside from the disruption caused by war or revolution, many countries find that their economic growth suffers due to corruption among the government officials who should be enforcing the law. For example, until 1991 the Indian government imposed many bureaucratic restrictions on businesses, which often had to bribe government officials to get approval for even routine activities—a tax on business, in effect. Economists have argued that a reduction in this burden of corruption is one reason Indian growth has been much faster in recent years than it was in the first 40 years after India gained independence in 1947.

The Brazilian Breadbasket

A wry Brazilian joke says that "Brazil is the country of the future—and always will be." The world's fifth most populous country has often been considered a possible major economic power, yet has never fulfilled that promise.

In recent years, however, Brazil's economy has made a better showing, especially in agriculture. This success depends on exploiting a natural resource, the tropical savanna land known as the *cerrado*. Until a quarter century ago, the land was considered unsuitable for farming. A combination of three factors changed that: technological progress due to research and development, improved economic policies, and greater physical capital.

The Brazilian Enterprise for Agricultural and Livestock Research, a government-run agency, developed the crucial technologies. It showed that adding lime and phosphorus made *cerrado* land productive, and it developed breeds of cattle and varieties of soybeans suited for the climate. (Now they're working on wheat.) Also, until the 1980s, Brazilian international trade policies discouraged exports, as did an overvalued exchange rate that made the country's goods more expensive to foreigners. After economic reform, investing in Brazilian agriculture became much more profitable and companies began putting in place the farm machinery, buildings, and other forms of physical capital needed to exploit the land.

What still limits Brazil's growth? Infrastructure. According to a report in the *New York Times*, Brazilian farmers are "concerned about the lack of reliable highways, railways and barge routes, which adds to the cost of doing business." Recognizing this, the Brazilian government is investing in infrastructure, and Brazilian agriculture is continuing to expand. The country has already overtaken the United States as the world's largest beef exporter and may not be far behind in soybeans.

Even when governments aren't corrupt, excessive government intervention can be a brake on economic growth. If large parts of the economy are supported by government subsidies, protected from imports, or otherwise insulated from competition, productivity tends to suffer because of a lack of incentives. As we saw in Module 38, excessive government intervention is one often-cited explanation for slow growth in Latin America.

Is World Growth Sustainable?

AP® Exam Tip

Understanding sustainability may be useful in answering free-response questions on the AP® exam.

Earlier, we described the views of Thomas Malthus, the nineteenth-century economist who warned that the pressure of population growth would tend to limit the standard of living. Malthus was right—about the past: for around 58 centuries, from the origins of civilization until his own time, limited land supplies effectively prevented any large rise in real incomes per capita. Since then, however, technological progress and rapid accumulation of physical and human capital have allowed the world to defy Malthusian pessimism.

But will this always be the case? Some skeptics have expressed doubt about whether long-run economic growth is **sustainable**—whether it can continue in the face of the limited supply of natural resources and the impact of growth on the environment.

Long-run economic growth is **sustainable** if it can continue in the face of the limited supply of natural resources and the impact of growth on the environment.

Natural Resources and Growth, Revisited

In 1972, a group of scientists called the Club of Rome made a big splash with a book titled *The Limits to Growth*, which argued that long-run economic growth wasn't sustainable due to limited supplies of nonrenewable resources such as oil and natural gas. These "neo-Malthusian" concerns at first seemed to be validated by a sharp rise in resource prices in the 1970s, then came to seem foolish when resource prices fell sharply in the 1980s. After 2005, however, resource prices rose sharply again, leading to renewed concern about resource limitations to growth. **Figure 39.2** shows the real price of oil—the price of oil adjusted for inflation in the rest of the economy. The rise and fall of concerns about resource-based limits to growth have more or less followed the rise and fall of oil prices shown in the figure.

Differing views about the impact of limited natural resources on long-run economic growth turn on the answers to three questions:

- How large are the supplies of key natural resources?
- How effective will technology be at providing alternatives to natural resources?
- Can long-run economic growth continue in the face of resource scarcity?

Figure 39.2 The Real Price of Oil, 1949–2013

The real price of natural resources, like oil, rose dramatically in the 1970s and then fell just as dramatically in the 1980s. Since 2005, however, the real prices of natural resources have soared.

Sources: Energy Information Administration, Bureau of Labor Statistics.

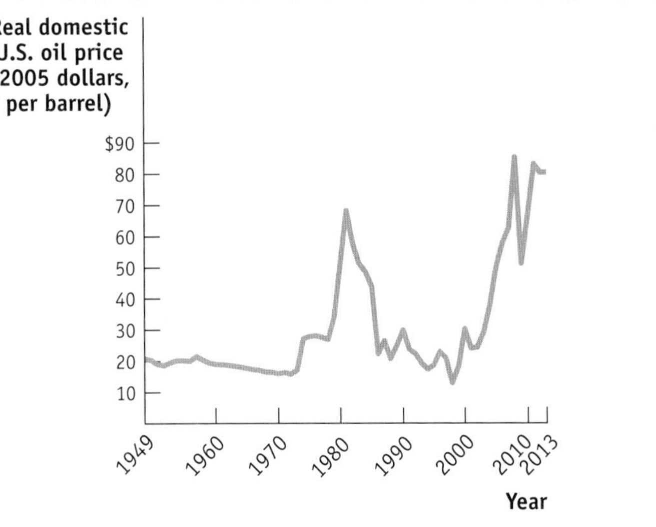

It's mainly up to geologists to answer the first question. Unfortunately, there's wide disagreement among the experts, especially about the prospects for future oil production. Some analysts believe that there is so much untapped oil in the ground that world oil production can continue to rise for several decades. Others—including a number of oil company executives—believe that the growing difficulty of finding new oil fields will cause oil production to plateau—that is, stop growing and eventually begin a gradual decline—in the fairly near future. Some analysts believe that we have already reached that plateau.

The answer to the second question, whether there are alternatives to certain natural resources, will come from engineers. There's no question that there are many alternatives to the natural resources currently being depleted, some of which are already being exploited. For example, "unconventional" oil extracted from Canadian tar sands is already making a significant contribution to world oil supplies, and electricity generated by wind turbines is rapidly becoming big business in the United States—a development highlighted by the fact that in 2009 the United States surpassed Germany to become the world's largest producer of wind energy.

The third question, whether economies can continue to grow in the face of resource scarcity, is mainly a question for economists. And most, though not all, economists are optimistic: they believe that modern economies can find ways to work around limits on the supply of natural resources. One reason for this optimism is the fact that resource scarcity leads to high resource prices. These high prices in turn provide strong incentives to conserve the scarce resource and to find alternatives.

For example, after the sharp increases in oil prices during the 1970s, American consumers turned to smaller, more fuel-efficient cars, and U.S. industry also greatly intensified its efforts to reduce energy bills. The result is shown in **Figure 39.3** on the next page, which compares the growth rates of real GDP per capita and oil consumption before and after the 1970s energy crisis. Before 1973, there seemed to be a more or less one-to-one relationship between economic growth and oil consumption, but after 1973 the U.S. economy continued to deliver growth in real GDP per capita even as it substantially reduced its use of oil. This move toward conservation paused after 1990, as low real oil prices

Photodisc/Getty Images

The Tehachapi Wind Farm, in Tehachapi, California, is the second largest collection of wind generators in the world. The turbines are operated by several private companies and collectively produce enough electricity to meet the needs of 350,000 people every year.

Figure 39.3 U.S. Oil Consumption and Growth over Time

Until 1973, the real price of oil was relatively low and there was a more or less one-to-one relationship between economic growth and oil consumption. Conservation efforts increased sharply after the spike in the real price of oil in the mid-1970s. Yet the U.S. economy was still able to grow despite cutting back on oil consumption.

Sources: Energy Information Administration; Bureau of Economic Analysis.

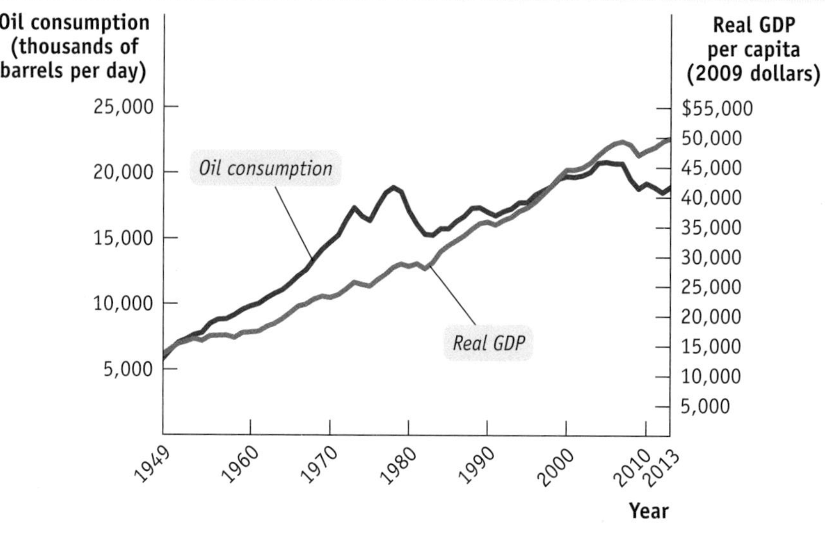

encouraged consumers to shift back to gas-greedy larger cars and SUVs. A sharp rise in oil prices from 2005 to 2008 encouraged renewed shifts toward oil conservation, although these shifts lost some steam as prices started falling again in late 2008.

Given such responses to prices, economists generally tend to see resource scarcity as a problem that modern economies handle fairly well, rather than a fundamental limit to long-run economic growth. Environmental issues, however, pose a more difficult problem because dealing with them requires effective political action.

Economic Growth and the Environment

Economic growth, other things equal, tends to increase the human impact on the environment. For example, China's spectacular economic growth has also brought a spectacular increase in air pollution in that nation's cities. It's important to realize, however, that other things aren't necessarily equal: countries can and do take action to protect their environments. In fact, air and water quality in today's advanced countries is generally much better than it was a few decades ago. London's famous "fog"—actually a form of air pollution, which killed 4,000 people during a two-week episode in 1952—is gone, thanks to regulations that virtually eliminated the use of coal heat. The equally famous smog of Los Angeles, although not extinguished, is far less severe than it was in the 1960s and early 1970s, again thanks to pollution regulations.

Despite these past environmental success stories, there is widespread concern today about the environmental impacts of continuing economic growth, reflecting a change in the scale of the problem. Environmental success stories have mainly involved dealing with *local* impacts of economic growth, such as the effect of widespread car ownership on air quality in the Los Angeles basin. Today, however, we are faced with *global* environmental issues—the adverse impacts on the environment of the Earth as a whole by worldwide economic growth. The biggest of these issues involves the impact of fossil-fuel consumption on the world's climate.

Burning coal and oil releases carbon dioxide into the atmosphere. There is broad scientific consensus that rising levels of carbon dioxide and other gases are causing a greenhouse effect on the Earth, trapping more of the sun's energy and raising the planet's overall temperature. And rising temperatures may impose high human and

Coal Comfort on Resources

Those who worry that exhaustion of natural resources will bring an end to economic growth can take some comfort from the story of William Stanley Jevons, a nineteenth-century British economist best known today for his role in the development of marginal analysis. In addition to his work in economic theory, Jevons worked on the real-world economic problems of the day, and in 1865 he published an influential book, *The Coal Question*, that foreshadowed many modern concerns about resources and growth. But his pessimism was proved wrong.

The Industrial Revolution was launched in Britain, and in 1865 Britain still had the world's richest major economy. But Jevons argued that Britain's economic success had depended on the availability of cheap coal and that the gradual exhaustion of Britain's coal resources, as miners were forced to dig ever deeper, would threaten the nation's long-run prosperity.

He was right about the exhaustion of Britain's coal: production peaked in 1913, and today the British coal industry is a shadow of its former self. But Britain was able to turn to alternative sources of energy, including imported coal and oil. And economic growth did not collapse: real GDP per capita in Britain today is about seven times its level in 1865.

economic costs: rising sea levels may flood coastal areas; changing climate may disrupt agriculture, especially in poor countries; and so on.

The problem of climate change is clearly linked to economic growth. **Figure 39.4** shows carbon dioxide emissions from the United States, Europe, and China since 1980. Historically, the wealthy nations have been responsible for the bulk of these emissions because they have consumed far more energy per person than poorer countries. As China and other emerging economies have grown, however, they have begun to consume much more energy and emit much more carbon dioxide.

Is it possible to continue long-run economic growth while curbing the emissions of greenhouse gases? The answer, according to most economists who have studied the issue, is yes. It should be possible to reduce greenhouse gas emissions in a wide variety of ways, ranging from the use of non-fossil-fuel energy sources such as wind, solar, and nuclear power; to preventive measures such as carbon sequestration (capturing carbon dioxide and storing it); to simpler things like designing buildings so that they're easier to keep warm in winter and cool in summer. Such measures would impose costs on the economy, but the best available estimates suggest that even a large reduction in greenhouse gas emissions over the next few decades would only modestly dent the long-term rise in real GDP per capita.

Figure 39.4 Climate Change and Growth

Greenhouse gas emissions are positively related to growth. As shown here by the United States and Europe, wealthy countries have historically been responsible for the great bulk of greenhouse gas emissions because of their richer and faster-growing economies. As China and other emerging economies have grown, they have begun to emit much more carbon dioxide.

Source: Energy Information Administration.

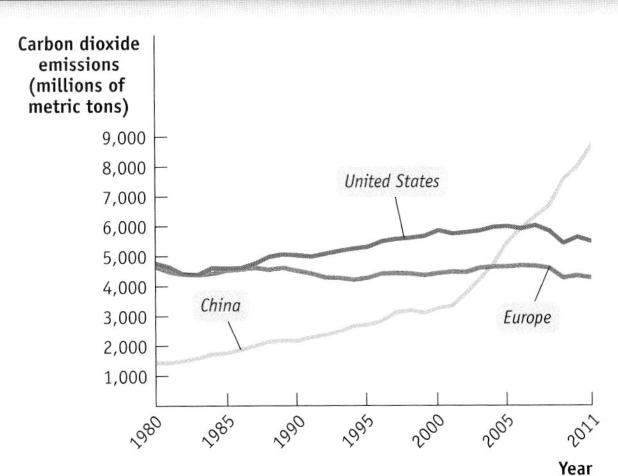

The problem is how to make all of this happen. Unlike resource scarcity, environmental problems don't automatically provide incentives for changed behavior. Pollution is an example of a *negative externality*, a cost that individuals or firms impose on others without having to offer compensation. In the absence of government intervention, individuals and firms have no incentive to reduce negative externalities, which is why it took regulation to reduce air pollution in America's cities. And as Nicholas Stern, the author of an influential report on climate change, put it, greenhouse gas emissions are "the mother of all externalities."

So there is a broad consensus among economists—although there are some dissenters—that government action is needed to deal with climate change. There is also broad consensus that this action should take the form of market-based incentives, either in the form of a carbon tax—a tax per unit of carbon emitted—or a cap and trade system in which the total amount of emissions is capped, and producers must buy licenses to emit greenhouse gases. However, there is considerable dispute about how much action is appropriate, reflecting both uncertainty about the costs and benefits and scientific uncertainty about the pace and extent of climate change.

There are also several aspects of the climate change problem that make it much more difficult to deal with than, say, smog in Los Angeles. One is the problem of taking the long view. The impact of greenhouse gas emissions on the climate is very gradual: carbon dioxide put into the atmosphere today won't have its full effect on the climate for several generations. As a result, there is the political problem of persuading voters to accept pain today in return for gains that will benefit their children, grandchildren, or even great-grandchildren.

The added problem of international burden sharing presents a stumbling block for consensus, as it did at the United Nations Climate Change Conference in 2013. As Figure 39.4 shows, today's rich countries have historically been responsible for most greenhouse gas emissions, but newly emerging economies like China are responsible for most of the recent growth. Inevitably, rich countries are reluctant to pay the price of reducing emissions only to have their efforts frustrated by rapidly growing emissions from new players. On the other hand, countries like China, which are still relatively poor, consider it unfair that they should be expected to bear the burden of protecting an environment threatened by the past actions of rich nations.

Despite political issues and the need for compromise, the general moral of this story is that it is possible to reconcile long-run economic growth with environmental protection. The main question is one of getting political consensus around the necessary policies.

The Cost of Climate Protection

In recent years, members of Congress have introduced a number of bills, some of them with bipartisan sponsorship, calling for ambitious, long-term efforts to reduce U.S. emissions of greenhouse gases. For example, a bill sponsored by Senators Joseph Lieberman and John McCain would use a cap and trade system to gradually reduce emissions over time, eventually—by 2050—reducing them to 60% below their 1990 level. Another bill, sponsored by Senators Barbara Boxer and Bernie Sanders, called for an 80% reduction by 2050.

Would implementing these bills put a stop to long-run economic growth? Not according to a comprehensive study by a team at MIT, which found that reducing emissions would impose significant but not overwhelming costs. Using an elaborate model of the interaction between environmental policy and the economy, the MIT group estimated that the Lieberman-McCain proposal would reduce real GDP per capita in 2050 by 1.11% and the more stringent Sanders-Boxer proposal would reduce real GDP per capita by 1.79%.

These may sound like big numbers—they would amount to between $200 billion and $250 billion today—but they would hardly make a dent in the economy's long-run growth rate. Remember that over the long run the U.S. economy has on average seen real GDP per capita rise by almost 2% a year. If the MIT group's estimates are correct, even a strong policy to avert climate change would, in effect, require that we give up less than one year's growth over the next four decades.

MODULE 39 Review

Check Your Understanding

1. Explain the link between a country's growth rate, its investment spending as a percent of GDP, and its domestic savings.
2. Which of the following is the better predictor of a future high long-run growth rate: a high standard of living today or high levels of savings and investment spending? Explain your answer.
3. Some economists think the best way to help African countries is for wealthier countries to provide more funds for basic infrastructure. Others think this policy will have no long-run effect unless African countries have the financial and political means to maintain this infrastructure. What policies would you suggest?
4. What is the link between greenhouse gas emissions and growth? What is the expected effect on growth from emissions reduction? Why is international burden sharing of greenhouse gas emissions reduction a contentious problem?

Tackle the Test: Multiple-Choice Questions

1. Economies experience more rapid economic growth when they do which of the following?
   - I. add physical capital
   - II. promote technological progress
   - III. limit human capital

   a. I only
   b. II only
   c. III only
   d. I and II only
   e. I, II, and III
2. Which of the following can lead to increases in physical capital in an economy?
   a. increased investment spending
   b. increased savings by domestic households
   c. increased savings from foreign households
   d. an inflow of foreign capital
   e. all of the above
3. Which of the following is true of sustainable long-run economic growth?
   a. Long-run growth can continue in the face of the limited supply of natural resources.
   b. It was predicted by Thomas Malthus.
   c. Modern economies handle resource scarcity problems poorly.
   d. It is less likely when we find alternatives to natural resources.
   e. All of the above are true.
4. Which of the following statements is true of environmental quality?
   a. It is typically not affected by government policy.
   b. Other things equal, it tends to improve with economic growth.
   c. There is broad scientific consensus that rising levels of carbon dioxide and other gases are raising the planet's overall temperature.
   d. Most economists believe it is not possible to reduce greenhouse gas emissions while economic growth continues.
   e. Most environmental success stories involve dealing with global, rather than local impacts.
5. According to the MIT study discussed in the module, a cap and trade system to reduce greenhouse gas emissions in the United States would lead to
   a. no significant costs.
   b. significant but not overwhelming costs.
   c. a loss of roughly three year's real GDP over the next 40 years.
   d. a reduction in real GDP per capita of over 10%.
   e. a loss of 5 years' worth of economic growth over the next 40 years.

Tackle the Test: Free-Response Questions

1. List and explain five different actions the government can take to promote long-run economic growth.

Rubric for FRQ 1 (10 points)

A maximum of 10 points can be earned for any 5 of the 6 possible actions/descriptions.

1 point: Build infrastructure

1 point: The government can provide roads, power lines, ports, rail lines, and related systems to support economic activity.

1 point: Invest in human capital

1 point: The government can improve access to quality education.

1 point: Invest in research and development

1 point: The government can promote technological progress by having government agencies support and participate in R&D.

1 point: Provide political stability

1 point: The government can create and maintain institutions that make and enforce laws that promote stability.

1 point: Establish and protect property rights

1 point: Growth is promoted by laws that define what property belongs to whom and by institutions that defend those property rights.

1 point: Minimize government intervention

1 point: The government can limit its intervention in the economy and promote competition.

2. What roles do physical capital, human capital, technology, and natural resources play in influencing the differences in long-run economic growth rates among countries?
(4 points)

Jetta Productions/Getty Images

MODULE 40 Economic Growth in Macroeconomic Models

In this Module, you will learn to:

- Explain how long-run economic growth is represented in macroeconomic models
- Model the effects of economic growth policies

Long-run economic growth is fundamental to solving many of today's most pressing economic problems. It is even more critical in poorer, less developed countries. But the policies we have studied in earlier sections to address short-run fluctuations and the business cycle may not encourage long-run economic growth. For example, an increase in household consumption can help an economy to recover from a recession. However, when households increase consumption, they decrease their savings, which leads to decreased investment spending and slows long-run economic growth.

In addition to understanding short-run stabilization policies, we need to understand the factors that influence economic growth and how choices by governments and individuals can promote or retard that growth in the long-run.

Long-run economic growth is the sustained rise in the quantity of goods and services the economy produces, as opposed to the short-run ups and downs of the business cycle. In Module 18, we looked at actual and potential output in the United States from 1989 to 2013. As shown in **Figure 40.1** on the next page, increases in potential output during that time represent long-run economic growth in the economy. The fluctuations of actual output compared to potential output are the result of the business cycle.

As we have seen throughout this section, long-run economic growth depends almost entirely on rising productivity. Good macroeconomic policy strives to foster increases in productivity, which in turn leads to long-run economic growth. In this module, we will learn how to evaluate the effects of long-run growth policies using the production possibilities curve and the aggregate demand and supply model.

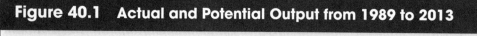

Figure 40.1 Actual and Potential Output from 1989 to 2013

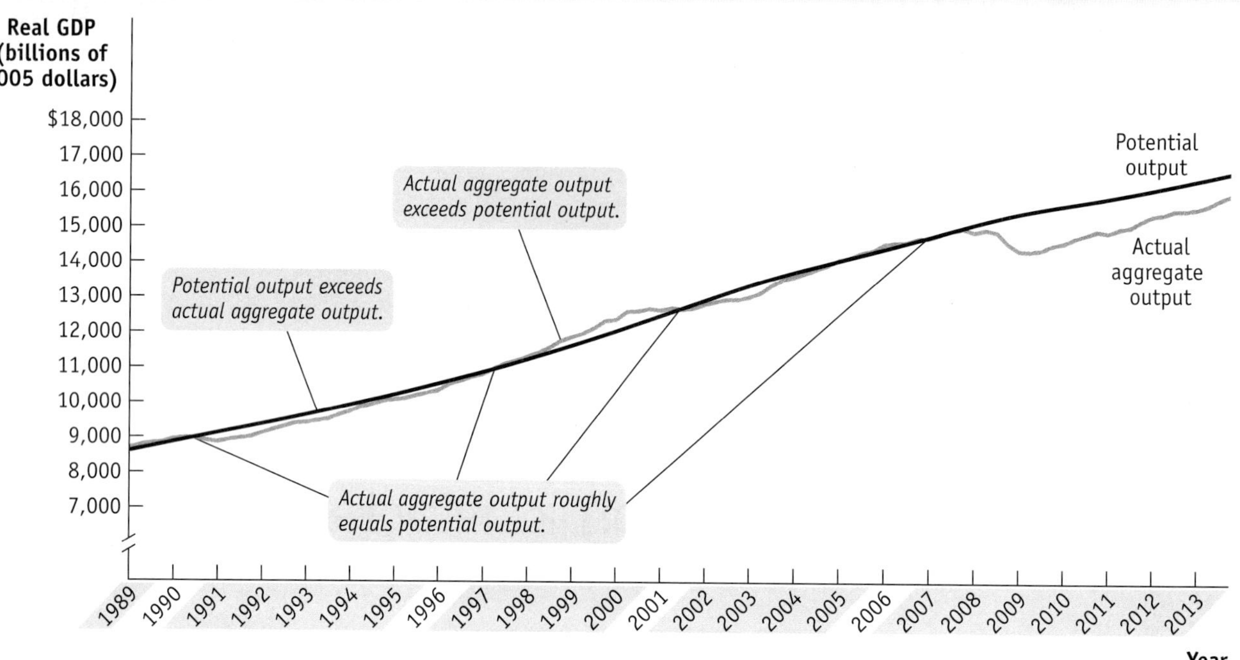

This figure shows the performance of actual and potential output in the United States from 1989 to 2013. The black line shows estimates, produced by the Congressional Budget Office, of U.S. potential output. The blue line shows actual aggregate output. The purple-shaded years are periods in which actual aggregate output fell below potential output, and the green-shaded years are periods in which actual aggregate output exceeded potential output. As shown, significant shortfalls occurred in the recessions of the early 1990s and after 2000. Actual aggregate output was significantly above potential output in the boom of the late 1990s.

Sources: Congressional Budget Office, Bureau of Economic Analysis.

AP® Exam Tip

The AP® exam has included questions on how to show economic growth on a graph. You should be able to draw a correctly labeled *PPC* and show economic growth with an outward shift.

Long-Run Economic Growth and the Production Possibilities Curve

Recall from Section 1 that we defined the production possibilities curve as a graph that illustrates the trade-offs facing an economy that produces only two goods. In our example, we developed the production possibilities curve for Tom, a castaway facing a trade-off between producing fish and coconuts. Looking at **Figure 40.2**, we see that economic growth is shown as an outward shift of the production possibilities curve. Now let's return to the production possibilities curve model and use a different example to illustrate how economic growth policies can lead to long-run economic growth.

Figure 40.3 shows a hypothetical production possibilities curve for a fictional country we'll call Kyland. In our previous production possibilities examples, the trade-off was between producing quantities of two different goods. In this example, our production possibilities curve illustrates Kyland's trade-off between two different *categories* of goods. The production possibilities curve shows the alternative combinations of investment goods and consumer goods that Kyland can produce. The consumer goods category includes everything purchased for consumption by households, such as food, clothing, and sporting goods. Investment goods include all forms of physical capital, that is, goods that are used to produce other goods. Kyland's production possibilities curve shows the trade-off between the production of consumer goods and

Figure 40.2 Economic Growth

Economic growth results in an *outward shift* of the production possibilities curve because production possibilities are expanded. The economy can now produce more of everything. For example, if production is initially at point *A* (20 fish and 25 coconuts), it could move to point *E* (25 fish and 30 coconuts).

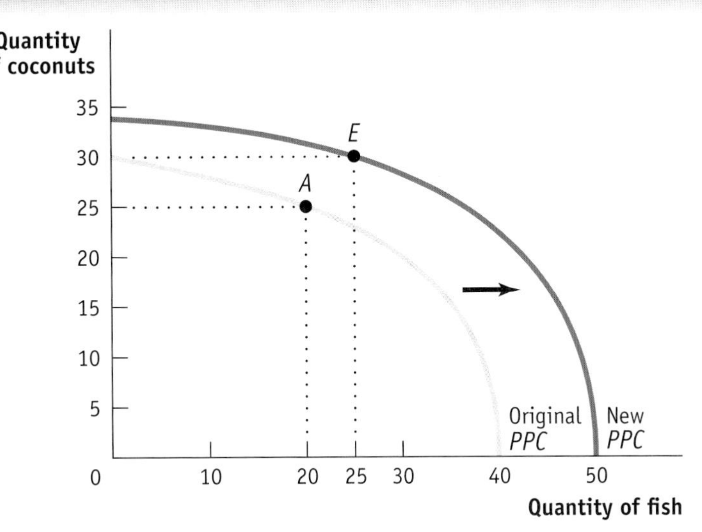

the production of investment goods. Recall that the bowed-out shape of the production possibilities curve reflects increasing opportunity cost.

Kyland's production possibilities curve shows all possible combinations of consumer and investment goods that can be produced with full and efficient use of all of Kyland's resources. However, the production possibilities curve model does not tell us which of the possible points Kyland *should* select.

Figure 40.3 illustrates four points on Kyland's production possibilities curve. At point *A*, Kyland is producing all investment goods and no consumer goods. Investment in physical capital, one of the economy's factors of production, causes the production possibilities curve to shift outward. Choosing to produce at a point on the production possibilities curve that creates more capital for the economy will result in greater

Figure 40.3 The Trade-off Between Investment and Consumer Goods

This production possibilities curve illustrates Kyland's trade-off between the production of investment goods and consumer goods. At point *A*, Kyland produces all investment goods and no consumer goods. At point *D*, Kyland produces all consumer goods and no investment goods. Points *B* and *C* represent two of the many possible combinations of investment goods and consumer goods.

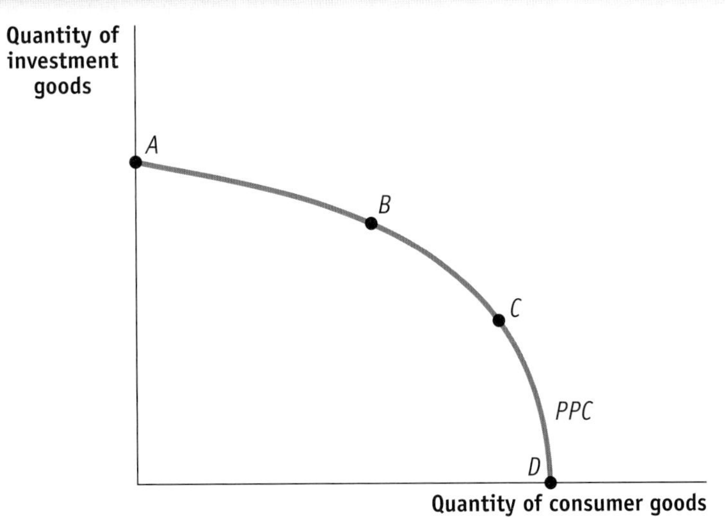

© Rosenfeld/Corbis

Investments in capital help the economy reach new heights of productivity.

production possibilities in the future. Note that at point *A*, there are no consumer goods being produced, a situation which the economy cannot survive.

At point *D*, Kyland is producing all consumer goods and no investment goods. While this point provides goods and services for consumers in Kyland, it does not include the production of any physical capital. Over time, as an economy produces more goods and services, some of its capital is used up in that production. A loss in the value of physical capital due to wear, age, or obsolescence is called **depreciation**. If Kyland were to produce at point *D* year after year, it would soon find its stock of physical capital depreciating and its production possibilities curve would shift inward over time, indicating a decrease in production possibilities. Points *B* and *C* represent a mix of consumer and investment goods for the economy. While we can see that points *A* and *D* would not be acceptable choices over a long period of time, the choice between points *B* and *C* would depend on the values, politics, and other details related to the economy and people of Kyland. What we do know is that the choice made by Kyland each year will affect the position of the production possibilities curve in the future. An emphasis on the production of consumer goods will make consumers better off in the short run but will prevent the production possibilities curve from moving farther out in the future. An emphasis on investment goods will lead the production possibilities curve to shift out farther in the future but will decrease the quantity of consumer goods available in the short run.

Depreciation occurs when the value of an asset is reduced by wear, age, or obsolescence.

So what does the production possibilities curve tell us about economic growth? Since long-run economic growth depends almost entirely on rising productivity, a country's decision regarding investment in physical capital, human capital, and technology affects its long-run economic growth. Governments can promote long-run economic growth, shifting the country's production possibilities curve outward over time, by investing in physical capital such as infrastructure. They can also encourage high rates of private investment in physical capital by promoting a well-functioning financial system, property rights, and political stability.

Long-Run Economic Growth and the Aggregate Demand–Aggregate Supply Model

AP® Exam Tip

Shifting *LRAS* is another way to show a change in economic growth because *LRAS* shows the potential output in an economy.

The aggregate demand and supply model we developed in Section 4 is another useful tool for understanding long-run economic growth. Recall that in the aggregate demand–aggregate supply model, the long-run aggregate supply curve shows the relationship between the aggregate price level and the quantity of aggregate output supplied when all prices, including nominal wages, are flexible. As shown in **Figure 40.4**, the long-run aggregate supply curve is vertical at the level of potential output. While actual real GDP is almost always above or below potential output, reflecting the current phase of the business cycle, potential output is the level of output around which actual aggregate output fluctuates. Potential output in the United States has risen steadily over time. This corresponds to a rightward shift of the long-run aggregate supply curve, as shown in **Figure 40.5**. Thus, the same government policies that promote an outward shift of the production possibilities curve promote a rightward shift of the long-run aggregate supply curve.

Distinguishing Between Long-Run Growth and Short-Run Fluctuations

When considering changes in real GDP, it is important to distinguish long-run growth from short-run fluctuations due to the business cycle. Both the production possibilities curve model and the aggregate demand–aggregate supply model can help us do this.

The points along a production possibilities curve are achievable if there is efficient use of the economy's resources. If the economy experiences a macroeconomic fluctuation

Figure 40.4 The Long-Run Aggregate Supply Curve

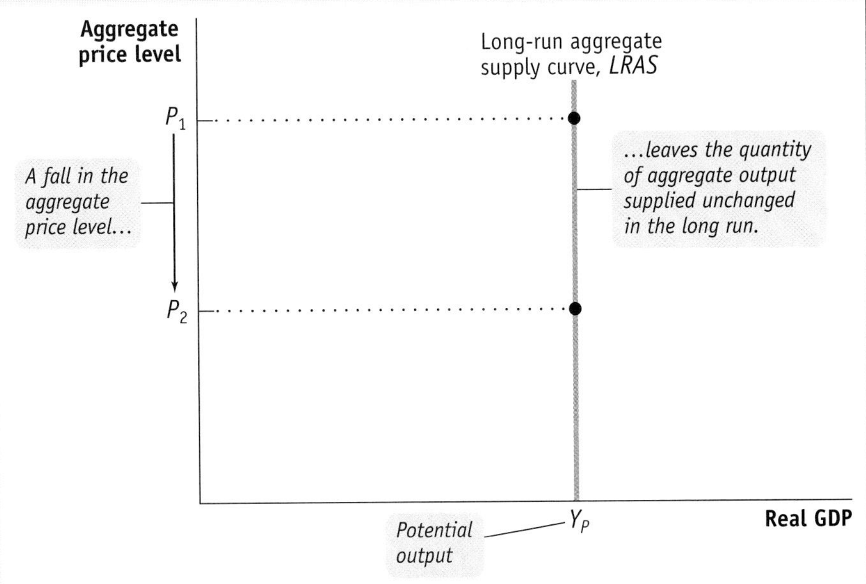

The long-run aggregate supply curve shows the quantity of aggregate output supplied when all prices, including nominal wages, are flexible. It is vertical at potential output, Y_P, because in the long run a change in the aggregate price level has no effect on the quantity of aggregate supplied.

due to the business cycle, such as unemployment due to a recession, production falls to a point inside the production possibilities curve. On the other hand, long-run growth will appear as an outward shift of the production possibilities curve.

In the aggregate demand–aggregate supply model, fluctuations of actual aggregate output around potential output are illustrated by shifts of aggregate demand or short-run aggregate supply that result in a short-run macroeconomic equilibrium above or below potential output. In both panels of **Figure 40.6** on the next page, E_1 indicates a short-run equilibrium that differs from long-run equilibrium due to the business cycle. In the case of short-run fluctuations like these, adjustments in nominal wages will eventually bring the equilibrium level of real GDP back to the potential level. By contrast, we saw in Figure 40.5 that long-run economic growth is represented by a rightward shift of the long-run aggregate supply curve and corresponds to an increase in the economy's level of potential output.

Figure 40.5 Long-Run Growth and the *LRAS* Curve

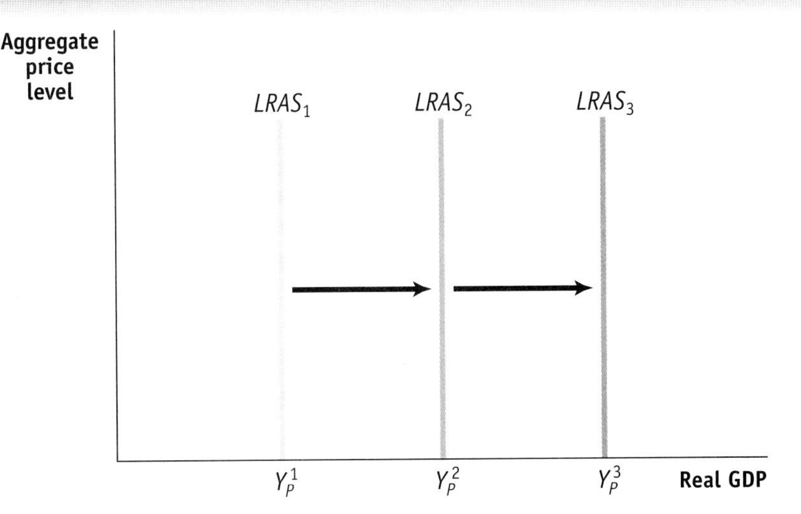

The growth in potential output over time can be shown as a rightward shift of the long-run aggregate supply curve.

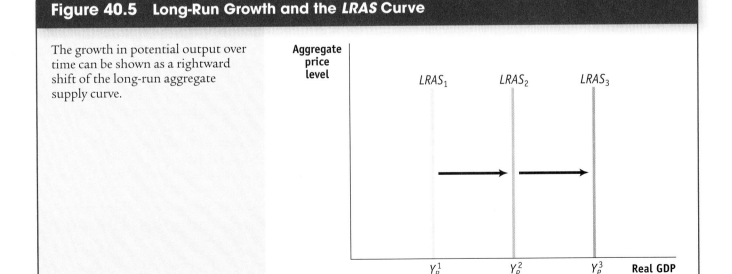

Figure 40.6 From the Short Run to the Long Run

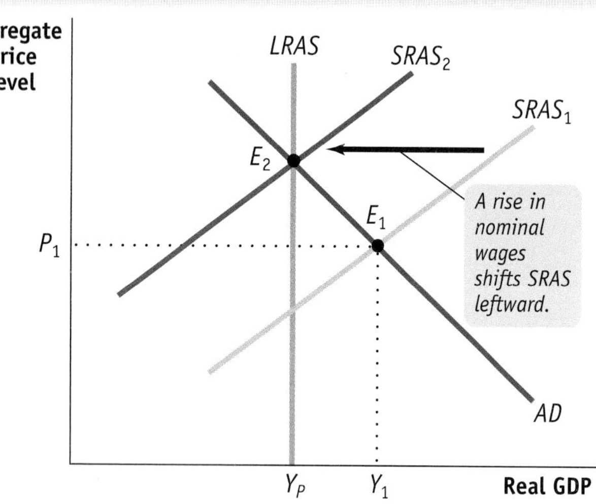

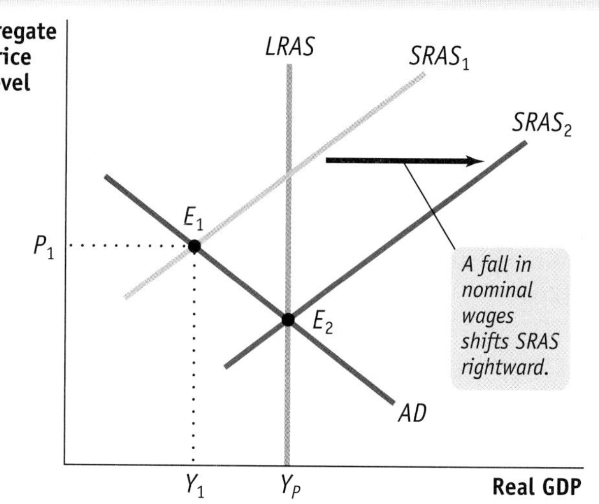

In panel (a), the initial equilibrium is E_1. At the aggregate price level, P_1, the quantity of aggregate output supplied, Y_1, exceeds potential output, Y_P. Eventually, low unemployment will cause nominal wages to rise, leading to a leftward shift of the short-run aggregate supply curve from $SRAS_1$ to $SRAS_2$ and a long-run equilibrium at E_2. In panel (b), the reverse happens: at the short-run equilibrium, E_1, the quantity of aggregate output supplied is less than potential output. High unemployment eventually leads to a fall in nominal wages over time and a rightward shift of the short-run aggregate supply curve. The end result is long-run equilibrium at E_2.

MODULE 40 Review

Check Your Understanding

1. How are long-run economic growth and short-run fluctuations during a business cycle represented using the production possibilities curve model?

2. How are long-run economic growth and short-run fluctuations during a business cycle represented using the aggregate demand–aggregate supply model?

Tackle the Test: Multiple-Choice Questions

1. Which of the following will shift the production possibilities curve outward?

- **I.** an increase in the production of investment goods
- **II.** an increase in the production of consumer goods
- **III.** technological progress

a. I only
b. II only
c. III only
d. I and III only
e. I, II, and III

2. In the production possibilities curve model, long-run economic growth is shown by a(n)

a. outward shift of the *PPC*.
b. inward shift of the *PPC*.
c. movement from a point below the *PPC* to a point on the *PPC*.
d. movement from a point on the *PPC* to a point below the *PPC*.
e. movement from a point on the *PPC* to a point beyond the *PPC*.

3. The reduction in the value of an asset due to wear and tear is known as
   a. depreciation.
   b. negative investment.
   c. economic decline.
   d. disinvestment.
   e. net investment.

4. In the aggregate demand–aggregate supply model, long-run economic growth is shown by a
   a. leftward shift of the aggregate demand curve.
   b. rightward shift of the aggregate demand curve.
   c. rightward shift of the long-run aggregate supply curve.
   d. rightward shift of the short-run aggregate supply curve.
   e. leftward shift of the short-run aggregate supply curve.

5. Which of the following is listed among the key sources of growth in potential output?
   a. expansionary fiscal policy
   b. expansionary monetary policy
   c. a rightward shift of the short-run aggregate supply curve
   d. investment in human capital
   e. both a and b

Tackle the Test: Free-Response Questions

1. Refer to the graph provided.

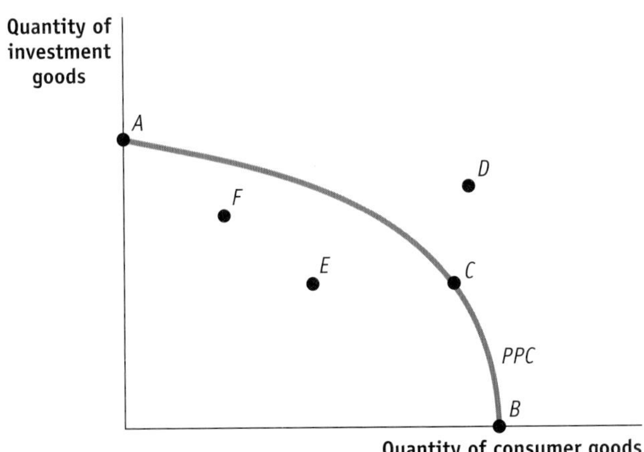

   a. Which point(s) could represent a downturn in the business cycle?
   b. Which point(s) represent efficient production?
   c. Which point(s) are attainable only after long-run economic growth?
   d. How would long-run economic growth be represented on this graph?
   e. Policy that results in an increase in the production of consumer goods without reducing the production of investment goods is represented by a movement from point ______ to point ______.
   f. Producing at which efficient point this year would lead to the most economic growth next year?

Rubric for FRQ 1 (9 points)

2 points: A downturn could be represented by points *E* or *F*.

3 points: Points *A*, *B*, and *C* represent efficient production.

1 point: Point *D* is attainable only after long-run economic growth.

1 point: Long-run economic growth would be represented by an outward shift of the curve.

1 point: Consumer goods increase and investment goods remain unchanged when moving from point *E* to point *C*.

1 point: Producing at point *A* would lead to the most economic growth.

2. Draw a separate, correctly labeled aggregate demand and supply graph to illustrate each of the following situations. On each of your graphs, include the relevant short-run aggregate supply curve(s), long-run aggregate supply curve(s), and aggregate demand curve(s).
   a. Expansionary fiscal policy moves the economy out of a recession.
   b. Investment in infrastructure by the government leads to long-run economic growth.
   (6 points)

SECTION 7 Review

 Section 7 Review Video

Module 37

1. Economic growth is a sustained increase in the productive capacity of an economy and can be measured as changes in real GDP per capita. This measurement eliminates the effects of changes in both the price level and population size. Levels of real GDP per capita vary greatly around the world: more than half of the world's population lives in countries that are still poorer than the United States was in 1910.

2. Growth rates of real GDP per capita also vary widely. According to the **Rule of 70**, the number of years it takes for real GDP per capita to double is equal to 70 divided by the annual growth rate of real GDP per capita.

3. The key to long-run economic growth is rising **labor productivity**, or just **productivity**, which is output per worker. Increases in productivity arise from increases in **physical capital** per worker and **human capital** per worker as well as advances in **technology**.

Module 38

4. The **aggregate production function** shows how real GDP per worker depends on physical capital per worker, human capital per worker, and technology. Other things equal, there are **diminishing returns to physical capital**: holding human capital per worker and technology fixed, each successive addition to physical capital per worker yields a smaller increase in productivity than the one before. Similarly, there are diminishing returns to human capital among other inputs. With **growth accounting**, which involves estimates of each factor's contribution to economic growth, economists have shown that rising **total factor productivity**, the amount of output produced from a given amount of factor inputs, is key to long-run growth. Rising total factor productivity is usually interpreted as the effect of technological progress. In most countries, natural resources are a less significant source of productivity growth today than in earlier times.

5. The world economy contains examples of success and failure in the effort to achieve long-run economic growth. East Asian economies have done many things right and achieved very high growth rates. In Latin America, where some important conditions are lacking, growth has generally been disappointing. In Africa, real GDP per capita declined for several decades, although there are recent signs of progress. The growth rates of economically advanced countries have converged, but the growth rates of countries across the world have not. This has led economists to believe that the **convergence hypothesis** fits the data only when factors that affect growth, such as education, infrastructure, and favorable policies and institutions, are held equal across countries.

Module 39

6. The large differences in countries' growth rates are largely due to differences in their rates of accumulation of physical and human capital, as well as differences in technological progress. A prime factor is differences in savings and investment rates, since most countries that have high investment in physical capital finance it by high domestic savings. Technological progress is largely a result of **research and development**, or **R&D**.

7. Government actions that contribute to growth include the building of **infrastructure**, particularly for transportation and public health; the creation and regulation of a well-functioning banking system that channels savings into investment spending; and the financing of both education and R&D. Government actions that slow growth are corruption, political instability, excessive government intervention, and the neglect or violation of property rights.

8. In regard to making economic growth **sustainable**, economists generally believe that environmental degradation poses a greater problem than natural resource scarcity does. Addressing environmental degradation requires effective governmental intervention, but the problem of natural resource scarcity is often well handled by the incentives created by market prices.

9. The emission of greenhouse gases is clearly linked to growth, and limiting emissions will require some reduction in growth. However, the best available estimates suggest that a large reduction in emissions would require only a modest reduction in the growth rate.

10. There is broad consensus that government action to address climate change and greenhouse gases should be in the form of market-based incentives, like a carbon tax or a cap and trade system. It will also require rich and poor countries to come to some agreement on how the cost of emissions reductions will be shared.

Module 40

11. Long-run economic growth can be analyzed using the production possibilities curve and the aggregate demand–aggregate supply model. In these models, long-run economic growth is represented by an outward shift of the production possibilities curve and a rightward shift of the long-run aggregate supply curve.

12. Physical capital **depreciates** with use. Therefore, over time, the production possibilities curve will shift inward and the long-run aggregate supply curve will shift to the left if the stock of capital is not replaced.

Key Terms

Rule of 70, p. 369
Labor productivity (productivity), p. 370
Physical capital, p. 371
Human capital, p. 371
Technology, p. 371
Aggregate production function, p. 373
Diminishing returns to physical capital, p. 374
Growth accounting, p. 375
Total factor productivity, p. 376
Convergence hypothesis, p. 380
Research and development (R&D), p. 385
Infrastructure, p. 386
Sustainable, p. 388
Depreciation, p. 398

AP® Exam Practice Questions

Multiple-Choice Questions

1. If real GDP grows by 5% per year, approximately how many years will it take for it to double?
   a. 150
   b. 75
   c. 35
   d. 15
   e. 5

2. What is the most important ingredient in long-run economic growth?
   a. increased labor productivity
   b. increased population
   c. low price level
   d. expansionary monetary and fiscal policies
   e. deficit spending

3. The technical means for the production of goods and services is known as
   a. physical capital.
   b. technology.
   c. human capital.
   d. productivity.
   e. machinery and equipment.

4. Which of the following is a major reason for productivity growth?
   a. financial investment
   b. an increase in the amount of capital available per worker
   c. a decrease in the amount of capital available per worker
   d. an increase in the price of capital
   e. technological progress

Refer to the following figure for Questions 5–6.

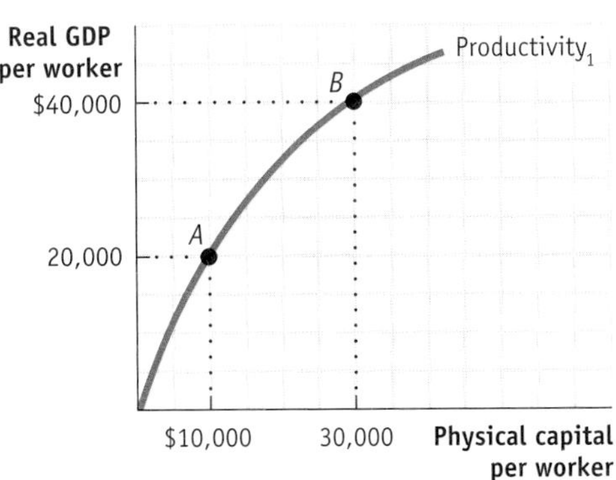

5. Assuming diminishing returns to physical capital, if physical capital per worker is 50,000, real GDP per worker will most likely equal which of the following?
   a. more than 60,000
   b. 60,000
   c. less than 60,000 but greater than 40,000
   d. 40,000
   e. 0

6. An upward shift of the curve shown could be caused by which of the following?
   a. an increase in real GDP per worker
   b. investment in physical capital
   c. diminishing returns to physical capital
   d. increases in population
   e. rising total factor productivity

7. Which of the following is true about the role of natural resources in productivity growth?
   a. They are a more important determinant of productivity than human or physical capital.
   b. They have played an increasingly prominent role in productivity growth in recent years.
   c. They play no role in determining productivity growth.
   d. They played a less important role in productivity growth in the 1800s.
   e. They result in higher productivity, other things equal.
8. According to the convergence hypothesis, over time, international differences in real GDP per capita will
   a. increase exponentially.
   b. increase slightly.
   c. decrease.
   d. remain the same.
   e. disappear.
9. When the government spends money to create and implement new technologies, it has invested in
   a. human capital.
   b. physical capital.
   c. infrastructure.
   d. research and development.
   e. political stability.
10. Which of the following is part of an economy's infrastructure?
   a. highways
   b. factories
   c. banks
   d. automobiles
   e. workers
11. If long-run economic growth can continue into the future despite limited natural resources, it is considered
   a. acceptable.
   b. equitable.
   c. economical.
   d. sustainable.
   e. expandable.
12. An outward shift of the production possibilities curve indicates which of the following?
   a. a decrease in cyclical unemployment
   b. long-run economic growth
   c. a reduction in productive resources
   d. a decrease in opportunity cost
   e. a decrease in potential output and the natural rate of unemployment
13. In the aggregate supply and demand model, a rightward shift of the *LRAS* curve indicates which of the following?
   a. long-run economic growth
   b. an increase in unemployment
   c. a decrease in real GDP
   d. an increase in the aggregate price level
   e. an economic recovery
14. Which of the following will lead to long-run economic growth?
   a. a decrease in nominal wages
   b. a decrease in the aggregate price level
   c. an increase in the production of consumer goods
   d. an increase in total factor productivity
   e. actual output that exceeds potential output
15. If an economy experiences long-run economic growth, which of the following is true of its potential output?
   a. It has increased.
   b. It has decreased.
   c. It is greater than actual output.
   d. It is less than actual output.
   e. It is no longer equal to *LRAS*.
16. Depreciation leads to
   a. a reduction in human capital.
   b. an increase in human capital.
   c. a reduction in physical capital.
   d. an advance in technology.
   e. an outward shift of the production possibilities curve.

Free-Response Question

1. Economic growth can be illustrated using macroeconomic models.
   a. Draw a correctly labeled production possibilities curve for an economy producing capital goods and consumer goods. Use your graph to illustrate economic growth.
   b. Draw a correctly labeled aggregate supply and demand graph showing an economy in long-run equilibrium. On your graph, illustrate economic growth.
   (6 points)

SECTION 8

The Open Economy: International Trade and Finance

A Roller Coaster Ride for the Exchange Rate

"You should see, when they come in the door, the shopping bags they hand off to the coat check. I mean, they're just spending. It's Monopoly money to them." So declared a New York restaurant manager, describing the European tourists who, in the summer of 2008, accounted for a large share of her business. Meanwhile, American tourists in Europe were suffering sticker shock. One American, whose family of four was visiting Paris, explained his changing vacation plans: "We might not stay as long. We might eat cheese sandwiches."

Bloomberg via Getty Images

It was quite a change from 2000, when an article in the *New York Times* bore the headline: "Dollar makes the good life a tourist bargain in Europe." What happened? The answer is that there was a large shift in the relative values of the euro, the currency used by much of Europe, and the U.S. dollar. At its low point in 2000, a euro was worth only about 85 cents. By mid-2008 it was worth more than \$1.50; in early 2010 its value had fallen again, to less than \$1.25. In early 2014, a euro was worth \$1.36.

What causes the ups and downs of the relative value of the dollar and the euro? What are the effects of such changes? These are among the questions addressed by *open-economy macroeconomics*, the branch of macroeconomics that deals with the relationships between national economies. In this section we'll learn about some of the key issues in open-economy macroeconomics: the determinants of a country's *balance of payments*, the factors affecting *exchange rates*, the different forms of *exchange rate policy* adopted by various countries, and the relationship between exchange rates and macroeconomic policy. In the final module we will apply what we have learned about macroeconomic modeling to conduct policy analysis.

Stockbyte/Thinkstock

MODULE 41

Capital Flows and the Balance of Payments

In this Module, you will learn to:

- Explain the meaning of the balance of payments accounts
- Identify the determinants of international capital flows

Capital Flows and the Balance of Payments

In 2012, people living in the United States sold about $3.5 trillion worth of stuff to people living in other countries and bought about $3.2 trillion worth of stuff in return. What kind of stuff? All kinds. Residents of the United States (including employees of firms operating in the United States) sold airplanes, bonds, wheat, and many other items to residents of other countries. Residents of the United States bought cars, stocks, oil, and many other items from residents of other countries.

How can we keep track of these transactions? Earlier we learned that economists keep track of the domestic economy using the national income and product accounts. Economists keep track of international transactions using a different but related set of numbers, the *balance of payments accounts*.

A country's **balance of payments accounts** are a summary of the country's transactions with other countries.

Balance of Payments Accounts

A country's **balance of payments accounts** are a summary of the country's transactions with other countries.

To understand the basic idea behind the balance of payments accounts, let's consider a small-scale example: not a country, but a family farm. Let's say that we know the following about how last year went financially for the Costas, who own a small artichoke farm in California:

Rob MacDougall/Getty Images

- They made $100,000 by selling artichokes.
- They spent $70,000 on running the farm, including purchases of new farm machinery, and another $40,000 buying food, paying utility bills for their home, replacing their worn-out car, and so on.

Table 41.1 The Costas' Financial Year

	Sources of cash	Uses of cash	Net
Purchases or sales of goods and services	Artichoke sales: $100,000	Farm operation and living expenses: $110,000	−$10,000
Interest payments	Interest received on bank account: $500	Interest paid on mortgage: $10,000	−$9,500
Loans and deposits	Funds received from new loan: $25,000	Funds deposited in bank: $5,500	+$19,500
Total	**$125,500**	**$125,500**	**$0**

- They received $500 in interest on their bank account but paid $10,000 in interest on their mortgage.
- They took out a new $25,000 loan to help pay for farm improvements but didn't use all the money immediately. So they put the extra in the bank.

How could we summarize the Costas' year? One way would be with a table like **Table 41.1**, which shows sources of cash coming in and money going out, characterized under a few broad headings. The first row of Table 41.1 shows sales and purchases of goods and services: sales of artichokes; purchases of farm machinery, groceries, heating oil, that new car, and so on. The second row shows interest payments: the interest the Costas received from their bank account and the interest they paid on their mortgage. The third row shows cash coming in from new borrowing versus money deposited in the bank.

In each row we show the net inflow of cash from that type of transaction. So the net in the first row is −$10,000 because the Costas spent $10,000 more than they earned. The net in the second row is −$9,500, the difference between the interest the Costas received on their bank account and the interest they paid on the mortgage. The net in the third row is $19,500: the Costas brought in $25,000 with their new loan but put only $5,500 of that sum in the bank.

The last row shows the sum of cash coming in from all sources and the sum of all cash used. These sums are equal, by definition: every dollar has a source, and every dollar received gets used somewhere. (What if the Costas hid money under the mattress? Then that would be counted as another "use" of cash.)

A country's balance of payments accounts summarize its transactions with the world using a table similar to the one we just used to summarize the Costas' financial year.

"This is how our new no risk pension scheme works."

Graham Chaffer/Cartoonstock

AP® Exam Tip

Remember that the current account includes goods and services and cash transfers such as foreign aid, gifts, and grants. You may be asked to identify these transactions on the AP® exam.

Table 41.2 The U.S. Balance of Payments in 2012 (billions of dollars)

	Payments from foreigners	Payments to foreigners	Net
1 Sales and purchases of goods and services	$2,211	$2,745	–$534
2 Factor income	776	552	224
3 Transfers	–	–	–130
Current account (1 + 2 + 3)			**–440**
4 Official asset sales and purchases	394	–81	475
5 Private sales and purchases of assets	150	178	–28
Financial account (4 + 5)			**447**
Total	–	–	7

Source: Bureau of Economic Analysis.

Table 41.2 shows a simplified version of the U.S. balance of payments accounts for 2012. Where the Costa family's accounts show sources and uses of cash, the balance of payments accounts show payments from foreigners—in effect, sources of cash for the United States as a whole—and payments to foreigners.

Row 1 of Table 41.2 shows payments that arise from sales and purchases of goods and services. For example, the value of U.S. wheat exports and the fees foreigners pay to U.S. consulting companies appear in the second column of row 1; the value of U.S. oil imports and the fees American companies pay to Indian call centers—the people who often answer your 1-800 calls—appear in the third column of row 1.

Row 2 shows *factor income*—payments for the use of factors of production owned by residents of other countries. Mostly this means investment income: interest paid on loans from overseas, the profits of foreign-owned corporations, and so on. For example, the profits earned by Disneyland Paris, which is owned by the U.S.-based Walt Disney Company, appear in the second column of row 2; the profits earned by the U.S. operations of Japanese auto companies appear in the third column. Factor income also includes labor income. For example, the wages of an American engineer who works temporarily on a construction site in Dubai are counted in the second column of row 2.

Row 3 shows *international transfers*—funds sent by residents of one country to residents of another. The main element here is the remittances that immigrants, such as the millions of Mexican-born workers employed in the United States, send to their families in their country of origin. Notice that Table 41.2 shows only the net value of transfers. That's because the U.S. government provides only an estimate of the net, not a breakdown between payments to foreigners and payments from foreigners.

The next two rows of Table 41.2 show payments resulting from sales and purchases of assets, broken down by who is doing the buying and selling. Row 4 shows transactions that involve governments or government agencies, mainly central banks. As we'll learn later, in 2012, most of the U.S. sales in this category involved the accumulation of *foreign exchange reserves* by the central banks of China and oil-exporting countries. Row 5 shows private sales and purchases of assets. For example, the 2012 purchase of the AMC cinema chain by the Chinese corporation Dalian Wanda showed up in the second column of row 5; purchases of European stocks by U.S. investors show up as positive values in the third column. However, because U.S. residents sold more foreign assets than they purchased in 2012, the value for this category is negative.

In laying out Table 41.2, we have separated rows 1, 2, and 3 into one group and rows 4 and 5 into another. This reflects a fundamental difference in how these two groups of transactions affect the future.

When a U.S. resident sells a good, such as wheat, to a foreigner, that's the end of the transaction. But a financial asset, such as a bond, is different. Remember, a bond is a promise to pay interest and principal in the future. So when a U.S. resident sells a bond to a foreigner, that sale creates a liability: the U.S. resident will have to pay interest and repay principal in the future. The balance of payments accounts distinguish between transactions that don't create liabilities and those that do.

Transactions that don't create liabilities are considered part of the **balance of payments on the current account**, often referred to simply as the **current account**: the balance of payments on goods and services plus factor income and net international transfer payments. The balance of row 1 of Table 41.2, -\$534 billion, corresponds to the most important part of the current account: **the balance of payments on goods and services**, the difference between the value of exports and the value of imports during a given period.

By the way, if you read news reports on the economy, you may well see references to another measure, the **merchandise trade balance**, sometimes referred to as the **trade balance** for short. This is the difference between a country's exports and imports of goods alone—not including services. Economists sometimes focus on the merchandise trade balance, even though it's an incomplete measure, because data on international trade in services aren't as accurate as data on trade in physical goods, and they are also slower to arrive.

The current account, as we've just learned, consists of international transactions that don't create liabilities. Transactions that involve the sale or purchase of assets, and therefore do create future liabilities, are considered part of the **balance of payments on the financial account**, or the **financial account** for short. (Until a few years ago, economists often referred to the financial account as the *capital account*. We'll use the modern term, but you may run across the older term.)

So how does it all add up? The shaded rows of Table 41.2 show the bottom lines: the overall U.S. current account and financial account for 2012. As you can see, in 2012, the United States ran a current account deficit: the amount it paid to foreigners for goods, services, factors, and transfers was greater than the amount it received. Simultaneously, it ran a financial account surplus: the value of the assets it sold to foreigners was greater than the value of the assets it bought from foreigners.

In the official data, the U.S. current account deficit and financial account surplus almost, but not quite, offset each other: the financial account surplus was \$7 billion larger than the current account deficit. But that's just a statistical error, reflecting the imperfection of official data. (And a \$7 billion error when you're measuring inflows and outflows of \$3.5 trillion isn't bad!) In fact, it's a basic rule of balance of payments accounting that the current account and the financial account must sum to zero:

$$\textbf{(41-1)} \quad \text{Current account } (CA) + \text{Financial account } (FA) = 0$$

or

$$CA = -FA$$

Why must Equation 41-1 be true? We already saw the fundamental explanation in Table 41.1, which showed the accounts of the Costa family: in total, the sources of cash must equal the uses of cash. The same applies to balance of payments accounts. **Figure 41.1** on the next page, a variant on the circular-flow diagram we have found useful in discussing domestic macroeconomics, may help you visualize how this adding up works.

Instead of showing the flow of money *within* a national economy, Figure 41.1 shows the flow of money *between* national economies. Money flows into the United States from the rest of the world as payment for U.S. exports of goods and services, as payment for the use of U.S.-owned factors of production, and as transfer payments. These flows (indicated by the lower green arrow) are the positive components of the U.S. current account. Money also flows into the United States from foreigners who purchase U.S. assets (as shown by the lower red arrow)—the positive component of the U.S. financial account.

At the same time, money flows from the United States to the rest of the world as payment for U.S. imports of goods and services, as

A country's **balance of payments on the current account**, or the **current account**, is its balance of payments on goods and services plus net international transfer payments and factor income.

A country's **balance of payments on goods and services** is the difference between the value of its exports and the value of its imports during a given period.

The **merchandise trade balance**, or **trade balance**, is the difference between a country's exports and imports of goods.

A country's **balance of payments on the financial account**, or simply the **financial account**, is the difference between its sales of assets to foreigners and its purchases of assets from foreigners during a given period.

AP® Exam Tip

Remember that the financial account tracks assets such as real estate, stocks, and bonds. Dividends and interest paid are not assets, so they are counted in the current account. You may be asked to identify these transactions on the AP® exam.

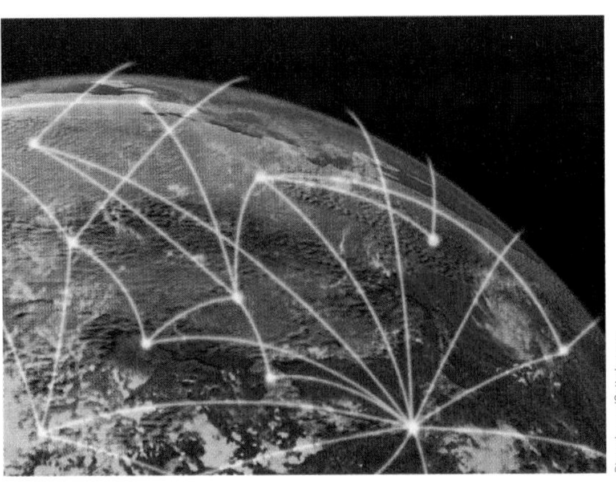

Bloomimage/Getty Images

Figure 41.1 The Balance of Payments

The green arrows represent payments that are counted in the current account. The red arrows represent payments that are counted in the financial account. Because the total flow into the United States must equal the total flow out of the United States, the sum of the current account plus the financial account is zero.

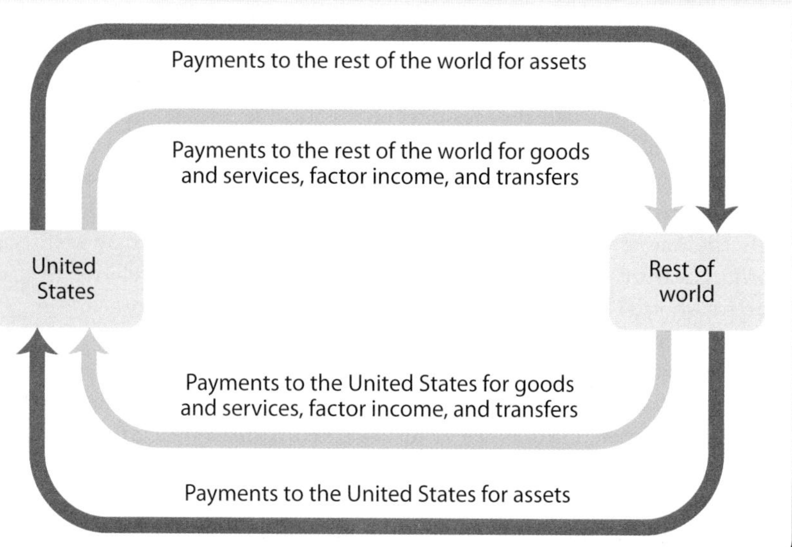

payment for the use of foreign-owned factors of production, and as transfer payments. These flows, indicated by the upper green arrow, are the negative components of the U.S. current account. Money also flows from the United States to purchase foreign assets, as shown by the upper red arrow—the negative component of the U.S. financial account. As in all circular-flow diagrams, the flow into a box and the flow out of a box are equal. This means that the sum of the red and green arrows going

FYI GDP, GNP, and the Current Account

When we discussed national income accounting, we derived the basic equation relating GDP to the components of spending:

$$Y = C + I + G + X - IM$$

where *X* and *IM* are exports and imports, respectively, of goods and services. But as we've learned, the balance of payments on goods and services is only one component of the current account balance. Why doesn't the national income equation use the current account as a whole?

The answer is that gross domestic product, which is the value of goods and services produced in a country, doesn't include two sources of income that are included in calculating the current account balance: international factor income and international transfers. The profits of Ford Motors U.K. aren't included in America's GDP, and the funds Latin American immigrants send home to their families aren't subtracted from GDP.

Shouldn't we have a broader measure that does include these sources of income? Actually, gross national product—GNP—does include international factor income. Estimates of U.S. GNP differ slightly from estimates of GDP because GNP adds in items such as the earnings of U.S. companies abroad and subtracts items such as the interest payments on bonds owned by residents of China and Japan. However, there isn't any regularly calculated measure that includes transfer payments.

Why do economists use GDP rather than a broader measure? Two reasons. First, the original purpose of the national accounts was to track production rather than income. Second, data on international factor income and transfer payments are generally considered somewhat unreliable. So if you're trying to keep track of movements in the economy, it makes sense to focus on GDP, which doesn't rely on these unreliable data.

Shutterstock

The funds Latin American immigrants send home through Western Union wires, as advertised on this billboard, aren't subtracted from GDP.

into the United States is equal to the sum of the red and green arrows going out of the United States. That is,

(41-2) Positive entries on the current account (lower green arrow) + Positive entries on the financial account (lower red arrow) = Negative entries on the current account (upper green arrow) + Negative entries on the financial account (upper red arrow)

AP® Exam Tip

The current and financial accounts balance each other out. If there is a surplus in one account, there is a deficit in the other.

Equation 41-2 can be rearranged as follows:

(41-3) Positive entries on the current account − Negative entries on the current account + Positive entries on the financial account − Negative entries on the financial account = 0

Equation 41-3 is equivalent to Equation 41-1: the current account plus the financial account—both equal to positive entries minus negative entries—is equal to zero.

But what determines the current account and the financial account?

Modeling the Financial Account

A country's financial account measures its net sales of assets, such as currencies, securities, and factories, to foreigners. Those assets are exchanged for a type of capital called *financial capital*, which is funds from savings that are available for investment spending. So we can think of the financial account as a measure of *capital inflows* in the form of foreign savings that become available to finance domestic investment spending.

What determines these capital inflows?

Part of our explanation will have to wait for a little while because some international capital flows are created by governments and central banks, which sometimes act very differently from private investors. But we can gain insight into the motivations for capital flows that are the result of private decisions by using the *loanable funds model* we developed previously. In using this model, we make two important simplifications:

- We simplify the reality of international capital flows by assuming that all flows are in the form of loans. In reality, capital flows take many forms, including purchases of shares of stock in foreign companies and foreign real estate as well as *foreign direct investment*, in which companies build factories or acquire other productive assets abroad.
- We also ignore the effects of expected changes in *exchange rates*, the relative values of different national currencies. We'll analyze the determination of exchange rates later.

Figure 41.2 on the next page recaps the loanable funds model for a closed economy. Equilibrium corresponds to point *E*, at an interest rate of 4%, at which the supply curve for loanable funds (*S*) intersects the demand curve for loanable funds (*D*). If international capital flows are possible, this diagram changes and *E* may no longer be the equilibrium. We can analyze the causes and effects of international capital flows using **Figure 41.3** on the next page, which places the loanable funds market diagrams for two countries side by side.

Figure 41.3 illustrates a world consisting of only two countries, the United States and Britain. Panel (a) shows the loanable funds market in the United States, where the equilibrium in the absence of international capital flows is at point E_{US} with an interest rate of 6%. Panel (b) shows the loanable funds market in Britain, where the equilibrium in the absence of international capital flows is at point E_B with an interest rate of 2%.

Will the actual interest rate in the United States remain at 6% and that in Britain at 2%? Not if it is easy for British residents to make loans to Americans. In that case, British lenders, attracted by high U.S. interest rates, will send some of their loanable funds to the United States. This capital inflow will increase the quantity of loanable funds supplied to American borrowers, pushing the U.S. interest rate down. At the same time, it will reduce the quantity of loanable funds supplied to British borrowers, pushing the British interest rate up. So international capital flows will narrow the gap between U.S. and British interest rates.

AP® Exam Tip

The financial account will have capital inflows and capital outflows based on changes in interest rates. This is financial capital and not capital in the form of machinery and equipment used in the production process.

Figure 41.2 The Loanable Funds Model Revisited

According to the loanable funds model of the interest rate, the equilibrium interest rate is determined by the intersection of the supply curve for loanable funds, *S*, and the demand curve for loanable funds, *D*. At point *E*, the equilibrium interest rate is 4%.

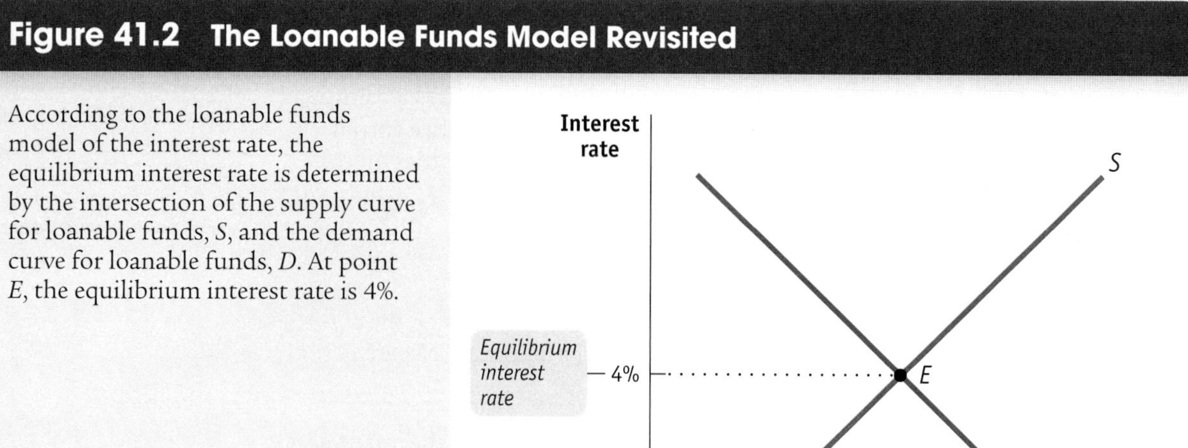

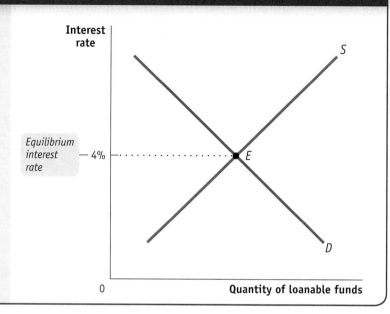

Let's further suppose that British lenders regard a loan to an American as being just as good as a loan to one of their own compatriots, and American borrowers regard a debt to a British lender as no more costly than a debt to an American lender. In that case, the flow of funds from Britain to the United States will continue until the gap between their interest rates is eliminated. In other words, international capital flows will equalize the interest rates in the two countries. **Figure 41.4** shows an international equilibrium in the loanable funds markets where the equilibrium interest rate is 4% in both the United States and Britain. At this interest rate, the quantity of loanable

Figure 41.3 Loanable Funds Markets in Two Countries

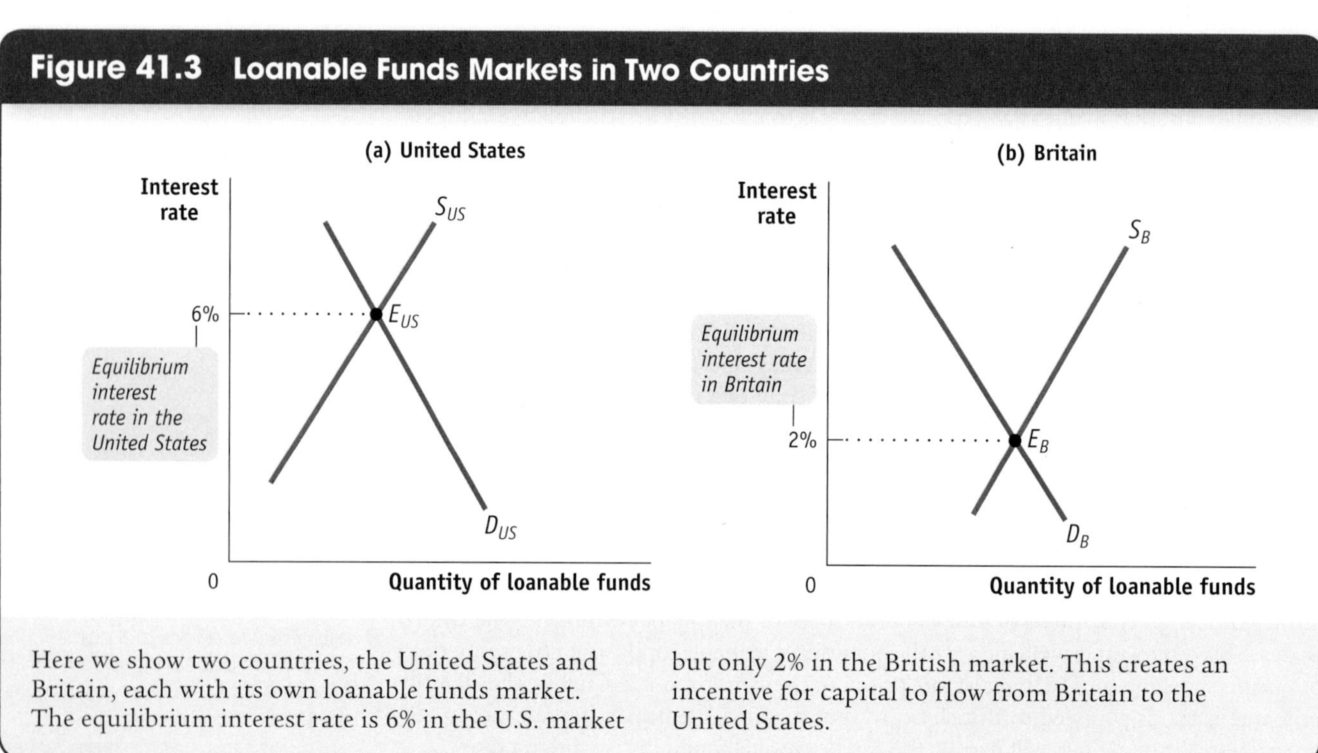

Here we show two countries, the United States and Britain, each with its own loanable funds market. The equilibrium interest rate is 6% in the U.S. market but only 2% in the British market. This creates an incentive for capital to flow from Britain to the United States.

Figure 41.4 International Capital Flows

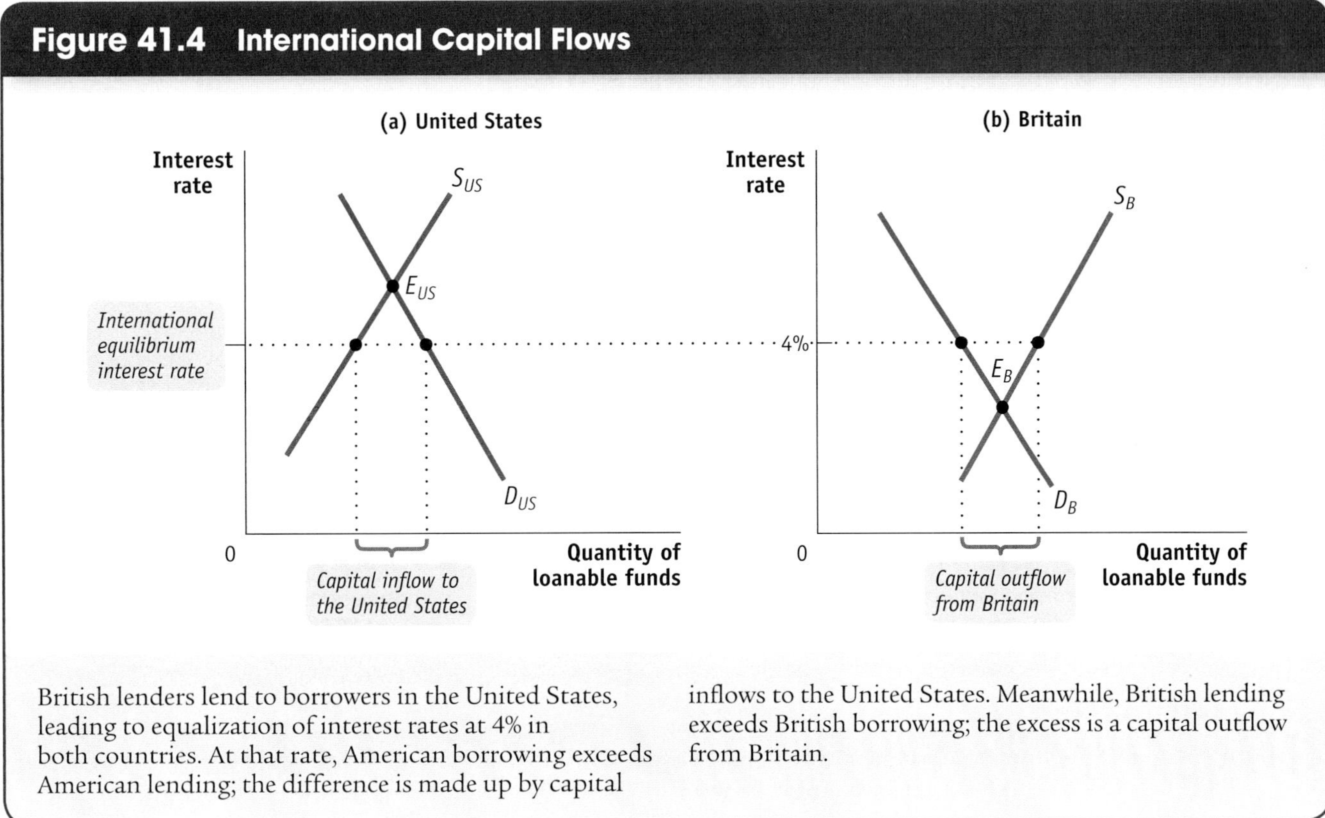

British lenders lend to borrowers in the United States, leading to equalization of interest rates at 4% in both countries. At that rate, American borrowing exceeds American lending; the difference is made up by capital inflows to the United States. Meanwhile, British lending exceeds British borrowing; the excess is a capital outflow from Britain.

funds demanded by American borrowers exceeds the quantity of loanable funds supplied by American lenders. This gap is filled by "imported" funds—a capital inflow from Britain. At the same time, the quantity of loanable funds supplied by British lenders is greater than the quantity of loanable funds demanded by British borrowers. This excess is "exported" in the form of a capital outflow to the United States. And the two markets are in equilibrium at a common interest rate of 4%. At that interest rate, the total quantity of loans demanded by borrowers across the two markets is equal to the total quantity of loans supplied by lenders across the two markets.

In short, international flows of capital are like international flows of goods and services. Capital moves from places where it would be cheap in the absence of international capital flows to places where it would be expensive in the absence of such flows.

Underlying Determinants of International Capital Flows

The open-economy version of the loanable funds model helps us understand international capital flows in terms of the supply and demand for funds. But what underlies differences across countries in the supply and demand for funds? And why, in the absence of international capital flows, would interest rates differ internationally, creating an incentive for international capital flows?

International differences in the demand for funds reflect underlying differences in investment opportunities. In particular, a country with a rapidly growing economy, other things equal, tends to offer more investment opportunities than a country with a slowly growing economy. So a rapidly growing economy typically—though not always—has a higher demand for capital and offers higher returns to investors than a slowly growing economy in the absence of capital flows. As a result, capital tends to flow from slowly growing to rapidly growing economies.

FYI A Global Savings Glut?

In the early years of the twenty-first century, the United States entered into a massive current account deficit, which meant that it became the recipient of huge capital inflows from the rest of the world, especially China, other Asian countries, and the Middle East. Why did that happen?

In an influential speech early in 2005, Ben Bernanke—who was at that time a governor of the Federal Reserve and who would soon become the Fed's chair—offered a hypothesis: the United States wasn't responsible. The "principal causes of the U.S. current account deficit," he declared, lie "outside the country's borders." Specifically, he argued that special factors had created a "global savings glut" that had pushed down interest rates worldwide and thereby led to an excess of investment spending over savings in the United States.

What caused this global savings glut? According to Bernanke, the main cause was the series of financial crises that began in Thailand in 1997, ricocheted across much of Asia, and then hit Russia in 1998, Brazil in 1999, and Argentina in 2002. The ensuing fear and economic devastation led to a fall in investment spending and a rise in savings in many relatively poor countries. As a result, a number of these countries, which had previously been the recipients of capital inflows from developed countries like the United States, began experiencing large capital outflows. For the most part, the capital flowed to the United States, perhaps because "the depth and sophistication of the country's financial markets" made it an attractive destination.

When Bernanke gave his speech, it was viewed as reassuring: basically, he argued that the United States was responding in a sensible way to the availability of cheap money in world financial markets. Later, however, it would become clear that the cheap money from abroad helped fuel a housing bubble, which caused widespread financial and economic damage when it burst.

The classic example is the flow of capital from Britain to the United States, among other countries, between 1870 and 1914. During that era, the U.S. economy was growing rapidly as the population increased and spread westward, and as the nation industrialized. This created a demand for investment spending on railroads, factories, and so on. Meanwhile, Britain had a much more slowly growing population, was already industrialized, and already had a railroad network covering the country. This left Britain with savings to spare, much of which were lent to the United States and other New World economies.

International differences in the supply of funds reflect differences in savings across countries. These may be the result of differences in private savings rates, which vary widely among countries. For example, in 2013, private savings were 27.1% of Japan's GDP but only 15.9% of U.S. GDP. They may also reflect differences in savings by governments. In particular, government budget deficits, which reduce overall national savings, can lead to capital inflows.

Andrew Holbrooke/Time Life Pictures/Getty Images

Nike, like many other companies, has opened plants in China to take advantage of low labor costs and to gain better access to the large Chinese market. Here, two Chinese employees assemble running shoes in a Nike factory in China.

Two-Way Capital Flows

The loanable funds model helps us understand the direction of *net* capital flows—the excess of inflows into a country over outflows, or vice versa. As we saw in Table 41.2, however, *gross* flows take place in both directions: for example, the United States both sells assets to foreigners and buys assets from foreigners. Why does capital move in both directions?

The answer to this question is that in the real world, as opposed to the simple model we've just constructed, there are other motives for international capital flows besides seeking a higher rate of interest. Individual investors often seek to diversify against risk by buying stocks in a number of countries. Stocks in Europe may do well when stocks in the United States do badly, or vice versa, so investors in Europe try to reduce their risk by buying some U.S. stocks, even as investors in the United States try to reduce their risk by buying some European stocks. The result is capital flows in both directions. Meanwhile, corporations often engage in international investment as part of their business strategy—for example, auto companies may find that they can compete better in a national market if they assemble some of their cars locally. Such business investments can also lead to two-way capital flows, as, say, European carmakers build plants in the United States even as U.S. computer companies open facilities in Europe.

Finally, some countries, including the United States, are international banking centers: people from all over the world put money in U.S. financial institutions, which then invest many of those funds overseas.

The result of these two-way flows is that modern economies are typically both debtors (countries that owe money to the rest of the world) and creditors (countries to which the rest of the world owes money). Due to years of both capital inflows and outflows, at the end of 2013, the United States had accumulated foreign assets worth $22 trillion and foreigners had accumulated assets in the United States worth $26.5 trillion.

MODULE 41 Review

Check Your Understanding

1. Which of the balance of payments accounts do the following events affect?
   - **a.** Boeing, a U.S.-based company, sells a newly built airplane to China.
   - **b.** Chinese investors buy stock in Boeing from Americans.
   - **c.** A Chinese company buys a used airplane from American Airlines and ships it to China.
   - **d.** A Chinese investor who owns property in the United States buys a corporate jet, which he will keep in the United States so he can travel around America.

Tackle the Test: Multiple-Choice Questions

1. The current account includes which of the following?
   - **I.** payments for goods and services
   - **II.** transfer payments
   - **III.** factor income
   - **a.** I only
   - **b.** II only
   - **c.** III only
   - **d.** I and II only
   - **e.** I, II, and III
2. The balance of payments on the current account plus the balance of payments on the financial account is equal to
   - **a.** zero.
   - **b.** one.
   - **c.** the trade balance.
   - **d.** net capital flows.
   - **e.** the size of the trade deficit.
3. The financial account was previously known as the
   - **a.** gross national product.
   - **b.** capital account.
   - **c.** trade deficit.
   - **d.** investment account.
   - **e.** trade balance.
4. The trade balance includes which of the following?
   - **I.** imports and exports of goods
   - **II.** imports and exports of services
   - **III.** net capital flows
   - **a.** I only
   - **b.** II only
   - **c.** III only
   - **d.** I and II only
   - **e.** I, II, and III
5. Which of the following will increase the demand for loanable funds in a country?
   - **a.** economic growth
   - **b.** decreased investment opportunities
   - **c.** a recession
   - **d.** decreased private savings rates
   - **e.** government budget surpluses

Tackle the Test: Free-Response Questions

1. **a.** How would a decrease in real income in the United States affect the U.S. current account balance? Explain.

   b. Suppose China financed a huge program of infrastructure spending by borrowing. How would this borrowing affect the U.S. balance of payments? Explain.

Rubric for FRQ 1 (4 points)

1 point: The current account balance would increase (or move toward a surplus).

1 point: The decrease in income would cause imports to decrease.

1 point: The increase in infrastructure spending in China would reduce the surplus in the U.S. financial account and reduce the deficit in the U.S. current account.

1 point: Because China is financing the program by borrowing, the demand for loanable funds in China would increase, causing an increase in the interest rate. It is likely that other countries would increase their lending to China, decreasing their lending to the United States. These capital outflows from the United States would reduce the U.S. surplus in the financial account and reduce the deficit in the current account.

2. Use two correctly labeled side-by-side graphs of the loanable funds market in the United States and China to show how a higher interest rate in the United States will lead to capital flows between the two countries. On your graphs, be sure to label the equilibrium interest rate in each country in the absence of international capital flows, the international equilibrium interest rate, and the size of the capital inflows and outflows.

   (6 points)

Udo Weitz/Bloomberg via Getty Images

MODULE 42 The Foreign Exchange Market

In this Module, you will learn to:

- Explain the role of the foreign exchange market and the exchange rate
- Discuss the importance of real exchange rates and their role in the current account

The Role of the Exchange Rate

We've just seen how differences in the supply of loanable funds from savings and the demand for loanable funds for investment spending lead to international capital flows. We've also learned that a country's balance of payments on the current account plus its balance of payments on the financial account add up to zero: a country that receives net capital inflows must run a matching current account deficit, and a country that generates net capital outflows must run a matching current account surplus.

The behavior of the financial account—reflecting inflows or outflows of capital—is best described as equilibrium in the international loanable funds market. At the same time, the balance of payments on goods and services, the main component of the current account, is determined by decisions in the international markets for goods and services. So given that the financial account reflects the movement of capital and the current account reflects the movement of goods and services, what ensures that the balance of payments really does balance? That is, what ensures that the two accounts actually offset each other?

The answer lies in the role of the *exchange rate*, which is determined in the *foreign exchange market.*

AP® Exam Tip

The foreign exchange market appears frequently on the AP® exam. You may be expected to graph and explain this market in the free-response section.

Understanding Exchange Rates

In general, goods, services, and assets produced in a country must be paid for in that country's currency. U.S. products must be paid for in dollars; most European products must be paid for in euros; Japanese products must be paid for in yen. Occasionally, sellers will accept payment in foreign currency, but they will then exchange that currency for domestic money.

International transactions, then, require a market—the **foreign exchange market**—in which currencies can be exchanged for each other. This market determines **exchange rates**, the prices at which currencies trade. (The foreign exchange market, in fact, is not

Currencies are traded in the **foreign exchange market**.

The prices at which currencies trade are known as **exchange rates**.

Table 42.1 Exchange Rates, April 3, 2014, 12:50 A.M.	U.S. dollars	Yen	Euros
One U.S. dollar exchanged for	1	103.97	0.7269
One yen exchanged for	0.0096	1	0.007
One euro exchanged for	1.3757	143.04	1

located in any one geographic spot. Rather, it is a global electronic market that traders around the world use to buy and sell currencies.)

Table 42.1 shows exchange rates among the world's three most important currencies as of 12:50 A.M., EST, on April 3, 2014. Each entry shows the price of the "row" currency in terms of the "column" currency. For example, at that time US$1 exchanged for €0.7269, so it took €0.7269 to buy US$1. Similarly, it took US$1.3757 to buy €1. These two numbers reflect the same rate of exchange between the euro and the U.S. dollar: 1/1.3757 = €0.7269.

There are two ways to write any given exchange rate. In this case, there were €0.7269 to US$1 and US$1.3757 to €1. Which is the correct way to write it? The answer is that there is no fixed rule. In most countries, people tend to express the exchange rate as the price of a dollar in domestic currency. However, this rule isn't universal, and the U.S. dollar–euro rate is commonly quoted both ways. The important thing is to be sure you know which one you are using!

When a currency becomes more valuable in terms of other currencies, it **appreciates**.

When a currency becomes less valuable in terms of other currencies, it **depreciates**.

When discussing movements in exchange rates, economists use specialized terms to avoid confusion. When a currency becomes more valuable in terms of other currencies, economists say that the currency **appreciates**. When a currency becomes less valuable in terms of other currencies, it **depreciates**. Suppose, for example, that the value of €1 went from $1 to $1.25, which means that the value of US$1 went from €1 to €0.80 (because 1/1.25 = 0.80). In this case, we would say that the euro appreciated and the U.S. dollar depreciated.

Movements in exchange rates, other things equal, affect the relative prices of goods, services, and assets in different countries. Suppose, for example, that the price of an American hotel room is US$100 and the price of a French hotel room is €100. If the exchange rate is €1 = US$1, these hotel rooms have the same price. If the exchange rate is €1.25 = US$1, however, the French hotel room is 20% cheaper than the American hotel room. If the exchange rate is €0.80 = US$1, the French hotel room is 25% more expensive than the American hotel room.

But what determines exchange rates? Supply and demand in the foreign exchange market.

The Equilibrium Exchange Rate

For the sake of simplicity, imagine that there are only two currencies in the world: U.S. dollars and euros. Europeans who want to purchase American goods, services, and assets come to the foreign exchange market to exchange euros for U.S. dollars. That is, Europeans demand U.S. dollars from the foreign exchange market and, correspondingly, supply euros to that market. Americans who want to buy European goods, services, and assets come to the foreign exchange market to exchange U.S. dollars for euros. That is, Americans supply U.S. dollars to the foreign exchange market and, correspondingly, demand euros from that market. International transfers and payments of factor income also enter into the foreign exchange market, but to make things simple, we'll ignore these.

Figure 42.1 shows how the foreign exchange market works. The quantity of dollars demanded and supplied at any given euro–U.S. dollar exchange rate is shown on the horizontal axis, and the euro–U.S. dollar exchange rate is shown on the vertical axis. The exchange rate plays the same role as the price of a good or service in an ordinary supply and demand diagram.

The figure shows two curves, the demand curve for U.S. dollars and the supply curve for U.S. dollars. The key to understanding the slopes of these curves is that the level of the exchange rate affects exports and imports. When a country's currency appreciates (becomes more valuable), exports fall and imports rise. When a country's currency depreciates (becomes less valuable), exports rise and imports fall. To understand why the demand curve for U.S. dollars slopes downward, recall that the exchange rate, other things equal, determines the prices of American goods, services, and assets relative to

Figure 42.1 The Foreign Exchange Market

The foreign exchange market matches up the demand for a currency from foreigners who want to buy domestic goods, services, and assets with the supply of a currency from domestic residents who want to buy foreign goods, services, and assets. Here the equilibrium in the market for dollars is at point *E*, corresponding to an equilibrium exchange rate of €0.95 per US$1.

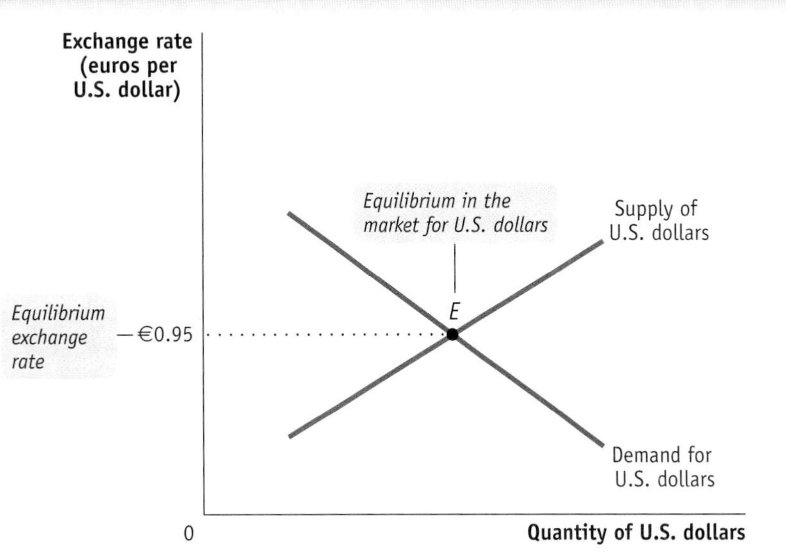

those of European goods, services, and assets. If the U.S. dollar rises against the euro (the dollar appreciates), American products will become more expensive to Europeans relative to European products. So Europeans will buy less from the United States and will acquire fewer dollars in the foreign exchange market: the quantity of U.S. dollars demanded falls as the number of euros needed to buy a U.S. dollar rises. If the U.S. dollar falls against the euro (the dollar depreciates), American products will become relatively cheaper for Europeans. Europeans will respond by buying more from the United States and acquiring more dollars in the foreign exchange market: the quantity of U.S. dollars demanded rises as the number of euros needed to buy a U.S. dollar falls.

A similar argument explains why the supply curve of U.S. dollars in Figure 42.1 slopes upward: the more euros required to buy a U.S. dollar, the more dollars Americans will supply. Again, the reason is the effect of the exchange rate on relative prices. If the U.S. dollar rises against the euro, European products look cheaper to Americans—who will demand more of them. This will require Americans to convert more dollars into euros.

The **equilibrium exchange rate** is the exchange rate at which the quantity of U.S. dollars demanded in the foreign exchange market is equal to the quantity of U.S. dollars supplied. In Figure 42.1, the equilibrium is at point *E*, and the equilibrium exchange rate is 0.95. That is, at an exchange rate of €0.95 per US$1, the quantity of U.S. dollars supplied to the foreign exchange market is equal to the quantity of U.S. dollars demanded.

The **equilibrium exchange rate** is the exchange rate at which the quantity of a currency demanded in the foreign exchange market is equal to the quantity supplied.

To understand the significance of the equilibrium exchange rate, it's helpful to consider a numerical example of what equilibrium in the foreign exchange market looks like. Such an example is shown in **Table 42.2** on the next page. (This is a hypothetical table that isn't intended to match real numbers.) The first row shows European purchases of U.S. dollars, either to buy U.S. goods and services or to buy U.S. assets such as real estate or shares of stock in U.S. companies. The second row shows U.S. sales of U.S. dollars, either to buy European goods and services or to buy European assets. At the equilibrium exchange rate, the total quantity of U.S. dollars Europeans want to buy is equal to the total quantity of U.S. dollars Americans want to sell.

Remember that the balance of payments accounts divide international transactions into two types. Purchases and sales of goods and services are counted in the current account. (Again, we're leaving out transfers and factor income to keep things simple.) Purchases and sales of assets are counted in the financial account. At the equilibrium exchange rate, then, we have the situation shown in Table 42.2: the sum of the balance of payments on the current account plus the balance of payments on the financial account is zero.

Table 42.2 Equilibrium in the Foreign Exchange Market: A Hypothetical Example

European purchases of U.S. dollars (trillions of U.S. dollars)	To buy U.S. goods and services: 1.0	To buy U.S. assets: 1.0	Total purchases of U.S. dollars: 2.0
U.S. sales of U.S. dollars (trillions of U.S. dollars)	To buy European goods and services: 1.5	To buy European assets: 0.5	Total sales of U.S. dollars: 2.0
	U.S. balance of payments on the current account: –0.5	U.S. balance of payments on the financial account: +0.5	

Now let's briefly consider how a shift in the demand for U.S. dollars affects equilibrium in the foreign exchange market. Suppose that for some reason capital flows from Europe to the United States increase—say, due to a change in the preferences of European investors. The effects are shown in **Figure 42.2**. The demand for U.S. dollars in the foreign exchange market increases as European investors convert euros into dollars to fund their new investments in the United States. This is shown by the shift of the demand curve from D_1 to D_2. As a result, the U.S. dollar appreciates: the number of euros per U.S. dollar at the equilibrium exchange rate rises from XR_1 to XR_2.

What are the consequences of this increased capital inflow for the balance of payments? The total quantity of U.S. dollars supplied to the foreign exchange market still must equal the total quantity of U.S. dollars demanded. So the increased capital inflow to the United States—an increase in the balance of payments on the financial account—must be matched by a decline in the balance of payments on the current account. What causes the balance of payments on the current account to decline? The appreciation of the U.S. dollar. A rise in the number of euros per U.S. dollar leads Americans to buy more European goods and services and Europeans to buy fewer American goods and services.

Table 42.3 shows how this might work. Europeans are buying more U.S. assets, increasing the balance of payments on the financial account from 0.5 to 1.0. This is offset by a reduction in European purchases of U.S. goods and services and a rise in U.S. purchases of European goods and services, both the result of the dollar's appreciation. *So any change in the U.S. balance of payments on the financial account generates an equal*

Figure 42.2 An Increase in the Demand for U.S. Dollars

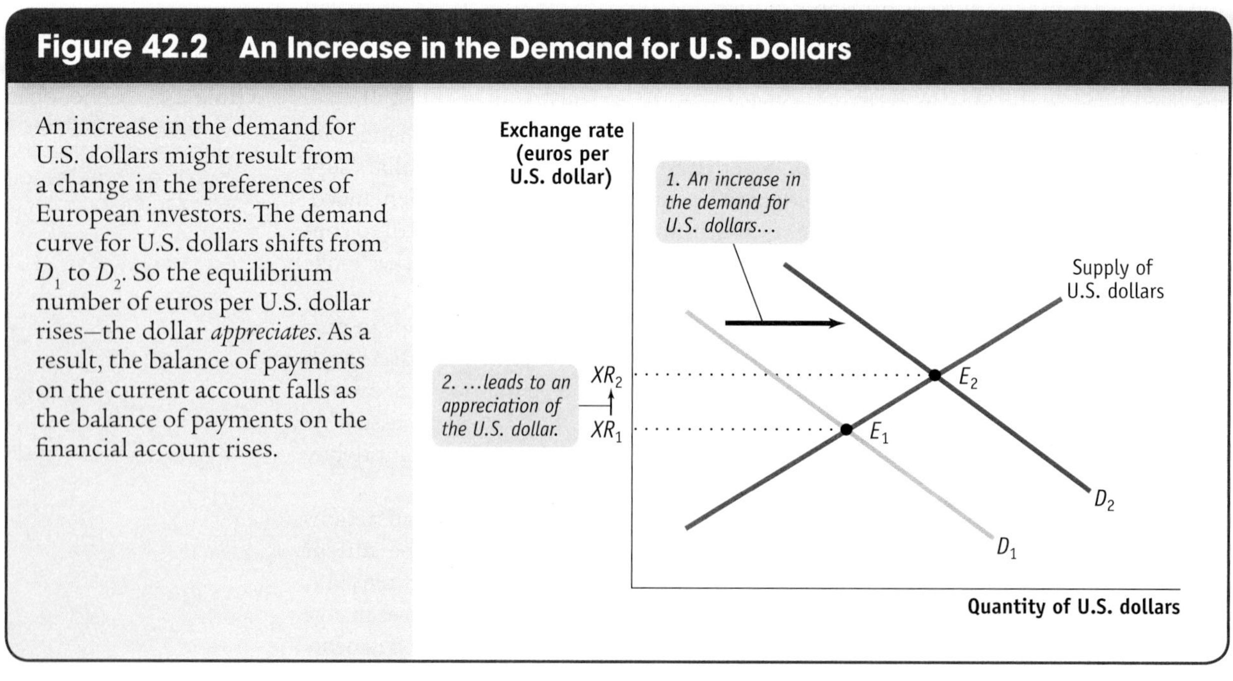

An increase in the demand for U.S. dollars might result from a change in the preferences of European investors. The demand curve for U.S. dollars shifts from D_1 to D_2. So the equilibrium number of euros per U.S. dollar rises—the dollar *appreciates*. As a result, the balance of payments on the current account falls as the balance of payments on the financial account rises.

Table 42.3 Effects of Increased Capital Inflows

European purchases of U.S. dollars (trillions of U.S. dollars)	To buy U.S. goods and services: 0.75 (down 0.25)	To buy U.S. assets: 1.5 (up 0.5)	Total purchases of U.S. dollars: 2.25
U.S. sales of U.S. dollars (trillions of U.S. dollars)	To buy European goods and services: 1.75 (up 0.25)	To buy European assets: 0.5 (no change)	Total sales of U.S. dollars: 2.25
	U.S. balance of payments on the current account: −1.0 (down 0.5)	U.S. balance of payments on the financial account: +1.0 (up 0.5)	

and opposite reaction in the balance of payments on the current account. Movements in the exchange rate ensure that changes in the financial account and in the current account offset each other.

Let's briefly run this process in reverse. Suppose there is a reduction in capital flows from Europe to the United States—again due to a change in the preferences of European investors. The demand for U.S. dollars in the foreign exchange market falls, and the dollar depreciates: the number of euros per U.S. dollar at the equilibrium exchange rate falls. This leads Americans to buy fewer European products and Europeans to buy more American products. Ultimately, this generates an increase in the U.S. balance of payments on the current account. So a fall in capital flows into the United States leads to a weaker dollar, which in turn generates an increase in U.S. net exports.

Inflation and Real Exchange Rates

Keith Dannemiller/Alamy

The exchange rates listed at currency exchange booths are nominal exchange rates. The current account responds only to changes in real exchange rates, which have been adjusted for differing levels of inflation.

In 1994, on average, one U.S. dollar exchanged for 3.4 Mexican pesos. By 2014, the peso had fallen against the dollar by almost 75%, with an average exchange rate in early 2014 of 13.3 pesos per dollar. Did Mexican products also become much cheaper relative to U.S. products over that 20-year period? Did the price of Mexican products expressed in terms of U.S. dollars also fall by almost 75%? The answer is no, because Mexico had much higher inflation than the United States over that period. In fact, the relative price of U.S. and Mexican products changed little between 1994 and 2014, although the exchange rate changed a lot.

To take account of the effects of differences in inflation rates, economists calculate **real exchange rates**, exchange rates adjusted for international differences in aggregate price levels. Suppose that the exchange rate we are looking at is the number of Mexican pesos per U.S. dollar. Let P_{US} and P_{Mex} be indexes of the aggregate price levels in the United States and Mexico, respectively. Then the real exchange rate between the Mexican peso and the U.S. dollar is defined as:

Real exchange rates are exchange rates adjusted for international differences in aggregate price levels.

$$\text{(42-1)} \qquad \text{Real exchange rate} = \text{Mexican pesos per U.S. dollar} \times \frac{P_{US}}{P_{Mex}}$$

To distinguish it from the real exchange rate, the exchange rate unadjusted for aggregate price levels is sometimes called the *nominal* exchange rate.

To understand the significance of the difference between the real and nominal exchange rates, let's consider the following example. Suppose that the Mexican peso depreciates against the U.S. dollar, with the exchange rate going from 10 pesos per U.S. dollar to 15 pesos per U.S. dollar, a 50% change. But suppose that at the same time the price of everything in Mexico, measured in pesos, increases by 50%, so that the Mexican price index rises from 100 to 150. We'll assume that there is no change in U.S. prices, so that the U.S. price index remains at 100. The initial real exchange rate is:

$$\text{Pesos per dollar} \times \frac{P_{US}}{P_{Mex}} = 10 \times \frac{100}{100} = 10$$

After the peso depreciates and the Mexican price level increases, the real exchange rate is:

$$\text{Pesos per dollar} \times \frac{P_{US}}{P_{Mex}} = 15 \times \frac{100}{150} = 10$$

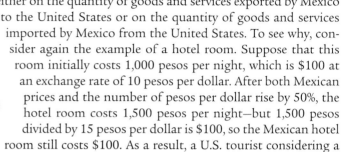

In this example, the peso has depreciated substantially in terms of the U.S. dollar, but the *real* exchange rate between the peso and the U.S. dollar hasn't changed at all. And because the real peso–U.S. dollar exchange rate hasn't changed, the nominal depreciation of the peso against the U.S. dollar will have no effect either on the quantity of goods and services exported by Mexico to the United States or on the quantity of goods and services imported by Mexico from the United States. To see why, consider again the example of a hotel room. Suppose that this room initially costs 1,000 pesos per night, which is $100 at an exchange rate of 10 pesos per dollar. After both Mexican prices and the number of pesos per dollar rise by 50%, the hotel room costs 1,500 pesos per night—but 1,500 pesos divided by 15 pesos per dollar is $100, so the Mexican hotel room still costs $100. As a result, a U.S. tourist considering a trip to Mexico will have no reason to change plans.

PhotoSpin, Inc/Alamy

The same is true for all goods and services that enter into trade: *the current account responds only to changes in the real exchange rate, not the nominal exchange rate.* A country's products become cheaper to foreigners only when that country's currency depreciates in real terms, and those products become more expensive to foreigners only when the currency appreciates in real terms. As a consequence, economists who analyze movements in exports and imports of goods and services focus on the real exchange rate, not the nominal exchange rate.

Figure 42.3 illustrates just how important it can be to distinguish between nominal and real exchange rates. The line labeled "Nominal exchange rate" shows the number of pesos exchanged for a U.S. dollar from 1990 to 2013. As you can see, the peso depreciated massively over that period. But the line labeled "Real exchange rate" indicates the cost of Mexican products to U.S. consumers: it was calculated using Equation 42.1, with price indexes for both Mexico and the United States set so that the value in 1990 was 100. In real terms, the peso depreciated between 1994 and 1995, and again in 2008, but not by nearly as much as the nominal depreciation. By 2013, the real peso–U.S. dollar exchange rate was just about back where it started.

Figure 42.3 Real Versus Nominal Exchange Rates, 1990–2013

Between 1990 and 2013, the price of a dollar in Mexican pesos increased dramatically. But because Mexico had higher inflation than the United States, the real exchange rate, which accounts for the relative price of Mexican goods and services, ended up roughly where it started.
Source: OECD.

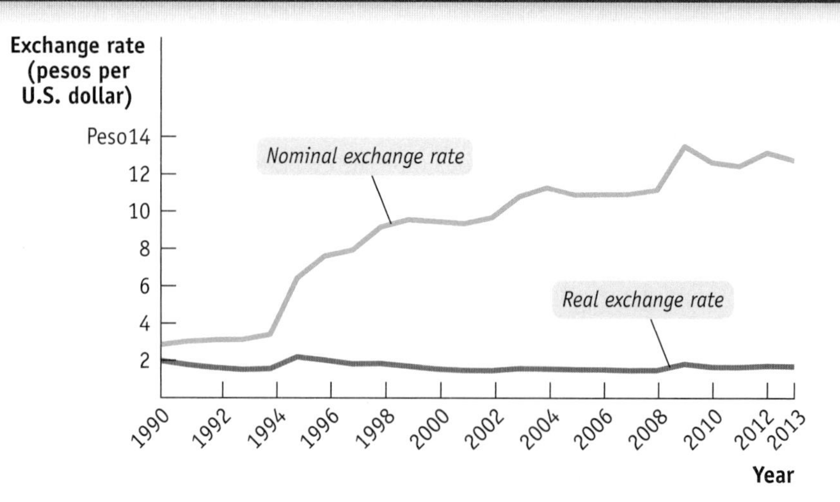

Purchasing Power Parity

A useful tool for analyzing exchange rates, closely connected to the concept of the real exchange rate, is known as *purchasing power parity*. The **purchasing power parity** between two countries' currencies is the nominal exchange rate at which a given basket of goods and services would cost the same amount in each country. For example, suppose that a basket of goods and services that costs $100 in the United States costs 1,000 pesos in Mexico. Then the purchasing power parity is 10 pesos per U.S. dollar: at that exchange rate, 1,000 pesos = $100, so the market basket costs the same amount in both countries.

The **purchasing power parity** between two countries' currencies is the nominal exchange rate at which a given basket of goods and services would cost the same amount in each country.

Calculations of purchasing power parities are usually made by estimating the cost of buying broad market baskets containing many goods and services—everything from automobiles and groceries to housing and telephone calls. But once a year the magazine *The Economist* publishes a list of purchasing power parities based on the cost of buying a market basket that contains only one item—a McDonald's Big Mac.

Nominal exchange rates almost always differ from purchasing power parities. Some of these differences are systematic: in general, aggregate price levels are lower in poor countries than in rich countries because services tend to be cheaper in poor countries. But even among countries at roughly the same level of economic development, nominal exchange rates vary quite a lot from purchasing power parity. **Figure 42.4** on the next page shows the nominal exchange rate between the Canadian dollar and the U.S. dollar, measured as the number of Canadian dollars per U.S. dollar, from 1990 to 2013, together with an estimate of the purchasing power parity exchange rate between the United States and Canada over the same period. The purchasing power parity didn't change much over the whole period because the United States and Canada had about the same rate of inflation. But at the beginning of the period the nominal exchange rate was below purchasing power parity, so a given market basket was more expensive in Canada than in the United States. By 2002, the nominal exchange rate was far above the purchasing power parity, so a market basket was much cheaper in Canada than in the United States.

Over the long run, however, purchasing power parities are pretty good at predicting actual changes in nominal exchange rates. In particular, nominal exchange rates

FYI Burgernomics

For a number of years the British magazine *The Economist* has produced an annual comparison of the cost in different countries of one particular consumption item that is found around the world—a McDonald's Big Mac. The magazine finds the price of a Big Mac in local currency, then computes two numbers: the price of a Big Mac in U.S. dollars using the prevailing exchange rate, and the exchange rate at which the price of a Big Mac would equal the U.S. price. If purchasing power parity held for Big Macs, the dollar price of a Big Mac would be the same everywhere. If purchasing power parity is a good theory for the long run, the exchange rate at which a Big Mac's price

Aleks Kend/Shutterstock

matches the U.S. price should offer some guidance about where the exchange rate will eventually end up.

In the January 2014 version of the Big Mac index, there were some wide variations in the dollar price of a Big Mac. In the U.S., the price was $4.62. In China, converting at the official exchange rate, a Big Mac cost only $2.74. In Switzerland, though, the price was $7.14.

The Big Mac index suggested that the euro would eventually fall against the dollar: a Big Mac on average cost €3.66, so that the purchasing power parity was $1.26 per €1 versus an actual market exchange rate of $1.38.

Serious economic studies of purchasing power parity require data on the prices of many goods and services. However, it turns out that estimates of purchasing power parity based on the Big Mac index usually aren't that different from more elaborate measures. Fast food seems to make for pretty good fast research.

Figure 42.4 Purchasing Power Parity Versus the Nominal Exchange Rate, 1990–2013

The purchasing power parity between the United States and Canada—the exchange rate at which a basket of goods and services would have cost the same amount in both countries—changed very little over the period shown, staying near C$1.20 per US$1. But the nominal exchange rate fluctuated widely.

Source: OECD.

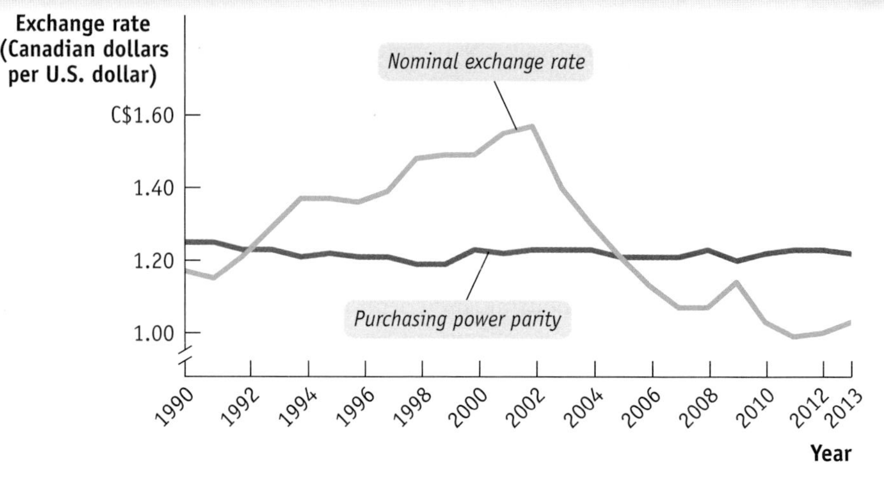

between countries at similar levels of economic development tend to fluctuate around levels that lead to similar costs for a given market basket. In fact, by July 2005, the nominal exchange rate between the United States and Canada was C$1.22 per US$1—just about the purchasing power parity. And by 2006, the cost of living was once again higher in Canada than in the United States.

FYI Low-Cost America

Does the exchange rate matter for business decisions? And how. Consider what European auto manufacturers were doing in 2008. One report from the University of Iowa summarized the situation as follows:

"While luxury German carmakers BMW and Mercedes have maintained plants in the American South since the 1990s, BMW aims to expand U.S. manufacturing in South Carolina by 50% during the next five years. Volvo of Sweden is in negotiations to build a plant in New Mexico. Analysts at Italian carmaker Fiat determined that it needs to build a North American factory to profit from the upcoming re-launch of its Alfa Romeo model. Tennessee recently closed a deal with Volkswagen to build a $1 billion factory by offering $577 million in incentives."

Why were European automakers flocking to America? To some extent because they were being offered special incentives, as the case of Volkswagen in Tennessee illustrates. But the big factor was the exchange rate. In the early 2000s, on average, one euro was worth less than a dollar; by the summer of 2008 the exchange rate was around €1 = $1.50. This change in the exchange rate made it substantially cheaper for European car manufacturers to produce in the United States than at home—especially if the cars were intended for the U.S. market.

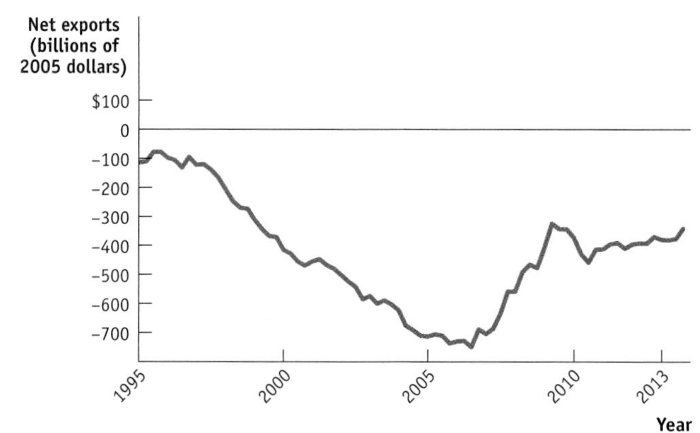

Source: Bureau of Economic Analysis.

Automobile manufacturing wasn't the only U.S. industry benefiting from the weak dollar; across the board, U.S. exports surged after 2006 while import growth fell off. The figure shows one measure of U.S. trade performance, real net exports of goods and services: exports minus imports, both measured in 2005 dollars. As you can see, this balance, after a long slide, turned sharply upward in 2006.

There was a modest reversal in 2009–2010, as the recovery from the 2007–2009 recession pulled in more imports, but a major narrowing of the trade gap remained in place.

MODULE 42 Review

Check Your Understanding

1. Suppose Mexico discovers huge reserves of oil and starts exporting oil to the United States. Describe how this would affect the following:
   - **a.** the nominal peso–U.S. dollar exchange rate
   - **b.** Mexican exports of other goods and services
   - **c.** Mexican imports of goods and services
2. Suppose a basket of goods and services that costs $100 in the United States costs 800 pesos in Mexico and the current nominal exchange rate is 10 pesos per U.S. dollar. Over the next five years, the cost of that market basket rises to $120 in the United States and to 1,200 pesos in Mexico, although the nominal exchange rate remains at 10 pesos per U.S. dollar. Calculate the following:
   - **a.** the real exchange rate now and five years from now, if today's price index in both countries is 100. [Reminder: Equation 15-1 provides the price index formula: (Cost of market basket in a given year/Cost of market basket in base year) × 100. For this problem, use the current year as the base year.]
   - **b.** purchasing power parity today and five years from now

Tackle the Test: Multiple-Choice Questions

1. When the U.S. dollar buys more Japanese yen, the U.S. dollar has
   - **I.** become more valuable in terms of the yen.
   - **II.** appreciated.
   - **III.** depreciated.
   - **a.** I only
   - **b.** II only
   - **c.** III only
   - **d.** I and II only
   - **e.** I and III only
2. The nominal exchange rate at which a given basket of goods and services would cost the same in each country describes
   - **a.** the international consumer price index.
   - **b.** appreciation.
   - **c.** depreciation.
   - **d.** purchasing power parity.
   - **e.** the balance of payments on the current account.
3. What happens to the real exchange rate between the euro and the U.S. dollar (expressed as euros per dollar) if the aggregate price levels in Europe and the United States both fall? It
   - **a.** is unaffected.
   - **b.** increases.
   - **c.** decreases.
   - **d.** may increase, decrease, or stay the same.
   - **e.** cannot be calculated.
4. Which of the following would cause the real exchange rate between pesos and U.S. dollars (in terms of pesos per dollar) to decrease?
   - **a.** an increase in net capital flows from Mexico to the United States
   - **b.** an increase in the real interest rate in Mexico relative to the United States
   - **c.** a doubling of prices in both Mexico and the United States
   - **d.** a decrease in oil exports from Mexico to the United States
   - **e.** an increase in the balance of payments on the current account in the United States
5. Which of the following will decrease the supply of U.S. dollars in the foreign exchange market?
   - **a.** U.S. residents increase their travel abroad.
   - **b.** U.S. consumers demand fewer imports.
   - **c.** Foreigners increase their demand for U.S. goods.
   - **d.** Foreigners increase their travel to the United States.
   - **e.** Foreign investors see increased investment opportunities in the United States.

Tackle the Test: Free-Response Questions

1. Draw a correctly labeled graph of the foreign exchange market showing the effect on the equilibrium exchange rate between the U.S. and Japan (the number of yen per U.S. dollar) if capital flows from Japan to the United States decrease due to a change in the preferences of Japanese investors. Has the U.S. dollar appreciated or depreciated?

Rubric for FRQ 1 (7 points)

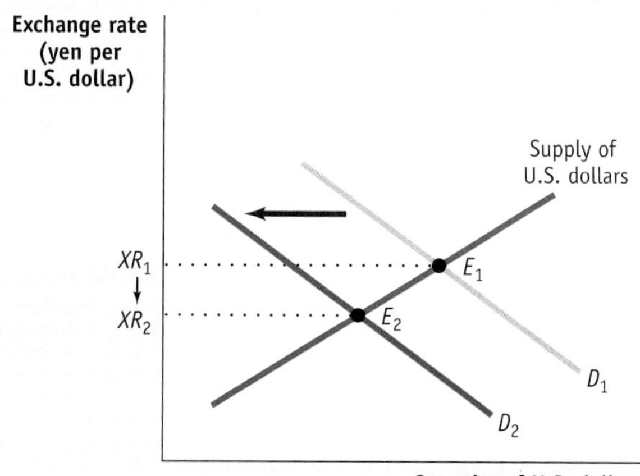

1 point: The vertical axis is labeled "Exchange rate (yen per U.S. dollar)" and the horizontal axis is labeled "Quantity of U.S. dollars."

1 point: The supply of U.S. dollars is labeled and slopes upward.

1 point: The demand for U.S. dollars is labeled and slopes downward.

1 point: The initial equilibrium exchange rate is found at the intersection of the initial supply and demand curves and is labeled on the vertical axis.

1 point: The new demand for U.S. dollars is to the left of the initial demand.

1 point: The new equilibrium exchange rate is found where the initial supply curve and new demand curve intersect and is labeled on the vertical axis.

1 point: The U.S. dollar has depreciated.

2. Use a correctly labeled graph of the foreign exchange market between the United States and Europe to illustrate what would happen to the value of the U.S. dollar if there were an increase in the U.S. demand for imports from Europe. Explain your answer.
(6 points)

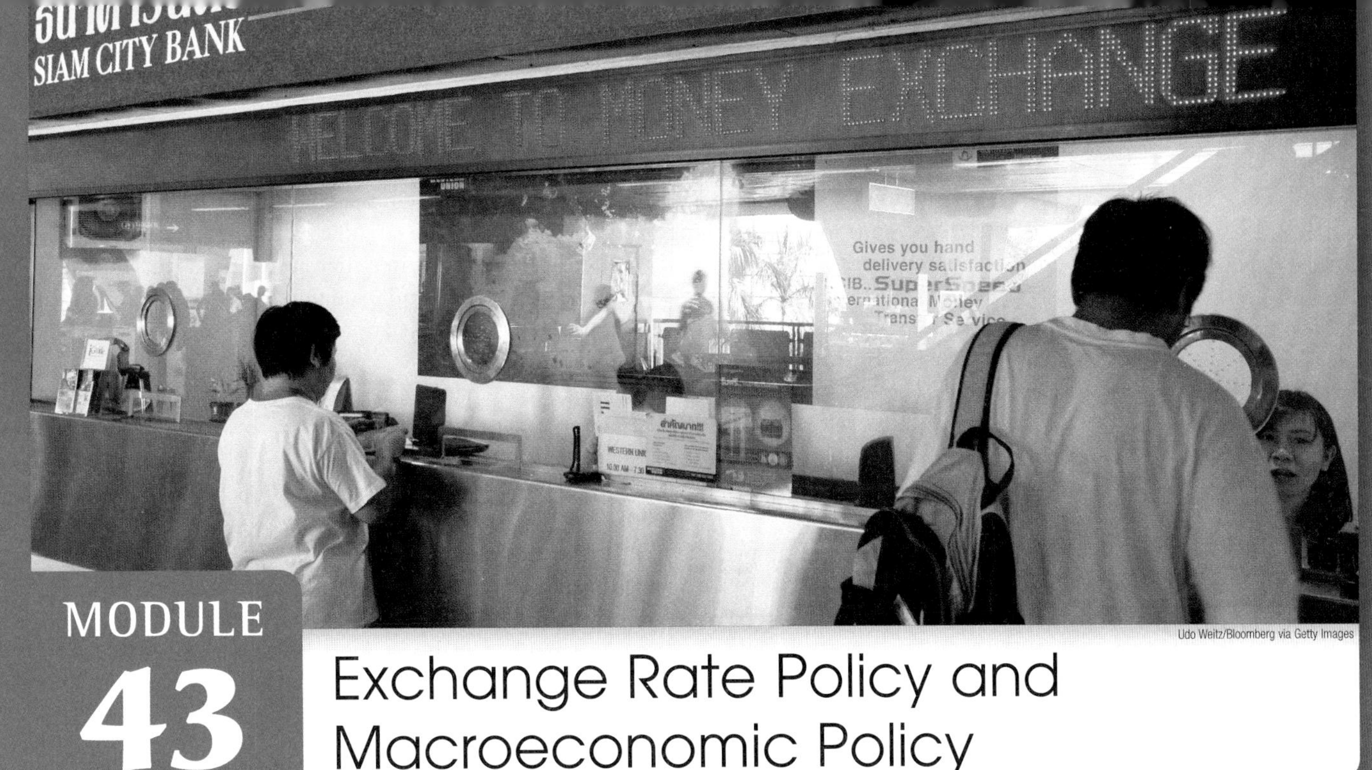

Udo Weitz/Bloomberg via Getty Images

MODULE 43 Exchange Rate Policy and Macroeconomic Policy

In this Module, you will learn to:

- Explain the difference between fixed exchange rates and floating exchange rates
- Discuss the considerations that lead countries to choose different exchange rate regimes
- Describe the effects of currency devaluation and revaluation under a fixed exchange rate regime
- Explain how macroeconomic policy affects exchange rates under a floating exchange rate regime

Exchange Rate Policy

The nominal exchange rate, like other prices, is determined by supply and demand. Unlike the price of wheat or oil, however, the exchange rate is the price of a country's money (in terms of another country's money). Money isn't a good or service produced by the private sector; it's an asset whose quantity is determined by government policy. As a result, governments have much more power to influence nominal exchange rates than they have to influence ordinary prices.

The nominal exchange rate is a very important price: the exchange rate determines the price of imports; it determines the price of exports; in economies where exports and imports are large relative to GDP, movements in the exchange rate can have major effects on aggregate output and the aggregate price level. What do governments do with their power to influence this important price?

The answer is, it depends. At different times and in different places, governments have adopted a variety of *exchange rate regimes*. Let's examine these regimes, how they are enforced, and how governments choose a regime. (From now on, we'll adopt the convention that we mean the nominal exchange rate when we refer to the exchange rate.)

Exchange Rate Regimes

An **exchange rate regime** is a rule governing policy toward the exchange rate. There are two main kinds of exchange rate regimes. A country has a **fixed exchange rate** when the government keeps the exchange rate against some other currency at or near a particular target. For example, Hong Kong has an official policy of setting an exchange rate of HK$7.80 per US$1. A country has a **floating exchange rate** when the government lets the exchange rate go wherever the market takes it. This is the policy followed by Britain, Canada, and the United States.

An **exchange rate regime** is a rule governing policy toward the exchange rate.

A country has a **fixed exchange rate** when the government keeps the exchange rate against some other currency at or near a particular target.

A country has a **floating exchange rate** when the government lets the exchange rate go wherever the market takes it.

Fixed exchange rates and floating exchange rates aren't the only possibilities. At various times, countries have adopted compromise policies that lie somewhere between fixed and floating exchange rates. These include exchange rates that are fixed at any given time but are adjusted frequently, exchange rates that aren't fixed but are "managed" by the government to avoid wide swings, and exchange rates that float within a "target zone" but are prevented from leaving that zone. In this book, however, we'll focus on the two main exchange rate regimes.

The immediate question about a fixed exchange rate is how it is possible for governments to fix the exchange rate when the exchange rate is determined by supply and demand.

How Can an Exchange Rate Be Held Fixed?

To understand how it is possible for a country to fix its exchange rate, let's consider a hypothetical country, Genovia, which for some reason has decided to fix the value of its currency, the geno, at US$1.50.

AP® Exam Tip

Think of a fixed exchange rate as a price ceiling or a price floor. That will help you understand if there is a shortage (ceiling) or surplus (floor) of a nation's currency.

The obvious problem is that $1.50 may not be the equilibrium exchange rate in the foreign exchange market: the equilibrium rate may be either higher or lower than the target exchange rate. **Figure 43.1** shows the foreign exchange market for genos, with the quantities of genos supplied and demanded on the horizontal axis and the exchange rate of the geno, measured in U.S. dollars per geno, on the vertical axis. Panel (a) shows the case in which the equilibrium value of the geno is *below* the target exchange rate. Panel (b) shows the case in which the equilibrium value of the geno is *above* the target exchange rate.

Consider first the case in which the equilibrium value of the geno is below the target exchange rate. As panel (a) shows, at the target exchange rate there is a surplus of genos in the foreign exchange market, which would normally push the value of the geno down. How can the Genovian government support the value of the geno to keep the rate where it wants? There are three possible answers, all of which have been used by governments at some point.

Figure 43.1 Exchange Market Intervention

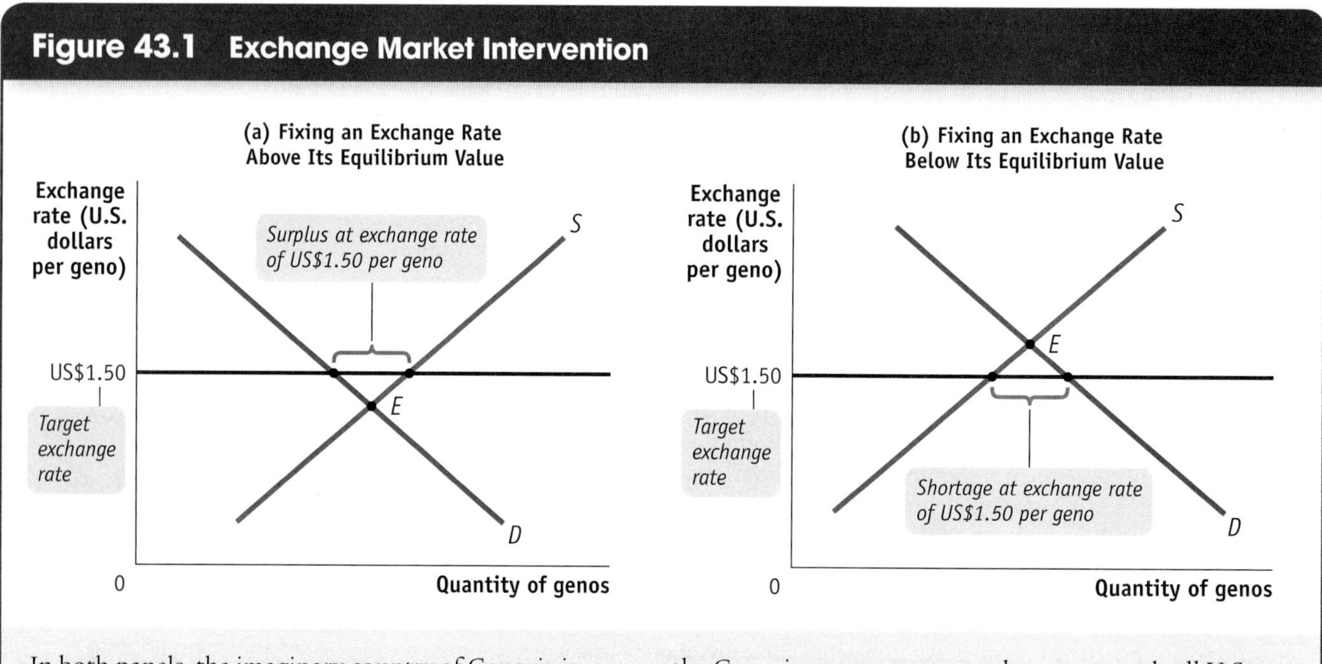

In both panels, the imaginary country of Genovia is trying to keep the value of its currency, the geno, fixed at US$1.50. In panel (a), there is a surplus of genos on the foreign exchange market. To keep the geno from falling, the Genovian government can buy genos and sell U.S. dollars. In panel (b), there is a shortage of genos. To keep the geno from rising, the Genovian government can sell genos and buy U.S. dollars.

One way the Genovian government can support the geno is to "soak up" the surplus of genos by buying its own currency in the foreign exchange market. Government purchases or sales of currency in the foreign exchange market are called **exchange market intervention**. To buy genos in the foreign exchange market, of course, the Genovian government must have U.S. dollars to exchange for genos. In fact, most countries maintain **foreign exchange reserves**, stocks of foreign currency (usually U.S. dollars or euros) that they can use to buy their own currency to support its price.

Government purchases or sales of currency in the foreign exchange market constitute **exchange market intervention**.

Foreign exchange reserves are stocks of foreign currency that governments maintain to buy their own currency on the foreign exchange market.

We mentioned earlier that an important part of international capital flows is the result of purchases and sales of foreign assets by governments and central banks. Now we can see why governments sell foreign assets: they are supporting their currency through exchange market intervention. As we'll see in a moment, governments that keep the value of their currency *down* through exchange market intervention must *buy* foreign assets. First, however, let's talk about the other ways governments fix exchange rates.

A second way for the Genovian government to support the geno is to try to shift the supply and demand curves for the geno in the foreign exchange market. Governments usually do this by changing monetary policy. For example, to support the geno, the Genovian central bank can raise the Genovian interest rate. This will increase capital flows into Genovia, increasing the demand for genos, at the same time that it reduces capital flows out of Genovia, reducing the supply of genos. So, other things equal, an increase in a country's interest rate will increase the value of its currency.

Third, the Genovian government can support the geno by reducing the supply of genos to the foreign exchange market. It can do this by requiring domestic residents who want to buy foreign currency to get a license and giving these licenses only to people engaging in approved transactions (such as the purchase of imported goods the Genovian government thinks are essential). Licensing systems that limit the right of individuals to buy foreign currency are called **foreign exchange controls**. Other things equal, foreign exchange controls increase the value of a country's currency.

Foreign exchange controls are licensing systems that limit the right of individuals to buy foreign currency.

So far we've been discussing a situation in which the government is trying to prevent a depreciation of the geno. Suppose, instead, that the situation is as shown in panel (b) of Figure 43.1, where the equilibrium value of the geno is *above* the target exchange rate and there is a shortage of genos. To maintain the target exchange rate, the Genovian government can apply the same three basic options in the reverse direction. It can intervene in the foreign exchange market, in this case *selling* genos and acquiring U.S. dollars, which it can add to its foreign exchange reserves. It can *reduce* interest rates to increase the supply of genos and reduce the demand. Or it can impose foreign exchange controls that limit the ability of foreigners to buy genos. All of these actions, other things equal, will reduce the value of the geno.

As we said, all three techniques have been used to manage fixed exchange rates. But we haven't said whether fixing the exchange rate is a good idea. In fact, the choice of exchange rate regime poses a dilemma for policy makers because fixed and floating exchange rates each have both advantages and disadvantages.

The Exchange Rate Regime Dilemma

Few questions in macroeconomics produce as many arguments as that of whether a country should adopt a fixed or a floating exchange rate. The reason there are so many arguments is that both sides have a case.

To understand the case for a fixed exchange rate, consider for a moment how easy it is to conduct business across state lines in the United States. There are a number of things that make interstate commerce trouble-free, but one of them is the absence of any uncertainty about the value of money: a dollar is a dollar, in both New York City and Los Angeles.

By contrast, a dollar isn't a dollar in transactions between New York City and Toronto. The exchange rate between the Canadian dollar and the U.S. dollar fluctuates, sometimes widely. If a U.S. firm promises to pay a Canadian firm a given number of U.S. dollars a year from now, the value of that promise in Canadian currency can vary by 10%

Robert Nickelsberg/Getty Images

Once you cross the border into Canada, a dollar is no longer worth a dollar.

or more. This uncertainty has the effect of deterring trade between the two countries. So one benefit of a fixed exchange rate is certainty about the future value of a currency.

In some cases, there is an additional benefit to adopting a fixed exchange rate: by committing itself to a fixed rate, a country is also committing itself not to engage in inflationary policies because such policies would destabilize the exchange rate. For example, in 1991, Argentina, which has a long history of irresponsible policies leading to severe inflation, adopted a fixed exchange rate of US$1 per Argentine peso in an attempt to commit itself to non-inflationary policies in the future. (Argentina's fixed exchange rate regime collapsed disastrously in late 2001. But that's another story.)

The point is that there is some economic value in having a stable exchange rate. Indeed, the presumed benefits of stable exchange rates motivated the international system of fixed exchange rates created after World War II. It was also a major reason for the creation of the euro.

However, there are also costs to fixing the exchange rate. To stabilize an exchange rate through intervention, a country must keep large quantities of foreign currency on hand, and that currency is usually a low-return investment. Furthermore, even large reserves can be quickly exhausted when there are large capital flows out of a country. If a country chooses to stabilize an exchange rate by adjusting monetary policy rather than through intervention, it must divert monetary policy from other goals, notably stabilizing the economy and managing the inflation rate. Finally, foreign exchange controls, like import quotas and tariffs, distort incentives for importing and exporting goods and services. They can also create substantial costs in terms of red tape and corruption.

So there's a dilemma. Should a country let its currency float, which leaves monetary policy available for macroeconomic stabilization but creates uncertainty for everyone affected by trade? Or should it fix the exchange rate, which eliminates the uncertainty but means giving up monetary policy, adopting exchange controls, or both? Different countries reach different conclusions at different times. Most European countries, except for Britain, have long believed that exchange rates among major European economies, which do most of their international trade with each other, should be fixed. But

FYI China Pegs the Yuan

In the early years of the twenty-first century, China provided a striking example of the lengths to which countries sometimes go to maintain a fixed exchange rate. Here's the background: China's spectacular success as an exporter led to a rising surplus on the current account. At the same time, non-Chinese private investors became increasingly eager to shift funds into China, to take advantage of its growing domestic economy. These capital flows were somewhat limited by foreign exchange controls—but kept coming in anyway. As a result of the current account surplus and private capital inflows, China found itself in the position described by panel (b) of Figure 43.1: at the target exchange rate, the demand for yuan exceeded the supply. Yet the Chinese government was determined to keep the exchange rate fixed (although it began allowing gradual appreciation in 2005).

To keep the rate fixed, China had to engage in large-scale exchange market intervention, selling yuan, buying up other countries' currencies (mainly U.S. dollars) on the foreign exchange market, and adding them to its reserves. During 2013, China added $510 billion to its foreign exchange reserves, bringing the year-end total to $3.8 trillion.

To get a sense of how big these totals are, you have to know that in 2013 China's nominal GDP, converted into U.S. dollars at the prevailing exchange rate, was $9.4 trillion. So in 2013, China bought U.S. dollars and other currencies equal to about 5.4% of its GDP. That's as if the U.S. government had bought $900 billion worth of yen and euros in just a single year—and was continuing to buy yen and euros even though it was already sitting on a $6.8 trillion pile of foreign currencies.

Chris Cameron/Alamy

China has a history of intervention in the foreign exchange market that kept its currency, and therefore its exports, relatively cheap for foreign consumers to buy.

Canada seems happy with a floating exchange rate with the United States, even though the United States accounts for most of Canada's trade.

Next we'll consider macroeconomic policy under each type of exchange rate regime.

Exchange Rates and Macroeconomic Policy

When the euro was created in 1999, there were celebrations across the nations of Europe—with a few notable exceptions. You see, some countries chose not to adopt the new currency. The most important of these was Britain, but other European countries, such as Switzerland and Sweden, also decided that the euro was not for them.

Why did Britain say no? Part of the answer was national pride: for example, if Britain gave up the pound, it would also have to give up currency that bears the portrait of the queen. But there were also serious economic concerns about giving up the pound in favor of the euro. British economists who favored adoption of the euro argued that if Britain used the same currency as its neighbors, the country's international trade would expand and its economy would become more productive. But other economists pointed out that adopting the euro would take away Britain's ability to have an independent monetary policy and might lead to macroeconomic problems.

As this discussion suggests, the fact that modern economies are open to international trade and capital flows adds a new level of complication to our analysis of macroeconomic policy. Let's look at three policy issues raised by open-economy macroeconomics.

Devaluation and Revaluation of Fixed Exchange Rates

Historically, fixed exchange rates haven't been permanent commitments. Sometimes countries with a fixed exchange rate switch to a floating rate. In other cases, they retain a fixed exchange rate regime but change the target exchange rate. Such adjustments in the target were common during the Bretton Woods era, discussed in the next FYI box. For example, in 1967, Britain changed the exchange rate of the pound against the U.S. dollar from US$2.80 per £1 to US$2.40 per £1. A modern example is Argentina, which maintained a fixed exchange rate against the dollar from 1991 to 2001, but switched to a floating exchange rate at the end of 2001.

A **devaluation** is a reduction in the value of a currency that is set under a fixed exchange rate regime.

A **revaluation** is an increase in the value of a currency that is set under a fixed exchange rate regime.

A reduction in the value of a currency that is set under a fixed exchange rate regime is called a **devaluation**. As we've already learned, a *depreciation* is a downward move in a currency. A devaluation is a depreciation that is due to a revision in a fixed exchange rate target. An increase in the value of a currency that is set under a fixed exchange rate regime is called a **revaluation**.

A devaluation, like any depreciation, makes domestic goods cheaper in terms of foreign currency, which leads to higher exports. At the same time, it makes foreign goods more expensive in terms of domestic currency, which reduces imports. The effect is to increase the balance of payments on the current account. Similarly, a revaluation makes domestic goods more expensive in terms of foreign currency, which reduces exports, and makes foreign goods cheaper in domestic currency, which increases imports. So a revaluation reduces the balance of payments on the current account.

AP® Exam Tip

A devaluation of a currency makes exports increase because they appear cheaper to foreign buyers, and a revaluation of a currency makes exports decrease because they appear more expensive to foreign buyers.

Devaluations and revaluations serve two purposes under a fixed exchange rate regime. First, they can be used to eliminate shortages or surpluses in the foreign exchange market. For example, in 2010, some economists urged China to revalue the yuan so that it would not have to buy up so many U.S. dollars on the foreign exchange market.

Second, devaluation and revaluation can be used as tools of macroeconomic policy. A devaluation, by increasing exports and reducing imports, increases aggregate demand. So a devaluation can be used to reduce or eliminate a recessionary gap. A revaluation has the opposite effect, reducing aggregate demand. So a revaluation can be used to reduce or eliminate an inflationary gap.

From Bretton Woods to the Euro

In 1944, while World War II was still raging, representatives of the Allied nations met in Bretton Woods, New Hampshire, to establish a postwar international monetary system of fixed exchange rates among major currencies. The system was highly successful at first, but it broke down in 1971. After a confusing interval during which policy makers tried unsuccessfully to establish a new fixed exchange rate system, by 1973 most economically advanced countries had moved to floating exchange rates.

In Europe, however, many policy makers were unhappy with floating exchange rates, which they believed created too much uncertainty for business. From the late 1970s onward they tried several times to create a system of more or less fixed exchange rates in Europe, culminating in an arrangement known as the Exchange Rate Mechanism. (The Exchange Rate Mechanism, strictly speaking, was a "target zone" system—exchange rates were free to move within a narrow band, but not outside it.) And in 1991 they agreed to move to the ultimate in fixed exchange rates: a common European currency, the euro. To the surprise of many analysts, they pulled it off: today most of Europe has abandoned national currencies for euros.

The accompanying figure illustrates the history of European exchange rate arrangements. It shows the exchange rate between the French franc and the German mark, measured as francs per mark, since 1971.

The exchange rate fluctuated widely at first. The "plateaus" you can see in the data—eras when the exchange rate fluctuated only modestly—are periods when attempts to restore fixed exchange rates were in process. The Exchange Rate Mechanism, after a couple of false starts, became effective in 1987, stabilizing the exchange rate at about 3.4 francs per mark. (The wobbles in the early 1990s reflect two currency crises—episodes in which widespread expectations of imminent devaluations led to large but temporary capital flows.)

In 1999 the exchange rate was "locked"—no further fluctuations were allowed as the countries prepared to switch from francs and marks to euros. At the end of 2001, the franc and the mark ceased to exist.

The transition to the euro has not been without costs. With most of Europe sharing the same currency, it must also share the same monetary policy. Yet economic conditions in the different countries aren't always the same.

For example, there were serious stresses within the eurozone between 2008 and 2012, when the global financial crisis hit some countries, such as Greece, Portugal, Spain, and Ireland, much more severely than it hit others, notably Germany.

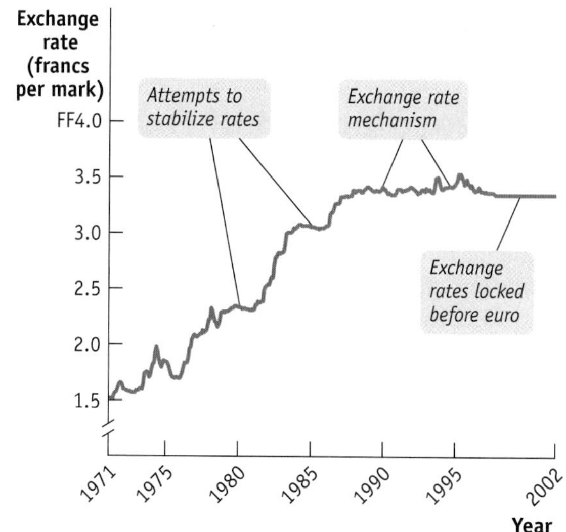

Source: Federal Reserve Bank of St. Louis.

Monetary Policy Under a Floating Exchange Rate Regime

Under a floating exchange rate regime, a country's central bank retains its ability to pursue independent monetary policy: it can increase aggregate demand by cutting the interest rate or decrease aggregate demand by raising the interest rate. But the exchange rate adds another dimension to the effects of monetary policy. To see why, let's return to the hypothetical country of Genovia and ask what happens if the central bank cuts the interest rate.

Just as in a closed economy, a lower interest rate leads to higher investment spending and higher consumer spending. But the decline in the interest rate also affects the foreign exchange market. Foreigners have less incentive to move funds into Genovia because they will receive a lower rate of return on their loans. As a result, they have less need to exchange U.S. dollars for genos, so the demand for genos falls. At the same time, Genovians have *more* incentive to move funds abroad because the rate of return on loans at home has fallen, making investments outside the country more attractive. Thus, they need to exchange more genos for U.S. dollars and the supply of genos rises.

Figure 43.2 shows the effect of an interest rate reduction on the foreign exchange market. The demand curve for genos shifts leftward, from D_1 to D_2, and the supply curve shifts rightward, from S_1 to S_2. The equilibrium exchange rate, as measured in U.S. dollars per geno, falls from XR_1 to XR_2. That is, a reduction in the Genovian interest rate causes the geno to *depreciate.*

The depreciation of the geno, in turn, affects aggregate demand. We've already seen that a devaluation—a depreciation that is the result of a change in a fixed exchange rate—increases exports and reduces imports, thereby increasing aggregate demand. A depreciation that results from an interest rate cut has the same effect: it increases exports and reduces imports, increasing aggregate demand.

In other words, monetary policy under floating rates has effects beyond those we've described in looking at closed economies. In a closed economy, a reduction in the interest rate leads to a rise in aggregate demand because it leads to more investment spending and consumer spending. In an open economy with a floating exchange rate, the interest rate reduction leads to increased investment spending and consumer spending, but it also increases aggregate demand in another way: it leads to a currency depreciation, which increases exports and reduces imports, further increasing aggregate demand.

International Business Cycles

Up to this point, we have discussed macroeconomics, even in an open economy, as if all demand changes or *shocks* originated from the domestic economy. In reality, however, economies sometimes face shocks coming from abroad. For example, recessions in the United States have historically led to recessions in Mexico.

Figure 43.2 Monetary Policy and the Exchange Rate

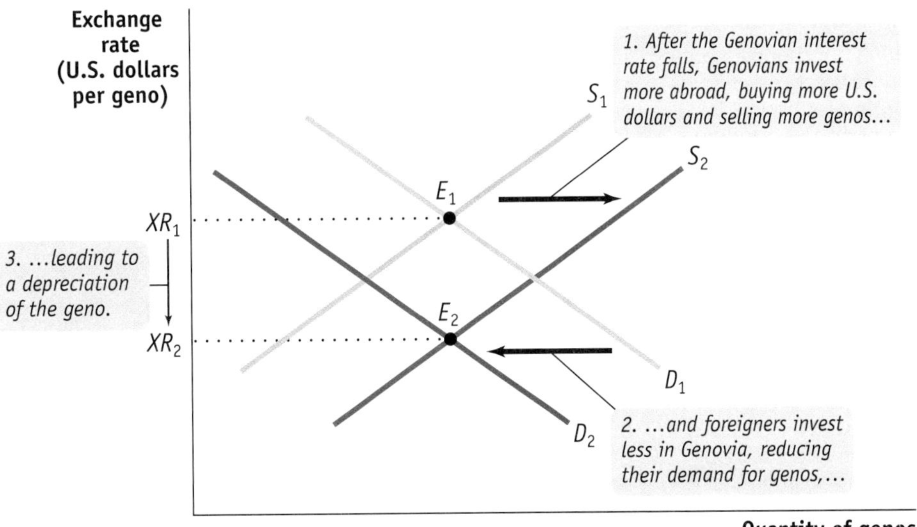
Exchange rate (U.S. dollars per geno)
1. After the Genovian interest rate falls, Genovians invest more abroad, buying more U.S. dollars and selling more genos...
S_1
S_2
E_1
XR_1
3. ...leading to a depreciation of the geno.
E_2
XR_2
D_1
D_2
2. ...and foreigners invest less in Genovia, reducing their demand for genos,...
Quantity of genos

Here we show what happens in the foreign exchange market if Genovia cuts its interest rate. Residents of Genovia have a reduced incentive to keep their funds at home, so they invest more abroad. As a result, the supply of genos shifts rightward, from S_1 to S_2. Meanwhile, foreigners have less incentive to put funds into Genovia, so the demand for genos shifts leftward, from D_1 to D_2. The geno depreciates: the equilibrium exchange rate falls from XR_1 to XR_2.

Sipa via AP Images

For better or worse, trading partners tend to import each other's business cycles in addition to each other's goods.

The key point is that changes in aggregate demand affect the demand for goods and services produced abroad as well as at home: other things equal, a recession leads to a fall in imports and an expansion leads to a rise in imports. And one country's imports are another country's exports. This link between aggregate demand in different national economies is one reason business cycles in different countries sometimes—but not always—seem to be synchronized. The prime example is the Great Depression, which affected countries around the world.

However, the extent of this link depends on the exchange rate regime. To see why, think about what happens if a recession abroad reduces the demand for Genovia's exports. A reduction in foreign demand for Genovian goods and services is also a reduction in demand for genos on the foreign exchange market. If Genovia has a fixed exchange rate, it responds to this decline with exchange market intervention. But if Genovia has a floating exchange rate, the geno depreciates. Because Genovian goods and services become cheaper to foreigners when the demand for exports falls, the quantity of goods and services exported doesn't fall by as much as it would under a fixed rate. At the same time, the fall in the geno makes imports more expensive to Genovians, leading to a fall in imports. Both effects limit the decline in Genovia's aggregate demand compared to what it would have been under a fixed exchange rate regime.

One of the virtues of floating exchange rates, according to their advocates, is that they help insulate countries from recessions originating abroad. This theory looked pretty good in the early 2000s: Britain, with a floating exchange rate, managed to stay

FYI The Joy of a Devalued Pound

The Exchange Rate Mechanism is the system of European fixed exchange rates that paved the way for the creation of the euro in 1999. Britain joined that system in 1990 but dropped out in 1992. The story of Britain's exit from the Exchange Rate Mechanism is a classic example of open-economy macroeconomic policy.

Britain originally fixed its exchange rate for both of the reasons we described earlier: British leaders believed that a fixed exchange rate would help promote international trade, and they also hoped that it would help fight inflation. But by 1992 Britain was suffering from high unemployment: the unemployment rate in September 1992 was over 10%. And as long as the country had a fixed exchange rate, there wasn't much the government could do. In particular, the government wasn't able to cut interest rates because it was using high interest rates to help support the value of the pound.

In the summer of 1992, investors began speculating against the pound—selling pounds in the expectation that the currency would drop in value. As its foreign reserves dwindled, this speculation forced the British government's hand. On September 16, 1992, Britain abandoned its fixed exchange rate. The pound promptly dropped 20% against the German mark, the most important European currency at the time.

At first, the devaluation of the pound greatly damaged the prestige of the British government. But the Chancellor of the Exchequer—the equivalent of the U.S. Treasury Secretary—claimed to be happy about it. "My wife has never before heard me singing in the bath," he told reporters. There were several reasons for his joy. One was that the British government would no longer have to engage in large-scale exchange market intervention to support the pound's value. Another was that devaluation increases aggregate demand, so the pound's fall would help reduce British unemployment. Finally, because Britain no longer had a fixed exchange rate, it was free to pursue an expansionary monetary policy to fight its slump.

Photodisc

Indeed, events made it clear that the chancellor's joy was well founded. British unemployment fell over the next two years, even as the unemployment rate rose in France and Germany. One person who did not share in the improving employment picture, however, was the chancellor himself. Soon after his remark about singing in the bath, he was fired.

out of a recession that affected the rest of Europe, and Canada, which also has a floating rate, suffered a less severe recession than the United States.

In 2008, however, a financial crisis that began in the United States produced a recession in virtually every country. In this case, it appears that the international linkages between financial markets were much stronger than any insulation from overseas disturbances provided by floating exchange rates.

MODULE 43 Review

Check Your Understanding

1. Draw a diagram, similar to Figure 43.1, representing the foreign exchange situation of China when it kept the exchange rate fixed at a target rate of $0.121 per yuan and the market equilibrium rate was higher than the target rate. Then show with a diagram how each of the following policy changes might eliminate the disequilibrium in the market.
   a. allowing the exchange rate to float more freely
   b. placing restrictions on foreigners who want to invest in China
   c. removing restrictions on Chinese who want to invest abroad
   d. imposing taxes on Chinese exports, such as clothing
2. In the late 1980s, Canadian economists argued that the high interest rate policies of the Bank of Canada weren't just causing high unemployment—they were also making it hard for Canadian manufacturers to compete with U.S. manufacturers. Explain this complaint, using our analysis of how monetary policy works under floating exchange rates.

Tackle the Test: Multiple-Choice Questions

1. Which of the following methods can be used to fix a country's exchange rate at a predetermined level?
   I. using foreign exchange reserves to buy its own currency
   II. using monetary policy to change interest rates
   III. implementing foreign exchange controls
   a. I only
   b. II only
   c. III only
   d. I and II only
   e. I, II, and III
2. The United States has which of the following exchange rate regimes?
   a. fixed
   b. floating
   c. fixed, but adjusted frequently
   d. fixed, but managed
   e. floating within a target zone
3. Devaluation of a currency occurs when which of the following happens?
   I. The supply of a currency with a floating exchange rate increases.
   II. The demand for a currency with a floating exchange rate decreases.
   III. The government decreases the fixed exchange rate.
   a. I only
   b. II only
   c. III only
   d. I and II only
   e. I, II, and III
4. Devaluation of a currency is used to achieve which of the following?
   a. an elimination of a surplus in the foreign exchange market
   b. an elimination of a shortage in the foreign exchange market
   c. a reduction in aggregate demand
   d. a lower inflation rate
   e. a floating exchange rate
5. Monetary policy that reduces the interest rate will do which of the following?
   a. appreciate the domestic currency
   b. decrease exports
   c. increase imports
   d. depreciate the domestic currency
   e. prevent inflation

Tackle the Test: Free-Response Questions

1. Suppose the United States and India were the only two countries in the world.
   a. Draw a correctly labeled graph of the foreign exchange market for U.S. dollars showing the equilibrium in the market.
   b. On your graph, indicate a fixed exchange rate set above the equilibrium exchange rate. Does the fixed exchange rate lead to a surplus or shortage of U.S. dollars? Explain and show the amount of the surplus/shortage on your graph.
   c. To bring the foreign exchange market back to an equilibrium at the fixed exchange rate, would the U.S. government need to buy or sell dollars? On your graph, illustrate how the government's buying or selling of dollars would bring the equilibrium exchange rate back to the desired fixed rate.

Rubric for FRQ 1 (9 points)

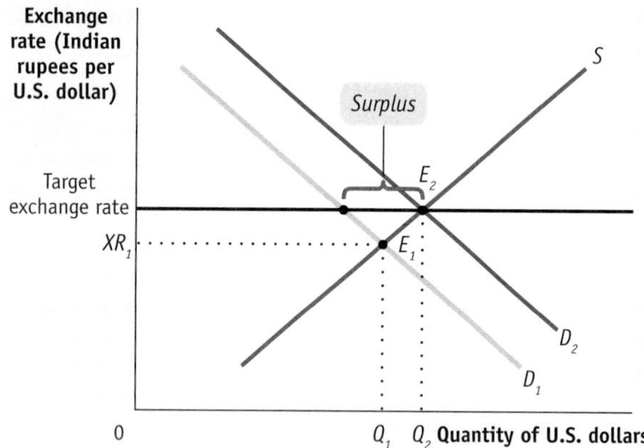

1 point: The vertical axis is labeled "Exchange rate (Indian rupees per U.S. dollar)" and the horizontal axis is labeled "Quantity of U.S. dollars."

1 point: Demand is downward-sloping and labeled, supply is upward-sloping and labeled.

1 point: The equilibrium exchange rate and the equilibrium quantity of dollars are labeled on the axes at the point where the supply and demand curves intersect.

1 point: The fixed exchange rate level is depicted above the equilibrium exchange rate.

1 point: Surplus

1 point: The quantity supplied exceeds the quantity demanded at the higher fixed exchange rate.

1 point: The surplus is labeled as the horizontal distance between the supply and demand curves at the fixed exchange rate.

1 point: Buy

1 point: The new demand curve is shown to the right of the old demand curve, crossing the supply curve at the fixed exchange rate.

2. Suppose the United States and Australia were the only two countries in the world, and that both countries pursued a floating exchange rate regime. Note that the currency in Australia is the Australian dollar.
   a. Draw a correctly labeled graph showing equilibrium in the foreign exchange market for U.S. dollars.
   b. If the Federal Reserve pursues expansionary monetary policy, what will happen to the U.S. interest rate and international capital flows? Explain.
   c. On your graph of the foreign exchange market, illustrate the effect of the Fed's policy on the supply of U.S. dollars, the demand for U.S. dollars, and the equilibrium exchange rate.
   d. How does the Fed's monetary policy affect U.S. aggregate demand? Explain.

   (10 points)

MODULE 44 Barriers to Trade

In this Module, you will learn to:

- Explain the pros and cons of protectionism
- Illustrate the effects of a tariff and an import quota

Trade Restrictions

It's natural for the citizens of a country to say, "We can make food, clothing, and almost everything we need. Why should we buy these goods from other countries and send our money overseas?" Module 4 explained the answer to this question: because specialization and trade make larger quantities of goods and services available to consumers. Yet the gains from trade are often overlooked, and many countries have experimented with a closed economy. Examples from the last century include Germany from 1933–1945, Spain from 1939–1959, Cambodia from 1975–1979, and Afghanistan from 1996–2001. The outcomes of these experiments were disappointing. By trying to make too many different products, these countries failed to specialize in what they were best at making; as a result, they ended up with less of most goods than trade would have provided.

Every country now has an open economy, although some economies are more open than others. **Figure 44.1** on the next page shows expenditures on imports as a percentage of GDP for select countries, which ranged from 14% in Brazil to 178% in Singapore. Several factors affect a country's approach to trade. Beyond the natural tendency for each country to want to make everything, special circumstances can limit the options for trade. For example, high transportation costs hinder trade for countries with primitive transportation systems as well as for countries that specialize in heavy, low-priced commodities such as bricks, drinking water, watermelons, or sand. Countries are wary of specialization that would make them overly reliant on other countries, because relationships with those countries could sour. And, as a matter of national pride, countries may prefer to make certain products on their own despite comparative disadvantages, such as food, art, weapons, and products that showcase technical know-how.

International trade can also have its casualties. As production shifts toward a country's comparative advantage, many workers in declining industries will lose their jobs, and will remain structurally unemployed until or unless they can obtain the skills required in other industries. For example, as the United States imported more clothing

Figure 44.1 Imports of Goods and Services as a Percentage of GDP

International trade is an important part of every country's economy, but some economies are more open than others. In 2012, imports as a percentage of GDP ranged from 14% in Brazil to 178% in Singapore.

Source: The World Bank.

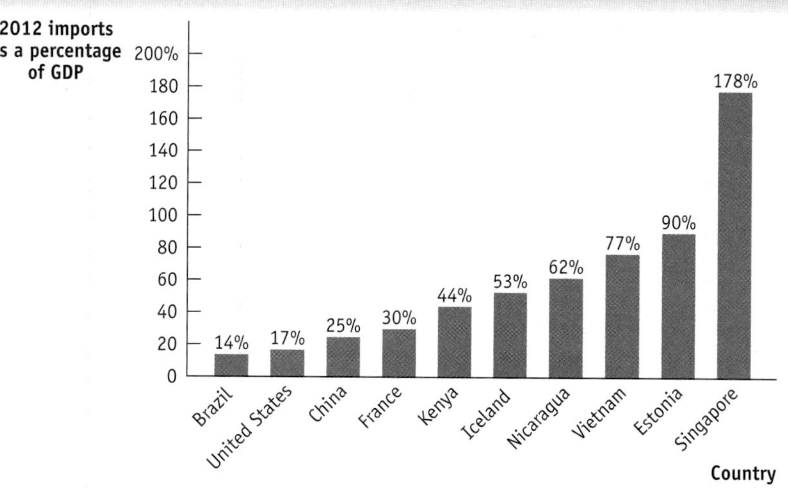

from countries with a comparative advantage in textiles, workers in the Fruit of the Loom factory in Campbellsville, Kentucky, were among many who lost their jobs. Fortunately, the unemployment rates in Campbellsville and in the United States as a whole rose only temporarily. Many of these workers were able to adapt to the requirements of growing industries such as construction, automotive parts, health care, and software design, and were able to secure new jobs as a result.

Protectionism is the practice of limiting trade to protect domestic industries.

Tariffs are taxes on imports.

Some industries may not initially be competitive at the international level, but they could attain a comparative advantage after a period of protection from lower-priced imports. This is the motivation for **protectionism**, the practice of limiting trade to protect domestic industries. *Tariffs* and *import quotas* are the primary tools of protectionism.

Tariffs

The imposition of **tariffs**, which are taxes on imports, helps domestic industries and provides revenue for the government. The bad news is that tariffs make prices higher for domestic consumers and can spark trade wars. Early in American history, tariffs provided a majority of the revenue for the U.S. government, reaching a high of 97.9% in 1825. As the benefits of free trade came to light, and income and payroll taxes were adopted in the early 1900s, the use of tariffs diminished. By 1944, tariff revenue amounted to only about 1% of federal government revenue, which is still the case today.

Shutterstock

Consider the U.S. market for ceramic plates, a hypothetical version of which is shown in **Figure 44.2**. The upward-sloping supply curve shows the supply from U.S. firms. The demand curve is for U.S. consumers only. If the United States had a closed economy, 5 million plates would sell for the no-trade equilibrium price of $15 each. However, suppose that an unlimited quantity of plates could be imported for the equilibrium price in the world market, $9. In the absence of trade restrictions, domestic firms would be unable to charge more than the world price. At the $9 world price, domestic firms would be willing to supply 3 million plates, but domestic consumers would demand 7 million. Four million imported plates would make up the difference between the 7 million plates demanded and the 3 million supplied in the domestic market.

AP® Exam Tip

The effects of tariffs and quotas can be shown on supply and demand graphs. You may need to illustrate or interpret a graph that involves trade barriers for the AP® exam.

Now suppose that the U.S. imposes a tariff of $3 per imported ceramic plate. As shown in **Figure 44.3**, that would effectively raise the curve that represents the supply from the rest of the world by $3. For every imported plate, the required payment would

Figure 44.2 The U.S. Ceramic Plate Market with Imports

Without trade, 5 million plates would be sold at the no-trade equilibrium price of $15. An unlimited quantity of plates can be imported at the equilibrium world price of $9. With unrestricted trade, domestic firms will be unable to charge more than the world price, for which they are willing to supply 3 million plates. Domestic consumers will demand 7 million plates at a price of $9 each. The difference between the domestic demand and the domestic supply, 4 million plates, will be imported.

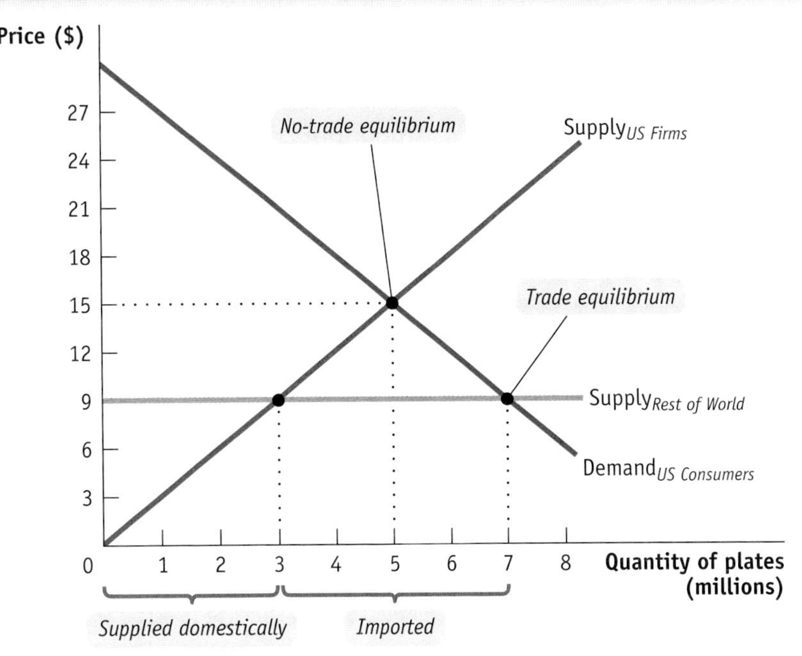

be $9 to the foreign suppliers plus $3 for the tariff, for a total of $12. Domestic firms would now be able to charge up to $12, for which they would be willing to supply 4 million plates, an increase of 1 million compared to the no-tariff situation. Domestic consumers would demand 6 million plates for $12, a decrease of 1 million from the no-tariff situation. Two million plates would be imported to make up the difference between the

Figure 44.3 A Tariff on Ceramic Plates

A tariff of $3 per imported ceramic plate effectively raises the curve that represents the supply from the rest of the world by $3. To receive an imported plate, one must pay $9 to the foreign suppliers plus $3 for the tariff, for a total of $12. Domestic firms can then charge up to $12, for which they are willing to supply 4 million plates. Domestic consumers demand 6 million plates for $12 each. Two million plates will be imported to make up the difference between the domestic supply and the domestic demand. This is 2 million less than the 4 million plates imported without the tariff.

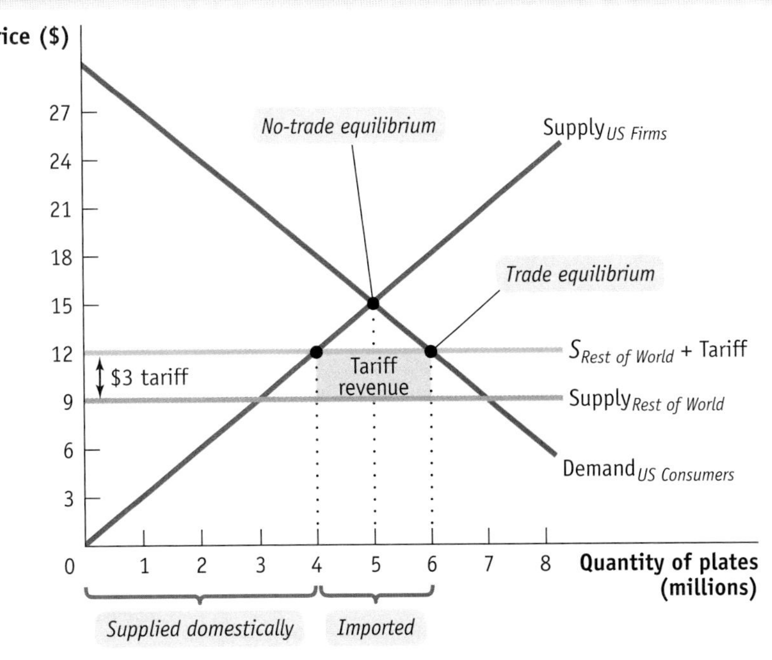

domestic supply of 4 million and the domestic demand of 6 million plates. Note that this is a drop of 2 million from the 4 million plates imported without the tariff. The tariff revenue would be 2 million × \$3 = \$6 million, as represented by the shaded rectangle in the figure.

Import Quotas

An **import quota** is a limit on the quantity of a good that can be imported within a given period.

AP® Exam Tip

Tariffs provide governments with revenues and quotas do not.

An **import quota** is a limit on the quantity of a good that can be imported within a given period. By restricting the supply of imports, import quotas reduce the equilibrium quantity and increase the equilibrium price. Like tariffs, quotas help domestic firms compete with foreign suppliers, but they also cause prices to be higher for domestic consumers. Consider sugar, which Americans consume at a rate of about 11 million tons per year. To protect domestic sugar cane and sugar beet farmers, the U.S. Department of Agriculture (USDA) sets a quota for the amount of sugar that can be imported—1.2 million tons in 2014—before a substantial tariff is applied.

Suppose that the United States imposes an import quota of 2 million ceramic plates. That quota would prevent a trade equilibrium at the intersection of U.S. consumers' demand and the supply from the rest of the world because, as we saw in Figure 44.2, that equilibrium would require imports of 4 million plates. Instead, consumers would face the pink supply curve in **Figure 44.4**, which represents the U.S. supply plus the 2 million plates that could be imported with the quota. Imports would not be available for less than \$9, so the pink U.S.-plus-quota supply curve does not extend below a price of \$9. The equilibrium price with the quota is \$12. Six million plates would be sold at that price, 4 million of which would be made domestically. Notice that the quota of 2 million plates would have the same effect on the price, imports, and domestic supply as the \$3 tariff. One difference is that with the quota, no tariff revenue would be collected.

The use of tariffs and import quotas is seldom one-sided. When one country erects a trade barrier against another, retaliation is common. For instance, after the

Figure 44.4 A Ceramic Plates Quota

With an import quota of 2 million ceramic plates, consumers face the pink supply curve made up of the U.S. supply plus the 2 million plates that can be imported. Imports are not available for less than \$9, so the pink U.S.-plus-quota supply curve does not extend below \$9. At the \$12 equilibrium price with the quota, a quantity of 6 million plates are purchased, 4 million of which are supplied domestically.

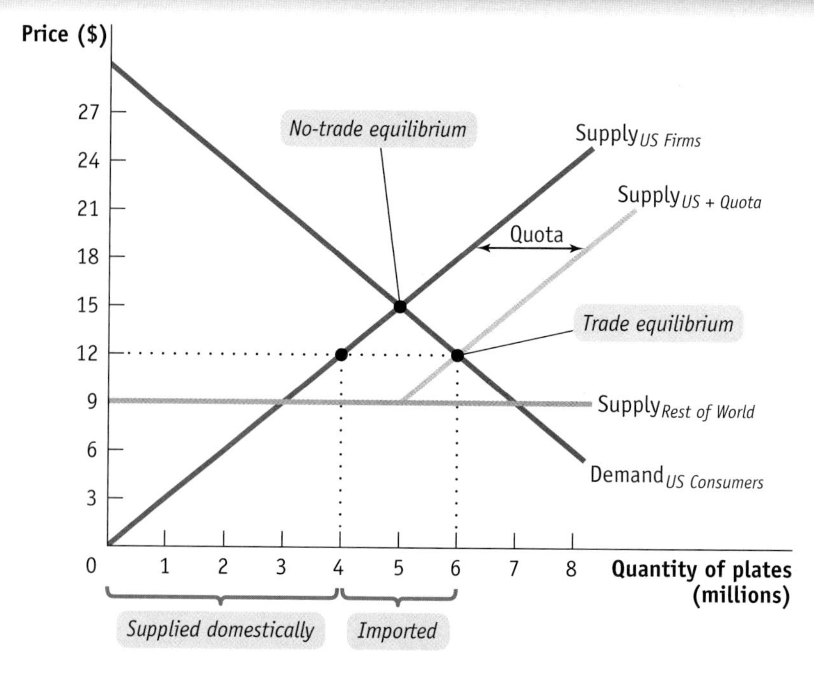

Obama administration imposed a tariff on tires imported from China, China threatened to cut off imports of chickens from the United States. Escalating trade wars can obliterate the gains from trade, which motivates many countries to move in the opposite direction and negotiate the elimination of trade barriers. Trade agreements such as the North American Free Trade Agreement and the Dominican Republic–Central America Free Trade Agreement limit the use of tariffs, quotas, regulations, and other impediments to trade among the economies involved. As discussed in the FYI that follows, these agreements can provide substantial benefits to citizens in the participating countries.

FYI Bringing Down the Walls

The United States and the European Union have the two largest economies in the world, and these economies trade more with each other than with any other economy. Yet trade barriers prevent this relationship from reaching its full potential. The average tariff between these two economies is 4%. Regulations and bureaucratic red tape add to the barriers that restrict transatlantic trade. For example, the United States and the European Union have differing regulations on food products and automobile safety that make it difficult to trade the affected products between the two economies. However, the Transatlantic Trade and Investment Partnership (TTIP) may bring these barriers down.

In March of 2014, representatives of the United States and the European Union completed their fourth round of talks on the details of the TTIP. Although it is relatively straightforward to eliminate tariffs as part of trade negotiations, differing regulations pose larger challenges. For example, regulations on genetically modified crops are stricter in the European Union than in the United States. And the European Union requires different safety tests for automobiles than the United States. Sometimes, mutually accepted revisions can close the gap between regulations. In the case of auto safety, the parties involved may determine that their differing approaches have the same effect of providing an acceptable level of consumer safety. And when the effect is the same, the trading partners can agree to accept each other's goods despite differences in the specific tests and guidelines imposed.

Analysts estimate that the TTIP could be a win-win for citizens of the United States and the European Union, adding between $545 and $900 to the disposable annual income of a typical family of four in each economy. Eighty percent of the gains are expected to come from cutting the costs imposed by regulations and bureaucracy.

The reduction of trade barriers also has its victims. For example, workers in industries protected by trade barriers may lose their jobs. To lessen this burden, the governments of the United States and European countries provide assistance to unemployed workers as they transition from industries that are contracting to industries that are growing.

Overall, the growing popularity of free-trade agreements reflects the demonstrated benefits of specialization and trade and the success of past experiments with free trade.

Paresh Nath/CagleCartoons.com

MODULE 44 Review

Check Your Understanding

Use the information provided in Figure 44.2 to answer the following questions:

1. What is the smallest tariff that would cause all plates to be supplied by U.S. firms?

2. What is the smallest import quota that would have no effect on international trade? Hint: You can think of the question this way: Every import quota smaller than what level would have an effect on international trade?

Tackle the Test: Multiple-Choice Questions

1. Which of the following is put forth as a reason for trade restrictions?
   a. National pride can take precedence over the gains from trade.
   b. Domestic industries need protection from foreign competition while they develop a comparative advantage.
   c. Citizens don't want to send their money overseas.
   d. Countries don't want to become overly reliant on other countries.
   e. All of the above.

2. The purpose of protectionism is to protect domestic
   a. resources.
   b. consumption levels.
   c. industries.
   d. exporters.
   e. all of the above.

3. Which of the following would result from a U.S. tariff on imported cars?
   a. The profit of U.S. car manufacturers would decrease.
   b. The price paid for cars in the U.S. would increase.
   c. More cars would be imported.
   d. Fewer domestically made cars would be sold in the United States.
   e. More cars from all sources would be sold in the United States.

4. An import quota is a
   a. minimum quantity of a good that may be imported.
   b. minimum quantity of a good that a factory must produce and sell overseas.
   c. maximum quantity of a good that may be imported.
   d. maximum quantity of a good that a factory may produce and sell overseas.
   e. maximum price that a company can charge for imports.

5. Which of the following would result if China imposed an import quota on telephones that influenced the amount of trade?
   a. The price of telephones in China would decrease.
   b. The Chinese government would collect more taxes on imported telephones.
   c. More telephones made outside of China would be sold in China.
   d. More telephones made in China would be sold in China.
   e. More telephones from all sources would be sold in China.

Tackle the Test: Free-Response Questions

1. Suppose that rice is traded in the world market at a price of $1 per pound, and that in the absence of trade, the equilibrium price of rice in Mexico is $1.25 per pound.
   a. Draw a correctly labeled graph that shows the domestic supply and demand for rice in Mexico.
   b. Label the no-trade equilibrium and the trade equilibrium.
   c. Use labeled brackets to indicate the portions of the horizontal axis that represent
      i. the quantity of rice imported at the world price.
      ii. the quantity of rice supplied domestically at the world price.
   d. Suppose that Mexico imposes a $0.15 tariff per pound of imported rice.
      i. Label the new trade equilibrium.
      ii. Shade the area that represents the total tariff revenue.

Rubric for FRQ 1 (6 points)

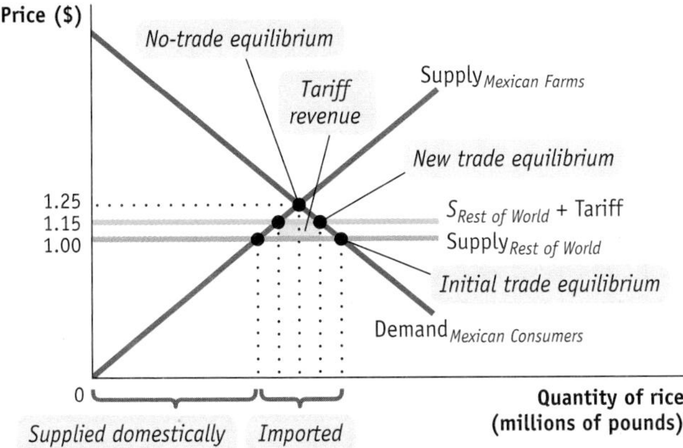

1 point: Graph with "Price" on the vertical axis, "Quantity of Rice" on the horizontal axis, downward-sloping demand, upward-sloping supply, and the no-trade equilibrium

1 point: Horizontal rest-of-world supply curve and trade equilibrium as shown in the figure

1 point: Correct indication of imported quantity

1 point: Correct indication of domestically supplied quantity

1 point: Horizontal rest-of-world supply + tariff curve and new trade equilibrium as in the figure

1 point: Shaded area that represents tariff revenue as in the figure

2. Suppose that cheese is traded in the world market at a price of €3 per pound. Assume that France has no trade barriers and has supply and demand curves for cheese as shown in the graph.

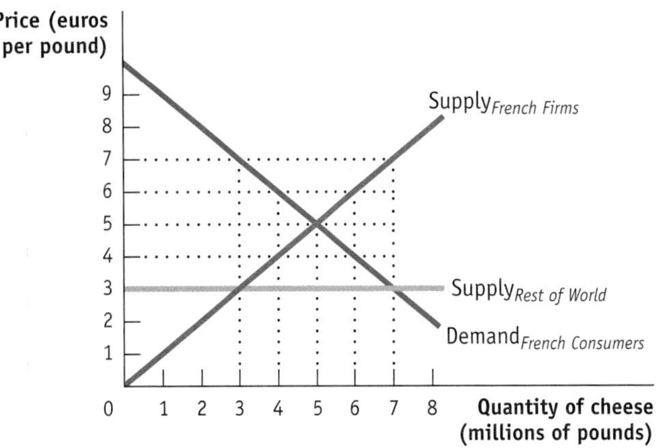

   a. How much cheese does France import?
   b. Suppose that France adopts an import quota of 2 million pounds of cheese.
      i. What will the price be at the new trade equilibrium?
      ii. How much cheese will French suppliers provide domestically with the quota in place?
      iii. If France imposed a tariff instead of a quota to restrict cheese imports, a tariff of what amount per pound would result in imports of 2 million pounds of cheese?
   c. Suppose that instead of any other trade restriction, France imposed a tariff of €4 per pound of cheese. How much cheese would France import? Explain.

   (6 points)

Istockphoto

MODULE 45 Putting It All Together

In this Module, you will learn to:

- Use macroeconomic models to conduct policy analysis
- Improve your approach to free-response macroeconomics questions

Having completed our study of the basic macroeconomic models, we can use them to analyze scenarios and evaluate policy recommendations. In this module we develop a step-by-step approach to macroeconomic analysis. You can adapt this approach to problems involving any macroeconomic model, including models of aggregate demand and supply, production possibilities, money markets, and the Phillips curve. By the end of this module you will be able to combine mastery of the principles of macroeconomics with problem solving skills to analyze a new scenario on your own.

A Structure for Macroeconomic Analysis

© ZUMA Press, Inc./Alamy

How will the Fed's monetary policy change nominal interest rates?

In our study of macroeconomics we have seen questions about the macroeconomy take many different forms. No matter what the specific question, most macroeconomic problems have the following components:

1. *A starting point.* To analyze any situation, you have to know where to start.
2. *A pivotal event.* This might be a change in the economy or a policy response to the initial situation.
3. *Initial effects of the event.* An event will generally have some initial, short-run effects.
4. *Secondary and long-run effects of the event.* After the short-run effects run their course, there are typically secondary effects and the economy will move toward its long-run equilibrium.

For example, you might be asked to consider the following scenario and answer the associated questions.

Assume the U.S. economy is currently operating at an aggregate output level above potential output. Draw a correctly labeled graph showing aggregate demand, short-run aggregate supply, long-run aggregate supply, equilibrium output, and the aggregate price level.

Now assume that the Federal Reserve conducts contractionary monetary policy. Identify the open-market operation the Fed would conduct, and draw a correctly labeled graph of the money market to show the effect of the monetary policy on the nominal interest rate.

Show and explain how the Fed's actions will affect equilibrium in the aggregate demand and supply graph you drew previously. Indicate the new aggregate price level on your graph.

Assume Canada is the largest trading partner of the United States. Draw a correctly labeled graph of the foreign exchange market for the U.S. dollar showing how the change in the aggregate price level you indicate on your graph above will affect the foreign exchange market. What will happen to the value of the U.S. dollar relative to the Canadian dollar?

How will the Federal Reserve's contractionary monetary policy affect the real interest rate in the United States in the long run? Explain.

Taken as a whole, this scenario and the associated questions can seem overwhelming. Let's start by breaking down our analysis into four components.

1. **The starting point**
   Assume the U.S. economy is currently operating at an aggregate output level above potential output.
2. **The pivotal event**
   Now assume that the Federal Reserve conducts contractionary monetary policy.
3. **Initial effects of the event**
   Show and explain how the Fed's actions will affect equilibrium.
4. **Secondary and long-run effects of the event**
   Assume Canada is the largest trading partner of the United States. What will happen to the value of the U.S. dollar relative to the Canadian dollar?
   How will the Federal Reserve's contractionary monetary policy affect the real interest rate in the United States in the long run? Explain.

Now we are ready to look at each of the steps and untangle this scenario.

The Starting Point

Assume the U.S. economy is currently operating at an aggregate output level above potential output. Draw a correctly labeled graph showing aggregate demand, short-run aggregate supply, long-run aggregate supply, equilibrium output, and the aggregate price level.

To analyze a situation, you have to know where to start. You will most often use the aggregate demand–aggregate supply model to evaluate macroeconomic scenarios. In this model, there are three possible starting points: long-run macroeconomic equilibrium, a recessionary gap, and an inflationary gap. This means that there are three possible "starting-point" graphs, as shown in **Figure 45.1** on the next page. The economy can be in long-run macroeconomic equilibrium with production at potential output as in panel (a); it can be in short-run macroeconomic equilibrium at an aggregate output level below potential output (creating a recessionary gap) as in panel (b); or it can be in short-run macroeconomic equilibrium at an aggregate output level above potential output (creating an inflationary gap) as in panel (c) and in our scenario.

The Pivotal Event

Now assume that the Federal Reserve conducts contractionary monetary policy.

It is the events in a scenario that make it interesting. Perhaps a country goes into or recovers from a recession, inflation catches consumers off guard or becomes expected, consumers or businesses become more or less confident, holdings of money or wealth change, trading partners prosper or falter, or oil prices plummet or spike. The event can also be expansionary or contractionary monetary or fiscal policy. With the infinite number of possible changes in policy, politics, the economy, and markets around the world, don't expect to analyze a familiar scenario on the exam.

While it's impossible to foresee all of the scenarios you might encounter, we can group the determinants of change into a reasonably small set of major factors that

Figure 45.1 Analysis Starting Points

(a) Long-Run Macroeconomic Equilibrium

Aggregate price level
LRAS
SRAS
P_E
E_{LR} — Long-run macroeconomic equilibrium
AD
Y_P
Real GDP
Potential output

(b) Short-Run Macroeconomic Equilibrium: Recessionary Gap

Aggregate price level
LRAS
SRAS
P_1
AD
Y_1 Y_P
Real GDP
Potential output

(c) Short-Run Macroeconomic Equilibrium: Inflationary Gap

Aggregate price level
LRAS
SRAS
P_1
AD
Y_P Y_1
Real GDP
Potential output

Panels (a), (b) and (c) represent the three basic starting points for analysis using the aggregate demand–aggregate supply model.

AP Photo/Gus Ruelas

You've seen the speech, now, how would you analyze the proposed policy?

influence macroeconomic models. **Table 45.1** matches major factors with the curves they affect. With these influences in mind, it is relatively easy to proceed through a problem by identifying how the given events affect these factors. Most hypothetical scenarios involve changes in just one or two major factors. Although the real world is more complex, it is largely the same factors that change—there are just more of them changing at once.

As shown in Table 45.1, many curves are shifted by changes in only two or three major factors. Even for the aggregate demand curve, which has the largest number of associated factors, you can simplify the task further by asking yourself, "Does the event influence consumer spending, investment spending, government spending, or net exports?" If so, aggregate demand shifts. A shift

Table 45.1 Major Factors that Shift Curves in Each Model

Aggregate Demand and Aggregate Supply

Aggregate Demand Curve	Short-Run Aggregate Supply Curve	Long-Run Aggregate Supply Curve
Expectations	Commodity prices	Productivity
Wealth	Nominal wages	Physical capital
Size of existing capital stock	Productivity	Human capital
Fiscal and monetary policy	Business taxes	Technology
Net exports		Quantity of resources
Interest rates		
Investment spending		

Supply and Demand

Demand Curve	Supply Curve
Income	Input prices
Prices of substitutes and complements	Prices of substitutes and complements in production
Tastes	Technology
Consumer expectations	Producer expectations
Number of consumers	Number of producers

Loanable Funds Market

Demand Curve	Supply Curve
Investment opportunities	Private saving behavior
Government borrowing	Capital inflows

Money Market

Demand Curve	Supply Curve
Aggregate price level	Set by the Federal Reserve
Real GDP	
Technology (related to money market)	
Institutions (related to money market)	

Foreign Exchange Market

Demand	Supply
Foreigners' purchases of domestic	Domestic residents' purchases of foreign
Goods	Goods
Services	Services
Assets	Assets

Note: It is the *real* exchange rate (adjusted for international differences in aggregate price levels) that affects imports and exports.

of the long-run aggregate supply curve is caused only by events that affect labor productivity or the number of workers.

In the supply and demand model there are five major factors that shift the demand curve and five major factors that shift the supply curve. Most examples using this model will represent a change in one of these ten factors. The loanable funds market, money market, and foreign exchange market have their own clearly identified factors that affect supply or demand. With this information you can link specific events to relevant factors in the models to see what changes will occur. Remember that having correctly labeled axes on your graphs is crucial to a correct analysis.

Often, as in our scenario, the event is a policy response to an undesirable starting point such as a recessionary or inflationary gap. Expansionary policy is used to combat a recession, and contractionary policy is used to combat inflationary pressures. To begin analyzing a policy response, you need to fully understand how the Federal Reserve can implement each type of monetary policy (e.g., increase or decrease the money supply) and how that policy eventually affects the economy. You also need to understand how the government can implement expansionary or contractionary fiscal policy by raising or lowering taxes or government spending.

The Initial Effect of the Event

Show and explain how the Fed's actions will affect equilibrium.

We have seen that events will create short-run effects in our models. In the short-run, fiscal and monetary policy both affect the economy by shifting the aggregate demand curve. As shown in panel (a) of **Figure 45.2**, expansionary policy shifts aggregate demand to the right, and as shown in panel (b), contractionary policy shifts aggregate demand to the left. To illustrate the effect of a policy response, shift the aggregate demand curve on your starting point graph and indicate the effects of the shift on the aggregate price level and aggregate output.

Secondary and Long-Run Effects of the Event

Assume Canada is the largest trading partner of the United States. What will happen to the value of the U.S. dollar relative to the Canadian dollar?

How will the Federal Reserve's contractionary monetary policy affect the real interest rate in the United States in the long run? Explain.

Secondary Effects In addition to the initial, short-run effects of any event, there will be secondary effects and the economy will move to its long-run equilibrium after the short-run effects run their course.

We have seen that negative or positive demand shocks (including those created by inappropriate monetary or fiscal policy) move the economy away from long-run macroeconomic equilibrium. As explained in Module 18, in the absence of policy responses,

Figure 45.2 Monetary and Fiscal Policy Close Output Gaps

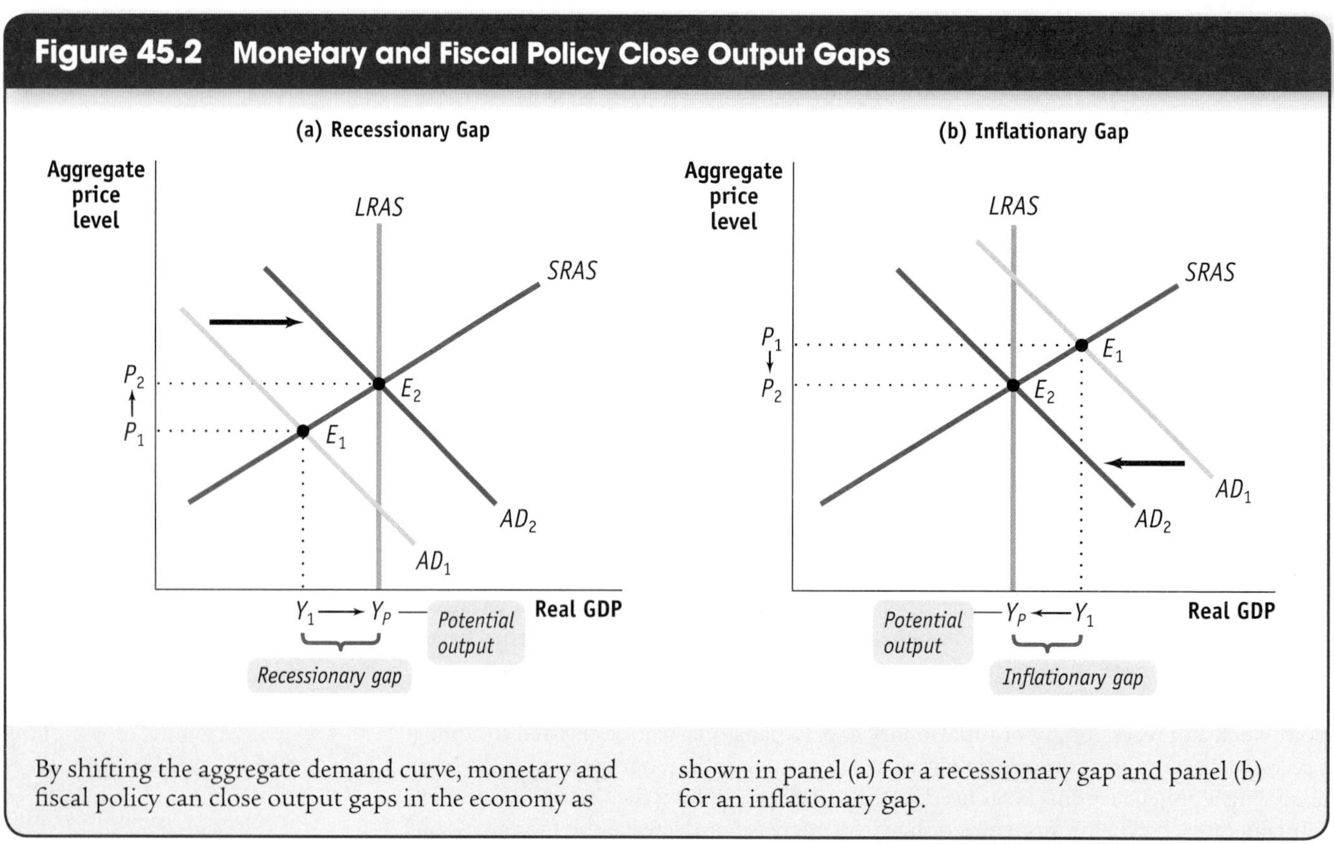

By shifting the aggregate demand curve, monetary and fiscal policy can close output gaps in the economy as shown in panel (a) for a recessionary gap and panel (b) for an inflationary gap.

such events will eventually be offset through changes in short-run aggregate supply resulting from changes in nominal wage rates. This will move the economy back to long-run macroeconomic equilibrium.

If the short-run effects of an action result in changes in the aggregate price level or real interest rate, there will also be secondary effects throughout the open economy. International capital flows and international trade will be affected as a result of the initial effects experienced in the economy. A price level decrease, as in our scenario, will encourage exports and discourage imports, causing an appreciation in the domestic currency on the foreign exchange market. A change in the interest rate affects aggregate demand through changes in investment spending and consumer spending. Interest rate changes also affect aggregate demand through changes in imports or exports caused by currency appreciation and depreciation. These secondary effects act to reinforce the effects of monetary policy.

Long-Run Effects While deviations from potential output are ironed out in the long run, other effects remain. For example, in the long run the use of fiscal policy affects the federal budget. Changes in taxes or government spending that lead to budget deficits (and increased federal debt) can "crowd out" private investment spending in the long run. The government's increased demand for loanable funds drives up the interest rate, decreases investment spending, and partially offsets the initial increase in aggregate demand. Of course, the deficit could be addressed by printing money, but that would lead to problems with inflation in the long run.

We know that in the long run, monetary policy affects only the aggregate price level, not real GDP. Because money is neutral, changes in the money supply have no effect on the real economy. The aggregate price level and nominal values will be affected by the same proportion, leaving real values (including the real interest rate as mentioned in our scenario) unchanged.

Analyzing Our Scenario

Now let's address the specific demands of our problem.

- *Draw a correctly labeled graph showing aggregate demand, short-run aggregate supply, long-run aggregate supply, equilibrium output, and the aggregate price level.*

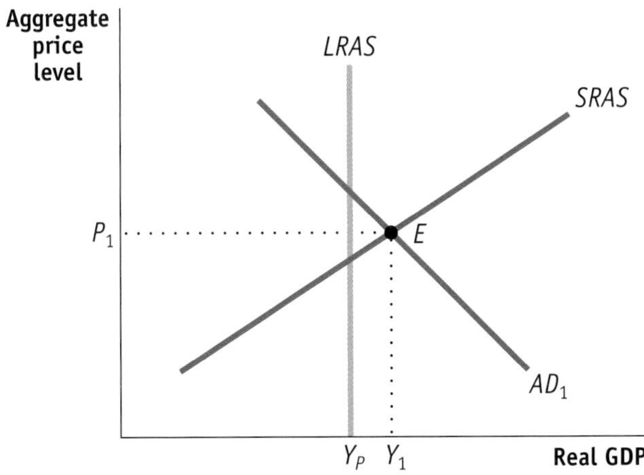

- *Identify the open-market operation the Fed would conduct.*

The Fed would sell U.S. Treasury securities (bonds, bills, or notes).

- *Draw a correctly labeled graph of the money market to show the effect of the monetary policy on the nominal interest rate.*

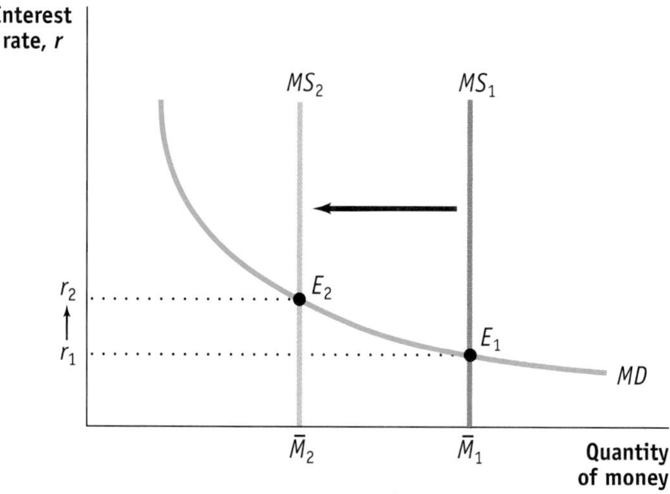

- *Show and explain how the Fed's actions will affect equilibrium in the aggregate demand and supply graph you drew previously. Indicate the new aggregate price level on your graph.*

A higher interest rate will lead to decreased investment and consumer spending, decreasing aggregate demand. The equilibrium price level and real GDP will fall.

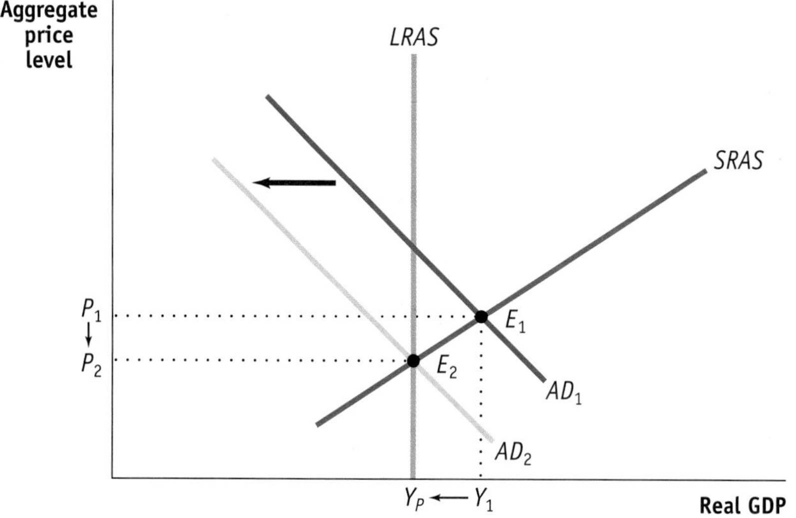

- *Draw a correctly labeled graph of the foreign exchange market for the U.S. dollar showing how the change in the aggregate price level you indicate on your graph above will affect the foreign exchange market.*

The decrease in the U.S. price level will make U.S. exports relatively inexpensive for Canadians to purchase and lead to an increase in demand for U.S. dollars with which to purchase those exports.

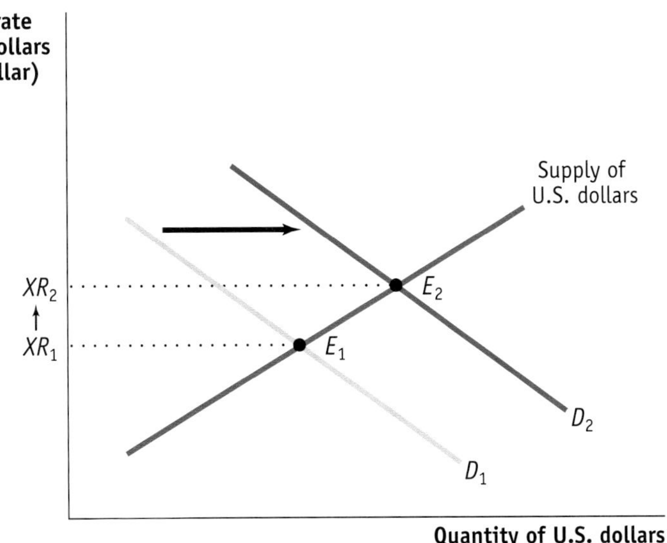

- *What will happen to the U.S. dollar relative to the Canadian dollar?*

The U.S. dollar will appreciate.

- *How will the Federal Reserve's contractionary monetary policy affect the real interest rate in the United States in the long run? Explain.*

There will be no effect on the real interest rate in the long run because, due to the neutrality of money, changes in the money supply do not affect real values in the long run.

MODULE 45 Review

Check Your Understanding

1. The economy is operating in long-run macroeconomic equilibrium.
   a. Illustrate this situation using a correctly labeled aggregate demand–aggregate supply graph.
   b. Use your graph to show the short-run effect on real GDP and the aggregate price level if there is a decrease in government spending.
   c. What will happen to the aggregate price level and real GDP in the long run? Explain.
   d. Suppose the government is experiencing a persistent budget deficit. How will the decrease in government spending affect that deficit? Use a correctly labeled graph of the loanable funds market to show the effect of a decrease in government spending on the interest rate.

Tackle the Test: Multiple-Choice Questions

Questions 1–5 refer to the following scenario:

The United States and Mexico are trading partners. Suppose a flu outbreak significantly decreases U.S. tourism in Mexico and causes the Mexican economy to enter a recession. Assume that the money that would have been spent by U.S. tourists in Mexico is, instead, not spent at all.

1. Which of the following occurs as a result of the recession in Mexico?

I. Output in Mexico decreases.
II. Aggregate demand in the United States decreases.
III. Output in the United States decreases.

a. I only
b. II only
c. III only
d. I and II only
e. I, II, and III

2. What is the effect of Mexico's falling income on the demand for money and the nominal interest rate in Mexico?

Demand for money	*Nominal interest rate*
a. increases	decreases
b. decreases	decreases
c. increases	increases
d. decreases	increases
e. increases	unchanged

3. Given what happens to the nominal interest rate, if the aggregate price level in Mexico decreases, what will happen to the real interest rate?

a. It will increase.
b. It will decrease.
c. It will be unchanged.
d. It will stabilize.
e. It cannot be determined.

4. Suppose the aggregate price level in Mexico decreases relative to that in the United States. What is the effect of this price level change on the demand, and on the exchange rate, for Mexican pesos?

Demand for pesos	*Exchange rate*
a. increases	appreciates
b. increases	depreciates
c. decreases	appreciates
d. decreases	depreciates
e. decreases	is unchanged

5. If the Mexican government pursues expansionary fiscal policy in response to the recession, what will happen to aggregate demand and aggregate supply in Mexico in the short run?

Aggregate demand	*Short-run aggregate supply*
a. increases	increases
b. increases	decreases
c. decreases	increases
d. decreases	decreases
e. increases	is unchanged

Tackle the Test: Free-Response Questions

1. Suppose the U.S. economy is experiencing a recession.

a. Draw a correctly labeled aggregate demand–aggregate supply graph showing the aggregate demand, short-run aggregate supply, long-run aggregate supply, equilibrium output, and aggregate price level.

b. Assume that energy prices increase in the United States. Show the effects of this increase on the equilibrium in your graph from part a.

c. According to your graph, how does the increase in energy prices affect unemployment and inflation in the economy?

d. Assume the United States and Canada are the only two countries in an open economy and that energy prices have remained unchanged in Canada. Draw a correctly labeled graph of the foreign exchange market for U.S. dollars, and use it to show the effect of increased U.S. energy prices on the demand for U.S. dollars. Explain.

Rubric for FRQ 1 (12 points)

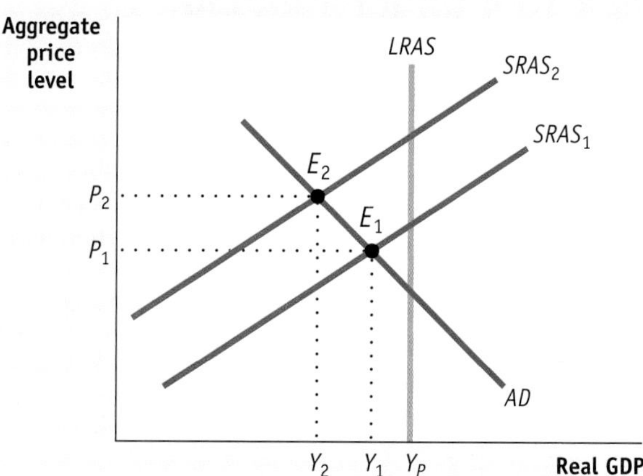

1 point: The vertical axis is labeled "Aggregate price level" and the horizontal axis is labeled "Aggregate output" or "Real GDP."

1 point: The *AD* curve slopes downward, the *SRAS* curve slopes upward, and the *LRAS* curve is vertical.

1 point: The equilibrium is found where the *SRAS* curve crosses the *AD* curve, and the equilibrium aggregate price level and aggregate output are shown on the axes at this point.

1 point: The equilibrium is to the left of the *LRAS* curve.

1 point: The *SRAS* curve shifts to the left.

1 point: The equilibrium aggregate price level and output are shown on the axes at the new equilibrium (increased aggregate price level, decreased aggregate output).

1 point: It increases unemployment.

1 point: It increases the aggregate price level (inflation).

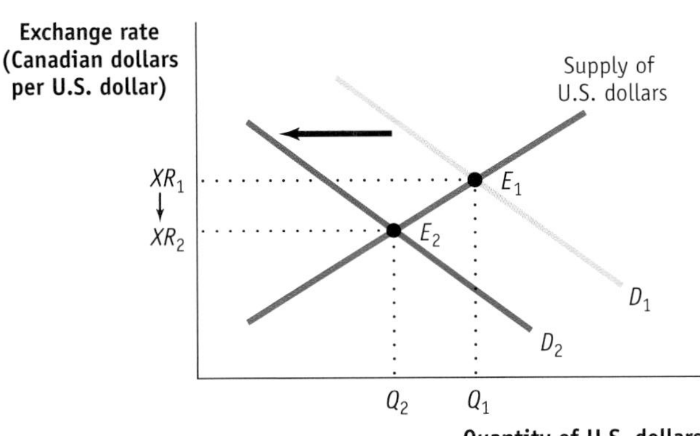

1 point: The vertical axis is labeled "Exchange rate (Canadian dollars per U.S. dollar)," and the horizontal axis is labeled "Quantity of U.S. dollars." Demand for U.S. dollars slopes downward and is labeled; supply of U.S. dollars slopes upward and is labeled.

1 point: The equilibrium exchange rate and quantity of U.S. dollars are shown on the axes at the intersection of the demand and supply curves.

1 point: The demand for U.S. dollars will decrease.

1 point: The inflation in the United States will lead to a decrease in the demand for U.S. exports (which must be purchased with U.S. dollars).

2. Assume the United States is operating below potential output.
- **a.** Draw a correctly labeled aggregate demand–aggregate supply graph showing equilibrium in the economy.
- **b.** Suppose the government decreases taxes. On your graph, show how the decrease in taxes will affect *AD*, *SRAS*, *LRAS*, equilibrium aggregate price level, and output.
- **c.** Assume the decrease in taxes led to an increased budget deficit and that the deficit spending was funded through government borrowing from the public. Use a correctly labeled graph of the market for loanable funds to show the effect of increased borrowing on the interest rate.
- **d.** Given the effect on the interest rate from part c, draw a correctly labeled graph of the foreign exchange market showing the effect of the change in the interest rate on the supply of U.S. dollars. Explain how the interest rate affects the supply of U.S. dollars.
- **e.** According to your graph from part d, what has happened to the value of the U.S. dollar? How will this affect U.S. exports and aggregate demand?

(12 points)

SECTION  Review

 **Section 8 Review Video**

Module 41

1. A country's **balance of payments accounts** summarize its transactions with the rest of the world. The **balance of payments on the current account**, or the **current account**, includes the **balance of payments on goods and services** together with balances on factor income and transfers. The **merchandise trade balance**, or **trade balance**, is a frequently cited component of the balance of payments on goods and services. The **balance of payments on the financial account**, or the **financial account**, measures capital flows. By definition, the balance of payments on the current account plus the balance of payments on the financial account is zero.

2. Capital flows respond to international differences in interest rates and other rates of return; they can be usefully analyzed using an international version of the loanable funds model, which shows how a country where the interest rate would be low in the absence of capital flows sends funds to a country where the interest rate would be high in the absence of capital flows. The underlying determinants of capital flows are international differences in savings and opportunities for investment spending.

Module 42

3. Currencies are traded in the **foreign exchange market**; the prices at which they are traded are **exchange rates**. When a currency rises against another currency, it **appreciates**; when it falls, it **depreciates**. The **equilibrium exchange rate** matches the quantity of that currency supplied to the foreign exchange market to the quantity demanded.
4. To correct for international differences in inflation rates, economists calculate **real exchange rates**, which multiply the exchange rate between two countries' respective currencies by the ratio of the countries' price levels. The current account responds only to changes in the real exchange rate, not the nominal exchange rate. **Purchasing power parity** is the exchange rate that makes the cost of a basket of goods and services equal in two countries. While purchasing power parity and the nominal exchange rate almost always differ, purchasing power parity is a good predictor of actual changes in the nominal exchange rate.

Module 43

5. Countries adopt different **exchange rate regimes**, rules governing exchange rate policy. The main types are **fixed exchange rates**, where the government takes action to keep the exchange rate at a target level, and **floating exchange rates**, where the exchange rate is free to fluctuate. Countries can fix exchange rates using **exchange market intervention**, which requires them to hold **foreign exchange reserves** that they use to buy any surplus of their currency. Alternatively, they can change domestic policies, especially monetary policy, to shift the demand and supply curves in the foreign exchange market. Finally, they can use **foreign exchange controls**.
6. Exchange rate policy poses a dilemma: there are economic payoffs to stable exchange rates, but the policies used to fix the exchange rate have costs. Exchange market intervention requires large reserves, and exchange controls distort incentives. If monetary policy is used to help fix the exchange rate, it isn't available to use for domestic policy.
7. Fixed exchange rates aren't always permanent commitments: countries with a fixed exchange rate sometimes engage in **devaluations** or **revaluations**. In addition to helping eliminate a surplus of domestic currency on the foreign exchange market, a devaluation increases aggregate demand. Similarly, a revaluation reduces shortages of domestic currency and reduces aggregate demand.
8. Under floating exchange rates, expansionary monetary policy works in part through the exchange rate: cutting domestic interest rates leads to a depreciation, and through that to higher exports and lower imports, which increases aggregate demand. Contractionary monetary policy has the reverse effect.
9. The fact that one country's imports are another country's exports creates a link between the business cycles in different countries. Floating exchange rates, however, may reduce the strength of that link.

Module 44

10. **Protectionism** is the practice of limiting trade to protect domestic industries. The idea is to allow domestic producers to gain enough strength to compete in global markets. Taxes on imports, known as **tariffs**, and limits of the quantities of goods that can be imported, known as **import quotas**, are the primary tools of protectionism.

Module 45

11. Most macroeconomic problems have a starting point, a pivotal event, initial effects of the event, and secondary and long-run effects of the event. A good approach is to consider these components sequentially: (1) if possible, draw a graph that illustrates the starting point; (2) show how the graph changes due to the pivotal event—often a curve shifts; (3) indicate the initial effects of the change; (4) analyze the secondary and long-run effects, as appropriate.

Key Terms

Balance of payments accounts, p. 406
Balance of payments on the current account (the current account), p. 408
Balance of payments on goods and services, p. 408
Merchandise trade balance (trade balance), p. 408
Balance of payments on the financial account (the financial account), p. 409
Foreign exchange market, p. 417
Exchange rates, p. 417
Appreciates, p. 418
Depreciates, p. 418
Equilibrium exchange rate, p. 419
Real exchange rate, p. 421
Purchasing power parity, p. 423
Exchange rate regime, p. 427
Fixed exchange rate, p. 427
Floating exchange rate, p. 427
Exchange market intervention, p. 429
Foreign exchange reserves, p. 429
Foreign exchange controls, p. 429
Devaluation, p. 431
Revaluation, p. 431
Protectionism, p. 438
Tariffs, p. 438
Import quota, p. 440

AP® Exam Practice Questions

Multiple-Choice Questions

1. Which of the following transactions is counted in the U.S. current account?
   a. A French importer buys a case of California wine.
   b. An American working for a Brazilian company deposits her paycheck.
   c. An American buys a bond from a Japanese company.
   d. An American charity sends money to an African aid agency.
   e. A Chinese national buys stock in a U.S. company.

2. The difference between a country's exports and imports of goods is that country's
   a. balance of payments on its current account.
   b. balance of payments on its financial account.
   c. balance of payments on its capital account.
   d. merchandise trade balance.
   e. balance of payments on goods and services.

3. Which of the following relationships between the current account (CA) and the financial account (FA) must be true?
   a. CA − FA = 0
   b. CA + FA = 0
   c. CA = FA
   d. CA = 1/FA
   e. (CA)(FA) = 1

4. Which of the following is a reason for capital to flow into a country?
   a. a rapidly growing economy
   b. government budget surpluses
   c. higher savings rates
   d. lower interest rates
   e. a relatively high supply of loanable funds

Refer to the following graphs and information for Questions 5–7.

Suppose that Northlandia and Southlandia are the only two trading countries in the world, that each nation runs a balance of payments on both the current account and the financial account equal to zero, and that each nation sees the other's assets as identical to its own.

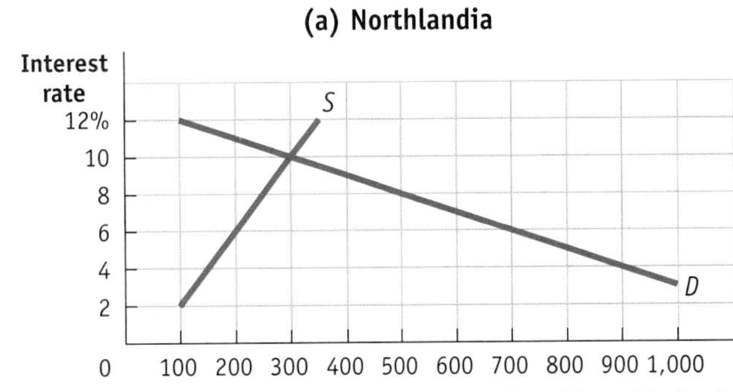

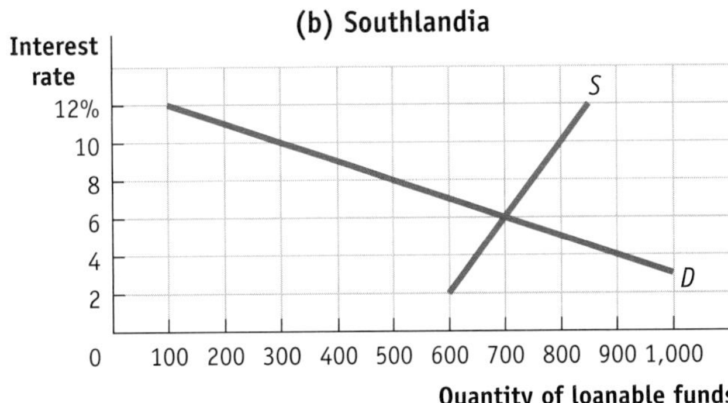

5. Given the situation depicted in the graphs, which of the following will happen?
   a. The interest rate in Northlandia will rise.
   b. The interest rate in Southlandia will fall.
   c. Capital will flow into Northlandia.
   d. Capital will flow into Southlandia.
   e. Southlandia will experience a balance of trade deficit.
6. Which of the following will happen in Southlandia?
   a. The quantity of loanable funds supplied will decrease.
   b. The supply of loanable funds will increase.
   c. The demand for loanable funds will decrease.
   d. The supply of loanable funds will decrease.
   e. The interest rate will decrease.
7. If the international equilibrium interest rate is 8%, which of the following will be true?
   a. Southlandia will experience a capital outflow of 250.
   b. Southlandia will experience a capital outflow of 700.
   c. Northlandia will experience a capital outflow of 250.
   d. Northlandia will experience a capital outflow of 300.
   e. The international equilibrium quantity of loanable funds will be 1,200.
8. Which of the following is traded in a foreign exchange market?
   a. imported goods only
   b. exported goods only
   c. both imported and exported goods
   d. international stocks and bonds
   e. currency
9. The price in a foreign exchange market is a(n)
   a. real interest rate.
   b. nominal interest rate.
   c. tariff.
   d. exchange rate.
   e. discount rate.

Refer to the following graph and information for Questions 10–11.

The graph shows the foreign exchange market for the bern, the currency used in the country of Albernia.

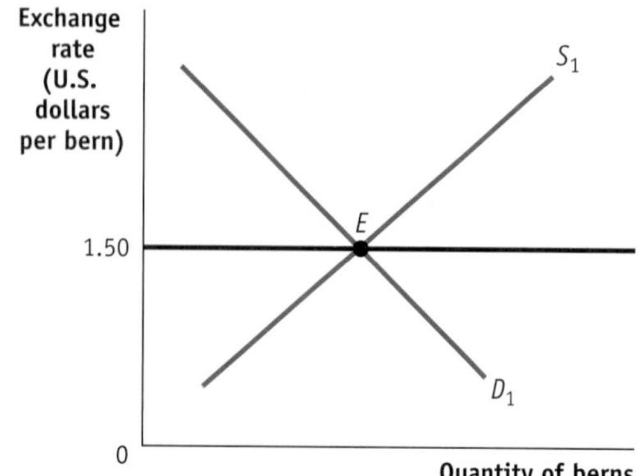

10. Given the equilibrium exchange rate on the graph, which of the following is true regarding the bern?
   a. It takes $1.50 to buy a bern.
   b. It takes $.75 to buy a bern.
   c. It takes $.67 to buy a bern.
   d. It takes 1.50 bern to buy a dollar.
   e. It takes .75 bern to buy a dollar.
11. How could depreciation of the bern be shown on the graph?
   a. a movement of the equilibrium exchange rate to 2
   b. a movement of the equilibrium exchange rate to 1
   c. a decrease in the equilibrium quantity of berns
   d. a rightward shift of the demand for berns
   e. a leftward shift of the supply of berns
12. Real exchange rates are adjusted for international differences in
   a. exchange rates.
   b. aggregate price levels.
   c. GDP per capita.
   d. capital flows.
   e. income.
13. Which of the following will occur in the foreign exchange market as a result of capital inflow to the United States?
   a. a decrease in the demand for dollars
   b. a decrease in the dollar exchange rate
   c. an increase in the supply of dollars
   d. appreciation of the dollar
   e. a decrease in the quantity of dollars exchanged
14. Which of the following is true if two countries have purchasing power parity?
   a. The two countries' real GDP per capita is the same.
   b. The two countries' imports equal their exports.
   c. The nominal exchange rate assures that goods cost the same amount in each country.
   d. There are no capital inflows or outflows between the two countries.
   e. The countries' exchange rates do not appreciate or depreciate.
15. When a government lets exchange rates be determined by foreign exchange markets, it is called
   a. an exchange rate regime.
   b. a fixed exchange rate.
   c. a floating exchange rate.
   d. a market exchange rate.
   e. a foreign exchange control.
16. Governments intervene to keep the value of their currency down in order to
   a. make domestic goods cheaper in the world market.
   b. decrease the price of imported goods.
   c. promote capital inflows.
   d. decrease exports.
   e. reduce aggregate demand.

17. A decrease in domestic interest rates will necessarily have which of the following effects in the foreign exchange market?

a. The supply of the domestic currency will decrease.
b. The demand for the domestic currency will decrease.
c. The exchange rate will increase.
d. The quantity of the domestic currency exchanged will rise.
e. The quantity of the domestic currency exchanged will fall.

18. An import quota on a good will do which of the following?

a. It will raise revenue for the government.
b. It will reduce the domestic price of the good.
c. It will raise the international price of the good.
d. It will reduce the quantity of the good sold domestically.
e. It will decrease domestic production of the good.

19. Which of the following is true of tariffs?

a. They are limits on the quantity of a good that can be imported.
b. They account for over 10% of federal government revenue in the United States.
c. They can result in trade wars between countries.
d. They do not protect domestic industries from competition.
e. They decrease the price of goods.

20. The goal of protectionism is to

a. generate revenue for the federal government.
b. lower the price of goods for domestic consumers.
c. increase world output through specialization and comparative advantage.
d. decrease competition for domestic industries.
e. raise the price of imported goods.

Free-Response Question

1. Draw a correctly labeled graph showing equilibrium in the U.S. foreign exchange market for Chinese yuan.

a. Assume the real interest rate in China falls relative to the real interest rate in the United States. Show the impact of the change in the real interest rate on each of the following.

i. The demand for Chinese yuan. Explain.
ii. The value of Chinese yuan relative to the U.S. dollar.

b. Assume that the U.S. current account balance is zero. Based on the change in the value of the yuan, will the U.S. current account balance move to a surplus, move to a deficit, or stay the same? Explain.

(6 points)

AP® Macroeconomics Exam Practice Test

Multiple-Choice Questions

Refer to the figure below to answer Question 1.

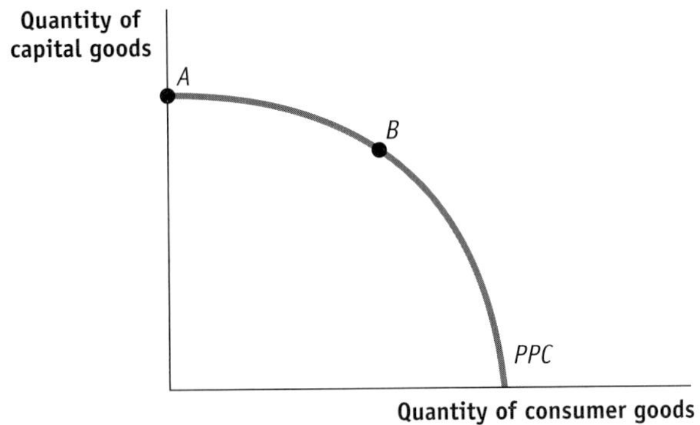

1. A movement from point *A* to point *B* illustrates which of the following?
   a. the opportunity cost of consumer goods
   b. an advance in technology
   c. an increase in available resources used to produce consumer goods
   d. an increase in the price of capital goods
   e. an increase in efficiency

Refer to the figure below to answer Question 2.

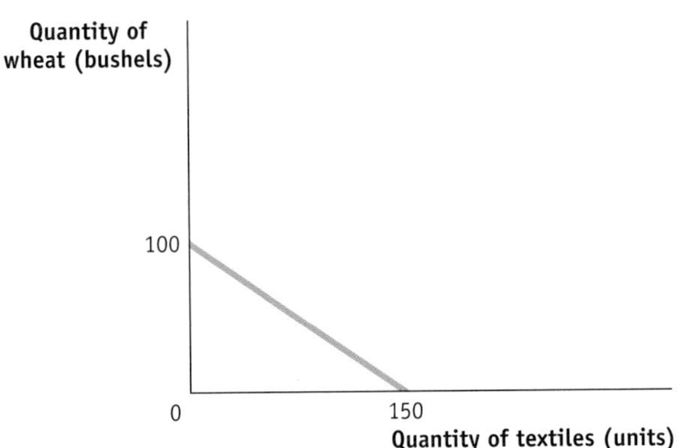

2. A country can produce either 100 bushels of wheat or 150 units of textiles, as shown on the graph above. If an advance in technology affects only the production of textiles, what happens to the slope of the production possibilities curve and the opportunity cost of wheat?

	Slope	*Opportunity cost of wheat*
a.	no change	no change
b.	decrease	decrease
c.	increase	increase
d.	no change	increase
e.	decrease	increase

3. According to the concept of comparative advantage, which of the following is true when countries specialize and trade?
   a. Each country obtains an absolute advantage.
   b. Total world output increases.
   c. The production possibilities curve for both countries shifts outward.
   d. Prices fall in both countries.
   e. Deadweight loss is created.

Refer to the figure below to answer Question 4.

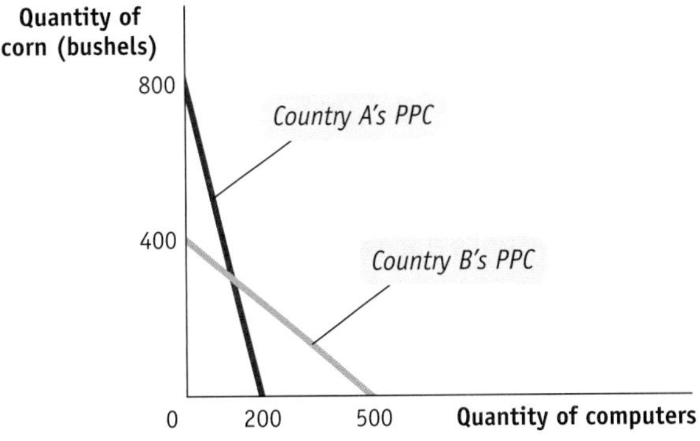

4. Using equal amounts of labor hours, two countries, Alpha and Beta, can produce corn and computers as shown. Based on the information provided, which of the following is true?
   a. Country A has an absolute advantage in the production of corn and computers.
   b. Country B has an absolute advantage in the production of corn and computers.
   c. Country A has a comparative advantage in the production of computers.
   d. Country B has a comparative advantage in the production of corn.
   e. Country A has an absolute advantage in the production of corn.

5. If the price of a substitute good increases, which of the following will happen to the price and the quantity sold in a market?

	Price	*Quantity sold*
a.	increase	increase
b.	increase	decrease
c.	decrease	increase
d.	decrease	decrease
e.	increase	no change

6. If the wages of workers producing a good increase, the price and quantity of the good sold will change in which of the following ways?

	Price	*Quantity*
a.	increase	increase
b.	increase	decrease
c.	decrease	increase
d.	decrease	decrease
e.	increase	no change

7. If real gross domestic product is declining, the economy is most likely experiencing which of the following?
   a. declining unemployment
   b. negative long-run economic growth
   c. inflationary pressures
   d. an increase in aggregate demand
   e. a recession

8. In the circular-flow model of an economy, which of the following is a leakage?
   a. savings
   b. investment
   c. wages
   d. government spending
   e. exports

9. Which of the following is not counted in a country's GDP?
   a. goods exported to other countries
   b. changes in inventories
   c. domestically produced capital goods
   d. financial assets, such as stocks and bonds
   e. newly produced services

10. Which of the following is true of the relationship between real GDP and nominal GDP?
   a. Real GDP is higher than nominal GDP when there is inflation in the economy.
   b. Real GDP is equal to nominal GDP when the economy is at full employment.
   c. Real GDP minus nominal GDP equals the rate of inflation.
   d. Real GDP is nominal GDP adjusted for changes in the price level.
   e. Real GDP increases when nominal GDP increases.

11. Which of the following transactions would be included in the calculation of GDP?
   a. Lee buys a used car.
   b. Kylie buys a new softball bat.
   c. Eric mows his own lawn rather than paying someone else $25.
   d. Ray resells his ticket to a football game.
   e. Kumar volunteers for 3 hours per week as a tutor at the local high school.

12. If the real interest rate is 2% and the nominal interest rate is 6%, the expected rate of inflation is
   a. 0%.
   b. 2%.
   c. 4%.
   d. 6%.
   e. 8%.

13. Suppose that last year the price level increased and the production of goods and services increased. Which of the following must be true? Nominal GDP
   a. increased but real GDP decreased.
   b. increased while the value of real GDP cannot be determined.
   c. stayed the same while real GDP increased.
   d. increased and real GDP increased.
   e. decreased while real GDP increased.

14. Given the information provided below, what is the unemployment rate?

Population	1,000
Labor force	800
Employment	600

   a. 20%
   b. 25%
   c. 33%
   d. 40%
   e. 50%

15. A worker laid off due to a recession is experiencing which type of unemployment?
   a. temporary
   b. frictional
   c. cyclical
   d. structural
   e. seasonal

16. Which of the following could lead the unemployment rate to be overstated?
   a. discouraged workers
   b. teenage workers
   c. part-time workers
   d. retired workers
   e. workers deciding which job offer to accept

17. Which of the following individuals is considered frictionally unemployed? A person who is not working and
   a. is in the process of looking for a new job.
   b. does not have the skills needed in the job market.
   c. was laid off during a recession.
   d. was laid off due to an increase in the minimum wage.
   e. has given up looking for a job.

18. If the general price level doubles and at the same time a worker's real wage rate doubles, what must be true of the worker's nominal wage rate?
a. It doubled.
b. It increased by 50%.
c. It quadrupled.
d. It decreased.
e. It did not change.

19. Which of the following is true of the natural rate of unemployment?
a. It equals the actual rate of unemployment in short-run equilibrium.
b. It includes both frictional and structural unemployment.
c. It measures cyclical unemployment.
d. It changes with the business cycle.
e. It increases over time.

20. A Canadian recession will affect the United States' aggregate supply and demand in which of the following ways?

Aggregate supply	*Aggregate demand*
a. increase	increase
b. increase	decrease
c. decrease	increase
d. decrease	decrease
e. no change	decrease

21. Which of the following will shift the aggregate demand curve to the left?
a. expansionary monetary policy
b. an increase in the aggregate price level
c. an increase in the value of household assets
d. an increase in the consumer confidence index
e. a decrease in planned business investment

22. If the marginal propensity to consume in an economy is 0.9 and the government increases spending by $10 million, GDP will increase by how much?
a. $9 million
b. $10 million
c. $19 million
d. $90 million
e. $100 million

23. In the short run, an increase in aggregate demand will change the price level and aggregate output in which of the following ways?

Price level	*Aggregate output*
a. increase	increase
b. increase	decrease
c. decrease	increase
d. decrease	decrease
e. increase	no change

24. Which of the following is the most likely to cause a leftward shift in the long-run aggregate supply curve?
a. a decrease in the wage rate
b. a decrease in short-run aggregate supply
c. contractionary fiscal policy
d. a deadly disease that decreases the size of the labor force
e. a long-term decrease in demand

25. If an economy is in long-run equilibrium, how will an increase in aggregate demand affect real GDP and nominal wages in the long run?

Real GDP	*Nominal wages*
a. increase	increase
b. increase	decrease
c. decrease	increase
d. decrease	decrease
e. no change	increase

26. The long-run aggregate supply curve is always
a. vertical and below potential output.
b. horizontal and at potential output.
c. upward-sloping at all output levels.
d. vertical and at potential output.
e. horizontal at all output levels.

27. An economy experiences inflationary pressures when the equilibrium level of output is
a. too low.
b. above the full employment level of output.
c. equal to the full employment level of output.
d. decreasing.
e. in long-run equilibrium.

28. Which of the following policies might provide a remedy when the equilibrium output in an economy is below the potential level of output?
a. Decrease government spending.
b. Raise the federal funds rate.
c. Reduce transfer payments.
d. Cut taxes.
e. Sell more government securities.

29. Which of the following would cause the aggregate demand curve to shift to the left?
a. a decrease in taxes
b. an increase in consumer wealth
c. a decrease in consumer confidence
d. an increase in exports
e. a decrease in savings

30. Which of the following is a liability for a commercial bank?
a. deposits
b. loans
c. reserves
d. Treasury securities
e. its building and equipment

31. If the interest rate is 2%, what is the present value of $1 paid to you in one year?
   a. less than $1
   b. $1
   c. $1.02
   d. $1.04
   e. $1.20

32. Which of the following is a component of the M1 money supply?
   a. gold
   b. cash
   c. savings deposits
   d. Treasury bills
   e. certificates of deposit

33. Which of the following will decrease the ability of the banking system to create money?
   a. a decrease in the amount of cash people hold
   b. a decrease in the reserve requirement
   c. an increase in the amount of excess reserves held by banks
   d. an increase in banks' willingness to make loans
   e. a decrease in the discount rate

34. If the reserve ratio is 5%, what is the maximum amount of money that could be created by a new deposit of $1,000?
   a. $1,000
   b. $1,020
   c. $1,050
   d. $10,000
   e. $20,000

35. Advances in information technology such as ATM machines have had what effect on the demand for money and the interest rate?

	Money demand	*Interest rate*
a.	increase	increase
b.	increase	decrease
c.	decrease	increase
d.	decrease	decrease
e.	no change	decrease

36. Which of the following will increase the demand for money?
   a. a decrease in the aggregate price level
   b. an increase in the use of mobile devices such as iPhones for payments
   c. a decrease in the interest rate
   d. an increase in the supply of money
   e. an increase in real GDP

37. Which of the following will increase the interest rate in the market for loanable funds?
   a. a decrease in the expected rate of return from investment spending
   b. an increase in government budget deficits
   c. an increase in the aggregate savings rate
   d. a decrease in expected inflation
   e. an increase in capital inflows

38. Which of the following is true of the money supply curve?
   a. It shifts to the right when the interest rate increases.
   b. It shifts to the left when the savings rate decreases.
   c. It is vertical.
   d. It shows a positive relationship between the interest rate and the quantity of loanable funds.
   e. It shifts to the left when the Federal Reserve buys Treasury bills.

39. When government borrowing increases interest rates, it is known as
   a. crowding out.
   b. fiscal policy.
   c. expansionary monetary policy.
   d. contractionary monetary policy.
   e. financial regulation.

40. According to the quantity theory of money, the money supply times the velocity of money is equal to
   a. nominal GDP.
   b. real GDP.
   c. full employment real GDP.
   d. the price level.
   e. a constant value.

41. An open market sale of securities by the Federal Reserve will lead to which of the following?
   a. an increase in the demand for money
   b. an increase in interest rates
   c. a decrease in investment demand
   d. an increase in aggregate demand
   e. an increase in the price level

42. The Federal Reserve will take actions that cause the federal funds rate to rise in an attempt to
   a. increase unemployment.
   b. increase the money supply.
   c. reduce inflation.
   d. increase real GDP.
   e. encourage investment.

43. An increase in expected inflation is likely to have which of the following effects?
   a. shift the long-run Phillips curve to the right
   b. shift the short-run Phillips curve downward
   c. increase the actual inflation rate
   d. decrease the unemployment rate
   e. shift the short-run aggregate supply curve to the right

44. Which of the following policies could the Federal Reserve implement to combat inflation created by expansionary fiscal policy?
   a. Lower the reserve requirement.
   b. Raise the discount rate.
   c. Buy Treasury securities.
   d. Raise taxes.
   e. Reduce government spending.

45. Which of the following is a contractionary fiscal policy?
- **a.** raising the reserve requirement
- **b.** decreasing transfer payments
- **c.** decreasing taxes
- **d.** raising government spending
- **e.** increasing the federal funds rate

46. If a country currently has a positive national debt and a balanced budget, how would a decrease in taxes affect the country's deficit and debt?

	Deficit	*Debt*
a.	increase	increase
b.	increase	decrease
c.	decrease	increase
d.	decrease	decrease
e.	decrease	no change

47. A country's national debt is
- **a.** the amount the country owes to foreigners.
- **b.** the difference between the country's tax revenue and government spending in a given year.
- **c.** the sum of the country's past deficits and surpluses.
- **d.** always positive.
- **e.** higher when gross domestic product is increasing.

48. Which of the following is an example of expansionary monetary policy?
- **a.** decreasing taxes
- **b.** increasing government spending
- **c.** raising the discount rate
- **d.** lowering the reserve requirement
- **e.** selling Treasury securities

49. During a recession, the Federal Reserve might ________ its purchase of Treasury bills in order to ________ the Federal funds rate and ________ aggregate demand.

	Treasury bill purchases	*Federal funds rate*	*Aggregate demand*
a.	increase	decrease	increase
b.	increase	decrease	decrease
c.	decrease	decrease	increase
d.	decrease	increase	increase
e.	decrease	increase	decrease

50. The short-run Phillips curve shows a ________ relationship between the unemployment rate and the rate of ________.
- **a.** negative; interest
- **b.** positive; interest
- **c.** negative; employment
- **d.** positive; GDP growth
- **e.** negative; inflation

51. Which of the following is true of the long-run Phillips curve?
- **a.** It shows a negative relationship between the unemployment rate and the inflation rate.
- **b.** It shows a negative relationship between the unemployment rate and the interest rate.
- **c.** It shifts upward when expected inflation increases.
- **d.** It is vertical at the natural rate of unemployment.
- **e.** It shifts to the right when the Federal Reserve pursues expansionary monetary policy.

52. An increase in which of the following over time best describes economic growth?
- **a.** nominal GDP
- **b.** real GDP per capita
- **c.** nominal GDP per capita
- **d.** the labor force
- **e.** aggregate demand

53. Which of the following is true of an increase in labor productivity in an economy?
- **a.** It will shift the long-run aggregate supply curve to the left.
- **b.** It will decrease the wages of workers.
- **c.** It will reduce the size of the labor force.
- **d.** It will shift the production possibilities curve outward.
- **e.** It results from a decrease in the availability of capital.

54. Which of the following is most likely to lead to long-run economic growth?
- **a.** a more restrictive immigration policy
- **b.** higher trade barriers
- **c.** increased government funding of education
- **d.** contractionary fiscal policy
- **e.** negative net investment

55. Which of the following transactions will be recorded in the financial account of the United States?
- **a.** A U.S. firm sells $100 million worth of its product to Mexico.
- **b.** Chinese imports to the United States increase by $200 million.
- **c.** The wages paid by U.S. firms to workers in India increase by $20 million.
- **d.** Canada purchases $50 million of new U.S. Treasury bills.
- **e.** The United States' trade balance moves from deficit to surplus.

56. The exchange rate is the price of
- **a.** goods expressed in terms of another nation's currency.
- **b.** one nation's currency expressed in terms of another's.
- **c.** the same basket of goods purchased in two countries.
- **d.** exported goods, adjusted for inflation.
- **e.** imported goods expressed in the other country's currency.

57. Which of the following would cause the U.S. dollar to appreciate relative to the Canadian dollar?

a. a decrease in net capital flows from Canada to the United States

b. a decrease in the real interest rate in Canada relative to the United States

c. a decrease in the balance of payments on the current account in the United States

d. a doubling of prices in both Canada and the United States

e. an increase in exports from Canada to the United States

58. If a country's inflation rate rises, which of the following will happen to the demand for the country's currency and the value of the country's currency on the foreign exchange market?

	Demand	*Value*
a.	shift right	depreciate
b.	shift right	appreciate
c.	shift left	appreciate
d.	shift left	depreciate
e.	no change	depreciate

59. If foreign investors increase investment in the United States, what will happen to the value of the dollar in the foreign exchange market and U.S. net exports?

	Value of the U.S. dollar	*U.S. net exports*
a.	appreciate	increase
b.	appreciate	decrease
c.	depreciate	increase
d.	depreciate	decrease
e.	no change	no change

60. Which of the following is an example of U.S. direct foreign investment?

a. a U.S. citizen spending while traveling abroad

b. a U.S. manufacturer building a factory overseas

c. a U.S. investor purchasing corporate bonds from a Mexican company

d. a U.S. worker sending money to a family member living abroad

e. a U.S. bank loaning money to an international company

Free-Response Questions

1. Assume the country of Apland is currently in long-run equilibrium.

(a) Draw a correctly labeled production possibilities curve if Apland produces only wheat and oil. On your graph, label point *X*, a point that illustrates a productively efficient output combination for Apland.

(b) Draw a correctly labeled aggregate supply and aggregate demand graph for Apland. Show each of the following:

(i) equilibrium output, labeled Y_1

(ii) equilibrium price level, labeled PL_1

(c) Assume the government of Apland has a balanced budget and decides to reduce income taxes.

(i) What effect will the reduction in taxes have on Apland's budget?

(ii) Show the short-run effect of the reduction in taxes on your graph from part (b), labeling the new equilibrium output and price level Y_2 and PL_2, respectively.

(d) Draw a correctly labeled graph of the loanable funds market. Suppose the government borrows money to pay for the tax cut. Show the effect of this borrowing on your graph from part (c).

(i) Label the equilibrium interest rate before the government borrowing i_1.

(ii) Label the equilibrium interest rate after the government borrowing i_2.

(e) How will the change in the interest rate depicted in your graph from part (d) affect real GDP in the long run? Explain.

(10 points)

2. Suppose a manufacturing firm in the United States sells $5 million worth of its output to consumers in Mexico.

(a) How will this transaction affect each of the following?

(i) Mexico's current account balance

(ii) the United States' current account balance

(iii) aggregate demand in Mexico

(b) Suppose there is an increase in U.S. financial investment in Mexico.

(i) Draw a correctly labeled graph of the foreign exchange market for Mexican pesos and show how an increase in U.S. financial investment in Mexico affects equilibrium in the market.

(ii) What happens to the value of the Mexican peso relative to the U.S. dollar?

(6 points)

3. Assume the expected rate of inflation is zero.

(a) Draw a correctly labeled graph showing the short-run and long-run Phillips curves. On your graph, identify each of the following:

(i) the nonaccelerating inflation rate of unemployment, labeled *N*

(ii) a point on the short-run Phillips curve indicating an unemployment rate below the natural rate of unemployment, labeled *A*

(b) Now assume the inflation rate associated with point *A* in part (a) is incorporated into inflationary expectations. Show the effect of this change in expectations on your graph from part (a).

(5 points)

Enrichment Module

Module A: Financial Markets and Crises

Economics by Example:

"What Is the Role of Government?"

Hopefully this sampling of economics has kindled your interest in more than just exam content. If you've wondered what the recent financial crisis was all about, you'll enjoy Enrichment Module A, which tells the story of the Great Recession. The Financial Literacy Handbook that follows it will help you navigate your own financial situation. And each chapter of the companion book, *Economics by Example*, applies economic analysis to a real-world dilemma. While these readings cover material in greater depth than is expected for the current AP® exam, they provide interesting background and insights for subsequent coursework, and they offer advice for making good economic decisions and developing sound financial habits.

Shutterstock

ENRICHMENT MODULE

A Financial Markets and Crises

In this Module, you will learn to:

- Describe the importance of a well-functioning financial system
- List the causes of financial crises in the economy
- Identify the macroeconomic consequences of financial crises
- Explain the factors leading to the financial crisis of 2008

The Role of Financial Markets

These days, almost everyone is connected in some way to *financial markets*. When you receive a paycheck, pay a bill, borrow money, or use a credit card, the financial markets assist with the transaction. And a recent FDIC study found that about 91% of U.S. households have some form of checking or savings account.

In Module 22, we learned about the three tasks of a financial system: to reduce transactions costs, to reduce risk, and to provide liquidity. The financial system performs these tasks largely through financial intermediaries, such as banks and mutual funds. In Module 25, we looked at what banks do and how problems in the banking system can adversely affect the economy. Past problems have led to financial regulations that help to ensure a safe and efficient financial system. But what happens in an economy when its financial markets do not function well—or even worse, collapse? In this module we will take another look at the role of financial markets in the economy and the causes and consequences of financial crises, including the 2008 financial crisis.

The Importance of an Efficient Financial System

Financial markets are the markets (banking, stock, and bond) that channel private saving into investment spending.

A well-functioning financial system promotes the saving and investing required for long-run economic growth. Depository institutions such as banks are a major part of an economy's financial system and are necessary to facilitate the flow of funds from lenders to borrowers. Let's take a look at the role the banking system and other **financial markets**—the markets that channel private saving into investment spending—play in an economy and how problems in the financial system can result in macroeconomic downturns.

The Purpose of the Banking System

Banks and other depository institutions are financial intermediaries that use liquid assets in the form of deposits to finance the illiquid investments of borrowers. When individuals deposit their savings in a depository institution, they are providing that institution with a short-term loan. In turn, the depository institution uses those funds to make long-term loans to other borrowers. Depositors are paid interest on their deposits and lenders pay interest on their loans. Because depository institutions receive the difference between the lower interest rate paid to depositors and the higher interest rate received from borrowers, they earn profits by converting their short-term deposit liabilities into long-term loans. This conversion is known as **maturity transformation**. Because deposits are short-term loans, depositors can demand to be repaid at any time. However, the loans made by depository institutions are long-term, and borrowers cannot be forced to repay their loans until the end of the loan period.

Maturity transformation is the conversion of short-term liabilities into long-term assets.

A **shadow bank** is a financial institution that engages in maturity transformation but does not accept deposits.

Other financial institutions also engage in maturity transformation and are part of the banking system. But instead of taking deposits, these institutions—known as **shadow banks**—borrow funds in short-term credit markets in order to invest in longer-term assets. Like depository institutions, shadow banks can earn profits as a result of the difference between the amount paid to borrow in the short-term credit market and the return received from the long-term asset. Increasing profits in the shadow banking market since 1980 have led to a steady increase in shadow banking in the United States.

You may recall seeing the maturity transformation function of financial markets in the circular-flow diagram. Financial markets take private savings that would otherwise leak out of the circular flow and inject it back into the economy through loans. In this way, financial markets facilitate the investment that drives economic growth.

Doug Menuez/Photodisc/Getty Images

Depository institutions earn profits by turning short-term deposits into long-term loans.

Risks of the Banking System: Banking Crises

Because a well-functioning financial system is crucial to economic growth, we need to understand the risk to an economy of a banking system failure. Individual bank failures are not uncommon; banks fail every year, as shown in **Figure A.1**. In 2013, the Federal Deposit Insurance Corporation reported 24 bank failures, down from 51 failures in 2012. Like other businesses in the economy, banks can fail for a variety of reasons. However, there is a big difference between the failure of a single bank and the failure of the banking system.

Figure A.1 Bank Failures

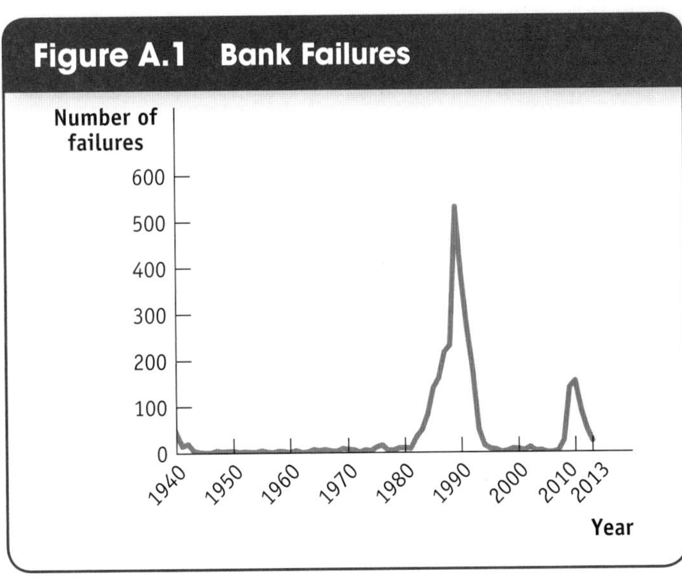

Fears of a bank failure can lead many depositors to panic and attempt to withdraw their funds at the same time, a phenomenon described in Module 25 as a *bank run*. The U.S. economy has experienced two periods of widespread bank failures: the National Banking era and the Great Depression. **Table A-1** on the next page shows the number of failures that occurred during each of those periods of panic. Current banking regulations protect U.S. depositors and the economy as a whole against bank runs. So modern bank failures generally take place through an orderly process overseen by regulators and often go largely unnoticed by depositors or the general public.

A *banking crisis* is much less common, and far more dangerous to the economy, than individual bank failures.

Table A.1 Bank Failures during the National Banking Era and the Great Depression

National Banking era (1883-1912)		Great Depression (1929-1941)	
Panic dates	**Number of failures**	**Panic dates**	**Number of failures**
September 1873	101	November–December 1930	806
May 1884	42	April–August 1931	573
November 1890	18	September–October 1931	827
May–August 1893	503	June–July 1932	283
October–December 1907	73*	February–March 1933	Bank Holiday

*This underestimates the scale of the 1907 crisis because it doesn't take into account the role of trusts.

A **banking crisis** occurs when a large part of the banking system fails.

A **banking crisis** occurs when a large part of the banking sector, either depository institutions or shadow banks, fails or threatens to fail. Banking crises that involve large segments of the banking system are comparatively rare. The failure of a large number of banks at the same time can occur either because many institutions make the same mistake or because mistakes from one institution spread to others through links in the financial system.

In an **asset bubble**, the price of an asset increases to a high level due to expectations of future price gains.

Banking crises often occur as a result of *asset bubbles.* In an **asset bubble**, the price of an asset, such as housing, is pushed above a reasonable level by investor expectations of future price increases. Eventually the market runs out of new buyers, the future price increases do not materialize, and the bubble bursts, leading to a decrease in the asset price. People who borrowed money to purchase the asset based on the expectation that prices would rise end up with a large debt when prices decrease instead. For example, individuals who borrow to purchase a house may find themselves "underwater," meaning that the value of their house is below the amount borrowed to purchase it.

Imagine that you purchase a house valued at $100,000 and pay for it with a $95,000 mortgage and a $5,000 down payment. At first, the value of your house increases, because investors demand more houses to resell at a profit after housing prices increase. In a few years, you have paid off some of your mortgage and you find yourself with a $93,000 mortgage on the same house; however, it is now worth $120,000! You have a more expensive house, but you didn't have to pay any more for it. You now have $27,000 of equity in your house. A few years later, the price increases that investors counted on for their profits end, so they stop buying houses. Demand in the housing market falls, and, with it, the value of your house. Now you find yourself living in the same house, but it is worth only $80,000. You have paid off more of your mortgage, but you still owe $90,000. You find yourself with a $90,000 mortgage on a house that is now worth $80,000. Your mortgage is underwater. If you stay in your house and continue to make your mortgage payments, being underwater may not make much difference to you. However, if you want or need to sell your house, it can become a real problem. The amount you would receive in the sale would not be enough to pay off your mortgage. You would actually have to *pay* to sell your house.

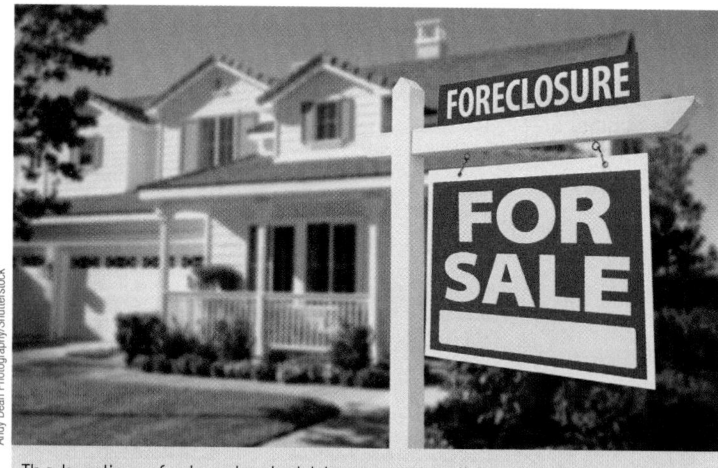

Andy Dean Photography/Shutterstock

The bursting of a housing bubble can cause the value of some homes to fall below the amount owed in loans for the homes. If the borrowers default on their loans, lenders take possession of the homes and sell them to recoup some of their losses.

The fall in asset prices from a bursting asset bubble exposes financial institutions to losses that can affect confidence in the financial system as a whole. For example, an economic downturn can cause people with underwater mortgages to default on them and abandon their houses rather than paying to sell them. When default rates on mortgages increase, financial institutions experience losses that undermine confidence in the financial system. If the loss in confidence is sufficiently severe, it can lead to an economy-wide banking crisis.

In an especially severe banking crisis, links in the financial system can increase the odds of even more bank failures. Bank failures can lead to a downward spiral, as each failure increases rumors and fears, thereby creating more bank failures. For example, when financial institutions have engaged in **leverage** by financing investments with borrowed funds, the institutions that loaned the funds may recall their loans if they are worried about default from failure of the borrowing institution. In addition, when financial institutions are in trouble, they try to reduce debt and raise cash by selling assets. When many banks try to sell similar assets at the same time, prices fall. The decrease in asset prices further hurts the financial position of banks, reinforcing the downward spiral in the banking system. Institutions in financial markets are linked to each other through their mutual dependence on confidence in the banking system and the value of long-term assets.

A financial institution engages in **leverage** when it finances its investments with borrowed funds.

As we have discussed, a well-developed financial system is a central part of a well-functioning economy. However, banking systems come with an inherent risk of banking crises. And banking crises, when left unchecked, can lead to a more widespread *financial crisis*.

Financial Crises: Consequences and Prevention

Some economists believe that to have a developed financial system is to face the risk of financial crises. Understanding the causes and consequences of financial crises is a key to understanding how they can be prevented.

What Is a Financial Crisis?

A **financial crisis** is a sudden and widespread disruption of financial markets. Such a crisis can occur when people suddenly lose faith in the ability of financial institutions to provide liquidity by bringing together those with cash to offer and those who need it. Since the banking system provides liquidity for buyers and sellers of everything from homes and cars to stocks and bonds, banking crises can easily turn into more widespread financial crises, as happened in 2008. In addition, an increase in the number and size of shadow banks in the economy can increase the scope and severity of financial crises, because shadow banks are not subject to the same regulations as depository institutions.

A **financial crisis** is a sudden and widespread disruption of financial markets.

The Consequences of Financial Crises

Financial crises have a significant negative effect on the economy and are closely associated with recessions. Historically, the origins of the worst economic downturns, such as the Great Depression, were tied to severe financial crises that led to decreased output and high unemployment (especially long-term unemployment). Recessions caused by financial crises tend to inflict sustained economic damage, and recovery from them can be very slow. **Figure A.2** on the next page shows the unemployment and duration associated with selected banking crises around the world.

When the financial system fails, there can be an economy-wide **credit crunch**, meaning that borrowers lose access to credit—either they cannot get credit at all, or they must pay high interest rates on loans. The lack of available or affordable credit in turn causes consumers and businesses to cut back on spending and investing, which leads to a recession. In addition, a financial crisis can lead to a recession because of a decrease in the price of assets. Decreases in housing prices are especially significant because real estate is often an individual's largest asset. Consumers who become poorer as a result of the decrease in the price of housing respond by reducing their spending to pay off debt and rebuild their assets, deepening the recession.

A **credit crunch** occurs when potential borrowers can't get credit or must pay very high interest rates.

Finally, financial crises can also lead to a decrease in the effectiveness of expansionary monetary policy intended to combat a recession. Typically, the Fed decreases the target interest rate to provide an incentive to increase spending during a recession.

Figure A.2 Episodes of Banking Crises and Unemployment

Economists Carmen Reinhart and Kenneth Rogoff have compared employment performance across several countries in the aftermath of a number of severe banking crises. For each country, the bar on the left shows the rise in the unemployment rate during and following the crisis, and the bar on the right shows how long it took for unemployment to begin to fall. On average, severe banking crises have been followed by a 7 percentage point rise in the unemployment rate, and in many cases it has taken four years or more before unemployment even begins to fall, let alone returns to precrisis levels.

Source: Carmen M. Reinhart and Kenneth S. Rogoff, "The Aftermath of Financial Crises," *American Economic Review* 99, no. 2 (2009): 466–472.

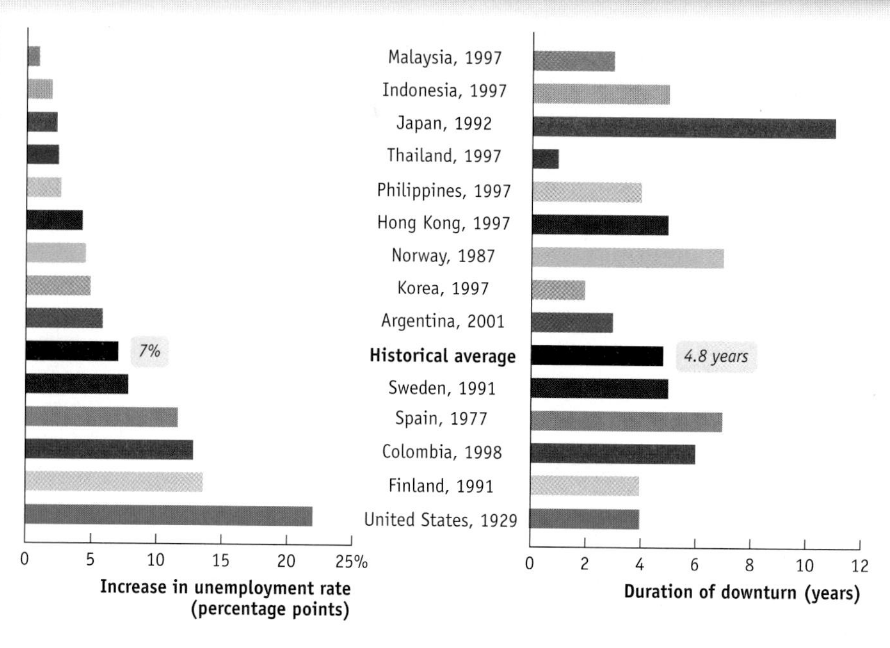

However, with a financial crisis, depositors, depository institutions, and borrowers all lose confidence in the system. As a result, even very low interest rates may not stimulate lending or borrowing in the economy.

Government Regulation of Financial Markets

Before the Great Depression, the government pursued a laissez-faire approach to banking. That is, the government let market forces determine the success or failure of banks, just as they did in other markets. However, since the Great Depression, considerable government regulation of financial markets has been implemented to prevent the severe economic downturns that can result from financial crises. Governments take three major actions to diminish the effects of banking crises: they act as a lender of last resort, guarantee deposits, and provide private credit market financing.

When governments act as a lender of last resort (usually through a central bank, such as the Federal Reserve), they provide funds to banks that are unable to borrow through private credit markets. Access to credit can help solvent banks—banks that have assets in excess of their liabilities—withstand bank runs without requiring them to sell off assets. In the case of financially unsound banks that are truly insolvent and will eventually go bankrupt, the government creates confidence in the banking system by guaranteeing the banks' liabilities. Deposit guarantees assure depositors that they will receive their deposits, preventing possible bank runs that would result from fear that deposits could be lost. Finally, governments have the ability to provide credit to shadow banks and to purchase private debt to keep the economy afloat when a banking crisis causes private credit markets to dry up.

The 2008 Financial Crisis

In 2008, the combination of a burst housing market bubble, a loss of faith in the liquidity of financial institutions, and an unregulated shadow banking system led to a widespread disruption of financial markets.

Causes of the 2008 Financial Crisis

The collapse of Lehman Brothers—a large shadow bank—set off the 2008 financial crisis, first in the United States and eventually across the globe. Although a number of factors led to the bank's collapse and the subsequent worldwide economic downturn, economists have identified four major causes of the 2008 financial crisis:

1. Macroeconomic conditions
2. A housing bubble
3. Financial system linkages
4. Failure of government regulation

The economy experienced a long period of low inflation, stable growth, and low global interest rates prior to the 2008 financial crisis. These macroeconomic conditions encouraged risk taking by shadow banks because they made it easy and cheap to borrow money. The banks searched for new ways to invest the funds they borrowed from short-term credit markets to earn higher returns in financial markets. One way to invest was through **securitization**, assembling a group of loans into a pool and selling shares of that pool to investors. Before the 2008 crisis, Lehman Brothers had been borrowing heavily in short-term credit markets and investing in subprime mortgages. **Subprime lending** had been a part of the banking industry for a long time, but subprime borrowing increased in the period leading up to the crisis. Subprime mortgages started to be packaged into so-called low-risk securities by pooling them together as **collateralized debt obligations**. These debt obligations are a type of financial **derivative**, a financial contract that has value based on the performance of another asset, index, or interest rate. Unfortunately, the shadow banks invested in these derivatives without accurately assessing their risk. When the real estate bubble burst, people began to default on their subprime mortgages and the value of the collateralized debt obligations fell. Because real estate markets represent a large part of the economy and shadow banks had invested heavily in subprime mortgages, the defaults quickly exposed the fragility of the financial system.

Securitization involves assembling a pool of loans and selling shares of that pool to investors.

Subprime lending involves lending to home-buyers who don't meet the usual criteria for being able to afford their payments.

A **collateralized debt obligation** is an asset-backed security tied to corporate debt or mortgages.

A **derivative** is a financial contract that has value based on the performance of another asset, index, or interest rate.

In 2008, when rumors of Lehman's exposure in the housing market spread, the shadow bank was no longer able to borrow in short-term credit markets to finance its long-term obligations. Without access to credit, Lehman Brothers went bankrupt.

Chains of debt linked Lehman to other financial institutions. **Credit default swaps** had been created to spread the risk of default on loans, but in fact they concentrated that risk. AIG was a large insurance company that provided those swaps. When the housing bubble burst, the large number of defaults caused AIG to collapse soon after Lehman Brothers.

A **credit default swap** is an agreement that the seller will compensate the buyer in the event of a loan default.

The 2008 crisis was like a traditional bank run—except that it was in the shadow banking system. The fall of Lehman Brothers led to a credit freeze, withdrawals of mutual funds, and a fall in derivative prices.

Finally, relaxed regulation of investment banks in the shadow banking sector failed to prevent the start and spread of the financial crisis. Prior to 2008, risk taking by shadow banks increased for several reasons. To begin with, given the vital importance of the financial system to the economy as a whole, many people thought the government would step in to prevent severe problems. That is, large financial institutions were considered "too big to fail." This led to the problem of **moral hazard**, which exists when a party takes excessive risks because it believes it will not bear all of the costs that could result. At the same time, the large profits earned by shadow banks further encouraged increased risk taking. Initially, the high-risk shadow banking activities were not a problem, because economic conditions were good. When the housing bubble burst, however, everything changed. It became clear that derivatives, which were thought to mitigate or eliminate default risk, only hid it. Because much of the existing government regulation did not apply to shadow banks, it could not prevent their activities from continuing to crisis.

Moral hazard involves a distortion of incentives when someone else bears the costs of lack of care or effort.

Figure A.3 Unemployment in the Aftermath of the 2008 Crisis

After 2008, the unemployment rate increased dramatically and remained high. Long-term unemployment, measured by the percentage of the unemployed who were out of work for 27 weeks or longer, increased at the same time. By 2011, almost half of all unemployed workers were long-term unemployed.

Source: Bureau of Labor Statistics.

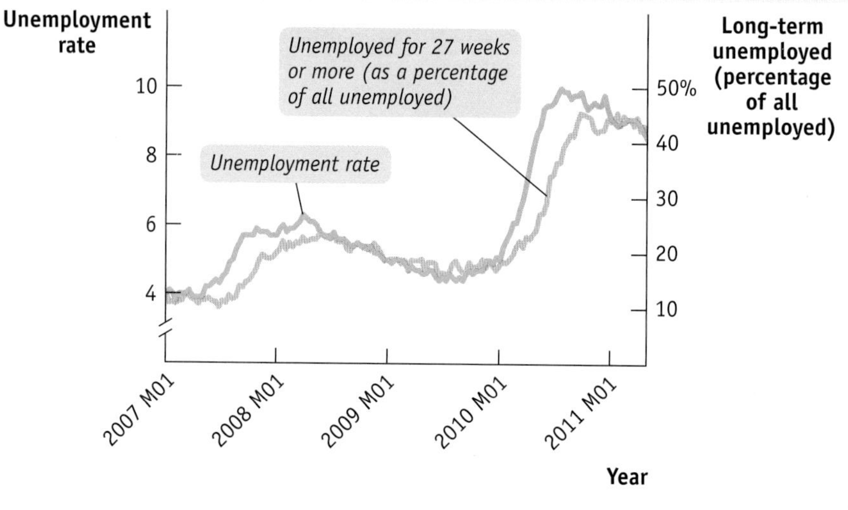

Consequences of the 2008 Financial Crisis

The 2008 financial crisis caused significant, prolonged damage to economies across the globe, with consequences that continued years later. For example, by the end of 2009, the United States' economy had lost over 7 million jobs, causing the unemployment rate to increase dramatically and remain high for years after, as shown in **Figure A.3**. In particular, the crisis led to an increase in long-term unemployment, which rose to almost half of the total unemployment in the economy.

The recession in the U.S. economy sent ripples throughout the world, and the years since the recession have seen only a weak recovery. For example, **Figure A.4** shows that it took more than five years for the United States to get back to the precrisis level of real GDP. In addition, in 2011–2012, fear of a second crisis related to public debt in Southern Europe and Ireland further hampered economic recovery from the crisis.

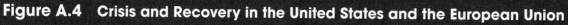

Figure A.4 Crisis and Recovery in the United States and the European Union

In the aftermath of the 2008 financial crisis, aggregate output in the European Union and in the United States fell dramatically. Real GDP, shown here as an index with each economy's peak precrisis quarter set to 100, declined by more than 5%. By late 2011, real GDP in the United States had only barely recovered to precrisis levels, and aggregate output in the European Union had still not reached its precrisis peak.

Sources: Bureau of Economic Analysis; Eurostat.

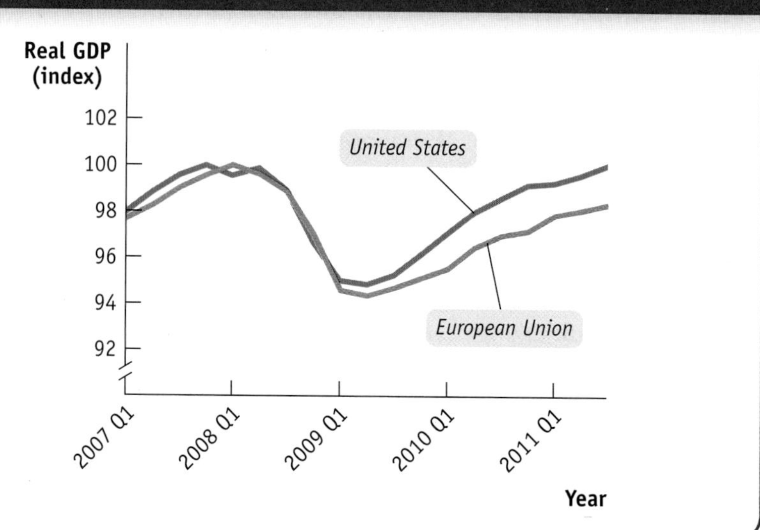

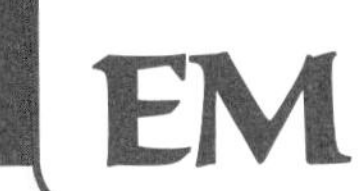

Government Response to the 2008 Financial Crisis

The intervention of the U.S. government and the Federal Reserve at the start of the financial crisis helped to calm financial markets. The federal government bailed out some failing financial institutions and instituted the Troubled Asset Relief Program (TARP), which involved the purchase of assets and equity from financial institutions to help strengthen the markets.

The Federal Reserve pursued an expansionary monetary policy, decreasing the federal funds rate to zero. The Fed also implemented programs to foster improved conditions in financial markets, significantly changing its own balance sheet. For example, the Fed acted as a lender of last resort by providing liquidity to financial institutions, it provided credit to borrowers and investors in key credit markets, and it put downward pressure on long-term interest rates by purchasing longer-term securities.

Financial Crises and the Future

The 2008 financial crisis highlighted the importance of financial markets and the need to ensure a well-functioning financial system. In 2010, the Wall Street Reform and Consumer Protection Act, known as the Dodd-Frank Act, was enacted to overhaul financial regulation in the aftermath of the crisis. The Dodd-Frank Act contains four main elements:

1. Consumer protection
2. Derivatives regulation
3. Shadow bank regulation
4. Resolution authority over nonbank financial institutions

Increases in the complexity of financial instruments played a large role in the financial crisis of 2008, as consumers purchased assets they either didn't understand or were not able to afford. The Consumer Financial Protection Bureau was created by the Dodd-Frank Act to protect borrowers from abusive practices that became prevalent due to the complexity of these instruments. The proliferation of derivatives was another important factor in the crisis, because derivatives, which had been designed to spread risk, worked to conceal risk prior to 2008. As a result, the new law also contains stipulations designed to make financial markets transparent so that asset risk is no longer concealed.

Shadow bank regulation and resolution authority extend government control during financial crises to cover nonbank financial institutions. The Dodd-Frank Act gives a special panel the ability to designate financial institutions that have the potential to create a banking crisis. These designated shadow banks are then subject to banklike regulation. In addition, the government now has the authority to seize control of financial institutions that require a bailout during a crisis, the way it already did with commercial banks. This power, called resolution authority, allows governments to guarantee a wide range of financial institution debts in a crisis.

Going forward, financial regulation faces several challenges. First of all, the idea that a financial institution can be "too big to fail" is still prevalent and the problem of moral hazard still exists. And, while new regulation has been put in place in the United States, it is not clear how these regulations can or will be applied in other countries. The 2008 financial crisis highlighted the global nature of financial markets and the worldwide linkages that must be acknowledged in order for regulation to be effective.

Finally, regulation that addresses what happened in 2008 may not be effective in addressing whatever financial crisis might loom in the future. World economies and world financial markets are ever changing; regulation must be dynamic and must be able to respond to the current situation, not merely the most recent crisis.

The Dodd-Frank Act created the Consumer Financial Protection Agency to protect borrowers from abusive practices that became more prevalent as financial instruments became more complex.

FYI The Day the Lights Went Out at Lehman

On Friday night, September 12, 2008, an urgent meeting was held in the New York Federal Reserve Bank's headquarters on Wall Street. In attendance were the outgoing Bush administration's Treasury secretary, Hank Paulson, and the then head of the New York Fed, Tim Geithner (later the Treasury secretary in the Obama administration), along with the heads of the country's largest investment banks. Lehman Brothers was rapidly imploding, and Paulson had called the meeting in the hope of pressing the investment bankers into a deal that would, like the LTCM bailout described in Module 26, avert a messy bankruptcy.

Since the forced sale six months earlier of the nearly bankrupt investment bank Bear Stearns to a healthier bank, Lehman had been under increasing pressure. Like Bear Stearns, Lehman had invested heavily in subprime mortgages and other assets tied to real estate. And when Bear Stearns fell as its creditors began calling in its loans and other banks refused to lend to it, many wondered if Lehman would fall next.

In July 2008, Lehman reported a \$2.8 billion loss for the second quarter of 2008 (the months April–June), precipitating a 54% fall in its stock price. As its share price fell, Lehman's sources of credit began to dry up and its trading operations withered. The CEO of Lehman, Richard Fuld, began a desperate search for a healthier bank to buy shares of Lehman and provide desperately needed funding. By early September 2008, Lehman's loss for the third quarter had risen to \$3.9 billion. On September 9, J.P. Morgan Chase, a far healthier investment bank that had been Lehman's major source of financing for its trades, demanded \$5 billion in cash as extra collateral or it would freeze Lehman's accounts and cut off its credit. Unable to come up with the cash, Lehman teetered on the edge of bankruptcy.

In the September 12 meeting, Treasury Secretary Paulson urged the investment bankers to put together a package to purchase Lehman's bad assets. But, fearing for their own survival in an extremely turbulent market, they refused unless Paulson would give them a government guarantee on the value of Lehman's assets. The Treasury had made the Bear Stearns sale possible by arranging a huge loan from the New York Fed to its purchaser. This time, facing a backlash from Congress over "bailing out profligate bankers," Paulson refused to provide government help. And in the wee hours of Monday morning, September 15, 2008, Lehman went down, declaring the most expensive bankruptcy in history.

Yet, as Fuld had earlier warned Paulson, the failure of Lehman unleashed the furies. That same day, the U.S. stock market fell 504 points, triggering an increase in bank borrowing costs and a run on money market funds and financial institutions around the world. By Tuesday, Paulson agreed to an \$85 billion bailout of another major corporation, the foundering AIG, at the time the world's largest insurer. Before the markets stabilized months later, the U.S. government made \$250 billion of capital infusions to bolster major U.S. banks. Whether or not Paulson made a catastrophic mistake by not acting to save Lehman is a matter likely to be debated for years to come.

Alex Wong/Getty Images News

Richard Fuld, the head of Lehman, testified before a congressional panel on how the collapse of Lehman precipitated a financial panic.

ENRICHMENT MODULE A Review

Check Your Understanding

1. Draw a circular-flow diagram that includes households, firms, factor markets, markets for goods and services, and financial markets. Circle the section of the diagram that illustrates maturity transformation and briefly explain the maturity transformation process.
2. What are the four major causes of the 2008 financial crisis? Briefly describe each one.
3. What are the four main elements of the Dodd-Frank Act? Briefly describe each one.

Discussion Starters

1. Explain why an efficient financial system is important.
2. What is a shadow bank? Give several specific examples of shadow banks.
3. Explain how an asset bubble can lead to an economy-wide banking crisis.
4. What are some of the possible consequences of a financial crisis?
5. Define moral hazard. Explain the role of moral hazard in the 2008 financial crisis.

Financial Literacy Handbook

By Laura Adams ("The Money Girl")

PART 1

Take It to the Bank

A bank account is a safe and convenient place to accumulate savings and to keep the money you need to pay bills and to make everyday cash purchases. Keeping a large amount of cash at home or in your wallet isn't as safe because your money could be lost or stolen.

Overview of Banks

Banks can be small community institutions that have just one or a few locations or they can be huge companies with thousands of branch locations all over the country. There are Internet-only banks with no physical location to visit and only a website address. In addition to holding your money, banks also offer a variety of services to help you manage your money.

Banks stay in business by using the money you deposit to make a profit by offering loans to other customers or businesses. They lend to customers who want to borrow money for big purchases like cars or homes. They also lend to small and large businesses for making purchases like inventory and equipment.

When you take a loan from a bank, you're charged interest, which is an additional charge on top of the amount you borrow. To stay profitable, a bank must receive more money in interest from borrowers than it pays out in the form of loans to customers.

Despite the benefits banking institutions offer, almost one-third of Americans are "unbanked" or "underbanked" and use no or few basic financial services. According to the Federal Deposit Insurance Corporation (FDIC), these individuals typically have low income. FDIC data shows that for households with annual income of less than $15,000 per year, 28% have no bank account and another 22% use less than a full range of banking services.

Consumers may not use banks for a variety of reasons, including the lack of a conveniently located branch office or the desire to avoid bank fees. However, some potential customers do not take advantage of the services banks offer because they don't understand how banks work or how much nonbank alternatives cost. In this section you'll learn why going without banking services is both expensive and inconvenient.

Finance Tip

You can use the Electronic Deposit Insurance Estimator (EDIE) at myfdicinsurance.gov to make sure your deposits in various bank accounts are fully covered by the FDIC.

Types of Financial Institutions

When you're ready to open a bank account, there are three main types of institutions to choose from: savings and loan associations, commercial banks, and credit unions.

Savings and Loan Associations and Commercial Banks

Savings and loan associations (S&Ls) and commercial banks operate under federal and state regulations. They specialize in taking deposits for checking and savings accounts, making home loans (known as mortgages) and other personal and business loans, facilitating the flow of money into and out of accounts, and providing various financial services for individuals and businesses.

Have you ever wondered what would happen to your money if your bank went out of business or failed? Most banks insure your deposits through the FDIC up to the maximum amount allowed by law, which is currently $250,000 per depositor per account type for each insured bank.

FDIC insurance means that if your bank closes for any reason, you won't lose your money. You'll know a bank is properly insured if it displays the FDIC logo at a local branch, on advertising materials, or online. To learn more, visit fdic.gov.

Credit Unions

Credit unions are nonprofit organizations owned by their customers, who are called members. Credit union members typically have something in common, like working for the same employer, working in the same profession, or living in the same geographic area. You must qualify to become a member of a credit union to be able to use its financial services.

Credit unions offer many of the same services as commercial banks and S&Ls. Most also offer insurance for your deposits through the National Credit Union Administration (NCUA), which gives the same coverage (up to $250,000 per depositor) as the FDIC. Just look for the official NCUA sign at credit union branches and websites. To learn more, visit ncua.gov.

Why Keep Money in a Bank?

While it's possible to keep your money at home and manage your personal finances using a cash-only system, here are five reasons why it's better to use an insured bank or credit union:

1. **Safety**: Money you deposit in a bank account is safe from loss, theft, or destruction. Even the best hiding places for money can be found by a thief or be susceptible to a flood or fire.
2. **Insurance**: Deposits covered by FDIC or NCUA insurance are protected by a fund backed by the full faith and credit of the U.S. government. So if your bank closes and can't return your money, the FDIC or NCUA will pay the insured portion of your deposits.
3. **Convenience**: Money in a bank account can be accessed in a variety of ways. You can make deposits by visiting a local branch or setting up electronic direct deposit. Some institutions have remote deposit services where you deposit a paper check by taking a picture of it with a mobile device or scanner and uploading it online. You can use online bill pay to send funds in the form of a paper check or electronic transfer.
4. **Low cost**: Different banks offer accounts with a variety of benefits, such as interest paid, debit cards, online banking, account alerts, bill pay, and overdraft protection. Many bank services are free, which makes using a bank to get cash or pay bills less expensive than alternatives, such as a check cashing service. Some check cashers charge a fee that's a percentage of the check value, plus an additional flat fee. For instance, cashing a $1,000 check at a check cashing service could cost 1.5%, or $15.
5. **Business relationship**: Building a relationship with a bank may give you the opportunity to qualify for premium banking services, loans, and credit cards that can improve your financial future.

Types of Bank Accounts

The two main types of bank accounts are deposit accounts and non-deposit accounts.

Deposit Accounts

Deposit accounts allow you to add money to or withdraw money from your account at any time. Examples of deposit accounts are checking, savings, and money market accounts.

Checking Account A checking account, also known as a payment account, is the most common type of bank account. It's a real workhorse that allows you to make purchases or pay bills using paper checks, a debit or check card, online bill pay, automatic transfer, or cash withdrawal from an automatic teller machine (**ATM**). The institution keeps a record of your deposits and withdrawals and sends you a monthly account statement. The best checking accounts offer no fees, no minimum balance requirement, and free checks.

Savings Account A savings account is a safe place to keep money, and it earns you interest. It doesn't give you as much flexibility or access to your money as a checking account. While there's typically no limit on the number of deposits you can make into a savings account, you can only make up to six withdrawals or transfers per month. Savings accounts typically don't come with paper checks, but they may offer a debit or ATM card that you can use a maximum of three times per month.

Finance Tip

Did you know that funds deposited electronically into your bank account are available sooner than those deposited by a paper check?

Finance Tip

Rewards checking accounts pay a relatively high rate of interest when you follow certain requirements, such as receiving e-statements, having at least one direct deposit per month, and using a debit card for a certain number of purchases each month.

Finance Tip

Use the power of the Internet to shop for the best bank accounts. Sites like checkingfinder.com and bankrate.com gather up-to-date information about the best offers nationwide.

If your balance dips below a certain amount, you may be charged a monthly fee. The institution keeps a record of your transactions and sends you a monthly account statement.

Savings accounts are perfect for your short-term savings goals, like a down payment on a car or holiday gift-giving. Interest rates on savings accounts vary, so it's important to shop around locally or online for the highest offers. Interest rates on savings accounts are variable, which means they're subject to change and can decrease after you open an account. (You'll learn more about compounded interest in Part 2 of this handbook.)

Money Market Account (MMA) A money market account has features of both a savings and a checking account. You can make up to six withdrawals or transfers per month, including payments by check, debit card, and online bill pay. You're paid relatively high interest rates, especially if you maintain a high minimum balance, such as $5,000 or more.

Money market accounts are a great choice when you start to accumulate more savings. Interest rates vary and are subject to change, so always do your research to find the best money market account offer.

There are also special types of deposit accounts known as *time deposits*, where you're restricted from withdrawing your money for a certain period of time.

Certificate of Deposit (CD) A certificate of deposit is a time deposit that requires you to give up the use of your money for a fixed term or period of time, such as 3 months, 12 months, or 5 years. In exchange for this restricted access, banks typically pay higher interest rates than for savings or money market accounts (where you can withdraw money on demand). In general, the longer the term of the CD, the higher the interest rate you receive.

For instance, a six-month CD might pay 1% interest and a five-year CD might pay 3.5%. If you take money out of a CD before the end of the term, or maturity date, you generally have to pay a penalty. So before putting money in a CD, be sure that you won't need it until after the maturity date and that you understand all the charges and fees associated with early withdrawals.

Non-deposit Accounts

Many banks offer non-deposit accounts that can be investments, such as stocks, bonds, or mutual funds. It's important to remember that non-deposit products are never insured by the FDIC or NCUA and may lose some or all of their value.

How Old Do You Have to Be to Open a Bank Account?

Many banks offer checking and savings accounts for young people. Some require you to open a joint account with a parent or guardian; however, some offer independent student accounts when you reach age 16.

The earlier you open up a bank account and start saving on a regular basis, the better. Having a checking and savings account established before you go to college will help you manage money and make necessary purchases. Money you earn from a job, get from a relative, or receive as a gift can be set aside for your future needs.

How to Maintain a Checking Account

It's important to maintain your checking account on a regular basis so you know exactly how much money you have at all times. You should reconcile each monthly statement's ending balance against your records so you never miss a transaction, such as an unexpected fee. Never write checks or make debit card purchases that exceed your balance.

Using ATM and Debit Cards

An ATM card allows you to use ATMs to make deposits, check your account balance, transfer funds between accounts, and make cash withdrawals 24 hours a day. You typically have to pay a fee for each ATM cash withdrawal at banks other than your own—unless your bank gives you free access to a network of ATMs or reimburses your ATM fees.

FYI What Is a Prepaid Card?

A prepaid card may look like a debit or credit card, but it isn't linked to a bank or credit account. Prepaid cards may come loaded with a set value or may require you to add money to the card. The card value goes down each time you make a purchase. Prepaid cards have many fees—such as a purchase fee, monthly fees, ATM withdrawal fees, transaction fees, balance inquiry fees, and more—which generally makes them more expensive to use than a bank debit card.

A debit card, also known as a check card, looks like a credit card because it typically has a MasterCard or VISA logo. A debit card can be used just like an ATM card or to make purchases where accepted by merchants. When you use a debit card, money is deducted immediately from your bank account and credited to the merchant's account. This reduces your available balance.

If you make a debit card purchase for more than your available balance, your transaction will be declined. However, if you enroll in overdraft protection, you authorize your bank to cover your transaction—but at the cost of a large service fee.

Writing Checks

With the popularity of debit cards and online banking, people don't use paper checks as much anymore. However, if you need to write one, it's easy to fill in the blanks. Always write clearly using dark ink and never cross out a mistake–it's better to start over with a fresh check.

Reconciling Your Checking Account

Each month you'll receive a statement that shows activity in your account. The statement

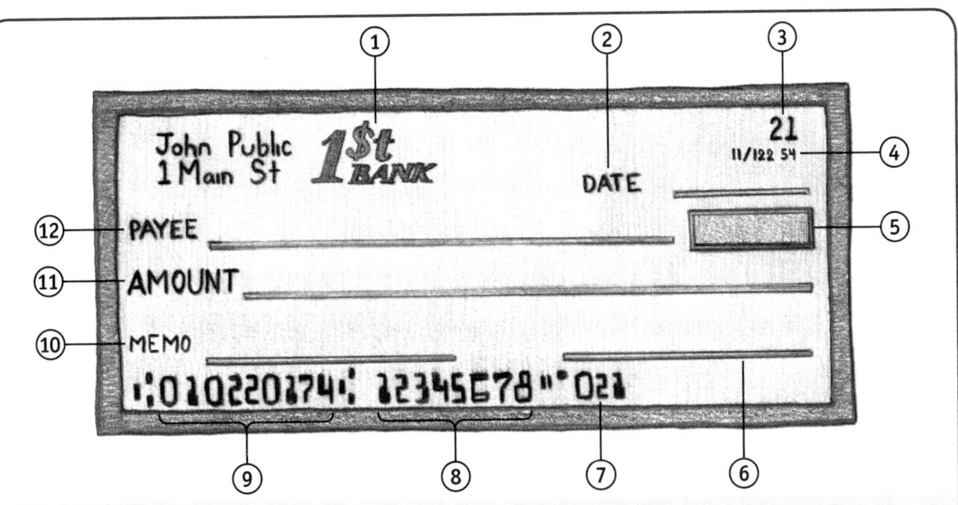

1. **Bank name**: This may be preprinted on each check.
2. **Date**: Enter the month, day, and year.
3. **Check number**: If your checks don't have preprinted numbers, label them with consecutive numbers.
4. **Bank ID numbers**: This may be preprinted on each check.
5. **Amount**: Enter the amount to pay in figures.
6. **Signature**: Sign your name exactly as you signed it on documents you completed when you opened the account.
7. **Check number**: This may be preprinted on each check.
8. **Account number**: This should be preprinted on each check.
9. **Bank routing number**: This should be preprinted on each check to identify your bank's unique routing number.
10. **Memo**: Write a quick note to remind yourself of the reason for the check.
11. **Amount**: Enter the amount to pay in words and draw a line over unused space so nothing can be added later.
12. **Payee**: Enter the person or company to pay.

Tips for Secure Mobile Banking

Online and mobile banking isn't particularly risky but it is important to be careful when making online transactions. Use these tips to avoid risk when you're making purchases or banking using a mobile device:

1. **Use a secured network** instead of public Wi-Fi so your personal information can't be exposed to a criminal. The web address of a secured network begins with "https" instead of "http."
2. **Guard your mobile device** like your wallet, because it may contain information to access your accounts if it were lost or stolen.
3. **Create strong passwords** for your devices (to turn them on or wake them from sleep mode) and for your online accounts that are at least 8 characters long and use a combination of letters, numbers, and symbols.
4. **Don't lend your mobile devices** or share your passwords with anyone you don't know or trust.
5. **Log off** from financial accounts and close the browser window or app when you finish using them.
6. **Only download trusted apps** from sources like your bank or other legitimate financial institutions.
7. **Delete text messages** from your bank once you've read them.
8. **Don't divulge personal information** such as your social security number or account number. A financial institution or authorized agency will never ask you for personal information over the Internet or even on the phone.

should include a reconciliation worksheet that you can follow. Reconciling or balancing your account is the process of making sure the information on the bank statement matches your records. Always keep track of your deposits, checks, debit card purchases, ATM withdrawals, and fees. You can use a paper or digital check register. Most financial software programs allow you to automatically download bank and credit card account transactions. Not having to enter each of your transactions manually saves time and makes account reconciliation simple.

Overdraft Protection

Having overdraft protection means your debit card purchases and ATM withdrawals will be processed, even if your bank account balance isn't high enough to cover them. You must give written permission for overdraft protection because using it comes with expensive nonsufficient funds (NSF) fees. However, you can opt out of overdraft protection and avoid the potential charges. This means that if you try to use your debit card and your account balance is too low, you will not be permitted to make the purchase.

How to Choose the Best Bank

Banks provide many financial services and may charge a fee for some of them. It's important to shop around to find a bank that charges the lowest fees for services you plan to use frequently and pays the highest rate of interest.

Common Banking Terms to Know

Banks use certain vocabulary that you should be familiar with so that you understand all you can about where your money is held. Here are several key banking terms to know:

account statement—a paper or electronic record of account activity, service charges, and fees, issued on a regular basis

bounced or **bad check**—slang for a check that is rejected due to insufficient funds in the account

check—a paper form that authorizes a bank to release funds from the payer's account to the payee

cleared or **canceled checks**—paper checks that have been processed and paid by a bank

deposit slip or **ticket**—a printed form you complete that lists cash and checks to be deposited into an account

direct deposit—an electronic payment method typically used by an employer or government agency

electronic payment or **transaction**—a deposit or charge to an account that happens without the use of a paper form

endorsement—the payee's signature on the back of a paper check that is required to deposit or to take cash out of an account

payee—the person or company to whom a check is made payable

payer—the person or company who writes a check or pays another party

reconciliation—the process of comparing a bank account statement to your records and resolving any differences until you determine an identical account balance

service charge (or maintenance charge)—a fee charged by a bank to maintain your account

Part 1 Review Questions

1. How do banks make money?
2. Describe the similarities and differences between commercial banks and credit unions. Why do you think someone would choose one over the other?
3. In your own words, describe why it's better to keep your money in a financial institution instead of holding large amounts of cash.
4. Give several reasons why someone would open more than one type of bank account.
5. Come up with at least five questions you should ask before deciding to put your money in a financial institution.

Project

Find and research several kinds of banks in your area. How many savings and loan associations, commercial banks, and credit unions are in your town? Speak to the manager of each financial institution. Approximately how many customers does each have? What services do they provide their customers? How do they attract new customers?

PART 2

Get Interested in Money Math

Whether you're shopping at the grocery store, choosing a car loan, or figuring out how much to invest for retirement, managing money comes down to the numbers. Making the best decisions for your personal finances always begins by doing some simple money math.

Pay Attention to Interest

When you borrow money by taking out a loan for college, a car, or any other loan, you'll be charged interest. Additionally, if you don't pay off a credit card balance in full by the statement due date, you'll also be charged interest on the balance owed. Lenders make money by charging interest to a borrower as a percentage of the amount of the loan, or the credit card balance due.

When you deposit money in a bank account that pays interest—for example, a savings account or CD—you become the lender and the bank is the borrower. The bank pays you interest for keeping money on deposit.

Interest is typically expressed as an annual percentage rate, or APR. To keep more of your money, it's wise to shop around and borrow at the lowest interest rates. Likewise, lend your money and deposit it in the bank that offers the highest possible interest rates, so you earn more.

How Simple and Compound Interest Work

But how does your money actually earn interest? There are two basic types of interest: simple interest and compound interest.

Simple Interest Simple interest is, well, pretty simple! That's because it's calculated on the original principal amount.

Say you borrow $100 from your friend John at a 5% annual rate of simple interest for a term of 3 years. Here's how the interest would be calculated for the loan:

Loan year	Principal amount (dollars)	APR (percent)	Annual interest earned (dollars)	Balance due (dollars)
1	$100	5%	$5	$105
2	100	5	5	110
3	100	5	5	115

Notice that the 5% APR is always calculated on the original principal amount of $100. At the end of the third year you have to pay $100 plus $15 in interest. In other words, your $100 loan cost a total of $115.

Compound Interest Compound interest is more complex because it's calculated on the original principal amount and also on the accumulated interest of a deposit or loan. Compound interest allows you to earn interest on a growing principal balance, which allows you to accumulate interest at a much faster rate. Interest can be compounded on any period of time, such as daily, monthly, semiannually, or annually.

Say you get the same loan of $100 for 3 years from your friend John, but this time he charges you 5% interest that compounds annually. Here's how the interest would be calculated:

Loan year	Principal amount (dollars)	APR (percent)	Annual interest earned (dollars)	Balance due (dollars)
1	$100	5%	$5	$105
2	105	5	5.25	110.25
3	110.25	5	5.51	115.76

Notice that the 5% APR is calculated on an increasing principal balance. At the end of the third year you'd owe the original

Table 1 Semiannual Compound Interest Calculation

Loan year	Principal amount (dollars)	Semiannual percentage rate (percent)	Annual interest earned (dollars)	Balance due (dollars)
1 (January)	$100	2.5%	$2.50	$102.50
1 (July)	102.50	2.5	2.56	105.06
2 (January)	105.06	2.5	2.63	107.69
2 (July)	107.69	2.5	2.69	110.38
3 (January)	110.38	2.5	2.76	113.14
3 (July)	113.14	2.5	2.83	115.97

amount of $100 plus interest of $15.76. Your $100 loan cost $115.76 with annual compounding interest. This table also shows you how much you'd earn if you deposited $100 in the bank and earned a 5% annual return that compounds annually.

Let's see how much you'd pay if John charged you 5% compounded semiannually, or every 6 months, shown in **Table 1**, above.

At the end of the third year you'd owe the original loan amount of $100 plus $15.97 of interest. With semiannual compounding your $100 loan would cost $115.97. Likewise, this table shows how much you could earn from $100 in savings if compounded semi-annually at a 5% annual rate of return.

Remember that the more frequent the compounding, the faster the interest grows.

Annual Percentage Yield (APY)

Annual percentage yield (APY) is the amount of interest you'll earn on an annual basis that includes the effect of compounding. APY is expressed as a percentage and will be higher the more often your money compounds.

What is the Rule of 72?

How long would it take you to double your money through savings and investments? It's easy to figure it out using a handy formula called the **Rule of 72**. If you divide 72 by the interest rate you earn, the answer is the number of years it will take for your initial savings amount to double in value.

For example, if you earn an average annual return of 1% on a bank savings account, dividing 1 into 72 tells you that your money will double in 72 years. But if you earn 6% on an investment, your money will take only 12 ($72 \div 6 = 12$) years to double.

You can also estimate the interest rate you'd need to earn to double your money within a set number of years by dividing 72 by the number of years. For instance, if you put $500 in an account that you want to grow to $1,000 in 12 years, you'll need an interest rate of 6% ($72 \div 12 = 6$).

Understand Credit Cards

Using credit cards without fully understanding the relevant money math is a recipe for financial disaster. Credit cards start charging interest the day you make a purchase, take a cash advance, or transfer a balance from another account.

You're typically charged a daily rate that's equal to the APR divided by 365 (the 365 days in a year). Rates may be different for each transaction category and depending on your credit rating. For instance, your APR could be 11.99% for new purchases, 23.99% for cash advances, and 5% for balance transfers. Balances accumulate day after day until you pay them off in full.

You can make a monthly minimum payment and carry over the remaining balance from month to month. But that's not a wise way to manage credit cards because the interest starts racking up. Additionally, if you make a late payment, you're charged a late fee that gets added to your outstanding balance—and interest is calculated on that amount too.

The bright spot in using a credit card wisely is that you're given a grace period for new purchases that allows you to avoid all

Finance Tip

Interest that you earn is considered income, and you may have to pay federal and state tax on it.

Finance Tip

When comparing different bank accounts, always compare APY instead of APR to know which one pays more interest on an annual basis.

Table 2 Amortization Schedule

Payment month	Loan balance (dollars)	Monthly payment (dollars)	Interest portion of payment (dollars)	Principal portion of payment (dollars)
1	$20,000	$617.54	$116.67	$500.88
2	19,499.12	617.54	113.74	503.80
3	18,995.32	617.54	110.81	506.74
4	18,488.58	617.54	107.85	509.69
5	17,978.89	617.54	104.88	512.67
6	17,466.22	617.54	101.89	515.66

interest charges—if you pay your balance in full by the billing statement due date. Note that there is generally no grace period for cash advances or balance transfers.

Credit cards are a powerful financial tool that can enhance your life if you use them responsibly. But abusing them by making purchases that you can't afford to pay off in full each month can be devastating to your financial future. It will also harm your credit report history if you make late payments. You'll learn more about how to establish and maintain a good credit history in Part 5.

Calculate Credit Card Payoff

Question: If you buy a TV for $2,000 using a credit card that charges 23.99% APR, how long would it take to pay off, if you only make minimum payments of 3% of your outstanding balance down to a minimum of $15 per month?

Answer: It would take over 16 years! So, if you're 17 years old right now, you'd celebrate your thirty-third birthday before you finally pay off the TV. Due to the high rate of credit card interest, the total cost of the TV would actually be $5,328. That's an increase of more than 266% on the TV's original purchase price. Only making minimum payments can easily double or triple the price of any item charged to a credit card, which is why it's so important to pay off credit card balances in full every month.

Finance Tip

To determine how long it would take to pay off a credit card if you only made the minimum payments, do a web search for "credit card minimum payment calculator" and enter your information.

Amortization

Gradually paying off a debt's principal and interest in regular installments over time is called amortization. Loans that amortize, such as a car loan or home mortgages, have fixed interest rates and charge equal monthly payments, though each payment is made up of a slightly different amount of principal and interest.

Take a look at **Table 2** to see how each payment is split up for the first six months on a three-year $20,000 car loan with an interest rate of 7%:

Notice that each month's beginning loan balance is reduced by the prior month's principal portion paid. The interest portion is slightly lower each month because it's calculated on an ever-decreasing principal balance.

How to Become a Millionaire

If you think that the only way to become a millionaire is to win the lottery, think again! Thanks to the power of compounding interest it's easy—if you get an early start. **Table 3** shows you how.

If you start saving and investing just $250 a month as soon as you get your first job, you could amass a million dollars by the time you're in your 60s. But if you wait until you're over 40 years old to get started and invest the same amount, you'd be close to 90 before becoming a millionaire!

Millionaire Case Study

Steve and Jessica are both 25 years old and work for the same company. They have the same financial goal: to retire at age 65 with one million dollars in savings. Steve starts contributing to his company's retirement plan right away, but Jessica waits 10 years, until she's 35 years old, to begin investing. Here's what happens: Steve can reach his million-dollar goal by contributing $400 a month and earning an average 7% annual

Table 3 At What Age Could You Become a Millionaire?

Age to begin saving	Amount to save each month (dollars)	Average APR (percent)	Years to become a millionaire	Age you're a millionaire!
18	$250	7%	46	64
20	250	7	46	66
25	250	7	45	70
30	250	7	45	75
40	250	7	45	86

return. But since Jessica gets a late start, she has to contribute much more than Steve. Jessica must contribute $850 a month with the same 7% rate of return to reach her million-dollar goal, as shown in **Figure 1**.

You'll notice that Steve only had to invest $192,000 over a 40-year period to amass over one million dollars. However, Jessica had to invest $306,000, or 60% more than Steve, over a 30-year period to accumulate approximately the same amount.

The Power of Saving Early Case Study

Sarah and Tom are both 25 years old, but they begin saving for retirement at different times. Sarah begins saving $200 per month right away, but Tom decides to buy a new car instead. Tom ends up delaying his retirement savings for 10 years. After his 35th birthday, he finally gets started and saves $300 per month. They both earn an average annual return of 8%.

Here's what happens: When Tom reaches age 65, he has almost $450,000. But Sarah has amassed close to $700,000. The benefit of choosing to invest earlier, rather than later, really pays off for Sarah because she has $250,000 more than Tom to spend during retirement, as demonstrated in **Figure 2** on the next page.

The sooner you start saving and investing, the more you will benefit from the power of compounding interest!

Figure 1 Saving To Be a Millionaire

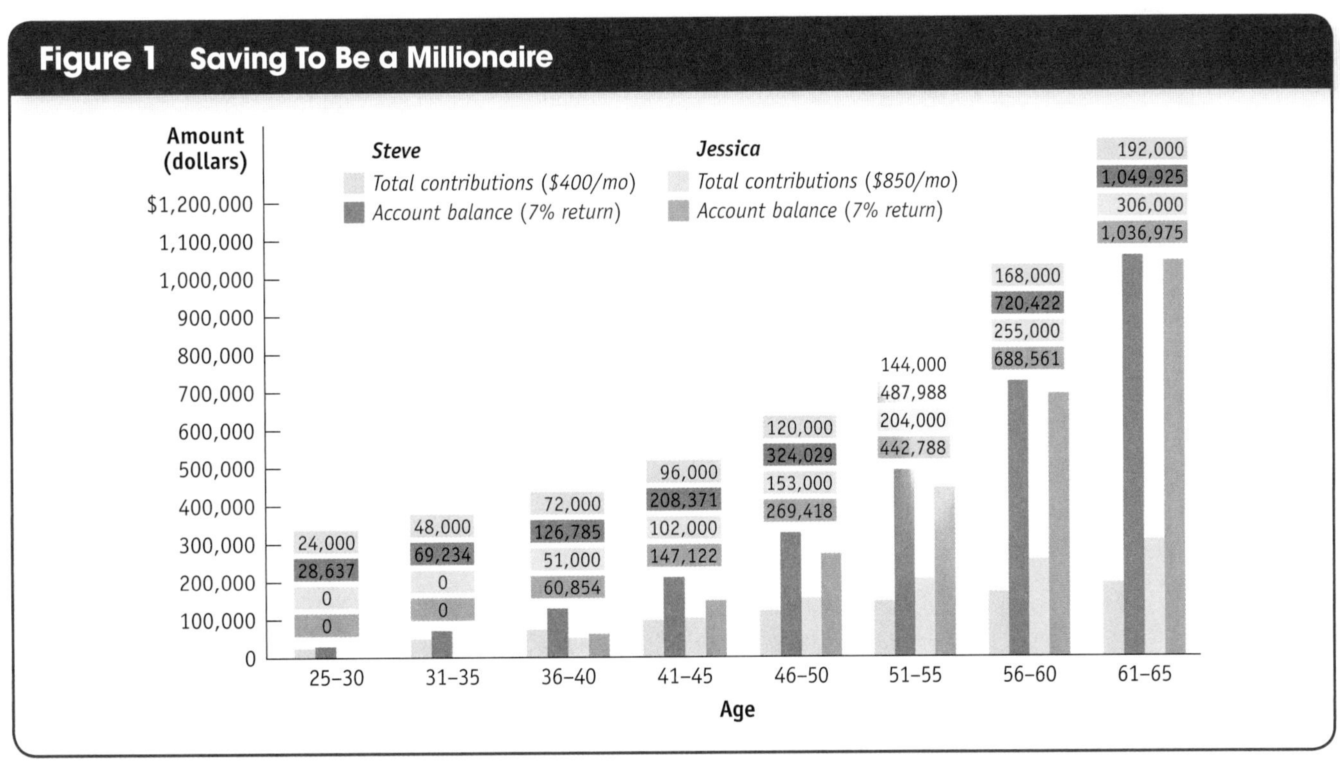

Figure 2 Saving for Retirement

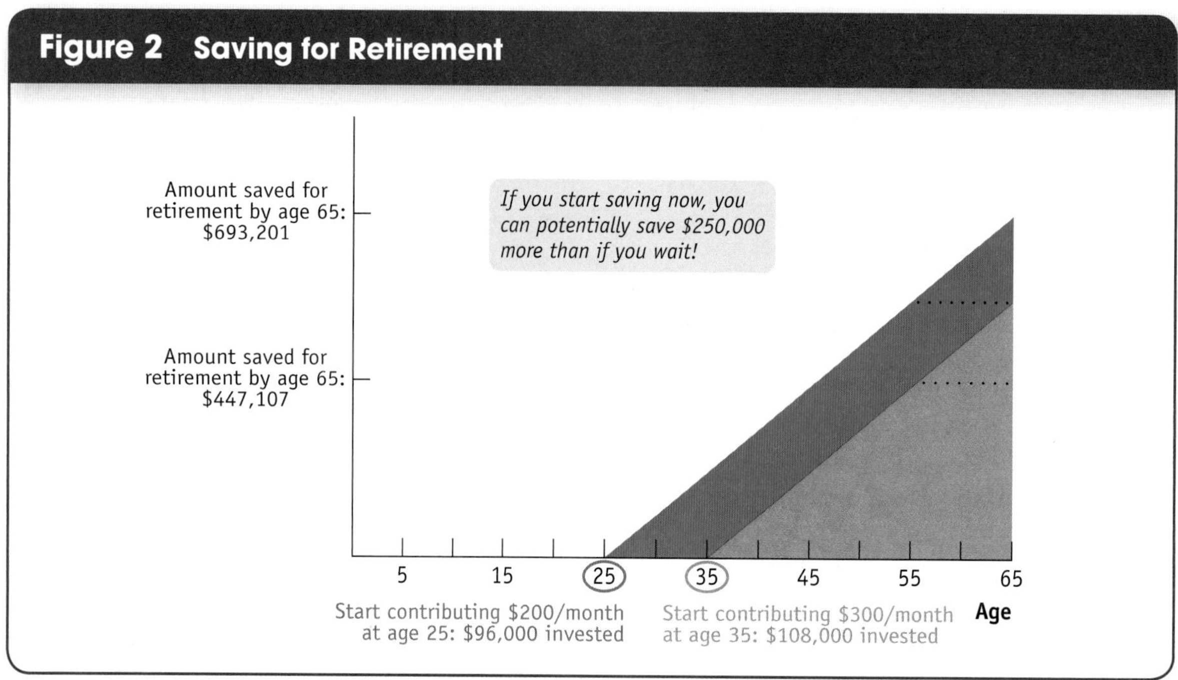

Amount saved for retirement by age 65: $693,201
Amount saved for retirement by age 65: $447,107
If you start saving now, you can potentially save $250,000 more than if you wait!
5
15
25
35
45
55
65
Age
Start contributing $200/month at age 25: $96,000 invested
Start contributing $300/month at age 35: $108,000 invested

Part 2 Review Questions

1. What is the difference between simple and compound interest?
2. Using the Rule of 72, how long will it take you to double your savings if you have $3,200 in an account making 4% interest?
3. Why is it generally a bad idea to make only minimum payments on your credit card?

Project

Imagine you deposit $125 in a savings account each month. It pays 3% annually, which is compounded monthly. How much interest will you earn for the year?

PART 3

Learn to Earn

How can you earn enough money to cover your expenses and save for the future? It starts by having the education and skills to get a good job or to start your own business. Every work experience builds your level of knowledge, boosts your resume, helps you know what work you like best, and makes you more attractive to potential employers.

What Is a Resume?

A resume is a summary of your education, skills, and work experience—that you submit to a potential employer in person, through the mail, or online—that highlights many of your outstanding traits and experiences. It should be a one-page document that is succinct and well written.

Employers typically conduct a background check to verify data in your resume, so never include any false information. Lying on a resume or job application can disqualify you for a job or cause an employer to fire you later on.

At the top of a resume, list your name, address, phone number, and e-mail address. The body should include sections titled "Objective," "Experience," "Skills," "Education," and "Honors or Awards." Tailor each resume to the particular job you apply for so the employer knows you have the skills to be successful.

If you have trouble creating a resume, ask for help from family, friends, or a professional resume writer, who can help you articulate the skills and experiences you have to offer a potential employer. You can also use free online resources such as careeronestop.org and myfuture.com.

What Is a Job Application?

In addition to your resume, many potential employers require you to complete a job or employment application. The application can be customized by the employer, but it typically asks for personal information, references, and specifics about the job you're applying for. Submitting an impressive resume and application will make you stand out from other applicants.

There are certain questions that an employer is not allowed to ask applicants under federal and some state and local laws. These may include topics such as your age, race, religion, citizenship status, and whether you are disabled, pregnant, or married. You can learn more about employment laws at the U.S. Department of Labor website at www.dol.gov.

Types of Income

The money you make falls into one of two basic categories: earned income and passive income.

Earned Income

Earned income is the income you receive by working for a company or someone who pays you, or from a business that you own and run. Earned income includes your hourly wages, salaries, tips, commissions, and bonuses. This is the most common way to make money. Of course, if you stop working, you stop earning. However, if you save and invest your earned income wisely, you can turn it into passive income.

Passive Income

Passive income is generated from assets you buy or create, such as financial investments, rental real estate, or something you have created, such as a book or a song. If you buy a house and rent it for more than your mortgage and other expenses, the profit is passive income. If you write and publish a book or a song that pays royalties, that is intellectual property that pays passive income. The benefit of passive income is that you get paid with little or no additional work on your part. That makes it possible to retire and still receive money to pay your everyday living expenses.

Although you must have income to meet your financial needs, it doesn't give you lasting wealth unless you save or invest some amount of it on a regular basis. Even those with high incomes can live paycheck to paycheck and end up with no true wealth. Likewise, those with modest incomes can save small amounts of money over a long period of time and accumulate a nest egg for a healthy financial future.

Getting a Paycheck

It might surprise you to know that if you get a job earning $600 a week, you don't actually receive $600 a week. Although your gross income or pay will be $600, you'll have payroll taxes deducted from each paycheck before you receive it, which include federal, state, Medicare, and Social Security taxes. You may also have voluntary deductions for workplace benefits such as health insurance, life insurance, and contributions to a retirement account. The remaining amount that you'll have to spend after taxes and deductions is called your net income or net pay.

When you take a new job, one of the forms you must complete is the W-4. It tells your employer how much tax should be taken out, or withheld, from each of your paychecks. If too little tax is withheld during the year, you'll owe money to the government's Internal Revenue Service (IRS) on tax day (which is usually April 15 unless it falls on a weekend or holiday). If too much tax is withheld, the IRS will pay a refund, but you will lose the use of your money until the refund payment arrives. So it is good to have your payroll withholding match the actual amount of tax you'll owe.

Significant events—such as marriage, divorce, the birth or adoption of a child, buying a home, or taking an additional job—will affect how much tax you owe. Additionally, earning income from savings accounts or investments affects the tax you owe. Any time your personal situation changes, you can file a new W-4 with your employer to make sure the right amount of tax is withheld so you don't have any surprises on tax day. You can learn more by visiting the IRS website at irs.gov and searching for Publication 919, How Do I Adjust My Tax Withholding?

Finance Tip

Employers are required to pay 50% of FICA on behalf of their employees. If you become your own boss, you must pay self-employment tax, which includes 100% of the Social Security and Medicare tax owed.

How Payroll Withholding Works

Employers are required to withhold four different types of tax from your paycheck:

1. **Federal income tax** is paid to the IRS for expenses such as salaries of elected officials, the military, welfare assistance programs, public education, and interest on the national debt.
2. **State income tax** is generally paid to your state's revenue department for expenses such as salaries of state employees and maintenance of state highways and parks. Depending on where you live, there may also be payroll deductions for county and city tax.
3. **Social Security tax** provides income for eligible taxpayers who are retired or disabled, or who survive a relative who was receiving benefits. The program's official name is OASDI, which stands for Old-Age, Survivors, and Disability Insurance.
4. **Medicare tax** provides hospital insurance benefits to eligible individuals who are over the age of 65 or have certain medical conditions. Social Security and Medicare taxes are collectively called the Federal Insurance Contributions Act (FICA) tax.

Filing an Income Tax Return

By April 15th of each year you must complete and file, by mail or electronically, a federal tax return to the IRS for income from the prior year. Most states also require a state tax return at the same time. Whether you must file a tax return depends on your income, tax filing status, age, and whether or not you are a dependent. The filing requirements apply even if you don't owe any tax.

If you don't file taxes on time, you'll be charged a late payment penalty, plus interest on any amount owed. Willfully failing to file a return is a serious matter because it's against the law and may result in criminal prosecution.

If you are an unmarried dependent student, you must file a tax return if your earned or unearned income exceeds certain limits. You may also owe tax on certain scholarships and fellowships for education. Tax rules are subject to change each year, so be sure to visit irs.gov and review IRS Publication 501, Exemptions, Standard Deduction and Filing Information, for income limits and up-to-date information.

In January and February each year, you'll receive official forms, like the sample shown below, from institutions that paid you, such as your employer, bank, or investment brokerage or firm. These forms provide the data you need to complete your taxes. Even if you don't receive these official tax documents, you must still declare all your income on a tax return. So be sure to request any missing information.

Even if your income is below a threshold set by the IRS and you do not have to file, you should file a tax return each year if you may be owed a refund—for instance, if you had income tax withheld from your pay or you qualify for refundable tax benefits.

In addition to individuals and families, the IRS (and certain states) also tax corporations, trusts, and estates.

How Much Income Tax Do You Pay?

The United States has a marginal or progressive tax system, which means that people with more earned income pay tax at a higher rate or percentage. A tax bracket is a range of income that's taxed at a certain rate. Currently, there are seven federal tax brackets that range from 10% up to 39.6%. So, someone with very little income may pay 10% while someone with high income could pay as much as 39.6% on their highest range of income for just federal income tax.

Every year the IRS adjusts many tax provisions as the cost of living goes up or down. They use the Consumer Price Index (CPI) to calculate the prior year's inflation rate and adjust income limits for tax brackets, tax deduction amounts, and tax credit values

Mom and Pop's Pizza Shop
1234 Main Street
Longview, NJ 99229

First Bank
Positano, NJ

233

18-1-1010

PAY TO THE ORDER OF **Jennifer Adams** $ 128.24

One hundred and twenty-eight and 24/100 DOLLARS

MEMO

Joseph Posentino

⑈000165⑈ ⑆1234567890⑆ 022⑈053304⑈

EMPLOYEE PAY STUB POSENTINO PIZZA SHOP CHECK NUMBER: 000233

Employee	SSN	Pay Period	Pay Date
Jennifer Adams	555-55-5555	04/06/2014–04/12/2014	04/18/2014

HOURS	Regular	OT
TP	20.00	0
YTD	160.00	0

EARNINGS	Regular	OT	Bonus	Other	Gross Pay
TP	$160.00	0	0	0	$160.00
YTD	$1,280.00	0	0	0	$1,280.00

DEDUCTIONS Pay	Social Security	Medicare	Federal	State	Retirement	Other	Net Pay
TP	$9.92	$2.24	$14.00	$5.60	0	0	$128.24
YTD	$79.36	$17.92	$112.00	$44.80	0	0	$1,025.92

Finance Tip

Use an online calculator at taxfoundation.org to find out how much federal tax you really pay (your effective tax rate) based on your income and tax filing status.

accordingly. All of these variables affect the net amount of tax you must pay.

Here's a table showing the federal income tax brackets and rates for 2014 for some different types of taxpayers:

2014 Federal Income Tax Brackets and Rates

Tax Rate	Single Filers	Married Joint Filers	Head Of Household Filers
10%	$0 - $9,075	$0 - $18,150	$0 - $12,950
15%	$9,076 - $36,900	$18,151 - $73,800	$12,951 - $49,400
25%	$36,901 - $89,350	$73,801 - $148,850	$49,401 - $127,550
28%	$89,351 - $186,350	$148,851 - $226,850	$127,551 - $206,600
33%	$186,351 - $405,100	$226,851 - $405,100	$206,601 - $405,100
35%	$405,101 - $406,750	$405,101 - $457,600	$405,101 - $432,200
39.6%	$406,751 +	$457,601 +	$432,201 +

You'll notice that if you're single and earn $40,000, you're in the 25% tax *bracket* for 2014. However, the following shows that your effective or net rate of federal tax rate would be only 15%:

Income Tax Bracket	Income Taxed	Federal Tax Rate	Federal Tax Due
$0 - $9,075	$9,075	10%	$908
$9,076 - $36,900	$27,825	15%	$4,174
$36,901 - $40,000	$3,100	25%	$775
Totals	$40,000		$5,857

Effective tax rate = $5,857 ÷ $40,000 = 15%

Although earning $40,000 means you're in the 25% tax bracket, your entire income is not taxed at this rate. A portion is taxed at 10%, another at 15%, and another at 25%, which generally makes your effective or net tax rate lower than your tax bracket rate.

There are four ways to file your federal and state tax returns:

1. Free File is tax preparation software provided free of charge at irs.gov for individuals with income below a certain amount. You're guided through a series of questions to calculate your tax liability, and your federal and state returns are filed electronically.
2. Fillable forms are free online tax forms at irs.gov that you can complete and file electronically without the help of software, regardless of your income. State tax forms are not included.
3. Tax software can be purchased to help you prepare your federal and state returns and file them electronically.
4. Tax preparers are tax professionals who prepare your federal and state returns and file electronically. Visit irs.gov for a list of authorized e-file providers or ask people you know to recommend a reputable tax accountant.

Not Every State Collects Income Tax

In addition to federal taxes, you may have to pay state tax on your income. Each state has its own tax system. The following nine states don't collect any tax from income that individuals earn: Alaska, Florida, Nevada, New Hampshire, South Dakota, Tennessee, Texas, Washington, and Wyoming.

Part 3 Review Questions

1. List several reasons that people work. What are some reasons people change jobs throughout their lifetime?
2. What are some "marketable skills" you possess? Think about skills you've developed and used in past jobs, volunteer opportunities, and even in school.
3. What are four different kinds of taxes withheld from your paycheck? What is the money ultimately used for?
4. Briefly describe the U.S. tax system.

Project

Research how the United States spent last year's tax dollars. What percentages went to discretionary spending, mandatory spending, and interest on federal debt? What does discretionary and mandatory spending pay for?

PART 4

Save and Invest Money

Going to college. Buying a car. Starting a business. Retiring from work. Any financial goal or dream that you have can become a reality if you get in the habit of consistently setting aside small amounts of money over time. Starting this routine at a young age will really pay off and allow you to control your financial future.

Though we tend to use the terms saving and investing interchangeably, they're not the same. The difference has to do with taking financial risk. Investors walk a line between wanting to make money and not wanting to lose money. Saving money in a bank keeps it completely safe but pays a lower rate of return than some other investments. Investments that pay higher rates of return come with higher risk—the chance you could lose some or all of your money.

It's important to understand that, most often, high-return investments come with higher risk. And low-return investments or savings usually come with low risk.

Types of Savings Accounts

You will probably earn only a small amount of interest on savings. But the purpose of having savings is to keep the funds completely safe and accessible. Money you need to spend in the short-term for planned purchases and emergencies should be kept in a federally-insured savings account, so you can't lose it.

There are three basic types of savings accounts you can open at most banks and credit unions: a savings account, a money market account, and a certificate of deposit. Review Part 1 of this handbook for an explanation of these accounts and the protection offered by the Federal Deposit Insurance Corporation, or FDIC.

Investing Basics

Looking at the period from 1928 to 2013, we see that investing money in the stock market has historically rewarded investors with average returns that exceed 11%. Even from 2004 to 2013—the decade that includes the most recent economic recession—investors earned approximately 9% on average.

So why would you put money in a bank savings account that might earn 0.1% to 2% instead? Because investing money always involves some amount of risk—the potential to lose money as well as the potential to make money.

Financial analysts make forecasts based on what happened in the past. But they include the disclaimer "Past performance does not guarantee future results." In other words, even the smartest analyst can't predict how much an investment will be worth in the future. Therefore, it's very important to invest with wisdom and caution.

The purpose of investing money is to increase your wealth over a long time period so you can achieve goals like paying for retirement or purchasing a home. Whether you should save or invest depends on your time horizon, which is the amount of time between now and when you'll actually need to spend the money. If you have a long time horizon—such as 10 years or more—investing makes sense. When you have a short time horizon—such as a year or less—many financial advisors recommend that you stick with an insured savings account.

What Is the Securities Investor's Protection Corporation (SIPC)?

Investments, or securities, are not guaranteed by any federal agency such as the FDIC. There is no insurance against losing money in an investment. However, the Securities

Investor Protection Corporation (SIPC) is a nongovernment entity that gives you limited protection in certain situations. They step in when an investment brokerage firm fails or fraud is the cause of investor loss. The SIPC replaces missing securities up to $500,000 per customer. You can learn more at sipc.org.

Types of Investments

The earlier you start investing, the more money you'll have to pay for your financial dreams and goals. There are four basic types of financial securities and products that you can purchase for your investment portfolio. They are stocks, bonds, mutual funds, and exchange-traded funds.

Stocks

Stocks are issued by companies—like Apple, Google, and Facebook—that want to raise money. When you buy shares of a stock, you purchase an ownership interest in a company and your shares can go up or down in value over time. Stocks are bought and sold on exchanges, like the New York Stock Exchange or the NASDAQ, and you can monitor their prices in real time online.

Stocks are one of the riskiest investments because the price per share can be volatile, swinging up or down in a short period of time. People can't be sure about which stocks will increase in value over the short or long term. However, historically, stocks have rewarded investors with higher returns than other major investment classes, like cash or bonds.

Bonds

Bonds are loans you give to a corporation or government entity, known as the issuer, who wants to raise money for a specific project. Projects paid for by a bond include things such as building a factory or a school. Bonds pay a fixed interest rate over a set period of time. The time can range from weeks to 30 years. In general, interest is higher for longer-term bond terms and for bonds issued by companies with better credit.

Bonds are also called fixed-income investments because the return is guaranteed. In return for a higher degree of safety than stocks, you receive a relatively low rate of return. (Remember that lower risk investments give you a lower return and higher risk investments typically offer higher returns.) But these conservative investments still have some risk. For example, a bond issuer can default on repayment. Agencies such as Standard and Poor's (standardandpoors.com) do research and offer a rating system of bond safety.

Mutual Funds

Mutual funds are products that bundle combinations of investments, such as stocks, bonds, and other securities. They're operated by professional money managers who invest the fund's money according to stated objectives, such as achieving maximum growth or earning fixed income. Mutual fund shares are purchased directly from the fund company or from investment brokers and can go up or down in value over time.

In general, mutual funds composed of stock have the greatest potential risk and reward; however, there's a wide range of risk within this category. Mutual funds composed of bonds also have a range of risk but are considered more conservative than stock funds.

Exchange-Traded Funds (ETFs)

Exchange-traded funds are products that bundle combinations of investments—just like mutual funds—but trade like a stock on an exchange throughout the day. These securities are growing in popularity due to their flexibility and low cost. The cost to operate an ETF is very low compared to many mutual funds.

Other Types of Investments

Other types of investments include real estate, precious metals (like gold and silver), and businesses, just to name a few. They generally require more expertise and skill to buy and sell than the four types of securities covered here. The drawback to alternative investments is that they aren't as liquid, or sold as easily, as mainstream investments.

Finance Tip

You can reduce risk by diversification, which means owning a variety of investments in your portfolio.

What Is Financial Risk?

To be a successful investor, you need to understand the financial risks of different types of investments and gauge your own tolerance for risk. Many brokerage firms offer a questionnaire that can help you determine this.

What seems safe to one person may be deemed very risky by another. Your tolerance for risk is how you react when your investments decline in value. Someone who doesn't like risk is considered risk averse. A risk-averse person is willing to miss out on higher rates of return in exchange for financial safety. A more risk-tolerant person is willing to accept investment losses in exchange for potential higher returns.

There is no right or wrong risk style that you should adopt. It just comes down to your personal feelings and preferences for how you want to manage your investments.

Ways to Invest

You have many choices when it comes to investing your money. The two most common are brokerage accounts and retirement accounts.

Brokerage Accounts

Brokerage accounts are available at local brokerage firms and firms that operate online that are licensed to place investment orders, such as buying or selling shares of a stock, a mutual fund, or an ETF. You own the assets in a brokerage account and must pay tax each year on the earnings, which are called capital gains.

Retirement Accounts

Retirement accounts are special accounts you can open at a variety of institutions, such as local or online banks and brokerage firms, that allow you to save for retirement. One of the advantages is that they allow you to pay less tax.

There are different kinds of retirement accounts available for individuals, as part of an employee benefit package at work, and for the self-employed. Investment options include many of the instruments already mentioned, such as stocks, bonds, mutual funds, ETFs, or even bank CDs.

When you invest through a retirement account—as opposed to a regular brokerage account—you defer, or avoid paying, tax on your earnings. That means you save money on taxes and have more money for retirement! However, if you withdraw funds from a retirement account that weren't previously taxed, you're typically subject to an early withdrawal penalty, in addition to ordinary income tax.

The most commonly used retirement accounts include individual retirement arrangements, the 401(k) plan, and the 403(b) plan. In order to have enough money to live comfortably for decades during retirement, it's important to get in the habit of saving money in a retirement account.

Individual Retirement Arrangement (IRA) The IRA is a personal account available to anyone, regardless of age, who has taxable income. You can begin making contributions to an IRA as soon as you get your first job. However, you're in charge of it, not your employer. With a traditional IRA you generally don't pay tax on contributions or earnings until after you retire and start taking withdrawals. In other words, taxes on the account are deferred until sometime in the future. With a Roth IRA, you pay tax on your contributions up front. However, you never pay tax on them again or on any amount of earnings. You get a huge tax benefit with a Roth because your entire account grows completely tax free.

401(k) Plan The 401(k) plan is a retirement account offered by many companies. You authorize a portion of your wages to be contributed to the plan before income tax is withheld from your paycheck. A 401(k) plan offers participants a set menu of investment choices. You can contribute amounts up to certain allowable limits each year.

403(b) Plan The 403(b) plan is a retirement account offered by certain organizations such as schools, churches, and hospitals. It's similar to a 401(k) in most aspects and also limits contributions each year.

Retirement Accounts for Employees

There are two main types of retirement programs found in the workplace: defined benefit plans and defined contribution plans.

- A **defined benefit plan** is funded and managed by an employer and is commonly known as a pension. Employees don't pay into the plan, pick investments, or manage the money in any way. Defined benefit plans give retired workers a specific, defined benefit, such as $800 per month for the rest of their life. The benefit paid depends on various factors, such as age, length of employment, and salary history. These plans have become rare in the workplace because they're expensive to operate. However, some large companies, government agencies, and labor unions offer them.
- A **defined contribution plan** is established by an employer but requires that the employee manage it. This type of plan includes the 401(k) and 403(b) plans. The retirement benefit that an employee will receive depends on the amount that's invested and the performance of the chosen investments over the years. Defined contribution plans are more common because they're less risky for an employer to administer.

What Is Employer Matching?

If you could earn a guaranteed 100% return on your money, would you be interested? Many employers match a certain amount of the money you put in a workplace retirement plan. Say your employer matches 100% of your contributions to a 401(k) up to 3% of your salary. If you earn $30,000 a year and contribute $75 a month or $900 a year, that's a contribution of 3% of your salary. With matching, your employer would also contribute $900. So you'd invest $900 and automatically get $900 from your company—an immediate 100% return on your money!

How Much Will Social Security Pay in Retirement?

As a young person, it's not possible to know exactly how much you'll receive in Social Security retirement benefits. They're calculated based on various factors, such as the current law, your future earnings, how long you pay payroll or self-employment taxes, the age you elect to start receiving benefits, and military service.

However, according to the Social Security Administration, the benefit replaces only about 40% of your preretirement earnings, if you have average income. As of June 2013, the average monthly benefit for a retired worker was $1,269. The maximum monthly benefit was $2,533; however, higher benefits may be possible if you choose to delay benefits and start receiving them after you reach full retirement age.

Therefore, it's important not to count on Social Security retirement benefits as your sole source of income during retirement. The program was created as a supplement for personal savings, not as a substitute for having a retirement plan.

Investing for Education

Just as there are special accounts that allow you to invest for retirement and pay less tax, there are two education savings accounts, or ESAs, to be familiar with: 529 plans and Coverdells.

- A **529 plan** is a savings or investment vehicle that allows you to contribute money to pay for a student's qualified expenses at a college, university, or vocational school. There are prepaid plans, where you prepay all or a portion of the future cost, and investment plans, where you choose specific investments. Contributions and earnings in a 529 plan grow tax free.
- A **Coverdell account** allows you to contribute money to pay for any level of education, from kindergarten through graduate school. It differs from a 529 plan in that it has more restrictions, such as how much can be contributed each year and the age of the student who will use the funds.

You can learn more about 529s and Coverdells at savingforcollege.com and finaid.org.

Part 4 Review Questions

1. What is the difference between *saving* and *investing*?
2. Briefly describe each of the four kinds of investments.
3. Briefly describe the different kinds of retirement accounts. Why is it a good idea to invest in retirement accounts as soon as you start working?

Project

What does it mean to "diversify" your savings plan? Research different kinds of savings and investments and come up with a plan that provides a good balance of both.

PART 5

Give Yourself Some Credit

How is it possible to make a major purchase, like a home, if you don't have the cash? The answer is credit. If you're "creditworthy," you can be trusted to borrow money and pay it back over time.

What Is Credit?

Credit is the ability to borrow money that you promise to repay with interest. Credit is an important part of your financial life because it allows you to do the following:

- **Make a large purchase and pay for it over time**. If you don't have enough money saved up to buy a car, having credit allows you to get a loan and repay it over a set period of time.
- **Stay safe in an emergency situation**. If your car breaks down and you don't have enough to pay for the repair, having a credit card or line of credit allows you to get back on the road and repay the balance over time.
- **Avoid having to carry cash or paper checks**. When you're making a large purchase, like a computer or furniture, using a credit card is safer than carrying around a large amount of cash or paper checks that could be stolen.
- **Make online purchases and reservations**. When you need to buy something over the Internet—like books, clothes, or travel reservations—it's convenient to use a credit card.

If you don't have credit, the only way to get a loan or credit card is to have someone with good credit cosign an account. A cosigner might be a family member or friend who guarantees to take full responsibility for the debt if you don't repay it.

How do you become creditworthy so a potential creditor—such as a bank or credit card company—will allow you to borrow money? While each institution has different guidelines for evaluating a potential borrower, the following five criteria are generally used:

1. **Credit score**: How likely are you to make on-time payments based on your credit history? In this section you'll learn more about what a credit score is.
2. **Income**: Do you have a steady job and have enough income to repay a debt?
3. **Debt**: Do you have existing debts? If so, will you have enough money to pay your current debt and make payments on a new debt?
4. **Financial ratios**: How much debt do you have relative to your income?
5. **Collateral**: Will you secure a debt by pledging property (like a car or home) that a lender could sell if you don't make payments?

Understanding Credit Reports

Your credit history is maintained by three major nationwide credit reporting agencies: Equifax (equifax.com), Experian (experian.com), and TransUnion (transunion.com). These agencies receive information about you from your creditors and list it on your credit report. They are interested in things such as whether you make payments on time, your outstanding debt balances, and your available credit limits. Credit reporting agencies don't make credit decisions; they simply report information provided to them on your credit reports.

Each of your credit reports from the three agencies is slightly different, but they generally contain the following four types of information:

1. **Personal information** includes your name, current and previous addresses, Social Security number, birth date, and employer.

2. **Account information** lists your open accounts and your closed accounts for up to a certain period of time.
3. **Credit inquiries** include a list of companies and employers that have made inquiries about you because you applied for a credit account or job.
4. **Public information** is data that's available in the public records about you, including bankruptcies, foreclosures, liens for unpaid income taxes, and legal judgments.

The information in your credit report sticks with you for a long time. Credit accounts with negative information (for example, late payments) remain on your credit report for seven years from the date your payment became past due, even after you close the account or pay it off in full. Credit accounts with positive information remain on your credit report for 10 years after you close the account or pay it off in full.

Understanding Credit Scores

Just as your schoolwork determines your final grade in various classes, the information in your credit reports is used to calculate your credit scores. One of the most confusing things about credit scores is that there isn't just one. Your credit score depends on the particular scoring model that's used to calculate it. Companies can create their own scoring systems or use brand-name scores calculated by other firms, like the FICO (Fair Isaac Corporation) Score or the VantageScore.

Your credit score is different from the final grade you receive for a class because it isn't figured once and filed away. Your credit score is calculated fresh every time it's requested. Therefore, it's a snapshot of your credit behavior up to that moment in time.

Poor credit may indicate that you've mismanaged your finances by making late payments or maxing out credit accounts. However, having too little credit history can also be a reason for having a low credit score.

Having poor credit means you'll be viewed as a risky customer who may not repay a debt. You'll either be turned down for credit or charged an interest rate that's higher than the rate offered to a customer with good credit. Why? In exchange for taking a financial risk on a customer with poor credit, lenders protect themselves financially by charging higher interest rates, which means you have to make higher monthly payments.

How Much Can Poor Credit Cost You?

Dora has excellent credit and goes to her bank to apply for a $15,000 car loan. After a few days the bank's lending representative calls her with good news—she's been approved! She can borrow $15,000 at 4% APR for a term of four years, which makes her monthly payment $338.69. The total amount of interest she'll pay on the loan principal is $1,256.92.

On the other hand, let's imagine Dora didn't have excellent credit and the bank charged her 12% APR instead of 4%. At this higher interest rate, her monthly payment would be $395.01. She'd pay a total of $3,960.36 in interest—or $2,703.44 more than if her credit was in good shape.

The larger a loan, the more poor credit costs you. **Table 1** below shows different scenarios for a home mortgage of $150,000 paid over 30 years. Not having excellent credit means you could pay an additional $127,493.41 in interest—on top of the original loan amount of $150,000.

Table 1 The Cost of Poor Credit

Credit status	APR (percent)	Monthly payment (dollars)	Total interest paid (dollars)	Cost of having poor credit (dollars)
Excellent	3.75%	$694.67	100,082.42	$0
Good	5.00	805.23	139,883.68	39,801.26
Average	7.50	1,048.82	227,575.83	127,493.41

Other Ways Having Poor Credit Hurts Your Finances

Did you know that having poor credit scores can cost you even if you don't want a loan or credit card? Here are five ways that having poor credit affects your personal finances:

1. **Paying high insurance premiums**: In most U.S. states, insurance companies are allowed to factor in your credit when setting car and home insurance rates. Having poor credit means you'll be quoted rates that could be double or triple the amount that someone with excellent credit would pay. That's because consumers with poor credit have been found to file more insurance claims.
2. **Paying high security deposits**: You may be asked to pay higher deposits for an apartment and for utilities such as power, gas, water, and phone accounts.
3. **Getting declined as a tenant**: You could be turned down for an apartment or house to rent because property managers prefer tenants who demonstrate good payment history.
4. **Getting turned down for government benefits**: You might not qualify for certain types of federal or state benefits that require a good credit history.
5. **Getting denied a job**: You might be turned down for a job by an employer who requires a credit check. Employers can't get your credit scores or see your entire credit report, but they can find out if you've had credit problems.

Finance Tip

To find out your credit score, you can visit the credit bureau websites mentioned earlier and purchase the information from them. You may also buy your FICO Score at myfico.com, or get several scores for free at creditkarma.com.

How to Establish Credit

The information in your credit report has a ripple effect throughout your entire financial life. How can you get started building good credit? Knowing how credit scores are calculated can help you improve them.

Each credit scoring model values the information in your credit report differently and uses a unique score range. The popular FICO Score uses a scale from 300 to 850 and values the following five factors:

1. **Payment history** (35%): making payments for bills and credit accounts on time
2. **Credit utilization** (30%): having lower amounts of debt relative to your available credit limits on credit cards and lines of credit
3. **Length of credit history** (15%): having credit accounts for a longer period of time
4. **Type of credit used** (10%): having a mix of credit types, including loans and credit cards
5. **Applications for credit** (10%): having fewer requests for new credit accounts

To build good credit, focus on actions within your control that have the biggest influence on typical scoring models. These include paying bills on time and not maxing out credit cards. But remember that it takes time to build good credit—it's a marathon, not a sprint.

Finance Tip

To stay on top of your credit more than once a year, space out your requests and get a free report from a different credit agency every four months at annualcreditreport.com.

How to Build Your Credit

It may be difficult to get approved for a credit card before you've established a good credit history. However, everyone over age 18 can get a secured credit card, which can help you build credit for the first time—as long as it reports payment transactions to the credit agencies. With a secured credit card, you must make a refundable upfront deposit (as little as $200) that serves as your credit limit.

How to Protect Your Credit

To protect the integrity of your credit, you should check your credit report on a regular basis. It's up to you to make sure that the information in your credit report is correct. Errors or fraudulent activity can hurt your credit scores without you knowing it.

Checking your credit reports is easy and it never hurts your credit scores. You can purchase your credit report from any of the three credit agencies, but you're entitled to a free report once a year at annualcreditreport.com. You can report inaccuracies or put a stop to fraud by placing a credit alert or credit freeze on your credit reports. The Fair Credit Reporting Act (FCRA) is a federal law that regulates how your credit information can be used and your consumer credit rights. You can learn more on the Federal Trade Commission website at ftc.gov.

Part 5 Review Questions

1. Briefly describe the criteria a creditor uses to evaluate a potential borrower.
2. Why is it important to maintain an excellent credit score? Name ways that bad credit can hurt someone. How can good credit help you achieve some of your own financial goals?
3. Why do you think lenders have an interest in your credit history?
4. Do you think it's fair that consumers with good credit scores typically pay less for credit accounts, such as credit cards and loans, and certain insurance products? Why or why not?

Project

Imagine that your best friend just got approved for a credit card with a $500 available credit limit. He or she is excited to use a credit card for the first time and wants to go on a shopping spree. If you know that he or she doesn't have much money to pay off the credit card bill, what advice would you offer?

PART 6

Borrow Without Sorrow

It can be easy to get into financial trouble if you borrow money that you can't repay. Getting behind on bills—such as payments for a car loan, student loan, or credit card—results in large late fees and long-term damage to your credit history. Therefore, it's important to know how to use debt responsibly and to make wise choices that are best for your financial future.

What to Know About Debt

Before you apply for credit or take on any amount of debt, ask yourself some important questions:

- Do I really need this item?
- Can I wait until I save enough cash to pay for it?
- What's the total cost of the credit, including interest and fees?
- Can I afford the monthly payments?

There are many different kinds of debt, but they fall into two main categories: installment loans and revolving credit.

Installment Loan Basics

An installment loan is an agreement you make with a creditor to borrow a certain amount of money and repay it in equal monthly payments, or installments, for a set period of time. The length or term of the loan could be very short or in excess of 30 years and may be secured or unsecured.

Secured loans are backed by collateral, which is something of value that you pledge to the lender. For instance, a car you finance is collateral for the car loan. And a house is collateral for a home loan, which is also known as a mortgage. Collateral protects lenders because they can sell it to repay your debt if you don't make payments as agreed.

Unsecured loans are not backed by any collateral. They're often called personal or signature loans because you sign an agreement where you promise to repay the debt. For instance, credit card debt and student loans are both forms of unsecured loans.

When you take an installment loan, your monthly payment will depend on three factors:

1. **Principal amount**: The less you borrow, the lower your monthly payment will be.
2. **Interest rate**: The lower the rate, the lower your monthly payment will be.
3. **Loan term**: The longer the term, the lower your monthly payment will be; however, this generally results in paying more total interest.

Common Types of Installment Loans

Installment loans give consumers money to buy many different products and services, like cars, homes, or a college education.

Consumer Loans

Consumer installment loans, also called personal or signature loans, are commonly used for small purchases, like buying a computer or paying for unexpected expenses. You can apply for an unsecured consumer loan from local banks, credit unions, or online lenders.

Auto Loans

Installment loans to buy a new or used vehicle are available from local banks, credit unions, online lenders, and some car dealers. You may be required to make a down payment on the purchase price—especially if you don't have good credit.

For example, if you want to buy a used car that costs $10,000, the lender may require that you pay 20% or $2,000 up front in order to borrow the remaining balance of $8,000.

As previously mentioned, a car you buy becomes collateral for the loan. If you don't make payments as agreed, the lender can repossess, or take back, the vehicle to pay off the outstanding loan balance. The lender typically holds the title of the car until the loan is paid off in full.

The term or repayment period for a car loan is typically 2 to 7 years. Choosing a longer loan term reduces the monthly payment but can significantly increase the amount of total interest you have to pay.

What's Being "Upside Down"? A new car depreciates, or loses its value, very quickly—especially in the first three years—depending on the make and model. For example, a $20,000 car might be worth only $15,000 after a year. But your outstanding loan balance could be over $16,000 if you made a low or no down payment (depending on the loan terms).

When you owe more for a car than it's worth, you're "upside down" on the loan. If you want to trade or sell the car, you have to pay extra out of pocket to pay off the loan. Making a down payment helps you avoid this common financial problem of being "upside down"—and helps reduce your monthly loan payment. So, even if you have good credit, it's wise to make a down payment on a car loan.

What's a Car Title? A car title is a document that shows who purchased a vehicle and lists information including the vehicle identification number (VIN), make, year of manufacture, purchase price, registered owner name and address, and the legal owner if any money is owed. When a car is sold, the title must be transferred to the new owner.

What's Vehicle Leasing? Instead of owning a car you can lease one for a set period of time. After the lease term (usually two, three, or four years) expires, you have to return the vehicle to the leasing company. Monthly lease payments may be less than a loan payment for the same vehicle and term. However, after you pay off a car loan the vehicle belongs to you. You can sell it for cash or continue to drive it for many years without having to make a car payment. Therefore, purchasing a car is more cost effective when you keep it for the long term.

Student Loans

Student loans are funds you can use for education expenses, such as tuition, books, room and board, and other living expenses while you attend college. There are two main types of unsecured installment loans that may be available to you or your parents: federal student loans and private student loans.

Federal student loans are issued by the federal government and most don't require a credit check for approval. Most students qualify for some type of federal loan, up to certain limits, depending on their income or their parents' financial qualifications. To apply, you must complete the Free Application for Federal Student Aid (FAFSA). You can submit it online at the U.S. Department of Education website at fafsa.ed.gov.

Here are three types of federal student loans:

- **Stafford Loan** is the main federal loan for students, which can be subsidized by the federal government or unsubsidized. To receive a subsidized Stafford Loan, you must demonstrate financial need. The government pays, or subsidizes, the interest on the loan while you're in school.

  Unsubsidized Stafford Loans require you to pay all the interest; however, you can defer making payments until after graduation. All students, regardless of financial need, can get an unsubsidized Stafford Loan.
- **Perkins Loan** is a subsidized federal loan given to students who have the most financial need. The government pays the loan interest during school and for a nine-month grace period.
- **Parent Loan for Undergraduate Students (PLUS)** is an unsubsidized federal loan for parents of students. A credit check is made to verify that the parents have no adverse credit history.

Private student loans originate from a private lender, such as an online institution, a local bank, or a credit union.

Finance Tip

The Kelley Blue Book at kbb.com is a guide that helps car buyers and sellers determine the market value of a new or used vehicle.

Finance Tip

Use the car loan calculator at dinkytown.com to find out how changing the down payment, loan amount, interest rate, and term of a loan results in different monthly payments.

Private education loans are generally used to bridge the gap between the cost of college and the amount you can borrow from the government.

Eligibility for a private loan depends on your or your parents' financial qualifications and credit scores. You submit an application directly to a private lender and don't have to complete any federal forms.

Private student loans typically have higher interest rates and less repayment flexibility than federal loans. Therefore, always apply for a federal student loan first.

Finance Tip

To learn more about completing the FAFSA and paying for college, finaid.org is a leading resource for financial aid—including loans, scholarships, grants, and fellowships.

Home Loans

You can get a home loan or mortgage from local banks, credit unions, or online lenders. They can be used to

- buy real estate, such as a house or condominium,
- buy a parcel of vacant land,
- build a home, or
- borrow against the equity or value of a home you already own.

There are three main types of home loans:

1. A **purchase loan** is used to buy a home and is secured by the property. You must make a down payment that's typically 5% to 20% of the purchase price. The loan term is typically 30 years, but 15- and 20-year mortgages are also common.
2. An **equity loan** is secured by your home and can be used for any purpose. **Equity** is the current market value of your property less the amount of outstanding debt you owe. For instance, if your home is worth $200,000 and your mortgage balance is $140,000, you have $60,000 in equity.
3. A **refinance loan** replaces an existing home loan by paying it off and creating a brand new loan that has better terms, such as a lower interest rate. Refinancing at a lower interest rate may allow you to lower your monthly payments and save money.

What Is Foreclosure? Foreclosure is a legal process a home lender uses to collect the balance of an unpaid debt when a borrower defaults or stops making loan payments as agreed. The lender can take legal title to the property, evict the borrower(s), and sell the property to pay off the debt, according to state laws.

Revolving Credit Basics

Revolving credit is different from an installment loan (such as a car or student loan) because it doesn't have a fixed number of payments or a final due date. The account revolves, or stays open indefinitely, as long as you make minimum monthly payments. The lender approves a maximum loan amount, or credit limit, to use at any time. Credit cards, retail store credit cards, and home equity lines of credit (HELOCs) are common types of revolving credit.

Applying for a Credit Card

If you're under age 21, you must show that you have income or an eligible cosigner to qualify for a credit card. The law requires that you receive a Federal Truth in Lending Disclosure Statement from any company that offers you credit. Be sure to read it carefully so you understand the terms and can compare cards based on these features:

- annual percentage rate (APR) for purchases, promotions, cash advances, and balance transfers
- your credit limit
- potential fees and penalties
- how balances are calculated
- rewards or rebates for purchases
- additional protections (such as travel insurance or extended warranties)

Managing a Credit Card

A credit card gives you the ability to make purchases now and pay for them later. For example, if you have a credit card with a $1,000 credit limit, you can use it to buy products or services, or take cash advances that total up to $1,000. However, you should never max out a credit card because that hurts your credit.

This flexibility makes credit cards powerful financial tools that can help you in an emergency situation. But credit cards can also devastate your finances if you get over your head in debt that you can't repay.

Because they're so convenient for consumers and come with unsecured risk for lenders, credit cards charge relatively high interest rates that can exceed 30%. Every time you make a credit card purchase, you're borrowing money that must be paid back. You'll also have to pay interest charges if you don't pay off your balance in full by the monthly statement due date.

Paying Your Credit Card

Credit cards issue an account statement each month that lists transactions from the previous month. The lowest amount you can pay—your "minimum payment"—varies depending on the card, but may range from 2% to 4% of your outstanding balance. For instance, if you owe $500, your minimum payment could be 3%, or $15. The remaining balance of $485 will continue to accrue interest, in addition to any new transactions you make or late fees that may apply.

However, if you pay off your entire credit card balance by the due date on your statement each month, you can use a credit card without paying any interest charges or late fees. That's because no interest charges accrue during this "grace period."

Tips to Reduce the Cost of Borrowing

The cost of borrowing money depends on several factors, such as the current interest rates, your credit rating, the APR you're offered, loan fees, and how long it takes you to repay the debt. Here are 10 tips to reduce the cost of borrowing:

1. **Shop around for the lowest APR** for a loan or credit card before you accept an offer.
2. **Finance an item based on the total price** (including interest) that you can afford—not just on a monthly payment amount.
3. **Repay loans over a shorter term** so you pay less total interest over the life of a loan.
4. **Pay off credit card purchases in full each month** so you're never charged interest or late fees.
5. **Make payments on time** so you're never penalized with expensive late fees or an increased APR on a credit card.
6. **Build a good credit history** so you have high credit scores and will be offered low interest rates by lenders and credit card companies. Establishing credit was covered in Part 5 of this handbook.
7. **Make a bigger down payment** so you'll owe less and receive lower APR offers from auto and home lenders.
8. **Take out federal student loans** before accepting private education loans so you qualify for the most favorable interest rates and repayment terms.
9. **Claim tax benefits** that come with education loans, such as the student loan interest tax deduction, which may allow you to reduce the amount of tax you owe.
10. **Never take a payday loan**, which is a short-term unsecured advance against your next paycheck. The interest rate for one of these loans can be over 15% for just two weeks—which translates into a sky-high APR that can exceed 400%!

Part 6 Review Questions

1. What do you think are the advantages and disadvantages of borrowing money?
2. What goals do you have that might require you to borrow money?
3. Briefly describe the different kinds of student loans. How can you be sure you don't borrow more than you can comfortably pay back, taking other lifetime financial burdens (such as buying a home or car, having children, etc.) into consideration?
4. What are some important rules to remember when it comes to managing a credit card the right way?
5. Why should credit cards and loans never be viewed as "free money"?

Project

Come up with five questions to ask when you are comparing different kinds of loans or credit. For example, one question can be "What is my minimum monthly payment?"

PART 7

Manage Your Money

Building wealth and creating financial security can be easy if you have a reliable income and manage your money wisely. Good money management starts with never spending more than you make each month. Your financial life will always be a balancing act between the short-term gratification of spending to fulfill your current wants versus the long-term benefit of saving. Striking the right balance will allow you to have enough money to fulfill your future wants and needs.

It's your job to have the willpower to resist unnecessary spending and get into the habit of saving for the future on a regular basis. If you use your financial resources responsibly, you'll be able to have a secure future and make your dreams a reality.

Setting Financial Goals

A financial goal is something you want to do with your money in a certain period of time. Goals can be short-term, like buying a car this year or taking a vacation next summer. Or goals can be long-term, like accumulating a large nest egg for retirement. Retirement is one of the most important goals for everyone. Why? Because as you grow older, you may neither want nor be able to work until the end of your life. The hope is that we save enough money so it's possible to enjoy life and pursue other interests besides work when desired.

In Part 3 you learned that Social Security benefits are likely to provide you with a small amount of income after you retire. However, you'll need additional savings for everyday expenses, such as housing, food, and medical costs—otherwise you won't have a comfortable lifestyle as you grow older.

Though you have many years to go, saving enough for retirement generally takes decades to achieve. That's why it's critical that you begin saving for the future as early as possible. Financial success doesn't happen overnight—so the earlier you start saving for retirement, the better.

What Is Social Security?

Social Security is a group of benefits paid to eligible taxpayers who are retired, disabled, or who survive a relative who was receiving benefits. The funds for Social Security come from taxes withheld from your paycheck. The amount you'll receive in retirement depends on how many years you work, how much payroll or self-employment tax you pay during your career, the age you elect to start receiving benefits, and the future financial health of the Social Security system. Visit ssa.gov for more information.

Creating a Budget

It's easy for everyday purchases like snacks, magazines, and music to get out of control if you're not watching them carefully. Keeping your expenses as low as possible can add up to huge savings over time. For instance, let's say bringing your lunch to work 4 days a week saves you $8 a day or $32 a week. If you invested $32 a week for 40 years at a moderate rate of return, that savings would grow to over $330,000.

The best way to take control of your money is to create a budget, also known as a spending plan. A spending plan helps you understand how much money you have and where it goes, so you can prioritize expenses and set objectives to achieve your short- and long-term financial goals.

Managing money the right way is all about making choices and sacrifices—like whether to spend money on a night out with friends or save it to buy a car. You'll always have many needs and wants competing for your limited financial resources.

You can apply an economic mindset to your financial planning too! It's up to you to choose your priorities and decide the best way to spend your money.

Four Steps to Preparing a Successful Budget

Knowing exactly how much you have to spend and where you spend it gives you power over your finances. You can keep track of your financial information on paper, using a computer spreadsheet or a mobile app, or by importing transactions from your bank or credit card accounts into a financial program like Quicken.

Here are four easy steps to creating a successful spending plan:

Step #1—Enter your net monthly income.

To stay in control of your money and reach your financial goals, you must know how much money you have coming in each month. Recall that net income, or take-home pay, is the amount you have left after taxes and other voluntary workplace deductions. Enter this amount at the top of your spending plan because it's what you actually have to spend each month.

Step #2—Enter your fixed and variable expenses.

Many people don't achieve financial success because they spend money carelessly. It's critical that you keep a close watch on your spending so it never exceeds your net income. Enter all your expenses below your income.

Fixed expenses don't change from month to month and may include your rent, insurance, phone, or a loan payment. Variable expenses can change each month or are discretionary, like dining out, transportation, or buying clothes.

Organize your expenses into major categories—such as rent, insurance, groceries, dining out, clothes, and entertainment—and enter the total amounts.

Step #3—Compare your income and expenses.

When you compare your total take-home pay to your total expenses, you may be pleased that you have money left over or be disappointed that there's none to spare. Discretionary income is the amount of money you have left over each month after all your essential living expenses are paid.

You must spend less than you make in order to have enough discretionary income to save and invest for your future. Living paycheck to paycheck may satisfy immediate wants and needs, but it won't empower you to achieve long-term financial success.

Step #4—Set priorities and make changes.

The final step is to create new spending guidelines. Decide how much you want to allocate toward each of your short- and long-term financial goals and enter them as separate categories in your spending plan. You may need to reduce spending in other categories or find ways to earn extra income to cover all your expenses.

It's up to you to figure out the best way to balance your spending and saving so you enjoy life today and put away enough money for a safe and secure tomorrow.

What Does "Pay Yourself First" Mean?

"Pay yourself first" is a common saying in personal finance that means saving money should be your top priority. Putting your savings on autopilot is the best way to remove the temptation to spend it! A portion of each paycheck can be deposited automatically in a savings or retirement account before you receive the balance. That way you pay yourself before paying your living expenses or making discretionary purchases.

Tracking Your Wealth

A spending plan is the perfect way to track your income and expenses. But to monitor the big picture of your finances, you need to know your net worth. Your net worth can be summed up in this simple equation:

$$\text{net worth} = \text{assets} - \text{liabilities}$$

Assets are items you own that have real value, such as cash in the bank, vehicles, investments, real estate, personal belongings, and money owed to you. Liabilities are your debts and financial obligations to others, such as a car loan, credit card debt, or money you borrowed from a friend.

If you have more assets than you owe in liabilities, your net worth will be a positive number. But if you owe more than you own, your net worth will be a negative number. The goal is to raise your net worth over time by increasing your assets or decreasing your liabilities, so you build wealth.

Paying Bills

Paying bills on time is one of the most important money management responsibilities. Late payments can result in expensive fees and damage to your credit. Thanks to online banking, it's never been easier to manage bills and pay them on time.

Most local and Internet-only banks offer free bill pay, which allows you to pay any company or individual with the click of a button. If a company you want to pay accepts electronic payments, your funds will transfer electronically. If not, the bill pay service prints and mails a paper check on your behalf to any payee in the United States that has a mailing address.

E-bills and e-statements can be sent to your e-mail, bill pay center, or both. You can set up a bill to be paid automatically on a certain date and e-mail you when the transaction is complete. Or you can log on to your bill pay center and manually initiate a payment for up to one year into the future. You can set up reminder alerts for all your recurring bills so no payment due date ever falls through the cracks.

Tips to Manage Money Like a Millionaire

One of the most surprising facts about wealthy people is that most of them weren't born that way. About 80% of the wealthiest people in the United States are first-generation millionaires. They accumulated wealth by working hard and saving and investing money. That means anyone who is disciplined with his or her money can achieve financial security. Here are 10 tips to manage your money like a millionaire:

1. **Live below your means**. Spending less than you make is a choice. Saving money, and not overspending, is how you build wealth.
2. **Know where your money goes**. If you don't have a spending plan to track your money, you won't know if you're making wise decisions. Getting ahead financially starts with taking control of your cash flow.
3. **Create an emergency fund**. Having money set aside for unexpected expenses is a safety net that you should never be without. That's how you'll make it through a financial rough patch, such as suddenly losing your job or having large unexpected expenses. Make a goal to accumulate at least six months' worth of your living expenses to keep on hand at all times.
4. **Focus on net worth instead of income**. No matter how much you earn, you can grow rich by slowly increasing your net worth over time. But even if you have a large income, you'll never grow rich if you don't get in the habit of setting aside money for the future.
5. **Have long-term financial goals**. Wealthy people know what they want to achieve and then work backward so they have a plan for what to do each year, month, week, or day to stay on track and meet their goals. Set objectives to achieve your goals.
6. **Begin saving for retirement early**. If you think you're too young to start saving for retirement, think again. Creating wealth for your future rarely happens overnight—unless you beat huge odds by having a winning lottery ticket or a big inheritance.
7. **Save and invest at least 15% of your income**. Make it a habit to save 15% to 20% of your income, starting with your first job, and adjust your lifestyle so you can easily live on the rest.
8. **Automate your savings and investments**. It's easier to save money that you never see. Participate in a workplace retirement account or have your paycheck split between a checking and savings account so your savings are on autopilot.
9. **View money as a tool**. Money is only as useful as what you do with it. So decide what's important to you and use money to achieve your needs and your dreams. Push away short-term gratification in favor of important, long-term goals like saving for retirement.
10. **Realize when you've made a money mistake**. Everyone makes mistakes with their money from time to time. If you overspend or make unwise decisions, stop and make the choice to get back on track right away.

Part 7 Review Questions

1. Do you think that writing down your goals and reviewing them on a regular basis could help increase your chances of accomplishing them? Why or why not?
2. What is the relationship between spending and the ability to build wealth?
3. Why does tracking how you spend money help you make better financial decisions?
4. What is the purpose of an emergency fund and how much should it be?

Project

Choose a savings goal that you'd like to achieve before the end of the summer. Create a savings plan and keep track of your progress over the next few months.

PART 8

Protect Yourself from Risk

Life is full of events that no one can predict. It's impossible to know if you'll get into a car accident, have your laptop stolen, or need to visit the emergency room for a broken bone. While you can't prevent these kinds of catastrophes, you can protect your personal finances by having enough of the right kinds of insurance.

Insurance is a special type of contract between you and an insurance company. The company agrees that when certain events occur, that are defined in an insurance policy, they'll meet certain expenses or provide a payout. For example, with a car insurance policy, the insurer agrees to pay some amount of the cost to repair it if you're in an accident. Health insurance pays a certain amount of your medical expenses if you need to go to the doctor.

Insurance eliminates or reduces the potential financial loss you could experience from an unforeseen event and protects the income and assets that you work hard for.

Types of Insurance

There are many different types of insurance products that can be purchased from an insurance company or a licensed insurance agent, either in person or online. The types you should have depend on your age and life circumstances. There are eight major types of insurance: health, disability, life, auto, homeowner's, renter's, long-term care, and umbrella.

Health Insurance

Without health insurance you could get stuck with a huge bill if you have any kind of medical need, from a broken bone to a chronic illness. Even a quick trip to the emergency room can cost thousands of dollars.

The Affordable Care Act (ACA), also known as Obamacare, is the nation's health reform law that was enacted in 2010. Starting in 2014, it requires most U.S. citizens and legal residents to purchase and maintain health insurance for themselves and their dependents, or to pay a penalty. The ACA may provide a financial subsidy, which reduces the monthly cost of health insurance, depending on your income and family size.

Many employers offer group health insurance, or you can purchase an individual policy on your own. You can stay on your parents' health policy until you're 26 years old—unless you're offered insurance at work.

Visit healthcare.gov to explore your health insurance options.

Disability Insurance

A disability is a physical or mental condition that limits your ability to perform various types of activities. If you're unable to work due to a disability, accident, or long-term illness, disability insurance replaces a portion of your income while you recuperate. Unless you have plenty of savings in an emergency fund, a disability could leave you unable to pay for everyday living expenses, such as housing or groceries. Remember that health insurance only covers a portion of your medical bills—not your everyday living expenses.

Many employers offer some type of disability coverage for employees, or if you're self-employed you can purchase an individual policy on your own. Professionals—like surgeons, athletes, or dancers—who want to protect their ability to do their job should always have disability coverage. Every disability policy is different, but there are two main types: short-term disability (STD) and long-term disability (LTD). A short-term policy usually pays you for a maximum of two years, while a long-term policy could provide benefits that last your entire life.

Life Insurance

Life insurance provides a lump-sum payment, known as a death benefit, to one or more named beneficiaries when the insured person dies. It's important to have life insurance when your death would cause a financial burden for those you leave behind—such as a spouse or child.

Many employers offer life insurance for employees, or you can purchase your own policy. There are two basic kinds of life insurance: term and permanent.

- **Term life insurance** provides less expensive coverage for a set period of time, such as 10 or 20 years, and pays the policy's death benefit amount to the beneficiary.
- **Permanent life insurance** provides lifetime coverage that pays a death benefit and accumulates a cash value that you can withdraw later in life. This type of policy is much more expensive that a term life policy.

A good rule of thumb is to purchase life insurance with a benefit that's 10 times your income. So if you make $50,000 a year, you might need coverage that would pay your beneficiary $500,000. However, factors such as your family size, debt, assets, and the lifetime income needs of a surviving partner, spouse, or child are critical considerations.

Auto Insurance

Most U.S. states require you to have some amount of insurance for vehicles such as cars, trucks, motorcycles, and recreational vehicles. The required insurance types and minimum amounts vary depending on the state in which you live.

Auto insurance is a package of coverages that may include the following:

- **Collision** pays for damage to your vehicle caused by getting into an accident with another vehicle, even if you are at fault.
- **Comprehensive** pays for damage to your vehicle due to something other than a collision, such as fire, hail, or theft.
- **Property damage liability** pays for damage you cause to someone else's property, such as their vehicle, a stop sign, or fence.
- **Bodily injury liability** pays for injuries you cause to another person. It's important to have enough liability because if you're involved in a serious accident, you could be sued for a large sum of money.
- **Personal injury protection** pays for medical expenses of the driver and passengers of the policyholder's car regardless of who's at fault, in certain states.
- **Uninsured and underinsured motorist coverage** pays when you're in an accident with an at-fault driver who has insufficient or no insurance to pay for your loss.

The cost of auto insurance varies depending on many factors, such as your age, driving record, credit history, vehicle, and the amount and type of coverage you choose. According to the most recent data, the Toyota Sienna is the least expensive car to insure, at $1,111 per year, and the Audi R8 Spyder Quattro Convertible is the most expensive, at $3,384 per year. So remember to factor in the cost of insurance when choosing a new ride.

Homeowner's Insurance

When you have a home mortgage, the lender requires you to purchase and maintain insurance for the property. Basic homeowner's insurance pays for damage to your property or personal belongings caused by a covered event, such as a natural disaster or theft. Homeowner's insurance also includes liability coverage that protects you if someone gets hurt while on your property.

Renter's Insurance

When you rent an apartment or home, your landlord's insurance doesn't cover your personal belongings or liability. Renter's insurance pays for damage to your possessions (such as clothes, jewelry, electronics, furniture, artwork, household goods, and sporting equipment) if they're damaged by a covered event, such as a natural disaster, wind storm, theft, or faulty plumbing. It can also reimburse your living expenses if you're forced to move out temporarily while repairs are being made. And as with homeowner's insurance, the liability protection keeps you safe if someone is injured on the property and involves you in a lawsuit.

If you rent a home or apartment, you should never go without renter's insurance. According to the National Association of Insurance Commissioners (NAIC), the national average cost of a renter's policy in 2011 was only $187. So it's a very inexpensive way to protect your finances from an unforeseen crisis!

Long-Term Care Insurance

If you have a long-term illness or disability that keeps you from taking care of yourself, long-term care (LTC) insurance pays a certain amount of day-to-day care that isn't covered by other types of insurance. Remember that disability insurance only replaces a portion of your lost income if you're unable to work due to a disability. And health insurance only pays for a portion of your medical bills.

Individuals who require long-term care may need help with activities of daily living, such as dressing, bathing, eating, and walking. Long-term care insurance generally covers care provided in your home by a visiting professional or in an assisted living facility.

Umbrella Insurance

As you build wealth, you may find that you need additional liability insurance protection to cover the total value of your assets. An umbrella policy gives you broad coverage from losses above the limits of your existing policies.

For instance, say you have $100,000 of auto insurance liability and a million dollar umbrella policy. If you were in a car accident that caused serious injuries to another driver that exceeded $100,000, your umbrella policy would give you protection up to one million dollars.

What Is an Insurance Deductible?

Many types of insurance—such as health, auto, renter's, and homeowner's—require you to pay a certain amount of expenses before the policy covers your remaining costs. This out-of-pocket expense is called your deductible. For example, if you have a medical bill for $2,000 and your deductible is $500, then you must pay $500 before the policy will pay all or a portion of the remaining $1,500 in covered benefits.

Extended Product Warranties

If you've ever purchased a product like a computer or a TV, the salesperson probably gave you a sales pitch for an extended product warranty. These warranties give you additional protection if something breaks after the manufacturer's warranty expires. They can also cover issues that the manufacturer doesn't.

While the added protection of an extended product warranty can come in handy, the cost can be very high. Product warranties are typically very profitable for retailers, who train salespeople to sell them aggressively. If the benefit isn't worth the cost, never let a salesperson talk you into buying something you don't need.

When to Purchase an Extended Product Warranty

Consider the following to know when you should purchase an extended product warranty:

- **Look at the price of the warranty versus the price of the product.** If you spend $100 for an MP3 player and the extended warranty is $40, that increases the price 40% for a relatively inexpensive product. However, spending $150 for a warranty on a $2,000 computer may be worthwhile, since it has many expensive parts that could break.
- **Consider the likelihood that you'll need extra coverage.** Will you use the product on a daily basis or in an environment where it could be damaged easily? Does the manufacturer have a reputation for making quality products?
- **Understand the coverage provided.** Does the warranty simply duplicate what's already available from the manufacturer, and how long does it

last? What about parts and labor? Are the rules of the warranty clear and do they make sense for your situation? If the coverage is thin or it's too difficult to file a claim, then the warranty would be useless.

- **Remember coverage offered by your credit card**. Many credit cards offer built-in extended warranty coverage as a card benefit. So it might make sense to purchase a product with your credit card to take advantage of the extra protection.

Identity Theft

Identity theft is a serious and growing crime. It happens when a criminal steals your personal information and uses it to commit fraud. A thief can use data—such as your name, date of birth, Social Security number, driver's license number, bank account number, or credit card number—to wreak havoc on your finances. An identity criminal can open new phone accounts, credit cards, or loans in your name, then go on a spending spree and leave you with a huge bill. Thieves have even filed fictitious tax returns and applied for driver's licenses in their victims' names.

Many insurance companies offer identity theft insurance to cover expenses that you may incur as a victim, such as lost wages, attorney fees, and certified mailing costs. You may have the option to add this protection to your homeowner's or renter's policy.

There are also companies that specialize in identity theft protection, credit monitoring, and identity restoration. These services may be sold through insurance agents, credit card companies, credit reporting agencies, or banks and credit unions. Be sure to read the fine print of these policies before signing up so you understand if do-it-yourself safeguards may be just as effective.

It's impossible to completely prevent identity theft; however, if you catch it early, you can stop it quickly and with less potential hassle and expense.

What To Do If You're the Victim of Identity Theft

Once your identity is jeopardized, getting it corrected can cost time and money. So be sure to keep an eye on your accounts and immediately take the following actions if you see any suspicious activity:

Step #1—Place an initial fraud alert on your credit report with one of the major credit reporting agencies (Equifax, Experian, TransUnion). They must inform the other two agencies on your behalf.

This makes it more difficult for a thief to open additional accounts in your name because a business must take additional steps to contact you directly to verify your identity. An initial fraud alert lasts for 90 days; however, you can renew it for free as needed.

Step #2—Request your credit reports from each of the three major credit reporting agencies. Placing a fraud alert also gives you access to free copies of your credit reports. It's a good idea to request copies that reveal only the last four digits of your Social Security number.

If you know which of your accounts have been compromised, contact those companies directly to discuss the fraudulent activity. Take notes about what actions are being taken and follow up in writing. Be sure to send all communication regarding an identity theft case by certified mail and ask for a return receipt. It's important to create a record that proves you have been diligent to resolve unauthorized charges on your account.

Step #3—Submit an identity theft report to the Federal Trade Commission (FTC) and then the local police. Having these formal reports will help you prove that you've been an identity theft victim to credit reporting agencies, businesses, and debt collectors. If a thief opened new accounts in your name and made large purchases, this could damage your credit history unless the creditor is willing to remove the account or the fraudulent charges from your report.

Visit the FTC website at consumer.ftc.gov to submit an identity theft report or to learn more.

Tips to Stay Safe from Identity Theft

Here are 10 tips to help you protect yourself and stay safe from identity theft:

1. **Never carry confidential information that you don't need.** Unless you plan to use them, remove your Social Security card, paper checks, and financial cards from your wallet and leave them at home so they can't be lost or stolen.
2. **Don't share your Social Security number.** There are only a few situations where you might need to provide it, such as for a new job, in tax-related matters, or when applying for credit or insurance. Never reveal your confidential information over the phone or Internet to any person or company that you don't trust entirely.
3. **Keep a close watch over your debit and credit cards.** When you hand a financial card to a store clerk or restaurant server, watch to make sure that it isn't copied and get it back as soon as possible. Also, never loan your financial cards to anyone.
4. **Shred all documents with personal information.** Make confetti out of receipts, financial account statements, and unwanted credit card offers before putting them in the garbage. Identity thieves dumpster dive for paperwork and can even use the last few digits of a confidential number against you.
5. **Check your credit reports once a year.** If an identity thief opens an account in your name, it will show up on your credit reports. That's why it's important to review them on a periodic basis at annualcreditreport.com.
6. **Resist clicking on links in e-mails.** Thieves can pose as a legitimate organization—such as the IRS, a bank, or PayPal—and send "phishing" e-mails with links to phony sites that ask for confidential information. Genuine companies never ask you for personal information over the phone or Internet. Instead of clicking on a hyperlink, enter a website address directly into an Internet browser.
7. **Use a secure Internet connection.** Don't access a website where you enter confidential information using a public computer or an open Wi-Fi connection. Hackers can track what you're doing over an unsecured Internet connection. Also, never send any personal information to a website unless the address begins with "https," which means that it's secure.
8. **Create strong online usernames and passwords.** Each password for your financial accounts should be unique, with no fewer than eight characters made up of uppercase and lowercase letters, numbers, and symbols. They should never include your Social Security number, name, address, or birth date.
9. **Opt for e-bills and e-statements when possible.** Criminals can change your mailing address so they receive your mail and have access to your personal information. Therefore, reducing the amount of paper documents you send and receive with confidential information is beneficial.
10. **Monitor your bank and credit card account activity.** Review your accounts online or view monthly statements to watch out for unauthorized transactions.

Part 8 Review Questions

1. Why do you think most U.S. states require drivers to have some amount of auto insurance for liability? Do you agree with this requirement? Why or why not?
2. Why does your driving record affect your auto insurance rates?
3. Imagine your best friend has enrolled in a photography program at a fine arts school. He was required to purchase nearly $3,000 worth of photography equipment for his courses and will be keeping it all in his new apartment. What kind of insurance would you suggest he get, if any, and why?
4. Who should have renter's insurance, and why is it a good idea?
5. Why do you think mortgage lenders require homeowners to have a certain amount of homeowner's insurance?
6. Describe several precautions you or your family take to stay safe from identity theft.

Project

Research health insurance plans online, taking into account your specific situation and needs. Start by making a list of how you use health insurance (frequency of doctor visits, need for special dental or vision services, etc.) and decide what kind of insurance policy would fit your needs best. Is it one with a high deductible but low monthly premium? Or is it different? Once you have selected the right fit, list the details of the plan and explain why this plan was the best fit for you.

Glossary

Italicized terms within definitions are key terms that are defined elsewhere in this glossary.

absolute advantage the advantage conferred by the ability to produce more of a good or service with a given amount of time and resources; not the same thing as *comparative advantage*. (p. 27)

absolute value the value of a number without a minus sign, whether or not the number was negative to begin with. (p. 42)

actual investment spending the sum of *planned investment spending* and *unplanned inventory investment*. (p. 168)

***AD–AS* model** *model* in which the *aggregate supply curve* and the *aggregate demand curve* are used together to analyze economic fluctuations. (p. 192)

aggregate consumption function the relationship for the *economy* as a whole between aggregate current *disposable income* and *aggregate consumer spending*. (p. 164)

aggregate demand curve shows the relationship between the *aggregate price level* and the quantity of *aggregate output* demanded by *households*, businesses, the government, and the rest of the world. (p. 172)

aggregate output the economy's total production of goods and services for a given time period. (pp. 12, 116)

aggregate price level a measure of the overall level of prices in the *economy*.(p. 146)

aggregate production function a hypothetical function that shows how *productivity* (output per worker) depends on the quantities of *physical capital* per worker and *human capital* per worker as well as the state of technology. (p. 373)

aggregate spending the total spending on domestically produced *final goods and services* in the *economy*; the sum of consumer spending, investment spending, government purchases of goods and services, and *exports* minus *imports*. (p. 109)

aggregate supply curve shows the relationship between the *aggregate price level* and the quantity of *aggregate output* supplied in the *economy*. (p. 180)

allocative efficiency achieved by an *economy* if it produces at the point along its *production possibilities curve* that makes consumers as well off as possible. (p. 18)

appreciation occurs when a currency becomes more valuable in terms of other currencies. (p. 418)

asset bubble situation in which the price of an asset increases to a high level due to expectations of future price gains; can cause a *banking crisis*. (p. EM-4)

automatic stabilizers government spending and taxation rules that cause *fiscal policy* to be automatically expansionary when the *economy* contracts and automatically contractionary when the economy expands. (p. 215)

autonomous change in aggregate spending an initial rise or fall in *aggregate spending* that is the cause, not the result, of a series of income and spending changes. (p. 161)

autonomous consumer spending the amount of money a *household* would spend if it had no *disposable income*. (p. 163)

balance of payments accounts a summary of a country's transactions with other countries. (p. 406)

balance of payments on goods and services the difference between the value of a country's exports and the value of its imports during a given period. (p. 409)

balance of payments on the current account (current account) a country's balance of payments on goods and services plus net international transfer payments and factor income. (p. 409)

balance of payments on the financial account (financial account) the difference between a country's sales of assets to foreigners and its purchases of assets from foreigners during a given period. (p. 409)

balanced budget multiplier the factor by which a change in both spending and taxes changes *real GDP*. (p. 213)

bank a *financial intermediary* that provides *liquid* assets in the form of *bank deposits* to lenders and uses those funds to finance borrowers' *investment spending* on *illiquid* assets. (p. 230)

bank deposit a claim on a bank that obliges the bank to give the depositor his or her cash when demanded. (p. 230)

bank reserves the currency that *banks* hold in their vaults plus their deposits at the Federal Reserve. (p. 244)

bank run a phenomenon in which many of a *bank's* depositors try to withdraw their funds due to fears of a bank failure. (p. 247)

banking crisis occurs when a large part of the banking system fails. (p. EM-4)

bar graph a graph that uses bars of various heights or lengths to indicate values of a variable. (p. 46)

black market a market in which goods or services are bought and sold illegally—either because it is illegal to sell them at all or because the prices charged are legally prohibited by a price ceiling. (p. 84)

bond a loan in the form of an IOU that pays interest. (p. 107)

budget balance the difference between tax revenue and government spending. (p. 224)

budget deficit the difference between tax revenue and government spending when government spending exceeds tax revenue. (p. 224)

budget surplus the difference between tax revenue and government spending when tax revenue exceeds government spending. (p. 224)

business cycle the alternation between economic downturns, known as *recessions*, and economic upturns, known as *expansions*. (p. 11)

capital manufactured goods used to make other goods and services. (p. 3)

capital inflow the total inflow of foreign funds minus the total outflow of domestic funds to other countries. (p. 225)

causal relationship a relationship between two *variables* in which the value taken by one variable directly influences or determines the value taken by the other variable. (p. 38)

central bank an institution that oversees and regulates the banking system and controls the *monetary base*. (p. 254)

chain-linking the method of calculating changes in *real GDP* using the average between the growth rate calculated using an early base year and the growth rate calculated using a late base year. (p. 118)

change in demand a shift of the demand curve, which changes the quantity demanded at any given price. (p. 52)

change in supply a shift of the supply curve, which changes the quantity supplied at any given price. (p. 61)

checkable bank deposits bank accounts on which people can write checks. (p. 233)

classical model of the price level *model* in which the real quantity of money is always at its *long-run equilibrium level*. (p. 319)

collateralized debt obligation an asset-backed security tied to corporate debt or mortgages. (p. EM-7)

command economy an *economy* in which industry is publicly owned and a central authority makes production and consumption decisions. (p. 2)

commercial bank a depository *bank* that accepts deposits and is covered by *deposit insurance*. (p. 258)

commodity money a good used as a *medium of exchange* that has intrinsic value in other uses. (p. 234)

commodity-backed money a *medium of exchange* with no intrinsic value whose ultimate value is guaranteed by a promise that it can be converted into valuable goods. (p. 234)

comparative advantage the advantage conferred by an individual if the *opportunity cost* of producing the good or service is lower for that individual than for other people. (p. 27)

competitive market a market in which there are many buyers and sellers of the same good or service, none of whom can influence the price at which the good or service is sold. (p. 49)

complements two goods (often consumed together) for which a rise in the price of one of the goods leads to a decrease in the demand for the other good. (p. 54)

consumer price index (CPI) measures the cost of the *market basket* of a typical urban American family. (p. 148)

consumer spending *household* spending on goods and services. (p. 106)

consumption function shows how a *household's* consumer spending varies with the household's current *disposable income*. (p. 163)

contractionary fiscal policy *fiscal policy* that reduces *aggregate demand*. (p. 207)

contractionary monetary policy *monetary policy* that reduces *aggregate demand*. (p. 307)

convergence hypothesis general principle stating that international differences in *real GDP* per capita tend to narrow over time. (p. 380)

cost-push inflation *inflation* that is caused by a significant increase in the price of an *input* with economy-wide importance. (p. 323)

credit crunch occurs when potential borrowers can't get credit or must pay very high interest rates. (p. EM-5)

credit default swap an agreement that the seller will compensate the buyer in the event of a loan default. (p. EM-7)

crowding out occurs when a government deficit drives up the *interest rate* and leads to reduced *investment spending*. (p. 280)

currency in circulation cash held by the public. (p. 233)

curve any line on a graph, regardless of whether it is a straight line or a curved line. (p. 38)

cyclical unemployment the deviation of the actual rate of *unemployment* from the natural rate. (p. 133)

cyclically adjusted budget balance an estimate of what the *budget balance* would be if *real GDP* were exactly equal to *potential output*. (p. 296)

deadweight loss the value of foregone mutually beneficial transactions. (p. 96)

debt deflation the reduction in *aggregate demand* arising from the increase in the real burden of outstanding debt caused by *deflation*. (p. 337)

debt-GDP ratio the government's debt as a percentage of *GDP*. (p. 299)

default when a borrower fails to make payments as specified by a *loan* or *bond* contract. (p. 228)

deflation a falling overall price level. (p. 13)

demand curve a graphical representation of the demand schedule. It shows the relationship between quantity demanded and price. (p. 51)

demand price the price of a given quantity at which consumers will demand that quantity. (p. 93)

demand schedule shows how much of a good or service consumers will be willing and able to buy at different prices. (p. 50)

demand shock an event that shifts the *aggregate demand curve*. (p. 193)

demand-pull inflation *inflation* that is caused by an increase in *aggregate demand*. (p. 323)

dependent variable in a *causal relationship*, the variable that is determined by the *independent variable*. (p. 38)

deposit insurance guarantees that a *bank's* depositors will be paid even if the bank can't come up with the funds, up to a maximum amount per account. (p. 247)

depreciation occurs when the value of an asset is reduced by wear, age, or obsolescence or when a currency becomes less valuable in terms of other currencies. (pp. 398, 418)

depression a very deep and prolonged downturn. (p. 11)

derivative a financial contract that has value based on the performance of another asset, index, or interest rate. (p. EM-7)

devaluation a reduction in the value of a currency that is set under a fixed *exchange rate regime*. (p. 431)

diminishing returns to physical capital in an *aggregate production function* when, holding the amount of *human capital* per worker and the state of technology fixed, each successive increase in the amount of *physical capital* per worker leads to a smaller increase in productivity. (p. 374)

discount rate the *interest rate* the Fed charges on *loans* to *banks*. (p. 262)

discount window the channel through which the Federal Reserve lends money to *banks*. (p. 247)

discouraged workers nonworking people who are capable of working but have given up looking for a job due to the state of the job market. (p. 123)

discretionary fiscal policy *fiscal policy* that is the result of deliberate actions by policy makers rather than rules. (p. 215)

discretionary monetary policy the use of changes in the *interest rate* or the *money supply* by the *central bank* to stabilize the *economy.* (p. 346)

disinflation the process of bringing the *inflation rate* down. (p. 143)

disposable income income plus *government transfers* minus taxes; the total amount of *household* income available to spend on consumption and to save. (p. 108)

diversification investment in several different assets with unrelated, or independent, risks. (p. 226)

economic aggregates economic measures that summarize data across many different markets. (p. 5)

economic growth an increase in the maximum amount of goods and services an *economy* can produce. (p. 13)

economics the study of scarcity and choice. (p. 2)

economy a system for coordinating a society's productive and consumptive activities. (p. 2)

efficiency wages wages that employers set above the equilibrium wage rate as an incentive for better employee performance. (p. 133)

efficient describes a market or *economy* in which there is no way to make anyone better off without making at least one person worse off. (p. 18)

employed people who are currently holding a job in the *economy*, either full time or part time. (p. 121)

employment the number of people who are currently working for pay in the *economy.* (p. 11)

entrepreneurship the efforts of entrepreneurs in organizing resources for production, taking risks to create new enterprises, and innovating to develop new products and production processes. (p. 3)

equilibrium an economic situation when no individual would be better off doing something different; a *competitive market* is in equilibrium when the price has moved to a level at which the quantity demanded of goods equals the quantity supplied of that good. (p. 69)

equilibrium exchange rate the exchange rate at which the quantity of a currency demanded in the foreign exchange market is equal to the quantity supplied. (p. 419)

equilibrium price (market-clearing price) the price of a good at which the quantity demanded of that good equals the quantity supplied of that good. (p. 70)

equilibrium quantity the quantity of a good bought and sold at its *equilibrium* price. (p. 70)

excess reserves a *bank's* reserves over and above its required reserves. (p. 250)

exchange market intervention government purchases or sales of currency in the *foreign exchange market.* (p. 429)

exchange rate regime a rule governing policy toward the exchange rate. (p. 427)

exchange rates the prices at which currencies trade. (p. 417)

expansion a period of economic upturn in which output and employment are rising; also referred to as recovery. (p. 11)

expansionary fiscal policy *fiscal policy* that increases *aggregate demand.* (p. 207)

expansionary monetary policy *monetary policy* that increases *aggregate demand.* (p. 307)

expenditure approach an approach to calculating *GDP* by adding up *aggregate spending* on domestically produced *final goods and services* in the *economy*—the sum of consumer spending, investment spending, government purchases of goods and services, and *exports* minus *imports.* (p. 109)

exports goods and services sold to other countries. (p. 108)

factor markets where *resources*, especially *capital* and *labor*, are bought and sold. (p. 106)

federal funds market allows *banks* that fall short of the *reserve requirement* to borrow funds from banks with *excess reserves.* (p. 262)

federal funds rate the *interest rate* that *banks* charge other banks for *loans*, as determined in the *federal funds market.* (p. 262)

fiat money a *medium of exchange* whose value derives entirely from its official status as a means of payment. (p. 235)

final goods and services goods and services sold to the final, or end, user. (p. 109)

financial asset a paper claim that entitles the buyer to future income from the seller. (p. 225)

financial crisis a sudden and widespread disruption of *financial markets.* (p. EM-5)

financial intermediary an institution that transforms the funds it gathers from many individuals into *financial assets.* (p. 229)

financial markets the markets (banking, *stock*, and *bond*) that channel *private savings* and foreign lending into *investment spending*, *government borrowing*, and foreign borrowing. (pp. 108, EM-2)

financial risk uncertainty about future outcomes that involve financial losses and gains. (p. 226)

firm an organization that produces goods and services for sale. (p. 106)

fiscal policy the use of government purchases of goods and services, government transfers, or tax policy to stabilize the *economy.* (p. 177)

fiscal year runs from October 1 to September 30 and is labeled according to the calendar year in which it ends. (p. 297)

Fisher effect the general principle that an increase in expected future *inflation* drives up the *nominal interest rate* by the same number of percentage points, leaving the expected *real interest rate* unchanged. (p. 282)

fixed exchange rate an *exchange rate regime* in which the government keeps the exchange rate against some other currency at or near a particular target. (p. 427)

floating exchange rate an *exchange rate regime* in which the government lets the exchange rate go wherever the market takes it. (p. 427)

foreign exchange controls licensing systems that limit the right of individuals to buy foreign currency. (p. 429)

foreign exchange market the market in which currencies are traded. (p. 417)

foreign exchange reserves stocks of foreign currency that governments maintain to buy their own currency on the foreign exchange market. (p. 429)

frictional unemployment *unemployment* due to the time workers spend in *job search.* (p. 130)

future value the amount to which some current amount of money will grow as interest accumulates over a specified period of time. (p. 239)

gains from trade an economic principle that states that people can get more of what they want through *trade* than they could if they tried to be self-sufficient; this increase in *output* is due to *specialization*. (p. 150)

GDP deflator (for a given year) 100 times the ratio of *nominal GDP* to *real GDP* in that year. (p. 150)

GDP per capita *GDP* divided by the size of the population; it is equivalent to the average *GDP* per person. (p. 118)

government borrowing the amount of funds borrowed by the government in the *financial markets*. (p. 108)

government debt the accumulation of past *budget deficits*, minus past *budget surpluses*. (p. 297)

Government purchases of goods and services total expenditures on goods and services by federal, state, and local governments. (p. 108)

government transfers payments that the government makes to individuals without expecting a good or service in return. (p. 108)

Gross domestic product (GDP) the total value of all final goods and services produced in the economy during a given year. (p. 109)

growth accounting estimates the contribution of each major factor in the *aggregate production function* to economic growth. (p. 375)

horizontal intercept indicates the value of the *x*-variable when the value of the *y*-variable is zero. (p. 39)

household a person or group of people who share income. (p. 106)

human capital the improvement in labor created by the education and knowledge of members of the workforce. (p. 371)

illiquid describes an asset if it cannot be quickly converted into cash without much loss of value. (p. 227)

implicit liabilities spending promises made by governments that are effectively a debt despite the fact that they are not included in the usual debt statistics. (p. 301)

import quota a limit on the quantity of a good that can be imported within a given period. (p. 440)

imports goods and services purchased from other countries. (p. 108)

incentives rewards or punishments that motivate particular choices. (p. 3)

income approach an approach to calculating *GDP* by adding up the total factor income earned by households from firms in the economy, including rent, wages, interest, and profit. (p. 109)

independent variable in a *causal relationship*, the variable that determines the *dependent variable*. (p. 38)

individual choice decisions by individuals about what to do, which necessarily involve decisions about what not to do. (p. 2)

individual demand curve illustrates the relationship between quantity demanded and price for an individual consumer. (p. 56)

individual supply curve illustrates the relationship between quantity supplied and price for an individual producer. (p. 65)

inefficient allocation of sales among sellers a form of inefficiency resulting from *price floors* in which those who would be willing to sell the good at the lowest price are not always those who manage to sell it. (p. 87)

inefficient allocation to consumers a form of inefficiency often resulting from *price ceilings* in which people who want a good badly and are willing to pay a high price don't get it, and those who care relatively little about the good and are only willing to pay a relatively low price do get it. (p. 83)

inefficiently high quality a form of inefficiency resulting from *price floors* in which sellers offer high-quality goods at a high price, even though buyers would prefer a lower quality at a lower price. (p. 88)

inefficiently low quality a form of inefficiency resulting from *price ceilings* in which sellers offer low-quality goods at a low price even though buyers would prefer a higher quality at a higher price. (p. 84)

inferior good when a rise in income decreases the demand for a good; usually considered less desirable than more expensive alternatives. (p. 55)

inflation a rising overall price level. (p. 13)

inflation rate the percentage increase in the overall level of prices per year. (p. 139)

inflation targeting occurs when the *central bank* sets an explicit target for the *inflation rate* and sets monetary policy in order to hit that target. (p. 309)

inflation tax a reduction, caused by *inflation*, in the value of money held by the public. (p. 322)

inflationary gap occurs when *aggregate output* is above *potential output*. (p. 198)

infrastructure roads, power lines, ports, information networks, and other underpinnings for economic activity. (p. 386)

input a good or service that is used to produce another good or service. (p. 63)

interest rate the price, calculated as a percentage of the amount borrowed, charged by lenders to borrowers for the use of their savings for one year. (p. 223)

interest rate effect of a change in the aggregate price level the change in investment and consumer spending caused by altered interest rates that result from changes in the demand for money. (p. 174)

intermediate goods and services goods and services bought from one firm by another firm to be used as inputs into the production of final goods and services. (p. 109)

inventories stocks of goods and raw materials held to facilitate business operations. (p. 109)

inventory investment the value of the change in total *inventories* held in the *economy* during a given period. (p. 168)

investment bank a *bank* that trades in *financial assets* and is not covered by *deposit insurance*. (p. 258)

investment spending spending on new productive physical capital, such as machinery and structures, and on changes in inventories. (p. 109)

job search when workers spend time looking for employment. (p. 130)

Keynesian economics set of ideas that focuses on the ability of shifts in *aggregate demand* to influence *aggregate output* in the short run. (p. 343)

labor the effort of workers. (p. 3)

labor force the number of people who are either actively employed for pay or unemployed and actively looking for work; the sum of employment and unemployment. (pp. 12, 122)

labor force participation rate the percentage of the population aged 16 or older that is in the labor force. (p. 122)

labor productivity (productivity) output per worker. (p. 370)

land all *resources* that come from nature, such as minerals, timber, and petroleum. (p. 3)

law of demand the "law" that a higher price for a good or service, other things being equal, leads people to demand a smaller quantity of that good or service. (p. 51)

law of supply the "law" that, other things being equal, the price and quantity supplied of a good are positively related. (p. 61)

leverage the degree to which a financial institution is financing its investments with borrowed funds. (p. EM-5)

liability a requirement to pay money in the future. (p. 225)

license gives its owner the right to supply a good or service; a form of quantity control, as only those who are licensed can supply the good or service. (p. 92)

life insurance company sells policies that guarantee a payment to a policyholder's beneficiaries when the policyholder dies. (p. 230)

linear relationship the relationship between two *variables* when the *curve* that shows their relationship is a straight line, or linear. (p. 38)

liquid describes an asset if it can be quickly converted into cash without much loss of value. (p. 227)

liquidity preference model of the interest rate *model* that says that the *interest rate* is determined by the supply and demand for money. (p. 272)

liquidity trap a situation in which conventional monetary policy is ineffective because *nominal interest rates* are up against the *zero bound*. (p. 337)

loan a lending agreement between an individual lender and an individual borrower. (p. 227)

loanable funds market a hypothetical market that brings together those who want to lend money and those who want to borrow money. (p. 276)

loan-backed security an asset created by pooling individual *loans* and selling shares in that pool. (p. 228)

long-run aggregate supply curve shows the relationship between the *aggregate price level* and the quantity of *aggregate output* supplied that would exist if all prices, including *nominal wages*, were fully flexible. (p. 186)

long-run macroeconomic equilibrium when the point of *short-run macroeconomic equilibrium* is on the *long-run aggregate supply curve*. (p. 196)

long-run Phillips curve (*LRPC*) shows the relationship between *unemployment* and *inflation* after expectations of inflation have had time to adjust to experience. (p. 334)

long-term interest rates *interest rates* on *financial assets* that mature a number of years in the future. (p. 269)

lump-sum taxes taxes that don't depend on the taxpayer's income. (p. 213)

macroeconomic policy activism the use of monetary and *fiscal policy* to smooth out the *business cycle*. (p. 344)

macroeconomics the branch of *economics* that is concerned with the overall ups and downs of the *economy*. (p. 5)

marginal analysis the study of the costs and benefits of doing a little bit more of an activity versus a little bit less. (p. 3)

marginal propensity to consume (*MPC*) the increase in consumer spending when *disposable income* rises by $1. (p. 160)

marginal propensity to save (*MPS*) the increase in household savings when *disposable income* rises by $1. (p. 160)

marginally attached workers would like to be employed and have looked for a job in the recent past but are not currently looking for work. (p. 123)

market basket a hypothetical set of consumer purchases of goods and services. (p. 147)

market economy an *economy* in which the decisions of individual producers and consumers largely determine what, how, and for whom to produce, with little government involvement in the decisions. (p. 2)

maturity transformation the conversion of short-term liabilities into long-term assets. (p. EM-3)

maximum the point along a *curve* with the largest value of *y*. (p. 42)

medium of exchange an asset that individuals acquire for the purpose of trading for goods and services rather than for their own consumption. (p. 233)

menu costs the real costs of changing listed prices. (p. 140)

merchandise trade balance (trade balance) the difference between a country's exports and imports of goods. (p. 409)

microeconomics the branch of *economics* that studies how individuals, households, and firms make decisions and how those decisions interact. (p. 5)

minimum the point along a *curve* with the smallest value of *y*. (p. 43)

minimum wage a legal floor on the hourly wage rate paid for a worker's labor. (p. 85)

model a simplified representation used to better understand a real-life situation. (p. 14)

monetarism asserts that *GDP* will grow steadily if the *money supply* grows steadily. (p. 346)

monetary aggregate an overall measure of the *money supply*. (p. 236)

monetary base the sum of currency in circulation and *bank reserves*. (p. 251)

monetary neutrality the concept that changes in the *money supply* have no real effects on the *economy*. (p. 314)

monetary policy the central bank's use of changes in the quantity of money or the interest rate to stabilize the *economy*. (p. 177)

monetary policy rule a formula that determines the *central bank's* actions. (p. 347)

money any asset that can easily be used to purchase goods and services. (p. 232)

money demand curve shows the relationship between the quantity of money demanded and the *interest rate*. (p. 270)

money multiplier the ratio of the *money supply* to the *monetary base*; indicates the total number of dollars created in the banking system by each $1 addition to the monetary base. (p. 251)

money supply the total value of *financial assets* in the economy that are considered *money*. (p. 233)

money supply curve shows the relationship between the quantity of money supplied and the *interest rate*. (p. 272)

moral hazard a distortion of incentives when someone else bears the costs of a lack of care or effort. (p. EM-7)

movement along the demand curve a change in the quantity demanded of a good that is the result of a change in that good's price. (p. 52)

movement along the supply curve a change in the quantity supplied of a good arising from a change in the good's price. (p. 62)

mutual fund a *financial intermediary* that creates a stock portfolio and then resells shares of this portfolio to individual investors. (p. 229)

national income and product accounts (national accounts) keep track of the flows of money among different sectors of the economy; calculated by the Bureau of Economic Analysis. (p. 105)

national savings the sum of private savings and the *budget balance*; the total amount of savings generated within the *economy*. (p. 224)

natural rate hypothesis to avoid accelerating *inflation* over time, the *unemployment rate* must be high enough that the actual *inflation rate* equals the expected inflation rate. (p. 348)

natural rate of unemployment the *unemployment rate* that arises from the effects of *frictional* plus *structural unemployment*. (p. 133)

near-moneys *financial assets* that can't be directly used as a *medium of exchange* but can be readily converted into cash or *checkable bank deposits*. (p. 236)

negative relationship the relationship between two *variables* when an increase in one variable is associated with a decrease in the other variable. (p. 39)

net exports the difference between the value of *exports* and the value of *imports* ($X - IM$). (p. 111)

net present value the *present value* of current and future benefits minus the present value of current and future costs. (p. 241)

new classical macroeconomics an approach to the *business cycle* that returns to the classical view that shifts in the *aggregate demand curve* affect only the *aggregate price level*, not *aggregate output*. (p. 349)

new Keynesian economics a set of ideas that argues that market imperfections can lead to price stickiness for the *economy* as a whole. (p. 350)

nominal GDP the total value of all *final goods and services* produced in the *economy* during a given year, calculated with the prices current in the year in which the *output* is produced. (p. 117)

nominal interest rate the interest rate actually paid for a loan. (p. 142)

nominal wage the dollar amount of the wage paid. (p. 181)

nonaccelerating inflation rate of unemployment (NAIRU) the *unemployment rate* at which *inflation* does not change over time. (p. 334)

nonlinear curve a *curve* along which the *slope* changes. (p. 41)

nonlinear relationship the relationship between two *variables* when the *curve* that shows their relationship is not a straight line, or is nonlinear. (p. 38)

normal good when a rise in income increases the demand for a good; most goods are normal goods. (p. 55)

normative economics the branch of economic analysis that makes prescriptions about the way the economy should work. (p. 6)

open-market operation a purchase or sale of government debt by the Fed. (p. 263)

opportunity cost the real cost of an item: what you must give up in order to get it. (p. 4)

origin the point where the (horizontal) x-axis and (vertical) y-axis meet. (p. 37)

other things equal assumption in the development of a *model*, the assumption that all other relevant factors remain unchanged; also known as the *ceteris paribus* assumption. (p. 14)

output the quantity of goods and services produced. (p. 12)

output gap the percentage difference between actual *aggregate output* and *potential output*. (p. 198)

pension fund a nonprofit institution that invests the savings of members and provides them with income when they retire. (p. 229)

physical asset a claim on a tangible object that gives the owner the right to dispose of the object as he or she wishes. (p. 225)

physical capital consists of human-made goods such as buildings and machines used to produce other goods and services. (p. 371)

pie chart a chart that shows the share of a total amount that is accounted for by various components, usually expressed in percentages. (p. 45)

planned investment spending the investment spending that businesses intend to undertake during a given period. (p. 166)

political business cycle unnecessary instability in the *economy* resulting from when politicians use *macroeconomic* policy to serve political ends. (p. 349)

positive economics the branch of economic analysis that describes the way the *economy* actually works. (p. 6)

positive relationship the relationship between two *variables* when an increase in one variable is associated with an increase in the other variable. (p. 39)

potential output the level of *real GDP* the *economy* would produce if all prices, including *nominal wages*, were fully flexible. (p. 187)

present value (of \$1 realized one year from now) $\$1/(1 + r)$; the amount of money you must lend out today in order to have \$1 in one year. It is the value to you today of \$1 realized one year from now. (p. 240)

price ceiling a maximum price that sellers are allowed to charge for a good or service. (p. 80)

price controls legal restrictions on how high or low a market price may go; typically take the form of either a *price ceiling* or a *price floor*. (p. 80)

price floor a minimum price that buyers are required to pay for a good or service. (p. 80)

price index measures the cost of purchasing a given market basket in a given year; the index value is normalized so that it is equal to 100 in the selected base year. (p. 147)

price stability when the overall price level is changing only slowly if at all. (p. 13)

private savings *disposable income* minus *consumer spending*; disposable income that is not spent on consumption but rather goes into *financial markets*. (p. 108)

producer price index (PPI) measures the prices of goods and services purchased by producers. (p. 150)

product markets where goods and services are bought and sold. (p. 106)

production possibilities curve illustrates the *trade-offs* facing an *economy* that produces only two goods; shows the maximum quantity of one good that can be produced for each possible quantity of the other good produced. (p. 17)

productive efficiency achieved by an *economy* if it produces at a point on its *production possibilities curve*. (p. 18)

property rights establish ownership and grant individuals the right to trade goods and services with each other. (p. 3)

protectionism the practice of limiting trade to protect domestic industries. (p. 438)

public debt *government debt* held by individuals and institutions outside the government. (p. 297)

purchasing power parity (between two countries' currencies) the nominal exchange rate at which a given basket of goods and services would cost the same amount in each country. (p. 423)

quantity control (quota) an upper limit on the quantity of some good that can be bought or sold. (p. 92)

quantity demanded the actual amount of a good or service consumers are willing and able to buy at some specific price. (p. 50)

quantity supplied the actual amount of a good or service people are willing to sell at some specific price. (p. 60)

Quantity Theory of Money emphasizes the positive relationship between the price level and the *money supply*; relies on the velocity equation ($M \times V = P \times Y$). (p. 347)

quota rent the earnings that accrue to the license-holder from ownership of the right to sell the good. (p. 95)

rate of return (on a project) is the profit earned on the project expressed as a percentage of its cost. (p. 277)

rational expectations the view that individuals and *firms* make decisions optimally, using all available information. (p. 350)

real business cycle theory claims that fluctuations in the rate of growth of total factor productivity cause the *business cycle*. (p. 350)

real exchange rates exchange rates adjusted for international differences in aggregate price levels. (p. 421)

real GDP the total value of all *final goods and services* produced in the *economy* during a given year, calculated using the prices of a selected base year in order to remove the effects of price changes. (p. 117)

real income income divided by the price level to adjust for the effects of inflation or deflation. (p. 139)

real interest rate the *nominal interest rate* minus the rate of *inflation*. (p. 142)

real wage the wage rate divided by the price level to adjust for the effects of inflation or deflation. (p. 139)

recession a period of economic downturn when output and employment are falling. (p. 11)

recessionary gap when *aggregate output* is below *potential output*. (p. 197)

required reserve ratio the smallest fraction of deposits that the Federal Reserve allows *banks* to hold. (p. 245)

research and development (R & D) spending to create and implement new technologies. (p. 385)

reserve ratio the fraction of *bank deposits* that a *bank* holds as reserves. (p. 245)

reserve requirements rules set by the Federal Reserve that determine the *required reserve ratio* for *banks*. (p. 247)

resource anything that can be used to produce something else. (p. 3)

revaluation an increase in the value of a currency that is set under a fixed *exchange rate regime*. (p. 431)

Rule of 70 a mathematical formula that tells us that the time it takes a variable that grows gradually over time to double is approximately 70 divided by that variable's annual growth rate. (p. 369)

savings and loan (thrift) a type of deposit-taking *bank*, usually specialized in issuing home *loans*. (p. 258)

savings-investment spending identity an accounting fact that states that savings and *investment spending* are always equal for the *economy* as a whole. (p. 224)

scarce in short supply; when a resource is not available in sufficient quantities to satisfy all the various ways a society wants to use it. (p. 3)

scatter diagram a diagram in which each point corresponds to an actual observation of the *x*-variable and the *y*-variable. (p. 45)

securitization involves assembling a pool of loans and selling shares of that pool to investors. (p. EM-7)

self-correcting describes the *economy* when shocks to *aggregate demand* affect *aggregate output* in the short run, but not the long run. (p. 198)

shadow bank a financial institution that engages in *maturity transformation* but does not accept deposits. (p. EM-3)

shoe-leather costs the increased costs of transactions caused by *inflation*. (p. 140)

shortage when the quantity of a good or service demanded exceeds the quantity supplied; occurs when the price is below its equilibrium level and is also known as *excess demand*. (p. 71)

short-run aggregate supply curve shows the relationship between the *aggregate price level* and the quantity of *aggregate output* supplied that exists in the short run, the time period when many production costs can be taken as fixed. (p. 182)

short-run equilibrium aggregate output the quantity of *aggregate output* produced in the *short-run macroeconomic equilibrium*. (p. 193)

short-run equilibrium aggregate price level the *aggregate price level* in the *short-run macroeconomic equilibrium*. (p. 193)

short-run macroeconomic equilibrium when the quantity of *aggregate output* supplied is equal to the quantity demanded. (p. 192)

short-run Phillips curve (*SRPC*) represents the negative short-run relationship between the *unemployment rate* and the *inflation rate*. (p. 328)

short-term interest rates the *interest rates* on *financial assets* that mature within a year. (p. 268)

slope a measure of how steep a *curve* is; indicates how sensitive the *y*-variable is to a change in the *x*-variable. (p. 39)

social insurance government programs intended to protect families against economic hardship. (p. 205)

specialization each person specializes in the task that he or she is good at performing. (p. 24)

spending multiplier the ratio of the total change in *real GDP* caused by an autonomous change in *aggregate spending* to the size of that autonomous change; indicates the total rise in *real GDP* that results from each $1 of an initial rise in spending. (p. 161)

stabilization policy the use of government policy to reduce the severity of *recessions* and rein in excessively strong expansions. (p. 201)

stagflation the combination of *inflation* and stagnating (or falling) *aggregate output*. (p. 195)

sticky wages *nominal wages* that are slow to fall even in the face of high *unemployment* and slow to rise even in the face of *labor* shortages. (p. 181)

stock a share in the ownership of a company held by a shareholder. (p. 107)

store of value a means of holding purchasing power over time. (p. 234)

structural unemployment *unemployment* that results when workers lack the skills required for the available jobs, or there are more people seeking jobs in a labor market than there are jobs available at the current wage rate. (p. 131)

subprime lending involves lending to home-buyers who don't meet the usual criteria for being able to afford their payments. (p. EM-7)

substitutes two goods for which a rise in the price of one of the goods leads to an increase in the demand for the other good. (p. 54)

supply and demand model *model* of how a competitive market works. (p. 50)

supply curve shows the relationship between the quantity supplied and the price. (p. 60)

supply price the price of a given quantity at which producers will supply that quantity. (p. 94)

supply schedule shows how much of a good or service producers would supply at different prices. (p. 60)

supply shock an event that shifts the *short-run aggregate supply curve*. (p. 194)

surplus when the quantity supplied of a good or service exceeds the quantity demanded; occurs when the price is above its equilibrium level and also known as *excess supply*. (p. 71)

sustainable describes *long-run economic growth* if it can continue in the face of the limited supply of natural resources and the impact of growth on the environment. (p. 388)

T-account a tool for analyzing a business's financial position by showing, in a single table, the business's assets (on the left) and *liabilities* (on the right). (p. 245)

target federal funds rate the Federal Reserve's desired level for the *federal funds rate*; the Federal Reserve can move the *interest rate* and achieve this target through open-market operations that shift the *money supply curve*. (p. 304)

tariffs taxes on imports. (p. 438)

tax multiplier the factor by which a change in tax collections changes *real GDP*. (p. 213)

Taylor rule for monetary policy a rule for setting the *federal funds rate* that takes into account both the *inflation rate* and the *output gap*. (p. 308)

technology the technical means for producing goods and services. (pp. 21, 371)

terms of trade indicate the rate at which one good can be exchanged for another. (p. 28)

time-series graph a graph with successive dates on the *horizontal (x-) axis* and the values of a variable that occurred on those dates on the *vertical (y-) axis*. (p. 44)

total factor productivity the amount of output that can be achieved with a given amount of factor inputs. (p. 376)

trade when individuals provide goods and services to others and receive goods and services in return. (p. 24)

trade-off when you give up something in order to have something else. (p. 16)

transaction costs the expenses of negotiating and executing a deal. (p. 226)

underemployed workers who would like to work more hours or who are overqualified for their jobs. (p. 123)

unemployed people who are actively looking for work but aren't currently employed. (p. 122)

unemployment the number of people who are actively looking for work but aren't currently employed. (p. 11)

unemployment rate the percentage of the labor force that is unemployed. (pp. 12, 122)

unit of account a measure used to set prices and make economic calculations. (p. 234)

unit-of-account costs arise from the way *inflation* makes money a less reliable unit of measurement. (p. 142)

unplanned inventory investment occurs when actual sales are lower than businesses expected, leading to unplanned increases in inventories; sales in excess of expectations result in negative unplanned inventory investment. (p. 168)

value added (of a producer) the value of a producer's sales minus the value of its purchases of inputs. (p. 110)

value-added approach an approach to calculating *GDP* by surveying firms and adding up their contributions to the value of *final goods and services*. (p. 109)

variable a measure that can take on more than one value. (p. 36)

velocity of money the ratio of *nominal GDP* to the *money supply*; a measure of the number of times the average dollar bill is spent per year. (p. 347)

vertical intercept indicates the value of the *y*-variable when the value of the *x*-variable is zero. (p. 39)

wasted resources a form of inefficiency in which people expend money, effort, and time to cope with the *shortages* caused by the *price ceiling* or *surpluses* caused by the *price floor*. (p. 83)

wealth the value of a *household's* accumulated savings. (p. 225)

wealth effect of a change in the aggregate price level the change in consumer spending caused by the altered purchasing power of consumers' assets. (p. 174)

wedge the difference between the *demand price* and the *supply price* of a good, often created by a quota. (p. 95)

x-axis the solid horizontal line on a graph that intersects with the *y-axis* at the *origin*; also called the horizontal axis. (p. 37)

y-axis the solid vertical line on a graph that intersects with the *x-axis* at the *origin*; also called the vertical axis. (p. 37)

zero bound the lower bound of zero on the nominal interest rate: it cannot go below zero. (p. 337)

Index

Note: **Boldface** type indicates key terms.